# Psychology

# Psychology
## THIRD EDITION

**Philip G. Zimbardo**
*Stanford University*

**Ann L. Weber**
*University of North Carolina at Asheville*

**Robert L. Johnson**
*Umpqua Community College*

Allyn and Bacon
Boston    London    Toronto    Sydney    Tokyo    Singapore

| | |
|---|---|
| Executive Editor: | Rebecca Pascal |
| Editorial Assistant: | Jill Jeffrey |
| Senior Editorial-Production Administrator: | Joe Sweeney |
| Editorial-Production Service: | Heckman & Pinette Editorial Services |
| Composition Buyer: | Linda Cox |
| Manufacturing Buyer: | Megan Cochran |
| Cover Administrator: | Linda Knowles |
| Text Design: | The Davis Group, Inc. |
| Text Composition: | Omegatype Typography, Inc. |

Allyn & Bacon
A Pearson Education Company
160 Gould Street
Needham Heights, MA 02494
www.abacon.com

LIBRARY OF CONGRESS CATALOGING-IN-PUBLICATION DATA
Zimbardo, Philip G.
   Psychology / Philip G. Zimbardo, Ann L. Weber, Robert L. Johnson.—3rd ed.
     p. cm.
   Includes bibliographical references and index.
   ISBN 0-321-03432-5 (alk. paper)
    1. Psychology.   I. Weber, Ann L.   II. Johnson, Robert L.   III. Title.
BF121.Z53 2000
150–dc21
                                                   99-051650

Printed in the United States of America

10 9 8 7 6 5 4 3 2  VHP  1 04 03 02 01 00 99

# Brief Contents

# Contents

## 6  Learning and Remembering    209

## 9    Stress, Health, and Well-Being        337

## 10    Personality        381

## 11   Intelligence and the Psychology of Differences     419

## 12   Social Psychology     455

## 13    Psychopathology    491

# 14 Therapies for Mental Disorder 533

# Preface

Psychological knowledge has exploded. As a result, introductory textbooks have grown to daunting proportions. Meanwhile our introductory courses remain the same length—with the material ever more densely packed. Even in a year-long course we cannot possibly introduce students to all the concepts, no matter how good our materials and presentation styles. Nor can students remember everything in the standard, encyclopedic introductory text. Accordingly, in the 3rd edition of *Psychology*, your authors have mercilessly pared the material that appeared in the previous editions to much more manageable proportions (although the professor may, of course, reintroduce old favorites!).

We also realize that the problem is not just one of sheer volume and information overload, it is also a problem of meaningfulness. To make the material more meaningful for students who use this edition of *Psychology*, we have found inspiration in a classic study of chess players. As you may recall, Adrian de Groot (1965) and his colleagues (Chase & Simon, 1973) showed that experts did no better than novices at remembering the locations of pieces on a chessboard when the pieces were placed at random. Only when the patterns made sense—because they represented actual game situations—did the experts show an advantage. Clearly, meaningful patterns are easier to remember than random arrangements. In applying this to *Psychology*, 3rd Edition, our goal has been to present the field of psychology in meaningful patterns that will help students take their first steps toward developing expertise. We have introduced several features to accomplish this:

- **Core Concepts**   We have organized each major section of every chapter around a single, clear idea that we call a *Core Concept*. For example, one of the four Core Concepts in the chapter on Development says:

  **Newborns begin life equipped to deal with three basic survival tasks: finding nourishment, making contacts with people, and avoiding harmful situations.**

To give another example, here is one of the three Core Concepts drawn from the chapter on Sensation and Perception:

> **Perception brings meaning to sensation, so perception produces an interpretation of the external world, not a perfect representation of it.**

To borrow an old saying, the Core Concepts become the "forest," while the details of the chapter become the "trees."

- **Key Questions**    Each Core Concept is introduced by a Key Question that serves as a main heading in the chapter. Here is an example from Chapter 4:

  **WHAT CAPABILITIES DOES THE NEWBORN POSSESS?**

  and one from Chapter 5:

  **WHAT IS THE RELATIONSHIP BETWEEN PERCEPTION AND SENSATION?**

  These questions help students anticipate the most important point in the section: the Core Concept. In fact, the Core Concept becomes the brief answer to the Key Question. All of the Key Questions and the Core Concepts are introduced in a chart on the first page of the chapter and are also used as the organizing framework for the Chapter Summary.

- **Psychology in Your Life**    Psychology has many connections with events in the news and in everyday life, and we have explored one of these connections at the end of each major section in every chapter. For example, in the chapter on Sensation and Perception, the Psychology in Your Life feature examines these topics:

  *Subliminal perception and subliminal persuasion*
  *The experience and control of pain*
  *Why seeing should not always be believing*

  Such connections, along with numerous briefer examples sprinkled throughout each chapter, make psychology come alive. They also promote critical thinking by helping students evaluate many of the psychological ideas that they will encounter in the popular press.

- **Do It Yourself!**    These active-learning exercises offer simple demonstrations of principles discussed in the text. Many are borrowed from demonstrations that we have used in our own classrooms. Examples include:

  *Playing with Children—Piagetian Style* (Chapter 4: Developmental Psychology)
  *Phosphenes Show That Your Brain Creates Sensations* (Chapter 5: Sensation and Perception)
  *Finding Your STM Capacity* (Chapter 6: Learning and Remembering)
  *Zooming In on Mental Images* (Chapter 7: Cognitive Processes)
  *Identifying Facial Expressions of Emotion* (Chapter 8: Emotion and Motivation)
  *What Makes a Samaritan Good or Bad?* (Chapter 12: Social Psychology)
  *Behavior Self-Modification* (Chapter 14: Therapies for Mental Disorder)

  Not only are these exercises fun, but each one reinforces an important psychological idea.

- **Using Psychology to Learn Psychology**    In a special section at the end of every chapter, we explain how some aspect of the chapter applies to studying and learning. For example, in Chapter 2, Biopsychology, we tell students how to put their knowledge of the brain to work for more efficient learning. In Chapter 8, Emotion and Motivation, we explain how they can use the concept of "flow" to motivate themselves. Thus, Using Psychology to Learn Psychology not only reinforces points that students have studied, it brings the material home with immediate and practical applications to their college lives.

- **Cross-Reference Arrows** Connections to important topics in other chapters are noted by a brief reference in the margin, accompanied by an arrow. Whenever possible, we have used this device instead of the intrusive phrase, "as we will see in Chapter 3." The explanatory note accompanying these cross-reference arrows gives the reader a quick preview of the discussion to be found in the referenced chapter. We intend this to convey to students the sense of psychology as a network of interconnecting ideas that can be entered from nearly any point. An example of these cross-reference arrows appears in this margin.

- **Marginal glossaries** In this 3rd edition of *Psychology*, the most important terms appear in **boldface**, with a glossary definition in the margin. Now, as many of you have requested, students will have clear definitions of important terms where they can easily access them as they study.

In addition to these new features, we have retained and refined the best of the 2nd edition:

- **Culture and Gender** Nearly every chapter brings in a cross-cultural, multicultural, or gender-related concept. We have not trivialized this material by setting it aside in special boxes or marking it with special icons. Rather, culture and gender have been fully integrated with psychology in the running text. Examples include:

    **Chapter 2:** *Biological influences on gender*
    **Chapter 4:** *Moral development across culture*
    **Chapter 5:** *Cultural influences on perception*
    **Chapter 7:** *Culture affects scripts, schemas, and cognitive maps*
    **Chapter 8:** *Cultural universals in facial expressions*
    **Chapter 12:** *The fundamental attribution error is not so fundamental in collectivistic cultures*
    **Chapter 13:** *Gender and cultural differences in the incidence of mental disorders*

- **Check Your Understanding** Reviewers have told us that they want a book that promotes active reader involvement. The 3rd edition of *Psychology* does this in many ways. For example, we have replaced the section summaries of the previous edition with a brief Check Your Understanding quiz at the end of each major chapter section. We have written these quizzes so that some of the questions call for simple *recall*, while others call for deeper *analysis* or *application* of the material. In addition, at least one of the questions in each Check Your Understanding quiz is aimed squarely at the Core Concept of the section.

- **Chapter Summaries** In the 3rd edition, the chapter summaries are organized according to the Key Question/Core Concept format. This approach is designed to help students move beyond the details so that they can glimpse the larger picture that the chapter paints. We have attempted to write the summaries in such a way that students will know that they are not a substitute for the chapter itself. Rather, they are a conceptual overview of the main ideas that link the Key Questions and the Core Concepts.

- **Chapter Review Tests** At the end of each chapter students will find a short, objective test with questions covering points across the entire chapter. These Chapter Review tests will help students assess their learning of the chapter as a whole.

- **If You're Interested**   This section invites students who are especially curious to go beyond the material presented in the text. Here, at the end of each chapter, we have listed provocative books and videos relating to topics covered by that chapter. Many were originally suggested to us by our students. All are readily available through libraries and video stores. Brief comments note the strengths or special relevance of each source listed.

By marrying these teaching/learning devices with a relaxed and spirited writing style, replete with examples, we believe that we have brought you a book that presents psychology in a fascinating and meaningful way. What you will not find here is a comprehensive catalog of terms and facts or a collection of independent "modules." Instead, our unique Key Question and Core Concept approach is designed with the goal of helping students finish the course with a broad understanding of psychology's most fundamental and important ideas. We think you'll like what you find here: It's all based on using psychology to teach and learn psychology.

## Helpful Supplemental Materials

The following supplements will also enhance teaching and learning for you and your students:

**INSTRUCTOR'S MANUAL**   Written by Anita Rosenfield and Philip Zimbardo, this helpful teaching companion includes chapter outlines and summaries, experiments and demonstrations, lecture launchers, class activities, a feature covering the use of concept maps, and plenty of teaching tips and course organization material.

**TEST BANK.**   Thomas Land, test bank author for the 3rd edition of *Psychology*, has provided a new, fully updated question bank, available in both print and computerized formats. The test bank offers 150 questions per chapter, including multiple choice, true-false, short answer, and essay questions.

**ALLYN & BACON TEST MANAGER—COMPUTERIZED TEST BANK**   (Available for Windows and Macintosh; DOS disk available upon request): Allyn & Bacon Test Manager is an integrated suite of testing and assessment tools for Windows and Macintosh. You can use Test Manager to create professional-looking exams in just minutes by building tests from the existing database of questions, editing questions, or adding your own. Course management features include a class roster, gradebook, and item analysis. Test Manager also has everything you need to create and administer online tests. For first-time users, there is a guided tour of the entire Test Manager system and screen wizards to walk you through each area.

**CALL-IN AND FAX TESTING**   One toll-free call to our testing center will have a finished, ready-to-duplicate test on its way to you within 48 hours, via mail or Fax.

**TRANSPARENCY PACKAGE (0-205-13273-1)**   A full set of color acetate transparencies is available to enhance classroom lectures and discussions.

**POWERPOINT PRESENTATION (CD-ROM)**   This book-specific presentation provides detailed outlines of key points for each chapter supported by charts, graphs, diagrams, and other visuals from the textbook. Resources from the Zimbardo/Weber/Johnson Companion Website are also integrated for easy access to the Website from your classroom.

**ALLYN & BACON DIGITAL MEDIA ARCHIVE CD-ROM FOR PSYCHOLOGY, 2.0 VERSION (0-205-32012-0)**   Allyn & Bacon provides an array of media products to help liven up your classroom presentations. The Digital Media Archive provides charts, graphs, tables, and figures electronically on one cross-platform CD-ROM. The Digital Media Archive also provides video and audio clips along with the electronic images that can be easily integrated into your lectures. This helpful resource extends the coverage found on the Zimbardo/Weber/Johnson Powerpoint Presentation CD-ROM.

**ALLYN & BACON MIND MATTERS CD-ROM (0–205–32179–8)**   This student CD-ROM features in-depth units on the history of psychology, research methodology, biopsychology, learning, memory, sensation, and perception. Each unit includes self-contained modules that cover core psychological concepts through a combination of text, graphics, humor, activities, and extensive assessment. The CD-ROM is available free, packaged with new copies of the Zimbardo/Weber/Johnson textbook.

**ALLYN & BACON MIND MATTERS FACULTY GUIDE (0–321–05452–0)**   This helpful instructor resource offers detailed overviews of each unit of the CD-ROM supplemented by additional test questions and chapter-by-chapter references correlating content from the CD-ROM with Allyn & Bacon introductory psychology textbooks. This in-depth guide makes it easy to integrate the Allyn & Bacon Mind Matters CD-ROM into your syllabus!

**THE PSYCHOLOGY PLACE WEBSITE**   *The Psychology Place* is a premier Web resource for introductory psychology that benefits both students and instructors. Instructors enjoy an extensive selection of teaching resources, access to recent research news, Web investigations, a wide variety of scientifically accurate and appropriate Web resources, integration of online investigative and collaborative learning activities, communication with other instructors, and the ability to share teaching ideas and challenges by participating in the Op Ed Forum. Students receive a six-month subscription that provides access to a wide range of helpful resources including extensive learning activities, news updates, research reports, Web links, and animations. Please visit www.abacon.com/zimbardo, or contact your local Allyn & Bacon publisher's representative for more information.

**ZIMBARDO/WEBER/JOHNSON COMPANION WEBSITE**   This helpful site contains a wide variety of valuable study tools for each chapter of the textbook, including learning objectives, chapter summaries, interactive online quizzes, and Web links to relevant psychology sites to reinforce learning. Each chapter of this Website is also accessible through the Zimbardo/Weber/Johnson Powerpoint Presentation CD-ROM, allowing for easy integration into your classroom lectures.

**PEARSON COURSE MANAGEMENT SYSTEM**   The PearsonCMS enables professors to easily create password-protected online courses and empowers professors to manage their courses in many ways. Each course Website contains the content of the highly popular and successful Allyn & Bacon Companion Website along with an integrated syllabus. Each site is PIN activated and password protected. PearsonCMS has been created in collaboration with the higher education community at every stage of its development. Please contact your Allyn & Bacon publisher's representative for more details.

**VIDEO PACKAGE**   A wide variety of videos are available upon adoption of Zimbardo/Weber/Johnson *Psychology*, 3rd Edition. Please contact your local Allyn & Bacon publisher's representative for more information.

**STUDENT STUDY GUIDE**   This study guide, written by Peter Gram of Pensacola Junior College, brings back many of the helpful features of the student guide for the 2nd edition of *Psychology*, along with many updates for the new edition. Features include material on how to do well in the course, page-referenced exploded outlines, key terms and definitions in flash-card format, practice test questions and answers, and experiments and demonstrations.

**PRACTICE TEST BOOKLET**   If students want extra help preparing for exams (and who doesn't?), this booklet provides sample multiple-choice tests, allowing students to practice what they have learned using a simulated classroom quiz. The booklet also includes answers and page references to the text. It is available packaged free with new copies of the Zimbardo/Weber/Johnson textbook.

**2000 INTERNET GUIDE**   Updated to reflect the most current URLs related to the study of psychology, this easy-to-read guide helps point you and your students in the right direction when looking at the tremendous array of information on the Internet as it relates to psychology. The guide is available free, packaged with new copies of the Zimbardo/Weber/Johnson textbook.

**EVALUATING PSYCHOLOGICAL INFORMATION**   The workbook *Sharpening Your Critical Thinking Skills*, 3rd Edition, developed by James Bell, focuses on helping students evaluate psychological research systematically and improving critical thinking skills.

**TOOLS OF CRITICAL THINKING**   This critical thinking text by David A. Levy provides tools and skills for approaching all forms of problem solving, particularly in psychology.

**HANDBOOK FOR PSYCHOLOGY**   This helpful handbook, created by Drew Appleby, provides students with a wide array of information ranging from majoring in psychology to graduate school and job opportunities with a psychology degree.

**HOW TO WRITE PSYCHOLOGY PAPERS, 2nd EDITION**   Les Parrot provides a brief overview for writing APA-style psychology papers, including information on overcoming paper panic, using the Internet, preparing a working reference list, avoiding plagiarism, and using inclusive language.

## A Note of Thanks

Nobody ever realizes the magnitude of the task when taking on a textbook-writing project. This fact was skillfully concealed by our friend and initial editor, Eric Stano, when the book was under the auspices of Addison-Wesley-Longman. As Acquisitions Editor, Eric helped us revise and refine our vision of this book, prodded us incessantly for new ideas, and provided unflagging support. When we moved to Allyn & Bacon, Rebecca Pascal moved with us and took up the cause seamlessly as our new Acquisitions Editor, guide, and advocate. Much thanks to them both.

The vision confronted reality under the guidance of Susan Messer, our Developmental Editor, whose instincts were (we can say now) always right. Susan did the difficult job of making our prose smooth and clear. She always let us know when it was good, and she was masterful at giving helpful and tactful suggestions when it was not.

The job of making the manuscript into a book fell to Joe Sweeney, Senior Editorial-Production Administrator, and Margaret Pinette, our Puckish copyeditor, in whom we met a stickler for style with a great sense of humor. We think they did an outstanding job—as did our tireless photo researcher, the tenacious Sarah Evertson, who had the class and brass to get photos from even the most reluctant of sources.

We are sure that none of the above would be offended if we reserve our deepest thanks for our spouses and closest colleagues. Phil thanks his wonderful wife, Christina Maslach, for her endless inspiration and for modeling what is best in academic psychology. He also acknowledges his appreciation to John Boyd for his constant research and teaching support, as well as to Jackie Wagner, whose passion for life is infectious, and whose dedication to always getting it "right" is so admirable.

Ann thanks her long-suffering spouse, John Quigley, for always and readily encouraging her efforts and assuring her that she's "the best." It will surprise no one who knows her that Ann also thanks her six cats and one perfect dog for their abiding, accepting love and for providing perspective and acceptance, no matter what. She also would like to thank her students and colleagues in the Department of Psychology at UNC Asheville for providing feedback, input, and inspiration of the teaching profession as well as the minutia of composing a book—lessons, examples, gimmicks, and especially ideas and images that don't work and so have to be deleted before the manuscript ever sees the light of publication!

Bob is grateful to his spouse and friend, Michelle, who proofread the rough drafts and made invaluable suggestions before we would let anyone else see them. Most of all, she has been a wellspring of understanding and loving support. His thanks, too, go to Rebecca, their daughter, who taught him the practical side of developmental psychology—and is now, much to her own astonishment, pursuing a graduate degree in psychology.

Many experts and teachers of introductory psychology also shared their constructive criticism with us on every chapter and feature of this text. We acknowledge here our reviewers and hope that they will recognize their valued input in all that is good in *Psychology*, 3rd Edition:

Gordon Allen, Miami University
Beth Barton, Coastal Carolina Community College
Linda Bastone, Purchase College, SUNY
Michael Bloch, University of San Francisco
Susan Beck, Wallace State College
John H. Brennecke, Mount San Antonio College
T. L. Brink, Crafton Hills College
Sally S. Carr, Lakeland Community College
Saundra Ciccarelli, Gulf Coast Community College
Authur Gonchar, University of LaVerne
Peter Gram, Pensacola Junior College
Mary Elizabeth Hannah, University of Detroit
Carol Hayes, Delta State University
Peter Horby, SUNY Plattsburgh
Laurel Krautwurst, Blue Ridge Community College
Judith Levine, SUNY Farmingdale
Margaret Lynch, San Francisco State University
Marc Martin, Palm Beach Community College
Steven Meier, University of Idaho
Yozan Dirk Mosig, University of Nebraska
Melinda Myers-Johnson, Humboldt State University
Michael Nikolakis, Faulkner State College
Faye Plascak-Craig, Marian College
Chris Robin, Madisonville Community College
Christina Sinisi, Charleston Southern University
Mario Sussman, Indiana University of Pennsylvania
John Teske, Elizabethtown College
Robert Wellman, Fitchburg State University

**IF You're Interested**

*If you're interested* in learning more about psychology as you do your course work and read *Psychology*, try to have some confidence and consult your own observations of human behavior. But if you're short on time or want to focus your search, let us recommend some worthwhile reading and viewing. At the end of each chapter in *Psychology*, 3rd Edition, you'll find a short section titled If You're Interested, in which we list our top picks of worthwhile books and rentable videos, both classics and more contemporary works.

If you have recommendations of your own that we should not overlook for the next edition of *Psychology*, please write to us! Address your comments to:

**Dr. Ann Weber**

**Department of Psychology, CPO#1960**

**UNC at Asheville**

**Asheville, NC 28804–8508**

. . . or send e-mail to:

**<weber@unca.edu>**

Thanks for your help–and enjoy pursuing your continuing interest in *Psychology*!

# Psychology

**CORE CONCEPTS**

**PSYCHOLOGY IN YOUR LIFE**

**WHAT IS PSYCHOLOGY, AND WHAT ARE ITS GOALS?**

Psychology is a science that seeks to describe, explain, predict, and control individual behavior and mental processes.

**Psychology as a Major:** If you're thinking about a career in psychology, you have lots of options.

**HOW DO PSYCHOLOGISTS LOOK AT BEHAVIOR AND MENTAL PROCESSES?**

Psychologists draw on six main perspectives: the cognitive, behavioral, psychodynamic, humanistic, biological, and sociocultural.

**The Effects of Your Own Culture:** You may not even notice your own culture. What may be perfectly acceptable behavior for an American might be unthinkable elsewhere.

**HOW DO PSYCHOLOGISTS DO RESEARCH?**

Psychologists, like all other scientists, use the scientific method to test ideas empirically.

**Become a Wiser Research Consumer:** If you can't check it out firsthand, then ask, "What's the evidence?"

**USING PSYCHOLOGY TO LEARN PSYCHOLOGY: STUDYING WITH THE KEY QUESTIONS AND CORE CONCEPTS**

# 1

# Mind, Behavior, & Science

*C*an a fourth grader be a scientist? Meet Emily Rosa of Loveland, Colorado, whose experimental results not only challenge the widely held belief in the power of therapeutic touch (TT), but made her the youngest author of a published article in the prestigious Journal of the American Medical Association (JAMA).

Emily describes her project this way: "I became interested in testing therapeutic touch because I really didn't know if nurses who do therapeutic touch were telling the truth about their ability to feel the human energy field. One day my mother, who is a nurse, was watching a video on nurses who practice therapeutic touch, and I wanted to find out for myself if they could really do it. . . . I also needed to think of an experiment for my science fair at school, and that was it" (Web site: Scientific American Frontiers, Ask the Scientists). Emily suspected that the nurses were really detecting their own beliefs and expectations, rather than the "human energy field."

Tens of thousands of TT practitioners claim that by moving their hands over a person's body without directly touching it, they can detect and manipulate the energy field that radiates from it. These health-care professionals claim that they can use TT to treat a wide range of medical and psychological problems from colic to cancer and arthritis to depression (Gorman, 1999). The technique is taught in more than 100 colleges and universities in 75 countries and used by nurses in at least 80 U.S. hospitals.

What Emily did was put their claims to a simple experimental test: Could TT practitioners accurately detect the presence of her hand when it was placed above one of their hands but out of sight? Emily predicted that they could not. To test her prediction, she invited each of 21 TT practitioners (varying in experience from one to 27 years) to determine which of their two hands (stuck through a screen palms up) was closest to one of hers (palm down a few inches from either of their hands). By a coin flip, Emily randomized the order of presenting her hand above either of the practitioners' hands. The test subjects' task was to say whether they felt energy from the girl's hand above their left or right hand. Emily knew that, just by guessing, nurses could be right 50 percent of the time. So, her subjects would have to perform significantly above the chance level to validate the claim that they can detect a "human energy field." But they did not; they were correct only 44% of the time (123

In her laboratory, psychologist Mary Ainsworth observes and records a child's behavior.

*of 280 trials). Length of experience slightly improved their score, but the effect was not significant (Rosa, Rosa, Sarner, & Barrett, 1998).*

*Some critics remain unconvinced by Rosa's results. They claim that TT depends on the transfer of emotional energy during a medical crisis, and because Emily was not sick she did not have disturbances in her energy field that could be detected by TT practitioners. However, Emily's curiosity and her use of the scientific method to probe the most basic claim of TT practitioners—that they can detect a person's energy field—surely raises doubt about their more elaborate treatment claims.*

*Emily's research earned her a check of $1,000.00 from the Skeptics Society and a plaque from The Guinness Book of Records editors for being the youngest researcher to have a paper published in a major medical journal. We, too, applaud her achievement, and we use her experiment to introduce you to psychological science for several reasons. First, we want to illustrate that some firmly entrenched beliefs and practices, such as TT, may be wrong or ineffective and thus cost people who blindly follow them money, time, and better treatment. Second, we want to reveal how open-minded skepticism and curiosity are at the core of the scientific enterprise in physical as well as social sciences. Finally, we want to inspire you to think critically when you encounter a seductive claim about how people think, feel, and act. Don't accept without question anything you hear, see, or read—even in this book!*

Emily Rosa has the mind-set of a good psychologist: curious, interested in human behavior and mental processes—and just a bit skeptical. "Show me," her experiment says. This is exactly the motto that will guide us on the journey through psychology that we begin in this chapter.

In a certain sense, everyone is a psychologist. That is, everyone studies people, analyzes their behavior, tries to understand what they are thinking and feeling, and attempts to predict what they will do next. But the difference between the casual, common-sense psychology of everyday life and the psychology you will learn about in this book lies in the "show me" approach. For the psychological scientist, as for Emily Rosa, common sense may be a good starting point, but it is not enough. A more reliable understanding requires objective evidence gained through observation and measurement. That is why **psychology,** at its core, is a *science*: the science of individual behavior and mental processes.

What psychological science has found may amaze you—as when you read of the discoveries made by researchers who study sleep and dreaming or the lessons learned from observing a railroad worker who survived a steel rod being blasted through his brain. Sometimes, when psychological science confirms what you had already suspected to be true about the mind and behavior, it will reassure you. And sometimes, especially when it contradicts long-held beliefs about, for example, the unconscious mind, IQ tests, or sexual orientation, it will perplex you. Always, it will be fascinating. Let us begin our journey through this challenging terrain with a broad sketch of what psychology is and what its goals are.

**Chapter 2
Biopsychology**

*Phineas Gage survived—but with major changes in his personality—after a steel rod pierced his frontal lobe.*

**KEY QUESTION** **WHAT IS PSYCHOLOGY, AND WHAT ARE ITS GOALS?**

Psychology is many things. People are drawn to it because they want to learn what psychologists have discovered about human problems, such as violence, addiction, prejudice, or mental disorder. Others turn to psychology for insights that can help them deal with stressful situations or deteriorating relationships. Still others simply find human behavior fascinating. In fact, psychology is a field brimming with hot topics: the unconscious, split brains, hypnosis, love, stress, sleep and dreaming, sexuality, drugs, creativity, intelligence, and child development. But psychology is much more than this.

**Psychology:** The science of individual behavior and mental processes.

Psychology is also about the components and processes that make up mind and behavior. It's about the brain. It's about how we sense and interpret the world. It's about learning, memory, and thinking. It's about motivation, emotion, stress, and personality. And it is about social interaction. But there is even more. . . .

As the *science* of behavior and mind, psychology gives us objective methods for checking our hunches and our common sense. Emily Rosa used some of these methods to test her suspicions about therapeutic touch. You may want to put some of your own ideas about mind and behavior under the light of science by taking our "Psychological Common-Sense Test" (see Do It Yourself, page 6).

In every chapter of this book, each major section is organized around a brief statement that captures the central idea of that section. We call these "Core Concepts." Your authors intend that these concepts will form the core around which you can organize the details of the chapter in your mind. They are based on the sound psychological principle that information is much easier to remember when it forms a meaningful pattern in memory. With this idea in mind, then, let us state the first Core Concept of this chapter:

 **CORE CONCEPT**   **Psychology is a science that seeks to describe, explain, predict, and control individual behavior and mental processes.**

We have already seen that psychology has a scientific basis, and we will return to that theme later in the chapter, when we take a detailed look at how psychologists do research. For now, let us concentrate on the four goals listed in our Core Concept. We will conclude this section by considering how these goals make psychology different from other disciplines that also study behavior and mental processes and what psychology as a major can offer you.

## The Four Goals of Psychology

What is it that psychologists hope to accomplish with their study of mind and behavior? Simply put, they have four goals: to describe, explain, predict, and control behavior and mental processes. Each of these requires some explanation.

**DESCRIBING WHAT HAPPENS**   You take the first step in understanding a psychological process by *describing* it as precisely and objectively as possible. Consider *love*. We could begin to construct a description of love by identifying exactly what we mean when we use this term: Can we define it in terms of objective, observable behaviors? Social psychologist Zick Rubin says that many objective behaviors signify love. For example, one way to tell when two people are in love is to measure how much time they spend looking into each other's eyes (Rubin, 1973). Lovers, he has observed, spend much more time gazing at each other than do mere acquaintances. Such a *behavioral* description of an otherwise fuzzy concept, like love, is an **operational definition.** Observations made of these behaviors become the "facts" of psychology, known as **data.** Our data on love, then, might show exactly how much time each couple in our study spends making eye contact.

In general, an operational definition of a concept defines how that concept is measured or what operations (procedures) will produce it. So, an operational definition of an A grade in one class may be "earning at least 90% of all possible test points." This definition tells you that the instructor adds the points each student earns and then calculates the percentage that represents all points possible—that is, the definition tells you the operation used to determine a particular grade. In Emily Rosa's study, the operation used to measure therapeutic touch involved subjects attempting to detect the location of the experimenter's hand.

Operational definitions are especially important in psychological research because many of psychology's terms are also words used in everyday language, and they

**Operational definition:** A definition of a concept stated in terms of how the concept is measured or what operations are used to produce it.

**Data:** Information, especially information gathered by a researcher to be used in testing a hypothesis. (Singular: *datum.*)

## Psychological Common-Sense Test

Indicate whether you think each of the items below is true or false. The answers are at the end, along with the chapter in which the scientific evidence relating to that item is discussed in more detail.

———— 1. Your brain makes a painkiller similar to heroin.

———— 2. Some unscrupulous merchants persuade their customers to buy merchandise by means of subliminal messages embedded in background music.

———— 3. What we call *colors*, *sounds*, *tastes*, *smells*, and *textures* exist only in our brains, not in the outside world.

———— 4. We are likely to forget ("repress") memories of experiences that make us anxious or events that were painful. These repressed memories then lurk in our unconscious minds and affect our thoughts and behavior beneath the level of our awareness.

———— 5. Nearly everyone dreams several times each night.

———— 6. Intelligence is a genetic trait that is fixed at the same level throughout a person's life.

———— 7. Damage to certain parts of your brain could prevent you from remembering any event that happens to you during the rest of your life.

———— 8. A good attitude can cure anything, even cancer.

———— 9. For people suffering from depression, psychotherapy can be just as effective as medications such as Prozac.

———— 10. Polygraph ("lie detector") machines are remarkably accurate in detecting physical responses that indicate when a suspect is lying.

*Answers:* All the odd-numbered items are true; the even-numbered items are false. The icons in the margin indicate the chapters in which each of these items is discussed further:

1. True: These chemicals are called *endorphins*. *(See Chapter 2.)*

2. False: There is no evidence that stimuli you cannot consciously detect can influence what you buy. *(See Chapter 5.)*

3. True: Strange as it may seem, these sensations are created entirely in our brains—although our brains are prompted to do so by stimuli from the outside world. *(See Chapter 5.)*

4. False: There is no solid, objective evidence that we repress painful memories. In fact, we are more likely to remember unpleasant events than those that do not provoke strong emotional reactions. *(See Chapter 6.)*

5. True: Most of us dream four to six times a night, although we often do not remember our dreams. *(See Chapter 3.)*

6. False: Intelligence is the result of both heredity and environment. Because it depends, in part, on environment, intelligence can change throughout our lifetimes. *(See Chapter 11.)*

7. True: This happened in the famous case of H. M., who now lives in the present moment, with recollections only of a past that ended nearly 50 years ago. *(See Chapter 6.)*

8. False: Although many people believe this, there is evidence to suggest that this is simply not true. We will also see that it may be a dangerous belief to harbor. *(See Chapter 9.)*

9. True: Psychotherapy has proved to be just as effective as medication—and sometimes better—for treating depression and many other disorders. *(See Chapter 9.)*

10. False: Even the most expert polygrapher can incorrectly classify a truth-teller as a liar or fail to identify someone who is lying. Objective evidence supporting the accuracy of lie detectors is conspicuously lacking. *(See Chapter 14.)*

lack scientific precision. For example, if a new drug promises to reduce "anxiety," what does that mean? The drug manufacturer's definition of anxiety may differ from yours. For you, anxiety could mean a cold sweat and a feeling of nervousness before a test. But for the pharmaceutical company's researchers, anxiety could refer to a hyperactive behavior observed among patients in psychiatric hospitals. A drug developed to reduce that kind of anxiety might not be appropriate for treating what you call anxiety. You and the drug company have different operational definitions.

Love and anxiety are much more than any of these operational definitions, you say? Of course they are—and those who study these psychological phenomena know that. But what they have chosen to do in their research is to study a small piece of a much larger concept. The idea is that when enough pieces of the larger puzzle have been found, the big picture will become clear. Here is the trade-off: What they lose in scope, they gain in precision and objectivity. That is the nature of scientific research.

**EXPLAINING WHAT HAPPENS**   The data can *describe* love or anxiety (or some other psychological process of interest), but by themselves they *explain* nothing. To achieve the second of psychology's goals—explanation—the psychologist must *interpret* the data. In Rubin's study of love, for example, this means explaining why people would want to spend a lot of time gazing into each other's eyes. This explanation is termed a **theory** (Kerlinger, 1985). Theories provide explanations for patterns observed or predicted in the data. For example, we might explain the prolonged eye contact of lovers with a *reward theory*—that is, an explanation stating that people spend more time looking at things they find rewarding than they do at things that don't offer them rewards. Thus, a reward theory of love suggests that people are attracted to each other (and gaze at each other) because they receive rewards from each other, such as gifts, attention, sexual favors, or social status (Aronson, 1995).

Chapter 12
**Social Psychology**
*Sometimes, however, people are attracted to relationships in which there are no rewards.*

Sometimes a psychological theory goes a step farther, by making an *inference*—a logical or reasonable judgment not based on direct observation—about a process that is happening inside an animal or human being. In the therapeutic touch study, for example, Emily Rosa's theory was that her subjects were responding to their own expectations, rather than detecting an external energy field. Such an inference often helps make the observed behavior more understandable. Rubin also made an inference when he suggested that prolonged eye contact signifies an internal condition called "love." To give another example, if your cat meows and paws at your ankles, and you notice that her food dish is empty, you may make an inference: "She must be hungry. No wonder she was trying to get my attention!" In this case, "hunger" is an inner state that cannot be directly observed.

Reward theory says we like people who reward us.

The inner states that psychologists make inferences about are often called *intervening variables*. **Intervening variables** are inner, unseen conditions that are assumed to link the observable stimulus and the individual's response. Examples of intervening variables include emotions such as love and anger and motives such as hunger. You cannot directly see love, anger, or hunger, but you can often observe the stimulus triggers, and you can measure the behavioral results. So, for example, if Joey insults Tommy, who hits Joey in return, we might suspect that anger was the intervening variable:

| *Stimulus* | *Intervening Variable* | *Response* |
|---|---|---|
| Insult $\longrightarrow$ | Anger $\longrightarrow$ | Hitting |

A word of caution: Take care in using the term *theory*. In everyday language, people often use the word *theory* to mean an unverified idea—an idea that has no

**Theory:** A body of interrelated principles used to explain or predict some psychological phenomenon.

**Intervening variables:** Inner, unseen conditions that are assumed to function as the links between the observable stimulus and the individual's response.

evidence to support it. "It's only a theory," we say. This is not the sense in which scientists use the term, however. In science, a theory is a testable explanation for a set of observations (Kukla, 1989). Some scientific theories have a great deal of evidence to support them, while others are highly speculative. Examples of well-supported theories include Einstein's theory of gravitation, the germ theory of disease, Darwin's theory of natural selection, and, in psychology, Pavlov's theory of classical conditioning, a common form of learning.

**Chapter 6**
**Learning and Remembering**
*Classical conditioning explains how fears and phobias can be learned.*

**PREDICTING WHAT WILL HAPPEN**   One of the best tests of a psychological theory lies in its ability to go beyond explanation to *predict* behavior—the third of psychology's goals. Thus, if you have a theory of attraction that can predict accurately who will fall in love with whom, it will be quite persuasive to other scientists. But no matter how successful it is, your theory would never be completely *proved*—because scientific theories are always tentative and subject to change. Even the most well-supported theories are never considered final, never accepted as absolute. It is always possible that you will find people whose attraction to each other does not fit your theory, suggesting that the theory needs to be modified or replaced.

Everyday life also requires predictions. For example, when you go to the dentist for a toothache, you are predicting that the dentist can stop the pain. In general, we need to predict what will happen in the future because our well-being and even our survival depend on making accurate judgments about situations that could be either dangerous or favorable. By contrast, making a scientific prediction is a more rigorous process, seeking to identify relationships between events, links between events and predictors, and signs of future occurrences. Scientific predictions must be worded precisely, communicated to other scientists, tested—and perhaps disconfirmed if the evidence fails to support them. In the TT experiment, Emily Rosa predicted that her subjects could not detect which hand she was holding her own hand near.

A common form of prediction starts with the assumption that a person's past actions are a good indicator of his or her future behavior. If you are not familiar with an individual's past record, you might consider the past behavior of similar people who were in the same situation. This is called a *base rate* prediction. A **base rate** is a statistic that identifies the normal frequency, or probability, of a given event. For example, automobile insurance companies use base-rate data about accidents to compute premiums. These data are intended to predict the likelihood of accidents in certain groups—such as males more than females and adolescents more than middle-aged drivers. Similarly, a psychologist studying depression might want to know the base rate of depression in males versus females or in certain age groups in order to pinpoint possible causes of depression.

**CONTROLLING WHAT HAPPENS**   The psychologist's fourth goal, *control,* sometimes frightens people, especially those who are wary of science and technology (Smith, 1992; Kipnis, 1987). Merely mentioning control raises the specter of manipulation, "brainwashing," and Orwell's novel, *1984,* in which the every move of the entire population was controlled and monitored by the government. Yet, there are several reasons why you need not be unduly alarmed about this goal, as envisioned by psychologists. For one thing, "control" can be interpreted in a positive sense: helping people to gain control over their own thoughts and behavior (e.g., nonassertive people, violent people, suicidal people, mentally retarded people, frightened people). In fact, gaining self-control is a common goal in counseling and psychotherapy. Another reason that softens the threat of psychological control lies in the fact that psychology is public knowledge: Psychologists publish their findings. They have no secret tricks for controlling people; everything known to psychology is available in the library and on the Internet. Third, learning about psychology can help you understand how other people (e.g., advertisers, politicians, lawyers, or even a potential lover) might try to influence your behavior. A knowledge of psychology

**Base rate:** A statistic that identifies the normal frequency, or probability, of a given event or process.

provides effective weapons to combat unwelcome attempts at manipulation and control. We also gain control in our lives when we discover—as in the TT experiment—that a widely used treatment has no basis in fact.

We should pause here to note that how we understand the term *control* depends on the culture in which we were raised. For example, Weisz, Rothbaum, and Blackburn (1984) have noted the contrasting meanings of control in the Japanese and American cultures. They point out that Americans generally think of control as dominance, assertiveness, or even aggression intended to effect change—controlling other people. On the other hand, the Japanese concept of control refers to finding ways to control oneself—one's own response to existing realities that cannot be changed. Throughout this book we will return to this theme of the cultural context, because culture is often a variable that affects how people think, feel, and act.

Psychology's goal of control involves helping people to learn how to control themselves.

PSYCHOLOGY IN YOUR LIFE

## Psychology as a Major

Most students taking an introductory psychology course have an interest in human behavior and mental processes. Many are considering psychology as a possible major. Let's see what it takes to become a psychologist, what kinds of psychologists there are, and how the four goals we have discussed above make psychology different from other disciplines that focus on behavior and/or mental processes.

WHAT IT TAKES TO BECOME A PSYCHOLOGIST   Being a psychologist requires graduate training. Psychologists typically hold master's or doctor's degrees, usually a PhD (Doctor of Philosophy), or in some cases an EdD (Doctor of Education) or a PsyD (Doctor of Psychology). In graduate school—after receiving a bachelor's degree—a psychology student takes advanced classes in one or more specialized areas and develops skills as a scholar, researcher, and perhaps as a practitioner.

Don't expect a psychologist to write a prescription, however. Although doctoral-level psychologists and physicians spend approximately the same amount of time in graduate school (about four to six years beyond the bachelor's degree), most psychologists have no medical training. Therefore, they cannot prescribe drugs or perform medical procedures. Their expertise lies elsewhere, in their broad understanding of behavior and mental processes. This distinction between psychology and medicine may soon become blurred, however. Some psychologists are calling for prescription privileges to be extended to psychologists with special training. A few psychologists are taking advantage of nurse-practitioner programs, which will earn them prescription privileges. And the U.S. Navy has begun a small program in which some of its psychologists are being trained to prescribe drugs for mental disorders (see Hayes & Heiby, 1996).

Satisfying careers are available at various levels of education in psychology. In most states, licensure as a psychologist requires a graduate degree, usually a doctorate, in some field of psychology. Most university teaching or research jobs also require a doctorate, although a master's degree, typically requiring two years of study beyond the bachelor's level, may qualify you for employment as a psychology instructor at the college or high school level or as an applied psychologist in certain specialties, such as counseling. Master's-level psychologists are common in human service agencies, as well as in private practice (although many states do not allow them to advertise themselves as "psychologists"). In addition, many practitioners with master's degrees in the related field of social work offer therapy for emotional problems. Those holding associate degrees and bachelor's degrees in psychology or related human services fields may find jobs as psychological aides and technicians in agencies, hospitals, nursing homes, and rehabilitation centers. A bachelor's degree in psychology, coupled with training in business or education, can also lead to interesting careers in personnel management or education.

If you would like further information about job prospects and salary levels for psychologists, the U.S. Department of Labor's *Occupational Outlook Handbook* is a good place to look. Your college's career or counseling center undoubtedly has a copy.

PSYCHOLOGICAL SPECIALTIES   Special fields of concentration within psychology provide students with an opportunity to study an area of interest in depth. Students
*Continued*

who decide to major in psychology can choose among many specialties and work settings, although they need be in no hurry to decide because intensive specialized study is usually reserved for graduate school. (See Figure 1.1). We will look at a sample of possibilities, drawn from two major categories: *experimental psychology* and *applied psychology*.

**Experimental psychologists** do research on psychological processes, usually at colleges and universities, where they typically also teach. A few are employed by private industry or the government. Research done by experimental psychologists has generated most of the scientific knowledge base for the field—knowledge used by experimental psychologists and applied psychologists alike. Most of the material you study in this book will involve discoveries made by experimental psychologists.

**Applied psychologists** use the knowledge developed by experimental psychologists to tackle human problems, such as training, equipment design, and psychological treatment, in a wide variety of places such as schools, clinics, factories, homes, airports, highways, hospitals, and even casinos. Applied psychology covers everything except **basic research,** which focuses on interesting psychological

**FIGURE 1.1:** Work Settings of Psychologists

Shown are percentages of psychologists working in particular settings, according to a survey of American Psychological Association (APA) members holding doctorate degrees in psychology.

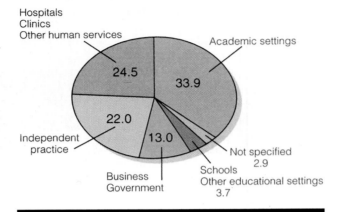

processes, but with no practical application in mind. All told, some 64% of the doctoral-level psychologists in the United States work primarily as applied psychologists, and that percentage has been steadily increasing since the 1950s (Rosenzweig, 1992; Stapp, Tucker, & VandenBos, 1985). Although applied psychologists may do research, their focus is typically different from their experimental colleagues. **Applied research** deals with practical problems. Some of the many specialties under the applied psychology

heading include *clinical and counseling psychology, industrial and organizational psychology, engineering psychology, school psychology,* and *rehabilitation psychology.*

- **Clinical psychologists** and **counseling psychologists** work with people who have problems with social and emotional adjustment or those who face difficult choices in marriages, careers, or education. Nearly half of all doctoral-level psychologists list clinical or counseling psychology as their specialty (American Psychological Association, 1996). The clinician is more likely to have a private practice involving psychological testing and long-term therapy, while the counselor is more likely to work for an agency or school and to spend fewer sessions with each client. (*See Chapter 14, Therapies for Mental Disorder.*)
- **Industrial and organizational psychologists** (often called *I/O psychologists*) specialize in modifying the work environment to maximize productivity and morale. Some I/O psychologists develop interview and testing procedures to help organizations select new employees. Some develop programs to train and retain employees. Other I/O psychologists specialize in market research.
- **Engineering psychologists** often design equipment, such as airplane instrument panels or computers, for easy and reliable human use. Or they may do psychological detective work to discover what went wrong in accidents attributed to "human error." Engineering psychologists usually work for private industry or the government on a team with other scientists.
- **School psychologists** have expertise in the problems of teaching and learning. Typically, they work for a school district, where they diagnose learning and behavior problems and consult with teachers, students, and parents. School psychologists may spend a good deal of time administering, scoring, and interpreting psychological tests.
- **Rehabilitation psychologists** serve with physicians, nurses, and social workers on teams that may treat patients with physical disorders, such as stroke, spinal

**Experimental psychologists:** Psychologists who do research on basic psychological processes—as contrasted with *applied* psychologists.

**Applied psychologists:** Psychologists who use the knowledge developed by experimental psychologists to solve human problems.

**Basic research:** Studies that focus on some process or phenomenon of interest to the researcher but with no practical application in mind.

**Applied research:** Research aimed at finding solutions to practical problems.

**Clinical psychologists:** Psychological practitioners who specialize in the treatment of mental disorders.

**Counseling psychologists:** Psychological practitioners who help people deal with a variety of problems, including relationships and vocational choice.

Counseling psychologists are less likely than clinical psychologists to do long-term therapy with persons having severe mental disorders.

**Industrial and organizational psychologists:** Applied psychologists who specialize in modifying the work environment to maximize productivity and morale. They are often called *I/O psychologists.*

**Engineering psychologists:** Applied psychologists who specialize in making objects and environments easier, more efficient, or more comfortable for people to use.

**School psychologists:** Applied psychologists with expertise in the problems of teaching and learning.

**Rehabilitation psychologists:** Applied psychologists who treat patients with physical disorders.

cord injury, alco-
holism, drug abuse, or
amputation. Some
work in a hospital set-
ting. Others work for
social service agencies
and for sheltered work-
shops that provide job
training for people
with disabilities.

A good source of further
information on the variety
of career possibilities in
psychology can be found
in *Psychology: Careers for
the Twenty-First Century*,
published by the Ameri-
can Psychological Associ-
ation (1996).

An engineering psychologist designs a "pilot-friendly" airplane instrument panel.

Thus, all the social sci-
ences share one or more
of psychology's goals: to
describe, explain, predict,
and control behavior and
mental processes. Psy-
chology, however, offers a
unique combination of
breadth of interest and a
focus on the individual.
Further, psychology is not
limited to people: It in-
cludes the study of animal
behavior, as well. But, because each of the social
sciences makes its own
contribution to our
knowledge, we suggest
that students who aspire
to become psychologists
should broaden their out-
look by taking some course work in each
of the social sciences.

### PSYCHOLOGY'S RELATION TO OTHER DISCIPLINES

While your au-
thors admit to some bias in favor of psychology (was it obvious?), we must quickly
tell you that each discipline that studies
people has its own emphasis and its own
unique contribution to make to our understanding. Among the *social sciences* that
study human behavior and mental
processes are the following:

- *Sociology* emphasizes the ways that social forces affect *groups* of people. For
example, sociologists study religious
groups, divorce rates, and causes of
poverty. Yet, no distinct boundary separates psychology from sociology; the
two meet in the specialty of *social psychology*, which looks at the interaction
of the individual with the group. (*See
Chapter 12, Social Psychology.*)
- *Anthropology* comes in two forms. One
involves the study of fossils and arti-
facts to solve the puzzles of human origins and ancient cultures, while the
other specializes in describing and
comparing existing cultures by observing and recording what people do. One
of the main lessons of anthropology
teaches us that culture can powerfully
influence behavior, as we saw in our
discussion of "control" above. Psychologists have noticed this work, and
*cross-cultural psychologists* have begun a
reexamination of psychology's database
to see which of its findings may have
universal validity and which may be
culture specific.
- *Economics* aims to describe, explain,
predict, and control human behavior in

the narrow, but important, realm of
production and consumption of goods,
services, money, credit, and capital. Recently psychologists have raised
provocative questions about the econo-
mists' assumption that people are rational decision-makers (Argyris, 1987;
Kirby & Hernstein, 1995; Staddon,
1992). Research clearly shows that
people sometimes make decisions based
largely on feelings and emotions, especially when they are choosing among
risky alternatives. It might be interesting to ask your economics professor
what impact this research has had on
the field of economics. (*See Chapter 7,
Cognitive Processes.*)
- *Political science* is the study of the ways
that people use power and control, especially in government. Why, political
scientists ask, do some political groups
thrive and others not? They also look
for the assumptions about human nature made by different forms of government, such as capitalistic democracy,
communism, and socialism. Political
scientists and psychologists have common interests in the study of motivation, persuasion, and leadership.
- *History* is a chronicle of human behavior that traditionally emphasizes the description and explanation of politics,
conquest, and discovery. Some historians view history as a social science,
while some see it as one of the humanities, more akin to literature and philosophy. The difference seems to be in
whether or not the historian emphasizes
a scientific analysis of historical data.

Medicine, too, has its specialties that
deal with understanding behavior and
mental processes—and therefore overlap
with the interests of psychology. We will
focus here on *psychiatry* and *psychoanalysis*:

- All **psychiatrists** have MD (Doctor of
Medicine) degrees plus specialized
training in treating mental and behavioral problems. Therefore, psychiatrists
can prescribe medicine and perform
other medical procedures. As you might
expect, the psychiatrist views patients
primarily from a medical or biological
perspective. Sometimes, however, the
public confuses psychiatry with *clinical
psychology*, because both professions
treat people having the same disorders
(Benjamin, 1986). Psychologists like to
point out that psychiatric training devotes relatively little time to important
psychological topics, such as perception, learning, psychological testing, developmental psychology, and social
psychology, in favor of a medical emphasis on mental "illnesses." (*See Chapter 14, Therapies for Mental Disorder.*)
- Most **psychoanalysts** train first as
physicians and then as psychiatrists.

**Psychiatrists:** Physicians who specialize in the treatment of mental
disorders.

**Psychoanalysts:** Specialists (usually psychiatrists) who use Freudian
methods of treating mental
disorders.

*Continued*

(Psychoanalytic training institutes also accept psychologists and social workers with doctorates, but the majority of those trained in psychoanalysis are MDs.) Finally, in their psychoanalytic training, they learn a particular "brand" of therapy based on the ideas of Sigmund Freud. With the lengthy Freudian method, an analyst directs the patient to relax and talk freely about dreams and fantasies, which the analyst interprets as reflections of unconscious problems. (*See Chapter 10, Personality.*)

From this description you can see that psychology, psychiatry, and psychoanalysis share a common interest in mental disorders and therapy. What makes psychology unique, however, lies in its broad range of concerns that have no overlap with the interests of psychiatry and psychoanalysis: Psychology is the study of *all* of the individual's behavior—not just of abnormality or mental illness.

As broad as psychology is, however, it is well to keep in mind that no single discipline has the whole truth about behavior and mental processes. Each has made valuable contributions to our knowledge. But your authors hope that you will agree that psychology is the most fascinating of them all.

## Check Your Understanding

1. **APPLICATION:** *Which of the following could be an operational definition of "fear"?*
   a. an intense feeling of terror and dread when thinking about some situation
   b. panic
   c. a desire to avoid something
   d. moving away from a stimulus

2. **RECALL:** *A theory is*
   a. an unsupported opinion.
   b. an interpretation of observational data.
   c. the opposite of a fact.
   d. a statement that has not yet been supported with facts.

3. **APPLICATION:** *In order to know whether depression is becoming more of a problem for people in the United States, you would need to know the _____ of depression.*
   a. base rate
   b. theory
   c. intervening variables
   d. cause

4. **RECALL:** *Psychologists are not allowed by law to*
   a. do psychotherapy with mentally disturbed individuals.
   b. prescribe medicine.

   c. call themselves "doctor."
   d. do basic research.

5. **RECALL:** *Which one would be considered an applied psychologist?*
   a. an I/O psychologist
   b. a psychologist doing basic research
   c. a professor of psychology at the university
   d. a psychiatrist

6. **UNDERSTANDING THE CORE CONCEPT:** *One of the main differences between psychology and the other social sciences is that psychology*
   a. aims to learn how to describe, explain, predict, and control behavior and mental processes.
   b. has a focus on the individual.
   c. is scientific.
   d. is primarily interested in mental disorders.

**ANSWERS:**   1. d   2. b   3. a   4. b   5. a   6. b

**KEY QUESTION**

## HOW DO PSYCHOLOGISTS LOOK AT BEHAVIOR AND MENTAL PROCESSES?

"Psychology has a long past, but only a short history," wrote one of the first experimental psychologists, Hermann Ebbinghaus (1908). While the formal start of modern psychology as a science can be traced to slightly over a century ago (quite recently in terms of human history), scholars and thinkers have long asked important questions about the nature of consciousness, how people perceive reality, and the origins of madness.

In 1879, Wilhelm Wundt (1832–1920) founded the first formal laboratory devoted to experimental psychology. He's shown here (center) in his laboratory in Leipzig in 1912.

In the fifth and fourth centuries B.C., the classical Greek philosophers Socrates, Plato, and Aristotle began puzzling over the workings of the mind. In the Middle Ages, however, this inquiry was squelched, as theologians taught that the mind and soul had free will and operated completely outside the natural laws that determined the actions of physical bodies and nonhuman creatures. In the Western world no scientific psychology was possible until this assumption finally was challenged in the seventeenth century, when the French philosopher René Descartes asserted that our sensations and responses were linked to activity in the nervous system.

The formal beginning of psychology as a modern science, however, did not come until 1879, when the German scientist Wilhelm Wundt (probably the first person to refer to himself as a "psychologist") founded the first laboratory devoted to experimental psychology. Soon, the idea of the new discipline of psychology spread across the Atlantic, where a young Harvard philosophy professor who had studied medicine and had strong interests in literature and religion developed a uniquely American psychological perspective. To summarize his views, William James wrote a two-volume work, *The Principles of Psychology* (1890), which many consider to be the first and most important psychology text ever written.

From these beginnings, the Western world (that is, Europe and North America) witnessed an explosion of new psychological ideas and applications. But, as we look closely, we will see that it has been an orderly explosion. Modern concepts of thought and behavior have formed around six often-competing psychological perspectives that trace their roots back to the differing viewpoints of psychology's founders. Our next Core Concept puts it this way:

 **CONCEPT**

**Psychologists draw on six main perspectives: the cognitive, behavioral, psychodynamic, humanistic, biological, and sociocultural.**

Throughout this book we will frequently encounter these six perspectives, as we look to them for help in understanding learning, thinking, motivation, perception, and the other components of modern psychology. Proponents of each of the six perspectives

## FIGURE 1.2: The Necker Cube

Look at the cube for a few moments, and you will suddenly see that your perspective changes (see text).

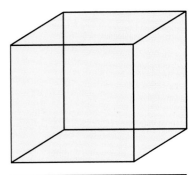

see behavior and mental processes in a different way—much like six painters portraying the same scene from different vantage points.

Students often wonder why we can't decide which of the six perspectives is the correct one. To help you understand why multiple perspectives are necessary in this field, it may be helpful for you to think of psychology as being something like the famous Necker cube (Figure 1.2): If you look at the cube for a few moments, you will find that you can see it from different perspectives—from above and to the right or from the lower left. (If you don't see this shift in perspectives, you may need to look for several minutes.) In fact, only by seeing it from multiple perspectives can you get the "true" and complete picture of the cube—the understanding that it is not just a two-dimensional drawing, but an object that presents a different face when seen from different viewpoints. Similarly, a complete view of psychology requires seeing behavior and mental processes from multiple viewpoints. Let's illustrate this concept with a real-life example.

### The Six Modern Perspectives in Psychology

One spring morning, on the day after he was suspended for having a firearm at school, 15-year-old Kip Kinkel fired more than 50 bullets into a group of 400 seniors attending a breakfast meeting at the Thurston High School cafeteria in Springfield, Oregon (Thill, 1998). Kinkel was quickly disarmed by a fellow student, who was wounded in the process. But the carnage left two students dead and 23 injured. And these weren't his only victims. When police searched his home, they found Kinkel's parents—dead—and a house booby-trapped with explosives.

Sadly, the Kinkel case was far from the first of its kind. And the more recent tragedy at Colombine High School in Littleton, Colorado, showed that it was not the last. A rash of schoolhouse shootings has been part of a rising tide of violence among youth (Nemecek, 1998; Sleek, 1998). In the past decade, homicides and suicides among teens have doubled. Yet, reports that overall violent crime had taken a downturn in the 1990s prevented most people from noticing that violent crime among youth had taken an unprecedented upturn, particularly in rural and suburban areas. Indeed, incidents of

Kip Kinkel confessed to a shooting spree at his high school in Springfield, Oregon.

school-related homicide have occurred in Arkansas, Florida, Kansas, Kentucky, Missouri, Oregon, Pennsylvania, South Carolina, Tennessee, Washington D.C., Washington state, and Colorado.

So, what has caused this deadly rampage? There was probably not a single cause. Even though many people seek simplistic answers, one of the great lessons of psychology's six perspectives is that complex problems usually have multiple causes. "One of the most frustrating things to me," says Jeff Sprague, codirector of the University of Oregon's Institute on Violence and Destructive Behavior, "is that everybody has a single solution—it's TV, it's our society, it's guns, or it's not guns. That single-solution kind of thinking makes me crazy" (Thill, 1998). Insisting on a single cause can blind us to other influences that may be at work. Also, different combinations of forces may cause different individuals to turn violent. Psychology, with its multiple perspectives, can help us look for a variety of possible causes. Let's begin with the perspective of biological psychology.

**THE BIOLOGICAL VIEW**    In general, the **biological view** in psychology searches for the causes of behavior in the functioning of genes, the brain and nervous system, and the endocrine (hormone) system. The biological approach would suggest examining Kip Kinkel and other violent individuals for signs of physical disorder in the brain and hormone system. Could Kinkel's behavior have been influenced by high levels of the "male hormone" testosterone, which has been associated with violence? Alternatively, could he, like the sniper who shot 14 people from the tower at the University of Texas three decades earlier, have a brain tumor that might have contributed to his aggression? In laboratory studies of aggression, abnormal activity in a brain structure called the amygdala has been associated with violent behavior in animals. At this point, however, we should note that no neurological evidence of brain disorder has come to light in the Kinkel case.

Chapter 2
Biopsychology
*The amygdala, a part of the limbic system, is involved in aggressive responses.*

As you might imagine, the biological view has strong roots in medicine and biological science. This approach makes three assumptions:

1. Psychological processes can be understood in terms of brain function and biochemical activity.
2. Behavior and mental processes can be modified by altering the underlying biology.
3. All behavior and mental processes, in the final analysis, are *determined* by their biological underpinnings.

This last assumption suggests that physical factors are the sole causes of our behavior and mental processes, an idea that we should examine more closely.

*DETERMINISM*    Biological psychology holds to the doctrine of **determinism,** the notion that physical, behavioral, and mental events are determined by specific causes, much as the motion of a ball across a pool table is determined by the forces acting on it. From this viewpoint, your behavior is completely accounted for by an interaction of your genetic tendencies and your experience. In general, determinism is essential to science because it assumes that physical reality can be completely understood in terms of natural forces involving matter and energy. Determinism says that there are no magical or miraculous forces that have physical effects on us. In its most extreme interpretation, "hard" determinism holds that behavior cannot be controlled by the individual—a challenge to the notion of **free will,** the supposed power each person has to direct his or her own behavior. Because of this, science may find itself at odds with the assumptions made by institutions such as the law, which are based on notions of free will.

Do we have free will, or are our "choices" determined by heredity and environment?

**Biological view:** The psychological perspective that searches for the causes of behavior in the functioning of genes, the brain and nervous system, and the endocrine (hormone) system.

**Determinism:** The assumption that physical, behavioral, and mental events are determined by specific causal factors—as opposed to *free will.*

**Free will:** The power of a person to direct his or her own behavior. The concept of free will is the antithesis of *determinism.*

The issue of free will vs. determinism is often an uncomfortable one for students first encountering it. Consider this: Could it be that the "choices" you make are not really choices after all? Could it be that your actions are determined entirely by your heredity and environment? A compromise position, sometimes called "soft" determinism, holds that we have some choice, even though heredity and environment exert strong

Chapter 4
Psychological Development
*The nature vs. nurture debate concerns the relative effects of heredity and environment.*

influences on us. It should be noted that no one has ever discovered a way to test which of these possibilities—hard determinism, soft determinism, or free will—is the way the world works. But we should also note that scientific psychology always assumes that behavior has natural causes.

*EVOLUTIONARY PSYCHOLOGY*    A new and controversial variation on the biological view, known as **evolutionary psychology,** emphasizes the genetic and evolutionary roots of behavior (Crawford & Anderson, 1989). To the evolutionary psychologist, conditions in our ancestral past have shaped our present behavior through the mechanisms of heredity. This happens because environmental forces "prune" the human family tree, allowing only those individuals with the most adaptive mental and physical characteristics to survive and reproduce. From this perspective, all human behavior—even the most destructive behavior, such as warfare, homicide, and racial discrimination—has grown out of tendencies that once may have helped humans adapt and survive. Evolutionary psychologists would point out that the ability to react violently may have helped our Stone Age ancestors who needed to fight for survival and for the opportunity to mate. This explanation suggests that Kip Kinkel's violent act may be genetically linked with behavior that gave his ancestors an advantage—but that no longer has survival value in most places in our modern world.

You may have guessed that these ideas originated with the work of the famous British scholar and naturalist, Charles Darwin. In his book, *On the Origin of Species,* published in 1859, Darwin proposed that environmental forces "naturally selected" certain biological traits when they provided an advantage in survival and procreation. Darwin (who lived before genes were discovered) theorized that organisms are always changing from generation to generation. Those inheriting advantageous features more often survive and pass their traits on to their offspring. In this way, the biological structure of a species would *evolve* (change) in the direction of characteristics that are more adaptive and that make them more competitive in the struggle to survive in particular environments.

Thus, the concept of behavioral and mental *adaptiveness* is the basis for an evolutionary perspective in psychology. But just because a behavior pattern is adaptive does not necessarily mean that it helps all members of the species. Adaptiveness means only that the genes carried in the individual who survives and reproduces will be replicated and further carried by surviving offspring and relatives.

Evolutionary psychologists also point out that, for most of human history, people lived under conditions that were much different from those we are accustomed to. For our remote ancestors, the world centered on small groups of hunter-gatherers. To understand the genetic basis of our own behavior, therefore, we must understand what behaviors would have helped our ancestors survive in their primitive, Stone Age environment. It is possible that some of our "natural" reactions to difficulty in modern life—defensiveness, anxiety, violence—are better suited to the dangers our ancestors faced many thousands of years ago.

**THE COGNITIVE VIEW**    The second of psychology's six perspectives says that we are more likely to understand ourselves if we look in our *minds.* According to the **cognitive view,** our actions are profoundly influenced by the way we *interpret* our experience. Consequently, cognitive psychologists emphasize mental processes, or **cognitions**—thoughts, expectations, perceptions, and memories.

A cognitive psychologist interviewing Kip Kinkel would probe for the expectations, goals, perceptions, and interpretations that lay behind his violent acts. What view did he have of his world? While very little about Kinkel's mental state has been made public, news reports indicate that other students thought him odd. Strikingly, Kinkel's middle-school yearbook described him as "Most Likely to Start World War III."

**Chapter 8**
**Emotion and Motivation**

*Evolutionary psychologists have developed controversial theories that explain gender differences.*

**Chapter 2**
**Biopsychology**

*Genes determine physical, mental, and behavioral characteristics.*

**Evolutionary psychology:** A new emphasis in biological psychology that views behavior in terms of genetic adaptations for survival and reproduction.

**Cognitive view:** The psychological perspective that emphasizes mental processing and interpretation of experience.

**Cognitions:** Mental processes, such as thinking, memory, sensation, and perception.

**Chapter 5**
**Sensation and Perception**
**Chapter 6**
**Learning and Remembering**

*Cognitive psychologists have done most of the existing research on perception and memory.*

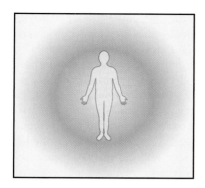

**Behavioral View:**
Emphasizes the power of the environment to influence behavior

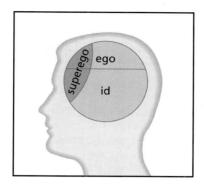

**Psychodynamic View:**
Emphasizes unconscious memories, needs, and conflicts as the causes of behavior

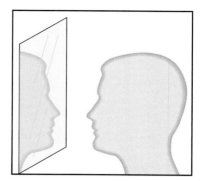

**Humanistic View:**
Emphasizes self-concept, free choice, and the potential for growth as the sources of behavior

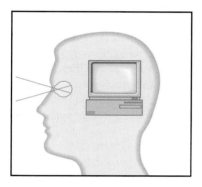

**Cognitive View:**
Emphasizes conscious thought, perception, and information processing as the causes of behavior

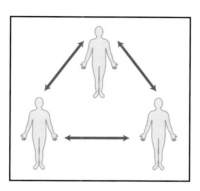

**Sociocultural View:**
Emphasizes social interaction and the cultural context of behavior

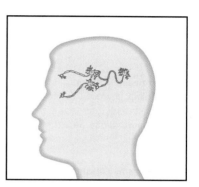

**Biological View:**
Emphasizes the influence of genetics and of physical processes occurring in the brain and the hormone system

Like biological psychologists, modern cognitive psychologists are *determinists* who view the brain as a sort of biological computer—a processor of information (Gardner, 1985; Gazzaniga, 1998; Sperry, 1988). Thus, they think of behavior as being controlled by mental programs, written by the environment into our memories and by heredity into our genes. In the "cognitive revolution" now under way, these psychologists are attempting to forge a synthesis between the cognitive and the biological views by searching for the biological foundations of perception, thought, and memory. Out of this synthesis is emerging an entirely new field known as **cognitive neuroscience** (Davis et al., 1988; Pribram, 1986; Rottschaefer, 1991). Appropriately, cognitive psychology itself is a synthesis of two ancestral traditions known as *structuralism* and *functionalism*.

*THE STRUCTURALIST TRADITION*   One of cognitive psychology's two historical traditions originated in the mid-1800s, when chemists discovered the periodic table

**Chapter 7
Cognitive Processes**

*The "cognitive revolution" has made cognitive psychology the dominant perspective in scientific psychology.*

**Cognitive neuroscience:** An emerging field that combines the cognitive and biological views.

of the chemical elements. All of science was excited and inspired by this discovery, which brought an elegant order to the previously chaotic field of chemistry. Perhaps a similar organizing principle could bring order to the emerging field of psychology, thought Wilhelm Wundt. Psychology would, he declared, search for "the elements of conscious experience." Thus, Wundt established **structuralism,** a "school" of psychology devoted to uncovering the basic structures that make up mind and thought. Accordingly, in his laboratory Wundt collected data using systematic and objective procedures, designed so that independent observers could repeat his experiments. Thus, Wundt's psychological tradition was characterized by a scientific emphasis on experimental methods (controlling conditions and observing psychological responses), precise measurement, and statistical analysis of data. In the laboratory, Wundt's students took the role of subjects, making simple, measurable responses (saying yes or no, pressing a button) to stimuli presented under varying conditions.

Structuralism emigrated to America when Edward Titchener, who had studied with Wundt in Germany, returned to the United States. He brought back with him Wundt's conviction that psychology should focus on consciousness and the elements of mental life. Significantly, his research method of choice involved *introspection*, a subject's systematic examination of his or her own thoughts and feelings about specific sensory experiences.

Wundt and Titchener's structuralism presumed that all human mental experience could be understood as the combination of simpler events or "elements." In a similar way, you make structuralist assumptions when you evaluate an experience by analyzing its parts, such as judging how good a movie is by its cast and director or deciding whether you want to try a dish by first asking what the ingredients are. Structuralist ideas in psychology include the assumption that some experiences are made up of combinations of separate thoughts, emotions, or motives. Yet, as appealing as this model may seem, structuralism was criticized as too simplistic, reducing complex experiences to basic sensations. Critics also considered it too "mentalistic," because it relied on unobservable and subjective inner processes and unverifiable verbal reports. Eventually these objections prevailed, and structuralism waned. But its interest in mental processes has remained in the modern viewpoint of cognitive psychology, which has developed more objective methods to study the makeup of conscious experience.

*THE FUNCTIONALIST TRADITION* Another of cognitive psychology's roots extends to a different group of psychologists called the *functionalists*. This group shared the structuralists' interest in the mind, but they disagreed with the search for the "elements" of consciousness. Instead, the functionalists believed that mental processes could best be understood in terms of their adaptive purpose and function. **Functionalism** gave primary importance to learned habits that enabled organisms to adapt to their environments and function effectively. (Note the influence of Darwin again here, with the emphasis on *adaptation*.)

Such ideas made a lot of sense to William James, a giant figure in American psychology, who tried to bridge both the structuralist and functionalist camps. James agreed with the functionalist idea that behavior must be adaptive and with the structuralist contention that consciousness must be central to psychology. He disagreed, however, with the structuralist search for mental "elements." Instead, James pictured consciousness as an ongoing "stream," a process of mind continually flowing, changing, and interacting with the environment. Human consciousness helped one to adjust to the environment; thus, the *functions* of mental processes—not the contents of the mind—were significant. In James's view, to understand a given thought or behavior, one should ask what function or purpose it served, not what its structure contained.

**Chapter 3
States of Mind**

*The technique of introspection has been criticized for its subjectivity.*

**Structuralism:** A historical school of psychology devoted to uncovering the basic structures that make up mind and thought. Structuralists sought the "elements" of conscious experience.

**Functionalism:** A historical school of psychology that believed mental processes could best be understood in terms of their adaptive purpose and function.

**Chapter 8
Emotion and Motivation**

*William James taught that our physical responses are the primary source of our emotions.*

**THE PSYCHODYNAMIC VIEW** Like cognitive psychologists, those adopting the **psychodynamic view** also attempt to understand the mind's covert operations. But, unlike their cognitive cousins, psychodynamic psychologists place heavy emphasis on motives and mental conflicts, especially unconscious motives and conflicts. (The term *psychodynamic* comes from the idea that the mind [*psyche*] is the source of behavioral energy [*dynamics*].) Modern psychodynamic psychology serves as an umbrella covering a whole spectrum of views that share an interest in the subjective, hidden forces at work in the mind. The psychodynamic view has always attracted many psychologists who specialize in counseling and psychotherapy. In general, these practitioners have emphasized the treatment of mental disorders over basic research.

Sigmund Freud founded *psychoanalysis,* by far the most influential and well-known of the psychodynamic theories. His approach portrayed the mind as a sort of mental boiler that holds the rising pressure of unconscious sexual and destructive desires, along with memories of traumatic events. But, said Freud, the unconscious mind cannot contain the pressure indefinitely. It needs a release. For most people, everyday activity acts as a kind of safety valve, blowing off energy by letting the psychodynamic "steam" escape from the unconscious. The disturbed mind, however, may require more dramatic or bizarre outlets.

A Freudian psychoanalyst, then, might conjecture that Kip Kinkel's problem arose from deep unresolved conflicts, unsatisfied needs, and smoldering anger. These problems festered in his unconscious mind, which finally spilled out its energy in the form of lethal behavior. To uncover the psychological root of the problem, a psychoanalyst would probe for pressures and tensions in Kinkel's family life—particularly his relationship with his parents. From all outward appearances, however, the parents were solid citizens, trying to do their best with a child they didn't know how to control and who was building bombs in his bedroom. From the Freudian perspective, it is especially significant that Kinkel assassinated his parents. This would suggest to a psychoanalyst the existence of severe and unconscious conflicts centering on unresolved jealousies and desires stemming from early childhood relationships with his parents.

**THE HUMANISTIC VIEW** Some psychologists have emphasized human ability, growth, and potential, rather than the threatening unconscious forces that figure so prominently in many of the psychodynamic theories. These are the *humanistic psychologists,* who, like Abraham Maslow (1968, 1970, 1971) and Carl Rogers (1951, 1961, 1977), have also rejected what they saw as the cold, rigid determinism of scientific psychology. In its place they have offered a model that portrays people as having the free will to make choices that affect their lives. Like their cognitive and psychodynamic colleagues, those who hold the **humanistic view** try to understand our thoughts, feelings, and self-concepts (Cushman, 1990). Unlike the psychoanalysts, however, humanistic psychologists assume that essentially healthy urges dwell inside us—even in a Kip Kinkel. As believers in free will, they assume that people make unhealthy choices when they perceive only unhealthy alternatives.

Thus, a humanistic psychologist viewing Kip Kinkel would look for the forces in his world that derailed his originally positive momentum and lowered his self-esteem. A humanist would note that Kinkel, like many other killers, was a loner and a bright underachiever who received a combination of As and Ds in school. "A kid who considers killing," says forensic psychologist Helen Smith, "usually feels like a nobody who desperately wants to be a somebody" (Witkin et al., 1998). From a humanistic perspective, Kinkel was an outsider looking in. Some cognitive psychologists disagree, however. While humanists might blame low self-esteem, psychologists Brad Bushman and Roy Baumeister believe that extreme *narcissism* (an excessively high opinion of oneself) drives such boys. Their research finds that narcissistic personalities act aggressively in order "to punish or defeat someone who has threatened their highly favorable views of themselves" (Bushman & Baumeister, 1998).

Chapter 3
**States of Mind**

*Some psychologists question the existence of a "dynamic" unconscious.*

Chapter 10
**Personality**

*Freud's psychoanalytic theory was the first comprehensive explanation of personality.*

Humanistic psychologists are more interested in discovering how self-actualizing individuals, such as Martin Luther King, are able to unleash their potential for leadership and creativity.

**Psychodynamic view:** A viewpoint that emphasizes the understanding of mental disorders in terms of unconscious needs, desires, memories, and conflicts.

**Humanistic view:** A viewpoint that emphasizes human ability, growth, potential, and free will.

What are the roots of humanistic psychology? This perspective did not grow primarily in the soil of science. Rather its roots extend from the humanistic tradition in philosophy, literature, and art—a tradition that celebrates human potential. Significantly, the humanistic perspective has had little effect on experimental psychology. Its impact, however, has been enormous on the practice of counseling and psychotherapy.

**THE BEHAVIORAL VIEW**    A very different approach to psychology says that the source of our behavior is more likely to be found in our environment than in our biology or our minds. This view, known as the **behavioral view** or **behaviorism,** originally arose because some psychologists disagreed with Wundt, Titchener, James, and their allies. These *behaviorists* believed that consciousness was too subjective to be studied scientifically. Instead, they said, the proper focus of psychology should be on observable *behavior* and on events in the *environment* that trigger behavior. B. F. Skinner, arguably the most influential of American behaviorists, claimed that the concept of "mind" has led psychology in circles, chasing something that cannot even be proved to exist (Skinner, 1987, 1989, 1990). (Think about it. Can you *prove* that you have a mind?). In brief, behaviorists look at the person entirely from the outside, emphasizing the effects of people, objects, and events on behavior, rather than the inner world of mental processes.

Behaviorists do share one thing in common with cognitive psychologists: They are *determinists*. Behaviorists, however, believe that the causes of behavior are *external stimuli* from the environment, rather than internal needs, desires, or thoughts. Thus, they search for the behavioral "laws" by which stimuli produce responses. A simple example: You may jump reflexively when you hear a sudden loud noise. For behaviorists, the stimulus–response connection says it all:

Stimulus ⟶ Response
(loud noise)    (jump)

You can see why we sometimes call this approach **stimulus–response psychology** or, simply, *S–R psychology*.

Hard-line behaviorists argue that covert thoughts, feelings, and motives play no role at all in directing behavior. How could this be? In their view, mental processes are the *result*, not the *cause*, of our responses to events. For example, behaviorists say that people do not cry because they feel sad—rather, they feel sad because events make them cry. Skinner lamented, "The crucial age-old mistake is the belief that . . . what we feel as we behave is the cause of our behaving" (Skinner, 1989, p. 17).

The first American behaviorist was John B. Watson, a professor and researcher whose ideas had been influenced by work that identified biological processes basic to *learning*. Watson concluded that mental events could not be studied scientifically. Therefore, he said, psychology must look not within the individual for the causes of behavior, but outside the individual, at the environment and the observable stimuli that lead to behavioral responses.

Watson's early groundwork was expanded upon by B. F. Skinner, who showed how the results of our actions—rewards and punishments—shape subsequent behavior, as when your studying produces a good grade, which in turn encourages more study behavior. Although Skinner and his disciples conducted their basic research with animal subjects (such as pigeons and rats), the principles of behaviorism they discovered have been widely applied to human problems. For example, behaviorists have advised parents and teachers how to encourage their children's desirable be-

**Chapter 14**
**Therapies for Mental Disorder**

*Humanistic therapy is one of the major forms of psychotherapy for mental disorders.*

**Behavioral view** or **behaviorism:**
A psychological perspective that finds the source of our actions in environmental stimuli, rather than in inner mental processes.

Through basic research conducted with animal subjects, B. F. Skinner (1904–1990) and his disciples developed the principles of behaviorism that have been so widely applied to human problems.

**Chapter 6**
**Learning and Remembering**

*Watson conducted controversial experiments that showed how fears and phobias could be learned.*

**Chapter 6**
**Learning and Remembering**

*Is punishment a less reliable means of changing behavior than reward?*

**Stimulus–response psychology:**
Another term for *behaviorism*.

havior with attention and eliminate unwanted behavior by ignoring it. Behavioral therapy for depression and other mental disorders also draws heavily on Skinner's ideas for changing behavior.

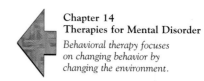

Chapter 14
**Therapies for Mental Disorder**
*Behavioral therapy focuses on changing behavior by changing the environment.*

So, how would behaviorists try to understand Kip Kinkel? Most likely, they would pay particular attention to the rewards and punishments that were offered in his environment. They would ask: How was his lethal behavior shaped and encouraged by the people, objects, and events around him? Was it, perhaps, a bid for attention—a powerful rewarding stimulus? Or, because punishment often produces aggression, they might ask: Was Kinkel's violence a response to the punishment of being suspended from school the day before? And, did anything else in his environment encourage his violent tendencies? According to newspaper reports, Kinkel's father had recently purchased a rifle to teach him gun safety.

**THE SOCIOCULTURAL VIEW**   A relative latecomer to psychology, the **sociocultural view** argues that other people influence our behavior just as powerfully as do our own internal thoughts, motives, and emotions. This social (or *anti*social) behavior arises, in part, from our social group, which specifies what behavior is appropriate or inappropriate. Until quite recently, however, most of psychology overlooked the effects of the larger social context of **culture,** a complex blend of language, beliefs, customs, values, and traditions developed by a group of people and communicated or shared with others in the same environment. It was as though psychology had always assumed that being Korean or Norwegian, Baptist or Buddhist, rich or poor, had no real effect on our basic psychological processes. This oversight was partly the result of mainstream psychology's origins in Europe and North America, where most psychologists lived and worked (Cole, 1984; Sexton & Misiak, 1984). In years past, only a few Western psychologists worried about how or whether their knowledge would transfer to African, Asian, Middle Eastern, and Latin American cultures.

*CROSS-CULTURAL PSYCHOLOGY*   Now the climate has begun to change. Although nearly half of the world's half-million psychologists still live and work in the United States, it is encouraging to note that interest in psychology is also growing in countries outside of Europe and North America (Pawlik & d'Ydewalle, 1996;

Cross-cultural psychologists, such as this researcher in Kenya, furnish important data for checking the validity of psychological knowledge.

**Sociocultural view:** A psychological perspective that emphasizes the importance of social interaction, social learning, and a multicultural perspective.

**Culture:** A term referring to a complex blend of language, beliefs, customs, values, and traditions developed by a group of people and shared with others in the same environment.

Rosenzweig, 1992). Even so, most of our psychological knowledge still has a North American/European flavor (Cushman, 1990). Recognizing this, cross-cultural psychologists have begun the long task of reexamining the "laws" of psychology across cultural and ethnic boundaries (Gergen et al., 1996; Triandis, 1994, 1995). They have found, for example, that the motives for individual achievement and independence, so strong in the United States, are not so powerful in some other successful countries, such as Japan, where the community may be seen as more important than the individual (Triandis, 1995).

The sociocultural perspective provides an important reminder that much of the psychology you will study in this text comes out of the *individualistic* cultural tradition of Western, Anglo-European values. In these societies—of which we authors and most of you, our readers, are a part—what is most prized is individual achievement, with special value awarded to independence, dominance, and competition. In contrast, in the *collectivist* societies that make up the majority of the world's cultures, different basic values apply. Collectivist cultures emphasize community over self, cooperation over competition, humility over winning, politeness at the expense of self-promotion, and devoting one's efforts to service rather than to individual achievement. These values lead not only to different social structures but also to alternative ways of relating to people, the environment, and one's self. Collectivist cultures are found in most parts of Asia, Africa, Latin America, and the Pacific islands, as well as among the native inhabitants of North America and Australia.

Incorporating other cultural perspectives into mainstream psychology, born of extremely individualistic traditions, is difficult. But it brings the field a greater diversity and breadth, as it addresses and involves more people (see Markus & Kitayama, 1994; Mays et al., 1996; Triandis, 1989, 1990). Incorporating other cultural perspectives also makes psychology more meaningful to people as our society becomes a more complex mixture of cultural traditions (Hall, 1997).

*SOCIAL LEARNING*   The sociocultural view also reminds us that we learn from observing other people's behavior, a process called **social learning.** It is based on the idea that learning is driven by our *expectations* of reward and punishments. Thus, social learning is like behaviorism—but with a cognitive and social twist.

The sociocultural view would remind us that Kinkel's social isolation—both his feelings of isolation and the absence of social controls exerted by others—may have played a part in his deviant behavior. A psychologist taking the sociocultural perspective might wonder: What other social pressures did Kinkel feel? Who were his role models? How well did he customarily get along with the people in his life? In this regard, it may be significant that he was reportedly angry about being teased by other students.

Imitation of media violence may also have been a factor in the Kinkel case. Abundant evidence tells us that violence on TV and in the movies is associated with violent behavior in real life. Sometimes the media can even set off a rash of copycat acts of violence (Witkin et al., 1998). The news of shockingly violent crimes spreads rapidly, and otherwise troubled children may decide to imitate. Still, this does not explain why it might have affected Kinkel more than other students. The results of psychological investigations of Kinkel have not been released, so we don't know if this was a factor in his shooting spree. We do know, however, that it was the sixth incident in eight months of a fatal shooting in America's public schools.

Now, to summarize the six perspectives we have just covered, please study Table 1.1. There you will find an overview of the main viewpoints that make up the spectrum of modern psychology. Taking a few moments to fix the six perspectives in your mind will pay big dividends in your understanding of the chapters that follow.

**Chapter 12**
**Social Psychology**
*Individualism vs. collectivism is the cultural difference that most affects psychological responses.*

**Chapter 6**
**Learning and Remembering**
*Social learning involves imitating responses of people whose behavior we see being rewarded or punished.*

**Social learning:** A process whereby we learn from observing others, rather than by directly receiving rewards and punishments for our actions.

**TABLE 1.1:** Six Major Perspectives in Modern Psychology

| PERSPECTIVE | VIEW OF HUMAN NATURE | WHAT DETERMINES BEHAVIOR | FOCUS OF STUDY |
|---|---|---|---|
| Biological | Essentially biological and deterministic; we are adapted to dealing with the problems of ancient human environments | Neural structures, biochemistry, and innate responses to external cues for survival and procreation | The role of the nervous system, endocrine system, and evolved hereditary mechanisms in behavior; biological/genetic disorders that cause abnormal behavior |
| Cognitive | We are information-processing animals | Stimulus conditions as interpreted by our mental processes | Mental processes, including sensation, perception, memory, language, and emotion |
| Psychodynamic | We are driven by unconscious motives that must be controlled | Unconscious needs, conflicts, repressed memories of early experiences, and unfinished business from earlier stages of development | Abnormal behavior as a reflection of unconscious motives; applications of psychodynamic theory to psychotherapy |
| Humanistic | We have free will and unlimited potential | The self-concept, perceptions, interpersonal relationships, and the need for personal growth | Life patterns, values, goals, self-actualizing individuals; applications of humanistic theory to counseling and psychotherapy |
| Behavioral | Deterministic; we are essentially reactive to stimulation | Stimulus cues in the environment control behavior | The "laws" connecting our responses to stimulus conditions in the environment |
| Sociocultural | People are essentially social animals; human behavior must be interpreted in its social context | Culture, social norms and expectations, and social learning. | Social interaction, socialization, and cross-cultural differences |

**PSYCHOLOGY IN YOUR LIFE**

## The Effects of Your Own Culture

Wearing shorts and a sleeveless top on a hot day might seem perfectly acceptable behavior for most American college women, for example, but might be forbidden for many Muslim women.

A cross-cultural psychologist would remind you that, surrounded by your own cultural influences, you may take them for granted or even not be able to recognize how what seems "natural" to you is alien or even shocking to others. Wearing shorts and a tank top on a hot day might seem perfectly acceptable behavior for most American college women, for example, but would be prohibited for many Muslim women. Crossing the street against a red traffic light is common for many New Yorkers, but it would be unthinkable among Japanese pedestrians in Tokyo. The sociocultural approach to psychology argues that, to predict individual behavior, it is necessary to see the individual as embedded in a social context that includes family, friends, coworkers, social organizations, the larger community, and the values and traditions of the culture.

At the same time, psychologists with multicultural interests are reminding us that we do not need to look outside our own country to find a variety of cultures and viewpoints (Garnets & Kimmel, 1991; Goodchilds, 1991; Jones, 1991; Sue, 1991; Tavris, 1991). Many distinctive cultural groups exist right here at home: Native Americans, Hispanics, Asians, and African Americans, to name a few. Similarly, gender has created its own subcultures. As a result, psychology is beginning to recognize the effects of gender and culture on thoughts and behavior. Indeed, the gender composition of psychology itself is rapidly shifting (Pion et al., 1996): The majority of doctorates in psychology are now being awarded to women. This important multicultural/cross-cultural/gender awakening in psychology will be a recurrent theme of this book.

*Continued*

Returning to the Kip Kinkel case, how influential do you suppose was the culture of the western United States, which emphasizes individual rights over group responsibilities and places a high value on the possession of firearms? We can never know for sure the extent to which such cultural factors contributed to this particular case. Nevertheless, we can see some suggestive clues. In Kinkel's home state of Oregon, for example, 53% of all households have guns. In fact, research has shown that violent behavior is much more prevalent in the southern and western states than it is in the rest of the United States (Cohen, 1998; Cohen et al., 1996; Nisbett, 1993). A multicultural approach suggests that we continue to look for cultural patterns in our attempt to understand violent behavior. *(See Chapter 10, Social Psychology.)*

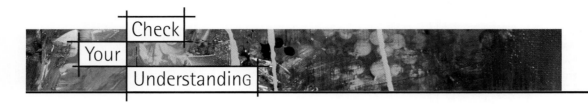

## Check Your Understanding

1. RECALL: *Which of the following terms is the opposite of determinism?*
   a. amygdala
   b. behaviorism
   c. covert
   d. free will

2. APPLICATION: *Which approach would say that the differences between the behavior of males and females are the result of different survival and reproduction pressures on the two sexes?*
   a. behavioral psychology
   b. evolutionary psychology
   c. humanistic psychology
   d. psychoanalysis

3. RECALL: *Mental processes, such as perception and remembering, are sometimes called*
   a. cognitions.
   b. affective events.
   c. neural nets.
   d. dependent variables.

4. RECALL: *One of the roots of cognitive psychology sought to identify the "elements of conscious experience." Adherents to this viewpoint were called*
   a. structuralists.
   b. functionalists.
   c. mentalists.
   d. behaviorists.

5. APPLICATION: *Suppose that your therapist tells you that your problems are caused by urges repressed in your unconscious mind. Which perspective is your therapist using?*
   a. the cognitive perspective
   b. the sociocultural perspective
   c. the humanistic perspective
   d. the psychodynamic perspective

6. RECALL: *Which of psychology's six perspectives would deny that mental events influence our actions?*
   a. the cognitive perspective
   b. the sociocultural perspective
   c. the behavioral perspective
   d. the humanistic perspective

7. RECALL: *In which of the following countries would you expect to encounter the influences of an individualistic culture?*
   a. the United States
   b. China
   c. Mexico
   d. Kenya

8. UNDERSTANDING THE CORE CONCEPT: *Which of psychology's six perspectives is least grounded in the scientific tradition?*
   a. the biological perspective
   b. the behavioral perspective
   c. the cognitive perspective
   d. the humanistic perspective

**ANSWERS:**  1. d  2. b  3. a  4. a  5. d  6. c  7. a  8. d

 **KEY QUESTION**

## HOW DO PSYCHOLOGISTS DO RESEARCH?

**Pseudoscience:** Any approach to explaining phenomena in the natural world that does not use empirical observation or other aspects of the scientific method.

Humanity has never suffered a shortage of people who claim to have special and mystical methods for revealing the secrets of human personality and behavior. As early as 1880, American psychology disputed the claims of spiritualists and psychics (Coon, 1992). Psychology still has many competitors from the realms of **pseudoscience,** including *astrology,* which claims to describe people's personalities and predict their fortunes from patterns found in the planets' movements among the constellations of the zodiac; *palmistry,* which attempts to decipher people's personalities and futures from patterns in the lines on their hands; *graphology*, which assumes that human personality reveals itself in people's handwriting styles; *biorhythm analysis*, which purports to analyze people's personality and fortunes based on regular physical, emotional, and intellectual cycles that are supposed to begin at the moment of birth. In addition there are many "psychics," "seers," and other mystics who claim to have special insights into people's personalities and to be able to predict their futures.

What makes scientific psychology different from the these pseudoscientific approaches to understanding people? Answer: None of the alternatives has survived trial by the *scientific method*, a way of rigorously testing ideas against objective observations. Astrology, palmistry, biorhythm analysis, graphology, numerology, consultation with spirit mediums, tea-leaf reading, crystal-ball gazing by fortune tellers, and the pronouncements of oracles and soothsayers are all based solely on speculation (and an intuitive understanding of human gullibility), rather than on evidence.

You might think this a snobbish view for psychologists to take. Why can't we make room for many different approaches to the understanding of people? In fact, psychologists have no problem accepting many other approaches to the study of human behavior and mental processes. They are quite willing to accept sociology, anthropology, economics, and political science as partners in the enterprise of understanding ourselves. Psychologists reject only those approaches that claim to be "scientific" but that really have only a scientific veneer. You see, the problem with the pseudosciences, such as astrology, is twofold. First, they usually insist that they possess the "truth," yet claims of absolute certainty are marks of pseudoscientific quackery. Science, on the other hand, always holds its explanations tentatively, realizing that new evidence could always upset the current understanding. Second, pseudosciences employ no objective method for testing their concepts and ideas against the evidence. The use of such a method is what really sets psychology apart from pseudoscientific approaches to mind and behavior. Our Core Concept for this section says:

**CORE CONCEPT**

**Psychologists, like all other scientists, use the scientific method to test ideas empirically.**

**Scientific method:** A five-step process for empirical investigation of a hypothesis under controlled conditions designed to control the observer's biases and subjectivity.

**Empirical investigation:** An approach to research that relies on sensory experience and observation as research data.

What is this marvelous method? Simply put, the **scientific method** is a process for catching and discarding compelling but mistaken ideas. And, as the Core Concept suggests, the heart of scientific investigation involves a process known as *empirical investigation*, the collecting of objective information firsthand. **Empirical investigation** is research that relies on sensory experience and observation as research data. To investigate a question empirically is to ask questions and collect information yourself, rather than consulting a secondhand reference or merely appealing to the opinion of "experts" or other authority figures. Literally, "empirical" means "experience-based," rather than based on faith, hope, armchair speculation, authority, or common sense. Empirical investigation is a useful approach for learning about every aspect of life in the natural world. Even if you never do psychological research, you will find that insisting on empirically obtained evidence will improve your critical-thinking skills.

To give an example of the value of empirical investigation, consider the antidrug education program DARE (Drug Abuse Resistance Education), used in schools to teach children to say "no" to drugs. Proponents claim that it works because parents, teachers, and students say they like the program and because it "makes sense." But does it really prevent drug use among children? When the program has been evaluated empirically to determine whether it actually had any effect on later drug-taking behavior, the outcome was

A police officer from the DARE program urges students to say "no" to drugs. Does it work?

**Chapter 3**
**States of Mind**

*Drug use has declined in recent years—but the decline cannot be attributed to drug-education programs.*

**Chapter 4**
**Psychological Development**

*Developmental psychologists have traced how our moral reasoning changes as we mature.*

quite different from most people's expectations. In fact, the evidence showed that DARE had *no* measurable impact on ability to resist drug use (Murray, 1997).

In contrast with the empirical approach of the scientific method, people sometimes rely on a personal hunch, their feelings, or scriptural revelations as the standard by which to judge truth or falsity of ideas. Is there anything wrong with that? The scientist would say that such subjective standards are quite appropriate for judging subjective ideas, as in questions of beauty, morality, and spirituality. Science, however, cannot speak to such issues.

Science cannot tell us, for example, whether abortion is morally right or wrong—although a scientist could study under what conditions people seek abortions and what the consequences are to their mental health. Likewise, science cannot tell us what the ideal standards for judging beauty should be—although a scientist could study how people judge a painting or a film. Nor can science give us answers to purely spiritual questions, such as the existence of God—although a scientist could study people's religious beliefs. Scientists, of course, may hold opinions on issues that are beyond the boundaries of science, but such opinions are not based strictly on the scientific method.

On the other hand, if one is interested in testing the truth or falsity of claims about the natural world—the world of objects, events, behavior, and other physical processes—science has the most appropriate method. It is the only means ever devised that puts ideas to an empirical test. Let's see how this method works.

## The Five Steps of the Scientific Method

In putting ideas to the test, the scientific method requires a set of five orderly steps. Its purpose is to establish an objective basis for accepting or rejecting ideas. The scientific method involves the same essential steps whether it is being applied in psychology, biology, chemistry, astronomy, or any other scientific discipline. It is the *method* that makes these fields scientific, not their subject matter. Ideally, the scientific method proceeds as follows:

**DEVELOPING A HYPOTHESIS**   Formulating an idea, a hunch, or guess about some variables of interest is the first step. Scientists call this idea a *hypothesis*. (The term "hypothesis" literally means "little theory.") Hypotheses can come from many sources, such as chance observations of interesting behavior, an article in the newspaper, a character in a novel, or a conversation with a friend. In Emily Rosa's experiment on therapeutic touch, you may remember that the hypotheses began to take shape this way:

> Emily suspected that the nurses were really detecting their own beliefs and expectations, rather than the "human energy field."

To give a more formal definition, a **hypothesis** is a statement predicting the outcome of a scientific study. (You can think of a hypothesis as a specific prediction that is derived from a larger theory.) For purposes of the study, everything in the hypothesis must be put in the form of *operational definitions* (which are stated in observable, measurable terms). Moreover, the hypothesis must be stated in such a way

**Hypothesis:** A statement predicting the outcome of a scientific study; a statement describing the relationship among variables in a study.

that it can be *falsified*—shown to be either correct or incorrect. Thus, Emily Rosa wondered:

> Could TT practitioners accurately detect the presence of her hand when it was placed above one of their hands but out of sight?

She hypothesized that they could not.

So far, so good—but a scientific study must not stop with a good hypothesis. (The pseudosciences, such as astrology, typically stop at the hypothesis, without going on to the other vital steps necessary to complete the study and verify or reject the hypothesis.) For a scientific hypothesis to be taken seriously by the scientific community, it must be subjected to rigorous testing.

Emily Rosa's experiment.

**PERFORMING A CONTROLLED TEST**   Before a new theory or hypothesis makes a difference in science, it must undergo an "ordeal of proof"—a controlled test. That is, the scientist designs a test that the hypothesis can either pass or fail. This is what Emily Rosa did:

> She invited each of 21 TT practitioners (varying in experience from one to 27 years) to determine which of their two hands (stuck through a screen palms up) was closest to one of hers (palm down a few inches from either of their hands).

This concept of a **controlled test** lies at the heart of scientific experimentation. In order to keep her experiment under control, Rosa varied only one aspect of the situation: whether her hand was above the subject's left or right hand on each trial. We call this variable condition the **independent variable.** It takes its name from the fact that it is a condition that the experimenter changes *independently* of all the other carefully controlled experimental conditions. The independent variable always involves the conditions that the experimenter is evaluating in a study. Thus, the placement of the experimenter's hand was the independent variable in Rosa's research. To give another example of an independent variable: In assessing a new drug, the independent variable would involve giving subjects either the new drug or a *placebo*, which looks like the real drug but contains no real medicines, allowing a comparison of the drug's physical effects against the effects of patients' expectations.

Rosa's control over the experimental conditions would have been incomplete, however, if she had simply put her hand alternately above the subjects' left and right hands or if she had used some other predictable pattern. Then, subjects might have just been responding to some pattern in her stimulus presentation. The solution was simple: **random** presentation of the stimulus.

> By a coin flip, Emily randomized the order of presenting her hand above either of the practitioners' hands.

Randomization means that chance alone determined the order in which the stimulus was presented. Randomization is one way of controlling experimenters' biases that can unexpectedly influence the results of a study. (We will see some other sources of bias later in the chapter.)

If the focus of her therapeutic touch study had been slightly different, Rosa might have also used randomization differently. Let's suppose that she had decided to study the effectiveness of TT by comparing it with standard massage therapy to see if those receiving TT got well faster than those receiving massage. In such a comparative study, she would have randomly assigned her research *subjects* to one of two conditions: One group would receive therapeutic touch, and another group would receive massage. This can be done in many ways, such as drawing names and assigning them alternately to each group. But whatever the means by which it is

**Chapter 5**
**Sensation and Perception**
*Placebos work because of the patient's expectations.*

**Controlled test:** A part of the scientific method that involves gathering data under conditions that are designed to control potentially confounding variables.

**Independent variable:** A stimulus condition that is so named because the experimenter changes it *independently* of all the other carefully controlled experimental conditions.

**Random:** Determined by chance.

**Experimental group:** Those subjects in an experiment who are exposed to the treatment of interest.

**Control group:** Those subjects who are used as a comparison for the experimental group. The control group is not given the special treatment of interest.

**Dependent variable:** The measured outcome of a study; the responses of the subjects in a study.

**Self-report measures:** Verbal answers, either written or spoken, to questions posed by researchers.

**Behavioral measures:** Responses consisting of overt, observable, and recordable actions.

**Physiological measures:** Data based on subjects' biological responses to stimuli.

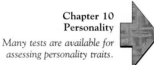

**Chapter 10
Personality**

*Many tests are available for assessing personality traits.*

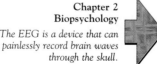

**Chapter 2
Biopsychology**

*The EEG is a device that can painlessly record brain waves through the skull.*

done, the purpose of random assignment of subjects is to minimize the chance that some pre-existing difference between the two groups (such as the severity of their illnesses) could account for the results of the experiment.

In such an experiment, those subjects exposed to the treatment of interest (therapeutic touch in this case) are said to make up the **experimental group.** The remaining subjects, the **control group,** offer a standard by which the experimental group can be compared. Without a control group, the experimenter would not be able to tell whether TT had made any real difference. Control groups are treated exactly like the experimental group in all respects except for the crucial treatment in which the experimenter is interested (touch versus massage, in our current case).

**GATHERING OBJECTIVE DATA**    In the third step of the scientific method the scientist collects objective, *empirical* data—the results of the study. Reputable scientists will find ways to gather objective data that do not depend on their own hopes, expectations, or personal impressions. Emily Rosa's data consisted of her subject's responses during the test:

> The test subjects' task was to say whether they felt energy from the girl's hand above their left or right hand.

These subjects' responses are referred to as the **dependent variable.** The term arises from the assumption that the subjects' responses are assumed to *depend* directly on how the subjects have been treated—that is, on how the independent variable has been manipulated. (In this sense, we can say that a hypothesis is a statement that describes the relationship among variables—particularly the dependent and independent variable.) In Emily Rosa's experiment, the dependent variable involved her subjects' guesses of "left" or "right." In other studies, more elaborate forms of testing may be used. In general, however, the methods of measurement employed by psychologists usually take one of three forms: *self-reports, behavior analysis,* and *physiological measures.*

**Self-report measures** are verbal answers, either written or spoken, to questions posed by researchers. When you tell a poll-taker your age, occupation, and political preferences, you are providing a self-report. Although self-reports cannot be obtained in some forms of research (for example, from nonhuman subjects or preverbal children), self-report measures such as questionnaires, surveys, personality tests, and interviews are popular because they are convenient, and the responses can be easily quantified.

**Behavioral measures** are used to study overt, observable, and recordable actions. Using this approach, an observer simply counts and records the frequency of certain behaviors, such as the number of times a child hits a playmate. This approach is especially useful in assessing the behavior of subjects in their everyday environments. To give another example, to use a behavioral measure in studying how college students form close relationships, you would begin by going where they go and watching them, tallying how often they make eye contact, how close they sit, and so on.

**Physiological measures** collect data based on subjects' biological responses. Such measures would be undertaken to gain access to information about less observable processes like brain activity, blood pressure, or perspiration. The researcher might use, for example, the *electroencephalograph (EEG)* for recording the electrical activity of the brain. The EEG patterns of waveforms, then, can provide clues about which parts of the brain are involved in various mental activities.

The foregoing is, of course, only a brief introduction to psychological measurement. As you progress through this book, you will learn more about how these methods are used. You will see that each branch of psychology has developed its own specialized instruments and techniques. For example, while research on the brain often involves high-tech devices, such as the EEG, studies of memory often involve simple, but clever, verbal probes of the mind. On another hand, research in social psychology frequently employs elaborate—almost theatrical—productions to disguise the researcher's real intent. We will see more of each in the chapters that follow.

### ANALYZING THE RESULTS AND ACCEPTING OR REJECTING THE HYPOTHESIS

In the fourth step of the scientific method, the scientist examines the results—the data—to see whether the hypothesis passed the test. Based on that analysis, the hypothesis is accepted or rejected. This part can be difficult, especially if the outcome requires a close call. For this reason, scientists usually rely on statistics to analyze their data. Statistical procedures can tell the researcher whether the observed results rise to the level of *significance*—that is, whether the results are likely due to the independent variable or merely due to chance. A detailed explanation of statistics is beyond the scope of this book. It is, in fact, a subject for a whole course in itself. Your authors have, however, provided a brief introduction to the use of statistics in the Statistical Appendix near the end of this book. There you will find a summary of key points and examples of how psychological concepts are *quantified* (measured and expressed as numbers) and how those quantities can provide meaning and understanding.

**Appendix**
**Understanding Statistics**
*A statistical analysis determines whether observed differences between groups are statistically significant.*

In Rosa's experiment, the statistical analysis was not complex. The chances of getting a correct answer by guessing was 50%: Half the time subjects could give the right answer even if they had no ability to sense the "human energy field." So, Rosa set this standard:

> Her subjects would have to perform significantly above the chance level to validate the claim that they can detect a "human energy field."

They did not, so she concluded that practitioners of therapeutic touch were not sensing "human energy fields."

### PUBLISHING, CRITICIZING, AND REPLICATING THE RESULTS

In the fifth step of the scientific method, scientists must find out whether their research can withstand the scrutiny and criticism of the scientific community. To do so, they announce their results to colleagues by publishing them in a professional journal, presenting a paper at a professional meeting, or writing a book. (You will recall that Emily Rosa published her results in *The Journal of the American Medical Association* [*JAMA*].) Then they wait for the inevitable criticism. If colleagues find the study of interest, they will look for flaws in the research design: Did the experimenter choose the subjects properly? Were the statistical analyses done correctly? Could other factors account for the results? As we noted earlier, in Rosa's experiment, some critics complained that her study was not an accurate representation of the conditions under which therapeutic touch is done:

> They claim that TT depends on the transfer of emotional energy during a medical crisis, and because Emily was not sick she did not have disturbances in her energy field that could be detected by TT practitioners.

They may try to check the work by *replicating* (redoing) the research, perhaps under different control conditions, to see whether they get the same results.

All this is a part of a thorough, and sometimes intimidating, screening process that goes on behind the scientific scenes to filter out poorly conceived and executed research. As a result, fewer than 2% of the papers submitted to psychological journals get into print without major revisions. In fact, the majority never see print at all (Eichorn &

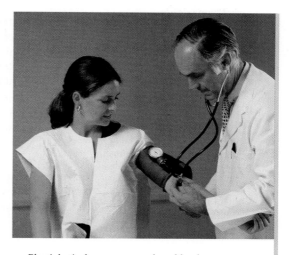

Physiological measures, such as blood pressure, can indicate subtle behavioral changes that reveal psychological states such as anxiety or arousal.

VandenBos, 1985). Journal editors and book publishers (including the publishers of this book) nearly always seek the opinion of several expert reviewers for each submission before agreeing to publish it. Different reviewers often will focus their criticism on different facets of the study (Fiske & Fogg, 1990). In this process, the author usually receives helpful, if sometimes painful, suggestions for revision. The result, the scientific community hopes, is the publication and acceptance of the best and most meaningful work. Only when a hypothesis has survived all these tests will other scholars tentatively accept it as scientific "truth." But, unlike astrology and other pseudoscientific dogma, the findings remain forever in jeopardy from a new study that calls for a new interpretation and relegates previous conclusions to the scientific scrap heap.

Now we ask you to turn, for a moment, to the alphabetized *References* section near the end of this book to find the full reference for Emily Rosa's published report. Throughout this text you will find we have listed one or more *citations*—authors' names and publication dates—to indicate the published source of ideas and arguments we are presenting here. In the text these are given by name and date in parenthesis, for example: (Rosa et al., 1998). The "et al." tells you that the source has several authors. Using these references, you can find the original source for any citation whose point seems especially interesting to you. A good library will have the resources you need to complete the search process and locate a copy of the original article, chapter, or book. You must track down such references in conducting a literature review, a preliminary step in pursuing any investigation. You will gain deeper understanding from doing a "reference check" from time to time.

## Types of Psychological Research

Now that you understand the basic steps of the scientific method, we should distinguish among several forms of psychological research. These include *experiments, correlational studies*, and *case studies*. We will look at each type in some detail because they differ in the kinds of conclusions to which they can lead.

**EXPERIMENTS**    Emily Rosa's study was an example of an **experiment,** a kind of research in which the researcher controls all the conditions and directly manipulates them, including the independent variable. Not only did Rosa and her colleagues design the apparatus used in their study, but they established the conditions under which subjects were tested. Virtually everything about the experiment was under their control.

Every experiment is designed to answer a question of this form: Does the independent variable *cause* a predicted change in the dependent variable? To determine this, the experimenter designs two or more ways of treating the subjects. In Emily Rosa's study, for example, she created two treatment conditions by varying which of her subjects' hands she placed her own hand near. By contrast, in an experiment designed to study a new drug's effectiveness, the two treatments would involve giving some subjects the experimental drug, while others receive a placebo. When two or more groups of subjects are used, those exposed to the special treatment are said to be in the **experimental condition** of the experiment. These subjects make up the *experimental group*. Meanwhile, subjects in the *control group* are placed in the **control condition,** where they may receive a placebo or no treatment at all. Thus, the control subjects can be used as a standard against which to compare the subjects in the experimental condition.

**CORRELATIONAL STUDIES**    Sometimes the degree of control described above cannot be achieved for practical or ethical reasons. Suppose, for example, that you wanted to test this hypothesis: Children who ingest lead-based paint (common in older homes, especially in low-income urban housing) suffer learning disabilities. You

**Experiment:** A kind of research in which the researcher controls all the conditions and directly manipulates the conditions, including the independent variable.

**Experimental condition:** The stimulus conditions involved in exposing those in the *experimental group* to the special treatment being investigated.

**Control condition:** The stimulus conditions for the control group—conditions that are identical to the experimental condition in every respect, except for the special treatment given to the experimental group.

Member,
Placebo Group

wouldn't do an *experiment* to verify this hypothesis. Why? In an experiment you would have to manipulate the independent variable: feeding toxic lead-based paint to an experimental group of children! Obviously, this would be dangerous and unethical.

Fortunately, we can find a way around this problem—but at the expense of some control over the research conditions. The alternative is a **correlational study.** In correlational research you, in effect, look for an "experiment" that has already been done by chance, not by design, in the world outside the laboratory. So, in a correlational study on the effects of ingesting lead-based paint, you would find a group of children who had already been exposed to leaded paint and compare them to another group who had not been exposed. As a control, you would try to match the groups so that they were comparable in every conceivable respect (age, family income, gender, etc.) *except* for their exposure to leaded paint.

Unfortunately, in such a study, you can never be sure that the groups are really similar in every way. Because you can't randomly assign subjects or manipulate the independent variable, you cannot say that the condition that interests you was the *cause* of the effects you observed. So, even if you observe more learning disabilities among children who were exposed to lead-based paint, you *cannot* conclude for certain that exposure to the paint *caused* the disabilities. The most you can say is that lead-based paint is *correlated* or associated with learning disabilities. Scientists put it this way: *Correlation does not imply causation.*

To determine the precise extent of a correlation between two variables, a researcher would first collect two sets of scores, one for each of the two variables. (In the example we used above, you might correlate lead levels in the blood with IQ test scores.) The next step is to calculate a statistic known as a *correlation coefficient,* often symbolized by the letter $r$. The **correlation coefficient** summarizes the relationship between the two variables. It can range from 0 to 1.0. If the two variables are perfectly correlated, they *always* occur together, and their correlation coefficient is 1.0. (In our example a correlation of 1.0 would mean that every child exposed to lead has a learning disability.) If they are related in the same direction—as one variable's scores increase, so do the other's—they are *positively* correlated. An example of a positive correlation is the moderate relationship between SAT scores and college grades (which is approximately +0.4). In contrast, if one variable decreases as the other increases, they are *negatively* correlated, and their coefficient would have a minus sign.

**Correlational study:** A form of research in which the relationship between variables is studied, but without the experimental manipulation of an independent variable. Correlational studies cannot determine cause-and-effect relationships.

**Correlation coefficient:** A statistic, $r$, that indicates the relationship between two variables. Correlation coefficients can range from –1.0 to 0 to +1.0.

**Appendix
Understanding Statistics**
*Correlation is a descriptive
statistical procedure.*

You would probably find a negative correlation between the amount of alcohol consumed by college students and their grade-point averages. If the variables have no relationship at all, their coefficient is 0. You would expect a zero correlation between hat size and GPA, for example.

Consider some variables in your own life that might be correlated. When you were a growing child, your age was probably positively correlated with your physical height. As you got older, you also grew taller: Records of your age and height at regular intervals would both steadily increase. On the other hand, some of your behaviors might be negatively correlated with other experiences. How is study time correlated with the amount of anxiety you feel just prior to taking a test? For most people, the *less* time spent studying for a test, the *more* anxiety they experience before and during the test session. If this is true for you, then the variable "study time" is negatively correlated with the variable "test anxiety."

It is important to note that a correlation can show a strong relationship, even when it is negative. Let us suppose that a measure of anxiety has a correlation of –0.7 with time spent studying. Even though it is a negative correlation, it shows a *stronger* relationship than, for example, a positive correlation of +0.4 between SAT scores and grades.

You will see throughout this book that correlational research comes in many forms. For example, a **survey** of attitudes, preferences, or behaviors can be part of a correlational study. Surveys typically ask people for their responses to a prepared set of verbal items. Then responses might be checked for correlations with age or scores on a test of vocabulary, for example. **Naturalistic observations** are another form of correlational research involving the observation of people or animals in their home surroundings—such as you might do to study the effect of various child-rearing practices.

CASE STUDIES    A third major kind of research, the **case study,** focuses on a few subjects (sometimes just one). The case study method is usually reserved for the in-depth study of unusual individuals with rare problems or unusual talents. Psychoanalysts have used this approach, also called the *clinical method,* to gather material from their psychotherapy patients and develop theories about mental disorder. The disadvantages of the case study method, of course, lie in its subjectivity and its small sample size, which limit the researcher's ability to draw conclusions that can be applied to other individuals. Nevertheless, the case study can sometimes give us valu-

**Survey:** A technique used in correlational research that typically involves seeking people's responses to a prepared set of verbal items.

**Naturalistic observations:** A form of correlational research involving *behavioral measures* of people or animals in their home surroundings.

**Case study:** Research that involves only a single subject (or, at most, a few subjects).

**Chapter 10**
**Personality**

Psychoanalytic theory *is Freud's explanation of personality and mental disorder.*

able insights that could be obtained by no other method. How else could we study the forces that shaped rare and talented individuals, such as Mother Teresa and Albert Einstein? And how else could we learn about the tragic circumstances that shaped Kip Kinkel?

## Sources of Bias

Think of an issue on which you have strong feelings and opinions—perhaps abortion, euthanasia, or capital punishment. Could you do research on such an issue and keep your biases in check? Scientists recognize that they cannot. No matter what type of research scientists are conducting, they must always be aware that their biases and expectations, and those of their subjects, can affect the outcome of their research. Thus, one of the hardest parts of doing research is remaining objective. Specifically, five sources of bias commonly challenge us:

Jane Goodall used the method of naturalistic observation to study chimpanzee behavior.

1. *External influences* such as culture or media can persuade people to accept a particular worldview. Can you spot biases in the news sources that you regularly read or watch? Are they liberal or conservative? Feminist? From a big city or a small town? For example, a social scientist who has strong opinions on gun control might not be objective in assessing the possible causes of Kip Kinkel's violent rampage.

2. *Personal bias* distorts one's ability to estimate or evaluate what is observed because of one's long-standing beliefs, characteristics, or past experiences. For example, in his book, *Even the Rat Was White*, psychologist Robert Guthrie (1998) criticizes much of the psychological literature because it is based on studies using mainly White subjects.

3. *Observer bias* occurs when one's prejudices or opinions act as "filters" to determine whether some events are noticed or seen as meaningful while others are not. For example, an observer studying aggressive behavior in grade school children may expect boys to be more aggressive than girls and so might not notice girls' aggressive behavior.

4. *Expectancy bias* affects observations when the observer expects—and looks for—certain outcomes to follow observed events. We find an expectancy bias in the teacher who believes a particular student will do outstanding work and thus awards her an A without really noticing that her performance did not deserve such a high grade. We can also see the expectancy bias in a classic study in which psychology students were asked to run groups of rats through a maze and record their times (Rosenthal & Jacobson, 1968). The experimenters told some students that their rats were especially bright; other students heard that their rats were slow learners. (In fact, the experimenters had randomly selected both groups of rats from the same litters). Amazingly, the students' data showed that rats believed to be bright outperformed their supposedly duller littermates. Obviously, expectations had influenced the students' observations.

5. Finally, a *placebo bias* occurs when people believe that a treatment is working when in fact there is no objective basis for its success. In reality, just believing in the power of a drug can lead to marked pain reduction, even though the "medication" is chemically inert, a sugar pill (see Roberts et al., 1993). The same placebo effect can occur for certain people when they believe that some treatment has the power to heal their pain or sickness. "Faith healing" probably works in this way. Emily Rosa's experiment might lead us to suspect that the healing power of therapeutic touch also comes from a placebo effect.

As we have seen, the best way to control biases and safeguard objectivity is to use various *control* procedures to keep hypothesis testing fair. One such control strategy is to keep research subjects experimentally *"blind,"* or uninformed about the real purpose of the research study or some key part of it. An even stronger strategy is for the researcher to have assistants conduct the study and to keep both the subjects and the assistants uninformed about the conditions of the research. When both researchers and subjects in an experiment are uninformed about the nature of the independent variable being administered, we have a **double-blind control.** So, in a double-blind drug study, for example, neither those administering the drug nor the volunteers taking the pills will know who is getting the real drug and who is receiving the placebo. Taking this precaution assures that the experimenters will not inadvertently treat the "real drug" subjects differently or scrutinize them more closely, and the subjects will not be able to detect any clue about how they are "supposed" to be responding to the pills.

"WE PLAN TO DETERMINE, ONCE AND FOR ALL, IF THERE REALLY ARE ANY CULTURAL DIFFERENCES BETWEEN THEM."

Finally, researchers must consider all possible influences on the behavior being studied. Recall that the independent variable is the stimulus condition assumed to influence the psychological process or event being studied, and the dependent variable is the influenced action or response. **Confounding variables,** then, are factors that could be confused with the independent variable and thus distort the results. For example, in a study of using a stimulant drug (such as Ritalin) to control hyperactive behavior among schoolchildren, what might be some confounding variables? The drug's effect might differ because of different body weights, eating schedules, and time, method, or setting of administration. Unless arrangements are made to control all such possible confounding variables—that is, to expose all the subjects to identical conditions—the researcher has no way of knowing what factors produced the results.

## Ethical Issues in Psychological Research

A final issue we should consider here involves the ethics of research. Ethics has to do with whether someone be hurt—mentally or physically—by participating in a psychological study. It's easy to imagine the distress subjects might feel in a study of fear, for example. So, is it ethical for scientists to cause someone distress, even if the distress is only temporary? Is a subject's psychological unease too high a price to pay for the knowledge gained from the experiment? These are difficult, but important, questions, and not all psychologists answer them in exactly the same way—although none would want a subject to suffer lasting distress.

To provide some guidelines and boundaries for psychological researchers, the American Psychological Association has published *Ethical Principles of Psychologists and Code of Conduct* (1992). This statement advises researchers of their ethical obligation to shield subjects from potentially harmful procedures. Further, the statement admonishes researchers that information acquired about people during a study must be

---

**Chapter 14
Therapies for Mental Disorder**

*Studies have shown stimulants to be effective in the treatment of children's hyperactive behavior syndrome.*

**Double-blind control:** An experimental procedure in which both researchers and subjects are uninformed about the nature of the independent variable being administered.

**Confounding variables:** Factors that could be confused with the independent variable and thus distort the results of a study.

held confidential and must not be published in such a way that individual rights to privacy are compromised. Nevertheless, gray areas still appear, making ethical problems of research a continuing issue (Kimmel, 1991; Pomerantz, 1994; Rosenthal, 1994).

The use of *deception* poses one such problem. Under most circumstances, the *Ethical Principles of Psychologists* states, participation in research should be voluntary and informed. That is, we should advise subjects of what they are in for and give them a real opportunity to opt out. But what if you are studying, for example, the conditions under which people will help a stranger in distress? If you contrive a phony emergency situation and then ask people if they are willing to participate in the research, you will spoil the very effect that you are trying to study. Consequently, the guidelines do allow for deception under some conditions, provided that no substantial risks accrue to the subjects. But who, you might ask, is to judge the risks? Most places where research is done now have watchdog committees that make these judgments by examining all studies proposed to be carried out under the sponsorship of the institution. When deception is used, the APA guidelines require that subjects be informed of the deception as soon as is possible without compromising the study's research goals. Subjects in deceptive research must also be *debriefed* after the study to make sure that they suffer no lasting ill effects. Despite these precautions, some psychologists oppose the use of deception in any form of psychological research (Baumrind, 1985; Bower, 1998).

Another long-standing ethical issue surrounds the use of laboratory animals, such as rats, pigeons, and monkeys. As far back as the mid-1800s, scientists used non-human animals for a variety of reasons, including the relative simplicity of their nervous systems and the relative ease with which a large number of subjects can be maintained under controlled conditions. Animals have also served as alternatives to human subjects when a procedure was deemed risky or outright harmful. Concerned about the issue as long ago as 1925, the American Psychological Association established a Committee on Precautions in Animal Experimentation, which adopted guidelines for animal research (Dewsbury, 1990). The American Psychological Association's *Ethical Principles of Psychologists* also directs researchers to provide decent living conditions for animal subjects and to weigh any discomfort caused them against the value of the information sought in the research. A 1985 federal law also imposes legal restrictions on animal research (Novak & Suomi, 1988).

Recent years have seen a renewal of concern, both inside and outside of psychology, about the use of animals as subjects, particularly when the research involves painful or damaging procedures, such as brain surgery, electrode implants, and pain

**Chapter 12
Social Psychology**

*Bystander intervention studies have found interesting reasons why people sometimes fail to help a person in distress.*

People are sharply divided on the use of laboratory animals in research.

studies. Some people feel that the limitations should be more stringent on studies using animals such as chimpanzees, which are most humanlike. Others believe that limitations or outright bans should apply to all animal research, including studies of simple animals like sea slugs (which are often used in neurological studies). Many psychologists, however, are staunch supporters of animal research, under the APA guidelines (Blum, 1994).

## PSYCHOLOGY IN YOUR LIFE

## Getting In Deeper

Whatever your intended major field of study, you should begin learning the professional role you intend to play in your field. Do this by taking out student memberships in professional organizations, attending events sponsored by your major department, getting to know your professors personally, and perusing the field's main magazines, journals, and newsletters. Specifically, if you are considering a major in psychology, you will want to investigate the following resources.

### PROFESSIONAL ORGANIZATIONS
The largest and oldest professional association for psychologists, the American Psychological Association (APA), has well over 150,000 members and affiliates (American Psychological Association, 1998). The American Psychological Society (APS) was recently formed to give a stronger voice to academic and research psychologists. Although the APS is a much smaller organization, it has won wide respect; many psychologists belong both to the APA and to the APS.

These groups have student memberships that include nearly all privileges at a fraction of full membership costs. If you are thinking of majoring in psychology, ask your instructor for information about student membership in a professional psychology association. Also consider attending a state, regional, or national convention to get a better view of what psychologists are really like. These conventions also offer an opportunity for students to present their own research. You could do this, too.

### PSYCHOLOGY-RELATED JOURNALS, MAGAZINES, AND NEWSLETTERS
Professional groups sponsor newsletters or journals that help keep their members abreast of new developments in the field. Psychology majors should begin looking over a few of the main ones every month. Some, like the *APA Monitor*, publish general and very readable articles, while others contain highly technical reports tailored for those with specialized advanced training. Take your first plunge into the psychological literature with these:

- *APA Monitor*—the monthly newspaper of the APA
- *Current Directions in Psychological Science*—a semimonthly APS journal that provides short reviews on trends and controversies in all areas of psychology
- *The American Psychologist*—the general journal of the APA
- *Psychological Science*—the general journal of the APS.

In addition, there are several popular magazines in which you may find articles of interest:

- *Discover*—a popular general-science magazine that often has articles on psychological topics
- *Scientific American*—another general-science magazine that often carries articles on important psychological topics
- *Science News*—a weekly magazine consisting of brief blurbs on new developments in science, including psychology
- *The Skeptical Inquirer*—a delightful pseudoscience-bashing magazine published by CSICOP, the Committee for the Scientific Investigation of Claims of the Paranormal.

Don't feel that you must keep up on the entire psychological literature. Nobody can. Read what interests you in these publications.

### ELECTRONIC RESOURCES IN PSYCHOLOGY
The printed psychological literature is vast and growing quickly. As a result, anyone wanting to find out what is known on a special topic must know how to access the information on the Internet and in an electronic database. There are several general databases available, such as CARL UnCover (http://uncweb.carl.org/) and Expanded Academic Index, along with some specializing just in psychology. One of the following may be available in your campus library:

- *PsychLit*—a database containing the recent psychology literature (on CD-ROM). Disks are updated every few months.
- *PsychInfo*—an online computer database closely related to PsychLit, but continuously updated.

In addition, much free information about psychology is available on the Internet. A good place to start looking would be the American Psychological Association's home page at http://www.apa.org or the American Psychological Society's home page at http://www.psychologicalscience.org/. Remember that Web addresses often change. Remember, also, that anyone can put anything on the Internet, so you will find some good information and some information of questionable repute. Be skeptical!

1. RECALL: *A scientific study should begin with*
   a. a controlled test.
   b. a hypothesis.
   c. data collection.
   d. risk/gain assessment.

2. ANALYSIS: *The conditions involving the independent variable could also be thought of as*
   a. stimuli.
   b. responses.
   c. cognitions.
   d. experimenter biases.

3. ANALYSIS: *Random assignment of subjects to different experimental conditions can control for differences between*
   a. the dependent variable and the independent variable.
   b. the experimental group and the control group.
   c. empirical data and subjective data.
   d. heredity and environment.

4. RECALL: *Which is the only form of research that can determine cause and effect?*
   a. a case study
   b. a correlational study
   c. a naturalistic observation
   d. an experimental study

5. ANALYSIS: *Which one of the following correlations shows the strongest relationship between two variables?*
   a. +0.4
   b. +0.38
   c. −0.7
   d. 0.05

6. RECALL: *In which kind of research does the scientist have the most control over variables that might affect the outcome of the study?*
   a. a case study
   b. a correlational study
   c. an experimental study
   d. a naturalistic observation

7. UNDERSTANDING THE CORE CONCEPT: *Unlike religion, art, the humanities, and the pseudosciences, a science (such as psychology) involves testing its theories against*
   a. firsthand observations.
   b. expert opinion.
   c. common sense.
   d. intuition and "gut" reactions.

**ANSWERS:**   1. b   2. a   3. b   4. d   5. c   6. c   7. a

# USING PSYCHOLOGY TO LEARN PSYCHOLOGY

## *Studying with the Key Questions and Core Concepts*

*L*earning anything new is difficult if it doesn't make sense—and easy if it does. To illustrate, let's turn to a simple demonstration. Examine the string of letters below for ten seconds:

### T W A I B M F B I C I A

Now look away and try to write down the letters in the correct order.

How did you do? Unless you saw some pattern or meaning in the letters, you probably had some difficulty with this task. A close look reveals that the letters are familiar initials of two businesses and two government agencies: TWA, IBM, FBI, and CIA. Discovering this meaning makes them much easier to remember.

In this book, your authors have attempted to help you find meaningful patterns in psychology. To do so, we have built in many learning devices. Among the most important are the Key Questions and the Core Concepts. Let us show you how using these features can make your study of psychology easier.

The Key Questions, which take the place of the familiar section headings in each chapter, give you a "heads up" by signaling what to watch for. For example, one of the Key Questions from this chapter asked, "How Do Psychologists Look at Behavior and Mental Processes?" It alerted you to the idea that psychologists have some special ways of looking at mind and behavior and that the following section would explain what they are. You are much more likely to remember these new ideas if you approach them with an appropriate question in mind (Bransford et al., 1986; Brown & Campione, 1986; Glaser, 1984). You can also use the Key Question as a review check of your understanding of each section before the next test. If you have a

study partner, try asking each other to respond to the key questions.

You may think of Core Concepts as brief responses to the Key Questions. They also highlight the central idea in each chapter section—previews of coming attractions. It is important to realize that a Core Concept is not a complete answer, but a capsule summary of ideas to be fleshed out. As you come to understand the meaning of a Core Concept, you will see that the details of the section will fall easily into place. And to reinforce your understanding, it is a good idea to revisit the Core Concept after you have finished reading the section. In fact, this is precisely what the brief end-of-section quizzes (Check Your Understanding) do.

Another good way to use the Core Concepts is to see if you can explain how the terms in boldface link to the Core Concepts. Let's take the second Core Concept in this chapter, which says:

> **Psychologists draw on six main perspectives: the cognitive, behavioral, psychodynamic, humanistic, biological, and sociocultural.**

Can you explain, for example, how the term **structuralism** relates to this Core Concept? (Sample answer: Structuralism is one of the cognitive perspective's historical roots.)

Together, then, the Key Questions and Core Concepts are designed to pose important questions that lead you to the big ideas in the chapter. They will help you step back from the details to see meaningful patterns. To rephrase an old saying: The Key Questions and Core Concepts will help you see the forest through the trees.

**WHAT IS PSYCHOLOGY, AND WHAT ARE ITS GOALS?**

- Psychology is a science. Its four goals include describing, explaining, predicting, and controlling individual behavior and mental processes. Professional psychologists specialize in various fields depending on the populations and problems of interest. Becoming a psychologist requires graduate study in one or more of psychology's many experimental and applied specialties. Despite having distinctive concerns, psychology also shares interests with other social, behavioral, biological, and health sciences.

**CORE CONCEPT**

Psychology is a science that seeks to describe, explain, predict, and control individual behavior and mental processes.

**HOW DO PSYCHOLOGISTS LOOK AT BEHAVIOR AND MENTAL PROCESSES?**

- Psychology has its roots in several often-conflicting traditions. Its formal beginning as a science is traced to the establishment of Wundt's laboratory in 1879. Modern psychology has six main viewpoints. The *biological view*, a deterministic approach, comes out of the medical and biological sciences. This approach looks for the causes of behavior in biological processes such as brain function and genetics. Evolutionary psychology represents a new emphasis within biological psychology, proposing that human mental and behavioral abilities are the result of genetic adaptation for survival and reproductive advantage. The *cognitive view* emphasizes mental processes and traces its beginnings to the structuralist and functionalist traditions. Structuralism advocated understanding mental processes such as consciousness by investigating their contents and structure. Functionalism argued that mental processes are best understood in terms of their adaptive purposes and functions. In the *psychodynamic view*, pioneered by Sigmund Freud, behavior and thought are influenced by inner, often unconscious, psychological forces and conflicts. The *humanistic view* characterizes human functioning as motivated by a desire to grow, be productive, and fulfill human potential. The *behavioral view* re-

jects mentalistic explanations and explains behavior in terms of observable stimuli and responses. The *sociocultural view* recognizes the power of society and cultural context on individual thought, feeling, and action, notably through social learning. Cross-cultural psychologists are working to incorporate information about other cultures into a field that has been dominated by psychologists from Europe and the United States.

**CORE CONCEPT**

Psychologists draw on six main perspectives: the cognitive, behavioral, psychodynamic, humanistic, biological, and sociocultural.

**HOW DO PSYCHOLOGISTS DO RESEARCH?**

- Psychology differs from the pseudosciences, such as astrology, in that it employs the scientific method to check its ideas empirically—based on firsthand observations. The scientific method consists of five steps: (1) developing a hypothesis, (2) performing a controlled test, (3) gathering objective data, (4) analyzing the results and accepting or rejecting the hypothesis, and (5) publishing, criticizing, and replicating the study. Although all science adheres to these steps, the scientific method allows for several types of research, including experiments, correlational studies, and case studies. These types of research differ in the amount of control the researcher has over the conditions being investigated.
- Everyone, including the scientist, has biases. Common types involve external influences, personal bias, observer bias, expectancy bias, and placebo bias. One way that scientists control for bias in their studies involves the double-blind control method.
- Psychologists must conduct their work by following a code of ethics, established by the American Psychological Association, for the humane treatment of subjects. Still, some areas of disagreement remain. These especially involve the use of deception and the use of animals as experimental subjects.

**CORE CONCEPT**

Psychologists, like all other scientists, use the scientific method to test ideas empirically.

For each of the following items, choose the single best answer. The answer key appears at the end.

1. Scientific psychology employs empirical investigation methods. This means that the data collected must be based on
   a. firsthand sensory evidence.
   b. reasoned speculation.
   c. the observer's subjective interpretation of events.
   d. established traditions of philosophical inquiry.

2. A college admissions officer examines an applicant's secondary school records in order to estimate the student's likelihood of performing well in college. The goal of psychology represented in this task is that of _____ behavior.
   a. controlling
   b. improving
   c. explaining
   d. predicting

3. Which of the following areas is *not* one of the applied psychology specialties?
   a. social psychology
   b. counseling psychology
   c. clinical psychology
   d. school psychology

4. Although "psychology has a long past," it has a short history. Its scientific origins are usually traced to the late nineteenth century, when _____ established the first psychological laboratory.
   a. William James
   b. Wilhelm Wundt
   c. Sigmund Freud
   d. John B. Watson

5. "To understand consciousness or behavior, you must focus on the probable purpose of an action or process." This statement reflects the arguments of
   a. humanism.
   b. functionalism.
   c. structuralism.
   d. behaviorism.

6. According to the _____ perspective in psychology, one's behavior and personality develop as a result of inner tensions and conflicts, created when selfish urges are restricted by societal controls.
   a. biological
   b. cognitive
   c. psychodynamic
   d. sociocultural

7. According to the evolutionary approach in modern psychology, human behavior has evolved in the direction of ever-greater
   a. cultural conformity.
   b. ability to process information.
   c. adaptation and genetic survival.
   d. conflict between individual goals and societal limits.

8. To study the effects of childhood abuse on adult adjustment patterns, you would do
   a. an experimental study.
   b. a correlational study.
   c. a double-blind study.
   d. an evolutionary study.

9. In psychological research, a _____ is a specific and testable prediction of the relationship between the events or variables being studied.
   a. model
   b. base rate
   c. hypothesis
   d. correlation

10. A researcher wonders how to stimulate young schoolchildren to be more creative. She randomly divides a class of first graders in half, reading stories to one group and having members of the other group take turns making up stories to go with the same set of titles. After two weeks, she finds that those who made up stories are producing more work in their reading, writing, and art classes than those who merely listened as she read stories to them. Which one of the following statements is *not* true about this study?
   a. The experimental group was the group that made up their own stories.
   b. The dependent variable involves the amount of work produced by the two groups of children.
   c. There are two levels or conditions in the independent variable.
   d. This is an example of a correlational investigation.

**ANSWERS:**   1. a   2. d   3. a   4. b   5. b   6. c
7. c   8. b   9. c   10. d

# IF YOU'RE INTERESTED . . .

## BOOKS

Burnie, D. (1999). *Get a grip on evolution.* New York: Time/Life.

*This short (190 pp.) paperback covers the basics of evolutionary theory and its applications.*

Colman, A. M. (1987). *Facts, fallacies, and frauds in psychology.* London: Hutchinson.

*This is a short, readable, and fascinating review of myths and realities in psychological theory and research.*

Collins, H. M., & Pinch, T. *The Golem: What you should know about science.* New York: Cambridge University Press.

*Named for the Jewish mythological creature, the Golem, who was powerful but clumsy, this brief and accessible paperback reviews some case studies of research that merit critical reevaluation, showing science in action as an imperfect but powerful approach to knowledge.*

Eysenck, H. J. (1988). *Fact and fiction in psychology.* Baltimore: Penguin Books.

*This engaging examination of what is and is not known in the realm of scientific psychology was written by one of the discipline's most articulate ambassadors to lay readers.*

Falcon, C. T. (1992). *Happiness and personal problems: Psychology made easy.* Lafayette, LA: Sensible Psychology Press.

*Falcon's interesting presentation of psychology applied to everyday life is divided into three sections: information and advice; solving personal problems; and seeking professional help. There are some questionable suggestions, but the author is refreshingly direct.*

Fancher, R. E. (1996). *Pioneers of psychology, 3rd ed.* New York: W. W. Norton & Co.

*Fancher has collected biographies of the women and men who established psychology and developed it as a scientific discipline.*

Fortey, R. (1998). *Life: A natural history of the first four billion years of life on earth.* New York: Knopf.

*A paleontologist describes the exhilaration of scientific discovery and explanation, with colorful imagery and appealing narration.*

Gardner, M. (1989). *Science: Good, bad, and bogus.* Prometheus Books.

*A follow-up to his earlier work* Fads and Fallacies in the Name of Science, *this book gives Martin Gardner an opportunity to review the emptiness of "evidence" for psychic powers, faith healing, and "mind control" that is nothing more than trickery. He includes emotional letters critiquing his earlier work, and responds to them.*

Gay, P. (1988). *Freud: A life for our time.* New York: W. W. Norton & Co.

*This definitive biography by the foremost expert on Freud's life and work is told sympathetically but realistically.*

Gonick, L., & Smith, W. (1993). *The cartoon guide to statistics.* New York: HarperPerennial.

*This helpful and entertaining comic book introduces probability, descriptive statistics, sampling, hypothesis testing, and experimental design. It "invites" the reader to "get it" and should be reassuring to even the most nervous student of research methods.*

Gould, S. J. (1997). *Full house: The spread of excellence from Plato to Darwin.* New York: Random House.

*Paleontologist and popular writer Stephen Jay Gould proposes that new species may be simpler than their parents, not more complex, and that the human mind offers amazing opportunities to make sense out of the world.*

Hilgard, E. R. (1987). *Psychology in America: A historical survey.* New York: Harcourt Brace Jovanovich.

*This interesting reference work describes the historical context, lives, and personal endeavors that have distinguished psychology in research, academia, and professional practice in the United States.*

Hunt, M. (1993). *The story of psychology.* New York: Doubleday.

*The author provides fascinating anecdotes, summaries, and documentation on the lives and times of what he calls "the Magellans of the mind," from ancient philosophy to modern research.*

James, W. (1890/1983). *Principles of psychology.* Cambridge, MA: Harvard University Press.

*The 1983 reissue, in one paperback volume, of the great text by William James, father of American psychology, is* still engaging and inspiring after more than a century of stunning growth and change in the discipline.

Randi, J. (1995). *An encyclopedia of claims, frauds, and hoaxes of the occult and supernatural: Decidedly skeptical definitions of alternate realities.* New York: St. Martin's Griffin.

This A to Z review of 666 people, fads, and fantasies that have captured the public imagination but defied the simplest scientific testing or scrutiny is written by the renowned professional magician and debunker of frauds and scams. Also worth reading by the same author is Conjuring (1992, New York: St. Martin's Press), a "definitive history" of magic, sorcery, wizardry, deception, and chicanery.

Sattler, D. N., & Shabatay, V. (Eds.). (1997). *Psychology in context: Voices and perspectives.* Boston: Houghton Mifflin.

Over 60 articles and essays explore topics all across the spectrum of psychology. The book includes excerpts by such names as Oliver Sacks, Diane Ackerman, Elizabeth Loftus, A. R. Luria, Helen Keller, Deborah Tannen, Annie Dillard, Dick Gregory, Mihaly Csikszentmihalyi, Arthur Ashe, and Studs Terkel.

Schick, T., Jr., & Vaughn, L. (1999). *How to think about weird things* (2nd ed.) Mountain View, CA: Mayfield.

This book is designed to help readers become good consumers of science by distinguishing good research from bad and keeping an open mind and high standards in evaluating explanations for baffling or troubling phenomena.

Shermer, M. (1997). *Why people believe weird things: Pseudoscience, superstition, and other confusions of our time.* New York: W. H. Freeman & Co.

Shermer presents powerful arguments for developing healthy skepticism about unbelievable and magical "explanations" and for debunking a wide range of bizarre beliefs, from alien abductions to antiscientific creationism and denial of the Holocaust.

Stanovich, K. E. (1996). *How to think straight about psychology* (4th ed.). Glenview, IL: Scott, Foresman.

This very practical handbook promotes surviving and thriving by using what you know about psychological research and applications.

Stec, A. M., & Bernstein, D. A. (Eds.). (1999). *Psychology: Fields of application.* Boston: Houghton Mifflin.

Each chapter is a view of one of psychology's applied fields, written by an expert in that specialty. Check this one out if you are interested in a career that combines psychology with any of these: health, education, consumer behavior, business, sports, law, the environment, product design, aviation, animal training, mental disorders, or paranormal phenomena.

Tavris, C. (1995). *Psychobabble & biobunk.* New York: HarperCollins.

In her usual lively style, Carol Tavris takes on various questionable beliefs and practices from the world that she calls "psychobabble": PMS, astrology, the "war" on drugs, the "gender wars," mistaken notions about sexual orientation, and the cult of self-esteem.

Wilson, E. O. (1998). *Consilience: The unity of knowledge.* New York: Knopf.

This call for an ethical and considered approach to science and life in the future was written by the enormously readable, award-winning biologist Edward O. Wilson.

Woods, P. (1987). *Is psychology the major for you?* Washington, DC: American Psychological Association.

Here is everything you ever wanted to know about how and why to major in psychology—and what kind of life and career you might expect after college.

Youngson, R. (1998). *Scientific blunders: A brief history of how wrong scientists can sometimes be.* New York: Carrol & Graf.

This work illustrates how science struggles to establish truth by a trial-and-error process that sometimes produces "explanations" that later seem obviously preposterous.

## VIDEOS

*Career encounters in psychology.* (1991, color, 30 min.)

Several psychologists with diverse careers describe their work in this American Psychological Association documentary.

*Fast, cheap, and out of control.* (1997, color, 82 min.). Directed by Errol Morris; starring Dave Hoover, George Mendonca, Ray Mendez, and Rodney Books.

This documentary interviews four eccentric "geniuses"—a lion tamer, a topiary gardener, an expert on the African naked mole rat, and an MIT robotics scientist—mixed with B-movie footage and running commentary on the nature of life, consciousness, expertise, inspiration, and motivation. Strange and wonderful!

*Inherit the wind.* (1960, B&W, 127 min.). Directed by Stanley Kramer; starring Spencer Tracy, Fredric March, Gene Kelly, Dick York.

This is a wonderful adaptation of the theatrical fictionalization of the 1925 "monkey trial" of John Scopes, a Dayton, Tennessee, schoolteacher prosecuted for teaching evolution in his public school class. Watch the movie—then research the facts about the real people behind the characters.

*King's Row.* (1942, B&W, 127 min.) Directed by Sam Wood; starring Robert Cummings, Ann Sheridan, Ronald Reagan, Claude Rains.

*In a small Midwestern town at the beginning of the twentieth century, a young man turns his life's lessons and losses into a determination to study psychiatry and heal broken minds. Soap-opera story features an outstanding score and a fine performance by Ronald Reagan—including his "Where's the rest of me?" speech—in his role as the hero's best friend.*

*The standard deviants: Psychology.* (1996, color, 122 min.) Produced by The Stimulating World of Psychology.

The Standard Deviants *takes students through major schools of psychology, the brain and nervous system, nature versus nurture, learning theories, psychoanalysis, cognitive science, experimentation, personality, and the scientific method. The film is funny as well as helpful for studying.*

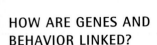 
**HOW ARE GENES AND BEHAVIOR LINKED?**

Behavior consistently found in a species is likely to have a genetic basis that evolved because the behavior has been adaptive.

**Choosing Your Children's Genes:** Within your lifetime parents may be able to select genes for their children. What price will we pay for these choices?

**HOW DOES THE BODY COMMUNICATE INTERNALLY?**

The body's twin communications systems, the nervous system and the endocrine system, both use chemical messengers to communicate with targets throughout the body.

**Side Effects of Psychoactive Drugs:** Chemicals that affect behavior usually mimic hormones or neurotransmitters. But they may stimulate unintended targets, where they produce unwanted side effects.

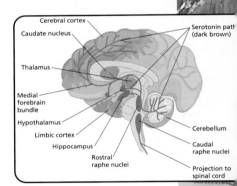

**HOW DOES THE BRAIN PRODUCE BEHAVIOR AND MENTAL PROCESSES?**

The brain is composed of many specialized and interconnected modules that work together to create mind and behavior.

**Brain Damage and Behavior:** Everyone knows somebody who has suffered brain damage from an accident, a tumor, or a stroke. The symptoms suggest which part of the brain was damaged.

**USING PSYCHOLOGY TO LEARN PSYCHOLOGY:**
**PUTTING YOUR KNOWLEDGE OF THE BRAIN TO WORK**

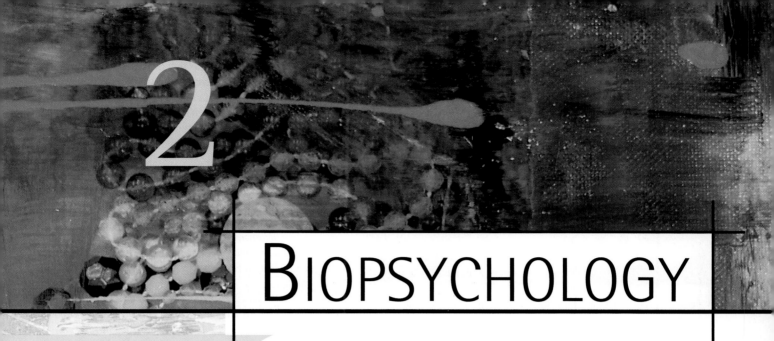

# 2

# BIOPSYCHOLOGY

*D*r. Frankenstein didn't fare well against his monster, and John Henry lost his cause against the steam drill. Now, in a modern version of the conflict between human and technology, Garry Kasparov has fallen to Deep Blue.

Who are these recent combatants? Until a short time ago, Garry Kasparov reigned as the undisputed champion of the world of chess. His adversary, Deep Blue, was a computer. Not just any computer, mind you, but a supercomputer designed specifically by the IBM corporation to topple the champ.

To accomplish this, IBM took on the task of building a machine that could outwit an impressive human brain. Blue's wits consisted of 256 separate, specially designed processors. With the aid of a huge software program, written by a committee of computer experts collaborating with rival chess experts, Blue's processors could "think" about 20 moves ahead at the speed of 200 million possible moves per second. (The human nervous system is much slower: You may have noticed that, after stubbing your toe, it takes about ½ second for the painful stimulus to register in your brain.)

What happened in the battle of silicon vs. biological wits? By all accounts, the turning point came in game two, when the computer seemed to overlook an obvious opportunity to move its queen into a powerful position. Instead, it opted for a subtle and unprecedented strategy that was to have far more devastating effects. At the time, Kasparov thought Deep Blue had made a mistake, but in fact it had seen more deeply into the game than its human opponent could. Kasparov later said, "Suddenly [Deep Blue] played like a god for one moment" (Levy, 1997a, p. 72). A demoralized Kasparov eventually lost not only that game but the six-game match as well. He had become a victim of his own humanity (Gelernter, 1997). Says Patrick Wolff, former U.S. chess champion, "What shocked me and most chess players who followed the match was how Kasparov simply fell apart at the end. He collapsed psychologically" (Peterson, 1997, p. 300). Onlookers sensed that he had become mentally fatigued by game four, while Blue's silicon circuits were always fresh and ready. In addition, Kasparov apparently became distracted by feelings of frustration, anger, and despair. Ironically, Deep Blue could feel no thrill at being on the top of the world's chess heap.

Where does Kasparov's defeat leave humanity? Are our brains becoming outmoded? Hardly. While computers like Deep Blue, or even their desktop cousins, can perform

Garry Kasparov and Deep Blue: How is the brain similar to (and different from) a computer?

*complex calculations at speeds that leave a biological brain in the digital dust, what they cannot do is even more remarkable (Bringsjord, 1998). Computers can't hold stimulating conversations—or even make sensible small talk. They can copy speech, but they can't understand it. They can't form any but the simplest concepts. They have no sense of humor or sense of the absurd (as when the checkout computer charges you $200 for a can of tuna). They don't make friends (although they have some enemies). They can't empathize. And, perhaps most of all, computers—with all their memory and all their power to manipulate data—have no "I" inside to appreciate the significance of their accomplishments or to want to do better next time. As one pundit put it, "Deep Blue took as little satisfaction from its win as does an espresso machine after producing the perfect latte." Even if we know that a computer such as Deep Blue has profound limitations, we can be forgiven for feelings of wounded pride when a computer defeats us on what was our own turf. The pundit continued, "A refrigerator doesn't think, either, but if one hits you on the head it still hurts" (Levy, 1997b, p. 84).*

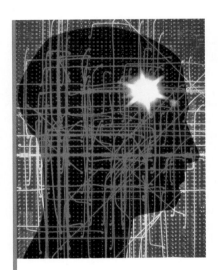

Early psychologists used the analogy of a telephone switchboard as an approach to understanding how the brain communicates information.

**Biopsychology:** The specialty in psychology that studies the interaction of biology, behavior, and the environment.

When fully matured, a brain like yours occupies a space the size of a grapefruit, weighs only 3 pounds, and consists of the most common chemical elements. Yet, despite its small size, the human brain is the most complex structure known. Its 100 billion nerve cells, designed to communicate and store information, far outnumber all the transistors and wires in the depths of the computer, Deep Blue. Indeed, the number of nerve cells in the human brain outnumbers the stars in our galaxy.

How can we even begin to understand such a complex object? Psychologists often think of the brain as a sort of biological computer, so powerful that it can learn, interpret, store, and communicate all the information that is possible for the brightest of us to know or the most sensitive of us to experience (Azar, 1997). Yet, as we have seen, it is much more—and less—than the most advanced computer on earth.

Evolutionary shaping of the brain has taken place over millions of years. And now the human brain has turned its attention on itself: This marvelous organ has become the subject of study for a new breed of researchers in **biopsychology,** a rapidly growing specialty that lies at the intersection of biology, behavior, and the environment. Biopsychologists seek to understand the biochemical processes behind the behavior of all living creatures. In general, they want to explain how the *nervous system* and its companion communication network, the *endocrine system,* cooperate to produce all human action. This field is the focus of the present chapter.

Like biopsychologists, we must use our brains to understand the brain and its mental processes. At first, these processes may seem to exist independently of the tissue inside our heads. But when disease, drugs, or accidents destroy brain cells, the biological basis of the human mind stands out in harsh relief. Then we are forced to recognize the physical matter from which spring sensation and perception, learning and memory, passion and pain, reason and madness.

In this chapter we will first set the scene for our look at the brain by examining how the twin forces of heredity and evolution influence our physical and mental characteristics. Next, we will examine the body's two internal communications systems: the endocrine system and the nervous system, of which the brain is the central component. Finally, we will study the structure and function of the brain itself. Along the way, you will encounter many new terms. We urge you to think of this chapter as a "journey" into the field of psychology. As with most journeys, you may at first find the new territory unfamiliar. But with persistence you will come to know the landmarks and place names of the new territory that lies inside you. On this journey we are asking you to look closely at yourself from a perspective that you may not have taken before—the perspective of biopsychology. By understanding your biological nature, you will better appreciate how brain, mind, behavior, and the environment interact to create the uniqueness of every human being.

 KEY QUESTION

## HOW ARE GENES AND BEHAVIOR LINKED?

Fish have an **innate** knack for swimming. Most birds are built for flight. And what about us? Humans, too, have many inborn behavioral tendencies. Our brains come already programmed for, among other things, language and social interaction. But how did these potentialities become woven into the fabric of the brain?

Understanding the marvelous piece of biology called the brain requires us first to consider **evolution,** the process by which species of organisms gradually change as they adapt to their environments. On a microscopic level, we can observe evolution in action, as we see bacteria adapt to antibiotics. Similarly, but over longer time spans, larger and more complex organisms (such as our ancestors) have also changed, as they adapted to changing temperatures, food supplies, and breeding opportunities. When the environment serves up severe challenges, only those most genetically prepared will survive and pass their genes on to their offspring. In this way, evolution also has an impact on both the physical attributes of a species and its genetically based behavior. This fact makes evolution an important force in psychology and the basis for the Core Concept for this section:

 **CORE** CONCEPT

**Behavior consistently found in a species is likely to have a genetic basis that evolved because the behavior has been adaptive.**

All through this book, the notion of an adaptive, evolutionary basis for behavior will help us understand otherwise puzzling psychological phenomena, including emotions, motives, and intelligence, as well as certain social behaviors and gender differences. After a closer look in the following paragraphs at the way evolution works, we will consider how it has influenced our behavior.

### How Evolution Works

About 170 years ago, British naturalist **Charles Darwin** set sail on HMS *Beagle*, an ocean research vessel commissioned to survey the coastline of South America. During the five-year trip, Darwin made detailed records of the many life-forms and fossils he encountered. The pattern that emerged in Darwin's mind was one of close relationships among species. He explained this pattern in his most famous book, *On the Origin of Species* (1859), where he set forth science's most fundamental and wide-sweeping biological theory, that of the evolution of life.

Darwin's observations convinced him that some natural mechanism influenced the breeding and survival of organisms from one generation to the next. Species ultimately either adapt to their environments and flourish, or they fail to adapt and die out. Thus the flowers of a plant, the colors of a butterfly's wings, or the hunting instincts of a cat prove adaptive to environmental conditions and are preserved, if the organism survives and breeds. Or, if the characteristics fail to help organisms adapt and reproduce, they may be "selected out." For the fortunate organisms whose ancestors had accumulated new traits that allowed them to adapt and survive, the result "would be the formation of a new species," claimed Darwin (1859).

 Chapter 1: Mind, Behavior, and Science
*The evolutionary perspective emphasizes the adaptive nature of traits.*

**Innate:** Inborn; present at birth; part of the organism's biological heritage.

**Evolution:** The gradual process of biological change that occurs in a species as it adapts to its environment.

**Charles Darwin:** The British naturalist who first described the evolutionary theory and provided overwhelming evidence for the process of natural selection.

"Evolution" is, of course, an emotionally loaded term, and many people have a mistaken notion of its meaning. For example, some mistakenly believe that Darwin's theory says humans "come from monkeys." But neither Darwin nor any other evolutionary scientist has ever stated this. Rather, they say we share a common ancestor—a big difference. Another common misconception holds that evolution occurs when an animal's behavior alters its genetic inheritance. According to this erroneous view, giraffes evolved long necks from stretching to reach leaves high in the trees. In truth, the ancestors of giraffes that, because of genetic variation, possessed slightly longer necks had a slight survival and reproductive advantage over their shorter-necked cousins. Consequently, the genetic variation behind longer necks came to dominate the gene pool. The real process of evolution is as biologically sound as it is simple and elegant.

More than 98% of our genetic material is also found in chimpanzees (Gibbons, 1998). This supports Darwin's idea that humans and apes had a common ancestor.

**NATURAL SELECTION**   You and your unique genetic traits may be an evolutionary dead end unless you have children who also survive and reproduce. According to Darwin's theory of **natural selection,** the driving force behind evolution is precisely this survival-and-reproduction interaction of organisms and their environment (Buss et al., 1998). Some members of a species produce more offspring that survive and reproduce than do others because environmental conditions favor their inheritable features. For example, birds with larger, stronger beaks may be more likely to survive and reproduce during times of scarcity because they can forage on tougher seeds (Weiner, 1994). Because this characteristic can be inherited, their offspring will carry this genetic advantage, too. In this fashion, individuals with the improved traits survive, reproduce, and pass their adaptive traits on to the next generation more often than do those with less-adaptive traits. Their offspring will, in turn, pass along the survival-promoting traits they possess, and their descendants will eventually outnumber those who have not inherited the helpful features. In evolutionary terms, successful organisms pass their genes along to succeeding generations, while unsuccessful organisms do not.

**THE HUMAN ADVANTAGE**   Hawks have better vision than we do. Dogs have keener noses. Cheetahs can run faster. Gorillas are stronger. So, what advantage do we have that allowed our species to survive? The marvelous piece of biology that is the human brain, with its capacity for learning, may be the feature that distinguishes us most clearly from other creatures (Harvey & Krebs, 1990). And which physical feature of the brain has contributed most to our survival? Neuroscientists call it **encephalization,** an evolutionary increase in brain size and in the proportion of specialized brain tissue.

As the human brain evolved and specialized, encephalization resulted in a particularly important milestone for our species: the advent of language (see Diamond, 1990). Language, a product of highly sophisticated brain processes, makes it possible for individuals to have interactions ranging from simple conversations to the exchange of complex ideas in art, music, and science. The specialized parts of our

**FIGURE 2.1:**   How Natural Selection Works

Environmental changes create competition for resources among species members. Individuals that inherit characteristics that promote survival will probably survive and reproduce. The next generation will then have a greater number of individuals possessing these advantageous genes.

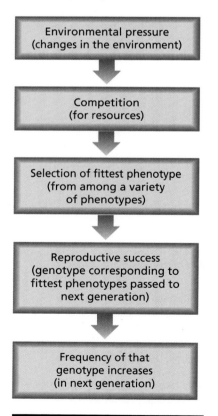

Environmental pressure
(changes in the environment)

↓

Competition
(for resources)

↓

Selection of fittest phenotype
(from among a variety
of phenotypes)

↓

Reproductive success
(genotype corresponding to
fittest phenotypes passed to
next generation)

↓

Frequency of that
genotype increases
(in next generation)

brain that give us the ability for language are part of the genetic blueprint that we inherited from our parents.

## Genes and Inheritance

What else did you inherit from your parents? Your physical characteristics, such as height, weight, facial features, and hair color, all come from the unique combination of your parents' genetic characteristics that were inscribed in every cell in your body. Yet, despite this genetic heritage, you are different from your parents. One source of this difference is the environment in which you grew up—distinct in time and sometimes place from that of your parents. Another source of difference arises from the unique combination of genes you possess, coming from both parents, yet different from either one of them.

A mother and father pass on to the offspring a random combination of the genetic traits that past generations of their family lines have given them. This inheritance results in a unique **genotype,** the organism's genetic structure, containing the complete biological blueprint and timetable for individual development. The study of this process—the inheritance of physical and psychological traits from ancestors—is called **genetics.**

Remarkably, Darwin knew nothing of **genes,** the molecular units that program our biological characteristics into every cell of our bodies. Although he correctly described the process of natural selection, he never knew that natural selection operates on the genes to drive evolutionary change. From our perspective 150 years later, we know that spontaneous genetic variations, or **mutations,** which occur at random in the genetic code, occasionally produce beneficial traits that aid survival. When this occurs, these newly developed genetic traits pass on to the succeeding generation's genetic reservoir. Occasionally, mutations will also produce troublesome genetic variations that generate problems such as mental retardation, hyperaggressiveness, or the extreme emotional turmoil of clinical depression. The same mechanism of mutation that produces beneficial traits may also produce maladaptive ones: Mutations are random, so they do not always work to the individual organism's advantage.

**CHROMOSOMES AND DNA** In the film *Jurassic Park*, the genetic code for dinosaurs was recovered from dinosaur blood trapped in fossil amber. Although the story was fiction, the film rested on an important fact: The nucleus of every cell in an organism's body contains the complete genetic code for that individual. In the nucleus a complex molecule, called **DNA** (deoxyribonucleic acid), contains the code of life: the genetic instructions for making proteins. These proteins, in turn, regulate the body's physiological processes and the expression of the body's **phenotype,** the observable or measurable expressions of an individual's genetic makeup. Thus, the proteins specified by the nuclear DNA exert biological control over body build, physical strength, intelligence, certain mental disorders, and many other behavior patterns—all of which are part of the individual's phenotype.

The complete package of DNA in a human cell contains approximately 100,000 genes. These genes are assembled end-to-end in long chains to form structures known as **chromosomes.** At the moment you were conceived, cells throughout your body inherited 46 chromosomes from your parents: 23 from your mother paired

**Chapter 4:**
**Psychological Development**
*Many developmental psychologists think that some language skills are built into the brain.*

**Chapter 4:**
**Psychological Development**
*Our genes influence both mental and physical development.*

**Natural selection:** The driving force behind evolution—by which the environment "selects" the fittest organisms.

**Encephalization:** An evolutionary increase in brain size and in the proportion of specialized brain tissue.

**Genotype:** An organism's genetic makeup.

**Genetics:** The study of the inheritance of physical and psychological traits.

**Genes:** Segments of a chromosome that encode the directions for the inherited physical and mental characteristics of an organism. Genes are the functional units of a chromosome.

**Mutations:** Genetic variations, which occur randomly, especially during the recombination of chromosomes in sexual reproduction.

**DNA:** A long, complex molecule that encodes genetic characteristics. The long name for DNA is *deoxyribonucleic acid.*

**Phenotype:** An organism's observable physical characteristics.

**Chromosomes:** Tightly coiled threadlike structures along which the genes are organized, like beads on a necklace. Chromosomes consist primarily of DNA.

# FIGURE 2.2: DNA, Genes, and Chromosomes

Each chromosome is made up of thousands of genes. Genes are segments of a long DNA molecule. Each gene contains the complete instructions for making a protein.

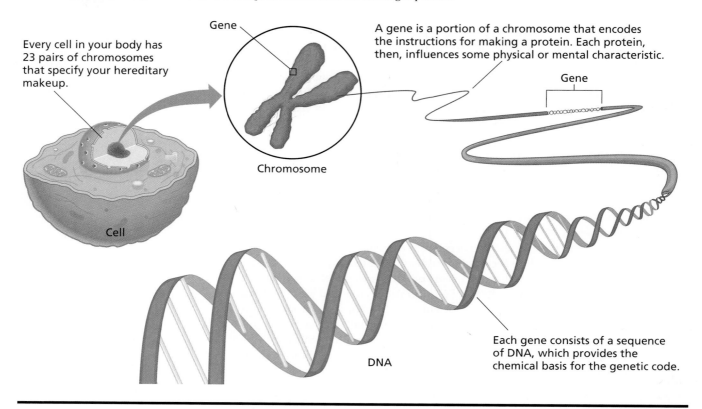

Every cell in your body has 23 pairs of chromosomes that specify your hereditary makeup.

**Gene**

**Chromosome**

A gene is a portion of a chromosome that encodes the instructions for making a protein. Each protein, then, influences some physical or mental characteristic.

**Gene**

**Cell**

**DNA**

Each gene consists of a sequence of DNA, which provides the chemical basis for the genetic code.

---

with 23 from your father. Each of these chromosomes contains thousands of genes. Genetic information in a special abbreviated form is written into the ova or sperm cells stored in your reproductive organs. (See Figure 2.2.)

The **sex chromosomes** warrant special mention because they contain genes for development of a male or female phenotype. An XX combination in this pair codes for femaleness, while an XY combination codes for maleness. Whatever your gender, you inherited one X chromosome from your biological mother. In addition, you received either an X (if you are female) or a Y (if you are male) from your biological father. Thus, your genotype determines your biological sex and the associated phenotypic characteristics in your body structure and chemistry that develop throughout your lifetime.

**GENETIC EXPLANATIONS FOR BEHAVIOR**  We should be cautious about assuming genetic explanations for all behavior, warns psychologist Jerome Kagan (1994). Yet, we know that genes exert considerable influence on intelligence, personality, certain mental disorders, and even on some reading disabilities (Bouchard, 1994; DeAngelis, 1997; Gelernter, 1994; Hamer, 1997; Plomin, Owen, & McGuffin, 1994; Plomin & Rende, 1991; Saudino, 1997). In the hybrid field of **behavior genetics,** geneticists and psychologists collaborate to uncover the genetic basis of still more behavioral characteristics (Plomin, 1997). They also develop environmental interventions, such as training programs, diet, and social interactions, that can modify genetically influenced behavior.

Research in behavior genetics has produced some practical results. Consider, for example, a condition called **Down syndrome,** caused by an extra 21st chromo-

**Sex chromosomes:** The X and Y chromosomes that determine our physical sex characteristics.

**Behavior genetics:** A new field bringing together geneticists and psychologists interested in the genetic basis of behavior and mental characteristics, such as intelligence, altruism, and psychological disorders.

**Down syndrome:** A genetic disorder that produces one form of mental retardation.

**Human Genome Project:** An international scientific effort to determine the complete human genetic code in all 23 pairs of chromosomes.

some fragment. The disorder involves markedly impaired psychomotor and physical development, as well as mental retardation. In an earlier day, people with Down syndrome faced a bleak and unproductive life in which they depended almost wholly on others to fulfill their basic needs. A deeper understanding of the disorder has now changed that outlook. Although no cure has been found, today we know that people with Down syndrome are capable of considerable learning, despite their genetic impairment. With special programs that teach life skills, those with Down syndrome now learn to care for themselves, work, and establish some personal independence.

The science of behavior genetics has had its most striking successes in identifying disorders that involve a single chromosome. To give another example, a rare pattern of impulsive violence found in several members of a Dutch family has been linked to a single gene (Brunner et al., 1993). However, many other genetically based disorders appear to involve multiple genes—or, sometimes, even more than one chromosome (Boomsma, Anokhin, & de Geus, 1997). This is probably the case with schizophrenia, a severe mental disorder, and with certain forms of Alzheimer's disease, a disorder involving deterioration of the brain and cognitive processes in some older individuals (Morrison-Bogorad & Phelps, 1997; Plomin, Owen, & McGuffin, 1994; Skoog et al., 1993).

The extra 21st chromosome fragment in Down syndrome underlies the mental retardation and the similar facial features of people with this genetic disorder. Special programs train such persons to lead productive lives.

**Chapter 13: Psychopathology**

*Schizophrenia is a psychotic disorder that affects about one out of 100 persons.*

PSYCHOLOGY IN YOUR LIFE

## Choosing Your Children's Genes

Scientists already have the ability to control and alter the genetics of animals, like Dolly, the famous fatherless sheep that was cloned from one of her mother's cells. But what are the prospects for genetic manipulation in people? As you read this, scientists are working on the **Human Genome Project,** a multibillion-dollar effort to decipher the complete human genetic code (Pennisi, E., 1998; Wade, 1998). Soon we will mine this knowledge for an understanding of the genetic basis for many physical and

Dolly was cloned from a single cell of her "mother," to which she is genetically identical.

*Continued*

mental disorders. But not all the promise of human genetics lies in the future. We can already sample fetal cells and search for certain genetic disorders, such as Down syndrome. The Human Genome Project will greatly expand this ability.

Within your lifetime, parents may be able to select genes for their children, much as you select the components of a deli sandwich. It is likely that we will learn to alter the DNA in a developing fetus in order to add or delete certain physical and mental traits (Henig, 1998). This will probably be done by infecting the fetus with a harmless virus containing desirable genes that will alter or replace the genetic blueprint in every cell of the body. But what will be the price of this technology?

Undoubtedly, parents in this brave new genetic world will want their children to be smart and good looking—but, we might wonder, by what standards will intelligence and looks be judged? And will everyone be able to afford to place an order for their children's genes—or only the very wealthy? What potential for conflict does this newfound "freedom" hold for our species? You can be certain that the problems we face will be simultaneously biological, psychological, political, and ethical. (*See Chapter 11, Intelligence and the Psychology of Differences.*)

The more we learn about behavior genetics, the more clearly we know about the powerful biological forces that determine human potential and life experience—and the power we will have when these genetic forces are completely understood. The American Psychological Association has identified genetics as one of the disciplines with the greatest promise for psychology's future (Plomin & McClearn, 1993). Already, psychologists are called on to provide guidance about how genetic knowledge can best be applied (Plomin, 1997), particularly in helping people assess genetic risks in connection with family planning. We invite you to assess your own concern with the genetics of parenting by answering the following questions:

- If you could select three genetic traits for your children, which ones would you select?
- How would you feel about raising children you have adopted or fostered but to whom you are not genetically related?
- If a biological child of yours might be born disabled or fatally ill because of your genetic heritage, would you have children anyway? What circumstances or conditions would affect your decision?
- If you knew you might carry a gene responsible for a serious medical or behavioral disorder, would you want to be tested before having children? Would it be fair for a prospective spouse to require you to be tested before conceiving children? Would it be fair for the state to make such a requirement?

## Check Your Understanding

1. RECALL: *Which of the following represent differences between the brain and a computer? (More than one may be correct.)*
   a. emotion
   b. accuracy of memory
   c. the ability to understand concepts
   d. the ability to make meaningful associations

2. RECALL: *Which of the following is a characteristic that might be a part of your phenotype?*
   a. your height and eye color
   b. the members of your family
   c. what you have learned in school
   d. the childhood diseases you have had

3. RECALL: *Which of the following statements expresses the correct relationship?*
   a. Genes are made of chromosomes.
   b. DNA is made of chromosomes.
   c. DNA is made of genes.
   d. Genes are made of DNA.

4. ANALYSIS: *In purely evolutionary terms, which one would be a measure of your own success as an organism?*
   a. your intellectual accomplishments
   b. the length of your life
   c. the number of children you have
   d. the contributions that you make to the happiness of humanity

5. UNDERSTANDING THE CORE CONCEPT: *Behavior consistently found in a species is likely to have a genetic basis that evolved because the behavior has been adaptive. Which of the following human behaviors illustrates this concept?*
   a. driving a car
   b. sending astronauts to the moon
   c. Down syndrome
   d. language

ANSWERS:   1. **all are correct**   2. **a**   3. **d**   4. **c**   5. **d**

## HOW DOES THE BODY COMMUNICATE INTERNALLY?

You are driving on a winding mountain road, and a car is coming directly at you. You and the other driver swerve in opposite directions at the last instant. Your heart is pounding—and it keeps pounding for several minutes after the danger has passed. Externally, you have avoided a potentially fatal accident. Internally, your body has responded to two kinds of messages from its two communication systems.

The fast-acting **nervous system,** a massive network of nerve cells that rapidly relays messages to and from the brain, came to your rescue first. The nervous system's messages rely on the production and release of *neurotransmitters*, chemicals that carry information between nerve cells. This is the system that initially sped up your heartbeat and sent messages to your muscles that you used to swerve the car out of danger.

The body's other communication system, the **endocrine system,** involves a network of glands that also manufacture chemical messengers and secrete them directly into the bloodstream. These chemical messengers, called **hormones,** affect the operation of other glands and organs. (See Figure 2.3 for the location of the body's endocrine glands.) Certain components of the slower endocrine system sent follow-up messages that kept your heart pounding, even after the emergency was past.

**Nervous system:** The entire network of neurons in the body, including the central nervous system, the peripheral nervous system, and their subdivisions.

**Endocrine system:** The hormone system—the body's chemical messenger system, including the following endocrine glands: pituitary, adrenals, gonads, thyroid, parathyroid, pancreas, ovaries, and testes.

**Hormones:** The chemical messengers used by the endocrine system. Many hormones also serve as neurotransmitters.

**FIGURE 2.3:** Endocrine Glands in Females and Males

The pituitary gland (shown at right) is the "master gland," regulating the endocrine glands, whose locations are illustrated at left. The pituitary gland is under the control of the hypothalamus, an important structure in the limbic system.

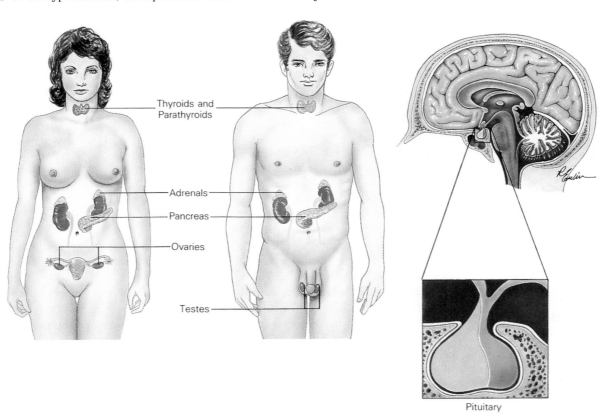

Thyroids and Parathyroids

Adrenals

Pancreas

Ovaries

Testes

Pituitary

In general, these two internal message systems work together to help us respond in emergencies. They also act in concert to produce our more usual, everyday behaviors. This is the Core Concept:

**CORE CONCEPT**

**The body's twin communications systems, the nervous system and the endocrine system, both use chemical messengers to communicate with targets throughout the body.**

**Chapter 13:**
**Psychopathology**
**Chapter 3:**
**States of Mind**

*Psychoactive drugs produce essentially the same chemical changes in the brain that occur in certain mental disorders.*

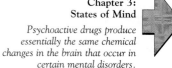

The brain is the "nerve center" of these two communication systems. All its incoming and outgoing messages rely on chemical signals. So do the brain's internal communications, which produce all our thoughts and feelings. As you might expect, psychoactive drugs work by altering these chemical communications. And in later chapters we will note that some psychological disorders also involve disturbances in these communication channels. For now, however, let's focus on the structure and function of the two communication systems: the nervous system and the endocrine system.

## The Nervous System

When you stub your toe, the body's fast communication network, the *nervous system*, carries the painful message from your toe to your brain. Processing this message may involve billions of highly specialized **nerve cells,** or **neurons.** These neurons are organized either into densely packed clusters (nuclei) or extended pathways (nerve fibers). Large clusters of nuclei make up much of the brain and spinal cord. Together with the nerve fibers extending throughout the body, these structures make up the entire *nervous system.*

**DIFFERENT PARTS HAVE DIFFERENT FUNCTIONS**    The nervous system has two major subsystems: the **central nervous system** (CNS) and the **peripheral nervous system.** The CNS is composed of all the neurons in the brain and spinal cord, while the peripheral nervous system is made up of all the nerve fibers that connect the CNS to the rest of the body. Figure 2.4 will help you conceptualize the relationship of the central and peripheral nervous systems.

Like an executive, the central nervous system integrates and coordinates all bodily functions, processes incoming neural messages, and sends out commands to different parts of the body. For example, if a vicious-looking dog approaches you, your CNS signals your legs to run. If a friend greets you, your CNS signals your arms to reach out and your voice to speak. The CNS sends and receives neural messages through the spinal cord, a trunk line of neurons that connects the brain to much of the peripheral nervous system. This trunk line is housed in the spinal column, the central tube running through your backbone.

The spinal cord also is responsible for simple, swift **reflexes** that do not involve the brain (such as the knee-jerk reflex that physicians elicit with a tap on the knee). We know that the brain is not involved in many simple reflexes, because an organism whose spinal cord has been severed from its brain can still respond, for example, by withdrawing its limb from a painful stimulus. Without direction from the brain, however, voluntary movements cannot occur. As a result, damage to the nerves of the spinal cord can produce paralysis of the legs or trunk, as seen in paraplegic individuals. The extent of paralysis depends on how high up on the spinal cord the damage occurred: the higher up the site of damage, the greater the extent of the paralysis. You may recall that, in 1995, American actor Christopher Reeve was paralyzed from the neck down by an injury sustained during a horseback riding accident. Physicians caring for Reeve emphasized that his **prognosis** (likely future condition) depended on the extent and location of damage to his spinal cord.

**Nerve cells** or **neurons:** Cells specialized to receive and transmit information to other cells in the body. Bundles of many neurons are called *nerves.*

**Central nervous system:** The brain and the spinal cord.

**Peripheral nervous system:** All parts of the nervous system lying outside the central nervous system. The peripheral nervous system includes the autonomic and somatic nervous systems.

**Reflexes:** Simple, unlearned responses triggered by stimuli—such as the knee-jerk reflex set off by tapping the tendon just below your kneecap.

**Prognosis:** Outlook, prediction.

**Chapter 5:**
**Sensation and Perception**

*Conscious sensations of pain are realized in the brain*

## FIGURE 2.4: Organization of the Nervous System

The sensory and motor nerves that make up the peripheral nervous system are linked to the brain by the spinal cord.

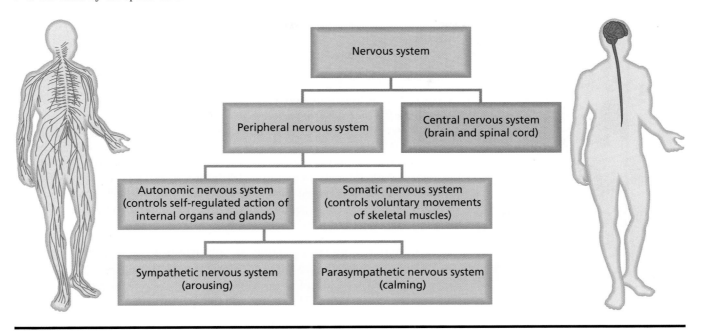

Nervous system

Peripheral nervous system

Central nervous system (brain and spinal cord)

Autonomic nervous system (controls self-regulated action of internal organs and glands)

Somatic nervous system (controls voluntary movements of skeletal muscles)

Sympathetic nervous system (arousing)

Parasympathetic nervous system (calming)

Despite their commanding position, the brain and spinal cord are isolated from any direct contact with the outside world. The central nervous system never directly experiences light waves, sound waves, or surface textures. Instead, it relies on the peripheral nervous system to provide information about the world from sensory receptors, such as those found in the eyes and ears. Likewise, the brain must control our actions by relaying commands through the peripheral nervous system to the muscles. This outgoing division of the peripheral nervous system is actually composed of two parts: the *somatic nervous system* and the *autonomic nervous system* (see Figure 2.4).

The **somatic nervous system** sends messages from the CNS to the body's skeletal muscles. For example, when you type a message on a keyboard, the instruction to move your fingers is carried by the somatic nervous system. As you plan what to type, your brain sends signals about which fingers to use on which keys, and your fingers return feedback about their position and movement. If you strike the wrong *kee,* the somatic nervous system informs the brain, which issues a correction so you can quickly delete the error and hit the right *key.*

The other part of the peripheral nervous system that conveys messages away from

Actor Christopher Reeve broke his neck in a horseback riding accident 1995. His paralysis was the result of damage to the spinal cord.

**Somatic nervous system:**
A portion of the peripheral nervous system that sends voluntary messages to the body's skeletal muscles.

The sympathetic nervous system responds to emergencies with a fight-or-flight response.

the brain is known as the **autonomic nervous system** (*autonomic* means self-regulating or independent). This network carries signals that coordinate largely involuntary functions of the internal organs. It operates constantly, regulating bodily processes we don't usually control consciously, such as respiration, digestion, and arousal. It also works during sleep and even sustains life processes during anesthesia and coma.

Complicating matters, the autonomic nervous system is itself subdivided into the *sympathetic* and *parasympathetic* nervous systems. These two systems work together, in an opposite but complementary fashion, to promote survival by maintaining basic bodily functions and preparing the body to respond to threat. The **sympathetic division** governs responses to stress under conditions of threat or emergency, when action must be quick and powerfully energized. This is the "fight-or-flight" nervous system. It energizes you to respond to a stressor quickly by either fighting what threatens you or taking flight from what you cannot fight. In contrast, the **parasympathetic division** monitors the routine operation of the body's internal functions. This "housekeeping" division returns the body to calmer functioning after sympathetic arousal. The separate duties of the sympathetic and parasympathetic nervous systems are illustrated in Figure 2.5.

**THE NEURON: BUILDING BLOCK OF THE NERVOUS SYSTEM**   How does the nervous system permit us to sense and respond to the world outside our bodies? To answer this question, we will look at the structure and function of the neuron, the basic unit of the nervous system. The neuron is a cell specialized to receive, process, and transmit information to other cells. Neurons vary in shape, size, chemical composition, and function. Although over 200 types have been identified in mammal brains, all neurons have the same basic structure (see Figure 2.8).

We are born with more neurons than we ever use, and many die in the first few years of life. By adolescence, however, the number of neurons stabilizes, and, although the brain apparently generates some new neurons throughout our lifetime, the total remains essentially constant throughout adulthood (Barinaga, 1998; Kempermann & Gage, 1999; Travis, 1998). This neural stability may be essential for the continuity of learning and memory over a long lifetime (Rakic, 1985). Surprisingly, however, human neurons do expire in astonishing numbers—about 200,000 will die every day of your life (Dowling, 1992). Fortunately, because we start out with so many neurons, we will lose less than 2% of our original supply in 70 years.

*TYPES OF NEURONS*   Biopsychologists distinguish three major classes of neurons: *sensory neurons, motor neurons,* and *interneurons.* **Sensory neurons,** also called **afferent neurons** (meaning "carrying toward"), transport messages from sense receptor cells toward the central nervous system. Receptor cells are highly specialized sensory neurons that are sensitive to light, sound, or other stimuli. By contrast, **motor neurons,** or **efferent neurons** (meaning "carrying from"), deliver messages from the central nervous system to the muscles and glands.

Except in the simplest of reflexive circuits (shown in Figure 2.6), sensory neurons do not communicate directly with motor neurons. Instead, they rely on the **interneurons** that make up most of the billions of cells in the brain and spinal cord. Interneurons relay messages from sensory neurons to other interneurons or to motor neurons. For every motor neuron in the body there are as many as 5,000 interneurons in the great intermediate network that forms the CNS's computational system (Nauta & Feirtag, 1979).

**Autonomic nervous system:** The portion of the peripheral nervous system that sends messages to the internal organs and glands.

**Sympathetic division:** The part of the autonomic nervous system that sends messages to internal organs and glands that help us respond to stressful and emergency situations.

**Parasympathetic division:** The part of the autonomic nervous system that monitors the routine operations of the internal organs and returns the body to calmer functioning after arousal by the sympathetic division.

**Sensory neurons** or **afferent neurons:** Nerve cells that carry messages from sense receptors toward the central nervous system.

**Motor neurons** or **efferent neurons:** Nerve cells that carry messages away from the central nervous system toward the muscles and glands.

**Interneurons:** Nerve cells that relay messages from between nerve cells, especially in the brain and spinal cord.

**FIGURE 2.5:** Divisions of the Autonomic Nervous System

The parasympathetic nervous system (diagramed at left) regulates day-to-day internal processes and behavior. The sympathetic nervous system (at right) regulates internal processes and behavior in stressful situations. On their way to and from the spinal cord, sympathetic nerve fibers make connections with specialized clusters of neurons called ganglia.

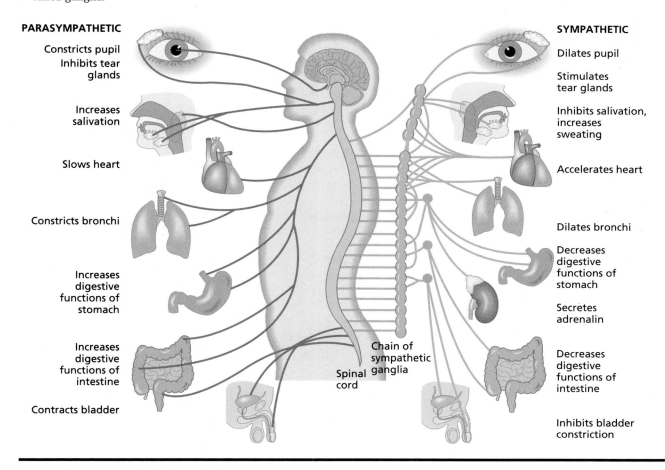

**PARASYMPATHETIC**

Constricts pupil
Inhibits tear glands

Increases salivation

Slows heart

Constricts bronchi

Increases digestive functions of stomach

Increases digestive functions of intestine

Contracts bladder

Spinal cord

Chain of sympathetic ganglia

**SYMPATHETIC**

Dilates pupil

Stimulates tear glands

Inhibits salivation, increases sweating

Accelerates heart

Dilates bronchi

Decreases digestive functions of stomach

Secretes adrenalin

Decreases digestive functions of intestine

Inhibits bladder constriction

*THE STRUCTURE OF A NEURON* Neurons typically take in information at one end and send out messages from the other. The parts of the cell that usually receive incoming signals consist of branched fibers called **dendrites,** which extend outward from the cell body. The dendrites receive stimulation from other neurons or sense receptors. (A look at Figure 2.7 will help you visualize the parts of a neuron.) The **cell body,** or **soma,** contains the nucleus of the cell and the surrounding material that sustains its life. The soma of a neuron also integrates information about the stimulation received from the dendrites (or in some cases received directly from another neuron) and passes it on to a single, extended fiber, the **axon,** which carries the neural message onward. In the case of neurons connecting the spinal cord and the toes, the axon can be several feet long, while many of those in the brain may be only a tiny fraction of an inch in length. When the neural message arrives at the far end of an axon it activates swollen, bulblike structures called **terminal buttons,** through which stimulation finally passes on to receptors in glands, muscles, or other neurons.

Neurons generally pass information in only one direction: from the dendrites through the soma to the axon to the terminal buttons. You can see this illustrated by the arrows in Figure 2.7. Because of this one-way flow of information, separate nerve

**Dendrites:** Branched fibers that extend outward from the main cell body and carry information into the neuron.

**Cell body** or **soma:** The part of a cell (such as a neuron) containing the nucleus—which includes the chromosomes.

**Axon:** In a nerve cell, an extended fiber that conducts information from the cell body to the terminal buttons. Information travels along the axon in the form of an electric charge.

**Terminal buttons:** Tiny bulblike structures at the end of the axon, which contain neurotransmitters that carry the neuron's message into the synapse.

**FIGURE 2.6:** Sensory and Motor Neurons and the Pain Withdrawal Reflex

Sensory neurons carry information, such as this painful stimulus, from the sense organs to the central nervous system by means of *affernet neurons*. Although the message is relayed to the brain by *interneurons* in the spinal cord, a painful stimulus may set off a simple withdrawal reflex, carried out by *motor neurons*.

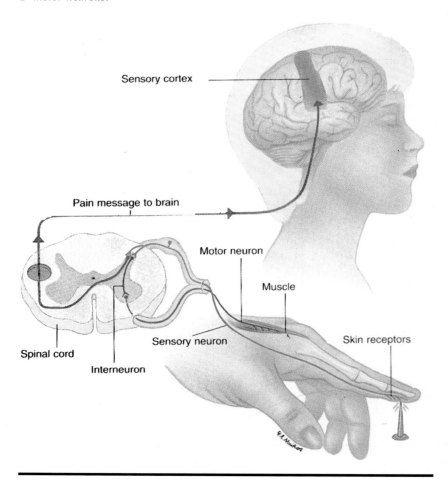

pathways are required to carry messages to and from each part of the body. The sensory and motor systems make up these separate one-way paths.

Interspersed among the brain's vast web of neurons are about five to ten times as many **glial cells.** The name comes from the Greek word for "glue," hinting at one of their major functions. The glia bind neurons to each other (without actually touching). Glial cells also form a **myelin sheath,** a fatty insulation around some types of axons, which interacts with the neuron to speed the conduction of internal impulses down the axon (see Figure 2.7). Certain diseases, such as multiple sclerosis, involve destruction of the myelin sheath, with disastrous consequences to neural communications.

*THE NEURAL IMPULSE*    The nervous system employs both electrical and chemical signals to process and transmit information. Together these electrical and chemical signals make up a **neural impulse,** the nerve cell's message. Every thought, sensation, or feeling that you have rides through your brain in the form of neural im-

**Glial cells:** These cells bind the neurons together. Glial cells also provide an insulating covering (the myelin sheath) of the axon for some neurons, which facilitates the electrical impulse.

**Myelin sheath:** A fatty insulation coating some types of neural axons, which biochemically speeds the conduction of neural impulses.

**Neural impulse:** An electrochemical process generated in a nerve cell to carry the cell's neural message.

## FIGURE 2.7: Major Structures of the Neuron

The neuron receives nerve impulses through its dendrites. These impulses are then transmitted through the cell body to the axon and to the terminal buttons, where neurotransmitters are released to stimulate other neurons.

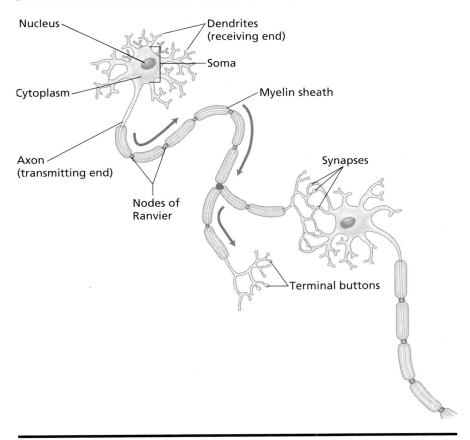

pulses. All of your actions arise from neural impulses delivered to your muscles. In addition, the effects of psychoactive drugs, such as tranquilizers, antidepressants, and painkillers, result from alterations of neural impulses. Typically, a message traveling through the nervous system will involve many neurons sending impulses in synchronized patterns (Deadwyler & Hampson, 1995; Ferster & Spruston, 1995).

At the level of the single neuron, the process begins when a stimulus, such as a sound or a pinprick, sets off a chemical reaction that causes the cell to become excited—much like a battery being charged. When it becomes sufficiently aroused, the neuron abruptly discharges, or "fires," sending an electrical charge, called the **action potential,** down the length of the axon. After firing, a powerful chemical mechanism quickly restores the neuron to a state of readiness. The whole process may take place in less than a hundredth of a second. But this is not the end of the matter, for the information carried by the action potential still has to traverse a tiny gap to another neuron.

Because no two neurons ever touch, they are always separated by a microscopic gap at a junction called the **synapse.** Arrival of the neural impulse at the terminal buttons sets off a whole new process designed to get the neuron's message across the synaptic gap (or *synaptic cleft*). In a remarkable sequence of events known as **synaptic transmission,** information from the electrical impulse in the axon is converted into a chemical message that can traverse the synaptic space between neurons (see Figure 2.8). This occurs in the following way.

**Chapter 3:
States of Mind**

*Most psychoactive drugs either amplify or inhibit communication between nerve cells in the brain.*

**Action potential:** The neural impulse—an electrical impulse that travels down the axon and carries the neural message.

**Synapse:** The junction between neurons or between a neuron and a muscle or gland. The synapse includes the terminal button, the synaptic cleft, and the receptor sites on the target cell. Neurotransmitters carry neural messages across the synaptic gap.

**Synaptic transmission:** The relaying of information across the synapse (from one neuron to another, for example) by means of chemical neurotransmitters.

## FIGURE 2.8: Synaptic Transmission

Firing in the presynaptic ("sending") neuron causes neurotransmitters to be released into the synaptic gap. After crossing the gap, these substances stimulate receptor molecules in the postsynaptic ("receiving") neuron. A single neuron may contain many different neurotransmitters.

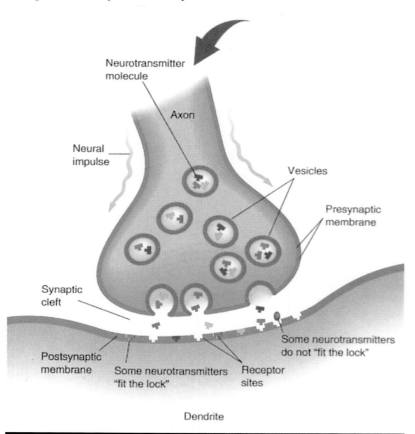

Muhammad Ali suffers from Parkinson's disease, caused by a deficiency of dopamine in his brain.

**Neurotransmitters:** Chemical messengers that relay neural messages across the synapse. Many neurotransmitters are also hormones.

**Chapter 3:**
**States of Mind**

*Psychoactive drugs often mimic neurotransmitters.*

*NEUROTRANSMITTERS* At the terminal buttons, the neural impulse activates small chemical packets containing **neurotransmitters,** biochemical substances that stimulate or suppress other neurons. When activated, these packets rupture, spilling their contents into the synaptic cleft. There some of the neurotransmitters attach themselves to the receiving neuron at its *receptor site*. If the neurotransmitter inputs are sufficiently stimulating at the receptor sites, the receiving neuron will experience a change (either being excited into firing or inhibited from firing). In this fashion, the message carried by the electrical impulse within the neuron can be relayed chemically from cell to cell.

More than 60 hormonelike chemicals are known or suspected to function as neurotransmitters in the brain. What is their practical importance for our understanding of human thought and behavior? All nervous system activity depends on synaptic transmission. And, as we will see, neurotransmitter imbalances probably underlie certain mental disorders, such as schizophrenia and depression. Moreover, treatment of these disorders may employ drugs that act like certain neurotransmitters in order to target certain brain pathways. Table 2.1 distinguishes six neurotransmitters that researchers have identified as important in daily brain functioning.

**TABLE 2.1:** Six Important Neurotransmitters

*Acetylcholine* is found in both the central and peripheral nervous systems. Peripherally, it is involved in muscle movement. In the brain, it appears to be associated with memory processes.

*GABA* (gamma-amino butyric acid) dampens the activity of other nerve cells. In addition, GABA interacts with a variety of drugs that cause sedation or reduction of anxiety by increasing levels of GABA in the synapses of the brain (Paul, Crawley, & Skolnick, 1986).

*Dopamine* and *norepinephrine* have been found to play important roles in psychological disorders such as schizophrenia and mood disturbances. Norepinephrine is also apparently involved in some forms of depression. Levels of dopamine that are higher than normal have been found in persons with schizophrenia, leading researchers to develop treatments that might decrease brain levels of dopamine (Wickelgren, 1998a).

*Serotonin* comes from neurons located in the brain stem, and it is involved with sleep and arousal. Lowered levels of serotonin are characteristic of forms of depression treated by the celebrated antidepressant drug Prozac. Hallucinogenic drugs, such as LSD, produce their bizarre sensory effects by making serotonin neurons more sensitive and ready to "fire" (Jacobs, 1987).

*Endorphins* are brain chemicals that, surprisingly, act like *opiates* (drugs derived from the opium poppy). Endorphins were discovered during experiments with morphine, a powerful sedative and addictive derivative of opium (Pert & Snyder, 1973). These neurotransmitters play an important role in the experience of emotion, pain, and pleasure. The pain relief provided by acupuncture or placebo effects may be caused by the release of endorphins (Fields & Levine, 1984; Hopson, 1988; Watkins & Mayer, 1982).

**Chapter 5:**
**Sensation and Perception**

*Placebos contain no real medicines. They work only because of the patient's expectations.*

Having completed our whirlwind tour of the nervous system, we now turn our attention to the body's other means of internal communication, the endocrine system. You will note that this system makes use of many of the same chemicals that neurons use for communication. In the case of the endocrine system, we call these chemicals *hormones*.

## The Endocrine System

Did you know that your blood carries *information*, along with oxygen and nutrients? It does so by serving as the information pathway for the endocrine system. The endocrine glands (which take their name from the Greek *endo* for "within" and *krinein* for "secrete") release hormones into the bloodstream, where they affect a wide array of bodily functions and behaviors. For example, hormones from the pituitary influence body growth; hormones from the ovaries and testes influence sexual development; hormones from the adrenals produce arousal; and hormones from the thyroid control metabolism (the body's rate of energy use). The endocrine glands don't operate independently, however. Their action is coordinated by hormones circulating in the bloodstream and by nerve impulses from the brain. Once secreted into the blood, hormones circulate throughout the body until delivered to their targets. Table 2.2 outlines the major glands and the body systems that they regulate.

**Chapter 4:**
**Psychological Development**
**Chapter 8:**
**Motivation and Emotion**

*Hormones are involved in the control of arousal, metabolism, and both physical and mental development.*

Significantly, endocrine communication not only sustains our normal bodily processes, it also helps the sympathetic nervous system respond in crises. When you encounter a stressor or an emergency (such as a car coming at you), the hormone adrenaline is released into the bloodstream, energizing your body for quick defensive action—for "fight or flight." Your heart pounds, your muscles tense, and you feel impelled to take whatever action your brain tells you makes sense.

**Chapter 9:**
**Stress, Health, and Well-Being**

*Hormones produce many of the effects of stress.*

DO IT Yourself!

## Neural Messages and Reaction Time

For only a dollar you can find out how long it takes for the brain to process information and initiate a response.

Hold a crisp dollar bill by the middle of the short side, so that it dangles downward. Have a friend put his or her thumb and index fingers on opposite sides and about an inch away from the center of the bill, as shown in the illustration. Instruct your friend to pinch the thumb and fingers together and attempt to catch the bill when you drop it.

If you drop the bill without warning (being careful not to signal your intentions), your friend's brain will not be able to process the information rapidly enough to get a response to the hand before the dollar bill has dropped safely away.

What does this demonstrate? The time it takes to respond reflects the time it takes for the sensory nervous system to take in the information, for the brain to process it, and for the motor system to produce a response. All of this involves millions of neurons, and even though they respond quickly, their responses do take time.

Do it yourself!

▌ Neural Messages and Reaction Time

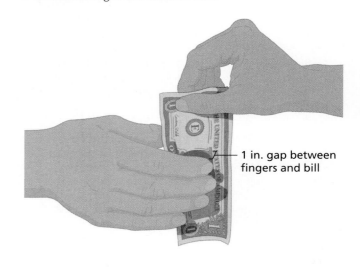

1 in. gap between fingers and bill

**TABLE 2.2:** Hormonal Functions of Major Endocrine Glands

| THESE ENDOCRINE GLANDS . . . | PRODUCE HORMONES THAT REGULATE . . . |
| --- | --- |
| Anterior pituitary | Ovaries and testes<br>Breast milk production<br>Metabolism<br>Reactions to stress |
| Posterior pituitary | Conservation of water in the body<br>Breast milk secretion<br>Uterus contractions |
| Thyroid | Metabolism<br>Physical growth and development |
| Parathyroid | Calcium levels in the body |
| Pancreas | Glucose (sugar) metabolism |
| Adrenal glands | Fight-or-flight response<br>Metabolism<br>Sexual desire (especially in women) |
| Ovaries | Development of female sexual characteristics<br>Production of ova (eggs) |
| Testes | Development of male sexual characteristics<br>Sperm production<br>Sexual desire (in men) |

The brain and the endocrine system have an intimate relationship. A small brain structure known as the *hypothalamus*, lying near the center of the brain, directs activity in the endocrine system. Specialized cells in the hypothalamus receive messages from other brain cells commanding it to release a number of different chemicals. These chemicals then influence the adjacent **pituitary gland,** the so-called master gland, which can either stimulate or inhibit the release of other glands' hormones. The pituitary gland also releases a hormone that directly influences bodily growth and development.

**Pituitary gland:** The master gland that produces hormones influencing the secretions of all other endocrine glands, as well as a hormone that influences growth. The pituitary is attached to the brain's hypothalamus, from which it takes its orders.

PSYCHOLOGY IN YOUR LIFE

*Side Effects of Psychoactive Drugs*

*M*ost **psychoactive drugs,** legal and illegal, mimic or inhibit the brain's neurotransmitters. Like neurotransmitters, these drugs either stimulate or inhibit nerve cells. In effect, they turn the message volume up or down in some part of the brain.

The well-known antidepressant Prozac does its work in the synapses of the brain's serotonin pathways, making more serotonin available (see Figure 2.9). Although Prozac (and related drugs with other brand names) is generally considered safe, undesirable symptoms occasionally occur in some people: anxiety, insomnia, changes in appetite, excitement (mania), seizures, and interference with cognitive performance (*Physician's Desk Reference*, 1999).

Why the unwanted side effects? A main reason involves the brain's design. Within the brain are many bundles of neurons—**neural pathways**—that connect regions having different functions. Each pathway employs only a few specific neurotransmitters. This fact allows drugs that mimic (or inhibit) certain transmitters to have a selective effect on brain pathways using those transmitters. Unfortunately for the drug-taking patient, several neural pathways may employ the same neurotransmitter for widely different functions. Thus, serotonin pathways, for example, affect not only mood but sleep, anxiety, and appetite. So, taking Prozac may treat depression but, at the same time, have side effects on other processes. This is the take-away lesson: No psychoactive drug exists that affects only one precise target in the brain.

**FIGURE 2.9:** Serotonin Pathways in the Brain

Each neurotransmitter is associated with certain neural pathways in the brain. In this cross section of the brain you see the main pathways for serotonin. Drugs that stimulate or inhibit serotonin will selectively affect the brain regions shown in this diagram.

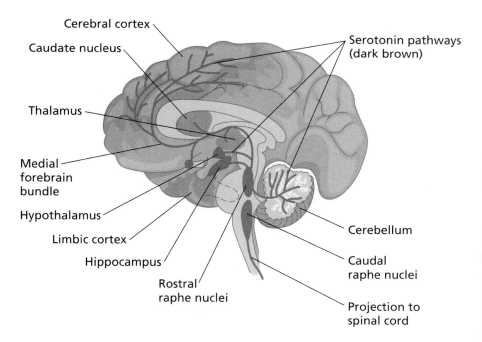

Cerebral cortex

Caudate nucleus

Serotonin pathways (dark brown)

Thalamus

Medial forebrain bundle

Hypothalamus

Limbic cortex

Hippocampus

Rostral raphe nuclei

Cerebellum

Caudal raphe nuclei

Projection to spinal cord

**Psychoactive drugs:** Chemicals that affect mental processes and behavior by their effects on neurons.

**Neural pathways:** Bundles of nerve cells that follow generally the same route and employ the same neurotransmitter.

1. **RECALL:** *Of the body's two main communication systems, the* _____ *is faster, and the* _____ *sends longer-lasting messages.*

2. **RECALL:** *The* _____ *division of the autonomic nervous system increases the heart rate during an emergency, while the* _____ *division slows the heart rate after an emergency is over.*

3. **RECALL:** *Which of the following might carry a neural impulse across the synapse?*
   **a.** an electrical charge
   **b.** dopamine
   **c.** the blood
   **d.** the cerebrospinal fluid

4. **RECALL:** *Which part of the brain communicates directly with the endocrine system?*
   **a.** the cortex
   **b.** the brain stem
   **c.** the cerebellum
   **d.** the hypothalamus

5. **RECALL:** *Make a sketch of two connecting neurons. Describe the location and function of the dendrites, soma, axon, myelin sheath, terminal buttons, synapse.*

6. **APPLICATION:** *Some people seem to have high blood pressure because they have an anxiety response while having their blood pressure taken at the doctor's office. Which part of the nervous system produces this anxiety response?*
   **a.** the somatic nervous system
   **b.** the sympathetic nervous system
   **c.** the parasympathetic nervous system
   **d.** the spinal cord

7. **UNDERSTANDING THE CORE CONCEPT:** *The chemical messengers in the brain are called* _____, *while in the endocrine system they are called* _____.

**ANSWERS:**    1. **nervous system/endocrine system**
2. **sympathetic/parasympathetic**    3. **b**    4. **d**
5. **See Figure 2.7**    6. **b**    7. **neurotransmitters/hormones**

---

 **KEY QUESTION** **HOW DOES THE BRAIN PRODUCE BEHAVIOR AND MENTAL PROCESSES?**

**Chapter 10: Personality**

*Asian cultures often do not see a "self" as an independent part of the personality.*

In September of 1848, a 25-year-old American railroad worker named Phineas Gage sustained a horrible head injury when a construction explosion blasted an iron rod up into his face and through his head. Amazingly, he recovered from this injury and lived another 12 years—but as a psychologically changed man. Those who knew him remarked that he had gone from being an efficient and capable manager to behaving in irresponsible, fitful, and even profane ways. In essence, he was no longer himself (Damasio et al., 1994). Had the site of his injury—the front and top of his brain—been the residence of his "old self"?

Humans have probably always recognized the existence of a link between body and mind. Even today one might speak of "giving one's heart" to another when falling in love, or of "not having the stomach" for something when describing disgust. Today we know that love does not reside in the heart, nor courage in the digestive system. We now know that emotions, desires, and thoughts flow from the brain. Neuroscientists are at last unraveling this complex neural knot, realizing that it evolved as distinct regions of tissue, each with a special function. This discovery becomes the Core Concept for this section of the chapter:

 **CORE CONCEPT**    **The brain is composed of many specialized and interconnected modules that work together to create mind and behavior.**

As you study the brain in the following pages, you will find that its components have specialized functions that contribute to our psychological makeup. Some specialize in sensory processes, such as vision and hearing. Some parts of the brain influence our emotional lives. Some contribute to memory. And some generate speech and other behaviors. The point is that these specialized parts of the brain usually manage to work together. And they normally do so automatically and without conscious direction. But, when something goes wrong with one or more of the brain's components, as happens to victims of stroke or Alzheimer's disease—or as happened to Phineas Gage—disorders of thought or behavior result.

Let's begin our journey through the brain with a look at the tools neuroscientists use to glimpse the operations of these brain modules.

## Windows on the Brain

What would you see if you could peer beneath the bony skull and behold the brain? Superficially, the gray-pinkish appearance of its surface gives no hint of the brain's internal structure or function. Much of what we know about its inner workings comes from disease and head injuries, as in the case of Phineas Gage. Unfortunate as they are, these problems offer the scientist an opportunity to make connections between the abilities lost by brain-injured patients and the site of damage.

We have also learned a great deal from mapping the brain's electrical activity. Using a device called the **EEG** (or **electroencephalograph**), researchers can—without opening the skull—record electrical **brain waves** picked up by electrodes pasted on the scalp. The EEG reveals which areas of the brain are most active during a particular task. It also traces abnormal brain waves caused by brain malfunctions, such as **epilepsy**, a disorder that arises from an electrical "storm" in the brain, often accompanied by seizures.

In the mid-20th century, Canadian neurologist Wilder Penfield opened another window on the brain by mapping its wrinkled surface with an electric probe. During a surgical procedure sometimes used to treat epilepsy, Penfield stimulated patients' exposed brains with an electrode (a thin wire that conducts a mild electric current) and recorded their responses. (Patients were kept awake, but under local anesthesia, so they felt no pain.) His medical purpose was to localize the origin of the seizures and to avoid making surgical **lesions** in other areas vital to the patient's functioning. In the process, he showed that different parts of the brain's surface have different functions. Stimulating a certain region might cause a particular body movement or sensory experience. Stimulating other areas would provoke a specific emotion or even a memory (Penfield & Baldwin, 1952). Later, Walter Hess pioneered the use of electrical stimulation to probe structures deeper in the brain. Hess found that deeply placed electrodes stimulated elaborate sequences of behavior and emotional activity.

Modern advances in brain science have developed even more complex and subtle technologies known as **brain scans.** Many of these techniques rest on the assumption that increased activity by cells in specific parts of the brain will lead to increased blood flow or other biochemical processes in those locations (Posner, 1993). With complex, computer-aided machines that detect and measure these brain events, scientists can study brain activity without needing to expose or physically invade the brain. Images from a brain scan show researchers how specific regions of the brain seem to "light up" when an individual performs certain activities, such as reading or speaking (Raichle, 1994). These methods also help neurosurgeons locate brain abnormalities such as tumors or stroke-related damage.

The most common brain-scanning methods currently used by researchers and clinicians are referred to as *CT scanning, PET scanning, MRI,* and *MEG* (Barinaga, 1997; Mogilner et al., 1993):

- **CT scanning,** or **computerized tomography,** creates a computerized image of the brain from X rays passed through the brain at various angles. Tomography (from the

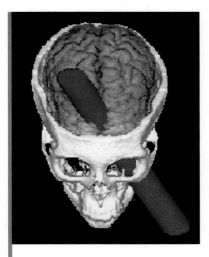

Phineas Gage became a different person after an iron bar blasted through his frontal lobes.

**EEG** or **electroencephalograph:** A device for recording brain waves, typically by electrodes placed on the scalp. The record produced is known as an *electroencephalogram* (also called an *EEG*).

**Brain waves:** Patterns of electrical activity generated by the brain. The EEG records brain waves.

**Epilepsy:** A brain disorder that is often marked by seizures and loss of consciousness. Epilepsy is caused by out-of-control electrical activity in the brain.

**Lesions:** Tissue damage that results from disease or injury. To study the connection between brain and behavior, biopsychologists make precise lesions in the brains of experimental animals and observe the changes in the animals' behavior.

**Brain scans:** Recordings of the brain's electrical or biochemical activity at specific sites. Typically, the data are formed into visual images by computer. Common brain scanning devices include MRI, CT, and PET.

**CT scanning** or **computerized tomography:** A computerized imaging technique that uses X rays passed through the brain at various angles and then combined into an image.

Greek *tomos*, "section") detects the soft-tissue structures of the brain that normal X rays do not reveal (see Figure 2.10).

- **PET scanning**, or **positron emission tomography**, detects brain cell activity by tracking the movement of radioactive substances in active regions of the brain. PET scans rely on the detection of atomic particles called *positrons* that are emitted by a radioactive dye administered to the patient.

- **MRI**, or **magnetic resonance imaging**, relies on the fact that different types of tissue give different responses to powerful pulses of magnetic energy. An even newer technique is *echo-planar MRI*, which produces high-resolution MRI images swiftly and clearly enough to distinguish more active tissues from less active ones (Alper, 1993). Thus, echo-planar MRI allows scientists to determine which parts of the brain are most active during various mental activities.

- **MEG**, or **magnetoencephalography**, measures the magnetic fields generated by electrical activity in the brain. Figure 2.11 shows that MEG is able to detect the brain sites where very brief sensations of touch are processed and can map these locations onto a larger picture provided by MRI.

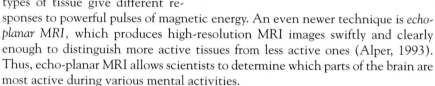

Magnetic resonance imaging produces an image that shows a slice of tissue through the brain. It does so by sensing the magnetic changes that occur when the patient is placed in a strong magnetic field.

**PET scanning** or **positron emission tomography:** An imaging technique that relies on the detection of radioactive sugar consumed by active brain cells.

**MRI** or **magnetic resonance imaging:** An imaging technique that relies on cells' responses in a high-intensity magnetic field.

**MEG** or **magnetoencephalography:** An imaging technique that measures magnetic fields generated by the electrical activity of the brain.

**Cognitive:** A term referring to information processing in the brain. Cognitive functions include learning, memory, thinking, sensation, and perception.

Figures 2.10 and 2.11 display the quality and detail possible with various brain scanning techniques. As you can see from the figure, each one provides a different "window" onto brain–mind connections.

Each scanning device also has its particular strengths and weaknesses. For example, PET is good at tracking the brain's activity, but not as good as MRI for distinguishing the fine details of brain structure. In addition, both PET and MRI techniques have difficulty scanning processes that occur at rates faster than hundreds of milliseconds. To track the very fast "conversations" brain cells are capable of conducting, the EEG or MEG is required, but they are limited in their detail and accuracy (Raichle, 1994). Currently, no single scanning technique gives biopsychologists the perfect "window" on the brain.

### Three Layers of the Brain

Brain scanning shows that some **cognitive** functions (mental processes) are widely distributed among different brain areas, while other functions are highly localized, or specific to a particular location of brain tissue (Posner, 1993). The picture that emerges shows the brain as a single organ made up of many components collaborating to produce human thought and behavior, as the Core Concept for this section suggests. In our study of the brain, we will recreate this picture by first looking at the brain as a whole and later taking a close-up look at its parts. A good place to begin is with the brain image in Figure 2.12, noting how it is composed of different but interconnected layers of tissue and structures.

Most psychologists would distinguish three especially important layers that appeared in the evolutionary sequence leading to the human brain. These layers consist of paired

**FIGURE 2.10:** Windows on the Mind

Images from brain-scanning devices. From top: PET, MRI, EEG. Each scanning and recording device has strengths and weaknesses.

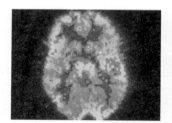

structures stacked like stereo components. In the bottom layer, at the base of the brain, lie the *brain stem* and *cerebellum,* which drive our vital functions, such as heart rate, breathing, digestion, and motor coordination. The next layer, the *limbic system,* elaborates on these vital functions by adding emotions, complex motives, and increased memory abilities. And at the top is the *cerebrum.* The brain's outermost layer of cells, known as the *cerebral cortex,* enables reasoning, planning, creating, and problem solving. It is the crowning achievement of the human brain's brain evolution. Within this cerebral cortex, networks of nerve cells integrate sensory information, control precise movements of the mouth and hands, and produce abstract thinking and reasoning. Let us examine more closely the structure and function of each of these three important layers.

**FIGURE 2.11:**    MEG Image of Sensory Sites in the Brain

Magnetoencephalography (MEG) records neural activity that is too brief to be detected by PET or MRI scans. This photo shows how MEG has identified the areas in the somatosensory cortex associated with the fingers of the right hand (see colored symbols).

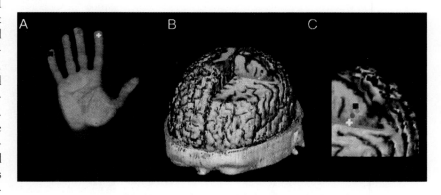

**THE BRAIN STEM AND CEREBELLUM**    If you have ever fought to stay awake in class, you have struggled with signals from the brain's most primitive layer, the **brain stem.** This part of the brain also contains modules that regulate the internal state of the body, plus many neural pathways that shuttle information between the brain and spinal cord (see Figure 2.13). Essentially the same equipment is found in the brain stems of all vertebrates (animals with backbones).

At the very top of the spinal cord you will note a slight bulge where the brain stem begins. This is the **medulla,** the region involved in regulating breathing and the

**Brain stem:** The most primitive of the brain's three major layers. It includes the medulla, pons, and the reticular activating system.

**Medulla:** A brain-stem region that controls breathing and heart rate. The sensory and motor pathways connecting the brain to the body cross in the medulla.

**FIGURE 2.12:**    Major Structures of the Brain

From an evolutionary perspective, the brain stem and cerebellum represent the oldest part of the brain; the limbic system evolved next; and the cerebral cortex is the most recent achievement in brain evolution.

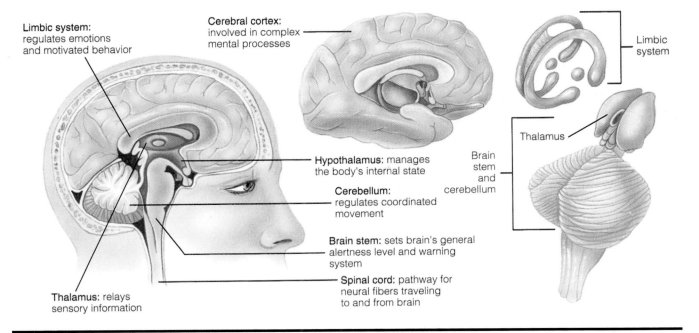

## FIGURE 2.13: The Brain Stem and Cerebellum

These structures in the central core of the brain are primarily involved with basic life processes: breathing, pulse, arousal, movement, balance, and early processing of sensory information.

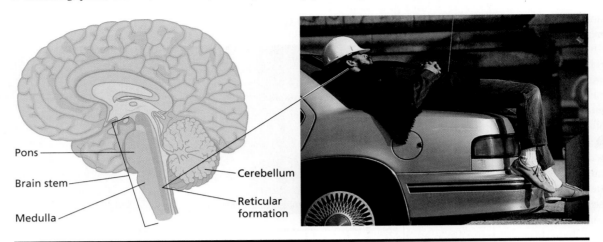

Pons

Brain stem

Medulla

Cerebellum

Reticular formation

**Pons:** A brain-stem region that regulates brain activity during sleep and dreaming. *Pons* derives from the Latin word for "bridge."

**Reticular activating system (RAS):** A pencil-shaped structure in the brain stem, situated between the medulla and the pons. The RAS arouses the cortex to keep the brain alert and to attend to new stimulation.

**Thalamus:** The brain's central "relay station," situated just atop the brain stem. Nearly all the messages going into or out of the brain go through the thalamus.

**Chapter 3:**
**States of Mind**
*How does the brain create consciousness?*

**Chapter 6:**
**Learning and Remembering**
*Classical conditioning links old responses to new stimuli.*

**Cerebellum:** The "little brain" attached to the brain stem. The cerebellum is responsible for coordinated movements.

**Limbic System:** The middle layer of the brain, involved in emotion and memory. The limbic system includes the amygdala, the hippocampus, the hypothalamus, and other structures.

beating of the heart. Significantly, nerve fibers connecting the brain and the body cross over at the medulla. Here the left side of the body makes a connection with the right side of the brain and the right side of the body links to the left side of the brain.

Directly above the medulla, the larger bulge of the **pons** regulates brain activity during sleep. Farther back, the **reticular activating system (RAS)** runs the length of the brain stem. This dense network of cells serves as the brain's sentinel by alerting the brain and helping it attend to new stimulation and to stimulation previously tagged as important. Activity in this structure diminishes when you become drowsy.

Nerve fibers run from the reticular activating system both down to the spinal cord and up through a small football-shaped structure called the **thalamus,** perched atop the brain stem. Here, at the very center of the brain, the thalamus serves much the same function as the central processing chip in a computer by receiving sensory information and channeling it to appropriate processing centers. For example, the thalamus relays visual information from the eyes to the visual processing regions at the back of the brain. The thalamus also relays messages from the motor control centers back to organs and muscles. In addition, this structure may play an essential role in learning and in combining sensations, emotions, and memories into the experience of consciousness.

The other major structure lying at the brain's base is a neural knot known as the **cerebellum.** Attached to the brain stem at the rear of the skull, the twin lobes of the cerebellum coordinate bodily motion, control posture, and maintain equilibrium (Wickelgren, 1998b). Your ability to walk, run, and dance reflects the functioning of the cerebellum. Recent research also implicates the cerebellum in an important type of learning, called *classical conditioning*, which involves learning to give reflexive responses to new cues—as when you begin salivating at the sound of the lunch bell (Raymond, Lisberger, & Mauk, 1996).

Taken together, the structures of the brain stem and cerebellum control the most basic functions of life. Note that much of their work is automatic and reflexive. That is, this part of the brain operates largely outside conscious awareness. The next two layers, however, have a heavier impact on our conscious states of mind.

**THE LIMBIC SYSTEM** All vertebrates have a brain stem and cerebellum, but only mammals and reptiles are equipped with the more recently evolved **limbic system.** (You can see it in Figures 2.12 and 2.14 as a structure that wraps around the thalamus in the shape of a pair of ram's horns.) The limbic system is yet another collection of brain modules with a variety of functions. Some of its components produce motivated behaviors, such as eating and sexual activity, while some create memories for specific events. Other parts operate more quietly in the background to regulate body temperature, blood pressure, and blood-sugar level. In addition, the limbic system contains "reward centers" that, when stimulated, produce sensations of pleasure. Because we tend to seek pleasure, these parts of the limbic system play a big part in determining which behaviors we choose.

It is the limbic system's role in emotion that may be its best-known feature. Here in the brain's middle layer lie the neural networks of fear, anger, ecstacy, and despair—the qualities that most clearly distinguish the human brain from the electronic network of a supercomputer such as Deep Blue. Neuroscientists are just now discovering how these emotional capabilities coordinate with rational thought processes to help us focus attention and tag important memories.

The largest of the limbic system's structures, the **hippocampus** (see Figure 2.14), helps with memory (Galluscio, 1990). The hippocampus gets its name from the ancient Greek word for "seahorse," referring to this structure's distinctively curved ridges. Hippocampal damage impairs the ability to lay down permanent records of newly acquired information. Evidence for this comes mostly from clinical research, notably from studies of a patient referred to as H. M., perhaps psychology's most famous case study (Hilts, 1996). At age 27, H. M. underwent surgery intended to reduce the frequency and severity of his epileptic seizures. During the operation, most of the hippocampus was removed on both sides of his brain. As a result, H. M. can remember only events prior to his surgery: The events of the rest of his life disappear from memory almost as soon as they occur. Long after surgery, H. M. continues to believe he is living in 1953, the year the operation was performed. Similar effects of hippocampal damage occur in monkeys and other experimental animals whose brains contain this structure (Squire, 1992).

The **amygdala,** another part of the limbic system, is known best for its roles in fear and aggression. It also participates in memory and certain basic motivations. Studies with several animal species, including humans, have shown that destroying parts of the amygdala has a calming effect on otherwise mean-spirited individuals, while electrically stimulating the amygdala can trigger aggressive behavior.

Hungry? Blame your **hypothalamus.** One of the smaller structures in the brain, the hypothalamus is also one of the most important. Composed of several bundles of nerve cells that continually monitor the blood, this limbic structure regulates a variety of emotional and motivated behaviors, including eating, drinking, temperature control, and sexual arousal. For example, when your body is running low on nutrients, the hypothalamus sends signals to prompt hunger and eating behavior. The hypothalamus also regulates the activities of the endocrine system and influences hormone production. In addition, it houses some of the brain's "reward centers," which generate the good feelings associated with gratifying the

**Hippocampus:** A component of the limbic system, involved in establishing long-term memories.

**Chapter 3:**
**States of Mind**

*"Reward centers" produce sensations of pleasure from certain psychoactive drugs.*

**Chapter 8:**
**Emotion and Motivation**

*The limbic system is a collection of brain structures involved in both motivation and emotion.*

**Chapter 6:**
**Learning and Remembering**

*The hippocampus is needed for making long-term memories of events.*

**Amygdala:** (a-MIG-da-la) A limbic system structure involved in memory and emotion, particularly aggression.

**Hypothalamus:** A limbic structure that serves as the brain's blood-testing laboratory, constantly monitoring the blood to determine the condition of the body.

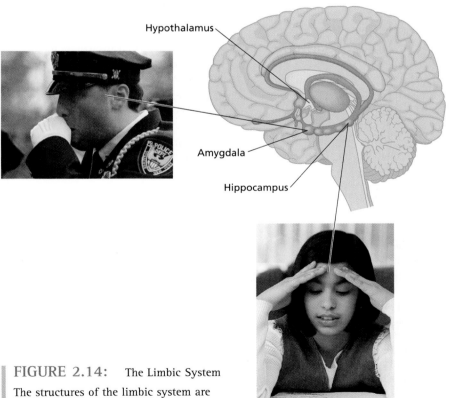

Hypothalamus

Amygdala

Hippocampus

FIGURE 2.14:    The Limbic System

The structures of the limbic system are involved with motivation, emotion, and certain memory processes.

## FIGURE 2.15: The Cerebral Cortex

Each of the two hemispheres of the cerebral cortex has four lobes. Different sensory and motor functions have been associated with specific parts of each lobe. The two hemispheres are connected by a thick bundle of fibers called the corpus callosum.

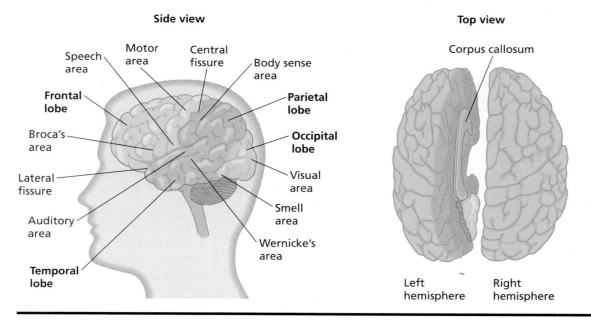

**Side view**

Speech area
Motor area
Central fissure
Body sense area
**Frontal lobe**
**Parietal lobe**
Broca's area
**Occipital lobe**
Lateral fissure
Visual area
Auditory area
Smell area
Wernicke's area
**Temporal lobe**

**Top view**

Corpus callosum

Left hemisphere
Right hemisphere

---

**Chapter 8:
Emotion and Motivation**

*The hypothalamus controls several homeostatic drives, such as hunger and thirst, to maintain a balanced condition in the body.*

**Homeostasis:** The body's tendency to maintain a biologically balanced condition, especially with regard to nutrients, water, and temperature.

**Cerebrum:** The topmost layer of the brain; the bulbous cap over the limbic system. The cerebrum, particularly the cerebral *cortex,* accounts for most of our thinking and processing of information from our environment.

**Cerebral cortex:** The thin grey-matter covering of the cerebrum, consisting of a ¼-inch layer dense with cell bodies of neurons. The cerebral cortex carries on the major portion of our "higher" mental processing, including thinking and perceiving.

**Cerebral hemispheres:** The two walnut-shaped halves of the cerebrum, connected by the corpus callosum.

**Corpus callosum:** The band of nerve cells that connects the two cerebral hemispheres.

hunger, thirst, and sex drives. Because the hypothalamus controls both the arousal of motives and the mechanisms for signaling satisfaction of these motives, it regulates the body's internal balance or equilibrium, a process called **homeostasis.** In general, all the limbic system structures (including the hippocampus, amygdala, and hypothalamus) work together to maintain balance, both within the body and between the individual and the environment.

**THE CEREBRUM** Evolution has designed the human **cerebrum,** the bulbous cap covering the limbic system, as the seat of higher cognitive functioning. Accounting for two-thirds of the total mass of the human brain, the cerebrum is the major reason why our brains are larger than those of most other species (see Figure 2.15). Its thin outer layer forms the **cerebral cortex** (*cortex* comes from the Latin for "bark" or "shell"). One unique aspect of this structure is its wrinkled or convoluted formation, folding in on itself to enable the billions of cells in this "thinking tissue" to be squeezed into the small space inside the skull.

The two nearly symmetrical halves of the cerebrum, known as the **cerebral hemispheres,** each mediate different cognitive and emotional functions. The two hemispheres normally work in harmony because they are connected by a thick mass of nerve fibers, collectively referred to as the **corpus callosum,** which carries messages back and forth between the hemispheres. (We will discuss the role of the corpus callosum and the distinct functions of the two hemispheres in more detail later in the chapter.)

## Four Lobes of the Cerebral Cortex

Neuroscientists have mapped the cortex of each hemisphere, using two important landmarks as their guides.

On each side of the brain, a groove called the **central fissure** divides the cortex almost vertically near the center of each hemisphere. The **lateral fissure** divides the cortex in each hemisphere horizontally. You can see both of these landmarks in Figure 2.15. These vertical and horizontal divisions roughly define four anatomical regions, or lobes, containing structures that serve specific functions. (Note: Each hemisphere has four lobes.) We will now take a closer look at these cortical lobes.

**THE FRONTAL LOBES** Your choice of major, your plans for the summer, and your ability to answer test questions all depend on the part of your brain lying above the lateral fissure and in front of the central fissure. Here we find the **frontal lobes,** which regulate motor movement and cognitive activities such as planning, deciding, and pursuing goals (Shimamura, 1996). The foundations for personality and temperament reside here, too. We know this from accidents that damage the frontal lobes and produce devastating effects, as we saw earlier in the famous case of Phineas Gage.

The frontal lobes have other functions, too. Located just in front of the central fissure, the **motor cortex** can send messages that control the body's more than 600 voluntary muscles. As you can see in Figure 2.16, the motor cortex contains an upside-down map of the body. Note, also, that the upper parts of the body (represented at the bottom of the cortical map) receive far more space on this motor strip than do the lower parts. One of the largest areas of the motor cortex is devoted to the fingers (especially the thumb), reflecting the importance of manipulating objects. Another major area sends messages to the muscles involved in speech. Oddly, although each frontal lobe has a strip of motor cortex, the **motor speech area** lies only in the left hemisphere in most people. With this exception, commands from the motor cortex on one side of the brain go to muscles on the opposite side of the body. Thus, it is the motor cortex in the right hemisphere of your brain that controls the muscles in your left foot.

**THE PARIETAL LOBES** If you sit on a tack, your **parietal lobes** will tell you. Located directly behind the central fissure toward the top of the head, these regions process certain incoming sensory information, especially touch and other skin senses. Located in the left and right parietal lobes, just behind the central fissure, the **somatosensory cortex** processes information about temperature, touch, body position, and pain. Like the motor cortex, the upper region of the somatosensory cortex relates to the lower parts of the body, and the lower part relates to the upper parts of the body. You will notice in Figure 2.16 that certain parts of the body are disproportionately represented in the somatosensory cortex, particularly the lips, tongue, thumb, and index fingers—the parts of the body that provide the most important input about touch. As with the motor cortex, the right half of the somatosensory cortex communicates with the left side of the body, and the left half with the right side of the body. Note the similarity between the motor cortex and the somatosensory cortex in Figure 2.16.

**THE OCCIPITAL LOBES** You see the world with the back of your brain, where the **occipital lobes** serve as the destination for incoming visual information. There we find the **visual cortex,** which processes sensations from the eyes. Input from the center part of the retina at the back of the eye, the area that transmits the most focused, detailed visual information, claims the greatest proportion of space in the visual cortex. Also within this region are highly specialized areas that process color, movement, shape, shading, and other aspects of visual stimulation, including a patch of cortex responsible solely for the recognition of human faces (Holden, 1997).

**THE TEMPORAL LOBES** When the phone rings or a horn honks, it registers in your **temporal lobes,** on the lower side of each cerebral hemisphere. There lies the **auditory cortex,** responsible for processing sounds. In most people, a specialized part of the auditory cortex found on

**Central fissure:** The prominent vertical groove in the cortex, separating the frontal from the parietal lobes in each hemisphere.

**Lateral fissure:** The prominent horizontal groove separating the frontal and temporal lobes in each hemisphere.

**Frontal lobes:** Regions at the front of the brain that are especially involved in movement and in thinking.

**Chapter 10: Personality**

*Psychologists have developed many explanations for personality and temperament.*

**Motor cortex:** A narrow vertical strip of cortex in the frontal lobes, just in front of the central fissure.

**Motor speech area:** A part of the left frontal lobe responsible for coordinating the muscles used in producing speech. It is often called Broca's area, after its discoverer.

**Parietal lobes:** Cortical lobes lying in the upper back of the brain and involved in touch sensation and in perceiving spatial relationships (the relationships of objects in space).

**Chapter 5: Sensation and Perception**

*The senses process stimulus information, which is passed on to the cortex in the form of nerve impulses.*

**Somatosensory cortex:** A strip of the parietal lobe lying just behind the central fissure. The somatosensory cortex is involved with sensations of touch.

**Occipital lobes:** The cortical lobes at the back of the brain, containing the visual cortex.

**Visual cortex:** The visual processing areas of cortex in the occipital lobes.

**Chapter 5: Sensation and Perception**

*Information about light and dark, color, shape, and movement is processed in separate areas of the visual cortex.*

**Chapter 5: Sensation and Perception**

*The auditory cortex extracts information about the frequency and pitch of sound waves.*

**Temporal lobes:** Cortical lobes that process sounds, including speech. The temporal lobes are probably involved in storing long-term memories.

**Auditory cortex:** Portions of the temporal lobe involved in hearing.

**FIGURE 2.16:** The Motor Cortex and the Somatosensory Cortex

Actions of the body's voluntary muscles are controlled by the motor cortex in the frontal lobe. The somatosensory cortex in the parietal lobe processes information about temperature, touch, body position, and pain. The diagram below shows the proportion of tissue devoted to various activities or sensitivities in each cortex.

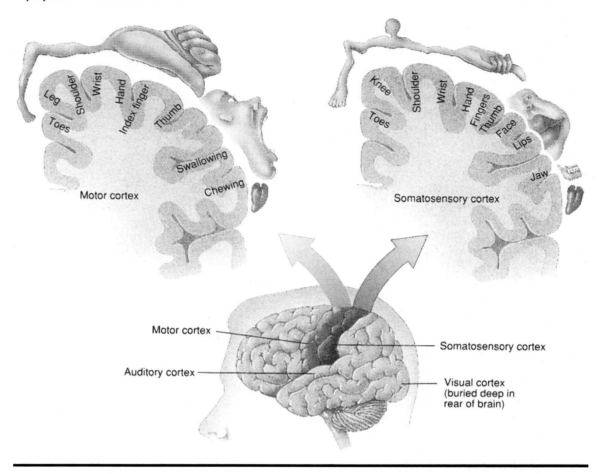

the left side of the brain processes speech sounds. Other parts of the temporal lobes may store long-term memories. This is not surprising, because the hippocampus, which we know to be involved in forming memories, lies directly beneath the temporal lobe.

### Cortical Cooperation and the Responsive Brain

No single brain lobe functions in isolation. For example, when you do something as simple as answering a ringing telephone, you hear it in your temporal lobes, visually locate it in your occipital lobes, grasp and handle the receiver with the help of your parietal lobes, and engage in thoughtful conversation through processes in your frontal lobes. The brain's structures normally work in concert to perform all complex functions, although specific structures appear to be necessary for specific activities, such as vision, hearing, language, and memory.

Not all the cerebral cortex, however, is devoted to processing sensory information and commanding the muscles to action. In fact, the largest proportion of the human cortex (those areas that are not specifically labeled in Figure 2.16) has the task of integrating information from various other parts of the brain. Collectively, these regions, known as the **association cortex,** process such mental activities as

**Association cortex:** Cortical regions that combine information from various other parts of the brain.

planning and decision making. We humans have more of the cerebral cortex area devoted to the association cortex than do nonhuman species. Consequently we show much greater flexibility in our behavior. This human associative ability underlies much of our species' adaptive ability to learn, think, anticipate, and solve problems.

Here is a more subtle point: Because of its flexibility, the very structure of the brain can be changed by its interactions with the outside world (Barinaga, 1996; Singer, 1995). For example, as a violin player gains expertise, the motor cortex reorganizes itself to devote a larger area to the fingers of the left hand (Juliano, 1998). Increased cortical representation also develops for the index finger used by a blind reader who learns to use Braille (Elbert et al., 1995). Usually these changes are adaptive, although accumulating evidence suggests that intensely traumatic experiences may also leave a biological imprint on the brain's ability to respond emotionally (Arnsten, 1998; Caldwell, 1995; Mukerjee, 1995). The brains of soldiers who experience combat or women who have been raped may undergo physical changes that can produce a hair-trigger responsiveness. This tends to make them overreact to mild stressors and even to merely unexpected surprises. In general, such findings indicate that the brain is a dynamic system capable of changing both its functions and its physical structure in response to the environment (Sapolsky, 1990).

**Chapter 9:**
**Stress, Health, and Well-Being**
*Extremely threatening experiences can cause post-traumatic stress disorder.*

## Cerebral Dominance

At about the same time that Phineas Gage sustained his frontal-lobe injury, a French neurosurgeon, Paul Broca, was studying the brain's role in language. His research initially focused on a man whose name was derived from the only word he had been able to speak, "Tan." When Tan died, Broca performed an autopsy, which revealed severe damage in the left front portion of Tan's brain. This finding led to the study of the brains of similarly injured patients, where Broca discovered that damage to the same region resulted in similar language impairments. He concluded that language ability depended on the functioning of structures in a specific region of the brain's left frontal lobe (see Figure 2.15). Broca's work was one of the early hints that the two sides of the brain have different tasks. Subsequent work has confirmed and extended Broca's findings:

- Patients suffering brain damage that paralyzes the right side of their bodies often develop speech disturbances, suggesting that speech production is localized in the left hemisphere.
- Patients suffering damage to the left hemisphere often develop problems using and understanding language.
- The left hemisphere is usually slightly larger than the right one.

Although the two hemispheres appear to be near-mirror-images of each other, both clinical and experimental evidence indicate dissimilar styles of processing information. This tendency for each hemisphere to dominate the control of different functions is called **cerebral dominance.** Yet, despite the fact that some processes are more under the control of the right hemisphere and others are left-hemisphere dominant, the brain typically functions in an integrated and harmonious fashion.

Much of our knowledge about cerebral dominance comes from observing people, like Tan, who have suffered brain damage on one side of the brain or people whose cerebral hemispheres could not communicate with each other. Patients with right-hemisphere damage are more likely to have perception and attention problems, which can include serious difficulties in **spatial orientation.** For example, they may feel lost in a previously familiar place or be unable to assemble a simple jigsaw puzzle. By contrast, patients with left-hemisphere damage are more likely to have problems with language and logic.

Similarly, studies of healthy individuals have shown that the left side of the brain is more involved in controlling speech and other verbal tasks, and the right side is more important in directing visual-spatial activities (see Bradshaw, 1989; Bryden,

**Cerebral dominance:** The tendency of each brain hemisphere to exert control over different functions, such as language or perception of spatial relationships.

**Spatial orientation:** (SPAY-shul) The process of locating one's body or other objects in space.

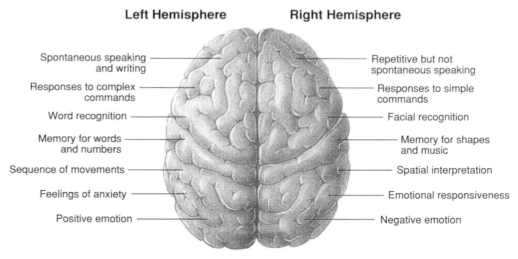

**Left Hemisphere**          **Right Hemisphere**

Spontaneous speaking and writing — Repetitive but not spontaneous speaking

Responses to complex commands — Responses to simple commands

Word recognition — Facial recognition

Memory for words and numbers — Memory for shapes and music

Sequence of movements — Spatial interpretation

Feelings of anxiety — Emotional responsiveness

Positive emotion — Negative emotion

1982; Davidson, 1992; Lempert & Kinsbourne, 1982; Posner & Raichle, 1994; Springer & Deutsch, 1993). However, the two hemispheres often make different contributions to the same task. That is, they seem to have different processing styles. For example, on matching tasks, the left hemisphere matches objects analytically and verbally—by similarity in function. The right hemisphere matches things that look alike or fit together to form a visual pattern (Gazzaniga, 1970; Sperry, 1968, 1982).

The differences between the two sides of the brain have captured popular interest in recent years, and many nonspecialists feel free to speculate whether someone is a "right-brain" or "left-brain" person. You should know, however, that such a distinction is simplistic and misleading. Research findings do not warrant categorizing people in this way. In reality, the differences between the two hemispheres do not outweigh their similarities. Both hemispheres are capable of either analytic (piece-by-piece) or holistic (as-a-whole) processing, and both use one mode or the other depending on the nature of the task (Trope et al., 1992). In their own ways, both hemispheres contribute to communication and memory functions, to perceptual–cognitive functions, and to emotional functions (see Figure 2.17). So, in most people, the hemispheres seem to complement rather than oppose each other.

There are some individuals, however, whose cerebral hemispheres do not work together—because they cannot. These are persons whose brains have been surgically "split." Let's see what their condition can tell us about specialization of the cerebral hemispheres.

## The Split Brain

The fact that the two cerebral hemispheres have different processing styles raises an intriguing question: Would each half of the brain act as a different conscious mind if it were, somehow, separated from the other? The answer to this question comes from a rare treatment to relieve the symptoms of severe epilepsy. In this procedure, surgeons sever the *corpus callosum*, the bundle of nerve fibers (discussed earlier) that transfers information between the two hemispheres (Figure 2.18). The goal of the surgery is to prevent abnormal electrical rhythms from echoing between the hemispheres and developing into a full-blown seizure (Trope et al., 1992; Wilson, Reeves, & Culver,

**FIGURE 2.18:**   The Corpus Callosum

Only the corpus callosum is severed when the brain is "split." This medical procedure prevents communication between the cerebral hemispheres. Strangely, split-brain patients act like people with normal brains under most conditions. Special laboratory tests, however, reveal a duality of consciousness in the split brain.

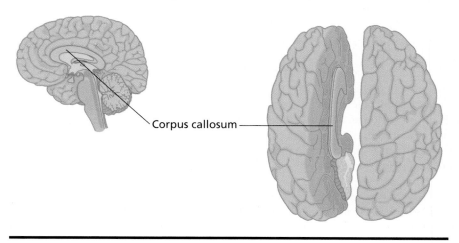

Corpus callosum

1977). After the operation, not only do the seizures usually diminish but the patient's subsequent behavior appears surprisingly normal under all but the most unusual conditions. People who undergo this type of surgery are often referred to as **split-brain patients.**

Early studies comparing the two sides of the brain had focused not on hemispheric independence but on the way the brain combines information. For example, sensory input from each eye automatically divides into two streams and flows to the opposite sides of the brain (right visual field to left hemisphere; left field to right hemisphere), as you can see in Figure 2.19. Thanks to the connecting pathways through the corpus callosum, the information is shared by both hemispheres in the intact brain.

But in the split-brain patient this sharing of information across the corpus callosum can't happen. Surprisingly, however, under conditions outside the laboratory, they get along very well when they can get input from both visual fields into both sides of the brain. (They normally do this by scanning across the visual field with their eyes.) By this means, they can function in their daily lives without noticeable difficulty. But when they must perform special tasks that involve different information presented to each visual field or each hand, the behavior of split-brain patients differs from that of people whose hemispheres can communicate with each other.

This was shown in a series of clever experiments by Roger Sperry (1968) and Michael Gazzaniga (1970). To test the capabilities of the separated hemispheres, Sperry and Gazzaniga devised situations that allowed visual information to be presented separately to each hemisphere (see Figure 2.20). But before they could find out what each side of the brain knew, they had to solve a communication problem: Because the left hemisphere has language, it could talk to the researchers, but the right hemisphere could not. The solution to this problem involved giving the right hemisphere manual tasks involving identification, matching, or assembly of objects—tasks that did not require the use of words. Once this communication mode was discovered, the right hemisphere turned out to be better than the left at solving problems involving spatial relationships and pattern recognition (Gazzaniga, 1995).

Because the brain is designed to function as a whole, the result of disconnecting the cerebral hemispheres is a striking **duality of consciousness.** In the split-brain patient, each hemisphere responds independently and simultaneously when stimuli are presented separately to each side. When stimuli are presented to only one side (as in Figure 2.20), responses tend to be more emotional or more analytic, depending on which hemisphere has the task of interpreting the message. Yet, we must be cautious about generalizing such findings from split-brain patients to conclusions about the way a normal brain functions. Does it function with a uniform central command system, or is it organized with specialized and independent functions for each hemisphere? Gazzaniga (1998) proposes that the human mind is neither a single entity nor a dual entity but rather a confederation of multiple mind-modules, each one specialized to process a specific kind of information. The input from these many separate "miniminds" is synthesized and coordinated for action by central, executive processors (Fodor, 1983; Hinton & Anderson, 1981; Ornstein, 1986a). Thus, we come full circle to a Core Concept that we encountered earlier in the chapter: *The brain is composed of many specialized modules that work together to create mind and behavior* (Baynes et al., 1998; Strauss, 1998).

**FIGURE 2.19:** The Neural Pathways for Visual Information

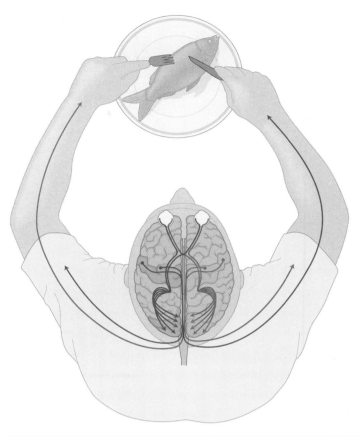

Chapter 3:
**States of Mind**
*The brain is capable of producing many states of consciousness.*

**Split-brain patients:** Individuals who have had the corpus callosum surgically severed, usually as a treatment for severe epilepsy.

**Duality of consciousness:** The condition in which a split-brain patient has a separate consciousness in each hemisphere. The intact brain does not exhibit this duality of consciousness.

**FIGURE 2.20:** Eye–Hand Coordination in Split-Brain Subjects

When a split-brain patient uses the left hand to find a match to an object appearing in the left visual field, eye–hand coordination is normal, because both are registered in the right hemisphere (left figure). But when asked to use the right hand to match an object seen in the left visual field, the patient cannot perform the task and mismatches a pear with a cup (right figure). This is because sensations from the right hand go to the left hemisphere, and there is no longer a connection between the two hemispheres.

Match

Mismatch

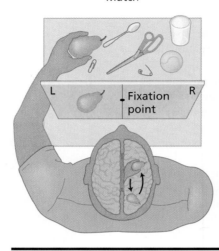
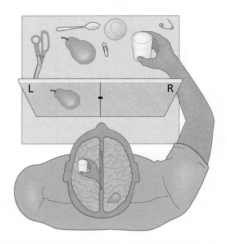

**Stroke:** An interruption of blood supply to a part of the brain.

## PSYCHOLOGY IN YOUR LIFE

### Brain Damage & Behavior

*n*early everybody knows someone who has suffered brain damage from an accident, a tumor, or a stroke. Your new knowledge of the brain and behavior will help you understand the problems such people must face. And if you know what abilities have been lost or altered, you can usually make a good guess as to which part of the brain sustained the damage—especially if you bear in mind two simple principles:

- Each side of the brain communicates with the opposite side of the body. Thus, if symptoms appear on one side of the body, it is likely that the other side of the brain was damaged. (See Figure 2.21.)
- For most people, speech is mainly a left-hemisphere function.

Now use your knowledge of the brain to guess where the damage probably occurred in the brains of these individuals:

1. Edna had a **stroke** (an interruption of blood supply to a part of the brain) and lost her ability to speak (although she could still understand speech). Where did the stroke most likely affect her brain?
2. Theo was in an auto accident, which left him with jerky, uncoordinated movements. Brain scans revealed no damage to his cerebral cortex.
3. Just prior to her seizures, Lydia has a strange sensation (an "aura") that feels like pinpricks on her left leg. What part of her brain generates this sensation?

What is the outlook for people such as these? Depending on her age, physical condition, the extent of the stroke, and

**FIGURE 2.21:** Effects of Damage to the Cerebral Hemispheres

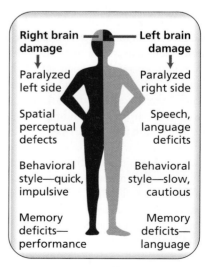

| Right brain damage | Left brain damage |
|---|---|
| ↓ | ↓ |
| Paralyzed left side | Paralyzed right side |
| Spatial perceptual defects | Speech, language deficits |
| Behavioral style—quick, impulsive | Behavioral style—slow, cautious |
| Memory deficits— performance | Memory deficits— language |

how quickly she received medical attention, Edna may get some or all of her speech back. Even if Broca's area in her left frontal lobe has been permanently damaged, other parts of her brain may be able to take over some of the lost function. Neuroscientists call this the **plasticity** of the brain. Long-term therapy for Edna will emphasize speech therapy.

Theo may also regain some or all of his abilities, especially if the affected neural cells in his cerebellum were merely injured but not severed or destroyed in the accident. Long-term treatment for him will in-

volve physical therapy. Both Edna and Theo may also need psychological therapy to help them cope with any permanent loss of function.

Lydia has epilepsy, originating in her right somatosensory cortex. Like most people with epilepsy, she will probably receive significant help from antiseizure medications. The chances are good that she will be completely symptom free when the drugs are properly adjusted.

A take-away message from all of these cases is that people who suffer from brain damage can often receive significant help.

Note, too, that help may come in many forms, both physical and mental. Perhaps the most important long-term therapy, however, is social support—a good thing to remember if you know someone who has sustained brain damage. (*See Chapter 9, Stress, Health, and Well-Being.*)

**Plasticity:** The ability of the brain to be modified or to compensate for damage.

## Check Your Understanding

1. RECALL: *Which technique for studying the brain relies on the brain's electrical activity?*
   a. EEG
   b. MRI
   c. PET
   d. CT

2. RECALL: *Name the three main layers in the human brain:*
   _____, _____, *and* _____.

3. RECALL: *Make a sketch showing the four lobes of the cerebral cortex. Indicate the main functions of each lobe. Which hemisphere of the brain controls language in most people? Which hemisphere of your brain controls your left hand?*

4. APPLICATION: *A brain tumor in the limbic system is most likely to produce changes in a person's*
   a. coordination.
   b. vision.
   c. sleep patterns.
   d. emotions.

5. RECALL: *In most people, speech is controlled by the brain's*
   a. left hemisphere.
   b. right hemisphere.
   c. corpus callosum.
   d. occipital lobe.

6. RECALL: *In the split-brain operation, what part of the brain is split?*
   a. the left hemisphere
   b. the right hemisphere
   c. the corpus callosum
   d. the occipital lobe

7. ANALYSIS: *The split-brain patient in Figure 2.20 has trouble using the* _____ *hand to select the object flashed on the left side of the screen.*
   a. right
   b. left
   (Hints: Which hemisphere controls each hand? Which hemisphere processes information from the left side of the visual field?)

8. RECALL: *Unlike the split-brain patient, we do not have two separate consciousnesses because the two hemispheres communicate through*
   a. the brain stem.
   b. the hypothalamus.
   c. the hippocampus.
   d. the corpus callosum.

9. UNDERSTANDING THE CORE CONCEPT: The brain is composed of many specialized and interconnected modules that work together to create mind and behavior. *Can you name at least two specialized parts of the brain that are known to work together? What is the result of the collaboration of the structures you have named?*

**ANSWERS:** 1. a   2. the brain stem and cerebellum, the limbic system, the cerebrum   3. See the location of the four lobes in **Figure 2.15. The left hemisphere controls language, and the right hemisphere controls your left hand.**   4. d   5. a   6. c   7. a   8. d   9. **Examples include the interaction of regions in the four lobes of the cerebral cortex when answering the phone. There are many other examples mentioned in this section.**

# USING PSYCHOLOGY TO LEARN PSYCHOLOGY

## *Putting Your Knowledge of the Brain to Work*

The idea that we use only 10% of our brains is bunk. Every part of the brain gets used every day—but not necessarily for intellectual purposes. Much of the brain merely controls basic biological functions. But is there a nugget in our knowledge of the brain that you can use to improve your intellectual power?

Consider the notion that the cerebral cortex contains many separate regions that are capable of communicating and coordinating with each other. If you can bring more of these cortical areas to bear on a lesson (about the brain, for example), more of your brain will lay down memories of the material. To be specific, reading the material in this book will help you form verbal memories. These can be strengthened by taking notes, which brings the motor cortex into play. Scanning the accompanying photos, charts, and drawings adds visual and spatial components of memory. In general, the more ways that you can deal with the material, the stronger will be your memories. Put your knowledge of the brain to work!

## CHAPTER SUMMARY

 **HOW ARE GENES AND BEHAVIOR LINKED?**

- Charles Darwin's theory of evolution explains behavior as the result of natural selection. Variation among individuals and competition for resources lead to survival of the most adaptive behavior, as well as the fittest features. This principle accounts for much of our own behavior. In particular, encephalization and language have given humans a distinct evolutionary advantage and promoted the development of human cultures.

 **CORE** CONCEPT

**Behavior consistently found in a species is likely to have a genetic basis that evolved because the behavior has been adaptive.**

 **HOW DOES THE BODY COMMUNICATE INTERNALLY?**

- The body's two communication systems are the nervous system and the endocrine system. The nervous system is composed of neurons organized into central and peripheral nervous systems. Each of these is further subdivided for different behavioral and bodily functions. The basic unit of the nervous system is the neuron, which fires when it is stimulated, causing neurotransmitters to be released. These neurotransmitters relay the impulse to other nerve cells throughout the system. The slower endocrine system secretes hormones into the bloodstream, influencing the activity of other glands and bodily structures.

 **CORE** CONCEPT

**The body's twin communications systems, the nervous system and the endocrine system, both use chemical messengers to communicate with targets throughout the body.**

 **HOW DOES THE BRAIN PRODUCE BEHAVIOR AND MENTAL PROCESSES?**

- Early medicine learned about the brain from the study of brain injuries. Later, studies of brain lesions helped to determine more precise brain localization. Recently, electrical stimulation and recording of brain activity have led to brain-scanning techniques that produce images that can reveal both brain structures and mental activity.

- We now know that the brain is organized in three integrated layers—the brain stem and cerebellum, the limbic system, and the cerebral cortex—each with distinct functions. Within each of these layers the brain contains many specialized modules, each performing a specific function automatically and without conscious direction.
- Different regions of the brain—notably the cerebral cortex—perform different and highly specialized tasks. Language, analytical thinking, and positive emotions are regulated by specific parts of the left hemisphere, while cortical centers in the right hemisphere control spatial interpretation, visual and musical memory, and negative emotions. If the hemispheres are surgically severed, each functions independently of the other and is not directly aware of stimulation or cognitive activities that affect the other.

 **CORE CONCEPT**

**The brain is composed of many specialized and interconnected modules that work together to create mind and behavior.**

# REVIEW TEST

For each of the following items, choose the single best answer. The correct answers appear at the end.

1. According to Darwin's theory of *natural selection,*
   a. the environment chooses organisms that are more complex and more advanced.
   b. some members of a species produce more offspring that survive and reproduce because the environment favors their inheritable characteristics.
   c. giraffes evolved longer necks because they were constantly reaching for the tender, higher leaves in the tall trees in their environment.
   d. evolution is a process whereby experience modifies an organism's genes.

2. In natural selection, an example of _____ is the many different genotypes and phenotypes that are represented in a population.
   a. variation
   b. environment
   c. competition
   d. cerebral dominance

3. Which one of the following is an example of behavior controlled primarily by the autonomic nervous system?
   a. typing a sentence accurately on a keyboard
   b. solving a mathematical problem
   c. breathing and swallowing while asleep
   d. feeling hungry

4. During a neural impulse, a neuron "fires" when
   a. it is physically contacted by another cell that is transmitting the signal.
   b. an electric charge travels down the axon.
   c. it contracts and releases powerful chemicals directly into the bloodstream.
   d. signals entering at the axon travel the length of the cell and exit through the dendrites.

5. Neurotransmitters are released by the terminal buttons into the _____, and hormones are released by the endocrine system into the

   _____.
   a. sympathetic nervous system/parasympathetic nervous system
   b. cortex/brain stem
   c. left hemisphere/right hemisphere
   d. synaptic cleft/bloodstream

6. Which form of brain scanning employs radioactive tracers to reveal the most active regions of the brain?
   a. EEG
   b. CT
   c. PET
   d. MRI

7. Which of the three brain layers is often thought of as the "emotional brain"?
   a. the brain stem and cerebellum
   b. the limbic system
   c. the autonomic nervous system
   d. the cerebrum

8. What part of the cerebral cortex is most involved with body movements?
   a. the frontal lobes
   b. the parietal lobes
   c. the temporal lobes
   d. the occipital lobes

9. Which of the following statements identifying the locations of important brain structures is true?
   a. The hypothalamus is part of the brain stem.
   b. The medulla is part of the limbic system.
   c. The occipital lobe is part of the cerebral cortex.
   d. All of the above.

**10.** The left hemisphere of the cerebral cortex is more involved than the right hemisphere in experiences such as
   **a.** recognizing and appreciating visual stimuli.
   **b.** enjoying and appreciating music.
   **c.** using spoken and written language.
   **d.** understanding spatial relationships.

ANSWERS:   1. b   2. a   3. c   4. b   5. d   6. c
7. b   8. a   9. c   10. c

# IF YOU'RE INTERESTED . . .

## BOOKS

Amen, D. G. (1999). *Change your brain, change your life.* New York: Random House.

> *Frustrated by a minority of his patients who seemed resistant to treatment, psychiatrist Daniel G. Amen found the answer through a brain-imaging technique called SPECT, concluding that it is brain dysfunction, not refusal to change, that traps people in unhappy and self-defeating ways of thinking and behaving.*

Calvin, W. H., & Ojeman, G. J. (1994). *Conversations with Neil's Brain: The neural nature of thought and language.* New York: Addison-Wesley.

> *Neil is preparing to have a brain operation, and his neurosurgeon explains to him what will happen. In the process, Neil (and the reader) painlessly and pleasurably learn a lot about the way the brain works.*

Edelman, G. M. (1992). *Bright air, brilliant fire: On the matter of the mind.* New York: Basic Books.

> *This is a Nobel Prize–winning immunologist's account— intended for the lay reader—of how the brain is designed not to mirror the world but to produce a mind that constructs consciousness.*

Gazzaniga, M. (1998). *The mind's past.* Berkeley: University of California Press.

> *One of the pioneers of split-brain research now tells us how the mind and brain reconstruct memories of our past. It is a process fraught with errors of perception and judgment.*

Gazzaniga, M. (1985). *The social brain: Discovering the networks of the mind.* New York: Basic Books.

> *A pioneer of split-brain research invites us to review modern brain research and its implications.*

Hilts, P. J. (1996). *Memory's ghost: The strange tale of Mr. M and the nature of memory.* New York: Touchstone.

> *This is a journalist's first-person account of meeting the legendary H. M., who lives a tragically distorted life without his hippocampi.*

Leakey, R., & Lewin, R. (1992). *Origins reconsidered: In search of what makes us human.* New York: Doubleday.

> *This review of archaeological evidence on the origins of the human species and its evolutionary development considers possible explanations for language, consciousness, and social violence.*

LeDoux, J. (1996). *The emotional brain: The mysterious underpinnings of emotional life.* New York: Touchstone.

> *This well-illustrated and reader-friendly work reviews some of the most complex questions about the human brain: Where do feelings come from, how are they controlled, and in what ways are our feelings distinctly human?*

Pinker, S. (1997). *How the mind works.* New York: W. W. Norton & Co.

> *Pinker is a brash young neuroscientist who has stirred up a controversy with this book, which suggests how evolution produced the brain and the mind.*

Posner, M. I., & Raichle, M. E. (1994). *Images of mind.* New York: W. H. Freeman.

> *This interesting and helpful book guides the reader through the development and use of the new brain scanning and imaging techniques.*

Ray, S. (1998). *5-HTP: Nature's serotonin solution.* Garden City Park, NY: Avery Publishing Group.

> *A medical doctor explains how the neurotransmitter serotonin affects a broad range of powerful mental and physical functions, including depression, weight loss, anxiety, and insomnia. The author cautiously recommends applications and treatments, citing case studies and side effects.*

Reeve, C. (1999). *Still Me.* New York: Ballantine Books.

> *Actor Christopher Reeve, rendered quadriplegic by a 1995 horseback riding accident, recounts how his life has changed, not changed, and even flourished since his injury. This is an affecting view of how one's body and self are related but not equal—and mutually limiting.*

Sacks, O. (1985). *The man who mistook his wife for a hat, and other clinical tales.* New York: Summit Books.

This fascinating series of clinical stories tells of patients with neurological disorders that have had extraordinary effects on their lives.

Sacks, O. (1995). *An anthropologist on Mars.* New York: Random House.

In his most recent collection of essays, neurologist Oliver Sacks explores how several individuals have sought to meet the challenges of unusual neurological disorders, including autism and Tourette's syndrome, by constructing extraordinarily "ordinary," adaptive lives.

Weiner, J. (1994). *The beak of the finch.* New York: Random House.

Weiner tells "the story of evolution in our time" with examples of classic and contemporary observations of species' adaptation to changing environmental challenges.

## VIDEOS

*Awakenings.* (1990, color, 121 min.). Directed by Penny Marshall; starring Robin Williams, Robert DeNiro, Julie Kavner.

Based on Oliver Sacks's collection of the same title, the movie focuses on the story of patients suffering from a mysterious "sleeping sickness," notably Leonard (DeNiro), whose lives are transformed—but only briefly—by the drug L-Dopa, a synthetic form of the neurotransmitter dopamine.

*My left foot.* (1989, color, 103 min.). Directed by James Sheridan; starring Daniel Day-Lewis, Brenda Fricker, Ray McAnally, Fiona Shaw.

This powerful and wonderful film, featuring Oscar-winning performances, is based on the true story of Christy Brown, an Irish artist-writer born with cerebral palsy.

*Phenomenon.* (1996, color, 124 min.). Directed by Jon Turtletaub; starring John Travolta, Kyra Sedgwick, Forest Whitaker, Robert Duvall, Brent Spiner.

This touching story relates how an ordinary man, seemingly struck by lightning, achieves supernormal brain development and intellectual feats—a blessing that turns out to be a curse.

*Regarding Henry.* (1991, color, 107 min.). Directed by Mike Nichols; starring Harrison Ford, Anette Bening, Bill Nunn, John Leguizamo.

A cold-hearted lawyer, shot in the head during a store holdup, undergoes a change of personality in the course of his rehabilitation. The film itself is somewhat cool and complacent but offers an intriguing view of how the brain might influence personality as well as intellectual function.

CORE CONCEPTS

PSYCHOLOGY IN YOUR LIFE

**WHAT IS THE NATURE OF CONSCIOUSNESS?**

Consciousness arises as the brain forms a model of the world that combines external stimulation with internal experience.

**The Unconscious Reconsidered:** An empirical look suggests a simpler unconscious than the one portrayed by Sigmund Freud.

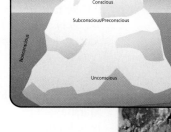

**WHAT ARE THE CYCLES OF EVERYDAY CONSCIOUSNESS?**

Consciousness changes in cycles that normally correspond to our biological rhythms and to the patterns of our environment.

**Sleep Disorders:** Insomnia, sleep apnea, narcolepsy, and daytime sleepiness can be hazardous to your health—and perhaps even to your life.

**WHAT OTHER FORMS CAN CONSCIOUSNESS TAKE?**

An altered state of consciousness occurs when some aspect of normal consciousness is modified by mental, behavioral, or chemical means.

**Drug Dependence and Addiction:** Psychoactive drugs alter brain chemistry, and they can produce physical or psychological addiction. But is addiction a disease or a character flaw?

**USING PSYCHOLOGY TO LEARN PSYCHOLOGY: HOW MUCH SLEEP DO YOU NEED TO LEARN EFFECTIVELY?**

# 3 States of Mind

## Chapter Outline

"One hundred, 99, 98, 97 . . ." Karen counted as the anesthetic flowed from the needle into her vein. Geometric patterns oscillated wildly before her. "Ninety-two, 91, 90 . . ." Darkness descended. Sensation and awareness shut down. Karen's surgery began.

Karen hadn't worried about this operation—it was only minor surgery to remove a cyst in her mouth. Minutes into the operation, however, the surgeon exclaimed, "Why, this may not be a cyst at all. It may be cancer!" Fortunately, the biopsy proved him wrong. In the recovery room the surgeon told Karen, who was still groggy and slightly nauseous, that everything was fine; the operation was a complete success.

That night, Karen felt anxious and had trouble falling asleep. She started crying for no apparent reason. Finally, when she did fall asleep, she dreamed about a puppy she couldn't get because of her allergy to dogs. Karen awoke feeling sad and was depressed all day. At first, she attributed her bad mood to her dream. But when all attempts to restore her usual good spirits failed and her depression worsened, Karen sought professional help. A therapist hypnotized Karen and asked her to lift her hand if something was disturbing her. Karen's hand rose, and the therapist suggested that she report what was disturbing her. Karen exclaimed, "The cyst may be cancerous!"

Karen's depression lifted after she received assurances that the cyst was benign. Consciously, Karen had not understood the source of her anxiety. But even in an unconscious, anesthetized state, some part of her mind had understood the surgeon's words. The dire meaning of that information became psychologically traumatic to Karen.

Karen's case is not unusual. Increasing evidence indicates that patients who are fully anesthetized and have no conscious recall of their operations may still hear what is going on during their surgery. Our hearing sensitivity appears to remain on alert even under adequate anesthesia. The reasons for this auditory alertness may be deeply rooted in our evolutionary history: Animals in the open have to respond swiftly to sounds of possible danger even when asleep. Whatever the reason, highly specialized cells in the auditory nerve make the signals passing along it exceptionally clear and hard to block out with anesthetics. Because of this sensitivity, even casual remarks in the operating room can be dangerous. Anesthetized patients may not be awake, but they are not entirely unaware: At some level they may perceive others' comments and react with shock or fear if those comments are frightening.

Consciousness can include a rich mixture of memory, fantasy, emotion, and external stimulation.

*Physicians and psychologists are intrigued by research findings on the capacity of anesthetized patients to learn and remember auditory information experienced during an operation. Such recall seems to occur despite patients' insistence of amnesia when they are conscious. Although not all research supports the operation of memory under general anesthesia, most recent, controlled experiments support several important conclusions (Ghoneim & Block, 1992). Patients under general anesthesia may not be oblivious to their operative experiences, partly because there is no adequate way to measure the depth of anesthesia while a patient is unconscious. Patients also perform well on experimental tasks that measure memory of information they were exposed to during anesthesia (Block et al., 1991; Kihlstrom et al., 1990). More important for patients' health are findings that unfavorable comments voiced about them during anesthesia may harm them, as in Karen's case (Blacher, 1987; Eich, Reeves, & Katz, 1985; Levinson, 1967). On the positive side, taped therapeutic suggestions played during surgical anesthesia improve patients' postoperative recovery, as shown by reduced use of morphine and earlier discharge (Evans & Richardson, 1988; McLintock et al., 1990).*

We know our ordinary, waking consciousness intimately. Yet when it changes, consciousness may suddenly seem strange and unfamiliar. Like a stream, consciousness flows continually, although it may flow in different channels when it takes on altered states such as meditation or hypnosis or when it comes under the influence of anesthesia or other drugs, as Karen's experience reminds us. But, perhaps the most dramatic change occurs every day during sleep, when consciousness seems to vanish, only to reemerge later in the bizarre world of dreams. No matter what form it takes, consciousness always seems to swirl around the center of our being, carrying with it everything we will remember about ourselves and our world.

 **KEY QUESTION** **WHAT IS THE NATURE OF CONSCIOUSNESS?**

Consciousness also poses psychology's greatest mystery. To understand the mystery, we invite you to try a "thought experiment." Relax. Get comfortable. Now reflect on the contents and boundaries of your conscious experience. What does it contain? And what does it exclude?

You will probably notice that the stream of consciousness sweeps up a mixture of events happening around you and combines them with your feelings, memories, interpretations, and other processes occurring in your brain. But did it occur to you that much of your brain activity (coordination of eye movements as you read this sentence, for example) takes place outside awareness? Likewise, your head is filled with information that is not caught up in consciousness—but could be, if you pulled it out of memory (the multiplication tables or the events of last night, for example).

Its private, ever-changing nature makes consciousness a difficult process to study. But perhaps the biggest challenge consciousness poses is to conceive of the mental processes that create it. For many people, consciousness seems like a theatre inside the head, where outside events, along with inner thoughts, appear on a sort of mental screen. But here's the problem with that metaphor: Who or what watches the screen? (And, is there another, still smaller, screen of consciousness inside that observer?)

Folk wisdom uses another metaphor by assigning consciousness to an *anima*, a soul or inner life force. A variation on this theme suggests that evil spirits or devils sometimes take over consciousness and cause bizarre behavior. Sigmund Freud's view represents another variant of the anima hypothesis: He put the **ego**—the rational de-

**Ego:** In Freud's psychoanalytic theory, the conscious, rational part of the mind.

cision-maker part of the mind—at the center of consciousness. There, said Freud, it attempts to keep the powerful forces of the unconscious in check. But was Freud right? While most psychologists today would say that his views were better as metaphors than as science, his ideas are still widely accepted by the general public.

Science first turned its spotlight on consciousness when experimental psychologists attempted to dissect conscious experience in their laboratories during the late 1800s and early 1900s. Using a simple technique called **introspection,** subjects were asked to look inside themselves at their own consciousness—much as you did a moment ago. While introspecting, these subjects performed various tasks and reported on the flow of events and ideas in their "stream of consciousness." Inspired by the concept of the periodic table of elements that had just revolutionized chemistry, experimental psychologists hoped to find the "elements" of consciousness. Unfortunately, this goal proved more elusive than they had supposed. The biggest problem was objectivity: How could an objective science study something so subjective and personal as consciousness?

Early in the 20th century, John Watson's approach to psychology gave up on consciousness altogether. Watson's behaviorism dismissed consciousness as little more than a by-product of behavior and scorned introspection as scientifically useless. In its place, he urged only direct observations of behavior, rather than a search for the mysterious mental processes hidden inside the organism. And, in the decades when behaviorism dominated American psychology—from the 1920s to the 1960s—scientists paid scant attention to consciousness.

Then, in the 1960s, a backlash against radical behaviorism began with a coalition of cognitive psychologists, neuroscientists, and computer scientists who accused the behaviorists of throwing out the mental baby with the unscientific bathwater (Gardner, 1985). They also began using new tools, especially computers, to do respectable scientific work on internal mental processes, such as memory, perception, and thought. This multidisciplinary effort is now called **cognitive neuroscience.** It eventually won over psychologists who viewed the conscious mind as a natural process occurring in the brain. After all, the brain has vast resources—approximately 100 billion neurons, each with thousands of interconnections. Surely, with this equipment, the human brain is capable of creating the universe of imagination we think of as consciousness (Chalmers, 1995; Churchland, 1995). Our Core Concept puts it this way:

Chapter 1
**Mind, Behavior, and Science**
Chapter 10
**Personality**

*Sigmund Freud's psychoanalytic theory says that most of the mind lies outside of consciousness.*

Chapter 1
**Mind, Behavior, and Science**

*Structuralism pioneered the use of introspection in its search for the "elements of conscious experience."*

Chapter 1
**Mind, Behavior, and Science**

*Watson's behaviorism banned consciousness from scientific psychology.*

**Introspection:** The process of looking inside to observe one's own mental state and conscious experience.

Chapter 2
**Biopsychology**

*Neurons are the biological basis for all mental processes.*

**Cognitive neuroscience:** A new, interdisciplinary field involving cognitive psychology, neuroscientists, computer scientists, and specialists from other fields who are interested in the connection between mental processes and the brain.

**CORE CONCEPT**

**Consciousness arises as the brain forms a model of the world that combines external stimulation with internal experience.**

The Nobel Prize–winning biochemist Francis Crick anticipates that most of us find it difficult to believe that brain activity is all there is to the mind. In the introduction to his book *The Astonishing Hypothesis: The Scientific Search for the Soul* (1994), Crick phrases the view of cognitive neuroscience in these words:

> The Astonishing Hypothesis is that "You," your joys and your sorrows, your memories and your ambitions, your sense of personal identity and free will, are in fact no more than the behavior of a vast assembly of nerve cells and their associated molecules. As Lewis Carroll's Alice might have phrased it: "You're nothing but a pack of neurons." This hypothesis is so alien to the ideas of most people alive today that it can truly be called astonishing. (p. 3)

Crick and other cognitive neuroscientists must defend their theories against critics who maintain that consciousness is too subjective to be studied scientifically (Wright, 1995b). They must also defend their ideas against many competing theories of

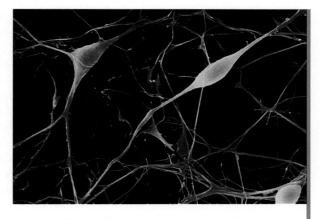

Crick's "Astonishing Hypothesis" says that you are "no more than the behavior of a vast assembly of nerve cells and their associated molecules."

consciousness that have appeared in the wake of the "cognitive revolution" in psychology. The one element that all these theories have in common is this: *Consciousness is a product of psychological processes based in the brain.* This consensus, then, offers the researcher a place to look for telltale traces of conscious experience (see Tononi & Edelman, 1998).

### How Consciousness Is Studied with the Tools of Science

High-technology tools, such as the MRI, PET, and EEG, have opened new windows through which researchers can look into the brain for the traces of consciousness. With these devices researchers can, at last, see which brain areas are active during different mental tasks. These imaging devices, of course, do not show the actual contents of conscious experience. To glimpse the underlying mental processes, psychologists have devised other ingenious techniques.

Suppose, for example, that you were asked to fill in the blanks to make a word from the following stem:

DEF ___ ___ ___

PET images can show which regions of the brain are most active in emotional states and when processing language.

**Chapter 2
Biopsychology**

*The EEG shows patterns of electrical activity in the brain.*

**Chapter 6
Learning and Remembering**

*Priming is a technique for probing unconscious mental processes.*

Using a technique called *priming*, psychologists can have some influence on the answers people give to such problems without subjects being aware that they were influenced. In the example just given, there are a number of possible ways to complete the word stem, including *define, defeat, defect, defile, deform, defray,* and *defuse.* But if you have recently read the last paragraph in the previous section, the chance that you might have filled in the blanks to make yet another word is slightly increased. There you were deliberately exposed (twice) to the word *defend* to "prime" your response. With priming methods such as this, psychologists have a powerful tool for probing the interaction of conscious and nonconscious processes. The technique might be used, for example, to study how patients, like Karen, can form memories while under surgical anesthesia.

Another approach employs a modern variation of introspection to get at the contents of consciousness. Subjects are asked to speak aloud as they work through puzzles, operate unfamiliar machines, or carry out other complex tasks. They report in as much detail as possible the sequence of thoughts they experience as they work (Ericsson & Simon, 1993; Newell & Simon, 1972). These reports are called **think-aloud protocols.**

Yet another method employs electronic pagers, which subjects wear as they go about their normal activities. Researchers arrange for subjects to be paged or signaled at prearranged or random moments in order to collect "samples" of their thoughts and feelings (Emmons, 1986; Hurlburt, 1979). In this **experience-sampling method,** subjects write down or tape-record what they are thinking and feeling whenever the pager signals. Subjects may also be asked to respond to questions such as "How well were you concentrating?" Researchers thus keep a running record of people's thoughts, awareness, and attention as they go about their everyday lives (Csikszentmihalyi, 1990). (Note to readers: Because we will see more of the work of Mihalyi Csikszentmihalyi, you may find it helpful to know that his name is pronounced *me-HIGH chick-SENT-me-high.*)

**Think-aloud protocols:** An introspective technique that has subjects describe their thought processes as they carry out complex tasks, such as solving puzzles.

**Experience-sampling method:** Another introspective technique that has subjects record what they are feeling at selected times—often signaled by the beeping of a pager.

This brief survey shows that psychologists have a variety of techniques for exploring and illuminating the private world of consciousness. With this in mind, let us turn now to a more detailed consideration of how consciousness is organized and how it works.

Chapter 8
Emotion and Motivation
*Csikszentmihalyi says that people in a "flow" state are more focused and creative.*

## The Functions and Structures of Consciousness

Ordinary waking consciousness consists of the immediate mental experiences that make up your perceptions, thoughts, feelings, and desires. Consciousness includes awareness of ourselves and of stimulation from our environment. We are usually conscious of what we are doing, why we are doing it, and the effect of our behavior on the environment. But neither the fact of consciousness nor a record of its contents tells us what purpose consciousness serves or how it operates. In tackling these problems we will first consider the *functions* of consciousness. Then we will review what research and theory can tell us about how consciousness is *organized*—its forms, structures, and dynamics—in order to perform its functions.

**WHAT CONSCIOUSNESS DOES FOR US** Imagine waking up to find yourself in a strange bed, being examined by white-coated strangers who tell you, "You've been in an accident, but you're in a hospital, and you're going to be all right." Your conscious abilities enable you to put this information together with your memories and recognize culturally meaningful information ("A hospital is a place where I will get medical care") to figure out what has happened. In general, consciousness helps us construct both personal realities and culturally shared realities.

Chapter 1
Mind, Behavior, and Science
Chapter 2
Biopsychology
*The evolutionary perspective emphasizes the function of behavior.*

The evolutionary perspective reminds us that this internal construction of reality must be highly adaptive to have become such a prominent feature of human cognition. What makes it adaptive? In brief, a conscious construction of reality allows us to integrate a huge amount of information from both internal cognitions and external stimulation. The following properties of consciousness facilitate this process:

- Consciousness restricts attention, controlling what we notice and think about; it allows us to attend only to what is relevant to our needs. In this way, consciousness keeps our brains from being overwhelmed by stimulation.
- Consciousness gives us not only a simplified view of the world, but a view that combines sensation with learning and memory. Thus, consciousness is an *interpretation* of the world.
- Consciousness helps us select and store in memory personally meaningful stimuli from the flow of all the input from our senses. In this way, consciousness helps us make a mental record of the most meaningful elements in our lives.
- Consciousness allows us to draw selectively on lessons stored in memory. Thus, we are not, like simpler organisms, prisoners of the moment. Rather, we can consider both the past and the future, as we evaluate alternative responses and imagine the effectiveness of their consequences.

You rely on these four dimensions of consciousness every day. For example, as part of your morning routine, you must restrict attention to certain immediate tasks, such as showering, dressing, and eating. The demands of attention may also rule out other, less pressing tasks, such as a second cup of coffee. Your consciousness also helps you select and store information from the daily weather forecast that helps you consider how to dress for the expected weather. It also helps you draw on memory in order to imagine the consequences of certain choices, such as carrying an umbrella or bringing books and other supplies with you. Consciousness is obviously handy. It offers humans the capacity for flexible, appropriate responses to life's changing demands (Baars, 1988; Baars & McGovern, 1994; Ornstein, 1986b; Rozin, 1976). Let us consider how consciousness is organized to perform these functions.

## FIGURE 3.1: Structures of Consciousness

If consciousness were represented as an iceberg, conscious processes would be those located above the water's surface, while the unconscious would be submerged. Subconscious and preconscious processes both lie beneath the surface but are accessible through special attention and recall. Nonconscious processes influence bodily processes but never become accessible to consciousness.

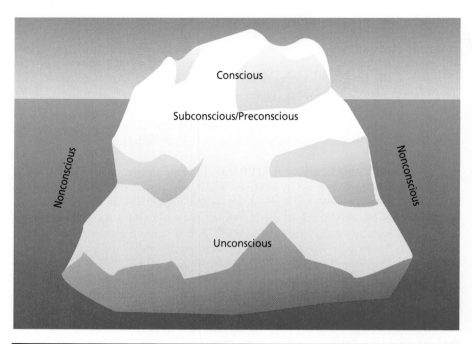

**LEVELS OF CONSCIOUSNESS**   Just now, were you aware of your heartbeat? Probably not, for controlling your heartbeat is a function that normally occurs outside of consciousness. Such **nonconscious processes** involve information processed in the brain but not represented in consciousness or memory. In general, the brain automatically and nonconsciously regulates the body's basic life-sustaining functions, such as breathing and the regulation of blood pressure. In addition, certain cognitive operations occur outside of consciousness but exert influence on consciousness. These include *preconsciousness*, the *subconscious*, and the *unconscious*.

*PRECONSCIOUSNESS*   Memories of events, such as your first kiss, have once been the focus of attention, but they are now accessible to consciousness only after something cues their recall. Psychologists call these **preconscious memories.** They lie in the background of your mind until they are needed, and they are retrieved with relative ease. We can bring to mind another example of a preconscious memory by asking: What did you have for breakfast this morning? If you can answer that question, some representation of your meal must have been stored in your mind. Although you did not expect to be quizzed about your breakfast, you not only ate it, but you thought about it and stored those thoughts at the preconscious level of awareness—until just now, when you pulled the memory out to answer the question (Baars & McGovern, 1994). Recalling something consciously is an attention-demanding act, requiring one to seek and shift information from preconsciousness to conscious memory (Jacoby, Woloshyn, & Kelley, 1989).

*SUBCONSCIOUS PROCESSING*   Just as you began reading this line, you were probably not thinking about background noises, like a clock ticking or traffic on nearby

**Nonconscious processes:** Any brain process that does not involve conscious processing. Examples include regulation of the heart rate, breathing, and control of the internal organs and glands.

**Preconscious memories:** Memories accessible to consciousness only after something calls attention to them.

streets. Constantly you must push much of the stimulation around you out of your mind so that you can focus attention on the small remainder that is relevant. But you may be surprised to learn that a great deal of nonattended stimulation gets registered and evaluated below the level of conscious awareness. Most of this **subconscious** information, however, never makes a permanent mark in long-term memory.

On the other hand, research indicates that ongoing consciousness can be influenced by events that have never commanded our attention (Kihlstrom, 1987). In fact, much cognitive processing seems to occur in this way—automatically and without awareness or effort, as when we correctly navigate a familiar route to work or school without apparent thought (Uleman & Bargh, 1989). Priming, which you experienced earlier, also involves subconscious processing. And, in the case that opened this chapter, Karen's depression was the result of a subconscious process.

*THE UNCONSCIOUS*   We use the term *unconscious* in common speech to refer to someone who has fainted, is comatose, or is under anesthesia. In psychology, however, the term **unconscious** has a special meaning. According to psychoanalytic theory, powerful unconscious forces block many of our motives, emotions, and memories from awareness. The founder of psychoanalysis, Sigmund Freud, taught that unconscious thoughts can shape our behavior even though we may have no awareness of their existence (Freud, 1925). According to Freud, the unconscious harbors memories, desires, and emotions that, at a conscious level, would cause one extreme anxiety. Such processes are assumed to stem from the need to *repress* (block) traumatic memories and taboo desires. In this view, the unconscious mind, then, serves as a mental storehouse where terrible urges and threatening memories can be kept out of consciousness. Let us look, however, at another perspective on the unconscious.

**Subconscious:** A store of information that was registered in memory without being consciously attended to.

**Unconscious:** In classic Freudian theory, a part of the mind that houses memories, desires, and feelings that would be threatening if brought to consciousness. Recently, many psychologists have come to believe in a simplified, "dumb" unconscious, which stores and processes some information outside of awareness.

**Chapter 6**
**Learning and Remembering**
*Priming techniques can tap information that reaches long-term memory without having been the focus of attention.*

**Chapter 10**
**Personality**
*Repression may make us forget unpleasant memories, said Freud*

---

**PSYCHOLOGY IN YOUR LIFE**

## The Unconscious Reconsidered

Ever since Freud, the art and literature of the Western world have been captivated by the notion of an unconscious filled with dark and sinister motives and memories. Joseph Conrad's *Heart of Darkness*, for example, tells a story of a person's internal and unconscious struggle with the most evil of desires. But is this the way our minds really work? Are we doomed to live in a mind divided against itself—consciousness against the unconscious? (*See Chapter 10, Personality.*)

Advances in research methods (such as priming) have made it possible to demonstrate and study nonconscious

thought processes in an **empirical** way (Kihlstrom, 1990; Kihlstrom, Barnhardt, & Tartaryn, 1992; Rozin, 1976). We now know with certainty what Freud was able to demonstrate only with conjecture: There is an unconscious aspect to your mind. But to cognitive psychologists it doesn't look much like Freud's vision. For one thing, the unconscious does not seem as dramatic or sinister as the Freud portrayal of it. For another, the new view of the unconscious suggests a much simpler structure than the complicated censoring and repressing system that Freud proposed (Greenwald, 1992).

In the cognitive view, the unconscious devotes its resources to simple background

tasks such as screening the incoming stream of sights, sounds, smells, and textures, rather than to repressing memories of traumatic experiences. Ironically, the new view of an unconscious that monitors, sorts, discards, and stores the flood of data we encounter may give this portion of the mind a larger role than Freud originally conceived. In this respect, the new view of the unconscious emphasizes the sort of *subconscious* processing that we discussed earlier.

**Empirical:** Relying on direct sensory observation rather than subjective judgment.

1. **RECALL:** *Who objected most strenuously to psychology being the science of consciousness?*
   a. the cognitive psychologists
   b. the behaviorists
   c. the psychoanalysts
   d. the neurologists

2. **RECALL:** *According to Francis Crick, what is the "astonishing hypothesis"?*
   a. Consciousness exists.
   b. Creativity arises from altered states of consciousness.
   c. Mental processes are nothing more than the activities of nerve cells and chemicals.
   d. The conscious mind has little access to the larger world of mental activity in the unconscious.

3. **APPLICATION:** *Suppose that you wanted to sample the contents of preconsciousness. Which technique would you use?*
   a. MRI
   b. recall

   c. priming
   d. psychoanalysis

4. **UNDERSTANDING THE CORE CONCEPT:** *Which of the following is a main function of consciousness suggested by the Core Concept for this section?*
   a. Consciousness combines sensation with learning and memory.
   b. Consciousness allows us to respond reflexively, without thinking.
   c. Consciousness controls the autonomic nervous system.
   d. Consciousness makes us more alert.

**ANSWERS:**  1. b   2. c   3. b   4. a

---

 **KEY QUESTION** **WHAT ARE THE CYCLES OF EVERYDAY CONSCIOUSNESS?**

If you are a "morning person," you are probably at your peak of alertness soon after you awaken. But this mental state doesn't last all day. Like most other people, you probably experience a period of mental lethargy in the afternoon. At this low point in the cycle of wakefulness, you may join much of the Latin world, which wisely takes a siesta. Later, your alertness increases for a time, only to fade again during the evening hours. Punctuating this cycle may be periods of heightened focus and attention (as when you are called on in class) and periods of reverie, known as daydreams. Finally, whether we are "morning" or "night" persons, we all eventually drift into that third of our lives spent asleep, where conscious contact with the outside world nearly ceases.

Psychologists have traced these cyclic changes in consciousness to find reliable patterns. We will see that the patterns they have found are rooted in our biological nature and in the recurring events of our lives. Our second Core Concept puts it this way:

 **CORE CONCEPT**

**Consciousness changes in cycles that normally correspond to our biological rhythms and to the patterns of our environment.**

In this section we will devote most of our attention to the cyclic changes in consciousness involved in sleep and nocturnal dreaming. First, however, we turn to the sort of dreams that occur while we are awake.

## Daydreaming

In the mild form of consciousness alteration known as **daydreaming,** attention shifts away from the external situation to focus internally on memories, expectations, and desires. Daydreaming occurs most often when people are alone, relaxed, engaged in a boring or routine task, or just about to fall asleep (Singer, 1966, 1975). But is daydreaming normal? Perhaps you will be relieved to know that most people daydream every day. In fact, it is abnormal if you do not! Research shows, however, that young adults report the most frequent daydreams, with the amount of daydreaming declining significantly with age (Singer & McCraven, 1961).

Daydreaming apparently serves valuable, healthy functions (Klinger, 1987). Research using the experience-sampling method shows that daydreams dwell on practical and current concerns in peoples lives: classes, goals (trivial or significant), and interpersonal relationships. Thus, daydreaming apparently helps us make plans and solve problems. It also gives us the opportunity for a creative time-out from the routine of daily life.

Fantasy is one form of daydreaming. When you fantasize—imagining unrealistic, unlikely, or impossible experiences—you are not necessarily escaping from life. Instead, you may actually be creatively confronting problems and working through difficulties. Fantasy may be the only way you can deal with feelings or motives that you might never act on in real life. For example, you may feel too shy to approach an attractive classmate about a date, yet fantasizing about the kind of interaction you might have is easy. Alternatively, daydreaming gives you the opportunity to rehearse your responses to events before they actually occur, as when you must talk to a professor about your grade—or when you decide to ask that attractive classmate for a date.

Sometimes people also have daydreams of a destructive nature, although they are less likely to tell us about these fantasies of breaking the rules, acting out aggression, or taking revenge on a wrongdoer. Perhaps you have imagined telling someone off in a particularly dramatic way. The effects of such fantasized conversations are, however, hard to predict: They might reduce the impulse to act too hastily, but they might just as easily become dress rehearsals for the real thing.

Now suppose that you decide to stop entertaining a particular wish or fantasy. What will happen? Research suggests that efforts to suppress unwanted thoughts are likely to backfire. In the "white bear" study (Wegner et al., 1987), subjects spoke into a tape recorder about anything that came to mind. They had been instructed, however, *not* to think about "a white bear." The results: despite their instructions, subjects mentioned a white bear about once per minute! Apparently, trying to suppress a thought or put something out of your mind can result in an obsession with the very thought you seek to escape. Ironically, when you allow your mind to roam freely, as daydreaming and fantasy naturally do, unwanted or upsetting thoughts usually become less intrusive and finally cease (Wegner, 1989).

And how do daydreams compare with dreams of the night? No matter how realistic our fantasies may be, daydreams are rarely as vivid as our most colorful night dreams. Neither are they as mysterious—because they are under our control. Nor do they occur (as do night dreams) under the influence of biological cycles and the strange world that we call sleep. It is to this world that we now turn our attention.

## Sleep and Dreaming

If you live to be 90, you will have slept for nearly 30 years. Although we spend about a third of our lives sleeping, most of us take this dramatic daily alteration of consciousness for granted. Once the province mainly of psychoanalysts, prophets, and psychics, dreams have now become a vital area of study for scientific researchers. They

Daydreaming, common among people of all ages, may be a source of creativity.

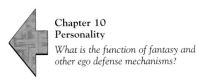

**Chapter 10
Personality**
*What is the function of fantasy and other ego defense mechanisms?*

**Daydreaming:** A mild form of consciousness alteration in which attention shifts to memories, expectations, desires, or fantasies and away from the immediate situation.

have shown that sleep must be understood as one among many natural biological rhythms. It is a consequence of our world's daylight–dark cycles interacting with our bodies' physical cycles (Beardsley, 1996). We begin our exploration of sleep and dreaming with an examination of these patterns.

**CIRCADIAN RHYTHMS**   Nearly all creatures fall under the influence of nature's cycles, especially the cycle of light and darkness. Among the most important for humans are those known as **circadian rhythms,** bodily patterns that repeat approximately every 24 hours. (*Circadian* comes from the Latin *circa* for "around" + *dies* for "a day.") Internal control of these circadian rhythms resides in a "biological clock" that sets the cadence of our metabolism, heart rate, body temperature, and hormonal activity. The "clock" itself is not a single mechanism but a coordinated set of physiological operations whose exact cycle may be dictated by an individual's genetic makeup (Dunlap, 1998; Page, 1994; Peretz, 1993). Coordination of these operations seems to be achieved by a group of cells in the thalamus. These thalamic cells are especially sensitive to the light–dark cycles of day and night.

Your normal circadian rhythms can be disrupted by air travel, mixed-shift work (work schedules that shift from day to night), and other disturbances in your sleep–wake habits (Moore-Ede, 1993). In fact, anything that throws off your biological clock affects how you feel and behave. Flying across several time zones results in **jet lag** because the internal circadian rhythm is disrupted by your new temporal environment. If it is 1:00 A.M. to your body but only 10:00 P.M. to the people around you, you must use energy and resources to adapt to your surroundings. The resulting symptoms of jet lag include fatigue, irresistible sleepiness, and temporary cognitive deficits. Air travelers should note that our biological clocks can adjust more readily to longer days than to shorter ones. Therefore, traveling eastbound (losing hours in your day) creates greater jet lag than traveling westbound (gaining hours). Apparently, it is easier to stay awake a bit longer than it is to fall asleep sooner than usual (Klein & Wegmann, 1974).

**THE MAIN EVENTS OF SLEEP**   For most of human history, sleep has been a mystery, made all the more perplexing by the fantastic pageant of our dreams. But now the use of the electroencephalogram (EEG) on sleeping subjects opens the door for researchers seeking an objective look at this formerly subjective world. With the EEG, sleep scientists have been able to record brain activity continuously through the night without disturbing the sleeper. They number among their discoveries the telltale changes in brain waves that begin at the onset of sleep and then cycle in predictable patterns during the rest of the night (Loomis et al., 1937).

The most significant discovery in sleep research first revealed itself in the eyes. About every 90 minutes during the night we enter a period marked by **rapid eye movements (REM)** that take place for several minutes beneath our closed eyelids (Aserinsky & Kleitman, 1953). The interim periods, without rapid eye movements, are known as **non-REM (NREM) sleep.** And what happens in the brain during these two different phases of sleep? To find out, researchers awakened sleepers either during REM sleep or NREM sleep and asked them to describe their mental activity (Dement & Kleitman, 1957). The NREM reports more often contained either no mental activity or brief descriptions of ordinary daily events, similar to waking thoughts. By contrast, most of the REM reports were filled with vivid cognitions, featuring fanciful, bizarre scenes. Such studies show that rapid eye movements are the best indicator of the mental activity we call dreaming. Strangely, while the eyes dance during REM sleep, the other voluntary muscles are immobile—paralyzed—a condition known as **sleep paralysis.** This

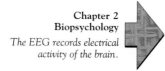
**Chapter 2
Biopsychology**
*The thalamus is the brain's
central "relay station."*

**Chapter 2
Biopsychology**
*The EEG records electrical
activity of the brain.*

**Circadian rhythms:** Physiological patterns that repeat approximately every 24 hours—such as the sleep-wakefulness cycle.

**Jet lag:** A biological and psychological disruption of the circadian rhythms produced by moving quickly across time zones and attempting to shift one's sleep-wakefulness cycle to the local time.

**Rapid eye movements (REM):** Quick bursts of eye movements occurring (under closed eyelids) at periodic intervals during sleep. REM sleep periods are associated with dreaming.

**Non-REM (NREM) sleep:** The recurring periods when a sleeper is not showing REM.

**Sleep paralysis:** A condition in which a sleeper is unable to move any of the voluntary muscles, except those controlling the eyes. Sleep paralysis normally occurs during REM sleep.

probably occurs to keep us from acting out our dreams. (In case you're wondering: Sleepwalking and sleep talking occur during NREM sleep.)

**THE SLEEP CYCLE** Now imagine that you are a subject in a laboratory specializing in sleep research. Already connected to EEG recording equipment, you have become comfortable with the wires linking your body to the machinery, and you are settling in for a night's sleep. At the moment, while you are awake and alert, the EEG shows your brain waves pulsing at a rate of about 14 cycles per second (cps). As you begin to you relax, they slow to about 8 to 12 cps. When you fall asleep, the EEG shows further changes. In fact, over the course of the night, your brain waves reveal a cycle of activity that repeats itself over and over. A closer look at the recording of this cycle the next morning will show several distinct stages, each with a characteristic EEG signature (see Figures 3.2 and 3.3):

- In Stage 1 sleep, the EEG displays fast brain waves similar to the waking state.
- During the next phase, Stage 2, the generally slower EEG is punctuated by *sleep spindles*—short bursts of fast electrical activity.
- In the following two stages (3 and 4), the sleeper enters a progressively deeper state of relaxed sleep. Brain waves slow dramatically, as do the heart rate and breathing rate. The deepest point in the sleep cycle occurs here, in Stage 4, about a half hour after sleep onset.
- As Stage 4 ends, the electrical activity of the brain increases, and the sleeper climbs back up through the stages in reverse order.
- As the brain reaches Stage 1 again, waves recorded by the EEG become fast. In addition, the sleeper now enters REM sleep for the first time (see Figure 3.2). Then, after a few minutes of REMing, the entire cycle begins to repeat itself.

Over the course of an average night's sleep, most people make the circuit through the stages of sleep four to six times. But in each successive cycle the amount of time spent in deep sleep (Stages 3 and 4) decreases, and the amount of time spent

**FIGURE 3.3:**  Stages of Sleep

During a typical night's sleep, one spends more time in the deepest stages of the early cycles. In later cycles, one spends more time in REM.

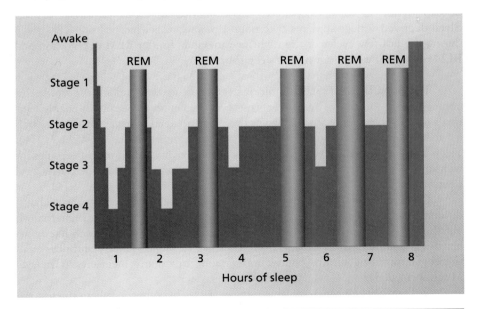

**FIGURE 3.2:**  EEG Patterns in Stages of Sleep

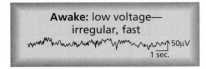

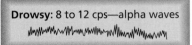

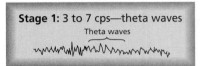

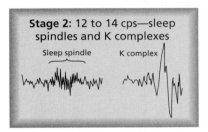

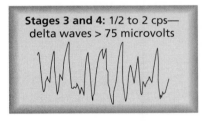

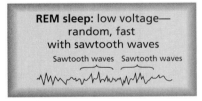

## Capture Your First Dream

Sleep researchers report that the first dream of the night is usually related to events of the previous day. Most often, however, we remember the *last* dream of the night—if we remember a dream at all. So, how can you capture the contents of the first dream? We know that a typical sleep cycle lasts about 90 minutes, followed by a REM period. So, set your alarm clock for about an hour and 40 minutes after the time you expect to get to sleep. When the alarm goes off, chances are that you will be a few minutes into a REM period. Put a pad and pencil by your bed so you can write down some of the events of the dream to cue your memory in the morning.

If you try this several times, you can gather enough data to perform a personal test of Cartwright's (1977) finding that the first dream of the night reflects events of the previous day. To carry your experiment further, you might also record, upon awakening, your final dream of the night. A comparison of the two dream records should show how, as the night progresses, your dreams become more and more disconnected from the previous day's experience.

in REM sleep increases. During the first cycle, the REM period may last only 10 minutes, while in the last cycle, we may spend as much as an hour REMing. See Figure 3.3 for the pattern of sleep through a typical night. Studying this cyclical pattern will not only help you understand your normal night's sleep but will also provide the framework for understanding the abnormal patterns found in sleep disorders. Again, note three features of normal sleep: (a) the 90-minute cycles, (b) the appearance of deepest sleep during the beginning of the night, and (c) the increase in REM duration as sleep progresses.

What do you suppose would happen if a person were deprived of a substantial part of REM sleep for a night? Laboratory studies show that REM-deprived subjects feel tired and irritable the next day. And, during the following night they spend much more time in REM sleep than usual, a condition known as **REM rebound.** This observation suggests that one of the functions of sleep is to satisfy a need for REM. Another function of REM sleep may be the maintenance of emotional balance. Sleep-deprived college students take note: Because we get most of our REM sleep during the last few cycles of the night, we inevitably suffer REM deprivation and REM rebound if we cut our night's sleep short.

**THE FUNCTION OF SLEEP**   Sleep serves at least two biological purposes: to conserve and to restore. Theorists suggest that sleep evolved because it enabled animals to conserve energy at times when there was no need to forage for food, search for mates, or work (Allison & Cicchetti, 1976; Cartwright, 1982; Webb, 1974). Sleep also enables the body to restore itself in several ways. During sleep, neurotransmitters build up to compensate for the quantities used in daily activities, and neurons return to their optimal level of sensitivity (Stern & Morgane, 1974).

Consciousness theorists Francis Crick and Graeme Mitchison propose an additional function for sleep. They believe that sleep and dreams help the brain to flush out the day's accumulation of unwanted and useless information—much like reformatting a computer disk. Dreams may also serve to reduce fantasy and obsession, thereby minimizing bizarre connections among our many memories (Crick & Mitchison, 1983).

William Shakespeare somewhat more elegantly hypothesized about the restorative function of sleep when he spoke of "Sleep that knits up the ravelled sleave of

**REM rebound:** A condition of increased REM sleep following a period of REM-sleep deprivation.

care." During sleep, unraveled material—loose ends of information—may be either integrated or eliminated. Less eloquently, sleep researcher Ernest Hartmann explains, "In the morning, sleep has done its thing. If you're in good shape your sleeve has been restored for the next day's wear" (*Discovering Psychology*, 1990, program 13).

**THE NEED FOR SLEEP** How much sleep we need depends on many factors. There is a genetically based need for sleep, different for each species. Sleep duration is also controlled by circadian rhythms, which are in turn linked to the hormone *melatonin* (Barinaga, 1997; Haimov & Lavie, 1996). But just as important for humans are volitional factors—that is, wanting to sleep. People may actively control sleep length in a number of ways, such as staying up late, drinking coffee, or using alarm clocks.

Sleep time also varies with personality. Those who sleep longer than average tend to be more nervous, worrisome, artistic, creative, and nonconforming, while short sleepers tend to be more energetic and extroverted (Hartmann, 1973). Strenuous physical activity during the day increases the amount of time spent in the slow-wave sleep of Stage 4, but, oddly, it has no effect on REM time (Horne, 1988).

Finally, sleep duration and the shape of the sleep cycle change over one's lifetime. As Figure 3.4 shows, we begin life by sleeping about 16 hours per day, with half that time devoted to REM. Young adults typically sleep seven to eight hours (although they may need more), with 20% REM. By old age, we sleep relatively less, with only 15% of sleep spent in REM.

**WHY WE DREAM** During every ordinary night of your life, you repeatedly experience an event staged only in the mind: the dream. Vivid, colorful, whimsical hallucinations, featuring complex miniplots that transform time, sequence, and place, take over the stage of your consciousness. Dreamers may feel as if they are behaving in unusual or impossible ways. They may talk, hear, and feel sexually excited, but, oddly, they cannot consciously process or sense smell, taste, or pain. Metaphorically, dreams may be characterized as theater of the absurd—chaotic dramas that appear illogical when analyzed in the rational light of our waking hours. What produces these fantastic cognitive spectacles?

As far back as history extends, people have attached significance to dreams. The ancient Israelites interpreted dreams as messages from God. Their Egyptian contemporaries attempted to influence dreams by sleeping in temples dedicated to the god of dreaming, Serapis. And in India, the sacred Vedas described the religious significance of dreams. Meanwhile, in China dreaming held an element of risk. During a dream, the ancient Chinese believed, the soul wandered about outside the body. For that reason they were reluctant to awaken a sleeper hastily, lest the soul not find its way back to the body (Dement, 1980). From the perspective of many African and Native American cultures, dreams were an extension of waking reality. Consequently, when

**FIGURE 3.4:** Patterns of Human Sleep Over a Lifetime

The graph shows changes with age in the total amounts of REM and NREM sleep and in the percentage of time spent in REM sleep. Note that, over the years, the amount of REM sleep decreases considerably, while NREM diminishes less sharply.

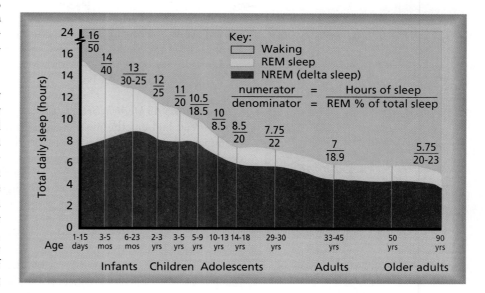

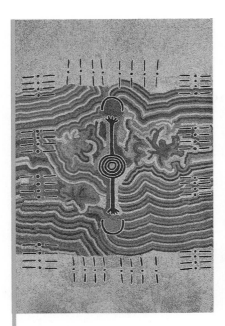

Much of the work by Australian Aboriginal painters depicts a time, long ago, when legend says that the physical features of the landscape were alive. They call this period *Dreamtime*. In the world of Aborigines, the act of making these paintings links the artist and the observer to the ancient Dreamtime. Such artwork has also been used for countless generations to instruct younger people in the ways of their ancestors. The Aborigines believe that those initiated into the mysteries of Dreamtime develop a new level of awareness, or consciousness, that connects the spiritual and material worlds.

**Manifest content:** In Freudian theory, the superficial and obvious meaning of a dream.

**Latent content:** In Freudian theory, the real and hidden meaning of a dream, disguised by symbolism.

traditional Cherokee Indians dreamed of snakebite, they received appropriate emergency treatment upon awakening. Likewise, when an African tribal chieftain dreamed of England, he ordered a set of European clothes, and upon appearing in the new togs, his friends congratulated him on making the trip (Dement, 1980).

In contrast with such folk theories, sleep scientists have approached dreaming with this question: What is the function of dreams? Some see dreams as meaningful mental events, having important cognitive functions or reflecting important events or fantasies in the dreamer's world. Others argue that dreams are merely the brain's random activity during sleep—and, therefore, their content may have no special meaning. We will consider both of these viewpoints.

DREAMS AS MEANINGFUL EVENTS    At the beginning of the 20th century, Sigmund Freud laid out the most complex and comprehensive theory of dreams and their meanings ever developed—a theory that has since enjoyed enormous influence, despite a lack of evidence to support it (Squier & Domhoff, 1998). In this view, dreams represent "the royal road to the unconscious," lined with clues to an individual's hidden mental life. Accordingly, Freud made the analysis of dreams the cornerstone of psychoanalysis with his classic book, *The Interpretation of Dreams* (1900).

In psychoanalytic theory, dreams have two main functions: to guard sleep (by disguising disruptive thoughts with symbols) and to serve as sources of wish fulfillment. Freud believed that dreams play their guardian role by relieving psychic tensions created during the day. They serve their wish-fulfillment function by allowing the dreamer to work through unconscious desires. He taught that interpreting dreams can help people to understand themselves better, and so dream analysis has became a central feature of psychoanalytic therapy.

Freud also theorized that dreams operate on two levels of meaning: **manifest content** and **latent content.** The manifest content refers to the dream's superficial meaning: the storyline of the dream. But, he said, the manifest content is really a disguise for the latent content—the dream's real, but hidden, meaning. In Freud's scheme, the latent meaning hides behind the symbols of the manifest story. For example, a child who is jealous of her parents' attention to a new baby sister might dream about squashing a bug. The manifest content, bug squashing, disguises the latent meaning of the dream, which is the child's wish to get rid of the younger rival.

Psychoanalytic therapists use this sort of dream analysis to understand their patients' problems. That is, they mine dreams for clues as to the motives and conflicts hidden in the patient's unconscious. In the tradition of psychoanalytic practice, however, dream analysis requires extensive training and careful detective work to avoid drawing the wrong conclusions about the meaning of dreams.

But is it really true that dreams are so hard to interpret that only a trained psychoanalyst could understand them? Your own experience probably says no. If awakened from a frightening dream, we can usually identify the life stressors that found their way into our sleeping thoughts. Many of our dreams have fairly obvious meanings because of their relevance to our waking lives and personal experiences. For example, a study of individuals depressed about divorce found their dreams were often fixed on past relationships (Cartwright, 1984). By analyzing the patterns and content of your own dreams, you may find it is not difficult to assign meaning to many of the images and actions you recall (Hall, 1953/1966; Van de Castle, 1994).

Freudian dream analysis has also been challenged on the grounds that Freud was not an experimentalist, nor was he always scrupulous in his data collection. So, for example, when he noted that boys frequently dream of strife with their fathers, he did no careful studies to verify his theoretical suspicions. Instead, he jumped to the conclusion that these dreams were signs of unconscious sexual jealousy. Many other explanations are possible, however, as anthropologists have shown by studying dreams of the Trobriand Islanders. Boys in that culture don't dream of their fathers so much as their uncles, who act as the disciplinarians in that society (Malinowski, 1927; Segall et al., 1990).

Unlike Freud, modern sleep scientists have accumulated much objective evidence about sleep and dreams. As a result, Freud's theory has now been largely supplanted by explanations based on firmer evidence—at least in scientific circles (see Domhoff, 1996). Psychologists now can point to research showing, for example, that the content of dreams varies by age, gender, and culture. Women everywhere more commonly dream of children, while men more often dream of aggression, weapons, and tools (Murray, 1995). The highly specific effects of culture can be seen in reports from the West African nation of Ghana, where dreamers often feature attacks by cows (Barnouw, 1963). Likewise, in their dreams, Americans frequently find themselves embarrassed by public nakedness, although such reports rarely occur in cultures where people customarily wear few clothes. Images of death appear more often in the dreams of Mexican-American college students than in the dreams of Anglo-American students, probably because concerns about death are more a part of life in Latin American cultures (Roll, Hinton, & Glazer, 1974). In general, the cross-cultural research lends support to Cartwright's hypothesis (1977) that dreams reflect life events that are important to the dreamer.

Researchers do content analyses of dreams by collecting subjects' detailed, written descriptions of recent dreams (Hall & Van de Castle, 1966). Then they categorize the settings, characters, objects, and actions described, looking for patterns based on subjects' gender, age group, or other classification. For example, dream researcher Calvin Hall found that, in a sample of over 1,800 dreams, women dreamed about both men and women, while men dreamed about men twice as often as about women. In another sample of over 1,300 dreams, Hall found that hostile interactions between characters outnumbered friendly exchanges, and that 64% of dreamed emotions had a negative complexion, such as anger and sadness (Hall, 1951, 1984). Children are more likely to dream about animals than adults are, and the animals in their dreams are more likely to be large, threatening, and wild. In contrast, college students dream more usually of small animals, pets, and tame creatures. This may mean that children feel less in control of their world than adults do and so may find that world depicted in scarier imagery while they sleep (Van de Castle, 1983, 1994).

Sleep research has also found that dream content frequently relates to recent experience. Typically, the first dream of the night connects with events of the previous day. Then, dreaming in the second REM period (90 minutes later) may build on a theme that emerged during the first REM period. And so it goes through the night—like the childhood game of whispering a message from person to person—the final dream that emerges may have only the remotest relationship to events of the previous day. Ironically, it is this final dream of the night that is most likely to be remembered (Cartwright, 1977; Kiester, 1980).

This connection between dreams and recent experience may belie yet another possible function of dreams. A comparison of subjects who were selectively deprived of REM sleep with those deprived of NREM sleep suggests that REM sleep helps us store information in long-term memory. Those who were deprived of REM sleep performed more poorly than NREM-deprived subjects on tests of material studied the previous day (Azar, 1997; Kinoshita, 1992; Winson, 1990). Thus, REM sleep may be a normal part of the process for storing memories and fitting recent experiences into networks of previous beliefs or memories (Barinaga, 1994; Cartwright, 1978; Dement, 1976; Karni et al., 1994).

### DREAMS AS STIMULATION FOR THE SLEEPING BRAIN

Not everyone believes that dream content has special importance. Among several such viewpoints, one of the most influential portrays dreams mainly as by-products of biological processes involved in sleep: The **activation-synthesis theory** says that dreams result when the sleeping brain tries to make sense of its own random biological activity (Leonard, 1998; Squier & Domhoff, 1998). According to this theory, the sleeping brain stem periodically emits random electrical discharges. As this energy sweeps over the cerebral cortex, the sleeper experiences impressions of sensation, memory, motivation,

**Chapter 10**
**Personality**
*Dream interpretation occupies a prominent place in Freudian psychoanalysis.*

**Chapter 6**
**Learning and Remembering**
*Long-term memory is a distinct stage in the memory system.*

**Activation-synthesis theory:** The theory that dreams begin with random electrical *activation* coming from the brain stem. Dreams, then, are the brain's attempt to make sense of—to *synthesize*—this random activity.

emotion, and movement. Although the cortical activation is random, and the images it generates may not be logically connected, the brain tries to make sense of the stimulation it receives. To do so, the brain *synthesizes* or pulls together the separate bursts of electrical *activation* by creating a coherent story—a dream.

The proponents of this theory, J. Allan Hobson and Robert McCarley (1977), argue that REM sleep furnishes the brain with an internal source of needed stimulation. This internal activation promotes the growth and development of the brain at the time when the sleeping brain has blocked out external stimulation. Dream content, therefore, results from brain activation, not unconscious wishes. While Hobson (1988) claims that meaning is added as a "brainstorm afterthought," he says that dream content may nevertheless have some psychological meaning in that the brain is reacting based on cortical patterns influenced by culture, gender, and personality factors. Thus, when activations are synthesized, dreams seem familiar and meaningful.

**PSYCHOLOGY IN YOUR LIFE**

## Sleep Disorders

*Y*ou may be among the more than 100 million Americans who get insufficient sleep. Sleep disturbances in various forms not only make us sleepy, they pose serious problems that can disrupt marriages, interfere with careers, and even shorten life. While some of these sleep disturbances seem to have a purely biological basis, many are job-related or the result of personal choices. Among people who work night shifts, for example, more than half nod off at least once a week on the job. And it may be no coincidence that some of the world's most serious accidents—the nuclear power plant disasters at Three Mile Island and Chernobyl, the toxic chemical discharge at Bhopal, and the massive oil spill from the tanker *Exxon Valdez*—have occurred during late evening hours when people are likely to be programmed for sleep. Sleep experts speculate that many accidents occur because key personnel fail

to function optimally as a result of insufficient sleep (Dement, 1976).

In the following paragraphs, we will examine a sampling of sleep problems of biological and psychological origin. Some are common, while some are both rare and bizarre. The single element that ties them together is a disruption in one or more parts of the normal sleep cycle.

**Insomnia,** the most common of sleep disorders, is usually the diagnosis when people are dissatisfied with the amount of sleep they get. Its symptoms are chronic inability to fall asleep quickly, frequent arousals during sleep, or early-morning awakening (Bootzin & Nicasio, 1978). Insomnia sufferers include one-third of all adults (Anch et al., 1988; Mellinger, Balter, & Uhlenhuth, 1985). Research shows it to be a complex disorder caused by a variety of psychological, environmental, and biological factors (Borkovec, 1982). So-called "sleeping pills" are a common cause because they disrupt the normal sleep cycle by cutting short our REM sleep (Dement, 1980).

When insomniac subjects are studied in sleep laboratories, researchers find that the quantity and quality of their sleep varies considerably (Anch et al., 1988). In fact, some people complaining of insomnia

Insomnia is a complex disorder caused by a variety of psychological, environmental, and biological factors. This college student anxiously contemplates her inability to get enough rest for the next day's classes.

actually show completely normal sleep patterns, a condition known as *subjective insomnia*. Equally curious is the finding that some people who show insomnia-like sleep disturbances report no complaints of insomnia (Trinder, 1988). The discrepan-

**Insomnia:** A disorder that involves insufficient sleep, the inability to fall asleep quickly, frequent arousals, or early awakenings.

cies may result from differences in the way people recall and interpret a state of light sleep.

**Sleep apnea,** another common disorder, may be apparent only in a person's complaints of daytime sleepiness and a sleep partner's complaints about snoring. Because sleep apnea involves problems in the upper respiratory tract, it interferes with breathing during sleep and frequently produces heroic snoring levels (Seligson, 1994). A common form results from collapse of the airway, when muscle tone relaxes during sleep. As a result, breathing stops, the blood's oxygen level drops, and emergency hormones course through the body, causing the sleeper to awaken briefly, begin breathing again, and then fall back to sleep.

While most of us have a few apnea episodes a night, someone with sleep apnea disorder may have hundreds, resulting in daytime sleepiness and other disruptions that spill over into the waking state. Remarkably, these apnea episodes usually make no impression on the sleeper (Guilleminault, 1989). Failure to recognize the nature of the problem can cause sufferers—and their families and co-workers—to interpret unusual daytime behavior as laziness or neglect. While this may be disruptive to relationships, sleep apnea can also have dangerous biological effects that include elevated blood pressure, which can put dangerous levels of stress on the blood vessels and heart (Anch et al., 1988; Stavish, 1994).

We should note that occasional episodes of sleep apnea are likely to occur in premature infants, who may need physical stimulation to start breathing again. Obviously, the problem can be lethal. Until their underdeveloped respiratory systems mature, these infants must remain attached to breathing monitors. For adults with sleep apnea, permanent breathing failure is not a strong concern. Treatment focuses on the hundreds of nightly apnea episodes, which can be alleviated by use of a device that pumps extra air into the lungs and keeps the airway open during sleep.

**Narcolepsy,** one of the most unusual of sleep disorders, produces sudden daytime sleep attacks, often without warning. These are no ordinary waves of drowsiness, however. So suddenly do narcoleptic sleep attacks appear that victims have reported falling asleep while base running in a soft-

ball game or while scuba diving under 20 feet of water. Oddly, anything exciting can trigger a narcoleptic attack. For example, patients commonly report that they fall asleep while laughing at a joke or while having sex. Obviously, narcolepsy can be dangerous—and not so good for intimate relationships, either.

A second main symptom of narcolepsy is **cataplexy,** a sudden loss of muscle control. These cataplectic episodes may occur just before the sleep attack, giving the narcoleptic patient the strange sensation of being awake and alert but unable to move. You may have already guessed what the cataplexy represents: REM sleep paralysis.

Assembling the pieces of the narcolepsy puzzle reveals a peculiar disorder of REM sleep. A sleep recording will clinch the diagnosis. It will show that the victim of narcolepsy has an abnormal sleep-onset REM period. Instead of waiting the usual 90 minutes for REM sleep to occur, the narcoleptic individual has a REM period as sleep begins.

Studies of narcoleptic animals show the disorder is a genetic problem based in the brain stem. It has no cure, but there are now effective treatments that rely on drugs to diminish the frequency of both the sleep attacks and the cataplexy. Happily, narcoleptic patients are no longer routinely placed in psychotherapy aimed at searching for the unconscious conflicts that were once assumed to cause the disorder.

**Daytime sleepiness** is a common annoyance and an inevitable consequence of not getting enough normal sleep. It may result from any of the sleep disorders we have already discussed, or it may be the result of deliberately choosing to abbreviate one's sleep. It is especially common in college students (Hicks, 1990). In the general population, about 4 to 5% report this condition (Roth et al., 1989). For all these sufferers, daytime sleepiness causes diminished alertness, delayed reaction times, and impaired performance of motor and cognitive tasks. Nearly half the individuals who report chronic sleepiness have had automobile accidents, and more than half have had on-the-job accidents.

You may wonder if it is an exaggeration to call sleepiness a disorder. Can't boring lectures, overheated rooms, heavy meals, or monotonous tasks cause daytime sleepiness? No, say the experts. These condi-

tions only obscure the presence of the biological urge to sleep; they do not cause it (Roth et al., 1989). (People who have had enough sleep and who are exposed to such conditions actually get fidgety, rather than sleepy.) Those who suffer from daytime sleepiness can benefit from learning how to get longer, more restful sleep.

If you show the signs of sleep deprivation and daytime sleepiness—dozing off rather than getting fidgety when bored, or falling instantly asleep when you finally do go to bed, for example—experts recommend several steps you can take to get the sleep you need (see Brody, 1994):

- Figure out how much sleep you need, and schedule your night to allow for it.
- Try a midafternoon nap, when your circadian rhythms make you especially sleepy. But avoid taking multiple catnaps throughout the day—a practice that will interrupt your ability to sleep at night.
- Stick to a routine by going to bed and getting up at the same times every day.
- Get daily physical exercise—but not within three hours of bedtime.

Remember that sleep deprivation is a real problem to be taken seriously. Pretending to be awake or relying on stimulants like caffeine to get you through the day will only mask the problem and allow it to worsen. The first step to solving the problem is admitting it exists—and understanding that you can solve it.

**Sleep apnea:** A respiratory disorder in which the person intermittently stops breathing while asleep.

**Narcolepsy:** A disorder of REM sleep, involving sudden REM-sleep attacks accompanied by cataplexy.

**Cataplexy:** A sudden loss of muscle control that may occur just before a narcoleptic sleep attack. Cataplexy is a waking form of sleep paralysis.

**Daytime sleepiness:** A sleep disorder, commonly caused by lifestyle or personal choice factors, which always comes from getting too little sleep.

1. RECALL: *Which statement is true about daydreaming?*
   a. Most people can easily suppress unwanted thoughts.
   b. Most people daydream every day.
   c. Daydreams usually serve as an escape from the concerns of real life.
   d. Daydreams are usually more vivid than night dreams.

2. RECALL: *All of the following are related to our circadian rhythms, except*
   a. sleep.
   b. dreaming.
   c. jet lag.
   d. daydreaming.

3. RECALL: *Suppose that you are working in a sleep laboratory, where you are monitoring a subject's sleep recording during the night. As the night progresses, you would expect to see that*
   a. the four-stage cycle gradually lengthens.
   b. REM periods become longer.
   c. Stage 3 and 4 sleep periods lengthen.
   d. dreaming becomes less frequent.

4. RECALL: *According to the activation-synthesis theory, dreams are*
   a. replays of events during the previous day.
   b. an attempt by the brain to make sense of random activity in the brain stem.
   c. a storylike episode that provides clues about problems in the unconscious mind.
   d. wish fulfillments.

5. APPLICATION: *Which of the following symptoms suggest the presence of a sleep disorder?*
   a. stopping breathing for several seconds three or four times a night
   b. a REM period at the beginning of sleep
   c. needing nine hours of sleep each night in order to feel rested
   d. not remembering your dreams

6. UNDERSTANDING THE CORE CONCEPT: *Our Core Concept states that* consciousness changes in cycles that normally correspond to our biological rhythms and to the patterns of our environment. *Which of the following illustrates this concept?*
   a. priming
   b. consciousness, preconsciousness, and the unconscious
   c. REM rebound
   d. sleep and dreaming

**ANSWERS:**   1. b   2. d   3. b   4. b   5. b   6. d

---

KEY QUESTION

## WHAT OTHER FORMS CAN CONSCIOUSNESS TAKE?

Children stand on their heads or spin around to make themselves dizzy. You may get much the same feeling on a wild theme-park ride. Why do we engage in these strange antics? One view says that "human beings are born with a drive to experience modes of awareness other than the normal waking one; from very young ages, children experiment with techniques to change consciousness" (Weil, 1977, p. 37). So, sleep, dreams, fantasies, and wild rides offer compelling alternatives to normal conscious experience. For some people, however, these alternatives may not be wild enough. Their search for mind-altering experiences may lead to drugs that change ordinary awareness. Among the legal substances that alter consciousness, they may be attracted to alcohol, tobacco, and caffeine. On the illegal side, they may turn to heroin, PCP, cannabis, amphetamines, or any of a number of other drugs that exert powerful mental effects. Purely psychological techniques can change consciousness, too. These include procedures such as hypnosis, relaxation training, and meditation.

A roller coaster ride is one way to alter your consciousness.

What is the idea that ties these altered or extended states of consciousness together? The Core Concept of this section says:

 **CONCEPT**

An altered state of consciousness occurs when some aspect of normal consciousness is modified by mental, behavioral, or chemical means.

The corollary idea says that altered states do *not* involve mysterious paranormal or New Age phenomena that defy explanation by science. Rather, altered states are modifications of ordinary consciousness that we can study with the tools of science. Specifically, let us see what these tools can tell us about hypnosis, meditation, and drug states.

## Hypnosis

Picture an individual being put into a hypnotic trance. The hypnotist is making suggestions to promote concentration and relaxation. Soon the subject appears to be asleep, although he or she can obviously hear suggestions and carry out requests. The subject also seems to have amazing powers to ignore pain, remember long-forgotten details, and create hallucinations. What mental processes make these things happen? To find out, we will explore the nature of hypnosis as a state of mind, its most important features, and some of its valid psychological uses.

The term "hypnosis" derives from *Hypnos*, the name of the Greek god of sleep. The EEG record tells us, however, that ordinary sleep plays no part in hypnosis, even though subjects may appear to be in a deeply relaxed, sleeplike state. (There is no unique EEG signature for hypnosis.) Rather, most authorities would say **hypnosis** involves a state of awareness characterized by deep relaxation, heightened suggestibility, and highly focused attention. When deeply hypnotized, some people—but not all—have the special ability to respond to suggestion with dramatic changes in perception, memory, motivation, and sense of self-control (Orne, 1980). After being hypnotized, subjects often report that they experienced heightened responsiveness to the hypnotist's suggestions and felt that their behavior was performed without intention or any conscious effort.

**HYPNOTIZABILITY** Dramatic stage performances of hypnosis give the impression that the power of hypnosis lies with the hypnotist. However, the real star is the person who is hypnotized. The hypnotist is more like an experienced guide showing the way. Some individuals can even practice self-hypnosis, or *autohypnosis*, by inducing the hypnotic state through self-administered suggestions.

The single most important factor in achieving a hypnotic state is a participant's susceptibility. Experts call this **hypnotizability,** and they measure it by a person's responsiveness to standardized suggestions. Individuals differ in this susceptibility, varying from no responsiveness to any suggestion to total responsiveness to virtually every suggestion. A highly hypnotizable person may respond to suggestions to change motor reactions, experience hallucinations, have amnesia for important memories, and become insensitive to painful stimuli.

Figure 3.5 shows the percentage of college-age subjects at various levels of hypnotizability the first time they were given a hypnotic induction test. For example, a hypnotist may test a new subject's acceptance of suggestion by saying, "Your right hand is lighter than air," and observing whether the subject allows his or her arm to float upward. High scorers are more likely than low scorers to experience pain relief, or **hypnotic analgesia,** and to respond to hypnotic suggestions for experiencing perceptual distortions.

**HYPNOSIS AS AN ALTERED STATE** We should maintain a scientific skepticism about the sensational claims made for hypnosis, especially when such claims are based

**FIGURE 3.5:** Level of Hypnosis Reached at First Induction

This graph shows the results achieved by 533 subjects hypnotized for the first time. (Hypnotizability was measured by the 12-item Stanford Hypnotic Susceptibility Scale.)

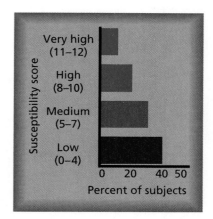

**Hypnosis:** An induced alternate state of awareness, characterized by heightened suggestibility and (usually) deep relaxation.

**Hypnotizability:** The degree to which an individual is responsive to hypnotic suggestions.

**Hypnotic analgesia:** Diminished sensitivity to pain while under hypnosis.

**Chapter 12
Social Psychology**

*Social roles and expectations exert a
profound influence on our behavior.*

on individual case reports or research that lacks proper control conditions (Barber, 1976, 1986). Even the experts disagree about the psychological mechanisms involved (Fromm & Shor, 1979). Some propose that hypnosis is simply heightened motivation (Barber, 1979). In this view, subjects are not entranced but merely motivated to focus their attention and to channel more energy into suggested activities. They are hypnotized because they want or expect to be, so they focus on expressing and achieving the responses the hypnotist tries to evoke. Other experts think that hypnosis involves social role playing, often to please the hypnotist (Sarbin & Coe, 1972). Still other researchers suggest that hypnosis is a fundamentally different state of consciousness (Fromm & Shor, 1979). Recent theories, however, bring these perspectives closer together by suggesting that hypnosis is actually a range of responses that cover all of these possibilities (Kirsch & Lynn, 1995).

**PRACTICAL USES OF HYPNOSIS**     Stage tricks aside, what is hypnosis good for? Studies show that hypnosis can exert a powerful influence on many psychological and bodily functions (Bowers, 1983; Burrows & Dennerstein, 1980; Hilgard, 1968, 1973; Miller & Bowers, 1993). This makes it a useful tool for researchers. So, instead of being limited to subjects who already have certain conditions or disorders, researchers can recruit normal volunteers and use hypnosis to create temporary mental states, such as anxiety, depression, or euphoria—or physical states, such as sensory loss. In one study, for example, subjects given the hypnotic suggestion to become deaf on cue reported feeling paranoid and excluded because they could not hear what other subjects were saying and assumed they were being deliberately whispered about and excluded (Zimbardo, Anderson, & Kabat, 1981).

Although hypnosis is not used extensively by psychologists or medical practitioners, it does have a place. The medical uses include pain control for procedures in which the patient may be hypersensitive to the usual anesthesia, although we should also note that not everyone can be hypnotized deeply enough for pain relief (Callahan, 1997; Miller & Bowers, 1993; Orne, 1980). In some cases, however, it has been demonstrated that hypnotized subjects can undergo treatments that would otherwise cause excruciating pain without anesthesia (Finer, 1980). For example, the Lamaze method of natural childbirth uses a hypnosis-like procedure as the primary means of pain control. And for some highly suggestible individuals, hypnosis may actually be superior to conventional anesthesia. One study found that, for selected subjects, hypnosis worked better than acupuncture, aspirin, Valium, or even morphine in

**Chapter 2
Biopsychology**

*Endorphins are brain chemicals
that act like opiates to reduce pain
or produce pleasurable sensations.*

Hypnosis can help to control pain in many individuals. Here, a woman is learning hypnotic techniques that she will use in natural childbirth.

masking intense pain (Stern et al., 1977). The mechanism by which hypnosis produces such effective pain relief is not known. Experiments show that endorphins, which account for the pain-relieving property of placebos, are *not* responsible for hypnotic analgesia (Grevert & Goldstein, 1985; Mayer, 1979; Watkins & Mayer, 1982).

In psychological treatment, hypnosis can be an effective tool in desensitizing phobic patients to fear-producing stimuli, such as snakes or heights. A variety of other unwanted responses may be eliminated by hypnotherapy, as well. Commonly, therapists taking this approach will make posthypnotic suggestions that influence the subject's later eating, drug using, or other behaviors, sometimes for several months (Barnier & McConkey, 1998; Kihlstrom, 1985). Hypnosis can also be a part of a relaxation training program designed to combat stress.

## Meditation

Many religions and traditional psychologies of the Asian and Pacific cultures purposely direct consciousness away from immediate worldly concerns and external stimulation. In doing so, they may seek to achieve an inner focus on the mental and spiritual self. In this quest, **meditation** is one technique employed to change consciousness. During meditative states, a person may learn to concentrate on a repetitive behavior (such as breathing), assume certain body positions (yogic postures), minimize external stimulation, and either generate specific mental images or free the mind of all thought.

To view meditation as an altered state of consciousness may reflect a particularly Western worldview, for Asian beliefs about the mind are typically very different from those of Western cultures. Buddhism, for example, teaches that the visible universe is an illusion of the senses. To become an enlightened being, a Buddhist tries to control bodily yearnings, to stop the ordinary experiences of the senses and mind, and to discover how to see things in their truest light. Thus, in the Buddhist view, meditation more accurately captures reality. In contrast, the Western scientist views meditation as the altered form of experience.

Meditation produces relaxation and, perhaps, new insights.

What exactly are the mental and physical effects of meditation? Certainly, it produces relaxation. Meditation also reduces anxiety, especially in those who function in stress-filled environments (Benson, 1975; Shapiro, 1985; van Dam, 1996). In some ways, meditating is like resting, because it has been found to reduce some measures of bodily arousal (Dillbeck & Orme-Johnson, 1987; Holmes, 1984; Morrell, 1986). As for some of the more subjective benefits attributed to meditation, such as its power to bring new understandings and meaning to one's life, researchers dispute whether these changes are measurable.

## Hallucinations

Sometimes people report distortions in consciousness that cause them to see or hear things that are not really present. Known as **hallucinations**, these experiences involve vivid perceptions that occur in the absence of objective external stimulation. To the cognitive psychologist they represent mental constructions of an individual's altered reality.

**Chapter 5**
**Sensation and Perception**
*Only some of the mechanisms that produce sensations of pain are well understood.*

**Chapter 14**
**Therapies for Mental Disorder**
*Desensitization therapy is a cognitive–behavioral therapy that is especially effective on phobias.*

**Meditation:** A form of consciousness change often induced by focusing on a repetitive behavior, assuming certain body positions, and minimizing external stimulation. Meditation is intended to enhance self-knowledge and well-being by reducing self-awareness.

**Hallucinations:** False perceptions that occur without external stimulation. Hallucinations may be the sign of drug states or of severe mental disorder.

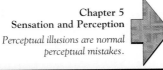

**Chapter 5**
**Sensation and Perception**

*Perceptual illusions are normal perceptual mistakes.*

The "phi phenomenon" produces the illusion of movement in sequences of flashing lights on a sign.

**Chapter 13**
**Psychopathology**

*Hallucinations may be a sign of a psychotic disorder.*

**Sensory deprivation:** A procedure that minimizes sensation by creating an environment that contains very little stimulation.

**Psychoactive drugs:** Chemicals that affect mental processes and behavior by their effects on the nervous system.

**Chapter 2**
**Biopsychology**

*The limbic system contains "reward centers" that produce sensations of pleasure when stimulated.*

Hallucinations differ from *illusions*, which are perceptual distortions or misinterpretations of real stimuli that are experienced by most people under similar conditions. For example, for most people, the sequence of flashing light bulbs on a theater marquee look like a single light zooming around the edge of the sign. On the other hand, if you "see" lights where there are none and where no one else sees them, you are experiencing a hallucination. Not all hallucinations are bizarre or even vivid, but they are all "false" in the sense that they are attributed to—but do not arise from—an external reality.

What causes hallucinations? As the phenomenon of REM rebound suggested to us earlier in the chapter, the brain requires constant stimulation. When deprived of stimulation, it may manufacture its own. In special environments that minimize all sensory stimulation, some subjects show a tendency to hallucinate. (Hallucinations are common, for example, among prisoners in solitary confinement.) Such **sensory deprivation** removes the external structure from our experience and forces subjects to restore meaning and stable orientation to their situation. Laboratory experiments with sensory deprivation suggest that hallucinations may be a way of reconstructing a reality in accordance with one's personality, past experiences, and the demands of the present setting (Suedfeld, 1980; Zubeck et al., 1961).

A more common form of hallucination may occur in young children who insist that they have imaginary friends—probably in response to social needs. Though rarer, similar adult experiences can occur in the wake of grief, as when one experiences a "visit" from a recently deceased loved one. In both children's and adults' experiences, such hallucinations may again be the mind's response to a loss or lack of stimulation, to loneliness or isolation (Siegel, 1992).

Just as insufficient stimulation might prompt hallucination, too much stimulation can also create hallucinations. Hallucinations can occur during high fever, epilepsy, and migraine headaches. They also occur in cases of severe mental disorders, especially *schizophrenia*. Such patients may respond to their private hallucinations as if they were external events. Many episodes of hallucinatory states also have been reported following overstimulating experiences, such as mob riots, religious revival meetings, prolonged dancing (such as that done by the religious sect of dervishes), extreme fright or panic, trance states, and moments of extreme emotion.

Finally, hallucinations may be induced by certain **psychoactive drugs,** such as peyote and LSD (lysergic acid diethylamide), as well as by withdrawal from alcohol in severe cases of alcoholism. Anthropologists and ethnologists note that some cultures, notably certain Native American groups, have employed natural *hallucinogenic* drugs derived from plants (such as the peyote cactus) as a way of experiencing hallucinations, either as an end in themselves, or as a means to self-discovery or spiritual awakening (Julien, 1995). We will see, however, that not all psychoactive drugs alter consciousness by producing hallucinations.

## Psychoactive Drug States

For millennia our ancestors have used alcohol, opium, cannabis, mescaline, coca, caffeine, and other drugs to alter their perceptions of reality. Especially under stress, individuals throughout the world take drugs to relax or avoid the unpleasantness of current realities. People also take drugs such as alcohol to help them feel comfortable with each other. And, as we have seen, some drugs such as LSD are taken by people seeking the hallucinations they produce.

To some extent, all psychoactive drugs impair the emotion-based brain mechanisms that usually help us make good decisions (Gazzaniga, 1998). In addition, we should note that the most widely abused illegal drugs—cocaine, heroin, and amphetamines—are attractive because they stimulate the brain's "reward centers." From an evolutionary perspective, we know that our brains are built to find pleasure in many substances (such as the taste of sweet or fatty foods) that helped our ancestors

When psychologists talk about drugs, they include legal substances such as tobacco and caffeine, two extremely popular stimulants in most cultures.

survive and reproduce. Cocaine, heroin, and amphetamines can trick us by exploiting these same mechanisms with strong pleasurable signals that makes our bodies "think" that these drugs are good for us (Nesse & Berridge, 1997).

Cultural trends influence drug-taking behavior, too. The United States saw this during the 1960s and 1970s, when the country entered a period of casual experimentation with recreational drugs and other mind-altering techniques. By 1989, nearly 55% of American high school seniors had reported using one or more illegal drugs in their senior year (Johnston, O'Malley, & Bachman, 1989). Of even more concern, the number of younger teenagers using drugs has increased. Since 1991, the number of eighth- and tenth-graders using illicit drugs has doubled. Recent figures, however, hint that the increases in drug use may be starting to level off (Martin, 1999). Credit for any decline in illicit drug use is often awarded to antidrug education programs, although the evidence does not show most of them to be especially effective (Murray, 1997).

Let us now have a closer look at the most commonly used and abused psychoactive drugs. We do so by grouping them in categories: *hallucinogens, opiates, depressants,* and *stimulants* (see Table 3.1). In general, we will find that all the drugs in each category will have similar effects on the mind and brain.

**HALLUCINOGENS**   Drugs known as **hallucinogens** or **psychedelics** produce changes in consciousness by altering perceptions of the external environment and inner awareness. They often create hallucinations and blur the boundary between self and the external world. For example, an individual experiencing hallucinogenic effects might listen to music and suddenly feel that he or she is producing the music or that the music is coming from within. Most hallucinogenic drugs act in the brain at specific receptor sites for the neurotransmitter serotonin (Jacobs, 1987).

Four of the commonly used hallucinogens are *mescaline* (from a type of cactus), *psilocybin* (from a mushroom), *LSD*, and *PCP* (phencyclidine). Both LSD and PCP are synthetic drugs made in chemical laboratories. PCP, or "angel dust," is a favorite of young people who use hallucinogens. This drug produces a strange dissociative reaction, in which the user feels disembodied or removed from parts of his or her personality. The user may become confused and insensitive to pain and feel separated from the surroundings.

**Cannabis,** derived from the hemp plant, is also usually classified as a hallucinogen. Its active ingredient is THC (tetrahydrocannabinol), found in both the plant's dried leaves and flowers (*marijuana*) and in the solidified resin of the plant (*hashish*). The experience derived from ingesting THC depends on its dose. Small doses create mild, pleasurable highs, and larger doses result in long hallucinogenic reactions. The positive effects include altered perception, sedation, pain relief, mild

**Chapter 2
Biopsychology**
*Serotonin is a neurotransmitter involved with sleep, memory, and depression.*

**Hallucinogens** or **psychedelics:** Drugs that alter perceptions the external environment and inner awareness.

**Cannabis:** A drug, derived from the hemp plant, whose effects include altered perception, sedation, pain relief, and mild euphoria. Cannabis is found in marijuana and hashish.

### TABLE 3.1: Psychoactive Drugs: Medical Uses, Effects, Likelihood of Dependence

| CATEGORY | MEDICAL USES | DURATION (HOURS) | DEPENDENCE PSYCHOLOGICAL | PHYSIOLOGICAL |
|---|---|---|---|---|
| **OPIATES** | | | | |
| Morphine | Painkiller, cough suppressant | 3–6 | High | High |
| Heroin | Under investigation | 3–6 | High | High |
| Codeine | Painkiller, cough suppressant | 3–6 | Moderate | Moderate |
| **HALLUCINOGENS** | | | | |
| LSD | None | 8–12 | None | Unknown |
| PCP | Veterinary anesthetic | Varies | Unknown | High |
| Mescaline | None | 8–12 | None | Unknown |
| Psilocybin | None | 4–6 | Unknown | Unknown |
| Cannabis | Reduces nausea from chemotherapy | 2–4 | Unknown | Moderate |
| **DEPRESSANTS** | | | | |
| Barbiturates | Sedative, sleep, anticonvulsant, anesthetic | 1–16 | Moderate–High | Moderate–High |
| Benzodiazepines | Antianxiety, sleep, anticonvulsant, sedative | 4–8 | Low–Moderate | Low–Moderate |
| Alcohol | Antiseptic | 1–5 | Moderate | Moderate |
| **STIMULANTS** | | | | |
| Amphetamines | Weight control, counteract anesthesia | 2–4 | High | High |
| Cocaine | Local anesthetic | 1–2 | High | High |
| Nicotine | Gum, patch for cessation of smoking | Varies | Low–High | Low–High |
| Caffeine | Weight control, stimulant in acute respiratory failure, analgesia | 4–6 | Unknown | Unknown |

euphoria, and distortions of space and time—quite similar in some respects to the effects of heroin, according to recent research (Wickelgren, 1997). However, depending on the social context and other factors, the psychological effects may also be negative: fear, anxiety, and confusion. Motor coordination is impaired with cannabis use (Julien, 1995), so those who work or drive under its influence suffer a higher risk of accidents (Moskowitz, 1985). Cannabis also produces temporary failures in memory.

**OPIATES**   The class of drugs known as **opiates**—derivatives of the opium poppy—includes *morphine, heroin,* and *codeine.* All are highly addictive drugs that suppress physical sensation and response to stimulation. Morphine and codeine have excellent analgesic (pain-relieving) properties that result from their similarity to the body's own pain-relieving chemicals, the *endorphins.* Morphine has long been used in postsurgical medicine, and codeine frequently finds application as a cough suppressant.

Made from morphine, heroin originally was developed in nineteenth-century Germany by the Bayer Company (of aspirin fame), but it was abandoned because it is even more highly addictive than morphine. For the intravenous heroin user, however, the drug has certain attractive effects that include a rush of pleasurable sensations. These feelings of euphoria supplant all worries and awareness of bodily needs, although—surprisingly—there are no major changes in cognitive abilities. Unfortunately, serious addiction is likely once a person begins to inject heroin. To avoid the pain and cravings of withdrawal, the heroin user must take the drug frequently—at least daily—making it a very expensive habit to maintain. Because addicts often steal to support their habit, the use of heroin causes a high proportion of property crime in cities around the world.

Paradoxically, patients who take opiates for pain under medical supervision rarely become addicted. The reason for the difference between the use of opiates for pleasure and for pain is unclear. It appears, however, that the presence of pain causes

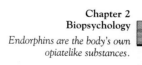

**Chapter 2 Biopsychology**
*Endorphins are the body's own opiatelike substances.*

**Opiates:** Highly addictive drugs, derived from opium, that can produce a profound sense of well-being and have strong pain-relieving properties.

opiates to affect parts of the brain other than the "reward centers" involved in pleasure. The practical point is this: There is little to fear from the legitimate medical use of these drugs for controlling pain (Melzack, 1990).

**DEPRESSANTS**   Drugs that slow down the mental and physical activity of the body by inhibiting central nervous system activity are collectively known as **depressants.** They include *barbiturates* (usually prescribed for sedation), *benzodiazepines* (antianxiety drugs), and *alcohol* (a social stimulant and nervous system depressant). By inhibiting the transmission of nerve impulses in the central nervous system, depressants tend to slow down the mental and physical activity of the body. In appropriate dosages, depressants relieve symptoms of pain or anxiety, but overuse or abuse of depressants is dangerous because these drugs impair reflexes and judgment. They may also be addictive.

Barbiturates, a common constituent of "sleeping pills," can induce sleep. Unfortunately, as we have seen, they have the little-known side effect of reducing REM-sleep time. This leaves the user feeling unrested, despite a full night's sleep. In addition, withdrawal from barbiturates causes severe REM rebound, filled with unpleasant dreams. Worse yet, overdoses of barbiturates may cause loss of all sensations, coma, and even death. Fatal reactions to barbiturates are made all the more likely because the lethal dose is relatively low, compared to the effective dose for inducing sleep or other effects. The chance of accidental overdose is further compounded by the additive effects of alcohol or other depressant drugs, which magnify the depressant action of barbiturates (Maisto, Galizio, & Connors, 1995).

The benzodiazepines (sometimes called "minor tranquilizers"), commonly prescribed to treat anxiety, are safer than barbiturates. Probably the best-known and most widely prescribed benzodiazepine is Valium. While the benzodiazepines (pronounced *BEN-zo-dye-AZ-a-peens*) can calm a patient without causing sleepiness or sedation, they, too, can be overused and abused. Overdoses may cause muscle incoordination, slurred speech, weakness, and irritability, while withdrawal symptoms include increased anxiety, muscle twitching, and sensitivity to sound and light. Because they are so commonly prescribed, and because they can be addictive, the benzodiazepines hold strong potential for abuse. However, these drugs are almost never used recreationally because people who are not anxious do not like their effects (Wesson, Smith, & Seymour, 1992).

Alcohol, another brain depressant, was one of the first psychoactive substances used by humankind. Under its influence, people have a variety of reactions that involve loosening of inhibitions. They may become talkative or quiet, friendly or abusive, ebullient or depressed. In very small dosages, alcohol can induce relaxation and even slightly improve an adult's reaction speed. However, the body breaks down alcohol at the rate of only one ounce per hour, and greater amounts consumed in short periods impair the central nervous system. When the level of alcohol in the blood reaches a mere 0.1% (1/1000 of the blood), an individual experiences deficits in thinking, memory, and judgment, along with emotional instability and motor incoordination. In most states this level of blood alcohol automatically qualifies a driver as being legally drunk.

Alcoholic beverage makers spend millions of dollars annually depicting the social and personal benefits of drinking alcoholic beverages. And, in fact, many adults use alcohol prudently. Yet, physical dependence, tolerance, and addiction all develop with prolonged heavy drinking—of the sort that often begins with binge drinking, common on many college campuses. When the amount and frequency of drinking alcohol interferes with job or school performance, impairs social and family relationships, and creates serious health problems, the diagnosis of *alcoholism* is appropriate (see Julien, 1995; Vallee, 1998). In general, the abuse of alcohol has become a significant problem for about one in ten Americans (National Institute on Alcohol Abuse and Alcoholism, 1993). The effects of the problem are much more

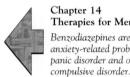

**Chapter 14**
**Therapies for Mental Disorder**
*Benzodiazepines are used to treat anxiety-related problems, such as panic disorder and obsessive-compulsive disorder.*

**Depressants:** Drugs that slow down mental and physical activity by inhibiting transmission of nerve impulses in the central nervous system.

widespread, however. Estimates suggest that 40% of Americans see the effects of alcohol abuse in a family member (Vallee, 1998). For many young Americans aged 15 to 25, the problem becomes a lethal one: Alcohol-related automobile accidents are the leading cause of death in this age group.

**Chapter 14**
**Therapies for Mental Disorder**
*Stimulants can help a child with ADHD to focus attention.*

**STIMULANTS**  In contrast with depressants, **stimulants** increase central nervous system activity. They speed up both mental and physical rates of activity and enhance attention. Medically, stimulants alleviate symptoms of certain sleep disorders and also *attention-deficit/hyperactivity disorder* (ADHD) in children. They are also used to treat sleep attacks in narcoleptic patients. Recreational users of stimulants such as *amphetamines* and *cocaine* seek other effects: intense pleasurable sensations, increased self-confidence, greater energy and alertness, and euphoria. Cocaine, in particular, packs what may be the most powerful reinforcing punch of any illegal drug (Landry, 1997). *Crack,* an especially addictive form of cocaine, produces a swift high that wears off quickly.

On the down side, heavy amphetamine and cocaine users may experience frightening hallucinations and paranoid delusions (beliefs that others are out to harm them). Special dangers of these drugs include the emotional roller coaster of euphoric highs and depressive lows, which lead users to increase the frequency and dosage, quickly making the use of these drugs spiral out of control. Yet another danger accrues to children who were exposed to cocaine while in the womb: Studies show that such children are at high risk for developing cognitive problems, emotional difficulties, and behavior-control disorders (Vogel, 1997).

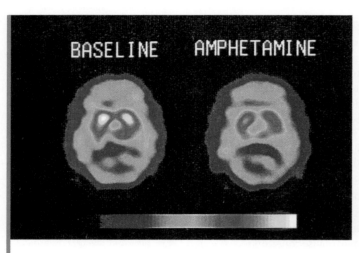

Brain changes during use of drugs can be seen on PET-scan images. Much less activity is seen in the limbic system of the brain under the influence of amphetamines.

Two other stimulants that you may not even think of as psychoactive drugs are *caffeine* and *nicotine.* Is it accurate to think of these commonplace, legal substances as "drugs"? Their effects are swift and powerful. Within ten minutes, two cups of strong coffee or tea administer enough caffeine to profoundly affect the heart, blood circulation, and the efficiency of the brain. Nicotine inhaled in tobacco smoke may have similar effects within just seconds. Both are addictive. Both augment the effects of the natural rewarding chemicals released by the brain. Thus, nicotine and caffeine stimulate the same neurons that make us feel good whenever we have done something that aids our survival or reproduction. In this way, both drugs tease the brain's reward centers into responding as if it were good for us to be using these substances. Fortunately, the negative effects of caffeine usage appear to be minor for most people. Further, caffeine has a built-in "braking" action that limits its intake: High dosages produce uncomfortable anxiety-like feelings.

On the other hand, nicotine is a much more dangerous drug because it is so addictive and because nicotine and the other ingredients in tobacco have been associated with a variety of health problems, including cancer, emphysema, and heart disease. In fact, the negative impact of smoking on health is greater than that of all other psychoactive drugs combined, including heroin, cocaine, and alcohol. According to the U.S. Public Health Service, smoking is the leading cause of preventable disease, with a human cost of more than 350,000 deaths annually. As a result, in 1995 the American Medical Association formally recommended that the U.S. Food and Drug Administration regard nicotine as a drug to be regulated. Currently, however, nicotine is both legal and actively promoted—with a $2.7 billion budget from the tobacco industry. Although antismoking campaigns have been somewhat effective in reducing the overall level of smoking in the United States, some 54 million Americans still smoke. Most worrisome is the fact that 3 million teenagers smoke, and their numbers are increasing by about 3,000 who start every day (Julien, 1995).

**Chapter 9**
**Stress, Health, and Well-Being**
*Smoking is an unhealthy response to stress.*

**Stimulants:** Drugs that arouse the central nervous system, speeding up mental and physical responses.

## Dependence and Addiction

The line between substance use and abuse is easy to cross for those who become addicted.

We have seen that powerful chemicals called psychoactive drugs can alter the functioning of neurons in your brain and, as a consequence, temporarily change your conscious awareness. Once in your brain, they usually act on synapses to block or stimulate neural messages. In this way, drugs profoundly alter the brain's communication system, affecting perception, memory, mood, and behavior.

The consequences of using these drugs, however, may go far beyond their immediate effects. For example, continued use of certain drugs, such as alcohol, lessens their psychoactive effect on the nervous system, so that greater dosages are required to achieve the same effect. Such reduced effectiveness with repeated use of a drug is called **tolerance.** Hand-in-hand with tolerance goes **physiological dependence**—a process in which the body adjusts to and becomes dependent on the substance, in part because the production of neurotransmitters in the brain is affected by the frequent presence of the drug (Wickelgren, 1998). **Addiction** is one unfortunate outcome of tolerance and dependence. A person with a physical addiction requires the drug in his or her body and may suffer unpleasant withdrawal symptoms if the drug is not present. **Withdrawal** symptoms can include physical trembling, perspiring, nausea, and, in the case of extreme alcohol withdrawal, even death. Although heroin and alcohol are the addictive drugs that most commonly come to mind, nicotine, caffeine, sleeping pills, and certain tranquilizing drugs actually claim more addicts.

With or without being physically addicted, individuals may find themselves craving or hungering for the drug and its effects. This is a result of **psychological dependence,** a pervasive desire to obtain or use a drug, irrespective of any physiological addiction. Psychological dependence can occur with any drug, including caffeine and nicotine, prescription medication, and over-the-counter drugs. In extreme cases, a person's lifestyle comes to revolve around drug use. In addition, as we have noted, the expense of maintaining an illegal drug habit drives many addicts to crime, including robbery, embezzlement, assault, prostitution, or drug peddling. On top of these problems lies the grave danger facing addicts who inject illegal drugs: the threat of infection with HIV, the virus that causes AIDS. By sharing hypodermic needles (a practice addicts rely on because syringes often cannot be obtained legally), intravenous drug users can unknowingly inject themselves with drops of bodily fluid from others with HIV.

Addiction, whether biological or psychological, ultimately affects the brain (Gazzaniga, 1998; Koob & Le Moal, 1997). Consequently, in the view of many public health professionals, this makes both forms of addiction brain diseases (Leshner, 1997). On the other hand, the general public has been reluctant to see drug addicts as people suffering from chronic illness. Instead, the public sees addicts as weak or bad individuals. What difference does this characterization of addiction make? When they are seen as persons suffering from a disease, addicts are most logically placed in treatment programs. By contrast, when they are seen as persons with defective characters, addicts are sent to prison for punishment—which does little to break the cycle of drug use, crime, and addiction.

Some observers, however, argue that viewing addiction as a disease may also interfere with the effective treatment of drug addicts. How? The addiction model, with its emphasis on biological causes and medical treatment, does little to deal with the social and economic context in which addictions develop. This may account for the fact that psychologically based treatment programs that treat alcohol abuse as a behavioral problem often work better than medically based programs (Miller & Brown, 1997). We can

**Tolerance:** The reduced effectiveness a drug has after repeated use.

**Physiological dependence:** A process by which the body adjusts to, and becomes dependent on, a drug.

**Addiction:** A physical condition that produces withdrawal when the body lacks a certain drug.

**Withdrawal:** After addiction, a pattern of painful physical symptoms and cravings experienced when the level of drug is decreased or the drug is eliminated.

**Psychological dependence:** A pervasive desire to obtain or use a drug—but without physical addiction.

also see the blind spots of the medical/addiction model by comparing the poor record of treatment programs for heroin addicts who have picked up their habits on the streets of the United States with the far greater success rate of treatment for the thousands of veterans who became addicted to heroin in Vietnam. What made the difference? The addicted veterans did not remain in the environment where they had become addicted (the wartime culture of Vietnam). Instead, they returned home to an environment that was not so supportive of a heroin habit. In contrast, heroin users who become addicted in the United States tend to return, after treatment, to the same environment that originally led to their addiction. For them there is no apparent way out: All the stimuli in their world are associated with the drug.

Whether physical or psychological, disease or character flaw, drug addiction poses many personal and social problems. Many psychoactive drugs have powerfully rewarding effects. And after a period of use, some generate powerfully punishing withdrawal effects. Unfortunately, the treatment techniques are often no match for this pull-push of reward and punishment, especially when the culture encourages drug use. Not surprisingly, the post-treatment relapse rate is high. Clearly, this is a field that has much room for new ideas and new research.

Check Your Understanding

1. RECALL: *Hypnosis is often used by psychological researchers to*
   a. study the effects of psychoactive drugs.
   b. induce amnesia for traumatic experiences.
   c. cure patients suffering from severe mental disorders.
   d. create mental states, such as anxiety or euphoria.

2. RECALL: *Psychoactive drugs usually create their effects by mimicking _____ in the brain.*
   a. dendrites
   b. neurotransmitters
   c. stress reactions
   d. memories

3. RECALL: *Unlike illusions, hallucinations arise entirely from*
   a. unexplained events in the environment.
   b. drugs.
   c. mental processes.
   d. severe mental disorders.

4. APPLICATION: *Which of the following groups of drugs have the opposite effects on the brain?*
   a. hallucinogens and stimulants
   b. opiates and sedatives
   c. stimulants and depressants
   d. depressants and opiates

5. UNDERSTANDING THE CORE CONCEPT: An altered state of consciousness occurs when some aspect of normal consciousness is modified either by mental, behavioral, or chemical means. *This suggests that:*
   a. some states of consciousness are mystical phenomena that cannot ever be explained.
   b. all states of consciousness are controlled by unconscious needs, desires, and memories.
   c. altered states of consciousness are the source of creativity in our minds.
   d. psychologists can study altered states of consciousness with scientific tools.

ANSWERS:    1. d    2. b    3. c    4. c    5. d

# USING PSYCHOLOGY TO LEARN PSYCHOLOGY

## *How Much Sleep Do You Need to Learn Effectively?*

*M*any college students operate in a chronic state of sleep deprivation. Because their schedules are crowded with study, work, and social events, students may convince themselves that they need only a few hours' sleep each night. And, in fact, the average college student sleeps only about 6.8 hours a night (Hicks, 1990). What sleep-deprived students do not understand are the effects this has on their powers of concentration, mental alertness, and learning. Does too little sleep really make a difference in how well you perform in your classes? Psychologist Cheryl Spinweber (1990) has found that sleep-deprived undergraduates get lower grades than their counterparts who get enough sleep.

So, how much sleep do you need? There is no one-size-fits-all answer. People vary in the amount of sleep they need for optimum functioning. While most adults need about eight hours, individual variations commonly range from about six to nine hours. Keep in mind that many people underestimate the amount of sleep they need and operate on a chronic sleep deficit, never realizing why they chronically feel tired and sleepy.

How can you tell if you need more sleep? Answer the following questions honestly:

- Do you often get sleepy in your classes?
- Do you sleep late on weekends?
- Do you awake in the morning feeling that you are not rested?
- Would you oversleep if you did not use an alarm clock to drive you out of bed?

If you answered "Yes" to any of these questions, chances are that you are shorting yourself on sleep. You may also be paying the price in the quality of your learning and in your grades. What's the cure? Get more sleep! For most students that requires reassessing priorities and eliminating activities that they can substitute with increased sleep time. We suggest experimenting with your sleep schedule until your answer to all of the questions above is "No."

## CHAPTER SUMMARY

 **WHAT IS THE NATURE OF CONSCIOUSNESS?**

- Consciousness represents one of the major mysteries of psychology. Cognitive psychologists theorize that consciousness is adaptive because it helps us integrate cognitions with external stimulation. It is also a process that has many distinct levels, including the preconscious, the subconscious, and the unconscious, as well as ordinary awareness. New technologies and techniques have opened windows on conscious processes for researchers. Increasingly, cognitive scientists are disputing the Freudian concept of an unconscious that works in opposition with the conscious mind.

 **CORE CONCEPT**

**Consciousness arises as the brain forms a model of the world that combines external stimulation with internal experience.**

 **WHAT ARE THE CYCLES OF EVERYDAY CONSCIOUSNESS?**

- Consciousness shifts and changes in everyday life, commonly taking the form of daydreaming, sleep, and nocturnal dreams. Sleep researchers have revealed the features of the normal sleep cycle, including the four stages of sleep, which change predictably over the course of the night. The sleep cycle also changes with age. Distortions of the sleep cycle define certain sleep disorders, including insomnia, sleep apnea, and narcolepsy. Chronic daytime sleepiness, common in college students, is also seen as a sleep disorder with many possible causes.

 **Consciousness changes in cycles that normally correspond to our biological rhythms and to the patterns of our environment.**

**KEY QUESTION** **WHAT OTHER FORMS CAN CONSCIOUSNESS TAKE?**

- Altered states of consciousness include not only sleep but hypnosis, meditation, hallucinations, and the effects of

psychoactive drugs. From a neuroscience perspective, these may involve changes in psychological processes rather than entirely new forms of awareness. Hypnosis remains a puzzle, although it is known to block pain and have other uses in therapy and research. Likewise, experts dispute whether meditation is a distinct state of consciousness, even though it has measurable effects on arousal. Hallucinations involve yet another alteration of conscious experience, arising from sensory deprivation, overstimulation, or drugs. But to understand the broader effects of psychoactive drugs, it is helpful to group them as hallucinogens, opiates, depressants, and stimulants. Most psychoactive drugs that are abused produce sensations of pleasure and well-being that make the drugs especially attractive and potentially addictive.

 **An altered state of consciousness occurs when some aspect of normal consciousness is modified by mental, behavioral, or chemical means.**

## REVIEW TEST

For each of the following items, choose the single correct or best answer. The correct answers appear at the end of the test.

1. What was the objection by Watson and other behaviorists to the study of consciousness?
   a. Conscious processes cannot be directly observed and measured.
   b. Consciousness could not be studied by means of introspection.
   c. Consciousness is not affected by rewards and punishments.
   d. Consciousness is the result of an inner life force, which they did not have the tools to study.

2. Imaging techniques, such as MRI and PET scans, allow cognitive scientists to connect mental activity with
   a. cognition.
   b. behavior.
   c. brain activity.
   d. priming.

3. Which of the following is *not* one of the functions of consciousness cited by your text?
   a. restricting attention to what is relevant
   b. selective attention and memory
   c. imagining and considering alternatives
   d. relinquishing control to enhance self-awareness

4. From a Freudian perspective, which of the following choices correctly pairs an example of an experience or process with its appropriate level of consciousness?
   a. unconscious: repressing traumatic experiences
   b. subconscious: regulation of blood pressure
   c. nonconscious: remembering how to tell time
   d. preconscious: preventing awareness of traumatic memories

5. Rapid eye movements are reliable behavioral signs that
   a. an individual has reached the deepest level of sleep.
   b. one has achieved a genuine meditative state.
   c. a sleeper's mental activity is centered on dreaming.
   d. a subject is very low in hypnotizability.

6. Which one of the following is a sleep disorder characterized by brief interruptions when the sleeper stops breathing, wakens, resumes breathing, and falls back asleep?
   a. apnea
   b. daytime sleepiness
   c. insomnia
   d. analgesia

7. Which of the following statements about hypnosis is true?
   a. Hypnosis is actually a form of NREM sleep.
   b. Hypnotizability relies on a subject's ability to respond to suggestion.
   c. Anyone can be hypnotized if the hypnotist knows the most effective techniques to use.
   d. The less intelligent or educated a person is, the more hypnotizable he or she will be.

8. Psychology has verified that meditation can be useful for producing
   a. a deeper understanding of oneself.
   b. enlightenment.
   c. a state of relaxation.
   d. heightened cognitive arousal.

9. Which of the following is a condition that would lead one to experience hallucinations?
   a. sensory isolation
   b. use of the drug mescaline
   c. withdrawal from alcohol in severe alcoholism
   d. all of the above

10. Three major effects sought by users of _____ are increased alertness, greater self-confidence, and euphoria.
   a. stimulants
   b. depressants
   c. opiates
   d. hallucinogens

**ANSWERS:**   1. a   2. c   3. d   4. a   5. c   6. a
7. b   8. c   9. d   10. a

# IF YOU'RE INTERESTED . . .

## Books

Bentov, I. (1998). *Stalking the wild pendulum: On the mechanics of consciousness.* Rochester, Vermont: Inner Traditions International.

*This work makes accessible ideas that are normally very complex—a theory of moral order based on a new idea about consciousness. Before his untimely death in 1979, Bentov was in the forefront of the new science of consciousness. With this book he questioned the traditional, materialistic view of mind—likewise questioning the human tendency to acquire and hoard—yet did so with imagination and captivating humor and optimism.*

Borbely, A. (1986). *Secrets of sleep.* New York: Basic Books.

*This book is an intriguing review of sleep research and its applications.*

Bowers, K. S. (1983). *Hypnosis for the seriously curious* (2nd ed.). New York: W. W. Norton & Co.

*This volume was written to inform the reader who is more than a layperson but less than a scholar. It is a good update on what is known and not yet known about hypnosis.*

Churchland, P. M. (1995). *The engine of reason, the seat of the soul: A philosophical journey into the brain.* Cambridge, MA: MIT Press.

*This neuroscientist argues that the brain represents a "quart-size universe" whose uncountable connections and processes more than account for the mysteries of the mind.*

Crick, F. (1994). *The astonishing hypothesis: The scientific search for the soul.* New York: Charles Scribner's Sons.

*Challenging but absorbing and interesting, Crick's work argues for the "astonishing hypothesis" that consciousness is ultimately an outcome of the brain's biochemistry.*

Davich, V. N. (1998). *The best guide to meditation.* Los Angeles: Audio Renaissance.

*An illustrated review of meditation's religious, therapeutic, and New Age origins and influences, the book or audio guides the reader through the basics of meditation irrespective of doctrine or any particular belief system.*

Dement, W. C., with Vaughn, C. (1999). *The promise of sleep: A pioneer in sleep medicine explains the vital connection between health, happiness, and a good night's sleep.* New York: Delacorte Press.

*As the title says, William C. Dement is probably the best-known expert on sleep today, and in The Promise of Sleep he asserts that we are a "sleep-sick" society and explains how we lost our gift for sleep, how we might get it back—and why we will be better for it.*

Dennett, D. C. (1992). *Consciousness explained.* Boston: Little, Brown & Co.

*We know a lot of things subjectively—how a favorite beverage tastes, what a piece of music "feels" like—that are extremely hard to explain. Maybe consciousness in these rich, personal forms cannot be "explained," but Dennet shows that it can be explored in a way that is engaging, humorous, and pleasurable to read.*

Du Maurier, G. (1894/1995). *Trilby*. New York: Oxford University Press.

> *George duMaurier's curious tale describes a young woman transformed from Parisian artist's model to great singer by the malevolent hypnotist Svengali. Not even remotely accurate about hypnosis, the novel nevertheless produced lasting images and prejudices about hypnotists' motives and methods.*

Gazzaniga, M. S. (1998). *The mind's past*. Berkeley: University of California Press.

> *What is the value of the distinctive human brain, with its disproportionately large cerebral cortex and capacities for language, forethought, and anxiety? Neuroscientist Michael S. Gazzaniga examines the whethers and whats of the brain's evolutionary advantages and the construction of personal identity and memory.*

Greenfield, S. A. (1995). *Journey to the centers of the mind*. New York: W. H. Freeman.

> *A neuroscientist offers "an accessible theory of consciousness" that seeks to link our comprehension of the brain as a physical and biological entity with philosophers' concepts of mental function and experience.*

Hobson, J. A. (1988). *The dreaming brain*. New York: Basic Books.

> *Hobson presents his own research and theory about the nature and meaning of dreams.*

Moore-Ede, M., LeVert, S., & Campbell, S. (1998). *The complete idiot's guide to getting a good night's sleep*. New York: Alpha Books.

> *Another in the Complete Idiot's series, this one addresses a serious problem for many people: the inability to fall and stay asleep. Whether your problem is chronic or occasional, you'll find these solutions practical, familiar, and helpful. Includes basic information about sleep medications, "natural" remedies, and light therapy.*

Peacock, R., & Gorman, R. (Eds.). (1998). *Sleep: Bedtime reading*. New York: Universe Publishing.

> *Wide awake and trying not to worry about it? Try some bedtime reading by the best authors. Includes writing by Alice Walker, John Updike, and others, as well as poetry, illustrations, photographs—all designed to take your mind off what's keeping you awake and help you make the transition to rest.*

Ramachandran, V. S., & Blakeslee, S. (1998). *Phantoms in the brain: Probing the mysteries of the human mind*. New York: William Morrow & Co.

> *Based on case studies of patients suffering from a wide array of neurological disorders—from phantom limb pain, blindsight, and stroke-induced disabilities—the authors capture the wonder of people's ability to assert life and individuality beyond the challenges to their bodies and brains. The writing is smart, caring, and funny, and addresses some powerful questions in a surprisingly absorbing way.*

Siegel, R. K. (1992). *Fire in the brain*. New York: Dutton.

> *Lyrically written and technically precise, this is a fascinating collection of case studies of hallucinations and the individuals who experienced them.*

Svengali (David Geliebter). (1998). *Fun with hypnosis: The complete how-to guide*. Phat Publications.

> *Admit it: You know this is serious stuff, but you can't help being fascinated and a little afrad of hypnosis. This guide makes hypnosis recognizable as the normal altered state of mind—hard to understand but as much a part of the human mind as sleeping and daydreaming. Disguised as a manual for the life of the party, this is really a demystifying review of an important, still mysterious ability of consciousness.*

Sark (Susan A. Rainbow Kennedy). (1999). *Change your life without getting out of bed: The ultimate nap book*. New York: Simon & Schuster.

> *Do you feel guilty when you try to catch up on sleep by napping? Reconsider your guilt: Naps can be good for you if you know how to begin them, enjoy them, and then wake up and do what needs to be done.*

Nørretranders, T. (1998). *The user illusion: Cutting consciousness down to size*. Translated by Johnathon Sydenham. New York: Viking Press.

> *In computing, the "user illusion" is the desktop graphic that conceals from the user the program's actual inner workings and dynamics. The author writes that our very consciousness is a similar illusion, discarding an astounding amount of information (what he calls "exformation") with a sort of fine-meshed filter. Just how much of reality are we missing out on, after all?*

## Videos

*Altered States*. (1980, color, 121 min.). Directed by Ken Russell; starring William Hurt, Blair Brown, Bob Balaban, Charles Haid.

> *Dated now but still a good, weird story—especially for a generation fond of "The X Files"—this film has a fantastic, high-end-vocabulary script by the late Paddy Chayefsky, based on his novel. A scientist experiments with sensory deprivation and mind expansion. There is no valid scientific information here, but good imagery and fun.*

*Bright Lights, Big City* (1988, color, 110 min). Directed by James Bridges; starring Michael J. Fox, Kiefer Sutherland, Phoebe Cates, Tracy Pollan.

> *This is a good cinematic translation of Jay McInerney's novel about a young Midwesterner transplanted to New*

*York yuppiedom and overwhelmed by nightlife and co-caine—and the need to maintain the addictive cycle.*

Clean and Sober. (1988, color, 125 min.). Directed by Glenn Gordon Caron; starring Michael Keaton, Kathy Baker, Morgan Freeman, M. Emmett Walsh.

*A man ducks out of his horribly troubled life into a drug re-habilitation program, hoping to hide out and avoid scrutiny for a while, but instead has to face his own cocaine addiction and the many problems it has created for him. Outstanding performances make it easier to watch a sometimes relentless story.*

Days of Wine and Roses. (1962, B&W, 117 min.). Directed by Blake Edwards; starring Jack Lemmon and Lee Remick.

*In a sentimental but not romanticized view, alcohol influences a romance, becomes a theme of the marriage, and ultimately destroys the relationship. The film has excellent performances and musical score.*

Freud. (1962, B&W, 120 min.). Directed by John Huston; starring Montgomery Clift, Susannah York.

*This popularized film biography of the founder of psycho-analysis features fascinating dream sequences with classic psychoanalytic symbolism and interpretation.*

I'm Dancing as Fast as I Can. (1982, color, 107 min.). Directed by Jack Hofsiss; starring Jill Clayburgh, Nicol Williamson, Dianne Wiest, Joe Pesci.

*The excellent cast performas in an okay story, based on personal memoir about the horror a woman experiences when she tries to quit her Valium addiction.*

The Lost Weekend. (1945, B&W, 101 min.). Directed by Billy Wilder; starring Ray Milland, Jane Wyman, Howard da Silva, Frank Faylen.

*Ray Milland's Oscar-winning performance riveted audi-ences with his painful assertion that, "I'm not a drinker— I'm a drunk." A drinking binge takes an articulate, intelligent man from his favorite bar to a psychiatric hospi-tal admission. Harsh and realistic, this was a landmark film in its stark depiction of alcohol abuse.*

KEY QUESTIONS

CORE CONCEPTS

PSYCHOLOGY IN YOUR LIFE

**HOW DO PSYCHOLOGISTS EXPLAIN DEVELOPMENT?**

Development is a process of growth and change brought about by an interaction of heredity and environment.

**Psychological Traits in Your Genes:** While genes contribute to your thoughts and behaviors, you shouldn't assume that biology is everything.

**WHAT CAPABILITIES DOES THE NEWBORN POSSESS?**

Newborns begin life equipped to deal with three basic survival tasks: finding nourishment, making contacts with people, and avoiding harmful situations.

**Milestones in a Child's Development:** The developmental milestones are averages, but children show great variation in their development.

**WHAT ARE THE DEVELOPMENTAL TASKS OF CHILDHOOD?**

Children face especially important developmental tasks in the areas of language, thought processes, and social relationships.

**Childhood Influences on Your Personality:** Erikson's theory says that your personality is shaped by a series of developmental crises.

**WHAT DEVELOPMENTAL CHANGES OCCUR IN ADOLESCENCE AND ADULTHOOD?**

Nature and nurture continue to produce changes in personality and mental processes throughout the life cycle.

**The Last Developmental Problems You Will Face:** The final years of life present a challenge, but a new picture of aging is emerging.

**USING PSYCHOLOGY TO LEARN PSYCHOLOGY: COGNITIVE DEVELOPMENT IN COLLEGE STUDENTS**

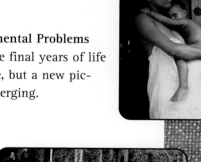

# 4

# Psychological Development

*N*ot long after their graduation from college in 1979, Shirley and Reuben ended their long engagement with a traditional church wedding ceremony at the campus chapel. Their first son, Bobby, was born later that year, and from day one he was the light of their lives. It seemed as if he were born to absorb everything around him with his inquiring eyes and irresistible smile. Although he did not cry often or fuss, the young parents jumped at his every sound, overreacting as many new parents tend to do, given their lack of experience "in the trenches." As he grew older, Bobby was equally happy leading other children in games or working alone on puzzles and taking things apart to see how they worked. He could be counted on never to make trouble, to be respectful of his elders, and to make sensible decisions that were never influenced solely by his emotions. He excelled in school at most subjects and went from being teachers' pet to high school valedictorian and on to college class president in a most natural progression.

A second child, Billy, was born in 1982. By now the proud parents knew a bit more about when to react to a baby's cries and when to sit them out. They knew they could count on Bobby to keep him in line and take care of him, as well as teach him some things. Billy Boy always seemed to be in the shadow of his big brother. They got along reasonably well, but Billy felt that nothing he did could quite measure up to what his big brother had done at any stage of their common development. That feeling may have influenced his progress, which always seemed a little slower on nearly every dimension: walking, talking, problem solving, forming relationships. When he entered school, it didn't help that teachers would remind him how really smart and responsible his big brother was. Billy Boy tried hard, was a good student, and had friends, but he could never do or achieve what Bobby did so seamlessly.

Two years after Billy, Benny was born, and with him the peace, quiet, and order of the family household went out the back door. He cried a lot, demanded to be heard, did whatever it took to get the attention of his parents and those two older lugs. Benny excelled at breaking things and messing up things. He found ever new ways to be alternately charming and irritating. But he made friends like bees make honey; he was the natural center of any group. What he lacked in smarts, Benny made up for in creativity and daring risk taking that produced novel consequences—some good, some . . . Don't ask.

117

At this writing, Bobby is majoring in physics. After he graduates from the university in only three years, he plans to be one of the first physicist-astronauts to work in a space station. Billy Boy is a college freshman with ambitions to own a car dealership in his hometown. Benny prefers the beach volleyball circuit but plans to finish up high school, if he can take time away from girls. But he has some interesting ideas about how to redesign Internet dating services and cyberspace courses that would replace boring teachers with ICIs—Ideally Cyber-Constructed Instructors. The problem is harnessing all that creative energy long enough for Benny to make a marketable product out of his many projects and to stay out of trouble long enough for that to happen.

On their recent 20th anniversary, Shirley and Reuben noted that all three boys have some of their own traits. But they worry that they didn't do everything right as parents and, therefore, may not have given their children—particularly Billy and Benny—the best start in life. They worry that they did not give as much attention and affection to Billy Boy as they had to their firstborn and maybe tried in vain to discipline their baby Benny too much in response to his emotional outbursts and mad antics. They wonder, as most parents do, what will become of their children, who seem so different to them even though they all grew up in the same, loving home environment.

One key to understanding the differences in the behavioral styles of Bobby, Billy, and Benny comes from the recent analysis of the impact of birth order on personality development. Birth-order expert Frank Sulloway (1996) argues that siblings learn to adapt to the power differences in the family by developing different strategies to compete for parental attention and favor. Firstborns, like Bobby, tend to become success-oriented, conservative, high achievers. Later-borns, like Benny, are "born to rebel," to challenge the status quo, needing to be different, deviant, and liberal. They are the most likely to be innovators, creating new theories and inventions. The middle-borns, like Billy, are the moderates on all these dimensions, being caught between the extremes of their older and younger siblings. Not everyone fits this pattern, of course, but Sulloway's large survey of thousands of biographies reveals that throughout history, eminent, successful people tend to be firstborns, like almost all the U.S. astronauts, while later-borns were most likely to lead rebellions and to propose radical theories or be the first to accept those of other scientists and philosophers.

People tend to agree about these birth order differences when asked to characterize those they know based on their sibling rank. The common belief is that firstborns are obedient, responsible, outgoing, intelligent, and unemotional. Last-borns are emotional, creative, irresponsible, and very outgoing. Middle-borns are ranked in the middle on these traits. Only-borns? People believe them to be spoiled, academic, and disagreeable (see Baskett, 1985; Musun-Miller, 1993; Nyman, 1995). These expectations, by themselves, can have powerful effects.

Bobby, Billy, and Benny also bring into focus some of the other forces that influence human development over the course of one's lifetime: heredity, family dynamics, and expectations. There are, of course, still other influences on how we grow and mature. Some, like birth order, family dynamics, peer pressure, culture, and economic circumstances, are part of a complex *environment* that shapes us. And, in addition, we are shaped by *heredity*, which includes all the genetic influences—both physical and behavioral—passed on to us from our parents.

To discover and understand how all these factors interact is the challenge facing developmental psychologists. Their field, **developmental psychology,** is concerned with the changes in cognition and behavior that occur from conception through the entire life span. Among the main concerns of developmental psychologists are the emergence of thought, language, emotional attachments, and morality—and how these processes change through life. We will begin our tour of developmental psychology by considering how psychologists think about development, starting with the

**Developmental psychology:** The psychological specialty that studies how organisms change over time as the result of biological and environmental influences.

study of newborns. Then we will follow the patterns of development across the life span, from infancy and childhood through adolescence and adulthood and to the end of life itself.

 **KEY QUESTION**

## HOW DO PSYCHOLOGISTS EXPLAIN DEVELOPMENT?

What have been the top ten changes in your life?

If you compare your personal list to those of others, you will find some broad similarities: You were born, formed relationships, attended school, and matured both physically and mentally. Your list may also hint at some of the ways in which you are distinctive: Perhaps you matured socially earlier than your friends, or perhaps you are more self-confident, verbal, artistic, or emotionally volatile than others you know. Your developmental story tells of both similarities and differences. It grows out of the most important influences on your life—both hereditary and environmental. The Core Concept for this section emphasizes the relationship between these two overreaching factors:

 **CORE CONCEPT**

**Development is a process of growth and change brought about by an interaction of heredity and environment.**

The most important word here is **interaction:** Heredity and environment are entwined in an inseparable relationship, often called the *nature–nurture* interaction. As we are about to see, the relative contributions of nature (heredity) and nurture (environment) have been the subject of continuing controversy. This much is certain: Neither operates alone.

### The Nature–Nurture Interaction

You are a product of your *genetic* inheritance (nature), the characteristics and physical features of your ancestors. But to what extent were you also shaped by your unique life experiences and opportunities (nurture)—especially by what you have *learned?* This **nature–nurture controversy** has been a long-standing debate among philosophers, psychologists, and educators.

In 1801 the nature–nurture debate erupted into public consciousness with the well-publicized discovery of the Wild Boy of Aveyron, a 12-year-old child who had lived alone in the forest near the village of Aveyron, France. Scientists hoped that this uncivilized, *feral* (wild) child—who had apparently never experienced a human environment—would hold the key to the fundamental questions of human nature and nurture (Candland, 1993). Accordingly, a young doctor, Jean Marie Itard, tried to civilize and educate the Wild Boy, whom he named Victor. At first Itard's training program seemed to work. Victor became affectionate and well-mannered, learning to follow instructions and eventually even learning to utter a few words. But after five intensive years, his progress stopped, and Itard reluctantly ended the "experiment" (Itard, reprinted, 1962; Shattuck, 1981). Victor continued to live with a caretaker until he died at about age 40.

Was it nature or nurture that failed Victor? Perhaps he had been abandoned as an infant because he was, by nature, developmentally slow. If that were so, training might have been expected to have only limited success. Alternatively, if Victor was capable of learning, then it was Itard's teaching program that failed—a nurture effect. A third explanation is also possible: Victor may have originally been able to learn the lessons of civilization. But, because he had spent the *critical period* for language development without human contact, he may have outgrown his receptivity to education by the time he was discovered.

 **Chapter 2 Biopsychology**
*Genes provide the hereditary blueprint for many physical characteristics and behaviors.*

 **Chapter 6 Learning and Remembering**
*Learning involves lasting changes in behavior and mental processes as a result of experience.*

**Interaction:** A process by which forces work together or influence each other—as in the interaction between the forces of heredity and environment.

**Nature–nurture controversy:** The long-standing dispute over the relative importance of nature (heredity) and nurture (environment) in their influence on behavior and mental processes.

So, which counts more in determining what we will become: nature or nurture? Although Itard's experiment with the Wild Boy was inconclusive, psychologists have finally answered this question (Azar, 1997a&b). It is *both*. Virtually every human characteristic (with the trivial exceptions of certain physical traits, such as eye color) is shaped by both an individual's biological inheritance and experience. Heredity and environment also have a continuing influence on each other throughout life. To reiterate: *Nature and nurture interact*. Your heredity establishes your potential, but your experiences determine how that potential will be realized. Although the nature–nurture debate continues on talk shows and in the popular press, psychologists today are more interested in understanding how heredity and environment work together to produce our personalities and our mental abilities (Bronfenbrenner & Ceci, 1994; Dannefer & Perlmutter, 1990).

Still, we might ask: Which of our characteristics does heredity affect most? And which are most heavily influenced by learning or other environmental factors (such as disease or nutrition)? It is worth noting that the answers to these questions pose some danger. For example, we know that certain genetic disorders, such as Down syndrome, can produce mental retardation, aggressive behavior, or social-emotional deficiencies, and there is no cure. Hearing this, the parents or teachers of children with such problems may simply give up hope. By focusing on the genetic cause, they may overlook effective learning-based treatments that can measurably improve the living skills of these individuals.

Mindful of the dangers, psychologists cautiously study the hereditary and environmental contributions to thought and behavior. To do so, they have invented several methods for weighing the effects of nature and nurture. These include studies of twins and studies of adopted children. Briefly, we will examine the strengths and weaknesses of these two methods.

**Chapter 2
Biopsychology**
*Down syndrome is a genetic disorder caused by an extra 21st chromosome fragment.*

**TWIN STUDIES**   Twins, especially when they have been separated since birth, can give us some tantalizing clues about the relative importance of nature and nurture. We must interpret these observations with great care, however (Phelps, Davies, & Schwartz, 1997). Consider, for example, the controversial case of the "Jim twins" (Jackson, 1980). Separated in infancy and reunited after nearly 40 years, Jim Springer

Twin studies are one way to study the relative importance of nature and nurture, but they must be interpreted with caution. This photo shows the identical "Bob Twins," who, like the "Jim Twins," grew up not knowing of each other's existance. Both sport mustaches and smoke a pipe; both have engineering degrees; and both married teachers named Brenda. It is unlikely that all the similarities—striking as they may be—are caused by genetics.

and Jim Lewis display some remarkable similarities. Both have been married twice, the first time to Lindas and the second time to women named Betty. Both owned dogs named Toy and worked as sheriff's deputies. Both smoke Salem cigarettes, drink Miller Lite beer, and make miniature furniture out of wood. Are these examples of heredity in action? There is no way to know for sure. Critics of **twin studies** correctly point out that the similarities found in *case studies*—no matter how astounding—may well be mere coincidences: Any two people are likely to have a number of things in common.

Less striking—but more scientifically robust—are findings that cut across many pairs of twins. These *correlational studies* give us a firmer basis for distinguishing the effects of heredity and environment. Correlational studies have found, for example, that twins are more similar than other siblings on measures of intelligence, personality, and interests, as well as in their facial expressions, gestures, and pace of speech (Bouchard et al., 1990; Jackson, 1980). Such findings strongly suggest that these characteristics have at least some genetic basis.

**Chapter 1**
**Mind, Behavior, and Science**
*Case studies offer the observer little control over factors that may have influenced the subject.*

**Chapter 1**
**Mind, Behavior, and Science**
*Correlational studies look for relationships among variables—but not cause and effect.*

**ADOPTION STUDIES**   If you adopted a baby, would it grow up to resemble you more than its biological parents? This is the sort of question asked by psychologists who do **adoption studies.** With this method, they compare the characteristics of adopted children with those of their biological and adoptive family members. Similarities with the biological family suggest the effects of nature, while similarities with the adoptive family point to the influence of nurture. This work has demonstrated, for example, a substantial (but not total) genetic contribution to intelligence and a small genetic influence on alcoholism (Bouchard, 1994). Because adopted children are easier to locate than are twins separated early in life, researchers more often use adoption studies to tease apart the effects of heredity and environment.

**Chapter 11**
**Intelligence and the Psychology of Differences**
*Intelligence is influenced by both heredity and environment.*

As scientists have come to understand more about genetics, especially during the past decade or so, we have all become more aware of genetic effects on behavior (Hamer, 1997; Plomin, Owen, & McGuffin, 1994; Pool, 1997; Sapolsky, 1997; Wright & Mahurin, 1997). Currently behavioral genetics is one of the hottest topics in psychology. Despite this enthusiasm—or, perhaps, because of it—we must guard against attributing any behavior entirely to heredity.

**Twin studies:** Developmental investigations in which twins, especially identical twins, are compared in the search for genetic and environmental effects.

**Adoption studies:** An alternative to twin studies in which the adopted child's characteristics are compared to those of the biological family and of the adoptive family.

### Gradual versus Abrupt Change

Taking its place alongside the nature–nurture controversy, a second major issue in developmental psychology deals with the *pattern* of development. Consider, for example, the process by which an infant forms an attachment to its parents or other

Many developmental changes, both physical and psychological, occur across the life span. Here we see Ronald Reagan as a boy, in his Hollywood years, and during his presidency.

## FIGURE 4.1:    Continuity versus Discontinuity

The continuity view sees development as a process of continual change, while the discontinuity view sees development as a series of "steps" or stages.

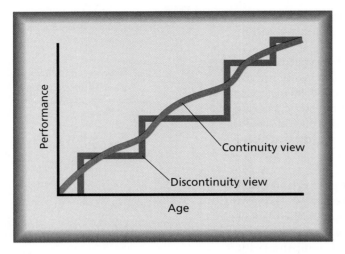

**Chapter 10
Personality**

*Freud's theory of personality development is a stage theory.*

**Continuity view:** The perspective that development is gradual and continuous—as opposed to the discontinuity (stage) view.

**Discontinuity view:** The perspective that development proceeds in an uneven (discontinuous) fashion—as opposed to the continuity view.

**Developmental stages:** Periods of life initiated by significant transitions or changes in physical or psychological functioning.

**Critical period:** A sensitive time in an organism's development, when it will acquire a particular behavior, such as language, if certain stimuli and experiences occur.

**Longitudinal method:** A type of developmental research that involves repeated observations of the same individuals over a period of time.

caregivers. Is this process gradual and ever-changing, or is it marked by clearly defined stages? According to the **continuity view,** we form social attachments and we become more skillful in thinking, talking, or acting in much the same way that we become taller: through a gradual developmental process. In contrast, psychologists who take a **discontinuity view** see development as a succession of changes that produce different behavior in different age-specific life periods, or *stages*, such as infancy, childhood, and adolescence. According to stage theories, particular aspects of development can be abrupt, or *discontinuous*. In this discontinuity view, a child enters a new developmental period when new abilities appear, often rather suddenly, as in the development of walking or talking.

You may have heard parents dismissing a child's misbehavior or moodiness as "just going through a stage," such as the "terrible twos," when children are becoming more mobile and independent. But for psychologists who subscribe to the discontinuity view, stages are not simply difficult times. These psychologists define **developmental stages** as periods of life initiated by distinct transitions (changes) in physical or psychological functioning. From a stage perspective, specific abilities, such as walking, talking, or abstract reasoning, appear at specific ages or life periods because different developmental processes come into play. In general, developmental psychologists who take the discontinuity view find that people go through the same stages in the same order—but not necessarily at the same rate.

**CRITICAL PERIODS**    Why is learning a foreign language so easy for young children and so hard for most adults? The swift and efficient development of language seems to require exposure to human language early in life. (This may have been part of Victor's problem.) Similarly, what we learn about social relationships during an especially impressionable period in childhood seems to set the stage for our adult relationships. In fact, many developmental tasks proceed much more efficiently if the individual is exposed to certain stimuli at just the right time—at a **critical period**—when the individual is most receptive. We may define a critical period as a sensitive time in an organism's development when the organism acquires a particular behavior, but only if it receives the appropriate stimulation. If the necessary stimulus conditions are not met, however, the individual will not develop the behavior and will have difficulty doing so later. As we have suggested, studies reveal critical periods for both language and attachment in humans. Similarly, when dogs and monkeys are raised in isolation for a few months after birth, they lack contact with their species during a critical period of social development. Then, even if they are reared with other normal animals, they behave in abnormal ways throughout the rest of their lives (Scott, 1963). Likewise, a female adult rhesus monkey who was initially reared in isolation will not react appropriately to signals for mating, and if she gives birth, she will not give her baby normal maternal care (Harlow & Harlow, 1966).

How do psychologists go about identifying stages, critical periods, and other developmental patterns? They have developed two main research methods for this purpose: the *longitudinal method* and the *cross-sectional method*. Let's look at the advantages and disadvantages of each.

**THE LONGITUDINAL METHOD**    In what ways are seven-year-olds different from four-year-olds? If we were to answer that question by using the **longitudinal method,** we would select a group of four-year-old children and study them repeatedly for three years. That is, with the longitudinal method, researchers observe and test the same subjects over a long period. By following a group of individuals as they grow older, developmental researchers can identify the characteristic changes associated with age. If different individuals show similar changes at similar times, the researcher cautiously assumes that such developments are caused by their ages rather than by coincidental environmental influences. Cognitive skills, moral development, and shyness have all been tested and tracked over time in this way (see Bullock, 1995). But ideal as longitudinal designs are, they are very expensive to carry out. And they require a long-term commitment from researchers, who find it difficult to track down subjects who move away or cease to participate. Fortunately, there is an alternative.

THE CROSS-SECTIONAL METHOD   Because longitudinal designs are not always practical, psychologists often turn to the **cross-sectional method** to study developmental changes. Using the cross-sectional method, researchers observe and compare groups of subjects at different age levels—a "cross section" of the population in which they are interested. For example, suppose we give the same task (a puzzle, perhaps) to a group of four-year-olds and another group of seven-year-olds. If the older children can perform the task with few errors, but the younger children are largely unable to complete the task, we might attribute the performance difference to their age difference.

The disadvantage of cross-sectional designs lies in the lack of control over other differences operating selectively on some age groups but not others. These selective influences are known as **cohort effects.** For example, the seven-year-olds may have been exposed to an environmental influence (such as a popular television show, a competitive game, or a specific classroom lesson) that was not available to the four-year-olds. Cross-sectional studies are also subject to bias resulting from larger historical events, such as the Vietnam War or the AIDS epidemic, which have selective effects on a particular age groups. Despite such problems, however, most developmental research uses a cross-sectional design because of its lower cost in both time and dollars.

**Chapter 11**
**Intelligence and the Psychology of Differences**
*Lewis Terman used the longitudinal method to study "gifted" people across the life span.*

**Cross-sectional method:** A type of developmental research in which groups of subjects of different ages are observed and compared at the same time; usually an economical alternative to the longitudinal method.

**Cohort effects:** Selective influences that affect one group (cohort) more than another.

---

**PSYCHOLOGY IN YOUR LIFE**

## Psychological Traits in Your Genes

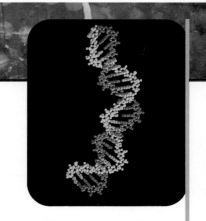

The genetic code, written in DNA, contains our complete hereditary blueprint, grouped into genes and chromosomes.

Eye color and the shape of your earlobes are purely genetic traits—but, as far as we know, heredity by itself determines none of our psychological characteristics (Horgan, 1993). In the psychological domain, heredity always acts in combination with environment. Nevertheless, developmental psychologists and biopsychologists often ask which characteristics have strong genetic links. In fact, they have found a number of traits that have a substantial hereditary basis—including some of your own attributes.

A genetic contribution to general intelligence, for example, is well established (although psychologists disagree over both the strength of heredity's role and the nature of "intelligence") (Plomin et al., 1994). There is also a good possibility that genes contribute to your sexual orientation (Hamer et al., 1993). And it just may be that an interest in skydiving, rock climbing, or other risky behavior has a genetic basis (Hamer, 1997). The evidence suggests that genes also contribute to your basic temperament and personality, including all of the "big five" personality factors (Bouchard, 1994; Plomin, 1997). (*See Chapter 10, Personality.*)

Some mental and behavioral disorders are associated with genetic abnormalities, too (Eley, 1997; Gibbs, 1995; Mann, 1994; Plomin et al., 1994). One of the first to be
*Continued*

discovered was *Huntington's disease*, a rare problem that causes aggressive behavior and mental deterioration beginning in midlife. Depression is among the more common emotional problems that can have an underlying genetic basis. Experts also believe that genetics contribute to *schizophrenia*, a major mental disorder. Fear can have a hereditary basis, as well, especially for those who have a condition known as *panic disorder*. So can repetitive rituals (such as compulsively checking and rechecking the alarm-clock setting) seen in *obsessive–compulsive disorder*. Likewise, the violence of an *antisocial personality* and the uncontrollable outbursts of *Tourette's syndrome* may originate in the genes. And, if you are older, you may worry that every instance of forgetting is a sign of *Alzheimer's disease*, which (in some forms) arises from a genetic flaw that first takes the memory and then the rest of the mind. (*See Chapter 13, Psychopathology.*)

Thus, it appears that many psychological traits, both desirable and undesirable, have a connection to our genes. But please note: Genetics is not everything. While heredity is involved in nearly all we do, most complex behaviors also contain a liberal portion of learning.

Unfortunately, people sometimes go to extremes and see hereditary effects everywhere. The danger in this lies in creating a sense of helplessness in those whose parents have undesirable characteristics, such as mental disorders or aggressive personalities. A strong hereditarian stance can also lead to unfair labeling of people as having "bad blood," if they come from troubled families. Just as disturbing, hereditarian expectations can create complacency and self-centeredness in those whose parents have desirable characteristics, such as high intelligence or good looks. Either way, expectations about genetic influences can also create a **self-fulfilling prophecy,** which leads people to live up (or down) to their expectations.

The main idea to remember is that heredity and environment *interact*. In the realm of behaviors and complex traits, neither one acts alone. Rather, genetics offers a basic plan, which learning always modifies.

1. RECALL: *Psychologists have resolved the nature–nurture controversy by saying that we are the products of*
   a. heredity.
   b. environment.
   c. both heredity and environment.
   d. neither heredity nor environment.

2. APPLICATION: *Which of the following statements is most accurate with regard to the "Jim twins"?*
   a. We cannot say for certain that their similarities are mainly genetic.
   b. It is reasonably certain that their similarities come from shared early experiences.
   c. It has been proven that their similarities are just chance.
   d. They are similar because they were raised in the same family environment.

3. RECALL: *Which one of the following is an alternative to twin studies in developmental research?*
   a. cross-sectional studies
   b. longitudinal studies

   c. scientific experiments
   d. adoption studies

4. RECALL: *Name one human behavior that involves a critical period.*

5. RECALL: *Which two techniques do researchers most often use to study stages and critical periods?*
   a. adoption studies and twin studies
   b. the longitudinal method and the cross-sectional method
   c. scientific experiments and case studies
   d. analysis and synthesis

6. UNDERSTANDING THE CORE CONCEPT: *Name a human characteristic that is caused by an interaction of heredity and environment.*

**ANSWERS:**   1. c    2. a    3. d    4. **Language and social attachments are two examples.**    5. b    6. **There are many, including language, temperament, and certain mental disorders.**

KEY QUESTION

## WHAT CAPABILITIES DOES THE NEWBORN POSSESS?

People used to think that babies began life completely helpless and dependent on their caregivers. In recent years, however, that picture has been changing. As we will see, psychologists now know that babies are born with a remarkable set of abilities that were programmed in their genes. These abilities are the focus of the Core Concept for this section:

**Self-fulfilling prophecy:** An expectation that becomes realized because it guides people's behaviors.

**CORE CONCEPT**

Newborns begin life equipped to deal with three basic survival tasks: finding nourishment, making contacts with people, and avoiding harmful situations.

To understand the origins and development of these abilities, we will consider four sets of underlying processes: (1) prenatal development and behavior, (2) maturation, (3) sensory development, and (4) how the developing infant builds on the neonatal blueprint.

## Prenatal Development and the Growth of the Brain

The **prenatal period** spans the time between conception and birth. Shortly after conception, an unrelenting flurry of development begins, as the **zygote** (fertilized egg) starts dividing. First one cell becomes two; two become four; and after about ten days, when the number reaches about 150, the zygote implants itself in the lining of the uterus. At this point it becomes an **embryo.**

During the short embryonic period, all the structures that are found in the newborn infant will begin to form. This occurs because the embryo's cells specialize, a process known as **differentiation.** At first, the embryo's cells form distinct layers. Eventually, those in the outer layer become the nervous system and the skin. Cells in the middle layer are programmed to become muscles, bones, blood vessels, and certain internal organs. Those in the inner layer differentiate on a path that will eventually make them into the digestive system, lungs, and glands. By the end of the first month the initial single cell of the zygote has developed into an embryo with millions of specialized cells. Eventually this process of cell division and differentiation, which continues throughout the prenatal period, produces all the tissues and organisms of the body.

The first "behavior"—a heartbeat—appears when the embryo is about three weeks old and a sixth of an inch long. A few weeks later, when it is not yet an inch in length, the embryo makes reflexive responses to stimulation. These behaviors occur long before the brain has developed to the point where it can command behaviors.

After the eighth week, the developing embryo is called a **fetus.** Spontaneous movements begin at about this time, although the mother doesn't usually feel these movements until the sixteenth week after conception (Carmichael, 1970; Humphrey, 1970). By this point, the fetus has grown to about 7 inches long (the average length at birth is 20 inches).

We also used to think that the womb shielded the developing organism from environmental assaults, but we now know better. Although the **placenta** (an organ that develops between the embryo/fetus and the mother) screens out many potentially dangerous substances, some can pass through this barrier. These toxic substances, called **teratogens,** include viruses, a variety of drugs, and other chemicals. Among the most common teratogens are nicotine and alcohol. The effects of these toxic substances vary from slight to devastating, depending on the amount of exposure and on the stage of prenatal development in which exposure occurs.

Prenatally, the brain grows new neurons at the amazing rate of up to 250,000 per

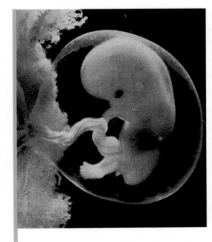

As the brain grows in the developing embryo, it generates 250,000 new neurons per minute.

**Prenatal period:** The developmental period before birth.

**Zygote:** A fertilized egg.

**Embryo:** In humans, the name for the developing organism during the first eight weeks after conception.

**Differentiation:** The process by which cells in the embryo take on specialized functions.

**Fetus:** In humans, the term for the developing organism between the embryonic stage and birth.

**Placenta:** The organ separating the embryo or fetus and the mother. The placenta separates the bloodstreams, but it allows the exchange of nutrients and waste products.

**Teratogen:** Any substance from the environment, including viruses, drugs, and other chemicals, that can damage the developing organism during the prenatal period.

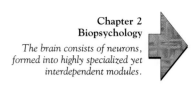

**Chapter 2
Biopsychology**

*The brain consists of neurons,
formed into highly specialized yet
interdependent modules.*

minute. By birth it has produced over 100 billion (Dowling, 1992). In addition to this cell proliferation, the neurons that build the brain actually migrate, moving into their genetically determined positions. Then, at birth, the brain shifts from producing new cells to a different mode of growth. In the newborn brain, a genetic program emphasizes the branching of axons and dendrites, in order to form the circuitry of the nervous system (Kolb, 1989). As the dendrites and axons grow and connect, the total mass of neural tissue in the brain continues to increase rapidly—by 50% in the first two years. By four years of age it has nearly doubled its birth size. However, the genetic program (along with the physical limitations imposed by the size of the skull) does not allow this tremendous growth to continue indefinitely. So, the brain's growth rate gradually diminishes, and finally, by about 11 years, the brain attains its ultimate mass.

All the while, the rest of the body is undergoing remarkable physical changes, too. In general, human growth has been viewed as a continuous process whose rate changes with age, slowing over time after a very rapid start in the early years. New research, however, indicates that at least one aspect of growth—the increase in length of infants' bodies—occurs in discontinuous "bursts," a pattern known as *saltation* (from the Latin *saltare*, "to leap"). These data suggest that human physical growth is based not on a single continuous process but on two processes: an inactive phase and a growth phase (Lampl, Veldhuis, & Johnson, 1992).

## Maturation

Like the growth of the brain, the appearance of walking, talking, the growth spurts of adolescence, and the onset of menopause all occur on their own biological time schedules. Psychologists use the term **maturation** for the unfolding of such genetically programmed processes of growth and development over time. When organisms are raised under adequate environmental conditions, their maturation follows a predictable pattern. It includes the systematic changes in bodily functioning and behavior that are influenced by both genetic factors and environmental factors, such as nutrition, touch, and gravity. In humans, maturation generates the sequences and patterns of behavior seen in Figure 4.2.

Most of what you do—your voluntary movement and action—requires physical maturation that gives you coordination and strength from many parts of your body. We see maturation in action when children sit without support by seven months of age, pull themselves up to a standing position a month or two later, and walk soon after their first birthday. Once the underlying physical structures are sufficiently developed, proficiency in these behaviors requires only a minimally adequate environment and a little practice.

We must always keep in mind, however, that the sequences of physical and mental growth involve the *interaction* of biology and environment—even though biology may often play the leading role. So, in the sequence for locomotion, as shown in Figure 4.2, a child learns to walk without special training following a time-ordered pattern that is typical of all physically capable members of our species. Indeed, in cultures where children are carried in cradle boards, walking occurs on a normal schedule (Dennis & Dennis, 1940). Despite this hereditary pattern, however, we find that environmental influences can sometimes have an influence on biological tendencies. So, in the West Indies, where infants receive vigorous massage after the daily bath and frequent practice in moving their legs while being held, children sit and walk a little earlier, on the average, than do children in the United States (Hopkins & Westra, 1988). On the other hand, lack of human contact can have the opposite effect: Infants who had spent their lives lying in cribs in Iranian orphanages were observed to be severely retarded in learning to sit and walk (Dennis, 1960).

## Innate Sensory and Motor Abilities

What is the sensory world like for the newborn? The father of American psychology, William James, declared that, to the newborn infant, everything must be an

**Maturation:** The process by which the genetic program manifests itself over time.

## FIGURE 4.2:  Maturational Timetable for Locomotion

The development of walking requires no specific training but follows a fixed
sequence typical of all physically capable human children. In cultures where there is
more stimulation, children begin to walk sooner.

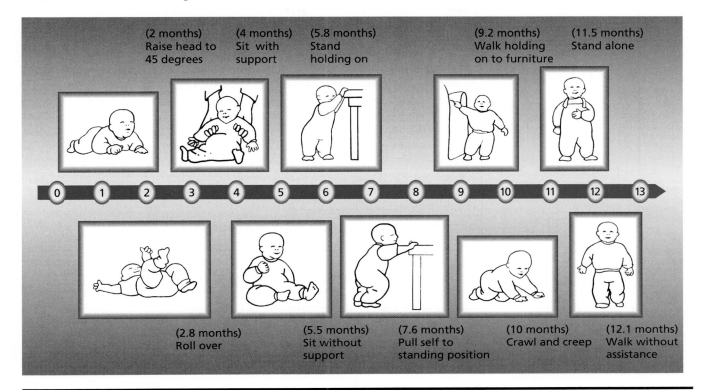

(2 months)
Raise head to
45 degrees

(4 months)
Sit with
support

(5.8 months)
Stand
holding on

(9.2 months)
Walk holding
on to furniture

(11.5 months)
Stand alone

(2.8 months)
Roll over

(5.5 months)
Sit without
support

(7.6 months)
Pull self to
standing position

(10 months)
Crawl and creep

(12.1 months)
Walk without
assistance

overwhelming jumble of stimuli—"One great blooming, buzzing confusion" (James,
1890). In 1928, behaviorist John Watson echoed James by describing the human infant as "a lively, squirming bit of flesh, capable of making a few simple responses." We
now know that their views grossly underestimated infants' capabilities. Long before
babies achieve motor coordination and locomotion, they take in vast amounts of information about their surroundings, filtering and processing stimulation that attracts,
interests, or upsets them. They also have an amazing behavioral repertoire that they
use to manipulate their environment.

During the **neonatal period** (newborn period), which
covers the time from birth to one month of age, neonates are
capable of responding to stimulation from all of their senses.
For example, newborn babies will turn their heads toward
anything that strokes their cheeks—a nipple or a finger—
and begin to suck it. They can also respond to taste: the
sweeter the fluid, the more continuously and forcefully an
infant will suck (Lipsitt et al., 1976). And, as early as 12
hours after birth, they show distinct signs of pleasure at the
taste of sugar water or vanilla.

What else can newborns do with their senses? Minutes
after birth, their eyes scan their surroundings. They turn in
the direction of a voice and search inquisitively for the
source of preferred sounds or stretch out an exploratory
hand. Neonates also express preferences, sometimes quite
unmistakably. They smile when they smell banana essence,

**Neonatal period:** In humans, the
neonatal (newborn) period extends
through the first month after birth.

**Chapter 5
Sensation and Perception**

*Sensation involves the initial stages
of information processing by the
sense organs and the brain.*

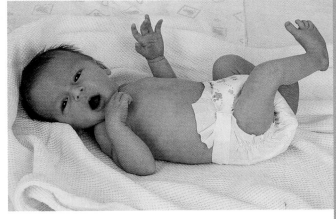

Is the world of the newborn a "blooming, buzzing confusion," as
William James claimed?

**Chapter 6**
**Learning and Remembering**

*Sucking on a plastic nipple is an operant behavior that can be used to determine the preferences of infants.*

**Chapter 2**
**Biopsychology**

*Reflexes are simple, innate behaviors activated by stimulation.*

**Chapter 6**
**Learning and Remembering**

*Through classical conditioning, organisms learn to associate two different stimuli.*

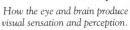

**Chapter 5**
**Sensation and Perception**

*How the eye and brain produce visual sensation and perception.*

**Chapter 2**
**Biopsychology**

*The occipital cortex is the brain's visual processing center.*

**Infancy:** In humans, infancy spans the time between the end of the neonatal period and the establishment of language—usually at about 18 months to two years.

and they prefer salted to unsalted cereal (Bernstein, 1990; Harris, Thomas, & Booth, 1990). However, they recoil from the taste of lemon or shrimp or the smell of rotten eggs. They prefer female voices; they attend to familiar sound patterns; and within a few weeks of birth they begin to recognize their mothers' voice (Carpenter, 1973; De-Casper & Fifer, 1980; DeCasper & Spence, 1986; Spelke & Owsley, 1979). In fact, recordings of fetal responses show that some functions, such as hearing, appear even before birth.

Aside from their sensory abilities, babies are born with a remarkable set of behavioral reflexes that sustain life and provide a biological platform for later development. Among these reflexes, the *postural reflex* allows babies to sit with support, and the *grasping reflex* enables them to cling to a caregiver. These and other reflexes equip babies with the essential tools for survival and "instinctive" know-how. In addition, babies are designed, as we have seen, to seek pleasurable sensations, such as sweetness, and to avoid or seek to escape unpleasant stimulation, such as loud noises, bitter tastes, bright lights, strong odors, and painful stimuli. All of this, of course, makes much evolutionary sense because these abilities are highly adaptive and promote survival.

## Building on the Neonatal Blueprint

Following the neonatal period, the child enters **infancy,** a period that lasts until about 18 months, when speech becomes well developed. (The Latin root *infans* means "incapable of speech.") It is a time of rapid, genetically programmed growth and reliance on the repertoire of reflexes and "instinctive" behaviors that we discussed above. But, it is also a period during which youngsters come to depend more and more on their abilities for learning new behaviors.

Hints of this ability to learn show up even in the neonatal period. Elliott Blass (1990) and his research team at Johns Hopkins University have shown that babies start to build up their knowledge of the world by observing relations between connected sensory events. This represents a fundamental form of learning called *classical conditioning*—the same sort of learning that makes your mouth water at the sight of a pizza. In their experiment, Blass's team taught newborns to anticipate pleasurably sweet sensations by first stroking the babies' foreheads and then giving them sugar water. After several trials, the stroking alone would cause the baby to turn its head in the direction from which the sweet fluid had been delivered—in anticipation of more of the same. What would you predict happened when the stroking was *not* followed by the pleasant taste of sugar water? The babies got upset. Almost all (seven of eight) newborns cried when the sweet fluid failed to arrive. In a control group not conditioned to expect sugar water after stroking, only one of 16 cried. It was as if the conditioned babies were responding emotionally to a violation of a reliable relationship that had been established (Blass, 1990). This experiment illustrates that babies can use both their inherited reflexes and their abilities for learning.

Despite all their innate abilities, babies have limits on their abilities, particularly their vision. In fact, babies are born "legally blind," with a visual acuity of about 20/500 (which means that they can discriminate at 20 feet stimuli that a normal older child can see clearly at 500 feet). Good vision requires the operation and coordination of a great many receptor cells in the eye's retina and in the occipital cortex of the brain. At birth, not enough of these connections are laid down. But these immature systems develop very rapidly, and the baby's visual abilities soon become evident (Banks & Bennett, 1988).

Early on, infants can perceive large objects that display a great deal of contrast. By one month a child can detect contours of a head at close distances. At seven weeks the baby can scan the features of the caregiver's face, and as the caregiver talks, the baby can scan his or her eyes. Just as heredity biases infants to prefer human voices over other sounds, it programs them to prefer human faces to most other visual patterns (Fantz, 1963). At as early as two months, the baby begins to see color, differentiating patterns of white, red, orange, and blue. At three months, the baby can perceive depth and is well on the way to enjoying the visual abilities of adults.

Babies are also designed to be sociable, and much of their development during infancy builds on that **innate** sociability. It is important to note that they not only respond to, but also interact with, their caregivers. Film studies of this interaction reveal a remarkable degree of *synchronicity*: close coordination between the gazing, vocalizing, touching, and smiling of mothers and infants (Martin, 1981). And while babies respond and learn, they also send out messages to those willing to listen to and love them. Studies also show that the feelings of mothers and infants are matched in a socially dynamic fashion (Fogel, 1991). So, a three-month-old infant may laugh when his or her mother laughs and frown or cry in response to her display of negative emotion (Tronick, Als, & Brazelton, 1980). Amazingly, even newborns will imitate simple facial expressions, such as sticking out the tongue or rounding the mouth (Meltzoff, 1998; Meltzoff & Moore, 1977, 1983, 1985, 1989).

In general, we have seen that babies seem to come equipped to accomplish three basic tasks of survival: finding sustenance (feeding), maintaining contact with people (for protection and care), and defense against harmful stimuli (withdrawing from pain or threat). These tasks require a set of innate abilities. These abilities form the foundation on which learning and maturation build the perceptual skills, the ability to understand experiences, and basic thinking skills that continue to develop throughout life (von Hofsten & Lindhagen, 1979).

**Innate:** Inborn.

## PSYCHOLOGY IN YOUR LIFE

## Milestones in a Child's Development

*I*t is risky to discuss the ages by which a child "should" achieve certain physical and mental skills. Children show great variation in their development (as we noted in the cases of Bobby, Billy, and Benny). So if your child, or a child you know, hasn't started walking and talking by age one, you shouldn't panic. Einstein was slow to talk, too. On the other hand, if a child still isn't beginning to walk and talk by age two, the caregiver should consult a specialist, such as a pediatrician or developmental psychologist, to see whether something is wrong. It is well to remember, also, that a delay in one area, such as the onset of speech, does not mean that the child is "retarded" or will be generally slow in other areas. Not only are there great variations among children, but variations occur normally within an individual child.

What developmental standards would a specialist use? Certainly, a child should be responsive to people almost from the moment of birth. All the major reflexes discussed in the previous section should be present. (These should be checked by the pediatrician.) Then, as the child develops, you will want to watch at the appropriate times for the abilities listed in Table 4.1 and Figure 4.2. Doing so will not only help you follow the child's progress, but it will make you more knowledgeable about the process of psychological development.

Children show great variation in development, but a child who departs greatly from the norms should be checked by a specialist.

## TABLE 4.1 Norms for Infant Mental and Motor Development (Based on the Bayley Scales)

**One month**
Responds to sound
Becomes quiet when picked up
Retains a large, easily grasped object placed in hand
Vocalizes occasionally

**Two months**
Smiles socially
Engages in anticipatory excitement (to feeding, being held)
Recognizes mother
Inspects surroundings
Blinks at object or shadow (flinches)
Lifts head and holds it erect and steady

**Three months**
Vocalizes to the smiles and talk of an adult
Searches for sound
Makes anticipatory adjustments to lifting
Reacts to disappearance of adult's face
Sits with support, head steady

**Four months**
Head follows dangling ring, vanishing spoon, and ball moved across table
Inspects and fingers own hands
Shows awareness of strange situations
Picks up cube with palm grasp
Sits with slight support

**Five months**
Discriminates strange from familiar persons
Makes distinctive vocalizations (e.g., pleasure, eagerness, satisfaction)
Turns from back to side
Has partial use of thumb in grasp

**Six months**
Reaches persistently, picks up cube deftly
Lifts cup and bangs it
Smiles at mirror image and likes frolicking
Reaches unilaterally for small object

**Seven months**
Makes playful responses to mirror
Retains two or three cubes offered
Sits alone steadily and well
Show clear thumb opposition in grasp
Scoops up pellet from table

**Eight months**
Vocalizes four different syllables (such as da-da, me, no)
Listens selectively to familiar words
Rings bell purposefully
Attempts to obtain three presented cubes
Shows early stepping movements (prewalking progression)

Note: This table shows the average age at which each behavior is performed up to eight months. Individual differences in rate of development are considerable, but most infants follow this sequence.

## Check Your Understanding

1. RECALL: *Which of the following does* not *appear before birth?*
   a. the heartbeat
   b. movement of limbs
   c. growth and migration of neurons
   d. vocalizations

2. RECALL: *After birth, brain development emphasizes*
   a. the migration of neurons.
   b. the development of connections among neurons.
   c. the development of the brain stem.
   d. the multiplication of neurons.

3. RECALL: *Which of the following is a behavior that appears largely because of maturation?*
   a. the onset of puberty
   b. starting school
   c. moving out of the parents' home
   d. sexual orientation

4. APPLICATION: *You would expect your newborn baby to*
   a. quickly learn to recognize the sound of its name.
   b. react negatively to a taste of lemon.
   c. prefer its father's deeper voice to its mother's higher voice.
   d. smile when it is eating.

5. UNDERSTANDING THE CORE CONCEPT: *Which one of the following is an innate ability that promotes survival?*
   a. the grasping reflex
   b. recognition of the mother's face
   c. toilet training
   d. sharp vision

**ANSWERS:**  1. d  2. b  3. a  4. b  5. a

# WHAT ARE THE DEVELOPMENTAL TASKS OF CHILDHOOD?

Three of the greatest accomplishments of your life include acquiring your native language, developing your ability to think and reason, and forming relationships with the important people in your life. Each of these achievements is part of the foundation for adulthood being laid by the child. And, we will see, as children work through these tasks, they undergo profound psychological changes. Our Core Concept states the idea this way:

## CORE CONCEPT

**Children face especially important developmental tasks in the areas of language, thought processes, and social relationships.**

In this section we will see that children are developmentally different from adults, but the differences they display in language, thought, and socialization are not simply the result of adults' greater experience or store of information. Rather, the differences between children and adults involve the unfolding of crucial developmental processes. Let us first observe these processes at work on the task of language acquisition.

## How Children Acquire Language

Infants know no words at all, yet in only a few years virtually all young children become fluent speakers of any language they hear spoken and have the opportunity to speak. What makes them such adept language learners? Apparently, human infants possess innate (inborn) abilities that help them learn language (Locke, 1994). Research shows, for example, that neonates come programmed to attend to language sounds. In addition, innate interest in social interaction strongly motivates children to learn language so they can communicate with others. Let's look more closely at the maturational factors known to assist children in learning language.

**BABBLING**   Beside their ability to perceive speech sounds, infants have a tendency to produce sequences of sounds that they will later use in speaking. Part of this tendency arises from a vocal apparatus that is biologically adapted for speech production. As a result, infants *babble*, producing speechlike sounds and syllables such as "mamama" or "beebee" well before they begin to use true words. Amazingly, during this **babbling stage,** babies make nearly all sounds heard in all languages. Eventually, however, the repertoire narrows down to the sounds of the language that the baby hears (Clark & Clark, 1977; Mowrer, 1960).

**INNATE LANGUAGE STRUCTURES IN THE BRAIN**   According to the **innateness theory of language,** children acquire language not merely by imitating but by following an inborn program of steps to acquire the vocabulary and grammar of the language in their environment. Psycholinguist Noam Chomsky (1965, 1975) says that children are born with mental structures—built into the brain—that make it possible to comprehend and produce speech. Many experts agree with Chomsky that innate mental machinery orchestrates children's language learning. One such mechanism, we have seen, lies in Broca's area, the motor speech "controller" in the cerebral cortex. Chomsky refers to these speech-enabling structures collectively as a **language acquisition device** or **LAD.**

In Chomsky's theory, the LAD—like a computer chip—contains some very basic rules of grammar, common to all human languages, built into its circuits. One such rule might be the distinction between nouns (for names of things) and verbs (for

**Babbling stage:** The time during the first year of life when an infant produces a wide range of sounds but not functional words.

**Innateness theory of language:** The view that children learn language mainly by following an inborn program for acquiring vocabulary and grammar.

**Language acquisition device or LAD:** A biologically organized mental structure in the brain that facilitates the learning of language because (says Chomsky) it is innately programmed with some of the fundamental rules of grammar.

**Chapter 2
Biopsychology**

*Broca's area, in the left frontal lobe, controls the muscles used in speech.*

## FIGURE 4.3: Growth in Children's Working Vocabulary

The number of words a child can use increases rapidly between 18 months and six years of age. This study shows children's average vocabularies at six-month intervals. (Source: B. A. Moskovitz, "The Acquisition of Language," *Scientific American*, Inc. All rights reserved; reprinted by permission.)

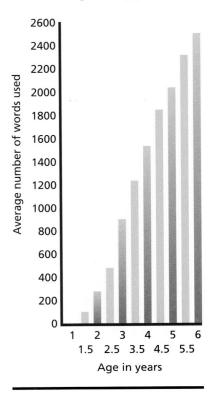

**Grammar:** The rules of a language, specifying how to use words, morphemes, and syntax to produce understandable sentences.

**One-word stage:** The first stage of true language, in which children communicate with single words, rather than sentences.

**Syntax:** Grammatical rules for word order.

**Two-word stage:** The second stage of true language, in which two words form rudimentary sentences—showing that the child is beginning to learn syntax.

actions). These innate rules, Chomsky argues, make it easier for children to discover patterns in languages to which they are exposed.

What other evidence does Chomsky have to suggest that the foundations of language are innate? For one thing, children worldwide proceed through very similar stages of learning their native languages. A logical hypothesis for explaining this pattern would be that children possess inborn "blueprints" for language development that unfold with time and experience. Despite the similarities in the sequence, however, language learning is not precisely the same across cultures. Such variations suggest that children's built-in capacity for language is not a rigid device but a set of lessons and "listening rules" or guidelines for perceiving language (Bee, 1994; Slobin, 1985a, 1985b). For example, babies pay attention to the sounds and rhythms of the sound strings they hear others speak (or in sign language, *see*), especially the beginnings, endings, and stressed syllables. Relying on their built-in "listening guides," young children deduce the patterns and rules for producing their own speech.

In general, language researchers have been impressed with the fact that most children are both ready to acquire language and flexible about its final form and context. This is equally true for children exposed to any of the world's 4,000 spoken languages, as well as to gestural communication systems, such as American Sign Language. Such adaptability suggests that the LAD in children is flexible, not rigidly programmed (Goldin-Meadow & Mylander, 1990; Meier, 1991).

**VOCABULARY AND GRAMMAR**  Acquiring a basic vocabulary represents an important project for children in their first few years of life, and young children are excellent word learners. By the age of six, the average child is estimated to understand an astounding 14,000 words (Templin, 1957). Assuming that most of these words are learned between the ages of 18 months and six years, this works out to about nine new words a day, or almost one word per waking hour (Bower, 1998; Carey, 1978). You can see the cumulative growth of a child's working vocabulary in Figure 4.3.

What is the pattern by which children develop vocabulary and **grammar**? Developmental psychologists recognize three initial stages: the *one-word stage*, the *two-word stage*, and *telegraphic speech*. During the **one-word stage,** which begins at about one year of age, children use only one word at a time (of course!), usually concrete nouns or verbs. Remember that the age at which talking begins can be quite variable, as we noted in the difference between Bobby and Billy in our opening case. Children use these single words to name objects that move, make noise, or can be handled, such as "mama," "ball," and "dog." They may also *overextend* words, using them incorrectly to cover a wide range of objects, such as using the word "dog" to refer to all animals. Overextension may simply result from having a still-limited vocabulary: A child who sees a goat for the first time may say "Kitty!" because she does not know the word "goat," but recognizes some common features (fuzzy, four-legged, smaller than a person) (Clark, 1983, 1987).

*NAMES AND WORD COMBINATIONS*  At around 18 months, children's word learning accelerates rapidly. At this age, children might point to every object in a room and ask, "What's that?" Researchers have called this phase the "naming explosion" because children begin to acquire new words, especially names for objects, at a rapidly increasing rate. Children also discern that some words are not names but actions (verbs) that describe how named objects and persons affect each other. As children experiment with verbs, they develop the beginnings of **syntax,** grammatical rules about combining words to indicate specific meanings (Naigles, 1990; Naigles & Kako, 1993). We will learn more about the development of grammar in a moment.

After the naming explosion occurs between about 18 months and two years of age, children begin to use one-word utterances in different sequences to convey more complex meanings. When they enter the **two-word stage,** the range of meanings children can convey increases tremendously. Studies of different languages show that, around the world, children's two-word utterances begin to divide the world into different categories of ideas. For example, ten children speaking different languages (English, Samoan, Finnish, Hebrew, and Swedish) were found to talk mostly about three categories of ideas: movers, movable objects, and locations (Braine, 1976). When young Alexis kicks a ball, for example, the mover is Alexis and the movable object is the ball. Alexis can express this relationship in the two-word sequence, "Alexi ball." It is in the two-word stage that children first develop the language rules called *grammar*. This allows them to move past simple naming and combine words into sentences.

*THE RULES OF GRAMMAR* Even if you have a limited vocabulary, you can combine the same words in different sequences to convey a rich variety of meanings. For example, "I saw him chasing a dog" and "I saw a dog chasing him" both use exactly the same words, but switching the order of the words "him" and "dog" yields completely different meanings. Grammar makes this possible: It is a language's set of rules about combining and ordering words to make understandable sentences. Different languages may use considerably different rules about grammatical combinations. In Japanese, for example, the verb always comes last, while English is much more lax about verb position.

In their early two-and three-word sentences, children's speech is *telegraphic*: short, simple sequences of nouns and verbs without plurals, tenses, or function words like "the" and "of." For example, "Ball hit Evie cry" is **telegraphic speech.** To develop full sentences, children must not only learn to use other forms of speech, such as modifiers (adjectives and adverbs) and articles (the, those), they must learn how to put words together—grammatically. In English, this means recognizing and producing the familiar subject-verb-object order, as in "The lamb followed Mary." It can become complicated when the same meaning is conveyed by alternative orders, such as "Mary was followed by the lamb."

Finally, children need to acquire grammatical skill in using **morphemes,** the meaningful units that make up words. Morphemes mark verbs to show tense (walk*ed*, walk*ing*) and mark nouns to show possession (Maria*'s*, the people*'s*) and plurality (fox*es*, child*ren*). Often, however, they make mistakes because they do not know the rule or apply an inappropriate one (Marcus, 1996). One common error, known as **overregularization,** applies a rule too widely and creates incorrect forms. For example, after learning to make past tense verb forms by adding *-d* or *-ed*, children may apply this "rule" even to its exceptions, the irregular verbs, creating such nonwords as "hitted" and "breaked." Learning to add *-s* or *-es* to make plurals, children may apply the rule to irregular nouns, as in "foots" or "mouses."

Children are not alone in their confusion about the rules of grammar. An adult may find it amusing or curious when young children have not yet mastered the irregular plurals of such common words as "women," "men," and "children." But adults also struggle with irregular words, mistakenly using terms like "data," "criteria," "stimuli," or "phenomena," as if they were singular forms, when in fact they are all plural. The grammar of one's own language can be a matter of lifelong learning.

Regardless of their formal education, most language-learners succeed well enough to be able to communicate for practical purposes. Yet this fact can be overlooked when researchers focus on errors rather than successes. They do so for good reason, however, because mistakes provide a glimpse into the detailed workings of language acquisition. By studying errors, researchers conclude that children's language learning depends on acquiring the general rules of grammar (and learning the exceptions) rather than merely imitating what adults say (Pinker, 1994; Slobin, 1979).

**OTHER LANGUAGE SKILLS** Words and the grammatical rules for combining them are only some of the ingredients of communication. To communicate well,

**Telegraphic speech:** Short, simple sentences, typical of young children, who omit plurals, tenses, and function words, such as "the" and "of"; so called because it sounds like a telegram.

**Morphemes:** The meaningful units of language that make up words. Some whole words are morphemes (example: "word"); other morphemes include grammatical components that alter a word's meaning (examples: "-ed," "-ing," and "un-").

**Overregularization:** Applying a grammatical rule too widely and creating incorrect forms.

**Chapter 8**
**Emotion and Motivation**

*Are facial expressions of emotion
the same around the world?*

children also need to learn the social rules of conversation. They must learn how to join a discussion, how to take turns talking and listening, and how to make contributions that are relevant. Adult speakers use body language, intonation, and facial expressions to enhance their communication. They also use feedback they get from listeners and are able to take the perspective of the listener. Children must master these skills in order to become successful communicators—to become part of a human language community.

As children grow older, they also begin to express more abstract meanings, going beyond their physical world to talk about their psychological world. For example, after the age of two, children begin to use words such as *dream, forget, pretend, believe, guess,* and *hope,* as they talk about internal states (Shatz, Wellman, & Silber, 1983). They also use words such as *happy, sad,* and *angry* to refer to emotional states. Finally, after cognitive advances that occur later in childhood, they understand and use highly abstract words such as *truth, justice,* and *idea.*

What is the major point that stands out amid the complexities of language acquisition? It is implied in our Core Concept: Language is a major developmental task of childhood—for which children are exquisitely prepared. And the way they acquire and use language suggests that becoming an adult involves a combination of learning and innate processes that unfold on their own developmental timetables.

## Cognitive Development

If you have ever known a toddler going through the naming explosion, you have seen that children have an insatiable appetite for labeling of things they know. Behind this labeling is their emerging ability for thinking, perceiving, and remembering. The next few pages will focus on the ways that these mental abilities emerge, a process called **cognitive development.**

**Chapter 7**
**Cognitive Processes**

*What are the components
of thought?*

Psychologists interested in cognitive development ask such questions as these: When do children realize that objects still exist even when they can't see them? Do they know that it is possible to believe in ideas that aren't true? Can they understand that people have desires and dreams, but objects do not? Developmental psychologists investigate not only *what* children think but *how* they think it.

In this section we will emphasize the pioneering work on cognitive development by the late Swiss psychologist Jean Piaget (although there are other points of view). For nearly 50 years, Piaget observed children's intellectual development. He saw the human mind as an active biological system that seeks, selects, interprets, and reorganizes environmental information to fit with its own existing mental structures.

Piaget began this quest to understand the nature of the child's mind by carefully observing the behavior of his own three children. His methods were simple: He would pose problems to them, observe their responses, slightly alter the situations, and once again observe their responses. Piaget attended especially to transitions and changes in his children's thinking, reasoning, and problem solving. This focus led to a *discontinuous stage model* of development, which emphasized Piaget's view that children undergo a revolution in thought at each stage. Three key ideas distinguish Piaget's approach: (1) *schemes,* (2) the interaction of *assimilation* and *accommodation,* and (3) the *stages of cognitive development.*

**SCHEMES** To illustrate the concept of *scheme,* think of a four-legged animal. Now think of one that is friendly. Now think of one that barks. You might have started by imagining elephants and tigers (both four-legged), then narrowed your choices down to cats and dogs (four-legged and friendly), and finally to just dogs (which bark). You could do this easily only because you have developed mental structures (mental programs) that enable you to interpret events and experiences. Piaget termed such mental structures **schemes.** We have schemes for concepts, such as "dog" and "development." We have schemes for actions, such as eating with chopsticks. We

**Cognitive development:** The process by which thinking changes over time.

**Schemes:** In Piaget's theory, mental structures or programs that guide a developing child's thought.

Although an infant will begin to suck a bottle just the way he or she sucked a breast (assimilation), the infant will soon discover that some changes are necessary (accommodation). The child will make an even greater accommodation in the transitions from bottle to cup.

also have schemes for solving problems, such as finding the area of a circle or dealing with a crying baby. In general, schemes are mental structures that guide thinking. According to Piaget, they are also the building blocks of developmental change. Our schemes change as we develop and organize our knowledge to deal with present experience and predict future events. Right now you are building a scheme about schemes!

**ASSIMILATION AND ACCOMMODATION** In Piaget's system, two dynamic processes underlie all cognitive growth: *assimilation* and *accommodation*. **Assimilation** is a mental process that modifies new information to fit with existing schemes—with what is already known. So, a baby reflexively knows how to suck from a nipple and will use assimilation to deal with new objects such as a finger or a new toy. Some adult examples: You, too, experience assimilation when you acquire more information about William Shakespeare or gain skill in using a word-processing program on the computer.

By contrast, **accommodation** is a process of restructuring or *modifying* schemes to incorporate new information. For example, a child's simplistic "bird" scheme, which includes any flying object, undergoes accommodation when the child learns that a butterfly is not a bird. Adults experience accommodation of their mental schemes, too. For example, many computer users in the 1990s had to modify their computer-using schemes when they made the transition from the older, text-based format (DOS) to the graphic Windows format. You, too, may need to modify a scheme when the professor in your psychology course says something that surprises you (such as, "Children have innate language abilities"). As a result, your scheme about newborn children may change to accommodate your new knowledge.

For Piaget, cognitive development results from this constant interweaving of assimilation and accommodation. Through these two processes, the individual's behavior and knowledge become less dependent on concrete external reality and more reliant on internal thought. In general, *assimilation* makes new information fit our existing views of the world, and *accommodation* changes our views to fit new information.

**PIAGET'S STAGES OF COGNITIVE DEVELOPMENT** The way a child thinks about the world progresses through four revolutionary changes. Piaget described these changes in terms of four *stages* of cognitive growth: the *sensorimotor stage* (infancy), the *preoperational stage* (early childhood), the *concrete operational stage* (middle childhood), and the *formal operational stage* (adolescence). At each stage, distinct styles of thinking emerge as the child progresses from sensory reaction to logical thought. It is important to note that all children progress through these stages in the same sequence, although one child may take longer to pass through a given stage than another.

*THE SENSORIMOTOR STAGE (Birth to about age two)* We have see that children enter the world equipped with many innate and reflexive behaviors, such as those for clinging, sucking, and crying. None of these require thought, in the sense of the complex mental activity seen in problem solving later in childhood. Instead, children in the **sensorimotor stage** give mainly reflexive or "instinctive" motor responses to stimulation, with very little "thinking" involved. Piaget called this

**Assimilation:** A mental process that modifies new information to fit it into existing schemes.

**Accommodation:** A mental process that restructures existing schemes so that new information is better understood.

**Sensorimotor stage:** The first stage in Piaget's theory, during which the child relies heavily on innate motor responses to stimuli.

Object permanence, the perception that objects exist independently of one's own actions or awareness, develops gradually during the first stage of cognitive development and is solidly formed before age one. The baby in these pictures clearly believes that the toy no longer exists once it is obscured by the screen.

**Sensorimotor intelligence:** The mental capacity shown in the first schemes an infant displays, which are mainly motor responses to stimuli, with a strong innate basis.

**Mental representation:** The ability to form internal images of objects and events.

**Object permanence:** The knowledge that objects exist independently of one's own actions or awareness.

**Preoperational stage:** The second stage in Piaget's theory, marked by well developed mental representation and the use of language.

**Egocentrism:** In Piaget's theory, the self-centered inability to realize that there are other viewpoints beside one's own.

**Animistic thinking:** A preoperational mode of thought in which inanimate objects are imagined to have life and mental processes.

**Centration:** A preoperational thought pattern involving the inability to take into account more than one factor at a time.

**sensorimotor intelligence.** Not everything is automatic, however. As we have seen, children at this stage are also capable of simple learning. They learn to recognize people they see frequently. And they learn to coordinate their body parts to grasp and explore attractive objects (a rattle, perhaps) or to avoid things that they dislike (such as the taste of a lemon wedge).

A major development of significance for later thinking and learning occurs in the second year: the ability to make internal **mental representations** of objects. With the power of mental representation, children can now form memories of objects and events that they retrieve later for use in thinking and problem solving. There is a vast mental difference, for example, between *pointing* to the toy one sees and *knowing* that an unseen toy must be somewhere so that it can be sought or asked for.

Gradually, the child takes mental representation one step farther, by realizing that objects continue to exist even when they are out of sight. This ability, called **object permanence,** liberates the child from the present and from its immediate surroundings. The basics are in place by one year of age, but the ability of object permanence continues to develop through the second year (Flavell, 1985). At the same time, language begins to appear, and so words become another way to make mental representations. Together these forms of representational thought become the major accomplishment of the sensorimotor stage.

*THE PREOPERATIONAL STAGE (From about two to six or seven years of age)* The cognitive advances in the next developmental stage, the **preoperational stage,** grow out of the ability to represent objects mentally. One of these advances involves the emerging sense of self as distinctive from other people and objects in the environment. Another advance involves the ability to solve simple problems using mental representation (such as searching different places for a lost toy). Yet, despite these abilities, the child cannot solve problems requiring logical thought. Three other important, limiting features of the child's mind in this period are *egocentrism, animistic thinking,* and *centration.*

- **Egocentrism,** a self-centered focus, causes children to see the world only in terms of themselves and their own position. Further, they assume that others see the world in the same way that they do. So, when talking to preoperational children on the phone, they may assume that you can see things on their end of the line. As a result of this egocentrism, they are not yet able to fully empathize with others or take others' points of view. For this reason children may act in ways that have destructive or hurtful consequences, even though they don't intend to upset or harm others.
- **Animistic thinking** involves the belief that inanimate objects have life and mental processes. For example, if a child slips and bangs her head on the table, she might complain about the "bad table," blaming it for hurting her. This is also the stage at which dolls and teddy bears come to life in the preoperational mind.
- **Centration** involves the inability to understand an event because the child focuses attention too narrowly, while ignoring other important information. So, for example, a thirsty child may insist on drinking a "big glass" of juice, preferring a tall narrow container to a short wide one, mistakenly assuming that the height of the glass ensures that it will hold more juice, while ignoring the other relevant dimension of width.

While we might see these as limitations, keep in mind that they are also the characteristics that make children at this stage most charming and interesting—and different from older children and adults.

*THE CONCRETE OPERATIONAL STAGE (From about seven to about eleven years of age)* At the next stage, children understand for the first time that many things may stay essentially the same, even when their superficial appearance changes. In this

This five-year-old girl is aware that the two containers have the same amount of colored liquid. However, when the liquid from one is poured into a taller container, she indicates that there is more liquid in the taller one. She has not yet grasped the concept of conservation, which she will understand by age six or seven.

**concrete operational stage,** they can understand that a short, wide glass can hold as much juice as a tall, narrow one. So, the short-wide versus tall-narrow glass problem that defeated the preoperational child now yields to a new understanding of the way that volume is *conserved*. Similarly, they now understand that a string of red beads is not longer than an identical string of blue beads, even though the red beads are stretched out in a line while the blue beads lie in a small pile. They realize that the beads *look* different in their grouping, but this does not mean that they *are* different in number. This new ability, called **conservation,** represents one of the most important cognitive breakthroughs that most seven-year-olds have made.

Along with the new ability to understand conservation, children at this stage acquire the capability for performing **mental operations.** Now they can solve problems by manipulating concepts entirely in their minds. This allows them to think things through before taking action. As a result, they may be less impulsive. They are also less gullible, giving up many "magical" notions, such as the belief in Santa Claus.

Using their ability for performing mental operations, concrete operational children begin to use simple logic and inference to solve problems. The symbols they use in reasoning are, however, still mainly symbols for concrete objects and events, not abstractions. The limitations of their concrete thinking are shown in the familiar game of "20 Questions," the goal of which is to determine the identity of an object by asking the fewest possible yes/no questions of the person who thinks up the object. A child of seven or eight usually sticks to very specific questions ("Is it a bird?" "Is it a cat?"), but does not ask the higher-level questions that more efficiently narrow down the possibilities for the correct answer ("Does it fly?" "Does it have hair?").

*THE FORMAL OPERATIONAL STAGE (From about age 12 on)* In the final stage of cognitive growth described by Piaget, the ability for abstract and complex thought appears. In this **formal operational stage** children also begin to ponder questions involving intangible concepts, such as truth, justice, relationships, and existence. Many adolescents begin, at last, to see that their particular reality is only one of several imaginable realities. With these formal operational reasoning powers, adolescents and adults now approach the "20 Questions" game in a way that demonstrates their ability to use abstractions and to adopt an information-processing strategy that is not merely random guesswork. They impose their own structures on the task, starting with broad categories and then formulating and testing hypotheses in light of their knowledge of categories and relationships. Their questioning moves from general categories ("Is it an animal?") to subcategories ("Does it fly?") and then to specific guesses ("Is it a bird?") (Bruner, Olver, & Greenfield, 1966).

**BEYOND PIAGET: CONTEMPORARY PERSPECTIVES ON COGNITIVE DEVELOPMENT** Most psychologists accept the broad picture that Piaget painted of the interplay between assimilation and accommodation (Flavell, 1996). However, newer research suggests that the transition between one stage and another is less abrupt than Piaget's theory implies. Also, researchers have shown that children are, in some ways, more intellectually sophisticated at each stage than Piaget had found (Munakata et

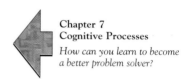

Chapter 7
Cognitive Processes
*How can you learn to become a better problem solver?*

**Concrete operational stage:** The third of Piaget's stages, when a child understands conservation, but still is incapable of abstract thought.

**Conservation:** The understanding that the physical properties of an object or substance do not change when appearances change but nothing is added or taken away.

**Mental operations:** Solving problems by manipulating images in one's mind.

**Formal operational stage:** The last of Piaget's stages, during which abstract thought appears.

## Playing with Children—Piagetian Style

If you have access to a child, you can try out some of the problems Piaget posed for his children in order to study their thinking. For example, with a preoperational or concrete operational child, it's always fun to give a conservation problem that involves pouring liquid from a tall, narrow container into a short, wide one. Begin by pouring the same amounts into two identical vessels, such as glass measuring cups. Get the child to agree that you are starting with the same amount in each. Then pour the liquid from one cup into a shallow pan. Ask the child, "Does one of these have more than the other, or are they both the same?" Then see if your child's responses fit with Piaget's observations.

Piaget found that the concrete operational child—who understands conservation—will know that the volume of liquid remains the same, regardless of the shape of the container. The preoperational child will think that the shallow pan has less because the liquid does not come up as far on the container. This shows that the younger child does not know that volume is conserved, regardless of the shape of the container. Piaget claimed that it also showed that the younger child cannot reason about both height and width simultaneously.

al., 1997). Recent research finds, for example, that some mental representation occurs as early as three months of age, rather than in the second year, as Piaget had thought (Gulya et al., 1998).

Some psychologists believe that what Piaget saw as limitations on preoperational thought may actually be the inability to *express* thoughts. So, preoperational children may actually *understand* some of the same concepts that older children do, but they may still lack the skills to perform accordingly. For example, a five-year-old child who has watched her father prepare breakfast in the past can watch him and understand what he is cooking, but may not be able to describe it to her visiting grandmother, or express why she likes her pancakes "the way Daddy fixes them." Researchers have found, in contrast with Piaget's notion of centration, that young children (ages three and four) understand that the "insides" of objects, although they are invisible, are not necessarily identical to their external appearances (Gelman & Wellman, 1991). And, in contrast with Piaget's claims about animistic thinking, three- to five-year-old children are consistently able to distinguish between real and purely mental (imaginary) entities (Wellman & Estes, 1986).

What is really needed, says Robert Siegler, is a new metaphor for development (Siegler, 1994). Instead of the abrupt changes implied by stage theories, he proposes that we think of "waves." The wave metaphor, he says, better fits both the scientific data and our everyday experience, which shows the variability of children's behavior. For example, a child may, during a single day, use several different strategies to solve the same linguistic problem: "I ate," "I eated," and "I ated." This is not the pattern we would find if a child were making a sudden leap from one stage to another. Instead, says Siegler, this is a pattern of overlapping developmental waves, where each wave can be thought of as the ebb and flow in the strength of a cognitive strategy (Azar, 1995).

### The Development of Moral Thinking

What shapes our sense of right and wrong? The best-known psychological approach to moral development comes from the late Lawrence Kohlberg (1964, 1981), who based his theory squarely on Piaget's theory of cognitive development. After all, reasoned Kohlberg, moral development is just a special form of cognitive develop-

**TABLE 4.2**  Kohlberg's Stages of Moral Reasoning

| LEVELS AND STAGES | REASONS FOR MORAL BEHAVIOR |
| --- | --- |
| I.   PRECONVENTIONAL MORALITY | |
|     Stage 1: Pleasure/pain orientation | Avoid pain or avoid getting caught |
|     Stage 2: Cost/benefit orientation; reciprocity ("an eye for an eye") | Achieve/receive rewards |
| II.   CONVENTIONAL MORALITY | |
|     Stage 3: "Good child" orientation | Gain acceptance, avoid disapproval |
|     Stage 4: Law-and-order orientation | Follow rules, avoid penalties |
| III.   POSTCONVENTIONAL (PRINCIPLED) MORALITY | |
|     Stage 5: Social contract orientation | Promote the welfare of one's society |
|     Stage 6: Ethical principle orientation | Achieve justice, avoid self-condemnation |

ment. Mirroring Piaget's views, each stage of moral reasoning proposed in Kohlberg's theory is based on a different moral standard. Table 4.2 summarizes these stages.

You can see how these stages of moral reasoning parallel the stages of Piaget's theory, as the individual moves from concrete, egocentric reasons to more other-oriented, abstract ideas of right and wrong. So, at the first stages, a child may not steal a cookie for fear of punishment, while at a more advanced level, the child may resist stealing for fear of not living up to the parents' expectations. In general, the earliest stages of moral reasoning are based on self-interest, while later, more advanced stages center on others' expectations or on broader standards of social good. Unfortunately, not all people attain the later, least egocentric stages. In fact, Kohlberg found, many adults never even reach Stage 4.

Does moral development follow the same rules everywhere? Yes, said Kohlberg. Cross-cultural work shows that individuals attain the same stages in the same order in all cultures studied, including Turkey, Taiwan, Guatemala, Japan, and the United States (Eckensberger, 1994). However, this research also hints at some limitations of the theory to explain moral development in other cultural contexts: the higher stages, as defined by Kohlberg, have not been found in all cultures. Even in his own culture, Kohlberg found that Stages 5 and 6 do not always appear. Their emergence appears to be associated with high levels of verbal ability and formal education (Rest & Thoma, 1976).

Kohlberg's theory of moral reasoning has generated considerable interest and much controversy. One of the most stinging criticisms has come from Carol Gilligan (1982), a colleague at Kohlberg's own campus. Gilligan has argued that Kohlberg's theory has a male bias and ignores uniquely feminine conceptions of morality. For women, says Gilligan, morality is embedded in social relationships and personal caring, which makes them appear to reach a plateau at Stage 3. To his credit, Kohlberg responded by taking a fresh look at his data for Stage 3 and Stage 4. As a result, he redefined Stage 4 by moving militant law-and-order responses (most often given by males) to Stage 3. Many subsequent studies have found no significant sex differences in moral reasoning (Walker, 1989, 1991; Walker & de Vries, 1985; Walker, de Vries, & Trevethan, 1987).

## Social and Emotional Development

Our moral development is closely linked to our abilities to get along with others. So is a child's very survival, which depends on forming meaningful, effective relationships. This means that children need to learn the rules that their society uses for governing its members' social and political interactions. They must also learn to deal with their own feelings and those of others.

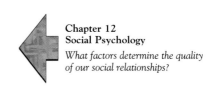

**Chapter 12
Social Psychology**
*What factors determine the quality of our social relationships?*

**Chapter 8**
**Emotion and Motivation**
*Some facial expressions of
emotion are universal.*

Smiling is one way people begin simple social and emotional interactions. So essential is a smile to human communication that a baby's first smile is probably generated automatically by genetically controlled processes. In fact, smiles occur in babies everywhere (Gazzaniga, 1998). The delight parents take in a baby's first smile represents the beginning of lifelong lessons in social behavior. People smile not only as a sign of positive feelings but also because their audience expects such a facial expression (Fridlund, 1990). However, social and emotional development involves much more than a winning smile. On the "nurture" side, psychologists have found many environmental factors that influence relationships, particularly the special social relationship called *attachment*. And on the "nature" side, they have found that an innate *temperament* influences our responsiveness to others. We will analyze these important concepts more deeply.

**Chapter 10**
**Personality**
**Chapter 13**
**Psychopathology**
*Patterns of shyness in adulthood*

**TEMPERAMENT**     Psychologists use the term **temperament** for an individual's inherited, enduring pattern of reacting to environmental stimuli and situations. Thus, temperament is the part of personality that is "wired in" at birth. Harvard researcher Jerome Kagan, who has studied temperament in thousands of children, has observed that about 10 to 15% of infants are "born shy" or "born bold" (Kagan, Resnick, & Suidman, 1994; Kagan & Snidman, 1991; Kagan, Resnick, & Snidman, 1986). The infants in these groups differ in sensitivity to physical and social stimulation. Specifically, the shy baby is more easily frightened and less socially responsive. As a result, people are less likely to interact and be playful with the shy baby, accentuating the child's initial disposition.

Shyness is a temperamental factor, according to Jerome Kagan.

Ironically, Kagan began his work on temperament with the assumption that reaction styles were best explained by social influences. He assumed, for example, that a shy child must have *learned* timidity as a result of unpleasant social experiences. Today, however, Kagan has adopted a position that gives much greater weight to biological predisposition (Gallagher, 1994; Kagan, 1994). In Kagan's new view, there are three basic temperament styles expressed in all people's behavior: fear, aggression, and sociability. Fearful children may have been born with a tendency to exaggerate the danger in the situations they encounter, and they grow to become avoidant, uncomfortable adults. Aggressive individuals approach problems by trying to fight them, becoming irritated, blaming others, and striking out at them. Sociable, outgoing children approach the world boldly and handle difficulties with equanimity. They are able to adapt to both surprise and disappointment without becoming either depressed or offensive.

**Chapter 6**
**Learning and Remembering**
*Learning by consequences is
called* operant conditioning.

While these temperaments are in place from birth, they are not written in stone (Kagan, 1996). Experience and parenting styles can modify the way a constitutional factor such as temperament expresses itself. For example, a bold child reared by bold parents will certainly experience and respond to the world differently from a bold child reared by timid or fearful parents. Likewise, if a shy baby's parents recognize the child's withdrawal and gently play with her and encourage her to interact, the child may become more outgoing than her temperament would otherwise have predicted. Thus family members and friends can teach every individual a variety of responses to the world, all within his or her temperamental range. Nor is one temperament ideal for all situations. We should "remember that in a complex society like ours, each temperamental type can find its adaptive niche" (Kagan, quoted in Gallagher, 1994, p. 47).

**Temperament:** An individual's characteristic manner of behavior or reaction—assumed to have a strong genetic basis.

**SOCIALIZATION AND ATTACHMENT**   In order to help children find the most adaptive niche for their abilities and temperament, parents *socialize* their offspring. **Socialization** is the lifelong process of shaping an individual's behavior patterns, values, standards, skills, attitudes, and motives to conform to those regarded as desirable in a particular society (Hetherington & Parke, 1975). Besides parents, many individuals and institutions exert pressure on the individual to adopt socially approved values. Among these, the family is certainly the most influential regulator of socialization, at least during childhood. The patterns of social responsiveness learned in the family form the basis of the individual's habitual style of relating to other people. And of these social response patterns, the most basic is learned in the infant's experience of *attachment.*

*INFANT ATTACHMENT*   Ideally, social development begins with the establishment of a close emotional relationship between a child and parent figure. This intense, enduring, relationship is called **attachment.** Developmental psychologists find that the attachment relationship is especially important because the quality of attachment lays the foundation for all other relationships that follow.

Attachment behaviors appear to occur "instinctively" in many species, but they are not necessarily limited to the infant's interactions with its biological parents. One striking example of instinctive attachment occurs in **imprinting,** the powerful attraction of infants of some species to the first moving object or individual they see. A baby chick hatched by a mother duck will form an attachment to this surrogate parent, staying close to her and following her right up to the water's edge when she and her ducklings go for a swim. The imprinting tendency is an innate predisposition, although the organism's environment and experience determine what form it will take. While imprinting occurs most clearly in birds, a similar, but more complex, process may account for the attachment between human infants and their caregivers.

**Chapter 8
Emotion and Motivation**
*"Instinct" refers to behaviors that have a strong genetic basis.*

Although humans apparently have an inborn need for attachment, there is no guarantee that parents will always respond to this need. What, then, can babies do to increase the chances of getting the contact they want? Unlike a baby chick, human babies are not mobile enough at birth to use their own locomotion to get closeness or attention from a caregiver. When they want to get close to the attachment figure (*e.g.,* their mother), they cannot simply crawl or move toward her. But they can emit signals—such as smiling, crying, and vocalizing—to promote responsive behavior (Campos et al., 1983). Who can resist a baby's smile? According to John Bowlby (1973), infants will form attachments to any individual who consistently and appropriately responds to their signals.

Some observers have suggested that attachment begins as early as the first few weeks (Bowlby, 1969, 1973; Ainsworth, 1973; Ainsworth et al., 1978). One study found, for example, that when mothers left the room, their two- to four-month-old babies' skin temperature dropped, a sign of emotional distress (Mizukami et al., 1990). In these youngsters, skin temperature dropped even more when a stranger replaced the mother. In contrast, skin temperature remained steady if the mother stayed in the room—even if the stranger was present. Apparently, children only a few months old rely on their caretakers as a "safe base," even before they can indicate attachment with crying or locomotion (Bee, 1994).

Developmental psychologist Mary Ainsworth has studied the various forms attachment takes by observing young children in a variety of "strange situations." She does this by separating them by a barrier from their mothers or by putting them in an unfamiliar room (Ainsworth, 1989; Ainsworth et al., 1978; Ainsworth & Wittig, 1969). Using

Konrad Lorenz (1903–1989), the researcher who pioneered the study of imprinting, graphically demonstrated what can happen when young animals become imprinted on someone other than their mother.

**Socialization:** The lifelong process of developing behavior patterns, values, standards, skills, attitudes, and motives that conform to those regarded as desirable in a society.

**Attachment:** The enduring social-emotional relationship between a child and a parent or other regular caregiver.

**Imprinting:** A primitive form of learning in which some young animals follow and form an attachment to the first moving object they see and hear.

Children become attached to their caregivers, and parents bond to their children. These bonds of love and responsibility help offset the daily struggles for survival faced by poor families the world over.

this method in a variety of cultures, Ainsworth found that the children's responses were of two main types: They were either *securely* or *insecurely* attached. Securely attached children felt close to their mothers, safe, and more willing to explore or tolerate a novel experience—confident that they could cry out for help or be reunited with the missing parent. Insecurely attached children were more likely to react to the "strange situation" in one of two ways: with anxiety and **ambivalence** or with avoidance. The anxious-ambivalent children wanted contact but cried with fear and anger when separated and proved difficult to console even when reunited with their mothers. The avoidant children acted as though they were unconcerned about being separated from their mothers, not crying when they left and not seeking contact when they returned. Avoidant children may be showing the effects of repeated rejection, no longer seeking attachment because their efforts have failed in the past (Shaver & Hazan, 1994).

Attachment fascinates researchers because patterns established in infancy seem to persist in a variety of childhood and even adult behaviors, influencing later-life job satisfaction, relationship choices, and intimacy experiences (Bower, 1997; Collins & Read, 1990; Hazan & Shaver, 1990, 1992; Shaver & Hazan, 1993, 1994). As children grow up and become adults, they no longer restrict their attachment to their primary caregiver. While they retain their childhood attachment style, they gradually widen their attachments to include peers, friends, teachers, coworkers, and others in their community. We should emphasize, however, that—powerful as attachment is—individuals who lack healthy attachments in infancy and childhood are not necessarily doomed to failure in life. While attachment problems are good predictors of later problems with social relationships, many people do succeed in overcoming attachment difficulties (Kagan, 1996, 1998). With that caution in mind, take the quiz on your own attachment style in *Do It Yourself! What's Your Attachment Style?*

*CONTACT COMFORT* Why and how do infants become attached to caregivers in the first place? An evolutionary explanation says that attachment safeguards an infant's survival by assuring the support and protection it requires. Through natural selection individuals with genetic tendencies to "attach" will survive, thrive, and pass those tendencies along to their own offspring.

In addition to protection, could attachment also be a child's way of encouraging the parents to provide food, an infant's most basic physical need? This has been dubbed the "cupboard theory" of attachment: Individuals become attached to those who provide the "cupboard" containing the food supply. This view has been a favorite of those who believe that nursing is the basis for healthy relationships. But does the cupboard theory really explain attachment?

Psychologists Harry and Margaret Harlow guessed that a more fundamental cause of attachment involves physical contact (Harlow, 1965; Harlow & Harlow, 1966). To see if they were right, they decided to test this idea against the cupboard theory in an animal model, using infant monkeys who had been

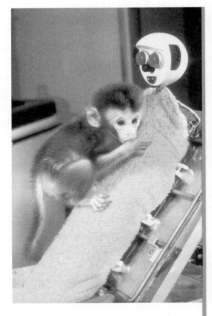

One of Harlow's monkeys and its artificial terry-cloth mother. Harlow found that the contact comfort mothers provide is essential for normal social development.

**Ambivalence:** Having conflicting thoughts or feelings.

## What's Your Attachment Style?

Identify which one of the following three self-descriptions you most agree with (adapted from Shaver & Hazan, 1994):

1. I am somewhat uncomfortable being close to others; I find it difficult to trust them completely, difficult to allow myself to depend on them. I am nervous when anyone gets too close, and often, love partners want me to be more intimate than I feel comfortable being.

2. I find that others are reluctant to get as close as I would like. I often worry that my partner doesn't really love me or won't want to stay with me. I want to get very close to my partner, and this sometimes scares people away.

3. I find it relatively easy to get close to others and am comfortable depending on them. I don't often worry about being abandoned or about someone getting to close to me.

### WHAT YOUR CHOICE MEANS

We realize that it is probably obvious to you which of the statements above is "best." Nevertheless, just considering the alternatives should help you understand attachment styles—and, perhaps, yourself—a little better. Here's our interpretation: If you selected the first statement, you agreed with the attitude that reflects an avoidant, insecure attachment. This style was chosen by 25% of Shaver and Hazan's respondent sample. The second statement reflects an anxious-ambivalent, insecure attachment style, selected by 20% of the sample. The third statement reflects a secure attachment style, the most common pattern identified, accounting for 55% of respondents (Shaver & Hazan, 1994).

What do these styles portend for later life? Through interviews, observations, and questionnaires, researchers have identified several consequences of attachment style, secure or insecure, in adulthood (see Ainsworth, 1989; Collins & Read, 1990; Hazan & Shaver, 1990; Kirkpatrick & Shaver, 1992; Shaver & Hazan, 1993, 1994; Simpson, 1990):

- Secure individuals have more positive self-concepts and believe that most other people are good-natured and well-intentioned. They see their personal relationships as trustworthy and satisfying.
- Secure respondents are satisfied with their job security, coworkers, income, and work activity. They put a higher value on relationships than on work and derive their greatest pleasure from connections to others.
- Insecure, anxious-ambivalent persons report emotional extremes and jealousy. They feel unappreciated, insecure, and unlikely to win professional advancement. They make less money than those with other attachment styles, working more for approval and recognition than financial gain. They fantasize about succeeding, but often slack off after receiving praise.
- Avoidant people fear intimacy and expect their relationships to fail. They place a higher value on work than on relationships and generally like their work and job security. They follow a workaholic pattern, but (not surprisingly) they are dissatisfied with their coworkers.
- Secure individuals tend to choose as partners others who are secure. After breakups, avoidant individuals claim to be less bothered by the loss of the relationship, although this may be a defensive claim, with distress showing up in other ways (e.g., physical symptoms).

separated from their mothers at birth. The Harlows placed orphaned baby monkeys in cages where they had access to two artificial **surrogate mothers.** One was a simple wire figure that provided milk through a nipple—a "cupboard," but little else. The other was a cloth-covered figure providing no milk but offering abundant stimulation from its soft terry-cloth cover. Confirming their expectations, the Harlows observed that their baby monkeys spent many hours nestled close to the cloth mother but little time with the wire model, despite the nourishment the latter provided. Moreover, when the baby monkeys were frightened, they sought comfort by clinging to the cloth figure. They also used it as a base of operations when exploring new situations. With these observations, then, the Harlows were able to show that the infant monkeys become attached to and prefer a "mother" figure that provides **contact comfort,** stimulation and reassurance derived from physical touch.

Human infants need contact comfort, too. The lack of a close, loving relationship in infancy even affects physical growth. We know this from observations of children in emotionally detached or hostile family environments: Such children have

**Surrogate mothers:** Mother substitutes, such as the cloth and wire dummies in Harlow's research.

**Contact comfort:** Stimulation and reassurance derived from the physical touch of a caregiver.

slower growth and bone development. They may grow again if removed from the poor environment, but their growth is stunted again if they are returned to it, a phenomenon known as *psychosocial dwarfism*. Accordingly, in some hospitals that recognize the power of contact comfort, premature infants and those born at risk (such as those born to crack-addicted mothers) are scheduled to receive regular holding and cuddling by staff members and volunteers. Clearly, a close, interactive relationship with loving adults is a child's first step toward healthy physical growth and normal socialization.

*EFFECTS OF DAY CARE*   As families make increasing use of day care for their children, many people have wondered: How necessary is it to have a full-time parent? The question is an urgent one in the United States, where over half of all mothers with children under age three are employed, and more children are cared for by paid providers than by relatives (Scarr, 1997; 1998). The research sends us mixed messages (Bower, 1996; Clarke-Stewart, 1989). First the good news: Most children thrive in day care. They do as well—sometimes better—both intellectually and socially as children raised at home by a parent. Now the bad news: Some day care experiences make children aggressive, depressed, or otherwise maladjusted. Fortunately, the overwhelming majority of day care centers do a fine job.

Even though negative effects of day care are rare, it is instructive to see what factors are associated with bad outcomes. The research shows that having multiple caregivers does *not* cause psychological problems. Instead, difficulties surface most often in poorly staffed centers where large numbers of children get little attention from only a few adult caregivers (Howes et al., 1988). Another problem results from the fact that children who are placed in the poorest-quality day care programs are most often from the poorest, most disorganized, and most highly stressed families. Developmental psychologist Laura Berk (1991) concludes that this volatile combination of inadequate day care and family pressures places some children at high risk. Yet, she says, using this evidence to curtail day care services would be mistaken, because forcing a parent on a marginal income to stay home may expose children to an even greater level of risk.

All this means that day care is, in itself, neither good nor bad. It is the *quality of care*, whether given by a parent or a paid provider, that makes all the difference. Development expert Sandra Scarr (1998) says:

> There is an extraordinary international consensus among child-care researchers and practitioners about what quality child care is: It is warm, supportive interactions with adults in a safe, healthy, and stimulating environment, where early education and trusting relationships combine to support individual children's physical, emotional, social, and intellectual development. . . . (p. 102)

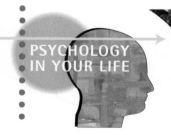

**PSYCHOLOGY IN YOUR LIFE**

## Childhood Influences on Your Personality

Your personality and your social relationships are a complex blend of your temperament, attachment style, and many other forces that have acted on you through life. But do these

factors produce predictable patterns across the life span? A theory of personality proposed by psychoanalyst Erik Erikson says yes. *(See also Chapter 10, Personality.)*

As a middle-aged immigrant to America, Erik Erikson (1963) became aware of conflicts and choices he faced because of

his new status. This caused him to reflect on the many such conflicts every individual must face in the continuing process of development. Before reading further, please take a moment to do as Erikson did: Recall some of the conflicts or crises you have experienced. These will give you

**TABLE 4.3** Erikson's Psychosocial Crises

| AGE/PERIOD (APPROXIMATE) | CRISIS | ADEQUATE RESOLUTION | INADEQUATE RESOLUTION |
|---|---|---|---|
| 0 to 1½ years | Trust vs. mistrust | Basic sense of safety, security; ability to rely on forces outside oneself | Insecurity, anxiety |
| 1½ to 3 years | Autonomy vs. self-doubt | Perception of self as agent; capable of controlling one's own body and making things happen | Feelings of inadequacy about self-control, control of events |
| 3 to 6 years | Initiative vs. guilt | Confidence in oneself as being able to initiate, create | Feeling of lack of self-worth |
| 6 years to puberty | Competence vs. inferiority | Adequacy in basic social and intellectual skills; acceptance by peers | Lack of self-confidence; feelings of failure |
| Adolescence | Identity vs. role confusion | Comfortable sense of self as a person, both unique and socially accepted | Sense of self as fragmented, shifting, unclear sense of self |
| Early adulthood | Intimacy vs. isolation | Capacity for closeness and commitment to another | Feeling of aloneness, loneliness, separation; denial of intimacy needs |
| Middle adulthood | Generativity vs. stagnation | Focus of concern beyond oneself, to family, society, future generations | Self-indulgent concerns; lack of future orientation |
| Late adulthood | Ego-integrity vs. despair | Sense of wholeness; basic satisfaction with life | Feelings of futility, disappointment |

a vantage point from which to understand Erikson's theory—and your own personality.

## ERIKSON'S THEORY OF PSYCHOSOCIAL DEVELOPMENT ACROSS THE LIFE SPAN

Erikson saw human development as a sequence of challenges that emerge at many stages in the life course, from infancy to old age. His theory says that when people face these **psychosocial crises** they make choices that influence the growth of their personalities across the entire life span. Positive choices—choices that bring people closer to others and enhance their self-esteem—lay the foundation for healthy growth during later stages of development. Negative choices lead to a shaky foundation for further development and consequent unhappiness.

What are the major psychosocial crises that shape our personalities? Erikson identified eight such challenges. With each, a particular conflict comes into focus, as shown in Table 4.3. The conflict must be sufficiently resolved at a given stage if an individual is to cope successfully with the new crises of later stages. Here we will review the psychosocial crises of childhood;

in the following section we will review the crises experienced in adolescence and adulthood.

**TRUST VERSUS MISTRUST** In the first stage of your psychosocial development, you needed to develop a basic sense of trust in your environment and in those who cared for you. This trust is a natural accompaniment to a strong attachment relationship with a caregiver who provides food, warmth, and the comfort of physical closeness. But if these basic needs were not met, Erikson suggested, you experienced a developmental crisis. At this stage, inconsistent handling, lack of physical closeness and warmth, or the frequent absence of a caring adult may produce a lasting sense of mistrust, insecurity, and anxiety. Children facing such conditions will not be prepared for the second stage in their psychological development. The healthy personality requires a foundation of trust from which the individual can become more adventurous.

**AUTONOMY VERSUS SELF-DOUBT** In the second stage, as you acquired skills in walking and talking, you expanded your exploration and manipulation of objects

(and sometimes of people). If you entered this stage with a sense of trust, these activities should have brought you a comfortable sense of **autonomy** (independence) and of being a capable and worthy person. Excessive restriction or criticism at this stage may have led to self-doubts. Demands made on you beyond your ability—such as attempting toilet training too early—could have discouraged your efforts to persevere in mastering new tasks. Such demands also can lead to stormy scenes of confrontation, disrupting the supportive parent–child relationship. In contrast, the two-year-old who affirms the right to do something without help, in response to appropriate demands, acts out of a need to affirm his or her autonomy and adequacy.

**Psychosocial crises:** In Erikson's theory, any of the eight major developmental challenges across the life span, which require an individual to rethink his or her orientation to self and others.

**Autonomy:** The ability to act independently.

*Continued*

**INITIATIVE VERSUS GUILT** If you developed a basic sense of trust and autonomy during your preschool days, you probably became a child who could comfortably initiate intellectual and motor tasks. For example, children in this stage want to do things for themselves, such as pour a glass of juice, choose what to wear, or get dressed. The danger at this stage is that overcontrolling adults will demand an impossible degree of self-control ("Why can't you sit still?"), and the child will be overcome by feelings of inadequacy and guilt. Caregivers' responses to self-initiated activities either encourage or discourage the freedom and self-confidence needed for the next stage.

**COMPETENCE VERSUS INFERIORITY** If you successfully resolved the crises of the

three earlier stages, you were ready to go beyond random exploration to develop your skills and competencies in a more systematic way. During the elementary school years, school and sports offer arenas for learning more complex intellectual and motor skills, while peer interaction offers the chance to develop social skills. Successful efforts in these pursuits lead to feelings of competence. Some youngsters, however, become discouraged spectators rather than performers, or they experience discouraging failure that leaves them with a sense of inferiority. Such children will find it more difficult to face continuing challenges and crises of psychosocial development.

**THE CURRENT STATUS OF ERIKSON'S THEORY** How much confidence should we

place in Erikson? Although widely accepted, his developmental theory does have some shortcomings. Based mainly on clinical observation, it lacks a rigorous scientific basis. Moreover, as some critics point out, Erikson's crises do not capture the problems faced by girls and women as well as they do those faced by boys and men, especially in the later periods of life, which we will cover in the next section. Despite these problems, however, Erikson's work should be seen as a comprehensive pioneering effort that has encouraged us to look at the life cycle as a whole, putting into perspective both the unfolding changes and the continuity of life experience.

## Check Your Understanding

1. RECALL: *Noam Chomsky has presented evidence supporting his theory that*
   a. children learn language by imitating their parents.
   b. children are born with some rules of grammar programmed into their brains.
   c. vocabulary is innate, but grammar is learned.
   d. different languages may have entirely different rules of grammar.

2. RECALL: *Match the ability/limitation with the Piagetian stage at which it appears.*
   a. centration
   b. abstract thought
   c. innate schemes
   d. conservation
   
   i. sensorimotor stage
   ii. preoperational stage
   iii. concrete operational stage
   iv. formal operational stage

3. RECALL: *According to Kohlberg, as moral reasoning advances, individuals become less*
   a. emotional.
   b. self-centered.
   c. ruled by instinct.
   d. attached to their parents.

4. RECALL: *Mary Ainsworth found two main types of attachment,*
   a. shy and bold.
   b. introverted and extraverted.
   c. secure and insecure.
   d. strong and weak.

5. APPLICATION: *You are a psychologist working in a pediatric hospital. What would you recommend as one of the most important things that the staff could do for newborn babies to promote their healthy development?*
   a. Talk to them.
   b. Touch them.
   c. Make eye contact with them.
   d. Feed them on demand.

6. UNDERSTANDING THE CORE CONCEPT: *Children are different from adults with respect to their language, their thought processes, and their social relationships. Can you name one way that young children are different from adults in each of these three areas?*

**ANSWERS:** 1. b  2. a. ii, b. iv, c. i, d. iii  3. b
4. c  5. b  6. Language: both vocabulary and grammar. Thought processes: for example, young children are not capable of abstract reasoning; Piaget's theory suggests other differences at each stage. Social relationships: adult attachments broaden to include peers, friends, coworkers, and others.

# WHAT DEVELOPMENTAL CHANGES OCCUR IN ADOLESCENCE AND ADULTHOOD?

Many cultures have initiation rites that signal a child's passage into adulthood. This photo shows the initiation ceremony of a young Lamaist monk.

Most early theorists assumed that the major work of development occurred before adolescence. After that, they believed, the psyche was set for life and would undergo few important changes. Modern research challenges such notions. It suggests that the long-term effects of early infant and childhood experiences are highly variable and continue to be influenced by later experiences. Psychologists now agree that we have a remarkable capacity for change throughout our life span (Kagan, 1996, 1998). This is the Core Concept of life-span development:

**Nature and nurture continue to produce changes in personality and mental processes throughout the life cycle.**

We will trace some of these changes below, as they occur through adolescence, adulthood, and at the end of life.

## The Transitions of Adolescence

Do you remember what event first made you think of yourself as an adolescent? Chances are that it had something to do with your sexual maturation, such as a first menstrual period or a nocturnal ejaculation. Psychologists pinpoint the beginning of **adolescence** at the onset of **puberty,** when sexual maturity, or the ability to reproduce, is attained. However, they cannot so precisely identify the point at which adolescence ends and adulthood begins. Variations among cultures compound the difficulty of delimiting the span of adolescence. Although the physical changes that take place at this stage are universal, the social and psychological dimensions of the adolescent experience depend heavily on the cultural context. For example, if you enter your teen years in a culture that celebrates puberty as the start of adult status and rewards you with the power to make responsible choices, you will have a very different experience from someone whose culture condemns teenagers as confused and potentially dangerous troublemakers.

Most nonindustrial societies do not identify an adolescent stage as we know it. Instead, children in these societies move directly into adulthood with **rites of passage.** These rituals usually take place around puberty and serve as a public acknowledgment of the transition from childhood to adulthood. Rites of passage vary widely among cultures, from extremely painful rituals to periods of instruction in sexual and cultural practices or periods of seclusion involving survival ordeals. For example, in some tribal cultures, the young person may be asked to take a meditative journey alone or to submit to symbolic scarring or circumcision surrounded by friends and family. Once individuals have completed the passage, there is no ambiguity about their status: They are adults, and the ties to their childhood have been severed.

Our own society has few transition rituals to help children clearly mark their new adolescent status or for adolescents to know when they have become young adults. One subtle rite of passage for many teenagers in our society is qualifying for a driver's license. Both symbolically and practically, being able to drive a car legally provides a young person with freedom, independence, and mobility that is not available to children.

Although many issues are important in adolescence, we will focus on a few of the most important developmental tasks that confront adolescents in Western society: coming to terms with physical maturity and adult sexuality; redefining social

**Adolescence:** In industrial societies, a developmental period beginning at puberty and ending (less clearly) at adulthood.

**Puberty:** The onset of sexual maturity.

**Rites of passage:** Social rituals that mark the transition between developmental stages, especially between childhood and adulthood.

Body image becomes especially important in the teenage years.

roles, including achieving autonomy from parents; and deciding upon occupational goals. Each of these issues is a component of the central task of establishing an integrated identity.

**PHYSICAL MATURATION** The first concrete indicator of the end of childhood is the *pubescent growth spurt.* Two to three years after the onset of the growth spurt, puberty, or sexual maturity, is reached. Puberty for males begins with the production of live sperm (usually about age 14 in the United States), while for girls it begins at **menarche,** the onset of menstruation (between ages 11 and 15).

Attractiveness influences the way we view each other (Hatfield & Rapson, 1993), and during adolescence an attractive appearance takes on vastly increased importance for many people. Part of achieving a personal identity involves coming to terms with one's physical self by developing a realistic yet accepting body image (one's personal and subjective view of one's own appearance). This image is dependent not only on measurable features, such as height and weight, but also on perceptions of other people's assessments and on cultural standards of physical beauty. During adolescence, dramatic physical changes and heightened emphasis on peer acceptance (especially peers of the opposite sex) can intensify concern with one's body image.

Approximately 44% of American adolescent girls and 23% of boys claimed that they "frequently felt ugly and unattractive"; similar data have been found across many cultures (Offer, Ostrov, & Howard, 1981; Offer et al., 1988). Physical appearance is clearly one of the biggest concerns among adolescents (Perkins & Lerner, 1995). Girls' self-concepts are particularly tied to perceptions of their physical attractiveness, while boys seem more concerned with their physical prowess, athletic ability, and effectiveness in achieving goals (Lerner, Orlos, & Knapp, 1976; Wade, 1991). Girls and women are more dissatisfied with their weight and shape than are males, and experience more conflict about food and eating (Rolls, Federoff, & Guthrie, 1991). These differences probably mirror a cultural preoccupation with female beauty and male strength—an inevitable source of concern because not all adolescents can embody the cultural ideals of attractiveness. There are also cultural influences on self-concept; some research indicates that the self-esteem of white adolescents of both sexes is more tied to physical attractiveness than is that of black adolescents (Wade, 1991). Over time, adolescents seem to become more accepting of their appearances. Nonetheless, the attainment of acceptable body images can be a difficult task.

**SEXUALITY** A new awareness of sexual feelings and impulses accompanies physical maturity. In one large study, the majority of American adolescent males and females said that they often think about sex (Offer et al., 1981). Yet many still lack adequate knowledge or have misconceptions about sex and sexuality—even if they are sexually active. Sex is a topic parents find difficult to discuss with children, so adolescents tend to be secretive about sexual concerns, making exchange of information and communication even more difficult. The development of a sexual identity that defines sexual orientation and guides sexual behavior thus becomes an important task of adolescence.

In early adolescence masturbation is the most common orgasmic expression of sexual impulses (Bell, Weinberg, & Hammersmith, 1981; Coles & Stokes, 1985; Wilson & Medora, 1990). Between 14 and 17% of teenage boys and half that many girls report some homosexual experiences (broadly defined as becoming sexually aroused with a person of the same sex), although most of these individuals ultimately identify with a heterosexual orientation (Hass, 1979; Sorensen, 1973; Wyatt, Peters, & Guthrie, 1988). Exclusively homosexual feelings are much more difficult to resolve during adolescence, when individuals are intensely concerned with the conventions and norms of their society. While most gay and lesbian individuals first become aware of their sexual orientation in early adolescence, many may not attain

**Chapter 8
Emotion and Motivation**
*Research has not been able to link sexual orientation to parenting styles.*

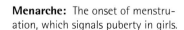

**Menarche:** The onset of menstruation, which signals puberty in girls.

self-acceptance of their sexual identities until their middle or late twenties (Newman & Muzzonigro, 1993; Riddle & Morin, 1977). The time lag undoubtedly reflects the relative lack of social support for a homosexual orientation and exemplifies the importance of society's role in all aspects of identity development.

The proportion of adolescents engaging in sexual intercourse rose substantially during the 1970s and 1980s but leveled off in the 1990s (Chilman, 1983; London et al., 1989; Reinisch, 1990; Zeman, 1990). Currently about half of all young people have engaged in intercourse before age 17, and about 75% have done so by the age of 20 (Harvey & Spigner, 1995). There is evidence that the initial sexual experiences of males and females differ substantially. For the vast majority of females emotional involvement is an important ingredient of sexual attraction. In contrast, for most males personal relationships appear to be less important than the sex act itself. In fact, the average male reports no emotional involvement with his first sexual partner (Miller & Simon, 1980).

**SOCIAL IDENTITY AND THE IDENTITY CRISIS**   Erik Erikson believed that the essential crisis of adolescence is discovering one's true *identity* amid the confusion of playing many different roles for different audiences in an expanding social world. Resolving this **identity crisis** helps the individual develop a sense of a coherent self. Failure to resolve the identity crisis adequately may result in a self-image that lacks a stable core. This was apparent in Benny's case, which we considered at the beginning of the chapter. Resolution of this issue is both a personal process and a social experience (Erikson, 1968). (Review Table 4.3 for Erikson's concept of the adolescent identity crisis.)

Chapter 10
Personality
*The self-concept is a core component of the personality, according to many theorists.*

According to Erikson, during the "identity crisis," adolescents must define their identities as individuals even as they seek the comfort and feeling of belonging that comes from being with friends and family. One compromise might be to experiment with different norms—such as clothing or hairstyles—within the security of supportive relationships with companions, cliques, or romantic partners.

Several factors influence the move toward an emerging self-identity. Family ties become stretched as the adolescent spends more time outside the home (Paikoff & Brooks-Gunn, 1991). Indeed, some developmental psychologists argue that the effects of parents, family, and childhood become nearly lost as the adolescent peer group gains influence (Harris, 1995). In American society, the adolescent encounters new values, receives less structure and adult guidance, and feels a strong need for peer acceptance. As a result, adolescents report spending more than four times as much time talking to peers as to adults (Csikszentmihalyi, Larson, & Prescott, 1977). With their peers, adolescents refine their social skills and try out different social behaviors. Gradually, they define their social identities, the kind of people they choose to be, and the sorts of relationships they will pursue.

Loneliness also becomes significant during adolescence: Between 15 and 25% of adolescents report feeling very lonely (Offer et al., 1981). Similarly, shyness reaches its highest level in early teenage years as the desire for social acceptance

**Identity crisis:** In Erikson's theory, the developmental crisis of adolescence.

Chapter 10
Personality
Chapter 13
Psychopathology
*Causes of shyness.*

markedly increases (Zimbardo, 1990). Studies of adolescent suicide show that the triggering experience for such a tragedy is often a shaming or humiliating event, such as failure in some achievement or a romantic rejection (Garland & Zigler, 1993). The intensity of a young person's social and personal motives can make it hard to keep perspective and recognize that even difficult times will pass and that everyone makes mistakes.

As the need for close friendships and peer acceptance becomes greater, anxiety about the possibility of rejection increases. Many young adolescents may choose the "safe" route of conformity and go along with their friends to avoid weakening those relationships. Females may be especially concerned with personal relationships, but they are less likely than males to give in to group pressure to behave antisocially (Berndt, 1979). Many parents worry that their teenagers will endanger themselves in proving their loyalty to unreasonable friends or norms. Fortunately, research suggests that most adolescents are able to "look before they leap" by considering the wisdom of committing risky acts (Berndt, 1992).

The dual forces of parents and peers at times exhibit conflicting influences on adolescents, intensifying the separation from parents and increasing identification with peers. But generally parents and peers serve complementary functions and fulfill different needs in adolescents' lives (Davis, 1985). For example, adolescents look to their families for structure and support, while they look to their friends for acceptance and approval. Ultimately, identity development involves establishing independent commitments that are sensitive to both parents and peers.

But, is adolescence inevitably a period of turmoil? For some, adolescence certainly presents overwhelming problems in relationships and in self-esteem. As a survey of the research has concluded, "The adolescent years mark the beginning of a downward spiral for some individuals" (Eccles et al., 1993, p. 90). For most teens, however, these years are *not* a time of anxiety and despair (Myers & Diener, 1995). While many parents anticipate that the relationship with their children will encounter a rocky road when the children enter adolescence, the more typical experience is relatively tranquil. In fact, the majority of adolescent youth say that they feel close to their parents (Galambos, 1992).

**OCCUPATIONAL CHOICES**   According to Erikson, deciding on a vocational commitment is a central issue of adolescent identity formation. The question, "What are you going to be when you grow up?" reflects the common assumption that what you *do* determines what you *are*. It also requires the ability to think about the future and to set realistic goals that are both achievable and likely to be satisfying. Anticipating the future—mentally imagining its possibilities—strongly influences adolescents' motivation and abilities to plan and evaluate life choices (Nurmi, 1991).

While many factors affect vocational interests and achievement, the clearest is socioeconomic background. Adolescents from families of higher socioeconomic status are more likely to pursue and complete education beyond high school and to aspire toward and achieve higher levels of personal and social success. Middle-class and upper-middle-class parents encourage higher achievement motivation in their children, model greater career success, and supply the economic resources unavailable to poorer children (Achenbach, 1982; Featherman, 1980; Gustafson & Magnusson, 1991). We saw another powerful factor in our chapter-opening case, where birth order and family position affected achievement motivation (Sulloway, 1996).

## The Developmental Challenges of Adulthood

The transition from adolescence to young adulthood is marked by decisions about advanced education, career, and intimate relationships. Making such decisions and adjusting to the consequences are major tasks of adulthood because they shape the course of adult psychological development. We might ask: What are the psychological forces that shape these decisions?

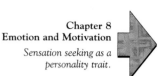

**Chapter 12**
**Social Psychology**
*Factors that influence conformity.*

**Chapter 8**
**Emotion and Motivation**
*Sensation seeking as a personality trait.*

**Chapter 8**
**Emotion and Motivation**
*McClelland studied the characteristics of people with a high need for achievement.*

**LOVE AND WORK**   According to Freud, adult development is driven by two basic needs: *love* and *work*. Abraham Maslow (1970) described these needs as *love* and *belonging*, which, when satisfied, develop into the needs for *success* and *esteem*. Other theorists divide the basic needs of adulthood into *affiliation* or *social acceptance* needs, *achievement* or *competence* needs, and *power* needs (McClelland, 1975, 1985; McClelland & Boyatzis, 1982). And in Erikson's theory, the early and middle adult years focus on needs for intimacy and "generativity."

**Chapter 8**
**Emotion and Motivation**
*Maslow puts the need for love and belonging in the middle of his hierarchy of needs.*

*INTIMACY VERSUS ISOLATION*   Erikson's psychosocial crisis of young adulthood poses the problem of establishing close relationships with loved ones (see Table 4.3). Erikson described intimacy as the capacity to make a full commitment—sexual, emotional, and moral—to another person. The individual must resolve the conflict between wanting to establish closeness to another and fearing the risks and losses such closeness can entail. Making intimate commitments requires compromising personal preferences, accepting responsibilities, and yielding some privacy and independence. Failure to resolve this crisis leads to isolation and the inability to connect to others in meaningful ways. Much research supports one of the most practical applications that you can take with you from this text: *Anything that isolates us from sources of social support—from a reliable network of friends and family—puts us at risk for a host of physical ills, mental problems, and even social pathologies.* We are social creatures, and we need each other's help and support to be effective and healthy (Basic Behavioral Science Task Force, 1996).

**Chapter 9**
**Stress, Health, and Well-Being**
*Social support affects your health and your ability to cope with stress.*

For Erikson, a young adult must consolidate a clear and comfortable sense of identity (resolving the crisis of adolescence) before being able to cope successfully with the risks and benefits of adult intimacy. In essence, you must know who and what you are before you can begin to love someone else and share your life with that person. However, the sequence from identity to intimacy that Erikson described may not accurately reflect present-day realities. The trend in recent years has been for young adults to live together before marrying, to delay making contractual commitments to lifelong intimacy with one person. Many individuals today must struggle with identity issues (for example, career choices) at the same time they are trying to deal with intimacy issues.

To complicate matters, marriage (one common route to the successful resolution of the search for intimacy) often occurs more than once in an individual's life. In fact, married adults in the United States are now divorcing at a rate four times greater than adults did 50 years ago. Half of all U.S. marriages end in divorce (Edwards, 1995). This situation may result from individuals seeking intimacy before they resolve their own identities. It may also result from unrealistic expectations that members of a couple have of each other and of what constitutes an ideal marriage and family structure (Cleek & Pearson, 1985). On the other hand, there is evidence that communication and affection between spouses is now better than it was in earlier times and that those who have learned good communications skills have substantially improved their chances of avoiding divorce (Caplow, 1982; Markman & Notarius, 1993).

In recent years, a growing tolerance for divorce has led many adults to change their ideas about traditional marriage. Communication and affection between modern spouses has also changed, improving over earlier times. Shown here on their wedding day are Ril and Sayoko Bandy with Ril's children from a previous marriage.

Married people at the change of the millennium are more likely to see each other as partners and friends and less likely to feel constrained by the stereotype of what society expects of a "husband" or "wife." Partners in "peer marriages" talk with and help each other in ways that work best for their relationship, irrespective of traditional ideas about the man being "boss" or the wife being responsible for "women's work" (Schwartz, 1994). The key to such a fair and satisfying relationship is communication in which both partners feel able to openly express their hopes and fears (Klagsbrun, 1985). A mushrooming of knowledge on how good communication can maintain relationships has helped our culture to view marriage as a worthwhile investment and therapy as a valuable option for supporting such efforts (Gottman, 1994; Notarius, 1996). In brief, relating is no longer viewed as a set of skills that "comes naturally" with the establishment of intimacy. Instead, close relationships are seen as lifelong works-in-progress, worthwhile investments of time and energy whose quality can be improved with clearer self-understanding, effective conflict resolution, and good communication.

*GENERATIVITY VERSUS STAGNATION*   According to Erikson, the next major opportunity for growth occurs in the **generativity** crisis of adult midlife. For those who have successfully met the earlier challenges of identity and intimacy, generativity brings a commitment to make a contribution to family, work, society, or future generations—a crucial challenge of one's thirties, forties, and fifties. Thus, people in this phase of life broaden their focus beyond self and partner, often as volunteers in community service groups. Research confirms that adults who express a strong sense of being generative and productive also report high life satisfaction (McAdams, de St. Aubin, & Logan, 1993). In contrast, those who have not resolved earlier crises of identity and intimacy may experience a "midlife crisis." Such people question past choices, becoming cynical and stagnant or, at the other extreme, self-indulgent and reckless.

**Generativity:**  In Erikson's theory, a process of making a commitment beyond oneself to family, work, society, or future generations.

PSYCHOLOGY IN YOUR LIFE

## The Last Developmental Problems You Will Face

At the beginning of this century, only 3% of the U.S. population was over 65. Today that figure is about 13%. When the baby-boom generation reaches this age in the next few years, nearly one-fourth of our population will be in this oldest group.

If you are now a 20-year-old college student, you will be 50 years old by the year 2030, and you will have witnessed a profound **demographic** shift. By that time, more than 80 million Americans will be over 60 years of age. For the first time in history, the number of people in the 60+ age group will outnumber those under 20 years of age. This represents a dramatic reversal of all previous demographics and a potentially significant shift away from today's youth-oriented culture (Pifer & Bronte, 1986). With such drastic changes in our society's age distribution, it is more essential than ever to understand the nature of aging as well as the abilities and needs of the elderly (Roush, 1996). The problem of dealing with an aging population is even more pressing in Third World countries, where incomes and standards of living are low

and where health care resources are minimal (Holden, 1996).

**EGO-INTEGRITY VERSUS DESPAIR**   According to Erikson, an increasing awareness of your own mortality and of the changes in your body, behavior, and social roles will set the stage for late adulthood. The crisis at this stage involves **ego-integrity,** the ability to look back on life without regrets and to enjoy a sense of wholeness. For those whose previous crises had unhealthy solutions, however, aspirations remain unfulfilled, and these individuals experience futility, despair, and self-deprecation. Sadly, they often then fail to resolve the crisis successfully at this final developmental stage.

In general, Erikson characterizes old age as a time of challenge. What are the tasks of old age, and what resources and limitations must we confront as we look ahead to the autumn of our lives? In a series of interviews with middle-aged and older men and women, Ryff (1989) found that both age groups and sexes defined "well-being" in terms of having an orientation toward others: being a caring, compassionate person and having good relationships. Respondents also empha-

sized the value of accepting change, enjoying life, and cultivating a sense of humor.

**NEW PERSPECTIVES ON AGING**   What does aging mean for us? From a biological perspective, aging typically means decline: Energy reserves are reduced, cells decay, and muscle tone diminishes. From a cognitive perspective, however, we know that aging is no longer synonymous with decline. In fact, many abilities, including expert skills and some aspects of memory, may improve with age (Azar, 1996; Krampe & Ericsson, 1996). A lifetime's accumulation of experience may finally culminate in wisdom—if the mind remains open and active. Theories of aging are models of balance or trade-offs: In old age, a person may lose energy reserve but gain an ability to control emotional experiences and thereby conserve energy. Thus, we can expect two kinds of changes—gains and losses—as we grow older (Baltes, 1987).

Some of the most obvious changes that occur with age affect people's physical appearances and abilities. As we grow older, we can expect our skin to wrinkle, our hair to thin and gray, and our height to decrease an inch or two. Our hearts and lungs operate less efficiently, so we expect decreased physical stamina. We can also expect some of our senses to dull. These changes occur and develop gradually, so we have ample opportunity to gauge them and try to adjust. Earlier psychological explanations characterized aging as a change from growth to decline, but a more accurate understanding of aging considers the joint influence of individual potential and realistic limits (Baltes, 1993). Consider how an individual might make the most of the resources he or she has, given each of the changes accompanying aging:

- **Vision** As we age, the lenses in our eyes become rigid and discolored, affecting both distance and color vision. Most people over 65 experience some loss of visual acuity, and without corrective lenses half of the elderly would be considered legally blind. Corrective lenses do aid in adjusting to these changes in vision, however, especially for night driving or close work such as reading. (*See Chapter 5, Sensation and Perception.*)
- **Hearing** Hearing loss is common among those 60 and older, especially the ability to hear high-frequency sounds. Problems can ensue if the loss is undetected or denied (Maher & Ross, 1984; Manschreck, 1989). A person may believe that others are deliberately whispering to avoid being heard, leading to a mild form of paranoia (belief that one is being victimized). Those with a hearing loss might explain others' actions inaccurately because they lack information and blame their misinterpretations on evil intentions instead of simple bad hearing (Zimbardo et al., 1981). Fortunately, early hearing-aid therapy can be more effective than later psychotherapy. Hearing aids can compensate for much of one's hearing loss. In addition, those close to someone with a probable hearing loss can help them by speaking in lower tones, enunciating clearly, and reducing background noise. (*See Chapter 13, Psychopathology.*)
- **Intelligence** A great fear about aging is that it is accompanied by the loss of mental abilities. Is this fear justified? In fact, there is little evidence that healthy older adults experience a decline in general cognitive abilities.

Older people who pursue high levels of environmental stimulation tend to maintain higher levels of cognitive abilities.

However, people do acquire information more slowly by the time they are in their seventies and eighties. Performance of tasks requiring imagination, such as vivid imagery strategies for memorizing, also decline with age (Baltes & Kliegl, 1992). However, more general losses are neither inevitable nor necessarily disruptive. There is even evidence that some aspects of intellectual functioning are superior in older people. For example, skilled musicians have been shown to improve well into their 90s (Krampe & Ericsson, 1996). Psychologists are now exploring age-related gains in wisdom, such as expertise in practical knowledge and life experience (Baltes, 1990). (*See Chapter 11, Intelligence and the Psychology of Differences.*)

- **Memory** A common complaint among older adults is that their ability to remember things is not as good as it used to be. Most of these age-related memory difficulties appear in a part of the memory system that processes and stores new information (Poon, 1985). Aging does *not* seem to diminish access to knowledge or events that occurred long ago. So, an elderly person may have to ask the name of a new acquaintance once or twice before finally remembering it, but may have no trouble recalling the names of old friends

or celebrities. A more important concern might be that people explain memory loss differently depending on the age of the forgetful person. Using a double standard, younger adults attribute other young adults' memory failures to lack of effort but those of older adults to loss of ability (Parr & Siegert, 1993). (*See Chapter 6, Learning and Remembering.*)

- **Sexual Functioning** One myth about aging is that elderly people cannot or should not be sexually active. Belief in such a myth can be a greater obstacle than any physical limitations to experiencing satisfying sex in late adulthood. There is no age, for either men or women, at which the capability for arousal or orgasm ceases. Sex loses its reproductive functions in late adulthood but not its capacity for providing pleasure. Regular sexual practice enhances healthy aging because it provides arousal, aerobic exercise, fantasy, and social interaction (Ornstein & Sobel, 1989). Experience and creativity clearly compensate for minor physical changes or losses of physical stamina. (*See Chapter 8, Emotion and Motivation.*)
- **Social Interaction** An unfortunate consequence of living a long life is outliving some friends and family members. In addition, the reduced mobility associated with aging can account for the fact that people become somewhat less active socially in later adulthood. While older adults reduce the extent of their social contacts, they remain more invested in those ties they choose to keep. Maintaining even a single intimate relationship can markedly improve personal health, as can living with a beloved pet (Siegel, 1990). Research shows that as people age, they tend to engage in **selective social interaction,** maintaining only the most

**Demographic:** Refers to population characteristics, such as age, gender, or income distribution.

**Ego-integrity:** In Erikson's theory, the ability to look back on life without regrets and to enjoy a sense of wholeness.

**Selective social interaction:** Choosing to restrict the number of one's social contacts to those who are the most gratifying.

*Continued*

rewarding contacts for the investment of precious physical and emotional energy (Carstensen, 1987, 1991; Lang & Carstensen, 1994). (*See Chapter 12, Social Psychology.*)

What can be done for those who experience trouble or personal difficulty in aging? Many elderly people have discovered particular strategies that help them age successfully. For example, older adults can remain both active and close to people by doing volunteer work in the community, joining clubs and classes, or spending time with grandchildren. In addition, we might learn lessons from other cultures where older citizens are respected and venerated for their wisdom. Before this happens, however, people must overcome stultifying stereotypes of the elderly as incapable and incompetent (Brewer, Dull, & Lui, 1981).

What, then, would be a good strategy for dealing with the challenges of aging? Perhaps successful aging consists of making the most of gains while minimizing the impact of losses. Additionally, it is helpful to realize that losses of specific abilities need not represent threats to one's sense of self. As one's physical and psychological resources change, so do one's goals (Carstensen & Freund, 1994). In this fashion, late adulthood may be a time not of increasing frustration, but of increasing fulfillment.

## Check Your Understanding

1. RECALL: *In recent years, psychologists have come to see that*
   a. adult development is a gradual process of decline of physical and cognitive functions until death.
   b. adults continue to develop in problem-solving skills but not emotionally.
   c. physical and mental development continue throughout the life cycle.
   d. most adults are mildly depressed about the passing of their youth.

2. RECALL: *Which one is a stage of life that is* not *recognized by many cultures?*
   a. childhood
   b. adolescence
   c. adulthood
   d. old age

3. RECALL: *Which one is associated with a major crisis of adolescence, according to Erikson?*
   a. identity
   b. intimacy
   c. generativity
   d. ego-integrity

4. APPLICATION: *Which of the following individuals is most likely to develop physical or mental problems?*
   a. Mary, who works long hours at a challenging job
   b. Joe, who has an easy job, but no friends
   c. Eduardo, who must study 10 hours a day in graduate school
   d. Lucy, who works in a fast-food restaurant all day and has no prospects for advancement

5. UNDERSTANDING THE CORE CONCEPT: Nature and nurture continue to produce changes in personality and mental processes throughout the life cycle. *In what way have you changed since you were in your previous stage of development?*

ANSWERS:    1. c    2. b    3. a    4. b    5. **Whatever you say is correct—but you should consider this: Does it jibe with Erikson's theory of life-span development?**

# USING PSYCHOLOGY TO LEARN PSYCHOLOGY

## Cognitive Development in College Students

*I*s the formal operational stage the end of the cognitive line—or will your thinking abilities continue to develop as you go through college? A study by developmental psychologist William Perry suggests that your perspective on learning will change and mature as your college experience unfolds. Of special note, in a sample of students that he followed through their undergraduate years at Harvard and Radcliffe, students' views of psychology and their other social science courses changed radically, as did their view of what they were there to learn (Perry, 1970, 1994).

Students in Perry's study had the most difficulty coming to grips with the diverse and conflicting viewpoints they encountered in their courses. For example, many confronted, for the first time, the idea that reasonable people can disagree—even about their most cherished "truths" concerning good and evil, God, nature, and human nature. Perry says:

> A few seemed to find the notion of multiple frames of reference wholly unintelligible. Others responded with violent shock to their confrontation in dormitory bull sessions, or in their academic work, or both. Others experienced a joyful sense of liberation. (Perry, 1970, p. 4)

In dealing with this academic culture shock, Perry's students passed through a series of distinct intellectual stages that were reminiscent of Piaget's stages. And, although they arrived at college at different levels of cognitive maturity and continued to develop at different rates, all progressed through the same intellectual stages in the same sequence. Here are some of the highlights of this intellectual journey:

- Students at first typically see a college or university as a storehouse of information—a place to learn the Right Answers. Thus, they believe it is the professor's job to help students find these answers.
- Sooner or later, students discover an unexpected diversity of opinion, even among the experts. At this stage they are likely to attribute conflicting opinions to confusion among poorly qualified experts.
- Eventually, students begin to accept diverse views as legitimate—but only in the fuzzy areas (such as psychology, other social sciences, and humanities) where experts haven't yet found the Right Answers. They decide that, in subjects where the Right Answers haven't been nailed down, professors grade them on "good expression" of their ideas.
- Next, some students discover that uncertainty and diversity of opinion are everywhere—not just in the social sciences and humanities. They solve this problem in their minds by dividing the academic world into two realms: (a) one in which Right Answers exist (even though they haven't all been discovered) and (b) another in which anyone's opinion is as good as anyone else's. Often, at this stage, they perceive math and the "hard" sciences as the realm of Right Answers, leaving the social sciences and humanities in the realm of opinion.
- Finally, the most mature students come to see that multiple perspectives exist in all fields of study.

The students who achieve this final stage begin to see "truth" as tentative. They now realize that knowledge is always building and changing—even in the "hard" sciences. And, they realize that a college education is not just learning an endless series of facts. Rather, it is learning about the important *questions* and major *concepts* of a field. In this book we have called them Key Questions and Core Concepts.

At what stage do you find yourself?

# CHAPTER SUMMARY

 **HOW DO PSYCHOLOGISTS EXPLAIN DEVELOPMENT?**

- Developmental psychologists study change and growth in physical and mental functioning throughout the life span. They have resolved the nature–nurture controversy by noting that nature and nurture interact. They employ a variety of methods, including observations of twins and adopted children, to assess the relative contributions of heredity and environment. The resulting studies show that many behaviors have a genetic component.

- Another controversy in developmental psychology involves continuity versus discontinuity. Researchers looking for these and other developmental patterns may perform cross-sectional and longitudinal studies.

 **Development is a process of growth and change brought about by an interaction of heredity and environment.**

 **WHAT CAPABILITIES DOES THE NEWBORN POSSESS?**

- Physical development, notably of the brain, proceeds at a rapid pace during the prenatal period and during the first few years after birth. Developmental research shows that infants are born with many sensory capabilities, preferences, and motor reflexes, plus the abilities to learn new responses. In addition, they are designed to be sociable. All of these characteristics make newborns highly interactive with the world around them.

 **Newborns begin life equipped to deal with three basic survival tasks: finding nourishment, making contacts with people, and avoiding harmful situations.**

 **WHAT ARE THE DEVELOPMENTAL TASKS OF CHILDHOOD?**

- Young children are biologically equipped to learn language and motivated to communicate. Many experts believe that children have "language acquisition devices" built into their brains. Psychologists find that language development proceeds in a predictable fashion, as children acquire both vocabulary and grammar at an almost unbelievable rate.

- Piaget's theory says that the twin processes of assimilation and accommodation underlie cognitive development. Piaget also proposed that children's cognitive development goes through four stages: the sensorimotor, the preoperational, the concrete operational, and the formal opera-

tional stages. New abilities mark the emergence of each stage. Newer theory and research have, however, modified many of Piaget's ideas. Kohlberg's theory of moral development, built on Piaget's foundation, is also a stage theory. In Kohlberg's view, lower stages involve concerns with personal consequences and higher stages have a broader focus on principles of ethical living.

- Social development is built on a foundation of temperament, but it is also strongly influenced by the process of attachment to the caregiver. Ainsworth finds that children may become either securely or insecurely attached. Attachment patterns established in infancy often persist into adulthood. Attachment probably evolved to give the infant protection. Harlow's research suggests that infants seek contact comfort in the attachment relationship.

- Erikson's theory proposes that personality develops through a series of crises, each focused on resolving an issue about oneself and others. These issues define four stages of psychosocial development in childhood.

 **Children face especially important developmental tasks in the areas of language, thought processes, and social relationships.**

 **WHAT DEVELOPMENTAL CHANGES OCCUR IN ADOLESCENCE AND ADULTHOOD?**

- The transitions of adolescence involve rapid physical maturation and development of sexual identity. Adolescents must also forge a social identity and make enduring occupational choices.

- The challenges of adulthood focus on achieving intimacy and a sense of generativity. In later adulthood, individuals must maintain a sense of integrity despite some physical changes and losses. Successful resolution of earlier life crises can enable one to face death and loss with acceptance and a willingness to cope.

- New perspectives on aging show that this period of life is marked by both gains and losses, notably in vision, hearing, intelligence, memory, sexual functioning, and social interaction. For some aging is very difficult, but for others it is a time of increasing fulfillment.

 **Nature and nurture continue to produce changes in personality and mental processes throughout the life cycle.**

For each of the following items, choose the single correct or best answer. The correct answers appear at the end.

1. Dr. Itard tried to educate Victor, the Wild Child. Itard's efforts could be called an example of
   a. heredity.
   b. nurture.
   c. discontinuity.
   d. the longitudinal method.

2. A psychologist taking the discontinuity view might see development as
   a. a gradual process.
   b. a matter of learning.
   c. entirely genetic.
   d. a series of stages.

3. Which of the following is true of the physical abilities of the newborn infant?
   a. At birth babies already have preferences for particular tastes and smells and dislikes for others.
   b. Just moments after birth a neonate turns in the direction of a voice or reaches out an exploring hand.
   c. While babies are born legally blind, they soon learn to detect large objects and high-contrast patterns.
   d. all of the above

4. A developmental researcher arranges to track the progress of a 30-member kindergarten class over the next ten years, maintaining contact with the children's teachers and families in order to test them annually. This ambitious plan illustrates the use of a _____ research design.
   a. normative
   b. longitudinal
   c. cross-sectional
   d. sequential

5. Which of the following utterances illustrates *overregularization* in language development?
   a. "Babababa."
   b. "Me gots two foots and two handses."
   c. "Drink milk, all gone."
   d. "Want cookie."

6. "Hey! That's not fair," complains Judi. "Tonio has more ice cream than me." Actually, both Judi and Tonio received a single scoop, but Tonio has stirred his around so it seems to fill the dish, while Judi's scoop is more compact. Judi's complaint indicates that she has not yet acquired the concept of

_____ that affects how children think about the physical properties of things.
   a. centration
   b. egocentrism
   c. conservation
   d. object permanence

7. Harry and Margaret Harlow conducted landmark studies of the behaviors of baby monkeys who were separated from their mothers and had access only to mother "dummies" in their cages. This work confirmed that
   a. genuine attachment is possible only with the infant's biological mother.
   b. contact comfort and physical touch are important for healthy early development.
   c. the "cupboard theory of attachment" is true for both humans and nonhumans.
   d. nonhuman infants will imprint on and restrict social behavior to the first visually prominent thing they see after birth.

8. For Erikson, the psychosocial crisis of _____ is addressed by skill development and social interaction during the elementary school years, when children must explore their abilities, talents, and peer relationships.
   a. trust versus mistrust
   b. autonomy versus doubt
   c. competence versus inferiority
   d. identity versus role confusion

9. The briefest summary of the concerns and crises of adult development might simply be
   a. success and security.
   b. power and conquest.
   c. youth and beauty.
   d. love and work.

10. In late adulthood, loss of _____ has often been associated with feelings of paranoia and social isolation.
    a. intellectual abilities
    b. sexual functioning
    c. one's spouse
    d. hearing

**ANSWERS:**   1. b   2. d   3. d   4. b   5. b   6. c   7. b   8. c   9. d   10. d

## BOOKS

Bruner, J. S. (1983). *Child's talk: Learning to use our language.* New York: W. W. Norton.

*This is a detailed and readable introduction to language development in children, by a renowned researcher and expert.*

Butterfield, F. (1995). *All God's children: The Bosket family and the American tradition of violence.* New York: Knopf.

*Willie Bosket is the hardest criminal the New York penal system has ever had. He comes from a long line of hard-luck tough guys, stretching back to the Civil War. But is it nature? His lineage was nurtured in the violent culture of honor (and insults to honor) in the American South. This is the book to read if you think you have all the answers to the problem of violence and crime.*

Candland, D. K. (1993). *Feral children and clever animals: Reflections on human nature.* New York: Oxford University Press.

*Candland chronicles the numerous wild children discovered in the past two centuries, the impact of these discoveries on cultural notions of nature and nurture, and what efforts were made to train or "civilize" the children themselves.*

Ceci, S. J., & Bruck, M. (1995). *Jeopardy in the courtroom: A scientific analysis of children's testimony.* Washington, DC: American Psychological Association.

*Are children believable witnesses in legal cases? Or are they too easily influenced by the wishes of the adults on either side? This scholarly review and resource is not sit-down reading but includes fascinating case histories, examples, a review of the history of research on witness suggestibility, and critiques of recent trends in children's testimony (e.g., using anatomically correct dolls for children's allegations of sexual abuse).*

DeBoer, R. (1994). *Losing Jessica.* New York: Doubleday.

*An unmarried woman gives her baby girl up for adoption, lying about her paternity. Later, she confesses to the biological father, who asserts his custodial rights and seeks to have the child removed from her adoptive home. Written simply and sentimentally by the adoptive mother, Robby, this book chronicles an unbelievable, maddening, and sad true story of the DeBoers' fight to keep baby Jessica. This is a sobering picture of the legal nonstatus of children and the conflict between children's "best interests" and parents' demands.*

de Hennezel, M. (1998). *Intimate death: How the dying teach us how to live.* (Translated by C. B. Janeway). Vintage Books.

*A bestseller in France, this book recounts lessons the author learned as a psychologist working in a hospital for the terminally ill in Paris, about how people relinquish their hold on life, sometimes with anguish, sometimes with dignity, always with meaning.*

Eagle, C. J. (1994). *All that she can be: Helping your daughter maintain her self-esteem.* New York: Fireside.

*Illustrated with anecdotes and sample conversations, this book is written in a lively style and aimed at parents concerned about the problems unique to adolescent girls, reviewing what is included in "normal" behavior and how to deal with issues of friendship, sexuality, and body self-awareness.*

Fisher, H. E. (1999). *First sex: The natural talents of women and how they are changing the world.* New York: Random House.

*Anthropologist Helen Fisher argues surprisingly that evolution has favored women, because they use contextual or "web thinking" more than men and have the leadership advantage in a global economy.*

Gilligan, C. (1982). *In a different voice: Psychological theory and women's development.* Cambridge, MA: Harvard University Press.

*This short, readable book by the researcher who first questioned Kohlberg's conclusions about gender differences in moral reasoning includes a brief summary of Kohlberg's original research strategy and early findings.*

Hayden, T. L. (1995). *One child.* New York: Avon Books.

*This is the story of an autistic, abused child whose life was turned around by a dedicated teacher who would not stop trying to reach her.*

Kagan, J., Snidman, N., Arcus, D., & Reznick, J. S. (1994). *Galen's prophecy.* New York: HarperCollins.

*These developmental psychologists present a fascinating exploration of temperament, its origins, varieties, and lifelong influence on behavior. Rich with examples and case studies, the book includes demonstrations of the distinctive interplay between an individual's environment and his or her distinctive readiness to respond in certain ways to that environment.*

Langford, L. (1998). *The big talk: Talking to your teen about sex and dating.* New York: John Wiley & Sons.

*Even if you don't have kids now, if you expect someday to be a parent, this is a worthwhile read both for future experience as a parent—and for current insight into how your own life has been affected by your feelings about your body, peer pressure, sex, and saving face.*

Miller, G. W. (1998). *Toy wars: The epic struggle between G.I. Joe, Barbie, and the companies that make them.* Holbrook, MA: Adams Media Corporation.

*Toys are not child's play—not from the perspective of the corporations that profit from sales to children and their parents. Reading like a mystery thriller, this true account of toy makers' competition reveals a perspective on children-as-consumers that is enlightening and a little scary.*

Pinker, S. (1994). *The language instinct.* New York: William Morrow.

*If you're interested in the origins of language and thought—and what they can tell you about your own brain—this one's for you.*

Rymer, R. (1993). *Genie: An abused child's flight from silence.* New York: HarperCollins.

*Rymer documents the efforts to teach a young adolescent, Genie, to talk and function normally after her parents had neglected, confined, and isolated her since birth. The book questions the power of training to make up for missed "critical periods" in a child's development and also raises ethical questions about the value of scientifically studying a child as a "case" versus rearing and loving her as any normal person.*

Segell, M. (1999). *Standup guy: Masculinity that works.* New York: Villard Books.

*When the traditional models of masculinity as dominance no longer work, what's a guy to live up to? Segell advocates a mixture of honest aggression tempered by heroic goals with a realistic admission that, in modern intimacy, power must be based on partnership. Though somewhat simplistic, this book provides an optimistic contrast with gloomier depictions of males as doomed dinosaurs.*

Seligman, M. E. P., Reivich, K., Jaycox, L., & Gillham, J. (1996). *The optimistic child.* New York: HarperPerennial.

*Martin Seligman's life work has taken him from the study of learned helplessness in animals to developing programs for preventing helplessness and depression in humans. In this book he focuses on the likely childhood causes of a pessimistic personality and how to prevent early cynicism in order to cultivate optimistic, hopeful, proactive thought and action in one's children and students.*

Sheehy, G. (1995). *New passages: Mapping your life across time.* New York: Random House.

*Sheehy follows up her earlier best-seller, Passages, with a collection of insights based on interviews about the challenges and crises of adult life, including the Tryout Twenties, Turbulent Thirties, Flourishing Forties, Flaming Fifties, Serene Sixties . . . and more! Engaging style, lots of good anecdotes, worthwhile humor, and wisdom compensate somewhat for still unresolved questions about the passages' generalizability to the larger population.*

Tiger, L. (1999). *The decline of males.* New York: Golden Books.

*Biological anthropologist Lionel Tiger posits that men have declined while women have ascended now that modern technology has made reproduction more of an option and less of a prison. As long as you accept biological or genetic explanations for such complex systems as gender roles, you may find this enlightening and refreshing.*

## VIDEOS

*The boy with green hair.* (1948, color, 82 min.). Directed by Joseph Losey; starring Dean Stockwell, Pat O'Brien.

*A war orphan raised by his grandfather becomes a social outcast when his hair inexplicably turns green, highlighting the fear of "differentness," the tragedies of war, and the dangers of mindless conformity.*

*Kramer versus Kramer.* (1979, color, 104 min.). Directed by Robert Benton; starring Dustin Hoffman, Meryl Streep, Justin Henry.

*An unhappy wife leaves her workaholic husband and their young son, only to return and seek custody later after father and son have bonded. This is a well-acted, powerful story about the conflicts between parents' personal goals and the best interests of the child.*

*Marvin's room.* (1996, color, 98 min.). Directed by Jerry Zaks; starring Meryl Streep, Diane Keaton, Leonardo Di Caprio.

*A woman who has become estranged from the rest of her family while caring for their sick father has her own health crisis and must call on her sister for help, while the sister herself is losing a battle with her own teenaged son. The tangle of family crises, feelings, insights, and oversights realistically summarizes real family entanglements in all their vividness.*

*On Golden Pond.* (1981, color, 109 min.). Directed by Mark Rydell; starring Katharine Hepburn, Henry Fonda, Jane Fonda, Doug McKeon, Dabney Coleman.

*An elderly couple summering at their lakefront home reflect on their lives, fears, and hopes as they "babysit" the son of their daughter's boyfriend. This sensitively portrayed story of conflict and communion across generations is based on Ernest Thompson's play.*

*Ordinary people.* (1980, color, 123 min.). Directed by Robert Redford; starring Donald Sutherland, Mary Tyler Moore, Timothy Hutton, Judd Hirsch.

*This vivid and stirring film of Judith Guest's novel looks at a family's deterioration after the death of the older son, especially as the death affects his surviving adolescent brother.*

*Three men and a cradle.* (1985, color, 106 min.; French: *Trois hommes et un couffin*). Directed by Coline Serreau; starring Roland Giraud, Michel Boujenah, Andre Dussolier.

*Much better than the 1987 U.S. remake, this film depicts a funny and instructive story of three bachelors whose lives and lifestyles are disrupted when a baby girl is left on the doorstep of the flat they share—and they become attached to her even as they try to get rid of her. There are some interesting insights on the demands of parenthood and the two-sided nature of attachment.*

*Welcome to the dollhouse.* (1996, color, 87 min.). Directed by Todd Solondz; starring Heather Matarazzo, Brandon Sexton, Jr., Daria Kalinina, Matthew Faber.

*The pain of puberty is depicted through the eyes of a young woman whose suburban parents are amazingly unsympathetic and favor her baby sister and whose school experience seems to be the Seventh Grade from Hell. There are good performances and a lot of humor.*

*The wild child.* (1969, French, B&W, 85 min.). Directed by François Truffaut; starring François Truffaut, Jean-Pierre Cargol, Jean Daste.

*This early effort by the brilliant French filmmaker Truffaut documents the story of Dr. Itard's work with Victor, the "wild boy" of Aveyron, in the early nineteenth century.*

## KEY QUESTIONS

### CORE CONCEPTS

### PSYCHOLOGY IN YOUR LIFE

**HOW DOES STIMULATION BECOME SENSATION?**

The brain senses the world indirectly because the sense organs convert stimulation into the language of the nervous system: neural impulses.

**A Critical Look at Subliminal Persuasion:** Subliminal perception occurs, but individual differences in perceptual thresholds make widespread use of subliminal persuasion unworkable.

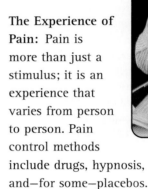

**HOW ARE THE SENSES ALIKE? AND HOW ARE THEY DIFFERENT?**

The senses all operate in much the same way, but each extracts different information and sends it to its own specialized processing region in the brain.

**The Experience of Pain:** Pain is more than just a stimulus; it is an experience that varies from person to person. Pain control methods include drugs, hypnosis, and—for some—placebos.

**WHAT IS THE RELATIONSHIP BETWEEN PERCEPTION AND SENSATION?**

Perception brings *meaning* to sensation, so perception produces an interpretation of the external world, not a perfect representation of it.

**Seeing and Believing:** Magicians and politicians rely on the fact that we don't merely sense the world, we perceive it.

**USING PSYCHOLOGY TO LEARN PSYCHOLOGY: STUDYING FOR THE GESTALT**

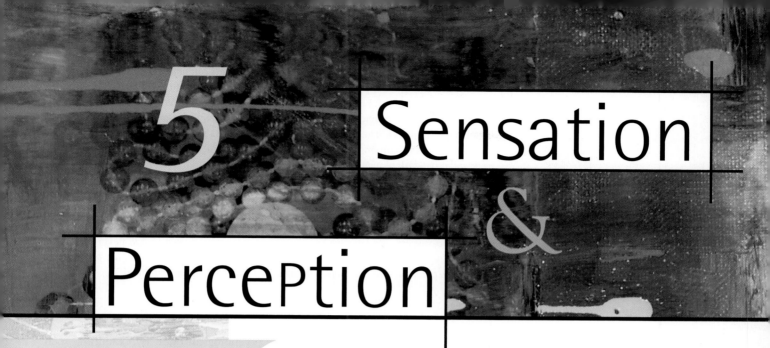

# 5 Sensation & Perception

## Chapter Outline

Can you imagine what your world would be like if you could no longer see colors? What if you awoke one morning and your normally color-filled world were clouded over into black, white, and gray? It might be a bit like watching your color television return to the old-fashioned black-and-white programming. But of course it would be so much worse—everything you saw, not only images on a TV screen, would be devoid of hue. Your food would be colorless; what would happen to your appetite? Your face in the mirror, and the faces of your loved ones, all would be gray. Rainbows, if you could detect them at all, would be colorless semicircles. Spring flowers would remain hidden in the grass, their vibrant colors indistinguishable from the flat grays of the landscape around you. Red traffic lights would look the same as green ones, so everyday tasks like driving and crossing a street would be risky at best. Your joy in life, and perhaps even your very survival, would be jeopardized.

Such a bizarre sensory loss actually befell Jonathan I., a 65-year-old New Yorker, following an automobile accident. Apparently the trauma of the crash caused damage to a region in his brain that processes color information. At first, Mr. I. also had some amnesia (memory loss) for reading letters of the alphabet, which all seemed like nonsensical markings to him. But after five days, his alexia, or inability to read, disappeared. However, his loss of color vision persisted as a permanent condition, known as cerebral achromatopsia (pronounced ay-kroma-TOP-see-a). As you might expect, Jonathan I. became depressed by this strange turn of events in his life. The problem was aggravated by his profession: Jonathan was a painter whose entire existence was based on representing his images of the world in vivid colors. He had been an art director, a commercial artist, and an abstract expressionist, adopting an artistic style that depends on color and unrealistic forms to express meaning and feelings. Now it was all gone, all drab, all "molded in lead." When he looked at his own paintings, which had seemed bursting with special meaning and emotional associations, all he now saw were unfamiliar and meaningless objects on canvas. Curiously, Jonathan also lost his memory of color, and eventually the names for colors. He could no longer even imagine, say, what "red" once looked like. "It was as if the brain's knowledge of color had been totally excised, leaving no trace, no inner evidence, of its existence behind" (Sacks, 1995, p. 13). What Jonathan I.'s experience dramatically demonstrated to the researchers and clinicians who studied him and tried to help him was the nonobvious *neurological truth that colors do not really exist "out there" in objects. Rather, our world of color is a construction of the sensory and perceptual processes of the brain.*

*Fortunately, Jonathan's story has a happy ending, one that reveals much about the resilience of the human spirit. First, Jonathan became a "night person," traveling and working at night, and socializing with other night people. (As we will see in this chapter, good color vision depends on bright illumination such as daylight; most people's color vision is not as acute in the dark of night.) Jonathan also became aware that what remained of his vision was remarkably good, enabling him to read license plates from four blocks away at night. He began to reinterpret his "loss" as a "gift" in which he was no longer distracted by color, so that he could now focus his work more intensely on shape, form, and content. Finally, Jonathan switched to painting only in black and white, and critics acclaimed his "new phase" as a success. He has also become good at sculpting, which he had never attempted before his accident. So as Jonathan's world of color died, a new world of "pure forms" was born in his perception of the people, objects, and events in his environment.*

Jonathan's experience shows that the brain has the flexibility to meet severe physical challenges and to adjust to daunting psychological ones. By examining such losses, we can momentarily slip outside the confines of our own experience. Jonathan and others who have suffered brain damage allow us to see more clearly how our mental machinery goes about sensing—and making sense of—our worlds. Although these very private processes extend deep into the mind and brain, we will begin this chapter's tour at the interface of body and environment. This is the territory of *sensory psychology*. Here we will witness the transformation of physical stimulation (such as light) into sensations (such as light and dark). Here we will find the basis for color, odor, sound, texture, and taste. Here we will learn why tomatoes and limes seem to have different colors, why a violin sounds different from a bass guitar, and why a pinprick feels different from a caress.

Our ultimate destination in this chapter lies in the realm of *perception*. There we will uncover the psychological processes that attach meaning and personal significance to the sensory messages entering our brains. Perceptual psychology will help us understand how we assemble a series of tones into a familiar melody or a collage of shapes and shadings into a familiar face. It will help us understand something of our preferences and prejudices. And, it will help us understand the profound differences in the ways people think.

Even more fundamentally, in this chapter we will learn that this inner world of sensation and perception is the only one we can ever know directly. No matter what we do, all the information we get about external events must always be secondhand, filtered through our sense organs and then combined with our unique mix of memories, emotions, motives, and expectations. We will also learn that many complex acts of sensing and perceiving occur behind the scenes, so effortlessly, continuously, and flawlessly that we pay them little conscious mind.

Under most conditions our sensory experience of external stimulation is highly reliable. So, when your alarm goes off in the morning or when you catch sight of a friend, the meaning usually registers clearly, immediately, and accurately. Sensation *has* to be reliable, if we are to survive. Nevertheless, we do have our sensory limitations. We humans lack the acute senses that many other species have perfected, such as the vision of hawks, the hearing of bats, the sense of smell of rodents, or the sensitivity to magnetic fields found in migratory birds. Instead, our own species has evolved the sensory equipment that enables us to process a wider range and variety of sensory input than any other creature.

Before going further, we should specify more exactly what we mean by "sensation" and "perception." Psychologists define **sensation** as the process by which a stimulated receptor (sensory neuron) creates a pattern of neural impulses that represent

**Sensation:** An early stage of perception in which neurons in a receptor create an internal pattern of nerve impulses that represent the conditions that stimulated it—either inside or outside the body.

To hunt small flying objects at night, bats rely on the sensory system of echolocation, a kind of sonar. Bats emit high-frequency sounds that bounce off insects, revealing their locations so the bats can find and eat them.

conditions inside or outside the body. For example, sensation represents the sound waves from a bell or the sharp irritation of a chili pepper. (It is important to realize that external stimulation, such as light or sound, never actually enters the brain.) Then, in a continuation of the process begun by sensation, **perception** elaborates and assigns meaning to the incoming sensory patterns. Perception creates an *interpretation* of the bell (near or far? church bell or door bell?) or of the chili pepper (hot or mild?).

As you can see, the boundary of sensation blurs into that of perception. In practice, psychologists treat sensation both as the neural pattern generated by the receptors responding to stimulation and the accompanying initial experience. Perception, then, is essentially a further interpretation and elaboration of sensation.

 KEY QUESTION

## HOW DOES STIMULATION BECOME SENSATION?

A thunderstorm is approaching, and you feel the electric charge in the air make the hair stand up on your head. Lightning flashes, and a split second later you hear the thunderclap. It was close by, and you smell the ozone left as the bolt sizzled through the air. Your senses are warning you of danger.

Our senses have other adaptive functions, as well. They aid our survival by directing us toward certain sensations, such as tasty foods, which provide nourishment, and sexual touch, which promotes procreation. In addition, through experiences that appeal to the eye, the ear, touch, taste, and smell, the senses involve us in the richness of life. This means that we cannot judge sensation merely by its accuracy—how perfectly it represents reality to us—or by its usefulness in everyday life. We must also appreciate it for the sensual pleasure that sensation affords us, even in the simplest experiences, such as breathing in the fragrance of fresh air, enjoying good food or music, or being soothed by the touch of a loved one.

How do our senses accomplish all this? The complete answer is complex, but it involves one simple idea that applies across the sensory landscape: Our sensory impressions of the world involve *neural representations* of stimuli—not the actual stimuli. The Core Concept puts it this way:

 CORE CONCEPT

**The brain senses the world indirectly because the sense organs convert stimulation into the language of the nervous system: neural impulses.**

The brain never receives stimulation directly from the outside world. Its experience of a tomato is not the same as the tomato itself—although we usually assume that the two are identical. The brain cannot receive light from a sunset, reach out and touch

**Perception:** A process that makes sensory patterns meaningful and more elaborate. Perception draws heavily on memory, motivation, emotion, and other psychological processes.

velvet, or inhale the fragrance of a rose. It must always rely on secondhand information from the go-between sensory system, which delivers only a coded neural message, out of which the brain must create its own experience.

To understand more deeply how stimulation becomes sensation, we will consider three attributes common to all the senses: *transduction, sensory adaptation*, and *thresholds*. They determine which stimuli will actually become sensation, what the quality and impact of that sensation will be, and whether it grabs our interest. These attributes determine whether a tomato actually registers in the sensory system strongly enough to enter our awareness, what its color and form appear to be, and how strongly it bids for our attention.

## Transduction

The idea that sensations, such as the redness and flavor of a tomato, are entirely creations of the sense organs and brain may seem incredible to you. How do we know that these qualities do not exist outside the nervous system? Remember that all sensory communication with the brain flows through neurons in the form of neural impulses: Neurons cannot transmit light or sound waves or any other external stimulus. Because of this constraint, none of the light bouncing off the tomato ever actually reaches the brain. It only gets as far as the back of the eyes, where the information it contains is converted to neural impulses. Neither do the chemicals that signal taste actually make their way into the brain; they go only as far as the tongue. In general, it is the job of the sensory receptors to convert stimulus information into electrochemical signals—neural impulses—the only language the brain comprehends. Sensations, such as "red" or "sweet" or "cold," occur when the neural signal reaches the cerebral cortex. In fact, it is here in the specialized regions of the cortex that sensory experience is created. The whole process seems so immediate and direct that it fools us into assuming that the sensation of redness is characteristic of a tomato or the sensation of cold is a characteristic of ice cream. But they are not!

Psychologists use the term **transduction** for the process that converts physical energy, such as light waves, into the form of neural impulses. Transduction begins

**Chapter 2:
Biopsychology**

*The brain receives information in
the form of neural impulses.*

---

**FIGURE 5.1:**   Stimulation Becomes Perception

For stimulation to become a percept it must undergo several transformations. First, physical stimulation (light waves from the butterfly) are *transduced* by the eye, where information about the wavelength and intensity of the light is coded into neural impulses. Second, the neural impulses travel to the sensory cortex of brain, where they become *sensations* of color, brightness, form, and movement. Finally, the process of *perception* interprets these sensations by making connections with memories, expectations, emotions, and motives in other parts of the brain.

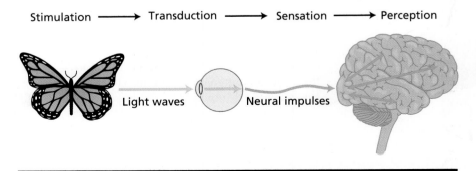

Stimulation ⟶ Transduction ⟶ Sensation ⟶ Perception

Light waves     Neural impulses

**Transduction:** Transformation of one form of energy into another—especially the transformation of stimulus information into nerve impulses.

## TABLE 5.1: Fundamental Features of Human Senses

| SENSE | STIMULUS | SENSE ORGAN | RECEPTOR | SENSATION |
|-------|----------|-------------|----------|-----------|
| Sight | Light waves | Eye | Rods and cones of retina | Colors, patterns, textures |
| Hearing | Sound waves | Ear | Hair cells of the basilar membrane | Noises, tones |
| Skin senses | External contact | Skin | Nerve endings in skin | Touch, warmth, cold |
| Smell | Volatile substances | Nose | Hair cells of olfactory epithelium | Odors (musky, flowery, burnt, minty, etc.) |
| Taste | Soluble substances | Tongue | Taste buds of tongue | Flavors (sweet, sour, salty, bitter) |
| Equilibrium | Mechanical and gravitational forces | Inner ear | Hair cells of semicircular canals and vestibule | Spatial movement, gravitational pull |
| Pain | Many intense or extreme stimuli: temperature, chemicals, mechanical stimuli, etc. | Net of pain fibers all over the body | Specialized pain receptors, overactive or abnormal neurons | Acute pain, chronic pain |

with the detection by a sensory neuron (in the ear, for example) of the physical stimulus (such as the sound wave made by a vibrating guitar string). When the appropriate stimulus reaches a sense organ, it activates specialized neurons, called **receptors,** which respond by converting their excitation into a *nerve impulse*. It is this impulse that carries a code of the sensory event in a form that can be further processed by the brain. This information-carrying impulse travels along a **sensory pathway** to specialized sensory processing areas in the brain (the auditory cortex, in the case of sounds). At this stage, the brain extracts information about the basic qualities of the stimulus, such as its intensity, pitch, and direction. Together, the incoming sensory pathways are known as the **afferent systems** (sensory systems) because they carry information coming *into* the brain. (*Afferent* comes from the Latin *ad* meaning "toward" + *ferens* meaning "carrying"). In contrast, the *motor systems* carry information *going out of* the brain to muscles and glands; these processes are known as **efferent systems** (from *ex* meaning "out" + *ferens*).

Table 5.1 summarizes the main stimuli and receptors for each sense. As you review this list, consider the enormous versatility of human receptors—the neurons that specialize in detecting and transforming stimuli into sensations as diverse as pungent odors, faint lights, and physical pressure. Please keep in mind that the stimulus itself terminates in the receptor: The only thing that continues on into the nervous system is *information*.

### Sensory Adaptation

If you have ever jumped into a cool pool on a hot day, you know that sensation is critically influenced by change. In fact, the main role of our stimulus detectors is to announce changes in the external world—a flash of light, a splash of water, a clap of thunder, the prick of a pin, or the burst of flavor from a dollop of salsa. Our sense organs are ultimately novelty detectors. Their receptors pump information about new and changing events into the barrage of neural messages that the brain uses to interpret environmental conditions.

The great quantity of incoming sensation would soon overwhelm us, if not for a specially evolved function of all sensory systems: *adaptation*. **Sensory adaptation** is the diminishing responsiveness of sensory systems to prolonged stimulation. Stimulation that does not change in intensity or some other quality tends to shift into the

**Chapter 2: Biopsychology**
*The brain gets all its information from nerve cells, or neurons.*

**Chapter 2: Biopsychology**
*Neural pathways involve bundles of neurons taking essentially the same route.*

**Receptors:** Specialized neurons that are activated by stimulation and transduce (convert) it into a nerve impulse.

**Sensory pathway:** Bundles of neurons that carry information from the sense organs to the brain.

**Afferent systems:** Sensory receptors and pathways that process information and carry it to the brain.

**Efferent systems:** Motor systems that process and carry information from the brain to muscles and glands.

**Sensory adaptation:** Loss of responsiveness in receptor cells after stimulation has remained unchanged for a while.

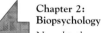

A swimmer must undergo sensory adaptation when jumping into cool water.

background of our awareness, unless it is quite intense or painful. For example, you probably did not realize—until you read these words and considered their meaning—that you had adapted to the press of furniture against your body at this moment. Until you refocused attention, you did not "feel" the chair against your posterior, the upholstery at your back, or the pillow under your neck. In a similar way, you do not notice the tension of socks or hose on your legs and feet, the concentration of cologne near your nose, or the unvarying drone of an air conditioner. As long as these streams of stimulation remain relatively constant, your attention shifts to other sensations. However, any change in the signals you are receiving (if the air conditioner suddenly becomes louder or higher-pitched, for example) will rivet your sensory attention. Incidentally, sensory adaptation is why the background music often played in stores is so boring: It has been selected and filtered to remove any large changes in volume or pitch that might distract our attention from the merchandise. (Do you see why you should not listen to interesting music while you are studying?)

## Thresholds

What is the weakest stimulus that an organism can detect? How dim can a light be, for instance, and still be visible? These questions refer to the **absolute threshold** for different types of stimulation: the minimum amount of physical energy needed to produce a sensory experience. In the laboratory, a psychologist would define this operationally as the intensity at which the stimulus is detected *half* of the time over many trials. Obviously, this threshold will vary from one person to another. So, if you point out a faint star to a friend who says he cannot see it, the star's light is above your absolute threshold (you can see it) but below that of your friend (who cannot). To give another example: If you have had your hearing tested, the clinician determined your absolute threshold for hearing sounds of various pitches.

A hearing test will also demonstrate that a faint stimulus does not abruptly become detectable as its intensity increases. Because of the fuzzy boundary between detection and nondetection, a person's absolute threshold is not absolute! Table 5.2 shows typical absolute threshold levels for several familiar natural stimuli.

We can illustrate another kind of threshold with the following imaginary experiment. Suppose you are relaxing by watching television on the one night you don't need to study, while your roommate busily prepares for an early morning exam. Your roommate asks you to "turn it down a little" to eliminate the distraction. You feel that

**Chapter 1:**
**Mind, Behavior, and Science**

*An operational definition describes a concept in terms of the operations required to produce, observe, or measure it.*

**Absolute threshold:** The amount of stimulation necessary for the stimulus to be detected. In practice, this means being detected half the time over a number of trials.

**TABLE 5.2:** Approximate Perceptual Thresholds of Five Senses

| SENSE MODALITY | DETECTION THRESHOLD |
|---|---|
| Light | A candle flame at 30 miles on a dark, clear night |
| Sound | The tick of a mechanical watch under quiet conditions at 20 feet |
| Taste | One teaspoon of sugar in 2 gallons of water |
| Smell | One drop of perfume diffused into the entire volume of a three-bedroom apartment |
| Touch | The wing of a bee falling on your cheek from a distance of one centimeter |

you should make some effort to comply but really wish to leave the volume as it is. What is the least amount you can lower the volume to prove your good intentions to your roommate while still keeping the volume clearly audible? Your ability to make judgments like this one depends on your **difference threshold,** the smallest physical difference between two stimuli that can still be recognized as a difference.

If you turn the volume knob as little as possible, your roommate might complain, "I don't hear any difference" or "You haven't turned it down enough." By "enough," your roommate probably means his or her difference threshold. Even if you have adjusted the volume downward slightly, the difference might not be large enough to detect. If you hear the difference, it exceeds your own difference threshold; if your roommate can hear the difference, it exceeds his or hers. Suppose you start adjusting the volume and ask your roommate to "say when"—to stop you when the adjustment is sufficient to be detected. This minimal amount of change in the signal that is still recognizable is the **just noticeable difference (JND).** The terms *difference threshold, just noticeable difference,* and *JND* are used interchangeably by psychologists.

Research on the JND for different senses has yielded some interesting glimpses of how human stimulus detection works. It turns out that *the JND is large when the stimulus intensity is high, and small when the stimulus intensity is low.* Psychologists refer to this notion, that the size of the JND is proportional to the intensity of the stimulus, as **Weber's law.** And what does Weber's law tell us about adjusting the TV volume? If you have the volume turned up very high, the JND for the next-lower volume will be large as well: You will have to turn the volume down a lot to make the difference noticeable. On the other hand, if you already have the volume set to a very low level, so that you can barely hear it if you listen carefully, a small adjustment will probably be noticeable enough for your roommate. The same principle operates across all our senses. Knowing this, you might guess that a weight lifter would notice the difference when small amounts are added to light weights, but it would take a much larger addition to be noticeable with heavy weights.

What does all this mean for our understanding of human sensation? It means that our senses send information to the brain about *relationships* among stimuli. Our senses compare the strength of a stimulus (or a change in a stimulus) against its background and send us a combined message. For humans, the meaning of what we sense begins in the relationships between stimuli and background. You can see how this works in the box, *Do It Yourself! An Enlightening Demonstration of Sensory Relationships.*

**Difference threshold:** The smallest amount by which a stimulus can be changed and the difference be detected half the time.

**Just noticeable difference (JND):** Same as the *difference threshold.*

**Weber's law:** This concept says that the size of a JND is proportional to the intensity of the stimulus; the JND is large when the stimulus intensity is high and small when the stimulus intensity is low.

## An Enlightening Demonstration of Sensory Relationships

In this simple demonstration, you will see how detection of change depends on the intensity of the background stimulation. Obtain a three-way lamp equipped with a bulb having equal wattage increments, such as a 50–100–150 watt bulb. (Wattage is closely related to brightness.) Then, in a dark room, switch the light on to 50 watts. This will unmistakably increase brightness. Changing from 50 to 100 watts will also seem like a large increase. But why does the last 50-watt increase (from 100 to 150 watts) appear only slightly brighter? Your sensory system does not give you a sensation of the exact brightness. Rather, it compares the stimulus *change* to the background stimulation, translating the jump from 100 to 150 watts as a mere 50% increase (50 watts added to 100) compared to the earlier 100% increase (50 watts added to 50). This illustrates how your brain computes *sensory relationships,* rather than absolutes.

## Signal Detection Theory

**Chapter 2: Biopsychology**

*MRIs are imaging devices that produce images of the brain by means of a powerful magnetic field.*

**Signal detection theory:** Explains perceptual judgment as a combination of sensation and decision-making processes. Signal detection theory adds observer characteristics to classical psychophysics.

Signal detection theory says that the background stimulation would make it less likely for you to hear someone calling your name on a busy downtown street than in a quiet park.

A modern improvement on the classical interpretation of absolute and difference thresholds comes from **signal detection theory** (Green & Swets, 1966). It works equally well for explaining human sensation and the electronic sensing of stimuli by devices such as your TV set or an MRI scanner. According to signal detection theory, sensation depends on the characteristics of the stimulus, the background stimulation, and the detector. In everyday life you may have noticed, for example, that you get more out of an 8 o'clock class if your nervous system has been aroused by a strong cup of coffee. Similarly, a person's interests and biases can affect what he or she notices on the evening news. Classical theory, however, ignored the effects of the perceiver's physical condition, judgments, or biases. In classical *psychophysics* (the study of stimulation and sensory experience), if a signal were intense enough to exceed one's absolute threshold, it would be sensed; if below threshold, it would be missed. In the view of the new signal detection theory, sensation is not a simple present/absent, "yes/no" experience.

What does signal detection theory offer psychology that was missing in classical psychophysics? One critical factor seems to be the variability involved in human judgment. The theory of signal detection states that a stimulus event (signal or noise) produces some neural activity in the sensory system. In deciding whether a stimulus is present, the observer compares the sensory experience with a personal standard. For example, perhaps you know that your telephone rings loudly enough for you to hear it even when you are in the shower. If the sound you thought you heard was not that loud, you may judge it to be noise, not a signal. But a sound might not be as loud as the telephone ringing and still be an important signal, such as a family member's cry for help. In such a case, you might be willing to risk a false alarm and jump prematurely out of the shower.

The signal detection theory approach now dominates modern psychophysics. It provides a model of decision making that can be used in everyday life. For example, if you judge that it would be worse to miss your date's call than to track water through the house while hurrying to the telephone, you risk a false alarm, rather than more conservatively guessing "no." Many everyday decisions involve rewards for every "hit" and correct rejection of a stimulus and penalties for every "miss" and responses to false alarm. The size and nature of these gains and losses influence your response biases.

**PSYCHOLOGY IN YOUR LIFE**

## A Critical Look at Subliminal Persuasion

*C*an extremely weak stimulation—stimulation that you don't even notice—affect your mind or behavior? The alluring promise that signals can be processed in your sensory system without awareness lies at the basis of the industry that sells "subliminal" tapes touted as remedies for obesity, shoplifting,

smoking, and low self-esteem. But before you put your money in the mail, let's look at a bit of history and some fundamentals of sensory psychology.

Almost 50 years ago, an advertising executive, James Vicary, dramatically announced to the press that he had discovered an almost irresistible sales technique now known as "subliminal advertising." Vicary said that his method consisted

of projecting very brief messages on the screen of a movie theater, urging the audience to "Drink Coke" and "Buy Popcorn." He claimed that the ads presented ideas so fleetingly that the conscious mind could not perceive them—yet the messages would still lodge in the unconscious mind, where they worked on the viewer's desires unnoticed. Vicary claimed that sales of Coca Cola and popcorn had soared at a New Jersey theater where he tested the technique.

The public was both fascinated and outraged. Subliminal perception became the subject of intense debate. People worried that they were being manipulated by powerful psychological forces without their consent. As a result, laws were proposed to quash the intolerable practice. But aside from the hysteria, was there any real cause for concern? For answers to that question we must return to the concept of *threshold,* the minimum amount of stimulation necessary to trigger a response. The word *subliminal* means "below the threshold" (*limen* = threshold). In the language of perceptual psychology, *subliminal* more specifically refers to stimuli lying below the absolute threshold. Such stimuli may, in fact, be strong enough to affect the sense organs and to enter the sensory system, without causing conscious awareness of the stimulus. But the real question is this: Can subliminal stimuli in this range influence our thoughts and behavior?

Several studies have found that subliminal words flashed briefly on a screen (for less than 1/100 second) can "prime" a person's later responses (Merikle & Reingold,

1990). For example, can you fill in the following blanks to make a word?

S N __ __ __ E L

If you had been subliminally primed by a brief presentation of the appropriate word, it would be more likely that a you would have found the right answer, even though you were not aware of the priming stimulus. (The answer, by the way, is "snorkel.") (*See Chapter 3, States of Mind.*)

Apparently people *do* respond to stimuli below the absolute threshold, under some circumstances (Reber, 1993). But here is the problem for would-be subliminal advertisers who would attempt to influence us in the uncontrolled world outside the laboratory: Different people have thresholds at different levels. So, what might be *subliminal* for me could well be *supraliminal* (above the threshold) for you. Consequently, the subliminal advertiser runs the risk that some in the audience will notice—and be angry about—a stimulus aimed slightly below the average person's threshold. In fact, *no controlled research has ever shown that subliminal messages delivered to a mass audience can influence people's buying habits.*

But what about those subliminal tapes that some stores play to prevent shoplifting? Again, no reputable study has ever demonstrated their effectiveness. A more likely explanation for any decrease in shoplifting accruing to these tapes lies in increased vigilance from employees who know that management is worried about shoplifting. The same goes for the tapes that claim to help you quit smoking, lose weight, become creative, or achieve other dozens of elusive dreams. In a comprehensive study of subliminal self-help techniques, the U.S. Army found all to be without foundation (Druckman & Bjork, 1991). The simplest explanation for rare successes lies in the purchasers' expectations of success and the desire to prove that they did not spend their money foolishly. And finally, to take the rest of the worry out of subliminal persuasion, you should know that James Vicary eventually admitted that his claims for subliminal advertising were a hoax (Druckman & Bjork, 1991).

## Check Your Understanding

1. RECALL: *The afferent systems carry information*
   a. from the brain to the muscles.
   b. from the sense organs to the brain.
   c. from the brain to the sense organs.
   d. from the central nervous system to the autonomic nervous system.

2. RECALL: *Which one refers to the least amount of stimulation that your perceptual system can detect half the time?*
   a. the stimulus threshold
   b. the difference threshold
   c. the absolute threshold
   d. the action threshold

3. APPLICATION: *Which one would involve sensory adaptation?*
   a. The water in a swimming pool seems cooler at first than it does after you have been in it for a while.
   b. The flavor of a spicy salsa on your taco seems hot by comparison with the blandness of the sour cream.

   c. You are unaware of a priming stimulus flashed on the screen at 1/100th of a second.
   d. You prefer the feel of silk to the feel of velvet.

4. RECALL: *Which of the following is a process that adds meaning to incoming information obtained by the sensory systems?*
   a. stimulation
   b. sensation
   c. sensory adaptation
   d. perception

5. UNDERSTANDING THE CORE CONCEPT: *When you hear the sound of a tree falling in the forest, the brain has received nothing but*
   a. sound waves from the air.
   b. neural impulses in the sensory pathways.
   c. the vibration of the eardrums.
   d. sound waves traveling through the sensory pathways.

**ANSWERS:**     1. b     2. c     3. a     4. d     5. b

# HOW ARE THE SENSES ALIKE? AND HOW ARE THEY DIFFERENT?

Vision, hearing, smell, taste, touch, pain, body position: In many respects all these senses work in the same ways. They all transduce stimulus energy into neural impulses. They are all more sensitive to change than to constant stimulation. And they all provide us information about the world—information that has survival value. So, how are they *different?* With the exception of pain, each sense taps a different form of stimulus energy, and each sends the information it extracts to a different part of the brain. These ideas lead us to the Core Concept of this section:

**CORE CONCEPT**

**The senses all operate in much the same way, but each extracts different information and sends it to its own specialized processing region in the brain.**

Each sense organ has a different design, but all of them send neural messages about stimulation to the brain. So, in the end, different sensations occur because different areas of the brain become activated. Whether you hear a bell or see a bell depends ultimately on which part of the brain receives stimulation. We will discover how this all works by looking at each of the senses in turn. First, we will find out how the visual system—the best understood of the senses—transduces light waves into visual sensations of color and brightness.

## Vision: How the Nervous System Processes Light

Animals with good vision have an enormous biological advantage. This fact has exerted evolutionary pressure to make vision the most complex, highly developed, and important sense for humans and most other mobile creatures. Good vision helps us detect desired targets, threats, and changes in our physical environment and adapt our behavior accordingly. How does the visual system accomplish this?

**THE ANATOMY OF VISUAL SENSATION**  You might think of the eye as the camera for the brain's motion pictures of the world (see Figure 5.2). But exactly how does the eye make its visual record? The eye gathers light (reflected from a moving ball, for example), focuses it, converts it to neural impulses, and sends these neural signals on their way for subsequent processing into a visual image. The unique characteristic of the eye is its ability to extract the information about the world from light waves—to transduce the characteristics of light into neural signals that the brain can process. This transduction happens in the **retina,** the light-sensitive layer of cells at the back of the eye that acts much like the film in a camera.

The light-sensitive cells in the retina are known as **photoreceptors.** These photoreceptors consist of specialized neurons that absorb light energy and respond by creating neural impulses—much as photographic film converts light into physical images. The retina does this with two types of photoreceptors known as **rods** and **cones** (see Figure 5.3). Why two kinds of photoreceptors? Because we sometimes function in darkness and sometimes in bright light, we have evolved two ways of processing light stimuli, with two distinct receptor cell types, named roughly for their shapes. The 125 million thin rods "see in the dark"—that is, they detect low intensities of light at night, though they cannot discriminate colors. The rods enable you to find a seat in a darkened movie theatre. The seven million fat cones dominate during the bright, color-filled day. Each cone is specialized to detect either the wavelengths corresponding to sensations of blue, red, or green hues. These cones allow us to distinguish red from green tomatoes in good light. The cones concentrate in the very

**Retina:** The light-sensitive layer at the back of the eyeball.

**Photoreceptors:** Light-sensitive cells in the retina that convert light energy to neural impulses.

**Rods:** Photoreceptors in the retina that are especially sensitive to dim light but not to colors.

**Cones:** Photoreceptors in the retina that are especially sensitive to colors but not to dim light.

**FIGURE 5.2:**   Structures of the Human Eye

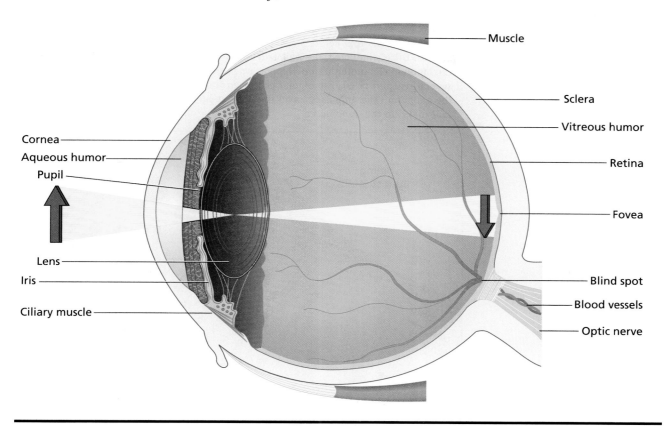

center of the retina, in a small region called the **fovea,** which gives us our sharpest vision. With the fovea you automatically scan whatever interests you visually—the features of a face or, perhaps, a flower.

Still other types of cells in the retina do not respond to light directly. Instead, they gather the responses from groups of nearby receptors. The *bipolar cells* collect impulses from many photoreceptors and send them on to *ganglion cells*. Bundled together, the axons of the ganglion cells make up the **optic nerve,** which carries visual information from the eye to the brain. (See Figures 5.3 and 5.4.)

At the point where the optic nerve exits each eye, there is a small area of the retina that has no layer of photoreceptors. This region, therefore, cannot detect light. The result is a gap in the visual field called the **blind spot.** You do not normally experience blindness there because what one eye misses is registered by the other eye, and the brain "fills in" the spot with information that matches the background. You can find your own blind spot by following the instructions in the *Do It Yourself!* box on page 174.

**PROCESSING VISUAL SENSATION IN THE BRAIN**   At the back of the brain lies a special area for processing incoming neural information from the eyes (see Figure 5.4). This area in the occipital lobe is known as the **visual cortex.** Here the brain transforms the signals from the eyes into visual sensations of color, form, boundary, and movement. Amazingly, the visual cortex also manages to take the two-dimensional images from each eye and assemble them into the three-dimensional world of depth (Barinaga, 1998; Dobbins et al., 1998). In addition, the cortex pulls these

**Fovea:** The area of sharpest vision in the retina.

**Optic nerve:** The bundle of neurons that carries visual information from the retina to the brain.

**Blind spot:** The point where the optic nerve exits the eye and where there are no photoreceptors.

**Visual cortex:** The part of the brain—the occipital cortex—where visual sensations are processed.

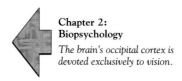

**Chapter 2: Biopsychology**
*The brain's occipital cortex is devoted exclusively to vision.*

## FIGURE 5.3:  Transduction of Light in the Retina

This simplified diagram shows the pathways that connect three layers of nerve cells in the retina. Incoming light passes through the ganglion cells and bipolar cells first before striking the photoreceptors at the back of the eyeball. Once stimulated, the rods and cones then transmit information to the bipolar cells (note that one bipolar cell combines information from several receptor cells). The bipolar cells then transmit neural impulses to the ganglion cells. Impulses travel from the ganglia to the brain via axons that make up the optic nerve.

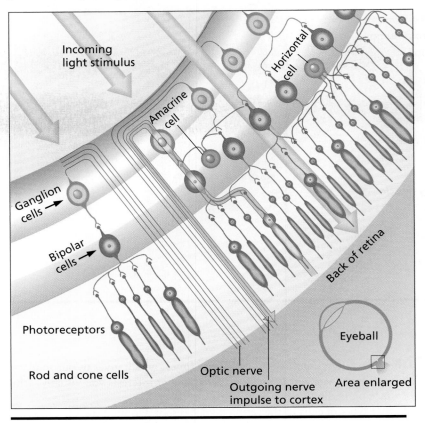

diverse visual sensations together, combining them with memories, motives, and emotions, to create a representation of the visual world that fits our current concerns and interests (Maunsell, 1995). This suggests why you are strongly attracted by the visual appeal of appetizing foods if you go grocery shopping when you are hungry. In short, we look with our eyes but we *see* with our brains.

*HOW THE VISUAL SYSTEM CREATES COLOR*  You may have been surprised to learn that a ripe tomato, itself, has no **color.** Physical objects seen in bright light *seem* to have the marvelous property of being awash with color, but as we have seen, the red tomatoes, green fir trees, blue oceans, and multihued rainbows are, themselves, actually quite colorless. Despite appearances, color does not exist in the external world. It exists only in the mind of the viewer. That is, color is a *psychological* property of your sensory experience, created when specialized areas of your brain process the wavelength information about a beam of light, which has been coded in neural impulses. To understand how this happens, we must first know something of the nature of light.

**Color:** The psychological sensation derived from the wavelength of visible light. Color, itself, is not a property of the external world.

## FIGURE 5.4: Neural Pathways in the Human Visual System

Light from the visual field projects onto the two retinas; neural messages from the retinas are sent to the two visual centers of each hemisphere.

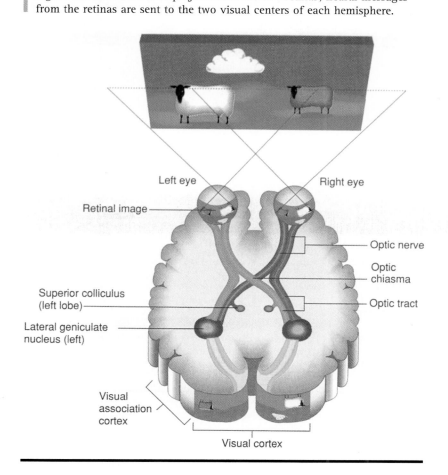

Left eye

Right eye

Retinal image

Optic nerve

Optic chiasma

Superior colliculus (left lobe)

Optic tract

Lateral geniculate nucleus (left)

Visual association cortex

Visual cortex

**Electromagnetic spectrum:** The entire range of electromagnetic energy, including radio waves, X rays, microwaves, and visible light.

**Visible spectrum:** The tiny part of the electromagnetic spectrum to which our eyes are sensitive.

Our eyes are designed to detect the special form of energy that we call visible light. Actually, the light we see occupies but a tiny segment of the vast **electromagnetic spectrum,** which also includes ultraviolet light, infrared light, X rays, microwaves, radio waves, and television waves. You can see how small our visual "window" is, in comparison with the whole electromagnetic spectrum, by examining Figure 5.6. Because we have no biological receptors sensitive to the other portions of the electromagnetic spectrum, we must employ special detection instruments, such as radios and TVs, to help us convert this energy into signals we can use.

Within the tiny portion of the electromagnetic spectrum that our eyes can detect, colors arise from a certain quality of light waves. The eyes are highly sensitive to differences in *wavelengths* of light in this **visible spectrum** (see Figure 5.6). It is the wavelength of light from which the eye extracts the information used by the brain to construct colors. Longer waves make us see a tomato as red, and medium-length waves give rise to the sensations of yellow and green in lemons and limes. Shorter waves from a clear sky stimulate sensations of blue.

Colors themselves are finally realized in a highly specialized region of the occipital cortex, where humans are capable of visually discriminating

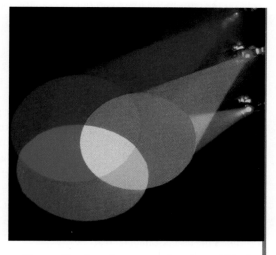

The combination of any two unique hues yields the complement of a third color. The combination of all three wavelengths produces white light, as does the combination of two complementary colors.

## Find Your Blind Spot

The "blind spot" occurs at the place on the retina where the neurons from the retina bunch together to exit the eyeball and form the optic nerve. There are no light-sensitive cells at this point on the retina. Consequently, you are "blind" in this small region of your visual field. The following demonstrations will help you determine where this blind spot occurs in your visual field.

**DEMONSTRATION 1:**   Hold the book at arm's length, close your right eye, and fix your left eye on the "bank" figure. Keep your right eye closed, and bring the book slowly closer. When it is about 10 to 12 inches away and the dollar sign is in your blind spot, the dollar sign will disappear—but you will not see a "hole" in your visual field. Instead, your visual system "fills in" the missing area with information from the white background. You have "lost" your money!

**DEMONSTRATION 2:**   To convince yourself that the brain fills in the missing part of the visual field with appropriate background, close your right eye again and focus on the cross in the lower part of Fig-

**FIGURE 5.5:**   Find Your Blind Spot

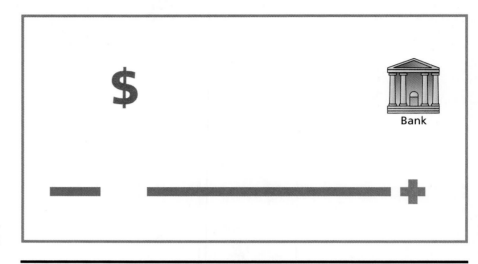

ure 5.5. Once again, keeping the right eye closed, bring the book closer to you as you focus your left eye on the cross. This time, the gap in the line will disappear and will be filled in with a continuation of the line on either side. This shows that what you see in your blind spot may not really exist!

among about five million different hues. Other nearby cortical areas are responsible for processing information about boundaries, shapes, and movements. Each of these regions is most sensitive to changing or contrasting stimulation. Remarkably, our experiences of color, form, position, and depth are all based on processing the same stream of sensory information from our eyes in different parts of the visual cortex.

**Color blindness:** Typically a genetic disorder (although sometimes the result of trauma) that prevents an individual from discriminating certain colors. The most common form is red-green color blindness.

*COLOR BLINDNESS*   Not everyone sees colors in the same way, because some people are born with a color deficiency. At the extreme, complete **color blindness** is the total inability to distinguish colors. (The *negative afterimage* effect of viewing the green, orange, and black flag in Figure 5.7 will not work if you are completely color blind.) Problems in distinguishing color come in different degrees and forms besides total color blindness. People with one form of *color weakness* can't distinguish pale colors, such as pink or tan. Most color weakness or blindness, however,

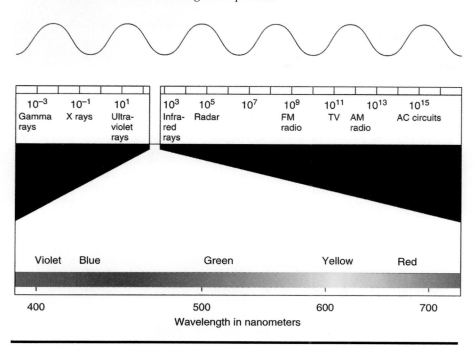

Wavelength in nanometers

involves a genetically based difficulty in distinguishing red from green, especially at weak saturations. Those who confuse yellows and blues are rare, about one or two people per thousand. Rarest of all are those who see no color at all and see only variations in brightness. In fact, only about 500 cases of this total color blindness have ever been reported—including Jonathan I., whom we met at the beginning of this chapter. To see whether you have a major color deficiency, look at Figure 5.8 and note what you see. If you see the number 26 in the dot pattern, your color vision is probably normal. If you see something else, you are probably at least partially color blind.

*HOW THE VISUAL SYSTEM CREATES BRIGHTNESS*   Understanding brightness is not so difficult as understanding color. Sensations of **brightness** come from the intensity of light. Our visual system determines brightness by how much light reaches the retina. A bright light creates much neural activity in the retina, while a dim light

TABLE 5.3:   Visual Stimulation Becomes Sensation

| PHYSICAL STIMULATION | PSYCHOLOGICAL SENSATION |
| --- | --- |
| wavelength | color |
| intensity (amplitude) | brightness |

Color and brightness are the psychological counterparts of the wavelength and intensity of a light wave. Wavelength and intensity are characteristics of physical light waves, while color and brightness exist only in the brain.

**Brightness:** A sensation caused by the intensity of light waves.

## The Amazing Afterimage

After you stare at a brightly colored object for a while and then turn away to look at a blank surface, you will see the object in complementary colors as a *visual afterimage*. You can experience this if you try our Patriotism Test. Stare at the dot in the center of the green, black, and orange flag in Figure 5.7 for at least 30 seconds. Take care to hold your eyes steady and not to let them scan over the image during this time. Then quickly shift your gaze to the center of a sheet of white paper or to a light-colored blank wall. What do you see? Have your friends take the Patriotism Test, too. Do they see the same afterimage?

**Afterimages** may be negative or positive. *Positive afterimages* are caused by a continuation of the receptor and neural processes following stimulation. They are brief. An example of positive afterimages occurs when you see the trail of a sparkler twirled by a Fourth of July reveler. *Negative afterimages* are the opposite or the reverse of the original experience, as in the flag example. They last longer. Negative afterimages are caused by the light temporarily

### FIGURE 5.7: The Patriotism Test

Stare at the dot at the center of the flag for at least 30 seconds, being careful not to let your eyes wander around the image. Then shift your gaze to the center of a sheet of white paper or to a light-colored, blank wall. What do you see? Do others see the same image when you have them take the test?

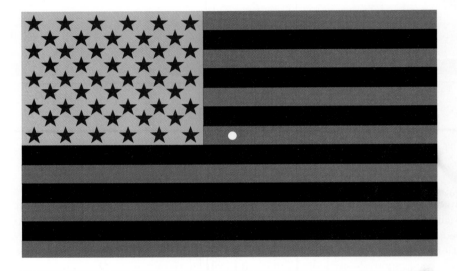

depleting the pigments in certain areas of the retina. As a result, white light subsequently coming into the eye can arouse only the previously unstimulated cone cells, which encode for the complementary colors.

does not. Ultimately, our brains sense brightness by the level of neural activity produced in the retina and passed along through the optic pathways.

**UNDERSTANDING WHAT HAPPENED TO JONATHAN**    After his accident, it seemed to Jonathan I. that the color had gone out of his world. In reality, however, the wavelength reflections that produce color were intact in the objects around him, but the "color"—the ability to sense different hues—was gone from Jonathan's visual system. His experience is consistent with the idea that color is not a quality of objects, but is an experience constructed in the brain of the viewer (Zeki, 1992). Such cases have also shown us that color and color vision have powerful personal and social meaning. A world without color is perceived as lifeless, gray, and even "dirty." Neurologist Oliver Sacks observes that Jonathan's greatest challenge was to overcome the psychological depression caused by his loss. As an artist, Jonathan might have given in to complete despair. Instead, he learned to use his artistic skill to reinterpret his view of the world:

**Afterimages:** Sensations that linger after the stimulus is removed. Most visual afterimages are *negative afterimages,* which appear in reversed colors.

Although Mr. I. does not deny his loss, and at some level still mourns it, he has come to feel that his vision has become "highly refined," "privileged," that he sees a world of pure form, uncluttered by color. . . . He feels he has been given "a whole new world," which the rest of us, distracted by color, are insensitive to. (Sacks, 1995, pp. 38–39)

## Hearing: If a Tree Falls in the Forest . . .

Although vision is the most thoroughly investigated of our senses, the study of hearing is also of great psychological importance. Imagine how your world would change if your ability to hear were suddenly and dramatically altered. You would soon realize that hearing, like vision, provides us with reliable spatial information over extended distances. In fact, hearing may be even more important than vision in orienting us toward distant events. We often hear things, such as footsteps coming up behind us, before we see the source of the sounds. Hearing may also tell us of events that we cannot see at all. You can remain seated in your room, studying for tomorrow's test, seeing only the words on the page, while your sense of hearing informs you about traffic outside your window, activity in the hall, and voices at the door. And, although you may take it for granted, you may use your auditory sense to determine what time it is, who is nearby, and what you should do.

Besides orienting us, hearing opens the gateway to spoken language. In this way, hearing is the principal sensory modality for most human communication. But the psychologist wants to go beyond the *functions* of hearing to learn *how* we hear sounds. We will review what sensory psychologists have discovered about the production of sound waves, how they are sensed, and how these sensations of sound are understood.

**THE PHYSICS OF SOUND**   Sound waves come from vibrating objects, such as guitar strings, bells, and vocal cords. The vibrational energy transfers to the surrounding medium—usually air—as the vibrating objects push the molecules of the medium back and forth. The resulting changes in pressure spread outward in the form of sound waves that can travel 1,100 feet per second in air. (Sound cannot travel in a true vacuum, such as outer space, because there is no medium there to carry the sound waves.)

A pure tone, such as made by a tuning fork, comes from a single, simple sound wave (see Figure 5.9). It has only two characteristics: *frequency* and *amplitude*, the physical properties that determine how it sounds to us. **Frequency** refers to the number of vibrations or cycles the wave completes in a given amount of time; it is usually expressed in *cycles per second (cps)* or *hertz (Hz)*. **Amplitude** measures the physical strength of the sound wave (shown in its peak-to-valley height); it is defined in units of sound pressure or energy. Thus, when you turn down the volume on your stereo, you decrease the amplitude of the sound waves. Most sounds, however, are produced not by pure tones but by complex waves containing a combination of frequencies and amplitudes. We hear different sound qualities from different sources (clarinet versus piano, for example) because the sounds contain different combinations of frequencies and amplitudes.

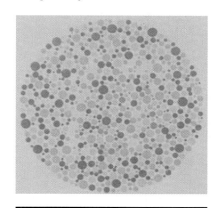

**FIGURE 5.8:**   The Ishihani Color Blindness Test

Someone who cannot discriminate between red and green hues will not be able to identify the number hidden in the figure. What do you see? If you see the number 15 in the dot pattern, your color vision is probably normal.

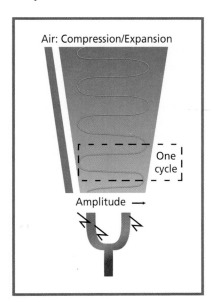

**FIGURE 5.9:**   Sound Waves

Sound waves produced by the vibration of a tuning fork create waves of compressed and expanded air.

Air: Compression/Expansion

One cycle

Amplitude →

**Frequency:**  The number of cycles completed by a wave in a given amount of time, usually a second.

**Amplitude:**  The physical strength of a wave. This is usually measured from peak (top) to trough (bottom) on a graph of the wave.

## FIGURE 5.10:   Structures of the Human Ear

Sound waves are channeled by the external ear (pinna) through the external canal, causing the tympanic membrane to vibrate. The vibration activates the tiny bones in the middle ear (hammer, anvil, and stirrup). These mechanical vibrations pass from the oval window to the cochlea, where they set internal fluid in motion. The fluid movement stimulates tiny hair cells along the basilar membrane, inside the cochlea, to transmit neural impulses from the ear to the brain along the auditory nerve.

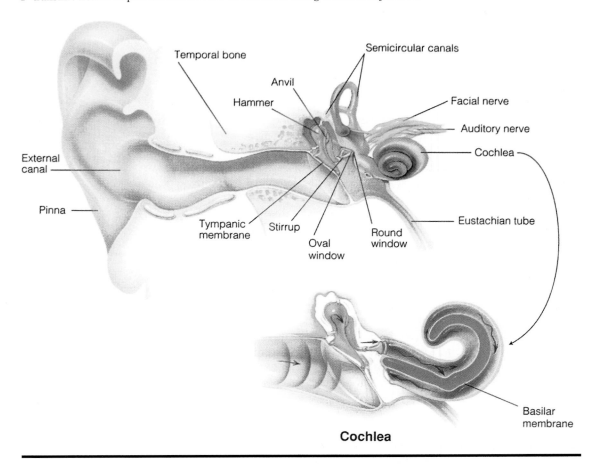

**Cochlea**

---

**HOW SOUND WAVES BECOME AUDITORY SENSATIONS**   The psychological sensation of sound requires that sound waves be transduced into neural impulses and sent to the brain. This happens in four steps:

1. *Airborne sound waves must be relayed to the inner ear.* In this initial transformation, vibrating air molecules enter the ears and strike the eardrum, or **tympanic membrane** (see Figure 5.10). The eardrum transmits the vibrations to three tiny bones: the hammer, anvil, and stirrup (named for their shapes). These bones pass the vibrations on to the primary organ of hearing, the **cochlea,** located in the inner ear.

2. *The cochlea focuses the vibrations on the basilar membrane.* Here in the cochlea, the formerly airborne sound wave becomes "seaborne," because the coiled tube of the cochlea is filled with fluid. As the bony stirrup vibrates against the oval window at the base of the cochlea, the vibrations set the fluid into wave motion. The fluid wave causes the **basilar membrane,** a thin strip of tissue running through the cochlea, to vibrate.

3. *The basilar membrane converts the vibrations into neural impulses.* Bending of tiny hair cells on the vibrating basilar membrane stimulates sensory nerve

**Tympanic membrane:** The eardrum.

**Cochlea:** The primary organ of hearing; a coiled tube in the inner ear, where sound waves are transduced into nerve impulses.

**Basilar membrane:** A thin strip of tissue sensitive to vibrations in the cochlea. The basilar membrane contains hair cells connected to neurons, which accomplish the final step of converting sound waves to nerve impulses.

endings connected to the hair cells. This transforms the mechanical vibrations of the basilar membrane into neural activity.

4. *Finally, the neural impulses travel to the auditory cortex.* Nerve impulses leave the cochlea in a bundle of neurons called the **auditory nerve.** The neurons from the two ears meet in the brain stem, which passes the auditory information to both sides of the brain. Ultimately, the signals arrive in the **auditory cortex** of the temporal lobes for higher-order processing.

If the auditory system seems complicated, you might think of it as a sensory "relay race." Sound waves are first funneled in by the outer ear, then handed off from the tissue of the eardrum to bones in the middle ear. Mechanical vibrations of these bones are then passed to the cochlea and basilar membrane, where they finally become neural impulses, which are, in turn, passed along to the brain. This series of steps transforms commonplace vibrations and shifts in air pressure into experiences as exquisite and varied as music, doorbells, whispers, shouts, and psychology lectures.

**THE PSYCHOLOGY OF PITCH, LOUDNESS, AND TIMBRE**   No matter whether they come from a concert, a cannon, or a coyote, sounds have only three qualities that we experience: *pitch, loudness,* and *timbre.* In the following discussion, we will learn how the two physical characteristics of a sound wave (frequency and amplitude) produce these three psychological sensations. As you read about psychology of sound, note the similarities between sound and the visual sensations discussed earlier.

*SENSATIONS OF PITCH*   A sound wave's *frequency* determines the highness or lowness of a sound—a quality known as **pitch.** High frequencies produce high pitch, and low frequencies produce low pitch (see Table 5.4). The full range of human auditory sensitivity extends from frequencies as low as 20 cps (the lowest range of a subwoofer in a good stereo system) to frequencies as high as 20,000 cps (produced by a stereo's high-frequency tweeter).

We derive a rich amount of information from the pitches of the sounds we hear. For example, we "read" people's voices: The pitch of a voice gives us clues about the age, gender, and mood of the speaker. A change to a higher-pitched voice warns us of alarm, while a lowering of pitch might mean calm—or a signal that one is about to stop speaking. Just as the visual system specializes in sensing color, the auditory system is particularly adept at distinguishing pitch.

How does the auditory apparatus produce sensations of pitch? Two auditory systems divide the task, affording us much greater sensory precision than either system alone could provide. Here's what happens:

- When sound waves are conducted through the inner ear, the basilar membrane vibrates (see Figure 5.10), as we have noted. Different frequencies activate different locations on the membrane. The pitch one hears depends, in part, on which basilar membrane site receives the greatest stimulation. Different *places* on the basilar membrane send neural codes for different pitches to the auditory cortex of the brain—an explanation of pitch perception known as the *place theory.* The place

**Chapter 2:**
**Biopsychology**
**Chapter 6:**
**Learning and Remembering**
*The temporal lobes process sounds and memories.*

**Chapter 2:**
**Biopsychology**
*The primary auditory cortex is in the upper region of the temporal lobes.*

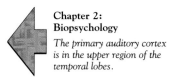

TABLE 5.4: Auditory Stimulation Becomes Sensation

| PHYSICAL STIMULATION | PSYCHOLOGICAL SENSATION |
|---|---|
| frequency (wavelength) | pitch |
| amplitude (intensity) | loudness |

Pitch and loudness are the psychological counterparts of the frequency and amplitude of a sound wave. Frequency and intensity are characteristics of the physical sound wave, while sensations of pitch and loudness exist only in the brain. Compare this table with Table 5.3 for vision.

**Auditory nerve:** The neural pathway connecting the ear and the brain.

**Auditory cortex:** A portion of the temporal lobe that processes sounds.

**Pitch:** A sensory characteristic of sound produced by the frequency of the sound wave.

theory accounts for our ability to hear high tones—above about 1,000 Hz (cycles per second).

- Neurons on the basilar membrane also respond with different firing rates for different frequencies. And so, the rate of firing provides another code for pitch perception in the brain. This *frequency theory* explains how the basilar membrane transduces frequencies below about 5,000 Hz. (Between 1,000 and 5,000 Hz, hearing is based on *both* place and frequency.)

Why does our auditory system seem designed for double duty for sounds within the range of 1,000 to 5,000 Hz? Not coincidentally, the frequency of human speech has a considerable overlap with this range. In addition, the shape of the auditory canal magnifies sounds within the speech range. It appears that the auditory system has evolved two mechanisms especially for hearing the human voice.

**Chapter 2: Biopsychology**
*Evolution occurs through natural selection, which favors adaptive traits.*

*SENSATIONS OF LOUDNESS* The **loudness** of a sound is determined by its physical strength or *amplitude* (much as brightness is determined by the intensity of light). We experience sound waves with large amplitudes (a shout) as loud and those with small amplitudes (a whisper) as soft. How soft a sound can we hear? As we saw in Table 5.2, the auditory system's sensitivity, under ideal conditions, can pick up the tick of a mechanical wristwatch at 20 feet: This is the system's absolute threshold. If our hearing were any more sensitive, we would hear the distracting sound of blood flowing in our ears. At the other extreme, a jet airliner taking off 100 yards away makes a sound wave so intense that it is actually painful. When we compare the two sounds in terms of physical units of sound pressure, the jet produces a sound wave with more than a billion times the energy of the ticking watch.

Because our range of hearing is so great, physical intensities of sound are usually expressed in ratios rather than absolute amounts. Specifically, loudness is measured in units called *decibels* (dB). Figure 5.11 shows the loudness of some representative natural sounds in decibel units. It also shows the corresponding sound pressures for comparison. Notice that sounds louder than about 90 dB can produce hearing loss, depending on how long one is exposed to them.

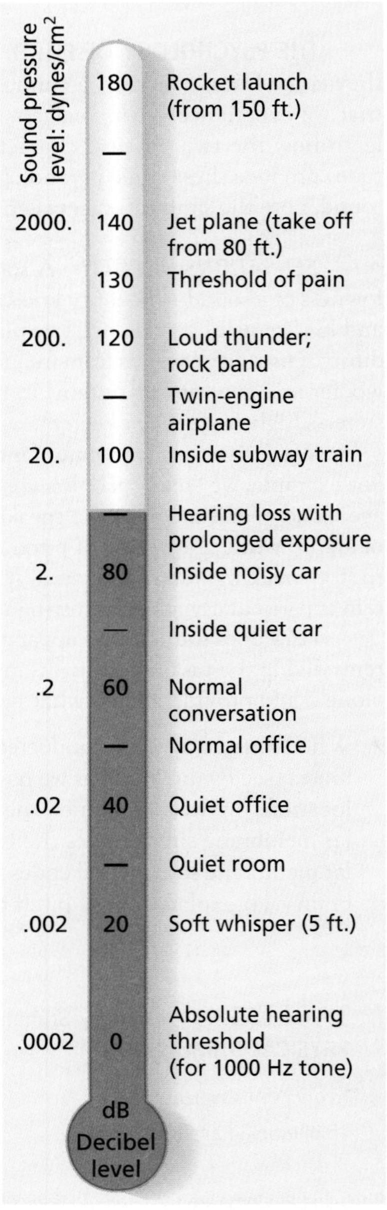

*SENSATIONS OF TIMBRE* The quality of a sound wave's complexity is its **timbre** (pronounced *TAM-b'r*). It is this property that distinguishes a guitar from a violin or one voice from another. Techni-

**Loudness:** A sensory characteristic of sound produced by the amplitude (intensity) of the sound wave.

**Timbre:** The quality of a sound wave that derives from the wave's complexity (combination of pure tones).

**FIGURE 5.11:** Loudness of Familiar Sounds

Sound pressure level: dynes/cm$^2$

| dynes/cm$^2$ | dB | |
|---|---|---|
| | 180 | Rocket launch (from 150 ft.) |
| | — | |
| 2000. | 140 | Jet plane (take off from 80 ft.) |
| | 130 | Threshold of pain |
| 200. | 120 | Loud thunder; rock band |
| | — | Twin-engine airplane |
| 20. | 100 | Inside subway train |
| | — | Hearing loss with prolonged exposure |
| 2. | 80 | Inside noisy car |
| | — | Inside quiet car |
| .2 | 60 | Normal conversation |
| | — | Normal office |
| .02 | 40 | Quiet office |
| | — | Quiet room |
| .002 | 20 | Soft whisper (5 ft.) |
| .0002 | 0 | Absolute hearing threshold (for 1000 Hz tone) |

dB Decibel level

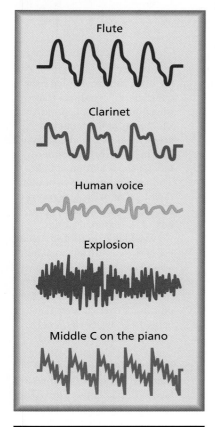

**FIGURE 5.12:** Waveforms of Familiar Sounds

Each sound is a distinctive combination of several pure tones.

Flute

Clarinet

Human voice

Explosion

Middle C on the piano

cally, timbre can be represented as a complex waveform made up of multiple pure tones. Figure 5.12 shows the waveforms that correspond to the timbre of several familiar sounds. Psychophysics has found that the human ear actually analyzes complex sound waves by breaking them down into their simpler component waves.

With this information in mind, we are in a position to answer an ancient riddle: If a tree falls in the forest and there is no ear there to hear it, is there a sound? Based on our knowledge of sensory psychology, we can say emphatically, "No." Even though a falling tree makes a physical *sound wave*, we know that it produces no physical sound because sound is not a physical phenomenon. Rather, sound is a purely *psychological sensation* that requires an ear (and the rest of the sensory system) to produce it.

**COMPARING AUDITORY AND VISUAL SENSATIONS**   Earlier we discussed how visual information is carried to the brain by the optic nerve in the form of neural impulses. Now, we find that auditory information is also conveyed to the brain as neural impulses—but by a different pathway. So, why do we "see" visual impulses and "hear" auditory impulses? As our Core Concept suggested, the answer lies in the region of the cortex receiving the neural message—not on some unique quality of the message itself. In brief, different regions of the brain are designed to produce different sensations. In the accompanying *Do It Yourself!* box, we will show you how to use visual sensations known as *phosphenes* to demonstrate this cortical specialization in your own brain.

## How the Other Senses Are Like Vision and Hearing

Of all our senses, vision and hearing have been studied the most. However, our survival depends on other senses, too. To conclude our discussion of sensation, we will briefly review the processes involved in our sense of (1) body position and movement, (2) smell, (3) taste, (4) the skin senses, and (5) pain. You will note that each gives us information about a different aspect of our internal or external environment. Yet each operates on similar principles. Each transduces physical stimuli into neural impulses, and each is more sensitive to change than to constant stimulation. And, as was the case with vision and hearing, each of these senses is distinguished by the type of information it extracts and by the specialized regions of the brain devoted to it.

**POSITION AND MOVEMENT**   To act purposefully and gracefully in our environment, we need constant information about where our limbs and other body parts are in relation to each other and to objects in the environment. Without this knowledge, even our simplest actions would be hopelessly uncoordinated. (You

## Phosphenes Show That Your Brain Creates Sensations

One of the simplest concepts in perceptual psychology is among the most difficult for most people to understand: The brain and its sensory systems create the colors, sounds, tastes, odors, textures, and pains that you sense. As we have discussed, the external world has no red or green or blue. Nor does it contain any of the other sensations that are so fundamentally a part of your everyday experience. These are all fabricated by the sensory processes in your brain. Moreover, the sensation you have depends more on which part of the brain has been stimulated than on the nature of the stimulus.

Skeptical? Think back on what we learned earlier about the nature of light and of visual sensation. Light has frequency and intensity—but light, itself, has no color or brightness. These *psychological sensations* are the amazing creations that the brain makes of neural impulses coming from your sense organs. We can demonstrate this with an odd perceptual phenomenon called the *phosphene*.

Try this experiment: Close your eyes and press gently with your finger on the inside corner of one eye. On the opposite side of your visual field you will "see" a

bright flash

pattern caused by the pressure of your finger—not by light. These **phosphenes** are visual images caused by fooling your visual system with pressure. Just as light does, the pressure on your eye stimulates the optic nerve, making it send messages to your brain, which misinterprets the signals as light. Direct electrical stimulation of the occipital lobe, sometimes done dur-

ing brain surgery, can have the same effect. This shows that what you sense depends on which part of the brain has been stimulated. It also shows that light waves are not necessary for the sensation of light. The sensory experience of light, therefore, must be a creation of the brain, rather than a property of the external world.

Would it be possible to make use of these artificial visual images to create visual sensations for people who have lost their sight? Work has been under way on this for over 20 years (Dobelle, 1977; Leutwyler, 1994). At this point, reearchers can connect a TV camera or computer to wires that have been surgically implanted on the surface of the occipital cortex. The "picture" sent to the brain actually consists of electrical impulses that the brain interprets as a scattered array of dots—something like a constellation of stars. While these are not detailed enough to convey complex images, patients can read messages encoded in phosphenes arranged in "cortical Braille" patterns, borrowed from the Braille alphabet that many blind people learn to read with their fingertips.

---

**Phosphenes:** Visual sensations that are not caused by light waves but by other forms of stimulation, such as pressure on the eyeball or electrical stimulation of the visual cortex.

**Vestibular sense:** The sense of body orientation with respect to gravity.

have probably had just this experience when you tried to walk on a leg that had "gone to sleep.")

The sense of body position and movement actually consists of two different systems. The **vestibular sense** is the body position sense that orients us with respect to gravity. It tells us how our bodies—especially our heads—are postured, whether straight, leaning, reclining, or upside down. The vestibular sense also tells us when we are moving or how our motion is changing. The receptors for this information are tiny hairs (much like those we found in the basilar membrane) in the *semicircular canals* of the inner ear (see Figure 5.10). These hairs respond to our movements by detecting corresponding movements in the fluid of the semicircular canals.

The **kinesthetic sense,** the other sense of body position and movement, keeps track of body parts relative to each other. Your kinesthetic sense (also called *kinesthesis*) makes you aware of crossing your legs, for example, and of which hand is closer to the telephone when it rings. Kinesthesis provides constant sensory feedback about what the body is doing during motor activities, such as whether to continue reaching for your cup of coffee or to stop before you knock it over. Without the kinesthetic sense, people could not coordinate most of the voluntary movements they usually make so effortlessly.

Receptors for kinesthesis can be found in the joints and in the muscles and tendons. These receptors, as well as those for the vestibular sense, connect to processing regions in the brain's parietal lobes—which, in general, help us understand the spatial relationship among objects and events. Because this processing is usually accomplished automatically and effortlessly, we most often take kinesthetic and vestibular information for granted and make automatic adjustments in our movements.

**SMELL**   The sense of smell, or **olfaction,** involves a chain of biochemical events. Odors, in the form of airborne chemical molecules, interact with receptor proteins on the membrane of tiny hairs in the nose (Axel, 1995; Buck & Axel, 1991). This stimulates associated nerve cells. Their impulses convey odor information to the **olfactory bulbs,** located on the underside of the brain just below the frontal lobes. Unlike all other sensory information, smell signals go directly to the olfactory bulbs, rather than first being relayed indirectly through the thalamus. This suggests that smell probably evolved before the other senses, which all go through the thalamus.

In humans, olfaction has an intimate connection with memory: Certain smells, such as a favorite perfume, may evoke emotion-laden memories (Azar, 1998a). Originally, however, smell was probably a system in primitive organisms for detecting and locating food (Moncrieff, 1951). A major factor in survival, smell is also used for detecting potential sources of danger. In addition, odors can be used for communication. Members of some species (for example, insects such as ants and termites and vertebrates such as dogs and cats) communicate with each other by

**Chapter 2:
Biopsychology**
*The parietal lobe keeps track of things—such as objects and body parts—in space.*

**Kinesthetic sense:** The sense of body position and movement of body parts relative to each other (also called *kinesthesis*).

**Olfaction:** The sense of smell.

**Chapter 2:
Biopsychology**
*The thalamus is the brain's "distribution center" for all senses—except smell.*

**Olfactory bulbs:** The brain sites of olfactory processing, located below the frontal lobes, where odor-sensitive receptors send their signals.

**FIGURE 5.13:**   Receptors for smell

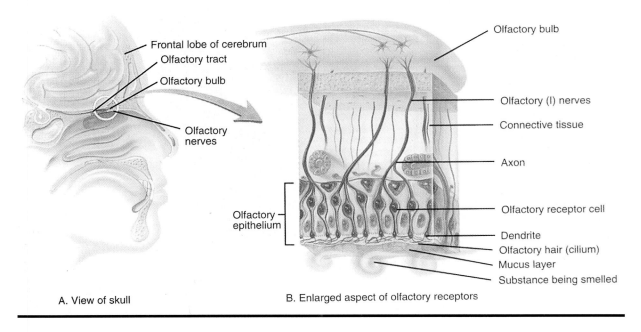

A. View of skull

Frontal lobe of cerebrum
Olfactory tract
Olfactory bulb
Olfactory nerves
Olfactory epithelium

Olfactory bulb
Olfactory (I) nerves
Connective tissue
Axon
Olfactory receptor cell
Dendrite
Olfactory hair (cilium)
Mucus layer
Substance being smelled

B. Enlarged aspect of olfactory receptors

secreting and detecting odorous signals. These signals, called **pheromones,** are chemical substances commonly used within a given species to signal sexual receptivity, danger, territorial boundaries, and food sources. Humans seem to use the sense of smell primarily in conjunction with taste to seek and sample food, but there is also some evidence that we may also secrete and sense sexual pheromones and pheromones that help us identify family members by smell (Azar, 1998b; Filsinger & Fabes, 1985; Holden, 1996).

**TASTE**    When you eat, the senses of taste and smell work together closely. Having a cold makes food seem tasteless because your nasal passages are blocked and you can't smell the food. Moreover, many of the subtle distinctions you may think of as flavors really come from odors. (Much of the "taste" of an onion is odor, not flavor.) Thus, your sense of taste, or **gustation,** is far from precise in its sensitivity. There are only four true, or primary, taste qualities: sweet, sour, bitter, and salty.

The taste receptor cells are gathered in the **taste buds,** receptors for taste that are located primarily on the upper side of the tongue. Taste buds cluster in very small mucous-membrane projections called *papillae,* as shown in Figure 5.14. Individuals vary in their sensitivity to taste sensations, a function of the density of these papil-

---

**FIGURE 5.14:**    Receptors for Taste

(A) Distribution of the papillae on the upper side of the tongue; (B) a single papilla enlarged so that the individual taste buds are visible; (C) one of the taste buds enlarged.

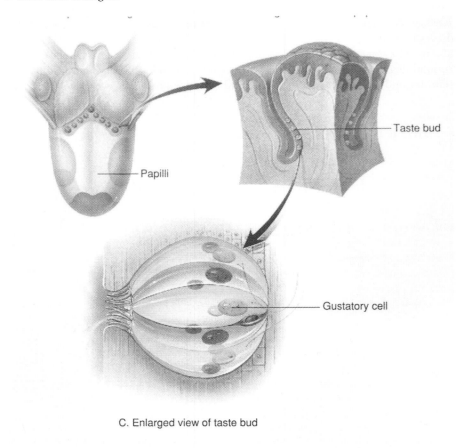

Taste bud

Papilli

Gustatory cell

C. Enlarged view of taste bud

**Pheromones:** Chemical signals released by organisms to communicate with other members of their species; often sexual attractors.

**Gustation:** The sense of taste.

**Taste buds:** Receptors for taste, located primarily on the upper side of the tongue.

lae on the tongue (Bartoshuk, Duffy, & Miller, 1994). Those with more taste buds for bitter flavors are "supertasters," more sensitive than regular tasters or extreme "non-tasters"—a survival advantage, because most poisons are bitter (Bartoshuk, 1993). Ultimately, taste is realized in a specialized region of the brain's parietal somatosensory cortex (adjacent to the area receiving touch stimulation from the face).

Taste sensitivity is exaggerated in infants and decreases with age. Consequently, many elderly people complain that food has lost its taste—which really means that they have lost much of their sensory ability to detect differences in the taste and smell of food. In addition, taste receptors can be easily damaged (by alcohol, smoke, acids, or hot foods). Fortunately, they are replaced every few days—even more frequently than the smell receptors. Because of this constant renewal, the taste system is the most resistant to permanent damage of all your senses, and a total loss of taste is extremely rare (Bartoshuk, 1990).

**THE SKIN SENSES** Consider the skin's remarkable versatility: It protects us against surface injury, holds in body fluids, and helps regulate body temperature. The skin also contains nerve endings that, when stimulated by contact with external objects, produce sensations of touch, warmth, and cold. These **skin senses** are ultimately realized in the somatosensory cortex located in the brain's parietal lobes.

The skin's sensitivity to stimulation varies tremendously over the body. For example, we are ten times more accurate in sensing the position of stimulation on our fingertips than the position of stimulation on our backs. In general, our sensitivity is greatest where we need it most—on our faces, tongues, and hands. Precise sensory feedback from these parts of the body permits effective eating, speaking, and grasping.

One aspect of skin sensitivity—touch—plays a central role in human relationships. Through touch we communicate our desire to give or receive comfort, support, love, and passion (Fisher, 1992; Givens, 1983; Harlow, 1965; Henley, 1977; Masters & Johnson, 1966; Morris, 1967). Touch also serves as a primary stimulus for sexual arousal in humans. And it is essential for healthy mental and physical development (Field & Schanberg, 1990). On the other hand, deprivation of touch stimulation has been shown to stunt the growth of rat babies and human children.

**Chapter 2:**
**Biopsychology**
*The somatosensory cortex identifies touch sensations from all parts of the body.*

**Skin senses:** Sensory systems for processing touch, warmth, and cold.

**PSYCHOLOGY IN YOUR LIFE**

## The Experience of Pain

If you are in pain, nothing else matters. The wound, the toothache, the spasm in your back, the ruptured appendix can dominate all other sensations. For many of us pain is only an occasional annoyance, but if you are among the one-third of Americans who suffer from persistent or recurring pain, the experience can be debilitating (Wallis, 1984). Depression and even suicide can result from the endless nagging of chronic pain. Yet, pain is also part of your body's adaptive mechanism that makes you respond to conditions that threaten damage to your body. Unlike other sensations, pain can arise from intense stimulation in various sensory pathways. Research points to the *anterior cingulate cortex*, located deep in the brain by the fissure separating the frontal lobes, as the site where pain signals from different pathways converge (Craig & Reiman, 1996; Vogel, 1996). *(See Chapter 2, Biopsychology.)*

Your response to pain is far from simple, involving an interplay between biochemistry, nerve impulses, and psychological and cultural factors. Remarkably, your attitudes, beliefs, emotions, and motives can influence the biological processes associated with pain (Turk, 1994). To a small child a bath can be a painful experience. And if someone unexpectedly touches you with an ice cube and says, "Hot!" you will feel it as a burn. In contrast, soldiers wounded in the excitement of battle may feel little or no pain from wounds that would, under other circumstances, cause great suffering. Painful stimuli can even be interpreted as pleasurable, as an aficionado of hot salsa or Thai

*Continued*

curry will testify. Thus, pain can be more than a mere signal of danger. Your reaction to pain also acts as a window into your state of mind. "It is useful to think of pain as a person's emotional experience of a distressing sensation; thus, morale and mood can be as important as the intensity of the feeling itself in determining the degree of pain." (Brody, 1986, p. 1)

The threshold of pain varies enormously from person to person. One study, for example, found that electric shocks had to be eight times more powerful to produce painful sensations in their least sensitive subjects as compared with their most sensitive subjects (Rollman & Harris, 1987). The same study also found that tolerance for intense pain varies by the same amount. This may explain why some people always demand Novocain at the dentist, while others may prefer dental work without the added hassle of an injection.

Pain comes in two main forms. *Acute pain* is sharp or sudden. Scientists study it experimentally in laboratories with paid volunteers, who experience varying degrees of a precisely regulated pain stimulus, such as heat applied briefly to a small area of the skin. This procedure can test a subject's tolerance for pain and measure responses to it without causing tissue damage. In contrast, *chronic pain* (prolonged or enduring pain) is typically studied in hospital research clinics as part of treatment programs designed to find new ways to alleviate such pain.

Wouldn't it be nice to banish the experience of pain altogether? Actually, such a condition could easily be deadly. People born with congenital insensitivity to pain do not feel what is hurting them, and their bodies often become scarred and their limbs become deformed from injuries that they could have avoided if their brains were able to warn them of

**Placebos:** Substances that appear to be drugs but are not.

**Placebo effect:** A response to a placebo (a fake drug), caused by subjects' belief that they are taking real drugs.

Pain is affected by experience and circumstance. A person who is unhappy may find the pain of a headache unbearable, while another individual, in a more satisfactory job, considers a headache merely annoying.

danger. In fact, because of their failure to notice and respond to tissue-damaging stimuli, these people tend to die young (Manfredi et al., 1981). In general, pain serves as an essential defense signal: It warns us of potential harm. It helps us to survive in hostile environments and to cope with sickness and injury.

What can you do if you are in pain? Analgesic drugs, ranging from over-the-counter remedies, such as aspirin and ibuprofen, to prescription narcotics, such as morphine, are widely used and effective. These act in a variety of ways. We have seen that morphine, for example, mimics your body's own pain control substances, the endorphins. All these drugs—especially the narcotics—can have unwanted side effects. If you use narcotics to control severe pain, the possibility of your becoming addicted, however, is far less than it would be if you were using narcotics recreationally (Melzack, 1990).

Because of its psychological qualities, you may also be able to control pain by treatments that use mental processes,

such as hypnosis, deep relaxation, and thought-distraction procedures. You also may be among the minority of people for whom pain can also be modified by **placebos,** phony drugs made to appear as real drugs. For example, a placebo may be an injection of mild saline solution (salt water) or a pill made of sugar. Such nothing-pills are routinely given to a control group in tests of new drugs. The reason, of course, involves the people's *belief* that they are getting real medicine. Because this **placebo effect** frequently occurs, any drug deemed effective must prove itself stronger than a placebo. (*See Chapter 3, States of Mind.*)

But exactly how do placebos produce their effects? Apparently the expectation of pain relief is enough to cause the brain to release painkilling endorphins. We believe this is so because those who respond to placebos report that their pain *increases* when they take the endorphin-blocking drug, *naltrexone* (Fields, 1978; Fields & Levine, 1984). It is likely that endorphins also produce the pain-relieving effects found in acupuncture (Watkins & Mayer, 1982; Price et al., 1984). (*See Chapter 2, Biopsychology.*)

In general, the way you perceive your pain, how you communicate it to others, and even the way you respond to pain-relieving treatments may reveal more about your psychological state—about the kind of inferences you are making—than about the intensity of the pain stimulus. What a pain means can depend on the individual's goals, developmental stage, and past experience. Consequently, pain may be more likely to cause distress and depression among patients who interpret its causes and consequences pessimistically than among those who are more hopeful about its meaning (e.g., Turk, 1995). For example, a patient who believes that pain signals a deteriorating or inoperable condition will experience more distress and more extreme pain than one who feels confident that the condition can be treated and the pain can be managed. This aspect of pain illustrates a general principle that we will see amplified in the last section of this chapter: *What you perceive may be different from—even independent of—what you sense.*

1. **RECALL:** *The eyes have two distinct types of photoreceptors: the* rods, *which detect* _____, *and the* cones, *which detect* _____.
   a. low-intensity light/wavelengths corresponding to colors
   b. motion/shape
   c. bright light/dim light
   d. stimuli in consciousness/stimuli outside of consciousness

2. **RECALL:** *The wavelength of light causes sensations of* _____, *while the* intensity *of light causes sensations of* _____.
   a. motion/shape
   b. color/brightness
   c. primary colors/secondary colors
   d. depth/color

3. **RECALL:** *The frequency theory best explains* _____ sounds, *while the* place theory best explains _____ sounds.
   a. low-pitched/high-pitched
   b. loud/soft
   c. pitch/timbre
   d. simple/complex

4. **RECALL:** *Which sense makes use of electromagnetic energy?*
   a. hearing
   b. taste
   c. pain
   d. vision

5. **SYNTHESIS:** *What do all of these forms of sensation have in common: vision, hearing, taste, smell, hearing, pain, equilibrium, and body position?*
   a. They all arise from stimulation that comes only from outside the body.
   b. They all involve location of stimulation in three-dimensional space.
   c. They all are conveyed to the brain in the form of nerve impulses.
   d. They all involve waves having frequency and amplitude.

6. **UNDERSTANDING THE CORE CONCEPT:** *Different senses give us different sensations mainly because*
   a. they involve different stimuli.
   b. they activate different sensory regions of the brain.
   c. they have different intensities.
   d. we have different memories associated with them.

**ANSWERS:**     1. a     2. b     3. a     4. d     5. c     6. b

---

**KEY QUESTION**

# WHAT IS THE RELATIONSHIP BETWEEN PERCEPTION AND SENSATION?

So, sensory signals have been transduced and transmitted to specific regions of your brain for further processing: Then what? You must employ the brain's *perceptual* machinery to understand what that sensory information *means* to you. Does a bitter taste mean poison? Does a red flag mean danger? Does a smile signify a friendly overture? The Core Concept of this section emphasizes this perceptual elaboration of sensory information:

**CORE CONCEPT**

**Perception brings *meaning* to sensation, so perception produces an interpretation of the external world, not a perfect representation of it.**

Perception is no mirror of reality, says psychologist Richard Gregory (1997). It involves many different mental processes: synthesizing elements into combinations; judging sizes, distances, intensities, and proportions; distinguishing known from unknown features; remembering past experiences; comparing different stimuli; and associating perceived qualities with appropriate ways of responding to them. In brief, we might say that the task of perception is to extract sensory input from the environment and organize it into stable, meaningful *percepts*. A **percept** is what is perceived—the experienced outcome of the process of perception. Not a simple task, perception must identify features of the world that are invariant (fixed and unchanging) by sorting through a continual flood of information. Consider how challenging it is to screen these ever-changing sensations in search of clear, reliable information about the real world. For example, as you move about the room, the sights in the environment create a rapidly changing, blurred sequence of images—yet you remain sure that it is you who are moving, while the objects around you remain stationary. As we study this complex process, we will first discuss how perception discerns what is real, and then we will consider the perceptual tasks of attention, organization, and identification.

## The Major Stages of Perceptual Processing

Imagine that you are the person in Figure 5.15A, seated in a furnished room. Light reflected by objects in the room enters your eyes, forming images on your retinas. In part B of Figure 5.15 you can see what would appear to your left eye as you sat in the room. How does this retinal image compare with the environment that produced it?

One important difference is that the retinal image is two-dimensional, whereas the environment it represents is three-dimensional (Dobbins et al., 1998; Barinaga, 1998). Compare the shapes of the physical objects out there in the world with the shapes of their corresponding retinal images. The shapes in Figure 5.15 that you "know" are rectangular do not necessarily cast rectangular images in your eyes. As

▌ FIGURE 5.15:   Interpreting Retinal Images

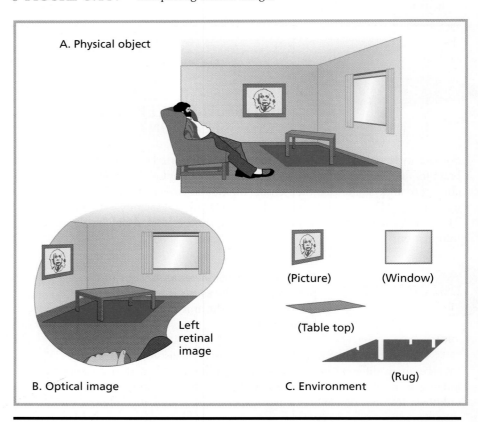

A. Physical object

Left retinal image

B. Optical image

(Picture)   (Window)

(Table top)

(Rug)

C. Environment

**Percept:** The meaningful product of perception—often an image that has been associated with concepts, memories of events, emotions, and motives.

you see in part C of Figure 5.15, only the window, viewed straight on, is sensed as an intact rectangle. The other shapes are distorted or are partially blocked by other objects. On reflection, it is amazing that you are able to see and recognize these shapes when their retinal images are so distorted and different from each other.

This ability to see an object as being the same shape from different angles or distances is an example of a **perceptual constancy.** The world rarely remains constant for long, as the patterns that we perceive continually change form and position. We must not only be able to recognize objects, but we must also be able to track them as they change. In fact, there are many kinds of perceptual constancies. These include *color constancy,* which allows us to see a flower as being the same color in the reddish light of sunset as in the white glare of midday. *Size constancy* allows us to perceive a person as the same size at different distances and also serves as a strong cue for depth perception. And the ability to see a door as remaining rectangular when it opens toward you (or the picture we discussed above seen as rectangular from different angles) is *shape constancy.*

There is more to perceiving a scene, however, than determining the physical properties of the stimulus, however. Besides accurately perceiving the shapes and colors of the objects, you interpret them in terms of your past experience with similar objects. You see objects as familiar and meaningful: a window, a picture, a table, and a rug. This process of identification and recognition is part of what you do automatically and almost constantly as you go about perceiving your environment.

We can use your imaginary encounter with the scene in Figure 5.15 to illustrate the entire sequence of steps in sensation and perception. Let's focus on the picture hanging on the wall: In the earliest sensory stage, this casts the image of a two-dimensional, distorted rectangle on your retina. As it becomes meaningful, you see this shape as a rectangle turned away from you in three-dimensional space. Finally, you recognize this rectangular object as a picture.

Figure 5.16 depicts a flow chart of this sequence of events. The processes that take information from one stage to the next are shown as arrows between the boxes. Note how the flow converges on identification/recognition both from the top (from the brain) and

**Perceptual constancy:** The ability to recognize the same object under different conditions, such as changes in illumination, distance, or location.

FIGURE 5.16:    Stages of Sensory and Perceptual Processing

In bottom-up processing, perception depends on the data originally provided in environmental stimulation. In top-down processing, perception is affected by an individual's knowledge, motivation, and expectations.

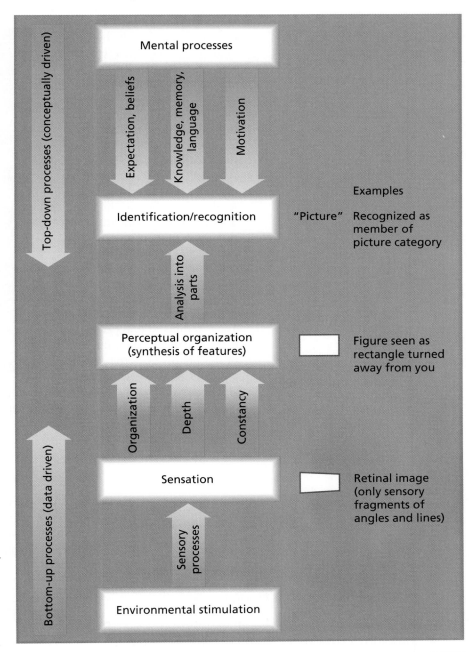

from the bottom (from the stimulation). Taking sensory data into the system through receptors and sending it "upward" for analysis based primarily on the characteristics of the stimulus is called **bottom-up processing.** This process is also known as *stimulus-driven* or *data-driven* because our final perception is determined, or "driven," by stimulus features. Many of the fundamental attributes of objects that we sense in our world clearly involve bottom-up processing. Examples include the motion of a ball, the colors of a banner, and the sound of a bell.

In support of the bottom-up view, research has shown that the brain contains specialized groups of cells that are dedicated to the detection of specific stimulus features, such as length, slant, color, and boundary (Heeger, 1994; Hubel & Wiesel, 1979; Lettvin et al., 1959; Maunsell, 1995; Zeki, 1992). There is even a special part of the occipital lobe that is charged with nothing but extracting features of human faces. Perceptual psychologists call these specialized cells **feature detectors.** One of

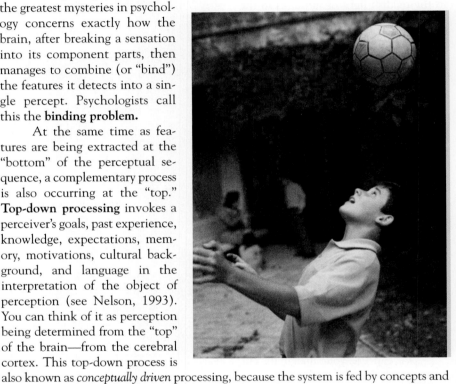

the greatest mysteries in psychology concerns exactly how the brain, after breaking a sensation into its component parts, then manages to combine (or "bind") the features it detects into a single percept. Psychologists call this the **binding problem.**

At the same time as features are being extracted at the "bottom" of the perceptual sequence, a complementary process is also occurring at the "top." **Top-down processing** invokes a perceiver's goals, past experience, knowledge, expectations, memory, motivations, cultural background, and language in the interpretation of the object of perception (see Nelson, 1993). You can think of it as perception being determined from the "top" of the brain—from the cerebral cortex. This top-down process is also known as *conceptually driven* processing, because the system is fed by concepts and other products of the perceiver's own thinking. Examples include recognizing a friend's face or hearing a familiar tune. The two types of processes—bottom-up and top-down—usually interact to enable us to perceive our environment in meaningful ways.

**Chapter 7:
Cognitive Processes**

*Concepts are fundamental units of thought.*

**Bottom-up processing:** Perceptual analysis that emphasizes characteristics of the stimulus, rather than internal concepts.

**Feature detectors:** Cells in the cortex that specialize in extracting certain features of a stimulus.

**Binding problem:** A major unsolved mystery in cognitive psychology, concerning the physical processes used by the brain to combine many aspects of sensation into a single percept.

**Top-down processing:** Perceptual analysis that emphasizes the perceiver's expectations, memories, and other cognitive factors, rather than being driven by the characteristics of the stimulus.

## Perceptual Ambiguity and Distortion

A primary goal of perception is to get an accurate "fix" on the world—to recognize predators, prey, possible opportunities, and dangers. Survival depends on accurately perceiving the environment, but the environment is not always easy to "read." We can illustrate this with the photo of black and white splotches in Figure 5.17. What is it? Try to extract the stimulus figure from the background: a Dalmatian sniffing at the ground. The dog is hard to find because it blends with the background. The same problem occurs when you try to single out a voice against a noisy background at a party.

What is depicted here? How do you know?

**LEARNING THE LESSONS OF ILLUSIONS**   Sometimes your senses can be fooled. When your senses deceive you into experiencing a stimulus pattern in a manner that is demonstrably incorrect, you are experiencing an **illusion,** as we shall see in some examples below (Figures 5.18 and 5.19). Psychologists who study perception appreciate illusions because they point out the discrepancy between our percepts and external reality. Illusions also can help us understand some fundamental properties of sensation and perception (Cohen & Girgus, 1978). Typically, illusions become more likely when the stimulus is unclear, when information is missing, when elements are combined in unusual ways, or when familiar patterns are not apparent.

First let's examine a remarkable illusion that works at the level of sensation: the black-and-white Hermann grid (Figure 5.18). As you stare at the center of the grid, note how dark, fuzzy spots appear at the intersections of the white bars. But when you focus on an intersection, the spot vanishes. Why? The answer lies in the way receptor cells in your eyes interact with each other. The firing of certain cells in the retina prevents or inhibits the firing of adjacent cells. This inhibiting process makes you see dark spots—the grayish areas—at white intersections just outside your focus. Even though you know the squares in the Hermann grid are black and the lines are white, this knowledge cannot overcome the illusion, which operates at the more basic, sensory level. Illusions at the sensory level generally occur because a pattern stimulates receptor processes in an unusual way that generates a distorted image.

To study illusions at the level of perception, psychologists rely on ambiguous figures—stimulus patterns that can be seen in two or more distinct ways. **Ambiguity** is an important concept in understanding perception because it shows that a single image at the level of sensation can result in multiple interpretations at the perceptual level. Figures 5.19A, B, and C all show examples of ambiguous figures. In A and

**Illusion:** The demonstrably incorrect experience of a stimulus pattern, shared by others in the same perceptual environment.

**Ambiguity:** Capable of more than one interpretation. *Ambiguous figures* demonstrate important principles of perception.

## FIGURE 5.19: Perceptual Illusions

A and B are illusions of perceptual interpretation. C is an illusion of recognition.

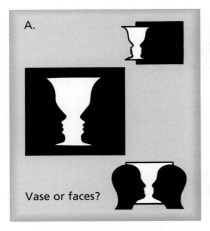

**A.**

Vase or faces?

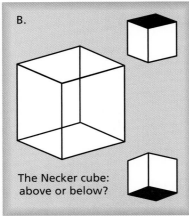

**B.**

The Necker cube: above or below?

**C.**

Duck or rabbit?

## FIGURE 5.18: The Hermann Grid

The Hermann grid is an example of an illusion that occurs at the sensory level (at the level of receptor cells).

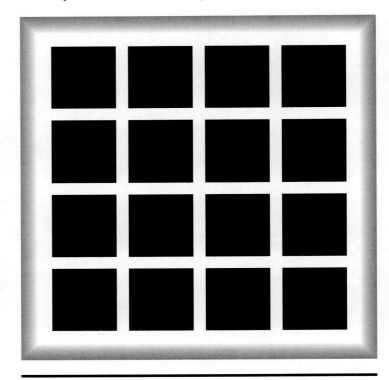

B, the illusions of the faces/vase and the Necker cube affect your interpretations, not your sensations. Each figure suggests two conflicting meanings. Look at each image until you can see it both ways. Once you have seen both, your perception will flip back and forth between them as you look at the figure. This perceptual instability of ambiguous figures is one of their most important characteristics. Your perceptual system cannot recognize both alternatives simultaneously.

The duck/rabbit figure in 5.19C is an example of ambiguity in recognition. You perceive the figure as one physical shape, but there is more than one possibility. Is it a duck or a rabbit? Transforming uncertainty about the environment into a clear interpretation is a fundamental property of everyday human perception. Fortunately, most stimuli are not so ambiguous. We use the same process to identify a familiar-looking face—but even then we sometimes make mistakes. Such errors and illusions remind us that what we "see" goes beyond the physical stimulus properties. The mind plays an active role in structuring our view of the world, and it is heavily influenced in this task by the context in which stimuli occur. When cues or context mislead us, we may as easily be tricked as is a desert traveler beguiled by the mirage of an oasis.

**APPLYING THE LESSONS OF ILLUSIONS** Several prominent modern artists, fascinated with the visual experiences created by ambiguity, have used perceptual illusion as a central artistic device in their work. Consider the two examples of art shown here. *Gestalt Bleue* by Victor Vasarely produces depth reversals like those in the Necker cube, with corners that alternately project and recede. In *Sky and Water* by M. C. Escher, you can see birds and fishes only through the process of figure–

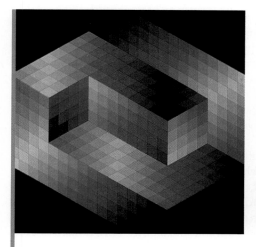

Two paintings using perceptual illusion as the central artistic device: Victor Vasarely's *Gestalt Bleue* (left) and M. C. Escher's *Sky and Water* (right).

ground reversal, as in the vase/faces illusion. The effect of these paintings on us underscores the function of human perception to make sense of the world and to fix on the best interpretation we can make.

In making sense of illusions, we draw on our personal experiences, learning, and motivation. Knowing this, those who understand the principles of perception often can control illusions to achieve desired effects far beyond the world of painting. Architects and interior designers, for example, create illusions that make spaces seem larger or smaller than they really are. So they may make a small apartment appear more spacious when it is painted in light colors and sparsely furnished. Similarly, set and lighting designers in movies and theatrical productions purposely create illusions on film and on stage. So, too, do many of us make everyday use of illusion in our choices of cosmetics and clothing (Dackman, 1986). Light-colored clothing and horizontal stripes can make our bodies seem larger, while dark-colored clothing and vertical stripes can make our bodies seem slimmer. In these ways, the judicious use of illusions can make our lives more pleasant.

## Theoretical Explanations for Perception

The constructive nature of perception and the fact that most people perceive illusions in essentially the same ways suggest that some fundamental psychological principles must be involved. In fact, psychologists looking for these fundamental principles have formulated theories that explain how perception works. Below we will examine two of the most prominent explanations: *learning-based inference* and the *Gestalt theory* of perception. We will see that these two theories arise from different positions on a familiar psychological issue—the nature–nurture controversy. Yet, we need both perspectives to understand the complexities of perception.

**INFERRING FROM LEARNING**    For almost a century, a dominant model among perception theorists was the view proposed by Hermann von Helmholtz. In 1866 Helmholtz pointed out the importance of learning from experience—or nurture—in perception. According to his theory of **learning-based inference,** an observer uses prior learning about the environment to interpret sensory information. Based on this learning the observer makes inferences—reasonable guesses or hunches—about what these sensations mean. Ordinarily these inferences are fairly accurate, but as we have seen, confusing sensations and ambiguous arrangements can create perceptual illu-

**Learning-based inference:** The view that perception is primarily shaped by learning (or experience), rather than innate factors.

**Chapter 4:**
**Psychological Development**
*The nature–nurture controversy centers on the relative importance of heredity and environment.*

**Chapter 6:**
**Learning and Remembering**
*Experiences that can be consciously recalled are stored in episodic memory.*

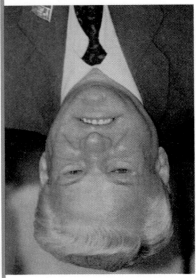

Although one of these photos clearly has been altered, they look similar when viewed this way. However, turn the book upside down and look again.

**Gestalt psychology:** A view of perception that originated in Germany. (*Gestalt* is a German word meaning "whole" or "form" or "configuration.") The Gestaltists believed that much of perception is shaped by innate factors built into the brain.

**Perceptual organization:** Refers to the mental processes by which sensory inputs are drawn together into a percept. The known aspects of perceptual organization include figure–ground, closure, and the Gestalt laws of perceptual grouping. The unknown details of how the brain accomplishes this are often referred to as the *binding problem*.

**Figure:** The part of a pattern that commands attention. The figure stands out against the ground.

**Ground:** The part of a pattern that does not command attention; the background.

sions and erroneous conclusions. Our perceptual interpretations are, in effect, hypotheses about our sensations. For example, as babies we learn to expect that faces have certain features in fixed arrangements (pair of eyes above nose, mouth below nose) and that expressions are most easily perceived in the right-side-up arrangement. In fact, we so thoroughly learn about faces in their usual orientation that we fail to "see" facial patterns that violate our expectations. When you look at the two upside-down portraits of Boris Yeltsin, do you detect any important differences between them? Turn the book upside down for a surprise.

**THE GESTALT APPROACH**    A different view of perception arose in Germany in the 1920s. Known as **Gestalt psychology,** this view maintained that percepts could be understood only as organized, structured wholes, and not in terms of their sensory components. The German word *Gestalt* (pronounced *gush-TAWLT*) roughly means *form, whole, configuration,* or *percept.* From the Gestalt perspective, many simple, but important, patterns are innate—built into the brain at birth by *nature.* That is, the Gestaltists believed that, in addition to things we have learned, the mind contains certain innate patterns that it imposes on sensory experience. Thus, the "whole" of a percept becomes more than just the sum of its sensory "parts" (Prinzmetal, 1995; Rock & Palmer, 1990). For example, a square is perceived as a single Gestalt, rather than four separate lines. Similarly, when you hear a familiar song, you do not remember the exact duration and pitch of each of its notes. Rather, you perceive the *melody,* which is your perception of the overall pattern of notes. This pattern has a meaning that the individual notes by themselves do not provide. The Gestaltists believed that we organize sensory information according to meaningfulness because this is the simplest, most economical way to package sensory input within the brain. Below we will study the mechanisms by which the Gestalt theory says we organize the elements of stimulation into percepts.

Which of these two views—Helmholtz's learning theory or the Gestaltists' innate theory—is correct? Both of them are. That is, our perceptual processes show the influence of both nature and nurture. While both emphasize top-down processes, Gestalt theory emphasizes that the brain is innately predisposed to influence perception in specific ways. But we can also say with confidence that perception is influenced by experience and learning, as Helmholtz's theory argues.

### How We Organize Many Sensations into a Percept

Imagine how confusing the world would be if we could not put together and organize the information available from the output of the millions of receptors in our sense organs. The feat of **perceptual organization** pulls sensory information together to give us the perception of coherence and meaning, as when we put together the shapes, colors, and boundaries that make up a face or a painting by Picasso. Psychologists don't understand the details of this process (which we earlier called the *binding problem*), but they have identified some of the principles involved. Perceiving an image requires first dividing it into *figure* and *ground,* then perceiving *contours* and *closure,* and, finally, *grouping* the perceptual elements into wholes. We will discuss each of these perceptual processes below.

**FIGURE AND GROUND**    One of the most basic of perceptual processes identified by Gestalt psychology divides a percept into *figure* and *ground.* A **figure** is a pattern that becomes the focus of attention, while everything else becomes **ground,** the backdrop against which

Picasso's *Weeping Woman* shows separation of figure and ground. One of the techniques pioneered by Picasso was the portrayal of a figure simultaneously from multiple perspectives.

we perceive the figure. Visually, the figure might be a word on the background of a page. In auditory perception, the figure might be a melody, heard against a background of complex harmonies. The ambiguous faces/vase in Figure 5.19A causes figure and ground to reverse, as the faces and vase alternatively become figure. When you perceive a region as a figure, boundaries between light and dark are interpreted as edges or contours belonging to the figure, and the ground seems to extend and continue behind these edges.

**FILLING IN THE BLANKS** In Figures 5.20 A and B, there seem to be three levels of organization: the pure white triangle—superimposed on red circles and black lines—and a larger white surface behind everything else. Perceptually you have divided the

DO IT Yourself!

## Figure Obscures Ground

The tendency to perceive a figure as being in *front* of a ground is strong. It is so strong, in fact, that you can even get this effect when the perceived figure doesn't actually exist! You can demonstrate this with an examination of Figure 5.20A. You probably perceive a fir-tree shape against a ground of red circles on a white surface. But, of course, there is no fir-tree figure printed on the page; the figure consists only of three solid red shapes and a black-line base. You perceive the illusory white triangle in front because the wedge-cuts in the red circles seem to be the corners of a solid white triangle. To see an illusory six-pointed star, look at Figure 5.20B. Here, the nonexistent "top" triangle appears to blot out parts of red circles and a black-lined triangle, when in fact none of these is depicted as such complete figures. Again, this demonstrates that we prefer to see the figure as an object that obscures the ground. (That's why we often call the ground a *background*.)

**FIGURE 5.20:** Subjective Contours
(A) A subjective fir tree; (B) a subjective 6-pointed star.

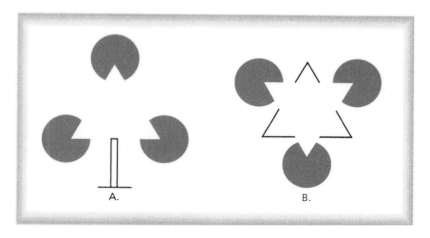

A.  B.

white area into two regions: the illusory triangle and the background. Where this division occurs you perceive **subjective contours:** boundaries that exist not in the stimulus but only in the subjective experience of your mind.

Your perception of these white triangles demonstrates another powerful organizing process identified by the Gestalt psychologists. **Closure** makes you see incomplete figures as complete and supplies the missing edges beyond gaps and barriers. So, when you see a face peeking around a corner, in your mind you automatically fill in the obscured parts of the face. In general, humans have a natural tendency to perceive stimuli as complete and balanced even when pieces are missing. (Does this ring a _____ with you?) Closure also fills in your "blind spot" (Ramachandran, 1992).

The perception of subjective contours and closure involves the brain's creation of percepts out of incomplete stimulation. Now let us turn to the perceptual laws that explain how we group the stimulus elements that are actually present.

**THE GESTALT LAWS OF PERCEPTUAL GROUPING**  How does your visual system accomplish this *perceptual grouping,* the perception that separate stimulus elements belong together? Grouping occurs when you mentally connect the line segments down the center of a road into a single line or when you put facial features together into a percept of a face. Gestalt psychologist Max Wertheimer (1923) studied this problem by presenting subjects with arrays of simple geometric figures. By varying a single factor and observing how it affected the way people perceived the structure of the array, he was able to formulate a set of **laws of perceptual grouping.** Figure 5.21 shows three of these Gestalt principles.

According to the **law of similarity,** we group things together that have a similar look (sound, feel, etc.). So, when you watch a football game, you can use the colors of the uniforms to group the players into two teams because of their similarity, even when

---

**FIGURE 5.21:**  Gestalt Principles of Perceptual Grouping

(A) similarity, (B) proximity (nearness), and (C) continuity. In (A) you most easily see the Xs grouped together, while Os form a separate Gestalt. So columns appear—not rows. The rows combine dissimilar elements and do not form patterns so easily. In (B) dissimilar elements easily group together when they are near each other. In (C), even though the lines cut each other into many discontinuous segments, it is easier to see just two lines—each of which appears to be continuous as a single line cutting through the figure.

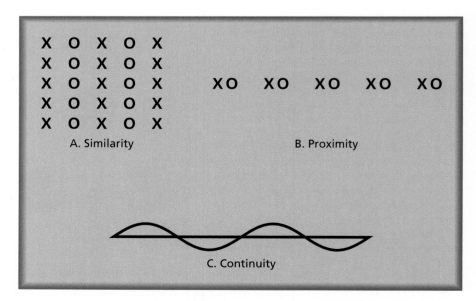

**Subjective contours:** Boundaries that are perceived but do not appear in the stimulus pattern.

**Closure:** The Gestalt principle that identifies the tendency to fill in gaps in figures and to see incomplete figures as complete.

**Laws of perceptual grouping:** The Gestalt principles of *similarity, proximity, continuation,* and *common fate.* These ideas suggest how stimulus elements are grouped together perceptually.

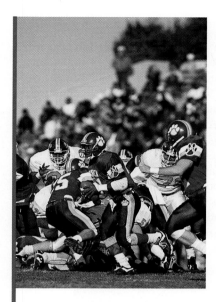

The law of similarity helps us group together players wearing the same color of uniform.

they are mixed together during a play. Likewise, in Figure 5.21 you see that the Xs and Os form distinct columns, rather than rows, because of similarity. Any such tendency to perceive things as belonging together because they share common features reflects the law of similarity. You can also hear the law of similarity echoed in the old proverb: "Birds of a feather flock together," which is a commentary not only on behavior but also on the assumptions we make about perceptual grouping.

Now, suppose that, on one drowsy morning, you mistakenly put on two different-colored socks because they were together in the drawer and you assumed that they were a pair. Your mistake was merely Wertheimer's **law of proximity** (nearness) at work. The proximity principle says that we group things together that are near each other, as you can see in the pairings of the Xs with the Os in Figure 5.21. On another level, your parents may have been worried about proximity when they cautioned you, "You're known by the company you keep."

The Gestalt **law of continuity** can be seen in Figure 5.21C, where the straight line is seen as a single, continuous line, even though it is cut repeatedly by the curved line. In much the same way, continuity makes us know that a car passing behind a tree remains whole, even though part of it is obscured by the tree. In general, the law of continuity says that we prefer smoothly connected and continuous figures to disjointed ones. Continuity also operates in the realm of person perception, where we make the assumption that a person we haven't seen for several days has continuity in his or her personality and is still essentially the same person we knew earlier.

There is another form of perceptual grouping that we cannot easily illustrate in a book because it involves motion. But you can conjure up a mental image that exemplifies the **law of common fate:** Imagine a gaggle of geese, a school of fish, or a marching band. When visual elements (the individual band members) are moving together, you perceive them as a single Gestalt. The same effect occurs when you see clusters of vehicles on a roadway all moving in the same direction together.

According to the Gestalt perspective, each of these examples illustrates the profound idea that perceptual groupings jibe with ideal patterns innately etched in the brain. These innate patterns, then, in a top-down fashion, determine the organization of the individual parts of the percept. In other words, the perceptual whole is more than the sum of the sensory parts. Gestalt psychologists believed that all these grouping laws are particular examples of a more general principle—the **law of Prägnanz** ("meaningfulness"), which says that we will perceive the simplest possible pattern, requiring the least cognitive effort. The most general of all the Gestalt principles, Prägnanz (pronounced *PRAYG-nonce*) has also been called the *minimum principle of perception.* The law of Prägnanz is what makes proofreading so hard to do, as you will find if you examine Figure 5.22.

**Law of similarity:** The Gestalt principle that we tend to group similar objects together in our perceptions.

**Law of proximity:** The Gestalt principle that we tend to group objects together when they are near each other.

**Law of continuity:** The Gestalt principle that we prefer perceptions of connected and continuous figures to disconnected and disjointed ones.

**Law of common fate:** The Gestalt principle that we tend to group similar objects together that share a common motion or destination.

**Law of Prägnanz:** The most general Gestalt principle, which states that the simplest organization, requiring the least cognitive effort, will emerge as the figure.

**Chapter 4: Psychological Development**
*Chomsky argues that patterns of language are also innate.*

**▌ FIGURE 5.22**

A BIRD IN THE THE HAND

We usually see what we expect to see— not what is really there. Look again.

## Connecting Sensation with Memory

The perceptual processes described so far explain how we get reasonably accurate knowledge about the position, size, shape, texture, and color of three-dimensional things in a three-dimensional world. With just this knowledge and some basic motor skills, you could manipulate objects, walk around without bumping into things, and make mental representations of your environment. Yet something would be missing. You would not know what the objects you encountered were or whether you had seen them before. Your experience might resemble a visit to an alien planet, where everything was new to you. You would not know what to eat, what to put on your head, what to run away from, or what to approach.

To get information about the things you perceive, you must first be able to identify or recognize them as objects or events you have encountered before and as members of the mental categories you have built from experience. In short, percepts must link with *concepts*. This happens through recognition and identification, which connect meaning to percepts. In this way, we recognize words on a page, the faces of

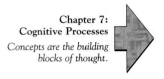

**Chapter 7:**
**Cognitive Processes**
*Concepts are the building*
*blocks of thought.*

Quickly scan this photo. Then look away and describe as much as you recall. Turn to the next page to learn what you, or other perceivers, might not have seen.

friends in a crowd, a familiar tune on the radio, or the smell of peppermint in a candy store. Recognition and identification also give our experiences continuity over time and across situations. In general, this stage of perception draws on memory, expectation, motivation, personality, and social experience to help us understand what we are perceiving.

What determines how successful we will be in recognizing and identifying a percept? The most important factors include the *context*, our *expectations*, and *perceptual set*. Each of these involves a way of narrowing our search of the vast store of concepts in long-term memory.

**CONTEXTS AND EXPECTATIONS**   Once you identify a *context*, you form *expectations* about what persons, objects, and events you are likely to see (Biederman, 1989). For example, you have probably experienced the problem of recognizing people you know in places where you didn't expect to see them, such as in a different city or an unusual social group. This experience makes you realize that it takes much longer to recognize people outside their usual context; sometimes you aren't even sure you really know them. The problem is not that they look different but that the context is unfamiliar: You didn't expect them to be there. Thus, perceptual identification depends on expectations as well as on an object's physical properties. To give a more immediate illustration of our expectations being influenced by the context, take a look at the following:

## THE CAT

It says THE CAT, right? Now look again at the middle letter of each word. Physically, these two letters are exactly the same, yet you perceived the first as an H and the second as an A. Why? Clearly, your perception was affected by what you know about words in English. The context provided by T__E makes an H highly likely and an A unlikely, whereas the reverse is true of the context of C__T (Selfridge, 1955). Context can fool you into misperceiving some stimuli, as in this demonstration. But context is an enormously useful cue to deciphering difficult stimuli, such as hard-to-read handwriting. If you receive a scenic postcard from a friend whose scrawled note describes "having a wonderful time on v_____," you rely on context cues to guess that the V-word is probably "vacation," and probably not a series of alternatives such as "vacuum," "viaduct," or "Venus"!

**PERCEPTUAL SET**   Another way context and expectation influence your perception comes from your *set*, or readiness to notice and respond to stimulus cues, like a sprinter waiting for the starter's pistol. In general, **perceptual set** is a readiness to detect a particular stimulus in a given context. For example, a new mother is perceptually set to hear the cries of her child. Often, a perceptual set leads you to transform an ambiguous stimulus into the one you were expecting.

To see how this works, read quickly through the series of words that follow in both rows:

FOX; OWL; SNAKE; TURKEY; SWAN; D?CK

BOB; RAY; DAVE; BILL; TOM; D?CK

Notice how the words in the two rows lead you to read D?CK differently in each row. The meanings of the words read prior to the ambiguous stimulus creates a perceptual

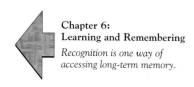

Chapter 6:
**Learning and Remembering**
*Recognition is one way of accessing long-term memory.*

Did you see a woman committing suicide in the photo, entitled "The Moment before Death," on the previous page? Most people have difficulty identifying the falling woman in the center of the photo because of the confusing background and because they have no perceptual schema that makes them expect to see a person positioned horizontally in midair.

**Perceptual set:** Readiness to detect a particular stimulus in a given context.

## You See What You're Set to See

Labels create a context that can impose a *perceptual set* for an ambiguous figure. Have a friend look carefully at the picture of the "young woman" in Figure 5.23A, and have another friend examine the "old woman" in Figure 5.23B. (Cover the other pictures while they do this.) Then, have them look together at Figure 5.23C. What do they see? Each will probably see something different, even though it's the same stimulus pattern. Prior exposure to the picture with a specific label will usually affect a person's perception of the ambiguous figure.

**▌ FIGURE 5.23:** Three Pictures of a Woman

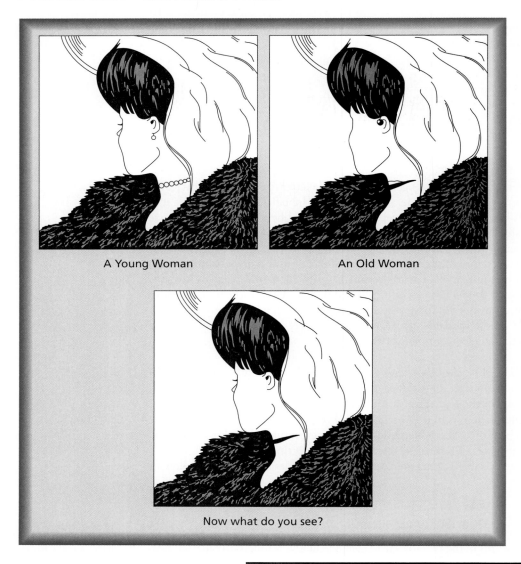

A Young Woman

An Old Woman

Now what do you see?

set. Words that refer to animals create a perceptual set that influences you to read D?CK as "DUCK." Names create a perceptual set leading you to see D?CK as DICK. Another illustration of perceptual set appears in the *Do It Yourself!* box.

People can also develop very different views of the same person when conditions have created different sets. For example, your perception of your psychology professor is probably quite different from that of someone who knows him or her primarily in a social setting. Likewise, context and perceptual set can influence attitudes toward groups of people. So, you can see that sets may underlie the social problem of prejudice. Those who have been taught that certain groups are strong, stupid, athletic, or musical may have developed perceptual sets that influence their attitudes and behaviors toward those groups.

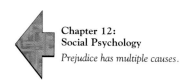

**Chapter 12:**
**Social Psychology**
*Prejudice has multiple causes.*

## Cultural Influences on Perception

Cross-cultural psychologists have shown that the different everyday experiences of people in different cultures create differences in their perceptions (Deregowski, 1980; Segall, 1994; Segall, Campbell, & Herskovits, 1966). People's responses to visual illusions have played an important part in many cross-cultural investigations. Consider, for example, the following figure, a version of the famous Ponzo illusion:

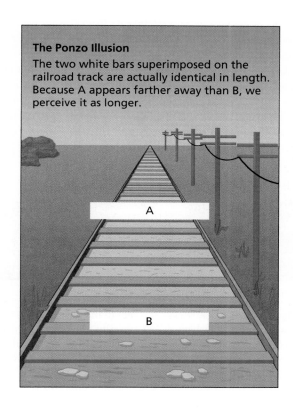

**The Ponzo Illusion**
The two white bars superimposed on the railroad track are actually identical in length. Because A appears farther away than B, we perceive it as longer.

The question for respondents looking at the figure is: "Which line is longer, the one on top (marked 'a') or the one on the bottom (marked 'b')?"

In actuality, both lines are the same length. Research shows, however, that responses to these figures depend strongly on culture-related experiences. Many readers of this book will report that the top line is longer than the bottom line. People from certain other cultural backgrounds are not so easily fooled by the Ponzo illusion. Why the difference?

People learn to use a variety of cues in judging size and distance. Thus, the world you have grown up in probably includes many structures with parallel lines, roadsides, edges, and borders, so your experience leaves you vulnerable to the Ponzo illusion. For example, when you look down a straight railroad track, the rails seem to converge in the distance. Yet you have learned from your everyday experience that railroad tracks do not actually converge or meet each other. The fact that the tracks seem to converge is a cue to distance. Similarly, in the Ponzo illusion illustrated, you may judge the top line to be longer because it seems to fill more of the space between the "parallel" lines. In addition, its higher position reinforces the suggestion that it is farther away along the converging edges or tracks. Intellectually, you know that far-off objects are bigger than they appear. Consequently, you apply this knowledge to judgments about the figures; however, in this instance, such a judgment is incorrect.

But what about people from cultures where individuals have had far less experience with this distance cue? Research on this issue has been carried out on the Pacific island of Guam, where there are no railroad tracks (Brislin, 1974, 1993). The roads there are winding, so people have few opportunities to see roadsides "converge" in the distance. There are several long runways for jet airplanes, but safety considerations prevent most people from standing at one end and looking into the distance. People who have spent their entire lives on Guam, then, have fewer opportunities to learn the strong perceptual cue that converging lines indicate distance.

As researchers had predicted, adult respondents on Guam were less susceptible to the Ponzo illusion than were respondents from the United States. Respondents from Guam were less likely to report that the top lines in the figures were longer. In addition, children 12 years of age and younger were less susceptible to the illusion in both Guam and the mainland United States. These data support the argument that people's experiences affect their perception. Children have had less time than adults to learn strong perceptual cues such as converging lines. Consequently, they will be less likely to use this cue when presented with stimuli that illustrate the Ponzo illusion.

**PSYCHOLOGY IN YOUR LIFE**

*Seeing & Believing*

If you assume, as most people do, that your senses give you an accurate and undistorted picture of the outside world, you are mistaken (Segall et al., 1990). Magicians, who base their careers on the difference between appearance and reality, count on people for whom "seeing is believing." You may have also noticed that politicians rely on influencing people's interpretations of events, too. We hope that this chapter has shaken your faith in your senses and perceptions . . . just a bit.

Unlike magicians and politicians, perceptual psychologists are happy to reveal how sensation and perception play tricks on all of us (Hyman, 1989). They have developed a number of demonstrations that show how your vivid impressions of the world are really highly processed and interpreted images. We have already seen this in many visual illusions presented in the chapter. But, to drive the point home, consider this statement (which, unfortunately, was printed backwards):

.rat eht saw tac ehT

Please turn it around in your mind: What does it say? At first most people see a sensible sentence that says, "The cat saw the rat." But take another look. The difficulty lies in the power of expectations to shape your interpretation of stimulation.

This demonstration illustrates how we don't merely *sense* the world as it is, we *perceive* it. That is, when we observe the outside world, we filter it, modify it, and interpret it. The whole point of the process by which stimulation becomes sensation and, finally, perception is to find meaning in our experience. But it is well to remember that you impose your own meanings on your sensory experience, especially the next time you get in a heated disagreement: Disputes are always about differing perceptions.

Differences in the ways we interpret our experiences explain why two people can look at the same sunset, the same presidential candidates, or the same religions and perceive them so differently. Perceptual differences make us unique individuals. An old Spanish proverb makes the point elegantly:

En este mundo traidor
No hay verdad ni mentira;
Todo es según el color
Del cristál con que se mira.

In this treacherous world
There is neither truth nor lie;
All is according to the color
Of the lens through which we spy.

Magicians count on the difference between appearance and reality.

1. RECALL: *Which of the following is an example of the kind of information that* top-down processing *contributes to perception?*
   a. seeing a face in a crowd and realizing it is a friend
   b. having to wait for your eyes to adjust to the dark in a theater
   c. hearing a painfully loud noise
   d. feeling a pinprick

2. RECALL: *The illusion in the Hermann grid (Figure 5.18) operates at the level of*
   a. stimulation.
   b. sensation.
   c. figure and ground.
   d. perception.

3. RECALL: *The Gestalt theory proposes that many of our perceptions are determined by*
   a. bottom-up factors.
   b. illusions.
   c. ambiguity.
   d. innate factors.

4. RECALL: *The faces/vase image (in Figure 5.19) illustrates*
   a. similarity.
   b. closure.

   c. figure and ground.
   d. attention as a gateway to consciousness.

5. APPLICATION: *When two close friends are talking, other people may not be able to follow their conversation because it has many gaps, which the friends can mentally fill in from their shared experience. Which Gestalt principle is illustrated by the friends' ability to fill in these conversational gaps?*
   a. similarity
   b. proximity
   c. closure
   d. common fate

6. UNDERSTANDING THE CORE CONCEPT: *Which of the following best illustrates the idea that perception is not an exact internal copy of the external world?*
   a. the sound of a familiar tune
   b. the Ponzo illusion
   c. a bright light
   d. jumping in response to a pinprick

**ANSWERS:**    1. a    2. b    3. d    4. c    5. c    6. b

# USING PSYCHOLOGY TO LEARN PSYCHOLOGY

## Studying for the Gestalt

One of the most mistaken notions about studying and learning is that students should set aside a certain amount of time for study every day. This is not to suggest that you shouldn't study regularly. Rather, it is to suggest that you shouldn't focus mainly on putting in your time. So where should you place your emphasis? (And what does this have to do with perceptual psychology?)

Recall the concept of *Gestalt*, the idea of the meaningful pattern, encountered earlier in this chapter. The Gestalt psychologists taught us that we have an innate tendency to understand our world in terms of meaningful pat-terns. Applied to your studying, this means that your emphasis should be on finding meaningful patterns—Gestalts—in your course work. In this chapter, for example, you will find that your authors have helped you by dividing the material into three major sections. You can think of each section as a conceptual Gestalt, built around a Core Concept that ties it together and gives it meaning. The psychological message is this: Organize your study around meaningful units of material. That is, identify a major concept or section of your book, and study that until it makes sense.

And forget about the clock.

## CHAPTER SUMMARY

 **KEY QUESTION** **HOW DOES STIMULATION BECOME SENSATION?**

- The most fundamental step in sensation transduces physical stimuli into neural events. Psychophysics has focused on identifying thresholds for sensations and for just-noticeable differences. A newer approach, signal detection theory, explains sensation as a process involving context, physical sensitivity, and judgment. Sensory adaptation occurs when the senses discontinue processing unchanging stimuli.

 **CORE CONCEPT** The brain senses the world indirectly because the sense organs convert stimulation into the language of the nervous system: neural impulses.

 **KEY QUESTION** **HOW ARE THE SENSES ALIKE? AND HOW ARE THEY DIFFERENT?**

- All the senses involve transduction of physical stimuli into nerve impulses. Vision and hearing have been the most thoroughly investigated by sensory psychologists. In vision, photoreceptors transduce light into neural codes, which are transmitted to the brain, where they become color sensations. In the ear, vibrations are transduced into neural energy and transmitted to the brain, where qualities of pitch and loudness are experienced. Other senses include position and movement (the vestibular and kinesthetic senses); smell; taste; the skin senses (touch, pressure, and temperature); and pain. Different sensations involve sensory processing by different regions of the brain.

  **CORE CONCEPT** The senses all operate in much the same way, but each extracts different information and sends it to its own specialized sensory processing region in the brain.

 **KEY QUESTION** WHAT IS THE RELATIONSHIP BETWEEN PERCEPTION AND SENSATION?

- Stimuli are organized and interpreted in stages that involve sensation, perceptual organization, and identification/recognition. We derive meaning from "bottom-up" stimulus cues and from "top-down" processes in the brain. By studying illusions, researchers can learn about the factors that influence and distort the construction of per-

ceptions. Perception has been explained by several theories, which differ in their accounts of the role of innate brain processes versus experience—nature versus nurture. The "binding problem," or how the pieces of perception are finally bound together meaningfully, remains unsolved. But we do know that certain organization processes in perception help us find meaning in sensation: to distinguish figure from ground, to identify contours and apply closure, and to group stimuli that are similar, near each other, or share a common fate. During identification and recognition, percepts are given meaning through processes involving context, expectation, perceptual set, and cultural and personal factors.

**CORE CONCEPT** Perception brings *meaning* to sensation, so perception produces an interpretation of the external world, not a perfect representation of it.

## REVIEW TEST

For each of the following items, choose the single correct or best answer. The correct answers appear at the end.

1. What is the process that converts physical energy, such as sound waves, into neural impulses?
   a. sensory adaptation
   b. psychophysics
   c. kinesthesis
   d. transduction

2. Luisa agrees to look after her friends' new baby while they run an errand. Luisa tries to read with the stereo on, but keeps listening for signs that the baby might be crying in the bedroom. Several times, Luisa thinks she can hear whimpering—but when she checks the baby, she finds her still sound asleep. Which of the following best explains why Luisa is hearing imaginary cries?
   a. classical absolute threshold theory
   b. signal detection theory
   c. the law of Prägnanz
   d. Weber's law

3. Which of these sensory structures does *not* belong with the others?
   a. lens
   b. ganglion cells
   c. basilar membrane
   d. visual cortex

4. Place theory and frequency theory are explanations for processes involved in the sensation of
   a. the hue created by a light's wavelength.
   b. the timbre of sound.
   c. different olfactory stimuli.
   d. the pitch of sound.

5. Which one of the following is the only sense that does not relay information through the thalamus?
   a. olfaction
   b. kinesthesis
   c. the vestibular sense
   d. vision

6. At a crime scene, a detective finds a slip of paper with three symbols printed on it in ink. She cannot identify the source of the figures or which orientation is up. Thus she cannot determine if the figures are the numbers *771* or the letters *ILL*. Because she has to guess at the meaning of the figures, her perception of them is
   a. data-driven.
   b. stimulus-driven.
   c. bottom-up.
   d. top-down.

7. Which one of the following is most commonly experienced when a stimulus is ambiguous, information is

missing, elements are combined in unusual ways, or familiar patterns are not apparent.
a. an illusion
b. closure
c. a false alarm
d. a correct rejection

8. According to Gestalt explanations of how perceptual processes work, when a person encounters an unfamiliar collection of stimuli, he or she will try to
a. judge whether each stimulus matches a familiar signal.
b. assemble the parts into a meaningful whole or pattern that makes sense.
c. analyze each stimulus component separately to ascertain its meaning.
d. make guesses about its symbolism until finding a matching concept.

9. Research has shown that cultural factors can influence people's perception of
a. distance.
b. timbre.
c. sensory adaptation.
d. subliminal stimulation.

10. Although the markings in the ceiling tiles are of all different shapes and sizes, you notice that the larger, darker spots seem to stand out against a background made up of the smaller, lighter ones. Which principle of perceptual grouping explains this distinction?
a. the law of similarity
b. the law of proximity
c. the law of common fate
d. the principle of closure

ANSWERS:   1. d   2. b   3. c   4. d   5. a   6. d
7. a   8. b   9. a   10. a

# IF YOU'RE INTERESTED . . .

## BOOKS

Ackerman, D. (1990). *A natural history of the senses.* New York: Vintage Books.
*Poet Diane Ackerman's collection of provocative and evocative essays discuss smell, touch, taste, hearing, vision, and synesthesia (experiencing a sensation in the "wrong" sense, such as seeing a sound or feeling a fragrance).*

Cytowic, R. E. (1993). *The man who tasted shapes: A bizarre medical mystery offers revolutionary insights into emotions, reasoning, and consciousness.* New York: Jeremy P. Tarcher.
*Inspired by a personal encounter with synesthesia (multiple sensations from a single stimulus), a neurologist documents instances and explanations of sensory experiences that appear to be hooked together. This fascinating story tells how a researcher transforms an idea into a question and a research program with widespread effect.*

Gregory, R. (1997). *Mirrors in mind.* New York: W. H. Freeman.
*A well-known expert synthesizes our knowledge of visual sensation and perception, using a deceptively simple mirror analogy for the mind.*

Hogan, K. L. (1998). *Tinnitus: Turning the volume down: Proven strategies for quieting the noise in your head.* Network 3000.
*Ringing in the ears or "noise in the head" is a very real and surprisingly common affliction. This book seeks to reassure sufferers by explaining the origins of this haunting distrac-*tion and recommending therapies and treatments that have been increasingly found to relieve the suffering.*

Jourdain, R. (1998). *Music, the brain, and ecstasy: How music captures our imagination.* New York: Avon Books.
*The author, a composer himself, examines the nature of sound, music, the experience of making and listening to music, and its links with emotional appeal, satisfaction, mood, and happiness.*

Lumet, S. (1995). *Making movies.* New York: Alfred A. Knopf.
*Award-winning film director Sidney Lumet (Twelve Angry Men, Serpico, Murder on the Orient Express, Dog Day Afternoon, Network—and many others) explains the art and science of cinema. This is an enjoyable presentation of filmmaking as a wonderful metaphor for perception, with separate contributions creating memory and meaning.*

Ornstein, R. E. (1998). *On the experience of time.* Boulder, CO: Westview Press.
*Through a series of experiments, consciousness expert Robert Ornstein demonstrates how the human mind uses a variety of sensations and perceptions in order to construct an experience of past, present, and future.*

Rodieck, R. W. (1998). *The first steps in seeing.* Sunderland, MA: Sinauer Associates.
*The author, a neuroanatomist, is most fascinated with the structure and power of the human retina but deals with the broadest range of biochemical and physiological processes— and challenges—involved in normal vision, providing clear*

explanations of the "eyeshow" the eyes and brain produce, highlighted with gorgeous illustrations.

Sacks, O. (1998). *The island of the colorblind.* New York: Vintage Books.

*The latest by the author of* The Man Who Mistook His Wife for a Hat *and* An Anthropologist on Mars, *this fascinating, touching, and funny book describes Sacks's journey to a small island in Micronesia, where all the residents are colorblind—yet experience and describe their world with richness, vividness, and acceptance.*

Schick, T., Jr., & Vaughn, L. (1995). *How to think about weird things: Critical thinking for a new age.* Mountain View, CA: Mayfield Publishing Co.

*This book hammers home the idea that we cannot uncritically trust our senses or even our most cherished beliefs. Schick and Vaughn take no prisoners as they attack both the New Age and age-old beliefs in ESP, UFO abductions, dowsing, creationism, near-death experiences, channeling, and miracle medical cures. In the process, they discuss how sensory and perceptual distortions can lead people to accept "weird things." Their prescription is a liberal dose of the scientific method, which they spell out in detail.*

Shepard, R. (1990). *Mind sights: Original visual illusions, ambiguities, and other anomalies, with a commentary on the play of mind in perception and art.* San Francisco: W. H. Freeman & Co.

*A well-known cognitive psychologist, Shepard is also a clever artist with the ability to show us some striking and playful examples of visual illusions—some familiar, some brand new. Both his sense of humor and his deep understanding of perception come bounding out of this volume.*

Süskind, P. (1991). *Perfume: The story of a murderer.* (Translated from the German *Das Parfum* by John E. Woods). New York: Pocket Books.

*A man with an exquisite sense of smell, devastated by the fact that he has no scent of his own, becomes a murderous "vampire of scent" in order to "acquire" it. Passionate, evocative, scary novel about the possible power of fragrance for self and in relationships.*

Valnet, J., & Tisserand, R. (Eds.). (1990). *The practice of aromatherapy: A classic compendium of plant medicines and their healing properties.* Beekman Publishing.

*How can natural aromas affect and even heal the body? As alternative therapies become more popular, it's worth taking a look at what is and is not yet known about smell, the most primitive and perhaps powerful sense, and the essences that stimulate it.*

## VIDEOS

*Babette's feast.* (1987, Danish, color, 102 min.). Directed by Gabriel Axel; starring Stéphane Audran, Jean-Philippe Lafont, Gudmar Wivesson, Jarl Kulle.

*This is a story of taste—the pleasures of eating, the limits of propriety. Set in a small seaside town in 19th-century Denmark, this beautiful tale contrasts the lives of two women, provincial minister's daughters, who use religion to hide from life, with that of their Parisian housekeeper, Babette. A refugee from the old regime in France, Babette unexpectedly wins a lottery back home—and decides to spend her fortune preparing a great feast for her employers and their friends. (This film may make you hungry!)*

*Immortal beloved.* (1995, color, 121 min.). Directed by Bernard Rose; starring Gary Oldman, Jeroen Krabbé, Isabella Rossellini, Johanna Ter Steege, Valeria Golino.

*After the death of composer Ludwig van Beethoven in 1827, his manager seeks to identify the love of Beethoven's life, whom he intended to be his true heir. This dramatic and beautiful film blends fiction and speculation with the facts of Beethoven's life. Note especially the filmmaker's theory of why Beethoven became deaf, Oldman's portrayal of how Beethoven coped with and sought to cover up his hearing loss, and the ultimate triumph of the composer's musical genius over his disability and early life trauma. (The soundtrack, conducted by Sir Georg Solti, is breathtaking, especially the Ninth Symphony, the "Ode to Joy," composed when Beethoven was completely deaf.)*

*Like water for chocolate.* (1992, Mexican, color, 113 min.). Directed by Alfonso Arau; starring Lumi Cavazos, Marco Leonardi, Regina Torne, Mario Ivan Martinez, Ada Carrasco.

*This is the evocative and provocative story of a young woman who, deprived of love and freedom by her domineering mother, expresses her passions and longings in the dramatic, sometimes magical effects of her cooking. The film is vivid, memorable, and funny.*

*The Miracle Worker* (1962, B&W, 107 min.). Directed by Arthur Penn; starring Patty Duke, Anne Bancroft, Victor Jory, Inga Swenson.

*This powerful film is an adaptation of William Gibson's play about Helen Keller (1880–1968), blind and deaf since infancy, and her relationship with Anne Sullivan, the young woman who taught her to perceive and communicate about the world through signing (and feeling the manual alphabet on her hands). Both Duke's and Bancroft's performances won Oscars.*

*Rashomon.* (1950, Japanese, B&W, 88 min.). Directed by Akira Kurosawa; starring Toshiro Mifune, Machiko Kyo, Masayuki Mori, Takashi Shimura.

*After a rape and murder, four witnesses provide vastly different accounts of the crime. The classic film is a wonderful illustration of how perception and memory are biased by individual motives and perspectives.*

CORE CONCEPTS

PSYCHOLOGY IN YOUR LIFE

**HOW DOES CLASSICAL CONDITIONING EXPLAIN LEARNING?**

In classical conditioning, the organism learns to give reflexive responses to new stimuli.

**Taste Aversions and Chemotherapy:** Your friend needs to avoid developing a food aversion when the medicine makes her feel sick.

**HOW DO WE LEARN NEW BEHAVIORS BY OPERANT CONDITIONING?**

In operant conditioning, the patterns of rewards, punishments, and other consequences encourage or discourage the behaviors they follow.

**A Checklist for Modifying Operant Behavior:** A combination of reinforcement and extinction is usually the best bet.

**HOW DOES COGNITIVE PSYCHOLOGY EXPLAIN LEARNING?**

Some forms of learning must be explained as changes in mental processes, rather than as changes in behavior alone.

**Violent Behavior and Imitation:** Violence is a complex problem, but observational learning is one important factor.

**HOW DOES MEMORY WORK?**

Memory is a cognitive system that operates constructively to encode, store, and retrieve information.

**Improving Your Memory with Mnemonics:** All the tricks for improving your memory are based on making things meaningful.

**USING PSYCHOLOGY TO LEARN PSYCHOLOGY: OPERANT CONDITIONING CAN HELP YOU STUDY MORE—AND ENJOY IT**

# 6 Learning & Remembering

## Chapter Outline

n the mid-1980s, 12-year-old Donna Smith began to suffer from severe migraine headaches, which left her sleepless and depressed. Her parents, Judee and Dan, agreed to seek therapy for her. During a psychiatric evaluation recommended by her therapist, Donna disclosed—for the first time—that she had been sexually molested at the age of three by a neighbor when the family lived in the Philippines. It was thought that memories of the assault, repressed and kept secret for so long, were probably responsible for some of Donna's current problems, so she continued with therapy.

In 1990 Donna, now a teenager, began work with a new therapist, Cathy M., a private social worker specializing in child abuse. In their first session, Donna was asked if she had been sexually abused by her own father. Donna denied this but did mention the neighbor's assault. The therapist, however, believed there must be more behind Donna's current problems. For many months, she repeatedly asked Donna whether her father hadn't actually abused her. Eventually Donna told her a lie, claiming her father had once "touched" her, hoping this false claim would enable her therapy to move on. The therapist immediately reported Donna's father to the local sheriff and to the Maryland Department of Social Services (ABC News, 1995).

When Donna realized the drastic consequences of her false claim, she tried to set the record straight, but Cathy M. dismissed Donna's confession, replying that all abuse victims recant their accusations once they learn their therapists are required to report such claims. Donna began to believe that it was her father, not the neighbor, who had assaulted her as a toddler, and that he had continued the abuse. Eventually the therapist suggested that Donna tell her story to county authorities. As a result, Donna was removed from her home and placed in foster care.

To Donna's parents, these sudden accusations were "like a bomb [had] hit"—and it got worse. Still in therapy, Donna became convinced her father had been a chronic abuser, and she began to hate him "wholeheartedly." Committed to another psychiatric hospital, Donna was diagnosed as having several different personalities, one of which claimed that her parents practiced ritual satanic abuse of Donna's younger brothers. The courts forbade Donna's parents to have contact with her. Judee Smith lost her license to run a day-care center. Dan Smith, a retired naval

The courts have sometimes been asked to rule in the controversy over recovered memories of abuse.

*officer, was arrested at his home and handcuffed in front of their two young sons. Financially ruined, Dan Smith was tried on charges of abuse, based solely on his daughter's testimony. His two-week trial ended in a hung jury and Dan Smith went free, but Donna moved to Michigan with her foster family.*

*In her new surroundings, far away from the system that had supported her fabricated story, Donna regained perspective and found the courage to tell the truth. She admitted the charges had all been fabrications, and her doctor recommended she be sent back to her family. The Smiths had a tearful reunion and began the slow process of rebuilding lost relationships and trust. "She's been a victim of this system, as much as we've been a victim," says Dan Smith. "You know, there's a lot of healing to be done."*

*Johns Hopkins psychiatrist Paul McHugh criticizes the practice of "recovering" long-repressed memories to use as evidence. He argues that such recollections are constructed from suggestions therapists offer in order to blame psychological problems on long-hidden trauma (ABC News, 1995). An expert on reconstructed memories, Elizabeth Loftus notes that some clinicians are prepared to believe in their clients' memories, even fantastic tales of ritualistic abuse (Loftus, 1993). In his book* Making Monsters, *social psychologist Richard Ofshe argues that clients can unknowingly tailor their recollections to fit their therapists' expectations, explaining that "therapists often encourage patients to redefine their life histories based on the new pseudo-memories and, by doing so, redefine their most basic understanding of their families and themselves" (Ofshe & Watters, 1994, p. 6).*

*Today Donna and her family are "in wonderful shape, back together." But the painful memories of the Smith family's ordeal will remain with them at some level for the rest of their lives. Fortunately, the same flexibility in human learning and remembering that created these problems can also provide the key to forgiving and healing.*

The ordeal that Donna and her family went through is rare. Still, such cases have surfaced often enough to alarm psychologists about the widespread misunderstanding people have about learning and memory. They know that these processes do not always make an accurate record of events. In fact, Donna's learning and memory processes probably work much like our own. Specifically:

**Chapter 5:
Sensation and Perception**

*Perception is an interpretation of experience.*

**Chapter 7:
Cognitive Processes**

*Concepts are the building blocks of thought.*

- Learning and memory normally serve us well, but they can be only as good as the information they received from the perceptual system—which provides an *interpretation* of our experience.
- We can learn both *concepts* (as Donna did when she came to believe that she had been sexually abused by her father) and *behaviors* (such as the different "personalities" she assumed after her commitment to the psychiatric hospital). Obviously, learning is not something that just occurs in a classroom.
- Memory does not maintain a continuous, complete, and objective record of our experiences—even though we may subjectively sense that it operates this way. It is not so much like a videotape as it is like a fragmented fossil record. When we remember, we recover pieces and fill in the gaps, sometimes even "remembering" events that never happened.

You may be wondering: Could learning and memory play tricks on you, too? The answer is "yes"—although we hope that the result will not be as traumatic for you as it was for Donna and her family. It is particularly easy to be fooled by the assumption that a vivid recollection assures that your learning and memory systems are giving you accurate information. At one time, Donna was sure of her false memories, too.

You may also be wondering why we have learning and memory systems that are so prone to distortion and error. The answer involves the reliance of these processes on sensation and perception. Our best defense against these quirks of learning and memory lies in understanding more about how they operate and what purposes they serve. As our first step in this direction, we will establish more precise definitions of these two processes. Then we will examine their adaptive functions to see how, despite their flaws, learning and memory serve us so well.

What do we mean by *learning*? Psychologists would say that learning takes place through our *experience*—our interaction with objects and events. Thus, we can define **learning** as a process through which experience produces a lasting change in behavior or mental processes. Reading this book, therefore, is part of your experience. So is attending your psychology class. Before we go on, however, let us pause to consider two aspects of our definition of learning that warrant further elaboration.

First, you will note that learning requires a *lasting change*. Thus, a simple, reflexive response, such as jumping when you hear a gunshot, doesn't qualify as learning because it involves nothing more than an inborn reflex, rather than a lasting change in response patterns. Reflexes, however, may become involved in learning: If, for example, the sight of a gun had been associated with the gunshot, you might later jump at the mere glimpse of a gun alone. This change in responding would indicate learning.

Second, our definition says that learning affects *behavior* or *mental processes*. In the gunshot example, it was easy to see how learning affected behavior. Mental processes are more difficult to demonstrate because we cannot directly observe internal events. This difficulty requires that the mental components of learning be inferred from changes in observable behavior. We will see that a certain group of psychologists, known as *behaviorists*, are reluctant to make inferences about mental processes that they cannot observe directly.

And, how do we distinguish *memory* from *learning*? Although our definition does not explicitly say so, learning also implies some sort of retention or storage for what has been learned. So, you might think of memory as the mental mechanism that stores learning for later use. Psychologists would define **memory** more broadly as a system that encodes, stores, and retrieves information (a definition that applies equally to an organism or a computer). In an organism, memory has an unobservable, internal component that must be inferred from behavior, as we saw with learning. We will reserve a more detailed analysis of the processes and problems involved in studying memory for the last section in the chapter.

So, what do learning and memory do for us? If you had no such capacities, you would have to rely entirely on the innate (inborn) behaviors that we often call "instincts." These genetically based patterns account for bird migrations, animal courtship rituals, and even a few human behaviors, such as nursing in the newborn. Learning and memory represent evolutionary advances over the limitations of innate behavior patterns because they allow animals to adapt to changing environments. Although most creatures, even simple ones such as worms and snails, are capable of some learning, most rely primarily on their repertoire of "wired-in" behaviors. Such unlearned behaviors help them locate food, escape from danger, and find a mate. In general, innate behaviors enable them to respond effectively to most conditions they encounter, although they offer little flexibility when conditions change. A salmon, for example, may have no alternative but to attempt a round trip to the ocean, even if it means a fatal plunge over a dam.

In contrast, we humans have made quite a different evolutionary bargain. We have developed enormous capacities for learning and memory—far beyond that of any other creature. Instead of responding automatically, we can consider which response best fits the conditions and adjust our behavior according to the results. This frees us from the limitations of an innate behavioral repertoire and gives us the potential for a selection of responses to stimuli in our environment. Learning and memory allow us to move into new environments—from the arctic to the tropics to outer space—and adapt to new dangers and take advantage of new opportunities. Everything that we call "culture" or "civilization" results from these abilities. Learning and

**Learning:** A lasting change in behavior or mental processes that results from experience.

**Memory:** A mental system that encodes, stores, and retrieves information that has been learned.

**Chapter 1:**
**Mind, Behavior, and Science**
*Behaviorism asserts that overt behavior is the only proper subject of study for psychology.*

**Chapter 8:**
**Emotion and Motivation**
*"Instinct" is a common—but imprecise—term referring to behavior that has a strong innate basis.*

**Chapter 1:**
**Mind, Behavior, and Science**
*Evolution involves genetic changes that help organisms adapt to their environments.*

memory also allow us to create music, discuss relationships, write books, carry grudges, make jokes, and negotiate business deals.

Part of our bargain, however, is an emphasis on approximation and interpretation over mindless, mechanical accuracy and precision. You have probably experienced this distinction when a computer didn't "know" that the file you were looking for was "mypaper" instead of "my paper." Unlike an accurate, but mindless, computer, we are built to assimilate the meaning—the gist of things. While this sometimes makes it difficult to learn and remember the exact details needed for an examination, the way we approach learning and memory gives us an interpretation of our world, the ability to see relationships, and the flexibility to try new responses to changing conditions.

In our exploration of learning and memory, the first two sections of the chapter will deal with two important forms of **behavioral learning,** known as *classical conditioning* and *operant conditioning*. Both deal with the psychological laws connecting stimuli and learned responses. In the third section of the chapter, the focus shifts from outside to inside—from behavior to cognition—as we look at the mental processes associated with learning. Then, in the final section of the chapter, we will look at *remembering*, the nat-

THE FAR SIDE    By GARY LARSON

*"Stimulus, response. Stimulus, response! Don't you ever think?"*

THE FAR SIDE, by Gary Larson.
© 1986. Universal Press Syndicate.

ural extension of the learning process. There you will discover not only how memory works but why memory sometimes fails. We will end on a practical note by considering some steps you can take to improve your memory.

## KEY QUESTION

# HOW DOES CLASSICAL CONDITIONING EXPLAIN LEARNING?

As young children, all three of your authors had bad experiences with specific foods. One of us got sick after eating pork and beans in the grade-school lunchroom. Another had been ill and experienced nausea after eating apple fritters. The third became demonstrably unwell after overdosing on olives. In all of these cases, we associated our sickness with the distinctive sight, smell, and taste of the food—not to anything else in our environment. Subsequently, the very smell or appearance of the "culprit" food set off reactions of nausea and avoidance. You may have had a similar reaction, which may have made you unable to eat a formerly favorite food.

Food aversions such as these are acquired by a special form of learning known as *classical conditioning*. It was discovered accidentally by the great Russian physiologist Ivan Pavlov (1849–1936) during his research on the digestive system. Here's his story.

To study the workings of digestion, Pavlov and his associates had surgically implanted tubes in dogs' glands and digestive organs to divert some of the body fluids into containers outside their bodies, where they then measured and analyzed the secretions (Dewsbury, 1997). To trigger these processes, the researchers routinely put powdered meat into the dogs' mouths. It was all carefully planned and executed, but the results didn't quite match the experimenters' expectations. Specifically, Pavlov

**Behavioral learning:** Forms of learning, such as classical conditioning and operant conditioning, that can be described in terms of stimuli and responses.

To study classical conditioning, Pavlov placed his dogs in a restraining apparatus. The dogs were then presented with a neutral stimulus, such as a tone. Through its association with food, the neutral stimulus became a conditioned stimulus eliciting salivation.

noticed that his dogs began salivating even *before* the powder was put in their mouths. Saliva would start to flow when they saw the food or the assistant who brought it. In fact, any stimulus that regularly preceded the presentation of food came to **elicit** salivation.

To Pavlov, this behavior was a puzzle. It did not make sense biologically: What, after all, is the survival value in salivating without food? Pavlov turned his attention to understanding these "psychic secretions"—automatic responses triggered by cues that had been learned. This turned out to be a bigger project than he had anticipated, and it diverted his attention from the work on digestion (for which he eventually won a Nobel prize). In so doing, Pavlov changed the course of psychology forever (Pavlov, 1928; Todes, 1997).

What was the importance of Pavlov's discovery? It went far beyond drooling dogs. The discovery of learned responses to previously neutral stimuli had implications for understanding a wide range of learned behaviors. He had stumbled on a model of *learning*—one that could be manipulated in the laboratory to tease out the subtleties of the connections among stimuli and responses. In subsequent research, Pavlov identified and described a number of important learning processes that are still being studied by modern psychologists.

Pavlov's discovery, now known as **classical conditioning,** is *a basic form of learning in which two stimuli become associated so that a neutral one acquires the power to elicit the same reflexive response as the other.* In brief, our Core Concept says:

**Elicit:** Evoke or draw out.

**Classical conditioning:** A form of behavioral learning in which a previously neutral stimulus (CS) acquires the power to elicit the same innate reflex produced by another stimulus.

 **CORE CONCEPT**

In classical conditioning, the organism learns to give reflexive responses to new stimuli.

More broadly, we will see that classical conditioning accounts for learning about cues that warn of danger, food, sexual opportunity, and other cues that promote survival and reproduction.

Although classical conditioning is normally beneficial and adaptive, we will see that it also accounts for certain unpleasant conditions, such as phobias. But, happily, behavior that has been learned can be unlearned, and therapists who understand classical conditioning have developed treatments that can eliminate learned anxieties and fears. We will see some of the tools they use as we examine the intricacies of classical conditioning below. But first we will spend a few moments on the methods Pavlov invented to study his newfound form of learning.

 **Chapter 14: Psychotherapy**

*Desensitization therapy uses classical conditioning to eliminate fears and phobias.*

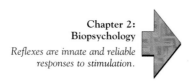

**Chapter 2:**
**Biopsychology**
*Reflexes are innate and reliable*
*responses to stimulation.*

## Pavlov's Experimental Approach

Pavlov's work focused on a simple behavior known as the *reflex* (Windholz, 1997). You may recall that reflexes are unlearned (innate) responses, such as salivation, pupil contraction, knee jerks, or eye blinks, that are naturally triggered by stimuli that have biological significance for the organism. Reflexes also help us deal with important events in the environment. For example, the blinking reflex protects the eyes; the salivation reflex aids digestion. What Pavlov found, however, was that reflexive responses could be connected to new stimuli that had no biological relevance. He could, for example, teach his dogs to salivate after hearing a certain sound, such as the tone produced by a tuning fork or a bell.

To understand how these "conditioned reflexes" worked, Pavlov knew that he would have to manipulate various aspects of his experimental setting and observe what effects would follow. The strategy was elegant and simple. He first placed an untrained dog in a harness. At intervals, a tone was sounded and the dog was given a bit of food. The dog's first reaction to the tone was only an *orienting response:* The dog pricked its ears and turned its head (oriented) to locate the source of the novel sound. But with repeated pairings of the tone and the food, the orienting response stopped, and salivation began. Pavlov found that this pattern could be produced by other pairs of stimuli, as well. In general, any **neutral stimulus** (one without any eliciting power, such as a tone or a light), when paired with a reflex-producing stimulus (food), will eventually elicit a learned response (salivation) very similar to the original reflex.

The same kind of conditioning occurs in kitchens everywhere, when a pet owner runs an electric can opener before dispensing dog or cat food: The pet, hearing the sound and associating it with food, salivates in preparation for a meal. To avoid later confusion, it is important to note that the animal may also exhibit another type of learned behavior—running to the food dish—but this is not *classically conditioned* behavior, because running is voluntary behavior, not an involuntary or "built-in" reflex like salivation. Thus, the pet has also been *operantly conditioned* to come running or begging for food because such actions have been rewarded in the past. We will discuss this other form of learning, operant conditioning, in more detail shortly: The point here is that different forms of learning are often interwoven to affect a broad range of behaviors, as we also saw in Donna Smith's story at the beginning of the chapter.

**Neutral stimulus:** Any stimulus that produces no response prior to learning.

**Unconditioned stimulus (UCS):** In classical conditioning, the stimulus that elicits an unconditioned response.

**Unconditioned response (UCR):** In classical conditioning, the response elicited by an unconditioned stimulus without prior learning.

### The Anatomy of Classical Conditioning

The main features of Pavlov's classical conditioning procedure are illustrated in Figure 6.1. At first glance, the terms used to describe them may sound a bit intimidating, but it will help you to learn them so that we can use them later to analyze real-life situations, such as the learning of fears, phobias, and aversions, that follow Pavlovian laws. Here we go . . .

The **unconditioned stimulus (UCS)** refers to any stimulus that, without any learning involved, automatically triggers a reflexive response, such as an eye blink or a knee jerk. In Pavlov's experiments, the food was the UCS because it provoked the reflexive behavior of salivating. The salivating behavior itself is called the **unconditioned response (UCR),** when it is elicited by the unconditioned stimulus. (To keep this barrage of terms straight, it will help to refer again to Figure 6.1.)

**FIGURE 6.1:** Basic Features of Classical Conditioning

Before conditioning, the UCS naturally elicits the UCR. A neutral stimulus (such as tone) has no eliciting effect. During conditioning, the neutral stimulus is paired with the UCS. Through its association with the UCS, the neutral stimulus becomes a CS and elicits a CR similar to the UCR.

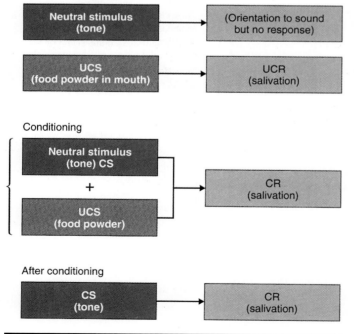

**FIGURE 6.2:** Acquisition, Extinction, and Spontaneous Recovery

During acquisition (CS + UCS), the strength of the CR increases rapidly. During extinction, when the UCS no longer follows the CS, the strength of the CR drops to zero. The CR may reappear after a brief rest period, even when the UCS is still not presented; only the CS alone appears. The reappearance of the CR is called "spontaneous recovery."

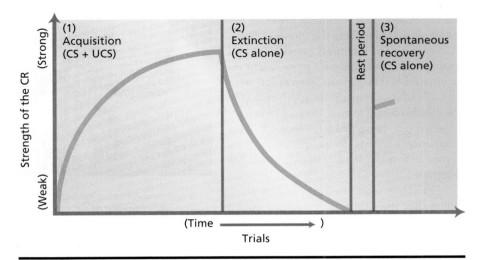

During conditioning, a neutral stimulus (a tone or a light, for example) is repeatedly paired with a UCS (such as food). After several trials, learning becomes apparent. When the neutral stimulus is presented alone, it now elicits the same response as the UCS does: salivation. The formerly neutral stimulus has now become a **conditioned stimulus (CS),** a stimulus that has acquired the power through learning to elicit the same response as the unconditioned stimulus. Although the response is essentially the same reflexive behavior (salivation), we refer to it as the **conditioned response (CR)** when it occurs in response to the CS alone.

Psychologists use the term **acquisition** for the process by which the CR is first elicited and then gradually increases in strength over repeated trials. The first panel in Figure 6.2 shows the acquisition phase of a hypothetical classical conditioning experiment. At first, only weak CRs are elicited by the CS. With continued CS–UCS pairings, however, the conditioned response is elicited with increasing strength.

In conditioning, as in telling a joke, *timing* is critical. The CS and UCS must be presented contiguously (close together in time) so that the organism perceives them as being related. The range of time intervals between the CS and UCS that will produce the best conditioning depends on the response being conditioned. For motor and skeletal responses, such as eye blinks, a short interval of a second or less is best. For visceral responses, such as heart rate and salivation, longer intervals of 5 to 15 seconds work best. Conditioned fear, which we will discuss below, usually requires longer intervals of many seconds or even minutes to develop.

## Variations on the Classical Conditioning Theme

Classical conditioning explains many learned behaviors across a wide range of species—from sea slugs to people. Not only does Pavlov's theory explain how these behaviors are acquired, it explains how they can be modified and eliminated. As we examine these variations on the theme of classical conditioning, let us begin with the conditioning of distastes and aversions.

**Conditioned stimulus (CS):** In classical conditioning, a previously neutral stimulus that comes to elicit the conditioned response.

**Conditioned response (CR):** In classical conditioning, a response elicited by a previously neutral stimulus that has become associated with the unconditioned stimulus.

**Acquisition:** The stage of classical conditioning in which a conditioned response is first elicited by the conditioned stimulus.

Chapter 2:
Biopsychology
*Voluntary motor responses involve the skeletal muscles, which move the body.*

**AVERSIVE CONDITIONING** Pavlov's use of meat powder in conditioning his dogs is an example of *appetitive conditioning*—conditioning in which the UCS is of positive value to an organism. However, another form of classical conditioning may result from an unpleasant UCS. **Aversive conditioning** occurs when the CS predicts the occurrence of an aversive UCS, as when the sight of a hypodermic needle (CS) precedes a painful injection (UCS). An organism's natural response to such stimuli is reflexive behavior aimed at reducing the intensity of the UCS or removing it entirely (as when a child screams and tries to escape a nurse intent on vaccination). Through its association with the UCS (the painful injection), the CS (the needle) also comes to elicit avoidance behavior when it is presented later by itself. This commonly happens to people who have learned to fear the sight of blood, which has become a CS.

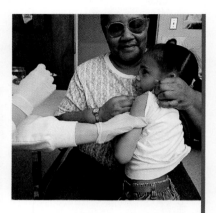

Aversive conditioning has occurred when the mere sight of an object, such as a hypodermic needle, causes an avoidance reaction.

Aversive conditioning studies have shown that the organism learns not only a specific conditioned muscle response (flinching or running) but also a generalized fear reaction that involves internal responses. Specifically, the aversive stimulus (the hypodermic needle) may produce responses in the autonomic nervous system that alter such things as heart rate and respiration. These changes, both internal and external, become part of an overall conditioned fear response produced by aversive conditioning.

When strong fear is involved, conditioning may take place after a single pairing of a neutral stimulus with the UCS. Traumatic events in our lives that may occur only once can condition us to respond with strong physical, emotional, and cognitive reactions that are highly resistant to elimination. Thus, conditioned fear is easy to acquire and sometimes difficult to eliminate—although it can be done, as we shall see next.

**EXTINCTION AND SPONTANEOUS RECOVERY** If you learn to fear spiders or salivate at the sound of the lunch bell, this does not have to become a permanent part of your behavioral repertoire. That is, a conditioned response need not last forever. Pavlov showed how such responses could be eliminated in experiments on a dog conditioned to salivate at a tone. His method was simple. After a few trials in which the tone was not followed by food, the dog stopped salivating. We call this **extinction.** In the language of classical conditioning, extinction occurs with repeated presentations of the CS (the tone), without the UCS (food). The result is that the CR (salivation) becomes weaker and weaker until it finally vanishes, as you see in Figure 6.2.

Now for the bad news: If your fear of spiders has been extinguished, it may spontaneously reappear, but in diminished intensity, sometime later when you happen to see a spider crawling across your desk (Figure 6.2, third panel). Pavlov referred to this later reappearance of the CR as **spontaneous recovery** of the conditioned response. Some cases require several extinction sessions before an unwanted response disappears completely. Each successive extinction period, however, is more rapid than the previous one.

**THE FAMOUS CASE OF LITTLE ALBERT** In 1920, psychologists John B. Watson and Rosalie Rayner conducted a classic study of conditioned fear with an infant named Albert. Watson and Rayner sought to discover whether fears could be learned

**Chapter 8:**
**Emotion and Motivation**

*Emotions (such as fear) include behavioral, biological, and cognitive components.*

**Chapter 2:**
**Biopsychology**

*The autonomic nervous system controls internal organs and glands.*

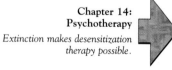

**Chapter 14:**
**Psychotherapy**

*Extinction makes desensitization therapy possible.*

**Aversive conditioning:** A type of classical conditioning in which the conditioned stimulus predicts the occurrence of an aversive or unpleasant unconditioned stimulus.

**Extinction:** In learning, the weakening of a conditioned association in the absence of an unconditioned stimulus or a reinforcer.

**Spontaneous recovery:** The reappearance of an extinguished conditioned response after a time delay.

through simple conditioning, and their experiment with "Little Albert," as he came to be known, confirmed they could. Using techniques that would never receive approval from modern research review committees, Watson and Rayner trained Albert to fear a white rat. They did so by pairing the rat with an aversive UCS—the sound of a loud gong struck just behind the child. The unconditioned startle response and the emotional distress caused by the noxious noise were the basis for Albert's learning, which proceeded quickly. It took only seven conditioning trials for him to react with fear at the appearance of the rat (CR) alone. Watson and Rayner also noted that the fear readily generalized from the rat to other furry objects, such as a rabbit, a dog, and even a Santa Claus mask (Harris, 1979).

Conditioned fear reactions may persist for years. For example, during World War II, the signal used to call sailors to battle stations aboard U.S. Navy ships was a gong sounding at the rate of 100 rings a minute. To personnel on board ships, the sound was associated with danger. Thus, it became a CS for strong emotional arousal, which showed its potency 15 years after the war. In a study conducted on the emotional reactions of hospitalized Navy and Army veterans to a series of 20 different auditory stimuli, the old "call to battle stations" still produced strong emotional arousal in the Navy veterans who had previously experienced combat (Edwards & Acker, 1962).

Like those veterans, we all retain a learned readiness to respond with fear, joy, or other emotions to old signals. When we are unaware of their origins, fear reactions that were once reasonable may be interpreted as anxiety. It may also add to our concern that we know our behavior to be irrational (Dollard & Miller, 1950). Even if it has been a long time since you encountered the conditioned stimuli for a fear response, your nervous system may retain reflexive patterns that leave you vulnerable to stimuli you thought you had forgotten. Thus you may find yourself feeling nervous "for no reason" or suspecting that a strange food will "make you sick" because of associations in your past experience. Some people harbor lifelong fears of snakes, spiders, or other, generally harmless, creatures without remembering the reason.

Fortunately, classical conditioning offers us tools for dealing with learned fears and anxieties (Wolpe & Plaud, 1997). The therapeutic strategy is to couple extinction of the undesirable CR with a new conditioned relaxation response to the CS. This *counterconditioning* therapy teaches the patient to respond in a relaxed manner in the presence of the CS. Such behavioral therapies have been particularly effective in dealing with phobias.

### WHAT FOOD AVERSIONS TELL US ABOUT CLASSICAL CONDITIONING

Your authors' experiences with learned food aversions, mentioned earlier, are not unusual. And, if you stop to think about it, learning to avoid foods associated with illness has real survival value. Because of this, humans and many other animals readily form an association between illness and food—much more readily than between illness and, say, a light or some other inedible stimulus. "Must have been something I ate!" we say. This tendency to connect illness specifically with food seems to run deep. In fact, **taste-aversion learning** appears to be a part of our genetic endowment. The interesting thing for our understanding of classical conditioning, however, is that studies of taste aversion seem to conflict with Pavlov's original conception of conditioning as a simple relationship among stimuli and responses. It makes much more sense when viewed as part of a species' adaptation to its natural environment.

Consider a rat that eats a small amount of poisoned bait. Many hours later, it becomes ill and vomits—but survives. After this single pairing, and despite the long interval (up to 12 hours) between tasting the food (CS) and vomiting (UCR) from poison (UCS), the rat learns an association between the food and the illness. It also learns to avoid other, similar-tasting foods. No simple stimulus–response formula can adequately explain either this one-trial learning or why such a long CS–UCS interval is effective in eliciting a CR.

John Watson and Rosalie Rayner conditioned Little Albert to fear furry objects like this Santa Claus mask (*Discovering Psychology*, 1990).

**Chapter 14:**
**Therapies for Mental Disorder**
Counterconditioning *is a behavioral therapy, based on classical conditioning, that is used to treat fears and phobias.*

**Taste-aversion learning:** A biological tendency in which an organism learns, after a single experience, to avoid a food with a certain taste, if eating it is followed by illness.

Bait shyness has survival value.

We have compelling evidence of an innate basis for food aversions from John Garcia's work. Specifically, Garcia and his colleagues showed that most stimuli present when the aversion was learned (such as a book on the table or the clothes you are wearing) are not avoided later—only those involving taste. Further, they found that some CS–UCS combinations can be easily learned through classical conditioning, while others apparently resist learning (Garcia & Koelling, 1966). For example, rats easily learn an association between the flavor of the bait and a later illness, but they do not learn to associate the flavor with a simultaneous pain. Similarly, they readily learn to associate sound and light cues with a shock-produced pain but do not connect these sensory cues with illness (see Figure 6.3). This probably makes "sense" to the rat's brain, because evolutionary pressure has programmed the rat's brain to know that illness can follow drinking and pain can follow an event involving light and noise. These results suggest that rats have an inborn bias to associate particular stimuli with particular consequences.

Even without conditioning, most animals show **bait shyness,** an unlearned reluctance to sample new foods or even familiar food in a strange environment. Apparently, evolution has provided organisms with a survival mechanism for avoiding foods that are toxic and thus illness-producing. Perhaps all unfamiliar foods are responded to as potentially toxic until proven otherwise. In an evolutionary sense, only "fools rush in" where wiser animals fear to eat.

So, what is the big lesson of taste aversions for our understanding of classical conditioning? Conditioning depends not only on the relationship among stimuli and responses but also on the way an organism is genetically predisposed toward stimuli in its environment (Barker, Best, & Domjan, 1978). What any organism can—and cannot—learn in a given setting is to some extent a product of its evolutionary history (Garcia, 1993).

**FIGURE 6.3:** Inborn Tendency to Associate Certain Cues with Certain Consequences

Rats possess an inborn bias to learn that certain cues predict certain outcomes. Rats avoided saccharine-flavored water when it predicted illness, but not when it predicted shock. They avoided the "bright-noisy" water when it predicted shock, but not when it predicted illness (Garcia & Koelling, 1966).

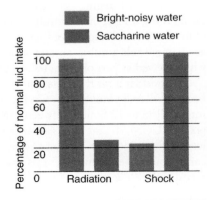

**Bait shyness:** An aversion to novel foods or to familiar foods in novel environments or conditions.

## Taste Aversions and Chemotherapy

*I*magine that your friend Jena is about to undergo her first round of chemotherapy, just to make sure that any stray cells from the tumor found in her breast will be destroyed. To her surprise, the nurse enters the lab, not with the expected syringe, but with a dish of licorice-flavored ice cream. "Is this a new kind of therapy?" she asks. The nurse replies that it is, indeed, explaining that most patients who undergo chemotherapy experience nausea, which can make them "go off their feed" and quit eating, just when their body needs nourishment to fight the disease. "But," says the nurse, "We have found that, if we give patients some unusual food before their chemotherapy, they will usually develop an aversion only to that food." She continued, "Did you ever hear of Pavlov's dogs?"

Cancer patients like Jena often develop aversions to normal foods in their diets to such an extent that they become anorectic and malnourished. In part, their aversions are a serious consequence of their chemotherapy treatments, which produce nausea and are often administered following

meals. Therapists try to prevent the development of aversions to nutritive foods by arranging for meals not to be given just before the chemotherapy and by presenting the patient with a "scapegoat" aversion. They are given unusually flavored candies or ice cream before the treatments so that the taste aversion becomes conditioned only to those special flavors. Extension of this practical solution to problems with chemotherapy may be a lifesaver for some patients (Bernstein, 1988, 1991).

The same principles of conditioned food aversion have also been applied to other problems. For example, conditioned food aversions can even be used to dissuade coyotes from their troublesome behavior of killing sheep. To accomplish this, Garcia and his colleagues put toxic lamb burgers wrapped in sheep skins on the outskirts of fenced-in areas of sheep ranches. The coyotes who ate these lamb burgers got sick, vomited, and developed an instant distaste for lamb meat. Their subsequent disgust at the mere sight of sheep made them back away instead of attack them (Garcia, 1990). Although field trials have demonstrated the effectiveness

If this child gets sick tonight she may develop a taste aversion to this unusual flavor of ice cream.

of this method for diminishing coyote predation on livestock, scientists have been unable to modify the behavior of sheep ranchers—who apparently have a strong aversion to feeding lamb to coyotes!

Check Your Understanding

1. RECALL: *Classical conditioning is especially useful for understanding which of the following kinds of learning?*
   a. a dog that has learned to "sit up" for a food reward
   b. a psychology student who is learning how memory works
   c. a child who, after a painful dental visit, has learned to fear the dentist
   d. an executive who is afraid that she will lose her job

2. RECALL: *The responses in classical conditioning are originally*
   a. innate reflexes.
   b. new behaviors.
   c. premeditated behaviors.
   d. random acts.

3. APPLICATION: *If you learned to fear electrical outlets after getting a painful shock, what would be the CS?*

   a. the electrical outlet
   b. the painful shock
   c. the fear
   d. the time period between seeing the outlet and getting the shock

4. UNDERSTANDING THE CORE CONCEPT: *Which of the following would be most likely to be an unconditioned stimulus (UCS) involved in classical conditioning?*
   a. food
   b. a flashing light
   c. music
   d. money

**ANSWERS:**    1. c    2. a    3. a    4. a

How do you suppose that Michael Jordan learned to be such a superb basketball player? Classical conditioning surely doesn't explain why he trained for hours nearly every day for years on end. Nor does it explain why you are taking a psychology class. Such behaviors are not a collection of simple reflexes, provoked like the salivation in Pavlov's dogs. From a learning perspective, the driving force behind Michael Jordan's performance, or your own, undoubtedly involves the *rewards* produced by these behaviors. That is, both you and Michael Jordan work hard because of the *consequences* of your behavior. In fact, it is the consequences of what we do that drives nearly everything that organisms voluntarily do. This idea becomes the Core Concept of this section:

**CORE CONCEPT**

**In operant conditioning, the patterns of rewards, punishments, and other consequences encourage or discourage the behaviors they follow.**

This is a powerful idea for at least two reasons. First, it involves a much wider spectrum of behavior than does classical conditioning. And second, it accounts for *new* behaviors—not just innate reflexes. Let's see where this concept of learning comes from.

### Trial-and-Error Learning

At about the same time that Pavlov was using classical conditioning to induce Russian dogs to salivate at the sound of a tone, Edward L. Thorndike (1898) was watching American cats trying to escape from "puzzle boxes" (see Figure 6.4). Unlike Pavlov's dogs, Thorndike's cats faced a problem: how to open the door in the puzzle box to get a food reward lying just outside. To do so, the cats had to use **trial-and-error learning,** rather than simple reflexes. Thorndike described a typical cat finding its way out of the puzzle box:

> The cat that is clawing all over the box in [its] impulsive struggle will probably claw the string or loop or button so as to open the door. And gradually . . . the particular impulse leading to the successful act will be *stamped in* by the resulting pleasure. . . . (Thorndike, 1898, p. 13).

For Thorndike's cats, learning was an association—not between two stimuli, as it was for Pavlov's dogs—but between a stimulus and a new response: a *stimulus–response connection (S–R)*. Thorndike pointed out that responses repeatedly followed by rewards brought satisfaction and were strengthened ("stamped in"). Unrewarded responses were weakened. As our Core Concept says, it is the *consequence* of the response that shapes behavior. Thorndike called this the **law of effect.**

**Chapter 2: Biopsychology**

*Natural selection is the mechanism that drives biological evolution.*

The law of effect has an important conceptual parallel to *natural selection* in evolution (Skinner, 1981). In natural selection, the environment determines which genes become more frequent in future populations. Similarly, the law of effect describes how the environment (the effects or consequences produced by behavior) determines which behaviors will be seen more frequently. Just as beneficial genetic traits are selected by the environment, so are behaviors that lead to satisfying or rewarding consequences. That is, they become more likely to occur than behaviors leading to unsatisfying or punishing consequences. For example, a small boy who whines for ice cream—and gets it—will be much more likely to whine again in the future.

## FIGURE 6.4: A Thorndike Puzzle Box

To escape the puzzle box and obtain food, Thorndike's cat had to operate a mechanism to release a weight that would pull the door open.

Thorndike based his theories on observations of animal learning, but he believed that the law of effect also applied to human learning. His ideas had a major impact on the field of educational psychology in his time. In his own work, however, Thorndike found that animal learning was easier to study scientifically than human learning was. His ultimate hope was that basic research with nonhumans would shed more light on the mysteries of human learning.

## Skinner Carries on the Behavioral Tradition

Thorndike's successor, B. F. Skinner, also embraced the view that environmental consequences influence the responses that preceded them. However, Skinner rejected any inferences about an organism's intentions, purposes, or goals. What an animal "wanted" or the "satisfaction" it felt were not important. As a radical behaviorist, Skinner refused to hypothesize about what happens inside an organism because such speculations could not be verified by observation. For example, while eating can be observed, we cannot observe hunger, the desire for food, or pleasure at eating.

Like Thorndike, Skinner concentrated on *operant responses*. An "operant" is an observable, voluntary behavior that an organism emits to "operate" or have an effect on the environment. (Compare this with Pavlov's emphasis on *involuntary* reflexes.) Not surprisingly, Skinner's system is called **operant conditioning.** Again, the main feature of operant conditioning lies in the effects of *consequences* of behavior, which come in the four main forms that we will analyze next.

## Four Kinds of Consequences

Significant events, or consequences, that follow and strengthen an organism's responses are called **reinforcers.** If an attractive classmate smiles at you when you come near, and you find yourself approaching more and more often, this winsome smile is your reinforcer. What other sorts of stimuli act as reinforcers? In general, pleasurable stimuli are reinforcing. Not so obviously, the *removal* of an unpleasant

**Trial-and-error learning:** An operant form of learning, described by Thorndike, in which the learner gradually discovers the correct response by attempting many behaviors and noting which ones produce the desired consequences.

**Law of effect:** Thorndike's law of learning, which states that the power of a stimulus to evoke a response is strengthened when the response is followed by a reward and weakened when it is not rewarded.

**Operant conditioning:** A form of behavioral learning in which the probability of a response is changed by its consequences—that is, by the stimuli that follow the response.

**Reinforcers:** Significant events that strengthen responses when they are delivered in connection with those responses.

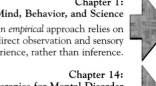

**Chapter 1:**
**Mind, Behavior, and Science**

*An empirical approach relies on direct observation and sensory experience, rather than inference.*

**Chapter 14:**
**Therapies for Mental Disorder**

*Behavioral therapy often focuses on changing the reinforcers in a person's environment.*

stimulus, such as a toothache, is also reinforcing. Strictly speaking, however, behaviorists don't determine what is reinforcing by how a stimulus makes us feel but by its observable effects on our behavior. That is, reinforcers are always defined *empirically*—in terms of their observable effects on the probability of a response. While reinforcers strengthen behavior, other kinds of consequences can *weaken* behavior by decreasing its frequency. These we usually think of as unpleasant or *punishing*. If you learn how all these consequences work, you will have a powerful tool kit for modifying behavior. Manipulating consequences will allow you (with a little more training) to teach rats to press levers, train porpoises to jump through hoops, modify your children's misbehavior, and (with lots more training) treat certain mental disorders. Let's examine the contents of this operant-conditioning tool kit.

**POSITIVE REINFORCERS**  Any stimulus that follows a behavior and increases the probability of that behavior over time is a **positive reinforcer.** A food pellet gives positive reinforcement for a rat's lever-pressing behavior. If you get a laugh for telling a joke, you have received positive reinforcement. Your obvious attention to your instructor's lecture positively reinforces the instructor for lecturing behavior (and, in turn, the instructor may give you some positive reinforcement for paying attention).

Naturally, any behavior that produces desirable consequences is reinforced and likely to be repeated. We can use this principle to identify exactly what is desirable to organisms that cannot communicate their desires. For example, newborn infants cannot directly tell researchers whether they recognize or prefer their own mothers' voices. Studies have shown, however, that newborns will learn a response (sucking on an artificial nipple) that gives them the opportunity to hear their mothers' voices instead of the voice of

B. F. Skinner is shown reinforcing the animal's behavior in an operant chamber, or "Skinner box." The apparatus allows the experimenter to control all the stimuli in the animal's environment.

another female (DeCasper & Fifer, 1980). In this way, the baby's behavior tells us that the mother's voice is preferred to other voices and is, therefore, reinforcing.

**Chapter 4:**
**Psychological Development**

*Sucking is an operant behavior that can be used to determine the preferences of babies (who cannot yet speak).*

**NEGATIVE REINFORCERS**  If removing, reducing, or preventing a particular (undesirable) stimulus increases the probability of a given behavior over time, the removal of the stimulus is a **negative reinforcer.** Thus, the process of removing or withholding such a stimulus following a response is called *negative reinforcement*. (Note that we did not call it *punishment!*) Using an umbrella to prevent getting wet during a downpour is a common example of a behavior that is maintained by negative reinforcement, because you prevent or terminate an unpleasant stimulus (getting wet) by using an umbrella. To give other examples: When a driver buckles the seat belt, the annoying sound of the seat belt buzzer stops. It is the stopping of the unpleasant sound that provides a negative reinforcement. Now, to see if you have the concept: What is the negative reinforcer when you take an aspirin for a pain in your shoulder? Answer: It's the removal of the pain.

To distinguish between positive and negative reinforcement, try to remember the following: Both positive and negative reinforcement will *reinforce*, or increase the probability of, the response they follow. Psychologists use "positive" and "negative" in the mathematical sense of "add" and "subtract." Thus, positive reinforcement involves adding or applying a desirable stimulus, such as giving someone candy or money or a smile. Negative reinforcement, on the other hand, involves removing an unpleasant stimulus, such as an annoying sound or a pain.

**Positive reinforcer:** A stimulus, received after a response, that increases the probability of that response happening again.

**Negative reinforcer:** The removal of an unpleasant or aversive stimulus, contingent upon a particular behavior. Compare with *punishment.*

We can see both positive and negative reinforcement in the case of Donna Smith at the beginning of the chapter. She explained her initial lie to the therapist by her hope that it would put an end to her therapist's repeated demands that she "admit" that the abuse had happened. In fact, when the therapist removed the pressure, Donna received negative reinforcement. Fabricating additional stories produced the same result with other social workers and clinicians. Later, the attention and approval Donna received once she took her case to the authorities provided positive reinforcement for maintaining her new pattern of relating stories of parental abuse. Whether Donna was seeking to reduce her therapist's nagging or to keep the rewarding approval she got from foster parents or other authorities, both consequences had the same reinforcing effect. Both increased her tendency to make up, tell, and later come to believe the false accusations against her parents.

Donna's case also points up the power of *social reinforcers*—both positive and negative. Much of people's behavior is fed and strengthened by the attention, praise, and support of significant others and of those considered influential. Thus, social reinforcement maybe just as powerful as the more tangible reinforcers of food, sex, and money.

Taking aspirin for pain usually results in negative reinforcement, because the pain diminishes.

**EXTINCTION**   Positive and negative reinforcement explain how many new behaviors are acquired and old ones maintained. Suppose, however, that you wanted to *eliminate* an existing operant behavior, such as child's temper tantrums. How would you do it? One good way is to *extinguish* the response.

If a response ceases to produce the reinforcing consequences it once led to, the response will likely diminish or disappear. In the language of conditioning, it will be *extinguished*. In different words, **operant extinction** is a procedure in which reinforcement is withheld in order to weaken the response to its original level. The effect on behavior is the same as we saw in the extinction of a classically conditioned response, but the procedure is slightly different. An example will show how it works.

Consider the factors that may encourage or discourage your professor to make eye contact with you during lecture. Smiling and nodding are behaviors you can use to reinforce your professor's tendency to make eye contact with you. Once you have the professor conditioned, you can try withholding these social reinforcers to extinguish the eye-contact behavior. But please note that extinction does not always require deliberate human manipulation. For example, if the light switch to your classroom stops working, students and instructors will eventually stop flicking the switch as they enter the room. Or have you ever had the experience of dropping money into a vending machine only to get nothing in return? If you kicked the machine and your soda or candy came out, kicking would be reinforced. However, if your kicking produced no soda, candy, or satisfaction, this useless response would soon be extinguished.

Kicking a vending machine would be reinforced if candy or soda came out as a result. If not, the kicking response is soon extinguished, unless it receives reinforcement from onlookers.

To extinguish an unwanted response, one must somehow withhold all possible reinforcers. Outside the control of the laboratory, this can be harder than you might think. In real life, many stimuli may strengthen or maintain a particular behavior. A parent, teacher, or work supervisor will not be able to identify easily—much less control—all the many reinforcers that maintain another person's unwanted response pattern. For this reason, extinction outside the laboratory is more likely to take effect when it can be combined with positive reinforcement of

**Operant extinction:** A form of extinction in which a response that has been learned by operant conditioning is weakened by removal of reinforcement.

the desired response. So, a child who throws public tantrums to get your attention is more likely to stop such misbehavior if (1) the rewarding attention is withheld (operant extinction) and (2) alternative behaviors are rewarded with attention and social approval (positive reinforcement of desired behavior). If a tantrum-pitching child learns that tantrums never work but that requests made in a polite voice do, the tantrums will be extinguished and replaced.

**PUNISHMENT** Another possible way to eliminate an undesirable behavior is through the use of **punishment.** This requires an aversive (unpleasant) condition that follows a response. Punishment is often created by the *application* of an unpleasant stimulus. If you touch a hot stove, for example, the pain punishes you and reduces the likelihood of your repeating that behavior. Punishment may also involve unpleasant conditions created by the *removal* of something desirable—as when parents take away a misbehaving teen's car keys. Either way, responses that are immediately punished tend to decrease in frequency. However, responses that produce delayed punishments may be suppressed only temporarily, if at all. If your misbehaving daughter is immediately punished, she is less likely to repeat the misbehavior; but if a babysitter delays punishment with a threat of "Wait till your parents get home!" the child may repeat her offense. Punishment must also be administered consistently or it loses effectiveness. In fact, *not punishing* unwanted behavior can have the effect of rewarding it. So, when a formerly punished response no longer produces aversive consequences, it tends to increase in frequency to prepunishment levels.

# Calvin and Hobbes

by Bill Watterson

HELLO, IS YOUR DAD THERE?

NO, HE ISNT.

OK, WILL YOU WRITE DOWN MY NUMBER AND HAVE HIM CALL ME?

HOLD ON. I NEED A PEN.

POW!

AGHH!! I'VE BEEN SHOT!

I HATE TAKING MESSAGES.

The probability of someone making another response can be decreased if the first response is followed by an aversive consequence, such as a loud noise or angry complaint.

*PUNISHMENT VERSUS NEGATIVE REINFORCEMENT* Please note that punishment is *not* the same as negative reinforcement, although these terms are often confused. While punishment and negative reinforcement share some features, they differ in important ways. By definition, punishment *decreases* a behavior, or reduces its probability of recurring. In contrast, negative reinforcement—like positive reinforcement—always *increases* a response's probability of occurring again. Despite some surface similarities (they both involve unpleasant stimuli), punishment and negative reinforcement have opposite effects on behavior (Baum, 1994). It is helpful to remember that the descriptors "positive" and "negative" are not synonyms for "pleasant" and "unpleasant," but rather for "add" and "remove." Thus, both positive reinforcement and one form of punishment involve administering or "adding" a stimulus. Negative reinforcement always involves withholding or removing a stimulus. See Table 6.1 for a summary of the distinctions between positive and negative reinforcement and punishment.

*THE USES AND ABUSES OF PUNISHMENT* To eliminate undesired behaviors, it is usually more effective and lasting to reinforce desirable behavior than to punish the unwanted behavior. So, if you want a child to stop reaching for food without asking permission first, you will get better results if you reinforce a desired behavior. Try praising the child for saying, "Please pass the broccoli" instead of scolding the child, smacking the outstretched hand, or sending the child from the table. Sometimes, however, people and institutions decide that such reinforcement is not practical or cannot be delivered expediently. If punishment is the only alternative and the un-

**Punishment:** The application of an aversive stimulus after an undesirable response. Compare with *negative reinforcement.*

## TABLE 6.1: Four Kinds of Consequences

| | APPLY STIMULUS (POSITIVE) | REMOVE/DO NOT APPLY STIMULUS (NEGATIVE) |
|---|---|---|
| **PLEASANT STIMULUS** | Positive reinforcement (reward: food, prize, award, praise, thanks, attention, money, sex, certain drugs) | Extinction (reward is withheld) and Punishment involving removal of desirable conditions. |
| **UNPLEASANT (AVERSIVE) STIMULUS** | Punishment involving application of aversive stimulus (pain, discomfort, fearful or offensive stimuli) | Negative reinforcement (removal of painful stimulus, discomfort, penalty) |

wanted response must be decreased, research shows that punishment will be most effective if it meets the conditions outlined below (Walters & Grusec, 1977):

- Punishment should be swift and brief; a delay will decrease its effectiveness.
- Punishment should be certain: administered every time the unwanted response occurs. (When punishment fails to occur, the effect can be rewarding.)
- Punishment should be limited in duration and intensity—just enough to stop the behavior.
- Punishment should clearly target the *behavior,* not the character of the person.
- Punishment should be limited to the situation in which the response occurred.
- Punishment should not give mixed messages to the punished person (e.g., "You are not permitted to hit others, but I am allowed to hit you").
- The most effective punishment usually consists of penalties (such as loss of privileges) rather than physical pain.

As you examine these recommendations, it may occur to you that most old-fashioned disciplinarians ignore these requirements. Unfortunately, it is widely accepted in this and other cultures that punishment is not only necessary but actually beneficial to character: "Spare the rod and spoil the child" (not a quote from the Bible, incidentally). Are the consequences of punishment, such as physically and verbally assaulting wrongdoers, serious enough that we should question such assumptions? When those in authority use punishment to control people's behavior, they show that they have failed to find constructive and rewarding ways to motivate others. Further, those who deliver punishment can lose control too easily and abuse their victims, especially children. Punishment causes physical harm, emotional scars, and hatred of the punisher. Worst of all, the punished person learns that aggression is an acceptable means of controlling others (Bongiovanni, 1977; Hyman, in Schmidt, 1987). Finally, when responses are punished, individuals may become helpless, defeated, and depressed. Because of these problems, punishment may be impossible to administer effectively, responsibly, and without costly side effects.

**Chapter 9:**
**Stress, Health, and Well-Being**
*Inescapable punishment causes* learned helplessness, *which results in depression.*

### Reinforcement Contingencies

Now that we have some operant tools to work with, let's return to the problem of encouraging new behaviors, rather than discouraging old ones. We know that positive reinforcement is by far the best tool for this job, but we have not yet addressed how much reinforcement might be needed and how often it should be applied. This raises the problem of *contingencies*. A **reinforcement contingency** is the relationship between a response and the rewards it produces.

Various contingencies are possible. For example, the reinforcement contingency that rewards a boy every time he practices the piano is quite different from that of a worker who is rewarded with a monthly paycheck. In both cases, the behavior is controlled by rewards, but the frequency of the rewards differs markedly. The worker

**Reinforcement contingency:** A consistent relationship between a response and the changes it produces in the environment.

Prison riots and other aggressive behavior may result from highly punitive conditions.

has to wait a whole month, while the boy gets something for every practice session. Using Skinner's work as a foundation, modern behavior analysts seek to understand how behavior is shaped and maintained by various reinforcement patterns.

By varying the **schedule of reinforcement**—the timing and frequency of reinforcements—behavior analysts can affect the rate at which any response is learned and how well it endures over time. Curiously, if you want to develop a hardy response that lasts, it is better to use **partial reinforcement**—that is, reinforcing sometimes, rather than all the time. Why would this be so? Under **continuous reinforcement**, as when a friend smiles every time you tell her a joke, the first time reinforcement doesn't occur (the first time you relate a joke but get no smile) you know that something is wrong. Perhaps your joking was in poor taste, or you told it badly. After continuous reinforcement, the first withholding of reinforcement weakens the response, so next time you see your friend, you feel hesitant to tell another joke.

In contrast, if the response was reinforced only intermittently, you have not developed an expectation that reward will follow every response. So, when reinforcement is withheld permanently, it may at first seem like just one more of the familiar delays in getting rewarded, and the response continues to be emitted for a longer period without reinforcement. You consider that perhaps your friend didn't smile at your joke because she had something on her mind: It may have had nothing to do with your joke or how you told it. So you try again and again before eventually giving up. This pattern of greater resistance to weakening of a learned response by training under partial reward conditions is known as the **partial reinforcement effect.** Because most of our social behaviors are "trained" with only occasional rewards—smiles, formal thanks, salary increases—we may persist in habits that no longer work well past the time when others have ceased reinforcing them, simply because we have become accustomed to such partial reinforcement in the past. Partial reinforcement may also explain the persistent behavior displayed in sexual harassment.

### Strategies for Eliciting New Behaviors

In general, reinforcers and punishers are the powers behind operant conditioning: They change or maintain behavior. *Contingent reinforcement* (reinforcement that is connected with the behavior that it follows) strengthens responding; contingent punishment suppresses responding. Noncontingent stimuli have little effect on behavior; if your behavior does not seem to be a condition for the good or bad things that befall you, you are unlikely to change it. In schools, clinics, hospitals, and prisons, psychologists employ a variety of contingency strategies to modify behavior. Here we will briefly discuss three such approaches: *conditioned reinforcers*, *preferred activities*, and *shaping*.

**CONDITIONED REINFORCERS**    In operant conditioning, neutral stimuli paired with **primary reinforcers,** such as food and water, acquire a reinforcing effect and become **conditioned reinforcers** for operant responses. Money, grades, praise, smiles of approval, gold stars, and various kinds of status symbols are among the many potent conditioned reinforcers that can influence our learning and behavior. Virtually any stimulus can become a conditioned reinforcer by being paired with a primary reinforcer. Conditioned reinforcers, such as money, status, or awards, may even come to serve as ends in themselves, substituting for the primary reinforcers that directly meet an organism's basic needs. Human behavior is influenced by a wide variety of conditioned reinforcers.

In some mental institutions, *token economies* have been set up to influence patients' behavior with conditioned reinforcers. Desired behaviors (grooming or taking medication, for example) are explicitly defined, and token payoffs are given by the staff when these behaviors are performed. Tokens can later be exchanged by the patients for a wide array of rewards and privileges (Ayllon & Azrin, 1965; Holden,

**Schedule of reinforcement:** A plan for the timing and frequency of reinforcements.

**Partial reinforcement:** A type of reinforcement schedule by which some, but not all, correct responses are reinforced.

**Continuous reinforcement:** A type of reinforcement schedule by which all correct responses are reinforced.

**Partial reinforcement effect:** The greater resistance to extinction produced by partial reinforcement, rather than continuous reinforcement.

**Primary reinforcers:** Reinforcers, such as food and sex, that have an innate basis because of their biological value to an organism.

**Conditioned reinforcers:** Stimuli, such as tokens or money, that acquire their reinforcing power by a learned association with primary reinforcers.

Chimpanzees will work for conditioned reinforcers. Here a chimp has earned plastic tokens, which it is depositing in a "chimp-o-mat" to obtain raisins, a primary reinforcer.

1978). These systems of reinforcement are especially effective in promoting patients' self-care, maintenance of their environment, and positive interactions with others. Humanistic psychologists, however, have criticized token economies as manipulative and as promoting materialistic values. And in fact, token economies do fall short of the goal of having individuals cultivate less egocentric value systems. But they provide useful strategies for teaching people how to act effectively in the world (Kazdin, 1994).

PREFERRED ACTIVITIES    Certain activities act just as effectively as food or drink for reinforcing behavior. Sex is an obvious example. Another involves exercise: People who work out regularly might use a daily run or fitness class as a "reward" for getting other tasks done. Teachers have even found that young children will learn to sit still if such behavior is reinforced with occasional permission to run around and make noise (Homme et al., 1963). The principle at work here says that a more probable activity (running around and making noise) can be used to reinforce a less likely one (schoolwork). Psychologists called this the **Premack principle,** after its discoverer, David Premack (1965). He found that water-deprived rats learned to increase their running in an exercise wheel when the running was followed by an opportunity to drink. Other rats that were not thirsty but exercise-deprived would learn to increase their drinking when that response was followed by a chance to run. According to the Premack principle, any activity that is often engaged in by the organism can act as a reinforcer for a less-frequent activity.

Parents and teachers often use the Premack principle to get children to engage in low-probability activities. For a shy child, the opportunity to read a new book could be used to reinforce the less-preferred activity of playing with other children. The preferred activity, used as a reinforcer, increases the probability that the individual will engage in an activity that is less preferred. Over time, the less-favored activities may even become more valued as exposure to them leads individuals to discover their intrinsic worth. The once-shy child might eventually enjoy playing with others and no longer require the promise of a preferred activity to reinforce social interaction.

PROMPTING AND SHAPING    A problem encountered by many behavior analysts is the difficulty of getting the organism to begin performing the desired behavior so that it can be reinforced. Suppose you want to train your dog to roll over on command. Must you wait and watch until the moment finally arrives when the dog spontaneously rolls over, so you can immediately reward this behavior? Chances are you will wait a long time for the animal to display such a specific sequence of actions purely by chance. A more efficient option is **prompting** the animal by moving it into the desired initial position and **shaping** its behavior by giving reinforcement in steps that get closer and closer to what you want—a complete sequence of rolling over on command. When shaping begins, any approximation of the target response is reinforced. Once this approximate response occurs regularly, only responses more like the

Chapter 14:
**Therapies for Mental Disorder**
*"Token economies" are a form of behavior modification therapy based on operant conditioning.*

**Premack principle:** The concept, developed by David Premack, that a more-preferred activity can be used to reinforce a less-preferred activity.

**Prompting:** Cuing a response in such a way that the subject knows what response is required. Prompting often involves touching or manipulating a body part to be moved in the desired response or modeling a part of the response.

**Shaping:** An operant learning technique in which a new behavior is produced by reinforcing responses that approach the desired performance; also called *learning by successive approximations.*

final goal response are reinforced. By reinforcing more and more specific versions of the target behavior, an experimenter can shape this higher-level action.

Suppose you wish to train a rat to press a lever in an **operant chamber.** The rat uses its paws in many ways but has probably never pressed a lever before. First, you would deprive the rat of food for a day, to make food a valuable reinforcer. (Remember: Skinner would not have said that the rat was "hungry.") Next, you would teach it to eat food pellets from the food tray in an operant chamber. When the rat is properly motivated and trained in finding food, you would begin the shaping process. First you deliver food only when the rat behaves in specific ways, such as moving toward the lever. Next, food is delivered only as the rat moves closer to the lever. Soon the requirement for reinforcement is for the rat actually to touch the lever. Finally, the rat must depress the lever to trigger food delivery. Now the chamber can be rigged to deliver food pellets automatically when the lever is pressed, and the rat can be left on its own; it has learned—one step at a time—that it can produce food by pressing the lever.

Animals can learn to do some surprising things (like water skiing!), with a little help from their human friends and the application of operant conditioning techniques.

Shaping is of interest to those who would influence human behavior as well. We often wish to get other people to make responses that might not appear spontaneously. For example, suppose a teacher wants to encourage class participation, especially among those students who don't usually offer answers or opinions. Could you devise a shaping procedure for an instructor to use to teach the quieter students first to volunteer answers, then to offer more assertive and thoughtful statements on a regular basis?

**Operant chamber:** A boxlike device that can be set up to deliver rewards or punishments contingent on specific behaviors, such as a food pellet for pressing a lever. Commonly, operant chambers are called "Skinner boxes."

Temper tantrums will last only as long as the child thinks that such displays will be rewarded.

## A Checklist for Modifying Operant Behavior

*T*hink of someone whose behavior you would like to change. For the sake of illustration, let's assume that you would like to change your nephew Johnny's temper tantrums that always seem to occur when you take him shopping. Operant conditioning offers a variety of tools that can help, provided you have some control over stimuli that are important to Johnny. Let's consider a checklist of these operant tools: positive reinforcement, punishment, negative reinforcement, and extinction.

- *Positive reinforcement* is a good bet, especially if you can find some desirable behavior to reinforce before the undesirable behavior occurs. Remember that attention is a powerful reinforcer. If Johnny has not been getting enough attention otherwise, he may produce a tantrum just for the attention.
- *Punishment* may be tempting, but it is always chancy. Unfortunately, it usually has a bad effect on the relationship between the punisher and the person being punished, so if that is important, think twice about using punishment. It is also dangerous because, unlike positive reinforcement, punishment must be done with unfailing consistency: Giving in to the tantrums just once

will strongly reinforce them. But if you must punish, do so swiftly, certainly, and without undue harshness. As we said earlier, restriction or loss of privileges is usually far more effective than physical punishment.

- *Negative reinforcement* has many of the same drawbacks as punishment because it involves unpleasant stimulation. Parents may try—most often unsuccessfully—to use negative reinforcement as a means of encouraging unlikely behavior that they value (doing homework, taking out the garbage, feeding the dog). In its most common form, the parents nag (an aversive stimulus) a child until the desired behavior occurs, whereupon the nagging presumably stops (negative reinforcement). This tactic rarely works to anyone's satisfaction. Nor is this approach well suited to temper tantrums or any other situation in which one person is trying to alter another's behavior. Negative reinforcement does work well, however, in situations where the aversive conditions were imposed by natural, impersonal conditions—as when taking aspirin removes the aversive stimulus of your headache.
- *Extinction* is a guaranteed solution, but only if you control the reinforcers. In Johnny's case, extinction simply means

not giving in to the temper tantrum and not letting him have what he wants (attention, candy, going home). Allow the tantrum to burn itself out. This may be embarrassing for you because children often pick public places for such displays—a sign that they are doing so for attention. The big problem with extinction, however, is that it may take a long time, so extinction is not a good option if the subject is engaging in dangerous behavior, such as playing in a busy street.

The best approach, often recommended by child psychologists, is to use a combination of tactics. Usually they will recommend both reinforcing desired behaviors and extinguishing the undesirable responses.

We recommend memorizing the four items on this checklist: positive reinforcement, punishment, negative reinforcement, and extinction. Whenever you are dealing with someone whose behavior is undesirable, go through the list and see if one or more of these operant tactics will do the trick. And remember: The behavior you may want to change could be your own!

## Check Your Understanding

1. RECALL: *Thorndike's* law of effect *said that animals will learn responses that are*
   a. rewarded.
   b. reflexive.
   c. prompted.
   d. preceded by a neutral stimulus.

2. APPLICATION: *Which one of the following is an example of* negative reinforcement?
   a. going to the dentist and having a toothache relieved
   b. spanking a child for swearing
   c. taking away a child's favorite toy when the child misbehaves
   d. making a child watch while another child is punished

*continued*

3. **APPLICATION:** *Suppose that you have taught your dog to roll over for the reward of a dog biscuit. Then, one day you run out of dog biscuits. Which schedule of reinforcement would keep your dog responding longer without a biscuit?*
   **a.** continuous reinforcement
   **b.** partial reinforcement
   **c.** negative reinforcement
   **d.** noncontingent reinforcement

4. **RECALL:** *Which one of the following is a* conditioned rein-forcer *for most people?*
   **a.** money
   **b.** food

**c.** sex
**d.** a sharp pain in the back

5. **UNDERSTANDING THE CORE CONCEPT:** *Operant condi-tioning, in contrast with classical conditioning, emphasizes events (such as rewards and punishments) that occur*
   **a.** before the behavior.
   **b.** after the behavior.
   **c.** during the behavior.
   **d.** at the same time as another stimulus.

**ANSWERS:**    1. **a**    2. **a**    3. **b**    4. **a**    5. **b**

---

**KEY QUESTION**

# HOW DOES COGNITIVE PSYCHOLOGY EXPLAIN LEARNING?

How do teenagers learn what styles of clothing to wear? This sort of learning certainly doesn't rely on the reflexive responses of classical conditioning. And the last thing most teens want to do is risk their reputations and social standing by trial-and-error. Rather, they learn how to dress in peer-acceptable clothing by careful observation and imitation.

The whole subject of imitation has raised troubling issues for a strict behavioral perspective because it is difficult to explain without resorting to mental concepts. People often imitate behavior for which they see *others* being reinforced. This does not cleanly fit into the behavioral model because it suggests that people's *expectations* are at work: They imitate behavior in the hope of being reinforced themselves. The problem is that expectations are *mental* and not directly observable. What's a be-haviorist to do?

While Skinner and his disciples insisted on building a psychology of learning based solely on observable stimulus–response events, another breed of psychologist has attempted to show that learning does not always result in changes in current be-havior. Instead, the immediate effects of learning may be only on mental processes (as when you read this book and take a test on the material next week). The Core Concept for this section deals with this mental aspect of learning:

**CORE CONCEPT**

**Some forms of learning must be explained as changes in mental processes, rather than as changes in behavior alone.**

At the heart of this sort of learning lies **cognition,** any mental activity in-volved in the representation and processing of knowledge. Cognitive activities include learning, thinking, remembering, perceiving, problem solving, and using language. Because cognition cannot be observed directly, its involvement in learn-ing must be inferred in a variety of ways. We will examine some of these cognitive methods below.

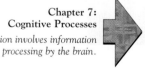

**Chapter 7: Cognitive Processes**

*Cognition involves information processing by the brain.*

**Cognition:** The mental processes involved in thinking, knowing, per-ceiving, learning, and remembering; also, the contents of these processes (e.g., thoughts, percepts, concepts).

## Insight Learning: Making the Light Go On

For Thorndike, solving problems required trial-and-error. Like cats in his puz-zle box, we solve problems by gradually learning correct responses and eliminating in-effective ones. Then along came the Gestalt psychologist Wolfgang Köhler and his clever chimpanzees to give us another perspective.

*"Well, you don't look like an experimental psychologist to me."*

Classic research by Köhler suggested that apes, like humans, could learn to solve problems by suddenly perceiving familiar objects in new forms or relationships, a thought process known as **insight learning** (Köhler, 1925). One ape, for example, had a flash of insight to stack boxes on which he could climb to reach food hung high in the cage. Another suddenly realized he could use a stick to pull in food placed just beyond the cage bars. According to insight theory, these animals could use the boxes or stick to reach the food only because they *perceived* those objects and their possible uses in a new way.

Behaviorism, in the mold of Pavlov, Watson, and Thorndike, had no convincing stimulus–response explanation for Kohler's demonstration. It appeared that the feats of his chimps demanded the *cognitive* explanation of perceptual reorganization. Similarly, research by a one-time behaviorist, Edward Tolman, also flew in the face of accepted behavioral doctrine.

### Cognitive Maps: Finding Out What's on a Rat's Mind

If you have ever tried to walk through your house in the dark or to give directions to someone, you have some idea of the **cognitive map** that Edward Tolman (1886–1959) introduced into psychology. While Tolman accepted the behaviorists' idea that psychologists must study observable behavior, he discovered many situations in which simple associations between stimuli and responses could not explain the behavior that he observed. Instead, Tolman found it necessary to use a cognitive analysis to explain certain behaviors of rats—at the time, a daring challenge to behaviorism (Kesner & Olton, 1990; Olton, 1992). For example, Tolman and his students performed a series of studies on **place learning.** They demonstrated that, in a maze, when an original goal path is blocked, an animal will take the shortest detour around the barrier, even though that particular response was never previously reinforced (Tolman & Honzik, 1930). Figure 6.5 shows the arrangement of one such maze. Rather than blindly exploring different parts of the maze through trial-and-error, the rats behaved as if they had an overview of the maze and were responding to an internal cognitive map, an inner representation of the learning situation as a whole.

In later research, Tolman (1948) observed that, before rats made a choice of detours around a blocked route, they paused and quietly engaged in what Tolman called "VTE"—**vicarious trial-and-error.** That is, the rats appeared to be pondering

**Insight learning:** A form of cognitive learning, originally described by the Gestalt psychologists, involving a sudden reorganization of perceptions.

**Cognitive map:** A mental representation of physical space.

**Place learning:** A type of cognitive learning in which the subject learns a cognitive map that it uses to get to a specific location or place, rather than just a sequence of behaviors.

**Vicarious trial-and-error:** Mentally trying alternative behaviors and thinking through their consequences before selecting a physical response. This concept was ridiculed by the behaviorists.

## FIGURE 6.5: Using Cognitive Maps in Maze Learning

Subjects preferred the direct path (Path 1) when it was open. When it was blocked at A, they preferred Path 2. When Path 2 was blocked at B, rats usually chose Path 3. Their behavior indicated that they had a cognitive map of the best route to the food box.

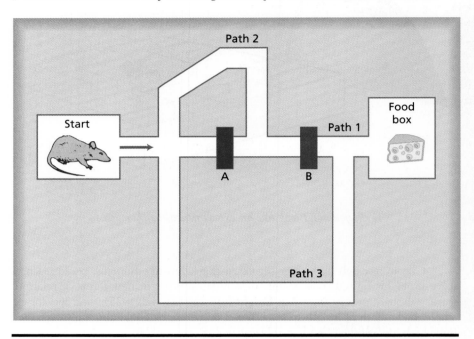

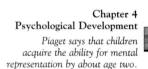

**Chapter 4**
**Psychological Development**

*Piaget says that children acquire the ability for mental representation by about age two.*

their options before choosing a new path! Tolman claimed that learning in these conditions involved not only a cognitive map, but also an *expectancy* about the consequences of the chosen response. The rats were not simply learning a rigid series of right and left turns, but they were acquiring some mental representation of the maze's spatial layout (Tolman, Ritchie, & Kalish, 1946). Subsequent experiments on cognitive maps in rats, chimpanzees, and humans have supported Tolman's findings (Menzel, 1978; Moar, 1980; Olton, 1979). Organisms learn the general layout of their environment by exploration, even if they are not reinforced for learning particular paths. The ability to learn and remember such lessons is obviously adaptive in foraging for food (Kamil, Krebs, & Pulliam, 1987).

In general, Tolman's work showed that we cannot always describe learning as a simple stimulus–response connection. We will see that even basic forms of learning such as conditioning may have cognitive features, such as expectancies, predictions, and judgments (Balsam & Tomie, 1985). For example, a student using a computer hears thunder outside and realizes a storm is brewing. She has learned that electrical storms can cause disruptions in power, so she saves the file to prevent the loss of her data, even though she personally may never have lost data during a storm. The precaution may not turn out to be necessary, but experience has taught her to use available information (for example, signs of a storm) to form expectations and predictions (for example, the computer could lose power, she might lose her file) and take appropriate action (for example, save the file). Such complex behavior is difficult to explain with operant or classical conditioning, but it makes much sense from a cognitive perspective. Thus, we can see that Tolman's pioneering work has led to a significant shift among psychologists from the behavioral viewpoint toward the cognitive approaches to learning.

## Rethinking Behavioral Learning

In the past few decades, cognitive psychologists have even ventured into the territory of classical conditioning and given it a more cognitive flavor. One of the big questions they have raised concerns the adaptive value of classical conditioning (Hollis, 1997). Particularly influential has been the work of Robert Rescorla, who has shown that the feature of the CS that most facilitates conditioning is its *informativeness*—its reliability in predicting the onset of the UCS (Rescorla, 1972; Rescorla & Wagner, 1972). In brief, the CS acts as a cue that signals the onset of the UCS, while other stimuli that are present at the same time may not serve this cuing function. As we saw in food aversions, a certain taste can serve as a warning of illness, while a flashing light will not. In the same vein, research by Leon Kamin (1969) has revealed that a learner will form a CS–CR connection only if the CS seems to provide unique information about the UCS. Some experiences are signaled not by a single stimulus but by a series of stimuli. Do you pay attention to *all* of them? According to Kamin, no: You learn to respond particularly to the stimuli that provide important *information*. For butterfly-eating birds this is fortunate because their aversion for monarch butterflies focuses on the unique markings and not on the less distinctive stimuli of shape or size. To give a more personal example, you may see smoke as well as smell the acrid odor of something burning before you actually see the flames of a fire. You have learned from experience that smoke is not always visible during a fire, but the *smell* of something burning is a telltale sign of fire. The smell provides better *information* about whether there is a fire, so you pay closer attention to the smell than to the sight of smoke.

Biological psychologists and other neuroscientists have also looked closely at classical conditioning, finding some of the neural mechanisms involved. This work shows, for example, that the cerebellum is often involved in classically conditioned reflexes (Daum & Schugens, 1996; Kim, Krupa, & Thompson, 1998; McCarthy, 1992; Steinmetz, 1998). On an even more basic level, Daniel Alkon (1983, 1984, 1989) has been able to pinpoint the neurons involved in classical conditioning in organisms with simple nervous systems. Alkon believes that all learning—even the learning you are acquiring as you read this book—relies on a similar neural mechanism.

**Chapter 2 Biopsychology**
*The cerebellum generates habitual motor responses.*

Neuroscientists Eric Kandel and Robert Hawkins (1992) have made a proposal that may be of truly momentous importance in bridging the gap between behavioral learning and cognitive learning. Their insight rests on the discovery that animals with relatively simple nervous systems have a single type of nerve circuit that enables them to learn simple motor responses. In the more complex brains of mammals, however, researchers have found a second type of learning circuitry that apparently facilitates higher forms of learning, such as memory for events.

What is the significance of this finding? Kandel and Hawkins speculate that the two types of learning circuits may divide the task of learning along the line that has long separated behavioral psychologists and cognitive psychologists. The simpler circuit seems to be responsible for the sort of "mindless" learning that occurs when a dog drools at the sound of a bell or when a person acquires a motor skill, such as riding a bike or swinging a golf club. (See also Clark & Squire, 1998.) This kind of learning occurs slowly and improves with repetition over many trials. Significantly, classical conditioning and much of operant learning fit this description. On the other hand, the second type of learning circuit seems to be responsible for more complex forms of learning that require conscious processing—the sort of learning that interests cognitive psychologists: concept formation, insight learning, and memory for events. If further research verifies that this division reflects a fundamental distinction in the nervous system, we will be able to say that those on the behavioral and cognitive extremes were both (partly) right. They were talking about fundamentally different forms of learning.

*D*oes observing violent behavior make viewers more likely to become violent? A classic study by Albert Bandura suggests that it does—at least in the children he invited to his lab. After watching adults model behavior of punching, hitting, and kicking an inflated, plastic clown (a BoBo doll), these children later showed a greater frequency of the same behaviors than did children in control conditions who had not observed the aggressive models (Bandura, Ross, & Ross, 1963). Subsequent studies showed that children imitated such behaviors just from watching filmed sequences of models, even when the models were cartoon characters.

An important implication of Bandura's study is that imitative learning can occur in situations where the learner has not had a chance to gather personal experience. Instead, he or she has had to rely on learning by *observation*—in this case by watching the behavior of another person, or *model*. If the model's actions appear successful, the observer seeks to behave in the same way; if it was unsuccessful, the observer avoids following the example. Thus, children may learn aggressive behavior through imitating aggressive role models who seem to be successful or admired or who seem to be enjoying themselves. Psychologists call it **social learning** or **observational learning**—the type of learning that occurs when someone uses observations of another person's actions and their consequences to guide his or her own future actions. (You will remember that we attributed teen fashions largely to observa-

**Social learning or observational learning:** A form of cognitive learning in which new responses are acquired after watching others' behavior and the consequences of their behavior.

In the BoBo doll experiment, a boy and girl imitate the aggressive behavior that they have seen from an adult.

tional learning.) While examples of observational learning abound among humans, it is also a common strategy for many nonhuman species. One study demonstrates that even a creature as simple as the octopus can learn by example from other octopi (Fiorito & Scotto, 1992). *(See also Chapter 12, Social Psychology.)*

As you might expect, much psychological research has been directed at assessing the impact that behavior modeled on film and video has on viewers (Huston, Watkins, & Kunkel, 1989; Williams, 1986). The issue is a controversial one (see Freedman, 1984, 1996). But correlational evidence from more than 50 studies shows that observing violence is associated with violent behavior, and experimental results from more than 100 studies point to a causal relationship (Huesmann & Moise, 1996; Primavera & Heron, 1996). The two major effects of dramatized violence were a reduction in emotional arousal and distress at viewing violence (conditions resulting in *psychic numbing*) and an increase in the likelihood of engaging in aggressive behavior (Murray & Kippax, 1979). Thus people are not impervious to the images of violence or trauma with which entertainment and news media bombard them. In fact, the greater the bombardment, the less noticeable and more acceptable such images and actions seem to become. *(See also Chapter 1, Mind, Behavior, and Science.)*

In general, however, there is little question that people learn much— both prosocial (helping) and antisocial (hurting) behaviors—through observation of models. This capacity to learn from watching enables us to acquire behaviors without going through tedious trial-and-error. So, while observational learning seems to be a factor in violent behavior, it also enables us to learn socially useful behaviors by profiting from the mistakes and successes of others.

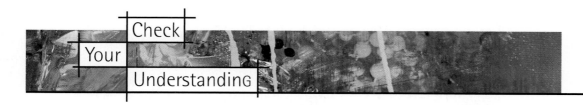
1. **RECALL:** *When their goal path was blocked, Tolman's rats would take the shortest detour around the barrier. This, said Tolman, showed that they had developed*
   a. trial-and-error learning.
   b. operant behavior.
   c. cognitive maps.
   d. observational learning.

2. **RECALL:** *Cognitive psychologist Robert Rescorla has reinterpreted the process of classical conditioning. In his view, the conditioned stimulus (CS) serves as*
   a. a cue that signals the onset of the UCS.
   b. a stimulus that follows the UCS.
   c. a negative reinforcement.
   d. a cognitive map.

3. **APPLICATION:** *If you were going to use Bandura's findings in developing a program to prevent violence among middle-school children, you might*

   a. have children watch videos of aggressive children who are not being reinforced for their aggressive behavior.
   b. have children role play nonaggressive solutions to inter-personal problems.
   c. have children punch a BoBo doll, to "get the aggression out of their system."
   d. punish children for aggressive acts performed at school.

4. **UNDERSTANDING THE CORE CONCEPT:** *Which of the following proved to be difficult to explain in purely behavioral terms?*
   a. a trained seal doing a trick for a fish
   b. a dog salivating at the sound of a bell
   c. a chimpanzee stacking boxes on which to climb for food hung high in its cage
   d. a cat learning to escape from a puzzle box

**ANSWERS:**    1. c    2. a    3. a    4. c

---

## KEY QUESTION  HOW DOES MEMORY WORK?

You will remember our opening case, which examined the experience of Donna, a young woman who claimed to remember abusive events that never happened. But, even though Donna's memories were fabricated, could a person have suffered a childhood trauma, tucked it away (*repressed* it) somewhere in memory, and then recalled the incident in flawless detail years later in therapy? This was Freud's contention, and it is based on a widely believed, but questionable, assumption about memory: the assumption that memory contains a record of everything that happens to us.

A strong blow to the Freudian theory of memory was struck by Elizabeth Loftus (1997a, 1997b) and her colleagues (Hyman, Husband, & Billings, 1995; Loftus & Ketcham, 1994), who demonstrated the ease with which college students could be misled into "remembering" false information, such as being lost in a shopping mall or spilling the punch bowl at a wedding. Such research flies in the face of the "common-sense" notion

Elizabeth Loftus and her colleagues have shown that college students can be influenced to have memories of incidents that never happened—such as this one.

of memory as a complete and accurate record of our personal experiences. Instead, cognitive psychology sees memory as a functional information storage system that is subject to the same influences and distortions as is perception (Payne et al., 1997). All memories—even the vivid "flashbulb" memories, such as the memory of your first kiss—become distorted over time by hopes, expectations, fantasies, motives, emotions,

**Chapter 5:**
**Sensation and Perception**
*Perception is a constructive process—not a mirror of the external world.*

needs, attitudes, and a host of other cognitive factors. We can state this succinctly in our Core Concept:

**CORE CONCEPT**

**Memory is a cognitive system that operates constructively to encode, store, and retrieve information.**

As a constructive process, memory actively shapes the material it keeps for us. In this way, human memory is more like an impressionist painting, rather than the nearly flawless, but "mindless," memory of a computer or a video recorder.

The explosion of the space shuttle *Challenger* was an emotionally shocking event. As a result, many adult Americans have a vivid "flashbulb" memory that includes not only the event but personal memories of where they were and what they were doing when they learned of it. You may have flashbulb memories of particularly emotional events in your life, such as a car accident, your first kiss, or the death of a loved one. Flashbulb memories show that emotion has an important role in memory.

### Never Forget Hermann Ebbinghaus

It is estimated that the average human mind can store 100 trillion bits of information, yet sometimes we can't recall where we left the car keys, or we forget that we promised to call home. We all would like to be able to improve our memories—for the material we study for tests and also for names, faces, jokes, and an assortment of trivial information. Finding ways to improve memory is one of the main reasons that psychologists have sought to understand how memory works. In fact, this fascination with human memory made it one of the first subjects investigated by scientific psychology when, more than a century ago, the scientific foundation for our modern view of memory was laid by a pioneering psychologist named Hermann Ebbinghaus.

Ebbinghaus was most interested in memory for verbal material. Hoping to work with a pure form of verbal memory that was not influenced by the meaningfulness of stimuli, Ebbinghaus gave his subjects wordlike stimuli, called *nonsense syllables*. Often he used himself as a subject. The task was to memorize a list of items presented one by one and recall it after a delay. He might begin by examining a list of nonsense syllables (such as POV, KEB, RUZ) and read through the items one at a time until he finished the list. Repeating this procedure again and again, he could eventually recite the items from memory in the correct order.

To measure how long the memory persisted, Ebbinghaus invented an ingenious method that required **relearning** the items on the original list after a delay, even after recall was impossible. Because he kept a record of the number of trials it took him to *relearn* the original list, he could compare this with the number of trials required to learn the list the first time. If it took fewer trials to relearn it than to learn it originally, this difference indicated a "savings" that could serve as a measure of memory. Using his **savings method,** Ebbinghaus recorded the degree of memory lost after different time intervals. The curve obtained when he plotted the data is shown in Figure 6.6. As you can see, he found a rapid initial loss of memory, followed by a declining rate of loss. Subsequent research shows that this **forgetting curve** captures the pattern by which we forget any relatively meaningless verbal material.

Modern psychologists have built on Ebbinghaus's work, but they are more interested than he was in how we remember *meaningful* material, such as information you

**Relearning:** A technique, invented by Herman Ebbinghaus, used in measuring memory retention by recording the number of trials necessary to relearn certain material. This is then compared with the number of trials necessary to learn the material originally (see *savings method*).

**Savings method:** Ebbinghaus's approach to measuring memory retention by calculating "savings" in number of trials necessary for relearning after varying amounts of time.

**Forgetting curve:** A graph plotting the amount of retention and forgetting over time for a certain batch of material, such as a list of nonsense syllables. The typical forgetting curve is steep at first, becoming flatter as time goes on.

read in a textbook. Most current work is based on a cognitive information-processing framework that had not been invented in Ebbinghaus's day. This view says that, in some respects, the mind handles information much like a computer. It also says that remembering something requires the three basic memory operations noted in our Core Concept: encoding, storage, and retrieval.

## Memory's Three Essential Functions

Any memory system, whether in a computer, a rat, or a person, must perform three essential functions. It must *encode* information in a useful format, it must *store* the information, and it must have a means of *accessing and retrieving* the stored data. Let's look more closely at each of these operations.

**Encoding** of memory in the brain requires that you first *select* some stimulus event from among the huge array of inputs nearly always available to you. Next you identify the distinctive features of that experienced event. Is the event a sound, a visual image, or a smell? If it's a sound, is it loud, soft, or harsh? Does it fit into some pattern that forms a name, a melody—or a cry for help? Is it a sound you have heard before? During encoding, you tag an experience with various labels, some specific and unique ("It's Minerva"), others describing a general category or class ("She's our cat"). This encoding process is usually so automatic and rapid that you are unaware you are doing it.

A further encoding process called **elaboration** relates the new input to other information you already have or to goals or purposes for which it might later prove useful. Retention is better when you can link new information with what you already know. Memories that are connected to other information are much more usable than isolated memory units. You can see that encoding and elaboration are closely associated with the processes of sensation and perception that we studied earlier.

**Storage** is the retention over time of encoded material. This information tends to be retained when it can be linked to information already stored, and lost if it is not. It also helps to rehearse or use the material periodically. The more meaningful some bit of information is and the more often it is rehearsed, the more likely it is to be retained.

**Access and retrieval** involve the recovery at a later time of the stored information. Retrieval is the payoff for all your earlier effort. When it works, it enables you to gain access—sometimes in a split second—to information you stored earlier in your memory banks. (Let's see if your access and retrieval mechanisms are working for the material we just covered. Can you remember which of the three memory functions comes before storage?) To understand the complexity of accessing material in memory, it is important to know that some retrieval tasks will necessarily be more difficult than others.

## Ways of Accessing Memory: Two Retrieval Tasks

You might, at first, assume that you either know something or you don't and that any method of testing what you know will give the same results. You can demonstrate to yourself that this assumption is wrong if you think about the relative difficulty of essay tests and multiple-choice tests. **Recall** (demanded by essay tests) is a retrieval task in which you must access memory with the help of only minimal cues. "What are the three memory operations?" is a recall question. **Recognition,** on the other hand, is a retrieval method in which you simply

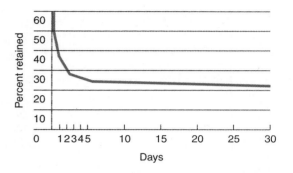

**Chapter 2:**
**Biopsychology**
*Cognitive theories often make use of the computer metaphor for the brain.*

## FIGURE 6.6: Ebbinghaus's Forgetting Curve

How many nonsense syllables can subjects remember when tested over a 30-day period? The curve shows that recall decreases rapidly and reaches a plateau, below which little more is forgotten. The fastest decrease in recall occurs during the first day after learning.

**Chapter 5:**
**Sensation and Perception**
*Sensory processes encode information as nerve impulses and perception adds meaning.*

**Encoding:** One of the three basic functions of memory, involving the modification of information to fit the preferred format for the memory system.

**Elaboration:** A form of encoding that adds meaning to information in working memory so that it can be more easily stored in long-term memory.

**Storage:** One of the three basic functions of memory, involving the retention of encoded material over time.

**Access and retrieval:** Together these form the third basic function of memory, involving the location and recovery of information from memory.

**Recall:** A retrieval method in which one must reproduce previously presented information.

**Recognition:** A retrieval method in which one must identify present stimuli as having been previously presented.

identify whether or not a stimulus has been previously experienced. Recognition is the retrieval method you employ when you answer the following multiple-choice question:

> Which of the following increases a behavioral response by removing an aversive stimulus?
> a. punishment
> b. extinction
> c. positive reinforcement
> d. negative reinforcement

Recognition is also the method employed when police ask an eyewitness to identify a suspected robber in a lineup. In both multiple-choice examinations and criminal investigations, the tested individual must determine whether—and which—immediate stimuli match those previously encountered. On examinations, recall questions usually give fewer and less specific cues than recognition questions, and thus seem "harder" to those taking the test.

There is another important difference between recognition and recall. For recognition, you need simply to match a stimulus from memory (the robber) against a present stimulus (a suspect in the lineup). In this case, both stimuli are in your consciousness. For recall, however, you must work with a fragmentary, *less-complete stimulus*. So, you must reconstruct from memory something that is not in the present environment and then describe it well enough that an observer can understand what is really in your mind—as when a witness works with a police artist to make a drawing of the suspect. That makes recall harder than recognition.

## The Three Memory Systems

Another similarity between your memory and that of a computer involves processing information in *stages*. In the standard model of human memory, information passes through three stages: sensory memory, working memory, and long-term memory. *Sensory memory* preserves fleeting impressions of sensory stimuli—sights, sounds, smells, and textures—for only a second or two, as when the sound of a television commercial seems to ring in your ears after you turn off the set. *Working memory* (or *short-term memory*), includes recollections of what you have recently perceived, such as a phone number you have just looked up. Such limited information lasts about 20 seconds, unless it receives special attention. *Long-term memory* preserves information for retrieval at any later time—up to an entire lifetime. Information in long-term memory constitutes our knowledge about the world and includes such varied material as the lyrics to your favorite song and the year that Wilhelm Wundt established the first psychology laboratory. (*Quiz:* What year was that? 18??) Figure 6.7 shows the hypothesized flow of information into and among these subsystems. We will focus our attention on each one in turn.

**FIGURE 6.7:** A Simplified Memory Model

The "standard model" says that memory is divided into three stages. Everything that goes into long-term storage must first be processed by sensory memory and working memory.

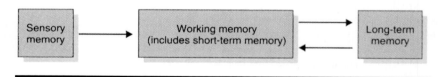

**Chapter 1:**
**Mind, Behavior, and Science**
*Wundt founded the "school" of psychology known as structuralism.*

**Sensory memory:** The first of three memory stages, preserving brief sensory impressions of stimuli; also called *sensory register.*

**SENSORY MEMORY**   A fleeting impression is formed in **sensory memory** from sensory input. Thus, sensory memory is a part of the sensory system, where it represents a primitive and brief kind of information storage for each sense. Sensory memory for vision, known as *iconic memory*, lasts about one-quarter second. An auditory memory, or *echoic memory*, may last several seconds (Neisser, 1967). You can easily demonstrate the difference between the sensory registers for yourself. When you turn off a radio, the sounds of the music literally echo in your head for a brief time

## FIGURE 6.8: Multiple Sensory Stores

We have a separate sensory memory for each of our sensory pathways. All feed into short-term (working) memory.

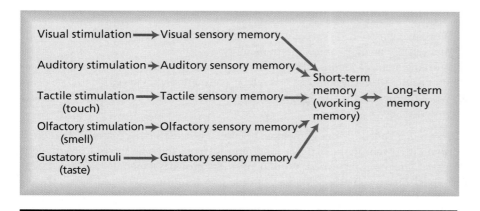

after the sound is gone, but if you pull down a window shade, the scene outside is gone almost at once. But without these fleeting sensations, we could see and hear stimuli only at the moment they were physically present, which would not be long enough for recognition to occur. Sensory memories are, therefore, essential for holding input until it is recognized and passed on for further processing.

Though of brief duration, your sensory storage capacity is large—more than your conscious mind can process at one time, as we shall see. Early researchers underestimated the amount of stimuli that sensory memory could store because they asked subjects to report large stimulus arrays. Subjects shown an array like the following for only a fraction of a second could report only about four items:

D J B

X H G

C L Y

But psychologist George Sperling guessed that most of the information actually entered the sensory system and then vanished before it could all be reported. To demonstrate this, Sperling concocted a clever experiment. Immediately after flashing an array of letters or numbers on a screen, he gave subjects an auditory cue that indicated which row of letters to report. Asked to give this smaller "partial report," subjects achieved almost perfect accuracy—no matter *which* row was signaled. Further research confirmed that, although reporting might be limited to three or four items, the actual capacity of sensory memory was much larger: nine or more items (Sperling, 1960, 1963). Thus, while the capacity of sensory memory is much larger than had been thought, its contents fade very rapidly.

Like visual memory, auditory memory holds more information than people can typically report before it disappears (Darwin, Turvey, & Crowder, 1972). Echoic memories may be necessary to process many subtle, simultaneously presented aspects of speech, such as intonation and emphasis. Would it be better if sensory memories lasted longer so that we would have more time to process them? Not really. New information is constantly coming in, and it must also be processed. Sensory memories last just long enough to give a sense of continuity but not long enough to interfere with new sensory impressions (Loftus, Duncan, & Gehrig, 1992).

**Chapter 5: Sensation and Perception**
*The sensory system begins the processing of incoming stimulus information.*

**WORKING MEMORY** Also called **short-term memory (STM), working memory** preserves recently perceived events or experiences (Beardsley, 1997; Goldman-Rakic, 1992). Working memory serves as the link between a fleeting sensory memory and the more permanent storage of a long-term memory. A number of interesting characteristics distinguish this second stage of memory:

- Working memory has a severely *limited capacity*, retaining less information than either sensory memory or long-term memory.
- Working memory retains material for a *short duration* of time; what is stored is lost after about 20 seconds, unless it is rehearsed (mentally reviewed).
- Working memory is the only memory system in which material is *consciously processed*.

This system is called "working" memory because it is here that the material transferred in from either sensory memory or long-term memory must be worked on, thought about, and mentally organized. Working memory provides a mental "working space" to help in sorting and processing new information (Shiffrin, 1993). Although the biological details remain obscure, neuroscientists have found that this part of memory involves brain mechanisms located in the frontal lobes (Beardsley, 1997).

Working memory is also an essential preliminary stage needed to form *explicit* long-term memories—that is, for memories that you *know* you know (Cowan, 1993). For example, after looking up an unfamiliar phone number, you may repeat it to yourself or recite it aloud until you dial it, in order to keep the digit sequence in working memory. After using the number, you may "discard" it and no longer find it in memory. But if the number proves to be useful or memorable, you can use rehearsal and associations to "upgrade" it to explicit long-term memory. Consequently, the next time you need the number, you will know that you don't have to look it up.

*ENCODING IN WORKING MEMORY* Information enters working memory as organized images and patterns that are recognized as familiar and meaningful. Verbal patterns entering working memory often seem to be held there in *acoustic* form—according to the way they sound—even when they come through an individual's eyes rather than ears. So, when subjects are asked to recall lists of letters they have just seen, the errors they make tend to be confusions of letters that *sound* similar—such as D and T—rather than letters that look similar—such as E and F (Conrad, 1964). Acoustic coding seems to be an essential part of the mechanism that allows us to learn spoken language (Schacter, 1999).

*STORAGE CAPACITY OF WORKING MEMORY* When the items to be remembered are *unrelated*, the capacity of working memory seems to be about seven (plus or minus two) items, such as letters, words, numbers, or almost any kind of meaningful information. When you try to force more than about seven items into working memory, earlier items are lost to accommodate more recent ones. This displacement process is similar to laying out a row of seven one-foot bricks on a seven-foot table. When an eighth brick is pushed on at one end, the brick at the opposite end is pushed off the table. The limited capacity of short-term/working memory is the smallest of the three memory systems. Thus, working memory is often viewed as the information "bottleneck" of the memory system (see Figure 6.9).

*PROCESSING IN WORKING MEMORY* We have two important ways to deal with the limited capacity of short-term

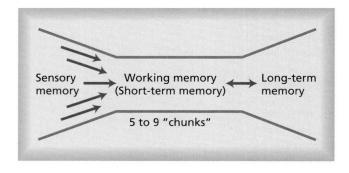

**Chapter 3: States of Mind**
*What is the nature of consciousness?*

**Working memory** or **short-term memory (STM):** The second of three memory stages, and most limited in capacity; preserves recently perceived events or experiences for less than a minute without rehearsal.

**FIGURE 6.9:** The STM Bottleneck

Caught in the middle, with a much smaller capacity than sensory and long-term memories, short-term memory (working memory) becomes an information bottleneck in the memory system. As a result, much incoming information from sensory memory is lost.

## Finding Your STM Capacity

Look at the following list of numbers and scan the four-digit number, the first number on the list. Don't try to memorize it. Just read it quickly; then look away from the page and try to recall the number. If you remember it correctly, go on to the next longer number, continuing down the list until you begin to make mistakes. How many digits are in the longest number that you can squeeze into your STM?

7 4 8 5

3 6 2 1 8

4 7 9 1 0 3

2 3 8 4 9 7 1

3 6 8 9 1 7 5 6

7 4 7 2 1 0 3 2 4

8 2 3 0 1 3 8 4 7 6

The result is your *digit span*, or your short-term (working) memory capacity for digits. Studies show that, under ideal testing conditions, most people can remember five to seven digits. If you got more, you may have been using special "chunking" techniques.

storage so that more of the information there can be transferred on through into long-term memory. These two methods—*chunking* and *rehearsal*—should be somewhat familiar to you since you already use them in other contexts.

In memory, a *chunk* is a meaningful unit of information. A chunk can be a single letter or number, a group of letters or other items, or even a group of words or an entire sentence. For example, the sequence 1-9-8-4 consists of four digits that could constitute four chunks, slightly smaller than the size of your working memory's capacity. However, if you see the four digits as a single meaningful sequence, they constitute only one chunk. For example, *1984* is the title of George Orwell's frightening futuristic novel (written in 1948, the last two digits transposed to suggest a distant future). **Chunking** is the process of recoding single separate bits of information into a single meaningful unit. When you memorize a seven-digit phone number (e.g., 5551212) as two shorter sequences of digits (555-1212, "five-five-five, one-two-one-two"), you have reduced seven bits to two chunks and have immediately freed up space in your remaining working memory.

Between looking up a needed telephone number and successfully dialing it, you probably repeat or recite the digits to yourself to keep them in mind. This technique is called **maintenance rehearsal.** Undistracted rehearsal appears to be essential to maintaining information in working memory. Rehearsal keeps information in working memory and prevents competing inputs from pushing it out. Unfortunately, maintenance rehearsal is not an efficient way to transfer information to long-term memory—although it is commonly used by people who don't know much about memory's workings.

To make sure that information is transferred to long-term memory, you need to engage in **elaborative rehearsal,** a process in which the information is not just repeated but actively analyzed and related to already stored knowledge. Suppose that you have a florist shop and you want people to remember your phone number. Because numbers are notoriously difficult to remember, you can help your customers with elaborative rehearsal by using a "number" that makes use of the letters on the phone buttons, such as 1-800-FLOWERS. The same principle can be used with more complex material, such as you are learning in psychology. For example, if you want to remember that the auditory component of sensory memory is *echoic* memory, you can elaborate this by thinking of an "echo" as an auditory sensation.

**Chunking:** Organizing pieces of information into a smaller number of meaningful units—a process which frees up space in working memory.

**Maintenance rehearsal:** A working-memory process in which information is merely repeated or reviewed to keep it from fading while in working memory. Maintenance rehearsal involves no active elaboration.

**Elaborative rehearsal:** A working-memory process in which information is actively reviewed and related to information already in long-term memory.

**LONG-TERM MEMORY**   Given the vast amount of information stored in this last of the three memory stages, **long-term memory (LTM),** it is a marvel that so much of it is so accessible. You can often get the exact information you want almost immediately:

- Who first developed classical conditioning?
- Name a play by Shakespeare.

Your responses to these requests probably came quickly because of a special feature of long-term memory: words and concepts are encoded by their *meanings,* which interconnect them with other stored items. Consequently, many different cues can help you retrieve exactly what you want from all that is in LTM.

Long-term memory has apparently unlimited capacity. It serves as the storehouse of all the experiences, events, information, emotions, skills, words, categories, rules, and judgments that have been transferred to it from working memory. LTM constitutes each person's total knowledge of the world and of the self. Material in longterm memory enables you to solve new problems, reason, keep future appointments, and use a variety of rules to manipulate abstract symbols, so that you can even think about situations you have never experienced or might be impossible. Much of this versatility of LTM arises from the contrasting functions of its two distinct partitions.

*TWO MAIN PARTITIONS OF LONG-TERM MEMORY*   We actually have two types of LTM: *procedural* memory and *declarative* memory. Each is distinguished by the kind of information it holds. **Procedural memory** stores memory for how things are done. We use it to acquire, retain, and employ perceptual, cognitive, and motor skills, such as riding a bicycle or tying shoelaces (Anderson, 1982; Tulving, 1983). Typically, you consciously recall the details of your skill memories only during the early phases of performance (when you first begin learning the skill). Experts, such as concert pianists, learn to perform tasks requiring advanced skills without conscious recall of the details of their appropriate skill memories, much as you more easily run down a flight of stairs without thinking about the movements of your feet. Thus, experts are often unable to think through their tasks consciously without hindering their performance.

The other division of LTM, **declarative memory** helps you remember specific information, such as facts and events. Remembering how to drive is a procedural process; recalling the directions for driving to a specific location requires declarative memory. Unlike procedural memory, which can involve easy or automatic retrieval, declarative memory involves at least some conscious effort. When people try to reproduce material from declarative memory, they may roll their eyes or make facial gestures to indicate such effort. As they do so, they are searching either of two subdivisions of declarative memory: *episodic* and *semantic* memory.

**Episodic memory** is a part of declarative memory that stores personal information—your memory for events, or "episodes" in your life—along with some *temporal coding* (or time tags) to identify when the event occurred and some *context* coding for where it took place. For example, memories of a happiest birthday or of a first love affair are stored in episodic memory. Episodic memory acts as your personal autobiographical record.

**Long-term memory (LTM):** The third of three memory stages, with the largest capacity and longest duration; LTM stores material organized according to meaning.

**Procedural memory:** A division of LTM that stores memories for how things are done.

**Declarative memory:** A division of LTM that stores explicit information; also known as *fact memory.* Declarative memory has two subdivisions: *episodic memory* and *semantic memory.*

**Episodic memory:** A subdivision of declarative memory that stores memory for personal events, or "episodes."

**FIGURE 6.10:**   A Model of Multiple Long-Term Memory Systems

Evidence from humans, rats, and monkeys suggests that semantic, episodic, and procedural memories involve distinct memory systems. Implicit memories in the semantic or procedural systems may influence behavior without conscious processing.

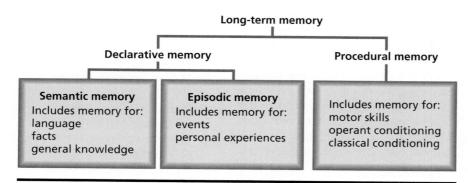

You consult episodic memory when someone says, "Where were you last Tuesday?" or "What did you do on your vacation?"

**Semantic memory** is another part of declarative memory that stores the basic *meanings* of words and concepts, without episodic reference to their time and place in the rememberer's experience. Semantic memory more closely resembles an encyclopedia or a database than an autobiography. Your semantic memory stores a vast array of generic facts about names, faces, grammar, history, musical composition, manners, scientific principles, and religious beliefs. The things you know and ideas you learn are stored in semantic memory. You consult semantic memory when someone asks you, "Who was the third President?" or "What are the two divisions of declarative memory?"

Alex Trebek, host of the television game show *Jeopardy*, challenges contestants to identify facts by drawing on the semantic division of declarative memory.

*THE TRAGIC CASE OF H. M.* Striking evidence of these several long-term memory systems comes from a famous surgical patient, now known only as H. M. As a result of a brain operation in 1953, H. M. lost most of his ability to form declarative memories (Hilts, 1995). More precisely, H. M.'s problem arose from the removal of the hippocampus and amygdala on both sides of the brain in an attempt to treat severe epileptic seizures (see Figure 6.11). Now, nearly 50 years after his surgery, H. M. would not remember meeting you five minutes ago. He has not been able to learn where he lives or who takes care of him. And he is always shocked to see an aging face when he looks in the mirror, expecting to see the younger man he had been a half century ago (Milner, Corkin, & Teuber, 1968; Rosenzweig, 1992).

To put H. M.'s problem another way, he can no longer transfer new information from working memory to LTM, a condition called **anterograde amnesia.** Although he can remember events prior to the surgery, he cannot add new material to episodic memory. Surprisingly, however, H. M.'s procedural memory remains intact, despite this massive disruption of memory for new events (Milner et al., 1968; Raymond, 1989). Researchers have found, for example, that H. M. can learn new and

**Chapter 2: Biopsychology**
*The hippocampus and amygdala are parts of the limbic system involved in memory.*

FIGURE 6.11: The Hippocampus and Amygdala

The hippocampus and amygdala were surgically removed from both sides of H. M.'s brain. To help yourself visualize where these structures lie, compare the drawing with the MRI image. The MRI shows the brain in cross section, with a slice through the hippocampus visible on each side.

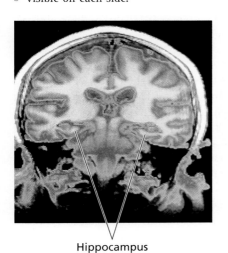

Hippocampus

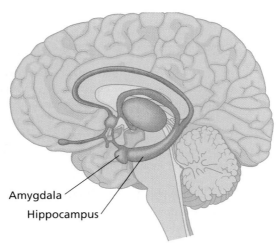

Amygdala
Hippocampus

**Semantic memory:** A subdivision of declarative memory that stores general knowledge, including the meanings of words and concepts.

**Anterograde amnesia:** The inability to form memories for new information (as opposed to *retrograde amnesia,* which involves the inability to remember information previously stored in memory).

complex motor skills, such as writing while looking in a mirror—yet he never remembers learning them.

Remarkably, after the operation H. M.'s IQ score actually rose from 101 to 118—probably as a result of fewer seizures. His working memory capacity for digits remained at 6–7, well within the normal range. He can still remember with reasonable accuracy the events of his youth and the concepts he learned before the operation. He can also use language well. When psychologist Brenda Milner tested his abilities to form new memories, she found that traces of events, objects, and people in working memory slip away before he can store them in long-term memory—much as you might forget a phone number that you just looked up. As a result of his severe memory problem, H. M. must live in a nursing home, where his caretakers and his surroundings forever appear unfamiliar. He reads the same magazines over and over. Tragically, although he knows who he is, he can never remember where he is, how he got there, who is there with him, or what he has experienced even moments before.

You don't have to have brain damage like H. M.'s to have discontinuities between episodic, semantic, and procedural memories. A normal memory has disconnected islands of information, too. As far back as 1886, Ebbinghaus realized that people can know something without knowing that they know it (Roediger, 1990). Memory expert Daniel Schacter (1992, 1996) calls this **implicit memory:** memory that can affect behavior, but of which we have no conscious awareness. Thus, semantic memory can be either *explicit* (typically learned through deliberate, conscious processing, such as in memorizing material for a test) or *implicit* (learned incidentally and without awareness). The central distinction between **explicit memory** and implicit memory lies in focusing *attention* on the material you are learning. As a result, you *know* that you know things in your explicit memory. Implicit memory, on the other hand, can affect your behavior without you realizing it. You should realize, however, that your implicit memories, like your explicit ones, can be biased and inaccurate (Seger, 1994).

H. M.'s case can also tell us something about the biological basis of memory. The surgery and the resulting memory deficits suggest that the hippocampus and/or amygdala serve as links that carry messages between STM and explicit LTM (see Figure 6.11). This has also been confirmed in studies of other individuals with comparable brain damage (Eichenbaum, 1997). However, the pathway destroyed in H. M.'s brain apparently carries information only one way: from STM to LTM—but not in the other direction. We know this because H. M. can retrieve old explicit memories, but he cannot store new ones. Thus, he cannot transfer new explicit memories from STM to LTM. Other work suggests that the hippocampus also plays an especially important role in place learning—of the sort that produced cognitive maps in Tolman's rats (Beardsley, 1997).

## Remembering Meaning and Context

We have seen that working memory records items in their order of arrival and often encodes them acoustically (in sounds). In contrast, LTM stores items according to their meanings and cross-references them with other stored information. Every item in LTM is connected by its meaning to many other indexes for retrieval. When people refer to "memory" in everyday, nonpsychological language, they usually mean the contents and processes of LTM. Because LTM is central to so much of psychology, we now take a closer look at how material in LTM is encoded, stored, and retrieved.

**MEANINGFUL ORGANIZATION**    The role that *meaningful organization* plays in long-term storage is demonstrated when you remember the gist or sense of an idea rather than the actual sentence you heard. For example, you may hear the sentence, "The book was returned to the library by Mary." Later, you are asked if you heard the sentence, "Mary returned the book to the library." You may indeed mistakenly re-

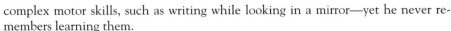

Chapter 3:
States of Mind
Chapter 5:
Sensation and Perception

*Priming is a technique used for studying unconscious processing and implicit memory.*

**Implicit memory:** A memory of which you are unaware but which can affect your behavior.

**Explicit memory:** Memory that has been processed with attention and can be consciously recalled.

member having "heard" the second sentence, because even though the two sentences are completely different utterances, they mean the same thing. Human LTM more accurately stores meaning than form (Bransford & Franks, 1971). The practical application of the fact that LTM is organized according to meaning is this: *If you want to store information in your LTM, you must make it meaningful while it is in working memory.* This means that you must connect new information with things you already know. That's why it is so important in your classes (such as psychology) to think of personal examples of the concepts you want to remember. On the other hand, the organization of LTM according to meaning is the source of memory distortion and inaccuracy because we remember things as we think they *should have been* rather than the way they actually happened. This, we shall see, can cause difficulties in eyewitness testimony.

**EYEWITNESS RECALL**   We saw earlier that memory is a constructive process based on perception. If so, how far should the memory of eyewitnesses be trusted in revealing the truth? A famous study by Elizabeth Loftus and John Palmer dealt with just this issue. After subjects watched a film of two cars colliding, Loftus and Palmer asked them to estimate how fast the cars had been moving. Subjects gave different speed estimates that depended on how the questions about the accident were worded (Loftus & Palmer, 1973; Loftus, 1979, 1984). The experimenters asked half their subjects, "How fast were the cars going when they *smashed* into each other?" These subjects' estimates were about 25% higher than those who were asked, "How fast were the cars going when they *hit* each other?" A week later, they asked the same subjects to recall the broken glass at the scene of the accident. (There was none.) More of the "smashed" subjects had memories of broken glass.

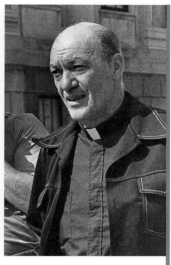

Because so much of our criminal justice system relies on eyewitness identifications and descriptions, the vulnerability of such memories to error and distortion has important implications for the law. Further research by Loftus and her colleagues (Lindsay, 1990, 1993; Loftus, 1992, 1993; Loftus & Ketcham, 1991, 1994; Weingardt, Loftus, & Lindsay, 1995) has identified several factors influencing the accuracy of eyewitness recall:

Our criminal justice system relies heavily on eyewitness identifications and descriptions. How well does this system work? You can judge for yourself in the case of a Catholic priest, Father Pagano (right), who was arrested and accused of a series of robberies. The police and the prosecutor were certain that they had the right man, because seven witnesses had identified him as the culprit. Father Pagano was finally exonerated during his trial, when the real robber (left)—hardly a look-alike—confessed.

- When the passage of time allows the original memory to fade, people are more likely to misremember information.
- People's recollections are more influenced by leading questions if they are not forewarned that interrogations can create bias.
- Age matters: Younger children and adults over 65 may be most susceptible to influence by misinformation in their efforts to recall (see Bruck & Ceci, 1997).
- Misinformation may not only distort reported recollections but also impair storage or retrieval of the original memory.
- Confidence does not predict accuracy: Misinformed subjects can actually come to believe the misinformation they claim to remember.

The process by which a person perceives an event, encodes that information, and recalls it at a later time is at the heart of psychological interest in learning and memory. Our human capacity for constructive memory not only increases the difficulty of getting accurate eyewitness testimony, it also shields people from some truths they do not want to accept. As we saw in the psychology of perception, we distort incoming information to fit our prejudices and remember what we expected rather than what really happened.

**Chapter 5:
Sensation and Perception**
*Perception is an* interpretation *of events.*

**RECOVERING REPRESSED MEMORIES**    In our opening case, the Smith family's ordeal began with Donna Smith's claim that she had been sexually abused by her father. Subsequently, Donna came to believe her own claims, although she now insists they were all lies—and at one time she herself knew they were lies. Research on eyewitness recall confirms that, as a result of misinformation or distortion, people not only report false memories, they come to believe them completely (Hyman et al., 1995; Loftus, 1997a, 1997b). Why do we, then, put so much stock in these reports of recovered *repressed* memories?

Chapter 10:
Personality

*Freud taught that most of our mind is not accessible to consciousness.*

The answer lies in the widespread belief in Sigmund Freud's theory of **repression.** Freud taught that threatening memories would be stored in the unconscious mind, where they could indirectly influence our thoughts and behavior. He also taught that the only way to be free of these repressed memories is to root them out during therapy—bringing them into the daylight of consciousness, where they can be dealt with rationally. In fact, the research suggests just the opposite: Memory for emotionally arousing events is especially well remembered (Shobe & Kihlstrom, 1997). Most people, however, are unaware of this fact, retaining a strong, but unfounded, belief in repression and in the Freudian unconscious. Donna Smith and her therapist were among the believers, and, at one point, she believed her recovered memories so completely that she "wholeheartedly hated" her father. Donna and her family got a second chance when she was able to face and admit the truth, away from the influences that had supported her false memories and accusations. Unfortunately, other stories of "recovered memories" have had less happy endings (Loftus & Ketcham, 1994).

**THE VALUE OF CONSTRUCTIVE MEMORY**    Despite its potential inaccuracies, constructive memory is an enormously positive feature of creative minds (Schacter, 1999). More often than not, it helps us make sense of our uncertain world by providing the right context in which to understand, interpret, remember, and act on minimal or fragmentary evidence. Without it, our memories would be little more than second-rate transcription services that could not assign any special significance to our many unique and personal experiences. This constructive ability, of course, also puts us at risk for distorted, changing, and false memories. Research on constructive memory continues to teach us about both its possibilities and limits and how such knowledge might be considered in applications in therapy and the law. It also has much to teach us about the ways that memory discards information—a topic to which we turn next.

## Forgetting

We all remember an enormous amount of material over long periods of time. College students can accurately recall details about the births of younger siblings, even when those events occurred 16 years earlier (Sheingold & Tenney, 1982). Knowledge in semantic memory (for example, knowing what historic event happened in the year 1492) is retrieved even better than knowledge in episodic memory (recalling where and when you first learned about 1492), regardless of the time that has elapsed since the actual gaining of the knowledge. In semantic memory, you will also retain generalizations longer than details. Unfortunately, however, even well-learned semantic material may become irretrievable over time. So, although we can remember an amazing amount of information, we forget an even greater amount of what we once knew. Why and how does this happen?

Early psychologists theorized that we forget because we suffer a gradual loss, or *decay,* of the memory traces in our minds. Modern psychologists still believe that memory decay causes loss in sensory memory and in working memory, when maintenance rehearsal is prevented. But simple decay does not jibe with the fact that LTM can retain some episodic memories clearly and accurately for a lifetime. Motor skills, too, are often retained substantially intact in procedural memory for many years, even

**Repression:** The Freudian defense mechanism of forgetting, by which painful or threatening material is blocked off in the unconscious and prevented from reaching consciousness.

without practice—"just like riding a bicycle." Trivia, commercial jingles, and odors from one's childhood all may persist in memory despite years of dormancy. Other explanations seem to account for forgetting better than the notion of mere physical decay does. Here we briefly examine two of those other perspectives on forgetting: *interference* and *retrieval failure*.

**INTERFERENCE**    Memories themselves can cause forgetting. That is, memories of other experiences can conflict with our learning and retention of new material. More precisely, **proactive interference** occurs when previously stored information prevents the learning of similar, new information. *Pro-* means "forward," and in this case old lessons move forward and block your ability to remember new ones. An example of proactive interference in procedural memory is shown when, after moving to a new home, you still look for items in "the old places" where you used to store them, although no such locations exist in your new environment. The old habit has proactively interfered with your efforts to retrieve the more recent memory of the new storage places.

**Proactive interference:** A cause of forgetting by which previously stored information prevents learning and remembering new information.

## FIGURE 6.12:    Two Types of Interference

In *proactive interference*, earlier learning (Spanish) interferes with memory for later information (French). In *retroactive interference*, new information (French) interferes with memory for information learned earlier (Spanish).

Spanish, learned beforehand, interferes proactively

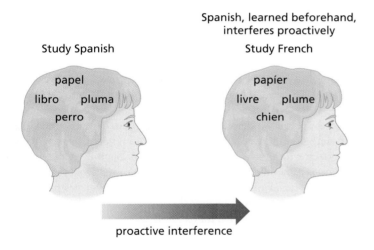

proactive interference

French, learned afterward, interferes retroactively

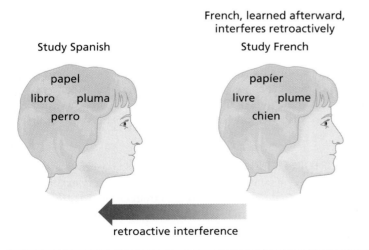

retroactive interference

**Retroactive interference** occurs when newly learned information prevents the retrieval of previously stored, similar material. *Retro-* means "backward"; the newer material seems to reach back into your memory to block access to old material. Retroactive interference describes what happens when studying for your Spanish test tomorrow makes it difficult for you to remember the French you learned in high school. Recent material retroactively interferes with your ability to retrieve an older memory.

Three general principles govern interference:

1. The greater the *similarity* between two sets of material, the greater the interference between them.
2. *Meaningless* material is more vulnerable to interference than meaningful material. (Interference would be more likely to affect your memory of the nonsense syllables ZAX, QOG, and KIV than the more meaningful TAX, FOG, and KIT.)
3. The more difficult the *intervening task* between learning and recall, the more it will interfere with memory of material learned earlier. (Between studying for a psychology test and taking it, you will forget more if you study for sociology than if you do your laundry, a simpler and less relevant distraction.)

The most obvious prediction that emerges from interference theory is that information undisturbed by new material will be recalled best. A classic study by Jenkins and Dallenbach (1924) provided support for this hypothesis. Subjects who went to sleep immediately after learning new material recalled it better the next morning than those who spent the same amount of time performing their usual activities after learning.

**RETRIEVAL FAILURE**   An apparent memory loss often turns out to be only a failure of retrieval. A question worded a little differently will guide us to the information, or a question requiring only recognition will reveal knowledge that we could not access and reproduce by recall. And, as Hermann Ebbinghaus demonstrated long ago, the demonstrable time savings involved in *relearning* can reveal the presence of the weakest memories, even when recall and recognition fail. Such evidence makes it clear that many failures to remember reflect poor encoding or inadequate retrieval cues rather than loss of memories. Failure to call up a memory is never positive proof that some fragmentary trace of the memory is not there.

But what causes retrieval failure? Why, for example, do we forget the names of many of our high-school classmates or even college teachers when we meet them away from school? When the setting is different from that in which we met those people originally, we have lost the *context* we once used to form memories for those acquaintances, so we lack the necessary retrieval cues (Reiser, Black, & Abelson, 1985). Typically, memories of people are formed around the social contexts in which we encounter them, and only later, with more interaction, do we add secondary retrieval cues based on the personality traits and personal attributes of those people (Bond & Brockett, 1987). Such cues are a part of encoding specificity, and they remind us that forgetting is influenced by the way material was first encoded into memory. Retrieval failure also reminds us that LTM is organized according to meaning.

**OTHER CAUSES OF FORGETTING**   Forgetting can have many causes other than decay, interference, and retrieval failure. These include what memory expert Daniel Schacter (1999) calls *absent-mindedness*, which results from failure to attend to important features of the forgotten material. For example, you are more likely to remember seeing the word TABLE if you are asked, "Is it a piece of furniture?" rather than "How many letters does it have?"

**Retroactive interference:** A cause of forgetting by which newly learned information prevents retrieval of previously stored material.

Memory errors are also caused by *misattribution*, as in the case of psychologist Donald Thomson (1988), who was accused of rape by a victim who gave an unmistakably detailed description of him as the assailant. At the time of the rape, however, Thomson was giving a live TV interview—which the victim had been watching. Ironically, the subject of the interview was memory distortions.

**Mnemonics:** Techniques for improving memory.

## Improving Your Memory with Mnemonics

To help yourself remember, you can use the same tricks the memory experts use: mental strategies called mnemonics (pronounced *nee-MON-ix*, from the Greek word meaning "remember"). **Mnemonics** are short, verbal devices that encode items to be remembered by associating them with familiar and previously encoded information. We will look at four types of mnemonic strategies: natural language mediators, the method of loci, visual imagery, and creating examples.

*Natural language mediators* are meanings or patterns of words that are already stored in LTM. These can easily be associated with new information. For instance, to remember a grocery list consisting of tuna, shampoo, and eggs, you can concoct a silly story linking the items: "The cat discovers I'm out of *tuna* so she interrupts me while I'm using the *shampoo* and meows to *egg* me on." The use of rhyming slogans and rhythmic musical jingles can make it easier to remember material as diverse as brand names ("Oscar Mayer has a way with . . . "), grammar rules ("I before E except after C"), and calendars ("Thirty days has September . . . "). Acronyms—words made up of initials—use natural language mediators to chunk unwieldy strings of words into pronounceable abbreviations, such as "Roy G. Biv" for the colors of the visible spectrum light (red, orange, yellow, green, blue, indigo, violet).

You can also remember lists of things by using the *method of loci* (pronounced *LOW-sigh*, from the Latin *locus*, "place"). Imagine a familiar sequence of places, such as the bed, desk, and chairs in your room. When memorizing a series of words

or names, you mentally put one in each of those places. To retrieve the series, you take a mental tour, examining those places to "see" what you have put in each one. To recall the grocery list, you might mentally picture a can of *tuna* on your bed, *shampoo* spilled on your desktop, and a box of *eggs* open on a chair. More bizarre or unconventional image combinations are usually easier to remember; a can of tuna in your bedroom will make a more memorable image than tuna in your kitchen (Bower, 1972).

The method of loci also involves the mnemonic power of *visual imagery*, one of the most effective forms of encoding. Mental images may work well because they use both verbal and visual memories simultaneously (Paivio, 1986). With visual imagery, you remember words by associating them with vivid, distinctive mental pictures. In the case of the grocery list, for example, you might simply combine mental images of tuna, shampoo, and eggs in a bizarre but memorable way: Picture a *tuna* floating on an enormous fried *egg* in a sea of foamy *shampoo*, for example. Or imagine a politician you dislike eating *tuna* from the can, his hair covered with *shampoo* suds, while you throw *eggs* at him.

Such techniques, however, do not help much with the material you must learn in your course work. Most of the information

Mnemonic strategies help us remember things by making them meaningful. Here an elementary school teacher helps students remember the letter "K" by showing that "K does karate."

you must learn in college consists of *concepts*—often abstract concepts, such as "operant conditioning" or "retroactive interference." The trick in remembering concepts is to make them meaningful by creating your own *examples* of the concepts—as we mentioned earlier. So, think of an example of operant conditioning or extinction in your own experience. (If you can't, try to visualize yourself in the examples that we have given you in this book.) This connects new information to the network of information already in your LTM, making it meaningful. (*See Chapter 7, Cognitive Processes.*)

In general, the use of mnemonics teaches us that memory is flexible, personal, and creative. It also teaches us that memory works by meaningful associations. With this knowledge and a little experimentation, you can devise techniques for encoding and retrieval that work well for you based on your own personal associations, regardless of what works for others.

1. RECALL: *Which one of the following statements best describes forgetting, as characterized by Ebbinghaus's forgetting curve?*
   a. We forget at a constant rate.
   b. We forget slowly at first and then more rapidly as time goes on.
   c. We forget rapidly at first and then more slowly as time goes on.
   d. Ebbinghaus's method of relearning showed that we never really forget.

2. RECALL: *Which of the following are the three essential functions of memory?*
   a. encoding, storage, access and retrieval
   b. sensory, working, and long-term
   c. remembering, forgetting, and repressing
   d. recall, recognition, and relearning

3. RECALL: *Which part of memory has the smallest capacity? (That is, which part of memory is considered the "bottleneck" in the memory system?)*
   a. sensory memory
   b. working memory
   c. long-term memory
   d. implicit memory

4. APPLICATION: *If you wanted to remember the major divisions of long-term memory, which method would be the most effective?*
   a. rehearsal: repeating them over and over to yourself
   b. elaboration: thinking of examples of each division
   c. acoustic encoding: trying to remember the sounds associated with each term
   d. temporal coding: identifying when you heard of each division

5. RECALL: *Which part of long-term memory stores autobiographical information?*
   a. semantic memory
   b. procedural memory
   c. recognition memory
   d. episodic memory

6. RECALL: *In order to get material into permanent storage, it must be made meaningful while it is in*
   a. sensory memory.
   b. working memory.
   c. long-term memory.
   d. recall memory.

7. APPLICATION: *Which kind of forgetting is involved when the sociology I studied yesterday makes it more difficult to learn and remember the psychology I am studying today?*
   a. decay
   b. retrieval failure
   c. proactive interference
   d. retroactive interference

8. UNDERSTANDING THE CORE CONCEPT: *Studies of eyewitness testimony and recovery of "repressed" memories show that*
   a. our unconscious minds remember events as they actually happened.
   b. memories can be severely distorted, even when we have confidence in them.
   c. distorted memories are a sign of mental disorder.
   d. the more confident we are of a memory, the more likely it is to be true.

**ANSWERS:**　1. c　2. a　3. b　4. b　5. d　6. b　7. c　8. b

# USING PSYCHOLOGY TO LEARN PSYCHOLOGY

## *Operant Conditioning Can Help You Study More—and Enjoy It*

*Y*ou may have tried the Premack principle to trick yourself into studying more, perhaps by denying yourself TV time or a trip to the refrigerator until your homework was done. It works for some people, but if it doesn't work for you, try making the studying itself more enjoyable and more reinforcing.

For most of us, being with people we like is reinforcing, regardless of the activity. So, make some (not all) of your studying a social activity. That is, schedule a time when you and another classmate or two can get together to identify and clarify important concepts and to try to predict what will be on the next test.

Don't just focus on vocabulary. Rather, try to discover the big picture—the overall meaning of each section of the chapter. The Core Concepts are a good place to start. Then you can discuss with your friends how the details fit in with the Core Concepts. You will most likely find that the social pressure of an upcoming study group will help motivate you to get your reading done and identify murky points. When you get together for your group study session, you will find that explaining what you have learned reinforces your own learning. The real reinforcement comes, however, from spending some time—studying—with your friends!

## CHAPTER SUMMARY

- Most human behavior reflects the influence of learning and remembering. Research on learning has long been influenced by the behaviorist emphasis on observable stimuli and responses. However, studies of both human and nonhuman subjects have contributed to cognitive views of learning.

ulus–response process. In general, classical conditioning affects basic, survival-oriented responses, including emotions and taste aversions.

 **CORE CONCEPT** In classical conditioning, the organism learns to give reflexive responses to new stimuli.

 **KEY QUESTION** **HOW DOES CLASSICAL CONDITIONING EXPLAIN LEARNING?**

- The earliest learning research focused on classical conditioning, beginning with Ivan Pavlov's discovery of how conditioned stimuli can elicit reflexive responses. His experiments showed how conditioned responses could be acquired, extinguished, and undergo spontaneous recovery in laboratory animals. John Watson extended this work to the human learning of fears in his famous experiment on Little Albert. Studies of taste aversions suggest, however, that classical conditioning is not a simple stim-

 **KEY QUESTION** **HOW DO WE LEARN NEW BEHAVIORS BY OPERANT CONDITIONING?**

- Trial-and-error learning was originally explored by Edward Thorndike, who developed the law of effect. B. F. Skinner expanded that work, now called operant conditioning, to explain how responses are influenced by their environmental consequences. His work examined positive and negative reinforcement, punishment, extinction, and various kinds of reinforcement contingencies. Operant conditioning has been applied extensively to both humans and nonhumans.

 **CORE CONCEPT**

In operant conditioning, the patterns of rewards, punishments, and other consequences encourage or discourage the behaviors they follow.

 **KEY QUESTION**

**HOW DOES COGNITIVE PSYCHOLOGY EXPLAIN LEARNING?**

- Much research now suggests that learning is not just a process that links stimuli and responses: Learning is also cognitive. This was shown in Köhler's work on insight learning in chimpanzees, in Tolman's studies of cognitive maps and place learning in rats, and in Bandura's research on social learning and imitation in humans. In recent years, cognitive scientists have reinterpreted behavioral learning, especially operant and classical conditioning, in cognitive terms.

 **CORE CONCEPT**

Some forms of learning must be explained as changes in mental processes, rather than as changes in behavior alone.

 **KEY QUESTION**

**HOW DOES MEMORY WORK?**

- Learned material is only usable if it is remembered. Memory involves cognitive processes for encoding new material, storing it, and allowing it to be retrieved. Hermann Ebbinghaus, who pioneered the study of memory, developed the forgetting curve and the savings method of measuring retention. Modern researchers have identified three different human memory systems. Sensory memory holds much material fleetingly. Working memory (short-term memory) processes information consciously, often with acoustic encoding; it has a small capacity. Information in long-term memory is encoded, stored, and retrieved according to the meaning and context of the material. LTM is divided into declarative memory (for facts and events) and procedural memory (for perceptual and motor skills). Declarative memory can be further divided into episodic and semantic systems. In LTM, information can be either explicit or implicit. Eyewitness accounts are subject to distortion, however, and even false memories may seem believable to the rememberer. Much forgetting can be attributed to interference or failure in retrieval. The key to remembering is making the material meaningful by means of elaborative rehearsal while it is in working memory.

 **CORE CONCEPT**

Memory is a cognitive system that operates constructively to encode, store, and retrieve information.

## REVIEW TEST

For each of the following items, choose the single correct or best answer. The correct answers appear at the end.

1. Which one of the following taught that psychology should involve only the analysis of observable stimuli and responses?
   a. Albert Bandura
   b. B. F. Skinner
   c. Sigmund Freud
   d. John Garcia

2. During classical conditioning, for an organism to learn a conditioned association between two stimuli, the UCS must seem to
   a. predict the CS.
   b. be predicted by the CS.
   c. be independent of the CS.
   d. follow the UCR.

3. According to Thorndike's *law of effect*, behavior is strengthened or not strengthened as a result of its
   a. consequences in the organism's environment.
   b. association with stimuli similar to those that have triggered it.
   c. purpose in the organism's efforts to survive.
   d. level of complexity in the organism's repertoire.

4. A _____ is a consistent relationship between a response and the changes in the environment it produces.
   a. behavior potential
   b. behavior analysis

c. reinforcement contingency

d. conditioned reinforcer

5. "The best part of going to the beach," your friend exclaims as you start your vacation, "is getting away from all the stress of work and school." If this is true, then your friend's vacation-taking behavior has been influenced by

a. positive reinforcement.

b. negative reinforcement.

c. extinction.

d. punishment.

6. Which of the following is *not* a good way to make punishment effective?

a. Make it swift and brief.

b. Make it intense.

c. Deliver it immediately.

d. Focus it on the undesirable behavior.

7. According to the Premack principle, a reinforcer can be anything that

a. changes behavior from its past norms.

b. rewards rather than penalizes behavior.

c. becomes associated with an unconditioned stimulus.

d. the organism does frequently.

8. In his research with rats running mazes, Edward C. Tolman concluded that place learning required each subject to rely on

a. a CS-UCS connection.

b. conditioned reinforcers.

c. a cognitive map.

d. spontaneous recovery.

9. Your knowledge of how to use a can opener, boot up your computer, address an envelope, and program a VCR are all examples of _____ memory.

a. procedural

b. semantic

c. sensory

d. constructive

10. Elise used to live in a house with a large kitchen, where all the silverware was stored in a drawer to the right of the sink. Since she moved to her new apartment, she finds that she habitually looks for the silverware in a drawer to the right of the sink, although no such drawer exists. Her behavior reflects forgetting due to

a. absence of appropriate retrieval cues.

b. retroactive interference.

c. proactive interference.

d. repression.

**ANSWERS:**   1. b   2. b   3. a   4. c   5. b   6. b
7. d   8. c   9. a   10. c

# IF YOU'RE INTERESTED . . .

## BOOKS

Artiss, K. L. (1996). *Mistake making*. Lanham, MD: University Press of America.

*Why doesn't everyone learn from experience? Some experiences may not be memorable—but certain types of people may also have difficulty making the adjustments necessary for each lesson, and, failing to learn, they end up suffering relentless punishment by repeating their errors and failures. Here's why it may happen—and what to do about it.*

Baum, W. M. (1994). *Understanding behaviorism: Science, behavior, and culture*. New York: HarperCollins.

*This short, readable text explains the specific goals and methods of behaviorism, with discussions of stimuli, reinforcement, and complex issues such as freedom, responsibility, and culture.*

Benne, B. (1988). *WASPLEG and other mnemonics*. Dallas, TX: Taylor Publishing.

*Benne presents handy strategies for remembering the seven deadly sins (Wrath, Avarice, Sloth, Pride, Lust, Envy, Gluttony) and other lists that might otherwise exceed the initial limits of memory.*

Greven, P. (1992). *Spare the child: The religious roots of punishment and the psychological impact of child abuse*. New York: Vintage Books.

*Imagine a world in which hitting a child is not only politically incorrect, it is also against the law of both man and God. Greven documents the great weight of evidence against any rationale for corporal punishment of children and asserts that we have a moral obligation to develop humane alternatives to beating our kids.*

Hilts, P. J. (1995). *Memory's ghost: The strange tale of Mr. M. and the nature of memory.* New York: Simon & Schuster.

This is the true story of Henry M., a young man who underwent experimental surgery for a severe epileptic condition in 1953 only to completely lose all ability to form new memories or learn new information. Based on numerous interviews with the subject, Hilts's book relates several stories: the abused ethics of medicine, the fragility of psychological reality, the complexity of mental life, and the centrality of memory to one's very sense of self.

Hyman, I. A. (1997). *The case against spanking: How to discipline your child without hitting.* San Francisco: Jossey-Bass.

Well-intentioned but frustrated parents need options in dealing with young children's misbehaviors. Because punishment such as hitting fails to change behavior, and often models aggression, families need strategies for "positive punishments," contingencies that will reduce unwanted behavior without teaching children even worse habits. Hyman also explores why children seem to know just what will most provoke their parents and argues firmly that the costs of corporal punishment vastly outweigh the flimsy justifications of convenience or power.

MacLean, H. N. (1993). *Once upon a time: A true story of memory, murder, and the law.* New York: Harper-Collins.

The true story of the case of Eileen Franklin, whose "recovered memories" led to the conviction of her father for the murder of her childhood friend. The book documents the trial of George Franklin, with the prosecution's case based totally on recollected testimony, and also explores whether Eileen's memories were not repressed but totally fabricated.

Ofshe, R., & Watters, E. (1994). *Making monsters: False memories, psychotherapy, and sexual hysteria.* New York: Charles Scribner's Sons.

Since the Eileen Franklin case (previous listing), the media have exploded with stories of long-repressed memories—of childhood molestation, satanic abuse, or murder—suddenly surfacing when victims enter therapy as adults. The authors examine how such memories may be constructed and shaped not by truth but by the suggestions of therapists and the victims' own prejudices.

Phillips, D., & Judd, R. (1978). *How to fall out of love.* New York: Fawcett Popular Library.

This book provides a short, useful, and practical application of behavioral modification techniques to getting over a painful romantic loss. Some techniques (e.g., thought-stopping, positive image building) can also be applied to various other intentional behavior changes.

Prochaska, J. O., Norcross, J. C., & Diclimente, C. C. (1995). *Changing for good.* New York: Avon Books.

This step-by-step behavior modification program is based on the conclusions of three psychologists that lasting behavior change depends not on fate or fortitude but on a process that can be learned and managed by anyone who can identify, first, what stage of change he or she is in, and next, the appropriate change strategy for that stage.

Rupp, R. (1998). *Committed to memory: How we remember and why we forget.* New York: Crown Publishing.

A biochemist well-versed in world literature explains what science knows about memory: how it begins, what goes in, what stays or leaves, why some things cannot be retrieved, and what we can do to improve our memory for the things that matter to us.

Schacter, D. L. (1996). *Searching for memory: The brain, the mind, and the past.* New York: Basic Books.

A famous memory researcher tells you about the state of his art. The book deals with both the biological and psychological mechanisms of memory and includes an excellent discussion of implicit memory.

Skinner, B. F. (1945/1976). *Walden two.* Boston: Allyn & Bacon.

Walden Two is a fictitious utopian community based on the science of human behavior. In this book, the world's most famous behaviorist tells us what the world would be like if he were in charge.

Wright, J. C., with Lashnits, J. W. (1994). *Is your cat crazy?* New York: Macmillan.

All right, this is a cat book, but John C. Wright is an animal behaviorist who documents interesting (and fun) case histories of "problem felines," some behavioral principles applied to modify their habits, and insights into the repertoires and instincts that influence what cats learn and do. Many of the principles could be applied to other companion animals—and companion humans!

## VIDEOS

*A clockwork orange.* (1971, color, 137 min.). Directed by Stanley Kubrick; starring Malcolm McDowell, Patrick Magee, Adrienne Corri, Aubrey Morris, James Marcus.

This fascinating, disturbing film is based on Anthony Burgess's novel about a futuristic society's efforts to reform a violent criminal by applying conditioning techniques.

*The crucible.* (1996, color, 123 min.). Directed by Nicholas Hytner; starring Daniel Day-Lewis, Winona Ryder, Joan Allen, Paul Scofield.

Based on Arthur Miller's play, whose subtext attacked the anticommunist "witch-hunts" of the U.S. House Un-

American Activities Committee in the 1950s, this is the classic tale of the tragedies of false memories and the accusations, hysteria, and trauma they create.

Groundhog Day. (1993, color, 103 min.). Directed by Harold Ramis; starring Bill Murray, Andie MacDowell, Chris Elliott.

*What if you were the only one around who had episodic memory for the recent past? That's the dramatic conflict in this funny fantasy about a cynical TV weatherman who must change his ways when he finds he mysteriously relives the same day over and over—but only he remembers "this day has happened before."*

Johnny mnemonic. (1995, color, 98 min.). Directed by Robert Longo; starring Keanu Reeves, Dolph Lundgren, Takeshi, Ice-T, Dina Meyer.

*This is the ugly futuristic tale of an "information" courier who travels the globe with messages stored in his head and who must elude an evil corporation after his latest cargo of "memories."*

Total recall. (1990, color, 109 min.). Directed by Paul Verhoeven; starring Arnold Schwarzenegger, Rachel Ticotin, Sharon Stone, Ronny Cox.

*In the 21st century, a man discovers that false memories—and a false identity—have been planted in his mind, so he travels to Mars to confront the perpetrators of the crime. Oscar-winning special effects highlight the film, based on science-fiction writer Phillip K. Dick's tale, "We Can Remember It for You Wholesale."*

## CORE CONCEPTS

## PSYCHOLOGY IN YOUR LIFE

**HOW DO COGNITIVE SCIENTISTS MEASURE THE MIND?**

Cognitive scientists have developed techniques that can link mental processes to stimuli, brain activity, and behavior.

**Turning It Over in Your Mind:** Mental rotation experiments show that this figure of speech may be literally correct.

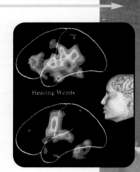

**WHAT DOES THINKING CONSIST OF?**

Thinking involves manipulation of mental representations, such as concepts, images, schemas, and scripts.

**Schemas and Scripts Help You Know What to Expect:** But sometimes they fill in the blanks—without your realizing it.

**DO WE THINK LOGICALLY— OR PSYCHOLOGICALLY?**

We are capable of logic, but our thinking is also influenced by such psychological factors as perceptions, emotions, motives, and personality.

**On Becoming a Creative Genius:** Such individuals have expertise, certain personality traits, and lots of motivation, but their thought processes are essentially the same as yours.

**USING PSYCHOLOGY TO LEARN PSYCHOLOGY: THINKING LIKE YOUR PROFESSOR**

# 7

# Cognitive Processes

*M*y Sicilian grandfather, Salvatore, loved the opera, but he was too poor ever to go to one in his adopted home, the United States. Instead, every Saturday he listened to The Opera from the Met *on a little radio in his shoe repair shop in the Bronx. He would play it full blast, and if it were an Italian opera, he would sing along with most of the tenor parts. He also felt he needed to educate "the Americans" to the joys of opera, so he would open his door and let the music blast out into the streets.*

*One Saturday his reverie was broken by a gang of toughs who were shouting offensive epithets at him: "Dirty wop!" "Guinea, go back to where you came from," and worse. Their shouting was so loud he could not hear his beloved opera, La Traviata. He cursed back, and they laughed and taunted him mercilessly. By the time they left, he could find no joy in listening to the end of the opera.*

*Next Saturday, like clockwork, the boys returned shouting and cursing. Grandpa Salvatore now went out front and said to them: "Boys, I did not appreciate what good voices you have. Please continue to shout and scream as loud as you can, and I will give each of you 25 cents for your performance." They did just that, screaming like banshees for nearly half an hour without intermission. He gave them their reward, and they left surprised but happy at this unexpected windfall of money for a movie and a Coke.*

*On the following Saturday when they returned, Grandpa Salvatore came out and said again how much he loved to hear their voices shouting even louder than the opera or the neighborhood garbage trucks, but since he was only a poor shoe repairman, he did not have enough money to pay them what they were worth. For today's show, he could give them only 10 cents each.*

*"What do you take us for, old man—suckers? We ain't gonna do no show for you for a measly dime. Take your money and shove it!" With that they sulked away, cursing as usual—but in modulated tones.*

*Next Saturday and all the ones after that, the ruffians refused to return to curse and shout at the old Italian shoemaker, whom they took for a cheapskate. Grandfather now could listen with undivided attention to his operas, play them loud and clear, and not worry about being interrupted and disturbed by this uncouth, prejudiced bunch of kids.*

This little story puts the human mind on center stage. It reveals some of its remarkable talents, such as appreciating art, making judgments, reasoning, developing beliefs, forming preferences, and solving problems. The quest to understand "how we know what we know" leads us to the study of cognitive processes. In this chapter we will investigate the many ways in which our mind transforms personal experience into information; sensory data into evidence; perception of events, people and relationships into knowledge; and accumulated knowledge into wisdom. But most of all, the human mind is designed to understand and communicate stories or accounts of how it and similar minds conspire to make the human connection.

—P.Z.

Only humans—because of their ability for thinking about what might be—can indulge in flights of fancy.

Only humans have the capacity to stretch their mental horizons to think about what was, will be, might be, and should be. And, perhaps most amazing of all, we humans have the ability to imagine what might be in each other's minds, as Grandpa Salvatore did so cleverly. What vehicle do we use for these mental flights? Thought: the cognitive processes operating in the private inner space of our brains, processes that enable us to form mental worlds containing things both realistic and fantastic.

And what does thought consist of? Its raw materials come from every cranny of our minds: from sensation, perception, learning, memory, emotion, motivation, and processes lying beyond the boundaries of consciousness. Thinking combines and manipulates these raw materials in many forms.

The thought processes called for in your college work involve selecting and storing important facts in long-term memory, of course. But you have probably discovered that education is about much more than crowding your memory with data. It also requires evaluating and organizing all the new information you are storing in memory. When you think in this way, you form networks of interrelated *concepts* (for example, "operant conditioning," "classical conditioning," "insight learning," "observational learning," . . . ). You also build complex cognitive structures that we will call *schemas* and *scripts* that pull together images, cognitive maps, concepts, and other components of thought. To help you do this, your professors ask those tough compare-and-contrast questions. They also ask you to go beyond facts and definitions to analyze and synthesize new information.

The value in learning these higher-level thinking skills may not always be obvious. College students, especially those juggling classes, jobs, and family obligations, sometimes express impatience with their professors' attempts to encourage thinking of the sort that experts in the field do. "Just tell us what you want us to know," they may say. Ironically, textbooks can reinforce this attitude. They may make it seem as though great thinkers—the Albert Einsteins, the Sigmund Freuds, the Emily Dickinsons—are a breed apart from the rest of us. But are they?

If you have ever wondered how such people think—and whether you could join their ranks—this chapter is for you. Here you will see how psychology has managed to peer inside the minds, not only of ordinary problem solvers, but also of experts and "geniuses." You will learn some of their cognitive tricks. In addition, you will also discover the most common obstacles to clear thinking that all of us face.

More broadly, this chapter takes us farther into the world of **cognitive psychology,** the scientific study of mental processes and mental structures. (See Figure 7.1.) Here you will see how cognitive psychologists investigate the ways people manipulate and transform information. We begin this chapter's exploration of cognitive processes by considering some of the ways in which researchers try to measure the elusive inner processes involved in thinking.

**Chapter 3: States of Mind**

*What is the nature of consciousness?*

**Cognitive psychology:** The branch of psychology specializing in the scientific study of mental processes and mental structures.

**FIGURE 7.1:** The Domain of Cognitive Psychology

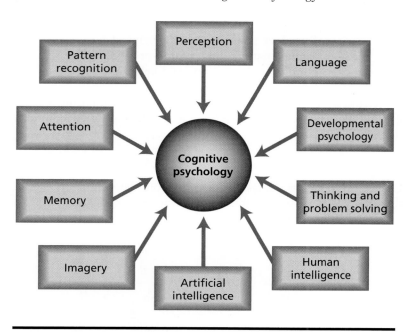

## HOW DO COGNITIVE SCIENTISTS MEASURE THE MIND?

Although it seems obvious that thinking should occupy a central position in psychology, it was not always so. During the decades when psychology was ruled by behaviorism, the field focused almost exclusively on examining the organism's behavioral responses to the external world. The behaviorists correctly pointed out that we cannot observe a person's thoughts objectively. Because thoughts and other mental processes are so private, they present a sticky problem for scientists, who want to develop objective knowledge. Nevertheless, a "science of the mind" did begin to emerge in the 1950s. At that time, a few scholars from cognitive psychology, neuroscience, philosophy, and computer science began to seek an understanding of the ways the mind and brain process information and give behavior its direction, meaning, and coherence (Gardner, 1985). The result has been a "cognitive revolution," a radical shift in the field of psychology in recent decades (see Figure 7.2). Today most psychologists accept the idea that a science of cognition is

**Chapter 6:**
**Learning and Remembering**

*Behaviorism focuses on observable stimuli and responses and refuses to speculate about internal mental processes.*

**FIGURE 7.2:** The Domain of Cognitive Science

The domain of cognitive science occupies the intersection of cognitive psychology, computer science (artificial intelligence), and neuroscience. It also includes study of the philosophy of the mind.

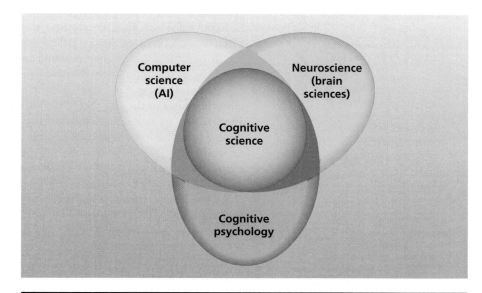

possible, based on the techniques of cognitive science and modern neuroscience. This is the Core Concept:

 **CORE CONCEPT**

**Cognitive scientists have developed techniques that can link mental processes to stimuli, brain activity, and behavior.**

Let us look more closely at some of the developments that made the cognitive revolution possible and allowed objective science to enter the previously hidden world of our private thoughts.

## Developments That Led to the Cognitive Revolution

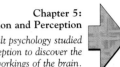
**Chapter 5: Sensation and Perception**

*Gestalt psychology studied perception to discover the workings of the brain.*

The Gestalt psychologists pioneered the science of cognition, but the effort stalled because their ideas were too far ahead of the available technology. They had no PET scanners or MRIs with which to image the living, functioning brain. And, perhaps more important, they had no computers to serve as a model of the mind.

A conceptual breakthrough occurred when computer scientists likened a computer to the brain. The computer is now a conceptual model of thought.

The modern conception of a computer as a "thinking machine," with built-in intelligence that is able to operate flexibly on internal instructions, came from the vision of a brilliant young American mathematician, John von Neumann. In 1945, it occurred to von Neumann that the electronic circuits of the newly invented digital computer were much like the brain's neurons. He also realized that the computer's lines of program code were much like memories stored in the brain. Inspired by von Neumann's insight, Herbert Simon and Allen Newell developed the first computer program that could simulate human problem solving. These conceptual breakthroughs provided wholly new ways of studying mental processes (Hinton, 1992; Newell, Shaw, & Simon, 1958). We glimpsed the success of this approach earlier in our discussion of the computer program called Deep Blue, which defeated world chess champion Garry Kasparov.

**Chapter 2: Biopsychology**

*Deep Blue, a computer program, can "think" well enough to play chess at a world-class level.*

**Chapter 4: Psychological Development**

*Piaget pioneered the psychology of cognitive development in children.*

Meanwhile, as American scientists were extending the frontiers of artificial intelligence (AI) in the computer, the Swiss psychologist Jean Piaget was pioneering another way to make inferences about mental processes. As we have seen, Piaget studied how children display predictable changes in their thinking about the physical world (Piaget, 1954). His notion of stages of cognitive development was based on clever observations of the mental tasks that children could perform at different ages.

**Chapter 5: Sensation and Perception**

*Feature detectors are specialized groups of brain cells that extract certain stimulus characteristics.*

Next, the 1960s brought a series of breakthroughs in neuroscience. In particular, David Hubel and Torsten Wiesel devised a way to implant tiny electrodes into the brains of animals and record the activity of single neurons. With this technology they mapped the visual cortex and found the "feature detectors" that underlie the previously hidden process of perception (Hubel & Wiesel, 1979). Shortly thereafter, other technology—PET and CAT scans and MRI machines—came on line and allowed neuroscientists to watch discrete regions of the brain in action through a variety of new electronic "windows." These developments made it possible, for the first time, to connect observed neural activity—the "mind" in action—directly with environmental events and behavior.

A fourth force behind the cognitive revolution came from linguistic researcher Noam Chomsky, who approached the problem of thought from a new direction. His focus was human language and how it reflects the workings of the mind and brain (Chomsky, 1957). Chomsky and other psycholinguists made the startling proposal that language is not altogether a product of learning. Rather, an innate language acquisition device (LAD), a sort of "language chip" in the brain, makes it possible for young children to understand the basic rules of grammar and to learn their native languages in the absence of any formal education or systematic reinforcement.

These four post-Gestalt approaches to human thought—breakthroughs in neuroscience, psycholinguistics, artificial (computer) intelligence, and the study of children's cognitive development—all boosted the scientific legitimacy of research on all forms of mental processes. In the intervening years, the cognitive perspective has developed into a pillar of modern psychology and its companion field, cognitive science (Mayer, 1981; Solso, 1991).

## Cognitive Science

The interdisciplinary field known as **cognitive science** (sometimes called *cognitive neuroscience*) studies the variety of systems and processes that manipulate information with the goal of understanding the mental processes in the human brain. Figure 7.2 shows that cognitive science draws on the three overlapping disciplines of cognitive psychology, computer science, and neuroscience (Farah, 1984). Cognitive science also receives input from other fields, such as linguistics and cultural anthropology. This emerging discipline seeks to explore classic questions of Western thought (Gardner, 1985): What is the nature of knowledge and thought, and how are they represented in the mind?

Researchers who study how information is represented and processed often build **conceptual models** to help them depict their understanding of cognitive processes. In cognitive science, conceptual models are explanatory metaphors that describe how information is detected, stored, and used by people and machines (Bower & Morrow, 1990). They may consist of descriptions, diagrams, or mathematical formulas. Conceptual models are useful because they can guide new research and make sense of existing knowledge. Although a model might seem correct, it must still withstand the "data test," which allows for new research to modify or discard the model.

The basic approach or cognitive model favored by most cognitive psychologists is the **information-processing model,** often called the *computer model* of information processing. This proposes that thinking and all other forms of cognition can be understood by organizing them into the component parts and processes of information flow, as in a computer. Incoming information goes through a series of stages from input to output. As information in the brain passes through all the processing systems, a variety of cognitive mechanisms analyzes the input, based on information already in the system. Each of these mechanisms then contributes to memories, feelings, and actions. In this way, you might think of cognition as an assembly-line process, building from primitive stages, such as basic sensations and perception, to more complex stages, such as naming, classifying, reasoning, and problem solving. Unlike most computers, however, the human mind works on parallel paths simultaneously. The mind can also make remote associations between thought units and come up with novel concepts and links between them that have never before been processed.

## Tools for Studying Thought

As they studied the inner world of thought, cognitive researchers have had to invent ways of measuring and mapping the territory of the mind with objectivity. We have hinted at some of these methods in our discussion of the breakthroughs in

**Chapter 4:**
**Psychological Development**
*The LAD is an innate brain structure that contains basic rules of grammar and facilitates language learning.*

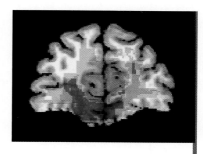

Neuroscientists can now see brain activity that corresponds to thought.

**Chapter 6:**
**Learning and Remembering**
*Information-processing theory is the basis for a three-stage model of human memory.*

**Cognitive science:** An interdisciplinary field that studies the variety of systems and processes that manipulate information.

**Conceptual model:** In cognitive science, an explanatory metaphor that describes how information is detected, stored, and used by people and machines.

**Information-processing model:** A cognitive perspective that proposes that thinking and all other forms of cognition can be understood by analyzing them as a flow of information, as in a computer.

**Event-related potentials:** Brain waves shown on the EEG in response to stimulation.

**Chapter 2:**
**Biopsychology**

*The EEG reveals changing patterns of "waves," of electrical activity generated by the brain.*

**Chapter 2:**
**Biopsychology**

*PET scans image the brain by showing the regions actively metabolizing glucose.*

**Chapter 2:**
**Biopsychology**

*The frontal lobes are involved in planning and directing behavior.*

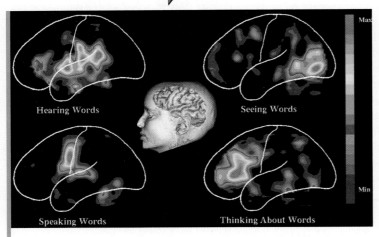

Hearing Words    Seeing Words

Speaking Words    Thinking About Words

Different kinds of mental activity can produce different patterns of brain activity.

neuroscience, computer science, cognitive development, and psycholinguistics that led to the cognitive revolution. In addition, we have seen in previous chapters that cognitive scientists have employed a variety of experimental tools in their study of consciousness, perception, cognitive learning, and memory. In this chapter we will explore the use of still other methods. As our Core Concept indicates, cognitive scientists have developed techniques that can now connect mental activity to activity in the brain (Beardsley, 1997).

For example, with the help of the computer, biological scientists have demonstrated that certain thoughts are associated with specific electrical wave patterns in the brain. They have demonstrated this by presenting a repeated stimulus (such as the word "dog" flashed on a screen) to a subject "wired" to record the brain's electrical responses. While the brain waves on one trial may show no clear pattern, a computer can average many brain wave responses to a single, repeated stimulus, eliminating the random background "noise" of the brain and isolating the unique brain wave pattern evoked by that stimulus (Donchin, 1975). These EEG patterns associated with particular stimuli are called **event-related potentials.**

Researchers who use event-related potentials can isolate and compare the level of brain activity devoted to specific tasks (Garnsey, 1993). The findings indicate that a single general task, such as reading, involves several subtasks addressed by different mental processes. For example, when a reader encounters an unexpected grammatical construction in a sentence, an event-related potential pattern is produced that is different from the pattern that occurs when the reader encounters an unexpected word (Osterhout & Holcomb, 1992).

Other methods can also tell us which parts of the brain switch on and off while we think. With the PET scanner and the MRI, neuroscientists have identified brain regions that become active during different kinds of mental tasks. Two broad findings have come from this work. First, thinking is an activity involving widely distributed areas of the brain—not just a single "thinking center." Second, brain scans have revealed the brain as a community of highly specialized modules each of which deals with different kinds of thought (Posner & McCandliss, 1993; Raichle, 1994; Solso, 1991). Thinking with words, for example, does not use the same parts of the brain required for thinking with visual images or with musical sounds. The picture of thought coming out of this work reveals a process composed of many elements.

Particularly exciting is the location of a part of the brain that seems to be associated with what we often call "common sense," or the ability to act on "intuition" (Bechara et al., 1997; Vogel, 1997). Psychologists have long known that when people make decisions—whether about buying a house or selecting a spouse—they draw on feelings, as well as reason. This emotional component of thinking apparently involves a region of the frontal lobes just above the eyes. This structure allows us unconsciously to add emotional "hunches" to our decisions in the form of information about past rewards and punishments. Individuals with damage to this part of the brain seem to display little emotion. They also lack "intuition"—the ability to know the value of something without conscious reasoning—and they frequently make unwise choices when faced with decisions.

In brief, various forms of brain scanning provide glimpses of cognitive processes through new windows. To understand what these glimpses mean, however, researchers still depend on each other to share information collected by various methods. The "big picture" of human cognitive processes is thus still emerging, piece by piece, just as you might assemble a jigsaw puzzle.

*Turning It Over in Your Mind*

A whole different approach to cognition—more in the venerable Gestalt tradition—can be seen in a famous experiment by Roger Shepard and Jacqueline Metzler (1971). They hypothesized that, when we think, we may literally turn images over in our minds. Using many pairs of images like those in Figure 7.3, Shepard and Metzler asked subjects to decide whether or not the two images in each pair portray the same object. They reasoned that, if people actually rotate these images in their minds to compare them, then subjects would take longer to respond when the difference between the angles of the images in each pair is increased. And that is exactly what they found. Most likely for you, too, it will take longer to respond to pair B—where the images have been rotated through a greater angle—than to pair A. (*See Chapter 5, Sensation and Perception.*)

In an experiment with a similar psychological twist, Stephen Kosslyn found that we use our cognitive machinery to "zoom in," camera-like, on details of our visual concepts. To demonstrate this, Kosslyn (1976) first asked subjects to think of objects, such as an elephant or a cat or a chair. Then he asked questions about details of the imagined object (for example, "Is it a black cat?" or "Does it have a long tail?"), recording how long it took for his subjects to answer. He discovered that the smaller the detail he asked for, the longer subjects needed for a response. Subjects required extra time, Kosslyn theorized, to make a closer examination of their mental images. Both the Shepard and Metzler and the Kosslyn experiments suggest that we mentally manipulate our visual images in much the same way that we might manipulate physical objects in the outside world (Kosslyn, 1983).

Further, cognitive psychologists believe that we use our ability for mental manipulation of images to construct mental models of stories that we read—creating our own "mental movie" of the narrative (Bower & Morrow, 1990). We

also construct mental models (or *schemas*) of how things work (Medin, 1989). For example, you probably have a mental model that explains why the light goes on when you open the refrigerator door and another that explains how a Thermos bottle keeps coffee hot. Likewise, you probably also have mental models that represent your explanation of how cars, computers, sewing machines, and VCRs work. We use these models to "run internal simulations" of processes in our minds and make predictions of the outcome. By running a mental model we can make predictions about the consequences of not gassing the car before a trip or of studying for a midterm exam or of voting for a particular candidate. Much of what we call "knowledge" is in the form of schemas (Oden, 1987). We will have a closer look at these components of thought in the next section of the chapter.

FIGURE 7.3: Figures similar to those used in Shepard & Metzler's mental rotation test.

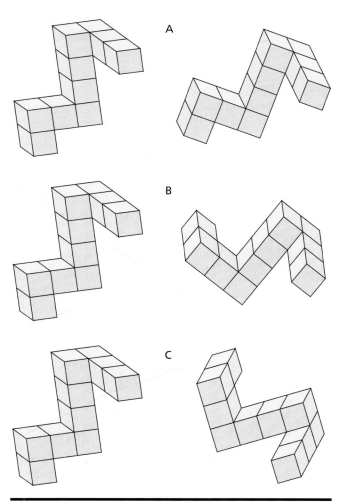

## DO IT Yourself!

## Zooming in on Mental Images

Ask a friend to close his or her eyes and imagine a house. Then, ask your subject to describe the color of the roof, the front door, and doorbell button. Using a watch or clock that displays seconds, record the amount of time it takes for your friend to answer. Based on Kosslyn's research,

which item would you predict would require the longest response time? The shortest?

You will probably find that the smaller the detail you ask for, the longer it takes your friend to respond. Kosslyn interpreted this to mean that people need the

extra time to "zoom in" on a mental image to resolve smaller features. In other words, we examine our mental images in the same way that we examine physical objects in the external world in order to perceive the "big picture" or the details.

## Check Your Understanding

1. RECALL: *Event-related potentials are records of*
   a. muscular responses initiated by the cerebral cortex.
   b. the brain's responses to an external stimulus.
   c. emotional reactions in the autonomic nervous system.
   d. the brain's processing of abstract concepts.

2. APPLICATION: *Suppose that you are doing a study based on Kosslyn's research (described in this section). You ask your subjects to form a mental image of one of the classes they are taking. Based on Kosslyn's results, you would predict that it would take longest for your subjects to respond to which one of the following demands?*
   a. Is it day or night?
   b. Is the professor male or female?
   c. What color is the chalkboard?
   d. Is the person next to you writing with a pen or a pencil?

3. UNDERSTANDING THE CORE CONCEPT: *All the following were major factors that encouraged the "cognitive revolution" in psychology, except one. Which one is the exception?*
   a. the development of behaviorism, which restricted psychology to the study of observable stimuli and responses
   b. advances in psycholinguistics, showing how language reflects brain organization
   c. the invention of the computer and its use as a model of information processing in the brain
   d. development of techniques for recording the activity of single neurons in the brain

**ANSWERS:**     1. **b**     2. **d**     3. **a**

**KEY QUESTION** **WHAT DOES THINKING CONSIST OF?**

**Thinking:** The cognitive process involved in forming a new mental representation by manipulating available information.

What do solving a math problem, deciding what to do Friday night, and indulging a private fantasy all have in common? All involve *thinking*. We can define **thinking** as the cognitive process involved in forming a new mental representation by manipulating available information. That transformation can invoke a spate of mental activities, such as inferring, abstracting, reasoning, imagining, judging, problem solving, and, at times, creativity. Thinking is especially remarkable because it may combine information that comes in several forms, as our Core Concept emphasizes:

**CORE CONCEPT**

**Thinking involves manipulation of mental representations, such as concepts, images, schemas, and scripts.**

**Chapter 4:**
**Psychological Development**
*Piaget found that children develop mental representations of their world by about age 2.*

In this section we will examine these components of thought. Please note that they consist not just of information but of information that has been organized to be meaningful and useful to the thinker.

## Concepts

You have probably had the experience known as *déjà vu* (from the French for "seen before"), the sensation that something you are perceiving now is also part of a memory of the past—that "this has happened before." Perhaps you visit a new place that seems oddly familiar or have a social conversation that seems repetitive. While this déjà vu feeling can be an illusion, it also reflects our brain-based capacity to treat new stimuli as instances of familiar categories—even if they are slightly different from anything we have encountered before. This ability to categorize individual experiences—to take the same action toward them or give them the same label—is regarded as one of the most basic abilities of thinking organisms (Mervis & Rosch, 1981). We call it *concept formation*.

The categories (mental groupings of related items) that we form are called **concepts.** Concepts are among the building blocks of thinking, because they enable us to organize knowledge in systematic ways (Goldman-Rakic, 1992). Concepts may represent objects, activities, or living organisms. They may also represent properties, (such as "red" or "large"), abstractions (such as "truth" or "love"), relations (such as "smarter than"), procedures (such as how to tie your shoes), or intentions (such as the intention to break into a conversation) (Smith & Medin, 1981). Because concepts are mental structures, researchers cannot observe them directly but must infer their influence in people's thinking indirectly by studying their observable effects on people's behavior or on brain activity. For example, you cannot be sure that someone you care about shares your concept of "red," but you can observe whether he or she responds in the same way you do to stimuli that you both call "red."

New ways of studying concepts have emerged from developments in brain imaging. For example, a certain brain wave signals intention to move before the movement is made (Fetz, 1997). Cognitive scientists can also visualize the parts of the brain that are most active when particular types of words and images are being used. These studies show, for example, that bilingual people use different parts of their brains for concepts when they switch languages (Barinaga, 1995).

Knowing which parts of the brain process certain concepts does not tell us *how* we form concepts, however. For that, we must turn to research of a more traditional nature. This work involves observing how people behave as they form concepts.

**TWO KINDS OF CONCEPTS**   Everyone conceptualizes the world in a unique way, so our concepts define who we are. Yet, behind this individual uniqueness, cognitive psychologists have found some fundamental similarities in the ways that people form concepts. For example, cognitive psychologists have found that we all make a distinction between two different types of concepts: *natural concepts* and *artificial concepts*. The distinction becomes evident when people are asked to explain their concepts of "bird" and "rectangle." (Take a moment to think about your own explanations of these concepts before reading further.)

**Natural concepts** are rather imprecise mental classifications that develop out of our everyday experiences in the world. So, you possess a natural concept of "bird"

**Concepts:** Mental representations of categories of items or ideas.

**Natural concepts:** Mental representations of objects and events drawn from our direct experience.

based on your experiences with birds. You also probably have natural concepts associated with Chevrolets, your mother's face, artichokes, and the Statue of Liberty. (Grandfather Salvatore also used natural concepts to think through his plan for handling the toughs who were disrupting his Saturday morning opera.) While each of these examples may involve words, natural concepts also characteristically involve visual images, emotions, and other nonverbal memories.

Most likely, your natural concept of "bird" invokes a mental **prototype,** a generic image that represents a typical bird from your experience (Hunt, 1989; Medin, 1989; Mervis & Rosch, 1981; Rosch & Mervis, 1975). To determine whether some object is a bird or not, you mentally compare the object to your bird prototype. The more sophisticated your prototype, the less trouble you will have with flightless birds, such as ostriches and penguins or with birdlike flying creatures, such as bats and moths, or with turtles, snakes, and platypuses, which lay eggs, as do birds. Natural concepts are sometimes called "fuzzy concepts" because of their imprecision (Kosko & Isaka, 1993).

By comparison, **artificial concepts,** such as your concept of "rectangle," are those defined by a set of rules or characteristics, such as dictionary definitions or mathematical formulas. Thus, they represent precisely defined ideals or abstractions rather than actual objects in the world. If you are a zoology major, you may also have an artificial concept of "bird," which defines it as a "feathered biped." In a similar fashion, your artificial concept of a "rectangle," is probably something like this: a closed figure with four straight sides and right-angle corners. Like these textbook definitions of birds and rectangles, most of the concepts you learn in school are artificial concepts. "Cognitive psychology" is an artificial concept; so is the concept of "concept"!

Most of the concepts in our everyday lives, however, are natural concepts. We can identify clusters of properties that are shared by different instances of a concept (for example, robins, penguins, and ostriches all are birds and all have feathers), but there may be no one property that is present in all instances. Still, we consider some instances as more representative of a concept—more typical of our mental prototype (more "birdlike")—than others. In support of this, studies show that people respond more quickly to typical members of a category than to more unusual ones (their reaction times are faster). For example, the reaction time to determine whether a robin is a bird is shorter than the reaction time to determine whether an ostrich is a bird, because robins resemble the common prototype of a bird more closely than ostriches do (Kintsch, 1981; Rosch et al., 1976). The prototype is formed on the basis of frequently experienced features. These features are stored in memory, and the more often they are perceived, the stronger their overall memory strength is. Thus, the prototype can be rapidly accessed and recalled.

The police use the general principle of the prototype when they help witnesses identify criminal suspects. They prepare a prototype face made of plastic overlays of different facial features of average dimensions (from a commercially prepared "Identi-Kit"). The witness then is asked to modify the prototype model until it is most similar to the suspect's face. Psychological researchers have borrowed this overlay technique to study memory for prototypes. In a typical exercise, subjects study a series of "exemplar faces" that represent variations on a few facial prototypes. In one study (Solso & McCarthy, 1981), subjects were shown a set of 12 exemplar faces made up as variations of three prototype faces. (Note: They saw only the variations, not the original prototypes.) Then they saw a second group of faces: some of the original exemplar faces, some new ones that were made deliberately different from the prototypes, and the original prototype faces (which they had never seen). The subjects' task was to rate their confidence in having seen each face earlier, during the first presentation. Three results were clear, as seen in the chart in Figure 7.4.

**Prototype:** An ideal or most representative example of a conceptual category.

**Artificial concepts:** Concepts defined by rules, such as word definitions and mathematical formulas.

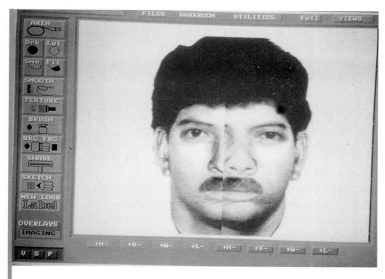

Witnesses' descriptions of criminal suspects can be transformed into composite sketches by assembling prototypical facial features and patterns.

## FIGURE 7.4: Prototype and Exemplar Faces

One hundred percent of the prototype face's features have been seen previously by subjects. The 75% face has all the features of the prototype except the mouth; the 50% face has different hair and eyes; the 25% face has only the eyes in common; and the 0% face has no features in common. Subjects had least confidence in recalling faces with unfamiliar features but, ironically, were most confident about the prototype face—which they had never actually seen.

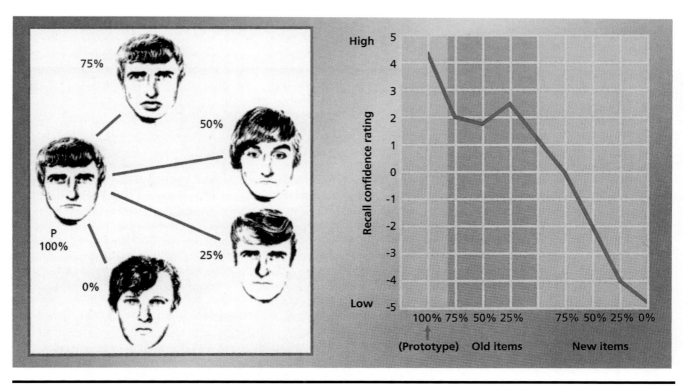

As you might expect, recall was accurate and confidence was high for the old items, which they had actually seen before. The new items were most often accurately identified as unfamiliar. But, a false confidence—a feeling of having seen them before—appeared as the items more closely resembled the prototype. Finally, the highest level of confidence was for the prototype face itself, although the subjects had never actually seen it before. The subjects' reaction here is known as **pseudomemory** (pronounced SUE-doe-memory), false memory of a new stimulus because its attributes were stored in memory (Solso & McCarthy, 1981).

**CONCEPT HIERARCHIES**   We organize much of our knowledge into **concept hierarchies,** from general to specific, as seen in Figure 7.5. For most people, the broad category of *animal* has several subcategories, such as *bird* and *fish,* which are subdivided, in turn, into their specific forms, such as *canary, ostrich, shark,* and *salmon.* The animal category may itself be a subcategory of the still larger category of *living beings.* We can think of these concepts and categories as arranged in a hierarchy of levels, with the most general and abstract at the top and the most specific and concrete at the bottom, as shown in the figure. They are also linked to many other concepts: Some birds are edible, some are endangered, some are national symbols. It may help you to understand this if you use the following conceptual model: The connections among concepts seem to work much like the hypertext links you see on your Internet browser.

Psychologists have identified a level in concept hierarchies at which people most easily categorize and think about objects. That level—called the *basic level*—can be retrieved from memory most quickly and used most efficiently. For example, the chair at your desk belongs to three obvious levels in a conceptual hierarchy: furniture, chair, and desk chair. The lower-level category, desk chair, would provide more detail than you generally need, whereas the higher-level category, furniture, would not be precise enough. When spontaneously identifying it, you would be more likely to call it a "chair" than a "piece of furniture" or a "desk chair"—so "chair"

**Pseudomemory:** False memory of a new stimulus pattern because its components were previously experienced separately.

**Concept hierarchies:** Levels of concepts, from most general to most specific, in which a more general level includes more specific concepts—as the concept of "animal" includes "dog," "giraffe," and "butterfly."

**FIGURE 7.5:**   Hierarchically Organized Structure of Concepts

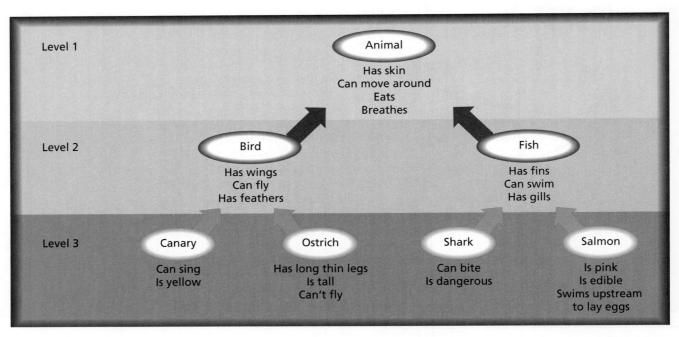

would be the basic level for that object. It is now believed that this dependence on basic levels of concepts is a fundamental aspect of thought. The higher-level concepts, however, are also essential because they help us see relationships among lower-level concepts that have similarities, even though they are not identical. The Core Concepts used in this book are higher-level concepts that connect the more basic ideas in a section of the chapter.

## Imagery and Cognitive Maps

Do you think only in words, or do you sometimes think in pictures and spatial relationships or other sensory images? If you take a moment to think of a face, a tune, or the smell of fresh bread, the answer is obvious. Sensory mental imagery revives information you previously perceived and stored in memory. This revival takes place without immediate sensory input and relies on internal representations of events and concepts in sensory forms, such as visual images. For example, consider the following question: What shape are a German shepherd's ears?

Assuming you answered correctly, how did you know? You probably have not intentionally memorized the shapes of dog ears or ever expected to be quizzed about such knowledge. To answer that a German shepherd has pointed ears, you probably consulted a visual image of a German shepherd stored in your memory. In general, thought based on imagery differs from verbal thought because it is stored in a different configuration in a different part of the brain (Kosslyn, 1983; Paivio, 1983).

**VISUAL THINKING**    Visual thought adds complexity and richness to our thinking, as do forms of thought that involve the other senses (sound, taste, smell, and touch). Visual thinking can be useful in solving problems in which relationships can be grasped more clearly in diagram form than in word form. Visual thought, for example, is useful in thinking about colors, shapes, or spatial relationships

A cognitive representation of physical space is a special form of visual concept called a cognitive map. You will remember that learning theorist Edward C. Tolman was the first to hypothesize that people form mental maps of their environment and that these internal maps guide their future actions toward desired goals. Cognitive maps help people get where they want to go, and they enable them to give directions to others. By using cognitive maps, people can move through their homes with their eyes closed or go to familiar destinations even when their usual routes are blocked (Hart & Moore, 1973; Thorndyke & Hayes-Roth, 1979). If you found the main door to the psychology classroom building locked, your cognitive map would tell you where to look for the back door or side entrance.

**Chapter 6:**
**Learning and Remembering**
*Tolman's rats behaved as though they had "cognitive maps" of the mazes they had learned.*

**CULTURAL INFLUENCES ON COGNITIVE MAPS**    Mental maps seem to reflect our subjective impressions of physical reality. The maps often mirror the view of the world that we have developed from the perspective of our own culture. For example, if you were asked to draw a world map, where would you begin and how would you represent the size, shape, and relations between various countries? This task was given to nearly 4,000 students from 71 cities in 49 countries as part of an international study of the way people of different nationalities visualize the world. The study found that the majority of maps had a Eurocentric world view: Europe was placed in the center of the map and the other countries were arranged around it (probably due to the dominance for many centuries of Eurocentric maps in geography books). But the study also yielded many interesting culture-biased maps, such as the ones by a Chicago student (Figure 7.6) and an Australian student (Figure 7.7). American students, incidentally, did poorly on this task, misrepresenting the placement of countries, while students from the former Soviet Union and Hungary made the most accurately detailed maps (Saarinen, 1987). This suggests that cultural differences—perhaps in education or worldview—have an impact on geographical thinking.

## FIGURE 7.6: Chicagocentric View of the World
How does this sketch compare with your view of the world?

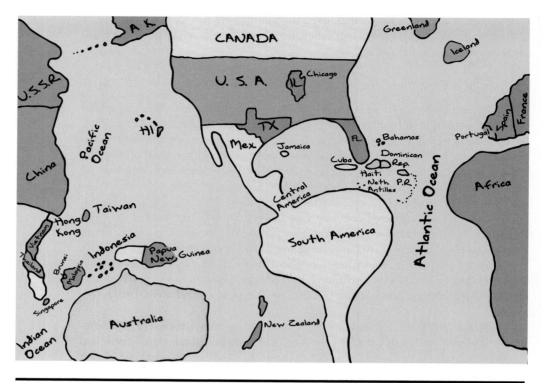

## FIGURE 7.7: Australiocentric View of the World
Now who's "down under"?

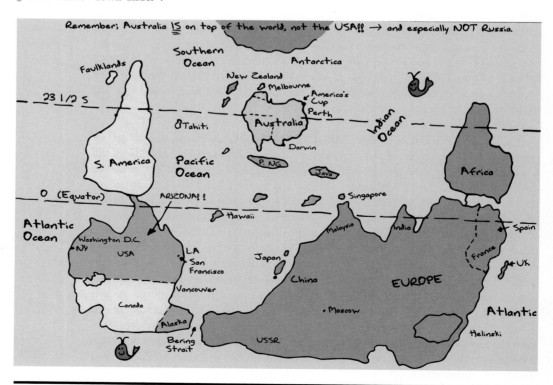

## Schemas and Scripts Help You Know What to Expect

Much of your knowledge is stored in your brain as *schemas*. A **schema** is a cluster of related concepts that provides a general conceptual framework for thinking about a topic, an event, an object, people, or a situation in one's life. You probably have schemas that represent "college" and "music," for example. Some of these schemas could contain an entire hierarchy of concepts. These knowledge clusters provide expectations about the features likely to be found when you encounter that concept or category, that person or situation. For example, to an airline passenger the word "terminal" probably conjures up a schema that includes scenes of crowds, long corridors, and airplanes. For a heart attack victim, however, the schema for "terminal" might include feelings of anxiety and thoughts of death.

MAKING INFERENCES   As noted, your schemas provide expectations about the features and effects that are typical of particular concepts or categories. New information, which is often incomplete or ambiguous, makes more sense when you can relate it to existing knowledge in our stored schemas. So schemas enable you to make inferences about missing information. Likewise, a mental schema also helped Grandpa Salvatore to predict the responses of the boys who were disrupting his music.

The following example will demonstrate how schemas help us make predictions and inferences. Consider this statement:

Tanya was upset to discover, upon opening the basket, that she'd forgotten the salt.

With no further information, what can you infer about this event? Salt implies that the basket is a picnic basket. The fact that Tanya is upset that the salt is missing suggests that the food in the basket is food that is usually salted, such as hard-boiled eggs or vegetables. You automatically know what other foods might be included and, equally important, what definitely is not: Everything in the world that is larger than a picnic basket and anything that would be inappropriate to take on a picnic—from a boa constrictor to bronze-plated baby shoes. The body of information you now have has been organized around a "picnic-basket" schema. By relating the statement about Tanya to your preestablished picnic-basket schema, you understand the statement better.

How important are schemas to you? Schemas are the primary mental structures that organize your knowledge (see Matlin, 1998). You comprehend new information by integrating consistent new input with what you already know. (Piaget called this *assimilation*.) If you find a discrepancy between new input and already stored schemas, you overcome it by changing what you know or ignoring the new input.

Do the following sentences make sense to you?

- The notes were sour because the seam was split.
- The haystack was important because the cloth ripped.

Taken alone, these sentences make little sense. What notes are being referred to, what is the seam, and how does a split seam cause sour notes? Why should ripped cloth make a haystack important?

Now, how does your thinking change with the addition of two words: *bagpipes* and *parachute*? Presto! The sentences suddenly become understandable. The notes were sour because the seam in the bag of the bagpipe was split. If you were falling from a plane in a torn parachute, the haystack could save your life. The sentences became comprehensible when you could integrate them into what you already knew—into appropriate schemas. They would remain confusing to anyone who did not know what a bagpipe or a parachute was. Here's the point: Thinking is a constructive process in which we draw on our existing mental structures to make as much sense as possible out of new information. We construct our subjective reality and personal world views of all the information we process. Once we interpret information as belonging to a particular schema, we may unwittingly change the information in our internal representation of it. To see how this transformation can occur, look at the *Do It Yourself!* box on the following page.

SCRIPTS AS EVENT SCHEMAS   We have schemas not only about objects and events but also about persons, roles, and ourselves. These schemas help us to decide what to expect or how people should behave under specific circumstances. An *event schema* or **script** is a cluster of knowledge about sequences of interrelated, specific events and actions expected to occur in a certain way in particular settings. We have scripts for going to a restaurant, using the library, listening to a lecture, going on a first date, and even making love.

Having a "picnic" schema enables one to make inferences about what is likely to be in a picnic basket as opposed to other sorts of baskets.

**Schemas:** Knowledge clusters and general conceptual frameworks that provide expectations about topics, events, objects, people, and situations in one's life.

**Script:** A cluster of knowledge about sequences of events and actions expected to occur in particular settings.

*continued*

Some scripts in other cultures differ from ours, such as the scripts that govern exchanging gifts, attending funerals, and ways of treating women. In Japan, for example, giving money is almost always an appropriate wedding present. Choosing a wedding gift is thus an extremely easy task. This contrasts sharply with custom in the United States, where many types of wedding gifts are appropriate and people often spend a great deal of time selecting a "good" gift. Cultural distinctions in scripts emerge in everyday life as well as on special occasions. For example, during the Persian Gulf War, American women stationed in Arab locales discovered that many behaviors they might take for granted at home—such as walking unescorted in public, wearing clothing that showed their faces and legs, or driving a car, were considered scandalously inappropriate by citizens of their host country. To maintain good relations, these servicewomen had to change their habits and plans to accommodate local customs. The rules that govern different cultures have developed from distinct schemas for viewing the world.

When all people in a given setting follow similar scripts, they feel comfortable because they have comprehended the

"meaning" of that situation in the same way and have the same expectations of each other (Abelson, 1981; Schank & Abelson, 1977). When people do not all follow similar scripts, however, they are made uncomfortable by the script "violation" and may have difficulty understanding why the scene was "misplayed." Conflicting scripts can sometimes produce much more than discomfort. They can lead to danger or trauma. For example, in a case of date rape, the rapist's script may tell him that she led him on and that she had no right to withdraw her "offer." Or his script may say that she really wants to be physically overpowered so she won't feel responsible for agreeing to sex. In contrast, the victim's script may tell her that a "no" should be respected. It may also tell her that the rapist's assault shows that he wants power, not intimacy, and that the experience is violent, not passionate.

Even in far less extreme situations, people may experience discomfort when they discover a potential conflict with another person's script. Thus, relatively unprejudiced people may avoid interaction with someone from another ethnic group because they fear that they will not understand what slang terms to use, what

Even though they are not prejudiced, people may avoid interactions with those of other ethnic groups because they don't understand each other's scripts.

music or food the other person favors, or what activities they might enjoy together. When scripts clash, people can say, "I tried to interact, but it was so awkward that I don't want to try again" (Brislin, 1993). Difficulties with scripts may also arise in situations that do not involve problematic relationships. For example, when a traffic delay prevents you from getting to a movie on time or an exam covers unexpected material, you may feel discomfort because events have not followed scripted patterns.

## DO IT Yourself!

## Your Memory for Concepts

Read the following passage carefully:

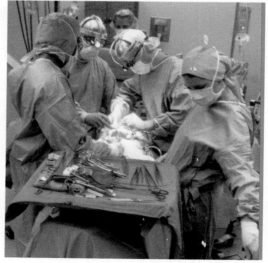

Chief Resident Jones adjusted his face mask while anxiously surveying a pale figure secured to the long gleaming table before him. One swift stroke of his small, sharp instrument and a thin red line appeared. Then the eager young assistant carefully extended the opening as another aide pushed aside glistening surface fat so that the vital parts were laid bare. Everyone stared in horror at the ugly growth too large for removal. He now knew it was pointless to continue.

In an experiment on the influence of schema-based expectations, subjects were asked to read a medical story. Because they had connected the story to their personal schemas for hospital surgery, the subjects "remembered" reading terms that were not in the story.

Stop! Without looking back, please complete the following exercise: Circle below the words that appeared in the passage:

| | |
|---|---|
| patient | scalpel |
| blood | tumor |
| cancer | nurse |
| disease | surgery |

In the original study, most of the subjects who read this passage circled the words patient, scalpel, and tumor. Did you? However, none of the words were there! Interpreting the story as a medical story made it more understandable, but also resulted in inaccurate recall (Lachman, Lachman, & Butterfield, 1979). Once the subjects had related the story to their schema for hospital surgery, they "remembered" labels from their schema that were not present in what they had read. Drawing on a schema not only gave the subjects an existing mental structure to tie the new material to but also led them to change the information to make it more consistent with their schema-based expectations.

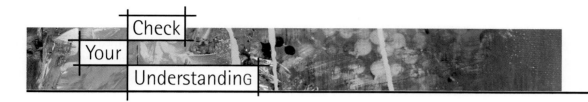

1. **APPLICATION:** *A dictionary definition would be an example of*
   **a.** an artificial concept.
   **b.** a natural concept.
   **c.** a core concept.
   **d.** an abstract concept.
2. **APPLICATION:** *Which one of the following would represent a concept hierarchy?*
   **a.** cat, dog, giraffe, elephant
   **b.** animal, mammal, dog, cocker spaniel
   **c.** woman, girl, man, boy
   **d.** lemur, monkey, chimpanzee, human
3. **APPLICATION:** *Knowing how to check out a book at the library is an example of*
   **a.** a natural concept.
   **b.** an event-related potential.
   **c.** a cognitive map.
   **d.** a script.
4. **UNDERSTANDING THE CORE CONCEPT:** *All of the following are components of thought* except
   **a.** concepts.
   **b.** images.
   **c.** schemas.
   **d.** stimuli.

**ANSWERS:**   1. **a**   2. **b**   3. **d**   4. **d**

**KEY QUESTION** ❓ **DO WE THINK LOGICALLY —OR PSYCHOLOGICALLY?**

The appeal of lotteries and casino games, in which our chances of winning are small, shows us that human thought is not always purely logical. Nevertheless, our *psychological* nature has some advantages: Our departures from logic allow us to fantasize, daydream, act creatively, react unconsciously, respond emotionally, and generate ideas that cannot be tested against reality. We are, of course, capable of careful reasoning: After all, our species did invent that most logical of devices, the computer. Still, the take-away lesson from the psychology of thinking is that we should not expect people to behave always in a strictly logical manner or that their best judgment will be based on reason alone. As our Core Concept says:

 **CORE CONCEPT**     **We are capable of logic, but our thinking is also influenced by such psychological factors as perceptions, emotions, motives, and personality.**

In order to see how far we humans normally depart from the standard of purely logical thought, we will first take a look at two types of formal reasoning, such as you might encounter in a logic class or a philosophy class. Then, we will look at how the human mind tempers logical thinking with psychological factors. In many ways, our departure from formal logic is adaptive because it helps us make decisions rapidly in a changing world that often gives us incomplete information. The downside, of course, is that this way of thinking can lead us to erroneous conclusions, as we shall see.

## Reasoning

Formal reasoning—of the sort that is required in mathematics, computer programming, or a logic class—is aimed at drawing logical conclusions from a set of data, facts, or assumptions. This sort of reasoning proceeds by rigidly defined rules. For our purposes we will divide formal reasoning into two main types: *deductive reasoning* and *inductive reasoning*.

**DEDUCTIVE REASONING**   Described over two millennia ago by the Greek logicians, **deductive reasoning** requires that we draw logical conclusions without going beyond the boundaries of the information we have and without bringing our preferences or values or experiences into play. The **syllogism** captures the essence of deductive reasoning. A syllogism is a logic statement that has two *premises* (assumptions) and a conclusion based on the premises. If we follow the rules of deductive logic, the conclusion will always be valid. Consider the following example.

| Major premise: | All people can think logically. |
| Minor premise: | Einstein was a person. |
| Valid conclusion: | Therefore, Einstein could think logically. |

If, however, the conclusion does not follow logically from the premises, it is invalid. Here is an example of an invalid conclusion to the syllogism above: *Therefore, Einstein always thought logically.* You can easily see that this conclusion doesn't necessarily follow from the premises, suggesting that deductive reasoning is a part of the kit of cognitive tools that most of us have (Rips, 1990).

Cognitive psychologists use valid and invalid syllogisms to study the errors people make in logic in order to understand their mental representations of premises and conclusions (Johnson-Laird & Byrne, 1989). Not surprisingly, errors are especially likely when an individual's personal beliefs about the premises and conclusions get in the way of logic. People tend to judge as valid those conclusions with which they agree and as invalid those with which they do not agree (Janis & Frick, 1943). If you have strong feelings on either side of the gun-control issue, for example, your thinking on this topic may not be altogether logical.

**INDUCTIVE REASONING**   After solving a difficult mystery, fictional detective Sherlock Holmes frequently explained to his companion, Dr. Watson, that his conclusions were based on observation and "deduction." About this, however, Holmes was wrong. In fact, his solutions involved shrewd *induction*: piecing together bits of data—clues in the case, and his own vast general knowledge—into a compelling web of evidence that eventually explains the manner and perpetrator of the crime. Like Holmes, we spend most of our lives jumping to conclusions. We do so in deciding for whom to vote, what major to select, and which car to buy. We have to operate this way in order to survive because the world does not always provide all the information we need for deductive reasoning. In general, **inductive reasoning** uses the available evidence to generate a conclusion about the likelihood—not a certainty—of something. When you reason inductively, you construct a hypothesis based on limited evidence and then test it against other evidence. The inferential leaps of inductive reasoning are accomplished by betting that past experience will predict the future.

**Deductive reasoning:** Drawing a conclusion intended to follow logically from a given set of assumptions (premises).

**Syllogism:** A particular form of deductive reasoning involving a major premise, a minor premise, and a deductive conclusion.

**Inductive reasoning:** Drawing a conclusion about the probability of an event or condition based on available, but incomplete, evidence and past experience.

Most scientific reasoning is inductive. And, while it is based on incomplete evidence, it can lead to valid conclusions, especially when we base those conclusions on information gathered under carefully controlled conditions. Much of our everyday reasoning, however, is not done under controlled conditions. That's where our perceptions, motives, emotions, and values come in to color our judgment, as we will see when we look at the errors people make when they solve problems.

## Problem Solving

Artists, inventors, Nobel Prize winners, great presidents, successful executives, world-class athletes, college students, and Italian shoemakers in the Bronx—all must be effective problem solvers. And what strategies do effective problem solvers use? No matter what the field, those who are repeatedly successful share certain fundamental skills that go beyond formal logic and reasoning. In particular, such people are good at (a) *identifying a problem* and (b) *selecting a strategy* to attack the problem. We will examine both of these skills with the aid of some examples.

Identifying the problem: Is it the fuel system or the electrical system that makes this car refuse to start?

**IDENTIFYING THE PROBLEM**    Suppose that you are driving along the freeway, and your car suddenly begins sputtering and then quits. As you coast over to the shoulder, you notice that the gas gauge says "empty." What do you do? Your action in this predicament depends on the problem you think you are solving. If you assume that you are out of fuel, you may hike to the nearest service station for a gallon of gas. But you may be disappointed. By representing the problem as "out of gas," you may fail to notice a loose battery cable that interrupts the supply of electricity both to the spark plugs and to the gas gauge.

Keeping in mind the idea that a successful solution depends on identifying the right problem, let's see how you do with a classic problem. Suppose that you are a physician working with a patient suffering from a small abdominal tumor. Suppose also that the patient's weak condition makes it risky to remove the tumor surgically. Therefore, you consider destroying it with radiation. The difficulty is that a beam of radiation powerful enough to kill the tumor will also destroy any healthy tissue in its path. How could you destroy the tumor with radiation and still spare the healthy tissue? After thinking about this problem awhile, compare your answer with the one given in Figure 7.8.

People who cannot find a good solution to the tumor problem usually try to solve the wrong problem, namely: How can I safely use a *single beam* of radiation to destroy the tumor? When they realize that the way they have defined the problem places unnecessary restrictions on them, they may be able to redefine the problem in such a way that alternative strategies immediately come to mind. Besides the solution given in Figure 7.8, they may also suggest implanting a radioactive pellet inside the tumor, which might destroy it with little effect on the surrounding tissue. The moral of the story is this: Merely being aware that a problem is poorly defined may be enough to help you see the situation in a new and more productive light.

**SELECTING A STRATEGY**    The second ingredient of successful problem solving requires selecting a strategy that fits the problem at hand (Wickelgren, 1974). As you would expect, solutions to problems in specialized fields, such as engineering or medicine, may require specialized knowledge and special techniques. Many of these are *algorithms*, described below. Even so, it is remarkable how often essentially the same problem-solving strategies pop up in different fields. Most of these general-purpose strategies are called *heuristics*. You will want some strategies of each sort in your own cognitive tool kit.

## FIGURE 7.8: The Inoperable Tumor Problem

Here is one possible solution to the problem of destroying the inoperable tumor with X rays. Instead of a single strong X-ray source, you could use several sources of lower intensity. Thus, the tumor is the only spot that receives a lethal dose (Duncker, 1945). Can you think of other ways to solve the problem?

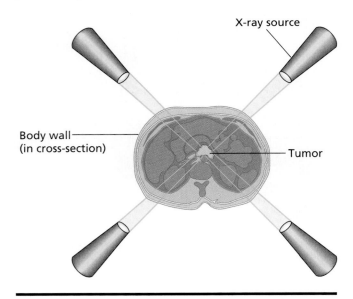

X-ray source

Body wall (in cross-section)

Tumor

*ALGORITHMS* Whether you are a psychology student or a rocket scientist, we can guarantee that **algorithms** will produce correct solutions for some of your problems. What are these miraculous strategies? Algorithms are formulas or procedures, like those you learned in math classes or in science labs, designed to solve particular kinds of problems. You can use algorithms to balance your checkbook, figure your gas mileage, and calculate your grade-point average. If applied correctly, an algorithm always works because you merely follow a step-by-step procedure that leads directly from the problem to the solution. Algorithms require only that you plug in the right data at the right places. In this respect, algorithms are tools of deductive logic, much like their cousin the syllogism.

Despite their usefulness, algorithms cannot solve all your problems. Problems of subjective values (Will you be happier with a red car or a white car? Or which is the best airline to take to Denver?) and problems that are just too complex for a formula (How can you get a promotion? What will the fish bite on today?) do not lend themselves to the use of algorithms. And that is why we also need the more flexible strategies called *heuristics*.

*HEURISTICS* Everyone makes a collection of **heuristics** while going through life. Examples: "Don't keep bananas in the refrigerator." "If it doesn't work, see if it's plugged in." "Feed a cold and starve a fever" (or, is it the other way around?). Heuristics are simple, basic rules—so-called "rules of thumb" that help us cut through the confusion of complicated situations. Unlike algorithms, heuristics do *not* guarantee a correct solution, but heuristics often give us a good start in the right direction. In this way, heuristics are tools of inductive reasoning. Some heuristics require special knowledge, such as training in medicine or physics or psychology. Other heuristics, such as those you will learn in the following paragraphs, are more widely applicable—and well worth learning.

**Algorithms:** Problem-solving procedures or formulas that guarantee a correct outcome, if correctly applied.

**Heuristics:** Cognitive strategies or "rules of thumb" used as shortcuts to solve complex mental tasks. Unlike algorithms, heuristics do not guarantee a correct solution.

Engineers use algorithms to determine exactly how much stress a structure can withstand.

**SOME USEFUL HEURISTIC STRATEGIES**  Here are three essential heuristics that should be in every problem-solver's tool kit. They require no specialized knowledge, yet they can help you in a wide variety of puzzling situations. The common element shared by all three of these heuristics involves getting the problem solver to approach a problem from a different perspective.

*WORKING BACKWARD*  Some problems, such as the maze seen in Figure 7.9, may baffle us because they present too many possibilities at the beginning. A good way to attack this sort of puzzle is by beginning at the end and **working backward.** (Who says that we must always begin at the beginning?) This strategy can eliminate the false starts and dead ends that we would otherwise stumble into by trial-and-error.

We also invite you to try the working-backward strategy on a famous puzzle that psychologists frequently use in studies of problem solving (Sternberg & Davidson, 1982, 1983):

> Suppose that a clump of water lilies doubles in size every day. It takes 60 days for the pond to be completely covered by water lilies. How many days does it take for the pond to become *half* covered?

You will have trouble with this problem if you merely guess or if you laboriously try to work out the areas covered by the lilies on Day 2, Day 3, and so on. In fact, working backward is the only way to solve it. If you have not already discovered the solution, try the working-backward strategy by imagining the pond on day 60 and then on day 59. The answer will come quickly. (Read no further, if you are still working on the problem. The solution: We know that the pond was half full on day 59, because when the lilies doubled again on day 60 the remaining half of the pond filled in.)

In general, working backward is an excellent strategy for problems in which the end-state or goal is clearly specified (e.g., a pond full of lilies). It can be especially valuable when the initial conditions are vague. Math students: Keep this strategy handy for doing proofs.

*SEARCHING FOR ANALOGIES*  Many problems we face are similar to those we have faced before, although the research shows that people are not always good at seeing the relationships without a lot of practice (Medin & Ross, 1992). When used successfully, however, the search for analogies involves exploiting familiar patterns in new problems. So, if you are an experienced cold-weather driver, you use this strategy to decide whether it is necessary to install tire chains on a snowy day: "Is the snow as deep as it was the last time I needed chains?" This is also the strategy that might alert a psychotherapist to the possibility of suicidal depression in a patient who complains of lack of friends and a life devoid of meaning. Likewise, the use of analogies figured prominently in the discovery of the chemical structure of DNA, the molecular basis of life. James Watson's (1968) account of the Nobel Prize winning discovery is filled with analogies that portray the life-giving molecule as a "backbone," a "spiral staircase," and "several . . . chains twisted about each other."

*BREAKING A BIG PROBLEM INTO SMALLER PROBLEMS*  Are you facing a huge problem, such as an extensive term paper? The best strategy in such cases may call for breaking the big problem down into smaller, more manageable steps. In writing a paper, you might break the problem into the subproblems of selecting a topic, doing your library research, outlining the paper, writing the first draft, and revising the paper. In this way, you will begin to organize the work and develop a plan for

**FIGURE 7.9:**   Working Backward

Mazes and math problems often lend themselves to the heuristic of working backward. Try solving this maze by starting at the finish and working backward to the start.

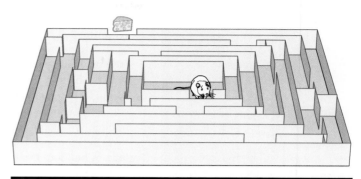

**Working backward:** A heuristic strategy that begins at the end (desired outcome) of the problem and proceeds backward.

Watson and Crick used the analogy of a spiral staircase to help them understand the structure of the DNA molecule and crack the genetic code.

attacking each part of the problem. And, by tackling a problem in a step-by-step fashion, a big problem will seem more manageable. Any large, complex problem—from writing a paper to designing an airplane—may benefit from this approach. In fact, the Wright brothers deliberately used this heuristic to break down their problem of powered human flight into components. Using a series of kites, gliders, and models, they studied the subproblems of lift, stability, power, and directional control before attempting powered human flight (Bradshaw, 1992).

The more experience you have at problem solving, the better you will get at judging which strategy fits which problem. Research, however, has uncovered an odd fact: Problem solvers often talk to themselves—silently or out loud—as they sort through their strategic tool kit. Surprisingly, such self-talk is not only normal, but it can actually help us solve problems. Laura Berk (1994) reports that young children frequently talk out loud about their ideas and strategies while grappling with a problem. By about age five, a silent, internal dialogue usually replaces this audible self-talk. What does this self-talk do? It apparently helps the problem solver to organize a problem and select a strategy of attack. Poor problem solvers, on the other hand, often display disturbances in their self-talk. For example, children whose private speech was immature (irrelevant or mainly an emotional reaction to the task) had less success in solving problems. Moreover, Berk found that such children often presented behavior problems in school. Her research aims at teaching these children how to talk to themselves more effectively. Says Professor Berk:

> Private speech is a problem-solving tool universally available to children who grow up in rich [stimulating], socially interactive environments. . . . We know that private speech is healthy, adaptive and essential behavior. . . . Still, many adults continue to regard private speech as meaningless, socially unacceptable conduct—even as a sign of mental illness. As a result, they often discourage children from talking to themselves. (p. 83)

Moral: When you have a problem, it is helpful to talk it over with yourself.

**OBSTACLES TO PROBLEM SOLVING**   Having a good repertoire of strategies is essential to successful problem solving, but people may also get stuck because they latch onto an ineffective strategy and refuse to give it up. For this reason, problem solvers must learn to recognize when they have encountered an obstacle that demands a new approach. In fact, becoming a successful problem solver has as much to do with recognizing such obstacles as it does with selecting the right algorithm or heuristic. Here are some of the most troublesome obstacles.

*MENTAL SET*   Sometimes you may persist with a less-than-ideal strategy simply because it has worked on other problems in the past. In psychological terms, you have an inappropriate **mental set**—a case of the search for analogies gone wrong. Let's illustrate this with the following problem.

Each of the groups of letters in the columns below is a common, but scrambled, word. See if you can unscramble them:

| | | | |
|---|---|---|---|
| nelin | frsca | raspe | tnsai |
| ensce | peshe | klsta | epslo |
| sdlen | nitra | nolem | naoce |
| lecam | macre | dlsco | tesle |
| slfal | elwha | hsfle | maste |
| dlchi | ytpar | naorg | egran |
| neque | htmou | egsta | eltab |

(adapted from Leeper & Madison, 1959)

**Mental set:** The tendency to respond to a new problem in the manner used for a previous problem.

Check your answers against the key in Figure 7.10.

## FIGURE 7.10:   Unscrambled Words

The words you found to solve the scrambled word problem may not jibe with the ones listed above—especially in the third and fourth columns. Most people, whether they are aware of it or not, develop an algorithm as they work on the first two columns. While the formula will work on all the words, it interferes with the problem solver's ability to see alternative solutions for the words in the last two columns.

| | | | |
|---|---|---|---|
| linen | scarf | pears | stain |
| scene | sheep | talks | poles |
| lends | train | melon | canoe |
| camel | cream | colds | steel |
| falls | whale | shelf | meats |
| child | party | groan | anger |
| queen | mouth | gates | bleat |

Most people, whether they realize it or not, eventually solve the scrambled word problem with an algorithm by rearranging the order of the letters in all the words in the same way, using the formula 3-4-5-2-1. Thus,

n e l i n          becomes          l i n e n
1 2 3 4 5                           3 4 5 2 1

Notice, however, that by using that algorithm, your answers for the last two columns won't agree with the "correct" ones given in Figure 7.10. A mental set that you developed early on prevented you from seeing that there is more than one answer for the last fourteen items. The lesson of this demonstration is that a mental set can make you approach new problems in old but restricted ways. While a mental set often does produce results, you should occasionally stop to ask yourself whether you have slipped into a rut that prevents your seeing another answer. (Now can you find some other possible answers to the scrambled words in the last two columns?)

When you think you need a screwdriver, but you don't realize that you could tighten the bolt with a dime, you have a special kind of mental set called **functional fixedness.** Under this condition, the *function* of a familiar object becomes so set, or *fixed*, in your mind that you cannot see a new function for it. To illustrate, consider this famous problem:

> Your psychology professor has offered you $5 if you can tie together two strings dangling from the ceiling (see Figure 7.11) without pulling them down. But when you grab the end of one string and pull it toward the other one, you find that you cannot quite reach the other string. The only objects available to you in the room are on the floor in the corner: a ping-pong ball, five screws, a screwdriver, a glass of water, and a paper bag. How can you reach both strings at once and tie them together?

**Chapter 6:**
**Learning and Remembering**
*Compare* functional fixedness *with* proactive interference.

**Functional fixedness:** The inability to perceive a new use for an object associated with a different purpose; a form of mental set.

## FIGURE 7.11: The Two-String Problem

How could you tie the two strings together, using only the objects found in the room?

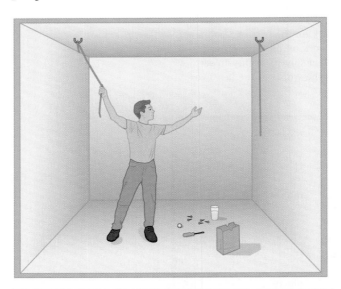

Read the following if you want a hint: In this problem you may have had functional fixedness with regard to the screwdriver. Did you realize that you could use the screwdriver as a pendulum weight to swing one of the strings toward you?

**SELF-IMPOSED LIMITATIONS** We can be our own worst enemies when we limit ourselves unnecessarily. The classic nine-dot problem in Figure 7.12 illustrates this neatly. To solve this one, you must connect all nine dots with no more than four connecting straight lines—that is, without lifting your pencil from the paper. The rules allow you to cross a line, but you may not retrace a line.

Most people begin by trial-and-error, connecting the dots in various ways, until they finally conclude that this random method will not produce a solution. At that point, some simply become discouraged and give up. Those who persist and succeed with the problem, however, will learn a great lesson: The biggest obstacles to problem solving can be those that we have unnecessarily placed in our own path. In the case of the nine-dot problem, most people place an unnecessary restriction on themselves by assuming that they cannot draw lines beyond the square made by the dots. Figure 7.13 gives two possible correct answers.

Translating the nine-dot problem into real-life terms, we can find many instances in which people impose unnecessary restric-

## FIGURE 7.12: The Nine-Dot Problem

Can you correct all nine dots with four connecting straight lines and without lifting your pencil from the paper?

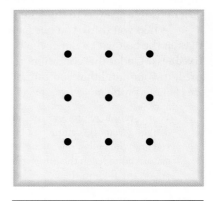

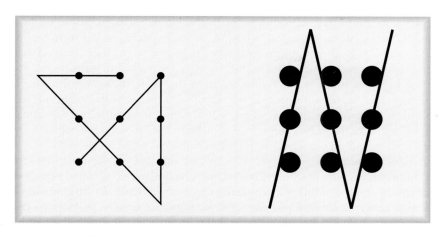

tions on themselves. Students may assume that they have no aptitude for math or science—thereby eliminating the possibility of a technical career. Because of gender stereotypes, a man may never consider that he could be a nurse or a grade-school teacher; a woman may assume that she must be a secretary, rather than an administrator. What real-life problems are you working on in which you have imposed unnecessary limitations on yourself?

*FAULTY HEURISTICS*    Amos Tversky and Daniel Kahneman made a career of showing how the heuristics that we call "common sense" sometimes lead to erroneous conclusions (Tversky & Kahneman, 1973, 1974). Here are some of their examples.

> Ask a few of your friends, one at a time, to give a quick, off-the-top-of-the-head guess at the answer to the following simple math problem:
>
> $$1 \times 2 \times 3 \times 4 \times 5 \times 6 \times 7 \times 8 = ?$$
>
> Make them give you an estimate without actually doing the calculation; give them only about five seconds to think about it. Then, give the problem in reverse to some other friends:
>
> $$8 \times 7 \times 6 \times 5 \times 4 \times 3 \times 2 \times 1 = ?$$

Are the results different for the two groups? Of course, nobody will give precisely the right answer, but we suspect that your friends will respond like Tversky and Kahneman's subjects, whose answers depended on whether the problem began with larger or smaller numbers. Those who saw the first problem gave a lower estimate than did those who were given the second problem. In Tversky and Kahneman's study, the average answer for the first group was 512, while the average for the second group was 2250. Apparently, their "first impression"—larger or smaller numbers at the beginning of the problem—biased their responses.

Tversky and Kahneman explain the difference between the two groups on the basis of an **anchoring bias.** That is, people apparently "anchor" their thinking to the higher or lower numbers that appear at the beginning of the problem. The first group was apparently more influenced by hearing the low numbers at the outset $(1 \times 2 \times 3 \dots)$ and, therefore, gave a lower total than the group that anchored its thinking to the higher numbers $(8 \times 7 \times 6 \dots)$. Multiply it out on your calculator to see how close your estimate is to the true answer.

**Anchoring bias:** A faulty heuristic caused by basing (anchoring) an estimate on a completely unrelated quantity.

Tversky and Kahneman found another example of anchoring bias when they asked people to estimate numbers that most people do not know with certainty (such as the percentage of African nations in the United Nations). Subjects first watched as the experimenters spun a "wheel of fortune," which gave a percentage between 0% and 100%. Then, subjects were asked to state whether they believed that the actual number was higher or lower. Finally, they were asked to estimate the actual value by moving upward or downward from the value shown on the wheel. Amazingly, the estimates were strongly correlated with the arbitrary numbers given by the wheel! For example, subjects who saw 10% come up on the wheel estimated, on the average, that the U.N.'s percentage of African nations was 25%, while those who saw 65% appear on the wheel gave estimates that averaged about 45%.

Besides the anchoring bias, problem solving may get off the track because people misunderstand the psychology of average behavior and exceptional behavior. For example, a group of military flight instructors noticed that when they praised a cadet's good performance on a maneuver, the performance usually deteriorated the next time. But when a cadet was reprimanded for a poor performance, the performance usually improved on the next trial. Before reading further: How would you explain this response pattern—particularly in light of the research on learning, which says that punishment usually has a detrimental effect on behavior?

In reality, the flight instructors had overestimated their impact on the students. That is, they had erroneously concluded that their praise had lowered performance and that their punishment had improved it. But they had ignored a fact that any observer of sports has seen repeatedly: Extremes of performance are more rare than average performance. When an athlete performs exceptionally well—or poorly—the chances are good that she or he will *regress* (return) toward an average performance on the next try. Basketball players, for example, have an especially "hot hand" only occasionally; baseball players don't usually stay in hitting slumps. Swings of performance from better to worse and back again are to be expected, and the more exceptional the performance, the more likely it is to be followed by a more average performance. Those who don't understand this are using a faulty heuristic strategy that we will call a misunderstanding of **regression to the average.** And so, returning to the case of the flight cadets, the instructors failed to realize that their students' variations in performance were simply normal fluctuations around average performance that they should have expected. The praises and reprimands probably had relatively little effect.

If you mistakenly assume that all blondes or ministers or psychology professors are the same, you have used the faulty **representativeness heuristic.** One reason we do so, however, is because it simplifies the complex task of social judgment. It involves the presumption that, once a person or event is "categorized," it shares all the features of other members in that category. The danger in this strategy, of course, is oversimplified thinking: People, events, and objects do not "belong" to categories simply because we find it mentally convenient to assign them to certain groups and labels. By relying on category memberships to organize our experiences, we risk ignoring or underestimating the tremendous diversity of individual cases and complexity of people.

**Chapter 6:
Learning and Remembering**
*Punishment encourages aggression and depression.*

Regression to the average: Exceptional performances—good or bad—are usually followed by more average performances the next time.

**Regression to the average:** A tendency for exceptional performances (either high or low) to be followed by more average performances—a concept often misunderstood, leading to faulty heuristic strategies.

**Representativeness heuristic:** A faulty cognitive strategy based on the presumption that, once a person or event is categorized, it shares all the features of other members in that category.

Does this woman represent enough of the characteristics of your concept of "vegetarians" to belong to that group?

When estimating the likelihood that a specific individual belongs to a certain category—"vegetarian," for example—we look to see whether it has the features found in a typical category member. For example, is your new acquaintance, Holly, a vegetarian? You've invited her to dinner but have not discussed her dietary restrictions. If she is a vegetarian, you do not want to offend her by serving her a cooked animal on a plate. Perhaps you could simply *ask* Holly her preference, but if that is not an option, you might guess based on what you *do* know about her. Does Holly resemble a "typical" vegetarian? Perhaps you believe that most vegetarians wear (nonleather) sandals, ride bicycles, and support liberal social causes. If Holly fits this description, you might feel safest guessing she must also be a vegetarian. In other words, you might judge Holly *represents* enough of the characteristics of your concept of "vegetarians" to belong to the same group.

But is such an analysis reasonable? Perhaps Holly wears sandals because when the weather is warm, sandals are the best footwear. She rides a bicycle as many other students do—although most are not vegetarians. And it's likely that, because most people are not vegetarians, then most people who support liberal social causes are not vegetarians. By ignoring the *base rate information*—the real probabilities that features of a given category occur or co-occur in the larger population—you have drawn erroneous conclusions. Holly may in fact be an omnivore like most of your acquaintances, although she will probably accept the cheese pizza and salad you offer her without complaint. The penalty for relying on the representativeness heuristic—judging people or events by what seems to be their "type"—may not be great in all instances, but small "acceptable" mistakes can accumulate over time into larger, painful misjudgments, such as in the numerous misjudgments people make regarding characteristics of minorities.

Yet another faulty heuristic comes from our tendency to judge probabilities of events by how readily examples come to mind. Psychologists call this the **availability heuristic.** We can illustrate this by asking you: Do more English words begin with "r" than have "r" in the third position? Most people think so because it is easier to think of words that begin with "r." That is, words beginning with "r" are more *available* to us from long-term memory. Similarly, people who watch a lot of television that features violent crime learn to judge their chances of being murdered or mugged as higher than do people who watch little television (Singer, Singer, & Rapaczynski, 1984).

There are many other obstacles to problem solving that we will simply mention, rather than discuss in detail. These include lack of specific knowledge required by the problem, lack of interest, low self-esteem, fatigue, and drugs (even legal drugs, such as cold medicines or sleeping pills). Arousal and the

Chapter 1:
**Mind, Behavior, and Science**
A base rate *is a statistic that identifies the normal frequency of a given event.*

**Availability heuristic:** A biased cognitive strategy that estimates probabilities based on information that can be recalled (made available) from personal experience.

The availability heuristic: People who watch lots of TV violence are apt to think the world is a violent place.

**Chapter 8:**
**Emotion and Motivation**
**Chapter 9:**
**Stress, Health, and Well-Being**

*Arousal and stress have an "inverted U" effect on performance.*

**Chapter 6:**
**Learning and Remembering**

*In operant conditioning the likelihood of a behavior recurring is controlled by its consequences.*

**Experts:** Individuals who possess well organized funds of knowledge, including the effective problem-solving strategies, in a field.

**Intuition:** The ability to find solutions to problems without going laboriously through a conscious reasoning process. Intuition is based on heuristic strategies.

**Preface**

*De Groot's study of chess experts was the inspiration for organizing the material in this book.*

accompanying stress represent another important stumbling block for would-be problem solvers. Arousal almost tripped up Grandpa Salvatore, who at first responded to the disruptions of his Saturday afternoon opera with curses at his tormenters. When he later calmed down, however, he was able to come up with a clever and effective strategy to solve his problem. When we study emotion and motivation, we will see that there is always an optimum arousal level for any task, be it basketball, brain surgery, or survival in the Bronx. Beyond that point, further arousal causes performance to deteriorate. Moderate levels of arousal actually facilitate problem solving, but high stress levels make problem solving impossible.

In general, our discussion of problem solving shows (as our Core Concept states) that we humans are thinkers who readily jump to conclusions, based on our knowledge and biased by our motives, emotions, and perceptions. In view of this, it is surprising that our thinking so often serves us well in day-to-day life. Yet, from another perspective it makes perfect sense: Most of our problem-solving efforts involve drawing on past experience to make predictions about future rewards and punishments. This is exactly what operant conditioning is about—which suggests that this mode of thinking is a fundamental part of our nature. Many of the "flaws" in our reasoning abilities, such as functional fixedness or the anchoring bias, are actually part of an adaptive (but necessarily imperfect) strategy that helps us use our previous experience to solve new problems.

In the remainder of this chapter we will see what we can learn from people who are especially adept at solving problems. We have labels for them: "creative," "expert," or even "genius." What abilities distinguish such people? And—could we learn enough about them to join their company?

## Intuition and Expertise

Obviously, **experts** are people who know a lot about a particular subject. But careful observations of experts in action show that, in addition to their knowledge, they possess two other qualities. The first of these we will call **intuition,** defined as the ability to find solutions to problems without plodding through a conscious reasoning process (Simon, 1992). While this may, at first, seem like a superhuman quality, the research we will examine below shows that it really is a heuristic ability that grows out of their fund of experience (Trotter, 1986). Unlike the novice, an expert confronting a problem does not have to start from scratch. Experts can often see a solution quickly because they have seen many similar (or *analogous*) problems before. The second difference that distinguishes expert thinkers from beginners lies in the way their knowledge is organized. While the beginner possesses only a collection of poorly organized facts and observations, experts have their knowledge well organized into elaborate *schemas* (Bédard & Chi, 1992; Bransford et al., 1986; Chi, Glaser, & Rees, 1982; Glaser, 1990; Greeno, 1989). We can see this quite clearly in a famous study of world-class chess players.

Dutch psychologist Adriaan de Groot found some striking differences when he compared the ways a group of grand master chess players and another group of merely good players responded to a chess problem.

Chess masters can remember pieces on a chess board better than merely good players—if the pieces are in a configuration that might appear during a game.

Allowed five seconds to view a configuration of pieces as they might appear on a chess board during a match, the grand masters were able to reproduce the pattern far more accurately than the less-expert subjects (de Groot, 1965). Does that mean that the grand masters had better visual memories? No. When confronted with a random pattern of pieces on the chess board—a pattern that would never happen in a match—the grand masters did no better than the other subjects. This suggests that the experts were able to draw on familiar patterns in memory, rather than trying to recall individual pieces and positions.

How does someone become an expert? Are experts born, or is expertise learned? Surprisingly, there is little evidence that inborn talent plays a substantial role in expert performance (Ericsson & Charness, 1994). On the other hand, people probably don't make the huge commitment of time and energy to become an expert in a field for which they do not have some innate aptitude.

So, could you, for example, become an expert? Perhaps. The research clearly shows that experts *learn* their expertise (Bédard & Chi, 1992). Specifically, experts acquire a great deal of knowledge about their fields, and that knowledge is well organized—not just an endless set of facts. Further, experts usually have a repertoire of multipurpose heuristics, such as those we discussed earlier. They also know the special problem-solving techniques, or "tricks of the trade," that are unique to their field of expertise. These heuristics help them find solutions more quickly, without having to follow so many blind leads (Gentner & Stevens, 1983; Simon 1992). But can these thinking skills and techniques be taught to ordinary people?

There was no question but that Albert Einstein was bright. He also had an independent streak, a sense of humor, an intense interest in the complex problem of gravity, and a willingness to restructure the problem. He also sought the stimulation of other physicists. But he probably did not use thought processes that were altogether different from those used by other thinkers.

A hint comes from an extensive study of problem solving in Venezuela (Hernstein et al., 1986). Over 400 Venezuelan seventh-graders and a group of matched controls, all from economically and educationally deprived families, were put to the test in an experiment on teaching thinking skills. Over the course of a year the experimental groups, in 12 different classrooms taught by 12 teachers, were given 56 lessons on reasoning, understanding language, verbal reasoning, problem solving, decision making, and inventive thinking. The results on a variety of tests of general mental abilities and of specific skills showed an impressive advantage for the experimental subjects, indicating that such skills can be taught.

Research on true experts, outstanding members of their fields, shows that learning general thinking skills is not enough to produce real expertise, however (Bransford et al., 1986; Glaser, 1984; Greeno, 1989; Mayer, 1983). This work suggests exactly what we have seen: Experts also possess a great deal of well-organized information about a field (the field's important *concepts*), which gives the expert both a fund of knowledge to apply to a problem and a familiarity with the field's common problems and solutions. How do you become an expert? Study and practice! But don't just focus on facts. Learn the schemas and the problem-solving strategies, as well. How long will it take? Research shows that achieving world-class status in any of a wide gamut of fields—from athletics to academics to chess to music—requires about ten years of intensive study and practice (Ericsson, Krampe, & Tesch-Römer, 1993; Gardner, 1993).

## On Becoming a Creative Genius

Everyone would agree that Einstein was a creative genius. So were Aristotle and Bach. But what about your Aunt Mabel who does crewel? What about Seth-the-second-grader who makes interesting finger paintings? These questions illustrate the big problem in this area: The experts cannot agree on an exact definition of creativity. Most, however, would go along with the slightly fuzzy notion that **creativity** is a process that produces novel responses that contribute to the solutions of problems. New Zealand psychologist John Nicholls (1972) would make the definition even more restrictive (if no more precise): Creativity produces "evidence of achievements that are original and make a meaningful contributions to culture." By extension, most would agree that a "genius" is someone whose insight and creativity are so great that they set that individual apart from ordinary folk. As in creativity, the boundary for genius is not well defined. But, whatever the definitions of creativity and genius we adopt, society obviously values these qualities.

Much of the literature equates creativity with **divergent thinking,** the ability to generate many responses to a problem, as opposed to **convergent thinking,** which homes in on a single, correct answer (Guilford, 1967). Consequently, many tests of creativity emphasize divergent thinking tasks, such as listing uses for a burned-out lightbulb or ways to improve a wristwatch. The assumption is that the more responses you can give, the more creative you are. Such tests, of course, put a premium on quantity and ignore the quality of the responses.

Hordes of consultants have made divergent thinking profitable by presenting seminars and workshops that purport to teach divergent thinking. They do this with a series of group exercises that encourage people to generate as many ideas as possible—the wilder, the better. The well-known technique of *brainstorming* (Osborn, 1953) is also based on the assumption that creativity arises from allowing many ideas to blossom, without making preliminary judgments on an idea's worth. Unfortunately, the evidence linking divergent thinking to other measures creativity is not impressive (Barron & Harrington, 1981; Nicholls, 1972).

So, where does this leave you in your quest to become a creative genius? Let's follow the lead of psychologist Robert Weisberg, who will restructure the problem (as a good problem solver should) by reexamining what is meant by "genius." What we will discover, with his help, is that such people are experts who also possess certain unusual, but quite human, personality characteristics.

CREATIVE GENIUS AS EXPERTISE   Are the rare people we call "geniuses" a breed apart from the rest of us? Do they have some extraordinary innate powers of thought that are unavailable to more ordinary mortals? Weisberg (1986) answers these questions this way:

> Our society holds a very romantic view about the origins of creative achievements. . . . This is the genius view, and at its core is the belief that creative achievements come about through great leaps of imagination which occur because creative individuals are capable of extraordinary thought processes. In addition to their intellectual capacities, creative individuals are assumed to possess extraordinary personality characteristics which also play a role in bringing about creative leaps. These intellectual and personality characteristics are what

is called "genius," and they are brought forth as the explanation for great creative achievements. (p. 1)

Because this idea is widely held, you may be surprised to learn that there is little evidence supporting the genius-as-a-breed-apart view of creativity. In fact, this conception may actually discourage creativity by making people feel that it is out of their reach. A more productive portrait, suggests Weisberg, represents the sort of thinking found in people we call geniuses to be "ordinary thought processes in ordinary individuals" (p. 11). Extraordinary creativity, he says, is grounded in expertise, motivation, and certain personal characteristics—not in terms of superhuman talents.

The literature generally agrees with Weisberg that the most highly creative individuals have highly developed expertise (Gardner, 1993). In fact, you cannot become highly creative without first becoming an expert: having extensive and organized knowledge of the field in which you will make your creative contribution. As we have seen, this knowledge extends beyond just the facts to include a repertoire of heuristic strategies (Weber, 1992). But such mastery is not easily achieved, and it belies a high level of motivation—the level of motivation that can sustain intense training and practice for the minimum of ten years required to master the knowledge and skills in a well-developed field (Ericsson et al., 1993; Sternberg & Lubart, 1991, 1992). *(See Chapter 8, Emotion and Motivation.)*

PERSONALITY CHARACTERISTICS AND CREATIVITY   In his book *Creating Minds,* Howard Gardner (1993) argues that the extraordinary creativity that we have seen in the work of Freud, Einstein, Picasso, and others is a combination of several factors that include not only expertise and motivation but certain patterns of abilities and personality characteristics. Highly creative individuals, he says, have aptitudes specific to certain domains. Freud, for example, had a facility for creating with words and understanding people; Einstein was especially good at logic and spatial re-

---

**Creativity:** A mental process that produces novel responses that contribute to the solutions of problems.

**Divergent thinking:** A problem-solving process aimed at producing many appropriate solutions to a single problem.

**Convergent thinking:** A problem-solving process aimed at producing a single correct answer to a problem.

lationships; and Picasso's abilities lay in a combination of spatial relationships and interpersonal perceptiveness. But along with these aptitudes, such individuals also must have a consuming interest in the subject matter with which they will be creative. This brings us back to the "ten-year rule": A person who would be highly creative must be willing to invest a minimum of ten years in intense learning and practice to position him- or herself for the first major creative breakthrough. This investment comes at a price, measured in terms of lost opportunities to explore other areas of interest, lost opportunities to invest in personal relationships, and lost opportunities for mere relaxation and fun. Are you willing to pay the price?

And what personality characteristics do highly creative people possess? The literature identifies several (Barron & Harrington, 1981). See how well they fit your personality.

- **Independence** Highly creative people have the ability to resist social pressure to conform to conventional ways of thinking, at least in their area of creative interest (Amabile, 1983, 1987). They can strike out on their own. Because of this, perhaps, many creative people (but not all) describe themselves as loners. (*See Chapter 12, Social Psychology.*)
- **Intense interest in a problem** Highly creative people are always tinkering, in their minds, with problems that interest them intensely (Weisberg, 1986). External motivators, such as money or a Nobel Prize, may add to their motivation, but the main motivators are internal; otherwise they could not sustain the long-term interest in a problem necessary for an original contribution. (*See Chapter 8, Emotion and Motivation.*)
- **Willingness to restructure the problem** Highly creative people not only grapple with problems, but they often question the way a problem is presented. (Recall our earlier discussion about defining the problem.) For example, students from the School of the Art Institute of Chicago who later became the most successful creative artists among their class members had one striking characteristic in common: They were always concerned about the way problems were presented. Before beginning a drawing, these students, more often than their less-creative counterparts, would experiment with various compositions and arrangements of materials. Frequently they would make major changes during their work. In short, the most creative students redefined the problems they were given (Getzels and Csikszentmihalyi, 1976). (Restructuring the problem was what Grandpa Salvatore did when he decided to change the behavior of his antioperatic tormentors by using decreasing "rewards" rather than punishments for their behavior.)
- **Preference for complexity** Creative people seem drawn to complexity—to what may appear to be messy or chaotic to others. Moreover, they revel in the challenge of looking for simplicity in complexity. Thus, they may be attracted to the largest, most difficult, and most complex problems in their fields. Robert Sternberg and Todd Lubart (1992) call this a "global" approach to problems.
- **Intelligence** This is a tricky issue: High intelligence does not necessarily produce creativity, but low intelligence may inhibit it. So, a person with an IQ of 70 is not likely to be as creative as a person with an IQ of 130, although the latter's intelligence carries no guarantee of creativity. In general, we can say that intelligence and creativity are distinct abilities (Barron & Harrington, 1981; Kershner & Ledger, 1985). We can find plodding, unimaginative persons at all IQ levels, and we can find highly creative persons with only average IQ scores. (*See also Chapter 11, Intelligence and the Psychology of Differences.*)
- **A need for stimulating interaction** Creativity of the highest order almost always grows out of an interaction of highly creative individuals (Gardner, 1993). Early in their careers, creative people usually find a *mentor*—a teacher who brings them up to the speed of the field. Highly creative individuals then go on to surpass their mentors and then find additional stimulation from the ideas of others like themselves. This may mean leaving behind family and former friends.

So, what is the take-home message in all of this for our understanding of creativity? Those who have looked closely at this domain agree on two particularly important points. First, creativity requires expertise or well-organized knowledge of the field in which the creative contribution will be made. Second, high-level creativity requires certain personal characteristics, such as independence and the motivation required to sustain an interest in an unsolved problem over a very long period of time.

That is your formula for becoming a creative genius.

Check Your Understanding

1. RECALL: *What is the first step in problem solving?*
   a. selecting a strategy
   b. avoiding pitfalls
   c. searching for analogies
   d. identifying the problem

2. RECALL: *Which kind of reasoning involves drawing a conclusion that goes beyond the available evidence?*
   a. deductive reasoning
   b. inductive reasoning

*continued*

c. strategic reasoning
d. functional fixedness

3. APPLICATION: *A math problem calls for finding the area of a triangle. You know the formula, so you multiply ½ the base times the height. You have used*
   a. an algorithm.
   b. a heuristic.
   c. functional fixedness.
   d. intuition.

4. RECALL: *Experts often use "tricks of the trade" or "rules of thumb" known as*
   a. algorithms.
   b. heuristics.
   c. trial-and-error.
   d. deductive reasoning.

5. APPLICATION: *Suppose that you are on the basketball team and you are averaging 18 points a game. Last night you had an exceptionally bad game, scoring only 12. What does your knowledge of regression tell you to expect from your performance at tonight's game?*
   a. You will probably score much higher than your average tonight to "balance out" your low score on the previous night.
   b. You may be in a slump, and you will probably score about as you did last night.
   c. You will probably score closer to your average number of points tonight.
   d. Your score on any given night is unrelated to your average.

6. RECALL: *A study of chess players' memory for pieces on a chess board showed that grand masters could remember the configuration better than ordinary players*
   a. regardless of the pattern.
   b. only when the pattern represented a pattern that might appear in a game.
   c. because they had better visual memories than the ordinary players.
   d. only if the board contained seven or fewer pieces.

7. RECALL: *Which of the following is* not *a characteristic that is consistently found among highly creative people?*
   a. independence
   b. a high level of motivation
   c. willingness to restructure the problem
   d. extremely high intelligence

8. UNDERSTANDING THE CORE CONCEPT: *Heuristic strategies show that our thinking is often based on*
   a. logic rather than emotion.
   b. experience rather than logic.
   c. trial-and-error rather than algorithms.
   d. deductive reasoning rather than inductive reasoning.

**ANSWERS:**  1. d  2. b  3. a  4. b  5. c  6. b  7. d  8. b

# USING PSYCHOLOGY TO LEARN PSYCHOLOGY

## *Thinking Like Your Professor*

When students enter a new course, their "cognitive maps" of the material are, at first, somewhat disorganized—as you might expect. Then, as the course progresses, their mental images of the field become simpler, organized around core concepts, and more like that of the experts: their professors. Cognitive scientists have discovered this using *path analysis*, a mathematical technique that shows the connections between concepts in our minds and how these connections change as we learn (Gonzalvo, Cañas, & Bajo, 1994).

The research examined how students and their professors saw the relationships among 30 important concepts in a history of psychology course. The students' cognitive map at the beginning of the course is shown on the left in Figure 7.14. By the end of the course it had changed, more closely matching the expert map, shown on the right. (Both are group averages.) Notice how the students and professors organized their thinking around quite different concepts. The professors' map reflects their expertise in its relative simplicity (not simple, but *simpler* than the students') and in its choice of the most important concepts—which you can see serve as organizing principles around which other concepts are clustered.

What does this suggest for your learning of psychology and other disciplines? You would do well to attend to the way your professors organize their courses. Consider such questions as the following:

• What are the terms that the professor keeps mentioning over and over? These might be such concepts as "cognitive science," "behaviorism," "developmental," "empiricism," "adaptive," or "alternative theoretical perspectives." For you they may be, at first, unfamiliar and abstract, but for the professor they may represent the core of the course. Make sure you know what the terms mean and why they are important.

## FIGURE 7.14:   Students' and Professors' Cognitive Maps

These show important terms in a history of psychology course. As the course proceeded, the students' maps more closely resembled those of the professors.

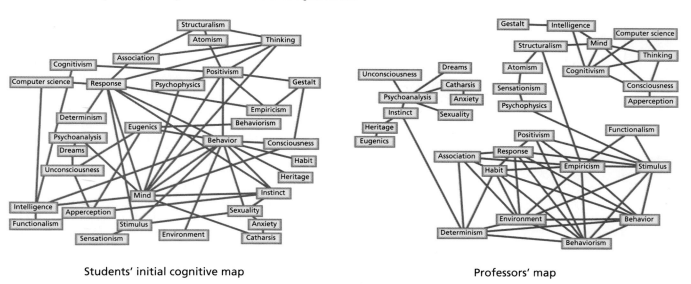

- Around what concepts is the course syllabus organized? What are the new terms that are associated with the main topics?
- Around what concepts is the textbook organized? You may be able to tell this quickly by looking at the table of contents. Alternatively, the authors may lay out the organizing points in the preface at the beginning of the book. (In this book, we have attempted to help you identify the organizing principles of each chapter in the form of Core Concepts.)

If you can identify the organizing principles for the course, they will simplify your studying. This makes sense, of course, in terms of our study of memory. Long-term memory (as you will remember!) is organized by meaningful associations: exactly what these cognitive maps are attempting to describe. Accordingly, when you have a simple and effective way of organizing the material, you will have a framework that will help you store and retain it in long-term memory.

## CHAPTER SUMMARY

**HOW DO COGNITIVE SCIENTISTS MEASURE THE MIND?**

- The field of cognitive science includes theories and research on the mental processes and structures that enable us to think, reason, solve problems, and make inferences and decisions. The "cognitive revolution" was made possible by advances in neuroscience, cognitive psychology, computer science, and psycholinguistics. Cognitive scientists often use an information-processing approach to explain cognition. Cognitive science has challenged behaviorism, taking a respected place as a science of mind, brain, and behavior. It employs a variety of techniques, ranging from neuroimaging to more traditional psychological experimentation.

**Cognitive scientists have developed techniques that can link mental processes to stimuli, brain activity, and behavior.**

**WHAT DOES THINKING CONSIST OF?**

- Thinking is a mental process that forms new mental representations by transforming available information. Natural concepts and artificial concepts are building blocks of thinking; they are formed by identifying properties that

are common to a class of objects or ideas. Concepts are often arranged in hierarchies, ranging from general to specific. Other mental structures that guide thinking include schemas, scripts, and visual imagery such as mental maps.

**Thinking involves manipulation of mental representations, such as concepts, images, schemas, and scripts.**

**DO WE THINK LOGICALLY—OR PSYCHOLOGICALLY?**

- We sometimes use deductive reasoning: drawing conclusions from premises on the basis of rules of logic. More often, we use inductive reasoning, which involves inferring a conclusion from evidence on the basis of its likelihood or probability. Forming and testing scientific hypotheses typically involves inductive reasoning. Much of our problem solving is influenced by perceptions, motives, and emotions. Two of the most crucial steps involve defining the problem and selecting a strategy. Useful strategies include algorithms and heuristics. Among the most useful heuristics are working backward, searching for analogies, and breaking a bigger problem into smaller problems. Common obstacles to problem solving include mental set, self-imposed limitations, and several types of faulty heuristics. Experts are effective problem solvers who have acquired a large fund of organized knowledge, including the algorithms and heuristics of their field. Those who are often called "creative geniuses" are highly motivated experts, who often have certain personality traits. They appear, however, to use ordinary thinking processes.

**CORE CONCEPT**

We are capable of logic, but our thinking is also influenced by such psychological factors as perceptions, emotions, motives, and personality.

## REVIEW TEST

For each of the following items, choose the single correct or best answer.

1. Which of the following were among the pioneers of psychology's "cognitive revolution"?
   a. behaviorists
   b. psychoanalysts
   c. humanists
   d. Gestaltists

2. The subject matter of cognitive science is
   a. information processing.
   b. unconscious motivation.
   c. understanding mental disorders.
   d. understanding human personality.

3. Which of the following statements about thinking is true?
   a. It transforms available information to form new mental representations.
   b. It cannot be inferred from observable behavior.
   c. It stores but does not manipulate one's knowledge.
   d. all of the above

4. An alien being from another galaxy has landed on Earth and is overwhelmed by the sensory input it must process. Eventually the alien simplifies its thinking by categorizing sets of experiences and objects according to common features. In other words, the alien learns to form
   a. algorithms.
   b. concepts.
   c. heuristics.
   d. hypotheses.

5. For most people, the idea of "bird" is
   a. a heuristic.
   b. a script.
   c. an artificial concept.
   d. a natural concept.

6. A mental _____ outlines the proper sequence in which actions and reactions might be expected to happen in given settings, as when you visit a new grocery store but are still able to shop and complete your purchases although you have never visited this particular location before.
   a. prototype
   b. script
   c. algorithm
   d. map

7. A syllogism is a form of _____ reasoning, in which a conclusion is drawn by applying rules relating the premises.
   a. inductive
   b. deductive
   c. heuristic
   d. algorithmic

8. Mack wants to estimate the total number of miles he will be driving during his vacation, so he carefully and tediously records every point-to-point mileage index in the road atlas between his hometown and his destination city. This slow but sure process is an example of
   a. a prototype.
   b. an algorithm.
   c. a mnemonic.
   d. a syllogism.

9. If you think your chances of being mugged are quite high because you watch a lot of violent videos, then your judgment is flawed because of
   a. mental set.
   b. functional fixedness.
   c. the availability heuristic.
   d. misunderstanding of regression.

10. Experts are different from novices because
   a. experts are more intelligent.
   b. experts are more highly motivated.
   c. expert knowledge is more highly organized.
   d. experts have more natural talent for their field.

**ANSWERS:** 1. d  2. a  3. a  4. b  5. d  6. b  7. b  8. b  9. c  10. c

## BOOKS

Adams, J. L. (1990). *Conceptual blockbusting: A guide to better ideas.* Reading, MA: Addison-Wesley.

*Engineer Adams discusses blocks to creative thinking and what to do about them. This book contains many classic problems used in the study of problem solving.*

Bryan, C. D. B. (1995). *Close encounters of the fourth kind: Alien abduction, UFOs, and the conference at MIT.* New York: Alfred A. Knopf.

*A journalist examines otherwise ordinary citizens' claims and convictions that they have been abducted by aliens, moving from skepticism to sympathy as he notes the "abductees" sincerity and consistency.*

Calvin, W. H. (1998). *The cerebral code: Thinking a thought in the mosaics of the mind.* Cambridge, MA: Bradford Books.

*Calvin presents a new theory of how the associative cortex works, building on Darwinian principles and seeking to explain not only concrete information processing but consciousness as well.*

Calvin, W. H., & Ojemann, G. A. (1994). *Conversations with Neil's brain: The neural nature of thought and language.* Reading, MA: Addison-Wesley.

*Neil is preparing to have a brain operation, and his neurosurgeon explains to him what will happen. In the process, Neil (and the reader) painlessly and pleasurably learn a lot about the way the brain goes about the process of thinking.*

Coles, R. (1989). *The call of stories: Teaching and the moral imagination.* Boston: Houghton Mifflin.

*Social scientist Robert Coles relates powerful stories and examines the storytelling process. Why do we pay better attention and enjoy a lesson more when it begins with a personal account or a fable? Are we basically narrative thinkers, arranging our thoughts and plans in plot lines? Coles identifies some common threads linking writers and readers, our human quest for order and comprehension.*

Feynman, R. P. (1985). *Surely you're joking, Mr. Feynman!* New York: W. W. Norton.

*Here's a collection of adventures from the life of—possibly—the world's smartest person. Nobel laureate physicist Feynman was a notorious prankster, who liked to play practical jokes on his buddies, while they were at Los Alamos inventing the atomic bomb. Not merely immensely entertaining, this book gives a rare glimpse into the mind of a genius at work . . . and at play.*

Frankl, V. E. (1984). *Man's search for meaning.* New York: Washington Square Books.

*This is the latest edition of psychologist Viktor Frankl's classic and moving memoir of surviving the Nazi concentration camps. Originally published in 1946 to introduce Frankl's system of "logotherapy," the book is based on the human need to find and construct meaning in life.*

Gardner, H. (1993). *Creating minds: An anatomy of creativity seen through the lives of Freud, Einstein, Picasso, Stravinsky, Eliot, Graham, and Gandhi.* New York: Basic Books.

*Indisputably creative, these seven minds were shapers of the 20th century, and—according to Gardner—all made a Faustian bargain in order to become giants in their fields. In Gardner's view, their creativity is due to a fortuitous misfit between each individual's special configuration of the seven intelligences and the state of the art or science in which they became creative.*

Hall, D., with Wecker, D. (1995). *Jump start your brain.* New York: Werner Books.

*With quotes, exercises, and advice, Doug Hall reviews several successful techniques for making yourself more creative. Contents include "Ten Commandments" for making dreams into reality; how humor can make your thinking more productive; ways to get out of a rut; and criteria for evaluating whether your ideas have "magic."*

Johnson, G. (1992). *In the palaces of memory: How we build the worlds inside our heads.* New York: Vintage Books.

*This is a rich and enlightening guide not only to how memory and conceptualization work but also to how science is conducted on processes at once intensely personal and not directly observable.*

Kerr, P. (1992). *A philosophical investigation.* New York: Penguin Books USA.

*A mystery that blends cognitive challenge with old-fashioned detective thrills, Philip Kerr's absorbing novel depicts a stunning scenario for the early 21st century. Governments routinely test young men for the sex-linked genetic clues that predict they will become serial killers. But one such man has used his knowledge of computer science and psychology to track and serially murder others who have also tested positive for this criminal trait. His nemesis is a woman named Jake, the detective who must identify the killer and prevent him from killing everyone on the list. This is a challenging, grim, suspenseful murder mystery.*

Lewis, D. (1983). *Thinking better*. New York: Holt, Rinehart & Winston.

This "how-to" manual for using your head is helpful and encouraging for those who would like to reason better and rely less on simple heuristics—especially when it's not always easy to remember what a "heuristic" is!

Pinker, S. (1999). *How the mind works*. New York: W. W. Norton & Co.

MIT psychologist Steven Pinker combines computer technology with evolutionary theory to review modern brain science, throwing in references to love, aggression, illusions, Star Wars, and The Far Side along the way.

Plous, S. (1993). *The psychology of judgment and decision making*. Philadelphia: Temple University Press.

Making the simple but elegant point that common sense is an unreliable guide to intelligent living, Scott Plous reviews the surprising and silly findings in the literature on how people "normally" make evaluations and choices. Focus is on applications in making decisions affecting war and international politics. This one is fun to read, with recommended antidotes for irrational thinking and illogical logic.

Randi, J. (1995). *An encyclopedia of claims, frauds, and hoaxes of the occult and supernatural: James Randi's decidedly skeptical definitions of alternate realities*. New York: St. Martin's Press.

The Amazing Randi, a professional illusionist and debunker of phony faith healers, psychics, and charlatans, reviews some of his more noteworthy exposés and explains "how people are deceived, and . . . how people deceive themselves" (Yam, 1995). The success of Randi and the group he founded, the Committee for the Scientific Investigation of Claims of the Paranormal (CSICOP), has earned him both acclaim and trouble—the latter from litigation brought by angry self-proclaimed healers and psychics and some of their committed flock. The ultimate guide to skeptical consumerism, Randi's book is a gold mine of stories, revelations, warnings, and advice.

Rothstein, E. (1995). *Emblems of mind: The inner life of music and mathematics*. New York: Random House.

A "speculative rumination" (according to its jacket) by the New York Times chief music critic about the interwoven human experiences of science and art in their respective forms of mathematics and music. Both begin in sensory experience and create abstraction, balancing proportion and size, analysis and synthesis. Rothstein shares his fascinating insights into how cultural mind-set determines both the discovery of symbol and the appreciation of rhythm, tone, and harmony.

Schick, T., Jr., & Vaughn, L. (1995). *How to think about weird things: Critical thinking for a new age*. Mountain View, CA: Mayfield.

These authors take on everyone's favorites: astrology, ESP, extraterrestrials, creationists, dowsers, near-death experiences, homeopaths, and the 100th monkey phenomenon— among others. Their prescription is a dose of skepticism and the scientific method.

Steward, I., & Cohen, J. (1997). *Figments of reality: The evolution of the curious mind*. New York: Cambridge University Press.

A mathematician and a biologist team up to argue that our brains interact with our distinct social cultures to produce what we call the "mind."

Watson, J. D. (1968). *The double helix: A personal account of the discovery of the structure of DNA*. New York: Signet Books.

The codiscoverer of the genetic code, Nobel Prize winner James Watson tells how this problem was solved. It's a classic mystery tale, full of science and insights into the personalities of scientists, including both Watson and Crick and their adversary, Linus Pauling.

Weisberg, R. (1986). *Creativity, genius, and other myths*. New York: Freeman.

Weisberg takes on the conventional wisdom about creativity and genius. In his view, both are products of ordinary thought processes, not superhuman abilities. He illustrates his points with anecdotes about famous creative personages, such as Mozart and Einstein.

## VIDEOS

*Apollo 13*. (1995, color, 140 min.). Directed by Ron Howard; starring Tom Hanks, Kevin Bacon, Bill Paxton, Gary Sinise, Kathleen Quinlan, Ed Harris.

"Houston, we have a problem . . . " This is a gripping docudrama of the real-life crisis of the Apollo 13 astronauts whose 1970 moon-bound flight was crippled—and nearly doomed—by a mysterious explosion and fuel loss. There are suspenseful portrayals of character, creativity, problem solving, and decision making by both crew and ground-control staff under conditions of unimaginable stress and pressure. Based on the book Lost Moon by crew commander Jim Lovell and coauthor Jeffrey Kluger (New York: Pocket Books, 1994), the film includes a brilliant scene in which flight control experts on Earth must solve a critical air-filtering problem using only the materials the astronauts have available to them 200,000 miles away in space.

*Nell*. (1994, color, 113 min.). Directed by Michael Apted; starring Jodie Foster, Liam Neeson, Natasha Richardson.

A small-town doctor discovers a young woman who has lived her life in isolation from the larger culture—and without recognizable language or sophistication. Includes some of the feral-child issues of whether such individuals should be left alone, should be "rescued," or are fair game for scrutiny and study.

## CORE CONCEPTS

## PSYCHOLOGY IN YOUR LIFE

**WHAT DO OUR EMOTIONS DO FOR US?**

Emotions mark situations that are important to us, command our attention, and arouse us to action; they also convey our intentions to others.

**Arousal, Performance, and the Inverted "U":** Increased arousal improves performance—but only up to a point. That point depends on the task.

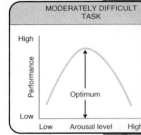

**WHERE DO OUR EMOTIONS COME FROM?**

Emotions result from an interaction of biological, mental, behavioral, and social/cultural processes.

**Emotional Differences between Men and Women Depend on Culture:** Culture and socialization account for many of the differences—but not for everything.

**HOW MUCH CONTROL DO WE HAVE OVER OUR EMOTIONS?**

Although emotional responses are not always consciously regulated, we can learn to control them.

**Controlling Anger:** A common misconception says that it is healthy to ventilate your anger.

**MOTIVATION: WHAT MAKES US ACT AS WE DO?**

Motivation takes many forms, but all involve inferred mental processes that select and direct our behavior.

**Rewards Can Squelch Motivation:** Sometimes extrinsic rewards can dampen intrinsic motivation.

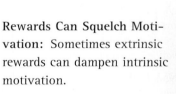

**HOW ARE ACHIEVEMENT, HUNGER, AND SEX ALIKE? DIFFERENT?**

No single theory accounts for all forms of motivation, because different motives involve different mixes of biological, mental, behavioral, and social/cultural influences.

**The Origins of Sexual Orientation:** We know more about what does *not* influence sexual orientation than what does.

**USING PSYCHOLOGY TO LEARN PSYCHOLOGY: MOTIVATING YOURSELF**

# 8

# Emotion & Motivation

*C*ut!" yelled the director, interrupting Jeff in midmonologue for the fifth time. "I want more intensity . . . more feeling!" Jeff, an acting student, had been struggling for weeks with a scene that calls for his character to explode with rage.

"It was a last resort," said director Dean Remick later. "I had tried everything else I knew, but the scene just wasn't working. Jeff is an easygoing guy, and he claimed he had never in his life been really angry. The script calls for his character to become angry, but he was just wimpy. I knew the audience would sense that he was acting the part, instead of feeling the emotion. So, I deliberately tried to make him angry."

"What really gets actors upset," said Remick, "is not being allowed to finish a bit that they've started. So I began interrupting him—insulting him with comments like, 'You're dragging this play down,' and 'You're the only one who can't do the character yet.' "

Finally, predictably, Jeff erupted in anger. Remick walked over to him and (maintaining a safe distance) exclaimed, "That's it! That's what I want you to do!" The actor immediately realized what his director had done: At last he knew how the emotion felt. From that point on, the scene worked.

As a teacher of theatre at a small college, Remick trains his actors to use a set of techniques that theatre people call "The Method." Developed by the legendary Russian director Konstantin Stanislavsky, "method acting" teaches players to focus on the characters' motives and emotions. Stanislavsky taught his actors that emotions and motives have intimate connections with our physical responses, with our most powerful and personal memories, and with our ability to communicate our intentions to others. Method actors like Meryl Streep, Dustin Hoffman, and Marlon Brando use Stanislavsky's insights to "get inside a character's head"—seeking to understand the internal motives and needs that drive the character—and by trying to respond to the situation in which their character has been immersed by the playwright. "If you can begin to respond to the situation in character," Remick asserts, "you will automatically feel the motives and emotions. So you don't have to 'act.' Sometimes, though, the right emotions don't come, and we have to resort to extraordinary tactics, like I used on Jeff."

Stanislavsky's method consisted of a whole bag of extraordinary tricks for eliciting emotions and motives. He was widely read in psychology, so many of these tricks

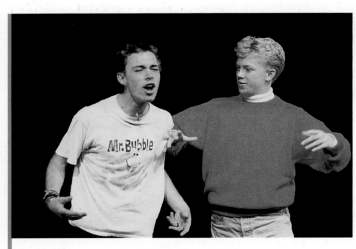

A method actor summons real emotions on stage.

drew on the famous theorists of his day: Ivan Pavlov, Sigmund Freud, and William James. The most famous of his techniques involves a process called "emotional recall." Using emotional recall, an actor retrieves a vivid and personal recollection of an incident that provoked the desired emotion, such as fear, anger, disgust, jealousy, or despair. Remick notes, "Odors are a powerful source of emotional memories, so I might have an actor wear a type of cologne that connects with an experience involving a feeling of lust or loss. And as an actor, I once stimulated the emotion of sorrow in myself by planting on the set a picture of a woman who broke my heart."

But you don't always have to feel the emotion before you can portray it, says Remick. "The act of slamming a door really hard can actually make you feel angry. Playing a romantic scene can get you into a romantic mood. So, actors sometimes use the action to bring out the emotion, and sometimes they use an emotion to help them get the right action."

What is the hardest emotional response to portray on stage? "Crying," claims Remick. "Crying is especially hard to do, if you want real tears. But what most people don't understand is that what we see most often—in real life—when we see a person crying, we're really seeing someone who is struggling to hold back the tears. So I teach my actors to cry by what Stanislavsky called 'practicing the opposite emotion'—by trying not to cry!"

Like method actors, psychologists see close connections among motives, emotions, and physical responses. They know that fear can make us pale and anger may make us gnash our teeth. But, unlike actors, the goal of psychologists is to develop a thorough understanding of the mechanisms behind our needs, desires, drives, and feelings. They want to understand, for example, the biochemical mechanisms that underlie depression and aggression—and how they can be controlled. Psychologists also seek to connect motivation and emotion to other behavior and mental processes, such as learning, perception, and memory. With the growth of cognitive science in recent years, this quest has become one of psychology's hottest topics. (See, for example, Damasio 1997; Davidson & Cacioppo, 1992; Lang, 1995; LeDoux, 1996; Mlot, 1998; van Goozen, van de Poll, & Sergeant, 1994)

**Chapter 7: Cognitive Processes**
*Cognitive science has largely ignored emotion and motivation until recently.*

How are emotion and motivation linked? Think of an emotion—fear, for example—and the behavior it motivates: fight or flight. Or, think about your own feelings for a person you love and the way these feelings make you act toward your loved one. In general, psychologists see such motives and emotions as complementary. The concept of emotion emphasizes arousal, both physical and mental, while motivation emphasizes how this arousal becomes action. Note that both words share a common root, "mot-," from the Latin *motus*, meaning "moved." The psychology of motivation and emotion has retained this meaning by viewing emotion and motivation as twin processes that arouse us to deal with important events.

In the first half of this chapter, we will concentrate on emotions. Here we will examine what emotional arousal does for the organism, where emotions come from, and how they can be controlled. Then, in the remainder of the chapter, we will turn to the complementary topic of motivation. There we will consider how organisms, once roused to action, go about selecting their responses and directing their energies into behavior. A concluding section will illustrate these processes with three motives: hunger, sex, and achievement. You can expect no simple answers to the questions of what drives people to act as they do or how they cope with both everyday and emergency emotions. Yet by the end of this chapter you will better understand the many factors that influence your own feelings and behavior.

# WHAT DO OUR EMOTIONS DO FOR US?

The death of a parent, an insult, rejection by a lover: All induce strong emotional arousal. This arousal may include subjective feelings of depression, despair, anger, puzzlement, or jealousy. In addition, emotional arousal may induce behavior, such as crying, grimacing, shouting, lashing out or running away. But—this is the important psychological question—what do such emotions *do* for us?

Sexual jealousy probably has an evolutionary basis because mate infidelity threatens the individual's chances of producing offspring.

Panic, anger, jealousy, envy, sorrow, disgust, and other troubling emotions paint our experiences in unpleasant tones. But that's not all. Cognitively, these emotional tones serve as mental markers pointing to memories of important events. In this way, negatively charged emotions tag memories of real or imagined objects and events to be avoided (such as a snarling dog or an angry neighbor). They label conditions to be changed (such as a failing relationship). And they identify opponents to be attacked (such as the opposing quarterback). In the same way, the more positive emotions such as love, joy, and ecstasy attract us, like magnets, to situations that promise us more of these pleasant feelings. Emotions are never neutral. They may cause us to approach or avoid, but they always direct our attention to something of perceived importance (Lang, 1995).

You can also see how emotion produces a disposition to act. The emotion of fear signals you to attend to an important situation (a car coming directly at you). It motivates you to take evasive action (swerving), and perhaps, to communicate your arousal to the other driver (with a honk or a gesture). So, besides putting a mental tag on important objects and events, emotions prepare us to respond to things of importance. In doing so, they also send a message to other individuals about our emotional state. These ideas become the basis for our Core Concept:

 **CONCEPT**

**Emotions mark situations that are important to us, command our attention, and arouse us to action; they also convey our intentions to others.**

In this section, we will look a little deeper into the adaptive functions of emotions. We will also examine how the universal language of emotional expression tells others of our emotional state. Finally, we will see how emotional arousal can affect our performance—say, on a test or in an athletic contest. Let's begin with the evolutionary advantages of emotions.

## The Evolution of Emotions

Whether they occur in humans, Holsteins, cats, or kangaroos, emotions serve as arousal states that help organisms cope with important recurring situations. Rage can help an animal answer a threat to its territory. Love may commit us to a family, which continues our genetic lineage. Sexual jealousy can be seen as a special mode that is "turned on" to deal with the important situation of mate infidelity, which threatens the individual's chances of producing offspring (Buss & Schmitt, 1993). Fear, to give another example, undoubtedly helped individuals in your family tree identify and react to situations in which they could have become a meal instead of an ancestor. Stanislavsky, too, understood the emotion-provoking power of the situation: He taught actors to follow their feelings by responding to the cues unfolding on stage, rather than trying to "act."

 **Chapter 1: Mind, Behavior, and Science**

*The evolutionary perspective says that behavior found across a species helped the species survive and reproduce.*

**Chapter 2:
Biopsychology**
*Genes encode both mental and
physical characteristics.*

Like other inherited characteristics, emotional tendencies enter the human genome through genetic variation and natural selection. Random genetic variations affecting emotional arousal continually occur as organisms reproduce. These genetic changes may alter, for example, the hormone system or the design of the emotional circuits in the brain. There they give the organism a tendency, perhaps, to be more fearful, more prone to anger, or more loving. When these genetic variations promote survival and reproduction, they will spread through the species in succeeding generations. In recent years, scientists have made progress in identifying the genetic basis for certain emotions, such as our response to stress (Gabbay, 1992).

## Emotional Expressions around the World

You can usually tell when your friends are happy or angry by the looks on their faces or by their actions. This is useful because reading their emotional expressions helps you to know how to respond to them: As our Core Concept suggests, emotional expressions aid social interaction. But, does raising the eyebrows and rounding the mouth say the same thing in Minneapolis as it does in Madagascar? Much of the research on emotional expression has centered on such questions of universal facial gestures.

According to Paul Ekman, the leading researcher in this area, people speak and understand substantially the same "facial language" the world around (Ekman, 1984, 1992; Ekman & Friesen, 1975). Studies by Ekman's group have demonstrated that humans share a set of universal emotional expressions, presumably because our species has a common biological heritage. Their cross-cultural research shows, for example, that smiles signal happiness and frowns indicate sadness on the faces of people in such far-flung places as Argentina, Japan, Spain, the jungles of New Guinea, and the Eskimo villages north of the Arctic Circle (Ekman et al., 1987; Izard, 1994). More generally, Ekman and his colleagues say that people everywhere

Facial expressions convey universal messages. Although their culture is very different, it is probably not hard for you to tell how these people from New Guinea are feeling.

can recognize at least seven basic emotions—sadness, fear, anger, disgust, contempt, happiness, and surprise (Ekman, 1993; Ekman & Friesen, 1971, 1986; Ekman,

## Identifying Facial Expressions of Emotion

Take the facial emotion identification test to see how well you can identify each of the seven emotions that Ekman claims are culturally universal. Do not read the answers until you have matched each of the following pictures with one of these emotions: disgust, happiness, anger, sorrow, surprise, fear, and contempt. Apparently, people everywhere in the world interpret these expressions in the same way. This tells us that certain facial expressions of emotion are probably rooted in our human genetic heritage.

▌ **FIGURE 8.1:** What Emotion Is Being Expressed in Each Face?

**ANSWERS:** The facial expressions in Figure 8.1 are (top row from left) surprise, disgust, happiness, and contempt; (bottom row) sadness, anger, and fear.

Sorenson, & Friesen, 1969; Ekman et al., 1987; Keating, 1994). Even babies, in their first day of life, produce facial expressions that communicate some of their feelings (Ganchrow, Steiner, & Daher, 1983). The ability to read facial expressions also develops early. Young children attend to facial expressions, and they nearly equal adults in their skill at reading people's faces by about age five (Nelson, 1987). This evidence all points to a biological basis for the expression and decoding of a basic set of human emotions. Moreover, as Charles Darwin pointed out over a century ago, some emotional expressions seem to appear across species boundaries. Darwin especially noted the similarity of our own facial expressions of fear and rage to those of chimpanzees and wolves (Darwin, 1998/1862; Ekman, 1984).

*What Do Our Emotions Do for Us?*  **299**

## FIGURE 8.2: The Emotion Wheel

Developed by Robert Plutchik, this model arranges eight basic emotions within a circle of opposites. Pairs of these adjacent primary emotions combine to form more complex emotions noted on the outside of the circle. For example, love is a combination of joy and acceptance, while remorse combines sadness and disgust. Secondary emotions emerge from basic emotions more remotely associated on the wheel.

Plutchik proposes that emotions are best separated from each other when they are at high intensities, such as loathing and grief, and least different when they are low in intensity, such as disgust and sadness. He also believes that each primary emotion is associated with an adaptive evolutionary response. Disgust is considered an evolutionary result of rejecting distasteful foods from the mouth, while joy is associated with reproductive capacities (Plutchik, 1980, 1984).

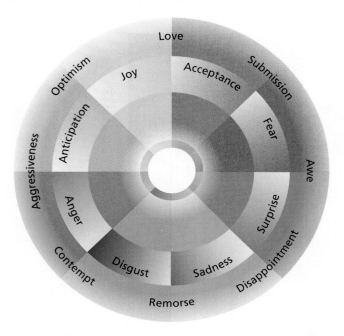

But are *all* emotional expressions universal? No. Cross-cultural studies of emotional expressions tell us that certain emotional responses differ from culture to culture (Ekman, 1992, 1994; Ellsworth, 1994). These, therefore, must be learned rather than innate. For example, what emotion do you suppose might be conveyed by sticking out the tongue? For Americans this might indicate disgust, while in China it can signify surprise. Likewise, a grin on an American face may indicate joy, while on a Japanese face it may just as easily mean embarrassment. Clearly, culture influences emotional expression.

But, whether a particular expression is universal or specific to a particular culture, it carries the potential to communicate the bearer's emotional state to others. This is normally adaptive because emotional cues allow people to anticipate each others' responses. In this way, emotional expressions help people live harmoniously in groups.

### Counting the Emotions

How many emotions have you felt? How many emotions are there? A long look in the dictionary turns up more than 500 different emotional terms (Averill, 1980). Most experts, however, see a more limited number of basic emotions. Often mentioned is Ekman's list of seven—anger, disgust, fear, happiness, sadness, contempt, and surprise—based on the universally recognized facial expressions. Robert Plutchik (1980, 1984) has argued for eight basic emotions that emerged from a mathematical analysis of people's ratings of a large number of emotional terms. You will see in Figure 8.2 that Plutchik's list is similar to Ekman's.

What about emotions that appear on none of these basic lists? What of love, optimism, awe, disappointment, humor, and the many other emotions that we feel? From the perspectives of Ekman, Plutchik, and others who argue for a simplified list of basic emotions, the wide range of human emotions involve complex blends of the more basic ones.

PSYCHOLOGY IN YOUR LIFE

*Arousal, Performance, and the Inverted "U"*

Sensation seekers thrive on stimulation that might terrify others.

*A*thletes always want to be "up" for a game—but how far up? Cheering sports fans might expect that increased arousal will improve performance—but that is not necessarily true. Too much arousal can make an athlete "choke" and performance falter. The same is true for you when you face an examination. Up to a point, increasing levels of arousal can motivate you to study and facilitate your recall during the test, but higher levels can produce test anxiety and a drop in your grade.

To frame the issue psychologically: What is the relation between emotional arousal and behavior? For hungry and thirsty rats used in experiments on learning, the curve of performance first rises and then later declines with the intensity of arousal. The same pattern holds for world-class athletes and for you. Psychologists call this the **inverted "U" function** (so named because the graph resembles an upside-down letter "U," as you can see in Figure 8.3). It suggests that either too little or too much arousal can impair performance.

The optimum amount of arousal varies with the task. As you can see in Figure 8.3, it takes more arousal to achieve peak performance on simple or habitual tasks than it does on complex tasks that require much thinking and planning. Thus, cheerleaders may boost performance at basketball games, but not in brain surgery.

The amount of stimulation needed to produce optimal arousal varies with the individual. In fact, some people seem to thrive on the thrill of dangerous sports, such as rock climbing and skydiving—activities that would produce immobilizing levels of arousal in most of us (Zuckerman, Buschsbaum, & Murphy, 1980; Zuckerman, Eysenck, & Eysenck, 1978). Marvin Zuckerman (1971, 1979), who has studied people he calls **sensation seekers,** believes that such individuals have a biological need for high levels of stimulation. You can test your own sensation-seeking tendencies with Zuckerman's scale, found in the *Do It Yourself!* box below.

**Inverted "U" function:** Describes the relationship between arousal and performance. Both low and high levels of arousal produce lower performance than does a moderate level of arousal.

**Sensation seekers:** In Zuckerman's theory, individuals who have a biological need for higher levels of stimulation than do other people.

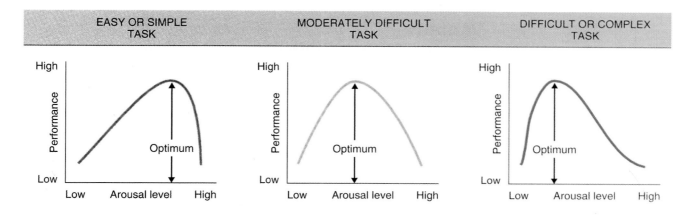

FIGURE 8.3:  The Inverted "U"

Performance varies with arousal level and task difficulty. For easy or well-practiced tasks, a higher level of motivation increases performance effectiveness. However, for difficult or complex tasks, a lower level of motivation is optimal. A moderate level of arousal is generally best for tasks of moderate difficulty. These inverted U-shaped functions show that performance is worst at both low and high extremes of motivation.

## Are You a Sensation Seeker?

From your score on the Sensation Seeking Scale below you can get a rough idea of your own level of sensation seeking. Marvin Zuckerman believes that this trait underlies the need for excitement, stimulation, and arousal.

In addition to the need for thrills, sensation seekers are impulsive, prefer new experiences, and are easily bored (Kohn, Barnes, & Hoffman, 1979; Malatesta, Sutker, & Treiber, 1981; Zuckerman, 1974).

You may want to give this scale to some of your friends. Do you suppose that most people choose friends who have sensation-seeking tendencies similar to their own? Wide differences in sensation-seeking tendencies may account for strain

*continued*

on close relationships, when one person is reluctant to take the risks that the other actively seeks.

## THE SENSATION-SEEKING SCALE

Choose A or B for each item, depending on which response better describes your preferences. The scoring key appears at the end.

1. A  I would like a job that requires a lot of traveling.
   B  I would prefer a job in one location.
2. A  I am invigorated by a brisk, cold day.
   B  I can't wait to get indoors on a cold day.
3. A  I get bored seeing the same old faces.
   B  I like the comfortable familiarity of everyday friends.
4. A  I would prefer living in an ideal society in which everyone is safe, secure, and happy.
   B  I would have preferred living in the unsettled days of our history.
5. A  I sometimes like to do things that are a little frightening.
   B  A sensible person avoids activities that are dangerous.

6. A  I would not like to be hypnotized.
   B  I would like to have the experience of being hypnotized.
7. A  The most important goal of life is to live it to the fullest and experience as much as possible.
   B  The most important goal of life is to find peace and happiness.
8. A  I would like to try parachute jumping.
   B  I would never want to try jumping out of a plane, with or without a parachute.
9. A  I enter cold water gradually, giving myself time to get used to it.
   B  I like to dive or jump right into the ocean or a cold pool.
10. A  When I go on a vacation, I prefer the comfort of a good room and bed.
    B  When I go on a vacation, I prefer the change of camping out.
11. A  I prefer people who are emotionally expressive even if they are a bit unstable.
    B  I prefer people who are calm and even-tempered.

12. A  A good painting should shock or jolt the senses.
    B  A good painting should give one a feeling of peace and security.
13. A  People who ride motorcycles must have some kind of unconscious need to hurt themselves.
    B  I would like to drive or ride a motorcycle.

### KEY

Each of the following answers earns one point: 1A, 2A, 3A, 4B, 5A, 6B, 7A, 8A, 9B, 10B, 11A, 12A, 13B. Compare your point total with the following norms for sensation-seeking:

| 0–3 | Very low |
| 4–5 | Low |
| 6–9 | Average |
| 10–11 | High |
| 12–13 | Very high |

Source: Zuckerman, M. (1978, February). The search for high sensation. *Psychology Today, 12*, 38–46. Copyright © 1978 by the American Psychological Association.

Check Your Understanding

1. RECALL: *From the evolutionary perspective, emotions help organisms identify*
   a. their parents.
   b. important and recurring situations.
   c. beauty and wonder in the world around them.
   d. locations in which to find food and mates.
2. RECALL: *Which one of the following is not one of the culturally universal emotions identified by Ekman's research?*
   a. anger
   b. surprise
   c. contempt
   d. regret
3. ANALYSIS: *Which one is a cognitive process influenced by emotion?*
   a. attention
   b. behavior
   c. threat
   d. rejection
4. UNDERSTANDING THE CORE CONCEPT: *According to this section of the chapter, what is the adaptive significance of communicating our emotional states?*
   a. It helps us understand our own needs better.
   b. It allows us to deceive others about our emotional states and get what we want.
   c. It allows people to anticipate each other's responses and so to live more easily in groups.
   d. Communicating our emotional state helps us get rid of strong negative emotions, such as fear and anger.

**ANSWERS:**    1. **b**    2. **d**    3. **a**    4. **c**

**KEY QUESTION**

# WHERE DO OUR EMOTIONS COME FROM?

What happens inside us when we feel fear, anger, envy, or ecstasy? These and other emotions have their biological roots in the hormone system and in certain parts of the brain. But these biological systems do not act by themselves. A full explanation of our emotional responses must also include a mental component that involves how we think, both about external events and about our own internal responses—as when we interpret a "Boo!" in a Halloween haunted house. The resulting emotion, as we have seen, can influence behavior, as seen in a person who jumps when startled. Many people are surprised to learn, however, that the reverse is also true: We will see that behavior can also influence emotions, just as Stanislavsky taught his actors. Finally, in this section, we will find that emotions have social/cultural roots that show up strongly in gender differences in emotional expression. This is the Core Concept:

 **CORE CONCEPT**

**Emotions result from an interaction of biological, mental, behavioral, and social/cultural processes.**

We turn now to a detailed look at these components of our emotions, beginning with the biology of arousal.

## The Biology of Emotional Arousal

Suppose someone crowds in front of you at the supermarket checkout, and you respond with a flash of anger. Internally, a series of electrical and chemical responses occur in your brain. Quickly, your endocrine system floods your body with anger-related hormones. These prime you for a response to the offender. In broad terms—whether the emotion is anger, fear, joy, or love—biological processes in the brain, autonomic nervous system, and the endocrine system provide the machinery by which emotions are realized both physically and mentally. Working together, the biological mechanisms of emotion allow us to make both physical and mental responses to objects, events, and thoughts that have significance for us. We will take a close-up look at some of these neural and hormonal components of emotion.

**THE RETICULAR ACTIVATING SYSTEM** Emotional reactions, such as anger, may begin with the nearly instantaneous arousal of the brain as a whole by the reticular activating system (RAS). This structure, strategically located in the brain stem, monitors the flow of incoming information. As important incoming sensory messages pass through the RAS, it acts as an early warning system. If the RAS detects a potential threat, it sets off a cascade of automatic responses that makes your heart accelerate, your respiration increase, your mouth get dry, and your muscles become tense. All these responses have evolved to mobilize the body quickly for an emergency reaction.

**OTHER BRAIN STRUCTURES** The hormonal and neural aspects of emotional arousal are integrated by the brain's limbic system. Situated above the brain stem, the limbic structures probably evolved originally as control systems for emotions and for patterns of attack, defense, and retreat: the "fight-or-flight" response (Caldwell, 1995; LeDoux, 1994, 1996). Evidence for this conjecture comes from lesioning (cutting) or electrically stimulating parts of the limbic system, which produces dramatic changes in emotional responding. Tame animals with altered limbic systems may become killers; prey and predators may become peaceful companions (Delgado, 1969).

**Chapter 2: Biopsychology**

*The endocrine system sends long-lasting chemical messages by means of hormones in the bloodstream.*

**Chapter 2: Biopsychology**

*The RAS is involved in attention and alerting the brain to important stimuli.*

**Chapter 2: Biopsychology**

*The limbic and the cerebral cortex are the middle and upper layers of the brain.*

**Lateralization of emotion:** Different influences of the two brain hemispheres on various emotions. The left hemisphere apparently influences positive emotions (for example, happiness), and the right hemisphere influences negative emotion (anger, for example).

In all complex human emotions, the cerebral cortex—the outermost layer of brain tissue, our "thinking cap"—also becomes involved. The cortex contributes the associations and memories that give meaning to biological experiences. Research suggests that distinct regions in the cortex process positive and negative emotions. In general, the left hemisphere seems to be more involved in positive emotions, such as happiness. The right hemisphere handles negative emotions, such as anger and depression (Davidson, 1984, 1992). This discovery—that the two cerebral hemispheres specialize in different classes of emotion—has been dubbed **lateralization of emotion.** Lateralization has also been found in EEG recordings of normal subjects' emotional reactions, as well as in studies relating specific disturbances in facial expressions to brain damage in the right or left hemisphere (Ahern & Schwartz, 1985; Borod et al., 1988).

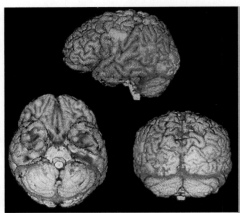

Auditory hallucinations in schizophrenia are audible only to the patient, but they may show up on the PET scan as especially active structures in the brain.

**Chapter 13: Psychopathology**

*Schizophrenia is a serious mental disorder involving emotional disturbances.*

Mental disorders can also tell us something about the source of emotions. Brain scans of volunteers suffering from schizophrenia (SKITS-oh-FREN-ya), a major disorder of thoughts and emotions, were made with PET scanning technology while the patients were hearing voices. These hallucinations, which the patients heard saying such things as, "How horrible!" and "Don't act stupid," showed up in the PET scans as brain regions of intense abnormal activity. At the same time, the part of the frontal lobes that normally verifies sensations showed diminished activation. Apparently, this distorted pattern of brain functioning allowed the patients' private mental experiences to career out of control (Begley, 1995; Silbersweig et al., 1995). The patients had no way of knowing whether their sensations were real or their emotional responses were reasonable. "The brain . . . is creating its own reality," commented one observer (Begley, 1995, p. 77).

**THE AUTONOMIC NERVOUS SYSTEM**    What makes your heart race when you are startled? A crucial link in the chain that produces the body's emotional responses lies in the autonomic nervous system (Levenson, 1992). With pleasant stimulation, its parasympathetic system dominates. When you are startled, or when you experience some other unpleasant stimulation, the sympathetic division is more active. While the stimulation may come from external events, such as a loud noise, memories also can provoke autonomic responses, as the "method" actor well knows. When an emergency—or the memory of an emergency—occurs (a speeding car is coming directly at you!), the brain responds by activating your body's sympathetic system. Swiftly and silently, it prepares you for potential danger. The sympathetic nervous system sends messages to the internal organs. It also directs the adrenal glands to release hormones. The torrent of hormones flows through the bloodstream to the internal organs. There they command the release of blood sugar, a rise in blood pressure, and an increase in sweating and salivation. What happens when the emergency has passed? The parasympathetic division takes over, calming you by inhibiting the release of emergency hormones. You may, however, remain aroused for some time after experiencing a strong emotional activation because hormones continue to circulate in the bloodstream. If the emotion-provoking situation is prolonged (as when you work every day for a boss whom you detest), the emergency response can sap your energy and cause both physical and mental deterioration.

**Chapter 2: Biopsychology**

*The sympathetic and parasympathetic nervous systems control automatic responses by internal organs and glands.*

**Chapter 9: Stress, Health, and Well-Being**

*Stress can produce both physical and mental disorders.*

**TABLE 8.1: RESPONSES ASSOCIATED WITH EMOTION**

| COMPONENT OF EMOTION | TYPE OF RESPONSE | EXAMPLE |
|---|---|---|
| Physiological arousal | Neural, hormonal, visceral, and muscular changes | Increased heart rate, blushing, becoming pale, sweating, rapid breathing |
| Subjective feelings | The private experience of one's internal affective state | Feelings of rage, sadness, happiness |
| Cognitive interpretation | Attaching meaning to the emotional experience by drawing on memory and perceptual processes | Blaming someone, perceiving a threat |
| Social/behavioral reactions | Expressing emotion through gestures, facial expressions, or other actions | Smiling, crying, screaming for help |

**HORMONES**   Your body produces dozens of hormones, but among the most important for your emotions are adrenaline, noradrenaline, and serotonin. Serotonin may be involved in feelings of depression; adrenaline is associated with fear; noradrenaline is more abundant in anger. Steroid hormones (which bodybuilders and other athletes sometimes use unwisely) can also exert a powerful influence on emotions. In addition to their effects on muscles, steroids act on nerve cells, causing them to change their excitability. This is a normal part of the body's response to emergency situations. But when additional doses of steroid drugs are ingested over extended periods, these potent chemicals can produce dangerous side effects, including tendencies to rage or depression (Majewska et al., 1986). The mood changes associated with stress, pregnancy, and the menstrual cycle may also be related to the effects that steroid hormones have on brain cells.

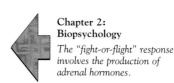

**Chapter 2: Biopsychology**
*The "fight-or-flight" response involves the production of adrenal hormones.*

### Theories of Emotion: Adding Behavior and Cognition to Biology

Biology accounts for a lot, but it is not the whole emotional show. A more complete theory of emotion must also include the mental and behavioral components of emotional experience. Such a theory would explain how feelings of anger can cause us to lash out, how fear can make us run, how love can make us send flowers to the object of our affections, and how embarrassment can dilate the blood vessels that make us blush. In short, a useful theory would explain how our emotions can produce physical reactions. But the earliest emotion theorists also raised a complementary issue, with which we will deal first: Could the emotional sequence ever be reversed? That is, can our physical responses produce emotional feelings?

**THE JAMES–LANGE THEORY OF PHYSICAL AROUSAL**   A century ago, William James taught that our physical responses are the primary source of our emotions. "We feel sorry *because* we cry, angry *because* we strike, afraid *because* we tremble," James said (1890, p. 1006). This view, simultaneously proposed by the Danish psychologist Carl Lange, became known as the **James-Lange theory of emotion.** It was this theory that dramatist Stanislavsky drew on to teach his actors that they could generate emotions by their actions.

Not only can our actions generate emotions, but our physical state can do so, as well. You may have noted edgy feelings after drinking too much coffee, grumpiness when sleepy or hungry, or feelings of well-being after a glass of wine. But, James and Lange were mistaken in thinking that physical changes always initiate our emotions. Nevertheless, they did have an important insight. This was clearly demonstrated in a classic experiment.

A female researcher interviewed male subjects who had just crossed one of two footbridges. One was a safe, sturdy structure; the other was wobbly and precarious—

**James–Lange theory of emotion:** The theory that an emotion-provoking stimulus produces a physical response that, in turn, produces an emotion.

guaranteed to produce physical arousal. The researcher, pretending to be interested in the effects of scenery on creativity, asked the men to write brief stories about an ambiguous picture of a woman. She also invited them to call her if they wanted more information about the research. As predicted, those men who had just crossed the wobbly bridge (and were, presumably, more physically aroused) wrote stories containing more sexual imagery than those who used the safer structure. And four times as many of them called the female researcher "to get more information"! Apparently, the men who had crossed the shaky bridge misinterpreted their increased arousal as emotional attraction to the female researcher (Dutton & Aron, 1974).

After crossing a scary bridge, your level of physiological arousal may be heightened. You might be more likely to misattribute your arousal to some other cause—and some other emotion, such as romantic attraction.

To strengthen their finding that arousal was really the independent variable influencing the emotional misinterpretation, the experimenters arranged for another group of men to be interviewed. A ten-minute delay after crossing the wobbly bridge gave this group enough time for their physical arousal symptoms to be reduced. Significantly, these unaroused men did not show the signs of sexual interest that the aroused men showed (Dutton & Aron, 1974).

What is the lesson to be learned from this study? James and Lange were right in their suggestion that physical arousal can generate emotional responses. But what they did not see clearly was the idea that a single physical state might give rise to several different emotions—depending on one's cognitive interpretation. In the bridge study, subjects' arousal conceivably could have been interpreted as anxiety or as sexual interest. In actuality, the subjects experienced sexual interest because they *misattributed* their physical arousal to the researcher rather than to the wobbly bridge. This research, along with many other subsequent studies, shows that we can easily mislabel our physical symptoms as an emotional state. In a similar way, the victim of phobic disorder may misattribute a feeling of arousal to a passing dog and develop a fear reaction. Likewise, being overheated can be misattributed to feeling angry; being physically aroused from exercise can be misinterpreted as being sexually aroused. This is the James-Lange theory with a cognitive twist, which we will see elaborated in the *two-factor theory* of emotion—next.

**THE TWO-FACTOR THEORY OF EMOTION**   According to Stanley Schachter (1971), the experience of emotion is the joint effect of physical arousal and cognitive appraisal of a situation, such as a ride on a scary roller coaster. So, how is this different from the James-Lange theory? Schachter places the emphasis on *cognition*, rather than on biological arousal. According to this view, when arousal occurs (as in the subject on the swinging bridge, the patient with panic disorder, or the passenger on the roller coaster), cognition determines how a person will label this ambiguous inner state (Mandler, 1984; Schacter & Singer, 1962). Thus, physical arousal may be

**Chapter 1:**
**Mind, Behavior, and Science**
*The independent variable involves the possible cause of a response being investigated in a study.*

**Chapter 13:**
**Psychopathology**
*Phobias are mental disorders involving extreme and irrational fear.*

attributed to whatever events or objects occupy the mind at the moment. So, the rickety-bridge-crosser attributed his arousal to the attractive researcher, rather than to the arousing experience of crossing the bridge. This position—that emotion involves the cognitive interpretation of physiological arousal and of the situation—has also become known as the **two-factor theory** of emotion.

Under what conditions are we most likely to misinterpret our emotions? Normally, external events confirm what our biology is telling us, without much need for elaborate interpretation—as when you feel fear during a roller-coaster ride. But what happens when we experience physical arousal from not-so-obvious sources, such as exercise, heat, or drugs? When we know (or think we know) that one of these is the source of our feelings, we will most likely make no emotional interpretation. Misattribution is much more likely in a complex environment where many stimuli are competing for our attention (as in the bridge study, above). It is also likely in an environment where we have faulty information about our physical arousal (as when the unsuspected caffeine in a soft drink makes us edgy).

The two-factor theory would predict that a decaffeinated-coffee drinker who accidentally drank coffee with caffeine could mistake the resulting physical arousal for an emotion.

Numerous attempts to test the two-factor theory have produced conflicting results (Leventhal & Tomarken, 1986; Sinclair et al., 1994). Suppose that you suddenly feel an increase in heart rate and respiration, and you are alone. How would you interpret it: excitement or anxiety? The majority of adult experimental subjects experiencing those arousal symptoms interpreted them as anxiety-based and negative—and searched for ways to control the feelings (Marshall & Zimbardo, 1979; Maslach, 1979). Other experiments show that people can apparently experience emotions without any physical arousal. For example, when confronted by emotion-provoking stimuli, such as an insult, experimental subjects who have received beta-blockers (drugs that reduce heart rate) still can experience intense anger or anxiety.

**FIGURE 8.4:** Comparison of James-Lange and Two-Factor Theories

The James-Lange theory accounts for emotional experiences in simple, unambiguous situations. The two-factor theory adds the second factor of cognitive appraisal, which can account for emotional responses in situations where conflicting stimuli are present.

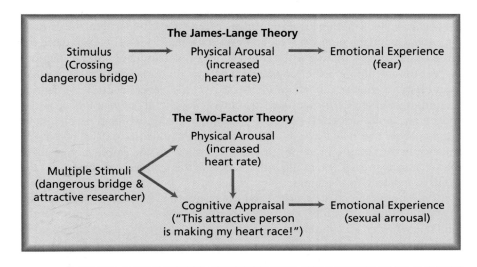

**Two-factor theory:** The proposal claiming that emotion results from the cognitive appraisal of both physical arousal (Factor #1) and an emotion-provoking stimulus (Factor #2).

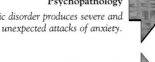

Depression is more common in women, but men are more prone to violence. This sketch is by Vincent Van Gogh, no stranger to depression himself.

**Chapter 13:**
**Psychopathology**
*Panic disorder produces severe and unexpected attacks of anxiety.*

**Chapter 14:**
**Therapies for Mental Disorder**
*Cognitive therapies assume a link between emotions and thoughts.*

This occurs despite their diminished physical arousal (Reisenzein, 1983). Such studies suggest that the two-factor theory is an incomplete explanation for emotion.

Perhaps the most sensible inference from such studies is that physical arousal does not always accompany our emotions. And, when we experience unexpected biological arousal, we may interpret it within the context of external events—but often negatively. Many times, however, as in the bridge study, arousal is not unexpected but merely misinterpreted. In any event, we continually monitor both our physiological arousal and the situation in an effort to identify our feelings, to determine which emotional label fits best, and to decide what our reaction means in that context.

**CURRENT ISSUES** Emotions sometimes overwhelm rational thinking. This is well known by politicians who seek votes by posturing on emotion-laden issues, such as crime, welfare, drugs, and school prayer. Recognizing this distortion of cognition by emotion, cognitive psychologists have traditionally viewed emotion as a nuisance—a monkey wrench in the machinery of thought. In recent years, however, they have changed their minds, coming to see emotion as an important influence on attention, perception, memory, and imagination (Kitayama & Markus, 1994; Oatley & Jenkins, 1992). Studies also show that moods filter the contents of our moment-to-moment consciousness (Posner, Rothbart, & Harman, 1994). So, when you feel happy, happy thoughts most easily come to mind, and when you have the blues, depressing thoughts overwhelm your consciousness. Health care professionals take note: A patient's emotional state will affect the symptoms the patient tells the examiner. So, a depressed individual is likely to describe more troublesome symptoms than is a happy patient (Goldman, Kraemer, & Salovey, 1996; Redelmeier, Rozin, & Kahneman, 1993).

What is still disputed among cognitive psychologists in the field of emotion today? The controversy over the relationship between cognition and emotional responses continues, but with a new emphasis. On one side of the debate, Robert Zajonc (his name rhymes with "science") (1980, 1984) and Carroll Izard (1989, 1993) argue that the brain mechanisms of emotion and cognition are independent of each other. In support, Zajonc and Izard note that emotions can be produced by electrical stimulation of the limbic system. If they are right that cognition and emotion involve independent systems, then cognition may not be a necessary ingredient of emotion. In that case, some of our emotional reactions can occur without cognitive appraisal (much as the James-Lange theory proposed). This may be what happens in panic disorder, for example, when a panic attack occurs in the absence of a situation that is judged as threatening.

On the opposing side of the controversy, Richard Lazarus (1984, 1991a, 1991b) takes the view of a therapist who helps people deal with their emotions. He asserts that cognition and emotion have an intimate connection. To illustrate, the way you think about a difficult professor ("He's an egotistical jerk!" versus "He has made the course challenging so that we will learn something") determines both the emotions you feel toward him and the long-term impact of the professor's course on you. Lazarus suggests that we can reduce the negative consequences of our self-defeating emotions if we change our cognitions. So, angry thoughts about your professor may produce an unpleasant stress response (and a low grade), while more charitable thoughts about him may leave you in a healthier emotional state (with better performance in the course). From this perspective, cognition and emotion are components of a single mental system. We will see more of this approach when we study the cognitive approach to therapy.

So, who is right? Are cognition and emotion separate, as Zajonc and Izard believe? Or are they intertwined, as Lazarus asserts? Both sides may own a piece of the truth. It may be that for some emotional responses (such as we found in panic disorder) cognition plays no causal role. At the same time, in other emotional reactions (such as the stage fright felt by a novice actor), cognition and emotion may be inseparable.

## PSYCHOLOGY IN YOUR LIFE

### Emotional Differences between Men and Women Depend on Culture

*I*f you felt depressed, would you tell your friends? Your answer to that question depends, in part, on your gender and your culture. In the United States, males and females often learn different lessons about emotional control. Stereotyped gender roles may dictate that men and boys receive reinforcement for emotional displays of dominance: anger and aggressive behavior (Fischer, 1993). On the other hand, they may be punished for emotional displays that show weakness: crying, depression, and sadness (Gottman, 1994). Meanwhile, the pattern of reinforcement and punishment may be reversed for females. Women and girls receive encouragement for emotions that show vulnerability. They may also be punished for displaying emotions that suggest dominance.

Not only does culture affect the emotional displays of men and women differently, but different cultures teach different **display rules**—the permissible ways of showing emotions (Ekman, 1984). It is noteworthy that researchers have found neither sex to be more emotionally expressive overall. Rather, cultures differ in emotional expression much more than do the sexes. Among the peoples of Europe, the Americas, and the Middle East, the display rules typically depend on the emotion being expressed. In Israel and Italy, for example, men more often than women hide their feelings of sadness. The opposite holds true in Britain, Spain, Switzerland, and Germany, where women are more likely than men to hide their emotions. In many Asian cultures both sexes learn to restrain all their emotional expressions (Wallbott, Ricc-Bitti, & Bänninger-Huber, 1986). Moreover, the power of the situation often overrides gender differences. Thus, an American man is just as likely as an American woman to control a flash of temper directed at a boss or other person of superior power. (*See Chapter 12, Social Psychology.*)

What is the source of the emotional differences between males and females? It

is difficult to distinguish biological from cultural influences. We know that men and women often give different emotional interpretations to the same situation—especially when the situation involves an encounter between a man and a woman (Lakoff, 1990; Stapley & Haviland, 1989). We also know that certain emotional disturbances, such as panic disorder and depression, occur more commonly in women. In addition, self-reports (see Figure 8.5) indicate that women cry more frequently than do men (Frey et al., 1983). On the other hand, men show more anger and display more physiological signs of emotional arousal during interpersonal conflicts than do women (Gottman, 1994; Gottman & Krokoff, 1989; Gottman & Levenson, 1986; Polefrone & Manuck,

1987; Rusting & Nolen-Hoeksema, 1998). Men also commit most of the world's violent acts.

So, what can we make of such diverse findings? The relative contributions of nature and culture remain clouded. Overall, we can say that the sexes often differ in their emotional experiences, both within and across cultures. We cannot conclude, however, that one sex has more emotional intensity than the other (Baumeister, Stillwell, & Wotman, 1990; Fischer et al., 1993; Oatley & Duncan, 1994; Shaver & Hazan, 1987; Shields, 1991).

**Display rules:** The permissible ways of displaying emotions in a particular society.

**FIGURE 8.5:** Episodes of Emotional Crying during One Month

In the first scientific investigation of adult crying behavior, 45 male and 286 female subjects judged to be psychiatrically normal kept records of their emotional crying behavior during a month. Duration of episodes for both groups was about six minutes, and the most frequent stimuli for crying involved interpersonal relations and media presentations. A high proportion of both groups said they felt better after crying.

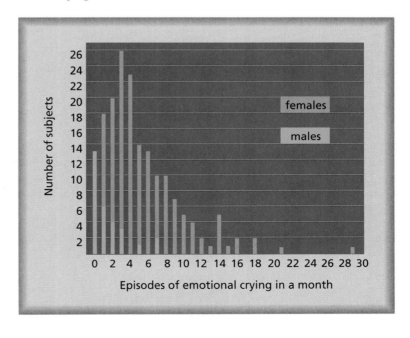

1. RECALL: *During emotional arousal, the _____ nervous system sends messages to the internal organs.*
   a. somatic
   b. sensory
   c. autonomic
   d. cerebellar

2. APPLICATION: *We would be most likely to misattribute the source of our arousal under which of the following circumstances?*
   a. taking a drug, such as a diet pill, that has the unexpected side effect of physical arousal
   b. taking a drug, such as caffeine, that we know produces arousal
   c. winning a race
   d. feeling depressed after the death of a loved one

3. RECALL: *In the field of emotion there is currently intense debate about whether*
   a. biological arousal can cause emotional responses.
   b. cognition can cause emotional arousal.
   c. cognition and emotion are independent of each other.
   d. men or women are more emotional.

4. RECALL: *In which respect do men and women differ in their emotional expressions?*
   a. Women are, overall, more emotionally expressive than men.
   b. Certain emotional disorders, such as depression, occur more often in women.
   c. In Asian countries, men are more open about their feelings than are women.
   d. Men are more rational than women.

5. UNDERSTANDING THE CORE CONCEPT: Emotions result from an interaction of biological, mental, behavioral, and social/cultural process. *Which two of these is emphasized in the two-factor theory of emotion?*
   a. biological and behavioral
   b. mental and behavioral
   c. biological and mental
   d. biological and social/cultural

**ANSWERS:**    1. c    2. a    3. c    4. b    5. c

---

KEY QUESTION

## HOW MUCH CONTROL DO WE HAVE OVER OUR EMOTIONS?

The boss says something critical of your work—unfairly, you think. Suddenly anger and defensiveness well up inside you. It's not prudent to express these emotions to the boss, but your face betrays your feelings. Is such a response as automatic and uncontrollable as the knee-jerk reflex? Richard Lazarus (1991a, 1991b) has shown that training can help people not only to modify and control their private feelings but also to control the expression of them. In many situations, aside from work, it may be desirable to mask or modify what you are feeling. If you dislike a professor, you might be wise to disguise your emotions. If you have strong romantic feelings toward someone, more than he or she realizes, it might be safest to reveal your feelings gradually as the relationship develops. In business negotiations, you will do better if you can prevent yourself from signaling too much emotional arousal. Even in leisure activities like playing poker or planning your next move in chess, you will be most successful if you keep your real feelings, beliefs, and intentions a secret.

In this section, we look at emotional control. We will begin with the concept of "emotional intelligence," the ability to understand your emotions and those of others, as well as to control the expression of potentially disruptive or harmful emotions and impulses. Then we will look at the other side of emotional control: the detection of deception—which is really a problem in detecting emotions that someone is trying to hide. Here is the *Core Concept* that ties these topics together:

CORE CONCEPT

**Although emotional responses are not always consciously regulated, people can learn to control them.**

The practical, take-away message from this section is that, while emotions do sometimes slip out of control, we are not simply at their mercy. Emotional control is a skill that can be learned.

## Developing Emotional Intelligence

Daniel Goleman (1995) claims that the ability to understand and control one's own emotions and, perhaps, those of others involves intelligent behavior. Moreover, he says, this sort of intelligence has been overshadowed by the academic intelligence encouraged in schools and valued by IQ tests. **Emotional intelligence,** says Goleman, involves the ability to use one's understanding of emotions effectively. Those with high emotional intelligence are not only tuned in to their emotions and those of others, but they can manage their unhealthy feelings and curtail the inappropriate expression of their impulses and desires. The power of this ability can be seen in the results of the "marshmallow test," a test of impulse control described in his book:

> Just imagine you're four years old, and someone makes the following proposal: If you'll wait until after he runs an errand, you can have two marshmallows for a treat. If you can't wait until then, you can have only one—but you can have it right now. It is a challenge sure to try the soul of any four-year-old, a microcosm of the eternal battle between impulse and restraint, id and ego, desire and self-control, gratification and delay. Which of these choices a child makes is a telling test; it offers a quick reading not just of character, but of the trajectory that the child will probably take through life.

How did the children in this experiment respond to the temptation of the marshmallow which sat before them, within reach, while the researcher was away? Goleman continues:

> Some four-year-olds were able to wait what must surely have seemed an endless fifteen to twenty minutes for the experimenter to return. To sustain themselves in their struggle they covered their eyes so they wouldn't have to stare at temptation, or rested their heads in their arms, talked to themselves, sang, played games with their hands and feet, even tried to go to sleep. These plucky preschoolers got the two-marshmallow reward. But others, more impulsive, grabbed the one marshmallow, almost always within seconds of the experimenter's leaving the room on his "errand." (pp. 80–81)

Remarkably, the power of the marshmallow test to predict later adjustment was revealed when these same children were tracked down in adolescence. As a group, those who had curbed their impulse to grab the single marshmallow were better off on all counts. They were more self-reliant, more effective in interpersonal relationships, better students, better able to handle frustration and stress. By contrast, the one-third of the subjects who had given in to temptation had lives marked by troubled relationships, shyness, stubbornness, and indecisiveness. They also were much more likely to hold low opinions of themselves, to be mistrustful of others, and to be easily provoked by frustrations. In the academic sphere, they were more likely to be disinterested in school. Astonishingly, the marshmallow test also correlated clearly with SAT scores: Those who, as four-year-olds, were able to delay gratification scored, on the average, 210 points higher than did their counterparts who had grabbed the single marshmallow years earlier.

Is this sort of savvy fixed by heredity or by early experience? Goleman believes that emotional intelligence is not rigid. Like academic intelligence, he says, emotional intelligence is a flexible ability that can be learned. Based on programs already in place in visionary schools across the country, Goleman has a plan for adding emotional training to the curriculum. The result, he predicts, will bring improved relationships, increased self-respect, and even, perhaps, gains in academic achievement.

But emotional control has its dark side, too. Just as some people get into trouble when they let their emotions—particularly negative emotions—go unchecked,

**Chapter 11:
Intelligence and the Psychology of Differences**
*IQ and "academic intelligence" involve logical thinking and problem solving.*

**Emotional intelligence:** In Goleman's theory, the ability to understand and control emotional responses.

others take emotional control to the opposite extreme. They become so guarded that they never convey affection, humor, or honest displeasure. Still others learn to control their emotions in order to deceive. This is the skill practiced by con artists. Their victims are people who believe that physical or behavioral cues are never-fail indicators of people's private feelings. Let's turn now to the branch of psychology that studies these deceptive tactics of emotional control.

## Detecting Deception

You might think you can spot deception when someone fails to "look you in the eye" or fidgets nervously. If so, you could be setting yourself up to be duped. Most of us are poor lie detectors—or truth detectors, for that matter. One reason is that social interactions often occur in familiar situations, where we pay little attention to nonverbal cues. Nevertheless, experts who study deception find that a person who deliberately tries to hoodwink us may "leak" uncontrolled nonverbal signals of deception. Knowing how to read these cues could be helpful in deciding whether a salesperson or a politician is lying to you or whether a physician might be concealing something about your medical condition.

The key to effective deception detection lies in perceiving patterns of a person's behavior over time. Without the chance for repeated observations, you are much less likely to be able to judge a person's honesty accurately (Marsh, 1988). Still, you may find yourself in a situation where even a little help in deception detection might be better than none at all—such as when buying a used car or listening to a political speech. Here are some helpful guidelines that psychology can offer (from Kleinke, 1975; Marsh, 1988; Zuckerman & DePaulo, 1981):

- When a lie involves false information, the effort to hide the truth costs the liar some cognitive effort. This results in heightened attention (evident in dilation of the pupils), longer pauses in speech (to choose words carefully), and more constrained movement and gesturing (in an attempt to avoid "giving away" the truth).
- Conversely, when a lie involves hiding one's true feelings, the liar may become physically and behaviorally more aroused. This becomes evident in postural shifts, speech errors, nervous gestures (such as preening by touching or stroking the hair or face), and shrugging (as if to dismiss the lie).
- The face is easier to control than the body, so a deceiver may work on keeping a "poker face" but forget to restrain bodily clues. A smart deception detective might therefore concentrate on a speaker's body movements: Are they rhythmic? Are they calculated? Do the hands move freely or nervously?
- The ability to "look you straight in the eye" is, in fact, a reasonably good indicator of truth-telling—but only when dealing with people who usually tell the truth. When they do lie, their amateurish efforts to deceive often show up in averted gaze, reduced blinking (indicating concentration of attention elsewhere), and less smiling. Remember, however, that a practiced liar can look you straight in the eye while relating complete fiction.

## Do "Lie Detectors" Really Work?

The **polygraph**, often called a "lie detector," relies on the assumption that people display physical signs of arousal when lying—even though this is not always true. The device really acts as an emotional arousal detector, rather than a direct indicator of truth or lies. Most such devices make a record of the suspect's heart rate, breathing rate, perspiration, and blood pressure. Occasionally, voice-print analysis is also employed.

Critics have pointed out several problems with the polygraphic procedure (Saxe, 1991, 1994). Subjects know when they are suspects, so some will give heightened responses to the critical questions, whether they are guilty or innocent. Some people, however, can give deceptive responses because they have learned to control or distort their emotional responses. To do so they may employ simple physical move-

**Polygraph:** A device that records or graphs many ("poly") measures of physical arousal, such as heart rate, breathing, perspiration, and blood pressure. A polygraph is often called a "lie detector," even though it is really an arousal detector.

**Biofeedback:** A clinical procedure in which people are given information (feedback) on their biological responses (such as perspiration).

The "lie detector" is really an emotional arousal detector. It can't distinguish between emotions such as fear, anger, anxiety, and guilt.

**Chapter 9:**
**Stress, Health, and Well-Being**
*Biofeedback is an operant conditioning procedure that can help people control stress responses.*

ments, drugs, or **biofeedback** training (Saxe, Dougherty, & Cross, 1985). Complicating matters, the profession of polygraphy has no generally accepted standards either for giving a polygraph examination or for interpreting the results. Without such standards, different examiners could examine the same evidence and arrive at different conclusions. Thus, a polygraph examiner risks incorrectly identifying innocent people as liars. For these reasons many courts have banned or severely restricted the use of polygraph examinations (Patrick & Iacono, 1991).

## PSYCHOLOGY IN YOUR LIFE

## Controlling Anger

" A nger has long been a problem for me," writes Melvyn Fein. "Over the years it has cost me a great deal of pain and denied me much happiness" (1993, p. ix). Failing at various efforts to control and constructively express his anger, Fein himself became a clinician and developed an approach to anger disorders. Fein's program, Integrated Anger Management (I.A.M.), involves five stages:

- Learning to express anger safely, so that it will not spin out of control;
- Developing tolerance by accepting feelings of anger without becoming enraged and violent;
- Identifying the underlying goals of one's anger, such as frustration with in-

justice or the inability to achieve a valued goal;
- Letting go of unrealistic goals that feed the anger, such as the naive belief that expressing anger will motivate others to "do the right thing"; and
- Using anger constructively to reach more realistic, achievable goals.

This analysis of anger represents an effort to correct the dangers created by popular myths about anger. On television talk shows, for example, you can see people attacking and humiliating others, as if the public venting of feelings and the act of revenge will eliminate their anger. In fact, retaliation for a real or imagined wrong is likely to bring only the most fleeting feeling of satisfaction. The overwhelming result of venting anger is to increase the tendency to become enraged at ever smaller provoca-

tions. Solid psychological research indicates that, when you are angry with someone, "getting it off your chest" by aggressively confronting or hurting that individual will *not* neutralize your bad feelings. Rather, it will more likely *intensify* them. And, from a social perspective, retaliation is not likely to end a feud but to fuel it—a reality obvious throughout human history, filled with wars about pride, power, status, and honor. A saner and safer strategy is to keep your feelings to yourself, at least until the passion of your anger has subsided and you can be more rational about the nature of your real complaint and what might really be done to solve the problem (Tavris, 1983, 1995). Often, all it takes to defuse a tense and angry situation is to communicate the facts and your feelings to the person toward whom you feel anger.

1. **RECALL:** *People with emotional intelligence*
   a. feel no emotions.
   b. are extremely emotionally responsive.
   c. know how to control their emotional responses.
   d. can deceive those with less emotional intelligence.

2. **RECALL:** *When lying by giving false information, you are likely to*
   a. become more animated in your gesturing.
   b. become more constrained in your gesturing.
   c. control your body more easily than you control your face.
   d. look someone "straight in the eye."

3. **RECALL:** *"Lie detectors" detect*
   a. feelings.
   b. arousal.
   c. motivation.
   d. untruthfulness.

4. **RECALL:** *Many psychologists have become concerned about the widespread use of polygraphy because*
   a. polygraph testing is not done under the supervision of qualified psychologists.
   b. hypnosis is much more accurate than polygraphy in the detection of lying.

c. innocent people can be incorrectly identified as lying.
d. people who are lying can be incorrectly identified as innocent.

5. **APPLICATION:** *Psychological research suggests that it might be best to handle your feelings of anger toward a friend by*
   a. hitting a punching bag.
   b. ventilating your anger by yelling at your friend.
   c. calmly telling your friend that you feel angry.
   d. doing nothing except "stewing" in your angry feelings.

6. **UNDERSTANDING THE CORE CONCEPT:** *Research suggests that the ability to control one's emotional responses is*
   a. a personality trait that varies from person to person.
   b. largely a matter of hormones.
   c. closely connected to IQ.
   d. a skill that can be learned.

**ANSWERS:**   1. c   2. b   3. b   4. c   5. c   6. d

---

 KEY QUESTION

## MOTIVATION: WHAT MAKES US ACT AS WE DO?

Why do some people climb mountains, rob banks, or join the Peace Corps? What drives anorectic individuals to starve themselves—sometimes to their deaths? Why do some of us feel a need to achieve, while others seek security? And for the method actor: What drives the characters in a play to behave as the playwright portrays them? Such questions lie in the domain of the psychology of motivation, which deals with the internal processes that cause us to move toward a goal or away from a situation that we judge to be unpleasant. As you will remember, motivation is the complement of emotion. While emotion emphasizes arousal, motivation channels that arousal into action.

**Motivation** is the general term for all the processes involved in starting, directing, and maintaining physical and psychological activities. Motivation includes the internal mechanisms involved in *preferring* one activity over another, the *strength* of responses, and the *persistence* of actions toward relevant goals. The highly motivated person seeks out certain activities over others, practices behaviors and perfects skills required to attain the objective, and focuses energy on reaching the goal despite frustrations.

The fact that some people do better in competition than others can be explained in part by different degrees of motivation. These men are participating in the international Games for the Disabled.

**Motivation:** Refers to all the processes involved in starting, directing, and maintaining physical and psychological activities.

Your internal motivational mechanisms determine which of many possible responses you will choose from the motivational menu of the moment. Will it be laughing or crying? Fight or flight? Studying or playing? The motivational menu always offers multiple choices. During a lifetime we must sort through a wide assortment of motives, ranging from the largely inborn mechanism that stimulates nursing in a newborn infant to the learned desires for money, fame, or expertise in the adult. The Core Concept for this section puts it this way:

**CORE CONCEPT**

**Motivation takes many forms, but all involve inferred mental processes that select and direct our behavior.**

We begin our study of motivation with an overview of some important types of motivation recognized by psychologists.

## Types of Motivation

Psychologists often distinguish between *motives* and *drives*. They prefer the term **drive** for motivation that is assumed to have a strong innate component and, therefore, plays an important role in survival or reproduction. Hunger and thirst are examples of innate biological drives that psychologists have studied intensively. In contrast, many (but not all) psychologists reserve the term **motive** for the mechanisms involving learned needs, such as the need for achievement or the desire to play video games. Obviously, however, many motivated behaviors—such as eating, drinking, and sexual behavior—can have roots in both biology and learning. We will see that the distinction between drive and motive is often not sharp.

Intrinsic motivation controls many behaviors.

Psychologists also distinguish between *intrinsic* and *extrinsic* motivation. **Intrinsic motivation** comes from within the individual, who engages in an activity for its own sake, in the absence of external reward. Leisure activities, such as cycling, kayaking, or playing the guitar, are usually intrinsically motivated. Intrinsic motivation arises from inner qualities, such as personality traits or special interests. On the other hand, **extrinsic motivation** comes from outside the person. It involves behavior aimed at some external consequence, such as money or praise, rather than at satisfying an internal need. Extrinsic motivation also comes from cultural expectations or social pressures, as when a college student undergoes a dangerous or humiliating "initiation" in order to join a fraternity. We will examine the effects of intrinsic and extrinsic motivation on achievement near the end of this chapter.

In addition, motives and drives can arise either from **conscious motivation** or **unconscious motivation.** That is, motivated individuals may or may not be aware of the drives or motives underlying their behavior. Can unconscious motives be brought into awareness? Freud taught that some motives lie so deeply buried in the unconscious that they are inaccessible to conscious experience except through special therapy techniques. Modern day psychologists, however, stand divided on this issue (See, for example, Bruner, 1992; Erdelyi, 1992; Greenwald, 1992; Jacoby, Lindsay, & Toth, 1992; Kihlstrom, Bernhardt, & Tartaryn, 1992; Loftus & Klinger, 1992).

**Drive:** Biologically instigated motivation.

**Motive:** An internal mechanism that selects and directs behavior. The term "motive" is often used in the narrower sense of a motivational process that is learned, rather than biologically based (as are drives).

**Intrinsic motivation:** The desire to engage in an activity for its own sake, rather than for some external consequence, such as a reward.

**Extrinsic motivation:** The desire to engage in an activity to achieve an external consequence, such as a reward.

**Conscious motivation:** Having the desire to engage in an activity and being aware of the desire.

**Unconscious motivation:** Having a desire to engage in an activity but being consciously unaware of the desire. Freud's psychoanalytic theory emphasized unconscious motivation.

## How Psychologists Use the Concept of Motivation

Professors may think that students who do poorly on exams are "not motivated enough." Sports commentators speculate that winning teams were "hungrier" or "more motivated" than their opponents. Detectives seek to establish motive in building a case against a criminal suspect. Millions of soap opera fans watch their favorite programs to see how the characters' motives—greed, envy, lust, or revenge—will affect the story line. In everyday language, we use the term "motivation" to refer to a variety of mental states involving intentions, energy, or effort.

Psychologists, like everyone else, often need to explain behavior that cannot be attributed to external conditions. Therefore, they may make inferences about internal processes that select and direct behavior. Their inferences are formalized in the concept of motivation, which they find useful in the following circumstances:

**Chapter 12:**
**Social Psychology**
*The common mistake of attributing behavior to personal characteristics (rather than the environment) is known as the* fundamental attribution error.

- *Motivation connects observable behavior to internal states.* When we see someone eating, we may infer that a hunger drive is causing the eating behavior. We must be careful about drawing such inferences too quickly, though, because eating might be caused by something other than a state of hunger (e.g., social pressure, the availability of a favorite food, or a desire to gain weight). So a motive, such as hunger, can be identified with confidence only when other influences have been ruled out.
- *Motivation accounts for variability in behavior.* Psychologists use motivational explanations when the variations in people's performances are not obviously due to differences in physical or mental abilities or to differing environmental demands. For example, the intensity of your motivation may explain why you play tennis well on one day but poorly on another. It also may explain why some people do better than others of comparable skill in competitive situations, such as in a basketball game.
- *Motivation explains perseverance despite adversity.* Motivation helps us understand why organisms can continue to perform reliably even under difficult or variable conditions. Motivation gets you to work on time, even when you had a sleepless night or had to drive through a blizzard. When highly motivated, you also persist to the best of your ability, even if you realize the chances of success are slim—as does one of your authors when facing a major whitewater challenge in his kayak.
- *Motives relate biology to behavior.* We are biological organisms with complex internal mechanisms that automatically regulate bodily functions to promote survival. States of deprivation (such as needing food) automatically trigger these mechanisms, which then influence bodily functioning (such as feeling hungry), creating motivational states.

In each of these cases, a motivational explanation proposes an internal process that channels the organism's energies into a particular pattern of behavior.

## Theories of Motivation

No single explanation of motivation adequately accounts for the whole gamut of human motives and drives. Hunger, for example, seems to obey different motivational rules from those regulating sex or achievement or attachment. Much of the difficulty arises because of our dual nature: We are simultaneously creatures driven by our biology (as when you are ravenous because you haven't eaten all day) and by learning (as when you associate the lunch bell with food). Let's first focus on the biological side of our nature with a look at the common ancestor of all modern motivational theories: the *instinct theory* of motivation.

**Instinct theory:** The now outmoded view that certain behaviors are determined entirely by innate factors. The instinct theory was flawed because it overlooked the effects of learning and because it employed instincts merely as labels, rather than as explanations for behavior.

**INSTINCT THEORY**     According to **instinct theory,** organisms are born with a set of biologically based behaviors essential for the survival of a species. Instinct accounts reasonably well for regular cycles of animal activity, as seen in salmon that travel thousands of miles back to the stream where they were spawned. Although such instinctive behavior does not depend heavily on learning, the environment can often modify the behavior. This is seen when bees communicate the location of food to other bees, army ants embark on synchronized hunting expeditions, or birds use landmarks in their annual migrations.

What role do instincts play in human behavior? Sigmund Freud (1915), the founder of psychoanalysis, thought that the instincts—which he grouped as *life instincts* (such as sex) and *death instincts* (such as aggression or destruction)—created tension within the organism in the form of a buildup of *psychic energy*. This uncomfortable condition, said Freud, drives us unconsciously toward activities or objects that will reduce the tension. We may find a modern example of the death instinct in "road rage." From a Freudian perspective, this extreme and lethal form of aggression occurs when people take their unconscious anger with them behind the wheel of a car.

The term "instinct" has migrated from the scientific vocabulary to the speech of everyday life. We speak casually of "maternal instincts," of an athlete who "instinctively catches the ball," and of a "killer instinct" in a competitive entrepreneur. In fact, we use the term in so many ways that its meaning has become vague and conflicted. The same problem has occurred in scientific discourse. By the 1920s, scholars interested in the concept of instinct had compiled a list of thousands (Bernard, 1924). As the list lengthened, they gradually recognized that these instincts were merely labels for common patterns of behavior (such as a "gregariousness" instinct for people who like people). These labels, of course, were not explanations for the behaviors. Further doubts about the instinct concept appeared as anthropologists began to report striking variations in human behavior from one culture to another (Benedict, 1959; Mead, 1939). These findings stood in contradiction to many assumptions about universal instinctive motivations. Finally, experiments demonstrated that much behavior, such as aggression, can be learned. As a result, the term "instinct" has dropped out of favor among psychologists. And ethologists, who study animal behavior in natural habitats, now prefer the term **fixed-action patterns,** more narrowly defined as unlearned behavior patterns that occur throughout a species and are triggered by identifiable stimuli. Examples of fixed-action patterns include bird migration and dominance displays in baboons.

Do instincts—perhaps in their new guise as fixed-action patterns—retain any value in explaining human behavior? They do seem to motivate some of the behaviors, such as nursing, that we see in newborns. But we stand on shakier ground when using the term to explain more complex human behaviors that receive strong influence from learning. So, while we might speculate that the motivation of a hard-driving executive could involve some basic biologically based instinct (such as we see in animals who stake out their hunting and breeding territories, perhaps), this explanation is weak, at best. Most human behavior seems to be too complex, too variable, and too affected by learning to be explained adequately by instinct theory. Such concerns have undermined instinct theories as explanations of human behavior.

**DRIVE THEORY** The concept of "drive" refers to the uncomfortable state of tension that moves an organism to meet a biological need (Woodworth, 1918). Thus, an animal that needs water is driven to drink. Likewise, a need for food drives it to eat. In drive theory, a biological **need** produces a drive. The drive, then, motivates the animal to act to reduce the drive level. You have felt this buildup and release of tension if you have been extremely thirsty and then drank your fill.

The desirable state, which organisms seek, is a balanced condition called **homeostasis** (Hull, 1943, 1952). According to drive theory, organisms that have a biological imbalance (caused, say, by lack of fluids) are driven to seek a homeostatic balance (by drinking). Similarly, we can understand hunger as an imbalance in the body's energy supply. This imbalance drives an animal that has been deprived of food to eat in order to restore a condition of equilibrium.

**Chapter 10: Personality**
*Sigmund Freud developed the psychoanalytic theory of personality and therapy.*

**Chapter 6: Learning and Remembering**
*Fixed-action patterns can put limitations on the kinds of behaviors an organism can learn.*

**Fixed-action patterns:** Genetically based behaviors, seen across a species, that can be set off by a specific stimulus. The concept of fixed-action patterns has replaced the older notion of instinct.

**Need:** In drive theory, a need is a biological imbalance (such as dehydration) that threatens survival, if the need is left unmet. Biological needs are believed to produce drives.

**Homeostasis:** The body's tendency to maintain a biologically balanced condition, especially with regard to nutrients, water, and temperature.

Unfortunately for drive theory, however, the complete story of motivation has proved not to be that simple. Both humans and other animals, in the absence of any apparent deprivation or drives, act merely to increase stimulation. For example, both humans and animals engage in play—behavior that is satisfying in itself, rather than a means of reducing a drive. Similarly, animals also explore and manipulate their environment simply for the sake of the experience. In the laboratory, for example, rats will cross an electrified grid to reach nothing on the other side, except a novel environment. Even animals deprived of food and water, when placed in unfamiliar surroundings with plenty of opportunities to eat or drink, may choose to explore instead. Only after they have satisfied their curiosity do they begin to satisfy their hunger and thirst (Berlyne, 1960; Fowler, 1965; Zimbardo & Montgomery, 1957). And, as for human motivation, it is hard to imagine a basic need or a biological drive that could propel people out of airplanes or force them up the face of Yosemite's El Capitán. Apparently, for both people and animals, exploring and taking an interest in the world are rewarding experiences in themselves. For these reasons, psychologists have concluded that drive theory does not hold all the answers to motivation. Still, they have been reluctant to abandon the concept of drive, which, as we noted earlier, has come to mean a biologically based motive that plays an important role in survival or reproduction.

**INCENTIVE THEORY**   While internal states can push us to eat, drink, or to achieve some goal, motivation can arise externally, too. You know this if you have been lured into a bakery by the aroma of bread fresh from the oven. Such external stimuli that trigger motives are known as **incentives.** The incentive value of a stimulus is often learned—as in the case of money as an incentive for work or other conditioned reinforcers.

Generally, we think of **incentive motivation** being aroused by external stimuli. In humans, however, incentive motivation may also be self-induced by mental imagery. Being able to picture your goal can motivate you to study for a good grade on the next exam or motivate an Olympic athlete to train for a gold medal. Incentive motivation can also be induced by *negative incentives,* such as fear of developing an addiction to drugs or feelings of shame for dropping out of a marathon race.

Advertisers know that incentive stimuli, such as a commercial for tasty tacos, can activate a biological drive, such as hunger. But it is also the case that incentives can motivate behavior in the absence of a biological need or drive. This has been observed in the behavior of one of your authors, who was recently seen buying unneeded gadgets in a bicycle shop.

**COGNITIVE THEORY AND LOCUS OF CONTROL**   We have seen that many of our motives depend more on learning and thinking than on biological drives or instincts. Watching TV, reading a book, listening to music, climbing a mountain: All these activities get their push from cognitive processes. One of the most influential of the cognitive theories emphasizes the importance of expectations in motivating behavior.

In his cognitive *social-learning theory* (1954), Julian Rotter (pronounced ROH-ter) asserted that the likelihood of someone engaging in a given behavior (such as studying for an exam instead of partying) is determined by two factors: (1) one's expectation of attaining a goal (getting a good grade) following that activity and (2) the personal value of that goal. But what determines these expectations? Rotter says that our expectations depend largely on our **locus of control,** our belief about our ability to control things that happen to us. If, for example, you believe that studying hard will lead to good grades, you have an *internal locus of control,* and you will behave differently from those who believe that grades depend on luck or on the teacher's biases. People who believe that their fate hangs on whim or luck have an *external locus of control.* Rotter's theory would also predict that people who exercise, save money, or

**Chapter 6:
Learning and Remembering**

*Conditioned reinforcers, such as tokens or money, acquire reinforcing power by association with primary reinforcers.*

**Incentives:** External stimuli that activate motives.

**Incentive motivation:** Motivation aroused by external stimuli.

**Locus of control:** An individual's sense of where his or her life influences originate—internally or externally.

use seat belts have an internal locus of control. Those who buy lottery tickets or smoke cigarettes have an external locus of control.

**MASLOW'S HUMANISTIC THEORY** How do you choose whether to eat, sleep, visit friends, or study? Abraham Maslow (1970) said that you act on your most pressing needs, and some of these needs take priority over others. Unlike the other theories of motivation we have considered, Maslow's humanistic theory attempts to span the whole gamut of human motivation from biological drives to social motives to creativity. Specifically, Maslow's theory proposes a **needs hierarchy** : a listing of needs arranged in priority order (Figure 8.6). The "higher" needs have little influence on our behavior, said Maslow, until the more basic needs are fulfilled:

- *Biological needs*, such as hunger and thirst, fall at the bottom of the hierarchy. They must be satisfied before higher needs make themselves felt. When biological needs are pressing, other concerns are put on hold.
- *Safety needs* motivate us to avoid danger, when biological needs are reasonably well satisfied. Note that a hungry animal (with unmet biological needs) may risk its physical safety for food, until it gets its belly full: Then the safety needs take over.
- *Attachment and affiliation needs* energize us when we are no longer concerned about danger. These needs make us want to belong, to affiliate with others, to love, and to be loved.
- *Esteem needs* follow next in the hierarchy. These include the needs to like oneself, to see oneself as competent and effective, and to do what is necessary to earn the respect of oneself and others.
- *Self-actualization* lies at the top of the needs hierarchy, motivating us to seek the fullest development of our creative human potential. Among their other positive attributes, self-actualizing persons are self-aware, self-accepting, socially responsive, spontaneous, and open to novelty and challenge.

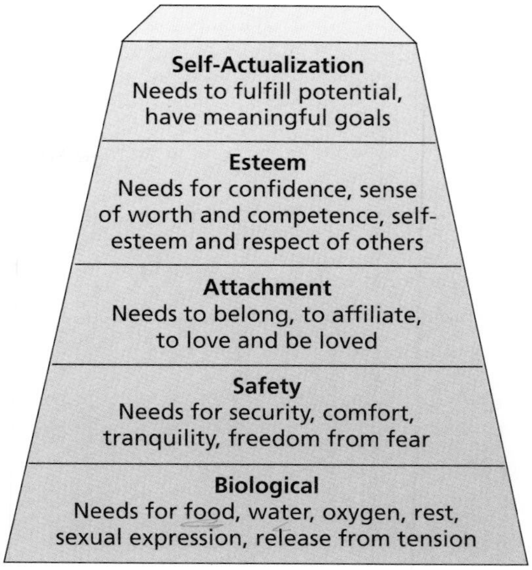

How does Maslow's theory square with the data? A great body of work now demonstrates people's needs for relationships with others (Brehm, 1992; Hatfield & Rapson, 1993; Kelley et al., 1983; Weber & Harvey, 1994). The kinds of attachments people form—best friends, playmates, coworkers, lovers, teammates, spouses, or members of the same club—and their reasons for forming them can be as varied as the individuals themselves. Most psychologists specializing in relationships now agree that this variety of liaisons and attachments arises from our fundamental motivation to "belong," as Maslow theorized (Baumeister & Leary, 1995).

Our happiness seems to depend also on the quality of our relationships. In a relevant study, a psychologist asked over 200 students to list the initials of people they knew and to rate each one on two dimensions: first for happiness–unhappiness and then for selfishness–unselfishness. Results showed that 70% of those judged to be unselfish seemed happy, but 95% of those deemed selfish seemed unhappy (Rimland, 1982). Individualistic cultures (such as is found in the United States) encourage individuals to promote their own happiness by acquiring things and seeking personal pleasure. Yet, research indicates, giving to and caring for others are surer roads to personal happiness—as well as social good. Why would unselfishness—sacrificing or depriving oneself of comfort or safety for others' sake—promote real happiness? Myers (1992) suggests that through altruism people can create a meaning in their lives that will survive death, thus incidentally promoting long-term self-preservation.

While such findings are generally supportive of Maslow, his theory has its critics. From a cross-cultural perspective, the theory has been criticized as applicable only to self-oriented (individualistic) cultures, rather than to group-oriented (collectivistic) cultures. Other critics point out that some important human behaviors do not fit

**Self-Actualization**
Needs to fulfill potential, have meaningful goals

**Esteem**
Needs for confidence, sense of worth and competence, self-esteem and respect of others

**Attachment**
Needs to belong, to affiliate, to love and be loved

**Safety**
Needs for security, comfort, tranquility, freedom from fear

**Biological**
Needs for food, water, oxygen, rest, sexual expression, release from tension

**FIGURE 8.6:** Maslow's Hierarchy of Needs

According to Maslow, needs at the lower level of the hierarchy dominate an individual's motivation as long as they are unsatisfied. Once these are adequately satisfied, the higher needs occupy an individual's attention.

**Chapter 9: Stress, Health, and Well-Being**

*Many of our common assumptions about happiness are based on myth or misunderstanding.*

**Needs hierarchy:** In Maslow's theory, the notion that needs occur in priority order, with the biological needs as the most basic.

Maslow's hierarchy. It fails to explain, for example, a soldier under fire who disregards personal safety to rescue a buddy. It fails to explain why you might miss a meal when you are absorbed in an interesting book. It fails to explain why sensation seekers, as we saw earlier, would pursue risky interests (such as whitewater kayaking) that override their safety needs. And it fails to explain the behavior of people who deliberately take their own lives. The critics will admit, however, that Maslow's theory was, at least, a step toward a comprehensive theory of motivation.

Overall, Maslow's influence has been greater in the spheres of psychotherapy and education than in motivational research. Business, too, has been especially receptive to Maslow's ideas. Many dollars have been made by consultants using this theory as the basis for seminars on motivating employees. The main idea they have promoted is that humans have an innate need to grow and actualize their highest potentials. Such an upbeat approach was also welcomed by psychologists who had wearied of the negative motivational emphasis on hunger, thirst, anxiety, and fear.

Chapter 10:
Personality
Chapter 14:
Therapies for Mental Disorder
*Humanistic psychotherapy draws on Maslow's ideas.*

## PSYCHOLOGY IN YOUR LIFE

## Rewards Can Squelch Motivation

Would you go to the dentist just for the fun of the visit? You will recall that psychologists use the term *extrinsic motivation* to explain behaviors (such as going to the dentist) that we engage in for some external consequence—usually to obtain a reward or to avoid an unpleasant situation. Taking vitamins, flinching at a pinprick, and marrying for money are also extrinsically motivated behaviors. When extrinsic factors are the sole source of motivation, behavior becomes instrumental (useful) for obtaining some desired outcome, not because the behavior itself is enjoyable. Because the laws of operant conditioning govern behavior produced by extrinsic motivation, such behavior is unlikely to occur for long in the absence of rewards or threats of punishment. This fact is of obvious concern to parents, teachers, employers, and others who wish to use extrinsic motivators to encourage high achievement and good behavior.

**Overjustification:** The process by which extrinsic (external) rewards displace internal motivation, as when a child receives money for playing video games.

What do you suppose might happen if children were given extrinsic rewards (praise, money, or other incentives) for behavior that they were already motivated intrinsically to produce—such as playing video games? Research indicates that, under such conditions, extrinsic rewards may actually squelch the behavior. The reason lies in **overjustification,** the process by which external reinforcement displaces internal sources of motivation. Under conditions of overjustification, play can become work. This was clearly shown in experiments by Mark Lepper and his colleagues (Lepper, Greene, & Nisbett, 1973). In these studies, children were given rewards (certificates) for activities they previously engaged in just for fun (drawing pictures). As a result of overjustification, the children's motivation changed from intrinsic to extrinsic, and they eventually spent less time drawing. When the extrinsic rewards were withdrawn, the children stopped the activity altogether because drawing had lost both its material value (the certificates) and its value as a source of intrinsic reinforcement (enjoyment) (Deci, 1975; Lepper, 1981; Lepper & Greene, 1978; Levine & Fasracht, 1974).

But do rewards always have this effect? A recent review of the literature shows

Overjustification occurs when extrinsic rewards for doing something enjoyable take the intrinsic fun out of the activity. It is likely that this person would not enjoy video games as much if he were paid for playing.

that the effect of rewards is variable, but they often have surprisingly desirable effects on behavior (Eisenberger & Cameron, 1996). While some studies show a decrease in behavior motivated extrinsically, others show that rewards can actually add interest to a task. This is consistent with the fact that many professionals both love their work and get paid

320    CHAPTER 8    *Emotion and Motivation*

for it. Eisenberger and Cameron claim that the only consistently negative effect of reward occurs when the reward is given without regard for quality of performance—as when employees are given year-end bonuses regardless of their work.

And what about threats? Extrinsic threats and constraints on people, such as high evaluation pressure or close surveillance during work, seem to have universally detrimental effects on motivation. Typically, students in courses where grades are heavily emphasized might find that their motivation, even for their favorite subjects, dwindles after the final exam because they were working only for the grade. In general, attempts to encourage a desired behavior with threats will backfire by discouraging the behavior when the threat is removed. Clearly, the use of extrinsic motivators is tricky business.

**Check Your Understanding**

1. RECALL: *Psychologists use the concept of motivation in several important ways. Which of the following is* not *among them?*
   a. to connect observable behavior to internal states
   b. to account for variability in behavior
   c. to explain perseverance despite adversity
   d. to explain reflexive responses

2. RECALL: *One reason the term "instinct" has dropped out of favor with psychologists is that*
   a. human behavior has no genetic basis.
   b. all behavior is learned.
   c. the term became a label for behavior, rather than an explanation for behavior.
   d. "instinct" applies to animal behavior, but not to human behavior.

3. ANALYSIS: *Incentives* are different from *drives* because
   a. incentives are external and drives are internal.
   b. incentives are homeostatic and drives are not.
   c. incentives are innate and drives are learned.
   d. incentives are emotions and drives are motives.

4. ANALYSIS: *What makes Maslow's theory of motivation different from most other theories?*
   a. It deals with biological motives.
   b. It deals with a wide range of motives.
   c. It helps us understand both animal behavior and human behavior.
   d. It deals with both emotion and motivation.

5. UNDERSTANDING THE CORE CONCEPT: Motivation takes many forms, but all involve inferred mental processes that select and direct our behavior. *Thus, the psychology of motivation attempts to explain why a certain* _____ *is selected.*
   a. emotion
   b. action
   c. sensation
   d. reward

**ANSWERS:**    1. d    2. c    3. a    4. b    5. b

**KEY QUESTION**

## HOW ARE ACHIEVEMENT, HUNGER, AND SEX ALIKE? DIFFERENT?

Now that we have reviewed some essential motivational concepts and theories, we will examine three diverse and important motives: achievement, hunger, and sex. We will see that each of these motives differs from the others, not just in the behavior it produces, but in deeper ways as well. The Core Concept expresses the point:

**CORE CONCEPT**    **No single theory accounts for all forms of motivation, because different motives involve different mixes of biological, mental, behavioral, and social/cultural influences.**

No one, not even Maslow, has yet been clever enough to concoct an explanation that encompasses all motivated behavior and still fits all the facts. For the moment,

**FIGURE 8.7:** Alternative Interpretations of a TAT Picture

*Story Showing High* n Ach: The boy has just finished his violin lesson. He's happy at the progress he is making and is beginning to believe that all his progress is making the sacrifices worthwhile. To become a concert violinist he will have to give up much of his social life and practice for many hours each day. Although he knows he could make more money by going into his father's business, he is more interested in being a great violinist and giving people joy with his music. He renews his personal commitment to do all it takes to make it.

*Story Showing Low* n Ach: The boy is holding his brother's violin and wishes he could play it. But he knows it isn't worth the time, energy, and money for lessons. He feels sorry for his brother, who has given up all the fun things in life to practice, practice, practice. It would be great to wake up one day and be a top-notch musician, but it doesn't happen that way. The reality is boring practice, no fun, and the likelihood that he'll become just another guy playing a musical instrument in a small-town band.

at least, we must be content with an array of theories targeted at different kinds of motives. The contrasts between hunger, sex, and achievement motivation will make this point clear.

### Achievement Motivation

Before you read further: What is your main goal in life? Sigmund Freud observed that a healthy life has two goals: love and work. We seek joy and satisfaction not only in pleasure or relationships, but also in a job well done. The desire to achieve one's goals, whether they involve getting an A in psychology or climbing to the top of a granite wall in Yosemite, is a psychological motive that empowers a wide variety of human actions. Unlike hunger and sex, achievement motives may be satisfied by the individual's knowledge that he or she has attained a goal of personal significance. Achievement may also be both motivated and satisfied by recognition, fame, praise, money, or other incentives. These motivators link an individual's goals and behaviors to feelings of self-worth.

**MEASURING THE NEED FOR ACHIEVEMENT** Psychologists Henry Murray and David McClelland pioneered the measurement of achievement motivation with a special instrument called the Thematic Apperception Test (TAT). On this test subjects are asked to tell stories in response to a series of ambiguous pictures. The stories, Murray and McClelland theorized, represent **projections** of the respondent's psychological needs. That is, they assumed that the stories would reflect the themes that were psychologically important for the storyteller. From responses to several of these TAT pictures, Murray and McClelland worked out measures of the **need for achievement (n Ach),** which they saw as the desire to attain a difficult, but desired, goal. The accompanying figure shows an example of how a high n Ach individual and a low n Ach individual might interpret a TAT picture.

What characteristics distinguish people with a high need for achievement? People high in n Ach show more persistence on difficult tasks (as long as they are meaningful tasks) than do people with low achievement needs (Cooper, 1983; French & Thomas, 1958; McClelland, 1985). In school, those with high n Ach tend to get better grades (Raynor, 1970). In their career paths, they take more competitive jobs (McClelland, 1965), assume leadership roles, and earn more rapid promotions (Andrews, 1967). As entrepreneurs, those with high n Ach become more successful (McClelland, 1987, 1993). In general, they are more likely than their low n Ach counterparts to delay short-term gratification in favor of long-range goals (Mischel, 1961). In a study of social mobility, not only were high-scoring n Ach people found to be more upwardly mobile than those with low scores, as you might expect, but their high n Ach sons were also more likely to rise above their fathers' occupational status than were low n Ach sons (McClelland et al., 1976).

In general, we may say that the need to achieve, like other motives, energizes and directs behavior. It also influences an individual's interpretations of situations and of other people's behavior. Even the economic growth of a society can be related to its encouragement of achievement motivation (McClelland, 1961, 1985).

**A CROSS-CULTURAL PERSPECTIVE ON ACHIEVEMENT** From a global viewpoint, our emphasis on achievement motivation may reflect a Western bias. Cross-cultural psychologist Harry Triandis points out that cultures differ in the value they place on achievement motivation. This difference, in turn, involves the most fundamental psychological distinction among cultures: their emphasis on *individualism* or *collectivism* (1990). Western cultures, including the United States, Canada, Britain, and Western Europe, emphasize **individualism.** People growing up in these cultures learn to place a high premium on individual achievement (along with the companion concepts of freedom and equality). By contrast, says Triandis, the cultures of Latin America, Asia, Africa, and the Middle East often emphasize **collectivism,** the values of group loyalty and subordination of self to the group. This means that the collectivistic cultures often discourage individual achievement. Even in the collectivist cultures of Japan, Hong Kong, and South Korea, where very high values are placed on achievement in school and business, the expectation is not of achieving individual honors but of bringing honor to the family.

Without a cross-cultural perspective, it would be easy for Americans to jump to the erroneous conclusion that motivation for individual achievement is a "natural" part of the human makeup. But Triandis's insight suggests that this is not true. Rather, collectivist cultures seem to value *group* achievement over *individual* achievement. More generally, cross-cultural research tells us that a complete understanding of motives—particularly those that involve learning—must always take cultural influences into account.

Chapter 4:
Psychological Development
Chapter 12:
Social Psychology

*Individualism and collectivism also have an effect on moral reasoning and on attributions.*

## Hunger Motivation

You will survive if you don't achieve, but you will die if you don't eat. Unlike achievement motivation, hunger serves as part of the body's own maintenance and survival mechanisms. And if eating were a behavior that had to be entirely learned, many people might starve to death before they mastered its complexities. When food is available and we are hungry, eating seems to come naturally. But, being "natural" does not make eating or hunger simple. In fact, hunger motivation and eating behavior have turned out to be far more complex than had originally been thought. Psychologists now incorporate the complexities of hunger and eating into a view we will call the *multiple systems approach.*

**THE MULTIPLE-SYSTEMS APPROACH TO HUNGER** In the current view, your brain combines hunger-related information of many kinds, including your body's energy requirements and nutritional state, your food preferences, food cues in your environment, and cultural demands. For example, your readiness to eat a slice of pizza depends on factors such as how long it has been since you last ate, whether you like pizza, what time of day it is (breakfast?), whether your friends are encouraging you to have a slice, and whether pizza is an acceptable food in your culture. Assembling all these data, the brain sends signals to neural, hormonal, organ, and muscle systems to start or stop food-seeking and eating. We will first touch on the main biological factors involved:

- Receptors in the brain monitor sugar and fat levels in the blood, sending signals to the *lateral hypothalamus*. If the sugar or fat levels in your blood are low, this brain structure sends out signals that produce the feeling of hunger (Nisbett, 1972).
- An internal biological "scale" continually weighs the body's fat stores and informs the central nervous system of the result. Whenever deposits stored

**Projection:** The process by which people attribute their own unconscious motives to other people or objects. The concept of projection originally comes from Freud's theory.

**Need for achievement (*n Ach*):** In Murray and McClelland's theory, a mental state that produces a psychological motive to excel or to reach some goal.

**Individualism:** The view, common in the Euro-American world, that places a high value on individual achievement and distinction.

**Collectivism:** The view, common in Asia, Africa, Latin America, and the Middle East, that values group loyalty and pride over individual distinction.

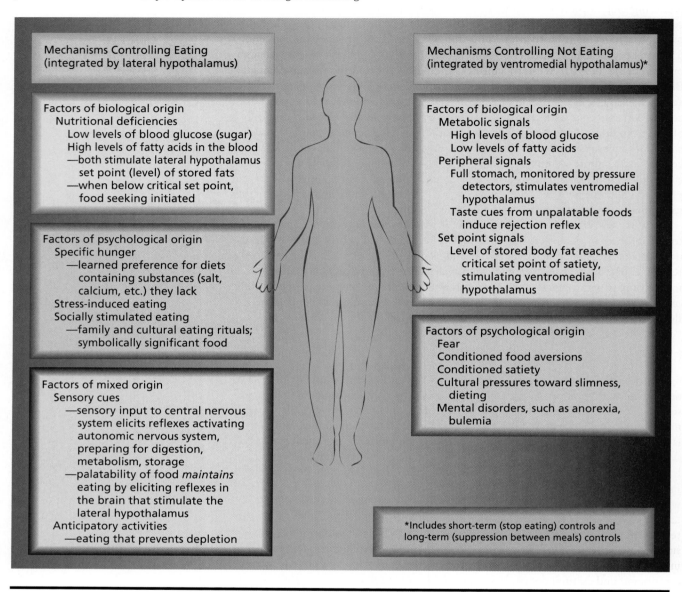

in specialized fat cells fall below a certain level, or **set point,** signals trigger eating behavior (Keesey & Powley, 1975). Recent work with mice suggests that one cause of obesity may be the lack of a protein that signals when the set point has been reached. Mice lacking this protein continue to eat even when not hungry (Adler & Salzhauer, 1995).

- Pressure detectors in the stomach signal fullness or a feeling of emptiness. These messages are sent to the brain, where they combine with information about blood nutrients and the status of the body's fat cells.
- Poorly understood mechanisms also give us preferences for sweet and high-fat foods. These preferences have a biological basis that evolved to steer our ancestors toward the calorie-dense foods that enabled them to survive when food supplies were unpredictable. This tendency has been exploited in modern times by the manufacturers of sweet and fatty snack foods.

**Set point:** Refers to the tendency of the body to maintain a certain level of body fat and body weight.

These hunger mechanisms work together to keep fat stores and body weight within a narrow range, specified by the biological set point. Different people have different set points, greatly influenced by genetics. Still, the set point is not the whole story of hunger and eating.

In addition to the biological mechanisms behind hunger, our emotional state can discourage or encourage eating. For example, both humans and animals refrain from eating when they are fearful. Other factors are at work, too. In many societies, such as the United States, social norms promote thinness. Images of ultra-thin fashion models can especially influence women and girls to believe they are "supposed" to look as if they do not eat much—a distorted ideal that has been linked to seriously self-destructive eating disorders, such as anorexia nervosa (Haller, 1992). Some situations become associated with eating through conditioning, so that they activate a hungry feeling, regardless of biological needs. This explains why you may feel a desire to snack when you watch TV or to have a third helping at Thanksgiving dinner. Thus, we eat not only when we are hungry, but we eat on cue. Observe your own responses to the lunch bell, watching others eat, or the sight and smell of food.

**Chapter 13: Psychopathology**
*Anorexia and bulimia are most common in Western cultures.*

**WEIGHT CONTROL** Many people, especially Americans, would like to lose weight for cosmetic or health reasons. At any given time, one-third of adult Americans say that they are on some sort of weight-control diet (Callaway, 1987; Jeffery, 1987). Truly, weight loss has become a national obsession (Brownell & Rodin, 1994). Yet, despite all we know about hunger, no one has yet discovered a weight-loss scheme that really works. Notwithstanding nationally advertised claims, no diet, surgical procedure, drug, or other weight-loss gimmick has ever produced long-term weight loss for a majority of the people who have tried it. Most experts would agree that, in the long run, body weight is largely determined by the biological set point, which can be set at vastly different levels in different people. Still, there is some good news for those who want to lose weight: Appetite and set point can be modified somewhat by a program of moderate exercise.

## Sexual Motivation

Sex is a most unusual drive. Unlike hunger or thirst, arousal of the sex drive is usually pleasurable. Even so, sexually aroused individuals typically seek to reduce the tension by sexual activity. And again unlike hunger and thirst, sex is not a homeostatic drive because it does not return the body to an equilibrium condition. Sexual motivation, however, can serve many other goals, including pleasure, reproduction, and social bonding.

In one respect, sexual motivation does have a kinship with hunger and thirst: It has its roots in survival. But even in this respect, sex is unique among biological drives because lack of sex poses no threat to the individual's survival. We can't live for long without food or water, but some people live their lives without sexual activity. Sexual motivation involves the survival of the *species*, not the individual.

All the biological drives—sex included—exert such powerful influences on behavior that they have become the focus of numerous social constraints and taboos. In the realm of sexuality we find extensive culture-specific rules and sanctions involving a wide variety of sexual practices. In fact, all societies regulate sexual activity, but the restrictions vary widely. For example, homosexuality has been historically suppressed in American culture, but it is widely accepted in Polynesian cultures. Even the discussion of sex can become mired in taboo, misinformation, and embarrassment. Scientists who study human sexuality have felt intense social and political pressures, which show no signs of abating in the present. The result is that the scientific understanding of sexuality, which we examine below, has been hard won.

Our cultural lessons and life experiences influence the meaning of sex in our lives.

**THE SCIENTIFIC STUDY OF SEXUALITY**   The first major scientific study of human sexuality was initiated by Alfred Kinsey and his colleagues (1948, 1953) in the mid-20th century, with interviews of some 17,000 Americans concerning their sexual behavior. To a generally shocked public these researchers revealed that many behaviors (oral sex, for example) previously considered rare, and even abnormal, were actually quite widespread—or at least reported to be. Kinsey's interview approach continues to be an important source of information about human sexual behavior, as seen in the major survey of American sexual behavior entitled *The Social Organization of Sexuality: Sexual Practices in the United States* (Laumann et al., 1994) and in a smaller, more readable companion volume called *Sex in America* (Michael et al., 1994). (See Table 8.2.)

But it was sex researchers William Masters and Virginia Johnson (1966, 1970, 1979) who really broke with tradition and taboo by bringing sex into their laboratory. There they studied sex by directly observing and recording the physiological patterns

**TABLE 8.2:**   Sexual Preferences and Behaviors of Adult Americans*

| FREQUENCY OF INTERCOURSE | NOT AT ALL | A FEW TIMES PER YEAR | A FEW TIMES PER MONTH | TWO OR MORE TIMES PER WEEK |
|---|---|---|---|---|
| Percentage by gender: | | | | |
| Men | 14 | 16 | 37 | 34 |
| Women | 10 | 18 | 36 | 37 |
| Percentage by age: | | | | |
| Men | | | | |
| 18–24 | 15 | 21 | 24 | 40 |
| 25–29 | 7 | 15 | 31 | 45 |
| 30–39 | 8 | 15 | 37 | 39 |
| 40–49 | 9 | 18 | 40 | 33 |
| 50–59 | 11 | 22 | 43 | 23 |
| Women | | | | |
| 18–24 | 11 | 16 | 32 | 41 |
| 25–29 | 5 | 10 | 38 | 47 |
| 30–39 | 9 | 16 | 36 | 39 |
| 40–49 | 15 | 16 | 44 | 25 |
| 50–59 | 30 | 22 | 35 | 14 |

| NUMBER OF SEXUAL PARTNERS SINCE AGE 18 | | | | | | |
|---|---|---|---|---|---|---|
| | 0 | 1 | 2–4 | 5–10 | 10–20 | 21+ |
| Percentage of Men | 3 | 20 | 21 | 23 | 16 | 17 |
| Percentage of Women | 3 | 31 | 31 | 20 | 6 | 3 |

| INFIDELITY WHILE MARRIED | |
|---|---|
| Men | 15.1% |
| Women | 2.7% |

| SEXUAL ORIENTATION | MALES | FEMALES |
|---|---|---|
| Heterosexual | 96.9 | 98.6 |
| Homosexual | 2.0 | .9 |
| Bisexual | .8 | .5 |

*Adapted from Michael et. al, 1994. Table based on survey of 3,432 scientifically selected adult respondents.

of people engaging in sexual activity of various types, including masturbation and intercourse. By doing so, they discovered not what people *said* about sex (which carries obvious problems of response bias) but how people actually *reacted physically* during sex. In the wake of Masters and Johnson's daring departure from tradition, the study of human sexual behavior has become much more accepted as a legitimate field of scientific inquiry.

Based on their observations, Masters and Johnson described four phases of human sexual responding, which they collectively called the **sexual response cycle** (see Figure 8.9). These are the distinguishing events of each phase:

- In the *excitement phase*, blood vessel changes in the pelvic region cause the clitoris to swell and the penis to become erect. Blood and other fluids also become congested in the testicles and vagina.

FIGURE 8.9:    Phases of Human Sexual Response

The phases of sexual response in males and females have similar patterns. The primary differences are in the time it takes for males and females to reach each phase and in the greater likelihood that females will achieve multiple orgasms.

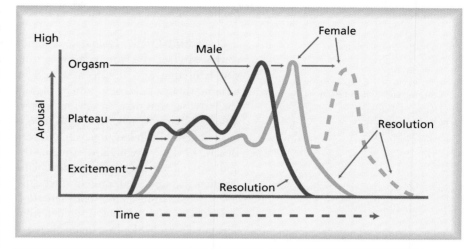

- During the *plateau phase*, a maximal level of arousal is reached. Rapid increases occur in heartbeat, respiration, blood pressure, glandular secretions, and muscle tension.
- When they reach the *orgasm phase*, males and females experience a very intense and pleasurable sense of release from the cumulative sexual tension. Orgasm, characterized by rhythmic genital contractions, culminates in ejaculation of semen in men and can involve clitoral and vaginal sensations in women.
- During the *resolution phase*, the body gradually returns to its preexcitement state, as fluids dissipate from the sex organs. At the same time, blood pressure and heart rate, which had increased dramatically during sexual arousal, drop to their customary levels. Note how similar men's and women's physical responses are at each phase of the sexual response cycle.

It is important to emphasize that Masters and Johnson focused on physiological arousal and responses. They did not emphasize the psychological aspects of sexuality—for example, emotional responses, sexual desire, or the motivation to seek out a partner or make oneself available for sexual experience. Still, from their biological observations of subjects' sexual behavior, Masters and Johnson were able to draw several significant conclusions:

- Men and women have remarkably similar patterns of biological response, regardless of the source of sexual arousal—whether it be intercourse or masturbation. This is clearly seen in the four phases of the sexual response cycle.
- Although the phases of the sexual response cycle are similar in the two sexes, women tend to respond more slowly but often remain aroused longer.
- Many women can have multiple orgasms in a short time period, while men rarely do.
- Size of the genitals or other physical sex characteristics (such as vagina, breasts, penis) is generally unrelated to any aspect of sexual performance (except, perhaps, attitude about one's sexual capability).

In addition, Masters & Johnson were able to use their discoveries about sexual behavior to develop effective behavioral therapies for a variety of sexual disorders, including

**Sexual response cycle:** The four-stage sequence of arousal, plateau, orgasm, and resolution occurring in both men and women.

**Chapter 14:**
**Therapies for Mental Disorder**

*Behavior therapy is effective for a variety of other problems, such as phobias and other anxiety disorders.*

**Chapter 6:**
**Learning and Remembering**

*Classical conditioning involves learning to give an old response to a new (conditioned) stimulus.*

**Chapter 3:**
**States of Mind**

*Altered states of consciousness also include sleep, hypnosis, meditation, and drug states.*

male erectile disorder (inability to achieve or maintain an erection), premature ejaculation, and female orgasmic disorder.

While Masters and Johnson focused on the physiological side of sex, other researchers have studied the cognitive and social components. Much of this work has emphasized how our sexual lives are influenced by learning. We see this, for example, in responses to cues that provoke sexual arousal.

**SEXUAL CUES**   Human sexual motivation does not come primarily from the genitals. In fact, the brain is the major human sex organ. What turns you on is what your brain finds sexually arousing, and how you respond is determined both by your inherited sexual tendencies and by what your brain has learned. The sequence of sexual activities that may lead to orgasm can begin with a single unconditioned stimulus—usually touch—but may also involve a variety of conditioned stimuli. In the form of genital caresses, touch is a universal component of sexual foreplay (Ford & Beach, 1951). Virtually any stimulus that becomes associated with genital touch and orgasm can become a conditioned stimulus that motivates sexual activity—whether the stimulus is present physically or only in memory or fantasy.

Research shows that both sensations (such as erotic pictures) and sexual fantasies during masturbation often determine what a person finds sexually stimulating (Storms, 1980, 1981). Inanimate objects, textures, sounds, visual images, odors—any tangible or imagined stimulus—can become the focus of arousal through this conditioned association. For reasons that are poorly understood, some people learn to become aroused only by conditioned stimuli, such as pain or the sight of undergarments (Rachman, 1966).

For most people, the goal of sexual activity is to achieve a cognitive state they associate with sexual satisfaction—a state that some compare to a profoundly altered state of consciousness (Davidson, 1980, 1981). The way we interpret experiences, the meaning we bring to specific sexual events, our sexual beliefs and values, our imagination, and our expectations all play parts in both our sexual behavior and the mental state we experience during sex (Byrne, 1981). Thus, sex seems to have the dual goals of meeting physiological needs and satisfying cognitive desires.

**SEXUAL SCRIPTS**   Generalized sexual arousal can be channeled into specific behaviors (such as kissing or masturbation) that depend on how the individual has learned to think about sexual matters. **Sexual scripts** are socially learned programs of sexual interpretation and responsiveness. How do you know how you are "supposed" to feel when aroused? What do you do when you feel that way? Your culture provides you with many clues from which you develop the sexual scripts for your own behavior. Images from movies and television suggest the importance of kissing and touching, and how to engage in these activities—or at least how beautiful actors and actresses (with many hours of "method" rehearsal) manage to engage in these displays. Advertisements, MTV, and gossip with acquaintances also contribute to many young people's sexual scripts. Unfortunately, while these scripts suggest images and goals, they seldom provide reliable and realistic information (Gagnon, 1977). We assemble aspects of these scripts through social interaction over a lifetime. The attitudes and values embodied in one's sexual scripts define one's general approach to sexuality.

When partners have different scripts for an interaction, adjustment problems can develop. For example, touch can have different meanings for men and women, depending on the sexual scripts they have acquired. Misunderstandings can arise when one person's comment or "friendly touch" is perceived by the other as a "sexual advance" (Nguyen, Heslin, & Nguyen, 1975).

**AN EVOLUTIONARY PERSPECTIVE ON SEXUALITY**   While the theory of sexual scripts says that sexual behavior patterns can be learned, the evolutionary perspective looks for the origins of sexual motivation in our genes. (In fact, both heredity

**Sexual scripts:** Socially learned programs of sexual interpretation and responsiveness.

and learning affect our sexual behaviors.) Some observers (Archer, 1996; Buss & Schmitt, 1993) argue that different genetic pressures have resulted in different mating strategies and, therefore, different gender roles, for males and females.

Biologically speaking, the goal of both sexes is to leave as many offspring as possible. Yet, the potential physical costs of mating are quite different for males and females. As a result, the sexes have evolved different—and sometimes conflicting—mating strategies. Because females can produce only a few children over a lifetime and because they make a huge biological investment in pregnancy and a substantial commitment of time and energy in child-rearing, the best sexual strategy for females involves caution in mate selection. For males, however, the costs and benefits are much different because they cannot become pregnant. For them, the theory says, the biggest payoff results from copulating as often as possible with mates who are in prime breeding condition. As a result, men tend to seek young and physically well-developed partners, while females may seek somewhat older mates who can offer resources, status, and protection for offspring. Not incidentally, these agendas often produce conflict, bringing all of the relationship problems associated with promiscuity and sexual jealousy.

Although the evolutionary perspective may seem cold and harsh in its view of sexual motivation, it does account for many of the gender differences in mating behaviors, such as the larger number of sexual partners reported by men than women. Even so, the evolutionary perspective does not require that we be prisoners of our biology. Neither does it preclude trusting and loving relationships. Biology does not prohibit the learning of alternative sex roles and scripts. Therefore, a complete understanding of sexual motivation must include both its evolutionary roots and, especially in humans, the many variations that occur through learning.

**Chapter 1:**
**Mind, Behavior, and Science**
*Evolutionary theory says that adaptive traits will spread through the population by natural selection.*

**Sexual orientation:** One's erotic attraction toward members of the same sex (a homosexual orientation), the opposite sex (heterosexual orientation), or both sexes (a bisexual orientation).

**PSYCHOLOGY IN YOUR LIFE**

## The Origins of Sexual Orientation

Heterosexuality and homosexuality represent two forms of **sexual orientation,** which refers to the direction or object of one's sexual interests. Ever since Alfred Kinsey's first reports, we have known that human sexual orientation is a complex issue. To complicate matters, cross-cultural studies reveal considerable variability in sexual orientation. In parts of New Guinea, for example, homosexuality is nearly universal among young males (Money, 1987). Among Americans, estimates put the figure between about 1 and 10 percent—depending on whether homosexuality is defined as one's primary orientation or as any same-sex erotic behavior during one's lifetime (see Table 8.2).

What does the available evidence tell us about the origins of sexual orientation? The notion that different parenting styles or family configurations cause children to turn toward heterosexuality or homosexuality has *not* found strong research support (see Bailey et al., 1995; Bell et al., 1981; Golombok & Tasker, 1996; Isay, 1990). Simi-

The origins of sexual orientation are unclear, although some evidence points to biological factors. What is clear is that research on sexual orientation often generates controversy.

*continued*

larly, researchers have come up empty handed in their attempts to link human sexual orientation to other specific environmental factors, such as early sexual experiences.

At the same time, attempts to identify biological origins of sexual feelings in the genes and the brain have shown some promise. For example, Richard Pillard and Michael Bailey (1991) did a genetic study of sexual orientation, involving male identical twins. They discovered that when one twin is homosexual the chances of the other being homosexual is about 50%—as compared with roughly 5 or 6% in the general population. This study also found that the rate drops to 22% for fraternal twins and 11% for adoptive brothers of homosexuals. Encouraged by these results, the researchers later studied female twin pairs—with essentially the same results (Bower, 1992).

Looking through a different biological window on sexual orientation, neurobiologist Simon LeVay (1991; LeVay & Hamer, 1995) found that a part of the hypothalamus in the brains of homosexual men was smaller than the same structure in heterosexual men. Critics of LeVay's research warn of confounding due to the fact that most of his homosexual subjects were AIDS victims and that the disease may have affected the structure under study.

Research in this area remains controversial because of the strong feelings and sexual politics involved. Further, it has attracted scientific criticism because it is correlational—rather than experimental— so the data cannot establish cause and effect with certainty. Also, some observers question whether gay men and lesbians should have to justify their behavior by seeking a biological root for it (Byne, 1995). On one small biological point all agree: Sexual orientation is *not* due to variations in levels of testosterone in adults (Meyer-Bahlburg, 1977, 1979). (*See Chapter 1, Mind, Behavior, and Science.*)

In general, psychological research has given us a deeper understanding of sexual orientation. We now see its development as a complex process that, in all probability, has no single or simple cause. While we currently know much about what does *not* influence sexual orientation, we can see that, with human sexuality in general, sexual orientation grows developmentally out of multiple influences in biology, conditioning, and culture.

1. RECALL: *Which of the following is often considered a* biological *drive?*
   a. hunger
   b. safety
   c. n Ach
   d. fear

2. RECALL: *How did Murray and McClelland measure* n Ach?
   a. with a polygraph
   b. with the Thematic Apperception Test
   c. by measuring achievement-related hormones in the blood
   d. by using grade-point averages (GPAs)

3. RECALL: *According to Masters and Johnson's research, the sexual response cycles of men and women are essentially the same, except for:*
   a. women's ability for multiple orgasms.
   b. men's sexual receptivity at any time of the month.
   c. men's responsiveness to many kinds of stimulation.
   d. women's need for commitment in a sexual relationship.

4. ANALYSIS: *Which of the following motives would most likely be influenced by living in an individualistic culture versus a collectivist culture?*
   a. hunger
   b. thirst
   c. sex
   d. n Ach

5. UNDERSTANDING THE CORE CONCEPT: *In which of the following would biological factors be* least *important in accounting for the motivational differences between individuals?*
   a. hunger
   b. thirst
   c. sex
   d. n Ach

ANSWERS: 1. a    2. b    3. a    4. d    5. d

# USING PSYCHOLOGY TO LEARN PSYCHOLOGY

## *Motivating Yourself*

Psychologists use the term "intrinsic motivation" to explain why people engage in activities that bring no external reward. Playing video games, singing in the shower, talking with friends, doing crossword puzzles, or keeping a secret diary are intrinsically motivated activities. Achievement of the highest order can stem from intrinsic motivation when a person becomes deeply interested in the job.

Intrinsically motivating activities have been described as producing a special state of mind called **flow,** a near-ecstatic state achieved by total focus on the present activity with an increase in creative ability (Csikszentmihalyi, 1990, 1998). (Note the parallel with Maslow's notion of *self-actualization.*) Flow experiences are characterized by a pleasurable loss of self-awareness and of any awareness of time, along with a deep concentration on the task rather than its outcomes. *(See Chapter 9, Stress, Health, and Well-Being.)* As you might expect, flow is inherent in the creative process. Although some people turn to drugs or alcohol to experience an artificial flow feeling, meaningful work produces more satisfying and more sustained flow experiences. In fact, one type of flow experience identified by Csikszentmihalyi (1990) is very similar to the goal of *n Ach* as identified by McClelland (1985), namely the intrinsic pleasure obtained from mastering a challenging task or doing something well.

What is the link with studying and learning? If you find yourself lacking in motivation to learn the material for some class, the extrinsic promise of grades may not be enough to prod you to study as much as necessary. You may, however, be able to trick yourself into developing some intrinsic motivation and "flow" by posing this question: In the field you are studying, what do people who are specialists find interesting? Among other things, the experts are fascinated by an unsolved mystery or an exciting practical application. A psychologist, for example, might wonder: What motivates violent behavior? Or how can we increase people's motivation to achieve?

If you find yourself lacking motivation in all your classes, it may be time to do some honest reassessment. Ask yourself: Are you embarking on a program that will be interesting enough to sustain your motivation for four years—and beyond, if graduate school is a requisite for your chosen field? One helpful source of information about your interests can be obtained from a good vocational interest inventory, which can tell you whether your pattern of interests (intrinsic motivation) is similar to people who are successful in the field you have chosen. The counseling or career center at your school should be able to give you such an instrument and help you interpret the results.

**Flow:** In Csikszentmihalyi's theory, an intense focus on an activity, accompanied by increased creativity and near-ecstatic feelings. Flow involves intrinsic motivation.

## *CHAPTER SUMMARY*

 **KEY QUESTION**

### WHAT DO OUR EMOTIONS DO FOR US?

- Emotion and motivation are complementary processes that arouse the organism and direct its behavior. Emotions are normally adaptive, but if too intense or prolonged they may be destructive. From an evolutionary standpoint, the function of motives and emotions is to help organisms make responses that promote their survival and reproduction. Socially, emotional expressions serve to communicate feelings and intentions. Research shows that certain basic facial expressions are understood across cultures.

 **CORE CONCEPT** Emotions mark situations that are important to us, command our attention, and arouse us to action; they also convey our intentions to others.

 **KEY QUESTION** WHERE DO OUR EMOTIONS COME FROM?

- Biologically, emotions come from arousal of portions of the nervous system and the endocrine system. Emotions also come from visceral and muscular changes. Cognitively, emotions come from appraisal of both external stimulus cues and internal signs of arousal. A current controversy involves the importance of cognition in emotion. Studies show that males and females may differ in their displays of emotion, although it is often difficult to tell whether these differences are mainly the result of biology or of social/cultural expectations.

 **CORE CONCEPT** Emotions result from an interaction of biological, mental, behavioral, and social/cultural process.

 **KEY QUESTION** HOW MUCH CONTROL DO WE HAVE OVER OUR EMOTIONS?

- People can learn to control their emotions, which can lead to intentional deception. No sure method of detecting deception exists. The polygraph industry, however, is built on the dubious premise that people who are lying will show signs of emotional arousal. On the other hand, *emotional intelligence*, the ability to keep one's emotions from getting out of control, is vital for maintaining good social relationships.

 **CORE CONCEPT** Although emotional responses are not always consciously regulated, we can learn to control them.

 **KEY QUESTION** MOTIVATION: WHAT MAKES US ACT AS WE DO?

- Psychologists use the concept of *motivation* to emphasize the processes that select and direct behavior. Theories of motivation have explained motivational processes in terms of instincts, drives, and cognitive factors. Maslow's humanistic theory attempted to bring together the whole range of human motives into a *hierarchy of needs*—with only partial success. Meanwhile, research has pointed out an often-overlooked factor in motivation: the dampening effect of *extrinsic* rewards.

 **CORE CONCEPT** Motivation takes many forms, but all involve inferred mental processes that select and direct our behavior.

 **KEY QUESTION** HOW ARE ACHIEVEMENT, HUNGER, AND SEX ALIKE? DIFFERENT?

- Achievement is primarily a cognitive motive. Individuals and societies vary greatly in their interest in achievement motivation. In contrast, eating is influenced at many levels —by biological processes, peripheral cues, social influences and learning. Many Americans are especially interested in the control of hunger and body weight, although no weight-loss system yet devised is effective with most people over the long run. Unlike hunger and weight control, the sexual drive is not homeostatic, even though sexual motivation has roots in biology. Human sexual behavior, particularly in humans, displays amazing variability. Much of the variability comes from the different sexual "scripts" that people learn. The available evidence suggests, however, that sexual orientation has a biological basis, although the roles of social influence and learning are disputed.

 **CORE CONCEPT** No single theory accounts for all forms of motivation, because different motives involve different mixes of biological, mental, behavioral, and social/cultural influences.

# REVIEW TEST

For each of the following items, choose the single best answer. The answer key appears at the end.

1. While emotion emphasizes _____, motivation emphasizes _____.
   a. behavior/cognition
   b. arousal/action
   c. neural activity/hormones
   d. needs/drives

2. According to the evolutionary perspective, emotions
   a. help organisms survive in important, recurring situations.
   b. add color and interest to our otherwise drab lives.
   c. give us strong feelings about our experiences.
   d. occur in humans, but not in "lower" animals.

3. Which of the following is a brain structure involved in emotions, attack, self-defense, and flight?
   a. the occipital cortex
   b. the limbic system
   c. the endocrine system
   d. the cerebellum

4. Which theory of emotion first called attention to the idea that our physical responses can influence our emotions?
   a. the instinct theory
   b. Maslow's theory
   c. Zajonc and Izard's theory
   d. the James-Lange theory

5. Psychologists use the concept of motivation for five basic purposes. Which of the following is *not* one of them?
   a. to relate behavior to internal biological mechanisms
   b. to infer internal states from observable behavior
   c. to explain perseverance despite adversity
   d. to make people work harder

6. Which approach is most compatible with the concept of *homeostasis*?
   a. instinct theory
   b. drive theory
   c. locus-of-control theory
   d. Maslow's humanistic theory

7. Which one of the following is an example of *intrinsic* motivation?
   a. studying because there is a test tomorrow
   b. studying because your friend asked you to study with her
   c. studying because you want to get good grades
   d. studying because you find the subject interesting

8. Unlike achievement motivation, hunger and sex have a strong _____ basis.
   a. cognitive
   b. environmental
   c. biological
   d. perceptual

9. Sexual motivation is different from the other basic drives because it
   a. is not a homeostatic drive.
   b. is more intense.
   c. has no biological basis.
   d. is the only drive for which satisfaction of the drive can be pleasurable.

10. People who are high in the need for achievement have been found to be more likely to
    a. demand immediate gratification for their desires.
    b. persist in monotonous tasks.
    c. have excellent interpersonal skills.
    d. get better grades in school.

ANSWERS:    1. b    2. a    3. b    4. d    5. d    6. b
7. d    8. c    9. a    10. d

# IF YOU'RE INTERESTED . . .

## BOOKS

Ackerman, D. (1994). *A natural history of love*. New York: Random House.

> Fascinating reading about a basic emotional experience by poet Ackerman, A Natural History looks at the history of love, ancient and modern ideas about how it influences behavior, its evolution and biochemistry, the intertwining of sex and love, courtship, and varieties of love—including love of children, strangers, and pets.

Barer-Stein, T. (1999). *You eat what you are: People, culture, and food traditions*. Toronto, Canada: Culture Concepts.

> Barer-Stein presents an exploration of how our culture determines not only what we eat but what we want to eat, how we hunger, and the role of food in our individual lives.

Csikszentmihalyi, M. (1990). *Flow: the psychology of optimal experience*. New York: Harper & Row.

> Using a combination of interviews and experience-sampling techniques, Csikszentmihalyi has managed to get some solid information about a subjective mental state.

Dalai Lama and Cutler, H. C. (1998). *The art of happiness: A handbook for living*. New York: Riverhead Books.

> Why are so many people unhappy and lonely, and how can the average person escape such pain without undergoing a major life change? Through a series of interviews, the authors explore questions of the meaning, motives, and interconnectedness of life.

Fein, M. L. (1993). *I.A.M.: A common sense guide to coping with anger (Integrated Anger Management)*. Westport, CT: Praeger/Greenwood.

> Fein has written a practical guide for people who want to manage their tempers.

Goleman, D. (1995). *Emotional intelligence*. New York: Bantam Books.

> Daniel Goleman, award-winning behavioral science reporter for the New York Times and former editor of Psychology Today, carefully documents the many forms, factors, and expressions of human emotion, including appropriate emotions and self-control, temperament, family and relationships, and whether (and how) emotional intelligence can be taught.

Goleman, D. (1998). *Working with emotional intelligence*. New York: Bantam Books.

> The concepts of Goleman's previous book (above) are applied to workplace experiences for virtually any job.

Hirschmann, J. R., & Munter, C. H. (1995). *When women stop hating their bodies*. New York: Fawcett Columbine.

> Subtitled "Freeing Yourself from Food and Weight Obsession," this book explores how the origins of many women's (and girls') addictions to diets and weight loss lie in their learned contempt for their own bodies and their desire to achieve an impossible "perfect" body. The solutions, the authors argue, are found in abandoning mindless acceptance of fashions or attitudes that suggest real bodies are somehow flawed and ugly and instead cultivating a solid sense of self-esteem based on realism, self-acceptance, and self-love.

Jamison, K. R. (1999). *On moods*. New York: Random House.

> The doctor-author who revolutionized writing about manic-depressive illness (bipolar disorder) in her book An Unquiet Mind now explores the range and power of lasting emotions and moods in general.

Lefkowitz, B. (1998). *Our guys: The Glen Ridge rape and the secret life of the perfect suburb*. New York: Vintage Books.

> Why did a group of popular, successful high-school football players take advantage of a young mentally retarded woman who was a fan—raping her with a baseball bat and a broomstick in the basement rec room where they had lured her? The author explores the influences and urges in the lives of young men who had been described as "pure gold" by the doting parents prior to the hideous assault that made national news.

Masson, J. M., & McCarthy, S. (1995). *When elephants weep: The emotional lives of animals*. New York: Delacorte Press.

> This manifesto and casebook by former psychoanalyst Masson and biologist McCarthy details the persuasive evidence of feelings—from fear and greed to love and altruism—among nonhuman species. Both scholarly and personal, this touching and affecting work will forever change the way you view your world, your diet, and what it means to be both human and humane.

Stacey, M. (1994). *Consumed*. New York: Simon & Schuster.

> Stacey provides a fascinating tour of the meanings of food to modern Americans: a chronology of cuisines; "healthy" obsessions and catchwords ("fiber," "low fat"); food fads (oat bran, junk food); and stories of "food designers," obsessive dieters, and scientists who feed pastry to rats. This is a thought-provoking essay on Americans' view of food not as sustenance or sensuality, but demon or angel.

Tannahill, R. (1992). *Sex in history*. New York: Scarborough House.

This illustrated volume (according to the Sunday Times [London]) is a treasure trove of historical information, history, cultural influences, customs, and rituals developed around sex worldwide. It makes for fascinating reading, not only about sex but about the origins of ideas and ideals of romantic love.

Thomas, E. M. (1993). *The hidden life of dogs*. New York: Simon & Schuster.

Thomas, E. M. (1994). *The tribe of tiger: Cats and their culture*. New York: Simon & Schuster.

Elizabeth Marshall Thomas's two best-selling works on our favorite companion animals explore the similarities and contrasts between domestic species and wild animals, as well as debunking many myths about the personalities, motives, and emotions of dogs and cats.

Tuan, Y.-F. (1998). *Escapism*. Baltimore: Johns Hopkins University Press.

"A human being," writes the author, "is an animal who is congenitally indisposed to accept reality as it is." When we cannot accept reality, we seek to escape—but from what? And how? Tuan finds this motivation to escape influencing a wide range of behaviors, from a sensible appreciation of nature to wild, impulsive, and irrational wishful thinking.

Weinrich, J. D. (1987). *Sexual landscapes: Why we are what we are, why we love whom we love*. New York: Charles Scribner's Sons.

Weinrich's provocative and sensible review of historical and scientific research includes such topics as sexual orientation and bisexuality, sexual taboos, pornography, sissies and tomboys, and the power of sexual arousal in everyday life and identity.

## VIDEOS

*The bear.* (1989, color, 93 min.). Directed by Jean Jacques Annaud; starring Douce, Bart, Tcheky Karyo, Jack Wallace, Andre Lacombe.

An orphaned grizzly cub and the adult male Kodiak bear who becomes his protector must survive and elude hunters in late-19th-century British Columbia. This award-winning film, based on the American novel The Grizzly King by James Oliver Curwood, is probably the best-ever cinematic presentation of wild animals' motivations and emotions and humans' difficulty in understanding them.

*Everything you always wanted to know about sex (but were afraid to ask).* (1972, color, 87 min.). Directed by Woody Allen; starring Woody Allen, Lou Jacobi, Louise Lasser, Tony Randall, Lynn Redgrave, Burt Reynolds, Gene Wilder.

This silly—but funny—film spoofs the overly serious tone of the book of the same name by Dr. David Reuben (but resembles the book only in occasional question-and-answer format). On a larger scale, it spoofs Americans' hypocritical and moralizing attitudes about sex—even as we are admittedly so fascinated by it.

*In & out.* (1997, color, 90 min.). Directed by Frank Oz; starring Kevin Kline, Joan Cusack, Tom Selleck, Matt Dillon.

A popular high school teacher in a small town is "outed" when a former student identifies him as gay just days before the teacher is to be married to his long-time fiancée. While maintaining a humorous and light tone, the film manages to explore confusion about sexual identity, stereotypes and prejudices, and the interrelationship of identity and intimacy.

**CORE** CONCEPTS

**PSYCHOLOGY IN YOUR LIFE**

IS IT THE STRESS OR
THE STRESSOR?

The effects of stress (an internal response) depend more on the intensity and duration of stress than on its source (the stressor).

**Change Can Be Hazardous to Your Health:** Some changes count more than others, but they all count.

HOW DOES STRESS AFFECT
US PHYSICALLY?

Stress can help us meet challenges and grow stronger, but too much stress—distress—can have harmful physical consequences.

**When Stress Is Good for You:** When stress is mild and brief it can becomes *eustress,* which has beneficial effects.

HOW DO WE RESPOND
PSYCHOLOGICALLY
TO STRESS?

Our psychological responses under stress depend on personality, perceptions, and the ways we have learned to respond.

**Ego Defenses under Stress:** Freud called our attention to some common reactions seen in people under stress.

HOW CAN WE COPE
EFFECTIVELY WITH STRESS?

All the factors that promote health and well-being will also combat distress—and they are largely under our control.

**Happiness and Well-Being:** As far as happiness is concerned, some things are more important than money.

USING PSYCHOLOGY TO LEARN PSYCHOLOGY:
COPING WITH TEST ANXIETY

# 9 Stress, Health, & Well-Being

*I*magine you are at a hospital visiting a sick friend who is suffering from much pain, is anxious about the prognosis for the illness, and is depressed over all the schoolwork being missed. Suddenly the door bursts open as the doctor in the white lab coat enters . . . wearing a red bulb nose, big squeaky shoes, a silly hat, and a wild tie that also makes noises. You can't help laughing, and so does your friend at this doctor-clown's outrageous antics. He violates every expectation about how doctors ought to act given their high status and the serious nature of their illness-treating profession.

But this is no ordinary physician; he is Hunter "Patch" Adams, a firm believer in the healing powers of humor, laughter, compassion, and the spiritual connection between patient and physician. Patch treats people, not just disease. He prescribes big belly laughs as well as a gaggle of giggles to give his patients a moment of relief from pain. He might appear on the ward dressed like a gorilla or fill a patient's room full of balloons or a bathtub brimming with noodles. Doing so clearly wipes away the professional distance and emotional detachment that is typical for doctors who regularly deal with sick patients. Instead, Patch is "in their face," openly showing his concern, empathy, friendship, and even love, of those who come to his medical center. In 1971 Patch and some colleagues formed the Gesundheit Institute (German for "health") in Virginia. This home-based family medical practice has worked with tens of thousands of people without any payment, malpractice insurance, or even formal facilities. (Royalties from the movie Patch Adams, starring Robin Williams, will help fund a 40-bed free hospital of the Gesundheit Institute.)

Patch's passion for helping others as a doctor started while he was institutionalized for clinical depression as a teenager. He became convinced that many sick patients suffer most from loneliness, boredom, and fear, which pills don't cure. Clearly Patch had to take many risks and to defy authority throughout his medical training and early career. Because he was not accepted as part of the medical system, he created a new system where a doctor could also clown around with patients and fulfill patients' fantasies. His inspiring books paint the portrait of the ideal medical practice that contributes to the creation of healthy, supportive, joy-filled communities by practicing the art of healing, listening, caring, and having fun with life (Adams, 1998; Adams & Mylander, 1998).

*Patch Adams understands the central message of this chapter—that negative emotional experiences and chronic stress impact adversely on the hormone system, nervous system, and immune system and create unhealthy changes in body and mind. He knows that emotions can trigger the release of neurotransmitters from neurons in the brain, altering the metabolic activity of cells in positive or negative directions (Pert, 1997). But—here is the bright spot—research has also shown that positive emotions, and especially laughter, can create neurochemical changes that buffer the immunosuppressive effects of stress, thereby promoting healthy reactions (Berk, 1996; Wooten, 1994, 1996). The following pages will give you the details of this emotional connection between mind and body.*

**Chapter 8:**
**Emotion and Motivation**

*Emotions are normally adaptive responses.*

Emotional arousal usually works to our advantage. It alerts us to important events and helps record them in memory; it moves us to action and, at the same time, communicates our intentions to others. More subjectively, the arousal of emotions also adds variety, pleasure, and intensity to our lives. Yet, with all their advantages, emotions have a dark side. Particularly in threatening situations, we can have emotional responses—such as fear, jealousy, envy, despair, or depression—that carry a potential threat to our mental and physical health. Physiologist Walter Canon originally introduced the term "stress" to refer to the physiological arousal that accompanies such negative emotions. We will see that modern psychologists have since broadened Canon's definition to include not only our physical responses but our mental responses.

Traffic can be a hassle—and a significant source of stress for some people.

Surprisingly, even the stress response is basically adaptive—helping us mobilize our defensive resources in the face of threat. But, under conditions of extreme or prolonged arousal, our stress defenses can turn against us, attacking body and mind. We can see this destructive form of the stress response—often called *distress*—at work among the frantic workers who have heart attacks in the pressure-cooker environment of corporate offices and air traffic control towers. We can also find the damaging consequences of stress in day-to-day living when people must cope with debilitating conditions in crime-ridden neighborhoods, stressful jobs, poverty, or chronic disease.

But have you ever wondered why some people roll easily through stressful events, while others are derailed by even minor hassles? Stuck in an endless traffic jam, some drivers calmly daydream or listen to their radios; others frantically hit their horns or crane their necks for a better view of the obstruction. The stressful effects of an unpleasant event are, to a large extent, a personal matter. How much stress we experience is determined not only by the quality and intensity of the stressful situation but by how we interpret it, the resources we have available to deal with it, and the consequent difficulty of meeting the demands placed on us. Figure 9.1 shows an overview of the whole stress process—stressors, stress, cognitive appraisal (mental evaluation of the situation), resources, and stress responses.

## FIGURE 9.1: A Model of Stress

Cognitive appraisal of the stress situation interacts with the stressor and the physical, social, and personal resources available for dealing with the stressor. Individuals respond to threats on various levels—physical, behavioral, emotional, and cognitive. Some responses are adaptive, and others are maladaptive or even lethal.

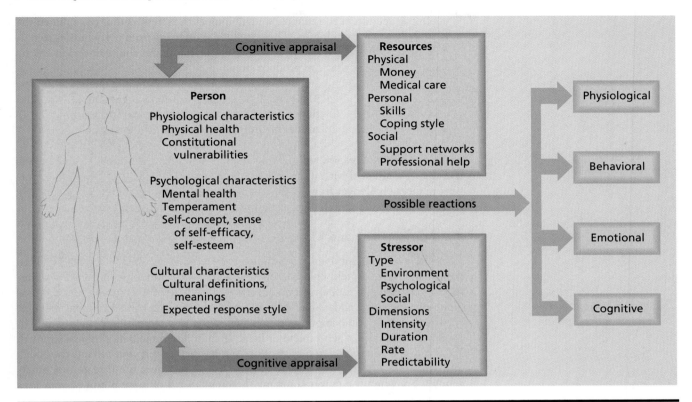

KEY QUESTION

## IS IT THE STRESS OR THE STRESSOR?

What images come to mind when you hear the word "stress"? Most people think of the pressures in their lives: difficult jobs, unhappy relationships, financial woes, health problems, final exams, grades, and scholarship deadlines. You may have some visceral associations with stress, too: a churning stomach, perspiration, headache, or high blood pressure. Patch Adams reminds us that stress is also linked with physical illness. In fact, stress is associated with many aspects of modern society, and it is also associated with our internal reactions. This is what makes stress a slippery concept.

We use the word "stress" loosely in everyday conversation (Lazarus et al.,1985). Confusion arises because the word has two meanings. In common usage, stress refers to a *situation*. For example, if your employer or professor has been giving you a difficult time, you may say that you are "under stress," as though you were being squashed by a heavy object. In this sense, stress means an external threat or pressure, an unpleasant event.

We psychologists, however, use the term in another way: For us, stress is a *response*. We see **stress** as the arousal—both physical and mental—that occurs in response to a challenging or threatening situation (Krantz, Grunberg, & Baum, 1985). This is not hair-splitting: we find it useful to make a distinction between stressful

**Stress:** A physical and mental response to a challenging or threatening situation.

stimuli or situations, which we call **stressors,** and the response to those stimuli, which we call *stress* or a *stress response*. So, a *stressor* is the large, angry man climbing out of the car you just bashed into; *stress* is your response to that large, angry man: the knot in your stomach, your racing heart, and the cold sweat on your palms. A *stressor* is your demanding boss; *stress* is your headache.

In this section of the chapter we will look at the stressors that have drawn the most attention of psychologists. These include everything from petty hassles to natural disasters. The Core Concept for this section emphasizes the connection among the many conditions that can produce stress:

**CORE CONCEPT**

The effects of stress (an internal response) depend more on the intensity and duration of stress than on its source (the stressor).

In the following pages, we will see that the problem is not stress, but *excessive* stress and the ways we deal with it. Basic stress is an unavoidable part of living. Every organism faces challenges from its external environment and from its personal needs; these are the challenges that organisms must solve to survive and thrive.

## Stressors Ancient and Modern

Early humans survived mortal dangers by responding quickly and decisively to potentially lethal attacks by predators or hostile tribes, and some of the ways we respond to stressors in modern times are the result of their evolutionary legacy. Modern life, of course, adds some new dangers: demanding jobs, financial worries, crowded airports, and computer crashes. Many of today's stressors are more likely to challenge our sense of self-esteem or lifestyle than our immediate physical survival. Yet, while we are exposed to new stressors, our basic stress response reflects the body's millennia-old tendency to become quickly aroused to meet life-threatening emergencies. So, when the power company threatens to cut off your power or your boss criticizes your work, your muscles may tighten, your hormones may surge, and you

**Stressors:** Stressful stimuli or situations.

Catastrophic events, like the Oklahoma City bombing, are particularly stressful because they are life threatening, out of our control, unpredictable, and difficult to explain.

may feel an urge to flee or fight. Unfortunately, these old remedies don't work as well with the new problems.

Some of the problems of our ancestors, however, are still with us—including war, famine, flood, fire, earthquake, and hurricane, to name a few. We will begin our survey of the human stress response by grouping these ancient and devastating maladies under the heading of *catastrophe*. We will see that certain distinctive behavior patterns emerge under catastrophic conditions. Yet, we will also see that people's responses to catastrophic events have much in common with their reactions to other sources of stress. The common themes are anxiety, frustration, physical symptoms, and sometimes even increased risk of death.

**CATASTROPHE**  Stress in the extreme can accompany catastrophic events. Anyone caught in a war, hurricane, fire, flood, or earthquake may suddenly lose loved ones and a lifetime of possessions. Clearly, catastrophic events can have extreme effects. What is not always obvious, however, is that our response to a catastrophic experience can also have a devastating effect on our physical and mental health.

Psychologists have learned much about stress from people who have undergone catastrophic losses and traumas (Baum, 1990). One such opportunity to understand how people respond to extreme ordeals presented itself just as the 1989 World Series was about to begin at San Francisco's Candlestick Park. As spectators settled into their seats, the band began to play. Suddenly, the entire stadium started to shake violently, the lights went out, and the scoreboard turned black. Sixty thousand fans fell silent. They had just experienced a major earthquake. Elsewhere in the city, fires erupted, a bridge collapsed, highways were crushed—and people were dying.

One week after the quake, a team of research psychologists began interviewing approximately 800 people chosen randomly from the San Francisco area and from several comparison cities some distance away. Subjects completed a ten-minute phone survey about their thoughts, social behavior, and health. For the next year, these same subjects were interviewed again every few weeks.

These surveys revealed a pattern: The lives of people who had been through the quake revolved around the disaster for about a month. After this period, the obsessive thoughts about the quake rather abruptly moved out of the center of consciousness. At about the same time, people began reporting an increase in other stress-related symptoms, such as earthquake dreams and troubled relationships. Most of these symptoms diminished during the ensuing one or two months, although as many as 20% of San Francisco area residents remained distressed about the quake a year later (Pennebaker & Harber, 1991).

In general, researchers have found that the psychological responses to disasters, such as the San Francisco quake, tend to occur in five stages (see Cohen & Ahearn, 1980):

- First, people typically experience a period of shock, confusion, and even *psychic numbness*, during which they cannot fully comprehend what has happened. This period may last only a few moments, or it can linger several days.
- In the next phase, people engage in *automatic action*, trying to respond to the disaster. They may behave adaptively but have little awareness of their actions and later show poor recall of these experiences. Depending on the nature of the crisis, the numbness of the first stage may quickly give way to automatic action or linger and paralyze victims into dangerous inaction. For example, when an earthquake shattered the city of Kobe, Japan, in January 1995, the citizens' shock and lack of preparedness prevented timely rescues. This delay in automatic action was later blamed for many of the almost 6,000 related deaths.
- In the third stage, people often have a sense of great accomplishment and a positive sense of *communal effort* toward a shared purpose. Also in this phase, they may feel weary and are aware that they are using up their reserves of energy. This

Confiding in others is helpful in working through feelings generated by trauma and loss.

phase builds on automatic action, but without conscious planning and collaboration people may lose hope and take no initiative in rebuilding their lives.

- During the fourth phase, people often experience a *letdown;* their energy is depleted, and they finally comprehend and feel the impact of the tragedy emotionally. For example, in recent years victims of hurricane damage have felt frustrated and abandoned when, weeks after the natural disasters occurred, the rest of the country turned its attention to other news events and appeared to forget about the continuing state of emergency in stricken communities.

- An extended final period of *recovery* follows, as people adapt to the changes brought about by the disaster. A flood may leave a small town so changed that some businesses are permanently shut down, while others move in and change the appearance and social activity of the postflood community.

Research indicates that, in the wake of catastrophic experiences such as earthquakes, floods, criminal attacks, relationship losses, crime, or serious personal injuries, we try to make sense of what happened: We formulate accounts, or stories, that characterize ourselves and others and explain what happened and what it means. The accounts we keep and relate about our losses and traumas are an important part of efforts to interact with and explain ourselves to each other. Forming and transmitting such accounts may even reflect a more general human need to tell our stories and be understood by those close to us (Harvey, 1996; Harvey, Weber, & Orbuch, 1990). While we formulate accounts and personal narratives about many life events, we seem especially likely to analyze and explain surprising and/or unpleasant experiences, such as trauma and loss (Holtzworth-Munroe & Jacobson, 1985). An important part of working through the pain of loss is formulating an account, and if possible, confiding it to one or more others (Weber & Harvey, 1994b).

The stress response under catastrophic conditions has a physical side, as well. This was reflected in the health records of people living in Othello, Washington, which was covered by a blanket of gray volcanic ash during the eruption of Mount Saint Helens in 1980. During the six months just after the eruption, these people had a nearly 200% increase in stress-related disorders. The death rate for the period also jumped by 19% (Adams & Adams, 1984). In general, people who undergo any sort of trauma become more susceptible to physical illness. We will look more closely at the physical basis for this response to stress in the second section of this chapter. Significantly, however, research shows that those who discuss the experience in detail with others suffer fewer health problems (Pennebaker, 1990; Pennebaker & Harber, 1993; Pennebaker, Barger, & Tiebout, 1989).

Studies showing how people typically respond to catastrophe can provide a model to help us predict what will happen the next time disaster strikes. This model enables rescue workers to anticipate and help victims deal with the problems that arise. Responses to events such as floods, tornadoes, airplane crashes, and factory explosions have all been shown to follow the model of disaster reactions sketched above.

**SOCIETAL STRESSORS**  Most of our stress comes not from sudden catastrophic events but from **societal stressors,** which are pressures in our social, cultural, and economic environment. These societal stressors often involve chronic home-, work-, or school-related difficulties. For example, a study of unemployed men revealed more depression, anxiety, and worries about health than in men who are employed. These symptoms usually disappeared, however, when the unemployed individuals found work (Liem & Rayman, 1982). In another investigation, high blood pressure among African Americans—long thought to be primarily genetic—was correlated with the chronic stress caused by low-status jobs, limited education, fruitless job seeking, and low socioeconomic status (Klag et al., 1991).

The times and circumstances into which we are born may deal us a hand of particularly difficult cards. Imagine for a moment the stress currently being experienced

**Societal stressors:** Stressful conditions arising from our social and cultural environment.

by people in Central Europe as they adjust to the tremendous social and economic up-heaval brought about by the end of the Soviet Union's control of their lives. Despite the suppression of individual initiative and the constant looming presence of police surveillance, most citizens enjoyed at least a predictable, stable status quo. With the transition to democratic government and capitalism have come personal freedom and new responsibilities—but also unemployment, loss of security, increased crime and violence, and, in some areas, the renewal of deadly ethnic conflicts (Myers, 1996). And how can an individual cope successfully with such enormous societal stressors? There are many ways, some of which we will consider at the end of this chapter.

**BURNOUT**   The greatest source of chronic stress for many people involves the pressures of work. Continually stressful work can lead to **burnout,** a syndrome of emotional exhaustion, depersonalization, and reduced personal accomplishment, says Christina Maslach (1998), a leading researcher on this widespread problem. It was first recognized in workers from professions that demand high-intensity interpersonal contact with patients, clients, or the public, but we now know that burnout can occur anywhere—even among college students. In the health-care field, practitioners experiencing job burnout begin to lose their caring and concern for patients and may come to treat them in detached and even dehumanized ways. The effect then feeds on itself, when these practitioners begin to feel bad about themselves and worry that they are failures. Regardless of the field, burnout is correlated with greater absenteeism and job turnover, impaired job performance, poor relations with coworkers, family problems, and poor personal health (Leiter & Maslach, 1988; Maslach, 1982; Maslach & Leiter, 1997; Schaufeli, Maslach, & Marek, 1993).

Why is health care a high-burnout profession?

Burnout can arise from a variety of conditions, including long working hours, high workloads, abusive managers or co-workers, and concerns about losing one's job. The extent of the problem can be seen in surveys showing that nearly three-quarters of all employees identify the worst aspect of their job as their immediate supervisor (Hogan, Curphy, & Hogan, 1994). One's personal life and relationships can also create burnout, so that one's friends, spouse, and children are seen as unreasonably demanding and draining of one's dwindling energy. For example, a majority of mothers of young children also work outside the home—yet few reliable changes have taken place *inside* the home to accommodate the needs of working mothers. Most household labor, especially that connected with meals and child care, is still regarded as the responsibility of wives. Consequently women with jobs as well as families may find their time divided between a hostile work environment where they are regarded as less valuable than male workers and an unsupportive home where they labor hard for no pay or appreciation (Long & Kahn, 1993). Burned-out spouses find their marriages unsatisfactory, and burned-out parents find less—perhaps no—joy in their children.

**Burnout:** A syndrome of emotional exhaustion, depersonalization, and reduced personal accomplishment—often related to work.

Every job, of course, has its stressors, and an employee's attitudes and **coping strategies** (ways of dealing with stressful situations) can make a big difference in how job stressors affect the individual. We will focus on these coping strategies—healthy and unhealthy—in the last two sections of the chapter. We should emphasize now, however, that the employee should not assume that burnout is a sign of personal weakness. Instead, it may signify a weakness in the organization. In an era of stiff competition and corporate "downsizing," employers may be reluctant to deal with obvious sources of stress and burnout, such as poor management and the threat of losing one's job. Often companies will use Band-Aid measures, such as providing stress-management workshops, rather than addressing the situations that cause the job stress. What this does, in effect, is to shift the blame for burnout from the company to the employees. Some employees may accept this shifted responsibility by assuming that it is, somehow, their own shortcoming for not being able to cope more effectively with job-related stress.

**HASSLES** It was a long day at work, and on the way home you stop at the grocery store, where they are out of the very thing you went there to buy. You get to the checkout with a consolation candy bar, and the clerk is impatient with your fumbling for change. These minor irritations and frustrations, known as **hassles,** don't seem like much in comparison to an earthquake or a burnout job. But, psychologists have found that their effects can accumulate, especially when they are frequent and involve interpersonal conflicts (Bolger et al., 1989).

Any annoying incident can be a hassle, but some of the most common hassles involve frustrations—the blocking of some desired goal—at home, at work, and at school. As you can see in Table 9.1, hassles can arise from a variety of sources, including time pressures, finances, health, and problem relationships.

You will recall that our Core Concept suggested that the cumulative impact of stress and our skills for coping with it matter more than its source. Thus, a life filled with hassles can exact a price as great as that of the more intense sources of stress we discussed earlier (Weinberger et al., 1987). If you interpret these hassles as important, harmful, or threatening to your well-being, they can affect you more than you might imagine (Lazarus, 1984). Some people may be especially prone to see the world as hassle-filled. One study showed that college students with a more

**Coping strategies:** Ways of dealing with stressful situations.

**Hassles:** Situations that cause minor irritation or frustration.

**TABLE 9.1:** Severity of Hassles as Perceived and Ranked by Four Groups

In these New Zealand samples, each group displayed its own pattern when ranking the severity of hassles. In the student group and the elderly group the rankings was almost opposite. For students time pressures were most important, while neighborhood and health pressures were the most important sources of hassles for the elderly. Note also the hassle rankings for mothers in this sample, who had one or more young children at home and no household help.

| HASSLE TYPE | STUDENTS (n561) | MOTHERS (n94) | COMMUNITY (n20) | ELDERLY (n50) |
|---|---|---|---|---|
| Time pressure | 1* | 2 | 3 | 4 |
| Future security | 2 | 4 | 1 | 3 |
| Finances | 3 | 1 | 2 | 4 |
| Household | 3 | 1 | 2 | 4 |
| Neighborhood | 4 | 3 | 2 | 1 |
| Health | 4 | 3 | 2 | 1 |

*A ranking of 1 means that this item was seen as the most severe hassle by this group.

pessimistic outlook experienced both more hassles and poorer health (Dykema, Bergbower, & Peterson, 1995).

In a diary study, a group of White, middle-class, middle-aged men and women kept track of their daily hassles over a one-year period. They also recorded major life changes and physical symptoms. A clear relationship emerged between hassles and health problems: The more frequent and intense the hassles people reported, the poorer was their health, both physical and mental (Lazarus, 1981; 1984). The opposite was also true: As daily hassles diminish, people's sense of well-being increases (Chamberlain & Zika, 1990).

What is a hassle or an annoyance to you, however, may be unnoticed—or even amusing—to someone else. If you find your life hassle-filled, reappraisal of the situations that provoke feelings of irritation can save you mental and physical wear and tear. In the last section of the chapter we will have more to say about how you might approach such cognitive reappraisal.

**Social Readjustment Rating Scale (SRRS):** A psychological rating scale designed to measure stress levels by means of values attached to common life changes.

## PSYCHOLOGY IN YOUR LIFE

# Change Can Be Hazardous to Your Health

The beginning or end of a relationship is always a time of tension and turmoil. Likewise, any change in your life can cause stress: a new job, starting college, even a vacation. Although change puts spice in our lives, all change demands some adjustment. But, did you realize that too much change of nearly any sort can jeopardize your health? Even events that we welcome may require major changes in our routines and adaptation to new requirements. Studies reveal that one of the most desired changes in a married couple's life, the birth of their first child, is also a source of major stress, contributing to reduced marital satisfaction for many couples (Cowan & Cowan, 1988). On the other hand, stress may result more from anticipating events than from living with them. For example, a review of research on the psychological responses to abortion reveals that distress is generally greatest *before* the abortion. Severe distress is low for most women following the abortion of an unwanted pregnancy, especially if they have had social support for their decision (Adler et al., 1990).

In general, significant levels of stress can result from any important life change

(Dohrenwend & Dohrenwend, 1974; Dohrenwend & Shrout, 1985; Holmes & Rahe, 1967), but people vary considerably in the ways they respond to change in their lives. Sometimes people can absorb stress and keep on functioning. Their reactions depend on their resources and the contexts in which stress occurs. If you have the money, time, and friends to help you pick up and go on after a disruption, you will certainly fare better than someone for whom more bad news is the last straw in a series of setbacks they have faced alone.

**THE SRRS**  How can we the measure stress of our everyday lives? And how much stress does it take before a person develops a stress-related illness? Thomas Holmes and Richard Rahe (1967) developed a psychological instrument, the **Social Readjustment Rating Scale (SRRS),** to answer these questions. Beginning with a list of 43 common stressful events, Holmes and Rahe assigned "marriage" an arbitrary middle value (50 on a 100-point scale) as a starting point. Then, they had a large number of people rate the other 42 events in comparison with the stress of marriage. The degree of stress associated with different kinds of change experienced in a given period was measured in *life-change units (LCU)*. To measure your current stress

level (and risk for stress-related problems) with the SRRS, you would merely total the LCU ratings accumulated in recent life experiences.

Holmes and Rahe found that the number of life-change units accumulated during the previous year became a modest predictor of changes in a person's health. Patients with heart disease, for example, had higher LCU scores than healthy subjects. Other studies reported that life stress increases a person's overall susceptibility to illness (Holmes & Masuda, 1974), and LCU values are also high for some time after an illness (Rahe & Arthur, 1978). Subsequent work has shown relationships between scores on the SRRS and heart attacks, bone fractures, diabetes, multiple sclerosis, tuberculosis, complications of pregnancy and birth, decline in academic performance, employee absenteeism, and many other difficulties (Holmes & Masuda, 1974). They even found that high SRRS scores among federal prisoners were associated with the length of their prison sentences. Note that these results are also consistent with our Core Concept, which emphasizes the cumulative impact of the stressors in our lives.

Although it was originally validated on an all-male sample, the SRRS has proved useful with both male and female subjects. Both sexes rate events with quite similar

*continued*

scores (Holmes & Masuda, 1974). In addition, the investigators have validated the ratings with Japanese, Latin American, European, and Malaysian samples. Remarkably, the SRRS has transferred well across cultures.

You can assess yourself on the SRRS in the *Do It Yourself!* box. You may want to compare your score with those of classmates and consider whether you detect the same sort of relationship between life changes and well-being that Holmes and Rahe found. Before you do so, though, please read the following critique of the SRRS.

**CRITICAL ANALYSIS OF THE HOLMES-RAHE SRRS** There is no doubt that the Holmes-Rahe scale and its successors have helped us learn about the relationship between stressful life changes and illness. In the first 15 years after it was published, the SRRS had been used in more than 1,000 studies worldwide (Holmes, 1979). Yet, the Holmes-Rahe scale has been criticized, particularly for the implication that stressful events might *cause* illness (Dohrenwend

& Shrout, 1985; Rabkin & Struening, 1976). In fact, the scale gives us *correlational* data. That is, it merely shows a relationship between certain life changes and health changes. (*See Chapter 1, Mind, Behavior, and Science.*) Even though the scale has some power to predict illness (Johnson & Sarason, 1979), the research does not show that life changes are the *cause* of illness. It could just as well be true that some as yet undiscovered factor might be the cause of *both* the life changes and illnesses.

For another thing, while the anchor point of the Holmes-Rahe SRRS is the stress of marriage, we now have substantial evidence that getting married is correlated with longer life. How can we reconcile this apparent contradiction? It appears that *getting married* can be a stressful experience, but once the stress of a wedding has dissipated, *being married* can provide a buffer against stress. In fact, any stable, long-term relationship seems to offer some protection against stress (Friedman et al., 1995). We will see, below, that other forms of social support also are associated with longevity.

Critics also point out that the correlations between life changes and health changes are moderate. A high score does not mean that illness is certain, nor does a low score guarantee health. Then too, certain groups, such as students, who are at change points in their lives, tend to get high scores, although it is not clear that they are more at risk for illness. Their youth may also offer some protection. In general, people's chances of incurring an illness may be more related to their *interpretations* and *responses* to life changes, rather than to the changes themselves (Lazarus et al., 1985). Different people have different abilities to deal with change, presumably because of genetic differences, general physical condition, healthy lifestyles, and good coping skills. The SRRS takes none of these factors into account—although we will do so in the final section of this chapter. Still, the SRRS does a fair job of measuring stress, and it remains the most widely used measure of stress that we have.

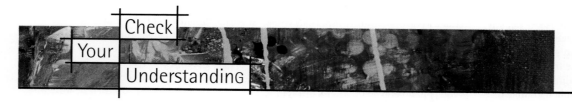

1. **RECALL:** *In everyday conversation people often think of stress as a _____, while psychologists refer to stress as a _____.*
   **a.** situation/mental and physical response
   **b.** response/stimulus
   **c.** disease/feeling
   **d.** result of heredity/result of environment

2. **RECALL:** *Burnout is a source of stress that comes from*
   **a.** catastrophic events.
   **b.** work.
   **c.** chronic disease.
   **d.** divorce.

3. **APPLICATION:** *You have taken the Holmes-Rahe SRRS and have a high score—say 400 points. How should you interpret this score?*
   **a.** You will almost certainly have a major health problem within the next year.
   **b.** Your chances of having a major health problem are low if you are married.

   **c.** Your chances of developing a health problem depend not only on your score but on your physical condition, lifestyle, and coping skills.
   **d.** There is no proven relationship between life changes and health.

4. **UNDERSTANDING THE CORE CONCEPT:** *Which of the following is most likely to cause a high level of stress?*
   **a.** a catastrophic event, such as a major earthquake
   **b.** burnout
   **c.** a large number of life changes
   **d.** all of the above may cause a high level of stress

**ANSWERS:**   1. **a**   2. **b**   3. **c**   4. **d**

# DO IT Yourself!

## The Social Readjustment Rating Scale

Marriage was given a score of 50 life change units on the SRRS.

For each of the following events that has occurred in your life during the past year, write the number of "life-change units" in the blank at the right. Then, add up your life-change units to determine your total score.

| | Life-Change Units | Your Score | | Life-Change Units | Your Score |
|---|---|---|---|---|---|
| Death of spouse | 100 | _____ | Son or daughter leaving home | 29 | _____ |
| Divorce | 73 | _____ | Trouble with in-laws | 29 | _____ |
| Marital separation | 65 | _____ | Outstanding personal achievement | 28 | _____ |
| Jail term | 63 | _____ | *Spouse beginning or stopping work | 26 | _____ |
| Death of close family member | 63 | _____ | Beginning or ending school | 26 | _____ |
| Personal injury or illness | 53 | _____ | Change in living conditions | 25 | _____ |
| Marriage | 50 | _____ | Revision of personal habits | 24 | _____ |
| Being fired | 47 | _____ | Trouble with one's boss | 23 | _____ |
| Marital reconciliation | 45 | _____ | Change in work hours or conditions | 20 | _____ |
| Retirement | 45 | _____ | Change in residence | 20 | _____ |
| Change in the health of family member | 44 | _____ | Change in schools | 20 | _____ |
| Pregnancy | 40 | _____ | Change in recreation | 19 | _____ |
| Sex difficulties | 39 | _____ | Change in church activities | 19 | _____ |
| Gain of new family member | 39 | _____ | Change in social activities | 18 | _____ |
| Business readjustment | 39 | _____ | *Mortgage or loan of less than $100,000 | 17 | _____ |
| Change in financial state | 38 | _____ | Change in sleeping habits | 16 | _____ |
| Death of close friend | 37 | _____ | Change in number of family get-togethers | 15 | _____ |
| Change to a different line of work | 36 | _____ | Change in eating habits | 15 | _____ |
| Change in number of arguments with spouse | 35 | _____ | Vacation | 13 | _____ |
| *Home mortgage over $100,000 | 31 | _____ | Celebrated Christmas | 13 | _____ |
| Foreclosure of a mortgage or loan | 30 | _____ | Minor violations of the law | 11 | _____ |
| Change in responsibilities at work | 29 | _____ | **Your total:** | | _____ |

How should you interpret your score? With caution. A total of 150 or less is good, suggesting a low level of stress in your life and a low probability of developing a stress-related disorder. But for people scoring between 150 and 200, Holmes and Masuda (1974) found a 50–50 chance of problems: Half the people they found in this range developed a significant physical or mental disorder in the next few months. About 70% of those scoring over 300 became ill. (Adapted from Holmes & Rahe, 1967.)

*These items have been updated.

# HOW DOES STRESS AFFECT US PHYSICALLY?

"Mind over matter" usually refers to the (supposed) psychic ability of the mind to influence physical objects—such as levitating a brick or influencing the roll of dice. If you think you have such paranormal powers, you should contact James "The Amazing" Randi, who promises to pay a cool million dollars to anyone who can demonstrate such abilities to his satisfaction. (See Mr. Randi's Web site at www.randi.org/ for details.) There is one influence of mind over matter, however, for which Randi will not pay because it does not fall into the category of paranormal or psychic powers: the influence of mental processes on the body.

The mind–body connection lies fully within mainstream psychological and medical science—not in the fantasy realm of magic or the paranormal. In fact, cognitive scientists assume that the mind and the body are one—not different substances. Mental processes occurring in the brain influence physical responses controlled by the brain. (This was Patch Adams's insight.) The way this happens when we are under stress is the subject of this section of the chapter. Here is the Core Concept:

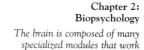

**Chapter 2: Biopsychology**

*The brain is composed of many specialized modules that work together create mind and behavior.*

**CORE CONCEPT**

**Stress can help us meet challenges and grow stronger, but too much stress—distress—can have harmful physical consequences.**

We have seen that stress has many sources, and it can have serious health consequences. Now we will learn *how* it works on us biologically and psychologically.

## Biological and Behavioral Responses to Stress

Imagine that you have a highly stressful job, such as being an air traffic controller at a busy metropolitan airport. On this job, you soon learn that keeping track of dozens of aircraft in a crowded airspace—knowing that hundreds of lives depend on your decisions—can extract a mental and physical toll. You may have more colds than you used to. You may find yourself taking medicine for indigestion and diarrhea more frequently. And, your friends may find you less jovial or more irritable. What is happening to you?

In this section, we will focus on the physical side of the response to stressful situations, such as your new job in air traffic control. (We will come back to the psychological consequences of stress after a few pages.) You are about to see that the physical response to nearly any stressor is likely to take four main forms: (1) an initial arousal, (2) a behavioral reaction called the "fight-or-flight" response, (3) an internal response of the autonomic nervous system and the endocrine system, and (4) decreased effectiveness of the immune system. We will examine each of these physical responses in turn.

**Acute stress:** A temporary pattern of arousal caused by a stressor with a clear onset and offset.

**Chronic stress:** A continuous state of stressful arousal persisting over time.

**Fight-or-flight response:** A sequence of internal processes that prepares the organism for struggle or escape and is triggered when a situation is interpreted as threatening.

**AROUSAL** If a stressful situation begins suddenly and intensely—as when an air traffic controller first hears a pilot's emergency call, "Mayday!"—the stress response is likely to begin with abrupt and intense arousal, including accelerated heart rate, quickened breathing, a jump in blood pressure, and profuse perspiration. Sometimes, however, arousal may merely fester, or it may grow slowly, as when jealousy first tugs at you, then distracts you, and finally disrupts your life with fear or outrage. The first example illustrates **acute stress,** a temporary pattern of arousal caused by a stressor with a clear

Working in an air traffic control tower at a busy airport is a high-stress occupation.

onset and a limited duration. The second case, of persistent strain, is an example of **chronic stress.** It involves a continuous state of stressful arousal persisting over time, in which demands are perceived to be greater than one's resources for dealing with them.

Arousal does us no good if it creates panic and confusion that keep us from responding to a threat. Fortunately, the human brain evolved to coordinate several simultaneous reactions involving the nervous system, the endocrine system, and the muscles. As a result, we are biologically equipped to make efficient and effective responses to changing environmental demands. So, when one perceives an external threat, these bodily mechanisms are set in motion. Many are automatic or reflexive because instant action and extra strength may be required if the organism is to survive. We turn now to the most easily observed and best known of such mechanisms, the *fight-or-flight response*.

The fight-or-flight response: For this rabbit, flight is a better strategy than fight.

**FIGHT OR FLIGHT** Consider this stressful situation: At a meeting for which you have thoroughly prepared, the chair criticizes you and accuses you of failing to attend to tasks that were, in reality, someone else's responsibility. As all eyes turn on you, you feel your face getting hot, your jaw tightening, and your fist clenching. You would not shout or hit anyone—doing so would only make things worse. But you feel like shouting or striking out. Now consider another stressful situation: You walk into class a few moments late, only to find everyone putting books and notes away—apparently preparing for a test you did not realize had been scheduled for today. Your heart seems to stop, your mouth is dry, your knees feel weak, and you momentarily consider hurrying back out the door. Your life is not really in danger, and running away will not solve your problem—so why should you feel a physical urge to escape?

These two scenarios illustrate the two poles of the **fight-or-flight response,** a sequence of internal processes that prepares the aroused organism for struggle or escape. It is triggered when a situation is interpreted as threatening. The resulting response depends on how the organism has *learned* to deal with threat, as well as on an *innate* fight-or-flight "program" built into the brain.

Evidence that the "fight" response can be learned is seen, for example, in studies showing that reactions to a perceived insult are strongly dependent on culture. In the United States this learned "fight" response has been nurtured in the "culture of honor" that developed in the South—which some experts believe may account for the southern states' much higher murder rate in comparison to the northern states (Nisbett, 1993). Learning can also affect our internal responses to stress. For example, in a study of patients with high blood pressure (which can be a stress response), those who took placebos along with their medication for high blood pressure maintained a healthy blood pressure after the medication was removed, as long as they continued taking the placebo (Ader & Cohen, 1993; Suchman & Ader, 1989). This suggests that the expectation that the placebos would control their blood pressure was enough to reduce the emergency response of the blood vessels.

**Chapter 5:**
**Sensation and Perception**
*Placebos contain no real medicines. They only work because of the patient's expectations.*

While the fight-or-flight response clearly can be learned, it also involves an innate reaction that operates largely outside consciousness. This was first recognized in the 1920s by physiologist Walter Canon, whose research showed that a threat stimulates a sequence of activities in the organism's nerves and glands. We now know that the hypothalamus controls this response by initiating a cascade of events in the autonomic nervous system (ANS), in the endocrine system, and in the immune system (Jansen et al., 1995).

**Chapter 2:**
**Biopsychology**
*The hypothalamus is a deep brain structure that controls many automatic responses.*

As you will recall, the autonomic nervous system regulates the activities of our internal organs. When an individual perceives a situation as threatening, this judgment

**Chapter 2:**
**Biopsychology**

*The autonomic nervous*
*system operates outside of*
*consciousness and sends messages*
*to the internal organs.*

causes the hypothalamus to send an emergency message to the ANS, which sets in motion several bodily reactions to stress. See Figure 9.2 for a detailed list of how the ANS and endocrine (internal gland) system prepare the body to respond with either fight or flight. This response is helpful when you need to escape a hungry bear or confront a hostile rival. It served our ancestors well, but it has a cost. As our Core Concept suggests, staying physiologically "on guard" against a threat eventually wears down the body's natural defenses. In this way, suffering from frequent stress—or frequently *interpreting* experiences as stressful—can create a serious health risk: an essentially healthy stress response can become *distress*.

In acute stress, these responses are helpful. They can save the life of a soldier in combat. They may also speed you out of danger if you think you might be mugged by the person following you on a dark street. But, as we have seen, modern living has produced a different class of stressors—*psychological stressors*—that act over far longer periods and threaten not our immediate survival but our status, lifestyles, health, or self-respect. In the face of psychological stressors, our physical fight-or-flight response may offer little help—or may even backfire. Again, stress may become *distress*.

While the fight-or-flight syndrome shows itself most obviously in our behavior, the accompanying autonomic and endocrine responses occur inside us. Like fight-or-flight, these internal processes are adaptive for dealing with acute, life-threatening stressors. But, if stress is chronic, our internal responses can produce the *general adaptation syndrome*—an insidious condition that can weaken us with its powerful attempts to counteract the stressors of life.

**│ FIGURE 9.2:**    Bodily Reactions to Stress

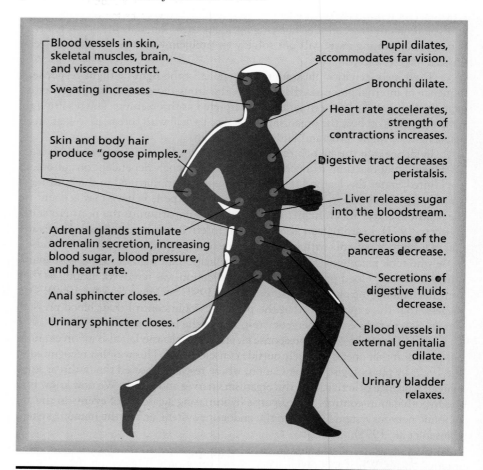

**THE GENERAL ADAPTATION SYNDROME** We turn now to one of the most provocative findings of modern psychology. It suggests that people who experience persistently negative emotional states (depression, anxiety, and hostility) are candidates for coronary disease, asthma, headache, gastric ulcers, arthritis, and a variety of other disorders (Friedman & Booth-Kewley, 1988). In general, chronic negative emotional states tend to produce disease-causing changes in the body, unhealthy behavior patterns, and poor personal relationships (Matthews, 1988).

The research that eventually led to these conclusions began with Hans Selye, a Canadian endocrinologist. In the late 1930s, Selye (pronounced *SELL-ya*) reported on a striking pattern that he had found in responses of laboratory animals to damaging agents such as bacterial infections, toxins, forced restraint, heat, and cold. Selye's great discovery was that many kinds of stress-producing agents all trigger essentially the same systemic reaction or *general* bodily response. Moreover, he found, all such stressors provoke some attempt at *adaptation*—adjustment of the body to the stressor and restoration of equilibrium, or homeostasis.

Selye termed this bodily response to stress the **general adaptation syndrome (GAS).** His model of the GAS describes a three-stage response to any threat, consisting of an *alarm reaction,* a stage of *resistance,* and a stage of *exhaustion* (Selye, 1956). These three stages of Selye's GAS are shown in Figure 9.3.

**General adaptation syndrome (GAS):** A general pattern of physical responses that takes essentially the same form in response to any serious, chronic stressor.

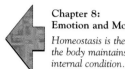

**Chapter 8:**
**Emotion and Motivation**
*Homeostasis is the process by which the body maintains a balanced internal condition.*

**FIGURE 9.3:** The General Adaptation Syndrome

Following exposure to a stressor, the body's resistance is diminished until the physiological changes of the corresponding alarm reaction bring it back up to the normal level. If the stressor continues, the bodily signs characteristic of the alarm reaction virtually disappear; resistance to the particular stressor rises above normal but drops for other stressors. This adaptive resistance returns the body to its normal level of functioning. Following prolonged exposure to the stressor, adaptation breaks down; signs of alarm reaction reappear, the stressor effects are irreversible, and the individual becomes ill and may die.

| *Stage I: Alarm reaction* (continuously repeated throughout life) | *Stage II: Resistance* (continuously repeated throughout life) | *Stage III: Exhaustion* |
|---|---|---|
| —Enlargement of adrenal cortex<br>—Enlargement of lymphatic system<br>—Increase in hormone levels<br>—Response to specific stressor<br>—Epinephrine release associated with high levels of physiological arousal and negative affect<br>—Greater susceptibility to increased intensity of stressor<br>—Heightened susceptibility to illness<br><br>(If prolonged, the slower components of the GAS are set into motion, beginning with Stage II.) | —Shrinkage of adrenal cortex<br>—Return of lymph nodes to normal size<br>—Sustaining of hormone levels<br>—High physiological arousal<br>—Counteraction of parasympathetic branch of ANS<br>—Enduring of stressor; resistance to further debilitating effects<br>—Heightened sensitivity to stress<br><br>(If stress continues at intense levels, hormonal reserves are depleted, fatigue sets in, and individual enters Stage III.) | —Enlargement/dysfunction of lymphatic structures<br>—Increase in hormone levels<br>—Depletion of adaptive hormones<br>—Decreased ability to resist either original or extraneous stressors<br>—Affective experience—often depression |

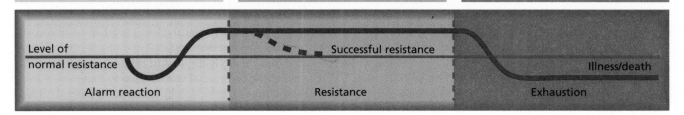

**Chapter 2:**
**Biopsychology**

*The hypothalamus connects the brain to the endocrine system and the autonomic nervous system.*

**Chapter 8:**
**Emotion and Motivation**

*The sympathetic nervous system carries messages that control the body's emergency reactions.*

**THE ALARM REACTION** In the first stage of stress, the body's warning system activates and begins to mobilize its resources against the stressor. Selye called this the **alarm reaction.** In this stage, the hypothalamus triggers an emergency response in the hormone system, especially in the adrenal glands, through the pathway shown in Figure 9.4. The result is a flood of steroid hormones into the bloodstream. These steroid hormones, incidentally, are the same ones that some athletes take to improve their performance. For the athlete, a dose of steroid hormones produces an artificial stress response, which fools the body into mobilizing for an "emergency" (such as a track meet). The stress hormones not only give the athlete a short-term boost in performance, they encourage the long-term buildup of stress-resisting tissues (including muscle).

While the hormone response of the alarm reaction is in progress, another mechanism is also at work. The hypothalamus sends parallel emergency messages through the sympathetic division of the autonomic nervous system to internal organs and glands. Those messages almost instantly arouse the body for action. In particular, the autonomic stimulation of the adrenal glands releases a charge of epinephrine (adrenaline) producing a surge of energy that can lead to greater-than-normal strength or speed. Everyone has heard stories of people under stress lifting massive objects, leaping high barriers, or running with extraordinary swiftness—feats that they could not duplicate later. Apparently, this is the mechanism that produces such amazing performances. This autonomic response acts through the pathways shown in Figure 9.5.

As our Core Concept suggests, if the stress lasts over a long period, this initially adaptive alarm reaction can become *distress*, as it depletes much of the body's energy and defensive resources. It can also cause high blood pressure, deterioration of the immune system, fatty deposits in the blood vessels, bleeding ulcers, and a variety of other symptoms. (Such physical deterioration is part of the reason that athletes should not take steroids to build muscle.) These reactions make the subject under stress a prime candidate for infections or other diseases, as well. In addition, studies also suggests that prolonged or repeated stress may produce long-term changes in the brain that provoke depression (Schulkin, 1994).

We should remember, however, that the alarm reaction is basically a good defense, especially against acute stress. We want our bodies to respond quickly when assaulted by a stressor. So, if a hungry bear comes your way, the alarm reaction gives you an epinephrine (adrenaline) boost that increases your heart rate and blood pressure, which combine to make your body ready for fight or flight. This is why Selye called it an *adaptation* syndrome: It is a mechanism by which the body *adapts* to a stressor. It becomes maladaptive only if our alarm-reaction defenses are weak or if the stressor is too intense or prolonged.

**THE STAGE OF RESISTANCE** If the stressor persists but is not so strong that it overwhelms the organism during the first stage, the subject begins to rebound during stage 2, the **stage of resistance.** Outwardly, the body appears to be gaining the advantage—resisting the stressor, as the symptoms of the alarm reaction fade. The adrenal glands, swollen earlier, now return to normal size, diminishing their output of emergency steroids. Yet, the hormone response does persist at a lower level, as an almost unnoticed internal struggle against the stressor continues.

Surprisingly, the resistance that the body displays in this stage applies *only* to the original stressor. When an experimental animal had adapted to a stressor, it soon died if Selye switched stressors (say, from electric shocks to cold). Apparently it had so depleted its resources that it could not mobilize a defense against the new stressor. In general, if a second stressor is introduced in the second stage of the GAS, the or-

**FIGURE 9.4:** The Alarm Reaction Pathway

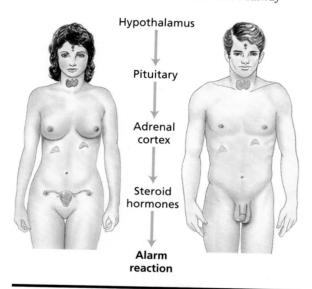

Hypothalamus

Pituitary

Adrenal cortex

Steroid hormones

**Alarm reaction**

**Alarm reaction:** The first stage of the GAS, during which the body mobilizes its resources to cope with a stressor.

**Stage of resistance:** The second stage of the GAS, during which the body seems to adapt to the presence of the stressor.

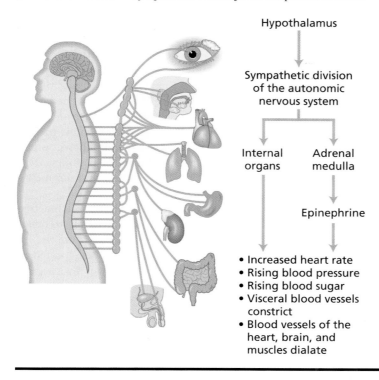

Hypothalamus

Sympathetic division of the autonomic nervous system

Internal organs

Adrenal medulla

Epinephrine

- Increased heart rate
- Rising blood pressure
- Rising blood sugar
- Visceral blood vessels constrict
- Blood vessels of the heart, brain, and muscles dialate

ganism may not be able to adapt. (Think of the "straw that broke the camel's back.") A human example might involve a soldier who suddenly dies in response to the new stress of a prison camp after surviving months of stressful combat.

*THE STAGE OF EXHAUSTION* If relief from the stressor doesn't arrive during the stage of resistance, the symptoms of the alarm reaction inevitably reappear. This time, however, a powerful autonomic response accompanies them. In this third stage, the **stage of exhaustion,** the autonomic nervous system overcompensates in its attempt to moderate the resurgent hormone response. Soon the organism may approach the point of no return: Exhaustion and eventual death overtake it if the stressor is not re-moved. You can see again why it is not healthy for an athlete to take high doses of

In a major forest fire, smoke jumpers may work under extremely hazardous conditions for long periods. In the process, they may experience all three stages of the general adaptation syndrome.

**Stage of exhaustion:** The third stage of the GAS, during which the body depletes its resources.

stress hormones for a long period. Prolonged use of steroids (except under certain medical conditions) can, in effect, put the body into Selye's Stage 3, a stage of perilous deterioration—even death.

**STRESS AND THE IMMUNE SYSTEM**     Since Selye, researchers have found other consequences of stress that underscore the influence of mental processes on the body. Scientists working on the immune system have found that the basis of the immune response lies in the ability of various types of white blood cells, formed in the bone marrow and the thymus gland, to counteract foreign cells and substances that enter the body. But they have also discovered the influences of our mental processes on the immune system—a finding that has established a new field known as **psychoneuroimmunology** (Ader & Cohen, 1993; Maier, Watkins, & Fleshner, 1994; Solvason, Ghanta, & Hiramoto, 1988). In brief, they have found that our mental states can influence the effectiveness of our immune responses.

How do mental processes affect the immune system? The brain sends messages to the autonomic nervous system and endocrine system, which have links to organs that produce the immune response. The brain also receives feedback from the immune system via endocrine pathways. Receptors for stress hormones, located on white blood cells, respond to the presence of a stressor by sending out a widespread chemical alarm, which alerts the brain.

As Patch Adams realized, disruption of these processes can have important effects on health (Adams, 1998; Adams & Mylander, 1998; Pert, 1997). For example, the dissolving of interpersonal relationships, such as happens following a death or divorce, can result in suppression of the immune response, making people more vulnerable to disease (Cohen & Syme, 1985; Kiecolt-Glaser & Glaser, 1987). Studies also show that men with wives dying of breast cancer and recently widowed women are less able to fight disease and face an increased risk of illness and premature death (Irwin et al., 1987; Schleifer et al., 1983). Similarly, depression has also been shown to produce **immunosuppression,** a diminished effectiveness of the immune response.

So, how does the immune system become compromised? When the stress response is activated, it mobilizes the individual to produce physical energy and channel it in three directions: toward muscular exertion (as we saw in the fight-or-flight response), toward activity of the nervous system and endocrine system (as we saw in the GAS), and toward activation of the immune system (Sapolsky, 1992). Consequently, the body's immune response and its other stress responses may have to compete with each other for limited energy resources. This is particularly likely to happen in states of chronic stress, when a new stressor (such as a virus) assaults an organism that has already invested most of its resources in combating another source of stress. As a result, the stress response may activate the organism's circulation and muscle systems and divert energy away from the immune response (Maier et al., 1994).

On a more hopeful note, research suggests that we may one day turn the same process that suppresses immune function into an advantage. In mice that are genetically prone to a lupuslike disease (an immune disorder), chemotherapy delays the onset of lupus symptoms. Remarkably, studies show that if flavored water is paired a few times with the chemotherapy, the flavored water alone provoked an immune response that was identical to that of the drug therapy. This discovery is important because chemotherapy often has unpleasant and toxic side effects. The hope is, then, that this procedure for Pavlovian conditioning of the immune system may one day allow human patients to substitute a neutral stimulus for part of their chemotherapy regimen (Maier et al., 1994).

An understanding of the general adaptation syndrome and immunosuppression has proven valuable in explaining disorders, such as heart disease, that formerly baffled physicians. However, most of this work has focused on reactions to *physical* stressors among experimental animals. As a result, it has had little to say about the *psychological* stressors so prevalent among humans. In the third section of this chapter, we will fill some of this gap.

**Psychoneuroimmunology:** A relatively new field that studies the influence of our mental states on the immune system.

**Immunosuppression:** Diminished effectiveness of the immune system caused by impairment (suppression) of the immune response.

**Chapter 6:**
**Learning and Remembering**
*In classical (Pavlovian) conditioning a previously neutral stimulus comes to elicit a reflexive response.*

## When Stress Is Good for You

Would this be eustress for you?

Sometimes stress can even be pleasurable, as when we play a game, visit an exotic culture, or take a thrilling white-water rafting trip. In fact, these episodes of relatively mild and brief stress can be healthful, rather than harmful. When we experience stress in this form, it actually strengthens us, both physically and mentally. Athletes use this principle to their advantage when they build their bodies with the brief intervals of stress they call "training." Unless overdone, such stress can make nearly anyone more resilient.

In his book *Stress without Distress*, Selye (1974) noted that it is not possible, or even desirable, to have a stress-free life. He later observed that "complete freedom from stress is death" (Selye, 1980, p. 128). Putting the point more positively: A modest level of stress motivates us to live, work, play, and love well, as our Core Concept implies. Selye (1980) called this optimal level of stress **eustress** (from the Greek prefix "eu," which means "good").

Not all of us respond to the stressors of life in the same way, of course. Selye believed that we can do little to change our basic biological responsiveness to stressful situations or the optimum level of stress that we need for healthy physical and mental growth. Although many psychologists disagree with Seyle on this point, everyone agrees that many strategies are available to help us cope more effectively with distressful events. We will look at some of those at the end of this chapter in the section labeled "Promoting Health and Well-Being."

For now, consider how you might apply the concept of "good" stress—*eustress*—in your own life. For example, if you are studying for a career in business management, think about how you might structure the work environment to reduce distress and increase eustress (Douglas, 1996). First, an employer should know the three most common sources of employee distress: (1) conflicting expectations from supervisors, (2) unclear expectations and goals, and (3) erratic changes in workload, swinging from overwork to underwork. The first suggests poor communication within management ranks, while the second problem involves poor communication between management and the work force. The third may have any of several causes, but it also calls for dialogue between workers and their managers to find ways of smoothing out the workload.

After addressing these problems, the employer should consider proactive steps to *create* eustress in the place of distress. For example, jobs can often be made more interesting and challenging, as when workers are assigned to teams that are given problems to solve, rather than management-imposed solutions. Under such circumstances, it is important to increase employees' authority as they are given increased responsibility.

In your personal life, you should remember that eustress can be an antidote for distress. For your own physical and mental health, it is wise to monitor your stress level. So, when you sense that stress is taking away your effectiveness, diminishing your emotional responsiveness, or making you feel generally "run down," it is time for a dose of eustress. Take a page from Patch Adams's book: Laugh, play, do something interesting; do something you don't *have* to do.

**Eustress:** An optimum level of stress; "good" stress.

Check Your Understanding

1. APPLICATION: *An oncoming car swerves into your lane and heads directly for you. At the last possible moment it swerves again, missing you by inches. Your heart pounds, your blood pressure rises, you begin perspiring. This is an example of*

   **a.** acute stress.
   **b.** eustress.
   **c.** chronic stress.
   **d.** the GAS.

*continued*

**2. RECALL:** *Which one of the following is most likely to be influenced by cultural factors?*

**a.** the fight-or-flight response
**b.** the general adaptation syndrome
**c.** the effect of stress on the immune system
**d.** the autonomic nervous system

**3. RECALL:** *If a chronic stressor is not removed, the stressed organism may eventually die during*

**a.** the alarm reaction.
**b.** the stage of resistance.
**c.** the stage of exhaustion.
**d.** eustress.

**4. UNDERSTANDING THE CORE CONCEPT:** *The biological mechanisms that helped our ancestors deal with stress are often poorly adapted to the _____ stress of the modern world.*

**a.** acute stress
**b.** eustress
**c.** chronic stress
**d.** autonomic

**ANSWERS:**     1. a     2. a     3. c     4. c

---

**KEY QUESTION**

# HOW DO WE RESPOND PSYCHOLOGICALLY TO STRESS?

The consequences of stress are not limited to the body. It is common for people to react to stressful situations, such as an upcoming surgical procedure or a final examination, with acute anxiety or depression. And, if the stress is extreme or prolonged, as in a rape or near-death automobile crash with serious injuries, the psychological consequences can be chronic and just as debilitating as the physical ones we examined earlier. As we have noted, such stress is often associated with anxiety, frustration, and other emotional responses. In this section we will emphasize several other, more complex psychological reactions to stressful situations. Our Core Concept suggests that these reactions vary widely:

**CORE CONCEPT**

**Our psychological responses under stress depend on personality, perceptions, and the ways we have learned to respond.**

Thus, different people may have quite different responses to the same stressful situation.

## Personality and Stress

Mr. A is an executive who always works over lunch. He makes business calls on his cellular phone as he drives to and from work. He carries a briefcase full of papers home every night, where he pours over them until bedtime, when he takes a pill to slow down his frenetic mind and get him to sleep. He would tell you that he thrives on stress. By contrast, Ms. B, who works in the same office, rarely takes work home, doesn't own a cell phone, and receives evaluations from her manager that are as good or better than Mr. A's. These two executives obviously have different working styles. If these styles are of long standing, if they are pervasive in these individuals' lives, and if they are similar to patterns found in many other people, we might be justified in calling them *personality types*. In fact, the two we have just described are representative of two opposite patterns known as *Type A* and *Type B*—patterns of behavior that have some intriguing associations with disease and health.

**Chapter 10:
Personality**

*Types are clusters of traits that are found in essentially the same pattern in many people.*

## Type A and B Behavior Patterns

When an upholsterer commented that the front edges of the chairs in their waiting rooms showed unusually high wear, cardiologists Meyer Friedman and Ray Rosenman (1974) realized that a certain coping style might be associated with heart disease. It was as if people with heart disease were always "on the edge of their seats."

A basketball coach displays some Type A behaviors.

Subsequent interviews with Friedman and Rosenman's patients revealed a striking pattern of impatience, competitiveness, aggressiveness, and hostility—all stress-related responses. Many said they were notorious workaholics. Friedman and Rosenman dubbed this the **Type A** behavior pattern. What is more important, they also found that this pattern was predictive of heart disease. In their studies, the Type A individual was found to have twice as much risk of heart disease as the **Type B,** an individual who takes a relaxed approach to life (Matthews, 1982).

Studies also show that Type A personalities tend to be ambitious, loners, and often highly dissatisfied with some aspect of their lives. Their behavior tends to be competitive, aggressive, and future oriented, at the expense of sensitivity to events in the present. For example, a Type A person might engage in *polyphasic* behavior, doing several things simultaneously, such as eating, "watching" television, writing a report, and talking on a cell phone.

Many Type A characteristics, however, are valued in our mobile, competitive society: Speed, perfectionism, and time-urgency may actually help one to succeed in the workplace and in the interpersonal "marketplace," where people are admired for being strong, independent, and self-promoting. But in the long run, the Type A style can be dysfunctional, unhealthy, and self-defeating. One study showed that Type A businessmen are stricken with coronary heart disease more than twice as often as men in the general population (Friedman & Rosenman, 1974; Jenkins, 1976). Other studies show that Type A individuals are at greater risk for all forms of cardiovascular disease, including heart attack and stroke (Dembroski et al., 1978; Dembroski & Costa, 1987; Haynes & Feinleib, 1980).

Not just an occupational hazard, the Type A pattern has also been observed among high school and college students, and even among grade-school children (Thoresen & Eagleston, 1983). In addition to cardiovascular risks, research links Type A habits to other illnesses: allergies, head colds, headaches, stomach disorders, and mononucleosis (Suls & Sanders, 1988; Suls & Marco, 1990). Currently researchers are focusing on identifying which specific dimensions of the Type A syndrome are its most deadly components. Hostility is particularly suspect (Whiteman & Fowkes, 1997). When a slow-moving vehicle blocks you in traffic, it is reasonable to become momentarily piqued, but it is Type A behavior—and potentially dangerous—to become enraged. Another risky Type A quality is perfectionism, which has been linked to anxiety (about reaching impossible goals) and depression (from failing to reach them) (Joiner & Schmidt, 1995).

How does the Type A behavior pattern get translated into a heart attack or other physical disease? The details are not yet clear, but a hint comes from another study by Friedman and Ulmer (1984). As the April 15th tax deadline approached, these researchers drew blood samples from a group of accountants. The closer they came to the filing date, the higher the accountants' cholesterol and clotting factors climbed, in many cases rising to dangerous levels. You will notice the similarity between this response to stress and the "alarm reaction" that Selye found in the first stage of the general adaptation syndrome, where his stressed laboratory animals developed fatty deposits in their blood vessels.

A word of caution: All the fuss in the popular press may lead you to conclude—erroneously—that you must be either a Type A or Type B. The truth is, most

**Type A:** A behavior pattern characterized by an intense, angry, competitive, or perfectionistic response to life.

**Type B:** A behavior pattern characterized by a relaxed, unruffled response to life.

People with Type A personality traits may be more likely to have a heart attack, but they are also more likely to take action to prevent a second one.

people have neither a Type A or Type B personality. The majority of us fall somewhere between these extremes.

Nor is it always bad to be a Type A. If you do have a heart attack, being Type A may save your life. In one study of 257 males who had heart attacks, death rates were equal among Type As and Type Bs. But among the first-day survivors, the Type As were twice as likely to be alive 13 years later. Stress experts suggest that the Type As may have an advantage because they are more aggressive about following medical advice to quit smoking, change their diets, and get more exercise than were the more easygoing Type Bs (Ragland & Brand, 1988).

An understanding of the Type A link with heart disease has led to the development of a remarkably effective approach to the prevention of second heart attacks. In a group of heart attack survivors, Friedman and Ulmer (1984) showed that those given stress management training had half as many heart attacks in the next three years as a control group who had received no such training. The researchers concluded: "No drug, food, or exercise program ever devised, not even a coronary bypass surgical program, could match the protection against recurrent heart attacks" afforded by learning to manage stress (p. 141). Similar success in preventing heart attacks was also reported in a similar study by Friedman, Thoresen, and Gill (1981).

More recently, a new personality pattern, dubbed *Type D,* has been associated with heart disease in a large Belgian study. The Type D personality is characterized by a need to suppress emotional distress. Among the 303 patients (268 men and 35 women) in the study, the risk of death from a heart attack was four times as high for those with Type D personalities (Denollet & Sys, 1996). Corroborating this finding in a sample of 83 women with heart disease, another study has found that those who react slowly to events and who suppress their anger are more likely to have fatal heart attacks (Powell, Shaker, & Jones, 1993). The results of these studies will need to be digested and replicated by other researchers. Stay tuned for further developments.

In summary, such reports have caused a stir, both among health professionals and in the popular press (Lesperance & Frasure-Smith, 1996). The evidence seemed clear cut. Hard workers were told to slow down and become more easygoing. Competitive people were told to relax, become less frantic. Then, the journals began to report mixed results. Many people with Type A or Type D behavior had no sign of heart disease! The last line of the Type A/B/D story has not been written yet. At this moment, however, it appears that those who are most at risk may be the ones who are depressed, those who display lots of anger, and (paradoxically) those who suppress their negative emotions (Friedman, Hawley, & Tucker, 1994; Whiteman & Fowkes, 1997; Wright, 1988).

**HARDINESS** Now consider another personality pattern that has received much attention as a stress moderator: **hardiness,** a resilient quality based on distinctive attitudes toward stress and how to manage it. In contrast with the Type A or D behavior patterns, this is one of the healthy coping styles, as shown in a study by psychologist Suzanne Kobasa (1984). She identified two groups of subjects from a pool of managers working for a big public utility in a large city. The members of one group experienced high levels of stress but were seldom ill, while the members of the second group had high stress and frequently experienced illness (Kobasa, Hilker, & Maddi, 1979). Those who were seldom ill possessed three distinctive attitudes or perspectives, called the "three C's of hardiness":

**Hardiness:** A resilient quality based on the "three Cs" of health: challenge (welcoming change), commitment (involvement in purposeful activity), and control (internal guide for actions).

- *Challenge:* Hardy people welcome change as a challenge, not necessarily a threat.
- *Commitment:* Hardy individuals make a focused commitment to engaging in purposeful activity, solving problems and meeting the challenges they face.
- *Control:* Hardy persons have an internal sense of control over their actions and experiences.

**Chapter 8:**
**Emotion and Motivation**
*Locus of control is a personality factor that predicts how much control a person senses over life events.*

For example, suppose that on the day you must prepare for a major test, a friend confides in you about a terrible problem and begs for your help. These two stressors—an important test and a needy friend—could be overwhelming, especially if you feel you are already stretching some of your resources to the limit. But a hardy individual would employ the "three C's" to reduce the stress of the situation: *challenge* ("I want to be fully prepared for this test; how can I reassure my friend that I'll help as well?"); *commitment* ("My friend is important to me, and so is this test; I'll find a way to meet my obligations in both areas"); and *control* ("I can't take time out from studying, but I can plan to spend the evening discussing the problem; once the test is over I can give my friend my undivided attention").

The key to hardiness is not luck or an inherited ability to face stress with a smile. Rather, hardiness is a learned approach to stress, based on *interpreting* or *perceiving* stressful events in an adaptive way (Kobasa, 1984). When you choose to see life circumstances as manageable rather than overwhelming, you enable yourself to face and solve most problems.

## Learned Helplessness

Another learned response follows a pattern that is very much the opposite of hardiness. Imagine a child who has grown up in a dysfunctional or abusive family—a child who received no emotional or intellectual support. All his life he has been told how "dumb" and "stupid" he was, and when he gets to school, he stumbles on his initial attempts with words and numbers. The teacher gives him poor grades; the other kids make fun of him. After only a few more such attempts he gives up permanently. This passive resignation following recurring failure or punishment is termed **learned helplessness.**

Evidence of learned helplessness originally came from animal studies performed by Martin Seligman and his colleagues. This work showed that dogs receiving inescapable electric shocks soon gave up their attempts to avoid the punishment and passively resigned themselves to their fate (Seligman, 1975, 1991; Seligman & Maier, 1967). Later, when given the opportunity to escape, the dogs typically did nothing but whimper and take the shock. In contrast, a control group of dogs that had not been subjected to previous punishment were quick to escape. Seligman concluded that the experimental group of animals had already learned that nothing they did mattered or altered the consequences, so they "gave up and lay down" (Seligman, 1991, p. 23) and passively accepted their fate (Seligman & Maier, 1967).

**Chapter 13:**
**Psychopathology**
*Learned helplessness can produce depression.*

An experiment by Donald Hiroto (1974) employed human subjects in a variation of Seligman's dog research. Subjects were first placed in a room where they were bombarded by a loud noise. Some quickly learned to turn off the noise by pressing buttons on a control panel, but for other subjects, the panel was rigged so that they could not find any pattern of button-pressing to stop the noise. When the subjects were placed in a new situation, in which a different annoying "whooshing" noise could be easily stopped by a simple hand movement, only those who had learned to stop the loud noise attempted to stop the whooshing sound. The veterans of inescapable noise just sat in the new room, making no effort to stop the latest stressor. They had already learned to be helpless. Seligman sees symptoms of the same learned helplessness syndrome in human populations, such as abused and discouraged children, battered wives, prisoners of war, and depressed patients (Seligman, 1975).

**Chapter 1:**
**Mind, Behavior, and Science**
*The experimental group (but not the control group) receives some special treatment.*

We also see learned helplessness in nursing homes (Baltes, 1995). In fact, we may overestimate the physical deterioration of older people in nursing homes because

**Learned helplessness:** A pattern of not responding to noxious stimuli after an organism learns that its behavior has no effect.

they have learned to feel and to act helpless, say Judith Rodin and Ellen Langer (Buie, 1988). Most nursing homes, geared to routine care of large numbers of patients, do not encourage patients to make decisions or take control of their lives. So, residents are awakened, fed, bathed, toileted, cached in front of television sets, and cycled back to bed, on a routine that offers little variety or choice. This treatment robs patients of individual responsibility and makes them seem incapable of even the simplest tasks.

But Rodin and Langer have shown that learned helplessness need not be hopeless. They arranged for an experimental group of elderly patients to make more choices about day-to-day events, such as meals and activities. Meanwhile, for a control group the staff took full charge of their care, as usual. After 18 months, the group

Nursing home patients who have some responsibility and choice about activities and meals are more active and alert. They also live longer.

given more responsibility were more active and alert and reported a more positive outlook than the controls. More significantly, during the follow-up period, 25% of the control group died, while deaths claimed only 15% of the group given increased responsibility (Rodin, 1986).

## Diminished Hedonic Capacity

Obviously, severe trauma, such as war and crime, can lower victims' post-trauma quality of life. But even garden-variety stress, such as that caused by persistent pressure and hassles, can rob one of **hedonic capacity,** the ability to experience emotions, particularly those of pleasure and joy. For those with diminished hedonic capacity, the defense against negative emotions, such as anxiety, irritation, depression, frustration, anger, and despair, is an emotional reserve—a numbness. College students, for example, report less pleasure in their everyday activities during final exam week than at a less stressful time (Berenbaum & Connelly, 1993). Stress especially reduces hedonic capacity for individuals whose families have a history of depression. You can see how such negative emotional responses can lead to a vicious cycle: Stress leads to joylessness, which prevents people from enjoying life or seeking pleasure, so that they lose hope that anything worth looking forward to will appear in their lives—which creates more stress.

## The Stockholm Syndrome

Victimization can also produce a bizarre stress response known as the **Stockholm syndrome.** This reaction occurs when people who have been hostages and prisoners come to identify and sympathize with their captors. The term refers to a 1974 bank robbery in Stockholm, Sweden, where after five days' imprisonment in the bank vault, the hostages expressed warmth, sympathy, and even attraction for the robbers who had locked them up. In a more recent example, Russian hostages in the breakaway republic of Chechnya had only kind words for their Chechen captors, whom they described as "good," "serious," and kind to children, but they had only harsh criticism for the Russian soldiers who stormed the town to liberate them (National Public Radio, 1995a).

What mysterious emotional process could be at work to make the captives bond so strongly to their captors? Remember that becoming the hostage or captive of terrorists is a grave trauma, a stressor that can place overwhelming demands on the captives' emotional repertoire. Even if other hostages are present, the captives' plight is

**Hedonic capacity:** The ability to experience pleasure and joy.

**Stockholm syndrome:** A psychological reaction in which hostages and prisoners identify and sympathize with their captors.

worsened by their isolation from the outside world. They know nothing of outsiders' efforts to free them, and they must depend on their captors for contact and information. Forming ties to and ultimately caring about their captors may be hostages' only effective way to respond to their fear and loss. In order to adjust to the new (if tragic) reality of their confinement, prisoners must begin to see their captors as human, approachable, and friendly (Auerbach et al., 1994). Only then might the captivity be endured and survived. A sad example of this process is found in the attachment abused children sometimes feel for their abusive parents (Goddard & Stanley, 1994).

## Posttraumatic Stress Disorder

Individuals who have undergone severe ordeals may experience a belated pattern of stress symptoms that can appear months, or even years, after their trauma. This **posttraumatic stress disorder (PTSD)** is a delayed stress reaction in which the individual reexperiences the mental and physical responses accompanying the trauma. In addition to the physical stress response, victims typically become distracted, disorganized, and experience memory difficulties (Arnsten, 1998). Emotionally, they suffer a psychic numbing in relation to everyday events (a reaction we also called *diminished hedonic capacity* earlier). They may also feel alienated from other people. The emotional pain of this reaction can result in various symptoms—such as problems with sleeping, guilt about surviving, difficulty concentrating, and an exaggerated "startle response" (wide-eyed, gasping, surprised behavior displayed when one perceives a sudden threat). Rape survivors, for example, may experience a barrage of psychological aftereffects, including feelings of betrayal by people close to them, anger about having been victimized, and fear of being alone (Baron & Straus, 1985; Cann et al., 1981).

Accumulating evidence suggests that posttraumatic stress disorder can also have lasting biological consequences (Arnsten, 1998; Caldwell, 1995; Mukerjee, 1995). Studies of the brains of humans and laboratory animals exposed to stress indicate that the brain may undergo physical changes when the stress is extreme in intensity or duration. Specifically, the pain-control system may become permanently overactive. In addition, the brain's system that governs the hormone response to stress develops a hair-trigger responsiveness, which tends to make the victim of posttraumatic stress disorder overreact to mild stressors or even to innocuous surprises or unexpected, but harmless, stimulation. Based on these clues, researchers are at work searching for a treatment that might counteract these malfunctioning brain pathways.

## Stress and Gender

Do men and women respond differently to stress? The earliest research on gender differences in coping suggested that women favored coping styles different from those of men: Men were found to use more active, problem-focused strategies, while women were thought to favor more passive and emotion-focused strategies. Newer work by Porter and Stone (1995) suggests that the difference lies not in gender-based coping styles but in the types of stressors individuals encounter. Specifically, the researchers asked individuals to categorize the hassles—mildly stressful daily events they most often encountered—and asked them to describe what action they took "to try to feel better or handle the problem" (that is, emotional-focused versus problem-focused strategies) (Porter & Stone, 1995, p. 190). They found that women most often described problems connected to themselves and close relationships (e.g., marriage, parenting). In contrast, the men reported more work-related problems. Despite this difference in focus, men and women did *not* report using different coping strategies. Notably, they did *not* respond in gender-stereotypical ways: Men were not more likely to "take action" to solve the problem, nor were women more likely to become emotionally distraught. Rather, suggested Porter & Stone, "it is the content of the problem rather than the gender of the individual that determines the selection of coping strategies" (p. 198).

**Chapter 13:**
**Psychopathology**
*Posttraumatic stress disorder is a psychological disorder with a delayed onset.*

**Posttraumatic stress disorder (PTSD):** A delayed stress reaction in which an individual involuntarily reexperiences emotional, cognitive, and behavioral aspects of past trauma.

## Ego Defenses under Stress

Some of our psychological defenses against threatening situations operate unconsciously, said that keen observer of human nature, Sigmund Freud. While many psychologists disagree with the details of Freud's explanation, most agree that he called our attention to some important reactions frequently seen in people under stress. Freud called these unconscious maneuvers **ego defense mechanisms.** (*See also Chapter 10, Personality.*) Most of them, he taught, are unhealthy because they don't really solve our problems but leave them to fester in the unconscious mind. Here are some of the commonest of the ego defense mechanisms identified by Freud:

- **Denial:** "I don't have a problem." This defense avoids a difficult situation by simply denying that it exists. Denial is a defense frequently seen, for example, in alcoholics, child abusers, people who have problems managing anger, and people who engage in risky behavior, such as casual, unprotected sex.
- **Rationalization:** A person using this defense mechanism gives socially acceptable reasons for actions that are really based on motives that they believe to be unacceptable. So, a student who feels stressed by academic pressures may decide to cheat on a test, rationalizing it by saying that "everyone does it."

- **Projection:** This one involves attributing one's own unacceptable motives to another person or thing. An example of projection might occur when two people are competing with each other for a promotion, and one accuses the other of trying to make her look bad in the supervisor's eyes.
- **Repression:** Many people deal with stressful situations by trying to put them out of their minds. If this is done deliberately and consciously, it is called *suppression*. Freud believed, however, that people may also *repress* memories by burying them in the unconscious mind. Freud thought that repressed memories could fester outside of consciousness, where they might cause symptoms of mental disorders, such as phobias, depression, or a psychotic break with reality. (*See also Chapter 6, Learning and Remembering.*)
- **Reaction formation:** This ego defense mechanism occurs when people act in exact opposition to their true feelings. Accordingly, people troubled by their own sexual desires may initiate a crusade against "dirty books" in the city library. Or a child with low self-esteem may become a bully.
- **Displacement:** When your boss makes you angry, you may later displace your anger by yelling at your mate or kicking the dog. This ego defense mechanism involves shifting your reaction from the real source of your distress to a safer individual or object.

People who engage in risky behavior, such as daredevil stunts or unprotected sex, may cope with the stress by the ego defense mechanism of denial: denying the amount of risk involved.

- **Regression:** Under stress, some people hide; others cry, throw things, or even wet their pants. That is, they adopt immature, juvenile behaviors that were effective ways of dealing with stress when they were younger.

Did you recognize yourself in this list? If so, the traditional remedy has been a long course of psychoanalysis, because Freud believed that these mechanisms must be carefully teased out of the unconscious. (*See Chapter 13, Therapies for Mental Disorder.*) While modern psychologists believe that Freud put his finger on some unhealthy responses that people often use under stress, they do not necessarily agree that these responses come from the unconscious. Therefore, contemporary psychologists are more likely to recommend a less extensive form of counseling or therapy—and, perhaps, a bit of eustress.

**Ego defense mechanisms:** According to Freud, these are unconscious strategies that we use to defend ourselves against threat and trauma, reduce internal conflict, and diminish anxiety.

**Denial:** Freud's ego defense mechanism that allows a person consciously to ignore a problem or to conclude that there is no problem at all.

**Rationalization:** Giving socially acceptable reasons for actions that are really based on motives that the person believes to be unacceptable.

**Projection:** Attributing one's own unacceptable motives to another person or thing.

**Repression:** Freud's ego defense mechanism responsible for forgetting.

**Reaction formation:** The ego defense mechanism that makes us overreact in a manner opposite to our unconscious desires.

**Displacement:** The ego defense mechanism by which we shift our reaction from the real source of distress to another individual or object.

**Regression:** The ego defense mechanism that makes us revert to immature behavior in the face of threat.

1. RECALL: *The Type A personality is most likely to be*
   a. aggressive and angry.
   b. humorous.
   c. calm and unruffled.
   d. disconnected from reality.

2. RECALL: *Which of the following are the "three C" characteristics of hardiness?*
   a. character, contentment, and charisma
   b. challenge, commitment, and control
   c. clarity, compassion, and cleverness
   d. careful, centered, and cautious

3. APPLICATION: *Which of the following persons would be most likely to develop a posttraumatic stress disorder?*
   a. a person who narrowly escaped an auto accident
   b. a soldier who had been in combat
   c. an air traffic controller at a busy airport
   d. a person who works for a difficult boss

4. RECALL: *Which ego defense mechanism is apt to make you speak sharply to a friend when you are angry at your supervisor?*
   a. repression
   b. reaction formation
   c. displacement
   d. regression

5. UNDERSTANDING THE CORE CONCEPT: *Which of the following best illustrates the Core Concept for this section?*
   a. Neither Mary nor Michiyo was worried about the upcoming exam, even though they knew that it would be difficult.
   b. They both knew the exam would be difficult, but Michiyo was confident, while Mary was a nervous wreck.
   c. The exam was easy, so both Mary and Michiyo were confident that they had done well.
   d. The exam was difficult, and neither Mary nor Michiyo felt that she would receive a good grade.

**ANSWERS:**    1. a    2. b    3. b    4. c    5. b

---

 **KEY QUESTION** **HOW CAN WE COPE EFFECTIVELY WITH STRESS?**

Do you want to live a long and healthy life? Or, would you prefer a shorter-than-average life ended by heart disease, cancer, stroke, diabetes, cirrhosis of the liver, AIDS, accident, or suicide? While some important factors, such as genetics and access to health care, can have an impact on your health and longevity, the two alternatives are, to a large extent, a matter of lifestyle choices (Elliott & Eisdorfer, 1982; Taylor, 1995). As you can see by "reading between the lines" in Table 9.2, many early deaths derive directly from lifestyle factors—that is, from behaviors that people have voluntarily selected. Stress, of course, is part of the lifestyle equation. For example, some of the risk factors that cause poor health and early death, including smoking and immoderate alcohol consumption, can be aggravated by stress. Others, such as poor diet and lack of exercise, may reduce our ability to handle stress. In this section of the chapter, we will explore some of the resources that we can call upon to pursue a healthier lifestyle and, in the process, help us cope more effectively with the stressors in our lives. As our Core Concept puts it:

 **CORE CONCEPT**     **All the factors that promote health and well-being will also combat distress—and they are largely under our control.**

We will begin this section of the chapter by examining some of our psychological options, such as social support and the power of humor. Then we will consider some of the physical options associated with stress reduction and disease prevention. Finally, we will look at the characteristics of people who say they have found happiness and a sense of well-being.

**TABLE 9.2:** Leading Causes of Death in the United States (1995)

| RANK | PERCENTAGE OF DEATHS | CAUSE OF DEATH | CONTRIBUTORS TO CAUSE OF DEATH (D = diet; S = smoking; A = alcohol) |
|---|---|---|---|
| 1 | 31.9 | Heart disease | DS |
| 2 | 23.3 | Cancers | DS |
| 3 | 6.8 | Strokes | DS |
| 4 | 4.4 | Chronic obstructive lung diseases | S |
| 4 | 4.0 | All accidents | A |
|  | 1.9 | Accidents; motor vehicles | A |
| 6 | 3.6 | Pneumonia and influenza | S |
| 7 | 2.6 | Diabetes | D |
| 8 | 1.9 | AIDS, HIV disease |  |
| 9 | 1.4 | Suicide | A |
| 10 | 1.1 | Chronic liver disease | A |

## Psychological Resources to Consider in Coping with Stress

Earlier in the chapter we saw how the Types A and D behavior patterns, learned helplessness, and certain ego defense mechanisms can aggravate the unhealthy effects of stress. But, as our Core Concept suggests, there are also many good techniques and resources for dealing with stress. We will examine a menu of possibilities below. Perhaps the most important fact is this: Nearly all the stress-related factors in our lives can be modified. We begin with a little help from our friends.

In addition to grief over lost comrades, delayed posttraumatic stress syndrome has been a special problem for Vietnam veterans. Feeling rejected by the American public seemed to heighten their difficulty in adjusting to civilian life.

**SOCIAL SUPPORT**   One of the best antidotes for stress is **social support:** the psychological and physical resources that others provide to help an individual cope with adversity. Research shows that people who encounter major life stresses, such as the loss of a spouse or job, come through the ordeal more easily if they have an effective network of friends or family for social support (Billings & Moos, 1985). By contrast, people with few close relationships die younger, on the average, than people with good social support networks (Berkman & Syme, 1979; Cohen, 1988; Gottlieb, 1981; House, Landis, & Umberson, 1988; Pilisuk & Parks, 1986). In fact, the lack of a reliable support network increases the risk of dying from disease, suicide, or accidents by about the same percentage as does smoking (House et al., 1988).

Social support can take many forms. First, *socioemotional support* gives you the message that you are loved, cared for, esteemed, and connected to other people in a network of communication and mutual obligation (Cobb, 1976; Cohen & Syme, 1985). At times, other people can also provide *tangible support* (money, transporta-

**Social support:** The resources others provide to help an individual cope with stress.

tion, housing) and *informational support* (advice, personal feedback, expert guidance). Anyone with whom you have a significant relationship can be part of your social support network in time of need.

Much research points to the power of social support in moderating vulnerability to a variety of stressful situations (Cohen & McKay, 1983). When people have other people they can turn to, they are psychologically better able to handle job stressors, unemployment, marital disruption, serious illness, and other catastrophes, as well as the everyday problems of living (Gottlieb, 1981; Pilisuk & Parks, 1986). In contrast, lack of a social support system clearly increases one's vulnerability to disease and death (Berkman & Syme, 1979). Moreover, decreased social support in family and work environments is related to increases in psychological problems.

Who is supportive? Health psychologist Shelley Taylor and her colleagues at UCLA have studied the effectiveness of different types of social support given to cancer patients. They found that the effects

Social support is helpful in preventing and coping with stress.

of the helpfulness depended on who the helper was. For example, patients appreciated information and advice from physicians but not from family members, and they valued a spouse's "just being there" but not a doctor's or nurse's mere presence (Dakof & Taylor, 1990; Taylor, 1995). Ironically, researchers have also found that attempts at support can sometimes backfire and actually *increase* the recipient's anxiety (Coyne, Wortman, & Lehman, 1988). Accordingly, if you prefer to attend a doctor's appointment alone, your mother's insistence on accompanying you might cause you to feel anxious, not relaxed. In that case, inappropriate social support may become intrusive and not helpful in the long run. On the other hand, a close other who is not supportive may leave you in greater stress than if you were alone. For example, the symptoms of depression are more likely to increase for a married person who cannot communicate well with his or her spouse than for another subject without a spouse (Weissman, 1987).

One's larger community can also be thought of as a potential support system. People belong to many organizations (neighborhood, religious, extended family)

Giving the elderly an opportunity to continue to make a difference in the lives of those around them greatly improves their health and mood.

that can identify those who require support and channel resources to them. In times of crisis, when a catastrophe strikes a community, both individual and collective efforts are necessary to save lives (Ursano, McCaughey, & Fullerton, 1994). As the human brain has evolved, we have inherited the capacity to connect with others as a way to promote our survival. Taking care of those who need help is an extension of self-protection motives: Our social relationships increase the support we all have available, both to give and receive (Shaffer & Anundsen, 1995).

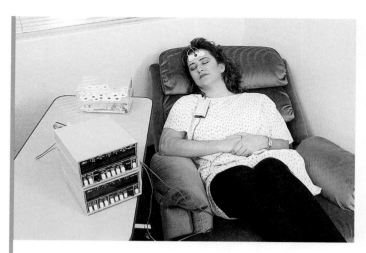

Biofeedback can help people learn how to relax.

**RELAXATION TRAINING AND BIOFEEDBACK** Another approach to coping with stress involves relaxation and leisure. The problem is that our ability to relax is, to a large extent, influenced by activity in the hormone system and the autonomic nervous system—neither of which is normally under direct voluntary control. One way around this problem relies on a technique called **biofeedback** to help people whose internal biological responses have surged out of control. Biofeedback devices measure a variety of physical responses, such as muscle tone, perspiration, skin temperature, and brain waves. The device then gives the user immediate information, or *feedback*, about subtle changes in these responses—changes of which they are not usually aware. With this feedback, subjects can learn relaxation techniques and see how they affect their physical responses.

How effective is biofeedback in learning to control stress? Despite some early, overblown claims for its effectiveness, biofeedback has not proved to be the cure-all that some hoped it would be. More realistically, it may be helpful as one component of a multidimensional therapy package (Miller & Brucker, 1979; Roberts, 1985) through which people learn to relax in the face of stress.

**Chapter 8:**
**Emotion and Motivation**

*Biofeedback devices sense physical signs of arousal—much like the polygraph.*

**OPTIMISTIC THINKING** An optimist sees the glass as half full, while the pessimist sees it as half empty. The optimist sees opportunity, where the pessimist sees potential disaster. The optimist enjoys the smooth sailing, as the pessimist sees only a calm before the storm. Which approach has the advantage under stress? "Life inflicts the same setbacks and tragedies on the optimist as on the pessimist," says psychologist Martin Seligman (1991), "but the optimist weathers them better."

A long-term research program by Seligman and his associates at the University of Pennsylvania indicates that an *optimistic style of thinking* has health benefits. This approach to life has three general characteristics:

- It attributes an unpleasant experience to *specific causes* rather than global problems: "I feel fine except for this headache."
- It blames problems on *external* rather than internal conditions: "I probably got the headache from reading too long without a break; next study session, I'll remember to stop and stretch every half hour."
- It assumes that the causes of pain or illness are *unstable* or temporary; for example, "I don't usually have headaches for very long, so I'm sure I'll feel better soon."

**Biofeedback:** A therapy technique for learning relaxation and new visceral responses to stress, involving devices that sense small physical changes and provide immediate feedback to the individual.

Seligman believes that an optimistic thinking style can be learned. Specifically, he advises those who feel depressed or helpless to acquire an optimistic outlook by *talking to themselves*. This self-talk, says Seligman, should concentrate on the meaning and causes of personal setbacks. For example, if a dieter splurges on a piece of dessert, instead of thinking, "Since I've ruined my whole diet—I might as well eat the whole cake!" she or he should think, "Well, I enjoyed that, but I'll stop with that piece, and I know I am strong enough to stick to this diet most of the time." In essence, Seligman argues that optimism is learned by adopting a *constructive* style of thinking, self-assessment, and behavioral planning.

**Chapter 14:**
**Psychotherapy**

*Psychotherapy includes a variety of psychological treatments for mental disorders.*

A psychotherapy technique, known as *cognitive restructuring*, is based on the constructive reappraisal of stressors. The approach recognizes two especially important factors in determining how people perceive stress: their *uncertainty* about impending events and their *sense of control* over them (Swets & Bjork, 1990). Consequently, two ways people can reduce stress are to reduce their uncertainty about stressful events by finding out as much as they can in advance and to increase their sense of control by learning healthy coping techniques. Cognitive restructuring is especially suitable for people who are having problems with chronic stress.

In general, the work on optimistic thinking and cognitive restructuring attests to the power of the mind to promote health and well-being. When you believe your problems are manageable and controllable, you are more likely to deal with them effectively—which averts the ravages of excessive stress. Consequently, optimistic people have fewer physical symptoms of illness, recover more quickly from certain disorders, are generally healthier, and live longer than pessimists do (Peterson, Seligman, & Vaillant, 1988).

You can apply the lesson of reappraisal if, for example, you are worried about giving a speech to a large, forbidding audience. Try imagining your potential critics in some ridiculous situation—say, sitting there in the nude—and they become less intimidating and perhaps more self-conscious than critical. If you are anxious about being shy at a social function you must attend, think about finding someone who is more shy than you and reducing his or her social anxiety by starting a conversation. You can learn to reappraise stressors by engaging the creative skills you already possess and by imagining and planning your life in more positive, constructive ways.

**THE POWER OF HUMOR**   Physicians like Patch Adams have long believed that people's mental attitudes can make a difference in the length of time they take to recover from an illness—or even *whether* they recover. In a famous book, *The Anatomy of an Illness* (1979), Norman Cousins described his refusal to succumb to the

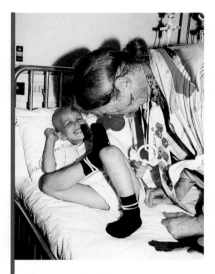

orthodox routine of hospital treatment for a grave form of rheumatoid arthritis. He objected to the regimen of painkilling and tranquilizing drugs and the bland hospital diet. Instead, with the help of a sympathetic physician, Cousins checked himself out of the hospital and into happier surroundings: a hotel room, where he stopped taking his painkillers and tranquilizers. In their place, he substituted large doses of vitamin C and a nearly continuous diet of old *Candid Camera* tapes, Marx Brothers films, and other favorite comedies. Remarkably, he not only survived, but he reversed many of his symptoms. Cousins credited his success to taking control over his environment and his illness and to replacing toxic negative emotions with healthful laughter. He concluded that laughter helps renew the adrenal glands, which can become exhausted from fighting disease.

Humor may be able to promote recovery from illness.

**EVALUATING THE EVIDENCE ON ATTITUDES AND HEALTH**   In evaluating the claims of Patch Adams and Norman Cousins, one must remember that their data consist primarily of their own experiences. They have not conducted controlled experiments. In Norman Cousins's case, other factors were at work that might have helped him recover just as rapidly had he remained in the hospital and followed the usual medical routine. Parallel studies lend some support to Adams's and Cousins's claims, however. For example, cancer patients given therapy aimed at boosting their morale develop stronger immune system defenses (Cousins, 1989). Canadian college students under high stress, but who had a good sense of humor, were less likely to get sick than were their more dour counterparts (Lefcourt & Martin, 1986).

On the opposite side of the issue, a study of 359 cancer patients surprised investigators when it turned up *no* evidence that a patient's attitude had any effect on

**Chapter 1:
Mind, Behavior, and Science**
*A controlled experiment often has a control group* against *which to compare the effects of the critical variable.*

the course of the disease (Cassileth et al., 1985). This finding prompted an editorial in the influential *New England Journal of Medicine*, labeling the attitude–disease connection as "myth" and "folklore" (Angell, 1985). While it may seem that a positive attitude can't hurt (even if it doesn't help), the editorial pointed out a hidden danger: What about patients who do *not* get better? Are they lacking a good attitude, a will to live, or some other strength of character? The editor noted that the happiness-will-make-you-healthy attitude can easily lead to blaming the patient for progression of the illness. Others, too, have noted a simplistic tendency to blame individuals when they become ill or fail to recover (Becker, 1993). Clearly, the issue is complex.

Critical thinking should cut both ways, however: We should also be critical of those who minimize the effects of attitudes on health. The study of cancer patents, cited above, must be weighed against the studies that *do* show a connection between mental states and physical health (Berk, 1996; Wooten, 1994, 1996). It seems likely that extremely negative attitudes can aggravate physical disease processes, while positive attitudes and laughter—in the Patch Adams and Norman Cousins style—can work with our bodies' natural tendencies to heal themselves. It is probably a mistake, however, to think that attitude is *everything*. It takes more than a healthy attitude to have a healthy body.

## Biophysical Resources to Consider in Coping with Stress

So far, we have looked primarily at psychological strategies for dealing with the adverse effects of stress. In addition to these, there are several physical and biological approaches to stress reduction. Some are highly effective. Others, we will see, must be approached with caution. We begin with the health-promoting effects of exercise.

**EXERCISE**   Unfortunately, we have bodies that are better adapted to the strenuous, Stone Age demands of hunting and foraging than to life in a digital, urban world. Spending our days in relative inactivity behind a desk or at computer terminal is not a formula for fitness or mental health. The result is a mind deprived of contact with the natural world and a body that loses muscle tone and accumulates fat under the skin and around the internal organs.

Without a doubt, a program of regular exercise can be good for you. Not only can it increase muscle tone and eliminate fat, but exercise can help you relax and interact with others. It can also reduce stress (McDonald, 1998). And, it may even prolong your life (Lloyd, 1993). A long-term study of 17,000 middle-aged men showed that those who were on an exercise regimen, the equivalent of walking five hours a week, had mortality rates that were almost one-third lower than their couch-potato

---

TABLE 9.3:   Ten Steps to Personal Wellness

1. Exercise regularly.
2. Eat nutritious, balanced meals (high in vegetables, fruits, and grains, low in fat and cholesterol).
3. Maintain a sensible weight.
4. Sleep 7 to 8 hours nightly; rest/relax daily.
5. Wear seat belts and bike helmets.
6. Do not smoke or use drugs.
7. Use alcohol in moderation, if at all.
8. Engage only in protected, safe sex.
9. Get regular medical/dental checkups; adhere to medical regimens.
10. Develop an optimistic perspective and supportive friendships.

Exercise is a good way to reduce stress and improve your general health.

counterparts (Paffenbarger et al., 1986). Even smokers who exercised reduced their death rate by about 30%. An exercise-for-health program has several big pluses. Exercise usually requires a change of environment, removing people from their usual daily hassles and other sources of stress. It also it has a physical training effect by putting short-term stress on the body, which causes the body to rebound and become physically stronger. (Remember *eustress?*)

In addition, it now appears that an exercise program can also make a person *mentally* stronger. In one study, regular aerobic exercise improved the emotional health of female college students who were mildly depressed (McCann & Holmes, 1984). Another study found that a 20-week physical fitness course could produce measurably lower levels of anxiety in sedentary women (Popejoy, 1967). Exercise programs have also been shown to have a positive effect on self-concept (Folkins & Sime, 1981).

Despite these advantages, most resolutions to get more exercise have short lives. People often find it difficult to maintain their motivation to stick with an exercise program. Nevertheless, studies show that people can *learn* to make exercise a regular part of their lives (Myers & Roth, 1997). The keys are (a) finding an activity you like to do, and (b) fitting exercise sessions into your schedule several times a week. Having an exercise partner often provides the extra social support people need to stick with their program.

**NUTRITION AND DIET**    Although a far greater variety of foods is available to us now, as compared to even a generation ago, diet-related disorders—particularly heart disease—are increasing. Undoubtedly part of the problem stems from the temptations of abundant fast foods, such as hamburgers, chips, and pizza. (Is it any wonder that a third of all American adults are currently trying to lose weight?) You can see in Table 9.4 that, among students surveyed in 21 European countries, only about half say they attempt to follow healthy eating practices. Note, also, that women are more likely to be conscious of good nutrition than are men.

**Chapter 8:
Emotion and Motivation**
*Weight control is an American national obsession.*

**TABLE 9.4:**  Eating Practices of European Students

| | PERCENTAGE WHO FOLLOW EACH PRACTICE | |
| --- | --- | --- |
| | MEN | WOMEN |
| Avoid fat | 29 | 49 |
| Eat fiber | 32 | 50 |
| Eat fruit daily | 43 | 62 |
| Limit red meat | 46 | 62 |
| Limit salt | 69 | 68 |

Based on Wardle et al. (1997) and a sample of 16,485 students from 21 European countries.

Nutrition and diet connect to psychology in two ways. First, an inadequate diet can cause mental, as well as physical, disabilities. Second, unhealthy dietary patterns are largely *learned*. Here are some specifics.

Studies of malnourished children show that nutritional deficiencies during early childhood, when the brain is growing fastest, can retard development (Stock & Smythe, 1963; Wurtman, 1982). Nutritional deficiencies can affect adults, too. For example, pernicious anemia, a failure to absorb vitamin $B_{12}$, causes physical and mental slowness. Potassium deficiency can cause listlessness and exhaustion. However, one should be cautious about going to the other extreme by ingesting large quantities of vitamins and minerals. Overdoses of certain vitamins (especially vitamin A) and minerals (such as iron) are easy to achieve and can cause problems that are even more severe than the deficiencies.

Hans Selye found that, for organisms under stress, a low-salt diet helps delay damage caused by clogging of the blood vessels. That prescription is now routinely given to human patients with heart disease and high blood pressure. Later research found that, under stress, a low-cholesterol diet also helps prevent arteriosclerosis. Stressed rats fed on a high-cholesterol diet were three times as likely to develop clogging of the arteries as were unstressed controls fed the same diet ("Stress–illness link," 1987).

What can you do to nurture your heath through nutrition? The categories in Table 9.4 are good places to start. We suggest, also, that you beware of nutritional fads, including dietary supplements that come with miraculous promises that seem almost too good to be true. Nutrition is a science in its infancy, and much remains to be discovered about its connections to physical and mental health.

**DRUGS AS STRESS RELIEVERS**   For millennia, people have used alcohol to help them cope with—or escape from—the stresses of their lives. Illicit drugs, such as cocaine, heroin, and methamphetamine can serve the same purpose. The problem, of course, is that the use of alcohol and other drugs can create new and even more stressful problems through their potential for dependency, addiction, and distortion of thought processes, not to mention their interpersonal and economic impact.

**Chapter 14: Psychotherapy**

*Minor tranquilizers (antianxiety drugs) have legitimate therapeutic uses.*

Physicians may prescribe *antianxiety drugs* (sometimes called "minor tranquilizers") to help their patients cope with stress. While there are valid medical reasons for prescribing these drugs, many psychologists believe that antianxiety drugs are too often given to patients who want only to ignore problems, rather than face them constructively. In addition to their potential for addiction, all such drugs reduce feelings of anxiety and stress at the cost of impaired cognition.

**Chapter 6: Learning and Remembering**

*The relief of nicotine withdrawal symptoms by smoking is an example of negative reinforcement.*

Smoking, too, can become a drug addiction, as well as a stress-related habit. Blood analysis shows that smokers smoke to maintain a constant nicotine level in their systems (Schachter, 1977). When nicotine levels drop, smokers begin to feel nervous, light-headed, and dizzy. They may develop cramps, tremors, heart palpitations, and cold sweats. The nicotine in a cigarette reverses these symptoms. Stress, however, increases the rate at which the body uses and excretes nicotine. Therefore, individuals addicted to nicotine must smoke more to maintain their accustomed level of this drug.

As a habit, smoking can also become associated with many aspects of a smoker's life that have nothing to do with stress. So, when a smoker attempts to quit, the world seems to come alive with stimulus cues that suggest smoking. Smoking becomes associated with finishing a meal, driving to work, taking a coffee break, going to a bar, watching television—with almost everything but showering and sleeping. Quitting, then, becomes both a matter of building new nonsmoking associations to all the situations in which the person once smoked and at the same time going through the biological discomfort of withdrawal. In recent years, the use of nicotine gum or a nicotine patch as a part of a plan for quitting has made it much easier for smokers to endure the withdrawal process.

As difficult as it is to quit, the majority of smokers who try to quit are eventually able to do so, although not necessarily on their first attempt (Schachter, 1977).

Most quit on their own. On the other hand, formal stop-smoking programs don't have a good record, probably because they get the most difficult cases, who have not been able to quit unassisted.

## Health Psychology and Behavioral Medicine

An amazing 93% of patients don't follow the treatment plans prescribed by their doctors (Taylor, 1990). Obviously, being told what to do and doing it are two different things, and we need to know what accounts for the difference. The desire to understand why people fail to take their medicine, get little exercise, eat too much fat, and cope poorly with stress has stimulated the development of two new fields: *behavioral medicine* and *health psychology*.

**Behavioral medicine** is the medical field specializing in the link between lifestyle and disease. **Health psychology** is the comparable psychological specialty. Practitioners in both fields are devoted to understanding the psychosocial factors influencing health and illness (Taylor, 1990, 1992). Among their many areas of concern are health promotion and maintenance; prevention and treatment of illness; causes and correlates of health, illness, and dysfunction; and improvement of the health care system and health policy information (Matarazzo, 1980).

Both fields are actively involved in the prevention and treatment of trauma and disease that result from stressful or dangerous environments and from poor choices with regard to nutrition, exercise, and drug use. Both are emerging disciplines in countries all over the world (Holtzman, 1992). As you might expect, behavioral medicine emphasizes physical causes of disease more than does health psychology. In practice, however, the two fields overlap, and any differences between health psychology and behavioral medicine are ones of emphasis. Psychologists have brought increased awareness of emotions and cognitive factors into behavioral medicine, making it an interdisciplinary field rather than an exclusively medical specialty (Miller, 1983; Rodin & Salovey, 1989). Both fields also recognize the interaction of mind and body and place emphasis on preventing illness, as well as changing unhealthy life styles after illness strikes (Taylor, 1986, 1990).

Helping patients to change their lifestyles is a difficult task. Persuasive strategies identified by social psychologists are now being used to encourage patients' cooperation with their health practitioners (Zimbardo & Leippe, 1991). For example, research shows that people are more likely to comply with requests when they feel they have freedom of choice. Therefore, instead of demanding that a patient strictly adhere to one course of treatment, a physician could be more effective by offering the patient several options, and asking him or her to choose one. Studies also suggest that treating patients in the context of a family or other social group can be productive: Patients are most likely to adhere to physicians' requests when they are informed of their options and get active social support from friends and family (Gottlieb, 1987; Patterson, 1985). In addition, patients are more satisfied with their health care—and are therefore more likely to comply with a treatment regimen—when they believe that the cost of treatment is outweighed by its effectiveness, and when their practitioners communicate clearly, act courteously, and convey caring and support. Based on this finding, some physicians who are critical of their profession argue that doctors' attitudes play a large role in their patients' noncompliance: From this perspective doctors must first be taught to *care* in order to *cure* (Siegel, 1988).

To continue advancing the quality of life into the 21st century, health practitioners must seek to decrease those deaths and disabilities associated with lifestyle factors (see Table 9.2). Smoking, weight problems, high intake of fat and cholesterol, unsafe sex, drug and alcohol abuse, and stress contribute to heart disease, AIDS, cancer, strokes, cirrhosis, accidents, and suicide. Changing the behaviors associated with these *diseases of civilization* will prevent much illness and premature death. People are more likely to stay well if they practice good health habits such as those listed in Table 9.3.

Smoking is a stress-related habit.

**Chapter 12:**
**Social Psychology**
*Social psychologists have studied the factors associated with persuasion, obedience, and compliance.*

**Behavioral medicine:** The medical field specializing in the link between lifestyle and disease.

**Health psychology:** The psychological specialty devoted to understanding how people stay healthy, why they become ill, and how they respond when ill.

### Prevention: The Example of Heart Disease

We can illustrate some of the problems and accomplishments of health psychology and behavioral medicine with a brief look at a major study to prevent heart disease that was conducted in three towns in California. The goals of the study were (1) to persuade people to reduce their cardiovascular risk via changes in smoking, diet, and exercise, and (2) to determine which method of persuasion was more effective. In one town a two-year advertising campaign was conducted through the mass media. A second town received the same two-year media campaign plus a series of special workshops on modifying health habits for high-risk individuals. The third town served as a control group and received no persuasive campaign. Results showed that the people in the town that had received only the mass-media campaign were more knowledgeable than the controls about the links between lifestyle and heart disease. But, as seen in Figure 9.6, the media blitz produced only modest changes in behaviors and health status. As compared with people in the other two groups, those in the town that received both the workshops and the media campaign showed more substantial and long-lasting effects in changing health habits, particularly in reducing smoking (Farquhar, Maccoby, & Solomon, 1984; Maccoby et al., 1977).

The good news from this study is that lifestyle factors can be modified. The bad news is that it is difficult and expensive to do so. Although mass-media campaigns are relatively inexpensive and can increase people's knowledge about healthy behaviors, apparently they are not very effective in changing behaviors.

### FIGURE 9.6: Promoting Healthy Change

Knowledge of cardiovascular disease risk factors was greater among residents of Town B, who were exposed to a two-year mass-media health campaign, than among residents of Town A, who were not exposed to the campaign. Knowledge gain was greater still in residents of Town C, who participated in intense workshops and instruction sessions for several months during the media blitz. As knowledge increased, bad health habits (risk behaviors) and signs (indicators) decreased, with Town C leading the way, followed by Town B.

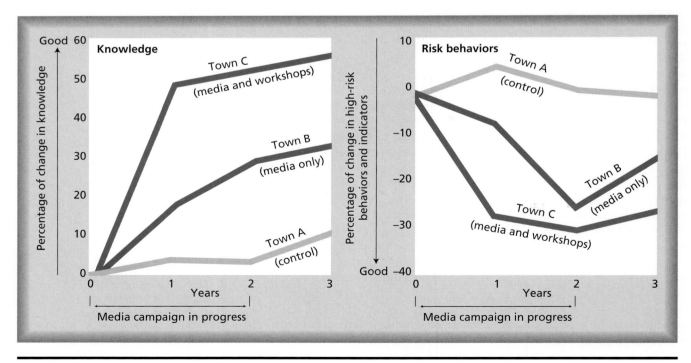

We have seen that heart disease is to some extent preventable with good exercise and nutrition programs. We have also seen that a stress-management program could reduce stress and, in turn, the likelihood of a second heart attack. Clearly, such measures can work for people who can be persuaded to adopt them. An ambitious program aimed at doing this with a group of more than a thousand cardiac patients has been under way since 1978. The project directors have tested several promising methods aimed at reversing the symptoms of the Type A personality, using different combinations of techniques with different groups of volunteer subjects. What have they found to be the best approach? The benefits from participating in small psychotherapy/discussion groups have been the most dramatic. After four and a half years of treatment, patients who had participated in the group therapy program had 44% fewer heart attacks than did a control group of cardiac patients enrolled in an educational program run by a cardiologist (Thoresen, 1990).

What can you do to make your own lifestyle more healthy—and, in the process, perhaps, prevent a heart attack? Table 9.3 gives some specific suggestions. Again, we would like to emphasize the idea contained in our Core Concept: The route to wellness is also the route that leads away from the debilitating effects of excessive stress.

**Subjective well-being (SWB):**
An individual's evaluative response to his or her life, including cognitive and emotional reactions.

## Happiness and Well-Being

Following the suggestions on the list in Table 9.3 can lead to a feeling-good state that researchers call **subjective well-being (SWB).** Do you usually have that feeling? Studies of SWB ask respondents to rate experiences in their lives or answer questions about factors that affect satisfaction, well-being, mood, or success (Diener, 1984; Diener & Diener, 1996). In an important review of decades of study, researchers David Myers and Ed Diener (1995) conclude that, despite many and important individual differences in the causes and expressions of SWB, it is defined by three central components:

- *Satisfaction with present life:* People who are high in SWB like their work and are satisfied with their current personal relationships. They are *sociable*, outgoing, and willing to open up to others (Pavot, Diener, & Fujita, 1990). Just as important, high SWB people *like themselves*, and they enjoy good health and high self-esteem (Janoff-Bulman, 1989, 1992).

- *Relative presence of positive emotions:* High SWBs more frequently feel pleasant emotions, mainly because they evaluate the world around them in a generally positive way. They have an *optimistic outlook*, and they expect success in what they undertake (Seligman, 1991).

- *Relative absence of negative emotions:* Individuals with a strong sense of subjective well-being experience fewer and less severe episodes of negative emotions such as anxiety, depression, and anger. On the positive side, they *like what they do*, have a good sense of control in life events, and are able to enjoy the "flow" of engaging work (Crohan et al., 1989; Csikszentmihalyi, 1990; Larson, 1989).

You can give yourself a quick SWB checkup by rating yourself on these three points.

So, who has feelings of subjective well-being and happiness? Before reading further, take a moment to consider whether you think some groups of people are happier than others. If so, which ones? (*See Chapter 8, Emotion and Motivation.*) From

their review of the SWB literature, Myers and Diener (1995) have exploded several myths and misunderstandings about happiness:

- *There is no "happiest age" of life.* SWB cannot be predicted from someone's age. Most age groups studied exhibit similar levels of life satisfaction, for example, although the causes of their happiness do change with age (Inglehart, 1990).

- *Happiness has no "gender gap."* While women are more likely than men to suffer from anxiety and depression, and men are more at risk for alcoholism and certain personality disorders, approximately equal numbers of men and women report being fairly satisfied with life (Fujita, Diener, & Sandvik, 1991; Haring, Stock, & Okun, 1984; Inglehart, 1990). (*See Chapter 13, Psychopathology.*)

- *There are minimal racial differences in happiness.* African Americans and European Americans report nearly the same levels of happiness, and African Americans are even slightly less vulnerable to depression (Diener et al., 1993). Despite racism and discrimination,

*continued*

members of disadvantaged minority groups generally seem to "think optimistically" by making realistic self-comparisons and attributing problems less to themselves than to unfair circumstances (Crocker & Major, 1989).

- *Money does not buy happiness.* At the level of nations, wealthier societies report greater well-being. But within countries—except for very poor, desperate nations such as Bangladesh and India—once the necessities of food, shelter, and safety are provided, there is only a very weak correlation between income and happiness. Having *no* money is a cause of misery, but wealth itself cannot guarantee happiness (Diener & Diener, 1996; Diener et al., 1993). The secret here is that happy people are not those who get what they want—but rather those who want what they have (Myers & Diener, 1995).

These findings tell us that life circumstances—one's age, sex, race, nationality, or income—do not predict happiness. Not surprisingly, considering that this is a psychology text, the key factors in subjective well-being appear to be psychological traits and processes. It is sometimes startling to

People who are high in SWB more frequently feel pleasant emotions because they evaluate the world in a positive way.

discover how well many people are able to adapt to major changes in their lives—and still feel happy. One study found, for example, that while the moods of victims of spinal cord injuries were extremely nega-

tive shortly after their accidents, several weeks later they reported feeling much happier than they had been *before* sustaining their injuries (Silver, 1983).

Life events can alter our moods, change and almost seem to destroy our lives. Not all life events can be forgotten; some people will find it daunting or impossible to recover from tragedies such as losing a loved one to war, violent crime, or diseases such as Alzheimer's (Bard & Sangrey, 1979; Janoff-Bulman, 1992; Silver, Boon, & Stones, 1983; Silver & Wortman, 1980; Vitaliano et al., 1991). Even more common losses such as the death of a spouse are likely to be deeply painful and sometimes require years for bereavement and healing. But studies of happiness and well-being show that people are exceedingly resilient. Those who have undergone severe stress usually manage to adapt after an initially strong and emotional response. Typically they return to a mood and level of well-being similar to—or even better than—that prior to the traumatic event (Headey & Wearing, 1992).

## Check Your Understanding

1. RECALL: *All the following are healthy ways to cope with stress, except*
   a. relaxation training.
   b. cognitive restructuring.
   c. exercise.
   **d.** reaction formation.

2. RECALL: *Biofeedback can help people learn*
   **a.** to relax.
   b. to get rid of ego defense mechanisms.
   c. to do an appraisal of their life goals.
   d. to engage in regular exercise.

3. RECALL: *Norman Cousins is well known for his belief in the healing power of*
   a. exercise.
   **b.** humor.
   c. social support.
   d. drugs.

4. APPLICATION: *If you have a very sick friend, you should avoid saying,*
   a. "Social support can help people cope with illness."
   b. "Good nutrition is an essential part of a healthy lifestyle."
   c. "Relaxation training and biofeedback can reduce stress."
   **d.** "A good attitude can make you well."

5. UNDERSTANDING THE CORE CONCEPT: *Exercise, good nutrition, social support, and relaxation training can help people*
   a. cope with stress.
   b. achieve a more healthy lifestyle.
   **c.** both a and b
   d. none of the above

**ANSWERS:** 1. d   2. a   3. b   4. d   5. c

## Coping with Test Anxiety

The test is being passed down the row, and your heart starts racing. You can feel your pulse pounding in your temples. A knot forms in the pit of your stomach. The pen feels slippery as your hands begin to perspire. You have studied for the test, but suddenly you can't remember "general adaptation syndrome" from "psychoneuroimmunology." You have a full-blown attack of test anxiety! What can you do?

Prevention rather than cure is the best way to deal with this problem: Take steps to prevent test anxiety from occurring in the first place. And that's where you can use psychology on yourself. Your authors recommend that you take the following steps well before the test:

- *Remember that a moderate degree of arousal is actually helpful.* It can perk up your brain and help you think more clearly. (Remember Selye's concept of *eustress*.) So, don't mistake a bit of nervousness for a debilitating attack of test anxiety.
- *Learn the material thoroughly.* Feeling confident that your head contains the information you need is a great anxiety reducer. To do so, you need to know not only the important terms but how these terms are connected to the important issues and concepts (such as the Core Concepts in this book). You will also want to "psych out" your profes-

sor: What does he or she see as the important terms, issues, and concepts? Learning the material and identifying the important concepts can be hard work—but not impossible. Don't be surprised if it requires two or more hours of study outside of class for every hour you spend in class.

- *Take advantage of social support.* Of all the techniques discussed in this chapter, this may be the most useful. You will find social support in other students who are taking the same course. Seek them out and schedule a few group study sessions. Use these sessions to clarify concepts and to anticipate what will be on the next examination.
- *Use relaxation training techniques.* Relaxation training will help you learn to calm both mind and body. It is likely that someone on your campus has some expertise in this area and would be happy to help you: Ask in your counseling center, psychology department, or learning resources center. Once you acquire some of the techniques, you will be able to apply them before a test or whenever you feel that anxiety threatens to run away with you.

It is also helpful to realize that test anxiety is a common problem. Nearly everyone has experienced it at one time or another. Perhaps it is most important to realize that test anxiety doesn't have to spiral out of control and ruin your grade. You can learn the techniques that will help you move from *distress* to *eustress*.

## CHAPTER SUMMARY

 **KEY QUESTION** **IS IT THE STRESS OR THE STRESSOR?**

- At the root of most stress is change and the need to adapt to environmental, physical, psychological, and social demands. Primitive stressors included mortal threats such as starvation, exposure to the elements, attack, and natural catastrophes. Modern life still may include catastrophes, but it also exposes us to the cumulative effects of stressors acting over the long term: societal stressors, hassles, burn-

out, and various life changes. The Holmes-Rahe SRRS has been used extensively to measure life changes and to correlate them with changes in health, although this work has been criticized on several counts.

 **CORE CONCEPT** The effects of stress (an internal response) depend more on the intensity and duration of stress than on its source (the stressor).

**KEY QUESTION** HOW DOES STRESS AFFECT US PHYSICALLY?

- Stress involves the effect of mental processes on the body. Stress arouses us physiologically and often produces a fight-or-flight response. This may serve us well in acute but not chronic stress. Selye found that chronic stress from any source produces the three stages of the general adaptation syndrome: the alarm reaction, resistance, and exhaustion. Stress can also have effects on the immune system—sometimes stimulating it and sometimes suppressing it. Selye also taught that some forms of stress—eustress—can have healthy effects by promoting growth and resilience.

**CORE CONCEPT**  **Stress can help us meet challenges and grow stronger, but too much stress—distress—can have harmful physical consequences.**

**KEY QUESTION** HOW DO WE RESPOND PSYCHOLOGICALLY TO STRESS?

- Certain personality variables can help or hinder an individual's ability to cope with stress. Those with Type A personality traits risk adverse stress reactions, although the specific traits associated with this risk are still under dispute. Some people, however, display a resistance to stress stemming from hardiness, a learned trait. When punishment or failure are unavoidable, the result is often learned helplessness and diminished hedonic capacity. There are no gender differences in coping styles, although there are differences in the causes of stress. Extreme stress sometimes produces a delayed stress reaction, known as posttraumatic stress disorder. Those who have undergone

a hostage ordeal may come to identify with their captors, a condition known as the Stockholm syndrome. Sigmund Freud identified several more common means of coping with threat that he called ego defense mechanisms. These include denial, rationalization, projection, repression, reaction formation, displacement, and regression.

**CORE CONCEPT**  **Our psychological responses under stress depend on personality, perceptions, and the ways we have learned to respond.**

**KEY QUESTION** HOW CAN WE COPE EFFECTIVELY WITH STRESS?

- Many psychological techniques and resources are available to help us cope with stress and promote a healthy lifestyle: social support, relaxation training, the modification of thought processes, optimism, and humor. Critics caution against uncritical acceptance of claims for the effects of attitudes on health. Among the physical factors that can help us cope with stress are exercise and good nutrition. Caution is in order, however, in using drugs to cope with stress. The relatively new fields of health psychology and behavioral medicine focus on coping with stress and encouraging healthy lifestyles. People who are happy or who have subjective well-being tend to have positive emotions and a general satisfaction with their lives. Happiness can be found in people of all ages, genders, racial groups, and income levels.

**CORE CONCEPT**  **All the factors that promote health and well-being will also combat distress—and they are largely under our control.**

## REVIEW TEST

For each of the following items, choose the single correct or best answer.

1. Which of the following would a psychologist call *stress?*
   a. an earthquake that destroys all your possessions
   b. an angry neighbor who is demanding that you turn down your stereo
   c. an adrenaline response that makes your heart pound, your face pale, and your palms sweaty
   d. an extremely frightening experience
2. Which of the following experiences would be considered a chronic *societal stressor?*
   a. an earthquake
   b. a jail term

c. being stuck in traffic

d. widespread unemployment

3. Which one would be most likely to produce *learned helplessness?*

a. frequent and inescapable punishment

b. as much money as you could ever spend

c. a situation in which you were fearful

d. the death of your spouse

4. Malcolm does not get upset when he encounters problems, seeing them as challenges to be overcome rather than threats to his well-being. Which of the following terms best describes Malcolm's approach to possible stressors?

a. hardiness

b. learned helplessness

c. the Type A personality

d. hedonic capacity

5. The fight-or-flight syndrome involves

a. PTSD.

b. ego defense mechanisms.

c. activity in the autonomic nervous system.

d. GAS stage 2.

6. Which of the following is *not* a stage in the general adaptation syndrome described by Hans Selye?

a. alarm

b. withdrawal

c. resistance

d. exhaustion

7. Nursing home patients had more positive moods, better health, and longer survival compared to others when they were provided with

a. round-the-clock medical care.

b. busywork and entertaining activities.

c. responsibilities that gave them perceived control.

d. service that relieved them of all aspects of self-care.

8. What is the medical specialty that is related to *health psychology?*

a. rehabilitation medicine

b. psychoneuroimmunology

c. behavioral medicine

d. eustress

9. A good friend of yours has recently suffered the loss of a close family member. To help your friend cope with this trauma, you should encourage her to

a. use her ego defense mechanisms.

b. hit a punching bag to "get it out of her system."

c. exercise until she is exhausted.

d. seek the social support of friends and relatives.

10. Research on subjective well-being indicates that
_____ are happier than _____.

a. women/men

b. wealthy Americans/middle-class Americans

c. young people/older adults

d. none of the above

ANSWERS:  1. c  2. d  3. a  4. a  5. c  6. b
7. c  8. c  9. d  10. d

# IF YOU'RE INTERESTED . . .

## BOOKS

Adams, P., and Mylander, M. (1998). *Gesundheit!: Bringing good health to you, the medical system, and society through physician service, complementary therapies, humor, and joy.* Rochester, VT: Healing Arts Press.

*The author, a doctor who dresses like a clown, tells the story of adding humor and compassion to medical care, founding the Gesundheit Institute (Gesundheit is German for "health"), and carrying the message of hopeful, humorous healing to other countries.*

Adams, P., with an introduction by Robin Williams. (1998). *House calls: How we can all heal the world one visit at a time.* San Francisco: Robert D. Reed.

*This primer on wellness includes suggestions to visit loved ones, how to make healthy choices, how to be a good doctor, and how to be a successful hospital patient. The key,*

*says Adams, is having a meaningful connection between doctor and patient—a healing bond for both of them.*

Cousins, N. (1979). *The anatomy of an illness as perceived by a patient: Reflections on healing and rejuvenation.* New York: W. W. Norton.

*Norman Cousins revolutionized popular and professional thinking about modern medicine when he reacted to a frightening diagnosis with his own self-prescription of happiness and laughter, contributing powerfully to the modern science of health promotion.*

Davidson, J. (1997). *The complete idiot's guide to managing stress.* New York: Alpha Books.

*Written in annotated outline form, illustrated with cartoons and diagrams, this lighthearted book is sensible and very helpful, not only for understanding and coping with your own stress, but for comprehending what is stressful for* others, the possible consequences, and how to take healthy preventive and responsive action.

Ellis, Carolyn. (1995). *Final negotiations: A story of love, loss, and chronic illness.* Philadelphia: Temple University Press.

*A remarkable work by a psychologist demonstrates both the account-making process "in action" and its therapeutic potential. Early in her academic career, Ellis had dealt with the tragic death of her brother in a plane crash. Years later, she watched her life partner of nine years die of emphysema—and then spent about as many years producing a book documenting her memories, grief, and struggles for meaning. Ellis candidly describes intimacy, withdrawal, agony, and relief. For Ellis, writing the book commemorated her love, structured her grieving, and gradually returned some control and hope to her life. "Opening up," therefore, is not a haphazard, indiscriminate act of disclosing to anyone who will listen or read; it is alternately private and public, a deliberate effort to sort through loss and reforge a sense of self.*

Gatto, R. P. (1993). *Controlling stress in the workplace: How you handle what happens.* San Diego: Pfeiffer and Company.

*We tend to be very work-identified—and much of our stress is specifically related to our job or workplace. This paperback discusses how to identify your stress level, organize your efforts to cope and control, identify your stress-management style, and change your own behavior.*

Hendricks, G. (1995). *Conscious breathing: Breathwork for health, stress release, and personal mastery.* New York: Bantam Books.

*A bit New-Agey in appearance, yet based on sound principles and practices, this well-illustrated workbook reviews techniques for relaxation, meditation, and body awareness/biofeedback that can be immediately applied to make one feel better, more focused and relaxed, and healthier.*

Klein, A. (1989). *The healing power of humor.* Los Angeles: Jeremy P. Tarcher.

*The subtitle is "Techniques for Getting through Loss, Setbacks, Upsets, Disappointments, Difficulties, Trials, Tribulations, and All That Not-So-Funny Stuff." It delivers on the promised techniques by reviewing what humor can (and cannot) be expected to accomplish; simple (if sometimes goofy) gimmicks for lightening things up; and explaining what research has shown about the connections between humor and well-being.*

Neeld, E. H. (1990). *Seven choices: Taking the steps to new life after losing someone you love.* New York: Delta.

*After her husband, a healthy and fit man, died suddenly while on an evening run, Elizabeth Neeld spent months observing and understanding her own and others' reactions to loss and grief, concluding that life after loss is conducted as a series of choices. Her story is also a guidebook for survivors of loss and those who wish to help bereaved loved ones.*

Paul, M., (1998). *The healing mind: The vital links between brain and behavior, immunity, and disease.* Dunne Books.

*A medical doctor, writing more like a novelist than a scientist, offers an overview of the connection between health and consciousness, ranging from topics as light as the benefits of keeping pets to those as heavy as dealing with terminal cancer.*

Plotkin, M. J. (1993). *Tales of a shaman's apprentice: An ethnobotanist searches for new medicines in the Amazon rain forest.* New York: Viking.

*"I had followed the old shaman through the jungle for three days and . . . we had developed an enigmatic relationship." Thus Mark Plotkin begins the story of his work with South American natives and their therapeutic uses of medicinal plants. This is a story not only of perspectives on healing but also of the changes and losses incurred when traditional cultures yield to "progress" and "development" by modern economic interests.*

Price, R. (1995). *A whole new life: An illness and a healing.* New York: Plume/Penguin.

*The celebrated novelist Reynolds Price reflects on his own experiences with the discovery of a cancerous tumor "certain to kill" him, his "refusal to die," and his explorations of traditional and alternative medicine, encounters with professionals and fellow patients, the callous and the sympathetic, and the challenges of weaving together the elements of his own life and past to face the crisis of his future.*

Sapolsky, R. M. (1998). *Why zebras don't get ulcers: An updated guide to stress-related diseases, and coping.* New York: W. H. Freeman.

*Cutting-edge research-based advice laced with humor and insight, this work examines the utterly human dilemma of life-threatening stress and how it can be understood, modified, and controlled.*

Seligman, M. E. P. (1991). *Learned optimism.* New York: Alfred A. Knopf.

*This well-written guide to developing a healthy, positive lifestyle and overcoming learned helplessness, mild depression, and pessimism includes self-assessment techniques and programs for acquiring optimistic, constructive life skills.*

Selzer, R. (1998). *The doctor stories.* New York: Picador USA.

*This selection of short fiction is written by physicians and surgeons, whose stories show the complex challenges and changes inherent in illness and the struggles of both patient and doctor to survive and heal.*

Siegel, B. S. (1986). *Love, medicine, and miracle.* New York: Harper & Row.

*These are stories of people who made remarkable recoveries, their new perspectives on life, and the characteristics that may have helped them to become survivors.*

## VIDEOS

*After the shock.* (1990 [made for cable], color, 100 min.). Directed by Gary Sherman; starring Jack Scalia, Yaphet Kotto, Scott Valentine, Rue McClanahan.

*This film provides moving depictions of ordinary citizens taking heroic action in rescue efforts following the 1989 San Francisco earthquake. Reenacted scenes are mixed with actual footage of the quake and its aftermath.*

*Born on the Fourth of July.* (1989, color, 144 min.). Directed by Oliver Stone; starring Tom Cruise, Willem Dafoe, Raymond J. Barry, Carolyn Kava, Kyra Sedgwick.

*This powerful true story tells of Ron Kovic, who joined the Marines as an eager volunteer during the Vietnam War and returned a paraplegic to face a hostile society, a family in denial, a torturous rehabilitation, and a complete political change of heart. The film is one of the best depictions of posttraumatic stress disorder (PTSD).*

*The doctor.* (1991, color, 123 min.). Directed by Randa Haines; starring William Hurt, Elizabeth Perkins, Christine Lahti, Mandy Patinkin.

*Before television's* Chicago Hope *and* ER, *one of the few recent film presentations of the roles played by physician and patient was this intriguing portrayal of a doctor who finds the tables turned on him. A successful but insensitive surgeon is diagnosed with throat cancer and forced to experience life from the patient's perspective. The film is based on the true story,* A Taste of My Own Medicine, *by Ed Rosenbaum, M.D.*

*Falling down.* (1993, color, 115 min.). Directed by Joel Schumacher; starring Michael Douglas, Robert Duvall, Barbara Hershey, Rachel Ticotin, Tuesday Weld.

*A stressed, repressed Californian abandons his car in a traffic jam and wanders Los Angeles in a frenzied, violent outburst. At one level, this is a movie about a man who has an incredibly bad day. But at another level, it is a review of how two men—the criminal and the police officer pursuing him—have responded so differently to the stressors and traumas of their lives. Well acted and realistic, it is also bleak and depressing.*

*Fearless.* (1993, color, 122 min.). Directed by Peter Weir; starring Jeff Bridges, Isabella Rossellini, Rosie Perez, Tom Hulce, John Turturro, John DeLancie.

*After he and a few others survive a devastating plane crash, a man loses perspective on the meaning of his life, work, and family. Suspecting that he has become indestructible, he engages in increasingly risky and careless—fearless—behavior, alienating everyone except fellow survivors who are similarly disoriented, traumatized, and guilt-ridden. The film displays great writing and acting and an intriguing look at what comes after surviving trauma.*

*God said, "Ha!"* (1999, color, 85 min.). Directed by Julia Sweeney; starring Julia Sweeney and Quentin Tarantino as themselves.

*Former Saturday Night Live cast comedian Julia Sweeney survived a terrible period during which both she and her brother were diagnosed with cancer, and their families' lives went into an upheaval of anxiety, relocation, and uncertainty that they characteristically treated with dark humor and comic hope. This film, her one-woman show, is based on her book of the same name (Bantam/Doubleday/Dell, 1998).*

*Hannah and her sisters.* (1986, color, 106 min.). Directed by Woody Allen; starring Woody Allen, Michael Caine, Mia Farrow, Barbara Hershey, Max von Sydow, Dianne Wiest.

*This is a funny, urbane story about three New York sisters and their convoluted relationships with men and with each other. A subplot involves the character of Mickey (played by Allen), an unhappy hypochondriac whose quest for meaning in life leads him to "shop" for religion and ultimately find what he needs in humor, self-acceptance, and love.*

*Heartsounds.* (1984, color, 135 min.). Directed by Glenn Jordan; starring Mary Tyler Moore, James Garner, Sam Wanamaker, Wendy Crewson.

*This touching and wrenching film is based on Martha Weinman Lear's novel about a woman whose husband, a physician, suffers a series of debilitating heart attacks. It is an outstanding presentation of the stresses and traumas that afflict not only the patient but family and friends who must meet and perhaps survive the challenges of illness and recovery.*

*Patch Adams.* (1998, color, 103 min.). Directed by Tom Shadyac; starring Robin Williams, Monica Potter, Daniel London, Bob Gunton, Peter Coyote.

*This film is based on the true story of Hunter "Patch" Adams, M.D., who became a physician despite his irreverence regarding the power and money of modern medicine and his desire to make medical care reassuring and even fun for patients. (See Adams's book recommendations, above).*

**WHAT FORCES SHAPE OUR PERSONALITIES?**

The psychodynamic, humanistic, and cognitive theories portray personality as a developmental process, shaped by our internal needs and cognitions and by external pressures from the social environment.

**Explaining Unusual People and Unusual Behavior:** You don't need a theory of personality to explain why people do the expected.

**WHAT PATTERNS ARE FOUND IN PERSONALITY?**

Some theories attribute personality to stable patterns known as traits, types, and temperaments.

**Finding Your Type:** When it comes to classifying personality according to types, a little caution may be in order.

**WHAT "THEORIES" DO PEOPLE USE TO UNDERSTAND EACH OTHER?**

People everywhere develop implicit assumptions ("folk theories") about personality, but these assumptions vary in important ways across cultures.

**Developing Your Own Theory of Personality:** You'll probably want to be eclectic.

**USING PSYCHOLOGY TO LEARN PSYCHOLOGY: YOUR ACADEMIC LOCUS OF CONTROL**

# 10

# Personality

*W*hat drove Margaret Sanger?

On a sweltering day in July of 1912, nurse Sanger was called to a slum in New York City's Lower East Side, to the cramped apartment of Jake Sachs and his family. Jake, a truck driver, had found his wife, Sadie, mother of their three small children, unconscious and bleeding on the kitchen floor after attempting a self-induced abortion. Days later, after Sanger and the doctor had successfully fought the infection that threatened Sadie Sachs's life, her immediate plea was, "Doctor, what can I do to stop having babies?" The doctor, kind, but no doubt frustrated at hearing this question asked too often, gruffly replied, "Better tell Jake to sleep on the roof" (Sanger, 1971).

In 1912, medical advice on sex was forbidden; condoms and diaphragms were virtually impossible to obtain. Reflecting the prevailing morality, legal codes outlawed any form of artificial birth control and condemned abortion. Nevertheless, up to 100,000 illegal abortions a year were performed in New York alone. People with education or money had always been able to prevent unwanted pregnancies. But among the poor and uneducated, those least able to bear the costliness of many children, little was known about sex, much less reproduction and family planning (Asbell, 1995). Furthermore, pregnancy was life-threatening. Between 1910 and 1925, more than 200,000 American women died in childbirth.

Sanger saw Sadie Sachs one last time: Three months later, pregnant once again, Sadie died of a back-alley abortion. After watching yet another needless death, Sanger resolved to find an answer to her patients' pleas for safe contraception, "no matter what it might cost" (Sanger, 1938, in Conway, 1992, p. 567).

The cost was high. Herself the mother of three children and happily married to an architect, Sanger left nursing and put her family in the background in order to research and promote contraception full-time. She chose the term "birth control" for her movement in order to shift the focus from sexuality and morality and place it firmly on humanity, choice, and population. When in 1914 she was threatened with a prison term for "indecency," Sanger fled to England until charges were dropped a year later. In 1916 she opened a public birth-control clinic and began to serve a series of jail sentences for illegally distributing information about contraception.

*For 40 years, Sanger persistently challenged laws making contraception a criminal act and insisted that women take control of—and responsibility for—their bodies, sexuality, and childbearing (Kennedy, 1970; Sanger, 1971). She had an acute sense for politics, but some criticized her as self-serving for breaking with political organizations that had promoted her early work when she saw those alliances as less to her advantage. Finally in 1952, Sanger, then in her 70s, joined forces with philanthropist Katharine McCormick to commission the development of an oral contraceptive, something that could be taken "like an aspirin." Without government backing or funding, Sanger convinced McCormick to provide financial support for the work of biological researcher Gregory Pincus and his staff. Pincus succeeded brilliantly—the first birth-control pills were approved for prescription in 1960—and he is credited as the "Father of the Pill." In view of its history, however, the Pill also had two mothers: passionate, persistent Margaret Sanger and philanthropist Katharine McCormick.*

*What drove Sanger to begin her crusade, and what personal qualities empowered her to endure punishment and sacrifice? Let's look more closely at some of the details of her life and work.*

- *Born in 1879, Margaret Higgins Sanger was the sixth of eleven children. She maintained a lifelong rivalry with a sister, Ethel Byrne, who was exceptionally pretty and their mother's obvious favorite.*
- *She was 19 when her mother died of tuberculosis. Although she remembered her father as generous and freethinking (and may well have acquired her habit of independent thought from him), she blamed him for exhausting her mother with children and household labor.*
- *Sanger's exile in England damaged her marriage irreparably. She had only just returned when her young daughter Peggy died of pneumonia. Stricken by guilt and grief, Sanger suffered a "nervous breakdown," recovering in time to face a trial on new charges of obscenity (Asbell, 1995).*
- *Divorced after 22 years of marriage, she married a wealthy businessman who adored her and supported her work, helping her to take her message to the powerful, affluent, and educated.*

Sanger's zeal was so strong and her efforts so effective that "the Pill" she sought was, at last, approved by the U.S. Food and Drug Administration in 1960—six years before her death. Thus, within her own lifetime, Sanger saw her life's mission begin, grow, and come to fruition. But why did she sacrifice so much to do it, when others who saw the same problems were willing to overlook them? Why give up a comfortable, anonymous life for notoriety, punishment, and disruption? Why, when she watched young Sadie Sachs die from a botched and illegal abortion, did she not walk away and forget about it? Like many health-care professionals who must deal with disease and death on a daily basis, Sanger could have disconnected herself from the Sachs tragedy. She could have rationalized the death, blaming Sadie herself, or her husband, or the impersonal cruelties of ignorance and poverty. She could then have gone back to her relatively comfortable and safe life. But something about Margaret Sanger's *personality* made it impossible for her to forgive and forget or to accept as inevitable so many unwanted births.

Did her personality also have a sinister side? Historians have criticized Margaret Sanger for seeking sole credit for the successes of the birth-control movement. However, as one biographer notes, "Her ambitions would be considered normal in a male reformer" (Conway, 1992, p. 550). Perhaps Sanger accomplished what she did, in part, because of her gender. Ultimately, however, it may have been another aspect of her personality—her compassion—that drove Margaret Sanger beyond gender to benefit all humankind.

You may wonder: Where do such qualities—compassion, selfishness, commitment to purpose, willingness to sacrifice, stubbornness, and obsessiveness—come

Personality is the thread of continuity in an individual in different situations.

from? And, how do these traits and life experiences produce the choices people make? In the following pages, we examine these questions of nature and nurture, and their consequences for who we are and what we do.

Psychologists describe personality in many ways, but common to all perspectives is the idea of *continuity*. Let us, therefore, define **personality** as the psychological qualities that bring continuity to an individual's thoughts and actions in different situations and at different times. The traits we develop and the sense of self we form are affected by both nature (our inherited tendencies) and nurture (our unique experiences and education). But, we shall see, personality is more than a list of traits and experiences: It is also a *process* that produces our choices and actions.

In this chapter we will examine a number of theoretical explanations for personality. As we do so, you will find that different theories are useful for dealing with different problems:

**Chapter 4:**
**Psychological Development**
*The nature versus nurture debate concerns the relative effects of heredity and environment.*

- If your goal is to understand a depressed friend, a troublesome child—any individual—as a developing, changing being, you will probably find one of the *psychodynamic, humanistic,* or *cognitive* theories of personality most helpful. These theories are described in the first part of the chapter.
- If what you need is a snapshot of a person's current personality characteristics—as you might want if you were screening job applicants for your company—a theory of *traits, types,* or *temperaments* may be your best bet. You will find these in the second section of the chapter.
- If you are most interested in how people understand each other—as you might want to if you were doing marriage counseling or conflict management—you will want to know the assumptions people make about each other, their *implicit theories* of personality, which we will consider in the third section of the chapter.
- And, if you are wondering whether people understand each other in the same ways the world around, you will want to know about the cross-cultural work in personality. Such issues are also considered in the last section of the chapter.

**KEY QUESTION ❓**

## WHAT FORCES SHAPE OUR PERSONALITIES?

If you have ever attended a family gathering or a high school reunion, you know that people relentlessly change and grow. They develop new interests and new friends, they move to new places, and they have new experiences. In this section we will consider

**Personality:** The psychological qualities that bring continuity to an individual's behavior in different situations and at different times

three ways of accounting for the paths their personalities take: the *psychodynamic,* the *humanistic,* and the *cognitive* theories. Each describes personality from a different perspective, but all portray it as a dynamic, developing process. And all emphasize the interplay of internal mental processes and social interactions—as our Core Concept says:

**CORE CONCEPT**

**The psychodynamic, humanistic, and cognitive theories portray personality as a developmental process, shaped by our internal needs and cognitions and by external pressures from the social environment.**

Although the three viewpoints we will consider in this section of the chapter share some common ground, each places emphasis on a different combinations of factors. The *psychodynamic theories* of personality call attention to the power of the unconscious and the lasting influence of early childhood experience. *Humanistic theories* put less emphasis on our past and more on our present, subjective reality: what we believe is important now and how we think of ourselves in relation to others. According to the *cognitive theories,* personality is influenced by perception and by social experience. Note that, in these respects, the three approaches complement rather than contradict each other: Our lives include past, present, and future; our minds have both conscious and unconscious levels; our behaviors are sometimes emotional and impulsive and at other times cooler and more calculated. Which theory we choose will depend, to some extent, on what aspect of personality and behavior we want to explain. Let us take a closer look at each perspective.

## Psychodynamic Theories

The psychodynamic approach originated in the late 1800s with a medical puzzle that was called *hysteria,* now known as *conversion disorder.* In this bizarre condition, the physician finds physical symptoms, such as a muscle weakness, loss of sensation in a part of the body, or even paralysis—but no apparent physical cause, such as nerve damage. The psychological nature of hysteria finally became apparent when the French physician, Jean Charcot, demonstrated that he could make hysterical symptoms disappear by suggestion. He did this while his patients were in a hypnotic trance.

Sigmund Freud (1856–1939), a young and curious doctor, heard of this work and traveled to Paris to watch Charcot's renowned hypnotic demonstrations. Inspired, Freud returned to Vienna, resolving to try the hypnotic cure on his own patients. But to his dismay, Dr. Freud found that many could not be hypnotized deeply enough to affect their symptoms. Moreover, even the ones who lost their symptoms under hypnosis regained them after the trance was lifted. Finally, a frustrated Freud resolved to find another way to understand and treat the mysterious illness. The new approach he created became known as **psychoanalysis.**

### FREUD'S PSYCHOANALYTIC THEORY

At center stage in the new psychoanalytic theory, Freud placed the concept of the **unconscious,** which he saw as the source of powerful impulses, drives, and conflicts that energize the personality. We are normally unaware of this psychic domain, said Freud, because its contents are too threatening and anxiety provoking. Only by using the special techniques

**Chapter 13:**
**Psychopathology**
*Conversion disorder is one of the somatoform disorders, which produce physical symptoms without a physical cause.*

**Psychoanalysis:** Freud's theory of personality and his system of treatment for mental disorders.

**Unconscious:** The psychic domain of which the individual is not aware but which is the storehouse of repressed impulses, drives, and conflicts that are unavailable to consciousness.

Sigmund Freud was the founder of psychoanalysis and the psychodynamic perspective. He is seen here walking with his daughter Anna Freud, who later became a psychoanalyst in her own right.

## FIGURE 10.1: Freud's Model of the Mind

For Freud, the mind is like an iceberg. Only a small portion, the Ego, is apparent, while the vast mass of the unconscious lurks beneath the surface.

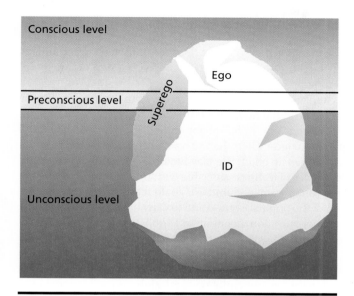

of psychoanalysis would we find that a person who had, for example, been sexually molested in childhood holds these memories in the unconscious. From there they may reemerge in disguised form—perhaps as a dream or a symptom of a mental disorder, such as depression or a phobia. Even in the healthiest of us, said Freud, behavior originates in unconscious drives that we don't want to acknowledge. Consequently, we go about our daily business without knowing the real motives behind our behavior. Today, many psychologists consider this concept of the unconscious to be Freud's most important contribution to psychology. (See Figure 10.1)

*DRIVES AND INSTINCTS*   The actions of the unconscious mind are powered by psychological energy—thought by Freud to be the mental equivalent of steam in a boiler. Psychoanalysis focuses on how mental energy is exchanged, transformed, and expressed. For example, the "mental steam" of the sex drive could be expressed directly through sexual activity or indirectly through joking or creative pursuits. Freud named this drive **Eros,** for the Greek god of passionate love. And the energy behind this drive he called **libido,** from the Latin word for "lust." It is libidinal energy that fuels not only our sexual behavior but our work and our leisure activities: skiing, skating, dancing, reading, body building—nearly everything we do.

But Eros did not explain everything that fascinated Freud. Specifically, it did not explain acts of human aggression and destruction. It also did not explain the symptoms of the war veterans he saw who continued to relive their wartime traumas in nightmares and hallucinations. Such misery could only be explained with another drive, which he called **Thanatos** (from the Greek word for "death"). Freud conceived of Thanatos as the "death instinct" that drives all the aggressive and destructive acts that humans commit against each other and against themselves.

Was Freud right about Eros and Thanatos? You might gauge his theory against your own experience. Have you observed any human behavior that could not, broadly speaking, be assigned to one of these two categories: life and death—or, if you prefer, creation and destruction?

*PSYCHIC DETERMINISM*   For the psychoanalyst, Freud's discoveries mean that the significance of symptoms such as fears and phobias must be interpreted as signs

**Chapter 14:**
**Therapies for Mental Disorder**

*Psychoanalysis is Freud's method of psychotherapy.*

**Chapter 13:**
**Psychopathology**

*There are also behavioral, cognitive, and biological explanations for phobias and depression.*

**Chapter 8:**
**Emotion and Motivation**

*Other drive theories are not based on unconscious motivation.*

**Eros:** The unconscious force that drives people toward acts that are sexual, life-giving, and creative.

**Libido:** The Freudian concept of psychic energy that drives individuals to experience sensual pleasure.

**Thanatos:** The unconscious force that drives people toward aggressive and destructive behaviors.

of unconscious difficulties. Similarly, a so-called **Freudian slip** occurs when "accidental" speech or behavior belies an unconscious conflict or desire. You might commit such a slip, as you leave a boring social function, by telling your host, "I have to go, but I really had a terrible—I mean *terrific*—time." Likewise, being consistently late for a date with a particular person is no accident, Freud would have said. Rather, it is an expression of the way you really feel unconsciously.

Freud believed that nothing we do is accidental. All our acts are determined by unconscious forces. This concept is known as the doctrine of **psychic determinism.** For example, consistently forgetting a certain person's name is a sign of inner conflicts or threatening memories.

In his work with hysterical patients, Freud observed that the particular physical symptom often seemed related to a traumatic event that had been "forgotten." For instance, a patient who was hysterically "blind" might, during therapy, suddenly recall seeing her parents having intercourse when she was a small child. How had this produced blindness? As she becomes an adult, she may have anticipated her first sexual encounter, which aroused powerful feelings associated with that upsetting memory. It occurred to Freud that the young woman's blindness could represent an unconscious attempt to undo her vision of the original event—and to deny her own sexual feelings. Blindness would also bring her attention, comfort, and sympathy from others. In this way, her inner psychic motives both determine and maintain her condition.

*EARLY CHILDHOOD EXPERIENCES*    Such cases also suggested to Freud that personality continues to develop throughout childhood and adolescence. He concluded, however, that experiences in infancy and early childhood have the strongest impact on personality formation and later behavior. These early experiences continue to influence the mind as the child progresses through a series of **psychosexual stages:** successive, instinctive patterns of associating pleasure with stimulation of specific bodily areas at different times of life. These stages are detailed in Table 10.1.

Among the problems that Freud was trying to solve with his theory of psychosexual development were those of gender identity and gender roles. Why is it that boys usually develop a masculine identity, even though most boys are raised primarily by their mothers? Why do girls, as they become adults, most often develop a sexual attraction to males—but most boys become attracted to females? And why do some *not* follow this pattern?

Freud's answers to these questions were convoluted and, many psychologists would say, contrived. His inside-the-mind perspective ignored the influence of vastly different forms of socialization for boys and girls. It also ignored the possibility of differences in genetic programming, about which little was known in Freud's day. Instead, he invoked the notion of the **Oedipus complex,** whereby boys displace (shift) an erotic attraction toward their mother to females of their own age and, at the same time, identify with their fathers. Girls, he proposed, develop **penis envy** (because they don't have one!) and are usually attracted to males (who do). Most psychologists today reject these Freudian notions of psychosexual development because they lack scientific support. It is important, however, to remember two things: First, these Freudian concepts continue to have a wide impact outside of psychology, particularly in the humanities. Second, while Freud may have been wrong about the details of psychosexual development, he may have been right about other aspects of human personality (Bower, 1998).

Freud might have been right, for example, in his assertion that certain difficulties early in life lead to **fixation:** arrested psychological development. An *oral stage*

**Chapter 4:**
**Psychological Development**

*Compare Freud's psychosexual stages with Erikson's psychosocial stages.*

**Chapter 8:**
**Emotion and Motivation**

*Most modern psychologists find that gender has a basis in both biology and in learning.*

**Freudian slip:** "Accidental" speech (a slip of the tongue) or behavior that reveals an unconscious desire.

**Psychic determinism:** Freud's assumption that all mental and behavioral reactions are caused by earlier life experiences.

**Psychosexual stages:** Successive, instinctive patterns of associating pleasure with stimulation of specific bodily areas at different times of life.

**Oedipus complex:** According to Freud, a largely unconscious process whereby boys displace an erotic attraction toward their mother to females of their own age and, at the same time, identify with their fathers.

**Penis envy:** According to Freud, the female desire to have a penis—a condition that usually results in their attraction to males.

**Fixation:** Occurs when psychosexual development is arrested at an immature stage.

**TABLE 10.1:** Freud's Stages of Psychosexual Development

| PSYCHOSEXUAL STAGE | | SIGNS OF PROBLEMS BEGINNING AT THIS STAGE |
|---|---|---|
| **Oral Stage** (1st year) | | Smoking |
| *Desires:* | Stimulation of oral erogenous zone through sucking, eating, crying, babbling | Nail-biting |
| | | Chewing |
| *Problem:* | Overcoming dependency | Gluttony |
| | | Obesity |
| | | Talkativeness |
| | | Dependency |
| | | Gullibility |
| **Anal Stage** (approximately 1–3 years) | | Messiness |
| *Desires:* | Stimulation of anal erogenous zone through bladder and bowel function | Temper tantrums |
| | | Destructiveness |
| *Problems:* | Toilet training | Cruelty |
| | Self-control | Excessive cleanliness |
| | | Stinginess |
| | | Coldness, distance, aloofness |
| **Phallic Stage** (approximately 3–6 years) | | Masturbation (not considered abnormal by modern psychology and psychiatry; see Chapter 8) |
| *Desires:* | Stimulation of genitals | Jealousy |
| *Problem:* | Resolving Oedipus complex, involving erotic attraction to parent of opposite sex and hostility to parent of same sex | Egocentric sex |
| | | Sexual conquests |
| | | Problems with parents |
| **Latency** (approximately 6 years to puberty) | | Excessive modesty |
| *Desires:* | Repression of sexual and aggressive desires, including those involved in the Oedipus complex | Prefers company of same sex |
| | | Homosexuality (considered by Freud to be a disorder, but not by modern psychology and psychiatry; see Chapter 8) |
| *Problems:* | Consciously: learning modesty and shame | |
| | Unconsciously: dealing with repressed Oedipal conflict | |
| **Genital Stage** (puberty and adulthood) | | (none) |
| *Desires:* | Mature sexual relationships | |
| *Problems:* | Displacement of energy into healthy activities | |
| | Establishing new relationship with parents | |

fixation, caused by a failure to throw off the dependency of the first year of life, may lead to dependency on others in later childhood and adulthood. We also see an oral fixation in certain behaviors involving the mouth, such as overeating, alcoholism, and tendencies toward sarcasm. Among these diverse problems we find a common theme: using the mouth as the way to connect with what one needs. Fixation in the *anal stage* is presumed come from problems associated with the second year of life when toilet training is a big issue. Anal fixations can result in a stubborn, compulsive, stingy, or excessively neat pattern of behavior—all related to common themes of "holding on" and not losing control of one's body or life. In Table 10.1 you will find examples of fixation at other developmental stages.

*PERSONALITY STRUCTURE*   Freud assembled these ideas about drives and stages into a theory that describes how the parts and processes of personality work together. In the resulting theory, Freud pictured a continuing battle between two antagonistic parts of the personality, the *id* and the *superego,* moderated by yet another part of the mind, the *ego.* (See Figure 10.1.)

During the phallic stage, a child must resolve feelings of conflict and anxiety by identifying more closely with the same-sex parent—said Freud.

**Id:** The primitive, unconscious portion of the personality that houses the most basic drives and stores repressed memories.

**Superego:** The mind's storehouse of values, including moral attitudes learned from parents and from society; roughly the same as the common notion of the conscience.

**Ego:** The conscious, rational part of the personality, charged with keeping peace between the superego and the id.

**Repression:** An unconscious process that excludes unacceptable thoughts and feelings from awareness and memory.

**Ego defense mechanisms:** Largely unconscious mental strategies employed to reduce the experience of conflict or anxiety.

He conceived of the **id** as the primitive, unconscious part of the personality that houses the basic drives. The id always acts on impulse and pushes for immediate gratification—especially sexual, physical, and emotional pleasures—to be experienced here and now without concern for consequences. It is the *only* part of the personality present at birth.

By contrast, the **superego** serves as the mind's "police force" in charge of values and morals learned from parents and from society. The superego corresponds roughly to our common notion of *conscience*. It develops as the child forms an internal set of rules based on the external rules imposed by parents and other adults. It is the inner voice of "shoulds" and "should nots." The superego also includes the *ego ideal*, an individual's view of the kind of person he or she should strive to become. Understandably, the superego frequently conflicts with the id's desires because the id wants to do what feels good, while the superego insists on doing what is right and moral.

Resolving these conflicts is the job of the third major part of the personality, the **ego**, which is the *conscious*, rational aspect of our minds. The ego must choose actions that will gratify the id's impulses but without violating one's moral principles or incurring undesirable consequences. For example, if you found that you had been given too much change at the grocery store, the superego would insist that you give it back, while the id might urge you to spend it on ice cream. The ego, then, would try to find a compromise, which might include returning the money and indulging a fantasy about the ice cream. That is, when the id and superego are in conflict, the ego tries to arrange a compromise

*"All right, deep down it's a cry for psychiatric help—but at one level it's a stick-up."*

that at least partially satisfies both. However, as pressures from the id, superego, and environment intensify, it becomes more difficult for the ego to find workable compromises. The result may be bizarre thoughts or behaviors that signify mental disorder.

*EGO DEFENSES*    If unconscious desires become too insistent, the ego may decide to solve the problem by "putting a lid on the id." To do so, the ego must push extreme desires and threatening memories out of conscious awareness and into the recesses of the unconscious mind. **Repression** is the name for this process that excludes unacceptable thoughts and feelings from awareness. Repression protects us from consciously experiencing anxiety or guilt about unacceptable or dangerous impulses, ideas, or memories. So, for example, repression may explain the behavior of a student who suspects she failed an important test and "forgets" to attend class the day the graded tests are returned. This unconscious memory lapse protects her from feeling upset or anxious—at least temporarily. In fact, that is the problem with repression and most of the other **ego defense mechanisms:** They solve the problem only for the moment, leaving the underlying conflict unresolved. You will remember that we saw a variety of ego defense mechanisms at work in our responses to stress, discussed in the previous chapter.

In Freudian theory, repression is the most basic of the ego defense mechanisms, all of which are preconscious mental strategies employed to reduce the experience of conflict or anxiety. The ego may use several of these defenses to deal with the daily conflict between the id's impulses to express primitive urges and the superego's demand to deny them. By using ego defense mechanisms, a person can main-

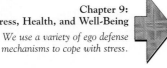

**Chapter 9:
Stress, Health, and Well-Being**

*We use a variety of ego defense mechanisms to cope with stress.*

**Chapter 3:
States of Mind**

*Preconscious processes operate just below the level of awareness.*

tain a favorable self-image and sustain an acceptable social image. For example, if a child has strong feelings of anger toward her father—which, if acted out, would risk severe punishment—repression may take over. The repressed hostile impulse can no longer consciously press for satisfaction. But, although the impulse is not consciously felt, it is not gone, said Freud. At an unconscious level it continues to influence behavior, but in less direct ways, perhaps disguised as dreams, fantasies, or symptoms of mental disorder. Thus, ego defense mechanisms are ultimately self-deceptive, even though at times they can be useful. When overused, they create more problems than they solve—steeping a person in denial, for example, and interfering with recovery after a painful experience.

To understand another important ego defense mechanism, consider the common experience of looking at a cloud and seeing a face or the shape of an animal. It is likely that a friend looking at the same cloud would see something different because the shape of the cloud is ambiguous and therefore open to several interpretations. What people see projected in the cloud, of course, are their own wishes, needs, or desires (Piotrowski, Sherry, & Keller, 1985; Piotrowski, Keller, & Ogawa, 1993). The underlying mechanism is the ego defense mechanism called **projection.** In a similar way, when we are upset or aroused, we may use the defense of projection to attribute our own unconscious desires to other people. This may occur, for example, when two people each accuse the other of provoking an argument or when golfers attribute their poor play to their "stupid clubs."

*PROJECTIVE TESTS*   Psychologists may take advantage of the human tendency to project our inner concerns onto external stimuli. Using a **projective test,** the psychologist asks a person to describe ambiguous stimuli, such as inkblots or pictures that can be interpreted in many ways. The respondent may be asked to say what the blots represent or tell stories about the drawings. Because the stimuli are vague, responses are determined by what the person brings to the situation—namely, inner feelings, motives, and conflicts that are *projected* onto the situations. What the disturbed person will see is a reflection of his or her unhealthy unconscious processes—perhaps the image of a threatening figure or a fearsome or destructive animal, such as a lion or a crocodile.

In the most famous of projective techniques, the **Rorschach test** (pronounced *ROAR-shock*), the ambiguous stimuli are symmetrical inkblots (Rorschach, 1942). The technique calls for showing the blots one at a time and asking the respondent, "What do you see? What does this seem to be?" The examiner usually interprets responses in light of psychoanalytic theory by noting how they might reflect unconscious sexual and aggressive impulses (Erdberg, 1990).

The Rorschach's value as a testing instrument has been questioned because objective studies of its accuracy have been disappointing (Anastasi, 1988; Wood, Nezworski, & Stejskal, 1996). Moreover, critics claim that the test is based on theoretical concepts (such as unconscious motives) that are impossible to demonstrate objectively. Despite these criticisms, many clinicians have continued to champion the Rorschach, arguing that it can provide unique insights as part of a broader personality assessment (Exner, 1974, 1978; Exner & Weiner, 1982).

By comparison, the **Thematic Apperception Test (TAT),** developed by Henry Murray, is a projective test that stands on somewhat firmer scientific ground. This test involves a series of ambiguous pictures, and respondents are instructed to generate a story about each (see Figure 10.2). The story should describe what the characters in the scenes are doing and thinking, what led up to each event, and how each situation will end. According to the theory behind the TAT, the respondent perceives the elements in the actual picture and further *apperceives* (fills in) personal interpretations and explanations, based on his or her own thoughts, feelings, and needs. The examiner then interprets the responses by looking for psychological themes,

**Projection:** An unconscious process by which we rid ourselves of tension, as we attribute our own impulses and fantasies to something or someone else.

**Projective test:** A personality assessment instrument based on Freud's concept of projection.

**Rorschach test:** A projective technique requiring subjects to respond to a series of ten inkblots.

**Thematic Apperception Test (TAT):** A projective test requiring subjects to make up stories that explain ambiguous pictures.

**Chapter 8:**
**Emotion and Motivation**

*The TAT is used to assess achievement motivation.*

such as aggression, sexual needs, and relationships among people mentioned in the stories. The TAT has proved to be especially useful for assessing achievement motivation (McClelland, 1985).

*EVALUATING FREUDIAN THEORY* Freud's observations were often astute, and his ideas have had an enormous impact on the way psychologists think about normal and abnormal aspects of personality (Fisher & Greenberg, 1985). Nevertheless, more psychologists today would probably criticize Freudian ideas than support them. One problem is that many Freudian concepts, such as "libido," "anal stage," or "repression," are vague. Because they lack clear operational defini-

**FIGURE 10.2:** Sample Card from the TAT

tions, much of the theory is difficult to evaluate scientifically. We have seen the results of this lack of objectivity in the controversy over recovery of repressed memories—a notion that arises directly from Freud's theory but that has no solid empirical support. Elizabeth Loftus warns that, by blithely accepting vague Freudian notions of repression and "recovery" of memories, society risks dangerous levels of paranoia, persecution of the innocent, and self-inflicted misery (Loftus & Ketcham, 1991, 1994).

A second criticism labels Freudian theory as passable history but poor science. That is, it does not reliably *predict* what will occur. Instead, it is applied *retrospectively*—to explain events that have already occurred. By overemphasizing historical origins of current behavior, the theory directs attention away from current events that may be responsible for maintaining the behavior.

A third criticism says that Freud gave short shrift to women. For example, we have seen that he portrayed women as suffering from "penis envy." In fact, Freud's theory may have been a description of the attitudes that permeated the male-dominated world of psychiatry of his time.

Much of Freud's appeal may be explained by his accessibility to nonpsychologists and by his "naughty" emphasis on sexuality. Freudian images and symbols abound in the art and literature of the 20th century. His ideas have had an enormous influence on marketing as well. For example, advertisers often promote new products by associating them with a sexy model and hinting that the product will bring sexual satisfaction to its owner. Alternatively, some advertisers capitalize on Freud's destructive instinct. Television commercials for everything from mouthwash and cake mix to laxatives and life insurance work by first reminding you of threats to your happiness (social rejection, irregularity, untimely death) and then offering products and services to reduce your anxiety and restore hope.

Among tough-minded scientists, Freudian ideas have long been regarded as suspect, primarily because of questions about his reliance on case studies rather than controlled observations. Yet, Freud's ideas have found a receptive audience with the public at large (Gray, 1993, p. 47). Unfortunately, this places most psychologists in the awkward position of disagreeing with ideas that have become "common sense."

**Chapter 1:**
**Mind, Behavior, and Science**

*Operational definitions are stated in objective, observable, and measurable terms.*

**Chapter 7:**
**Learning and Remembering**

*Evidence for recovery of long-repressed memories is anecdotal.*

Let us end our discussion of Freud by seeing whether his theory can give us a new perspective on Margaret Sanger. A psychoanalyst interpreting her drive and sense of mission would examine her childhood, looking for conflicts with parents and anxiety about sexual feelings. The analyst might also focus on her mother's death, which occurred when Sanger was 19, and on her later claim that she blamed her father for exhausting her mother with so many births. Unresolved anger toward her mother (a vestige of the phallic stage of psychosexual development) would be transformed into guilt over her mother's death. By projecting blame onto her father, she removed her conscious sense of guilt. Perhaps Sanger took up the banner of birth control in order to deal with the presence of her now-unconscious guilt and anxiety about unhappy family experiences. Or perhaps she identified with her mother's sacrifice and sought to punish her father and other would-be fathers by depriving them of their control over women's reproductive fate. As is usual with psychoanalysis, these guesses are guided by hindsight—and cannot be either proved or disproved.

**CARL JUNG: EXTENDING THE UNCONSCIOUS**   Freud attracted many disciples, but none more famous than Carl Jung (pronounced YUNG), a member of the inner circle of colleagues who helped Freud develop and refine psychoanalytic theory during the first decade of the 1900s. For a time, Freud viewed Jung as his "crown prince" and probable successor, but Freud's paternal attitude increasingly vexed Jung, who was developing theoretical ideas of his own (Carver & Scheier, 1992). Eventually this personality conflict—which Freud interpreted as Jung's unconscious wish to usurp his authority—caused a split in their relationship.

For Jung, the break with Freud centered on two issues. First, Jung thought that his mentor had overemphasized sexuality at the expense of other unconscious impulses: He believed spirituality, for example, to be a fundamental human motive, coequal with sexuality. Second, he disputed the very structure of the unconscious itself. This new vision of the unconscious, Jung's most famous invention, warrants closer examination.

Jungian archetypes can be found in ancient art and literature, such as in this depiction of the archetypal hero from classical Greece. In this picture, Heracles, clad in the cured hide of the Nemean lion he had previously defeated, battles the serpent Hydra, the many-headed reptilian embodiment of evil.

*THE COLLECTIVE UNCONSCIOUS*   In place of the Freudian id, Jung installed a two-part unconscious, consisting of both a **personal unconscious** and a **collective unconscious.** While the Jungian personal unconscious spanned essentially the same territory as the Freudian id, its collective twin was another matter—and wholly a Jungian creation. He saw in the collective unconscious a reservoir for instinctive "memories" held by people everywhere—in much the same way that we have a universal basis for language built into our brains. The collective memories tie together countless generations of human history and give us the ancient images, called **archetypes,** that appear and reappear in art, literature, and folk tales around the world (Jung 1959).

Among these archetypal memories Jung identified the **animus** and the **anima,** representing the masculine and feminine sides of our nature. Other archetypes give us the universal concepts of mother, father, birth, death, the hero, the trickster, God, and the self. On the darker side of the self

**Personal unconscious:** Jung's term for that portion of the unconscious corresponding roughly to the Freudian id.

**Collective unconscious:** Jung's addition to the unconscious, involving a reservoir for instinctive "memories," including the archetypes, which exist in all people.

**Archetypes:** The ancient memory images in the collective unconscious. Archetypes appear and reappear in art, literature, and folk tales around the world.

**Animus:** The male archetype.

**Anima:** The female archetype.

Chapter 4:
**Psychological Development**
*Chomsky says that some of our knowledge of grammar is innate.*

lurks the **shadow,** representing the destructive and aggressive tendencies that we don't want to recognize in our personalities. You can recognize your shadow at work the next time you take an instantaneous dislike to someone: This occurs when the other person reminds you of your shadow characteristics. For Jung, the causes of mental disorder include not only repressed traumas and conflicts in the personal unconscious but failure to acknowledge the archetypes we find unacceptable in our collective unconscious. Applying Jungian theory to the case of Margaret Sanger, a therapist might suspect that Sanger's aggressiveness might have originated in conflicts between the masculine and feminine sides of her nature: the animus and anima. Another Jungian possibility would be that her mother's early death made her deny her own maternal archetype, resulting in her obsession with birth control.

*PERSONALITY TYPES*    Jung's **principle of opposites** portrays each personality as a balance between opposing pairs of unconscious tendencies. The most famous of these pairs is **introversion** versus **extraversion.** *Extraverts* turn attention outward, on external experience. As a result, extraverts are more in tune with people and things in the world around them than they are with their inner needs. They tend to be outgoing and unaffected by self-consciousness. *Introverts*, by contrast, focus on inner experience—their own thoughts and feelings—which makes them less sociable. Few people have all pairs of forces in perfect balance. Instead, one or another dominates, giving rise to different personality types (Jung, 1971).

*EVALUATING JUNG*    Like Freud, Jung's influence is strongest outside of psychology, especially in literature and the popular press. Psychology has not found Jung so attractive, mainly because his ideas, like Freud's, do not lend themselves to objective observation and testing. In two respects, however, Jung has impacted psychological thinking. First, he challenged Freud and thereby opened the door to a spate of alternative personality theories. Second, his notion of *personality types* makes Jung not only a psychodynamic theorist but one of the pillars of the trait/type/temperament approach that we will review in the middle segment of this chapter. There you will see that Jung's type theory is the basis for the most widely used psychological test in the world.

## KAREN HORNEY: A FEMINIST VOICE IN PSYCHODYNAMIC PSYCHOLOGY

Karen Horney (HOR-nye) and Anna Freud, Sigmund Freud's daughter, represent virtually the only feminine voices within the early psychoanalytic movement. In this role Horney disputed the elder Freud's notion of the Oedipus complex, an erotic attachment of the child to its mother, and his assertion that women may suffer from penis envy, a desire to be a man (Horney, 1939). Instead, said Horney, women want the same opportunities and rights that men enjoy. She saw that many of the differences between males and females were the result of socially defined roles, not unconscious urges. She also disputed Freud's contention that personality is determined by unconscious urges and early childhood experiences. For Horney, normal growth involves the full development of social relationships and of one's potential. This development, however, may be blocked by a sense of uncertainty and isolation that she called *basic anxiety*. It is this basic anxiety that leads to adjustment problems and mental disorder. The neurotic person, she said, suffers from "unconscious strivings developed in order to cope with life despite fears, helplessness, and isolation" (1942, p. 40).

*NEUROTIC TRENDS*    Horney identified three neurotic patterns that people use to deal with basic anxiety: moving toward others, against others, or away from others. Those who move *toward others* in a neurotic fashion have a pathological need for constant reminders of love and approval. Such persons may need someone to help,

---

**Shadow:** The archetype representing the destructive and aggressive tendencies that we don't want to recognize in ourselves.

**Principle of opposites:** A Jungian concept that portrays each personality as a balance between opposing pairs of unconscious tendencies, such as introversion and extroversion.

**Introversion:** The Jungian dimension that focuses on inner experience—one's own thoughts and feelings, making the introvert less outgoing and sociable than the extravert.

**Extraversion:** The Jungian personality dimension involving turning one's attention outward, toward others.

to take care of, or for whom to "sacrifice" themselves. Alternatively, they may seek someone on whom they can become dependent. They may end up behaving passively and feeling victimized. In contrast, those who move *against others* earn power and respect by competing or attacking successfully, but they risk being feared and ending up "lonely at the top." Those who take the third route, moving *away from others* to protect themselves from imagined hurt and rejection, are likely to close themselves off from intimacy and support.

What analysis would Horney have made of Margaret Sanger? We suspect that she would have focused on Sanger's achievements, attempting to determine whether they were the result of a healthy drive to fulfill her potential or a neurotic need for power, status, self-respect, achievement, and independence. Undoubtedly, Horney would have reminded us that society often praises these needs in men and punishes them in women. So, from this point of view, it is likely that Horney may have seen in Sanger a robust and healthy personality.

*EVALUATING HORNEY'S WORK*   Neglect engulfed Karen Horney's ideas during midcentury (Monte, 1980). Then, her 1967 book, *Feminine Psychology*, appeared at just the right time to elevate her among those seeking a feminist perspective within psychology and psychiatry. But, having attracted renewed interest, will Horney eventually slip again into oblivion? Her theory suffers from the same flaw that plagues the other psychodynamic theories: a weak scientific foundation. It awaits someone to translate her concepts into verifiable form so that they can be put to a scientific test.

**OTHER POST-FREUDIAN THEORIES**   Sigmund Freud's revolutionary ideas attracted many others to the psychoanalytic movement—some of whom, like Erik Erikson and Alfred Adler, also broke away from Freud to develop their own ideas in different directions. For the most part, the post-Freudian theorists accepted the basic psychodynamic notions of psychic determinism and unconscious motivation. But they did not always agree with Freud on the details, especially about the sex and death instincts or the indelible nature of early life experiences. In general, the post-Freudians made several significant changes in the course of psychoanalysis:

- They put greater emphasis on ego functions, including ego defenses, development of the self, and conscious thought—whereas Freud focused primarily on the unconscious.
- They viewed social variables (culture, family, and peers) as playing a greater role in shaping personality—whereas Freud focused mainly on instinctive urges.
- They extended personality development beyond childhood to include the importance of experiences across the entire life span—whereas Freud focused mainly on early childhood experiences.

In doing so, the post-Freudians broke Freud's monopoly on personality theory and paved the way for new ideas from the humanistic and cognitive theorists.

## Humanistic Theories

With its emphasis on internal conflict and mental disorder, psychoanalysis failed to provide a workable theory of the healthy personality. The humanistic perspective arose to fulfill that need. Its theories are optimistic about the core of human nature. For humanists, personality is not driven by unconscious conflicts and defenses against anxiety, but rather by needs to adapt, learn, grow, and excel.

Mental disorders, when they do occur, are seen by the humanists as stemming from unhealthy situations, low self-esteem, and unmet needs, rather than unhealthy *individuals*. Once people are freed from negative situations and negative self-evaluations,

How would Karen Horney have interpreted Margaret Sanger's personality? Margaret Sanger had a flair for publicity. Here she has her lips sealed with tape so that she cannot be accused of preaching birth control in Boston—where she will write her message on a blackboard.

**Chapter 4:**
**Psychological Development**
*Erikson proposed a life-span theory of psychosocial development.*

the tendency to be healthy should actively guide them to make life-enhancing choices. And, in fact, the whole idea of personal choice was an idea most prominently developed by humanistic psychology. This idea brought with it a new respect for the individual's own internal and subjective view of reality rather than the external perspective of an observer or therapist.

**Chapter 1:**
**Mind, Behavior, and Science**
*Behaviorism asserts that our actions are controlled by the environment, rather than by free will.*

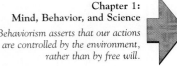

**ABRAHAM MASLOW AND THE HEALTHY PERSONALITY**  Maslow often referred to the humanistic view as psychology's "third force," to contrast his ideas with the Freudian and behavioristic movements that had dominated psychology during most of his lifetime. He was especially concerned by the Freudian fixation on mental disturbance and maladjustment. Instead, Maslow argued, we need a theory that describes mental health as something more than just the absence of illness. That theoretical need became his life's quest. He sought the ingredients of the healthy personality where no one had ever looked for them before: in people who had lived especially full and productive lives.

Maslow's subjects included the historical figures Abraham Lincoln and Thomas Jefferson, plus several persons of stature during his own lifetime: Albert Einstein, Albert Schweitzer, and Eleanor Roosevelt. In these individuals Maslow found personalities whose basic needs had been met (e.g., needs for food, shelter, love, and respect) and who had become free to pursue an interest in "higher" ideals, such as truth, justice, and beauty—a penchant that sometimes engaged them in causes about which they felt deeply. (We hope you're thinking about Margaret Sanger at this point.) They could act independently because they had no neurotic need for the approval of others. Maslow called these people **self-actualizing personalities.** He found his self-actualizers to be creative, full of good humor, and given to spontaneity—but, at the same time, accepting of their own limitations and those of others. In brief, self-actualizers are those who feel free to fulfill their potentialities.

Maslow considered Eleanor Roosevelt to be a self-actualizing person.

Although Maslow was most interested in the healthy, self-actualizing personality, his theory of a *hierarchy of needs* also offers an explanation of maladjustment. A long-unfulfilled "deficiency" need, such as a need for love or esteem, can produce maladjustment, while freedom from such needs allows the person to pursue interests that promote growth and fulfillment of one's potential. Indeed, the research shows that people who are self-accepting lead happier lives, while people who have low self-esteem may go through life feeling fearful, angry, or depressed (Baumeister, 1993; Brown, 1991).

**Chapter 8:**
**Emotion and Motivation**
*Maslow's theory of motivation is based on a hierarchy of needs.*

**Self-actualizing personalities:** Healthy individuals who have met their basic needs and are free to pursue an interest in "higher" ideals, such as truth, justice, and beauty.

**Fully functioning person:** Carl Rogers's term for a self-actualizing individual, who has a self-concept that is both positive and congruent with reality.

**Incongruence:** Occurs when a negative emotional experience affects one's ability to perceive accurately.

**CARL ROGERS'S FULLY-FUNCTIONING PERSON**  Carl Rogers brought the light of an optimistic humanism to bear on human suffering. In contrast with Maslow (with whom he fundamentally agreed), Rogers was a therapist who often worked with dysfunctional people rather than self-actualizers. Here we will examine the assumptions of his *person-centered theory* of human personality (1951, 1961, 1980).

Like Maslow, Rogers was fascinated by the healthy personality, which he called the **fully functioning person.** Such a person is distinguished by a self-concept that is *positive* and *congruent* with reality. That is, the fully functioning person has high self-esteem, which is consistent (congruent) with the messages he or she receives from others, who express their approval, friendship, and love. Negative experiences, however, can produce **incongruence,** a threat to one's self-esteem. For example, a boy who thinks of himself as "smart" has a positive self-concept, but he experiences incongruence when the teacher returns his paper with a C on it.

Expressions of affection and pride are an important way for parents to demonstrate unconditional positive regard and love to their children.

Rogers insisted that psychology recognize the reality of perceptions and feelings, which he called the **phenomenal field.** We respond, he said, to this phenomenal field, not to an "objective" reality. Thus, how a student reacts to a grade depends entirely on the student's perception: Receiving a C may shock a superior student but thrill one who has been failing. In Rogers's system, the phenomenal field becomes a part of the personality. It contains our interpretations of both the external world and our inner experience. It also contains the *self,* the humanists' version of the Freudian *ego,* which is the part of the phenomenal field that defines who we are.

Rogers believed that everyone has the capacity for growth in a supportive and nurturing environment. This assumption probably grew from his reaction to an isolated and unhappy childhood dominated by the rigid rules of his parents' strict religious beliefs. So restrictive was this environment that he even felt "wicked" when he first tasted a bottle of pop without his parents' knowledge (Rogers, 1961). Later, from an adult perspective, Rogers concluded that children from homes where parental love is *conditional* (dependent) on good behavior may grow up with anxiety and a strong sense of guilt that leads to low self-esteem and mental disorder. Instead of guilt-mongers, he believed, we need people in our lives who can give us **unconditional positive regard**—love without conditions attached.

Rogers, Maslow, and other humanistic personality theorists emphasized motivation. But, unlike the psychodynamic theorists who focused on unhealthy, self-destructive motives, the humanists believe that our deepest motives are for positive growth. In its healthiest form, self-actualization is a striving to realize one's potential—to develop fully one's capacities and talents. According to the humanistic theorists, this innate quest for self-fulfillment and the realization of one's unique potential is a constructive, guiding force that moves each person toward positive behaviors and the enhancement of the self.

How would humanistic theorists characterize Margaret Sanger? They would probably begin by asking, "How does Margaret Sanger see her world? What matters to her? Where is she, where does she want to be, and how does she believe she can get there?" The answers to these questions would identify her motives. Perhaps Sanger saw her life as an opportunity to change the miserable and often deadly consequences of unwanted pregnancy. But why, then, did she claim credit for the success of the birth-control movement, despite the fact that it was a team effort? A humanistic perspective would not assume that her motives were necessarily self-centered. If she believed the cause needed a figurehead, she may have felt that too many personalities associated with the movement would diffuse the effort. Ultimately, they would judge her healthy if her motives were healthy, that is, if she were self-actualizing. In everyday language this means "doing the right thing for the right reasons."

**EVALUATING THE HUMANISTIC THEORIES** The upbeat humanistic view of personality brought a welcome change for many therapists who had become accustomed to the more pessimistic Freudian perspective, with its emphasis on unspeakable desires and repressed traumas. They liked its focus on making one's present and

Chapter 8:
**Emotion and Motivation**
*The most basic levels in Maslow's hierarchy must be met before the person is motivated by self-actualization.*

**Phenomenal field:** Our psychological reality, composed of perceptions.

**Unconditional positive regard:** Love or caring without conditions attached.

future life more palatable, rather than dredging up painful memories of an unalterable past. They also liked its attention to mental health rather than mental disorder.

But not everyone jumped on the humanists' bandwagon. Behaviorists criticized humanistic concepts for being fuzzy: What exactly is "self-actualization," they asked? Is it an inborn tendency or is it created by one's culture? The behaviorists also noted that humanistic psychologists had neglected the influence of important environmental variables by emphasizing the role of the self in behavior. Experimental psychologists contended that too many concepts in humanistic psychology are so unclear that they defy objective testing. And the psychoanalytic theorists criticized the humanistic emphasis on present conscious experience, arguing that the humanistic approach does not recognize the power of the unconscious. Finally, cross-cultural psychologists criticized the humanists' emphasis on the *self*—as in *self*-concept, *self*-esteem, and *self*-actualization. This "self-centered" picture of personality may simply be the viewpoint of observers looking through the lens of an individualistic Western culture.

So, is there an alternative view that overcomes the problems we have seen in the psychodynamic and the humanistic theories? Let's consider the cognitive approach.

## Cognitive Theories

Neither the humanists or psychoanalysts showed much interest in putting their ideas on a firm experimental foundation. Their work came more out of a clinical tradition of working with individuals who sought their help. Cognitive psychology, however, arose from a different source—a solidly scientific tradition with an emphasis on research. The trade-off is that the cognitive theories are not as comprehensive as those of the humanists or psychodynamic theorists. The cognitive approach zeroes in on specific influences on personality and behavior, without assuming to explain everything, as we shall see in our sampling of cognitive ideas below.

**SOCIAL LEARNING AND PERSONALITY**    In Albert Bandura's view, we are driven not by inner forces or environmental influences alone but also by our *expectations* of how our actions might affect other people, the environment, and ourselves (Bandura, 1986). A distinctive feature of the human personality is the ability to foresee the consequences of actions without having to actually experience them. So, you don't have to yell "Fire!" in a crowded theatre to know what would happen if you did. In addition, we have the ability to learn *vicariously* (by observing other people) to see what rewards and punishments their behaviors bring. Thus, our personalities are shaped by our interactions with others—by *social* learning.

Perhaps the most important contribution of Bandura's theory is this focus on **observational learning,** the process by which people learn new responses by watching each others' behavior. Through observational learning, children and adults acquire an enormous range of information about their social environment—what gets rewarded and what gets punished or ignored. Skills, attitudes, and beliefs may be acquired simply by noting what others do and the consequences that follow. In this vein, psychological problems, then, can be acquired by observing poor role models or by exposure to environments that reward unhealthy behaviors.

Note how Bandura's theory points to an interaction of cognitions, behavior, and the environment. Each of these three factors can influence or change the others, and the direction of change is rarely one way; it is *reciprocal* or bidirectional. Bandura calls this **reciprocal determinism.** It is a process in which cognitions, behavior, and the environment mutually influence each other (Bandura, 1981). The simple but powerful relationship of these variables is summarized in Figure 10.3. How does it work in real life? If, for example, you like sailing, your interest (a cognition) will probably lead you to spend time on the waterfront (an environment) interacting with people (social

**Chapter 6:**
**Learning and Remembering**

*The behaviorists have emphasized that psychology should include only those things that we can observe and measure.*

Children develop a clearer sense of identity by observing how men and women behave in their culture.

**Chapter 6:**
**Learning and Remembering**

*Bandura's "Bobo doll" experiment showed the power of observational learning.*

**Observational learning:** The process of learning new responses by watching others' behavior.

**Reciprocal determinism:** The process in which the environment, cognition, and behavior mutually influence each other.

**FIGURE 10.3:** Reciprocal Determinism

In reciprocal determinism, the individual's cognitions, behavior, and the environment all interact.

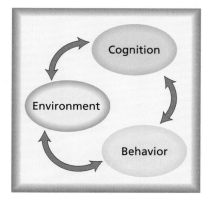

behavior) who share your interest. To the extent that this is stimulating and rewarding, this activity will reciprocally strengthen your interest in sailing and encourage you to spend more time with your friends on the waterfront. This, then, is one instance of the reciprocal determinism among cognition (interest in sailing), environment (the waterfront) and behavior (interacting with other sailors).

**LOCUS OF CONTROL** Another cognitive psychologist, Julian Rotter (rhymes with *voter*) tells us that the way we act depends on our sense of personal power or **locus of control.** Consider the grade you expect to receive in your psychology class. Do you have a sense that you can control the grade that you achieve? If so, you have an *internal* locus of control, and you probably work hard to get good grades. If you have the feeling that the professor will arbitrarily give you whatever she or he wants you to have—regardless of how much studying you do or the quality of your work—you have an *external* locus of control, and you probably study relatively little.

Scores on Rotter's *Internal-External Locus of Control Scale* correlate with people's emotions and behavior in many situations (Rotter, 1990). For example, those with an internal locus of control are not only more likely to get good grades, but they also are more likely to exercise and watch their diets than are externals (Balch & Ross, 1975; Findley & Cooper, 1983). As you might expect, externals are more likely to be depressed (Benassi, Sweeney, & Dufour, 1988).

While we may feel more in control of certain situations than others, many studies suggest that locus of control is frequently a pervasive characteristic of our personalities. In general, people approach different situations with the same general assumptions about their ability to control their fate. Therefore, an internal or external disposition seems to be a reliable characteristic of personality—although Rotter resists calling this a *trait* because he believes the term conveys the erroneous idea that internality–externality is fixed and unchangeable. You can evaluate your own locus of control by following the instructions in the *Do It Yourself!* box on the next page.

**EVALUATING THE COGNITIVE APPROACH TO PERSONALITY** Critics argue that the cognitive theories generally overemphasize rational information processing and overlook *emotion* as an important component of personality. For those who feel that emotions and motives are more central to the functioning of human personality, the cognitive approaches to personality are flawed. However, because emotion has assumed a greater role in cognitive psychology recently, we can anticipate a new generation of cognitive theories of personality that do take emotion into account.

How would a cognitive psychologist explain Margaret Sanger? A cognitive interpretation of Sanger's work and personality would focus on how she interpreted the rewards and punishments she experienced and how these interpretations shaped her behavior. Each time she gave a public lecture about birth-control methods or printed and distributed an illegal pamphlet, Sanger's actions brought punitive consequences—but she was also rewarded with public attention and admiration, press coverage, and ultimately the revocation of unjust laws. Margaret Sanger learned that by enduring the hardships she invited by violating "obscenity" laws, she raised public awareness and changed the social climate. In turn, these successes shaped her, making her less a private citizen and more a public figure.

Chapter 8:
**Emotion and Motivation**
*Rotter's locus-of-control theory is also a motivational theory.*

Chapter 9:
**Stress, Health, and Well-Being**
*Compare external locus of control with Seligman's concept of learned helplessness.*

Chapter 7:
**Cognitive Processes**
*Emotion is increasingly recognized as a component of cognition.*

**Locus of control:** An individual's sense of where his or her life influences originate.

## Finding Your Locus of Control

Julian Rotter (1966) has developed a test that assesses a person's sense of internal or external control over events. The test items consist of pairs of contrasting statements, and subjects must choose one statement with which they most agree from each pair. This format is called a *forced choice test*. Unlike the MMPI-2, the scoring for each item on Rotter's Internal–External Scale is transparent: The test-taker can easily tell in which direction most items are scored. Here are some items from a preliminary version of the test (Rotter, 1971):

1a. Promotions are earned through hard work and persistence.

1b. Making a lot of money is largely a matter of getting the right breaks.

2a. In my experience I have noticed that there is usually a direct connection between how hard I study and the grades I get.

2b. Many times the reactions of teachers seem haphazard to me.

3a. If one knows how to deal with people they are really quite easily led.

3b. I have little influence over the way other people behave.

4a. People like me can change the course of world affairs if we make ourselves heard.

4b. It is only wishful thinking to believe that one can really influence what happens in society at large.

5a. I am the master of my fate.

5b. A great deal that happens to me is probably a matter of chance.

You can see which direction you lean by counting up the number of statements with which you agreed in each column. Agreement with those in the left column suggests an internal locus of control.

A cognitive personality theorist would also call attention to the lessons Sanger learned in her social relationships. As she became a celebrity—someone whom others saw as a symbol of a movement rather than a mere individual—she acquired a sense of personal power and an internal locus of control that had eluded her in her early efforts to speak about health education. In her 1938 autobiography, she styled herself as a heroine and martyr, interweaving fanciful stories with accurate information about her life. A cognitive theorist would wonder whether she had come to believe the legendary side of the personality that she had strived to create.

### Current Trends in Personality Theory

Gone are the days when Freud, Jung, Erikson, Horney, and others were building the grand, sweeping theories of personality that attempted to explain everything we humans do. From the perspective of a new millennium, such a task looks impossible. Everything appears more complex now, thanks to the humanistic and cognitive theorists who have pointed out blind spots in the older psychodynamic theories. The emphasis, however, has shifted again, as psychologists have brought together elements of the psychodynamic, humanistic, and cognitive perspectives with new knowledge about the impact of culture, gender, and family dynamics. You should be especially aware of three important trends that, in the last decade or so, have had an impact on our thinking about personality.

In *family systems theory*, for example, the basic unit of analysis is not the individual but the family (Gilbert, 1992). This perspective says that personality is shaped by the ways people interacted first in the family and, later, in the peer group. While Freud and others did recognize that parents influence children, the new emphasis is on *interaction*—on the ways that members of the family or the peer group influence each other. This has led to viewing people with psychological problems as individuals embedded in dysfunctional groups, rather than as "sick" persons. This emphasis has also given us a new interpersonal language for personality. We often speak now of *codependence* (instead of *dependent* personalities) and *communication* (instead of mere *talk*). We also have a heightened awareness of *relationships* and *process* (the changes that occur as relationships develop).

A second trend comes from psychology's increasing awareness of cultural differences. As Stanley Sue (1991) reminds us, our society is becoming ethnically more diverse. We can no longer assume that the old perspectives on personality will fit people from all cultural backgrounds. No longer can we assume that everyone shares the same cultural experience or the same values. Harry Triandis (1995) has warned us, for example, that people who grow up in *collectivistic* societies may not have the need for individual achievement learned by those who grow up in *individualistic* societies. Triandis also tell us that no culture's approach is superior to the others: They are merely different. We will consider the question of personality differences across cultures in more detail near the end of this chapter. Suffice it to say here that none of the classic theories of personality has taken such cultural differences into account.

A third trend comes from an increasing appreciation of gender influences. While we do not know the weights to assign nature and nurture in our attempts to understand gender differences, we do know that males and females often perceive situations differently (Tavris, 1991). For example, males tend to be more physically aggressive than females. Females tend to form close relationships in small, equal-status groups, while males tend to connect in larger groups (teams) organized hierarchically with leaders and followers.

Together these three trends have enlarged our understanding of the forces that shape personality. The new emphasis is on diversity and on group processes, rather than on commonalities and on individuals. As a result, the picture of personality has become much more complex—but it has undoubtedly become far more accurate.

**Chapter 12:**
**Social Psychology**
*Individualism and collectivism represent one of the fundamental differences among cultures.*

**Chapter 8:**
**Emotion and Motivation**
*There are gender differences in the ways that people express emotions.*

---

PSYCHOLOGY IN YOUR LIFE

## Explaining Unusual People and Unusual Behavior

A theory of personality is helpful in understanding unusual personalities.

You don't need a theory of personality to explain why people usually get to work on time, go to concerts, or spend weekends with their family and friends. That is, you don't need a theory of personality to explain why people do what you would expect them to do. But when they behave in odd and unexpected ways, that is when a personality theory becomes handy. A good theory can help you understand interesting and unusual people whom you read about in the newspaper—those who risk their lives to save another, politicians embroiled in scandal, a serial killer, the charismatic leader of a religious cult, and the controversial CEO of a Fortune 500 company.

Which approach to personality is the best? Unfortunately, none has the whole truth. But each perspective we have covered so far—the psychodynamic, the humanistic, and the cognitive—can help you see personality from a different angle, so you will need to use them all to get the whole picture. To illustrate, let's suppose that you are a counseling psychologist, working at a college counseling center, and one of your clients, a young woman, tells you that she is contemplating suicide. How can your knowledge of personality help you understand her?

The cognitive perspective, with its emphasis on perception and social learning, would suggest that her difficulty may lie in her interpretation of some depressing or threatening event. It also would alert you to the possibility that her suicidal thoughts reflect a suicidal role model—perhaps a friend or a family member.

The humanistic view suggests that you explore her unmet needs, such as feeling

*continued*

alone, unloved, or not respected. This view also calls your attention to the possibility of suicidal thoughts arising from low self-esteem.

The psychodynamic perspective suggests that you consider your client's internal motivation. Is she a hostile person who has turned her hostility on herself? Does

she have some unfinished emotional business from an earlier developmental stage, such as guilt for angry feelings toward her parents? Does she have an unresolved identity crisis?

No one has a simple answer to the problem of understanding why people do what they do. That is for the counselor

and client to work out together. What these theories of personality can do, however, is help you find places to start looking and to call your attention to factors you might otherwise overlook.

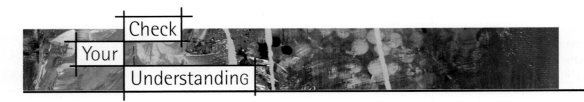

## Check Your Understanding

1. **RECALL:** *The psychodynamic theories emphasize*
   a. motivation.
   b. learning.
   c. consciousness.
   d. the logical basis of behavior.

2. **RECALL:** *Freud believed that mental disorders stem from conflicts and drives that are repressed in the*
   a. ego.
   b. superego.
   c. id.
   d. Eros.

3. **APPLICATION:** *Which of the following behaviors would a Freudian say is driven by Thanatos?*
   a. sexual intercourse
   b. a violent assault
   c. dreaming
   d. flying an airplane

4. **RECALL:** *What is the ego defense mechanism on which the Rorschach and TAT are based?*
   a. displacement
   b. fantasy
   c. regression
   d. projection

5. **APPLICATION:** *If you react strongly to angry outbursts in others, you may be struggling with which Jungian archetype?*
   a. the anima
   b. the shadow
   c. introversion
   d. the hero

6. **RECALL:** *Karen Horney believed that the main forces behind our behaviors are*
   a. social.
   b. sexual.
   c. aggressive and destructive.
   d. the result of the Oedipus complex.

7. **RECALL:** *The humanistic theorists were very different from the psychodynamic theorists because of their emphasis on*
   a. the cognitive forces behind behavior.
   b. the healthy personality.
   c. mental disorder.
   d. emotional intelligence.

8. **RECALL:** *Our expectations of reward, punishment, and control over forces in our environment play a major role in*
   a. the psychodynamic theories.
   b. the humanistic theories.
   c. the cognitive theories.
   d. none of the above theories of personality.

9. **UNDERSTANDING THE CORE CONCEPT:** *What do the psychodynamic, humanistic, and cognitive theories of personality have in common?*
   a. They all view personality as largely unconscious.
   b. They all acknowledge the internal mental processes underlying our personality characteristics.
   c. They all say that men and women have entirely different motives underlying their behaviors.
   d. They all have a strong basis in psychological research.

**ANSWERS:**   1. **a**   2. **c**   3. **b**   4. **d**   5. **b**   6. **a**
7. **b**   8. **c**   9. **b**

**KEY QUESTION** **WHAT PATTERNS ARE FOUND IN PERSONALITY?**

Long before academic psychology appeared, people were classifying each other according to four *temperaments,* based on a theory proposed by the Greek physician Hippocrates. A person's temperament, he suggested, resulted from the balance of the four

**humors,** or fluids, secreted by the body. A *sanguine*, or cheerful, person was characterized by strong, warm blood. A *choleric* temperament, marked by anger, came from yellow bile (called *choler*), believed to flow from the liver. Hippocrates thought that the liver also produced black bile, from which arose a *melancholic*, or depressed, temperament. Finally, if the body's dominant fluid is phlegm, or mucus, the person will have a *phlegmatic* temperament: cool, aloof, slow, and unemotional. Hippocrates' biology may have been a little off the mark, but his notion of different temperaments established themselves as "common sense." Even today you will occasionally encounter his terms *sanguine*, *melancholy*, *choleric*, and *phlegmatic* used to describe people's temperaments.

Since the days of Hippocrates, many other personality classification systems have been developed to link simple, highly visible characteristics and behaviors that can be expected from people that share the same attributes. If fat, then jolly; if an engineer, then conservative; if female, then sympathetic. Such systems have traditionally had much popular appeal—and they still do in the mass media. Unfortunately, they oversimplify the very complicated problem of understanding the patterns found in personality.

But there seems to be something in human nature that encourages us to group people by categories, according to certain distinguishing features. This habit is apparently universal—although the specific characteristics and categories may vary. For college students, the most important features may include college class, major, sex, ethnicity, and qualities such as honesty, shyness, or sense of humor. In modern psychology, some personality theorists describe people in terms of *traits*, enduring characteristics in the personality. Others group people according to their personality *types*, or clusters of traits. Amid this confusion, however, there seems to be some agreement on the fundamental dimensions of personality. Our Core Concept says:

 **CORE CONCEPT**     **Some theories attribute personality to stable patterns known as traits, types, and temperaments.**

It is important to note that the trait, type, and temperament theories all give us a "snapshot" of the personality, portraying it as relatively fixed and unchanging. Unlike the developmental perspectives we considered in the first part of the chapter, the trait, type, and temperament theories typically say little about how the personality works—about the underlying mechanisms or *processes*. As a result, these approaches are of more interest to personnel managers and others who would like to screen individuals and select those having certain characteristics. Because they take a "content" view of personality, the trait, type, and temperament theories are of less value in counseling and psychotherapy than are the psychodynamic, or "process," theories, considered earlier in this chapter.

## Personality and Temperament

Psychologists define **temperament** as the inherited personality dispositions that are apparent in early childhood and that establish the tempo and mood of the individual's behaviors (Hogan, Hogan, & Roberts, 1996; Mischel, 1993). When they speak of temperaments, psychologists are usually referring to a single, dominant "theme," such as shyness or moodiness, that characterizes a person's personality. Modern psychology has, of course, abandoned the old humor theory of temperament, but it has retained its most basic concept: Biological factors do affect our basic personalities. In support of this view, psychologists can point to parts of the brain that are known to regulate fundamental aspects of personality. You will recall, for example, the case of Phineas Gage, who gave himself an accidental lobotomy and thereby demonstrated the role of the frontal lobes in social interaction and the suppression of impulsive behavior.

**Chapter 13: Psychopathology**
*Hippocrates' theory also explained mental disorders.*

**Humors:** Four body fluids—blood, phlegm, black bile, and yellow bile—that, according to an ancient theory, control personality by their relative abundance.

**Temperament:** The basic, inherited personality dispositions that are apparent in early childhood and that establish the tempo and mood of the individual's behaviors.

 **Chapter 2: Biopsychology**
*Phineas Gage had a dramatic change in his personality when an iron rod blasted through his frontal lobes.*

**Chapter 2: Biopsychology**

*Neurotransmitters are chemicals used for communication between neurons.*

**Chapter 13: Psychpathology**

*Shyness is not a mental disorder, but there are effective therapies for overcoming it.*

Biological psychologists now suspect that some individual differences in disposition also arise from the balance of chemicals in the brain, which may also have a genetic basis (Sapolsky, 1992). In this sense, the theory of humors still lives, but in different clothes: Modern biological psychology has replaced the humors with neurotransmitters. So, depression—which is characteristic of most suicidal people—may result from a relative abundance or deficiency of transmitters. Likewise, anxiety, anger, and euphoria may each arise from other neurochemical patterns. As developmental psychologist Jerome Kagan says (in Stavish, 1994), "We all have the same neurotransmitters, but each of us has a slightly different mix" (p. 7). That, says Kagan, is what accounts for many of the temperamental differences among people, especially with regard to negative traits, such as fearfulness, sadness, and shyness.

In fact, Kagan runs a fascinating research program focusing on the inherited basis of shyness (Kagan et al., 1994). This program has clearly demonstrated that on the very first day of life, newborns already differ in the degree to which they are "inhibited" or "uninhibited"—that is, shy versus bold. About 10 to 15% of all children appear to be born shy or introverted, while a similar percentage appear to be born bold or extraverted, as assessed by a variety of measures. These initial differences in temperament persist over time, with the majority of children being classified with the same temperament in measurements taken over an 11-year interval. On the other hand, we know that the percentage of shy college-age students—40% or more—is much higher than the percentage of shy children (Zimbardo, 1990). It is thus reasonable to assume that some shyness is inherited, while some is learned through negative experiences in one's social life. It is also the case that if a child is withdrawn, startles easily, is unlikely to smile, and is fearful of both strangers and novelty, then that child will create an environment that is not friendly, playful, or supportive. In this way, heredity and environment interact, with initially inherited characteristics becoming amplified—or perhaps muted—over time, because they produce social signals telling others to either approach or stay away.

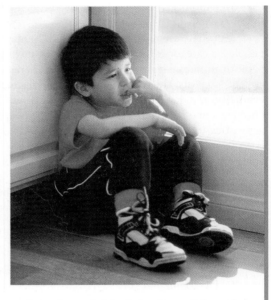

Some shyness is inherited and some is learned through experience.

So does biology determine your destiny? An inherited temperament may set the *range* of your responses to some life situations. However, temperament by itself does not fully determine your life experiences. Even among your biological relatives, your unique family position, experiences, and sense of self guarantee that your personality pattern is unlike that of anyone else (Bouchard & McGue, 1990).

## Personality as a Composite of Traits

If you were to describe a friend, you might speak of temperament—a single dominant theme in his or her personality. But it is also likely that you would describe your friend on several dimensions, using the language of *traits*: moody, cheerful, melancholy, enthusiastic, volatile, friendly, or smart. **Traits** are stable personality characteristics that are presumed to exist within the individual and guide his or her thoughts

**Traits:** Stable personality characteristics that are presumed to exist within the individual and guide his or her thoughts and actions under various conditions.

and actions under various conditions. An individual can have several traits, and these traits appear across different situations, giving consistency to the personality.

We can see the close kinship between trait theory and biological psychology in the book *The Biological Basis of Personality,* by British trait theorist Hans Eysenck (1967). In this manifesto Eysenck declares, "Personality is determined to a large extent by a person's genes" (p. 20). He believes that especially strong evidence points to a biological basis for the traits of introversion and extraversion and for emotional stability (Eysenck, 1992; Eysenck & Eysenck, 1985).

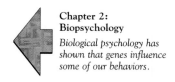

**Chapter 2:**
**Biopsychology**
*Biological psychology has shown that genes influence some of our behaviors.*

**THE "BIG FIVE" TRAITS**  By restricting the definition of personality to motivational and emotional characteristics (excluding such attributes as IQ, skills, and creativity), trait theorists are building a consensus on the major components of personality. Using the mathematical tool of *factor analysis* (which helps an investigator look for relationships, or clusters, among personality test items), many researchers have found five dominant personality factors, sometimes called the "**Big Five**" (Digman, 1990; Goldberg, 1981, 1993). These are the five fundamental traits mentioned in the Core Concept for this section. As yet, we have no universally accepted names for these factors, although the first term in the list below may be the most widely used. (You will note that each dimension is *bipolar,* describing a range from high to low on that trait. The first term we have listed is a label referring to the "high" pole for each trait.)

- *Extraversion* (also called *social adaptability, assertiveness, sociability, power,* or *interpersonal involvement,* and at the opposite pole, *introversion*)
- *Agreeableness* (also called *conformity, likability, friendly compliance, love, social interest*)
- *Neuroticism* (also called *anxiety,* or at the opposite pole, *emotional stability* or *emotional control* )
- *Openness to Experience* (also called *inquiring intellect, curiosity, independence*)
- *Conscientiousness* (also called *dependability, self-control, need for achievement, superego strength, prudence, constraint,* or *task interest,* or at the opposite pole, *impulsiveness*)

The five-factor theory is important because it greatly simplifies a formerly confusing picture. Various theorists, such as Freud, Jung, Adler, Horney, Erikson, and Maslow, had suggested a wide array of "fundamental" personality dimensions. In addition, the dictionary gives us several hundred terms commonly used to describe personality (Allport & Odbert, 1936). While psychologists had attempted to simplify this daunting list of personality characteristics, it wasn't until the last decade or so that agreement has emerged on which traits were fundamental. Although debate still continues about the details, a broad coalition of theorists has now concluded that we can describe people with reasonable accuracy by specifying their position on each of these five dimensions. The five-factor theory also offers the advantage of describing personality in the familiar terms of everyday language.

Significantly, the five-factor model also seems to have validity across cultures. An Israeli sample produced the same five factors as those found in Americans (Birenbaum & Montag, 1986). A study drawing on subjects from Canada, Germany, Finland, and Poland also supported the five-factor theory (Paunonen et al., 1992), as did still other studies of Japanese university students (Bond, Nakazato, & Shiraishi, 1975) and Filipino students (Guthrie & Bennet, 1970). Note that the same five factors stood out in each of these cultures as the basic framework of personality. Digman (1990) notes that these strikingly consistent results, coming in from such widely diverse cultures, lead to the suspicion "that something quite fundamental is involved here" (p. 433).

**ASSESSING TRAITS**  If you were a clinical or counseling psychologist, you would have your choice of dozens of instruments for measuring personality. We have already

**Big Five:** A group of apparently fundamental personality traits: Extraversion, Agreeableness, Conscientiousness, Emotional Stability, and Openness to New Experience.

met some of these in our discussion of the Rorschach Inkblot Technique, along with its projective cousin, the TAT, which came to us from the psychodynamic perspective. Now, let us examine some of the personality tests spawned by the trait theories.

One of the newest trait-based instruments comes from the five-factor theory: the NEO-PI or "Big Five Inventory" (Caprara et al., 1993; Costa & McCrae, 1992a, 1992b). This personality assessment device has been used to study personality stability across the life span and the relationship of personality characteristics to physical health and various life events. It is also useful in career counseling.

The most widely used of the trait inventories is the Minnesota Multiphasic Personality Inventory, usually called the **MMPI-2** (Boone, 1994; Butcher et al., 1989; Butcher & Williams, 1992; Dahlstrom, Welch, & Dahlstrom, 1975; Greene, 1991; Helmes & Reddon, 1993; Svanum, McGrew, & Ehrman, 1994). (The "2" refers to a revised form of the original MMPI.) The test consists of 567 statements dealing with attitudes, habits, fears, preferences, physical health, beliefs, and general outlook. Here are some items similar to those found on the MMPI-2:

- I am often bothered by thoughts about sex.
- Sometimes I like to stir up some excitement.
- If people had not judged me unfairly, I would have been far more successful.

Respondents are asked to indicate whether each statement describes them, and their answers are scored on the ten clinical dimensions listed in Table 10.2.

Attempting to fake a good or bad score on the MMPI-2 is not a smart idea. The test has four "lie" scales that will most likely signal that something is amiss in the responses of those who try to falsify their test profiles. All are sensitive to unusual responses. Here are some items similar to those on the lie scales:

- Sometimes I put off doing things I know I ought to do.
- On occasion I have passed on some gossip.
- Once in a while, I find a dirty joke amusing.

Too many attempts to make yourself look good or bad will boost your lie scale scores up into the questionable range.

As a diagnostic instrument, the MMPI-2 has a good record—although it must be used with care in non-Western cultures (Lonner, 1990). Clinicians should also be cautious when giving the MMPI-2 to members of ethnic minorities in the United States, because minority groups were not well represented in the original sample used

**Chapter 9:**
**Stress, Health, and Well-Being**
*Personality variables are related to people's physical and mental responses under stress.*

**MMPI-2:** A widely used personality assessment instrument that gives scores on ten important clinical traits. Also called the *Minnesota Multiphasic Personality Inventory.*

**TABLE 10.2:** MMPI-2 Clinical Scales

**Hypochondriasis** (Hs): Abnormal concern with bodily functions

**Depression** (D): Pessimism; hopelessness; slowing of action and thought

**Conversion hysteria** (Hy): Unconscious use of mental problems to avoid conflicts or responsibility

**Psychopathic deviate** (Pd): Disregard for social custom; shallow emotions; inability to profit from experience

**Masculinity–femininity** (Mf): Differences between men and women

**Paranoia** (Pa): Suspiciousness; delusions of grandeur or persecution

**Psychasthenia** (Pt): Obsessions; compulsions; fears; low self-esteem; guilt; indecisiveness

**Schizophrenia** (Sc): Bizarre, unusual thoughts or behavior; withdrawal; hallucinations; delusions

**Hypomania** (Ma): Emotional excitement; flight of ideas; overactivity

**Social introversion** (Si): Shyness; disinterest in others; insecurity

in developing the test (Butcher & Williams, 1992; Graham, 1990). Nevertheless, the instrument does a credible job of identifying depressed or psychotic persons (Greene, 1991). On the other hand, the MMPI-2 is of less value in understanding the normal personality because the items were developed to measure serious mental problems.

**EVALUATING TRAIT AND TEMPERAMENT THEORIES** The biggest criticisms of trait theories are that (1) they portray personality as fixed and static, rather than as a dynamic and changing process, and (2) they oversimplify our complex natures by describing personality on just a few dimensions. As evolution scholar Stephen Jay Gould has remarked, "The world does not come to us in neat little packages" (1996, p. 188). And what would we gain, for example, by judging Margaret Sanger as "passionate" or by finding that she scored high on traits such as outgoingness and dominance but low on agreeableness or conventional thinking? Such judgments would validate others' observations of her, and even her own self-descriptions. But brief labels and concise categories also leave out important detail. Although many women may have possessed similar traits, no one else did what Margaret Sanger did when she did it. A simpler picture of personality cannot provide the insight of a more complex portrait.

On the positive side, trait theory, as used to construct trait-based personality tests, gives us some ability to *predict* behavior in common situations, such as work settings. But how good is trait theory as an *explanation* of behavior? On this score, you can see that trait theories suffer from the same problem as the instinct theories. Both *describe* behavior with a label but do not really *explain* it. For example, we can attribute depression to a depressive trait or an outgoing personality to extraversion without really understanding the behavior. In short, trait theories identify common traits, but they do not tell us much about their source or how they interact (McAdams, 1992; Pervin, 1985). Going beyond labels, we need to know whether traits are mainly genetic or mainly learned or whether some traits become dominant over others in certain situations. Moreover, because most people display a trait only to a moderate degree, we must ask how useful traits are for understanding all but the extreme cases. In contrast, dynamic theories of personality (which we examined in the first part of this chapter) emphasize changing, developing forces within the individual and in the environment.

Finally, with trait theory we again encounter the problem of the *self-fulfilling prophecy*. When given trait labels, people may begin to act as those labels suggest, making it more difficult for them to make needed changes in their behavior. A child labeled "shy," for example, may have to struggle against both the label and the trait.

**TRAITS AND THE PERSON–SITUATION DEBATE**
Cognitive theorist Walter Mischel dropped a scientific bombshell on the trait theorists with evidence suggesting that we behave far less consistently from one situation to another than most had assumed (1968, 1973). A person who is extraverted in one situation can become shy and retiring in another; an emotionally stable person may fall apart when the situation changes radically. Therefore, Mischel argued, knowledge of the *situation* is more important in predicting behavior than knowing a person's traits. The ensuing tumult within the field has become known as the **person–situation controversy** (Pervin, 1985).

Mischel's position had wide repercussions because it challenged the very foundations of most personality theories. After all, if people do act inconsistently in different situations, then what good is a theory of personality? Critics mounted withering

**Chapter 13:**
**Psychopathology**
*Depression, paranoia, hypochondriasis, hysteria, and schizophrenia are examples of serious mental disorders.*

**Chapter 8:**
**Emotion and Motivation**
*The instinct theory foundered because it merely labeled behavior, rather than explaining it.*

**Person–situation controversy:** A theoretical dispute concerning the relative contribution of personality factors and situational factors in controlling behavior.

**Chapter 4:**
**Psychological Development**
*A self-fulfilling prophecy can come true because expectations can influence behavior.*

Often the situation is a more powerful predictor of behavior than are personality traits.

Extraversion is thought by some to represent a major personality type.

Chapter 1:
Mind, Behavior, and Science

*A correlation is a relationship—but not necessarily a causal relationship—among variables.*

**THE FAR SIDE**                    By GARY LARSON

"The glass is half full!"

"The glass is half empty."

"Half full... No! Wait! Half empty!... No, half... what was the question?"

"Hey! I ordered a cheeseburger!"

© 1990 FarWorks, Inc./Dist. by Universal Press Syndicate

THE FAR SIDE by Gary Larson/Universal Press Syndicate

**The four basic personality types**

attacks on Mischel's thesis, pointing out that his methods underestimated a thread of consistency across situations (Epstein, 1980). Bem and Allen (1974) have also pointed out that some people behave more consistently than others. Moreover, people are most consistent when others are watching (Kenrick & Stringfield, 1980) and when in familiar situations (Funder, 1983a, b; Funder & Ozer, 1983).

Nevertheless, it is true that personality traits as measured by personality tests typically account for less than 10% of all the factors that affect behavior (Digman, 1990)—a small number, indeed! But don't make the mistake of assuming that the situation accounts for the remaining 90%. Correlations between situations and behaviors are relatively weak, too. The lesson to be learned here is that the majority of factors affecting behavior simply cannot be assigned to one category or the other. Behavior seems to result from an *interaction* of trait and situational variables (Kenrick & Funder, 1988). In fact, Mischel has never suggested that we abandon theories of personality. Rather, he sees behavior as a function of the situation, the individual's *interpretation* of the situation, and personality (1990; Mischel & Shoda, 1995).

Mischel has argued that personality variables will have their greatest impact on behavior when cues in the situation are *weak* or *ambiguous*. When situations are strong and clear, there will be less individual variation in response. For example, suppose that one day when you are in class, a student collapses, apparently unconscious, onto the floor. After a stunned silence, the instructor asks the class to keep their seats and then points *at you*, demanding loudly, "Go to the office, call 911, and get an ambulance here!" What do you do? This is a "strong" situation: Someone is in control, an instructor you already see as an authority figure; that person has told you unambiguously what to do. You will most likely quickly comply—as would most people in that situation. In Mischel's characterization of person–situation interactions, there would be very little variation in how individuals respond to these circumstances.

But now suppose instead that you are walking leisurely through campus and you see a crowd gathered to listen to a figure giving an impassioned speech. Will you stop to listen? This is a "weak" situation, and your actions are likely to depend more strongly on your interests and on such personality variables as independence, curiosity, and extraversion.

The notion of **type** refers to especially important dimensions or clusters of traits that are found in essentially the same pattern in many people. As we saw earlier, Carl Jung made the concept of type a feature of his theory of personality. (Thus, we can see Jung as both a psychodynamic theorist and a trait/type theorist.) Jung's typology scheme, especially his notions of introversion and extraversion, have enjoyed wide influence and, as we have seen, is now recognized as one of the Big Five trait dimensions. Of particular importance is the use of Jung's typology as the foundation for the world's most widely used test of personality: the Myers-Briggs Type Indicator.

It is likely that you have taken the **Myers-Briggs Type Indicator (MBTI)** because it is given to nearly two million people each year (Druckman & Bjork, 1991). It is used in many college counseling centers, where students may be advised to select a career that fits with their personality type. It is also used in relationship counseling, where couples are taught to accommodate to each other's personality styles. And, the MBTI is commonly used by consultants in management training sessions to convey the message that different people may have distinct personality patterns that make them suited for different kinds of jobs.

We pause to give the MBTI a close look for two reasons. First, as the only objective measure of personality based on Jung's type theory, it presents an opportunity to examine some of his ideas critically. Second, as one of the most widely used of psychological instruments, the MBTI deserves critical scrutiny. We suggest that there are some good reasons to be cautious when interpreting the results on an MBTI profile.

On the Myers-Briggs test, subjects will answer a series of questions that ask how they make judgments, perceive the world, and relate to others (Myers, 1962, 1976, 1980, 1987). Based on these responses, a scoring system assigns an individual to a four-dimensional personality type, derived from the Jungian dimensions of *Introversion–Extraversion, Thinking–Feeling, Sensation–Intuition*, and *Judgment–Perception*. Remember that, according to Jung, personality types are stable patterns over time.

So, what does the Myers-Briggs Type Indicator tell us about the stability or **reliability** of types? A *reliable* test gives consistent results, but the reliability of the MBTI is not altogether encouraging for Jungians. While the test assesses people on four dimensions, many people receive a significantly different score on at least one or two of those dimensions when they are retested some time later. One study found that less than half of those tested on the *MBTI* had exactly the same type when retested five weeks later (McCarley & Carskadon, 1983). Another study found a change in at least one of the four type categories in about 75% of respondents (see Druckman & Bjork, 1991). Such results certainly raise questions about the fundamental concept of "type" in Jung's theory and about the value of the MBTI itself.

A second issue concerns the **validity** of the Myers-Briggs test (Pittenger, 1993). A *valid* test actually measures what it is being used to measure. And again the research on the MBTI gives a mixed picture (Druckman & Bjork, 1991). As you might expect, people who work with people— entertainers, counselors, managers, and sellers—tend to score higher on extraversion. By comparison, librarians, computer specialists, and physicians number many introverts in their ranks. The danger lies, however, in turning averages into stereotypes. In actual fact, the data show a diversity of types within occupations. Further, we have a conspicuous lack of evidence documenting a relationship between personality type and occupational success. Although proponents of the MBTI claim that it is useful in vocational counseling, a review of the literature by a team from the National Academy of Sciences found no relationship between personality type, as revealed by the MBTI, and performance on a particular job (Druckman & Bjork, 1991). This report has, however, been hotly disputed by users of the instrument (Pearman, 1991). Clearly, the Myers-Briggs Type Indicator needs more validity work before we can confidently encourage people to make life choices on the basis of its results.

Counselors using the Myers-Briggs to assess Jungian personality types often argue that its value lies not in its accuracy but in its ability to suggest new avenues for exploration. And those who take the test often report that they have gained insight into themselves from the experience. Thus, the instrument may have some value in counseling, especially when counselors resist the temptation to interpret the results rigidly. Unfortunately, no research has been done that documents these benefits over the long term. Says the National Academy of Sciences Report (Druckman & Bjork, 1991), "Lacking such evidence, it is a curiosity why the instrument is used so widely" (p. 99).

**Type:** Refers to especially important dimensions or clusters of traits that are not only central to a person's personality but are found with essentially the same pattern in many people.

**Myers-Briggs Type Indicator (MBTI):** A widely used personality test based on Jungian types.

**Reliability:** An attribute of a psychological test that gives consistent results.

**Validity:** An attribute of a psychological test that actually measures what it is being used to measure.

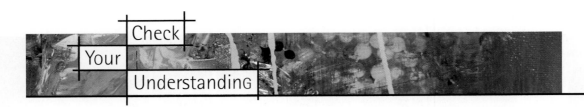
1. **RECALL:** *Temperament refers to personality characteristics that*
   **a.** cause people to be "nervous" or unpredictable.
   **b.** are learned, especially from one's parents and peers.
   **c.** have a substantial biological basis.
   **d.** cause mental disorders.

2. **APPLICATION:** *A friend of yours always seems calm and unruffled, even in circumstances where other people feel stress. Which one of the Big Five traits applies to this characteristic of your friend?*
   **a.** Introversion
   **b.** Agreeableness
   **c.** Emotional stability
   **d.** Conscientiousness

3. **RECALL:** *Walter Mischel argues that* _____ *is (are) less important than* _____ .
   **a.** traits/the situation
   **b.** traits/temperament

   **c.** the conscious mind/the unconscious
   **d.** emotions/reason

4. **UNDERSTANDING THE CORE CONCEPT:** *What is found in most psychodynamic, humanistic, and cognitive theories, but is not found in most trait, type, and temperament theories?*
   **a.** a description of the components of the personality
   **b.** labels for common mental disorders
   **c.** concepts that are useful for individuals involved in personnel selection decisions
   **d.** a description of the processes of development and change underlying personality

**ANSWERS:**    1. **c**    2. **c**    3. **a**    4. **d**

---

 **KEY QUESTION**

## WHAT "THEORIES" DO PEOPLE USE TO UNDERSTAND EACH OTHER?

We have seen how psychologists view personality. But how do people who are *not* psychologists think about people? This is an important matter because we all regularly make assumptions—right or wrong—about other people's personalities. You do so when you meet someone new at a party, when you apply for a job, and when you form your first impression of a new professor or classmate. We might also ask whether people make the same assumptions about each other in different cultures. These questions are significant because the "folk theories," or *implicit personality theories,* that people use to understand each other can support or undermine relationships among individuals—or even among nations. Our Core Concept says:

 **CORE CONCEPT**

**People everywhere develop implicit assumptions ("folk theories") about personality, but these assumptions vary in important ways across cultures.**

In this section we will examine the assumptions commonly found in these implicit theories.

### Implicit Personality Theories

Think of someone who has been a role model for you. Now think of someone you can't stand to be around. In both cases, what immediately springs to mind are personal attributes—traits—that you have learned to use to describe people: honesty, reliability, sense of humor, generosity, outgoing attitude, aggressiveness, moodiness, or pessimism, for example. Even as a child, you used your own rudimentary system for appraising personality. You tried to determine which new acquaintances would be friend or foe; you worked out ways of dealing with your parents or teachers based on how you read their personalities. You have probably also spent a great deal of time trying to get a handle on who *you* are—on what qualities distinguish you from others, which ones to develop, and which to discard.

In each case, your judgments were personality assessments reflecting your **implicit personality theory**, your personal explanation of how people's qualities and experiences influence their response patterns. Implicit theories simplify the task of understanding other people (Fiske & Neuberg, 1990; Macrae et al., 1994). Some observers believe that certain aspects of our implicit theories are innate, especially the tendency to interpret others' mental states (Lillard, 1997).

Implicit theories often rely on naive assumptions about traits. For example, people tend to assume that certain clusters of traits go together—creativity and emotional sensitivity, for example. Consequently, when they observe one of these traits, they may assume that the person possesses the other (Hochwalder, 1995). Your personal experiences and motives can also influence your judgment of others. So, if you have had your heart broken by someone who was attractive but unwilling to make a commitment, you may quickly judge other attractive persons to be "insincere" or "untrustworthy."

Americans and Europeans also tend to make the **fundamental attribution error,** the assumption that another person's behavior, especially clumsy, inappropriate, or otherwise undesirable behavior, is the result of a flaw in the personality, rather than in the situation. For example, if you spill your coffee in an American restaurant, people are liable to assume that you are a clumsy person, rather than assuming that some external cause, such as someone bumping you, caused the spill. Cross-cultural research shows that the fundamental attribution error is less common in group-oriented "collectivistic" cultures, such as are found in China and India (Lillard, 1997; Miller, 1984; Morris & Peng, 1994).

## Personality across Cultures

The very concept of personality theory is a Western (Euro-American) invention (Draguns, 1979). Therefore, it is not surprising that all formal theories of personality have been created by people trained in the framework of the Western social sciences, with a built-in bias toward individualism (Guisinger & Blatt, 1994). Other cultures, however, address many of the same issues in their own ways. Most of these non-Western perspectives have originated in religion (Walsh, 1984). Hindus, for example, see personality as a union of opposing characteristics (Murphy & Murphy, 1968). The Chinese concept of complementary opposite forces, *yin* and *yang,* provides a similar perspective (which influenced Carl Jung's *principle of opposites*). We see another theme in non-Western views that minimizes "normal" conscious experience and emphasizes "higher" levels of consciousness, to be achieved through meditation or ritual activity.

According to Harry Triandis (1989, 1990, 1994), cultures differ most fundamentally on the dimension of *individualism* versus *collectivism,* which we alluded to above. For those raised in the Euro-American tradition, the individual is the basic unit of society, while those raised in many Asian and African cultures emphasize the family or other social groups. In *collectivistic cultures* people tend to form identities that blend harmoniously with the group, and they expect that others are motivated to do the same. In *individualistic cultures,* a person tends to form a unique identity and assume that others are similarly motivated to stand out from the crowd (Pedersen, 1979). Thus, for Euro-Americans, the self is a whole, while for many Asians and Africans the self is only a part (Markus & Kitayama, 1994). For Euro-Americans, a group is composed of separate individuals; when they work together they become a "team" of individuals. By contrast, for Asians and Africans the group is the natural unit, rather than the individual; the individual is incomplete without the group. Much of the conflict and misunderstanding arising from business dealings and political negotiations across cultures stems from different expectations about personality and the individual's relationship to the group.

**Implicit personality theory:**
Assumptions about personality that are held by people (especially nonpsychologists) to simplify the task of understanding others.

**Fundamental attribution error:**
The assumption that another person's behavior, especially clumsy, inappropriate, or otherwise undesirable behavior, is the result of a flaw in the personality, rather than in the situation.

**Chapter 12:**
**Social Psychology**
*The fundamental attribution error is not so fundamental in some other cultures.*

**Chapter 8:**
**Emotion and Motivation**
*Achievement motivation is affected by the culture's tendency toward individualism or collectivism.*

Most Asian cultures have a collectivist tradition that affirms the group, rather than the individual, as the fundamental social unit.

**Chapter 12: Social Psychology**

*The American assumption of romantic love as the basis for a long-term commitment is not universal.*

Many aspects of peoples' personalities and behavior are related to their culture's position on the individualism versus collectivism dimension. We have already seen how the fundamental attribution error is more common in individualistic cultures. Two other topics related to individualism versus collectivism and to personality have received special emphasis by cross-cultural psychologists: (1) competition versus cooperation and (2) the need for achievement. In brief, when given the choice of competition or cooperation, individualistic Americans characteristically choose to compete (Gallo & McClintock, 1965). Americans, on the average, also score higher on measures of need for achievement than do people in collectivist cultures.

Cultural change that produces a clash between the values of individualism and collectivism may also cause conflict *within* a culture. One can see this conflict developing in Japan, the archetypal collectivist culture, as its youth experiments with individualist values imported along with American music, television, and film. One can also find generational conflicts over individualistic and collectivistic values in Hispanic, Asian, and Afro-American groups in the Unites States.

Other personality-related dimensions on which cultures differ, but that are not so obviously related to individualism–collectivism, include:

- *Status of different age groups, sexes:* The status of the elderly is higher in many Asian cultures than in the United States; women have second-class status in the Arab world and many other societies (Segall et al., 1990).
- *Romantic love:* The assumption that romantic love should be the basis for marriage is a recent European invention and is most often found in individualistic cultures (Rosenblatt, 1966).
- *Stoicism:* Asian cultures teach people to suppress the expression of intense feelings (Tsai & Uemura, 1988), while Euro-Americans are much more likely to express strong emotions (although there are pronounced gender differences).
- *Locus of control:* Persons in industrialized nations, such as the United States and Canada, more often have an internal locus of control than those in developing countries, such as Mexico or China (Berry et al., 1992; Draguns, 1979).
- *Thinking versus feeling:* Many cultures (e.g., in Latin America) do not make the strong distinction between thoughts and emotions that Americans do (Fajans, 1985; Lutz, 1988).

Even the ideal personality is different in different cultures. In the Western psychological tradition, mental health consists of integrating opposite and conflicting parts of the personality. This can be seen especially clearly in Freudian and Jungian theory. By contrast, some Asian psychologies, particularly those associated with Buddhism, seek the opposite: to dissociate consciousness from sensation and from memories of worldly experience (Pedersen, 1979).

Despite these differences, can we say that people are fundamentally the same the world over? On the level of neurons and brain circuits, the answer is almost certainly "Yes." But personality is also locked in the embrace of culture, so a more comprehensive answer would be "No—but perhaps they can be described on the same Big Five dimensions." In the words of Erika Bourguignon (1979), "It is one of the major intellectual developments of the twentieth century . . . to call into question the concept of a universal human nature."

Even though personality and culture are partners in a perpetual dance, we can make this distinction between them:

> "Culture" refers to those aspects of a society that all its members share, are familiar with, and pass on to the next generation. "Personality" refers to unique combinations of traits (which all people in a culture know about, even though a given trait does not describe a given person) which differentiate individuals within a culture. (Brislin, 1981, pp. 51–52)

But don't forget that culture and personality also interact. A culture shapes the personalities of the individuals within it, just as individuals can influence a culture (Draguns, 1979). So, your personality is, to a certain extent, a product of your society's values, attitudes, beliefs, and customs about morality, work, child-rearing, aggression, achievement, competition, death, and dozens of other matters important to humans everywhere. And, in a larger sense, a culture is the personality of a society (Benedict, 1934).

**Eclectic:** Either switching theories to explain different situations or building one's own theory of personality from pieces borrowed from many perspectives.

## Developing Your Own Theory of Personality

None of the theories we have examined can explain everything. Consequently, most psychologists become **eclectic**. That is, they either switch theories to fit different situations or construct a theory of personality by borrowing ideas from many perspectives. While an eclectic approach may appear to offer the easiest route, it presents difficulties that arise from certain fundamental conflicts among theories. To give one example: How could we reconcile Freud's concept of our behavior being driven by

**TABLE 10.3:** Comparison of the Major Psychological Theories of Personality

| PERSPECTIVE | EMPHASIS | CAUSES OF PSYCHOLOGICAL DISORDER | MAJOR FIGURES | IMPORTANT TERMS |
|---|---|---|---|---|
| Psychodynamic theories | Unhealthy motivation | Unconscious drives and conflicts | Sigmund Freud | Id, ego, superego<br>Ego defense mechanisms: repression, projection<br>Rorschach, TAT<br>Eros, Thanatos, libido<br>Psychic determinism<br>Psychosexual stages |
| | | | Carl Jung | Collective unconscious<br>Archetypes<br>Introversion, extraversion<br>Personality types |
| | | | Erik Erikson | Psychosocial stages |
| Humanistic theories | Healthy motivation | Unhealthy situations, low self-esteem, unmet needs | Abraham Maslow<br>Carl Rogers | Hierarchy of needs<br>Self-actualization<br>Self-esteem |
| Cognitive theories | Cognitive learning, expectations | Poor role models, unhealthy situations | Albert Bandura<br><br>Julian Rotter<br>Walter Mischel | Observational learning<br>Reciprocal determinism<br>Locus of control<br>Person–situation controversy |
| Trait, type, and temperament theories | Enduring personality characteristics | Maladaptive traits, conflicts of different personality types, extremes of temperament | Jerome Kagan<br>Hans Eysenck<br><br>Various theorists | Temperament<br>Extraversion, neuroticism, psychoticism<br>"Big Five" personality traits<br>MMPI-2<br>MBTI |
| Implicit and cross-cultural theories | "Common sense" theories<br>Cultural differences | Many views— depending on culture | Harry Triandis | Individualistic versus collectivistic cultures<br>Fundamental attribution error |

*continued*

vulgar instincts with humanism's assumption of the innate goodness of our nature?

It may help to think of a personality theory as a map showing the major pathways through the psychological landscape. As you formulate your own theory, you must decide how to weight the forces that determine which paths we select—the forces of conditioning, motivation and emotion, heredity and environment, individualism and collectivism, cognition, traits, culture, self-concept, and potential. We propose the following questions, which will help you sort out the assumptions in your implicit theory of personality.

- In your opinion, are people more rational and logical (as the cognitive theories contend), or do they more often act on the basis of feelings and emotions (as the psychodynamic theories argue)?
- Are people usually conscious of the reasons for their behavior, as many of the post-Freudians claimed? Or, are their actions mainly caused by uncon-

Some views of personality assert that anger comes from an inner drive that arises in the unconscious mind. Other views emphasize conscious cognitions of environmental stimuli. Do you think these people are conscious of the reasons for their behavior?

scious needs, desires, and urges (as Freud suggested)?
- What are the basic motives behind human behavior: sex, aggression, power, love, spiritual needs . . . ?

- Are human motives essentially egocentric and self-serving? Or, on the other hand, can people act on the basis of altruism, unmotivated by the desire for personal gain (as the humanists suggest)?
- When you try to understand another person's actions, which of the following do you consider to be most important: the situation (as Mischel says); the person's inner needs, drives, motives, and emotions (as the psychodynamic theories say); or the person's basic personality characteristics (as the trait and type theories say)?
- Is our basic, inner nature essentially healthy and good (as the humanists see it) or composed of vulgar and self-serving desires (as Freud saw it)?

No one has yet found the "right" answers, but the answers *you* give say a great deal about your own personality.

## Check Your Understanding

1. APPLICATION: *You would expect to find the concept of* self *emphasized in*
   a. the culture of an industrialized society.
   b. a wealthy culture.
   c. an individualistic culture.
   d. a collectivistic culture.

2. RECALL: *Cross-cultural psychologists say that the most basic distinction among cultures is their emphasis on*
   a. capitalism or socialism.
   b. external or internal locus of control.
   c. thoughts or feelings.
   d. individualism or collectivism.

3. APPLICATION: *You are making the* fundamental attribution error *(which is not so fundamental, after all) when*
   a. you decide to dislike someone who speaks angrily to you.
   b. you see someone who is nice looking and assume that she is self-centered and arrogant.

   c. you go to a foreign country and assume that everyone thinks the same way you do.
   d. you think someone is clumsy when he trips and drops his books.

4. UNDERSTANDING THE CORE CONCEPT: *Implicit personality theories involve*
   a. the assumptions that people make about each other's motivations and intentions.
   b. assumptions about themselves that people want to hide from others.
   c. unconscious instincts, memories, and conflicts.
   d. opinions that people privately hold about others but will not say openly.

**ANSWERS:**    1. c    2. d    3. d    4. a

# USING PSYCHOLOGY TO LEARN PSYCHOLOGY

## Your Academic Locus of Control

Although an internal or external locus of control can be a central feature of your personality, your perceived locus of control can also change from situation to situation. When you are speaking in front of a group, for example, you may feel that the situation is beyond your control, but when you are on skis, you may feel that your are fully the master of your fate. And what about your education? Do you have a sense of internal or external control with regard to, say, your grade in psychology?

An external locus of control concerning grades poses a danger for the college student because college life is so full of distractions and temptations. If you believe that your grades are largely beyond your control, you can easily be driven by the enticements of the moment and let your studies slide. This attitude can, of course, become a self-fulfilling prophecy that ruins your grades not only in psychology but across the board.

The following questions will help you discover your academic locus of control.

1. On a test do you often find that, even if you know the material, anxiety will wipe the information from your memory?
2. On a test do you often know the material well but find that the test is unfair or covers material that the teacher did not indicate would be on the test?
3. Do you feel poorly motivated to cope with college-level work?
4. Are you so easily distracted that you can never quite get around to studying?
5. Do you believe that some people are born to be good students and some are not?
6. Do you feel that you have no control over the grades you receive?
7. Do you feel that you are not smart enough to cope with college-level work?
8. Do you feel that success in college is largely a matter of luck?

If you answered "yes" to several of these questions, then you probably have an *external* locus of control with respect to your college work—an attitude that can put you at risk for college success. What can be done? Nothing, if you are completely convinced that your success in college is beyond your control. If, however, you are open to the idea of establishing more control over your college experience, here are several suggestions.

- Get help with test anxiety from your counseling center or learning resources center.
- Find a tutor either among friends or at your learning resources center.
- Talk to your professors individually: Ask them to give you some pointers on what they consider to be especially important (and testable) in their classes.
- Go to your counseling center or learning resources center and get an assessment of your strengths and weaknesses and of your interest patterns. Then make a plan to correct your weaknesses (e.g., with remedial classes in your weak areas) and build on your strengths. Select a major that capitalizes on your interests.

We would wish you good luck—but that's only of concern to externalizers!

# CHAPTER SUMMARY

 **WHAT FORCES SHAPE OUR PERSONALITIES?**

- The psychodynamic, humanistic, and cognitive theories all seek to explain the influences that mold our personalities. Psychodynamic theories, such as those proposed by Freud, Jung, and Horney, assume that personality is driven by unconscious forces and shaped by early childhood experience. Humanistic theories, such as those of Maslow and Rogers, argue that people are naturally driven toward self-actualization, but this tendency can be suppressed by unhealthy conditions and perceptions. According to the cognitive theories, such as those of Bandura and Rotter, behavior is a function of situational and personal variables, direct and observational learning, and expectations.

 **CORE CONCEPT** The psychodynamic, humanistic, and cognitive theories portray personality as a developmental process, shaped by our internal needs and cognitions and by external pressures from the social environment.

 **WHAT PATTERNS ARE FOUND IN PERSONALITY?**

- Type, trait, and temperament theories are descriptive approaches to personality with a long history stretching back to the ancient Greeks. Modern trait/type/temperament theories are frequently used as the basis for diagnosis, personnel selection, and psychological testing. Temperament

refers to innate personality dispositions, which may be tied to factors in the brain. Traits give personality consistency across situations and may be influenced by both heredity and learning. Many psychologists now agree on the Big Five traits. The person–situation controversy, however, has raised questions about the relative contribution of personality traits and situations to behavior. Type theory is seen especially in the controversial and widely used MBTI, based on Jung's personality typology.

 **CORE CONCEPT** Some theories attribute personality to stable patterns known as traits, types, and temperaments.

 **WHAT "THEORIES" DO PEOPLE USE TO UNDERSTAND EACH OTHER?**

- People everywhere deal with each other on the basis of their implicit personality theories, which simplify the task of understanding others. Implicit theories may rely on naive assumptions, such as the fundamental attribution error. Moreover, cross-cultural psychologists have found that the assumptions people make about personality and behavior vary widely across cultures.

 **CORE CONCEPT** People everywhere develop implicit assumptions ("folk theories") about personality, but these assumptions vary in important ways across cultures.

# REVIEW TEST

For each of the following items, choose the single best answer. The correct answers appear at the end.

1. Which sort of personality theory would most likely emphasize unconscious motivation?

    **a.** psychodynamic theory
    **b.** trait theory
    **c.** humanistic theory
    **d.** cognitive theory

2. Which one of the following is an ego defense mechanism that causes us to forget unpleasant or threatening experiences?
   a. displacement
   b. projection
   c. regression
   d. repression
3. Critics fault Freud's psychoanalytic theory because
   a. it does not explain the source of mental disorders.
   b. it has no theory of psychological development.
   c. it has little basis in scientific research.
   d. it has had little impact on popular culture.
4. One of the biggest differences between Freud and Jung can be seen in Jung's idea of
   a. the collective unconscious.
   b. locus of control.
   c. implicit personality theories.
   d. shyness.
5. The humanistic theorists were the first to emphasize
   a. unconscious motives.
   b. mental disorder.
   c. the healthy personality.
   d. how people are similar to other animals.
6. According to Rogers, children may grow up with feelings of guilt and anxiety in homes where
   a. parents are not good role models.
   b. one of the parents is absent most of the time.
   c. parental love is conditional on good behavior.
   d. the parents are in conflict with each other.
7. Reciprocal determinism involves the interaction of
   a. the id, ego, and superego.
   b. self-actualization, unconditional positive regard, and the phenomenal field.

   c. the conscious mind, the conscience, and the collective unconscious.
   d. cognitions, behavior, and the environment.
8. Explaining why a new classmate does not seem attractive, your friend remarks, "I don't much like thin people, because they're too nervous!" This assumption reveals that your friend favors a _____ theory of personality.
   a. type
   b. psychodynamic
   c. cognitive
   d. collectivistic
9. Which of the following is *not* one of the Big Five personality factors?
   a. neuroticism
   b. intelligence
   c. conscientiousness
   d. openness to experience
10. Your *implicit theory of personality* would help you
   a. know that a friend needs comforting when she loses her job.
   b. laugh at a joke.
   c. shout at a friend when you are angry at your employer.
   d. feel rewarded when you receive your paycheck.

ANSWERS:   1. a   2. d   3. c   4. a   5. c   6. c
7. d   8. a   9. b   10. a

# IF YOU'RE INTERESTED . . .

## BOOKS

Angier, N. (1999). *Woman: An intimate geography.* Boston: Houghton Mifflin.

> *Pulitzer Prize–winning writer Natalie Angier discusses, with wit and expertise, how the female body distinguishes the development of the "feminine" personality and the experience of becoming and being a woman.*

Asbell, B. (1995). *The Pill: A biography of the drug that changed the world.* New York: Random House.

> *This vivid and powerful account of the people as well as the processes involved in producing the first reliable, effective,*

> *safe oral contraceptive includes stories of the lives of Margaret Sanger, Katharine McCormick, Russell Marker, Carl Djerassi, Gregory Pincus, John Rock, and Anne Biezanek, and the roles of feminism and antifeminism, science, the Catholic Church, the sexual revolution, and the revolution in biotechnology.*

Beattie, M. (1997). *Stop being mean to yourself: A story about finding the true meaning of self-love.* HarperSanFranciso.

> *The author of Co-Dependent No More blends the story of her travels in North Africa with reflections on adventures, mishaps, instincts, cultures, and competence.*

Berne, E. (1996). *Games people play.* New York: Ballentine Books.

Berne recasts Freudian theory in more contemporary terms, as an interplay among the Parent, Adult, and Child aspects of our personalities and those of others. He calls these "ego states," but they bear a striking resemblance to the superego, ego, and id. Berne claims that we get into trouble when we play "games," which are dishonest transactions that the Parent and Child initiate with other people. This leads to such games as "Alcoholic," "Look How Hard I've Tried," "Let's You and Him Fight," and "Now I've Got You, You S.O.B." Berne's system of Transactional Analysis (TA) is widely used in marriage counseling and group therapy.

Campbell, J., & Moyers, B. (1988). *The power of myth.* New York: Doubleday.

The companion book to the successful PBS television series of interviews between mythologist Joseph Campbell and journalist Bill Moyers examines the persistence and value of mythic symbols from primitive human origins and early religions through modern popular cultural phenomena such as the Star Wars films. This is an excellent introduction to the power of story in constructing personal identity and making life choices.

Carducci, B. J., with Golant, S. (1999). *Shyness: A bold new approach.* New York: HarperCollins.

This is not a workbook for "changing" shy people into extraverts but rather a set of strategies for living a "successfully shy life," including managing shyness when meeting others, working, falling in love, making small talk, and caring for shy children.

Dreikurs, R. (1964). *Children: The challenge.* New York: Hawthorn Books.

Alfred Adler was one of Freud's inner circle, who broke ranks to form a theory that puts the individual in a social context, motivated by a healthy goal of social interest or a neurotic goal of personal power and superiority. Rudolph Dreikurs was Adler's leading disciple in America, who established many family counseling programs, based on Adler's methods, across the country. This book gives the essentials of this approach. Highly readable, the book offers sensible, practical advice for parents.

Fiffer, S. (1999). *Three quarters, two dimes, and a nickel: A memoir of becoming whole.* New York: Free Press.

Paralyzed from the neck down by a high-school wrestling accident, Steve Fiffer (pronounced FYE-fer) dealt with denial, deceit (no one told him the extent of his injuries for weeks), depression, and rejection before he finally found a coach and mentor who could bully him into independent movement and mobility. The title refers to his response to a woman who had broken up with him, that she might not be getting a dollar, but she would get three quarters, two dimes and a nickel—he might be different, but he was whole.

Gay, P. (1990). *Freud: A life for our time.* New York: W. W. Norton and Co.

This comprehensive, revealing biography by historian Peter Gay includes stories of Freud's influences and relationships and photographs of the people and places important to the development of psychoanalytic theory.

Grealy, L. (1994). *Autobiography of a face.* Boston: Houghton Mifflin.

As a child, Lucy Grealy survived cancer of the jaw—and a series of disfiguring facial surgeries. This short, frank, beautiful book reflects on her memories of her illness, treatment, many plastic surgeries, and the efforts of her family to give her unconditional love as a beautiful person, irrespective of her facial beauty. A powerful and touching memoir of the part of the self that one sees through others' eyes.

Hales, D. (1999). *Just like a woman: How gender science is redefining what makes us female.* New York: Bantam.

Writer Diane Hales reviews research findings regarding differences and similarities between the genders, with an emphasis on how women can overcome stereotypes and prejudices that block their potential for growth.

Rosenbaum, R. (1999). *Explaining Hitler: The search for the origins of evil.* New York: HarperCollins.

Instead of another biography or history of the life of the Nazi dictator, this book seeks to understand why Adolf Hitler became the monster behind the war and Holocaust. What emerges is no single, comprehensive explanation, but many faces of one man, much like any other person with private and public personas.

Sulloway, F. J. (1992). *Freud, biologist of the mind: Beyond the psychoanalytic legend.* Cambridge, MA: Harvard University Press.

This book argues that Freud was a genius, but that he also took an active interest in creating his own legend. In Sulloway's view, Freud portrayed himself as a lone hero bucking an entrenched establishment—but perhaps his ideas weren't quite that far outside the mainstream of his time.

Sulloway, F. J. (1996). *Born to rebel: Birth order, family dynamics, and creative lives.* New York: Pantheon Books.

Sulloway argues that birth order is a big factor in personality and in achievement. It's not the only factor, mind you, but it is important, and it has been largely overlooked.

Trillin, C. (1993). *Remembering Denny.* New York: Farrar, Straus & Giroux.

Eloquent essayist Calvin Trillin's reflections on the life and times of his late friend Denny Hansen, a promising fellow member of Yale's Class of 1957 who somehow never became a superstar as his friends predicted. Trillin speculates on the social and personal stressors that shaped Denny's life, causing him to be "depressed all of his life," and eventually to commit suicide in 1991 at the age of 55. Also of *interest are the contrasting views of Denny offered by his many friends, from his college days and later on, offering different "windows" into a single personality and life.*

Zimbardo, P. G. (1990). *Shyness: What it is and what to do about it.* Reading, MA: Perseus Books.

*This is a re-issue of Zimbardo's popular book on shyness. The focus is on helping college students deal with the problem of shyness.*

## VIDEOS

*Choices of the heart: The Margaret Sanger story.* (1995, made for cable, color, 100 min.). Starring Dana Delany, Rod Steiger.

*This dramatization is based on the early career of Margaret Sanger, who coined the term "birth control" in the movement she founded for reproductive freedom and who ultimately commissioned the research that developed the oral contraceptive pill. The film focuses on the conditions and experiences that shaped her struggles against New York's Comstock laws.*

*Freud.* (1962, B&W, 120 min.). Directed by John Huston; starring Montgomery Clift, Susannah York, Larry Parks.

*An engrossing dramatization of Sigmund Freud's early life and work, this film focuses on his use of hypnosis and dream analysis in treating hysteria. An interesting story-in-a-story dramatizes influences on Freud's own personality and his efforts to understand himself.*

*Gattaca.* (1997, color, 112 min.). Directed by Andrew Niccol; starring Ethan Hawke, Uma Thurman, Jude Law, Alan Arkin, Tony Shalhoub.

*In this sci-fi view of the future, parents can eliminate genetic defects from their unborn children so that they will be "Valid" for their destinies. An "In-Valid" (genetically imperfect) young man dreams of becoming an astronaut, so swaps identities with a Valid acquaintance in order to qualify—and must now elude detection as well as penalties for "passing" as perfect.*

*La cage aux folles (Birds of a feather).* (1978, color, 91 min., French-Italian). Directed by Edouard Molinaro; starring Ugo Tognazzi, Michel Serrault, Michel Galabru, Claire Maurier.

*Somewhat better than the 1996 U.S. remake* The Birdcage, *the story of a boy raised by his gay father and his father's effeminate partner, who try to pose as a straight couple to impress the conservative parents of their son's fianceé. Some outrageous and some touching scenes about the difficulty of changing one's role or behavior through an act of will alone.*

*Lust for life.* (1956, color, 122 min.). Directed by Vincente Minnelli; starring Kirk Douglas, Anthony Quinn, James Donald, Pamela Brown.

*This is a moving and visually stunning adaptation of Irving Stone's biography of post-impressionist painter Vincent Van Gogh, who sold but one work in his lifetime and died of a self-inflicted gunshot wound. The film presents strong images of the influences and anguish that moved this great artist.*

*The Truman Show.* (1998, color, 102 min.). Directed by Peter Weir; starring Jim Carrey, Laura Linney, Ed Harris, Noah Emmerich.

*Truman Burbank was born and raised on a TV production set, an enormous sound stage peopled entirely by actors and extras, all so his life (with him unaware that this is all show) can be broadcast 24 hours a day on television. The film raises more questions than it answers about what makes him the person he is, given that his "parents," "friends" and "teachers" are all constantly conning and persuading him. Nonetheless, the film is eerie, well-acted, and absorbing.*

*What's eating Gilbert Grape?* (1993, color, 117 min.). Directed by Lasse Hallström; starring Johnny Depp, Leonardo DiCaprio, Juliette Lewis, Mary Steenburgen.

*No dramatic crisis is presented, but a slice-of-life depiction of the feelings and experiences of a young man in a small town who is stuck caring for a retarded younger brother and dealing with his agoraphobic, obese mother.*

**CORE CONCEPTS**

**PSYCHOLOGY IN YOUR LIFE**

HOW HAVE
PSYCHOLOGISTS
DESCRIBED AND
MEASURED INTELLIGENCE?

Intelligence testing has a history of controversy, but most psychologists now assume that intelligence is a stable, normally distributed trait that can be measured by performance on a variety of mental tasks—both verbal and nonverbal.

**What Can You Do for an Exceptional Child?** In both mental retardation and giftedness, children should be encouraged to capitalize on their abilities.

WHAT ARE THE
COMPONENTS OF
INTELLIGENCE?

Psychologists have long disagreed about the makeup of intelligence—particularly whether it is best described as a single, general factor or a collection of distinct abilities.

**IQ and the Self-Fulfilling Prophecy:** An IQ score can create expectations that have a life of their own.

HOW DO PSYCHOLOGISTS
EXPLAIN IQ DIFFERENCES
AMONG SOCIAL AND
RACIAL GROUPS?

While most psychologists agree that both heredity and environment affect intelligence, they disagree on the source of IQ differences among racial and social groups.

**Helping Others Think Critically about Group Differences:** There are many reasons why the heritability of intelligence doesn't mean that group differences are genetic.

USING PSYCHOLOGY TO LEARN PSYCHOLOGY:
PSYCHOLOGICAL ASSESSMENT AND CAREER PLANNING

# 11 Intelligence & the Psychology of Differences

## Chapter Outline

*A*t the age of 37, newspaper and magazine columnist Bob Greene started to suspect that he "was dumber than [he] had been in high school" (Greene, 1985). At 17 he had been able to add, subtract, and multiply without using a calculator. Twenty years later, those skills seemed to have disappeared completely. To see if he could still make the grade, Greene decided to retake the Scholastic Aptitude Test (SAT), the three-hour examination of verbal and mathematical abilities that many colleges use to select students for admission. Greene sent in his fee, and on the designated Saturday morning, he showed up at his local high school with six sharpened No. 2 pencils in his pocket. After one hour, "all of us looked dazed, unhappy, and disoriented, although I believe that I was the only student to go to the water fountain and take an Inderal for his blood pressure" (Greene, 1985).

The SAT was designed as a standardized measure of high school students' academic aptitudes. Admissions officers had had difficulty interpreting grade-point averages from thousands of high schools with different standards and grading policies. Although the tests were intended to be objective evaluations, they have been accused of bias, and, despite many revisions over the years, it has been difficult to quell those accusations. Across all ethnic groups, average SAT scores increase as family income goes up. Whites and Asian Americans consistently outperform Mexican Americans, Puerto Ricans, and African Americans (Hacker, 1986). Men on the average score higher than women (Gordon, 1990).

However, the SAT is changing. Consider the commonplace use of calculators, for example. When the SAT was introduced in 1941, pocket calculators did not even exist. In the mid-1980s, when Greene took the test for the second time, the proctor instructed that "Calculators or wristwatches with calculator functions may not be used." Later, in 1994, students were permitted to use calculators for the first time, and 20% of the math questions were constructed to require students to produce their own responses rather than merely select from a set of multiple-choice alternatives. Test-takers would have to come up with their own answers for questions such as "If the population of a certain country is increasing at the rate of one person every 12 seconds, by how many persons does it increase every half hour?" (Educational Testing Service, 1990a).

*When Greene's test results finally arrived in the mail, his hands were shaking. He felt ridiculous. After all, he already had a college degree and a successful career. Nevertheless, he nervously ripped open the envelope. Greene's verbal score had gone up 56 points, not surprising for a writer. But in math, over the two decades since Greene first took the test, his score had nosedived by 200 points!*

*Just as it is difficult to know why some groups perform better than others on the SAT, it is impossible to know with certainty why Bob Greene's math score plummeted. Wasn't the test supposed to measure his basic* aptitude *for math—what he understood, and not just what he had learned? Perhaps his math aptitude had decreased because, in his work as a writer, he no longer used the math he had once practiced regularly in high school. Or perhaps the test itself didn't measure Bob Greene's aptitude or potential to learn and use math. Instead, perhaps the test actually measured his recent accomplishments and practice in the subjects covered on the test—accomplishments made possible because his adult life experience as a professional writer had enhanced his verbal ability, but seldom required use of his early math skills.*

*Greene (1985) wrote about his experiences with the SAT to document some problems that exist with this system of testing. Standardized group tests—paper-and-pencil instruments, uniformly administered to vast numbers of people—are heavily relied upon, for better or worse, by most college and university admissions offices. Consequently, tests such as the SAT are centrally important to the academic lives of millions of students.*

No wonder Bob Greene was anxious. He was trained—as most of us have been trained—to have tests tell us what we know, where our talents lie, and even who we are. Our society seems obsessed with tests: SAT tests, IQ tests, achievement tests, abilities tests, interest tests, personality tests—not to mention all the tests in math, history, literature, and biology that we take in high school and college. To get a driver's license, you must pass a driving test. And, it is likely that you are reading this book, at least in part, because you anticipate a test on it.

In the opinion of some, the use of psychological tests to assess differences between individuals' mental abilities is "one of psychology's unquestioned success stories" (Tyler, 1988). At their best, psychological tests compare people on various dimensions according to objective standards that are not filtered through the whims and biases of subjective interpreters. They are supposed to be fair comparisons of the mental capacities of all individuals taking the same test under the same conditions. Such tests have been perceived as "tools of democracy," allowing selection of individuals for education and employment to be based on *what* those individuals know and can show, rather than on *whom* they know and what their family can show (Sokol, 1987).

Some people, however, see another side of psychological tests. In their view, a test may be little more than a sophisticated way of labeling people or even discriminating against them. And, we will see that they have a point. Tests have been used unfairly—wittingly or unwittingly—to hold people back from opportunities that they might otherwise have seized.

Any test can be said to work well if it accurately predicts performance in future situations. Test results from the SAT, for example, *are* generally good predictors of later academic grades, just as tests used in personnel selection can predict some types of job performance. When a person's aptitudes, interests, attitudes, and personality are accurately and objectively taken into account, the chances of a good fit between person and school or person and job greatly increase—to the benefit of all concerned. In the case of Bob Greene, however, it is not clear whether his SAT score represents his innate *aptitude* or what he has *learned*—an important distinction for people such as high-school graduates, whose scores will determine their access to future opportunities.

Bob Greene's SAT scores do clearly show that people's performance improves on the tasks they practice and worsens in the tasks they neglect. Practicing test-taking can also improve test performance. In fact, the Educational Testing Service, which designs and distributes the SAT, markets test-taking courses for high schools and how-to-succeed testing books for the general public. Because scores can be improved with practice, schools have sometimes been accused of "teaching the test" rather than enabling students to master the material. Some students worried about the SAT also take private "prep courses" that they hope will improve their performance. Such practices underscore the significance of tests in our culture and in our lives.

In judging the whole enterprise of assessment, we should also bear in mind that psychological testing is big business. Many psychologists spend a great deal of time on the construction, evaluation, administration, and interpretation of psychological tests. Testing supports a multimillion-dollar industry: Thousands of children and adults regularly take some form of the many tests distributed by more than 40 major U.S. test publishers. Virtually everyone in our society who has attended school, gone to work, joined the military services, or registered in a mental health clinic has undergone some kind of psychological testing.

Cultures differ in the emphasis they place on formal education. Japanese children, for example, spend many more hours in school than do American children. Their parents are also more likely to attribute academic success to hard work, rather than to high intelligence.

In this chapter we will examine the foundations and applications of psychological assessment with a critical eye. First, we will see where this strong tradition of testing comes from and what its purposes are—especially in the area of intelligence testing. Our emphasis on intelligence reflects the historical weight placed on intelligence in American education and the American public's belief that intelligence is the main ingredient of academic success (Stevenson, 1992). Next, we will examine what intelligence is made of—or, more precisely, the makeup of various theories of intelligence. Finally, we will consider the politics of IQ: why intelligence testing has generated so much controversy. Along with learning about individual differences, we will also learn something about evaluating tests: what makes any test useful, how tests work, why tests may not always do the job they were intended to do, and how tests might be misinterpreted. Perhaps most important, we will see how tests have been used and misused to assess differences among groups of people. We begin with the measurement of intelligence.

 **KEY QUESTION**

## HOW HAVE PSYCHOLOGISTS DESCRIBED AND MEASURED INTELLIGENCE?

The assessment of individual differences did not begin with modern psychology. Chinese records show that sophisticated assessment techniques were commonplace in ancient China. In fact, the Chinese employed a well-planned program of civil service testing over 4,000 years ago, when officials were required to demonstrate their competence every third year at an oral examination. Two thousand years later, the Han dynasty used written civil service tests to assess competence in the areas of law, the military, agriculture, and geography. Later, during the Ming dynasty (1368–1644), public officials were chosen on the basis of their performance at three stages of an objective selection procedure, involving several days of examinations and written work. British diplomats and missionaries in the early 1800s described China's selection procedures admiringly. As a result, the British, and later the Americans, adopted modified versions of China's system for the selection of civil service personnel (Wiggins, 1973).

Unlike the historical Chinese, modern Americans seem to be more interested in how "smart" people are, as opposed to how much they have learned. It is the interest in this sort of "native intelligence" that spurred the development of psychological testing as we know it today. But, despite the long history of mental testing and the widespread use of intelligence tests in our society, the meaning of the term *intelligence* is still disputed. In everyday language, we may call people "intelligent" who have done clever things, who are witty, or who are creative. Nor are psychologists agreed on a precise definition of the term (Neisser et al., 1996). As we will find, they cannot even agree whether intelligence is one or many abilities. Unfortunately, therefore, we cannot give you a definition of intelligence that is both precise and agreeable to everyone. But, for our working definition, let us say that **intelligence** is the mental capacity to acquire knowledge, reason, and solve problems effectively. Note, however, that intelligence is also a relative term: An individual's level of intelligence is always defined in relation to the same abilities in a comparison group, usually of the same age range. We should also note that intelligence is a **hypothetical construct:** a characteristic that is not directly observable, but is, instead, inferred from behavior. In practice, this means that intelligence is measured from an individual's responses on an intelligence test, and it is such tests that are the focus of the first section of this chapter. Our Core Concept says:

**CORE CONCEPT**

Intelligence testing has a history of controversy, but most psychologists now assume that intelligence is a stable, normally distributed trait that can be measured by performance on a variety of mental tasks—both verbal and nonverbal.

We begin our survey of intelligence and intelligence testing by introducing you to Sir Francis Galton, a charismatic scholar whose controversial ideas about intelligence and genius set psychology's original course through the territory of individual differences.

## Galton and the Eugenics Movement

Sir Francis Galton (1822–1911) was a man obsessed by numbers. Believing that anything could be **quantified,** Galton converted even his subjective impressions into numbers, which he then treated as fact. This habit led to a system for rating the beauty of English women. (London had the fairest.) He also worked on a measure of boredom by timing the twitches of restless colleagues at meetings of the Royal Geographical Society. And, on a loftier level, Galton even monitored the attentiveness of God with a statistical study on the effects of prayer (Gould, 1996). Not surprisingly, this influential English gentleman also played his fast-and-loose numbers game with intelligence, which he believed to be a single, hereditary trait that could account for most differences among people. His theories caught the popular imagination at the 1884 International Exhibition in London, where thousands paid threepence to have Galton assess their mental abilities, based on his measurements of skull size and other physical tests.

While Galton's ideas may seem strange from the perspective of the 21st century, we should see him both as a founding figure in intelligence testing and as a product of his time. Influenced by his cousin, Charles Darwin, Galton attempted to apply evolutionary theory to the study of human behavior, becoming especially interested in how and why people differ so greatly in their abilities. Because Galton was a respected scientist, his theories, published in an 1869 book entitled *Hereditary Genius*, profoundly influenced subsequent thinking on the theories, methods, and practices of testing.

**Intelligence:** The mental capacity to acquire knowledge, reason, and solve problems effectively.

**Hypothetical construct:** A characteristic that is not directly observable but is, instead, inferred from behavior.

**Quantified:** Converted to numbers.

**Chapter 2:**
**Biopsychology**

*Darwin said that evolution favors individuals with the most adaptive traits.*

Among his more sensible ideas, Galton postulated that intelligence is *measurable*. More specifically, he argued that intelligence is **normally distributed,** meaning that it was spread through the population in varying degrees and that few people possessed extremely high or low intelligence, while most people clustered around the middle of the range. These notions about the measurement and distribution of intelligence proved to be of lasting value, even though some of Galton's other ideas were a bit fanciful or even downright bizarre.

At the upper end of the intelligence distribution, Galton proclaimed, lay the region occupied by "genius," which he believed to be inherited (Galton, 1869). Great intellectual ability, he said, was passed through generations of families, with nurture having only a minimal effect. But Galton didn't stop there: he also concluded that intelligence was related to "moral worth" (Galton, 1884). That is, people deemed less intelligent were (in his view) more likely to engage in immoral or criminal behavior.

Galton's ideas found an eager audience among the British aristocracy, who so much liked the implication that high intelligence runs in prominent families that they knighted him for this work. These hereditarian convictions also led Galton to found the **eugenics** movement (from the Greek *eugenes*, "well-born"), which advocated the regulation of marriage (and, therefore, of breeding) based on measurements of people's mental and physical traits. Supporters of the eugenics movement encouraged biologically superior people to interbreed and sought to discourage biologically inferior people from having offspring.

Today such an assumption that one's moral worthiness is determined by inherited factors rather than one's own responsible actions may seem preposterous. But in Galton's time the policies of eugenics won many adherents among policy makers and wealthy social leaders. Protesting the shortsightedness of his critics, Galton wrote, "There exists a sentiment, for the most part quite unreasonable, against the gradual extinction of an inferior race" (Galton, 1907 p. 200). Yet, in the end, genetics held the ultimate irony: Galton was unable to have children.

Galton's controversial ideas were endorsed and later expanded on by others. These disciples argued forcefully that the intellectually superior race (usually those of wealth and power) should propagate at the expense of those with inferior minds (the poor and the powerless). Such notions have led to forced sterilizations of the retarded and other "unfit" persons. At its most extreme, the eugenics movement added fuel to the fires of the Nazi Holocaust in the 1930s and 1940s, when millions of people were exterminated for being "inferior" to the ideals of the Aryan "race." Even today, groups of white supremacists promote these ideas with arguments for "racial purity" and "ethnic cleansing," even though they lack both logic and any scientific support.[1]

## Binet and Simon's Challenge

Galton's views did not sway everybody, particularly a Parisian named Alfred Binet, who saw intelligence as less fixed—less determined by heredity—than did Galton. In 1904 Binet (Bi-NAY) stepped into history when a new law required all children to attend school, and the French government asked him to devise a means of identifying those who needed remedial help. Binet and his colleague Théodore Simon turned to a short mental test consisting of 30 problems that sampled a variety of

[1]Biologists tell us that there are no biological characteristics that cleanly separate people into racial categories. In particular, there is no physical characteristic that reliably distinguishes the brain of a person of one geographic region or ethnic origin from that of another. Because of this, the concept of "race" cannot be defined biologically with precision. In fact, race is primarily a socially defined term, rather than a biological one (Jones, 1991). Alternatively, the concept of "culture," not "race," serves as a far better explanation for much of human diversity (Cohen, 1998).

**Appendix:
Understanding Graphs and Statistics: Analyzing Data and Forming Conclusions**
*The distribution of many psychological characteristics can be described by the normal curve.*

**Normally distributed:** Spread through the population in varying degrees, so that few people fall into the high or low ranges, while most people cluster around the middle.

**Eugenics:** A philosophy and a political movement that encouraged biologically superior people to interbreed and sought to discourage biologically inferior people from having offspring.

On the original Binet-Simon test, a child was asked to perform tasks such as the following:

- Name various common objects (such as a clock or a cat) shown in pictures.
- Repeat a 15-word sentence given by the examiner.
- Give a word that rhymes with one given by the examiner.
- Imitate gestures (such as pointing to an object).
- Comply with simple commands (such as moving a block from one location to another).
- Explain the differences between two common objects.
- Use three words (given by the examiner) in a sentence.
- Define abstract terms (such as "friendship").

abilities that seemed necessary for school (Figure 11.1). The new approach was a success. It did, indeed, predict which children could handle normal schoolwork.

Curiously, Binet and Simon offered no definition of the mental abilities measured by the test. Nor did they offer a theoretical explanation of the origin and development of intelligence. They wrote:

> Our purpose is to be able to measure the intellectual capacity of a child who is brought to us in order to know whether he is normal or retarded. We should, therefore, study his condition at the time and that only. We have nothing to do either with his past history or with his future. . . . (cited in Gould, 1996, p. 182)

If it worked, that was enough for Binet and Simon.

Four important features distinguish the Binet-Simon approach to testing intellectual ability:

1. Binet and Simon interpreted scores on their test as an estimate of *current performance* and not as a measure of innate intelligence.
2. They wanted the test scores to be used to identify children who needed special help and not merely to label them.
3. They emphasized that training and opportunity could affect intelligence, and they wanted to identify areas of performance in which special education could help these children.
4. Binet and Simon constructed their test *empirically*—based on how children were observed to perform—rather than tying it to a particular theory of intelligence.

**Chapter 1:**
**Mind, Behavior, and Science**

*An empirical investigation relies on observational data.*

For their test, Binet and Simon designed age-appropriate problems or test items on which many children's responses could be compared (see Figure 11.1). The problems on the test were chosen so that they could be scored objectively. They also emphasized judgment and reasoning rather than rote memory (Binet, 1911). In addition, Binet and Simon deliberately chose items that were not heavily influenced by differences in children's environments.

**Appendix:**
**Understanding Graphs and Statistics: Analyzing Data and Forming Conclusions**

*The mean (average) is the sum of all scores divided by the number of scores.*

On this test, children of various ages were assessed, and the average for normal children at each age was computed. Then, each individual child's performance was compared to the average for other children of that age. Test results were expressed in terms of **mental age (MA):** the average age at which normal (average) individuals achieve a particular score. So, when a child's score was the same as the average score for a group of five-year-olds, for example, the child was said to have a mental age of five, regardless of his or her actual **chronological age (CA),** the number of years since the individual's birth. Binet and Simon then operationally defined "retardation" as being two MA years behind CA.

## IQ Testing

After Binet and Simon began the standardized assessment of intellectual ability, statistics-minded psychologists took their idea and ran. In the United States, they modified the Binet and Simon scoring procedure, improved the reliability of the tests, and studied the scores drawn from large normative groups of people. Soon intelligence testing was a technique by which Americans were defining themselves—and each other.

**THE APPEAL OF INTELLIGENCE TESTING IN AMERICA**   Why did intelligence testing become so popular in the United States? Three forces that were changing the face of the country early in the 20th century conspired to make intelligence testing seem like an orderly way out of growing turmoil and uncertainty. First, the United States was experiencing an unprecedented wave of immigration, resulting from global economic, social, and political crises. Second, new laws requiring universal education—schooling for all children—were flooding schools with students. And third, when World War I began, the military needed a way of assessing and classifying the new recruits. Together, these events—massive immigration, new education laws, and World War I—resulted in a need for large numbers of people to be identified, documented, and classified (Chapman, 1988). At the time, "intelligence test results were used not only to differentiate [among] children experiencing academic problems, but also as a measuring stick to organize an entire society" (Hale, 1983, p. 373). Assessment was seen not only as a way to bring some order to the tumult of rapid social change, but as an inexpensive, democratic way to separate those who could benefit from education or military leadership training from those who could not.

In 1917, when the United States declared war on Germany and joined the massive military campaign of World War I, the government commissioned a group of illustrious psychologists, including Lewis Terman, Edward Thorndike, and Robert Yerkes, to develop psychological instruments that could be used to assess the mental abilities of large numbers of people quickly. They responded by developing the necessary tests in only one month (Lennon, 1985). These new group-administered tests of mental ability were eventually used to evaluate over 1.7 million recruits.

One consequence of this large-scale group-testing program was that the American public came to accept the idea that intelligence tests could differentiate people in terms of mental ability. This acceptance led to the widespread use of tests in schools and industry. Another, more unfortunate, consequence was that the tests reinforced prevailing prejudices, because the Army reports indicated that differences in test scores were linked to race and country of origin (Yerkes, 1921). Of course, the same statistics *could* have been used to demonstrate that environmental disadvantages limit the full development of people's intellectual abilities. But instead, the data were used to support racist ideology. Immigrants with limited facility in English or even little understanding of how to take such tests were found to be "morons," "idiots," and "imbeciles" (terms used at the time to specify different degrees of mental retardation). Immigrants from Northern Europe did much better than those from Southern Europe, who had lower educational levels and less familiarity with English.

While these problems are more obvious to us now, at the time they were obscured by the fact that the tests did what most people wanted them to do: Mental tests were simple to administer, and they provided a means of assessing and classifying people according to their scores. Never mind that there were some biases and that some people were treated unfairly. In general, the public perceived that the tests were fair and democratic.

**Chapter 1:**
**Mind, Behavior, and Science**
*Operational definitions are stated in objective, observable, and measurable terms.*

**Chapter 6:**
**Learning and Remembering**
*Thorndike also first recognized trial-and-error learning.*

**Mental age (MA):** The average age at which normal (average) individuals achieve a particular score.

**Chronological age (CA):** The number of years since the individual's birth.

**THE STANFORD-BINET INTELLIGENCE SCALE AND THE CONCEPT OF IQ** Realizing that the early efforts at testing intelligence were crude, American psychologist Lewis Terman began to develop a more precise instrument—one that would be administered individually rather than in groups. Although this was not so economical as were the old group tests, individual testing proved to be more accurate and consistent. It was also better suited for spotting learning problems. Even more importantly, Terman's test was designed for children, as well as adults. This opened the doors of schools all over America to intelligence testing.

Terman's approach was to adapt the Binet and Simon test for U.S. schoolchildren by standardizing its administration and its age-level norms. The result was the Stanford Revision of the Binet Tests (named after Stanford University, where Terman worked). It is commonly referred to as the Stanford-Binet Intelligence Scale (Terman, 1916), and it soon became the standard by which other measures of intelligence were judged.

With this new test, Terman introduced the concept of the **intelligence quotient (IQ),** a term coined originally by German psychologist Wilhelm Stern in 1914. The IQ was the ratio of mental age (MA) to chronological age (CA), multiplied by 100 (to eliminate decimals):

$$IQ = \frac{MA}{CA} \times 100$$

Please follow us through the IQ equation with this example: Consider a child with a CA of eight years, whose test scores revealed an MA of 10. Dividing the mental age by chronological age (MA/CA = 10/8) gives us 1.25. Multiplying that result by 100, we obtain an IQ of 125. A child of that same chronological age who performed at the level of an average six-year-old has an IQ of 6/8 × 100 = 75 according to the formula. Those who perform at the mental age equivalent to their chronological age have IQs of 100, considered to be the average or "normal" IQ.

Within a short time, the new Stanford-Binet test became a popular instrument in clinical psychology, psychiatry, and educational counseling. With the publication of this test Terman also promulgated his belief that intelligence was largely hereditary and that his IQ test could measure it. The implicit message was that an IQ score reflected something fundamental and unchanging about people.

Although the Stanford-Binet was the "gold standard" of intelligence testing, it had its critics. The loudest objection was that it was based on a fuzzy concept of intelligence because the test measured different mental abilities at different ages. For example, two- to four-year-olds were tested on their ability to manipulate objects, whereas adults were tested almost exclusively on verbal items. Test makers heeded these criticisms, and as the scientific understanding of intelligence increased, psychologists found it increasingly important to measure *several* intellectual abilities at *all* age levels. A modern revision of the Stanford-Binet now provides separate scores for several mental skills (Vernon, 1987).

**THE WECHSLER INTELLIGENCE SCALES** Terman's competitor, David Wechsler of Bellevue Hospital in New York, set out to correct the Stanford-Binet's dependence on verbal items in the assessment of adult intelligence. In 1939, he published the Wechsler-Bellevue Intelligence Scale, which combined *verbal* subtests with nonverbal or *performance* subtests. Thus, in addition to an overall IQ score, subjects were given separate estimates of verbal IQ and nonverbal IQ. After a few changes, the test was retitled the Wechsler Adult Intelligence Scale (WAIS) in 1955, and later the revised WAIS-R (Wechsler, 1981).

Verbal intelligence, as measured by the WAIS-R, has six components: Information, Vocabulary, Comprehension, Arithmetic, Similarities (stating how two things are alike), and Digit Span (repeating a series of digits after the examiner).

**Intelligence quotient (IQ):** A numerical score on an intelligence test, originally computed by dividing the person's mental age by chronological age and multiplying by 100.

These verbal tests are both written and oral. By contrast, the performance components of intelligence emphasize manipulation of materials and have little or no verbal content. In the block design test, for example, a subject tries to reproduce designs shown on cards by fitting together blocks with colored sides. The Digit Symbol test provides a key that matches nine symbols to nine numeric digits, and the task is to write the appropriate digits under the symbols on another page. Other performance tests involve Picture Arrangement, Picture Completion, and Object Assembly. If you were to take the WAIS-R, you would perform all 11 subtests, and receive three scores: a verbal IQ, a performance IQ, and an overall or full-scale IQ.

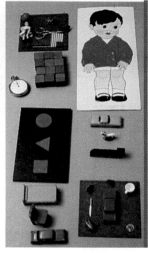

A psychologist administers an intelligence test to a four-year-old child. The performance part of this test includes a block design task, an object completion task, and a shape identification task.

The WAIS-R is designed for people 18 years or older, but similar tests have been developed for children. The Wechsler Intelligence Scale for Children, Revised (WISC-R) is suited to children ages 6 to 17, and the Wechsler Preschool and Primary Scale of Intelligence (WPPSI) for children ages 4 to 6 years. Some subtests were specially created for use with children, but most have a direct counterpart in the WAIS-R (Wechsler, 1989, 1991).

The WAIS-R, the WISC-R, and the WPPSI form a family of intelligence tests that yield a verbal IQ, a performance IQ, and a full-scale IQ at all age levels. In addition, they provide comparable subtest scores that allow researchers to track the development of even more specific intellectual abilities as the individual moves out of one test's age range and into another. For this reason, the Wechsler scales are particularly valuable when the same individual is to be tested over time, at different ages.

**GROUP TESTS OF INTELLIGENCE** In addition to the individually administered Stanford-Binet and Wechsler scales, psychologists have devised many other intelligence tests designed to be given in groups. These are much more refined than the old tests given to World War I recruits. Of all forms of intelligence testing, you are probably most familiar and experienced with these group tests: The chances are good that you took several of them during your earlier school years. Some students take as many as 20 standardized group tests of their abilities before graduating from high school (Seligman, 1988).

While individual tests are often used to diagnose learning difficulties in specific individuals, it is often less clear why group tests are given across the board to large numbers of children. Sometimes the scores are simply used to screen the upper and lower ends of the IQ spectrum for special classes. Making all children take IQ tests for such purposes is hard to justify, especially in view of the potential for labeling that may occur when students are tagged by teachers as "average" or "slow," based on their test scores.[2]

The primary benefits of group tests are that they require no special training to administer, they can be given to a large group in relatively little time, and they are quickly and accurately scored by computer. These tests are ideal when a large number of people are to be tested in an economical way. Two of the most popular group tests of intelligence are the Cognitive Abilities Test (CAT) (Thorndike & Hagen, 1978) and the School and College Ability Tests (SCAT) (Educational Testing Service, 1990b). They provide separate verbal and quantitative (math) scores, and the

[2]Whereas IQ tests are often conceived as measures of innate ability or academic potential, "achievement" tests are designed as measures of *learning*. Thus, achievement tests given to groups of schoolchildren may be valuable in determining how the *school* is doing.

## Do It Yourself!

## Sample IQ Test Items

Try your hand at the following items that have been adapted from group tests of intelligence. Some of the items are more challenging than others. You will find the correct answers at the end.

**VOCABULARY**   Select the best definition for each word:

1. **viable**    a. traveled       b. capable of living
              c. "v"-shaped     d. can be bent

2. **imminent**  a. defenseless    b. expensive
              c. impending      d. notorious

**ANALOGIES**   Examine the relationship between the first two words. Then, find an answer that has the same relationship with the word in **bold letters:**

3. Washington: Lincoln
   **July**:      a. January     b. April
              c. May         d. October

4. ocean: canoe
   **verse**:     a. poem        b. pen
              c. water       d. serve

**SIMILARITIES**   Which figure on the right belongs to the same category as the one on the left?

5. **J     A M S Z T**

6. **A     S T U V X**

**SEQUENCES**   Choose the answer that best completes the sequence:

7. a z b y c x d?      e      s      u      w      f

8. 1 3 6 10 15?      16      18      21      27      128

**MATHEMATICAL REASONING**

9. Portland and Seattle are actually 150 miles apart, but on a map they are two inches apart. If Chicago and Norfolk are five inches apart on the same map, what is the actual distance between those two cities?

   a. 125 miles      b. 250 miles.      c. 375 miles      d. 525 miles

**ANSWERS:**    1. **b**    2. **c**    3. **d (October comes after July)**    4. **d (***verse* and *serve* have the same letters)**    5. **S (the only one with a curve in it)**    6. **U (the only vowel)**    7. **W**    8. **21**    9. **375**

**Chapter 10: Personality**

Validity: *Does the test measure what it is intended to measure?*
Reliability: *Does the test show consistency for people's scores?*

CAT also provides a nonverbal score. The developers of these tests maintain that they are *valid* predictors of school achievement and are as *reliable* as the Stanford-Binet and the Wechsler tests. On the other hand, the lack of individual detail makes such application limited. Individualized tests provide detail that group tests cannot assess, such as firsthand observation of how a person tackles a problem or which tasks someone most enjoys (Lennon, 1985).

## Problems with the IQ Formula

A problem in calculating IQ scores became apparent as soon as psychologists began to use their formula with adults. Here's what happens: Throughout childhood, most children get more and more IQ test questions right as they get older. The improvement, however, begins to slow down, and scores level off in the mid- to late teenage years. This causes mental age to reach a plateau. So, mental age fails to keep pace with birthdays, as chronological age continues to increase. As a result, the formula used for computing IQs makes normal children seem to develop into retarded adults! Note what happens to the average 30-year-old's score if mental age stays the same as it was at 15.

$$IQ = \frac{\text{Mental Age}}{\text{Chronological Age}} = \frac{15}{30} \times 100 = 50$$

Psychologists quickly realized that this is a mathematical fluke. People do not become less intelligent as adults (even though their children sometimes think so). Rather adults develop in different directions, which their IQ scores do not necessarily reflect. Prudently, psychologists decided to abandon the original IQ formula and to find another means of calculating IQs. Their solution was similar to the familiar practice of "grading on the curve." This famous curve demands some explanation.

## Standard Scores and Normal Distributions: A New IQ Formula

Behind the new method for calculating IQs lay Francis Galton's assumption that intelligence is *normally distributed*, like many physical traits, including height, weight, or shoe size. If you were to measure any of these variables in a large number of people, you would probably get a set of scores that follow the same "curve" teachers use when they grade "on the curve." Let us take women's heights as an example.

Imagine that you have *randomly* selected a large number of adult women and arranged them in single-file columns, according to their heights (everybody 5' tall in one column, 5' 1" in the next, 5' 2" in the next, and so on). You would find most of the women in the columns near the group's *average* height (see Figure 11.2). Only a few would fall in the columns containing extremely tall women or extremely short women. We could easily describe the number of women at each height by a curve that follows the boundary of each column. We call this bell-shaped curve a *normal distribution*.

Applying this same concept to intelligence, psychologists find that people's IQ test scores (like the women's heights we considered above) fit a normal distribution. (See Figure 11.3.) Specifically, when tests are given to large numbers of individuals, the scores of those at each age level are normally distributed. (Adults are placed in one group, and the distribution of their scores also fits the bell-shaped curve.) Instead of using the old IQ formula (which divides MA by CA), IQs are determined from tables, which indicate where test scores fall on the normal curve. The raw test scores are statistically adjusted so that the average for each age group is set at 100 and the middle two-thirds of the distribution falls between approximately 85 and 115 IQ points. This, then, becomes the **normal range.** At the extreme ends of the distribution, scores below 70 are often said to be in the *mentally retarded* range, while those above 130 are sometimes said to indicate *giftedness*.

Thus, IQ scores are no longer derived by dividing mental age by chronological age, although the concept of a "ratio" expressed as a multiple of 100 (a percentage-like number that is

**Chapter 1:**
**Mind, Behavior, and Science**
*Random selection means that all potential subjects have an equal chance of being selected.*

**Normal range:** Scores falling in (approximately) the middle two-thirds of a normal distribution.

**FIGURE 11.2:**  An (imaginary) normal distribution of women's heights

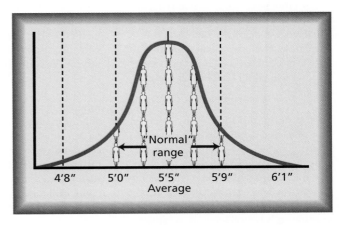

easy to understand) is retained. This solves the problem of calculating adult IQs by comparing adults with adults. Scores between 90 and 110 are now labeled "normal" (see Figure 11.3).

**▌ FIGURE 11.3:** The Normal Distribution of IQ Scores among a Large Sample

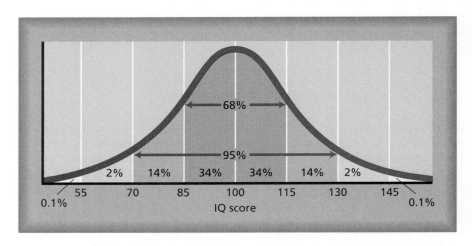

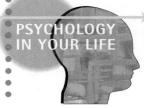

**PSYCHOLOGY IN YOUR LIFE**

## What Can You Do for an Exceptional Child?

The Special Olympics offers mentally retarded children (and others with disabilities) an opportunity to capitalize on their abilities and to build self-esteem.

*M*ental retardation and *giftedness* lie at the opposite ends of the intelligence spectrum. As usually conceived, **mental retardation** occupies the IQ range below IQ 70—taking in the scores achieved by approximately 2% of the population (see Figure 11.3). Arbitrarily, **giftedness** begins 30 points above average, at 130 IQ points. Similarly, the gifted range comprises about 2% of the population. Now, bearing in mind all we have learned about the limitations of IQ tests, we will take a brief look at these two groups.

MENTAL RETARDATION   The most current view of mental retardation deemphasizes IQ scores by focusing on abilities to get along in the world (Baumeister, 1987). In fact, the American Association of Mental Retardation now offers a definition of mental retardation that does not even mention an IQ cutoff score. According to this new perspective, mental retardation

involves "significantly sub-average intellectual functioning" that becomes apparent before age 18. It also involves limitations in at least two of the following areas: "communication, self-care, home living, social skills, community use, self direction, health and safety, functional academics, leisure and work" (Turkington, 1993, p. 26).

CAUSES OF MENTAL RETARDATION   Mental retardation has many causes (Scott & Carran, 1987). Some are known to be genetic because we can point to a specific genetically controlled defect, as we have seen in the cases of Down syndrome (*See Chapter 2, Biopsychology.*). Some are environmental, as in *fetal alcohol syndrome*, involving brain damage incurred before birth, caused by the mother's abuse of alcohol during pregnancy. Other environmental causes include postnatal accidents that damage the cognitive regions of the brain. Still other causes involve conditions of deprivation or neglect, which fail to give the developing child the experiences needed for advancement up the in-

tellectual ladder. Some cases have no known cause.

DEALING WITH MENTAL RETARDATION
For most cases of mental retardation we have no cures, although research has found ways to prevent certain forms from occurring. For example, a simple test performed routinely on newborn babies can identify a genetic disorder known as PKU. If detected early, the mental retardation associated with PKU can be prevented by a special diet. More generally, genetic counseling, pregnancy care ser-

vices, and education of new mothers are simple preventive measures for which there is a great need (Scott & Carran, 1987).

In addition to prevention, biological scientists hope that one day they will be able to treat certain genetically based forms of mental retardation with genetic therapies that are just now being developed. This tactic will probably involve splicing a healthy gene into a virus that will "infect" all of a retarded person's cells and replace the defective gene. Genetic therapy is now being tried experimentally for the treatment of certain physical diseases, but it is at least a few years away in the treatment of mental retardation.

For now, what can you do if you have a mentally retarded child? Dealing with mental retardation usually means making the best of a difficult situation. Parents of a retarded child should realize that, because the nervous system is so immature at birth and because so much physical development occurs during the first years of life, interventions that begin early will have the greatest payoffs. While some interventions have a biological focus (in PKU, for example), psychological approaches that involve sensory stimulation and social interaction can be enormously important. In fact, an enriched environment may be just as helpful to a mentally retarded child as it is to a gifted child. Teams of special education teachers, speech therapists, educational psychologists, physicians, and other specialists can devise programs that allow mentally retarded persons to capitalize on the abilities they have, rather than being held a prisoner of their disabilities (see Schroeder, Schroeder, & Landsman, 1987). Behavior modification programs, based on operant conditioning, have been especially successful. *(See Chapter 6, Learning and Remembering, and Chapter 14, Therapies for Mental Disorder.)* As a result, many retarded citizens have learned to care for themselves and have learned vocational skills that enable them to live independently (Landesman & Butterfield, 1987).

GIFTEDNESS    At the other end of the intelligence spectrum we find the "gifted," with their especially high IQs (typically defined as being in the top 1 or 2%). But, you might wonder, what do such people eventually do with their superior intellectual abilities? Does a high IQ give its owner an advantage in life? A 70-year look at gifted individuals suggests that it does.

TERMAN'S STUDIES OF GIFTEDNESS    The most extensive project ever undertaken to study gifted individuals began in 1921 under the direction of Lewis Terman (the same person who brought Binet and Simon's IQ test to the United States). From a large pool of children tested in the California schools, Terman selected 1,528 children who scored near the top of the IQ range. His longitudinal research program followed these children as they went through school and on into adulthood. Periodically through their lives, Terman retested them and gathered other information on their achievements and adjustment patterns. The resulting decades of data have taught us much about the nature of giftedness. Almost uniformly, Terman's gifted children excelled in school—as one might expect from the strong correlation between IQ and academic achievement. Terman was also struck by the good health and happiness of the children in his sample. Apparently, a healthy mind and a healthy body often go together.

As they moved into adulthood, the gifted group continued on the path of success. An unusually high number of scientists, writers, and professionals emerged from its ranks. Together they published more than 2,000 scientific articles, patented 235 inventions, and wrote 92 books. By middle age, more than 86% of the men in Terman's sample had entered high-status professions (Terman & Oden, 1959).

Yet, for all their achievements, no one in this high-IQ sample achieved the level of an Einstein, a Picasso, or a Martha Graham. Nor did a high IQ turn out to be a guarantee of wealth or stature. In fact, many from Terman's sample led ordinary, undistinguished lives. The ones who were most visibly successful seemed to have, in addition to their high IQs, extraordinary motivation and someone at home or at school who was especially encouraging to them (Goleman, 1980; Oden, 1968).

DEALING WITH GIFTEDNESS    Imagine that you are the parent of a child with a very high IQ score, say 145. Which one of the following would be best for your child?

a) Enroll your child in special after-school classes.

b) Hire a tutor to help the child with his or her homework.
c) Send the child to a private school.
d) Do nothing special.

What do the experts say?

Don't rush out to enroll your child in special classes or provide other "help" because of his or her IQ score, counsels Csikszentmihalyi (Csikszentmihalyi et al., 1993; Wong & Csikszentmihalyi, 1991). He warns that parents can destroy the spark of curiosity by pushing a child toward goals that do not hold the child's interest. Chances are you have already provided an environment in which your child's native ability could thrive. So, do not make any rash and radical changes.

Above all, avoid making the child feel like a freak because of the high IQ score. And do not feel smug about your genetic contribution to your child's intellect. Remember that IQ tests sample only a small fraction of human abilities. Other people's kids may have equally amazing abilities in untested regions of their intellects.

Remember, also, that a high IQ is no guarantee of high motivation, high creativity, or success in life. All it guarantees is an intellectual opportunity. Ironically, you could suppress that opportunity with parental pressure, warns Csikszentmihalyi. Your high expectations could trigger a backlash, if the child decides to rebel against your insistence on intellectual achievement.

So, what should you do with a bright child? Nothing special that you would not have done before you knew the IQ score.

**Mental retardation:** Often conceived as representing the lower 2% of the IQ range, commencing about 30 points below average (below about 70 points). More sophisticated definitions also take into account an individual's level of social functioning and other abilities.

**Giftedness:** Often conceived as representing the upper 2% of the IQ range, commencing about 30 points above average—at about 130 IQ points.

1. **RECALL:** *Francis Galton coined the term "eugenics" for his political movement, which advocated*
   a. cloning of intelligent people.
   b. discouraging biologically inferior people from breeding.
   c. searching for a gene that was imagined to control intelligence.
   d. higher pay for brighter workers.

2. **RECALL:** *One of Binet's great ideas was that of mental age, which was defined as*
   a. the average age at which normal individuals achieve a particular score on an intelligence test.
   b. an individual's biological age plus the score he/she achieves on a mental test.
   c. an individual's level of emotional maturity, as judged by the examiner.
   d. the variability in scores seen when an individual is tested repeatedly.

3. **APPLICATION:** *You have tested a 12-year-old child and found that she has a mental age of 15. Using the original IQ formula, what is her IQ?*
   a. 75
   b. 100
   c. 115
   d. 125

4. **RECALL:** *The problem with the original IQ formula is that it gave a distorted picture of the intellectual abilities of*
   a. adults.
   b. children.
   c. retarded persons.
   d. gifted students.

5. **UNDERSTANDING THE CORE CONCEPT:** *If intelligence is a normally distributed characteristic, then you would expect to find it*
   a. to be different abilities in different people.
   b. to be spread throughout the population, but with most people clustered near the middle of the range.
   c. to a significant degree only in people whose IQ scores are above 100.
   d. to be determined entirely by hereditary factors.

**ANSWERS:**      1. b      2. a      3. d      4. a      5. b

---

**KEY QUESTION**

## WHAT ARE THE COMPONENTS OF INTELLIGENCE?

People who show aptitude in one area—language, for example—often score high on other dimensions, such as mathematics or spatial relationships. This fact argues for the idea of a single, general intellectual ability. But there are some glaring exceptions. Persons with **savant syndrome** represent the most extreme cases of this sort. These individuals have a remarkable talent (such as the ability to multiply numbers quickly in their heads or to determine the day of the week for any given date) even though they are mentally slow in other domains. (You may remember Dustin Hoffman's portrayal of one such person in the film *Rain Man.*) These cases raise a serious question about the whole concept of a single, general intelligence factor. Obviously, there is no simple answer to the question of one or many intelligences. Different psychologists have dealt with this issue in different ways, as our Core Concept suggests:

**Savant syndrome:** Found in individuals having a remarkable talent (such as the ability to multiply numbers in their heads or to determine the day of the week for any given date) even though they are mentally slow in other domains.

**CORE CONCEPT**

**Psychologists have long disagreed about the makeup of intelligence—particularly whether it is best described as a single, general factor or a collection of distinct abilities.**

By themselves, IQ scores do not tell how much people know or what they can do. A high-school student with an IQ of 100 has knowledge and skills that a fourth-grader with a higher IQ of 120 does not have. Likewise, individuals labeled "retarded" or "developmentally disabled" on the basis of their IQ scores vary considerably in what they can do and what they can learn. And when we look at the abilities of elderly persons we find that they may perform more poorly than the young on test items where speed is important, while showing measurably greater wisdom in many other domains (Baltes, 1990). Do these widely different patterns of performance come from a single intellectual ability?

## Psychometric Theories

Although the theories we will examine in the following pages portray intelligence as many things—from logic to musical ability to "street smarts"—the fundamental difference among these diverse perspectives is whether intelligence is viewed as a single ability or multiple abilities. We begin with two theories representing the two extremes: One conceptualizes intelligence as a single factor, while the other sees it as having 150 separate components. Both views grew out of **psychometrics,** the field that was born of the IQ testing movement.

**SPEARMAN'S "G" FACTOR** Charles Spearman of England, an early-1900s figure in assessment, used mathematical analysis of test scores to show that an individual's performances on a variety of mental tests are often highly correlated (1927). This, he said, points to a single, common factor of *general intelligence* underlying people's performance across all intellectual domains. He did not deny that some people have outstanding talents or deficits in certain areas. But, he said, these individual differences should not blind us to a general intelligence factor at work behind all our mental activity. Spearman called this common intellectual ability the **g factor,** a general intelligence factor assumed to be the individual's basic intellectual ability. Like Galton, Terman, and others before him, Spearman also assumed that this general factor is innate. "It was almost universally assumed by psychologists and by the general public in these early years that individual differences in intelligence were innately determined. One's intellectual level was a characteristic one must accept rather than try to change" (Tyler, 1988, p. 128).

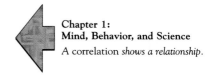

Chapter 1:
**Mind, Behavior, and Science**
A correlation *shows a relationship*.

**GUILFORD'S STRUCTURE-OF-INTELLECT** Going to the opposite extreme, J. P. Guilford carried the idea of intelligence as a collection of separate abilities farther than anyone else by proposing 150 specific components. His model of intelligence (see Figure 11.4) looks like a cube, but you can also think of it as Guilford's attempt to create psychology's "periodic table" of the intellect. How did Guilford arrive at 150 components of intelligence? To begin, he proposed that all intellectual tasks involve three broad attributes (Guilford, 1973, 1985):

- *Operations*—which refers to the kind of thinking required (e.g., looking for "correct" answers, as opposed to "creative" answers)
- *Contents*—which refers to the kind of information that must be used (e.g., visual, verbal, or mathematical information)
- *Products*—which refers to the form that the product of thought will take (e.g., a written report, a painting, or a new surgical procedure)

But Guilford did not stop there. His theory further subdivides the above categories into five kinds of mental operations, five classes of contents, and six types of intellectual products. Thus, each of the 150 small cubes in **Guilford's structure-of-intellect** contains a different combination of these 16 factors. To give an example: The children's TV program, *Sesame Street*, often presents viewers with a group of objects (e.g., shirt, socks, shoes, pencil) and asks, "Which one is not like the others?" In Guilford's terms, this problem requires *evaluation* (an operation), *semantic* information (one type of content), and organization of information into *classes* (a product).

**Psychometrics:** The field of mental testing.

**g factor:** A general ability, proposed by Spearman as the main factor underlying all intelligent mental activity.

**Guilford's structure-of-intellect:** J. P. Guilford's model of intelligence, consisting of some 150 separate factors, generated by five kinds of mental *operations,* five classes of *contents,* and six types of intellectual *products.*

Guilford's structure-of-intellect model

Guilford's three dimensions of intellect—operations, contents, and products—may be arranged in various combinations to produce 180 separate factors of intellect.

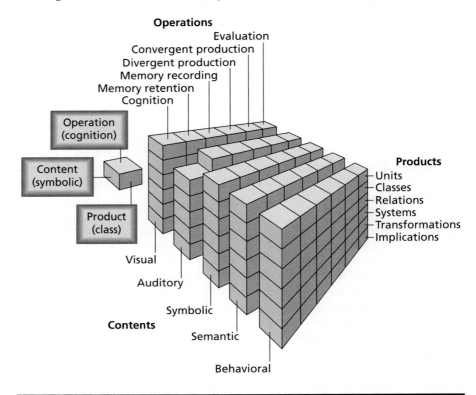

**Convergent thinking:** The form of intelligence, proposed by Guilford, that is used to find "correct" answers.

**Divergent thinking:** The form of intelligence, proposed by Guilford, that is used to generate creative responses.

**Chapter 7: Cognitive Processes**

*Many tests of creativity are based on Guilford's notion of divergent thinking.*

**Chapter 1: Mind, Behavior, and Science**

*The cognitive view emphasizes mental processes, such as learning, memory, and perception.*

**Practical intelligence (also called** *contextual intelligence***):** According to Sternberg, this is the ability to cope with the environment; sometimes called "street smarts."

While Guilford's model represents the most detailed theory of intelligence yet proposed, it has had little real impact on the practice of intelligence testing. Even so, the structure-of-intellect model has helped us realize that there are many ways to be smart. Perhaps Guilford's most influential contribution lies in his distinction between two kinds of mental operations: **convergent thinking** (used to find a correct answer) and **divergent thinking** (used to find creative solutions to problems that can have many answers).

## Cognitive Theories

As the cognitive view became a force in psychology, cognitive psychologists (who had never been part of the psychometric tradition) began to develop radical new perspectives on intelligence. In brief, their broader definition of intelligence went well beyond the emphasis on vocabulary, logic, problem solving, and other skills that had been used to predict school success. *Intelligence*, they said, involves cognitive processes that contribute to success in many areas of life—not just school. We will concentrate on two of these cognitive theories.

**STERNBERG'S TRIARCHIC THEORY**   You may know someone who seems to have plenty of "book smarts," but who has never been very successful in life. Such people often don't know how to "read" others or to deal with unexpected events. Psychologist Robert Sternberg says that they lack **practical intelligence** (also called *contextual intelligence*): the ability to cope with their environment. It is sometimes called "street smarts," although it applies just as well at home, on the job, or at school as it does on the street. One study suggests that it can also be thought of as "horse sense": researchers found that, among regular visitors to racetracks, those who were most successful at picking winning horses had IQs no higher than those who were less successful, suggesting that their ability is different from the sort of intelligence measured on standard IQ tests (Ceci & Liker, 1986).

In contrast with practical intelligence, Sternberg refers to the ability measured by most IQ tests as **logical reasoning** (also called *componential intelligence*). It includes the ability to analyze problems and find correct answers. Your grades in college are likely to be closely related to your logical reasoning abilities.

A third form of intelligence described in Sternberg's theory is called **experiential intelligence**—involving insight and creativity. This form of intelligence helps people see new relationships among concepts. For example, experiential intelligence is thought to be what Picasso used to develop the new form of painting called Cubism. It is also the form of intelligence that Sternberg used to develop his new theory of intelligence.

Sternberg's formulation is often called the **triarchic theory** because it combines three (*tri* = three) intelligences. For Sternberg each one in this trio of abilities—practical intelligence, logical reasoning, and experiential intelligence—is relatively independent of the others. That is, a person's ability in one of the three areas doesn't necessarily predict his or her intelligence in the other two. Each represents a different dimension for describing and evaluating human performance.

Sternberg's triarchic theory reminds us that it is inaccurate to think of a single IQ score as summarizing all that is important or valuable in people's intelligence (Sternberg et al., 1995). Traditional measures of IQ tell only part of the story—the componential (logical) part. Further, says Sternberg, intelligence can be *learned:* People can improve their experiential, practical, and logical abilities (Sternberg, 1986). Thus, the three intelligences are not solely the result of an innate blueprint, etched in the genes. All can be enhanced with the right kind of training—which Sternberg's research program is now trying to identify.

Sternberg expects to demonstrate that many students who do poorly in school do not lack intelligence of the traditional (logical) sort. Rather, they do poorly because they have not picked up the skills for adapting to new situations (practical intelligence)—skills that are rarely taught deliberately in school. So, they may never have learned when to speak up and when to keep quiet, how to make friends and allies, how to hand in neat papers, or how to budget time so as to get work completed on schedule. Ultimately, he would like to develop a test that can help any student identify both strengths and weaknesses. Then, based on the test results, a student could enter a program tailored to teaching the missing skills (Sternberg, 1994).

**GARDNER'S SEVEN INTELLIGENCES**  Like Sternberg, Howard Gardner also believes that traditional IQ tests measure only a limited range of human mental abilities. He finds that we have at least seven separate intelligences or **frames of mind** (Ellison, 1984; Gardner, 1983, 1999):

1. *Linguistic ability*—often measured on traditional IQ tests by vocabulary tests and tests of reading comprehension.
2. *Logical-mathematical ability*—also measured on most IQ tests with analogies, math problems, and logic problems.
3. *Spatial ability*—the ability to form mental images of objects and to think about their relationships in space.
4. *Musical ability*—the ability to perceive and create patterns of rhythms and pitches.
5. *Bodily-kinesthetic ability*—involves movement and coordination, such as that needed by a dancer or a surgeon.

**Logical reasoning (also called *componential intelligence*):** According to Sternberg, this is the ability measured by most IQ tests; includes the ability to analyze problems and find correct answers.

**Experiential intelligence:** According to Sternberg, the form of intelligence that helps people see new relationships among concepts; involves insight and creativity.

**Triarchic theory:** The term for Sternberg's theory; so called because it combines three main forms of intelligence.

**Frames of mind:** A term sometimes used to refer to Gardner's seven forms of intelligence.

Chapter 2:
Biopsychology

*The brain is composed of many specialized modules that work together to create mind and behavior.*

6. *Interpersonal ability*—understanding other people's emotions, motives, and actions.

7. *Intrapersonal ability*—the ability to know oneself and to develop a sense of identity.

Each of these intelligences arises from a separate module in the brain, says Gardner.

Like Sternberg, Gardner sees each component of intelligence as equally important. Yet, the value of each is also culturally determined, according to what is needed by, useful to, and prized by a given society. Gardner notes that Western society promotes the first two intelligences, while other societies value one or more of the other kinds of intelligence. For example, in small island societies, people place a high value on getting along with others (Gardner's *interpersonal ability*). In these restricted social settings, people have no place to go if they get into a quarrel and want to escape or part ways. People cannot move 100 miles away if they live on an island 10 miles in diameter. In such societies, people avoid quarrels by recognizing potential problems at an early stage and modifying behaviors to solve problems quickly.

Assessing these kinds of intelligence demands more than paper-and-pencil tests and simple quantified measures. Gardner's tests of intelligence require that the subject be observed and assessed in a variety of life situations as well as in the artificial samples of life depicted in traditional intelligence tests. On its face, the theory appears to be sound, but it awaits verification through tests still in the process of development.

### Cultural Definitions of Intelligence

One of Gardner's seven intelligences is bodily-kinesthetic intelligence, the ability to coordinate one's body movements with grace and control, as demonstrated by dancers.

If you had been socialized in a Pacific island culture, which would matter more: your SAT scores or your ability to navigate a boat on the open ocean? Cross-cultural psychologists tell us that the notion of "intelligence" can have different meanings in different cultures (Kleinfeld, 1994; Neisser et al., 1997; Rogoff, 1990; Segall et al., 1990; Serpell, 1994; Vernon, 1969). While intelligence is almost universally associated with the ability to solve problems, many Western cultures associate intelligence specifically with *quick* solutions to problems. The Buganda people in Uganda, on the other hand, associate intelligence with slow and thoughtful responses. The Djerma-Sonhai in Niger (West Africa) think of intelligence as a combination of social skills and good memory. And for the Chinese, intelligence involves, among other things, extensive knowledge, determination, social responsibility, and ability for imitation.

John Berry (1992) has extensively studied the kinds of mental abilities considered valuable among Native Americans. Berry began by asking adult interviewees among the Cree in northern Ontario to provide him with Cree words that describe aspects of thinking, starting with examples like "smart" or "intelligent." The most frequent responses translate roughly to "wise, thinks hard, and thinks carefully." He also asked his respondents to sort all the words he had gathered according to their similarity. Closely related were terms such as "smartness displayed at school," "understands new things," and "accumulated knowledge." Although Cree children attend schools introduced by the dominant Anglo (English-European) culture, the Cree themselves make a distinction between "school" intelligence and the kind of "good thinking" valued in the Cree culture.

Another term the Cree consistently offered was "respectful." As one respondent explained, intelligence "is being respectful in the Indian sense. You need to really know the other person and respect them for what they are" (Berry, 1992, p. 79). The element of "respect for others" is widespread in Native American cultures. Whereas the general Anglo culture may consider this a pleasant but optional social attitude, Native American traditions regard it as essential to civilized living—an aspect of adaptive intelligence.

One term Berry's respondents offered as an example of the opposite of intelligence translates as "lives like a White," referring to behaviors the Cree have observed among some Anglo people. In analyzing reasons for this negative term, Berry notes that the Cree rate "lives like a White" as similar to "stupid" and "backwards knowledge." A "stupid" person does not know the necessary skills for survival and does not learn by respecting and listening to elders. One has "backwards knowledge" if he or she disrupts relationships, creating disharmony instead of encouraging smooth interactions with others. Such disruption is not necessarily intentional: Well-meaning outsiders often create disruptions without being aware of the effects of their actions. For example, an English teacher may ask Cree students to write an essay that would *persuade others* to change certain behaviors. However, in the Cree culture the concept of "persuading" can interfere with the traditional Cree value of "accepting others *as they are*." By encouraging such questioning of elders and traditions—a common practice in Anglo education—the teacher promotes disruption, which may be a path to "wisdom" in Anglo culture, but is "backward" in Cree views of intelligence.

As you can see from these examples, different cultures define intelligence and adaptive living differently. In order to understand and cooperate with people of diverse heritage, we would be most "intelligent" if we resisted the impulse to impose our own definition of "intelligence" on others. Instead, watch and listen, and try to discern what is considered valuable—and negative—in other people's experience.

## Other Measures of Mental Ability

We have seen that psychologists have developed a variety of tests to assess people's intelligence and personality. In addition, psychologists have developed tests for assessing many other human characteristics. You have probably had firsthand experience, for example, with instruments designed to measure academic skills, such as reading, writing, and mathematics. And, the Using Psychology to Learn Psychology section in this chapter encourages you to learn more about career interest tests (as you learn more about yourself.)

What is not always obvious amid all this testing is that psychological tests reveal no single, best pattern of abilities. Employers, schools, community organizations, and potential life partners look for a wide variety of abilities and characteristics. Equally important is the fact that none of the psychological attributes that distinguish one person from another is unchangeable. Aptitude, achievement, intelligence, motivation, interests—all can be modified by experience.

We do not have space for a detailed look at all the ways that psychologists assess mental abilities. We will, however, refocus for a moment on the college-entrance test known as the SAT, which was the subject of our chapter-opening vignette. As we look at the SAT, you will see that it has much in common with the tests of intelligence that we have been discussing.

**ACADEMIC ABILITIES AND THE SAT**   The test that reporter Bob Greene took, the Scholastic Aptitude Test (now known as the Scholastic Achievement Test and often called the SAT or the "College Boards," after the group that publishes it), was designed specifically to predict success in college. It has often been thought of as an **aptitude** test, which meant that it is supposed to measure potential ability. In reality, the SAT is as much of an **achievement** test—a test of learning—as it is an aptitude test. It most directly measures what students already know, although it does give an indirect assessment of what students have the capability to learn. And it is among the best predictive instruments we have for forecasting academic success. The unhappy side is that it does not have as much predictive power as we might wish: SAT scores account for less than half of all the factors, such as interest, motivation, and stress level, that make a contribution to college success. Further, as we saw in Bob Greene's case, SAT scores can change over time with new experiences. Again, this shows us that our abilities (like our interests) are fluid, rather than fixed.

**Chapter 10: Personality**
*Personality tests include the MMPI-2, the Rorschach, and the TAT.*

**Aptitude test:** A test designed to measure a person's potential for acquiring various skills—not necessarily present performance, but how well she or he will be able to perform in the future, with adequate training.

**Achievement test:** A test designed to measure current skills or how much an individual has learned.

**IQ AND THE SAT**    Scores on the SAT also correlate with IQ test scores, making the SAT an IQ test of sorts. Unlike most IQ tests, which set an average score of 100 points, the "average" SAT score was originally pegged at 500 points, based on a group of about 10,000 students who took the first SAT in 1941. (A perfect score is 800.) Mysteriously, since the early 1960s scores on the SAT have been on a downhill slide until the mid-1990s, when they leveled off. Paradoxically, this has happened as scores on IQ tests have been on the rise (Neisser et al., 1996). What causes this apparent contradiction in the trends of SAT scores and IQ scores is one of the biggest unsolved problems in the psychology of assessment.

Many educators look for an explanation of the SAT score decline in the **demographics**—the population characteristics, such as income level, family size, and ethnic background—of those taking the college entrance tests (Williams & Ceci, 1997; Zajonc & Mullally, 1997). Beginning in the 1960s, the number of people taking the SATs swelled as college attendance grew dramatically. Many of those people were less prepared for postsecondary work than were their predecessors. Many were minority students representing cultural backgrounds in which formal education had never been an option. Some educators also blame eroding academic standards in elementary and secondary schools. They claim that reading assignments have been "dumbed down" so that students do not have to work so hard and, incidentally, do not learn as much. Others blame television, which eats up time that might have been devoted to studies.

The gradual, worldwide *rise* in IQ scores—about three points per decade—is also unexplained. No one really believes that people today are more intelligent than their grandparents, although a literal interpretation of the data suggests this. Many psychologists think that part of the answer lies in the emphasis society places on tests, causing people to become better test takers (Horgan, 1995). Another part of the answer probably involves the increasing demands being made on people as society becomes more complex (Neisser et al., 1996). One thing seems certain, notes Robert Sternberg: "Environment has a very strong effect on whatever is measured by I.Q." (Shea, 1996)

**Demographics:** Population characteristics, such as the number of people at various income levels, from families of different sizes, and from various ethnic backgrounds.

## Test Scores and the Self-Fulfilling Prophecy

The self-fulfilling prophecy: Teachers' expectations can powerfully affect how well children do in school.

If you have ever been called "dumb" or "slow," "shy," "plain," "bossy," or "uncoordinated," you know, firsthand, the powerful effect that labels and expectations can have. An IQ score is a label, too, and in our test-conscious society, an IQ score can make or break a life. We are a nation of test takers and we sometimes forget that our test scores are, at best, statistical measures of our current functioning. People too often think of themselves as *being* "an IQ of 110" or "a B student," as if the scores were labels

stamped permanently on their foreheads. Such labels may become barriers to advancement, as people come to believe that their mental and personal qualities are unchangeable—that they cannot improve their lot in life. Two classic studies brought this fact (which Terman never understood) into stark relief.

Robert Rosenthal and Lenore Jacobson (1968a, b) asked psychology students to run groups of rats through a maze and record their times. The experimenters told some students that their rats were especially bright; other students heard that their rats were slow learners. (In fact,

Rosenthal and Jacobson had randomly assigned rats to the groups from the same litters). Amazingly, the students' data showed that rats *believed* to be bright outperformed their supposedly duller littermates. Obviously, expectations had influenced the students' observations.

So, Rosenthal and Jacobson wondered: Could a teacher's expectations similarly affect evaluations of a student's performance in school? To find out, they arranged to give grade-school teachers erroneous information about the academic potential of about 20% of their students (approximately five in each classroom). Specifically, the teachers heard that some students had been identified by a standardized test as "spurters," who would blossom academically during the coming year. In fact, testing had revealed no such thing; the "spurters" had been randomly selected by the experimenters. Knowing what happened to the rats, you can guess what happened to these children. Those whom the teachers expected to blossom

did so. The teachers also rated them as being more curious and having more potential for success in life than the other children. Socially, the teachers saw them as happier, more interesting, better adjusted, more affectionate, and needing less social approval. Significantly, when the children again took the original test (actually an IQ test) a year later, the children in the experimental group (who had been arbitrarily assigned a high expectation of mental growth) actually made dramatic gains in IQ points, far outstripping their counterparts who were not so labeled. The gains were especially pronounced among first and second graders.

Rosenthal and Jacobson call this effect a **self-fulfilling prophecy.** You can see it operating anywhere that people live up

(or down) to the expectations of others—or of themselves. So, did the self-fulfilling prophecy apply to the students not labeled as possible academic "spurters?" Many of these children also gained IQ points during the year of the experiment, but they gained fewer points, and they were rated less favorably by their teachers. Apparently, *not* receiving a promising prophecy can create negative expectations, just as a positive label can create positive expectations.

Remember the self-fulfilling prophecy the next time someone puts a label on you.

**Self-fulfilling prophecy:** Observations or behaviors that result primarily from expectations.

Check Your UnderstandinG

1. RECALL: *Guilford's structure-of-intellect model says that creative solutions to problems are found through*
   a. a "g" factor.
   b. divergent thinking.
   c. convergent thinking.
   d. contextual intelligence.

2. APPLICATION: *A friend tells you that he has found a way to improve his grades by stopping by his psychology professor's office once a week to ask questions about the reading. If this is successful, you could say that your friend has shown*
   a. practical intelligence.
   b. logical reasoning.
   c. experiential intelligence.
   d. convergent thinking.

3. RECALL: *Which of Gardner's seven intelligences is most like that measured on standard IQ tests?*
   a. linguistic ability
   b. bodily-kinesthetic ability
   c. interpersonal ability
   d. intrapersonal ability

4. RECALL: *A self-fulfilling prophecy comes true because of*
   a. innate factors.
   b. most people's lack of substantial logical-mathematical ability.
   c. the lack of precision of IQ tests.
   d. people's expectations.

5. RECALL: *A test of your _____ is intended to measure what you have learned.*
   a. interests
   b. aptitudes
   c. achievement
   d. intellect

6. RECALL: *One of the biggest puzzles in the field of assessment concerns the observations that*
   a. abilities do not always coincide with interests.
   b. a test can be fair, yet it can lead to labeling.
   c. IQ scores have been falling and SAT scores have been rising.
   d. SAT scores have been falling and IQ scores have been rising.

7. UNDERSTANDING THE CORE CONCEPT: *Which of the following most sharply characterizes the current debate about intelligence?*
   a. divergent versus convergent
   b. single versus multiple
   c. practical versus logical
   d. cognitive versus behavioral

**ANSWERS:**   1. b   2. a   3. a   4. d   5. c   6. d
7. b

# HOW DO PSYCHOLOGISTS EXPLAIN IQ DIFFERENCES AMONG SOCIAL AND RACIAL GROUPS?

It is a fact that a gap of approximately 15 points exists between the average IQ scores of African Americans and Caucasian Americans (Brody, 1985; Humphreys, 1988; Vincent, 1991). A similar IQ gap separates children from middle-income homes and low-income homes (Jensen & Figueroa, 1975; Oakland & Glutting, 1990). Nobody disputes that these gaps exist. What the experts disagree about are the causes. As we will see, the disagreement is another manifestation of the nature–nurture controversy. Our Core Concept describes the issue this way:

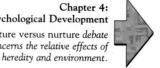

**Chapter 4:
Psychological Development**

*The* nature versus nurture *debate concerns the relative effects of heredity and environment.*

**CORE CONCEPT**

**While most psychologists agree that both heredity and environment affect intelligence, they disagree on the source of IQ differences among racial and social groups.**

The controversy over the source of intelligence is potentially of great importance for people's lives—and a politically hot issue. If we assume that intelligence is primarily the result of innate (hereditary) factors, we will most likely conclude that it is fixed and unchangeable. This leads some to the mistaken conclusion that a group having low IQ scores must be inferior and should be treated as second-class citizens. On the other hand, if we conclude that intelligence is shaped largely by experience (environment), we are more likely to make a range of educational opportunities available for everyone and to view people of all ethnic, cultural, and economic groups as equals. Either way, our conclusion may become a self-fulfilling prophecy.

In fact, neither the hereditarian nor environmentalist view is completely right. Repeatedly in this book we have seen that psychologists now recognize that *both* heredity and environment play a role in all our behavior and mental processes. But there is more to the issue of group differences than this. In this chapter we add another important dimension to the heredity-environment interaction: While every individual's intelligence is determined in part by heredity, this fact does *not* mean that the IQ differences among *groups* have a genetic basis. On the contrary, many psychologists have argued that group differences are environmental—although this is disputed, as our Core Concept suggests. You will find out why this is so in the following pages.

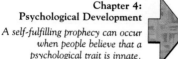

**Chapter 4:
Psychological Development**

*A* self-fulfilling prophecy *can occur when people believe that a psychological trait is innate.*

## Intelligence and the Politics of Immigration

In the early 1900s, Henry Goddard, an influential psychologist who believed that intelligence is a hereditary trait, proposed mental testing for all immigrants and the selective exclusion of those who were found to be "mentally defective." With encouragement from Goddard and some other assessment-minded psychologists, Congress passed the 1924 Immigration Restriction Act, designed to restrict immigration of groups and nationalities in which people had been "proven" to be of inferior intellect—based largely on Goddard's data. Among the groups restricted were Jews, Italians, Russians, and others of southern and eastern Europe. What Goddard and the U.S. Congress ignored were the differences between the groups in their familiarity with the English language and the dominant culture.

**THE "BAD SEED" CONCEPT**   Many Americans supported the immigration policy because they feared that the restricted groups would bring with them bad genetic stock, producing not only people of inferior intellect but a spate of serious social problems. Thus, the belief in the intellectual inferiority of certain racial and ethnic groups was compounded by the erroneous belief that linked low intelligence with crime, disease, poverty, and moral degeneracy. As Goddard's colleague Lewis Terman (author of the Stanford-Binet test) said:

> Not all criminals are feeble-minded, but all feeble-minded persons are at least potential criminals. That every feeble-minded woman is a potential prostitute would hardly be disputed by anyone. Moral judgment, like business judgment, social judgment, or any other kind of higher thought process, is a function of intelligence. Morality cannot flower and fruit if intelligence remains infantile. (1916, p. 11)

His solution: Remove the mentally unfit from society to permanent custodial care. Fortunately, more cautious heads quietly abandoned Terman's solution.

Immigrants being processed at Ellis Island early in the 20th century.

**THE JUKES AND KALLIKAKS: CASE STUDIES IN BAD SCIENCE** So, Goddard (1917), Terman, and others went beyond merely associating low IQ with hereditary racial and ethnic origins. They added moral worthlessness, mental deficiency, and immoral social behavior to the mix of negatives related to low IQ. To reinforce their view they cited pedigree studies of two infamous families: the Jukes and the Kallikaks. These families were traced back for many generations to show, allegedly, that "bad seeds" planted in family genes will yield defective human offspring.

The Juke family obviously had its problems, and psychology portrayed it as a long line of congenital misfits. In all, over 2,000 family members were identified, many with flagrant records of developmental disability, delinquency, and crime. Of these family members, 458 were found to be developmentally disabled in school performance, 171 were classified as criminals, and hundreds of their kin were labeled, rather vaguely, as "paupers, intemperates, and harlots." The conclusion was that heredity was responsible for the disreputable development of members of this family and, presumably, other ne'er-do-wells.

Goddard drew a similar conclusion from his own case study of another family—the Kallikaks—with a "good seed" on one side of its family tree and a "bad seed" on the other. (In his report, Goddard changed the family's real name to *Kallikak*, which means "good–bad" in Greek.) The common ancestor in the two branches of the family tree was Martin Kallikak, a Revolutionary War soldier who had an illegitimate son with a woman who would be described today as "developmentally disabled" or "mentally retarded." Their union eventually produced 480 descendants. Goddard classified 143 of them as "defective" and only 46 as "normal." He found crime, alcoholism, mental disorders, and illegitimacy common among the rest of the family members. By contrast, when Martin later married a "good woman," their union produced 496 descendants, only 3 of whom were classified as "defective." Goddard also found that many offspring from this quality union had become "eminent"—recognized as talented and productive members of society (Goddard, 1914).

On the basis of such evidence, Goddard and others came to believe that heredity determined intelligence, genius, and eminence on the positive side and delinquency, alcoholism, sexual immorality, developmental disability, and maybe even poverty on the negative side (McPherson, 1985). But it is important for us to realize that his research violated the basic requirements of the scientific method. Goddard ignored the effects of poverty and other environmental factors that might have contaminated his observations. Thus, his "results" were nothing more than a reflection of his own biases. Nevertheless, his blemished conclusions found an eager and receptive audience that used his work to reinforce their own prejudices.

Today we know that heredity does have an effect on an *individual's* intelligence, although experience does, too. At the same time, we know that Goddard was mistaken in his conclusion that heredity accounts for *group* differences in intelligence. To see how both of these statements could be true, we need to look first at the evidence

**Chapter 1:
Mind, Behavior, and Science**
*The scientific method requires control of confounding variables.*

The IQ scores of identical twins show a strong influence of genetics. The identical twins in this photo have gathered for the Twins Days Festival in Twinsburg, Ohio.

**Chapter 4:**
**Psychological Development**

*Twin studies and adoption studies help psychologists identify hereditary and environmental effects.*

supporting the hereditarian and environmentalist arguments. Then we will be in a position to understand the important, and often misunderstood, concept of *heritability*.

### Argument: Intelligence Is Inherited

Many lines of research point to a hereditary influence on intelligence. For example, studies comparing the IQ scores of identical twins with fraternal twins and other siblings show a strong genetic correlation. Another common approach compares adopted children with their biological and adoptive families. These studies find that the correlation between the IQs of children and their biological parents is greater than that with their adoptive parents. As Table 11.1 shows, the closer the genetic relationship—from cousins to siblings to twins—the closer the relationship of IQ scores. In general, work on twins and adopted children shows genetic influences on a wide range of attributes as diverse as heart functioning (Brown, 1990), personality traits (Tellegen et al., 1988), hypnotizability (Morgan, Hilgard, & Davert, 1970), and intellectual functioning (Chorney et al., 1998; McClearn et al., 1997; Neisser et al., 1996; Petrill et al., 1998).

While psychologists agree that heredity plays an important part in determining an individual's IQ scores, they also agree that it remains difficult to estimate the relative weights of heredity and environment (Plomin, 1989; Scarr, 1988; Stevenson et al., 1987). One reason for this is that children who live in the same family setting do not necessarily share precisely the same psychological environment. First children, for example, are treated differently from the youngest. You probably are aware of this fact if you have siblings with interests and lifestyles that differ from yours.

### Counterargument: Intelligence Is Environmentally Determined

The evidence that the environment influences our intellectual development is also persuasive. Even when we look for genetic effects, we find greater similarities of IQ among those who have been reared together than those reared apart. And, in lab-

**TABLE 11.1:** Correlation of IQ Scores with Genetic Relationship

| GENETIC RELATIONSHIP | CORRELATION BETWEEN IQ SCORES |
|---|---|
| Identical twins | |
| Reared together | 0.86 |
| Reared apart | 0.72 |
| Fraternal twins | |
| Reared together | 0.60 |
| Siblings | |
| Reared together | 0.47 |
| Reared apart | 0.24 |
| Parent/child | 0.40 |
| Foster parent/child | 0.31 |
| Cousins | 0.15 |

Note: A correlation shows the degree of association between variables—in this case, between the IQs of pairs of individuals. The closer to 1.0, the closer the connection. For example, we can see that the IQ scores of identical twins reared together are more closely correlated (.86) than the IQs of mere siblings reared together (.24). The data strongly suggest a genetic component that contributes to intelligence.

oratory animals, a stimulus-enriched habitat early in life has been shown to result in a more complex, complete development of brain cells and cortical regions. The superior performance of these animals on a range of tasks persists until late in life. In other experiments, we find that young monkeys who are trained to solve problems and are offered the companionship of other monkeys display more active curiosity and higher intelligence than those reared without this environmental stimulation.

These findings hint that we might boost the intellectual functioning of human infants by enriching their environments. Indeed, we will see that early enrichment programs, such as Head Start, can raise children's IQ scores. Regular schooling also may boost IQ scores: The amount of schooling children get is directly correlated with their IQ scores (Ceci & Williams, 1997), although we must be cautious about interpreting correlational data. Even in adulthood, environmental factors, such as the cognitive complexity and intellectual demands of one's job, can influence mental abilities throughout life (Dixon, Kramer, & Baltes, 1985). You will recall that columnist Bob Greene's verbal SAT scores increased, undoubtedly because his work called for using verbal skills, while his math SAT scores plummeted, probably due to neglect of his math skills.

## Heritability and Group Differences

Let us acknowledge, then, that heredity has an influence—perhaps a substantial influence—on intelligence. But we should also be clear about *heritability*, a concept that is crucial for understanding our claim that hereditary differences among *individuals* do not imply that heredity accounts for the differences we observe among *groups*. **Heritability** refers to the amount of trait variation *within a group* that can be attributed to genetic differences. It is important to realize that we can speak of heritable differences *only within a group of individuals who have shared the same environment*.

To illustrate, suppose that we examine a group of children who were all raised in an intellectually stimulating environment, with devoted parents who spent lots of time interacting with them and reading to them—things we know improve intellectual abilities. Among these children we would find variation in intellectual abilities. Because they were all treated in essentially the same fashion, however, we could attribute much of the differences in their IQ scores to the effects of heredity. In this group, IQ would have a *high heritability*.

In contrast, suppose that we examine a group of children who had been raised under conditions of neglect (given mere custodial care in an orphanage, with no intellectual stimulation from their caregivers). We would most likely find that these children have relatively little variability among their IQ scores because they are all intellectually stunted. For this group, intelligence would have *low heritability*—because the poor environment did not offer an opportunity for these children's genetic potential to be realized.

Now, what about the differences *between* the two groups? The IQ differences are real. But—this is the important part—our observations tell us nothing about the genetic differences (if any) between the groups. For all we know they could have the same genetic potential. But because the environments were so different we cannot tell what role genetics played in determining their IQ scores. By extrapolating this notion to groups of people who are exposed to different cultural traditions or experience different levels of wealth or discrimination, you can see that we have no way to evaluate what proportion of the differences between the groups should be attributed to heredity or to environment. To reiterate: *Heritability is a concept that refers to within-group differences, not between-group differences*. Just because intelligence may be highly heritable does not mean that the environment has no impact (Neisser et al., 1996).

**THE JENSEN CONTROVERSY** Despite the concerns we have cited, a few psychologists remain unconvinced that group differences in IQ can be accounted for by environmental factors. In particular, Harvard psychologist Arthur Jensen (1969)

**Heritability:** The amount of trait variation *within a group,* raised under the same conditions, that can be attributed to genetic differences. Heritability tells us nothing about between-group differences.

stirred up a hornets' nest of controversy with his Galton-like contention that racial differences in IQ have a genetic basis. We can boost IQ scores to some extent, said Jensen, by helping the poor and disadvantaged, but there are limits imposed by heredity.

In support of his thesis, Jensen cited several studies showing a strong influence of heredity on IQ. He also presented a complex statistical argument that showed only a weak environmental effect on IQ and achievement. Then, turning his attention to government programs that had attempted to give extra help to disadvantaged Black children, Jensen claimed that, while most had shown some positive effects, none had erased racial differences in performance. What remained must be a genetic difference in abilities, he maintained.

Over the next five years more than 100 published articles responded to Jensen's challenge. Sometimes it seemed that the Jensen controversy had generated far more heat than light. The protest occasionally became ugly, with charges of bigotry and racism nearly drowning the scientific debate. Nevertheless, it did have the positive effect of stimulating a new wave of research and theory aimed at gaining greater understanding of Black–White IQ differences.

Critics pointed out several factors that Jensen had minimized or ignored, including the effects of racism, lower teacher expectations for Black children, lack of opportunity, low self-esteem, and a White, middle-class bias built into IQ and achievement tests. While Jensen holds to his original position (Jensen, 1980, 1985), many (but not all) psychologists now agree that a combination of environmental factors can explain the differences on which Jensen built his case. Let us now look at some of the post-Jensen discoveries, beginning with a study of children whose environment had been altered by adoption.

The personal attention children receive can affect their intelligence. This contemporary parent is deeply involved in his children's education.

**THE SCARR AND WEINBERG ADOPTION STUDY**   A monumental study by Sandra Scarr and Richard Weinberg confronted the issue head-on by comparing Black and White children who had been adopted into similar home environments (1976, 1978). Their research focused on educational records and IQ test scores from both the biological families and adoptive families of a 115 White children and 176 Black children who had been adopted in Minnesota during the 1950s. All the children had been adopted into White families. For both groups of children, the biological parents had average IQ scores (near 100), while the adoptive parents' IQs were somewhat higher, averaging above 115.

What did Scarr and Weinberg find when they examined the IQ scores of these two groups of adoptees in late adolescence? There were *no* differences! *Both* the Black group and the White group of adoptees had scores that averaged about 110, significantly higher than their biological parents, although not quite as high as their adoptive parents. Such results testify to a powerful effect of the environment on IQ. The results also contradict Jensen's claim that group differences are genetic.

**SOCIAL CLASS AND IQ**   Research on the relationship between social class and IQ shows similar environmental effects. Socioeconomic class (as reflected in an individual's financial status and lifestyle) is clearly correlated with IQ. While affluence is associated with higher IQ scores, groups with the lowest average IQ scores are those for whom poverty, illiteracy, and hopelessness are most widespread. Supporters of the environmental position claim that racism and discrimination initially landed many minorities in the impoverished inner cities, and these same factors continue to keep them there today.

How does social class affect IQ? Poverty creates circumstances that limit individual potential in many ways, particularly in terms of nutrition, health care, and education (Brown & Pollitt, 1996; Neisser et al., 1996). Poverty means less-adequate health care, so it should not surprise you that researchers have traced poor health during pregnancy and low birth weight to low mental ability in children. Poverty also means less of other factors known to promote intellectual development. Poor nutrition, lack of access to books and computers, and job schedules that leave parents little time to stimulate a child's intellect all correlate with poverty and can be detrimental to performance on tasks such as those demanded by IQ tests (for example, vocabulary or sentence comprehension). Research also shows that a significant proportion of children with low IQs have been adversely affected by "environmental insults," such as living in homes with lead-based paint chips peeling from walls, causing toxic lead levels in the blood (Needleman et al., 1990).

Poverty has other crippling effects, too. In most parts of the United States, public schools are funded by revenue from local property taxes. Thus, wealthy neighborhoods can provide bigger and better school facilities and amenities, while poorer districts may suffer from crowding, physically deteriorating structures, threats to personal safety, and few "extras" such as media centers or computers. In such environments, even children with the aptitude to learn may find it difficult to rise above their mean circumstances. Proponents of the view that environment has a strong influence on intelligence usually support equal-opportunity legislation, better schools, and intervention programs, such as Head Start, which help disadvantaged children build self-confidence and learn the skills necessary to succeed in school (Zigler & Muenchow, 1992; Zigler & Styfco, 1994).

Launched in the 1960s as a part of the "war on poverty," **Head Start** is a program that provides educational enrichment for children of poor families. It grew from the assumption that children from disadvantaged families needed a preschool intellectual boost to prepare them to learn at the same level as children from less deprived families. The program was intended to head off problems on several fronts by serving children's physical as well as mental needs with nutritional and medical support, plus a year or two of preschool education. Wisely, Head Start also involved parents in making policy, planning programs, working in classrooms, and learning about parenting and child development. Head Start centers around the country currently serve about 600,000 children yearly—less than a third of the number who need it (Kantrowitz, 1992).

Does it work? Again, there is some controversy (Jensen, 1969; Kantrowitz, 1992), although a great deal of research suggests that Head Start does, indeed, help disadvantaged children get ready for school (Lazar & Darlington, 1982; Lee, Brooks-Gunn, & Schnur, 1988; Schweinhart & Weikart, 1986; Smith, 1991). Children who were enrolled in the program score higher on IQ tests and have higher school achievement during the early grades than matched control groups who receive no such intervention (Zigler & Styfco, 1994). More important, however, their head start lasts. Although the differences between the Head Start children and the control group diminish over time, the effects are still detectable in adolescence. Compared to the control group, Head Start children are less likely to be placed in special education classes, less likely to fail a grade, and more likely to graduate from high school.

It now appears, however, that such attempts to raise IQ by special environmental interventions may not start early enough. Studies indicate that early educational intervention, starting in the first months of life, can raise infants' scores on intelligence tests by as much as 30% compared to control groups (Ramey & Ramey, 1998a; Wickelgren, 1999). Although the gains may diminish with time, especially if

Chapter 1:
Mind Behavior, and Science
*A well-designed experiment has a control condition to serve as a basis of comparison.*

**Head Start:** A program providing educational enrichment for children of poor families, launched in the 1960s as a part of the "war on poverty."

supportive programs are withdrawn, significant differences remain when intervention starts in infancy. The effectiveness of such early-intervention strategies has been shown most clearly by a long-term experimental study at the University of North Carolina at Chapel Hill, where clear effects of early intervention strategies have been demonstrated in children from high-risk families (Ramey & Ramey, 1998b). The best way to summarize these and other relevant findings is to say that the earlier the individual is immersed in an enriched environment, the better.

**TESTS AND TESTING BIASES**     Still other forces influence IQ scores and contribute to differences among groups. A portion of the difference between the average IQ scores of Black and White children may reside in problems with the IQ tests themselves. Many psychologists argue that IQ test questions have built-in biases toward a middle- or upper-class background—which favors the White child (Garcia, 1981; Helms, 1992; Miller-Jones, 1989). One source of bias stems from the fact that most IQ tests rely heavily on vocabulary level. This gives an advantage to middle-class children who have been read to and who are encouraged to read. We can see a related bias in a well-known IQ test that asks for a definition of "opulent" (rich), a term one is far less likely to hear in a poor household. Another example of bias emerged from a study which found that children's IQ scores were correlated to experience with a popular—and expensive—game that featured remarkable similarities to items on the IQ test (Dirks, 1982).

Because expectations can also affect IQ scores, psychologists have argued that lowered expectations among some minority groups about their own potential can affect racial differences in IQ scores (Schwartz, 1997). One study found that merely being asked to identify their race produced lower scores for minority students on a test of academic abilities (Steele, 1997). In another study, a group of Black women faltered on an IQ test when they were told that White women usually do better on the test. The women, who expected to do poorly, received IQ scores that averaged a full 10 points lower than another group who were told that Black women usually receive high scores (Thomas, 1991).

Yet another source of bias has to do with the examiner. Not only does the examiner's attitude influence IQ scores, but so does his or her gender and race. Studies have found that Black children receive higher scores when tested by a Black examiner (Bodmer & Cavalli-Sforza, 1970; Sattler, 1970). In brief, test takers do best when they perceive the examiner to be similar to themselves.

Finally, Janet Helms (1992) has pointed out that the attempt to explain why African American children deviate from the Caucasian American norm may rest on the biased assumption that one culture is superior to another. Specifically, she says, it "assumes that White-American culture defines the most intellectually rich environment" (p. 1086). Seldom do we ask how well White children learn the norms of other cultures. Helms asks: Why should the Caucasian-American norm be the standard by which everyone else is judged?

**THE BELL CURVE: THE LATEST HEREDITARIAN OFFENSIVE**     The dispute over causes of racial differences in IQ flared again in 1994 with the publication of *The Bell Curve: Intelligence and Class Structure in American Life* by Richard Herrnstein and Charles Murray. In this book, named for the shape of the "normal distribution" of IQ scores among the population (see the bell-shaped graph in Figure 11.3), Herrnstein and Murray argue that genetic differences in IQ threaten to turn the United States into a split society, with a largely White "elite" at the top of the IQ range and the less intelligent masses at the other end, comprised mainly of African Americans and other minorities. Herrnstein and Murray suggest that acknowledging innate group differences in IQ could lead to more enlightened and humane social policies. Critics immediately identified not only a racist bias but pointed to unsound "science" at the core of *The Bell Curve*.

How is *The Bell Curve*'s argument flawed? The answer will be familiar to you by now: While there is no doubt that heredity influences individual intelligence, Herrnstein and Murray, like hereditarians before them, have offered no proof that differences *between groups* have a hereditary basis (see Coughlin, 1994; Fraser, 1995). Further, much of the "evidence" that they offer is suspect (Kamin, 1994). One study, cited by Herrnstein and Murray, claimed to document the low IQs of Black Africans, but it employed tests given in English—a language in which the Zulu subjects of the study were not fluent (Kamin, 1995). The test used in that study also assumed that subjects were familiar with electrical appliances found in urban middle-class homes (rather than Zulu villages) and equipment, such as microscopes, not typically found in Zulu schools. Compounding the problems in their analysis of the evidence, Herrnstein and Murray commit a scientific blunder about which you learned early in this book: They confuse correlation with causation. As psychologist Leon Kamin put it:

**Chapter 1:**
**Mind, Behavior, and Science**
*A correlation does not mean that one variable causes the other.*

> Not surprisingly [the data] indicate that there is an association within each race between IQ and socioeconomic status. Herrnstein and Murray labor mightily to show that low IQ is the cause of low socioeconomic status, and not vice versa. The argument is decked out in all the trappings of science—a veritable barrage of charts, graphs, tables, appendices and appeals to statistical techniques that are unknown to many readers. But on close examination, this scientific emperor is wearing no clothes. (Kamin, 1995, p. 101)

In fact, the Herrnstein and Murray argument is just as plausible when turned around: Poverty and all of the social and economic disadvantages that go with it could just as well be important causes of low IQ scores.

Despite its pseudoscience and flawed logic, *The Bell Curve* may have struck a chord with many Americans. Not only does it pander to existing prejudices, but it resonates with our preference for simple genetic "causes" for behavior rather than more complex explanations. When asked to account for a child's academic success, American respondents predictably emphasize "innate ability," whereas Asian respondents emphasize the importance of "studying hard" (Stevenson, Chen, & Lee, 1993). Perhaps by blaming genetics we excuse ourselves for failure ("It's not my fault, I just didn't inherit the same ability as other people"). Blaming genetics also exonerates us from guilt ("It's too bad that others aren't doing as well as my group, but there's nothing I can do to help them"). However, scientific evidence supports the view that intelligence, like other human qualities, is the product of both inherited and experience factors. Instead of rationalizing injustice and prejudice, we might find ways to develop individual potential while respecting diversity, whatever its influences and origins.

**PSYCHOLOGY IN YOUR LIFE**

## Helping Others Think Critically about Group Differences

So, if someone you know were to claim that the discrepancy between IQ scores of Whites and Blacks is proof of the genetic intellectual superiority of Whites, how would you respond? You might begin with the argument that the influence of genetics on *individual* intelligence tells us nothing about the influence of genetics on *group* differences. You could also point to the evidence showing that, while the group average IQ for African Americans is as much as 10 to 15 IQ points below the group average for U.S. Whites, there is much overlapping of scores. The difference *between* groups is small compared to the spread of scores of individuals *within* each group (Loehlin, Lindzey, & Spuhler, 1975). And, you could say that biologists have taught us that "race" is not even a valid biological concept. Even if we use a social definition, where people define their
*continued*

own racial group, the differences between the gene pools of people who claim to be of different racial groups are very small compared to the genetic differences among individual members of the same group (Gould, 1996; see also Zuckerman, 1990).

Perhaps the most persuasive argument against the genetic interpretation of group differences is that many other variables are confounded with race, including racism, poverty, self-fulfilling prophecies, and differential opportunities for education—each of which can influence IQ scores. For example, in a large-scale, longitudinal study of more than 26,000 children, the best predictors of a child's IQ at age four, for both black and white children, were the family's socioeconomic status and the level of the mother's education (Broman, Nichols, & Kennedy, 1975). When opportunities are made more equal, as we saw in the Scarr-Weinberg study, the differences disappear.

Unfortunately, the fact of group differences in IQ scores has been interpreted as a genetic difference and used to justify racist views. Even today, such data are used to justify discrimination against the disadvantaged poor, women, minorities, and immigrants in providing educational and career opportunities and in formulating public policy (Gould, 1996; Hirsch, Harrington, & Mahler, 1990; Kamin, 1974). In the extreme, racist interpreters of the genetic argument support eugenics programs (which promote the propagation of "superior" races) to limit "breeding" by undesirable groups, laws restricting the immigration of certain groups, and legal inequality that favors the group in power. But the science just doesn't support these distorted views.

In the "separate but equal" schoolroom of 1940s Tennessee, African American children received little attention and a poor education.

## Check Your Understanding

1. RECALL: *Most early American psychologists working on intelligence believed that the dominant influence on intelligence was*
   a. heredity.
   b. experience.
   c. gender.
   d. the size of one's brain.

2. ANALYSIS: *The studies of the Jukes and the Kallikaks were scientifically flawed because they failed to take into account*
   a. heredity.
   b. environmental factors.
   c. gender.
   d. the moral standards of the individuals involved.

3. RECALL: *The concept of heritability refers to genetic variation on a trait*
   a. within an individual's sperm cells or ova.
   b. between one group and another.

   c. within an individual's immediate family.
   d. within a group of individuals that have been treated the same.

4. UNDERSTANDING THE CORE CONCEPT: *Although everyone agrees that heredity affects _____ intelligence, there is no evidence that it accounts for differences among _____.*

   a. individual/groups
   b. group/individuals
   c. high/the mentally retarded
   d. academic/practical

**ANSWERS:**     1. a     2. b     3. d     4. a

# USING PSYCHOLOGY TO LEARN PSYCHOLOGY

## Psychological Assessment and Career Planning

Even if you do not yet know what career you might like best, you probably want a job that suits your interests and serves goals that you consider worthwhile. If you are like many college students, you may have little idea of what people in many occupations actually do. Consequently, you may not really know how their job activities relate to your personal values and goals. You may also be unsure about the nature of your own interests, abilities, values, and goals. A number of tests have been designed to help people assess themselves on these dimensions so that they can make appropriate career decisions. You can probably take such a test and have it interpreted for you by a professional at your school's career center or counseling center. Doing so is not only a good way to find out more about yourself; it is also a good way to get a firsthand look at psychological testing.

One of the most useful tests is an instrument often used tests for measuring career interests: the Strong-Camp-

bell Interest Inventory. The test is based on an empirical approach, similar to that used to develop the Binet-Simon test (in that both rely on how well the test predicts measurable behaviors). In developing his test of career interests, Edward Strong studied groups of men in different occupations who answered items about activities they liked or disliked. The answers of those who were successful in particular occupations were then compared with the answers of men in general to create a scale. Subsequent versions of the test have added scales relevant to women and to newer occupations. With your results from this test, a career counselor could tell you what types of jobs are often held by people with interests similar to yours.

Like your other psychological characteristics, however, your interests are not fixed. Almost certainly, they will shift and broaden as a result of your experiences, especially your college and work experiences. Therefore, our advice is to use the results of interest tests, but don't feel that you should be bound by them.

## CHAPTER SUMMARY

 **HOW HAVE PSYCHOLOGISTS DESCRIBED AND MEASURED INTELLIGENCE?**

- The measurement of intelligence is both common and controversial. Assessment of mental ability has an ancient human history but was not based on scientific practice until the 20th century. Sir Francis Galton's conviction that intelligence was normally distributed and genius was inherited inspired important developments in testing—as well as some racist applications of the eugenics movement. In 1904, Binet and Simon developed the first workable test of intelligence, based on the assumption that education can modify intellectual performance. In America, IQ testing

became widespread for the assessment of Army recruits, immigrants, and schoolchildren. The original IQ calculation was abandoned in favor of standard scores based on the normal distribution. IQ scores are a key ingredient in identifying mental retardation and giftedness, which are often seen as occupying the extremes of the IQ distribution.

 **CORE CONCEPT**

**Intelligence testing has a history of controversy, but most psychologists now assume that intelligence is a stable, normally distributed trait that can be measured by performance on a variety of mental tasks—both verbal and nonverbal.**

**KEY QUESTION**

## WHAT ARE THE COMPONENTS OF INTELLIGENCE?

- Among the psychometric theories of intelligence Spearman's "g" emphasized a single, common factor. Others, such as Guilford, believed that intelligence was composed of many mental abilities. Cognitive approaches agreed that intelligence involves many abilities, but they extended the definition of intelligence beyond school-related tasks. Cross-cultural psychologists have pointed out that "intelligence" has different meanings in different cultures. In addition to IQ tests, psychologists have developed many ways of assessing mental abilities, including the SAT, which is both an aptitude test and an achievement test. Psychologists are puzzled, however, by the simultaneous decline in SAT scores and rise in IQ scores. The United States places much emphasis on mental tests. A big danger lies in test scores becoming mere labels that influence people's behavior through the self-fulfilling prophecy.

**CORE CONCEPT**

Psychologists have long disagreed about the makeup of intelligence—particularly whether it is best described as a single, general factor or a collection of distinct abilities.

**KEY QUESTION**

## HOW DO PSYCHOLOGISTS EXPLAIN IQ DIFFERENCES AMONG SOCIAL AND RACIAL GROUPS?

- Hereditarian arguments maintain that intelligence is substantially influenced by genetics. Environmental approaches argue that intelligence can be dramatically shaped by influences such as health, economics, and education. Hereditarian arguments and poorly designed case studies (such as those of the Jukes and Kallikaks) persuaded the U.S. government to use IQ tests to restrict immigration early in the 20th century. Most psychologists currently agree that intelligence is heritable. Heritability, however, refers to variation within a group and does not imply that between-group differences are the result of hereditary factors. Nevertheless, the dispute over the nature and nurture of group differences in intelligence flared again in 1969, when Jensen argued that the evidence favored a strong genetic influence. This argument was echoed in the 1994 book *The Bell Curve*. Critics have pointed out that much of the research cited by those taking the extreme hereditarian position is flawed. In addition, intelligence testing itself may be biased in favor of those with particular language and cultural experiences. Hereditarian claims, however, have stimulated much research, such as Scarr and Weinberg's research on adopted children and follow-up studies of the Head Start program. This research has shown that the racial and class differences in IQ scores can be eliminated by environmental changes.

**CORE CONCEPT**

While most psychologists agree that both heredity and environment affect intelligence, they disagree on the source of IQ differences among racial and social groups.

## REVIEW TEST

For each of the following items, choose the single correct or best answer.

1. Which of the following best expresses the opinions of early supporters of the eugenics movement?
   a. A supportive and stimulating environment can overcome most genetic disadvantages.
   b. It is immoral for superior races to attempt to extinguish inferior races.
   c. Only the fittest and brightest individuals should be encouraged to reproduce.
   d. Individual accomplishments depend more on circumstance than on genetic inheritance.

2. Galton believed that intelligence is *normally distributed*, which means that
   a. people are evenly spread across the entire spectrum of intelligence, from low to high.
   b. few people possess extremely high or low intelligence, while most people are clustered around the middle of the range.
   c. high intelligence is inherited.
   d. most people are of rather low intellectual ability.

3. Unlike Galton, Binet and Simon assumed that
   a. intelligence is inherited.
   b. mental age does not increase as fast as chronological age.
   c. social class differences in intelligence should be remedied by governmental programs.
   d. training and opportunity could affect intelligence.

4. Early in the 20th century, IQ testing was used extensively in the United States to
   a. assess and classify immigrants.
   b. identify children for accelerated classes.
   c. identify candidates for graduate programs.
   d. support the widespread assumption that group differences in IQ were the result of different environmental influences.

5. A child with a chronological age of 12 takes an intelligence test that shows a mental age of 15. According to Lewis Terman's mathematical formula, this child's IQ is
   a. 103.
   b. 120.
   c. 125.
   d. 150.

6. Which one of Robert Sternberg's types of intelligence is also known as "business sense" or "street smarts"?
   a. practical
   b. componential
   c. experiential
   d. interpersonal

7. According to Howard Gardner, there are actually seven "intelligences" instead of just one. Which one is most like an ability assessed by traditional IQ tests?
   a. musical
   b. kinesthetic
   c. linguistic
   d. intrapersonal

8. The fact that intelligence is heritable has sometimes been misunderstood by those taking an extreme hereditarian view as meaning that _____ explains _____ differences in IQ scores.
   a. environment/individual
   b. genetics/group
   c. environment/group
   d. genetics/individual

9. The Scarr and Weinberg study supports the idea that racial differences in IQ scores are the result of
   a. genetic differences.
   b. environmental differences.
   c. test biases.
   d. unknown factors.

10. A(n) _____ measures a person's potential for acquiring some skill, not necessarily how well that person presently performs related tasks.
    a. achievement test
    b. interest test
    c. job analysis
    d. aptitude test

ANSWERS:     1. c     2. b     3. d     4. a     5. c     6. a
7. c     8. b     9. b     10. d

## IF YOU'RE INTERESTED . . .

## BOOKS

Fraser, S. (Ed.). (1995). *The bell curve wars: Race, intelligence, and the future of America*. New York: Basic Books.

*This penetrating collection of reviews was prompted by the controversial publication in 1994 of* The Bell Curve: Intelligence and Class Structure in American Life *by Richard J. Herrnstein and Charles J. Murray. Among other authors featured, evolutionist Stephen Jay Gould critiques the questionable methodology of* The Bell Curve, *psychologist Howard Gardner points out that social class is not genetically determined, Jacqueline Jones questions any effort to genetically "justify" racism, and Orlando Patterson exposes a series of assumptions—not all warranted—that Herrnstein and Murray have accepted about intelligence, IQ, and the nature of racial differences.*

Gardner, H. (1983). *Frames of mind: The theory of multiple intelligences.* New York: Basic Books.

*Here Howard Gardner argues why it makes sense to think of seven intelligences, instead of a single general "g." The seven include linguistic, musical, logical-mathematical, spatial, bodily-kinesthetic, and two personal intelligences. This idea, claims Gardner, is solidly grounded in research on the brain, cognition, and behavior.*

Gleick, J. (1992). *Genius: The life and science of Richard Feynman.* New York: Random House.

*What's it like to be (arguably) the world's smartest person? This book captures much of the astonishing mind and unique personality of physicist and Nobel Prize winner Richard Feynman. You don't have to be a physicist to understand this biography.*

Gould, S. J. (1996). *The mismeasure of man* (2nd ed). New York: Norton.

*Never one to pull his punches, Gould attacks the entrenched view that claims intelligence to be a single, unitary characteristic determined mainly by heredity. This new edition was spurred by publication of Herrnstein and Murray's The Bell Curve (see below).*

Herrnstein, R. J., & Murray, C. (1994). *The bell curve: Intelligence and class structure in American life.* New York: Free Press.

*This is the book that recently renewed the controversy over the role of heredity in IQ. The thesis is that it is intelligence—determined primarily by heredity—and not poverty, lack of education, or lack of opportunity that lie at the root of many of our social problems. The authors imply that IQ differences among "races" have a biological basis. As indicated in this chapter, nearly everything in this book has been widely criticized.*

Janda, L. H. (1996). *The psychologist's book of self-tests: 25 love, sex, intelligence, career, and personality tests developed by professionals to reveal the real you.* New York: Perigee Press.

*Just remember that any self-report technique depends on your responses—meaning that, to a large extent, you already know or can somewhat control the "outcome." Nonetheless, well-constructed, valid, and reliable psychological assessments can cast individual data in a new light according to various theories of development, individual difference, and aptitude—and the experience, once understood, can be fun as well as helpful.*

Tavris, C. (1992). *The mismeasure of woman.* New York: Simon & Schuster.

*Psychologist Carol Tavris reviews how, when "man is the measure" of human pursuits, woman is left forever trying (and failing) to measure up. She examines why women are neither inferior nor superior to men; tend to be misdiag-*nosed as sick or handicapped; and are disadvantaged not by genetic endowment but by social myths and unevenly distributed power and resources.

## VIDEOS

*Broadcast news.* (1987, color, 131 min.). Directed by James L. Brooks; starring William Hurt, Holly Hunter, Albert Brooks, Joan Cusack, Jack Nicholson.

*Three network news coworkers—an intense producer, a smart reporter, and a pretty-boy anchor—form the triangle at the center of this story of how abilities and ethics affect work and relationships. Albert Brooks is outstanding as a brilliant journalist and writer who utterly lacks the social skills and "camera presence" to be an anchor, and William Hurt seems disturbingly familiar as the affable "talking head" who has presence and social skills, but little substance and few scruples.*

*Charly.* (1968, color, 103 min.). Directed by Ralph Nelson; starring Cliff Robertson, Claire Bloom, Lilia Skala, Leon Janney.

*This powerful, provocative fantasy is based on Daniel Keyes's short story, "Flowers for Algernon," about a retarded man who volunteers for experimental surgery that transforms him rapidly into a genius. The film examines the stigma of labels and the complex relationship of intelligence to other human abilities—and to one's overall sense of self.*

*Higher learning.* (1995, color, 127 min.). Directed by John Singleton; starring Omar Epps, Kristy Swanson, Laurence Fishburne, Jennifer Connelly, Ice Cube.

*An African American college athlete suffers from confusion and rage about how to respond to racism and to social injustice. A Black political science professor tries to guide him toward a more realistic view of the world—and his abilities to live in it. Except for a simplistic subplot about evil skinheads, this is an involving and well-done film about how racism corrupts our promise and possibilities.*

*Little man Tate.* (1991, color, 99 min.). Directed by Jodie Foster; starring Jodie Foster, Dianne Wiest, Adam Hann-Byrd, David Hyde Pierce, Harry Connick, Jr.

*A working-class single mother must determine how best to bring up her son, a child genius whose abilities challenge the good intentions and resources of the adults who care about him. Moving, involving, and not simplistic, this exploration of what "intelligence" means in a complete life is also well produced and boasts a great jazz score.*

*Rain man.* (1988, color, 140 min.). Directed by Barry Levinson; starring Dustin Hoffman, Tom Cruise, Valeria Golino, Jerry Molden, Jack Murdock, Michael D. Roberts.

*After his wealthy father's death, a selfish, high-living young man discovers he has an older brother, institutionalized* most of his life, who is an autistic savant: He cannot function well in the outside world but is capable of remarkable feats of memory and calculation. The relationship they develop—as men, brothers, and persons with very different individual abilities—highlights important questions about the intelligence, personal qualities, and personal relationships essential to a happy life.

Roxanne. (1987, color, 107 min.). Directed by Fred Schepisi; starring Steve Martin, Daryl Hannah, Rick Rossovich, Shelley Duvall, Damon Wayans, Kevin Nealon.

A modern, comic retelling of Rostand's Cyrano de Bergerac, with Martin as C. D., a funny, smart fire chief afflicted with a big nose and a big crush on a beautiful astronomer visiting his small resort town. When she shows interest in a cute but dumb friend, C. D. agrees to write the letters and speak the words that will win her heart. A light, funny story of the ironies of seeking beauty while respecting intelligence. What if you can't get everything in one package?

Searching for Bobby Fischer. (1993, color, 110 min.). Directed by Steven Zaillian; starring Joe Mantegna, Max Pomeranc, Joan Allen, Ben Kingsley, Laurence Fishburne.

Based on a true story, this film shows a father who promotes his young son's genius for chess, entering him in competitions and soon eroding the boy's spirit and original enjoyment of the game. The film is touching, brilliantly acted, well done. Considers the implications of talent and competition for a person's peace of mind and love of life.

Stand and deliver. (1987, color, 105 min.). Directed by Ramon Menendez; starring Edward James Olmos, Lou Diamond Phillips, Rosana de Soto, Andy Garcia.

This film is based on the true story of a tough, demanding high-school teacher who leads his impoverished, cynical students out of their East L.A. rut by training them for an Advanced Placement Calculus Test—and what comes after.

CORE CONCEPTS

PSYCHOLOGY IN YOUR LIFE

**HOW DOES THE SITUATION AFFECT OUR BEHAVIOR?**

We usually adapt our behavior to the demands of the social situation, and in ambiguous situations we take our cues from the behavior of others.

**Need Help? Ask for It!** In an emergency, giving simple instructions can turn bystander bewilderment into helping behavior.

**HOW DO WE CONSTRUCT OUR SOCIAL REALITY?**

Our social reality depends on our cognitive interpretation of situations and the people in them.

**Loving Relation-ships:** The end of a relationship can be difficult for everyone. Social psychologists have begun to study what it takes to keep people together.

**WHAT CAN PSYCHOLOGY TELL US ABOUT RESOLVING CONFLICTS?**

By changing the situation, we may be able to alter the incompatible social realities that lead to conflict.

**Resolving Real-Life Conflicts:** An experiment on groups of Boy Scouts holds lessons for dealing with conflict in the Middle East and with your loved ones.

USING PSYCHOLOGY TO LEARN PSYCHOLOGY:
THE SOCIAL PSYCHOLOGY OF GETTING INTO GRADUATE SCHOOL

# Social Psychology

*On a summer Sunday in California, a siren shattered the serenity of college student Tommy Whitlow's morning. A police car screeched to a halt in front of his home. Within minutes, Tommy was charged with a felony, informed of his constitutional rights, frisked, and handcuffed. After he was booked and fingerprinted, Tommy was blindfolded and transported to the Stanford County Prison, where he was stripped, sprayed with disinfectant, and issued a smock-type uniform with an I.D. number on the front and back. Tommy became Prisoner 647. Eight other college students were also arrested and assigned numbers.*

*The prison guards were not identified by name, and their anonymity was enhanced by khaki uniforms and reflector sunglasses—Prisoner 647 never saw their eyes. He referred to each of his jailers as "Mr. Correctional Officer, Sir"; to them, he was only number 647.*

*The guards insisted that prisoners obey all rules without question or hesitation. Failure to do so led to the loss of a privilege. At first, privileges included opportunities to read, write, or talk to other inmates. Later on, the slightest protest resulted in the loss of the "privileges" of eating, sleeping, and washing. Failure to obey rules also resulted in the assignment of menial, unpleasant work such as cleaning toilets with bare hands, doing push-ups while a guard stepped on the prisoner's back, and spending hours in solitary confinement. The guards were always devising new strategies to make the prisoners feel worthless. Every guard Prisoner 647 encountered engaged in abusive, authoritarian behavior at some point during his incarceration; the only difference was in the frequency and regularity of their hostility toward the prisoners.*

*Less than 36 hours after the mass arrest, prisoner 8412, one of the ringleaders of an aborted prisoner rebellion that morning, began to cry uncontrollably. He experienced fits of rage, disorganized thinking, and severe depression. On successive days, three more prisoners developed similar stress-related symptoms. A fifth prisoner developed a psychosomatic rash all over his body when the parole board rejected his appeal.*

*At night, Prisoner 647 tried to remember what Tommy Whitlow had been like before he became a prisoner. He also tried to imagine his tormentors before they became guards. He reminded himself that he was a college student who had answered a newspaper ad and agreed to be a subject in a two-week experiment on prison life. He had thought it would be fun to do something unusual, and he could always use some extra money.*

*Everyone in the prison, guard and prisoner alike, had been selected from a large pool of student volunteers. On the basis of extensive psychological tests and interviews, the volunteers had been judged as law-abiding, emotionally stable, physically healthy, and "normal-average" on all psychological measures. In this mock prison experiment, assignment of participants to "guard" or "prisoner" roles had been randomly determined by the flip of a coin. The prisoners lived in the jail around the clock and the guards worked standard eight-hour shifts.*

*As guards, students who had been pacifists and "nice guys" in their usual life settings behaved aggressively—sometimes even sadistically. As prisoners, psychologically stable students soon behaved pathologically, passively resigning themselves to their unexpected fate of learned helplessness. The power of the simulated prison situation had created a new social reality—a real prison—in the minds of the jailers and their captives.*

*Because of the dramatic and unexpected emotional and behavioral effects the researchers observed, those prisoners with extreme stress reactions were released early from their "pretrial detention" in this unusual prison, and the psychologists decided to terminate the two-week study after only six days. Although Tommy Whitlow said he wouldn't want to go through it again, he valued the personal experience because he learned so much about himself and about human nature. Fortunately, he and the other students were basically healthy, and they readily bounced back from that highly charged situation. Follow-ups over many years revealed no lasting negative effects. The participants had all learned an important lesson: Never underestimate the power of a bad situation to overwhelm the personalities and good upbringing of even the best and brightest among us (Haney, Banks, & Zimbardo, 1973; Haney & Zimbardo, 1998; Zimbardo, 1973, 1975; Zimbardo, Maslach, & Haney, in press; replicated in Australia by Lovibond, Adams, & Adams, 1979).*

Scenes from the Stanford prison experiment.

Suppose *you* had been a subject in the Stanford prison experiment. Would you have been a "nice guy" guard—or a sadist? A model prisoner—or a rebel? Could you have resisted the pressures and stresses of these powerful circumstances? We'd all like to believe we would be good guards and heroic prisoners—and maybe we would be. But the best bet is that we would react the way other people like ourselves actually behaved in such a setting. In all likelihood, many of us would fall short of our own standards.

Welcome to *social psychology*, the field that investigates how individuals affect each other. It may be a relief to hear that not all of social psychology brings such bad news about ourselves as does the Stanford prison experiment. It also tells us about the forces that bring people together for friendships and loving relationships. As you study about **social psychology** in this chapter, you will learn how people's thoughts, feelings, perceptions, motives, and behavior are influenced by interactions with others. That is, social psychologists try to understand behavior within its *social context*. Defined broadly, this context includes the real, imagined, or symbolic *presence of other people*; the *activities and interactions* that take place among people; the *settings* in which behavior occurs; and the *expectations and norms* governing behavior in a given setting (Sherif, 1981).

Most of all, the Stanford prison experiment conducted by Philip Zimbardo (one of your authors) underscores the *power of social situations* to control human behavior. This is a major theme to emerge from the research that social psychologists have conducted over the past 50 years. In the first part of this chapter, you will see the power of the situation in research that shows how seemingly minor features of social settings can have a huge impact on what we think and how we feel and act. In these studies you will see how the situation can produce conformity to group standards—even when the group is clearly "wrong." Other studies will demonstrate how the situation can lead people blindly to follow orders—perhaps even orders to harm others.

Yet, as powerful as the situation can be, psychologists know that it is not objective reality to which we respond. Rather, we respond to our *subjective interpretation* of the situation, which can sometimes be quite different for different individuals. This, then, is the second great theme in social psychology: the construction of a *subjective social reality*. It is this world of expectations and perceptions that we must grasp in order to understand the attractive forces at work in friendships and romantic relationships, as well as the repulsive forces underlying prejudice.

Our examination of prejudice will set the stage for a third theme that will combine the first two. We will see how social psychologists have experimented with altering the situation to change subjective social reality. This, we will discover, has important implications for resolving conflicts among individuals, groups, and even nations. We begin now with the first of these three themes, the power of the situation.

**Chapter 5:
Sensation and Perception**
*Perception normally gives us useful—but not always entirely accurate—interpretations of events.*

## HOW DOES THE SITUATION AFFECT OUR BEHAVIOR?

Suppose that you have just graduated from college. You find yourself in an interview, with the very real possibility of being hired for the job of your dreams. Afterward, the department head suggests that you go to lunch together in the company cafeteria. Will you order a sandwich, a salad, or a full-course meal? Will you leave the plastic tray under your plate as you eat? Will you put the tiny paper napkin in your lap? If you are like most people in an unfamiliar situation such as this, you will take your cues from those around you.

Social psychologists believe that, even when the situation is a familiar one, such as a college classroom, the primary determinant of individual behavior is the nature of the social situation in which that behavior occurs. So powerful is the situation that it can sometimes dominate our personalities and override our past history of learning, values, and beliefs. We will see that the pressures of the situation can create powerful psychological effects, such as prejudice, blind obedience, and violence. Situational aspects that appear trivial to many observers—social roles, competition, or the mere presence of others—can profoundly influence how we behave. Often,

**Social psychology:** The branch of psychology that studies the effects of social variables and cognitions on individual behavior and social interactions.

these subtle situational variables affect us without our awareness. Our Core Concept emphasizes this point:

**CORE CONCEPT**

We usually adapt our behavior to the demands of the social situation, and in ambiguous situations we take our cues from the behavior of others.

In this section, we will review some research that explores this concept, called **situationism** by social psychologists. Situationism assumes that the environment can have both subtle and forceful effects on people's thoughts, feelings, and behaviors. Here we will look particularly at the power of the situation to create conformity, obedience, and sometimes even the willingness to inflict harm on others.

### Social Standards of Behavior

A job interview, such as the one we discussed above, provides an example of a situational influence on your behavior. Another would be the pressure of a salesperson who is trying to get you to buy a car. You will also notice the power of the situation when you compare the way students talk to their friends versus their professors. That is, most people learn to size up their social circumstances and conform their behavior to situational demands. The responses they make depend heavily on two factors: the *social roles* they play and *norms* of the group. Let us look at both of these more closely.

**SOCIAL ROLES**   Whether you are at a football game, a department meeting, or a pizza parlor, you will see that people operate by different rules, depending on their *social roles*. You can see this more clearly by responding to the question: Who are you? Almost certainly you and other readers of this book are students or professors of psychology—social roles that imply different sets of behaviors. (One, for example, takes exams, the other grades them.) It is likely that you take on several other social roles, too. Are you a part-time employee? Someone's parent? A cyclist? A body builder? A friend? A **social role** is one of several socially defined patterns of behavior that are expected of persons in a given setting or group. The roles you assume may be the result of your interests, abilities, and goals—or they may be imposed on you by the group or by cultural, economic, or biological conditions beyond your control. In any case, social roles prescribe your behavior.

The situations in which you live and function also determine the roles that are available to you and the behaviors others expect of you. Being a college student, for example, is a social role that carries certain implicit assumptions about attending classes, studying, and handing in papers. In addition, the adoption of this role makes other roles less likely. Thus, your role as college student diminishes the chances that you will assume the role of homeless person, drug pusher, or shaman, for example. By the same token, because you have college experience, numerous other roles (such as manager, teacher, airline pilot, and politician) are available to you.

The Stanford prison experiment cast guards and prisoners in different social roles. Yet, just a week before, their roles (college students) were very similar. Chance, in the form of random assignment, had decided their new roles as guards or prisoners, and these roles created status and power differences that came out in several ways in the prison situation.

Remember that no one taught the participants to play their roles. Each student called upon *scripts* about those roles. A **script** involves a person's knowledge about the sequence of events and actions that are expected of a particular social role. So,

Social norms can define rigid dress codes for group members.

**Situationism:** The view that environmental conditions influence people's behavior as much or more than their personal dispositions do.

**Social role:** One of several socially defined patterns of behavior that are expected of persons in a given setting or group.

**Script:** Knowledge about the sequence of events and actions that is expected in a particular setting.

if an individual understands the role of "guard" as someone who uses coercive rules to limit the freedom of "prisoners," then that person is likely to use a script derived from that schema to become an authoritarian guard under conditions such as the Stanford prison experiment. In fact, many students in the guard role were surprised at how easy it was for them to enjoy controlling other people: Just putting on the uniform transformed them from college-student research subjects into "prison guards" ready to manage "inmates."

In trying to understand what happened in the Stanford prison experiment, we should note that all the prisoners and guards were male. Would it have made any difference if women had been in the roles of prisoner and guard? We will never know because the unanticipated negative impact of the experiment on both the guards and prisoners would make it unethical to do the experiment again. The possibility of gender differences, however, is raised by this fact: The experiment was called off after a female graduate student, Christina Maslach, visited the "prison" and was shocked by what she saw. Immediately she conferred with Dr. Zimbardo, whom she implored to end the study. After some discussion, he agreed to do so. (Drs. Maslach and Zimbardo were later married.)

**Chapter 6:**
**Learning and Remembering**

Schemas *are cognitive structures that integrate knowledge and expectations about a topic or concept.*

**SOCIAL NORMS**   In addition to specific social roles, groups develop many "unwritten rules" for the ways that all their members should act. These expectations, called **social norms,** dictate socially appropriate attitudes and behaviors for members of a group. Social norms can be broad guidelines, such as ideas about which political or religious attitudes are considered acceptable. Social norms can also be quite specific, embodying specific standards of conduct, such as being quiet in the library or shining your shoes for a job interview. Norms can guide conversation, as when they restrict discussion of sensitive or taboo subjects in certain company. And norms can define dress codes for group members, whether requiring uniforms or business suits or prohibiting shorts and tank tops. In the Stanford prison experiment, the guards quickly developed norms for abusive behavior.

When a person joins a new group, such as a work group or a group of friends, there is always an adjustment period during which the individual tries to discover how best to fit in. Adjustment to a group typically involves discovering the set of social norms that regulates desired behavior in the group setting.

*"GOSH, ACKERMAN, DIDN'T ANYONE IN PERSONNEL TELL YOU ABOUT OUR CORPORATE CULTURE?"*

Individuals experience this adjustment in two ways: by noticing the *uniformities* in certain behaviors of all or most members and by observing the *negative consequences* when someone behaves in a nonnormative way, violating a social norm. For example, a child whose parents move her to a new school sees that her new classmates all wear jeans and baggy T-shirts. If a child violates this social norm, the others may laugh at her, penalizing her "mistake."

We can also see the power of social norms in a famous study of students attending Vermont's Bennington College in the 1930s. At that time, Bennington's campus culture had a prevailing norm of political and economic liberalism, encouraged by a young, dynamic, and liberal faculty. By contrast, most of the young women attending Bennington came from privileged, conservative homes—and brought decidedly nonliberal values with them. Social psychologist Theodore Newcomb wondered: Which forces would prevail in shaping the students' attitudes? His data showed that the norms of the campus won the war of influence against the norms of the family. In most women, the initial attitude of conservatism steadily waned as they

**Chapter 6:**
**Learning and Remembering**

*Bandura demonstrated that we acquire many social behaviors through observational learning.*

**Social norms:** A group's expectations regarding what is appropriate and acceptable for its members' attitudes and behaviors.

progressed through their college years, so that by their senior year they had clearly converted to liberal thinking and causes (Newcomb, 1943).

Twenty years later, the marks of the Bennington experience were still evident, Newcomb discovered. Women who had graduated as liberals were still liberals; those who had resisted the prevailing liberal norm had remained conservative. Most had married husbands with values similar to their own and created supportive new home environments. In the 1960 presidential election, the liberal Bennington allegiance was evident when 60% of the class Newcomb had studied voted for liberal John F. Kennedy, rather than conservative Richard M. Nixon—in contrast to less than 30% support for Kennedy among graduates of comparable colleges at that time (Newcomb et al., 1967).

Campus culture is not the only source of norms and group pressure, of course. One's workplace, neighborhood, religious group, and family can all communicate standards for behavior to the individual—and threaten sanctions (such as firing, social rejection, or excommunication) for violating the norms of that particular community. But a college or university environment can have a powerful impact on young people. This is especially true if they have had narrow life experiences and not previously encountered attitudes radically different from their own. For example, a new student may adopt classmates' political opinions, as in the Bennington study, as well as religious beliefs and attitudes about sex and alcohol (Prentice & Miller, 1993; Schroeder & Prentice, 1995).

## Conformity

How powerful are these social pressures to conform? We can see the effects of social pressure in clothing styles. We can also see social pressure in the political attitudes of Bennington College students. In these examples, social pressures shaped people's attitudes and opinions. But we might ask: Can social influence be strong enough to make them follow a group norm that is clearly and objectively wrong? That is the question posed by Solomon Asch's classic study of conformity.

**THE ASCH STUDIES**   Imagine that you were part of a group asked to judge some aspect of physical reality, such as the color of a tomato, and you found that the rest of the group saw the tomato differently from you—*wrongly*, in fact. Could the power of that situation prove stronger than the evidence of your own eyes? Solomon Asch (1940; 1956) set out to answer just such a question with a group rigged to make subjects think that their eyes were deceiving them.

In Asch's study, male college students were told they would be participating in a study of visual perception. They were shown cards with three lines of differing lengths and asked to indicate which of the three lines was the same length as a separate, standard line (see Figure 12.1). The problem was simple: The lines were different enough so that mistakes were rare in subjects responding alone. But in a group of seven to nine students, where others had been coached to give wrong answers, everything changed.

Here's how the experiment worked. On the first three trials, everyone agreed on the correct answer. But the first person to respond on the fourth trial reported an obviously incorrect judgment, reporting as equal two lines that were clearly different. So did the next person and so on, until all members of the group but the remaining one (the only real subject in the experiment) had unanimously agreed on an erroneous judgment. The subject then had to decide whether to go along with everyone else's view of the situation and conform, or remain independent, standing by the evidence of his own eyes. This group pressure was imposed on 12 of the 18 trials.

What did he and others in his position finally do? As you might expect, subjects showed signs of disbelief and discomfort when faced with a majority who saw the world so differently from the way they did. But the group pressure usually pre-

## FIGURE 12.1: Conformity in the Asch Experiments

In this photo from Asch's study, the naive subject, number 6, displays obvious concern about the majority's erroneous judgment. At top right, you see a typical stimulus array. At top left, the graph illustrates conformity across 12 critical trials, when subjects were grouped with a unanimous majority, or had the support of a single dissenting partner. (A lower percentage of correct estimates indicates a greater degree of conformity with the group's false judgment.)

vailed. Three-quarters of the subjects conformed to the false judgment of the group one or more times, while only one-fourth remained completely independent on all trials. In various related studies, between 50 and 80% of the subjects conformed with the majority's false estimate at least once; a third of the subjects yielded to the majority's wrong judgments on half or more of the critical trials. Social psychologists call this the **Asch effect:** the influence of a group majority on the judgments of an individual. The Asch effect has become the classic illustration of **conformity**—the tendency for people to adopt the behavior and opinions presented by other group members. Even though subjects were judging matters of fact, not merely personal opinions, most caved in to conformity pressures.

**Asch effect:** A form of conformity in which a group majority influences individual judgments.

**Conformity:** The tendency for people to adopt the behaviors, attitudes, and opinions of other members of a group.

Conformity isn't always a bad thing, especially in heavy traffic. Much of the harmony in any social situation is the result of conformity to group norms.

At the same time, we should be sure to recognize that the Asch effect, powerful as it is, still does not make everyone conform. Conformity researchers do regularly find "independents," individuals who are bothered and even dismayed to find themselves in disagreement with the majority, but who nonetheless stand their ground and "call 'em as they see 'em"—even to the point of deliberately giving a wrong answer when the group gives a correct one (Friend, Rafferty, & Bramel, 1990).

**GROUP CHARACTERISTICS THAT PRODUCE CONFORMITY** In further experiments, Asch identified three factors that influence whether a person will yield to group pressure: (1) *the size of the majority*, (2) *the presence of a partner who dissented* from the majority, and (3) *the size of the discrepancy* between the correct answer and the majority's position. He found that subjects tended to conform with a unanimous majority of as few as three people, but not if they faced only one or two confederates. However, even in a large group, giving the subject one ally who dissented from the majority opinion sharply reduced conformity (as shown in Figure 12.1). With such a "partner," nearly all subjects were able to resist the pressures to conform to the majority. Remarkably, however, a certain proportion of individuals continued to yield to the group even with a partner present. All who yielded underestimated the influence of the social pressure and the frequency of their conformity; some even claimed that they really had *seen* the lines as the majority had claimed (Asch, 1955, 1956).

Numerous studies have revealed additional factors that influence conformity. (These experiments have included both female and male subjects.) Specifically, a person is likely to conform under the following circumstances:

- When a judgment task is difficult or ambiguous (Deutsch & Gerard, 1955; Lott & Lott, 1961; Saltzstein & Sandberg, 1979);
- When the group members are perceived as especially competent;
- When responses are given publicly rather than privately;
- When the group majority is unanimous: Once that unanimity is broken, the rate of conformity drops dramatically (Allen & Levine, 1969; Morris & Miller, 1975).

For example, when you vote in a group, as is common in clubs or on boards of directors, you are more likely to go along with the majority if: (a) the issue being decided is complex or confusing, (b) others in the group seem to know what they are talking about, (c) you must vote by raising your hand instead of casting an anonymous ballot, and (d) the entire group, without exception, votes in a certain way. In this circumstance, you may not even realize how much others in the group have influenced you.

The Asch situation has given us abundant information about the conditions that produce conformity to group pressure. Now let us take the question of social influence a step farther: Under what conditions will social pressure produce *obedience*? Specifically, could a situation be contrived in which ordinary people would be willing to follow orders that would cause harm to another person? The answer to these questions, unfortunately, is "Yes."

### Obedience

So far, we have seen how groups influence individuals. But the arrow of influence also points the other way: Certain individuals, such as leaders and authorities, can command the obedience of groups—even large masses of people. The ultimate demonstration of this effect was seen in the World War II era, with the emergence of Adolf Hitler in Germany and Benito Mussolini in Italy. These dictators were able to transform the rational citizens of whole nations into loyal followers of a hideous fascist ideology bent on world conquest. Their success was so great that the resulting regimes threatened democracies and freedom everywhere.

Modern social psychology had its origins in this wartime crucible of fear and prejudice. In contrast with the current emphasis on the power of the situation, early social psychologists looked for answers in the personalities of people drawn into fascist groups. Specifically, they looked for an *authoritarian personality* behind the fascist group mentality (Adorno et al., 1950). Later research by Stanley Milgram shifted the attention of social psychologists to the situation in order to learn how individuals become so blindly obedient to the commands of authority figures. But before we look at Milgram's work, let us reflect for a moment on some more recent examples of unquestioning obedience to authority.

In 1978, a group of American citizens left California to relocate their Peoples Temple in South America. There they carved an isolated retreat out of the jungle and named it Jonestown, after their charismatic leader, Reverend Jim Jones. Responding to publicity about the group, now called a "cult" in the press, an investigation team from the U.S. Congress flew to Jonestown on a fact-finding mission. There one of the team members was murdered on orders from Jones. Knowing that his community would soon be under siege, Rev. Jones proclaimed that it was time for all in the community to die. Following his orders, over 900 members of the Peoples Temple willingly administered lethal doses of cyanide to their children and then to themselves.

In 1993, 100 members of a religious sect in Waco, Texas, joined their leader, David Koresh, in defying federal agents who had surrounded their compound. After a standoff of several weeks, the Branch Davidians set fire to their quarters rather than surrender to authorities. In the resulting conflagration, scores of men, women, and their children perished. Did Jonestown and Waco represent isolated incidents? Apparently not. Four years later the members of another group calling itself Heaven's Gate followed their leader's command to commit mass suicide in order to achieve a "higher plane" of being.

Now let's get personal: How about *you?* Are there any conditions under which you would blindly obey an order from a person you love and respect (or fear)? Could you imagine, for example, participating in the American military massacre of hundreds of civilians in the Vietnamese village of My Lai on the orders of your commanding officer (Hersh, 1971; Opton, 1970, 1973)? Or would you obey an authority figure who told you to electrocute a stranger?

Your answer is most likely, "No! What kind of person do you think I am?" After reading this chapter, you may be more likely to answer, "I hope not—but I don't know for sure." Experiments suggest that, depending on the social forces at work, you might well do what others have done in those situations—however horrible and alien their actions may seem outside that context. The study of obedience, as nothing else in psychology, brings into critical focus the power of the social situation to shape our behavior. It is our hope that your thoughtful consideration of this topic will help you question the forces that sometime produce knee-jerk obedience in others.

On that note, let us now turn to the most convincing demonstration of situational power ever created in the laboratory. In a dramatic experiment, Stanley Milgram (1965, 1974) showed that a willingness to follow brutal, and even potentially lethal, orders is not confined to a few extreme personalities or deranged individuals. Rather, it is a response of which any of us may be capable—given the wrong circumstances. This finding, along with certain ethical issues that the experiment raises, places Milgram's work at the center of one of the biggest controversies in psychology (Blass, 1996; Miller, 1986; Ross & Nisbett, 1991). Let us begin with a look at the controversial methods Milgram used.

**Chapter 6:
Learning and Remembering**

*At the time of Milgram's
studies, we already knew that
punishment inhibits the
learning of new responses.*

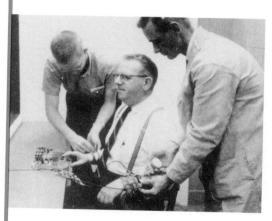

Milgram's obedience experiment, from top to
bottom: the "teacher" instructed by the authority,
the shock generator, and the "learner" being
strapped into his electrified chair. Experts incorrectly
predicted the behavior of Milgram's subjects because
they failed to consider the influence of the special
situation created in the experiment. Although many
of the subjects in Milgram's study dissented verbally,
the majority obeyed.

**MILGRAM'S OBEDIENCE EXPERIMENT**   The volunteers thought that they
were participating in a scientific study of memory and learning. Specifically, the experimenter told them that the purpose of the experiment was to discover how learning and memory could be improved through the proper balance of reward and
punishment. Cast in the role of "teacher," a volunteer subject was instructed to punish memory errors made by another person (actually a confederate of the
experimenter) playing the role of "learner." To administer punishment,
the teacher was told to throw a switch that would deliver an electric shock
to the learner each time the learner made an error. Moreover, the teacher
was told to increase the level of shock by a fixed amount for every new
error. Overseeing the whole procedure was a white-coated experimenter.
This authority figure presented the rules, arranged for the assignment of
roles (by a rigged drawing of lots), and ordered the teachers to do their job
whenever they hesitated or dissented.

The real question driving the experiment was this: How far would
subjects go before they defied the authority figure by refusing to obey? The
dependent variable was the subject's response, measured by the shock level
the subject was willing to deliver. The level of shock could be clearly seen
on a "shock generator" that featured a row of 30 switches that apparently
could deliver shocks in 15-volt steps up to an whopping 450 volts.

To make the situation realistic, Milgram gave each "teacher" a mild
sample shock. This convinced his subjects that the apparatus was actually
delivering shocks and that they would be causing the "learner" increasing
pain and suffering each time they flipped a switch. Except for this demonstration shock, however, no shocks were actually administered: You will remember that the learner was actually a part of the experimental team.

The part of the learner was played by a pleasant, mild-mannered
man, about 50 years old. He mentioned having a "heart condition" but said
he was willing to go along with the procedure. The experimenter obliged
by strapping him into an "electric chair" in the next room. As the learner,
his task was to memorize pairs of words, then choose the correct response
for each stimulus word from a multiple-choice listing. Following the experimental script, the learner soon began making mistakes.

At 75 volts, the script called for the learner to moan and grunt; at
150 volts he would demand to be released from the experiment. At 180
volts he would cry out that he could not stand the pain any longer. The
plan then called for the learner's protests to increase with increasing shock
levels. For any subjects still delivering punishment at the 300-volt level,
the learner would shout that he would no longer take part in the experiment and must be freed. He would also whimper about a heart condition
and refuse to reply any further. As you might imagine, this situation was
stressful. If the teacher hesitated or protested about delivering the required
shock at any level, the experimenter would interrupt, stating that the experiment "must continue" and asking the teacher to "please continue."
The experiment would end only when the shock level reached the 450-volt
maximum—or when the teacher refused to obey.

**THE SHOCKING RESULTS**   Suppose for a moment that *you* were the
subject-teacher. Ask yourself the following questions:

- How far up the shock scale would you go?
- At which level of shock would you refuse to continue?

In fact, the majority of subjects obeyed the authority fully! Nearly
two-thirds delivered the maximum 450 volts to the learner. Even most of
those who refused to give the maximum shock obeyed until reaching about

300 volts. And never did any subject who got within five switches of the end refuse to go all the way. By then their resistance was broken; they had resolved their own conflicts and just tried to get it over with as quickly as possible.

It is important to note, however, that these were not sadistic people who obeyed happily. Most dissented verbally, even though they continued to deliver shocks. One subject complained to the unwavering experimenter, "He can't stand it! I'm not going to kill that man in there! You hear him hollering? He's hollering . . . Who is going to take the responsibility if anything happens to that gentleman?" Clearly upset, this subject added, "You mean I've got to keep going up with that scale? No sir, I'm not going to kill that man!" (1965, p. 67). But, even though such verbal protests were common, the shocks continued. When the learner simply stopped responding to the teacher's questions, some subjects called out to him, urging him to get the answer right so they would not have to continue shocking him. All the while they protested loudly to the experimenter, but the experimenter insisted that the teacher continue: "Rules are rules!" Even when there was only silence from the learner's room, the teacher was ordered to keep shocking him more and more strongly, all the way up to the button that was marked "Danger: Severe Shock XXX (450 volts)." Most subjects obeyed.

We should remind you that no actual shocks were ever delivered to the learner. The "victim" of the "shocks" was an accomplished actor who congenially chatted with his "teacher" after the experiment and assured him he was fine and had never felt any shocks at all. The controversy about Milgram's research concerns the ethics of inflicting potential mental harm on the teachers by allowing them to believe (before debriefing) that they were actually shocking the learner. Consider this dilemma: Is it important to know the potential we might have for obediently harming others— even if, to gain that knowledge, we must subject people to psychological pain and discomfort and perhaps unpleasant realizations about themselves?

**WHY DO WE OBEY AUTHORITY?**    You may wonder whether Milgram's subjects were unusual in some way. His initial obedience experiments were conducted at Yale University with male college students and then with male residents of New Haven who received payment for their participation. In later variations, Milgram set up a storefront research unit in Bridgeport, Connecticut, recruiting through newspaper ads a broad cross section of the population. Subjects eventually included both sexes and varied widely in age, occupation, and education. In all, Milgram tested more than 1,000 subjects.

From the many variations Milgram conducted on his original study, we can conclude that subjects tended to be obedient under the following conditions (Milgram, 1965, 1974; Rosenhan, 1969):

- *When a peer modeled obedience* by complying with the authority figure's commands
- *When the victim was remote from the subject* and could not be seen or heard
- *When the teacher was under direct surveillance of the authority figure* so that the teacher was aware of the authority's presence
- *When a subject acted as an intermediary bystander*—merely "assisting" the one who was delivering the shock, rather than actually throwing the switches
- *When the authority figure had higher relative status than the subject*, as when the subject was a student and the experimenter was billed as "professor" or "doctor"

If you carefully review these conditions (Figure 12.2), you can see that the obedience effect results from situational variables and not personality variables. In fact, personality tests administered

This Chinese man risked his life by defying authority. Would you have done so?

## FIGURE 12.2: Obedience in Milgram's Experiments

The graph shows a profile of weak to strong obedience effects across situational variations of Milgram's study of obedience to authority.

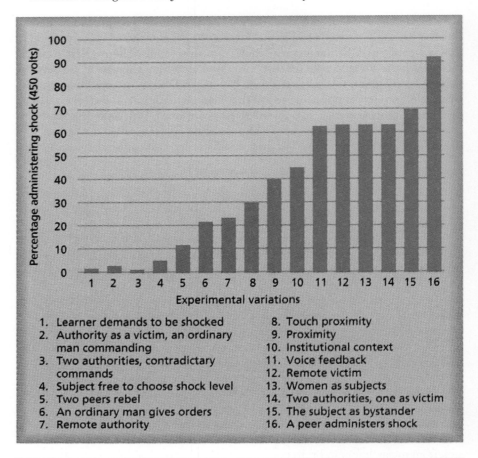

1. Learner demands to be shocked
2. Authority as a victim, an ordinary man commanding
3. Two authorities, contradictary commands
4. Subject free to choose shock level
5. Two peers rebel
6. An ordinary man gives orders
7. Remote authority
8. Touch proximity
9. Proximity
10. Institutional context
11. Voice feedback
12. Remote victim
13. Women as subjects
14. Two authorities, one as victim
15. The subject as bystander
16. A peer administers shock

to the subjects did *not* reveal any traits that differentiated those who obeyed from those who refused, nor did they identify any psychological disturbance or abnormality in the obedient punishers. These findings enable us to rule out personality as a variable in obedient behavior. And what about gender? Milgram found that women were just as obedient as men (Milgram, 1974).

Like the Stanford prison study, obedience research challenges the myth that evil lurks in the minds of evil people—that the bad "they" are different dispositionally from the good "us" who would never do such things. The purpose in recounting these findings is not to debase human nature or to excuse evil deeds, but to make clear that even normal, well-meaning individuals are subject to the human potential for giving in to strong situational and social influences to do wrong. As TV's kindly neighbor, Mr. Rogers, tells his little viewers, "Sometimes even nice people do bad things." What he doesn't add, but you now know, is that *it depends on the power of the situation.*

### The Bystander Problem

Harm doesn't always come from a hurtful act. It can also come from *inaction* when someone needs help. We can illustrate this fact with a news event that stunned the nation and loosed a flood of psychological research: In Queens, New York, 38 ordinary citizens watched a man stalk and stab Kitty Genovese for more than half an hour, in three separate attacks. Two times the sound of the bystanders' voices and the sudden glow of their bedroom lights interrupted the assailant and frightened him. Each time, however, he returned and stabbed her again. Not a single person telephoned the police during the assault. Only one witness called the police—after the woman was dead (*New York Times*, March 13, 1964, cited in Darley & Latané, 1968). The newspaper and TV accounts of this murder played up the angle of bystander "apathy" and bewildered a nation that could not accept the idea of such indifference on the part of its responsible citizenry. The outrage over the Kitty Genovese murder drew unprecedented attention to the problem of bystander apathy.

Why didn't bystanders help? Is it something in the *person* or something in the *situation*? Come let us see again how social psychology is done.

**CONTRIVED EMERGENCIES**    Soon after hearing of the Kitty Genovese murder and the analysis in the press, social psychologists Bibb Latané and John Darley began a series of studies of the bystander intervention problem. These studies all ingeniously created laboratory analogues of the problem faced by bystanders in real emergency situations. In one such experiment, a college student, placed alone in a room with an intercom, was led to believe that he was communicating with one or more students in adjacent rooms. During the course of a discussion about personal problems, the subject heard what sounded like one of the other students was having a seizure and gasping for help. During the "seizure" it was impossible for the subject to talk to the other students or to find out what, if anything, they were doing about the emergency. The dependent variable—the response of interest in the experiment—was the speed with which he reported the emergency to the experimenter. The independent variable was the number of people he believed were in the discussion group with him.

It turned out that the speed of response by subjects in this situation depended on the number of bystanders they thought were present. The more other people they believed to be listening in on the situation in other rooms, the slower they were to report the seizure, if they did so at all. As you can see in Figure 12.3, all subjects in a two-person situation intervened within 160 seconds, but nearly 40% of those who believed they were part of a larger group never even bothered to inform the experimenter that another student was seriously ill (Latané & Darley, 1968).

Was it the person or the situation? Personality tests showed no significant relationship between particular personality characteristics and speed or likelihood of intervening. The best predictor of bystander intervention was the situational variable of *size of the group* present. By way of explanation, Darley and Latané proposed that the likelihood of intervention *decreases* as the group *increases* in size, because each person assumes that others will help, so he or she does not have to make that commitment. Individuals who perceive themselves as part of a large group of potential interveners experience a **diffusion of responsibility:** a dilution or weakening of each group member's obligation to help, as total responsibility is shared with all group members. You may have experienced moments of diffused responsibility if you have driven past a disabled car beside a busy highway because "surely someone else" would stop and help. In contrast, if you believe you are the only bystander to know of a victim's plight, you will feel a greater degree of responsibility—and opportunity—for providing assistance.

Another factor was undoubtedly also at work: conformity. As you will remember from our Core Concept and from Asch's studies of conformity, when people don't know what to do, they take their cues from others. The same thing occurred in the bystander studies, where subjects who failed to intervene were observing and conforming to the behavior of other people who were doing nothing. Thus, the bystander problem is, in part, a problem of conformity to group norms.

**DOES TRAINING ENCOURAGE HELPING?**    Two studies suggest that the bystander problem can be countered with appropriate training. Ted Huston and his colleagues (1981) found no personality traits that distinguished people who had helped in actual emergency situations from those who had not. But they did find that helpers more often had had some medical, police, first-aid, or CPR training in dealing with

Kitty Genovese was murdered in her neighborhood, while 38 of her neighbors watched. Why didn't somebody help? The answer is not what most people think.

**Chapter 1:**
**Mind, Behavior, and Science**
*The* independent variable *refers to the various conditions for different groups in an experiment.*

**Diffusion of responsibility:** Dilution or weakening of each group member's obligation to act when responsibility is perceived to be shared with all group members.

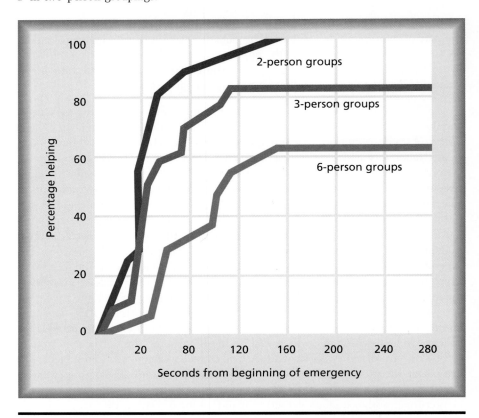

FIGURE 12.3:   Bystander Intervention in an Emergency

The more people present in a crisis, the less likely it is that any one bystander will intervene. As this summary of research findings shows, bystanders act most quickly in two-person groupings.

emergency situations. And another study shows that even a psychology class lecture on the bystander problem can help (Beaman et al., 1978). Students had an opportunity to help a "victim" slumped in a doorway while walking by with a nonresponsive confederate of the experimenter. Those who had attended a lecture on bystander intervention were twice as likely to stop and attempt to help as those who did not receive the lecture on helping. Education apparently makes a difference.

## What Makes a Samaritan Good or Bad?

Now that you know something about bystander intervention, let's see how good you are at picking the crucial variable out of a bystander situation inspired by the bib-

lical tale of the Good Samaritan (see Luke 10:30–37). In the biblical account, several important people are too busy to help a stranger in distress. He is finally assisted by

an outsider, a Samaritan, who takes the time to offer aid. Could the failure of the distressed individual's countrymen to help be due to character flaws or personal dispositions? Or was it determined by the situation?

Social psychologists decided to put students at the Princeton Theological Seminary into a similar situation. It was made all the more ironic because they thought that they were being evaluated on the quality of their sermons—which were assigned to highlight the parable of the Good Samaritan. Let's see what happened when these seminarians were given an opportunity to help someone in distress.

With sermon in hand, each was directed to a nearby building where the sermon was to be recorded. But as a subject walked down an alley between the two buildings, he came upon a man slumped in a doorway, in obvious need of help. The student now had the chance to practice what he was about to preach. What would you guess was the crucial variable that predicted how likely a seminarian—ready to preach about the Good Samaritan—was to help a person in distress? Choose one:

a. how religious the seminarian was (as rated by his classmates)
b. how "neurotic" the seminarian was (as rated on the "Big Five" personality traits)

## FIGURE 12.4: Results of the "Good Samaritan" Study

Even with a sermon on the Good Samaritan in hand, seminary students who were in a hurry didn't usually stop to help.

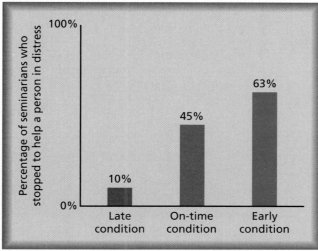

c. how much of a hurry the seminarian was in
d. how old the seminarian was

Let's see . . .

All of the *dispositional variables* (personal characteristics) of the seminarians were controlled by random assignment of subjects to three different conditions. Thus, we know that personality was not the determining factor. Rather, it was a

*situational variable:* time. Before subjects left the briefing room to have their sermons recorded in a nearby building, each was told how much time he had to get to the studio. Some were assigned to a *late condition,* in which they had to hurry to make the next session; others to an *on-time condition,* in which they would make the next session just on time; and a third group to an *early condition,* in which they had a few spare minutes before they would be recorded.

What were the results? Of those who were in a hurry, only 10% helped. Ninety percent failed to act as Good Samaritans! If they were on time, 45% helped the stranger. The greatest bystander intervention came from those who were not in any time bind—63% of these seminarians acted as Good Samaritans (Darley & Batson, 1973).

Remarkably, the manipulation of time urgency made those in the "late" condition six times less likely to help than those in the "early" condition. It is likely that the "late" subjects, while fulfilling their obligation to the researcher to hurry and not be late for their appointment, held a single-minded purpose that blinded them to other events around them. It is the power of the situation.

## PSYCHOLOGY IN YOUR LIFE

## Need Help? Ask for It!

To demonstrate the positive effects of situational power, social psychologist Tom Moriarity (1975) arranged two fascinating experiments. In the first study, New Yorkers watched as a thief snatched a woman's suitcase in a restaurant when she left her table. In the second, they watched a thief grab a portable radio from a beach blanket when the owner left it for a few minutes. What did these onlookers do? Some did nothing, letting the thief go on his merry way. But others did intervene. What were the conditions under which some helped and others did not?

In each experiment, the would-be theft victim (the experimenter's accomplice) had first asked the soon-to-be observer of the crime either "Do you have the time?" or "Will you please keep an eye on my bag (radio) while I'm gone?" The first interaction elicited no personal responsibility, and the bystander stood by idly as the theft unfolded. However, of those who had agreed to watch the victim's property, almost every bystander intervened. They called for help, and some even tackled the runaway thief on the beach.

*continued*

The encouraging message is that we can convert apathy to action and transform callousness to kindness just by asking for it. The act of requesting a favor forges a special human bond that involves other people in ways that materially change the situation. It makes them responsible to you, and thereby responsible for what happens in your shared social world. You can use this knowledge to increase your chances of getting aid from would-be helpers in several ways (Schroeder et al., 1995):

- *Ask for help*. Let others know you need it rather than assuming they realize your need or know what is required.
- *Reduce the ambiguity* of the situation by clearly explaining the problem and what should be done: "She's fainted! Call an ambulance right away and help me keep her warm," or "Someone broke into my house—call the police and give them this address!"
- *Identify specific individuals* so they do not diffuse responsibility with others present: "You, in the red shirt: Call 911!" or

"Will the person in the blue Toyota please call for a tow truck right away?"

None of these tactics guarantees the safety of your person or possessions, of course. (Kitty Genovese did call for help.) Nevertheless they probably represent your best hope if you find yourself, alone in a crowd, facing a real emergency.

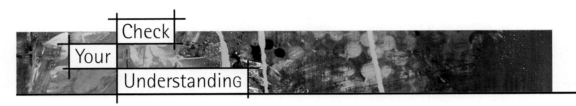

1. RECALL: *The Stanford prison experiment illustrates the power of _____ to influence people's behavior.*
   a. personality
   b. heredity
   c. childhood experiences
   d. the situation

2. RECALL: *Which one of the following would be a social role?*
   a. prisoner
   b. student
   c. professor
   d. all of the above

3. RECALL: *In the Asch studies, which of the following produced a decrease in conformity?*
   a. The task was seen as difficult or ambiguous.
   b. The subject had to respond publicly, rather than privately.
   c. The majority was not unanimous in its judgment.
   d. The group was very large.

4. RECALL: *In Milgram's original study, about what proportion of the subjects gave the maximum shock?*
   a. about two-thirds
   b. about 10%

   c. about 3%
   d. nearly all

5. APPLICATION: *In an emergency situation, you would have the best chance of getting help from*
   a. a lone bystander.
   b. a large group of people.
   c. a group of people who are friends of each other.
   d. a group of six people.

6. UNDERSTANDING THE CORE CONCEPT: *Which of the following best illustrates how people in ambiguous situations take their cues from others?*
   a. the majority of subjects in the Asch experiments
   b. those who disobeyed Milgram
   c. helpers who have had CPR training
   d. the experimenter in the Latané & Darley study of bystander intervention

**ANSWERS:**    1. d    2. d    3. c    4. a    5. a    6. a

KEY QUESTION

## HOW DO WE CONSTRUCT OUR SOCIAL REALITY?

In the first part of the chapter we saw that people often respond to situations in predictable ways, as shown experiments on conformity, obedience, and bystander intervention. But, powerful as it is, the situation doesn't account for everything. For example, it does not account for the individual differences we see in people's choices of friends and romantic partners, nor does it account for their prejudices. To explain the patterns we find in social interaction, we must also look at cognitive processes.

In the language of social psychology, we need to understand how we construct our **social reality**—our subjective interpretations of other people and of our relationships. Thus, the social reality that we construct determines whom we find attractive, whom we find threatening, whom we seek out, and whom we avoid. This, then, leads us to the second lesson of social psychology, captured in our next Core Concept:

 **CORE CONCEPT**
Our social reality depends on our cognitive interpretation of situations and the people in them.

We will illustrate how these cognitive factors operate by analyzing how they affect our attitudes toward other people. We will commence on the positive end of the scale by asking a simple question: What makes people like each other? Then we will move to the opposite end with a look at the negative feelings that lie at the heart of *prejudice*.

## Interpersonal Attraction

It is no surprise that we are attracted to people who have something to offer us (Brehm, 1992; Simpson & Harris, 1994). We like those who give us gifts, agree with us, act friendly toward us, share our interests, entertain us, and help us in times of need—unless, of course, we suspect that their behavior is self-serving. Although we don't necessarily mind giving something back—a social exchange—we may shrink from relationships that merely take from us and offer nothing in return. In the best of relationships—be it a friendship, partnership, marriage, or business relationship—both parties receive rewards. You might consider whether this is true in your own relationships as we look at the reward theory of attraction in the following paragraphs.

**REWARD THEORY: WE (USUALLY) PREFER REWARDING RELATIONSHIPS** We can formalize the idea of mutual advantage by saying that most relationships can be seen as an exchange of benefits (Batson, 1987; Clark, Mills, & Corcoran, 1989). The benefits could be some combination of money, cars, clothes, or other material possessions. Or the exchange might involve something intangible like praise, status, information, sex, or emotional support.

Social psychologist Elliot Aronson (1995) summarizes this in a **reward theory of attraction,** which says that attraction is a form of social learning. By looking at the social costs and benefits, claims Aronson, we can usually understand why people are attracted to each other. In brief, reward theory says that we like best those who give us maximum rewards at minimum cost. After we look at the evidence, we think you will agree that this theory explains (almost) everything about interpersonal attraction.

What is it about another person that we find most rewarding? Social psychologists have found four especially powerful sources of reward that predict interpersonal attraction: *proximity, similarity, self-disclosure,* and *physical attractiveness*. Most of us choose our friends, associates, and lovers because they offer some combination of these factors at a relatively low social cost. Let's see how each of these affects our relationships.

*PROXIMITY* An old saying advises, "Absence makes the heart grow fonder." Another contradicts with "Out of sight, out of mind." Which one is correct? Studies show that frequent contact is the best predictor of our closest relationships (Simpson & Harris, 1994). In college dormitories, residents more often become close friends with the person who lives in the next room than they do with the person who lives two doors down (Priest & Sawyer, 1967). Residents of apartments make more friendships among people who live on the same floor than among those who live on other floors (Nahemow & Lawton, 1975). Those who live in neighborhoods more often become friends with the occupants of the house next door than with people living

 **Chapter 6:**
**Learning and Remembering**
*Social learning involves expectations of rewards and punishments learned through social interaction and the observation of others.*

**Social reality:** An individual's subjective interpretation of other people and of relationships with them.

**Reward theory of attraction:** A social learning view that says we like best those who give us maximum rewards at minimum cost.

The principle of proximity predicts that coworkers are likely to become friends.

two houses away (Festinger, Schachter, & Back, 1950). This **principle of proximity** (nearness) also accounts for the fact that many people end up married to the boy or girl next door (Ineichen, 1979). And it correctly predicts that people at work will make more friends among those with whom they have the most contact (Segal, 1974).

Although you don't have to like your neighbors, the proximity rule says that when you know two individuals who are equally attractive, you will probably find it easier to make friends with the nearest one: The rewards are equal, but the cost is less in time and trouble. Apparently, the old saying that familiarity breeds contempt should be revised in light of social psychological research: Familiarity more often breeds friendship. Increased contact, itself, often increases peoples' liking for each other (Bornstein, 1989).

*SIMILARITY*   People usually find it more rewarding to strike up a friendship with someone who shares their attitudes, interests, values, and experiences than to have their thinking challenged by people who are disagreeable or merely different (Hatfield & Rapson, 1993; Hendrick & Hendrick, 1992; Kelley et al., 1983; Simpson & Harris, 1994). If we have just discovered that we share tastes in music, politics, and attitudes toward education, we will probably hit it off because we have, in effect, exchanged compliments that reward each other for our tastes and attitudes (Byrne, 1969). The **similarity principle** also explains why teenagers are most likely to make friends among those who share their political and religious views, educational aspirations, and attitudes toward alcohol and drugs (Kandel, 1978). Likewise, similarity accounts for the fact that most people find marriage partners of the same age, race, social status, attitudes, and values (Brehm, 1992; Hendrick & Hendrick, 1992). In general, similarity—like proximity—makes the heart grow fonder.

*SELF-DISCLOSURE*   Good friends and lovers share intimate details about themselves (Sternberg, 1998). This practice not only allows people to know each other more deeply, but it sends signals of trust. It is as if I say, "Here is a piece of information that I want you to know about me, and I trust you not to hurt me with it." Friends and lovers usually find such exchanges highly rewarding. When you observe people exchanging confidences and details about their lives, you can predict that they are becoming more and more attracted to each other.

*PHYSICAL ATTRACTIVENESS*   A cliché tells us that beauty is only skin deep. Nevertheless, people usually find it more rewarding to associate with people whom they consider to be physically attractive than with those whom they consider to be plain or homely (Patzer, 1985). This may result from the expectation that others will like us more if they see us with attractive companions, or it may simply occur because we prefer looking at more attractive people than at less attractive ones. Whatever the reasons—fair or not—good looks are a real social asset. Potential employers, for example, prefer good-looking job candidates to plainer applicants (Cash & Janda, 1984). Looks also affect people's judgments of children. Attractive children are judged as happier and more competent than their peers (Dion, 1986; Eagly et al., 1991; Hatfield & Sprecher, 1986). Even babies judge people by their appearances. We know this because babies gaze longer at pictures of normal faces than at those of distorted faces (Langlois et al., 1987).

Most people are repelled by the idea that they might make judgments based only on looks. Indeed, when asked what they look for in a dating partner, college students rank physical attractiveness last (Tesser & Brodie, 1971). But what people *say*

**Principle of proximity:** The notion that people at work will make more friends among those who are nearby—with whom they have the most contact. *Proximity* means "nearness."

**Similarity principle:** The notion that people are attracted to those who are most similar to themselves.

does not match their actions, as psychologists have shown with people's reaction to randomly paired blind dates (Walster et al., 1966). When subjects rate their blind dates, physical attractiveness emerges as the single most important factor used in deciding whether a person wants to arrange a second date. At least as far as first impressions go, physical attractiveness dominates everything else (Feingold, 1990).

Other research shows that the principle of attractiveness applies equally to same-sex relationships and opposite-sex relationships (Maruyama & Miller, 1975). Gender differences do exist, however. While both males and females are strongly influenced by physical attractiveness, men seem to be *more* influenced by looks than are women (Cash & Killcullen, 1985; Feingold, 1990; Folkes, 1982; Hatfield & Sprecher, 1986).

These findings may come as bad news for the majority of us, who consider ourselves rather average-looking—or worse. But we can take some comfort in a study that suggests that people actually consider "average" features to be the most attractive. Investigators fed images of many students' faces into a computer that allowed them to manipulate the facial features. Surprisingly, they found that people usually liked best the images having features closest to the average size and shape (Langlois & Roggman, 1990; Langlois, Roggman, & Musselman, 1994).

Now some bad news for exceptionally attractive readers: While we usually associate positive qualities with attractive individuals (Calvert, 1988), studies show that extreme attractiveness can also be a liability. Although physically attractive people are seen as more poised, interesting, sociable, independent, exciting, sexual, intelligent, well-adjusted, and successful, they are also perceived as more vain and materialistic (Brigham, 1980; Cash & Duncan, 1984; Hassebrauck, 1988; Moore, Graziano, & Millar, 1987). A "double standard" also comes into play. For example, the public favors good-looking male politicians but disparages their attractive female counterparts (Sigelman et al., 1986).

These studies on the effects of physical attractiveness hint that reward, as powerful as it is, does not account for everything. We will see this more clearly below, as we explore some important exceptions to the reward theory of attraction. In particular, we will explore some interesting (and sometimes tragic) conditions in which people feel most attracted to those who do *not* offer the greatest rewards at the least cost.

**Matching hypothesis:** The prediction that most people will find friends and mates that are of about their same level of attractiveness.

**EXCEPTIONS TO THE REWARD THEORY OF ATTRACTION**   While the rules of proximity, similarity, self-disclosure, and physical attractiveness may explain a lot about interpersonal attraction, a casual look around reveals lots of relationships that don't seem especially rewarding. Why, for example, might a woman be attracted to a man who abuses her? Or, why would a person want to join an organization that requires a difficult or degrading initiation ritual? Such relationships pose most interesting puzzles (Aronson, 1995). Could it be that, under some circumstances, people actually feel *more* attraction when they find that another person has *less* to offer them? Let's try to uncover the principles of social cognition operating behind some interesting exceptions to a reward theory of attraction.

*EXPECTATIONS AND THE INFLUENCE OF SELF-ESTEEM*
We have seen that reward theory predicts our attraction to smart, good-looking, talented, witty, wealthy, nearby, self-disclosing, like-minded, and powerful people. Yet, you have probably observed that most people end up with friends and mates that you would judge to be of about their same level of attractiveness—the so-called **matching hypothesis**

The matching hypothesis predicts that most people will have friends and mates that you would judge to be of about their same level of attractiveness.

(Feingold, 1988). How does this happen? Is our selection of associates the result of a sort of bargaining for the best we can get in the interpersonal marketplace?

Yes, says **expectancy-value theory.** People usually decide whether or not to pursue a relationship by weighing the *value* they see in another person (including such qualities as physical attractiveness, wit, interests, and intelligence) against their *expectation* of success in the relationship (Will the other person be attracted to me?). Most of us don't waste too much time on interpersonal causes we think are lost. Rather, we initiate relationships with the most attractive people we think will probably like us in return. In this sense, expectancy-value theory is not so much a competitor of reward theory as it is a refinement of it.

One noteworthy exception to this argument involves people who suffer from low self-esteem. Sadly, people with low opinions of themselves tend to establish relationships with people who share their views—that is, with people who devalue them. Such individuals generally feel a stronger commitment to a relationship when their partner thinks poorly of them than they do when the partner thinks well of them (Swann, Hixon, & De La Ronde, 1992).

Those individuals who appear to be extremely competent can also be losers in the expectancy-value game. Why? Most of us keep such people at a distance—probably because we fear that they will reject our approaches. But, if you happen to be one of these stunningly superior people, do not despair: Social psychologists have found hope! When highly competent individuals commit minor blunders—spilling a drink or dropping a sheaf of papers—other people actually like them *better*, probably because blunders bring them down to everyone else's level (Aronson, Willerman, & Floyd, 1966; Aronson, Helmreich, & LeFan, 1970). Don't count on this, however, unless you are so awesomely competent as to be unapproachable. The latté-in-the-lap trick only makes most of us look like klutzes that people like *less*.

Cognitive dissonance theory predicts that these recruits will increase their loyalty to the Marine Corps as a result of their basic training ordeal.

*ATTRACTION AND SELF-JUSTIFICATION* "Semper fidelis," says the Marine Corps motto: "Always faithful." Considering the discomforting experiences that people must go through to become Marines (grueling physical conditioning, loss of sleep, lack of privacy, being yelled at, suffering punishment for small infractions of rules), it may seem remarkable that recruits routinely develop so much loyalty to their organization. How can a three-month ordeal under the often painful, exhausting, and humiliating conditions of basic training foster fondness for the organization that gave them such rough treatment? Obviously, some powerfully attractive and interesting forces are at work to make them justify their loyalty.

*Cognitive dissonance theory* offers a compelling explanation for the mental adjustments that occur in people who voluntarily undergo unpleasant experiences (Festinger, 1957). The theory says that when people voluntarily act in ways that produce discomfort or otherwise clash with their attitudes and values, they develop a highly motivating mental state, called **cognitive dissonance.** A Republican politician who makes a public statement agreeing with a Democratic opponent is likely to feel cognitive dissonance. The same holds true for people who find themselves acting in ways that cause them physical discomfort. Thus, our Marine recruits may feel cognitive dissonance when they find that they have volunteered for an experience that is far more punishing than they had imagined.

According to cognitive dissonance theory, people are motivated to avoid the uncomfortable state of dissonance. If they find themselves experiencing cognitive dissonance, they will attempt to reduce it in ways that are predictable—if not always

**Expectancy-value theory:** A theory in social psychology that states how people decide whether or not to pursue a relationship by weighing the potential *value* of the relationship against their *expectation* of success in establishing the relationship.

**Cognitive dissonance:** A highly motivating state in which people have conflicting cognitions, especially when their voluntary *actions* conflict with their *attitudes.*

entirely logical. The two main ways of reducing dissonance are to change either one's behavior or one's cognitions. So, in civilian life, if the boss is abusive, you might avoid dissonance by simply finding find another job. But in the case of a Marine recruit, changing jobs is not an option: It is too late to turn back once basic training has started. A recruit experiencing cognitive dissonance therefore is motivated to adjust his or her thinking. One possibility is to decide, "This is a horrible experience, and I am a fool for volunteering." But this self-deprecation is painful, too. Therefore, it is more likely that the recruit will resolve the dissonance by rationalizing the experience ("It's tough, but it builds character!") and by developing a stronger loyalty to the organization ("Being a member of such an elite group is worth all the suffering!").

In general, cognitive dissonance theory says that, *when people's cognitions and actions are in conflict (dissonance), they often reduce the conflict by changing their thinking to fit their behavior.* This is a powerful concept about which psychologists have learned a great deal. In fact, cognitive dissonance theory has spawned more than a thousand published articles (Cooper & Fazio, 1984; Tesser & Shaffer, 1990).

Cognitive dissonance theory explains many things that people do to justify their behavior and thereby avoid dissonance. For example, it explains why smokers so often rationalize their habit. It explains why people who have put their efforts into a project, whether it be volunteering for the Red Cross or writing a letter of recommendation, become more committed to the cause as time goes on—in order to justify their effort. It also explains why, if you have just decided to buy a Chevrolet, you will attend to new information supporting your choice (such as Chevrolet commercials on TV), but you will tend to ignore dissonance-producing information (such as a Chevy broken down alongside the freeway).

Cognitive dissonance theory also helps us understand certain puzzling social relationships—for example, a woman who is attracted to a man who abuses her. Her dissonance might be summed up in this thought: "Why am I staying with someone who hurts me?" Her powerful drive for self-justification may make her reduce the dissonance by focusing on his good points and minimizing the abuse. And, if she has low self-esteem, she may also tell herself that she deserved his abuse. In this way, she justifies her decision to remain with him and, in the process, may find him even more attractive than before. To put the matter in more general terms: *Cognitive dissonance theory predicts that people are attracted to those for whom they have agreed to suffer.* A general reward theory, by contrast, would never have predicted that outcome.

To sum up our discussion on interpersonal attraction: You usually will not go far wrong if you use a reward theory to understand why people are attracted to each other. People initiate social relationships because they expect some sort of benefit. It may be an outright reward, such as money or status or sex, or it may be an avoidance of some feared consequence, such as pain. But social psychology also shows that a simple reward theory cannot, by itself, account for all the subtlety of human social interaction. A more sophisticated and useful understanding of attraction must take into account such cognitive factors as expectations, self-esteem, and cognitive dissonance. That is, a complete theory must take into account the ways that we *interpret* our social environment. This notion of interpretation also underlies other judgments that we make about people, as we shall see next in our discussion of *attributions*.

## Making Attributions

We are always trying to explain to ourselves why people do what they do. Suppose that you are riding on a bus, when a middle-aged woman with an armload of packages gets on and, in the process of finding a seat, drops everything on the floor as the bus starts up. How do you explain her behavior? Do you think of her as the victim of circumstances—or is she a klutz?

Social psychologists have found that we tend to *attribute* other people's actions and misfortunes to their personal traits, rather than to situational forces, such as the unpredictable lurching of the bus. This helps explain why we often hear attributions of laziness or low intelligence to the poor or homeless, rather than an externally imposed lack of opportunity (Furnham, 1982; Pandey et al., 1982; Zucker & Weiner, 1993). It also helps us understand why most commentators on the Kitty Genovese murder attributed the inaction of the bystanders to defects in character, rather than to social influence. As you might expect, such negative attributions usually make people seem less attractive to us. (The only exception, you may remember, occurs when a person who is seen as uncommonly competent commits a minor blunder and is thereby seen as *more* attractive.)

On the other side of the attributional coin, we find that people use the same process to explain each other's successes. So, you may ascribe the success of a favorite singer, athlete, or family member to personal traits, such as exceptional talent or intense motivation. In doing so, we tend to ignore the effects of situational forces, such as the influence of family, coaches, a marketing blitz, or just a "lucky break." Again, as you might expect, such positive trait attributions make people seem more attractive to us.

Psychologists call this tendency to emphasize personal traits and ignore situational influences the **fundamental attribution error.** Despite its name, however, the fundamental attribution error is not as fundamental as psychologists at first thought. Cross-cultural research has suggested that it is more pervasive in individualistic cultures, as found in the U.S. or Canada, than in collectivist cultures, as found in Japan or China (Brehm & Kassin, 1990; Fletcher & Ward, 1988; Miller, 1984; Ross, 1977; Triandis, 1996).

The fundamental attribution error (FAE) is not always an "error," of course. If the causes really are dispositional, the observer's guess is correct. So the FAE is best thought of as a *bias* rather than a mistake. However, the FAE is an error in the sense that an observer may overlook legitimate, situational explanations for another's actions. For example, if the car in front of you brakes suddenly so that you almost collide, your first impression may be that the other driver is at fault, a dispositional judgment. But what if the driver slowed down in order to avoid hitting a dog that ran into the road? Then the explanation for the near-accident would be situational, not dispositional. By reminding ourselves that there may be circumstances that account for seemingly inexplicable actions, we are less likely to commit the FAE.

Oddly, you probably judge yourself by a different standard—depending on whether you have experienced success or failure. When things go well, most people

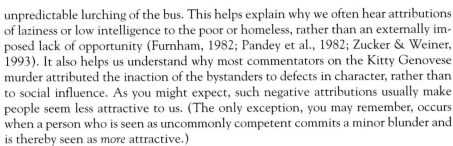

**Chapter 4:**
**Psychological Development**

*Collectivist cultures socialize people to put the needs of the group before the desires of the individual.*

**Fundamental attribution error:**
The tendency to emphasize internal causes and ignore external pressures. The FAE is more common in individualistic cultures than in collectivistic cultures.

If this observer attributes his blunder to clumsiness or carelessness, he commits the fundamental attribution error. This is more likely in Western cultures, such as those of Canada and the United States, than in Eastern cultures, such as those of China and Japan.

attribute their own success to internal factors, such as motivation, talent, or skill ("I am good at taking multiple-choice tests."). But when things go poorly, they attribute failure to external factors beyond their control ("The professor asked trick questions.") (Smith & Ellsworth, 1987). Psychologists have dubbed this tendency the **self-serving bias** (Bradley, 1978; Fletcher & Ward, 1988). Self-serving biases are probably rooted in the need for self-esteem, a preference for interpretations that save face and cast our actions in the best possible light (Epstein & Feist, 1988; Ickes & Layden, 1978; Schlenker, Weingold, & Hallam, 1990). Social pressures to excel as an individual make the self-serving bias, like the fundamental attribution error, more common in individualist cultures than in collectivist cultures (Markus & Kitayama, 1994).

## Prejudice and Discrimination

While attribution can be positive or negative, prejudice, as social psychologists use the term, is always negative. Prejudice can make an employer discriminate against women (or men) for a management job. It can make a teacher expect poor work from a minority student. And, some places in the world, it can still lead to *genocide*, the systematic extermination of a group of people because of their racial or ethnic origins. We will define **prejudice** as a negative attitude toward an individual based solely on his or her membership in a particular group. Prejudice may be expressed as negative emotions (such as dislike or fear), negative attributions or stereotypes that

justify the attitude, and/or the attempt to avoid, control, dominate, or eliminate those in the target group. Prejudiced attitudes serve as filters that influence the way others are perceived and treated. Thus, prejudice exerts a powerful force for selectively processing, organizing, and remembering pertinent information about people.

We should distinguish prejudice from *discrimination*, a related concept. While prejudice is an *attitude*, discrimination is a *behavior*. We will define **discrimination,** then, as a negative action taken against an individual as a result of his or her group membership. While discrimination can arise from prejudice, we will see that this is not always the case.

**CAUSES OF PREJUDICE** Prejudice and discrimination can grow from many sources (Aronson, 1995). Some of these attitudes and behaviors are taught to us at an early age. Some are defensive reactions when we feel threatened. Some are the result of conformity to social customs. An understanding of these sources of prejudice and discrimination will provide us with the foundation necessary for thinking about possible "cures." Here are some of the common sources that have links with concepts we have already studied.

*DISSIMILARITY AND SOCIAL DISTANCE* If similarity breeds liking, then dissimilarity can breed disdain. So, if you wear baggy shorts and a nose ring, it's a good bet that some middle-aged people from a traditional background feel just a bit uncomfortable around you. They are likely to perceive you as a part of a social group that flaunts values and behaviors quite distinct from those of their own group. This perceived difference can easily become fertile ground for the growth of prejudice.

What psychological principles are at work? When you perceive someone to be unlike the people in your **in-group,** you mentally place that person at a greater **social distance** than members of your own group. You are then less likely to view that

**Chapter 4:
Psychological Development
Chapter 8:
Emotion and Motivations**
*Individualism and collectivism also have an effect on moral reasoning and on achievement motivation.*

**Self-serving bias:** An attributional pattern in which one takes credit for success but denies responsibility for failure. (Compare with the *fundamental attribution error*.)

**Prejudice:** A negative *attitude* toward an individual based solely on his or her membership in a particular group.

**Discrimination:** A negative action taken against an individual as a result of his or her group membership.

**In-group:** The group with which an individual identifies.

**Social distance:** The perceived difference or similarity between oneself and another person.

**Chapter 6:
Learning and Memory**
*Aggression often results from punishment or the threat of punishment.*

Probable causes of prejudice at work here include conformity to group norms, role models, and a sense of threat.

individual as a social equal (Turner & Oakes, 1989). This inequality easily translates into inferiority, making it easier for you to treat members of an **out-group** with contempt. Historically, more powerful groups have discriminated against out-groups by withholding privileges, sending members of out-groups to different schools, making them sit in the back of the bus, forcing them into low-wage jobs, and otherwise treating them harshly.

*ECONOMIC COMPETITION* Highly competitive situations, where one group wins economic benefits or jobs at the other group's expense, can easily fan the flames of prejudice. For example, in the Pacific Northwest, where competition over old-growth forests threatens jobs and wildlife habitat, prejudice breeds among both timber workers and environmentalists. Likewise, prejudice may develop between groups of adults who see themselves in competition for the same jobs, especially if one group seems to have received preferential treatment. Such a situation often fans the flames of race or gender prejudice. Surveys have found, for example, prejudice against Black Americans to be greatest among White groups poised at an economic level just above the Black American average—precisely the ones who would feel their jobs most threatened by the possibility of losing their jobs to Black Americans (Greeley & Sheatsley, 1971).

*SCAPEGOATING* The Hebrew priests of old performed a ritual that symbolically transferred the sins of the people to a goat—the *scapegoat*. The animal was then driven into the desert to carry its burden of guilt away from the community. The term "scapegoat" has been applied in modern times to an innocent person or group who receives blame when others feel threatened. You may have seen, for example, an angry boss who suffered a business setback taking anger out on an unfortunate employee. On a far larger and more horrifying scale, German Jews served as scapegoats for the Nazis in World War II. **Scapegoating** may also explain why the number of lynchings in the southern United States between 1882 and 1930 was related to the price of cotton. When cotton prices dropped, lynchings increased, and when cotton prices rallied, the number of lynchings fell (Hovland & Sears, 1940).

*CONFORMITY TO SOCIAL NORMS* Perhaps the most pervasive source of discrimination and prejudice against women and minority groups is not a deliberate agenda based on conscious prejudice. Rather, it is an unthinking tendency to maintain conditions the way they are—even when those conditions involve unfair assumptions, prejudices, and customs (see Aronson, 1995). For example, in many offices it is the norm for secretaries to be female and executives to be male. Because of this norm, it may be difficult for a woman to break into the executive ranks. We may find the same process leading to discrimination where the norm says that nurses should be females, engineers should be males, or basketball players should be African Americans.

So, conformity to social norms can cause discrimination, but can this behavior also affect the attitudes that people hold about the group against which they are discriminating? That is, can discrimination cause prejudice? Imagine that you were the male executive who discriminated against a woman applying for an executive position. Or, imagine that you were the White bus driver in the mid-20th-century South who routinely sent Black passengers to a special section in the back of the bus. In either case, you would have had to justify your own behavior to yourself. After all, most people are taught to "Be nice to people" and "Treat other people as you want them to treat you." But if you have just treated people as a second-class citizens because of their gender or ethnicity, it will be difficult—perhaps impossible—for you to think of them as anything other than inferior beings (without having a severe attack of cognitive dissonance). In this way, your discriminatory behavior can cause or strengthen prejudices.

*MEDIA STEREOTYPES* The images used to depict groups of people in film, in print, and on television may reflect and reinforce prejudicial social norms. But they

**Out-group:** Those outside the group with which an individual identifies.

**Scapegoating:** Blaming an innocent person or a group for one's own troubles.

can also change those norms. Until the Black Power movement gained media attention, Africans and African Americans were most often portrayed in movies and on TV as simple, slow, comic characters, perpetuating the "Sambo" image that many Whites held. While the most blatant racial stereotypes have disappeared from the national media in the past few decades, other stereotypes remain. For example, the sexes still appear in stereotypical roles. If you examine the older textbooks still used in American grade schools, you will find that Nancy appears as a nurse, but never as a doctor. Native Americans, too, are cast as chiefs, braves, and squaws, but never architects or accountants. Such images are far from harmless, because people learn many of their prejudices from the stereotypes they see on TV and in books, movies, and magazines (Greenberg, 1986).

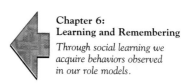

**Chapter 6:
Learning and Remembering**
*Through social learning we acquire behaviors observed in our role models.*

**COMBATING PREJUDICE**   During the civil rights struggles of the 1950s and 1960s, educators expressed a belief that prejudice could be overcome through a gradual process of information campaigns and education. The idea was to change prejudiced attitudes, and then a change in discriminatory behavior would follow. But experience provided no encouragement for this hope, at least where the traditional classroom tools of textbooks, movies, lectures, and discussions were concerned. In fact, these approaches have been found to be among the *least effective* tools for combating prejudice. The reason? Prejudiced people (like everyone else) usually avoid information that conflicts with their view of the world. Even for those who want to change their prejudiced attitudes, erasing the emotions associated with long-standing prejudices is difficult (Devine & Zuwerink, 1994). The process is even more difficult for those who cherish their prejudices.

So, how can one attack the prejudices of people who do not want to listen to another viewpoint? Research in social psychology suggests several possibilities. Among them are the use of *new role models, equal status contact,* and (surprisingly) *legislation.*

*NEW ROLE MODELS*   Tiger Woods, Connie Chung, and many others serve as role models in prestigious jobs and leadership positions where few of their race or gender have appeared before. Certainly having such role models must encourage people in these groups who might never have considered such careers. What we do not know much about, however, is the ability of role models to change the minds of people who are already prejudiced. Role models may serve better to prevent prejudice than to cure it.

Golfer Tiger Woods is a new role model in a sport that has traditionally had few representatives of minority groups.

*EQUAL STATUS CONTACT*   Slave owners have always had plenty of contact with their slaves, but they have always managed to hang onto their prejudices. Obviously, mere contact with people from an out-group is not enough to erase prejudices against them. Evidence, however, from integrated public housing (where the economic threat of lowered property values is not an issue) suggests that when people are placed together under conditions of equal status, where neither wields power over the other, the chances of developing understanding increases (Deutsch & Collins, 1951; Wilner, Walkey, & Cook, 1955).

*LEGISLATION*   You can't legislate morality. Right? The evidence of several studies suggests, however, that the old cliché may be wrong (Aronson, 1995). One of the most convincing of these studies was an experiment, done in the late 1940s, comparing the attitudes of White tenants toward Black tenants in public housing projects. In one project, White and Black occupants were assigned to different buildings—that is, the project was racially segregated. In another project the two racial groups were mixed (integrated) by being assigned housing in the same buildings. Only in the racially integrated project did prejudicial attitudes sharply decrease after moving into the housing projects (Deutsch & Collins, 1951). This result strongly suggests that rules requiring equal-status contact can diminish prejudice.

This notion is reinforced by a larger social "experiment" that, unfortunately for social psychologists, was done under far less controlled conditions. During the last half century, the United States has adopted laws abolishing racial discrimination. The consequences were sometimes unhappy, even violent, but prejudice and discrimination have gradually diminished (although they have not been eliminated). Evidence for this shift comes from polls showing that, in the 1940s, fewer than 30% of White Americans favored desegregation. That percentage has steadily climbed to well above 90% today (Aronson, 1995).

Because these changes in public opinion were not part of a carefully controlled experiment, we cannot say that the data *proves* that legislation has *caused* peoples' prejudices to diminish. Nevertheless, we can argue that the increased number of White Americans favoring desegregation is exactly what one might predict from cognitive dissonance theory: When the law requires people to *act* in a less discriminatory fashion, people will have to justify their new behavior. If, at the same time, threats are kept to a minimum, they will probably respond by softening their prejudiced attitudes. From this vantage point, it appears that legislation can affect prejudiced attitudes, after all (Aronson, 1995).

**Romantic love:** A temporary and highly emotional condition based on infatuation and sexual desire.

**Triangular theory of love:** A theory that describes various kinds of love in terms of three components: passion (erotic attraction), intimacy (sharing feelings and confidences), and commitment (dedication to putting this relationship first in one's life).

## PSYCHOLOGY IN YOUR LIFE

### Loving Relationships

We return to the positive end of the attitude spectrum to consider the form of attraction called "love." How do we know when attraction becomes love? To a large extent, our culture tells us. That is, each culture has certain *common themes defining love*—such as sexual arousal, attachment, concern for the other's welfare, and a willingness to make a commitment. It is important to realize that the idea of "love" can vary greatly from culture to culture (Aron & Aron, 1994; Beall & Sternberg, 1995; Berscheid, 1988; Fehr, 1988; Hatfield, 1988; Sprecher & McKinney, 1994; Sternberg, 1998).

It is also important to note that there are many kinds of love. The love that a parent has for a child is different from the love that longtime friends have for each other. Both are different from the commitment found, say, in a loving couple who have been married for 40 years. Yet, for many Americans, the term "love" brings to mind yet another form of attraction based on infatuation and sexual desire: **romantic love,** a temporary and highly emotional condition that generally fades after a few months at most (Hatfield, Rapson, & Rapson, 1995; Hatfield & Rapson, 1993). But the American assumption of romantic love as the basis for a long-term intimate commitment is not universal. In many other cultures marriage is seen as an economic bond or, perhaps, as a political relationship linking families.

A well-known view, proposed by Robert Sternberg (1998) in his **triangular theory of love,** says that love can have three components: passion (erotic attraction), intimacy (sharing feelings and confidences), and commitment (dedication

to putting this relationship first in one's life). Various forms of love can be understood in terms of different combinations of these three components. Thus, Sternberg suggests that

- *Romantic love* is high on passion and intimacy, but low on commitment
- *Liking* and *friendship* are characterized by intimacy, but not by passion and commitment
- *Infatuation* has a high level of passion, but it has not developed into intimacy or a committed relationship
- *Complete love (consummate love)* involves all three: passion, intimacy, and commitment

The need to understand what strengthens and what weakens loving relationships in our own culture has acquired some urgency because of the "divorce epidemic" in the United States (Brehm, 1992). If current rates hold, approximately half of all today's first marriages—and up to 60% of second marriages—will end in divorce. Much of the research stimulated by concern about high divorce rates has focused on the effects of divorce on children (Ahrons, 1994; Edwards, 1995).

In the last decade or so, however, research emphasis has shifted to the processes by which couples maintain loving relationships (for a review, see Brehm, 1992; Duck, 1992; and Hatfield & Rapson, 1993). We now know, for example, that for a relationship to stay healthy and to thrive both partners must see it as rewarding and equitable. As we saw in our discussion of reward theory, both must, over the long run, feel that they are getting something out of the relationship, not just giving. What they get—the rewards of the relationship—can involve many things, including adventure, status, laughter, mental stimulation, and material goods, as well as nurturance, love, and social support.

In addition, for a relationship to thrive communication between partners must be open, ongoing, and mutually validating (Gottman & Silver, 1994; Monaghan, 1999). Research shows that couples in lasting relationships have five times more positive interactions than negative ones—including exchanges of smiles, loving touches, laughing together, and compli-

Is it love? Social psychologists have been exploring the psychology of the human heart, collecting and interpreting data about how people fall in love and strengthen their bonds of intimacy. Most recently the emphasis has shifted to the factors that keep relationships together.

menting each other (Gottman, 1994). Yet, because every relationship experiences an occasional communication breakdown, the partners must know how to deal with conflicts effectively. Conflicts must be faced early and resolved fairly and effectively. Ultimately, each partner must take responsibility for his or her own identity, self-esteem, and commitment to the relationship—rather than expect the partner to engage in mind reading or self-sacrifice. (We will have more to say about dealing with conflicts in the next section of the chapter.)

This has been the briefest sampling from the growing social psychology of relationships. Such research has practical applications. Teachers familiar with research findings can now inform their students about the basic principles of healthy relationships with friends and partners. Therapists apply these principles in advising clients on how to communicate with partners, negotiate the terms of their relationships, and resolve inevitable conflicts. More immediately, as you yourself learn about the factors that influence how you perceive and relate to others, you should gain a greater sense of self-control and well-being in your own intimate connections with others (Harvey, 1996; Harvey et al., 1990).

Check Your Understanding

1. RECALL: *According to Aronson, we can explain almost everything about interpersonal attraction with a theory of*
   a. love.
   b. rewards.
   c. genetics.
   d. gender.
2. RECALL: *Which of the following does the research say is most important in predicting initial attraction?*
   a. physical attractiveness
   b. money
   c. personality
   d. nurturing qualities
3. RECALL: *Which theory of attraction best explains why people who are considered to be extremely competent are often not the people we are most attracted to?*
   a. reward theory
   b. expectancy-value theory

   c. cognitive dissonance theory
   d. psychoanalytic theory
4. APPLICATION: *According to cognitive dissonance theory, which of the following would be the best strategy for getting people to like you?*
   a. Give them presents.
   b. Show interest in their interests.
   c. Tell them that you like them.
   d. Persuade them to perform a difficult or unpleasant task for you.
5. RECALL: *Prejudice is a(n)* _____, *while discrimination is a(n)* _____.
   a. behavior/attitude
   b. instinct/choice
   c. attitude/behavior
   d. stimulus/response

*continued*

6. RECALL: *The evidence suggests that one of the most effective techniques for eliminating racial prejudice has been*
   a. education.
   b. threat and force.
   c. legislation.
   d. tax incentives.

7. UNDERSTANDING THE CORE CONCEPT: *Reward theory, expectancy-value theory, cognitive dissonance theory, and attribution theory all tell us that we respond not just to situations but to*

a. our cognitive interpretations.
b. our social instincts.
c. the intensity of the stimuli.
d. our biological needs and drives.

ANSWERS:   1. b   2. a   3. b   4. d   5. c   6. c   7. a

---

**KEY QUESTION**

## WHAT CAN PSYCHOLOGY TELL US ABOUT RESOLVING CONFLICTS?

From domestic disputes to war, most human problems involve social conflict. From the viewpoint of social psychology, **conflict** occurs when people pursue opposing goals based on incompatible social realities. Sometimes conflict occurs between individuals, as when you and your friend can't agree on which movie to see. Sometimes it occurs between groups, as when two governments try to occupy the same territory. Conflict can lead to hostile attitudes that undermine or destroy relationships. It can also lead to aggression and violence.

We have already seen many potential causes of conflict, particularly in our discussion of prejudice. And there are many more. Our focus in this section, however, will be on dealing constructively with conflict. In doing so, we will highlight the two great themes of social psychology: the *power of the situation* and the *cognitive construction of social reality*. Here we bring these two themes together in our Core Concept:

**CORE CONCEPT**

By changing the situation, we may be able to alter the incompatible social realities that lead to conflict.

We will explore this idea first in one of psychology's most famous experiments. Then we will glimpse how one social psychologist is attempting to apply his understanding of conflict to the real-life problems involved in international tensions.

### The Robbers' Cave: An Experiment in Conflict

The "laboratory" used by Muzafer Sherif and his colleagues (1961) to study conflict was a Boy Scout Camp known as the Robbers' Cave. The subjects, normal 11- to 12-year-old boys who had signed up for a summer camp, were placed randomly in two groups, dubbed the Eagles and the Rattlers. The research design called for competitive games and other conditions that the experimenters hoped would encourage rivalry and conflict between the two groups. Then, after discord was well established, the plan was to try out various techniques that the experimenters hoped would break down the animosities between the groups. The first part of the plan proved exceptionally easy to implement.

Initially, the experimenters kept the Eagles and Rattlers separated, and they used within-group activities to promote group **cohesiveness** (solidarity, loyalty, and a sense of group membership). Later the two groups were brought together for a series of competitive activities, such as tug-of-war and football. Prizes for the winners heightened the competition. The final straw was a "party" at which the experimenters arranged to have the Eagles arrive an hour early. Half of the food was mouthwatering, and half was deliberately ugly and unappealing. As you might expect, when the Rattlers arrived they found that the other group had taken the appealing food for itself. Name calling and scuffling soon escalated into a vicious food fight.

**Conflict:** In social psychology, an interpersonal difficulty that occurs when people pursue opposing goals based on incompatible social realities.

**Cohesiveness:** Solidarity, loyalty, and a sense of group membership.

With a rancorous atmosphere well established, Sherif and his colleagues tried to reverse the process and promote cooperation between the Eagles and their archenemies, the Rattlers. Before you read further, try to imagine what you might have done to turn this conflict into cooperation.

Several tactics tried by the Sherif team were spectacular failures. In particular, it did *not* help merely to bring the two groups together for pleasant social events, such as movies or eating in the same dining room. Such occasions just offered opportunities for more food fights and other displays of intergroup hostility.

What *did* help was to remove the rewards for competition and to contrive situations in which the groups had to cooperate in order to serve their own interests. First, the experimenters called a halt to the competitive games. Then, they brought the boys together to inform them of a "problem" that had developed with the camp's vital water line. Both groups agreed to search the line for the trouble spot, which they did together—harmoniously. On another day, the experimenters arranged for the camp truck to break down—meaning that it could not go to town for food. In order to get the truck running, the two groups had to work together by pulling it with the same rope previously used for the divisive tug-of-war game. In order to get what each group wanted, it had no choice but to cooperate with the "enemy." Under these new conditions, the groups no longer had incompatible social realities; no longer did they need to pursue conflicting goals.

It took several of these shared crises to break down the hostile barriers between the two groups and to build a sense of **mutual interdependence** based on shared goals. But, in the end, the groups actively sought opportunities to mingle with each other, and friendships developed between members of the Eagles and Rattlers. One group even used its own money to buy treats for members of the other group.

What psychological principles were at work here? As we noted, a change in social realities occurred. It began when the experimenters altered the situation to minimize competition and to provide greater rewards for cooperation than for conflict. Cognitive dissonance also undoubtedly played a part. Note that, as hostilities changed to friendliness, the boys first behaved cooperatively (during the emergencies) and then later changed their attitudes toward the other group. Why? If you voluntarily cooperate with someone you do not like, you will feel cognitive dissonance. At that point, the least painful way to reduce the dissonance is to change your attitude toward the other person. The Eagles and Rattlers justified their cooperation with former rivals by deciding that they weren't such bad guys after all.

Competition can promote aggressive behavior.

**Mutual interdependence:** A shared sense that individuals or groups need each other in order to achieve common goals.

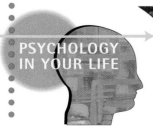

**PSYCHOLOGY IN YOUR LIFE**

*Resolving Real-Life Conflicts*

The Sherif experiment shows that finding common goals and establishing mutual interdependence had the capacity to reduce conflicts among Boy Scouts. But it is a great leap from the Robbers' Cave to the "real world." Could the lesson of the Eagles and the Rattlers apply, for example, to conflicts on the international stage?

The hope that the psychology of cooperation and conflict reduction might ease international tensions lies behind a quiet program currently operating in Israel. There Herbert Kelman applies what we have learned about competition and common goals to the long-standing hostilities and prejudices between the Israelis and the Palestinians (Kelman, 1997; Rouhana & Kelman, 1994). His approach involves bringing community leaders from both sides together for small-group discussions of mutual problems. Not just anyone could
*continued*

have started such a program: Kelman's credibility with both sides is a product of his stature as a scholar and the prestige of his affiliation with Harvard University.

Kelman's approach was carefully planned around a situation designed to encourage cooperation and minimize the rewards for hostile behaviors. Representatives of both groups were invited to attend a series of meetings together. These are not the usual, high-profile public negotiation sessions, however. Kelman finds that the process has the most impact on the community when the participants are mid-level community leaders, who have some power and status but who are in close touch with ordinary, grassroots citizens. Also important is the fact that meetings are held in private to avoid aggressive posturing for the press. Removed from the public spotlight, tensions between the two factions have eased, and earnest communication has developed.

Proof that this approach works is difficult to come by, although Kelman can recite case studies in which old hatreds have

been soothed. In fact, several participants in these workshops have later become involved in other peace efforts in their communities. While the method is inspired by solid science, Kelman is performing no laboratory experiment. Rather, he is applying principles of social psychology to the world beyond the laboratory, where most of the variables remain uncontrolled.

Could the same lessons be used to deal with conflicts closer to home—say in your own relationships? Suppose that you and a friend are planning a vacation together for spring break. You both want to get some sun, but you can't agree on whether to go to Baja or to Belize. You will probably be able to find an agreement, unless you both decide that you have to have your own way. But if you don't agree, you may have a conflict on the order of the Eagles and Rattlers or the Palestinians and Israelis. Your dispute now has nothing to do with the original problem of where to vacation. Instead, it has everything to do with pride, with saving face, with winning and losing.

In the Robbers' Cave experiment, the experimenters helped the boys resolve their conflict by focusing on mutually compatible goals. Kelman is doing much the same in the Middle East, where he is helping community leaders work together on common problems by finding shared social realities. Similarly, you and your friend would be more likely to work out your differences if you could focus on the common goal of spending a great vacation together in the sun. To do so, one of you could take steps to alter your environment and your social realities. It may help to meet in neutral territory or, perhaps even better, in a situation that both of you like, such as a favorite restaurant for dinner. Then, taking care to avoid provoking further disagreement or assigning blame, lay both problems on the table: the problem of finding a vacation site and the problem of winning. Also indicate your willingness to find a compromise. Then, as conflict expert John Gottman (1999) says, take a deep breath and listen.

Check Your Understanding

1. **RECALL:** *Conflict between the groups in the Robbers' Cave experiment was encouraged by*
   a. punishing nonaggressive boys.
   b. showing movies featuring hostile role models.
   c. competitive games.
   d. putting a particularly aggressive boy in charge of each group.
2. *In Kelman's work in the Middle East, he removed much of the incentive for competitive responses by*
   a. punishing those who responded competitively.
   b. holding the meetings in private.
   c. taking hostages from both sides.
   d. publicly denouncing those who responded competitively.

3. UNDERSTANDING THE CORE CONCEPT: *In both the Robbers' Cave experiment and Kelman's work in the Middle East, helping people to build a sense of mutual interdependence encouraged them to*
   a. alter their perceptions of each other.
   b. punish those who had encouraged hostilities.
   c. become more creative.
   d. adopt new personality traits.

**ANSWERS:**    1. **c**     2. **b**     3. **a**

# USING PSYCHOLOGY TO LEARN PSYCHOLOGY

## The Social Psychology of Getting into Graduate School

*I*f you're planning to do graduate study in psychology (or any other discipline), you should realize that getting into graduate school is like getting into any other group. It helps to know somebody.

Good grades and test scores are certainly a "must," but they are no more important than good recommendations. So, while you are completing your undergraduate work, take advantage of opportunities to get to know some faculty members—and to let them get to know you. Then, when you are ready to gather your recommendations for the graduate school application packet, you can count on professors who will know you as more than a face in a class.

What kinds of opportunities should you look for? For one thing, consider joining the Psi Beta or Psi Chi psychology honorary society on your campus. (Ask your professor or department secretary for details.) Another thing that looks

good on the resume is some research experience, so you might look for a professor who is working on a problem of interest to you and who needs a research assistant. Expect your first research experience to involve simple data entry or other clerical "dirty work"—but realize that you are starting on the ground floor. Some students even manage to parlay this experience into a coauthorship of a published study during their undergraduate career.

Such tactics, of course, make use of the psychology of interpersonal attraction. The reward theory predicts that your professors will like you if you show interest in their interests. It also suggests that serving as a volunteer on their research projects will increase their liking for you. Then, when you ask them for the favor of a letter of recommendation, they will be more likely to justify their efforts with a glowing recommendation—just as cognitive dissonance theory would predict.

## CHAPTER SUMMARY

 **HOW DOES THE SITUATION AFFECT OUR BEHAVIOR?**

- The Stanford prison experiment demonstrated how norms and social roles can be major sources of situational influence. The Asch studies demonstrated the powerful effect of the group to produce conformity, even when the group is clearly wrong. Another shocking demonstration of situational power came from Stanley Milgram's controversial experiments on obedience to authority. Situational influence can also lead to inaction: The bystander studies showed that individuals are inhibited by the number of bystanders, the ambiguity of the situation, and their resultant perception of their social role and responsibility.

 **CORE CONCEPT**

We usually adapt our behavior to the demands of the social situation, and in ambiguous situations we take our cues from the behavior of others.

 **HOW DO WE CONSTRUCT OUR SOCIAL REALITY?**

- The situation, by itself, does not determine behavior. Rather it is our *interpretation* of the situation—our constructed social reality—that regulates behavior, including our social interactions. Usually we are attracted to relationships that we find rewarding, although there are exceptions, predicted by expectancy-value theory and cognitive dissonance theory. Attribution theory predicts that we will attribute other people's blunders to their traits (the fundamental attribution error) and our own to the situation (the self-serving bias), although this tendency depends on one's culture. Prejudice and discrimination also demonstrate how we construct our own social reality through such cognitive processes as the perception of social distance and threats, the influence of media stereotypes, scapegoating, and self-justification. Healthy loving relationships also demonstrate the social construction of reality, because there are many kinds of love and many cultural variations in the understanding of love.

 **Our social reality depends on our cognitive interpretation of situations and the people in them.**

 **WHAT CAN PSYCHOLOGY TELL US ABOUT RESOLVING CONFLICTS?**

- In the Robbers' Cave experiment, contriving situations that fostered mutual interdependence and common goals reduced conflict between groups. On the international scene, such discoveries about conflict resolution lie behind an ongoing effort that is opening a dialogue between Israeli and Palestinian community leaders. The same principles can help to resolve conflicts involving family and friends.

 **By changing the situation, we may be able to alter the incompatible social realities that lead to conflict.**

## REVIEW TEST

For each of the following items, choose the single correct or best answer. The answer key appears at the end.

1. Which of the following is the social psychological principle illustrated by the Stanford prison experiment and its findings about participants' behavior?
   a. Social situations have powerful influences on human behavior.
   b. An experience is only socially real when the group is unanimous about interpreting it.
   c. Because everyone is basically different, no two people will respond to the same circumstances in the same way.
   d. Even in healthy circumstances, disturbed people will behave in unhealthy ways.

2. Theodore Newcomb's study of the attitudes of Bennington College students showed that, 20 years after they were first studied,
   a. all the women had gradually shifted to more conservative attitudes.
   b. all the women had gradually shifted to more liberal attitudes.
   c. the liberals were still liberal, and the conservatives still conservative.
   d. none of the above.

3. According to research on the Asch effect, which of the following is *not* a condition that encourages greater conformity?

   a. The task being judged is difficult or ambiguous.
   b. Each group member votes privately and anonymously.
   c. The group is extremely cohesive.
   d. The group members perceive each other to be highly competent.

4. Which of the following statements about Milgram's obedience experiments is true?
   a. All subjects were unable to resist the authority figure's orders, no matter how high the level of shock they believed they were administering.
   b. The majority of subjects delivered increasingly intense shocks until the learner complained of a heart condition, at which point most subjects refused to go on.
   c. Although most subjects verbally dissented and complained, most obeyed.
   d. Despite predictions by human nature experts that no one would comply, subjects enjoyed the experiment and had no trouble obeying the authority figure's commands.

5. Research on the factors that influence helping behavior suggests that the best predictor of bystander intervention is
   a. each individual's measurable level of personal altruism.
   b. the appearance or attractiveness of the victim.

c. an individual's degree of religiousness or agreement with conventional religious values.

d. the size of the group of bystanders to the emergency.

6. According to research on interpersonal attraction and close relationships, which of the following is *false*?

a. The more you interact with someone, the more likely you are to like him or her.

b. We form friendships on the basis of our similarity of backgrounds and attitudes.

c. As far as first impressions go, a pleasing personality counts more than good looks.

d. If you voluntarily undergo a hardship or suffering at someone's request, you will probably like them more than you did before.

7. Which of the following situations would likely create a feeling of cognitive dissonance in the mind of the individual described?

a. A woman who has said she is on a diet declines the offer of dessert.

b. A young man who says he loves his girlfriend spends a great deal of time choosing just the right valentine card to send her.

c. When a man finds out the car he wants costs more than he can afford, he decides not to buy it and looks instead for a less expensive vehicle.

d. A woman with a prejudice against Jews finds herself agreeing to do a favor for a Jewish neighbor.

8. Which of the following illustrates the effects of the fundamental attribution error?

a. Explaining why he is turning his paper in late, a student tells the professor that he had car trouble on the way to campus.

b. Watching an acquaintance hurry from the dining hall, a woman remarks, "Amy's in such a hurry— she must be a pretty impatient person."

c. After waiting an unusually long time to be waited on in a restaurant, a customer thinks there must be something wrong in the kitchen that is interfering with the waitress's ability to work as quickly as usual.

d. All of the above illustrate the fundamental attribution error.

9. In the Robbers' Cave experiment, hostility between the groups was reduced by

a. having the groups engage in social activities with each other.

b. creating crisis situations that the groups had to work on cooperatively.

c. punishing aggressive behavior.

d. allowing the groups to take out their hostilities in competitive sports.

10. In an application of social psychological findings on promoting cooperation between hostile groups, Herbert Kelman has

a. used the power of conformity (the Asch effect) to reduce hostilities.

b. advocated the use of rewards for peaceful actions and punishments for hostile actions.

c. brought community officials on both sides together for private discussions of mutual problems.

d. promoted "friendly" athletic competition as a means of displacing harmful aggressions and "burning off" energy that could explode into violence.

**ANSWERS:**  1. a    2. c    3. b    4. c    5. d    6. c
7. d    8. b    9. b    10. c

# IF YOU'RE INTERESTED . . .

## BOOKS

Aronson, E. (1995). *The social animal* (7th ed.). New York: W. H. Freeman & Co.

> *Aronson is one of the best writers and one of the best social psychologists around. His book tells you everything you wanted to know about aggression, conformity, persuasion, interpersonal attraction, and cognitive dissonance.*

Butterfield, F. (1995). *All God's children: The Bosket family and the American tradition of violence.* New York: Knopf.

> *We mentioned this one before, but because it is such a thought-provoking book and because it speaks to the big person–situation issue of social psychology, we'll mention it again here. Willie Bosket is the hardest criminal the New York penal system has ever had. He comes from a long line of hard-luck tough guys, stretching back to the Civil War. But is it nature? His lineage was nurtured in the violent, culture of honor (and insults to honor) in the American South. This is the book to read if you think you have all the answers to the problem of violence and crime.*

Canada, G. (1995). *Fist stick knife gun: A personal history of violence in America.* Boston: Beacon Press.

*Reflecting on his own life and upbringing in the inner city's culture of violence, Geoffrey Canada presents powerful arguments about what causes aggressive criminal behavior, how aggression must be rechanneled, how at-risk children must be cared for, and what specific changes can and must be made in society's laws, attitudes, and norms.*

Friday, N. (1996). *Our looks, our lives: Sex, beauty, power, and the need to be seen.* New York: Harper.

*Best-selling author Nancy Friday takes a careful, critical look at life in the "age of the Empty Package," when looks take precedence over personal qualities, and everyone lusts for Beauty.*

Gay, P. (1994). *The cultivation of hatred.* New York: W. W. Norton & Co.

*Volume 3 of a series exploring the bourgeois experience at the turn of the last century, Peter Gay's book examines the ambivalence of Victorians about aggression, so that it was channeled into sports, duels, wars of "honor," fantasies of "manliness," and finally old-fashioned warfare, prejudice, racism, sexism, and repression.*

Guthrie, R. V. (1998). *Even the rat was white: A historical view of psychology* (2nd ed.). Boston: Allyn and Bacon.

*A Black psychologist takes a look at the historical White bias that has permeated psychology. The book also features contributions to the field made by Black psychologists.*

Judah, T. (1998). *The Serbs, history, myth and the destruction of Yugoslavia.* New Haven, CT: Yale University Press.

*Maligned as the chief villains in the Bosnian and Kosovar conflicts, the Serbs remain a little-known people not much different from other cultures struggling with internal problems, manipulative dictators, and persistent prejudice-based hostilities.*

Kohn, A. (1990). *The brighter side of human nature: Altruism and empathy in everyday life.* New York: Basic Books.

*Uplifting review of the many ways in which people help and cooperate with each other, and the challenges this poses for more cynical views of human nature as essentially aggressive and competitive. The appendix includes The Seville Statement on Violence, UNESCO's manifesto of the incorrectness of brutish or defeatist views of human nature. Rich with examples and case histories as well as practical suggestions for living more helpful, collaborative lives.*

Lorenz, K. (1966). *On aggression.* New York: Bantam Books.

*In this classic, Nobel laureate Konrad Lorenz explores aggression from the point of view of a naturalist and ethologist, asking: What is the function of aggression? And is aggression an inevitable part of human nature?*

Malcolm, N. (1998). *Kosovo: A short history.* New York University Press.

*This 55-mile plateau in southern Serbia should be a political backwater, argues the author, but for its symbolism in an ages-old cultural conflict. He provides a good review of the human sources—individual and societal—of prejudice and war.*

Moghaddam, F. M., Taylor, D. M., & Wright, S. C. (1993). *Social psychology in cross-cultural perspective.* New York: W. H. Freeman and Company.

*An introduction to the cross-cultural revolution that is taking place in social psychology. This book brings together findings on a variety of topics, including attitudes, attribution, social influence, relationships, aggression, and prosocial behavior. A final chapter looks at the social psychology of people making contact across cultures.*

Sternberg, R. J. (1998). *Cupid's arrow: The course of love through time.* New York: Cambridge University Press.

*This is the latest psychological scoop on why people fall in and out of love. Sternberg attempts to bring it all together with his "triangular" theory of love. (The vertices of the triangle are passion, intimacy, and commitment.)*

Tannen, D. (1998). *The argument culture: Moving from debate to dialogue.* New York: Random House.

*Unquestionably, we slip too easily from disagreements to fights, from fights to warfare. What can we do to stop the escalation? Best-selling author of* You Just Don't Understand *and* That's Not What I Meant, *psycholinguist Deborah Tannen shows how our culture encourages us to be adversarial, and just what the cost is in human misery and destruction. Beyond an examination of the elements of our argument culture, Tannen also goes into how we can change—and why we must.*

Watson, L. (1995). *Dark nature: A natural history of evil.* New York: HarperCollins.

*A biologist examines the destructive, aggressive, and otherwise "evil" acts found all over the animal kingdom in an attempt to define an "ecology of evil." The ultimate application, of course, is to human nature. You be the judge of his success.*

## VIDEOS

*The birdman of Alcatraz.* (1962, B&W, 143 min.). Directed by John Frankenheimer; starring Burt Lancaster, Karl Malden, Thelma Ritter, Betty Field, Telly Savalas.

*This is the absorbing true story of convicted murderer Robert Stroud, who devoted his sentence of life in prison to the study of diseases afflicting birds and how to treat them. The film is not a whitewash of Stroud's original character or crimes, but an affecting reflection on society's choice be-*

*tween punishment and rehabilitation and the consequences of that choice for individual and society alike.*

Guyana tragedy: The story of Jim Jones. (1980 [made for TV], color, 192 min.). Directed by William A Graham; starring Powers Boothe, Ned Beatty, Veronica Cartwright, Brad Dourif, LeVar Burton, Randy Quaid, Diana Scarwid, James Earl Jones.

*This is the powerful, detailed recreation of the 1979 mass suicide of over 900 members of Rev. Jim Jones's Peoples Temple in Jonestown, Guyana, and the events in Jones's life and ministry that led the cult to form, leave the United States, and follow Jones to their deaths. It provides vivid reminders of how easily individuals seek meaning and comfort in groups—and the subsequent pressure they feel to conform to group norms, even to disastrous extremes.*

The Ox-Bow incident. (1943, B&W, 75 min.). Directed by William A. Wellman; starring Henry Fonda, Dana Andrews, Anthony Quinn, Harry Morgan, Harry Davenport.

*A group of frontier citizens, outraged by rumors of a murder, takes the law into their own hands and threatens to become a lynch mob. Upsetting and familiar story of how emotion overrules reason when individuals lose their sense of personal responsibility and yield to the brutality of the group mind.*

Six degrees of separation. (1993, color, 111 min.). Directed by Fred Schepisi; starring Stockard Channing, Donald Sutherland, Will Smith, Ian McKellen, Mary Beth Hurt, Bruce Davison, Richard Masur, Anthony Michael Hall.

*Years ago, social psychologists gave people envelopes addressed to strangers in all parts of the world and asked them to use their social networks to have the letters hand-delivered, from friend to friend, in order to reach the addressee. It took the senders on average only five "connector" people between sender and recipient—thus each sender was separated from any randomly identified stranger in the world by only six degrees. Similarly, this film explores the possible connections among those who seem socially unconnected. Based on a true incident, the plot deals with how an affluent New York couple are conned by a young man who claims to be a celebrity's son. Like it or not, the world is perhaps much smaller than we thought.*

Sliding doors. (1998, color, 108 min.). Directed by Peter Howitt; starring Gwyneth Paltrow, John Hannah, John Lynch, Jeanne Tripplehorn, Zara Turner.

*This romantic comedy explores how situations and chance events—like catching or not catching a subway home—can set in motion a sequence of life-changing events. Two parallel stories are told of a woman's experiences after she either does or does not get through the sliding doors in time to catch the departing train.*

The Stepford wives. (1975, color, 115 min.). Directed by Bryan Forbes; starring Katharine Ross, Paula Prentiss, Peter Masterson, Patrick O'Neal.

*What happens when your aspirational reference group's norms require you to sacrifice your identity? After moving to a suburban community, two housewives are pressured to yield to community standards of traditional gender roles, mindlessness, and subservience to their husbands. This is an eerie story of "suburban body snatchers," in which the invaders are not aliens or communists, but social pressures to conform.*

12 angry men. (1957, B&W, 95 min.). Directed by Sidney Lumet; starring Henry Fonda, Lee J. Cobb, E. G. Marshall, Ed Begley, Jack Klugman, Jack Warden, Robert Webber.

*This absorbing drama examines jurors' deliberation over the outcome of a murder trial, in which one outnumbered man argues for acquittal. Though all the action takes place in the jury room without flashbacks, the jurors' recollection of the evidence and eyewitnesses' accounts creates a vivid impression of the trial. This is an elegant portrayal of many social psychological processes: person perception, prejudice, norms, group pressure, and reconstructive memory.*

Welcome to Sarajevo. (1997, color, 101 min.). Directed by Michael Winterbottom; starring Stephen Dillane, Woody Harrelson, Marisa Tomei.

*This realistic look at reporters covering the Bosnian war in Sarajevo in the former Yugoslavia depicts the dilemmas of "studying" social tragedies and war while trying to maintain objectivity—and how hard it is for human beings not to care about others, regardless of efforts not to get involved.*

## CORE CONCEPTS

## PSYCHOLOGY IN YOUR LIFE

**WHAT IS MENTAL DISORDER?**

The medical model takes a "disease" view, while psychology sees mental disorder as an interaction of biological, cognitive, social, and other environmental factors.

**A Caution to Readers:** If you find that you have some signs of mental disorder, don't jump to conclusions.

**HOW ARE MENTAL DISORDERS CLASSIFIED?**

The most widely used system, found in the *DSM-IV*, classifies disorders by their mental and behavioral symptoms.

**Shyness:** If you have it, it doesn't have to be permanent. (And, by the way, it's not a mental disorder.)

**WHAT ARE THE CONSEQUENCES OF LABELING?**

Ideally, accurate diagnoses lead to proper treatments, but diagnoses may also become labels that depersonalize people and ignore the social and cultural contexts in which their problems arise.

**The Plea of Insanity:** It's not a psychological or psychiatric term, and, contrary to popular opinion, it is a defense that is seldom used.

**USING PSYCHOLOGY TO LEARN PSYCHOLOGY: DIAGNOSING YOUR FRIENDS AND FAMILY**

# 13

# Psychopathology

## Chapter Outline

*T*he volunteers knew they were on their own. If they managed to get into the hospital, the five men and three women could only get out by convincing the staff that they were sane. None had ever been diagnosed with a mental illness, but perhaps they were not so "normal" after all: Would a normal person lie to get into such a place? In fact, all were collaborators in an experiment designed to find out whether normality would be recognized in a mental hospital.

The experimenter, David Rosenhan—himself one of the pseudopatients—suspected that terms such as "sanity," "insanity," "schizophrenia," "mental illness," and "abnormal" might have fuzzier boundaries than the psychiatric community thought. He also suspected that some strange behaviors seen in mental patients might originate in the abnormal atmosphere of the mental hospital, rather than in the patients themselves. To test these ideas, Rosenhan and his collaborators decided to see how mental hospital personnel would deal with patients who were not mentally ill.

Individually, they applied for admission at different hospitals, complaining that they had recently heard voices that seemed to say "empty," "hollow," and "thud." Aside from this, they claimed no other symptoms of mental disorder. All used false names, and the four who were mental health professionals gave false occupations—but apart from these fibs, the subjects answered all questions truthfully. They tried to act normally, although the prospect of entering the alien hospital environment made them feel anxious; they also worried about not being admitted and—worse yet—being exposed as frauds. Their concerns vanished quickly, for all readily gained admittance at 12 different hospitals (some did it twice). All but one were diagnosed with "schizophrenia," a major mental disorder often accompanied by hearing imaginary voices.

After admission, the pseudopatients made no further claims of hearing voices or any other abnormal symptoms. Indeed, all wanted to be on their best behavior to gain release. Their only apparent "deviance" involved taking notes on the experience—at first privately and later publicly, when they found that the staff paid little attention. The nursing records indicated that, when the staff did notice, they interpreted the note-taking as part of the patient's illness. (One comment: "Patient engages in writing behavior.") But in spite of the absence of abnormal symptoms, it took an average of 19 days for the pseudopatients to convince the hospital staff that they were ready for discharge. One unfortunate subject wasn't released for almost two months.

Two main findings from this classic study jarred the psychiatric community to its core. First, *no professional staff member at any of the hospitals ever realized that any of Rosenhan's pseudopatients was a fraud.* Of course, the staff may have assumed that the patients had been ill at the time of admission and had improved during their hospitalization. But that possibility did not let the professionals off Rosenhan's hook: Despite apparently normal behavior, not one of the pseudopatients was ever labeled as "normal" or "well" while in the hospital. And, upon discharge, they were still seen as having schizophrenia—but "in remission."

The mistaken diagnosis does not suggest that the hospital staff members were unskilled or unfeeling. The fact that they did not detect the pseudopatients' normal behavior is probably because they spent little time observing and interacting with the patients. Most of the time they kept to themselves in a glassed-in central office that patients called "the cage." As Rosenhan (1973) said:

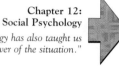

Chapter 12:
Social Psychology

*Social psychology has also taught us about the "power of the situation."*

> It could be a mistake, and a very unfortunate one, to consider that what happened to us derived from malice or stupidity on the part of the staff. Quite the contrary, our overwhelming impression of them was of people who really cared, who were committed and who were uncommonly intelligent. Where they failed, as they sometimes did painfully, it would be more accurate to attribute those failures to the environment in which they, too, found themselves than to personal callousness. Their perceptions and behavior were controlled by the situation. . . . (p. 257)

A second finding tells us volumes about the patients and the nature of mental disorder itself: To everyone's surprise, *the hospital patients readily detected the ruse, even though the professional staff did not.* The pseudopatients reported that the other patients regularly voiced their suspicions: "You're not crazy. You're a journalist or a professor. . . . You're checking up on the hospital." In his report of this experience, entitled "On Being Sane in Insane Places," Rosenhan (1973) noted dryly: "The fact that the patients often recognized normality when staff did not raises important questions" (p. 252). You will hear the echo of these "important questions" as we critically examine of the medical view of mental disorder in this chapter.

Please note that Rosenhan did not deny the existence of mental abnormalities. People *do* suffer the anguish of psychopathology. According to a study conducted by the National Institutes of Mental Health, at any time about 15.4% of the population suffers from diagnosable mental health problems. Another study found that, during any given year, the behaviors of over 56 million Americans meet the criteria for a diagnosable mental disorder (Carson, Butcher, & Mineka, 1996; Regier et al., 1993). Over the life span, as many as 32% of Americans will suffer from some psychological disorder (Regier et al., 1988).

Neither did Rosenhan deny that the initial diagnoses given his pseudopatients were justified. After all, they claimed to be hearing voices—a strong indicator of abnormality. The problem was that their caretakers never did see anything but abnormality. Rosenhan's quarrel with mental hospitals and with the psychiatric establishment was aimed at the dehumanizing hospital environment and the dehumanizing assumptions and expectations made about mental "illness." Those assumptions, he argued, blind mental health professionals to the needs of their patients. As we look at the problem of diagnosing and describing mental disorder in this chapter, it will be helpful to keep Rosenhan's study in mind.

Advertisements, like the one shown here, have gone a long way toward correcting our views of mental illness and creating sympathy for its sufferers.

## WHAT IS MENTAL DISORDER?

Distinguishing "normal" from "abnormal" is no simple task. Consider, for example, how you would classify such eccentric personalities as Robin Williams or Madonna or Dennis Rodman. And what about a soldier who risks his or her life in combat: Is that "normal"? Or consider a grief-stricken woman who is unable to return to her normal routine three months after her husband died: Does she have a mental disorder?

Three classic symptoms suggest severe mental disorder: *hallucinations, delusions,* and extreme *affective disturbances.* **Hallucinations** are false sensory experiences, such as hearing nonexistent voices (as Rosenhan's pseudopatients said they did). **Delusions** are disorders of logical thinking. If you think you are the President of the United States (and you are not), you have a symptom of psychopathology. Similarly, those whose **affect** (emotion) is, for no apparent reason, depressed, anxious, or manic—or those who seems to have no emotional response at all—have yet other signs of mental disorder. The clinician, however, must be aware that any of these may also arise from other causes, such as drug reactions.

Beyond such signs of distress, the experts do not always agree, however. What is abnormal and what is not becomes a judgment call, a judgment made more difficult because no sharp boundary separates normal from abnormal thought and behavior. It may be helpful to think of mental disorder as part of a *continuum* ranging from the absence of disorder to severe disorder, as shown in Figure 13.1.

The "abnormal" region of this continuum is sometimes referred to as the region of *psychopathology* or *mental disorder*—or even *mental illness.* In general, we can define **psychopathology** as any pattern of emotions, behaviors, or thoughts inappropriate to the situation and leading to personal distress or the inability to achieve important goals. In everyday terms, this may mean unhappiness, anxiety, despair, worries, addiction, anger, or loss of contact with the surrounding world. Of course, occasional periods of worry, self-doubt, sadness, and escapism are all part of normal life. But taken to excess, these same experiences become symptoms of mental disorder. It is a matter of degree; it is a matter of judgment.

In this section of the chapter, we will focus on two contrasting views of mental disorder. One, coming to us from the profession of psychiatry, is sometimes called the "medical model" of mental disorder. It portrays mental problems much as it does

**Hallucinations:** False sensory experiences suggestive of mental disorder. Hallucinations can also be caused by drugs.

**Delusions:** Disorders of logical thinking. Delusions are the hallmark of paranoid disorders.

**Affect:** A term referring to emotion or mood.

**Psychopathology:** Any pattern of emotions, behaviors, or thoughts inappropriate to the situation and leading to personal distress or the inability to achieve important goals.

FIGURE 13.1: The Spectrum of Mental Disorder

Mental disorder occurs on a spectrum that ranges from the absence of signs of pathology to severe disturbances, such as is found in schizophrenia. The important point is that there is *no* sharp distinction that divides those with mental disorders from those who are "normal."

| No disorder | Mild disorder | Moderate disorder | Severe disorder |
|---|---|---|---|
| • Absence of signs of mental disorder<br>• Absence of behavior problems<br>• No problems with interpersonal relationships | • Few signs of unease or distress<br>• Few problem behaviors<br>• Few difficulties in interpersonal relationships | • Signs of unease or distress that are more pronounced or occur more frequently<br>• More distinct behavior problems<br>• More frequent difficulties with relationships | • Clear signs of mental disorder meeting *DSM-IV* criteria<br>• Severe behavior problems meeting *DSM-IV* criteria<br>• Many poor relationships or lack of relationships with others |

physical disorders: as sickness that occurs largely within the afflicted person. The other view, a psychological view, sees mental disorders as the result of multiple factors both inside and outside the person. As our Core Concept puts it:

**CORE CONCEPT**

The medical model takes a "disease" view, while psychology sees mental disorder as an interaction of biological, cognitive, social, and other environmental factors.

No matter how we conceptualize psychopathology, nearly everyone agrees that mental disorder is widespread. It touches the daily lives of millions. It can be insidious, working its way into thoughts and feelings, diminishing its victims' emotional and physical well-being, along with their personal and family relationships. And it can create an enormous financial burden through lost productivity, lost wages, and the high costs of prolonged treatment. Yet, the way people conceptualize psychopathology does have a consequence: It determines how they will attempt to treat it—with drugs, charms, rituals, talk, torture, surgery, hospitalization, or commitment to an "insane asylum."

In this section of the chapter, we will find that the two main ways of looking at psychopathology, the medical model and the psychological view, are often at odds. Some of this conflict is territorial, resulting from professional infighting over turf. But some of the conflict has historical roots, as we shall see next.

## Evolving Concepts of Mental Disorder

In the ancient world, people assumed that supernatural powers were everywhere, accounting for good fortune, disease, and disaster—even for the rise and fall of nations. In this context, psychopathology was caused by demons and spirits that had taken possession of the person's mind and body (Sprock & Blashfield, 1991). If you had been living at that time, your daily routine would have included rituals aimed at outwitting or placating these supernatural beings.

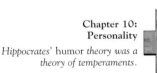

**Chapter 10: Personality**

*Hippocrates' humor theory was a theory of temperaments.*

In about 400 B.C., the Greek physician Hippocrates (Hip-POCK-ra-teez) may have taken humanity's first step toward a scientific view of mental disturbance when he declared that abnormal behavior has physical causes. He taught his disciples to interpret the symptoms of psychopathology as an imbalance among four body fluids called "humors": blood, phlegm (mucus), black bile, and yellow bile. Those with an excess of black bile, for example, were inclined to melancholy or depression, while those who had an abundance of blood were sanguine, or warmhearted. With this revolutionary idea, Hippocrates incorporated mental disorder into medicine, and his view influenced educated people in the Western world until the end of the Roman Empire.

Then, in the Middle Ages, superstition eclipsed the Hippocratic model of mental disorder. Under the influence of the Church, physicians and clergy reverted to the old ways of explaining abnormality in terms of demons and witchcraft. In these harsh times, the Inquisition was driven by the belief that unusual behavior was the work of the Devil. The "cure" involved attempts to drive out the demons who possessed the unfortunate victim's soul. This mind-set resulted in thousands of mentally disturbed people being tortured and executed all across the European continent. And in 1692, the same view of mental disorder led the young colony in Salem, Massachusetts, to place a group of its residents on trial for witchcraft (Karlsen, 1987). A group of young girls had frightened the community with a rash of convulsions and reports of sensory disturbances. Convinced that these were signs of demonic possession, the court convicted and executed twenty of those the girls accused of "possessing" them. A modern analysis of the Salem witch trials has concluded that the girls were probably suffering from poisoning by a fungus growing on rye grain—the same fungus that produces the hallucinogenic drug LSD (Caporeal, 1976; Matossian, 1982, 1989).

Even today the ancient ideas about spirit possession, witchcraft, and mental disturbance hold sway in some quarters. A well-known American evangelist recently declared on television that the Devil causes mental illness. Many other Americans believe that the full moon drives people to "lunacy." (It does not.) Similar folk beliefs permeate many cultures. Some Africans, for example, believe that mental disorder results from sorcery (Sow, 1977); the Haitian belief in voodoo has the same origins. Likewise, Thais assert that clever spirits called *pi* can create mental disturbances, while peoples of the northern Mediterranean credit the "evil eye" with supernatural powers that cause physical or mental affliction.

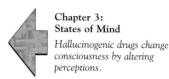
**THE MEDICAL MODEL**  In the latter part of the eighteenth century, the "illness" view that originated with Hippocrates reemerged with the rise of science. The resulting **medical model** held that mental disorders are *diseases* of the mind that, like ordinary physical diseases, have objective causes, and require specific treatments. People began to perceive individuals with psychological problems as *sick* (suffering from illness), rather than as demon-possessed or immoral. And what a difference a new theory made! It no longer made sense to treat mental disorder by torture and abuse. The new view of mental illness brought sweeping reforms that were implemented in "asylums" for the "insane." In this supportive atmosphere, many patients actually improved—even thrived—on rest, contemplation, and simple but useful work (Maher & Maher, 1985). Unfortunately, the initially therapeutic asylums turned into warehouses of neglect, as a result of overcrowding and political pressures.

A painting of the Salem witchcraft trials, Salem, Massachusetts, 1692. Twenty people were executed before the hysteria subsided.

Despite such problems, however, the medical model was unquestionably an improvement over the demon model. Yet, modern psychologists think that the medical model has its own weaknesses. They point out that the assumption of "illness" leads to a doctor-knows-best approach in which the therapist takes all the responsibility for diagnosing the illness and prescribing treatment. Under the traditional medical model, a "mental patient" would have no part in planning a treatment program. The patient becomes a passive recipient of medication and advice, rather than an active treatment participant learning how to manage his or her thoughts and behaviors. Psychologists believe that this attitude wrongly encourages dependency on the doctor, encourages unnecessary drug therapy, and does little to help the patient develop good coping skills.

Not incidentally, the doctor-knows-best approach also takes responsibility away from psychologists and gives it to psychiatrists. Psychologists bristle at the medical model's implication that their treatment of mental "illnesses" should be done under the supervision of a physician. In effect, the medical model assigns psychologists to second-class professional status. As you can see, ownership of the whole territory of mental disorder is hotly contested.

**PSYCHOLOGICAL MODELS**  What do psychologists have to offer in place of the medical model? The psychological alternative gives equal footing to cognitive, environmental, and biological explanations. Thus, if you are depressed, your problem

**Medical model:** The view that mental disorders are diseases that, like ordinary physical diseases, have objective causes and require specific treatments.

is seen as a disorder of thought and circumstances, as well as the brain. This view opens up the possibility of treatment on many fronts.

Like the medical model, this psychological perspective began to emerge most clearly at the end of the eighteenth century, helped along by the flamboyant work of Franz Anton Mesmer (1734–1815). Mesmer believed (incorrectly) that many disorders were caused by disruptions in the flow of a mysterious force that he called *animal magnetism*. He unveiled several new techniques to study animal magnetism, including one originally called *mesmerism*—which we now call hypnosis (Darnton, 1968; Pattie, 1994).

Mesmer's animal magnetism theory was eventually discredited by scientists, but his hypnotic techniques were embraced by many clinicians, including a prominent French neurologist, Jean-Martin Charcot (1825–1893). With the aid of hypnosis, Charcot dramatically demonstrated that he could remove the symptoms of "hysteria," a mysterious disorder that presented physical symptoms, such as paralysis of a limb, but no neurological disease. Moreover, Charcot showed that hypnosis had the power to produce the symptoms of hysteria even in healthy individuals. This work suggested that the disorder was **psychogenic** (psychologically caused).

One of Charcot's students, the brilliant young Sigmund Freud, began his own experiments with hypnosis. These experiments eventually led to Freud's revolutionary idea that psychopathology arises from pressures originating in the unconscious mind. Eventually Freud abandoned hypnosis, replacing it with his "talking cure," which he claimed to be a more effective system for revealing unconscious conflicts and for treating psychological disorders. However, he continued to teach that mental illness arose from desires, conflicts, and traumatic memories in the unconscious.

The modern psychological approach, however, goes well beyond these prescientific theories. Their primary legacy in clinical psychology is the conviction that psychopathology involves disturbances in thoughts and emotions—disturbances that the victim may not fully understand. In the place of Freud's psychoanalytic theory of mental disorder, most clinical psychologists have now turned to two other psychological perspectives: *behaviorism* and *cognitive psychology*—both of which have a solid base in scientific research. We will look at both of these more closely.

*THE COGNITIVE–BEHAVIORAL APPROACH*  A new understanding of psychopathology combines what were once the two warring camps of cognitive psychology and behaviorism. In brief, cognitive psychology looks inward, emphasizing mental processes, while behaviorism looks outward, emphasizing the influence of the environment. A major shift in psychological thinking in recent years sees these two traditions as opposite sides of the same coin.

The **behavioral perspective** tells us that abnormal behaviors can be acquired in the same fashion as healthy behaviors—through behavioral learning. This view focuses on our behavior and the environmental conditions, such as rewards and punishments, that maintain it. For example, the behavioral perspective would suggest that a fear of public speaking could be the result of a humiliating public speaking experience and a subsequent avoidance of any opportunity to develop public speaking skills.

By discovering the conditions that initiate and maintain an undesirable behavior, the clinician can recommend an effective treatment (Emmelkamp, 1986). Thus, a behavioral therapist treating a fear of public speaking would focus on the conditions under which the individual felt fearful. Does the fear occur in a group of friends or only with strangers? How big does the group have to be in order to produce symptoms? Is the fearful response rewarded in some way—with attention or sympathy? In general, behavioral therapy emphasizes identifying problem behaviors, analyzing the conditions that keep them in place, and identifying ways to encourage new behaviors, especially through reinforcement. Instead of probing for memories of long-repressed traumas, as a Freudian analyst might do, the behavioral perspective deals with the present conditions that keep the disorder alive.

**Chapter 3**
**States of Mind**

*When hypnotized, some people respond to suggestion with changes in perception, memory, and motivation.*

**Chapter 14:**
**Therapies for Mental Disorder**

*Freud's "talking cure" was also called "psychoanalysis."*

**Chapter 10:**
**Personality**

*Freud proposed that unconscious needs and conflicts drive much of our behavior.*

**Chapter 6:**
**Learning and Remembering**

*Behavioral learning includes operant conditioning and classical conditioning.*

**Psychogenic:** Caused by psychological factors.

**Behavioral perspective:** The psychological view suggesting that abnormal behaviors can be acquired through behavioral learning, especially by operant conditioning and classical conditioning.

The **cognitive perspective,** the other half of the new cognitive–behavioral view, suggests that we must also consider how people *perceive* or *think* about themselves and their relations with other people. Among the important cognitive variables are these: whether people believe they have control over events in their lives (an internal or external locus of control), their ability to cope with threat and stress, and their patterns of attributing behavior to either situational or personal factors (Bandura, 1986).

The **cognitive–behavioral approach,** then combines both the cognitive and the behavioral perspectives. From this view, then, a fear of public speaking can be understood in terms of both behavioral and cognitive learning. The complete picture of the problem requires looking for contributing factors both inside and outside the person.

*THE BIOPSYCHOLOGY OF MADNESS*  Although most psychologists reject the medical model, they do not deny the influence of biology on thought and behavior. Modern biopsychology assumes that mental disturbances involve the biology of the brain or nervous system in some way, and this view is taking an increasingly prominent position alongside the cognitive–behavioral approach in our understanding of psychopathology. An explosion of research in neuroscience during the last decade makes it impossible to ignore the role of the brain as a complex organ whose mental functions depend on a delicate balance of chemicals and ever-changing circuits. Subtle alterations in the brain's tissue or in its chemical messengers—the neurotransmitters—can profoundly alter thoughts and behaviors. Genetic factors, brain injury, infection, and learning are a few of the factors that can tip the balance toward psychopathology.

Many links between psychological disorders and specific brain abnormalities have been revealed by brain scanning techniques, such as PET scans and MRI (Gur & Pearlson, 1993). Such work has, for example, linked extreme tendencies toward violence with brain tumors located in the amygdala, a part of the limbic system known to be associated with aggressive behavior. Psychology also recognizes that drug therapies can alleviate certain symptoms of psychological disorders (Elkin et al., 1989; Kane & Marder, 1993; Papolos & Papolos, 1987; Schatzberg, 1991).

On the heredity front, advances in the field of behavioral genetics may eventually allow researchers to identify genes associated with specific psychological disorders (Joyce, 1989; Kelsoe et al., 1993; Kendler & Diehl, 1993; Rutter et al., 1990). So far, however, only a few genetic abnormalities have been linked with specific mental problems despite the fact that some of the most severe pathologies, such as schizophrenia and bipolar disorder, do run in families. It is likely that most such disorders are the result of multiple genes interacting with forces in the environment (Boomsma, Anokhin, & de Geus, 1997). Stay tuned for further developments on the genetics of psychopathology.

*AN INTERACTIONIST VIEW*  Psychologists today increasingly view psychopathology as the product of an *interaction* among biological, behavioral, and cognitive factors (Cowan, 1988). For example, a genetic predisposition may make a person vulnerable to depression by affecting neurotransmitter levels or hormone levels. At the same time, psychological or social stressors, such as the loss of a love or certain learned grief behaviors, may be required for the disorder to develop fully. And why does one person seem to get over a relationship breakup fairly quickly, while another suffers prolonged grief reaction? A quick recovery may be attributable to a supportive social environment, mental "hardiness," or good coping skills. Additionally, one individual may be genetically better equipped than another to deal with stress. Effective treatment must, therefore, reflect these individual differences in biology, cognition, and environment.

**Chapter 10:**
**Personality**

*Rotter's locus-of-control theory comes from the cognitive perspective on learning and personality.*

**Chapter 6:**
**Learning and Remembering**

*Behavioral learning emphasizes the environment, and cognitive learning emphasizes mental processes.*

**Chapter 2:**
**Biopsychology**

*Neurotransmitters are chemicals used for communication between neurons across the synapse.*

**Chapter 2:**
**Biopsychology**

*The field of behavior genetics searches for the genetic basis of personality and mental disorder.*

**Cognitive perspective:** The psychological view suggesting that abnormal behaviors are influenced by mental processes—by how people perceive or think about themselves and their relations with other people.

**Cognitive–behavioral approach:** A psychological view that combines both the cognitive and the behavioral perspectives in attempting to understand behavior and mental processes.

**Chapter 9:**
**Stress, Health, and Well-Being**

*Social support and hardiness allow some people to deal with stress better than others.*

## Indicators of Abnormality

Clinicians often disagree about the causes of mental disorders. Yet they may look for the same indicators of abnormality when they diagnose psychopathology (Rosenhan & Seligman, 1995). What are these indicators?

1. *Distress.* Does the individual show unusual or prolonged levels of unease or anxiety? For example, almost anyone will get nervous before an important test, but feeling so overwhelmed with unpleasant emotions that concentration becomes impossible is a sign of abnormality.
2. *Maladaptiveness.* Does the person act in ways that interfere with his or her well-being or the needs of society? We can see this, for example, in someone who drinks so heavily that she or he cannot hold down a job or drive a car without endangering others.
3. *Irrationality.* Does the person act or talk in ways that are irrational or incomprehensible to others? A woman who converses with her long-dead sister, whose voice she hears in her head, is behaving irrationally. Likewise, behavior or emotional responses that are inappropriate to the situation, such as laughing at the scene of a tragedy, show irrational loss of contact with one's social environment.
4. *Unpredictability.* Does the individual behave erratically and inconsistently at different times or from one situation to another, as if experiencing a loss of control? For example, a child who suddenly smashes a fragile toy with his fist for no apparent reason is behaving unpredictably. Similarly, a manager who treats employees compassionately one day and abusively the next is acting unpredictably.
5. *Unconventionality and undesirable behavior.* Does the person behave in ways that are statistically rare and violate social norms of what is legally or morally acceptable or desirable? Being merely "unusual" is not a sign of abnormality—so feel free to dye your hair red and green and stroll through the mall at Christmastime. But if you decide to take rare behavior beyond the bounds of social acceptability by strolling naked in the mall, that would be considered abnormal.
6. *Observer discomfort.* Does the person create discomfort in others by making them feel threatened or distressed in some way? Bullying behavior is abnormal on this count. So is the behavior of a stranger who sits down beside you in a restaurant and begins to question you loudly.

Is the presence of just one indicator enough to demonstrate abnormality? In fact, clinicians are more confident in labeling behavior as "abnormal" when two or more of the six indicators are present. Moreover, none of these six criteria is a condition shared by all forms of disorder. Different diagnoses, we shall see later in the chapter, include different combinations from the above list. The more extreme and prevalent the indicators are, the more confident psychologists can be about identifying an abnormal condition.

While these indicators may suggest abnormality, the clinician still must make a diagnosis by deciding which disorder it is. This can be a difficult task because psychopathology takes many forms. Some disorders may have a familiar ring: *depression, phobias,* and *panic disorder.* You may be less well acquainted with others, such as *Tourette's disorder, conversion disorder,* or *catatonic schizophrenia.* In all, a bewildering 300-plus varieties of psychopathology are

Behaviors that make other people feel uncomfortable or threatened may be a sign of abnormality.

described in the *Diagnostic and Statistical Manual of Mental Disorders* (4th edition), known by clinicians and researchers as the **DSM-IV** ("DSM-four"), used by mental health professionals of all backgrounds to describe and diagnose psychopathology. So influential is this system that we will devote the entire middle section of this chapter to an explanation of it.

**DSM-IV:** The latest revision of the *Diagnostic and Statistical Manual of Mental Disorders,* published by the American Psychiatric Association; the most widely accepted classification system in the United States.

## PSYCHOLOGY IN YOUR LIFE

## A Caution to Readers

As you read about the symptoms of mental disorder, you are likely to begin wondering about your own mental health. This is a hazard that all students studying abnormal psychology face. To see what we mean, you might answer the following questions, which are based on the six indicators of abnormality discussed earlier.

1. Have you had periods of time when you felt "blue" for no apparent reason? (distress)
2. Have you ever gone to a party on a night when you knew you should be studying? (maladaptiveness)
3. Have you had an experience in which you thought you heard or saw something that wasn't really there? (irrationality)
4. Have you had a flash of temper in which you said something that you later regretted? (unpredictability)
5. Have you had unusual thoughts that you told no one about? (unconventionality)

6. Have you made someone else distressed because of something you said or did? (observer discomfort)

The fact is that almost everyone will answer "yes" to at least one—and perhaps all—of these questions. This does not necessarily mean abnormality. Whether you, or anyone else, is normal or abnormal is a matter of degree and frequency—and opinion.

So, as we begin to take a close look at specific mental disorders in the next section of the chapter, you will most likely find some symptoms that you have experienced. So will your classmates. Even though they may not say so, most other students will find themselves in one or more of the disorders that we will be studying. (A similar problem is common among medical students, who begin to notice that they, too, have symptoms of the physical diseases they learn about.) You should realize that *this is normal,* although it may cause readers some distress. One reason, of course, that you may see yourself in this chapter arises from the fact that no sharp line separates psychopathology from normalcy. All psychological disorders in-

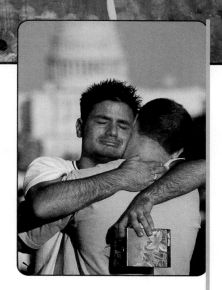

Sadness or crying is not necessarily a sign of abnormality. Some occasions call for sadness and tears.

volve exaggerations of quite normal tendencies. Healthy people may become depressed, for example—although they do not *stay* depressed or develop the depths of despair that clinically depressed people do. We are not suggesting that concerns about mental disorder should be taken lightly, however. If, after reading this chapter, you suspect that you may have a problem, you should discuss it with a professional.

## Check Your Understanding

1. RECALL: *In Rosenhan's study, who discovered that the "pseudopatients" were feigning mental illness?*
   a. psychiatrists
   b. psychologists
   c. nurses and aides working on the ward
   d. other patients

*continued*

2. **APPLICATION:** *Which of the following symptoms most clearly suggests the presence of abnormality?*
   **a.** hallucinations
   **b.** worries
   **c.** unusual behavior
   **d.** creativity

3. **RECALL:** *Hippocrates proposed that mental disorder was caused by*
   **a.** possession by demons.
   **b.** an imbalance in four body fluids.
   **c.** a fungus growing on rye grain.
   **d.** traumatic memories in the unconscious.

4. **RECALL:** *The behavioral perspective emphasizes the influence of _____, while the cognitive perspective emphasizes _____.*
   **a.** the environment/mental processes
   **b.** conscious processes/unconscious processes

   **c.** heredity/environment
   **d.** medical factors/psychological factors

5. **UNDERSTANDING THE CORE CONCEPT:** *Which of the following would be least likely to be noticed by a clinician using strictly the medical model of mental disorder?*
   **a.** delusions
   **b.** severe disturbances in affect
   **c.** an unhealthy family environment
   **d.** a degenerative brain disease

**ANSWERS:**     1. d     2. a     3. b     4. a     5. c

---

## HOW ARE MENTAL DISORDERS CLASSIFIED?

Imagine that you have entered a music store looking for a particular CD. Anything you could possibly want is there, but the employees do not bother grouping albums by musical category: They just dump everything randomly into the bins. With so many selections, but no organization, shopping there would pose an impossible problem—which is why record stores never operate this way. Instead, they organize selections into a small number of categories, such as rock, blues, classical, rap, country, and jazz. In much the same way, the *Diagnostic and Statistical Manual of Mental Disorders* (4th ed.) brings order to the profusion of more than 300 recognized mental disorders by organizing them into categories. Because it is the most widely used system for classifying mental disorders, we will use it as the scheme for organizing the disorders discussed in this chapter.

What is the organizing pattern employed by the *DSM-IV?* Symptoms, not causes or treatments, are the key. It groups nearly all the recognized forms of psychopathology into categories, according to mental and behavioral symptoms, such as anxiety, depression, sexual problems, and substance abuse. Our Core Concept states:

 **The most widely used system, found in the *DSM-IV,* classifies disorders by their mental and behavioral symptoms.**

It would be impossible to cover all the recognized mental disorders in this chapter. Therefore we must focus on those that you are most likely to encounter in daily life and in the study of psychopathology in more advanced courses. All of the disorders discussed in this chapter appear in Table 13.1. (Please note, however, that Table 13.1 also includes disorders that are discussed elsewhere in this book.)

### Overview of the *DSM-IV* Classification System

The latest revision of the *Diagnostic and Statistical Manual of Mental Disorders,* the *DSM-IV,* was published in 1994 by the American Psychiatric Association. It offers practitioners the substantial advantage of a common and concise language for the description of mental disorders. It also contains specific criteria for diagnosing each one of the more than 300 disorders included between its covers. Even though the

TABLE 13.1: Some Important *DSM-IV* Disorders

| *DSM-IV* CATEGORY | PRIMARY SYMPTOMS |
|---|---|
| **AFFECTIVE DISORDERS**<br>Depressive disorders<br>Bipolar disorder | Excitement or depression (extreme forms may be psychotic) |
| **ANXIETY DISORDERS**<br>Panic disorder<br>Agoraphobia<br>Specific phobias<br>Obsessive–compulsive disorder<br>Posttraumatic stress disorder (Chapter 9) | Fears, panic attacks, anxiety |
| **SOMATOFORM DISORDERS**<br>Conversion disorders<br>Hypochondriasis | Physical symptoms or overconcern with physical health |
| **DISSOCIATIVE DISORDERS**<br>Dissociative fugue<br>Depersonalization disorder<br>Dissociative identity disorder | Nonpsychotic fragmentation of the personality |
| **EATING DISORDERS**<br>Anorexia nervosa<br>Bulimia | Extreme dieting or binging and purging |
| **SCHIZOPHRENIA AND OTHER PSYCHOTIC DISORDERS**<br>Disorganized schizophrenia<br>Catatonic schizophrenia<br>Paranoid schizophrenia<br>Undifferentiated schizophrenia | Psychotic deterioration of the personality or paranoid disturbances of logic and reasoning |
| **PERSONALITY DISORDERS**<br>Narcissistic personality disorder<br>Antisocial personality disorder | Chronic disorders affecting all parts of the personality |
| **ADJUSTMENT DISORDERS AND OTHER CONDITIONS THAT MAY BE A FOCUS OF CLINICAL ATTENTION** | The patient has problems, but not a major mental disorder |

manual was developed primarily by psychiatrists, its terminology has been adopted by clinicians of all stripes, including psychiatrists, psychologists, and social workers. In addition, its terminology is considered to be the standard by most health insurance companies in determining what treatments they will pay for—a fact that gives the *DSM-IV* enormous economic influence.

The fourth edition of the *DSM* has brought with it some big changes in the way we describe mental disorder. For example, it has banished the term "neurosis" from the official language of psychiatry (although you will frequently hear the term used in more casual conversation). Originally, a **neurotic disorder** or **neurosis** was conceived of as a relatively common pattern of subjective distress or self-defeating behavior which did not show signs of brain abnormalities or grossly irrational thinking. In short, a "neurotic" was someone who might be unhappy or dissatisfied, but not considered dangerously ill or out of touch with reality. In the *DSM-IV*, the term "neurosis" has been replaced by the term "disorder" (Carson et al., 1996; Holmes, 1994).

In contrast, a **psychotic disorder** or **psychosis** was previously thought to differ from neurosis in both the quality and severity of symptoms. A condition was

**Neurotic disorder** or **neurosis:**
Before the *DSM-IV*, these were terms used to describe a pattern of subjective distress or self-defeating behavior that did not show signs of brain abnormalities or grossly irrational thinking.

**Psychotic disorder** or **psychosis:**
A disorder involving profound disturbances in perception, rational thinking, or affect.

designated as psychotic if it involved profound disturbances in perception, rational thinking or affect (emotion). Using previous editions of the *DSM*, a clinician would have been more likely to diagnose severe depression, for example, as "psychotic." In the *DSM-IV,* the term "psychotic" is restricted mainly to a loss of contact with reality, as is found in the *schizophrenic* disorders, which we shall discuss below (Carson et al., 1996; Holmes, 1994).

As you may have surmised from its origins in psychiatry, the *DSM-IV* has close ties to the medical model of mental illness. Although psychologists were invited to participate in the development of the *DSM-IV,* the project was dominated by psychiatry. Its language is the language of medicine—symptoms, syndromes, diagnoses, and diseases—and its final form is a curious mixture of science and tradition. (Note: It contains no diagnosis of "normal.") Yet, in contrast with early versions of the manual, which had a distinctly Freudian flavor, the *DSM-IV* manages, for the most part, to avoid endorsing theories of cause or treatment. It also differs from early versions of the *DSM* by giving extensive and specific descriptions of the symptoms of each disorder. So, while the *DSM-IV* has its critics, the need for a common language of mental disorder has brought it wide acceptance. For better or worse, it currently serves as the standard system for diagnosing and classifying mental disorders in the United States.

Let us turn now to a sampling of disorders described in the *DSM-IV.* A look at Table 13.1 will help you understand how the manual classifies these disorders. We begin with those that involve extremes of mood: the *affective disorders*.

## Affective Disorders

Everyone, of course, experiences occasional strong or unpleasant emotional reactions. Emotionality is a normal part of our ability to interpret and adapt to our world. However, when moods career out of control, soaring to extreme elation or plunging to deep depression, the diagnosis will probably be one of the **affective disorders.** The clinician will also suspect an affective disorder when an individual's moods are consistently inappropriate to the situation. Here we will discuss the two best-known of these affective disturbances: *bipolar disorder* and *unipolar depression*.

**BIPOLAR DISORDER**  Wide swings of mood, unexplained by events in a person's life, signify a form of mood disturbance, often called *manic–depressive disorder.* The *DSM-IV* calls it **bipolar disorder.** The alternating periods of **mania** (excessive elation or manic excitement) and the profound sadness of **depression** represent the two "poles." During the manic phase, the individual becomes euphoric, energetic, hyperactive, talkative, and emotionally wound tight like a spring.

It is not unusual for people, swept up in mania, to spend their life savings on extravagant purchases or to engage promiscuously in a number of sexual liaisons or other potentially high-risk actions. When the mania begins to diminish, they are left trying to deal with the damage and predicaments they have created during their frenetic period. Soon, in the depressive phase, a dark wave of depression sweeps over the mind, producing symptoms indistinguishable from the "unipolar" depression we will discuss below. Biologically speaking, however, these two forms of depression are different: We know this because the antidepressant drugs that work well on unipolar depression are not usually effective for bipolar disorder.

The duration and frequency of the mood disturbances in bipolar disorder vary from person to person. Some people experience long periods of normal functioning punctuated by occasional, brief manic or depressive episodes. A small percentage of unfortunate individuals go right from manic episodes to clinical depression and back again in continuous, unending cycles that are devastating to them, their families, their friends, and their coworkers.

A genetic component in bipolar disorder is well established, although the exact genes involved have not been pinpointed (Plomin, Owen, & McGuffin, 1994).

**Chapter 8:**
**Emotion and Motivation**

*Mental disorders tell psychologists much about emotional processes.*

**Affective disorders:** Abnormal disturbances in emotion or mood, including bipolar disorder and unipolar disorder.

**Bipolar disorder:** A mental abnormality involving swings of mood from mania to depression.

**Mania:** Pathologically excessive elation or manic excitement.

**Depression:** Pathological sadness or despair.

**Chapter 14:**
**Therapies for Mental Disorder**

*Antidepressant drugs are now used to treat a variety of disorders.*

While only 1% of the general population has bipolar attacks, having an identical twin afflicted with the problem inflates one's chances to about 70% (Allen, 1976; Tsuang & Faraone, 1990). The fact that bipolar disorder usually responds well to medication also suggests biological factors at work.

**UNIPOLAR DEPRESSION**   If you fail an important examination, lose a job, or lose a love, it is normal to feel depressed. If a close friend dies, it is also normal to feel depressed. But if you remain depressed for weeks or months, long after the depressing event has passed, then you may have the clinically significant depressive disorder called **unipolar depression,** the commonest of all major mental disturbances. Novelist William Styron (1990) writes movingly about his own experience with severe depression. The pain he endured convinced him that clinical depression is much more than a bad mood: He characterized it as "a daily presence, blowing over me in cold gusts" and "a veritable howling tempest in the brain" that can begin with a "gray drizzle of horror." Unipolar depression does not give way to manic periods.

Psychologist Martin Seligman (1973, 1975) has called depression the "common cold" of psychological problems because nearly everyone has suffered it at some time. In the United States, depression accounts for the majority of all mental hospital admissions, but it is still believed to be underdiagnosed and undertreated (Robins, Locke, & Regier, 1991). *The Wall Street Journal* estimates that depression costs Americans about $43 billion each year, including the costs of hospitalization, therapy, and lost productivity (Miller, 1993). But the human cost cannot be measured in dollars. Countless people in the throes of depression may feel worthless, lack appetite, withdraw from friends and family, have difficulty sleeping, lose their jobs, and become agitated or lethargic. In severe cases, they may also have psychotic distortions of reality. Most worrisome of all, depressed persons run a high risk of suicide.

Cross-cultural studies indicate that the incidence of major depression varies widely throughout the world, as Table 13.2 shows. While some of the variation may be the result of differences in reporting and in readiness or reluctance to seek help for depression, other factors seem to be at work, too. In Taiwan and Korea, for example, these include low rates of marital separation and divorce—factors known to be associated with high risk of depression in virtually all cultures. On the other hand, the stresses of war have undoubtedly inflated the rate of depression in Lebanon (Horgan, 1996; Weissman et al., 1996).

Dutch artist Vincent Van Gogh showed signs of bipolar disorder. This problem seems to have a high incidence among highly creative people.

**TABLE 13.2:**   Lifetime Risk of a Depressive Episode Lasting a Year or More

| | |
|---|---|
| Taiwan | 1.5% |
| Korea | 2.9% |
| Puerto Rico | 4.3% |
| United States | 5.2% |
| Germany | 9.2% |
| Canada | 9.6% |
| New Zealand | 11.6% |
| France | 16.4% |
| Lebanon | 19% |

**Unipolar depression:** A form of depression that does not alternate with mania.

FIGURE 13.2:  Seasonal Affective Disorder

People who suffer from seasonal affective disorder are most likely to experience symptoms of depression during months with shortened periods of sunlight.

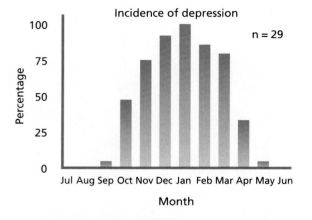

Incidence of depression

n = 29

Percentage (y-axis: 0, 25, 50, 75, 100)

Month: Jul Aug Sep Oct Nov Dec Jan Feb Mar Apr May Jun

**Chapter 3:
States of Mind**

*The "biological clock," located in the thalamus, regulates our circadian rhythms.*

**Chapter 9:
Stress, Health and Well-Being**

*People suffering from* learned helplessness *passively accept unpleasant conditions.*

**Chapter 12:
Social Psychology**

*Compare this attribution style with the* self-serving bias *of nondepressed individuals.*

**Seasonal affective disorder** or **SAD:** A form of depression believed to be caused by deprivation of sunlight.

Some cases of unipolar depression, however, almost certainly have a genetic predisposition. Severe bouts with depression often run in families (Andreasen et al., 1987; Plomin, Owen, & McGuffin, 1994; Weissman et al., 1986). Further indication of a biological basis for depression comes from the favorable response that many depressed patients have to drugs that affect the brain's neurotransmitters norepinephrine, serotonin, and dopamine (Hirschfeld & Goodwin, 1988; Nemeroff, 1998). Evidence also indicates that depression is related to lower brain wave activity in the left frontal lobe (Davidson, 1992). In a few cases, depression may be caused by viral infection (Bower, 1995). Such evidence leads some observers to believe that depression is really a collection of disorders having a variety of causes (Kendler & Gardner, 1998).

A special form of unipolar depression seems to be related to sunlight deprivation. It appears most frequently among people who live in high latitudes. There, during the long, dark winter months, the incidence of depression runs high (Wehr & Rosenthal, 1989). Aptly named, **seasonal affective disorder,** or **SAD,** is related to levels of the light-sensitive hormone *melatonin*, which regulates our internal biological clocks (Campbell & Murphy, 1998; Oren & Terman, 1998). Based on this knowledge, researchers have developed an effective therapy that regulates melatonin by exposing SAD sufferers daily to bright artificial light (Lewy et al., 1987).

Biology alone cannot entirely explain depression, however. We must also understand it as a mental and a behavioral condition. Initially, a negative event, such as losing a job, can make anyone feel depressed, but low self-esteem and a pessimistic attitude can fuel a cycle (Figure 13.3) that keeps some individuals caught up in depressive thought patterns (Abramson, Matalsky, & Alloy, 1989; Sweeney et al., 1986; Wood, Saltzberg, & Goldsant, 1990a; Wood et al., 1990b). Probably because of low self-esteem, depression-prone people are more likely to perpetuate the depression cycle by attributing negative events to their own personal flaws or to external conditions that they feel helpless to change (Azar, 1994; Robins, 1988; Seligman, 1991; Seligman et al., 1979). Martin Seligman calls this *learned helplessness*. The resulting negative self-evaluation generates a depressed mode, which leads in turn to negative behaviors such as crying. These behaviors encourage others to avoid the depressed individual. Consequently, depressed people feel rejected and lonely, which also feeds the cycle of their despair (Coyne, Burchill, & Stiles, 1991).

A study of college students supports the notion that depressed people have a negative attribution style. Those who were depressed and who failed a test attributed their failure to a personal flaw—their lack of ability—while those depressed students who passed the test attributed their successes to luck. In comparison, nondepressed students took more credit for successes and blamed failures on external factors and on bad luck (Barthe & Hammen, 1981). Moreover, students who have a negative attribution style have been found to earn lower grade point averages than their less-negative-thinking classmates (Peterson & Barrett, 1987).

The cognitive approach to depression points out that negative thinking styles are learned and modifiable. This implies that, if you work on changing the way you *think*, perhaps blaming yourself less and focusing more on constructive plans for doing better, you can ultimately change your feelings and your performance. Indeed, Peter Lewinsohn and his colleagues (1975, 1980, 1990) have found that they can treat many cases of depression effectively with cognitive–behavioral techniques. Their approach intervenes at several points in the cycle of depression to teach people how to change their helpless thinking, to cope adaptively with unpleasant situations, and to build more rewards into their lives.

**FIGURE 13.3:** The Cognitive–Behavioral Cycle of Depression

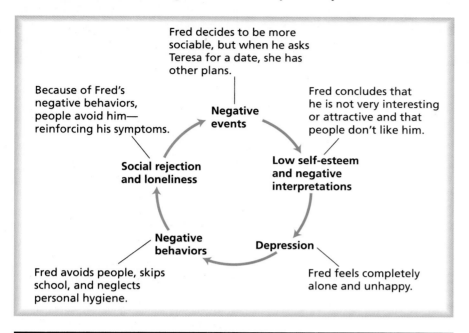

Clinicians have noted that depression rates are higher for women than for men (Leutwyler, 1995; Strickland, 1992; Turkington, 1992; Weissman et al., 1996). According to Susan Nolen-Hoeksema (1987, 1990), the response styles of men and women once they begin to experience negative moods may account for the difference. In this view, when women experience sadness, they tend to think about the possible causes and implications of their feelings. In contrast, men attempt to distract themselves from depressed feelings, either by shifting their attention to something else or by engaging in a physical activity that will take their minds off their current mood state. This model suggests that the more *ruminative* response of women—characterized by a tendency to concentrate on problems—increases women's vulnerability to depression (Shea, 1998). From a cognitive approach, paying attention to one's negative moods can increase thoughts of negative events, which eventually increases the quantity and/or intensity of negative feelings.

It is also noteworthy that the incidence of depression and the age at which it strikes are changing—at least in the United States. According to Martin Seligman, depression is between 10 and 20 times as common as it was 50 years ago (National Press Club, 1999). At midcentury, most casualties of depression were middle-aged women, but now it has become a teenage problem—still more prevalent in females than in males. Currently, the average age of individuals diagnosed with depression in the United States is between 14 and 15 years. Seligman blames this increase in occurrence and decrease in age to three factors: (1) an out-of-control individualism and self-centeredness that focuses on individual success and failure, rather than group accomplishments; (2) the self-esteem movement, which has taught a generation of schoolchildren that they should feel good about themselves, irrespective of their efforts and achievements; and (3) a culture of *victimology*, which reflexively points the finger of blame at someone or something else.

Chapter 12:
Social Psychology

*The self-serving bias, which attributes mistakes and failures to external causes, is more common in individualistic cultures.*

### Anxiety Disorders

Would you pick up a snake or let a tarantula rest on your shoulder? For some people the mere thought of snakes or spiders is enough to send chills of fear down

## A Depression Check

Most people think that depression is marked by outward signs of sadness, such as weeping. But depression affects other aspects of thought and behavior, as well. For a quick check on your own tendencies to depression, please answer "yes" or "no" to each of the following questions, all adapted from the *DSM-IV*:

1. Do you feel deeply depressed, sad, or hopeless most of the day?
2. Do you feel you have lost interest in most or all activities?
3. Have you experienced any major change in appetite or body weight, though not from dieting?
4. Have you experienced a significant change in your sleeping patterns?
5. Do you feel more restless than usual—or more sluggish than usual?
6. Do you feel more fatigued than you ought to?
7. Do you feel persistently hopeless or inappropriately guilty?
8. Have you been finding it increasingly difficult to think or concentrate?
9. Do you have recurrent thoughts of death or suicide?

Your answers to these items do not constitute any proof that you are or are not depressed. While there is no "magic number" of items you must answer "yes" to in order to qualify as depressed, if you answered "yes" to some of them and if you are concerned, it might be a good idea to seek a professional opinion. Remember that it is the *pattern* and the *quality* of your life, experience, and behavior that determine whether or not you are depressed. Remember also that self-report is always subject to some bias. A competent examination by a mental health professional would take into account not only your self-descriptions but also observable behaviors and performance.

---

their spines. Everyone, of course, has experienced anxiety or fear in threatening or dangerous situations. But pathological anxiety is far more severe than the normal anxiety associated with life's challenges. It is also relatively common. One estimate says that 15% of the general population has, at some time, experienced the symptoms that are serious enough to qualify as one of the **anxiety disorders** recognized in the DSM (Regier et al., 1988).

Here we will review three major problems that have anxiety as their main feature: (1) panic disorder, (2) phobic disorder, and (3) obsessive–compulsive disorder. You will note that the major difference among them has to do with the focus of anxiety. Does the anxiety seem to come from nowhere—unrelated to the individual's environment or behavior? Does it come from an external object or situation, such as the sight of blood or a snake? Does it involve the victim's own ritualistic behavior, as in a person who compulsively avoids stepping on cracks in the sidewalk?

**PANIC DISORDER**   While calmly eating lunch, an unexpected wave of panic sweeps over you, seemingly from nowhere. Nothing really threatens you, but your heart begins to race, your body begins shaking, you feel dizzy, your hands feel clammy and sweaty, you are afraid that you might be dying. You are having a *panic attack*.

The distinguishing feature of **panic disorder** is a feeling of panic that has no connection with events in the person's present experience. The feeling is one of "free-floating anxiety." Attacks usually last for only a few minutes and then subside; they can recur without warning (McNally, 1994). Because of the unexpected nature of these "hit-and-run" attacks, *anticipatory anxiety* often develops as an added complication in panic disorders. The dread of the next attack and of being helpless and suddenly out of control can lead a person to avoid public places, yet fear being left alone. Cognitive–behavioral theorists view panic attacks as conditioned responses to

**Anxiety disorders:** Mental problems characterized mainly by anxiety. Anxiety disorders include panic disorder, phobias, and obsessive–compulsive disorder.

**Panic disorder:** A disturbance marked by panic attacks that have no connection with events in the person's present experience.

physical sensations that may have initially been learned during a period of stress (Antony, Brown, & Barlow, 1992).

Biologically, the mechanism for these attacks may lie in the brain's limbic system, especially in the amygdala, which shows up as abnormal on PET scans of some patients with this disorder (Resnick, 1992). There is evidence that a fearful experience can cause overstimulation of the brain's fear circuits, producing physical changes that make the individual susceptible to further anxiety attacks (Rosen & Schulkin, 1998). We also have evidence of an underlying genetic influence (Plomin et al., 1994).

To complicate matters, many victims of panic disorder have additional symptoms of **agoraphobia.** This condition involves panic that develops when they find themselves in situations from which they cannot easily escape, such as public places or open spaces (Antony et al., 1992). The term "agoraphobia" is a literal translation from the ancient Greek for "fear of the marketplace," generalized to include all public places and open spaces. Individuals with agoraphobia experience anxiety in crowded rooms, malls, buses, airplanes, freeways, and open fields (Magee et al., 1996). They often fear that, if they experience an attack in one of these locations, help might not be available or the situation will be embarrassing to them. These fears deprive afflicted persons of their freedom, and some become prisoners in their own homes. If the disorder becomes this extreme, they cannot hold a job or carry on normal daily activities.

You may know someone who has panic disorder or agoraphobia. These disorders occur in about 2% of the population (McNally, 1994) and are much more common in women than in men. Fortunately, the treatment outlook is good. Medical therapy involves antianxiety drugs to relieve the panic attacks. Purely psychological treatment is also effective: Psychologist David Barlow has shown that cognitive–behavioral therapy, a form of therapy that attempts to change both thoughts and behaviors, may outperform drug therapy in reducing or eliminating panic attacks ("Cognitive–Behavior Therapy," 1991).

**Chapter 2: Biopsychology**
*The limbic system, in a layer between the brain stem and the cortex, regulates emotion and memory.*

**PHOBIC DISORDERS**   In contrast with panic disorder, **phobia,** or **phobic disorder,** involves a persistent and irrational fear of a specific object, activity, or situation. A phobia is an exaggerated fear or anxiety response that grows all out of proportion to the circumstances. Many of us respond fearfully to certain stimuli, such as spiders or snakes—or perhaps to multiple-choice tests! But these emotional responses become full-fledged phobic disorders only when they cause substantial disruption to our lives.

This may be the worst nightmare for a person with a snake phobia.

Phobias are a relatively common psychological problem. Studies suggest that 12.5% of Americans suffer from some form of phobia at some point in their lives (Regier et al., 1988). Some phobias are oddly specific, such as a fear of a certain type of insect; others are so common, such as fear of public speaking, that they seem almost normal (Stein, Walker, & Ford, 1996). Nearly any stimulus can come to generate a phobic avoidance reaction (see Table 13.3), although some phobias are much more common than others. Among the most common phobic disorders are *social phobias,* irrational fears of normal social situations such as interacting with others or appearing in front of a group (Magee et al.,

**Agoraphobia:** A fear of public places and open spaces, commonly accompanying panic disorder.

**Phobia** or **phobic disorder:** An anxiety disorder involving a pathological fear of a specific object or situation.

## TABLE 13.3: Phobias

| | OBJECT/SITUATION | APPROXIMATE PERCENTAGE OF ALL PHOBIAS | GENDER DIFFERENCES | TYPICAL AGE OF FIRST OCCURRENCE |
|---|---|---|---|---|
| Agoraphobia | Crowds, open spaces | 10–50 | Large majority among women | Early adulthood |
| Social phobias | Fear of being observed or doing something humiliating | 10 | Majority are women | Adolescence |
| Specific phobias<br>*Animals* | Cats (ailurophobia)<br>Dogs (cynophobia)<br>Insects (insectophobia)<br>Spiders (arachnophobia)<br>Birds (avisophobia)<br>Horses (equinophobia)<br>Snakes (ophidiophobia)<br>Rodents (rodentophobia) | 5–15 | Vast majority are women | Childhood |
| *Inanimate objects or situations* | Closed spaces (claustrophobia)<br>Dirt (mysophobia)<br>Thunder (brontophobia)<br>Lightning (astraphobia)<br>Heights (acrophobia)<br>Darkness (nyctophobia)<br>Fire (pyrophobia) | 20 | None | Any age |
| *Illness-injury* | (nosophobia)<br>Death (thanatophobia)<br>Sight of blood (hematophobia)<br>Cancer (cancerophobia)<br>Venereal disease (venerophobia) | 15–25 | None | Middle age |
| *Other specific phobias* | Numbers (numerophobia)<br>The number 13 (triskaidekaphobia)<br>Strangers, foreigners (xenophobia)<br>String (linonophobia)<br>Books (bibliophobia)<br>Work (ergophobia) | rare | | |

Note: Hundreds of phobias have been described and given scientific names; this table provides only a sample. Some of the rare and strange-sounding phobias may have been observed in a single patient.

**Chapter 6:**
**Learning and Remembering**

*Watson's infamous experiment with Little Albert showed that fears could be learned by classical conditioning.*

**Chapter 2:**
**Biopsychology**

*Natural selection favors organisms possessing genetic traits that have survival value.*

**Preparedness hypothesis:** The notion that we have an innate tendency, acquired through natural selection, to respond quickly and automatically to stimuli that posed a survival threat to our ancestors.

1996). Phobic responses to heights (acrophobia), snakes (ophidiophobia), and closed-in spaces (claustrophobia) are also common.

What causes phobias? Long ago, John Watson demonstrated that fears can be learned. We also have abundant evidence that fears and phobias can be *unlearned* through cognitive–behavioral therapy based on conditioning. But learning may not tell the whole story. Martin Seligman (1971) contends that humans are biologically disposed to learn some kinds of fears more easily than others. This **preparedness hypothesis** suggests that we carry an innate tendency, acquired through natural selection, to respond quickly and automatically to stimuli that posed a survival threat to our ancestors (Seligman, 1971). This explains why we develop phobias for snakes and lightning much more easily that we develop fears for automobiles and electrical outlets—objects that have posed a danger only in recent times.

**OBSESSIVE–COMPULSIVE DISORDER**    Just a year ago, 17-year-old Jim seemed to be a normal adolescent with many talents and interests. Then, almost overnight, he was transformed into a lonely outsider, excluded from social life by his psychological disabilities. Specifically, he developed an obsession with washing. Haunted by the notion that he was dirty—in spite of what his senses told him—Jim began to spend more and more of his time cleansing himself of imaginary dirt. At first his ritual ablutions were confined to weekends and evenings, but soon they began to consume all his time, forcing him to drop out of school (Rapoport, 1989).

Jim is suffering from a condition known as **obsessive–compulsive disorder,** a condition characterized by patterns of persistent, unwanted thoughts and behaviors. Obsessive–compulsive disorder (OCD) is estimated to affect 2.5% of Americans at some point during their lives (Regier et al., 1988). Nearly everyone has had some of its symptoms in a mild form.

The *obsession* component of OCD consists of thoughts, images, or impulses that recur or persist despite a person's efforts to suppress them. For example, a person with an obsessive fear of germs may avoid using bathrooms outside his or her home or refuse to shake hands with strangers. Obsessions are experienced as an unwanted invasion of consciousness. To the victim these thoughts seem to be senseless and perhaps even repugnant. Consequently, the individual may take great pains to avoid the situations that relate to the content of the obsessions. And, because sufferers realize that their obsessive thoughts and compulsive rituals are senseless, they often go to great lengths to hide their compulsive behavior from other people. This, of course, places restrictions on their domestic, social, and work lives. Not surprisingly, OCD patients have extremely high divorce rates.

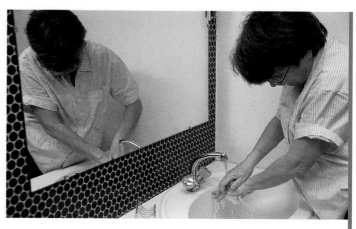

Obsessive–compulsive disorder makes people engage in senseless, ritualistic behaviors, such as repetitive handwashing.

You probably have had some sort of mild obsessional experience, such as petty worries ("Did I remember to lock the door?" or "Did I forget to turn off the oven?") or the persistence of a haunting phrase or melody that kept running through your mind. Such thoughts are normal if they occur only occasionally and have not caused significant disruptions of your life. By contrast, the thoughts of the obsessive–compulsive sufferer are much more compelling and cause much more distress. As we have noted in other disorders, it is a matter of degree.

*Compulsions*, the other half of obsessive–compulsive disorder, are repetitive, purposeful acts performed according to certain private "rules," in response to an obsession. Victims feel that their compulsive behavior will reduce the tension associated with their obsessions. Typical compulsions include irresistible urges to clean, to check that lights or appliances have been turned off, and to count objects or possessions. People with obsessive–compulsive disorder initially resist carrying out their compulsions. When they are calm, they view the compulsion as senseless, but when their anxiety rises, the power of the compulsive behavior ritual to relieve tension seems irresistible. The action must be performed. Part of the pain experienced by people with this problem is that they are frustrated by the irrationality of their obsessions and their powerlessness to eliminate them.

The tendency for OCD to run in families suggests a genetic link. Another hint comes from the finding that many people with OCD also display **tics,** unwanted involuntary movements, such as exaggerated eye blinks. In these patients, brain imaging often shows oddities in the deep motor control areas, suggesting something amiss in the brain (Resnick, 1992). OCD expert Judith Rapoport tells us to think of compulsions as "fixed software packages" programmed in the brain. Once activated, she theorizes, the patient gets caught in a behavioral "loop" that cannot be switched off (Rapoport, 1989).

Curiously, certain drugs that are commonly prescribed for depression can alleviate both the obsessions and the compulsive rituals (Poling, Gadow, & Cleary, 1991). In further support of a biological basis for OCD, investigators have found that

**Obsessive–compulsive disorder:** A condition characterized by patterns of persistent, unwanted thoughts and behaviors.

**Tics:** Unwanted involuntary movements and twitches, such as exaggerated eye blinks.

**Chapter 6:**
**Learning and Remembering**
*This is slightly different from Pavlov's original form of extinction: It calls for presenting the conditioned stimulus without allowing the conditioned response.*

these drugs can reverse compulsive behavior in dogs that display a compulsion for grooming themselves (Ross, 1992). Again, however, we must note that biology cannot explain everything. Behavioral therapy, too, is effective in reducing compulsive actions. The behavioral strategy for treating compulsive hand-washing, for example, calls for a form of extinction, in which the therapist soils the patient's hands and prevents him or her from washing them for progressively longer periods of time. Indeed, behavioral therapy can produce changes that show up in PET scans of OCD sufferers' brains (Schwartz, Stoessel, & Phelps, 1996). Thus, when we change behavior, we inevitably change the wiring of the obsessive–compulsive brain. This disorder shows us, once again, that biology and behavior are inseparable.

## Somatoform Disorders

"Soma" means *body*. Thus, we use the term **somatoform disorders** for psychological problems appearing in the form of bodily symptoms or physical complaints, such as weakness or excessive worry about disease. Because these symptoms have no apparent biological cause, clinicians call them *psychogenic:* The cause originates in the mind. The *DSM-IV* recognizes several types of somatoform disorders, but we will cover only two: *conversion disorder* and *hypochondriasis*. (Note that the *DSM-IV* places the *psychosomatic disorders*, in which mental conditions—especially stress—lead to physical disease, under a separate heading called Psychological Factors Affecting Medical Condition.)

**Chapter 9:**
**Stress, Health, and Well-Being**
*Stress demonstrates the effect of the mind (psyche) on the body (soma).*

**CONVERSION DISORDER** Paralysis, weakness, or loss of sensation—with no discernible physical cause—distinguishes **conversion disorder** (formerly called "hysterical neurosis"). Patients with this diagnosis may, for example, be blind, deaf, unable to walk, or insensitive to touch in part of their bodies. Yet they have no organic disease that shows up on neurological examinations, laboratory tests, or X rays. In conversion disorder, the problem really is "all in the mind."

"Glove anesthesia" represents a classic form of conversion disorder. As you can see in Figure 13.4, the pattern of insensitivity to touch or pain fits the patient "like a glove." The tip-off that the problem is psychogenic, not physical, comes from the pattern of the patient's symptoms: The symptoms do not match any possible pattern of nerve impairment. Other cases, however, are not always so clear-cut. Therefore, conversion disorder may be merely a convenient diagnosis when the neurologist has ruled out everything else. Some physicians, too, may be quick to diagnose conversion disorder when they are confronted with baffling symptoms or especially difficult patients. Concluding that it is "all in their heads" conveniently gets rid of the problem by tossing it into somebody else's ballpark. Women, particularly, have charged that physicians may not take their physical complaints seriously, dismissing them as "just a hysterical reaction" and referring the patient

### FIGURE 13.4: Glove Anesthesia

The form of conversion disorder know as "glove anesthesia" (a) involves a loss of sensation in the hand, as though the patient were wearing a thick glove. This cannot be a neurological disorder because the pattern of "anesthesia" does not correspond to the actual pattern of nerves in the hand, shown in (b).

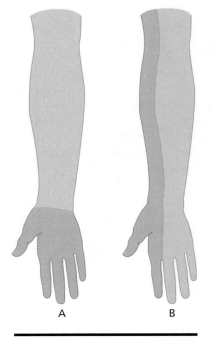

A          B

**Somatoform disorders:** Psychological problems appearing in the form of bodily symptoms or physical complaints, such as weakness or excessive worry about disease. The somatoform disorders include conversion disorder and hypochondriasis.

**Conversion disorder:** A type of somatoform disorder, marked by paralysis, weakness, or loss of sensation, but with no discernible physical cause.

to a psychiatrist. Clearly, conversion disorder, like many other labels for mental problems, is a diagnosis that can be abused.

We should point out that the term "conversion disorder" carries with it some baggage from the Freudian past. "Conversion" implies an unconscious displacement (conversion) of anxiety into physical symptoms—although many clinicians no longer subscribe to that explanation. Some cases of conversion disorder are now thought to be physical stress responses.

Mysteriously, conversion disorder was much commoner several decades ago in Europe and the United States. As we saw earlier, both Charcot and Freud diagnosed many cases of conversion disorder. For unknown reasons, the problem has declined in the industrialized countries (American Psychiatric Association, 1994), but it still occurs frequently in economically undeveloped regions, such as China (Spitzer et al., 1989) and Africa (Binitie, 1975).

**Chapter 10: Personality**

*Freud began his work in psychopathology by attempting to explain hysteria—now called conversion disorder.*

**HYPOCHONDRIASIS**   "Hypochondriacs" worry about getting sick. Every ache and pain signals a disease. Because of their exaggerated concern about illness, patients with **hypochondriasis** often bounce from physician to physician until they find one who will listen to their complaints and prescribe some sort of treatment—often tranquilizers or placebos. Naturally, these individuals represent easy marks for health fads and scams. They also find their way to the fringes of the medical community, where they may buy extensive treatment packages from herbalists, naturopaths, and homeopathic physicians.

The flip side of the problem is a mistaken diagnosis of hypochondriasis (similar to the problem we found with conversion disorder). Clinicians may sometimes be too ready to conclude that the patient's concerns are imaginary. This can have disastrous consequences, such as overlooking the symptoms of very real and very serious physical diseases, such as cancer or a chronic infection.

## Dissociative Disorders

The common denominator for all the **dissociative disorders** is "fragmentation" of the personality—a sense that some parts of the personality have detached (dissociated) from other parts. Among the dissociative disorders, we find some of the most fascinating forms of mental pathology, including *dissociative fugue, depersonalization disorder,* and the controversial *dissociative identity disorder* (formerly called "multiple personality"), made famous by the fictional Dr. Jekyll and Mr. Hyde. Their underlying causes remain unclear.

## Dissociative Fugue

Consider the case of "Jane Doe," a woman who was found to be incoherent, suffering the effects of exposure, and near death in a Florida park. She had no memory of her identity nor any ability to read or write. Therapy revealed general information about the kind of past she must have had, but no good clues to her origins. After a nationwide television appeal, Jane Doe and her doctors were flooded with calls from possible relatives, the most promising of which was an Illinois couple, certain she was their daughter. They had not heard from her for over four years, since she had moved from Illinois to Florida. Despite their confidence that they had found her, she was never able to remember her past or what had happened to her (Carson et al., 1996).

Jane Doe had **dissociative fugue,** which is a combination of **amnesia** and *fugue,* or "flight." Persons with dissociative fugue not only lose their sense of identity, but they abruptly flee their homes, families, and jobs. Some appear disoriented and perplexed. Others may travel to distant locations and take up new lives, appearing unconcerned about the unremembered past. Usually the fugue state lasts only hours or days, followed by complete and rapid recovery. A few cases may continue for months—or, as with Jane Doe, for years.

**Hypochondriasis:** A somatoform disorder involving excessive concern about health and disease.

**Dissociative disorders:** A group of pathologies involving "fragmentation" of the personality, in which some parts of the personality have become detached, or dissociated from other parts. Forms of dissociative disorder include amnesia, fugue, depersonalization disorder, and dissociative identity disorder.

**Dissociative fugue:** Essentially the same as dissociative amnesia, but with the addition of "flight" from one's home, family, and job. "Fugue" means "flight."

**Amnesia:** A loss of memory for personal information, such as one's identity or residence.

**Chapter 6: Learning and Remembering**

*Compare with anterograde amnesia in the case of H. M.*

**Chapter 6:
Learning and Remembering**

*Recovery of repressed memories
is a controversial topic.*

Heavy alcohol use may predispose a person to dissociative fugue. This suggests that it may involve some physical impairment of the brain—although no certain cause has been established. Like dissociative amnesia, fugue occurs more often in those under prolonged high stress, especially in times of war and other calamities. Some psychologists also suspect memory dissociation and repression accompany instances of sexual and physical childhood abuse (Spiegel & Cardeña, 1991). This conjecture, however, is disputed.

**DEPERSONALIZATION DISORDER**   Yet another form of dissociation involves a sensation that mind and body have separated. Patients with **depersonalization disorder** commonly report "out-of-body experiences" or feelings of being external observers of their own bodies. Some patients report that they feel as if they were in a dream. People undergoing severe physical trauma, such as a life-threatening injury in an auto accident, may report symptoms of depersonalization, as do some patients who have had near-death experiences. Usually the sensation passes quickly, although it can recur. Investigators have attributed the disorder to hallucinations and to natural changes in the brain that occur during shock (Siegel, 1980).

**DISSOCIATIVE IDENTITY DISORDER**   Robert Louis Stevenson's famous story of Dr. Jekyll and Mr. Hyde has become a misleading stereotype of **dissociative identity disorder.** In reality, most cases of dissociative identity disorder are women, and most display more than two identities (Ross, Norton, & Wozney, 1989). Unlike the homicidal Mr. Hyde, rarely do they pose a danger to others.

Once thought to be rare, some specialists now believe that dissociative identity disorder has always been common, but hidden or misdiagnosed. It usually first appears in childhood (Vincent & Pickering, 1988), and its victims frequently report having been sexually abused (Putnam et al., 1986; Ross et al., 1990). The formation of multiple identities or selves may be a form of defense by the dominant self to protect itself from terrifying events.

Dissociative identity disorder (DID) has now become a familiar diagnosis because of its portrayal in fact-based books and movies, such as *The Three Faces of Eve* (Thigpen & Cleckley, 1957), *Sybil* (Schreiber, 1973), and *The Flock* (Casey & Wilson, 1991). Although the original personality is unaware of the others, the others are

**Depersonalization disorder:** An abnormality involving the sensation that mind and body have separated, as in an "out-of-body" experience.

**Dissociative identity disorder:** A condition in which an individual displays multiple identities, or personalities; formerly called "multiple personality disorder."

These two paintings by Sybil, a dissociative identity disorder (DID) victim, illustrate the differences between the personalities. The painting on the left was done by Peggy, Sybil's angry, fearful personality. The painting above was done by Mary, a home-loving personality.

usually aware of the host and often of each other. Each emerging personality contrasts in some significant way with the original self. For example, they might be outgoing if the original personality is shy, tough if the original is weak, and sexually assertive if the other is fearful and sexually naive. Each personality has a unique identity, name, behavior pattern, and even characteristic brain-wave activity. In some cases, dozens of characters emerge to help the person deal with a difficult life situation. The emergence of these alternate personalities, each with its own consciousness, is sudden and is usually precipitated by stress.

What lies behind this mysterious disturbance? Psychodynamic theories explain it as a fracturing of the ego, as a result of ego defense mechanisms that do not allow energy from conflicts and traumas to escape from the unconscious mind. Cognitive theories see it as a form of role-playing. Others suggest that at least some cases are frauds (as in the case of a student, charged with plagiarizing a term paper, who claimed that he had multiple personalities and that one of them copied the paper without the knowledge of his dominant personality).

Until about 30 years ago, only some 100 cases had been documented worldwide. Since then the numbers have gone up rapidly, possibly because more patients are being misdiagnosed with DID or more are feigning the symptoms—or because the trauma and abuse associated with the syndrome have increased along with a variety of other societal "sicknesses" (Carson et al., 1996). Alternatively, through social learning people may become convinced that they have DID when they hear of it on talk shows and see it featured in television soap operas.

**Chapter 6:**
**Learning and Remembering**
*Social learning, or observational learning, involves expectations of rewards and punishments learned through social interaction and the observation of others.*

In an unfortunate choice of terms, dissociative identity disorder is sometimes called "split personality." This causes confusion because *schizophrenia,* which literally means "split mind," has no relationship to dissociative identity disorder. In schizophrenia, the "split" refers to a psychotic split from reality, not to a fracturing of one personality into many personalities. Dissociative identity disorder, on the other hand, is *not* a psychotic disorder. We suggest that the reader avoid confusion by avoiding the term "split personality."

We might add a note of caution here about what is and is not yet understood about dissociative disorders. There is an ongoing debate in psychology, psychiatry, and the public arena about the validity of the recent increase in cases of DID that are based on adult women's claims to have been abused as children. Some observers have even suggested that the disorder exists only in the minds of a few therapists (Piper, 1998). In this view, patients may initially be led by the suggestive questioning of their therapists, who seek to uncover what they suspect are repressed memories of trauma and molestation. Then, based on the therapists' expectations, some patients may be reinforced for generating not only repressed memories but also multiple personalities (Loftus, 1993; Loftus & Ketcham, 1994; Ofshe & Watters, 1994).

**Chapter 6:**
**Learning and Remembering**
*Recall the case of Donna, who fabricated memories of abuse.*

## Eating Disorders

Like a drug addiction, Carla's eating disorder is so powerful that she cannot resume healthy eating patterns without great difficulty. She (it is usually a *she*) has always felt overweight, and recently she has put herself on a severe diet—a starvation diet. Little does Carla realize that she has become the victim of an eating disorder that will ultimately alter her body in undesirable, and even lethal, ways. After some months, she may become dangerously underweight. Food has become repugnant. Her appetite is gone, so she feels "full" after eating only a bite or two. The original motivation may have been the same with Carla's friend Jennifer, but Jennifer has resorted to another extreme method of weight control: She often overeats, but she makes herself vomit after a meal. In the short run, it works. But Jennifer does not realize that her teeth and the tissues in her mouth and esophagus will come under attack by the action of refluxed stomach acid. Nor does Jennifer realize that she, like Carla, may become dangerously malnourished.

Significantly, such eating disorders are most prevalent in Western cultures in which hunger is not a widespread problem. They are especially likely to develop among middle-class and upper-middle-class young women. Here we examine the two best-known eating disorders, exemplified in the cases above: *anorexia nervosa* and *bulimia*.

**ANOREXIA NERVOSA**  The condition called *anorexia* (persistent lack of appetite) may develop as a consequence of certain physical diseases or conditions, such as shock, nausea, or allergic reactions. However, when loss of appetite that endangers an individual's health stems from emotional or psychological reasons rather than from these organic causes, the syndrome is called **anorexia nervosa** ("nervous anorexia"). A person suffering from anorexia nervosa may act as though she is unconcerned with her condition, although she is visibly undernourished and emaciated. Commonly, anorexia nervosa is associated with extreme dieting, as in Carla's case. (Normal dieters, by contrast, have an increased desire for food.)

What causes anorexia nervosa? A strong hint comes from the finding that most anorectic persons are young White females from middle-class American homes. They typically have backgrounds of good behavior and academic success, but their case histories show that they starve themselves, hoping to become acceptably thin and attractive (Brumberg, 1988; Gilbert & DeBlassie, 1984). While cultural ideals of feminine beauty change over time, in recent decades the mass media—including

**Chapter 8: Emotion and Motivation**

*Anorexia nervosa shows that cognitions and emotional states can affect the hunger drive.*

**FIGURE 13.5:**  Women's Body Images

April Fallon and Paul Rozin (1985) asked female college students to give their current weight, their ideal weight, and the weight they believed men would consider ideal. The results showed that the average woman felt that her current weight was significantly higher than her ideal weight—and higher than the weight she thought men would like best. To make matters worse, women also see their bodies as looking larger than they actually are (Thompson, 1986). When men were asked to rate themselves on a similar questionnaire, Fallon and Rozin found no such discrepancies between ideal and actual weights. But, when asked what they saw as the ideal weight for women, they chose a higher weight than women did. In light of these findings, it is no wonder that women go on diets more often than men and are more likely than men to have a major eating disorder (Mintz & Betz, 1986; Striegel-Moore, Silberstein, & Rodin, 1986).

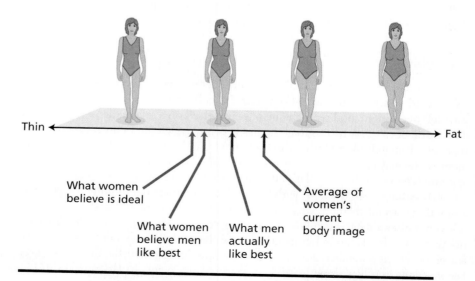

**Anorexia nervosa:** An eating disorder involving persistent loss of appetite that endangers an individual's health and stemming from emotional or psychological reasons rather than from organic causes.

fashion magazines and MTV—have promoted images of unrealistically slim models and celebrities (Andersen & DiDomenico, 1992; Rolls et al., 1991). Especially during adolescence, when people tend to evaluate themselves in terms of physical attractiveness, they judge themselves harshly for failing to live up to cultural ideals (Conger & Petersen, 1984). A victim of anorexia typically holds a distorted body image, believing herself to be unattractively fat, and rejects others' reassurances that she is not overweight (Bruch, 1978; Fallon & Rozin, 1985). In an effort to lose imagined "excess" weight, the anorectic victim rigidly suppresses her appetite, feeling rewarded for such self-control when she does lose pounds and inches—but never feeling quite thin enough.

BULIMIA    A related disorder, known as **bulimia,** involves a "binge-and-purge" syndrome in which the sufferer indulges in episodes of overeating (binges) followed by efforts to lose weight (purging) by means of self-induced vomiting (as in Jennifer's case), laxative use, or fasting (Rand & Kuldau, 1992). Those who suffer from bulimia usually keep their disorder inconspicuous and may even be supported in their behavior patterns by peers and by competitive norms in their academic, social, and athletic lives (Polivy & Herman, 1993; Rodin, Striegel-Moore, & Silberstein, 1985; Squire, 1983; Striegel-Moore, Silberstein, & Rodin, 1993).

Eating disorders are often associated with other forms of psychopathology. For example, bulimia is a predictor of depression (Walters et al., 1992). Further, while hungry normal people look forward to eating and enjoying a good meal, eating-disordered individuals do not associate pleasure with food and may even dread having to eat. In comparison with control subjects, bulimic patients in one study took longer to begin eating a scheduled meal, ate more slowly, and reported significantly more negative moods during eating (Hetherington et al., 1993). Although their original rationale might have been to lose weight, anorectic and bulimic individuals apparently take little joy in their slimmer states. Ironically, their extreme behaviors may eventually attract the attention of friends and family members who can urge them to seek professional treatment for their disorder.

Cognitive explanations for eating disorders analyze how the individual sees herself and thinks about food, eating, and weight. Anorectic persons may exhibit more mental rigidity (less flexibility in their thinking) than normal people (Korkina et al., 1992). Among bulimia victims, those who purge more often than others have been found to have more trouble in performing certain cognitive tasks (Cooper & Fairburn, 1993). Findings such as these suggest that eating-disordered individuals have distorted ways of perceiving and thinking. Accordingly, many successful treatments of eating disorders are based on cognitive strategies that focus first on building up self-esteem and self-efficacy (Baell & Wertheim, 1992).

Diana, Princess of Wales, publicly divulged her struggle with bulimia, an eating disorder in which the sufferer overeats (binges), and then purges, through self-induced vomiting, laxatives, or fasting.

## Schizophrenic Disorders

Literally, the word *schizophrenia* means "split or broken mind." In psychological terms, a **schizophrenia** is a severe form of psychopathology in which personality seems to disintegrate and perception is distorted. Schizophrenia is the disorder we usually mean when we refer to "madness," "psychosis," or "insanity."

For the victim of schizophrenia, the mind is distorted in terrible ways. The world may become bleak and devoid of meaning, or it may become so filled with sensation that everything appears in a confusion of multiple realities layered with hallucinations and delusions. In schizophrenia, emotions may become blunted, thoughts turn bizarre, and language takes strange twists. The disorder breaks the unity of the mind, sending its victims on meaningless mental detours, riding trains of "clang"

**Bulimia** (pronounced *boo-LEE-me-uh*): An eating disorder characterized by eating binges followed by "purges," induced by vomiting or laxatives; typically initiated as a weight-control measure.

**Schizophrenia** (pronounced *skits-o-FRENNY-a*): A psychotic disorder involving distortions in thoughts, perceptions, and/or emotions.

associations (associations involving similar-sounding words), and producing confused verbalizations that clinicians call "word salads." Here is an example of schizophrenic speech:

> The lion will have to change from dogs into cats until I can meet my father and mother and we dispart some rats. I live on the front of Whitton's head. You have to work hard if you don't get into bed . . . It's all over for a squab true tray and there ain't no squabs, there ain't no men, there ain't no music, there ain't no nothing besides my mother and my father who stand alone upon the Island of Capri where is no ice. Well it's my suitcase sir. (Rogers, 1982)

Those suffering from the catatonic type of schizophrenia may hold unusual poses for long periods . . . as if frozen in action.

Between two and three million living Americans have suffered from this tragic mental disorder (Regier et al., 1988). In a lifetime, more than one of every 100 Americans—approximately two million over the age of 18—will become afflicted (Holmes, 1994; Regier et al., 1993). For as yet unknown reasons, the first occurrence of schizophrenia typically occurs for men before they are 25 and for women between 25 and 45 years of age (Lewine, Straus, & Gift, 1981).

For years, schizophrenia has consistently been the primary diagnosis for about 40% of all patient admissions to public mental hospitals—far out of proportion to all other possible categories of mental illness (Manderscheid et al., 1985). Because schizophrenic patients require prolonged or recurrent treatment, they can be expected to occupy about half of all mental hospital beds in the nation (Carson et al., 1996). Most sobering, about one-third of all schizophrenic patients will never fully recover, even with the best therapy available.

**MAJOR TYPES OF SCHIZOPHRENIA** Many investigators consider schizophrenia a constellation of separate disorders. Here are the five most commonly recognized forms:

- **Disorganized type** represents everyone's image of mental illness, featuring incoherent speech, hallucinations, delusions, and bizarre behavior. A patient who talks to imaginary people most likely has this diagnosis.
- **Catatonic type,** involving a spectrum of motor dysfunctions, appears in two forms. Persons with the more common *catatonic stupor* may remain motionless for hours—even days—sometimes holding rigid, statuelike postures. In the other form, called *catatonic excitement,* patients become agitated and hyperactive.
- **Paranoid type** features delusions and hallucinations, but no catatonic symptoms and none of the incoherence of disorganized schizophrenia. The delusions found in paranoid schizophrenia are typically less well organized—more illogical—than those of the patient with a purely delusional disorder.
- **Undifferentiated type** serves as a catchall category for schizophrenic symptoms that do not clearly meet the requirements for any of the other categories above.
- **Residual type** is the diagnosis for individuals who have suffered from a schizophrenic episode in the past but currently have no major symptoms such as hallucinations or delusional thinking. Instead, their thinking is mildly disturbed, or their emotional lives are impoverished. The diagnosis of residual type may indicate that the disease is entering *remission,* or becoming dormant.

Our understanding of schizophrenia suffers from the fact that most schizophrenic patients display such a hodgepodge of symptoms that they drop into the "undifferentiated" category. Trying to make more sense of the problem, many investigators

**Disorganized type:** A form of schizophrenia featuring incoherent speech, hallucinations, delusions, and bizarre behavior.

**Catatonic type:** A form of schizophrenia involving stupor or extreme excitement.

**Paranoid type:** A form of schizophrenia in which a combination of delusions and hallucinations is the prominent feature.

**Undifferentiated type:** A category used to designate persons displaying a combination of schizophrenic symptoms that do not clearly fit in one of the other categories of schizophrenia.

**Residual type:** A diagnostic category used for individuals who have suffered from a past episode of schizophrenia but are currently free of positive symptoms.

now merely divide the schizophrenias into "positive" and "negative" types. **Positive schizophrenia** involves active symptoms, such as delusions and hallucinations, while **negative schizophrenia** is distinguished by deficits, such as social withdrawal and poverty of thought processes. Patient responses to drug therapy support this division: Those with positive schizophrenia usually respond to antipsychotic drugs, while those with negative schizophrenia do not (Heinrichs, 1993). But even this distinction has its problems. Negative schizophrenia often looks like major depression. In addition, both positive and negative symptoms may occur in a single patient. All these difficulties have led some researchers to conclude that schizophrenia is a name for many separate disturbances.

**Chapter 14: Therapies for Mental Disorder**

*Antipsychotic drugs work by reducing the activity of the neurotransmitter dopamine in the brain.*

**POSSIBLE CAUSES OF SCHIZOPHRENIA**   No longer do most theorists look through the Freudian lens to see schizophrenia as the result of defective parenting or repressed childhood trauma (Johnson, 1989). Solid evidence against the poor-parenting hypothesis comes from studies showing that adopted children, with *no* family history of the disorder, run no increased risk of developing schizophrenia when placed in a home with a schizophrenic parent (Gottesman, 1991). Instead, an emerging consensus among psychiatrists and psychologists alike views schizophrenia as fundamentally a brain disorder—or a group of disorders.

Support for this brain-disorder view comes from many quarters. As we have noted, the antipsychotic drugs (sometimes called *major tranquilizers*)—which interfere with the brain's dopamine receptors—can suppress the symptoms of positive schizophrenia (Carlsson, 1978; Snyder, 1986). On the other hand, drugs that stimulate dopamine production (e.g., the amphetamines) can actually produce schizophrenic symptoms. Other evidence of a biological basis for schizophrenia comes in the form of brain abnormalities shown by computerized imaging techniques (Mesulam, 1990; Raz & Raz, 1990; Resnick, 1992; Suddath et al., 1990).

Yet another line of evidence for the biological basis of schizophrenia comes from family studies (Plomin et al., 1994). As we found with the mood disorders, the closer one's relationship to a person with schizophrenia, the greater one's chances of developing the disorder (Gottesman, 1991; Heston, 1970; Nicol and Gottesman, 1983). This conclusion comes from impressive studies of identical twins reared apart and from adoption studies of children having schizophrenic blood relatives. While only about 1% of us in the general population become schizophrenic, the

**FIGURE 13.6:**   MRI Scans of a Twin with Schizophrenia and a Twin without Schizophrenia

The normal twin is on the left. Note the enlarged ventricles in the brain of the schizophrenic twin on the right.

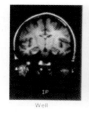
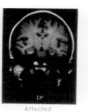
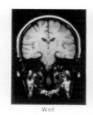
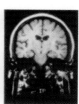
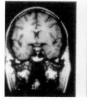
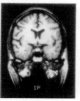
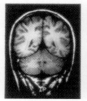
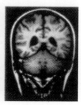

child of a schizophrenic parent incurs a risk about 14 times higher. The worst case would be to have an identical twin who has developed the condition. In that event, the other twin's chances of becoming schizophrenic jump to nearly 50%.

As with the mood disorders, genetics does not tell the whole story of schizophrenia. We can see the effect of the environment, for example, in the fact that 90% of the relatives of schizophrenic patients do not have schizophrenia (Barnes, 1987). Even in identical twins who share *exactly* the same genes, the **concordance rate** for schizophrenia is only about 50%. That is, in half the cases in which schizophrenia strikes identical twins, it leaves one twin untouched. A hopeful Finnish study found that being raised in a healthy family environment can actually lower the risk of schizophrenia in adopted children having a genetic predisposition to the disease (Tienari et al., 1987). Apparently, schizophrenia requires both a biological predisposition plus some unknown environmental agent to "turn on" the hereditary tendency (Cromwell, 1993; Iacono & Grove, 1993). This agent could be some chemical toxin,

**Positive schizophrenia:** Any form of schizophrenia in which the person displays active symptoms, such as delusions or hallucinations.

**Negative schizophrenia:** Any form of schizophrenia distinguished by deficits, such as withdrawal and poverty of thought processes, rather than by active symptoms.

**Concordance rate:** The percentage of relatives who show the same trait.

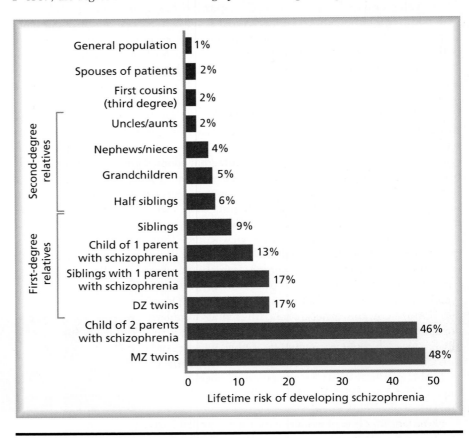

## FIGURE 13.7: Genetic Risk of Developing Schizophrenia

The graph shows average risks for developing schizophrenia. Data were compiled from family and twin studies conducted in European populations between 1920 and 1987; the degree of risk correlates highly with the degree of genetic relatedness.

it could be stress, or it could be some factor that we have not yet dreamed of. Taken as a whole, this research suggests that genetic factors may contribute to schizophrenia but may not by themselves be sufficient for the development of the disorder (Nicol & Gottesman, 1983). Despite all the biological evidence, we must remember that mental disorder is always an interaction of biological, cognitive, and environmental factors, as our first Core Concept of the chapter suggested.

This broader perspective is often called the **diathesis–stress hypothesis.** It says that biological factors may place the individual at risk, but environmental stressors transform this potential into an actual schizophrenic disorder (Walker & Diforio, 1997). (The word *diathesis* refers to a predisposition or physical condition that makes one susceptible to disease.) Thus, schizophrenia can be seen as a stress response. On the other hand, individuals who are genetically predisposed to develop schizophrenia may never do so if they do not experience certain damaging conditions or stressors that push them "over the edge."

### Personality Disorders

A way of life characterized by distrust, lack of feelings for others, attention-seeking, hypersensitivity, submissiveness, perfectionism, impulsivity, unstable relationships, or a pathological need for admiration suggests one of the **personality disorders.** These conditions involve a chronic, pervasive, inflexible, and maladaptive

---

**Chapter 9:
Stress, Health, and Well-Being**

*Stress can cause both physical and mental disorders.*

**Diathesis–stress hypothesis:** In reference to schizophrenia, the proposal says that genetic factors place the individual at risk, but environmental stress factors transform this potential into an actual schizophrenic disorder.

**Personality disorders:** Conditions involving a chronic, pervasive, inflexible, and maladaptive pattern of thinking, emotion, social relationships, or impulse control.

pattern of thinking, emotion, social relationships, or impulse control. The key is that the condition derives from a personality pattern of long standing. These patterns can seriously impair an individual's ability to function in social or work settings and can cause significant distress.

There are many types of personality disorders (ten types are recognized in the *DSM-IV*). They are usually recognizable by the time a person reaches adolescence or early adulthood. Here we will consider two of the better known: *narcissistic personality disorder* and *antisocial personality disorder*.

People with a **narcissistic personality disorder** have a grandiose sense of self-importance, a preoccupation with fantasies of success or power, and a need for constant attention or admiration. These people often respond inappropriately to criticism or minor defeat, either by acting indifferent to criticism or by overreacting. They have problems in interpersonal relationships, feeling entitled to favors without obligations, exploiting others selfishly, and having difficulty understanding how others feel. For example, an individual with narcissistic personality disorder might express annoyance—but not empathy—when a friend has to cancel a date because of a death in the family.

Serial killer Jeffrey Dahmer admitted killing at least 17 people and ghoulishly keeping parts of their bodies in his apartment. He fits the criteria for an antisocial personality.

**Antisocial personality disorder** is marked by a long-standing pattern of irresponsible or harmful behavior that indicates a lack of conscience and a diminished sense of responsibility to others. Chronic lying, stealing, and fighting are common signs. People with antisocial personality disorder may not experience shame or any other sort of intense emotion. They can "keep cool" in situations that would arouse and upset normal people. Violations of social norms begin early in their lives—disrupting class, getting into fights, and running away from home. Individuals who show a criminal pattern of antisocial personality disorder, such as committing murders and other serious crimes, are popularly referred to as "psychopaths" or "sociopaths."

Although carriers of the antisocial type of personality disorder can be found among street criminals and con artists, they are also well represented among successful politicians and businesspeople who put career, money, and power above everything and everyone. Two to three percent of the population in the United States may have antisocial personality disorder. Men are four times more likely to be so diagnosed than women (Regier et al., 1988, 1993).

## Adjustment Disorders and Other Conditions

Although the large majority of everyday psychological problems involve making choices and dealing with confusion, frustration, and loss, the *DSM-IV* gives these problems short shrift under **adjustment disorders** and under the awkwardly named **"other conditions that may be a focus of clinical attention."** Together, these categories represent a catch basin for relatively mild problems that do not fit well under other headings. They span a diverse range of conditions that include mild depression,

**Chapter 10:**
**Personality**
*Personality brings continuity to a person's thoughts and actions in different situations.*

**Narcissistic personality disorder:** Characterized by a grandiose sense of self-importance, a preoccupation with fantasies of success or power, and a need for constant attention or admiration.

**Antisocial personality disorder:** Characterized by a long-standing pattern of irresponsible behavior indicating a lack of conscience and a diminished sense of responsibility to others.

**Adjustment disorders** and **other conditions that may be a focus of clinical attention:** A diverse group of relatively mild problems that do not fit under other headings. These categories include mild depression, physical complaints, marital problems, academic problems, job problems, parent–child problems, bereavement, malingering, and a number of other conditions.

*"Wait! Come back! I was just kidding about wanting to be happy."*

physical complaints, marital problems, academic problems, job problems, parent–child problems, bereavement, and even *malingering* (faking an illness). Consequently, the largest group of people suffering from mental problems may fit these headings—even though the *DSM-IV* devotes disproportionately little space to them.

No one is immune from the commonplace problems of adjustment, because we all have to confront unpleasant events and make difficult choices. In this sense, adjustment disorders are neither unusual nor "abnormal." Nor are they as disabling as some of the more celebrated and exotic disorders that we discussed earlier. Still, some people with adjustment problems seek professional help, even though they may be essentially healthy individuals caught in difficult circumstances. Because these adjustment difficulties are so prevalent, sufferers who turn to psychologists and psychiatrists account for a large proportion of the patient load seen by professionals in private practice.

## PSYCHOLOGY IN YOUR LIFE

## Shyness

Shyness may be painful, but it is not a *DSM-IV* disorder.

Being shy is a common problem, but it is not a *DSM-IV* disorder. Rather, **shyness** is a distressing pattern of avoiding or withdrawing from social contact. Shy behavior may resemble the social phobias, as afflicted individuals seek to limit or escape from social interactions. As we have seen many times before, it is a matter of degree. Shy people are not utterly incapacitated by fear, yet they may suffer from loneliness and from lost opportunities to pursue interests and relationships.

What are the origins of this painful problem? For some people it may begin at birth: Shyness is one of three basic temperaments that have been observed among infants and traced through adult life (Kagan et al., 1988, 1994). (*See Chapter 4, Psychological Developemnt.*) But there is also evidence that shyness and other forms of social anxiety are *learned* responses, so that even those who are not "born shy" can acquire shy behavior patterns. Several social forces and societal changes in recent

decades have reduced people's experience of daily, casual, face-to-face interaction. Adults are less likely to engage in conversations, and children are less likely to learn interaction skills, either firsthand or by observation. Consider five social forces that have diminished social contact among Americans (National Public Radio, 1995b; Zimbardo, 1995):

- *Automation* in the workplace and in human services replaces people with more efficient, but nonhuman, computer chips. We conduct transactions with ATMs (automatic teller machines) instead of human bank tellers, and we fill our gas tanks by sliding credit cards into automated gas pumps without having to speak to a clerk or mechanic.
- *The perception of widespread, uncontrolled crime* has frightened citizens into hiding indoors. Fearful for their children's safety, parents either restrict their outdoor play or supervise them closely. Turning to video games instead, children are lulled into passivity by television and may even come to regard their computers as their "best friends."
- *Changes in family structure* such as divorce, single parenting, and households where both parents work outside the home have led many children to be-

come "prematurely mature." Because they see less interaction among their parents or other adults, they end up with no real-life models for their own social behavior and may rely too much on stereotyped media imagery.

- *Perceptions of a culture-wide "time crunch"* lead individuals to feel busier and more pressured than ever—an irony since we have more time-saving options than any previous generation. When we make and take less time for hobbies, social groups, leisure, and household chores, we lose valuable opportunities

**Shyness:** A distressing pattern of avoiding or withdrawing from social contact; not a *DSM-IV* disorder.

for unique interactions with family and friends. We also develop a prejudice against such socializing as time-wasting and unproductive, so we continue to minimize its value in our lives.

- *Computer technology and the Internet* make it possible for people to engage in faster and more numerous exchanges with people they never actually meet, see, or touch. Faxes and electronic mail enable us to focus on others' words without the experience of their facial expressions, tone of voice, or nonverbal gestures.

This mixture of social forces leaves many people alienated and lonely. With diminished opportunity to acquire interpersonal skills, more and more people seem to be responding to their discomfort with shyness. Since the mid-1980s, the number of Americans who describe themselves as shy has increased from 40% to almost 50% (Carducci & Zimbardo, 1995). It appears that the conveniences of high technology and the challenges of living in a complex society have *taught* people to be shy.

On a hopeful note, we should emphasize that shyness does not have to be a permanent condition. Many people overcome it on their own. Organizations such as Toastmasters exist to help people build verbal skills and confidence in social situations. And many others have found the help they need in cognitive–behavioral therapy groups. If you suffer from shyness, we recommend Dr. Philip Zimbardo's (1990) book *Shyness* as a good place to start looking for help.

Check Your Understanding

1. RECALL: *The DSM-IV is based on*
   a. the cognitive perspective.
   b. the behavioral perspective.
   c. the medical model.
   d. the psychoanalytic view.

2. RECALL: *Which disorder involves extreme swings of mood from elation to depression?*
   a. panic disorder
   b. bipolar disorder
   c. schizophrenia
   d. unipolar depression

3. APPLICATION: *According to the biological preparedness hypothesis, which (one) of the following phobias would you expect to be most common?*
   a. fear of snakes (ophidophobia)
   b. fear of cancer (cancerophobia)
   c. fear of horses (equinophobia)
   d. fear of the number 13 (triskaidekaphobia)

4. RECALL: *Which of the following disorders involves a deficiency in memory?*
   a. phobia
   b. antisocial personality
   c. dissociative fugue
   d. obsessive–compulsive disorder

5. RECALL: *Which one is a disorder in which the individual displays more than one distinct personality?*
   a. schizophrenia
   b. depersonalization disorder
   c. bipolar disorder
   d. dissociative identity disorder

6. RECALL: *Which one is primarily a disorder of young American women?*
   a. bipolar disorder
   b. schizophrenia
   c. anorexia nervosa
   d. antisocial personality disorder

7. RECALL: *Which category of disorder is most common?*
   a. schizophrenic disorders
   b. dissociative disorders
   c. eating disorders
   d. the adjustment disorders and "other conditions that may be a focus of clinical attention"

8. RECALL: *Hallucinations and delusions are symptoms of*
   a. positive schizophrenia.
   b. negative schizophrenia.
   c. anxiety disorders.
   d. depersonalization disorder.

9. UNDERSTANDING THE CORE CONCEPT: *The DSM-IV groups most mental disorders by their*
   a. treatments.
   b. causes.
   c. symptoms.
   d. theoretical basis.

**ANSWERS:** 1. c    2. b    3. a    4. c    5. d    6. c
7. d    8. a    9. c

## The Insanity Plea: How Big Is the Problem?

How often is the plea of insanity used? Before you read about the insanity defense in the next part of the chapter, try to guess the approximate percentage of accused criminals in the United States who use a plea of insanity in court: _____%.

You will find the correct answer in the *Psychology in Your Life* section below. (An answer within 10% indicates that you have an exceptionally clear grasp of reality!)

*Hint:* Research shows that the public has an exaggerated impression of the problem.

 **KEY QUESTION** **WHAT ARE THE CONSEQUENCES OF LABELING?**

Mad. Maniac. Mentally ill. Crazy. Insane. Disturbed. Psychotic. Neurotic. These, along with all the diagnostic terms that appear in the *DSM-IV*, are labels used by the public, the courts, and mental health professionals to describe people who display mental disturbances. Ideally, an accurate diagnosis leads to an effective treatment program for the afflicted individual. Sometimes, however, labels can create more confusion and hurt than understanding. The problem is that labels can turn people into stereotypes, masking their personal characteristics and the unique circumstances that contribute to their disorders. And, if that is not enough, labels can provoke prejudices and social rejection.

In this section we will begin with the problem of labeling as it affects the individual. Then we will pursue the issue of labeling in a larger context: Does mental disorder mean the same thing in all cultures? Finally, we will take a critical look at the label "insanity" used by the courts. The Core Concept, around which all of this is organized, says:

 **CORE CONCEPT**

**Ideally, accurate diagnoses lead to proper treatments, but diagnoses may also become labels that depersonalize people and ignore the social and cultural contexts in which their problems arise.**

### Labeling and the Individual

Labels for people are deceptive in their simplicity, but they can have far-reaching effects. We saw a hint of this at the beginning of the chapter, in Rosenhan's "pseudopatient" study, where the glaring fact of normalcy was obscured by a diagnosis of schizophrenia. But there is yet another danger. The **depersonalization**—the stripping away of individuality—described by Rosenhan came from several sources in the hospital environment: from lack of privacy, from loss of legal rights at the time of commitment, and from the physical barriers that separated the staff from the patients. It also came from the hospital "pecking order," with the doctor on top and the patient on the bottom. The sources of depersonalization are numerous, but none was more powerful that the power of words—the diagnostic labels put on mental-hospital patients.

**Depersonalization:** The denying or stripping away of a person's individual character; treating the person as a label or a stereotype.

Labeling a person as mentally disturbed can have both serious and long-lasting consequences, aside from the mental disturbance itself. People may suffer a broken leg or an attack of appendicitis, but when they recover the diagnosis moves into the past. Not so with mental disorders. A label of "depression" or "mania" or "schizophrenia" can follow a person forever. But what about a *mistaken* diagnosis? As Rosenhan pointed out, a mistaken diagnosis of cancer is cause for celebration, but almost never is a diagnosis of mental disorder found to be wrong.

The diagnostic label may also become part of a cycle of neglect resulting from the inferior status accorded people with mental disorders. There is little doubt that in our society, to be mentally disordered is to be publicly degraded and personally devalued. This, of course, lowers self-esteem and reinforces disordered behavior. Thus, society extracts costly penalties from those who deviate from its norms (see Figure 13.8)—and in the process it perpetuates the problem of mental disorder.

Perhaps the most extreme reaction against labeling comes from radical psychiatrist Thomas Szasz, who says that mental illness does not exist; it is a "myth" (1961, 1977). Szasz argues that the symptoms used as evidence of mental illness are merely medical labels that give an excuse for professional intervention into what are really social problems: deviant people violating social norms. Once labeled, these

**FIGURE 13.8:**  Penalties for Unacceptable Behavior

This figure illustrates a continuum of behaviors that are deemed increasingly unacceptable and are responded to with increasing severity. In essence, each reaction is a punishment for deviance. Thus behavior toward those who suffer from psychopathology can be seen to resemble behavior toward criminals or other deviants.

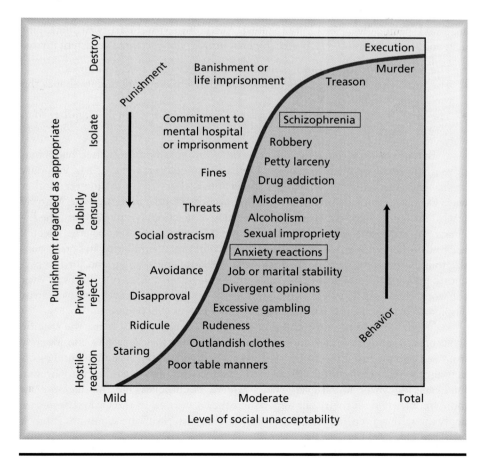

people can be treated for their "problem of being different," with no threat of disturbing the existing order.

We must keep in mind, therefore, that the goal of diagnosis is not simply to fit a person into a diagnostic box and think that we have understood his or her difficulty. Instead, a diagnosis should initiate a process that leads to a greater understanding of a person and to the development of a plan to help. A diagnosis should be a beginning, not an end.

## Diagnostic Labels and the Social–Cultural Context

Few other clinicians would go as far as Thomas Szasz, but many advocate an *ecological model* that takes the individual's external world into account (Levine & Perkins, 1987). In this model, abnormality is viewed as an interaction between individuals and the social and cultural context. Disorder results from a mismatch between a person's abilities and the needs of the situation. If you are a private investigator, for example, it might pay to have a slightly suspicious, or "paranoid," complexion to your personality, but if you are a nurse, this same characteristic might be called "deviant."

In support of an ecological model, studies show that culture influences both the prevalence of mental disorders and the symptoms that disturbed people show. For example, work done by the World Health Organization (1973, 1979) in Columbia, Czechoslovakia, Denmark, India, Nigeria, Taiwan, Britain, the United States, and the then-USSR established that the incidence of schizophrenia varies substantially from culture to culture. It also showed that schizophrenic symptoms, such as auditory hallucinations, also show cultural variability.

There are signs that psychiatry, too, is beginning to broaden its horizons and to note the effects of culture on psychopathology. The *DSM-IV*, in fact, has a section devoted to culture-specific disorders (although this section recognizes no disorders that are found specifically in the United States). According to psychiatrists Arthur Kleinman and Alex Cohen (1997), psychiatry has clung too long to three persistent myths:

- The myth that mental disorders have a similar prevalence in all cultures
- The myth that biology creates mental disorder, while culture merely shapes the way a person experiences it
- The myth that culture-specific disorders occur only in exotic places, rather than here at home

But, are cultural differences so great that certain symptoms such as hallucinations might earn you a label of schizophrenia in our culture, and a title of visionary or *shaman* (a medicine man or woman or seer) in another? To put the matter another way: Do all cultures distinguish between psychotics and prophets? Jane Murphy (1976) set out to answer this question in a study of two non-Western groups, the Eskimos of northwest Alaska and the Yorubas of rural tropical Nigeria, societies selected because of their wide geographic separation and cultural dissimilarity. In both groups she found separate terms and distinct social roles for the shaman and for the psychotic individual. Similar findings have since come from studies of cultures all over the world (Draguns, 1980). If mental illness is a socially defined myth, as psychiatrist Thomas Szasz asserts, it is a myth cherished by cultures everywhere.

While all cultures apparently recognize severe mental disorders, the specific symptoms of many disorders and people's explanations for them vary considerably from one group to another (Manson, 1994). The incidence of specific mental disorders also varies among cultures. Abundant evidence shows that, while schizophrenia, for example, can be found everywhere, American clinicians use the diagnosis far more frequently than their counterparts in other countries. In the United States we apply the schizophrenic label to nearly all patients with psychotic symptoms (Sprock & Blashfield, 1991).

## The Plea of Insanity

The plea of insanity is used less than most people realize.

*N*ow let's look at another label: the plea of insanity. What is your opinion: Does the insanity plea really excuse criminal behavior and put thousands of dangerous people back on the streets? Let's look at the facts.

In 1843, Daniel M'Naughten, a deranged woodcutter from Glasgow, thought he had received "instructions from God" to kill the British Prime Minister, Robert Peel. Fortunately for Peel, this would-be assassin struck down his secretary by mistake. Apprehended and tried, M'Naughten was found "not guilty by reason of insanity." The court reasoned that M'Naughten's mental condition prevented him from knowing right from wrong. The public responded with outrage. Neither did the public like the outcome of the modern-day case involving John Hinckley, the young man who shot and wounded then-President Ronald Reagan. Hinckley pled insanity, and the court agreed. As a result, he was placed in a mental hospital, where he remains today.

Such infamous cases have molded a low public opinion of the insanity defense. The citizenry blames psychologists and psychiatrists for clogging the courts with insanity pleas, allowing homicidal maniacs back on the streets, and letting criminals go to hospitals for "treatment" instead of prisons for punishment. But there are several problems with this public image of insanity.

For one thing, "insanity" appears nowhere among the *DSM-IV* listing of disorders recognized by psychologists and psychiatrists. Technically, **insanity** is not a psychological nor psychiatric term. It is a *legal* term, which only a court—not psychologists or psychiatrists—can officially apply. By law, insanity can include not only psychosis, but jealous rage, mental retardation, and a wide variety of other conditions in which a person might not be able to control his or her behavior or distinguish right from wrong (Thio, 1995).

So, why can we not simply abolish the laws that allow this technicality? The answer to that question turns on the definition of a crime. Legally, a crime requires two elements: (1) an illegal *act* (just wanting to commit a crime is not enough) and (2) the *intent* to commit the act. Merely wishing your boss dead is no crime (because you committed no illegal act). Neither is flattening the boss who accidentally steps in front of your moving car in the parking lot (assuming you had not planned the deed). But, if you lie in wait and willfully run over the scoundrel, you have committed an intentional and illegal act—and the courts can convict you of murder.

From this example, you can see why no one wants to give up the legal requirement of intent. You can also see why this safeguard leaves the door open for the controversial plea of insanity. The law will not hold you responsible if you can convince the court that it was an accident or that you did not know right from wrong or that you acted on an irresistible impulse. So-called "crimes of passion" fall in this latter category.

With these things in mind, take a moment to recall your estimate of the percentage of accused criminals who use the insanity plea. (See the earlier *Do It Your-*self! box.) In reality, the problem of the insanity defense receives more press than it deserves, because accused criminals use the insanity defense far less often than the public realizes. According to David Rosenhan (1983), it occurs in only about two of 1,000 criminal cases, and of this tiny number, only a fraction are successful. Also contrary to popular belief, most successful insanity pleas do *not* occur in murder cases. Still, public concern about abuses of the insanity plea have led several states to experiment with alternatives. Some now require separate verdicts on the act and the intent, allowing a jury to reach a verdict of "guilty but mentally ill" (Savitsky & Lindblom, 1986).

**Insanity:** A legal term, not a psychological or psychiatric one, referring to a person who is unable, because of a mental disorder or defect, to conform his or her behavior to the law.

1. RECALL: *Which one of the following statements is true?*
   a. Mental disorders have a similar prevalence in all cultures.
   b. In general, biology creates mental disorder, while culture merely shapes the way a person experiences it.
   c. Culture-specific disorders occur primarily in undeveloped countries.
   d. Cultures around the world seem to distinguish between people with mental disorders and people who are visionaries or prophets.

2. RECALL: *The term "insanity"*
   a. is a psychological term.
   b. is a psychiatric term, found in the *DSM-IV* under "psychotic disorders."
   c. is a legal term.
   d. is a term that refers either to "neurotic" or "psychotic" symptoms.

3. UNDERSTANDING THE CORE CONCEPT: *This section of the chapter emphasizes one of the unfortunate consequences of diagnosing mental disorders,*
   a. the inaccuracy of diagnosis.
   b. depersonalization.
   c. adding to the already overcrowded conditions in mental hospitals.
   d. some cultures do not recognize mental disorders.

ANSWERS:    1. d    2. c    3. b

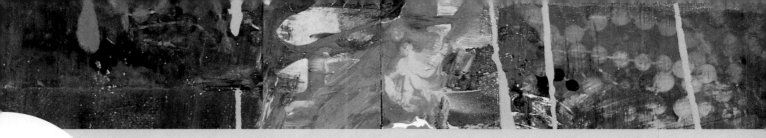

# USING PSYCHOLOGY TO LEARN PSYCHOLOGY

## *Diagnosing Your Friends and Family*

on't do it! Don't use your new knowledge of mental disorders to diagnose your family and friends. This is a common source of grief among psychology students.

We realize how tempting it is to apply what you are learning to the people in your life. Some of the disorders that we have considered here are common, so it would be surprising if they sounded completely alien. As you go through this chapter, you will almost certainly notice signs of anxiety, paranoia, depression, mania, and various other impairments of perception, memory, or emotion in your friends and relatives. It is a variation on the tendency, discussed earlier, to see signs of mental disorder in oneself. You should recognize this as a sign that you are assimilating some new knowledge of mental disorder. But we suggest that you keep these thoughts to yourself.

You must remember that reading one chapter does not make you an expert on psychopathology. So, you should be cautious about making amateur diagnoses. What you especially should *not* do is to tell someone that you think he or she *is* schizophrenic, bipolar, obsessive–compulsive—or any other diagnostic label.

Having said that, we should also note that erring too far in the opposite direction by ignoring signs of pathology could also be hazardous. If someone you know is struggling with significant mental problems—and if he or she asks for your opinion—you should refrain from putting a label on the problem, but you can encourage that person to see a competent professional for diagnosis and possible treatment. We will discuss more about how that is done—in the next chapter.

## CHAPTER SUMMARY

 **WHAT IS MENTAL DISORDER?**

- Our conception of abnormality has evolved from that of demon possession to the current medical model, which sees psychopathology as "illness," and the broader psychological model, which includes mental and contextual factors as well as biological ones. In practice, abnormality is judged by the degree to which a person's actions resemble a set of indicators that include distress, maladaptiveness, irrationality, unpredictability, unconventionality, and observer discomfort.

 **CORE CONCEPT**

**The medical model takes a "disease" view, while psychology sees mental disorder as an interaction of biological, cognitive, social, and other environmental factors.**

 **HOW ARE MENTAL DISORDERS CLASSIFIED?**

- The most widely used system for classifying mental disorders is the *DSM-IV*, which derives from psychiatry and has a bias toward the medical model. The *DSM-IV* recognizes more than 300 specific disorders, categorized by symptom patterns, but it has no category for "normal" functioning.

- Among the *DSM-IV* categories are the *affective disorders*, which involve disturbances of mood. Unipolar depression is the most common affective disorder, while bipolar disorder is much rarer. The *anxiety disorders* include panic disorder, phobic disorders, and obsessive–compulsive disorder. The *somatoform disorders* involve the mind–body relationship in various ways. Those with conversion disorder have physical symptoms, but no organic disease, while those with hypochondriasis suffer from exaggerated concern about illness. The *dissociative disorders* include dissociative amnesia, fugue, depersonalization disorder, and dissociative identity disorder. All disrupt the integrated functioning of memory, consciousness, or personal identity. There are two common patterns of *eating disorders:* anorexia nervosa (self-starvation) and bulimia (binging and purging). Both are related to unrealistic, negative body images and are difficult to treat. *Schizophrenia* is characterized by extreme distortions in perception, thinking, emotion, behavior, and language. Schizophrenia takes five forms: disorganized, catatonic, paranoid, undifferentiated, and residual types. Evidence for the causes of schizophrenia has been found in a variety of factors including genetics, abnormal brain structure, and biochemistry. *Personality disorders* are patterns of perception, thinking, or behavior that are long-standing and inflexible and that impair an individual's functioning. The most common forms of disorder are classified in the *DSM-IV* as the *adjustment disorders* and *"other conditions that may be a focus of clinical attention."* These include a wide range of problems in living. *Shyness* is a widespread problem—and a treatable one—but it is not officially a disorder, unless it goes to the extreme of a social phobia.

 **The most widely used system, found in the *DSM-IV,* classifies disorders by their mental and behavioral symptoms.**

**KEY QUESTION** **WHAT ARE THE CONSEQUENCES OF LABELING?**

- Labeling someone as psychologically or mentally disordered is ultimately a matter of human judgment. Therefore, even professional judgments can be biased by prejudices. Those labeled with psychological disorders are often depersonalized in ways that most physically ill people are not. Culture has an effect on whether a behavior is called normal, abnormal, or merely unusual. Cross-cultural research suggests that people everywhere distinguish between psychotic individuals and those that they label shamans, prophets, or visionaries. Insanity, however, is a special sort of label that is awarded by the courts: Insanity is not a psychological or psychiatric term.

 **Ideally, accurate diagnoses lead to proper treatments, but diagnoses may also become labels that depersonalize people and ignore the social and cultural contexts in which their problems arise.**

---

# *REVIEW TEST*

For each of the following items, choose the single correct or best answer. The answer key appears at the end.

1. The medical model views mental disorder as
   a. a character defect.
   b. a disease or illness.
   c. an interaction of biological, cognitive, behavioral, social, and cultural factors.
   d. normal behavior in an abnormal context.

2. Which of the following is *not* one of the six indicators of possible abnormality agreed upon by psychologists?
   a. chronic physical illness
   b. observer discomfort
   c. unconventionality
   d. irrationality

3. The *DSM-IV* refers to
   a. a personality inventory.
   b. the most widely used classification system for mental disorders.

   c. the neurochemical implicated in anxiety disorders.
   d. a class of psychoactive drugs effective in the treatment of schizophrenia.

4. A long-standing pattern of irresponsible behavior that hurts others without causing feelings of guilt or remorse is typical of
   a. an obsessive–compulsive disorder.
   b. an antisocial personality disorder.
   c. a narcissistic personality disorder.
   d. paranoid schizophrenia.

5. A young woman wanders into a hospital, claiming not to know who she is, where she came from, or how she got there. Her symptoms indicate that she might be suffering from a(n) _____ disorder.
   a. anxiety
   b. affective
   c. personality
   d. dissociative

**6.** Which of the following statements about phobic disorders is true?
  **a.** Any extreme and irrational fear, such as of spiders, is considered a "phobia."
  **b.** The "preparedness hypothesis" suggests that some people learn their fears from their parents at an early age.
  **c.** Phobias represent one form of affective disorders.
  **d.** all of the above

**7.** _____ has been called the "common cold of psychopathology," because it occurs so frequently and because almost everyone has experienced it at some time.
  **a.** Obsessive–compulsive disorder
  **b.** Bipolar disorder
  **c.** Unipolar depression
  **d.** Paranoid schizophrenia

**8.** A person who suffers from _____ cannot eat normally but engages in a ritual of "binging"—overeating fattening foods—followed by "purging" with induced vomiting or use of laxatives.
  **a.** anorexia nervosa
  **b.** bulimia

  **c.** inhibition
  **d.** mania

**9.** The _____ type of schizophrenia is characterized by delusions.
  **a.** disorganized
  **b.** catatonic
  **c.** paranoid
  **d.** undifferentiated

**10.** Rosenhan believes that his "pseudopatients" were not recognized as normal is because
  **a.** the staff members in the mental hospitals were stupid and foolish.
  **b.** the staff members in the mental hospitals were just as disturbed as the patients.
  **c.** mental illness is a myth.
  **d.** many situational factors depersonalize mental patients.

**ANSWERS:**  1. b   2. a   3. b   4. b   5. d   6. a
7. c   8. b   9. c   10. d

---

## IF YOU'RE INTERESTED . . .

### BOOKS

Alvarez, A. (1971). *The savage god: A study of suicide.* New York: W. W. Norton & Company.

*Somewhat high-level, this fascinating study of famous suicides presents a history of social, religious, literary, and "romantic" attitudes toward suicide and theories of its causes and influences, from medieval to modern times.*

American Psychiatric Association. (1994). *Diagnostic and statistical manual of mental disorders* (4th ed.). Washington, DC: American Psychiatric Association.

*As long as you are studying about the DSM-IV, you might as well meet it face-to-face. Although some of the language is technical, you will find it readable after you have studied this chapter. Your library probably has a copy.*

Colas, E. (1998). *Just checking: Scenes from the life of an obsessive–compulsive.* New York: Pocket Books.

*The author frankly and humorously discusses her incessant worrying about everything, one hallmark of the obsessive–compulsive personality, who may be unable to resist the urge to check and double-check every threat and possible*

*action in everyday life, from electric lights and appliances to the dangers of driving accidents.*

Jamison, K. R. (1995). *An unquiet mind: A memoir of moods and madness.* New York: Alfred A. Knopf.

*Kay Redfield Jamison, a doctor and professor of psychiatry specializing in manic–depressive (bipolar) disorder, reflects with drama and clarity on her own struggle with that very illness. The book charts the development of her illness from her adolescence—through college and graduate school, passionate love and desperate loss, bouts of violence and even attempted suicide. She candidly explores how the energy of her "high highs" led her to resist medications that might reduce the intensity of both her highs and lows. The book is beautifully written and personal.*

Lyden, J. (1997). *Daughter of the Queen of Sheba: A memoir.* Boston: Houghton Mifflin.

*National Public Radio journalist Jacki Lyden turns her journalistic attention to her own childhood, growing up with a "mad mother" whose bipolar disorder made her by turns impossible to live with and hysterically funny and delightful.*

Pipher, M. (1994). *Reviving Ophelia: Saving the selves of adolescent girls.* New York: Grosset/Putnam.

*This book presents an involving account of the paradoxical challenges facing adolescent women today: with more opportunities and freedoms than women of any previous generation, they also struggle with vicious, ironic assaults on self-esteem, drops in intelligence, relationship conflicts and impasses, and risk for a variety of psychopathologies ranging from depression and obsession to life-threatening eating disorders.*

Secunda, V. (1998). *When madness comes home: Help and hope for the children, siblings, and partners of the mentally ill.* New York: Hyperion.

*This well-researched and well-written book describes what can be expected by the loved ones of those afflicted by psychological disorders and presents strategies for coping, by a sympathetic author whose own sister is schizophrenic.*

Sheehan, S. (1982). *Is there no place on earth for me?* New York: Vintage.

*In a book originally published as a series of articles in* The New Yorker, *Susan Sheehan reports her impressions and the experiences of a young schizophrenic woman, "Sylvia Frumkin," with whom she lived and spent time in order to better understand the nature of thought disorders and the difficulties of treating them.*

Siegel, R. K. (1992). *Fire in the brain: Clinical tales of hallucination.* New York: Dutton.

*Written very much in the manner of Oliver Sacks (The man who mistook his wife for a hat), this is a book of clinical tales involving hallucinations from various causes, psychological, neurological, and drug-induced. Hallucinations are a window opening onto the inner workings of the mind.*

Styron, W. (1990). *Darkness visible: A memoir of madness.* New York: Random House.

*In this brief, poetic essay, the author of Sophie's Choice documents his own plunge into clinical depression and his gradual progress back to the light.*

Torrey, E. F. (1995). *Surviving schizophrenia: A manual for families, consumers, and providers.* New York: Harper-Perennial.

*Psychiatrist E. Fuller Torrey's "indispensable" manual presents every aspect of the causes, manifestations, and treatments of schizophrenia, as they affect the patients and those who care for and about them.*

Zimbardo, P. G. (1990). *Shyness: What it is and what to do about it.* Reading, MA: Perseus Books.

*Dr. Zimbardo, one of your authors, has made an extensive study of shyness, and this book will tell you what he has discovered. It is highly recommended for those who want to understand their shyness and want to do something about it.*

## VIDEOS

➤ *As good as it gets.* (1997, color, 138 min.). Directed by James L. Brooks; starring Jack Nicholson, Helen Hunt, Greg Kinnear, Cuba Gooding, Jr.

*Jack Nicholson portrays a lonely and insufferable OCD sufferer. Helen Hunt becomes his reluctant girlfriend, who has to put up with his difficult obsessions and compulsions.*

*The Caine mutiny.* (1954, color, 125 min.). Directed by Edward Dmytryk; starring Humphrey Bogart, Jose Ferrer, Van Johnson, Fred MacMurray, E. G. Marshall.

*Based on Herman Wouk's prizewinning novel, this is the story of a U.S. Navy court martial and the events that led to it. Humphrey Bogart is outstanding as the paranoid Captain Queeg, whose nervous habits and delusional thinking frighten his officers into taking mutinous action.*

*The fisher king.* (1991, color, 137 min.). Directed by Terry Gilliam; starring Robin Williams, Jeff Bridges, Amanda Plummer, Mercedes Ruehl, Michael Jeter.

*When a talk-radio announcer's flip remark to an unstable caller has tragic consequences, he seeks to make amends by helping one of the victims. The film presents powerful imagery of fantastic visions, paranoid delusions, and post-traumatic stress—with poignant and comic moments, too.*

*Invasion of the body snatchers.* (1956, B&W 80 min.). Directed by Don Siegel; starring Kevin McCarthy, Dana Wynter, King Donovan, Carolyn Jones.

*This is the first and best science fiction/paranoia story about the aliens who conquer the world, one individual at a time, in the form of plant "pods" that somehow take over the minds and bodies of their human hosts. Two themes to watch for are the loneliness of the one man who knows about the danger but cannot save his community in time, and the importance of being ever vigilant so that "they"— the nation's enemies, alien ideologies, and Big Brother—do not "possess" their unwitting and unprepared victims (an allusion to the Senate's anticommunist hearings in the late 1940s and early 1950s). This version is much better than the 1978 remake.*

*One flew over the cuckoo's nest.* (1975, color, 133 min.). Directed by Milos Forman; starring Jack Nicholson, Louise Fletcher, Brad Dourif, Will Sampson, Danny DeVito, Christopher Lloyd, Scatman Crothers.

*This captivating (and Oscar-capturing) film is based on Ken Kesey's novel about the confrontation created by a criminal's entry into a psychiatric hospital, his relationships with voluntary patients, and his doomed struggle against institutional authority. There are gross inaccuracies about* everything from nurses' power in psychiatric settings to the uses and abuses of psychosurgery; but with those cautions in mind, the viewer enjoys terrific insights into the nature of mental disorders, the complexity of deciding who is "normal," and what to do about individuals who are not.

*Promise.* (1986 [made for TV], color, 100 min.). Directed by Glenn Jordan; starring James Garner, James Woods, Piper Laurie, Peter Michael Goetz, Michael Alldredge, Alan Rosenberg.

*When his mother dies, a middle-aged bachelor must honor a promise he made to her to care for his schizophrenic younger brother. Wonderfully written, the story does not gloss over the real problems of living with (and being) someone who is thought-disordered. The film presents outstanding portrayals of personalities, feelings, and the delicate balance between freedom, love, and responsibility.*

*The ruling class* (1972, color, 154 min.). Directed by Peter Medak; starring Peter O'Toole, Alastair Sim, Arthur Lowe, Harry Andrews, Coral Brown.

*This funny and irreverent dark comedy tells of an English aristocrat with undeniable disorders and the delusion that he is Jesus Christ.*

*Sling blade.* (1996, color, 134 min.). Directed by Billy Bob Thornton; starring Billy Bob Thornton, Dwight Yoakam, J. T. Walsh, John Ritter, Lucas Black, Natalie Canerday.

*A fascinating picture depicts a mentally deficient man, a lifelong victim of abuse, whose devotion to his first friend outside an institution has violent consequences. Superb performances sharpen this film, which won the Oscar for Best Screenplay Adaptation.*

*The three faces of eve.* (1957, B&W, 91 min.). Directed by Nunnally Johnson; starring Joanne Woodward, Lee J. Cobb, David Wayne.

*Based on fact, this is the story of a woman found to have at least three distinct personalities and the efforts she and her therapists make to find the source—and the resolution—of her disorder.*

*Vertigo.* (1958, color, 128 min.). Directed by Alfred Hitchcock; starring James Stewart, Kim Novak, Barbara Bel Geddes.

*A police detective with a fear of heights (acrophobia) is lured into a mysterious romance and then a crime in this dramatic cinematic portrayal of anxiety and terror.*

CORE CONCEPTS

PSYCHOLOGY IN YOUR LIFE

**WHAT IS THERAPY?**

Therapy takes a variety of forms, but the common element is a relationship focused on altering behavior or mental processes.

**Paraprofessionals Do Therapy, Too:** Some studies show that amount of training is not the main factor in therapeutic effectiveness.

**HOW DO PSYCHOLOGISTS TREAT MENTAL DISORDERS?**

Psychologists employ two main forms of treatment: the behavioral therapies and the insight therapies.

**Where Do Most People Get Help?** A lot of therapy is done by friends, hairdressers, and bartenders.

**HOW DO THE BIOMEDICAL THERAPIES APPROACH MENTAL DISORDERS?**

The biomedical therapies alter the structure or function of the brain through drugs, surgery, or electrical stimulation.

**What Sort of Therapy Would You Recommend?** If a friend asks for a recommendation, you have a wide range of therapeutic possibilities to consider.

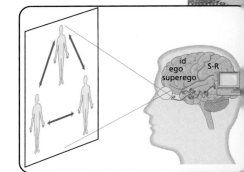

**USING PSYCHOLOGY TO LEARN PSYCHOLOGY: HOW IS EDUCATION LIKE THERAPY?**

# 14 Therapies for Mental Disorder

## Chapter Outline

*K*en had always loved school. It was the place where he excelled, as head of every class, pet of every teacher, and envy of every student. He was "Straight-A Ken." It embarrassed him a little when his parents called him that—but it also pleased him a lot.

Soon after he went away to college, Ken's image changed as his grades began to slip. He had difficulty concentrating because he was experiencing three disturbing symptoms, each of which distracted him from studying and interfered with being fully alert in class. When the symptoms worsened and became a source of chronic concern, Ken reluctantly went to see the psychotherapist at the Student Health Center.

He told the therapist that he had been losing weight because he was unable to eat properly and would get nauseous, often vomiting whatever he had eaten. This food–weight problem was weakening him, and it made it difficult to study. Problem number two was more awkward for him to talk about to a stranger, especially a female therapist. Ken had a sexual difficulty: He often could not get or maintain an erection. This bothered him a lot. He was worried about getting into an intimate relationship, and he was beginning to question his masculinity. These worries also made it difficult to keep his attention on schoolwork. But maybe symptom three was even more distressing. Whenever anyone disagreed with him about anything, however trivial, Ken couldn't keep from imagining horrible things happening to them: auto accidents, suicides, shootings . . . These fantasies extended to his close friends and roommates and made it difficult to discuss any topic on which they might disagree. Of course, such troublesome thoughts affected studying and further contributed to his academic decline. He desperately wanted the therapist to help him overcome these symptoms so that he could return to his normal state of well-being and effective intellectual functioning.

One of the first things the therapist wanted to know was when each of his symptoms had started. Because Ken believed they were the cause of his poor freshman grades, the therapist wanted to establish which came first: the symptoms or the negative grade reports. Before their next therapy session, she obtained a copy of Ken's grade transcript.

The therapist showed sympathy for Ken's plight and compassion for his distress, but she also laid out the time line for him to reflect upon. The poor grades came first, it turned out; then the physical and mental symptoms started. The therapist suggested that Ken

533

*had developed the symptoms as a result of his fall from academic perfection—not the other way around. She believed that the three symptoms were modifiable through therapy. She was less clear about the true cause of his academic distress. It may have been due to fear, or it may have been a lack of interest, preparation, or ability to get As in this new, high-powered academic environment. Whatever it was, the therapist was certain that Ken was making matters worse with his worrying and with what might be impossibly high standards that he had set for himself. As they discussed the possibilities, it became clear that Ken's expectations about being academically perfect were of equal concern with the other three symptoms. Academic excellence, the therapist discovered, was also of overwhelming importance to Ken's parents, who wanted him to become a physician. Together, Ken and the therapist talked about Ken establishing his own goals and searching for a career that really interested him. They also discussed taking an alternative approach to his college work: focusing on enjoyment of his classes and building intrinsic motivation instead of an excessive emphasis on grades. In less than a month, each of Ken's symptoms diminished and stopped bothering him. His grades actually began to go up, too. At this point, a year later, he is well on his way to a bachelor's degree in journalism.*

**Chapter 13: Psychopathology**

*The DSM-IV contains the most widely accepted listing of mental disorders.*

How typical is Ken's case? While the overwhelming majority of people who seek **therapy** receive significant help, each individual who seeks treatment is different. Not only do they come to therapy with the full range of problems found in the *DSM-IV*, but they come from diverse backgrounds and with varied goals for therapy. These are some of the things that make evaluating therapy difficult.

Not everyone who enters therapy, of course, becomes a success case. Some people wait too long, until their problems become intractable. Some do not end up with the right sort of therapy for their problems. And many people who could benefit from therapy do not have access to it because of financial constraints. Yet, despite these shortfalls, the development of a wide range of effective therapies is one of the success stories in modern psychology.

In this last chapter of our journey through *Psychology*, we begin our overview of therapy by discussing what it is: who seeks it, what sorts of problems they bring to therapy, and who the therapists are. We will also see how therapeutic practices are influenced by history and culture. In the second section of the chapter, we consider the major types of psychological treatments currently used and how well they work. In the final section we will look at medical treatments for mental disorders, including drug therapy, psychosurgery, and "shock treatment." We will also consider when it is appropriate to place people who need treatment in institutions, such as mental hospitals, as opposed to delivering therapy in the community. As you read through the chapter, we hope that you will weigh the advantages and disadvantages of each therapy, keeping in mind that you may sometime be asked by a friend or relative to use what you have learned here to recommend an appropriate therapy.

Many people could benefit from some form of therapy. Most people who enter therapy receive significant help.

**KEY QUESTION**

## WHAT IS THERAPY?

**Therapy:** A general term for any treatment process; in psychology and psychiatry, "therapy" refers to a variety of psychological and biomedical techniques.

When you think of "therapy," chances are that a stereotypic scene, taken from countless cartoons and movies, pops into mind: a "neurotic" patient lying on the analyst's couch, with a bearded therapist sitting at the patient's head, scribbling notes and

*"You are a very sick rabbit."*

making interpretations. In fact, this is a scene from classic Freudian therapy, which is a rarity today. The reality of modern therapy differs from the stereotype on several counts. First, most therapists don't use a couch. Second, people now seek therapeutic help for a wide range of problems: making difficult choices, dealing with academic problems, and coping with unhappy relationships. And third, many forms of therapy involve far more than talk and interpretation.

In modern therapy for mental disorders—as with physical illnesses—the form that treatment takes is determined by the nature and severity of the problem. Some difficulties, such as schizophrenia, are so serious that they may require long-term, intensive treatment in special institutional settings. A less overwhelming problem, such as making a career decision, may require only short-term counseling. Many people with mild difficulties in everyday living might mention them to a family doctor, ask advice from friends, and ultimately find effective solutions that do not involve help from a trained therapist. Between the extremes of severe and mild lie a variety of disorders. Because the experience of abnormality affects each individual uniquely and subjectively, people's willingness to consider therapy will vary widely even for similar problems. As we will see in this chapter, when it is appropriate for the problem, therapy can be a great source of help and reassurance.

For those who do seek therapy, help may appear in a bewildering menu of possibilities, which can involve talk and interpretation, behavior modification, drugs, and, in some cases, even "shock treatment," or brain surgery. No matter what form therapy takes, however, there is one constant, as our Core Concept suggests:

**Therapy takes a variety of forms, but the common element is a relationship focused on altering behavior or mental processes.**

In this chapter, as we examine a sampling of the therapeutic universe, we will see that each form of therapy is based on different assumptions about mental disorder. Yet, as we highlight the differences, it is well to keep in mind that all involve relationships designed to change that person's functioning in some way. Let's begin our exploration of therapy by looking more closely at the variety of people who enter treatment and the problems they bring with them to the therapeutic relationship.

**cathy®**  by Cathy Guisewite

## Entering Therapy

Why would *you* go into therapy? Why would anyone? Most often, people enter therapy when they have a problem that they are unable to resolve by themselves. They may seek therapy on their own initiative after trying ineffectively to cope with their problems, or they may be advised to do so by family, friends, a physician, or a coworker.

The problems that people bring to therapy run the gamut of life's difficulties. People seek therapy to cope with sudden life changes due to unemployment, death of a loved one, or a divorce. They seek treatment for help with problems associated with long-term physical illnesses. Students who seek therapy from college mental health facilities often do so because of difficulties in their interpersonal relationships and concerns about academic performance. In a few cases, persons whose behavior is judged as dangerous to themselves or others can be committed by a state court to a mental institution for therapy.

Obviously, you don't have to be "crazy" to seek therapy. If you do enter therapy, however, you may be referred to as either a *patient* or a *client*. The term "patient" is often used by professionals who take a biological or medical approach to the treatment of mental disorders and for those who are hospitalized for their treatment. The term "client" may be used by professionals who think of psychological disorders not as mental *illnesses* but rather as *problems in living* for which people seek the assistance of professionals trained in various forms of **psychotherapy** (Rogers, 1951; Szasz, 1961).

One's ability to obtain therapy can be affected by a variety of factors. As we have noted, therapy is far easier to obtain if you have money or adequate health insurance. The poor, especially poor ethnic minorities, often lack access to adequate mental health care (Bower, 1998; Nemecek, 1999). Part of the problem can be lack of qualified therapists. In many communities, it is still much easier to get help from a medical doctor for physical health problems than it is to find a qualified mental health worker who has time to provide needed, affordable psychological help. Even the nature of a person's psychological problems can interfere with getting help. An individual with agoraphobia, for example, finds it hard, even impossible, to leave home to seek therapy. Paranoid persons may not seek help because they don't trust mental health professionals. And extremely shy people cannot call for an appointment or go to an initial diagnostic interview precisely because of the problem for which they desire help.

## The Therapeutic Relationship and the Goals of Therapy

Is a therapist just a "paid friend?" Sometimes you may only need to talk out a problem with a sympathetic companion, perhaps to "hear yourself think" or to receive reassurance that he or she still cares for you. But friends have needs and agen-

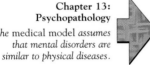

**Chapter 13:
Psychopathology**

*The* medical model *assumes that mental disorders are similar to physical diseases.*

**Chapter 13:
Psychopathology**

*Agoraphobia* commonly *involves a fear of public places and open spaces, from which there is no easy escape.*

**Psychotherapy:** A term for any of the psychologically based therapies, including behavioral therapies and insight therapies.

das of their own that may not always coincide with those of the person seeking assistance. Sometimes they may be a part of the problem. For whatever reason, when friends or family cannot offer the help you need, it may be appropriate to seek the help of a professionally trained therapist. You might also want professional help if you wish to keep your problems and concerns confidential. Moreover, professional therapists have expertise in identifying mental disorders and in using therapeutic techniques that a friend would probably not know about and certainly would not have the skills to employ. In all these ways, a professional relationship with a therapist is different from a friendship.

Despite the differences between therapy and friendship, however, the essence of therapy is still a *relationship* between the therapist and the patient/client seeking assistance—as our Core Concept indicates. You must be able to trust your therapist, just as you would a reliable friend. You and your therapist must be able to work as *allies*, on the same side, joining forces to cope with and solve the problems that have brought you to therapy (Horvath & Luborsky, 1993). And you must share concerns, values, and goals with the therapist. It also helps if you *believe* that therapy will be effective for your problem.

In addition to the relationship between therapist and client, the therapeutic process typically involves the following four tasks or goals:

1. *Identifying the problem.* This may mean merely agreeing on a simple description of circumstances or feelings to be changed, or, in the case of a *DSM-IV* disorder, this step may call for a formal *diagnosis* about what is wrong.
2. *Identifying the etiology, or cause, of the problem.* This involves identifying its probable origins, its development, and the reasons for the symptoms.
3. *Making a prognosis.* This is the prediction of the course the problem will take and the outlook for improvement or recovery.
4. *Deciding on and carrying out some form of treatment.* This involves selecting a specific type of therapy designed to minimize or eliminate the troublesome symptoms and, perhaps, also their sources.

Although more people seek out therapy now than in the past, people usually turn to trained mental health professionals only when their psychological problems become severe or persist for extended periods of time. When they do, they usually choose one of seven main types of professional therapists: counseling psychologists, clinical psychologists, psychiatrists, psychoanalysts, psychiatric nurse practitioners, clinical social workers, or pastoral counselors. The differences among these specialties are detailed in Table 14.1. As you examine that table, note that each has its area of emphasis and special expertise. For example, the only therapists licensed to prescribe drugs are psychiatrists, psychoanalysts (with medical degrees), and psychiatric nurse practitioners. Currently some psychologists are seeking to obtain prescription privileges, but this is a highly political issue that is not likely to be resolved soon (Clay, 1998; Sleek, 1996). On the other hand, we will see later in the chapter that psychologists have developed therapeutic alternatives that are in many cases equal or superior to drug treatment.

Incidentally, we should note that little practical difference exists between the processes called *counseling* and *psychotherapy*. Some see counseling as a shorter problem-solving process, while psychotherapy involves a longer-term overhaul of the personality. The difference, if any, is one of degree.

## Therapy in Historical and Cultural Context

People with psychological problems may encounter anything from sympathetic understanding to avoidance to scorn and even abuse. How we respond depends on the way we think about mental disorder. Do you believe, for example, that mental problems are diseases, the mark of a character flaw, a "problem in living," or a sign of

TABLE 14.1: Types of Mental Health Care Professionals

| PROFESSIONAL TITLE | SPECIALTY AND COMMON WORK SETTINGS | CREDENTIALS AND QUALIFICATIONS |
|---|---|---|
| Counseling psychologist | Provides help in dealing with the common problems of normal living, such as relationship problems, childrearing, occupational choice, and school problems. Typically counselors work in schools, clinics, or other institutions. | master's in counseling, PhD (Doctor of Philosophy), EdD (Doctor of Education), or PsyD (Doctor of Psychology) |
| Clinical psychologist | Trained primarily to work with those who have more severe disorders; practice often overlaps considerably with that of all other mental health professionals. Usually in private practice or employed by mental health agencies or by hospitals. Not licensed to prescribe drugs. | Phd or PsyD |
| Psychiatrist | A specialty of medicine; deals with severe mental problems—most often by means of drug therapies. May be in private practice or employed by clinics or mental hospitals. | MD (Doctor of Medicine) |
| Psychoanalyst | Practitioners of Freudian therapy. Usually in private practice. | MD—In the United States, psychoanalysts are usually psychiatrists who have taken additional training in psychoanalysis. |
| Psychiatric nurse practitioner | A nursing specialty; licensed to prescribe drugs for mental disorders. May work in private practice or in clinics and hospitals. | RN (Registered Nurse)—Plus special training in treating mental disorders and prescribing drugs. |
| Clinical social worker | Social workers with a specialty in dealing with mental disorders, especially from the viewpoint of the social and environmental context of the problem. | MSW (Master of Social Work) |
| Pastoral counselor | A member of a religious order or ministry who specializes in treatment of psychological disorders. Combines spiritual guidance with practical counseling. | varies |

demon possession? How society responds—including the treatment options it provides—depends on its prevailing beliefs about mental disorders and on the economic resources it has available for treatment.

**CONTEMPORARY APPROACHES TO THERAPY**  Modern mental health professionals have abandoned the old demon model and frankly abusive treatments in favor of therapies based on psychological and biological theories of mind and behavior. Yet the professionals often disagree on the exact causes and appropriate treatments. This situation is reflected in the abundance of therapies available: Each theory and its accompanying treatment emphasizes some aspects of mind and behavior and deemphasizes others. To help you sort them out, here is a preliminary sketch of the modern therapeutic landscape—a picture that will also serve as a preview of things to come in this chapter.

The **psychological therapies,** as we have noted, are often collectively called simply "psychotherapy." They focus on changing disordered thoughts, feelings, and behavior using psychological techniques rather than biological interventions. No matter what the name, all the psychological therapies consist principally of (a) helping people change their behavior or (b) helping people achieve *insight* into their problems. Let's look at some specific differences among the psychological therapies.

**Chapter 13: Psychopathology**
*Demon possession was the medieval explanation for mental disorder.*

**Psychological therapies:** Therapies based on psychological principles (rather than on the biomedical approach); often called "psychotherapy."

In this engraving from the 1730s, we see the chaos of a cell in the London hospital St. Mary of Bethlehem. Here the upper classes have paid to see the horrors, the fiddler who entertains, and the mental patients chained, tortured, and dehumanized. The chaos of Bethlehem eventually became synonymous with the corruption of its name—Bedlam.

*Behavioral therapy* treats the problem behaviors themselves as disturbances that must be modified. Disorders are viewed as learned habit patterns rather than as the symptoms of some underlying mental disease. Behavior therapists believe that changing problematic behavior corrects the disorder.

Among the insight therapies, *cognitive therapy* tries to restructure how a person thinks by altering distorted self-statements a person makes about the causes of a problem. Cognitions (including thoughts, beliefs, emotions, and attitudes) are viewed as the focus of therapy. As compared with behavior therapy, the emphasis in cognitive therapy is internal, rather than on external circumstances and behaviors.

Another group of insight therapies, the *psychodynamic approaches*, view mental disorders as the outer symptoms of unresolved childhood traumas and inner conflicts. The best-known psychodynamic treatment is Freudian *psychoanalysis*, the so-called "talking cure" in which a therapist helps a person develop insights about the relationship between the overt symptoms and the unresolved hidden conflicts that are presumably causing those symptoms.

Insight therapies emerging from the humanistic tradition emphasize the self-concept, needs, and values of the patient. *Humanistic therapies* are directed toward self-actualization and psychological growth. Humanistic therapists emphasize the development of more meaningful interpersonal relationships and the enhancement of freedom of choice and a healthier view of oneself.

In contrast with psychotherapy, the **biomedical therapies** focus on treating mental problems by changing the underlying biology of the brain. To do so, a physician or nurse practitioner can call on a variety of drugs, including antidepressants, "tranquilizers," and stimulants. Occasionally the brain may be treated with electrical stimulation or even surgery. In general, biomedical therapies try to alter brain functioning with chemical or physical interventions.

**Biomedical therapies:** Treatments that focus on altering the brain, especially with drugs, psychosurgery, or electroconvulsive therapy.

**Chapter 6:**
**Learning and Remembering**
*Behavioral therapy is based on the principles of behavioral learning.*

**Chapter 7:**
**Cognitive Processes**
*Cognitive therapy is based on the principles of cognitive science.*

**Chapter 10:**
**Personality**
*Psychoanalysis is based on Freud's theory of personality.*

**Chapter 10:**
**Personality**
*The hierarchy of needs is part of Maslow's humanistic theory of personality.*

**Chapter 2:**
**Biopsychology**
*The brain has two communication systems: the peripheral nervous system and the endocrine system.*

In Mozambique, a Femba tribe's medicine woman, one of their *curandeiros* or healers, "catches the bad spirit" of her patient.

As we have noted, laws specify which professions are licensed to provide biomedical therapy, but most mental health practitioners collaborate to meet both the legal requirements and their patients' needs. So, clinical psychologists, who cannot prescribe medicine but may give therapy to individuals who need medical treatment, often work closely with physicians in making diagnoses and recommendations for the proper course of medication.

**HEALING IN CULTURAL CONTEXT**   Modern Western (European and North American) views and practices generally regard psychological disorders to be the result of disease processes, abnormal genetics, distorted mental processes, unhealthy environments, or stressors. But other cultures often have quite different perspectives (Triandis, 1990). For example, a common African conception portrays mental disorder not as an individual characteristic but in terms of becoming estranged from nature and from the community, including the community of ancestral spirits (Nobles, 1976; Sow, 1977). In such cultures, treatment of mentally disturbed individuals by removing them from society is unthinkable. Instead, healing takes place in a social context, emphasizing a distressed person's beliefs, family, work, and life environment. The African use of group support in therapy has been expanded into a procedure called "network therapy," where a patient's entire network of relatives, coworkers, and friends becomes involved in the treatment (Lambo, 1978). Similar views have begun to work their way into therapies in the United States and other individualistic countries. A focus on *family context* and *supportive community* are especially evident in therapeutic approaches that emphasize social support networks and family therapy.

In many places around the world, the treatment of mental and physical disease is also bound up with religion and the supernatural. Certain persons—priests, ministers, shamans, sorcerers, and witches—are assumed to have special mystical powers to help distressed fellow beings. Their methods involve ceremonies and rituals that infuse special emotional intensity and meaning into the healing process. These practices heighten patients' suggestibility and sense of personal importance. Combined with the use of symbols, they connect the individual sufferer, the shaman, and the society to supernatural forces to be won over in the battle against madness (Devereux, 1981; Wallace, 1959). In some cases this approach is similar to the old demon-possession model that was dominant in medieval Europe, although we should note that attributing disorders to supernatural forces has more often led to personal blame and abusive treatment in individualist cultures than in collectivist societies.

**PSYCHOLOGY IN YOUR LIFE**

## Paraprofessionals Do Therapy, Too

*D*oes the best therapy always require a highly trained (and expensive) professional? Or can *paraprofessionals*—who have received on-the-job training in place of graduate training and certification—be effective therapists? If you are seeking treatment, these questions are important because hospitals, clinics, and agencies are increasingly turning to paraprofessionals as a cost-cutting measure: Those who lack full professional credentials can be hired at a fraction of the cost of those with professional degrees. They are often called "aides" or "counselors" (although many counselors do have professional credentials).

Surprisingly, a review of the literature has failed to find substantial differences in the effectiveness of the two groups across a wide spectrum of psychological problems (Christensen & Jacobson, 1994). The implications of this conclusion are not yet clear, but it is good news in the sense that the need for mental health services is far greater than the number of professional therapists can possibly provide. And, because paraprofessional therapists can be effective, highly trained professionals may be freed for other roles, including prevention and community education programs, assessment of patients, training and supervision of paraprofessionals, and research. The reader should be cautioned about over-interpreting this finding, however.

Professionals and paraprofessionals have been found to be equivalent only in the realm of the insight therapies (Zilbergeld, 1986). Such differences have not been demonstrated in the areas of behavioral therapies, which require extensive knowledge of operant and classical conditioning and of social learning theory.

More and more therapy is being done by paraprofessionals.

**Check Your Understanding**

1. RECALL: *People in collectivist cultures are likely to view mental disorder as a symptom of something wrong in*
   a. the unconscious mind.
   b. the person's behavior, rather than in the mind.
   c. the family or the community.
   d. a person's character.

2. RECALL: *A therapist, but not necessarily a friend, can be relied on to*
   a. maintain confidentiality.
   b. give you good advice.
   c. offer sympathy when you are feeling depressed.
   d. give you social support.

3. APPLICATION: *Which of the following therapists would be most likely to treat an unwanted response, such as nail biting, as merely a bad habit, rather than as a symptom of an underlying disorder?*
   a. a psychoanalyst
   b. a psychiatrist

   c. a humanistic therapist
   d. a behavioral therapist

4. UNDERSTANDING THE CORE CONCEPT: *All therapies are alike in this respect:*
   a. All may be legally administered only by licensed, trained professionals.
   b. All make use of insight into a patient's problems.
   c. All involve the aim of altering the mind or behavior.
   d. All focus on discovering the underlying cause of the patient's problem, which is often hidden in the unconscious mind.

**ANSWERS:**    1. c    2. a    3. d    4. c

**KEY QUESTION**    **HOW DO PSYCHOLOGISTS TREAT MENTAL DISORDERS?**

Psychologists have developed an impressive array of therapies. Some are based on the assumption that psychopathology is learned—and can be unlearned. Others emphasize the roles of emotion, personality traits, or the social context. The boundaries between the various forms of therapies, however, are becoming blurred. As therapists become more *eclectic*, they are assembling their therapeutic tool kits with a blend of

**Chapter 10: Personality**

*An eclectic theorist combines ideas from many different perspectives.*

methods borrowed from a variety of sources. These include the psychodynamic theories, cognitive theories, existential–humanistic theories, and the behavioral learning theories—all of which we have studied earlier in this book. Our Core Concept will help you organize in your mind the many approaches to therapy that we will cover in this section:

 **CORE CONCEPT**

**Psychologists employ two main forms of treatment: the behavioral therapies and the insight therapies.**

The insight therapies, we shall see, were the first truly psychological treatments developed. And, for a long time they were the only psychological therapies available. But in recent years they have been joined by the behavioral therapies, which are now in many cases the most effective tools we have. Frequently they equal or surpass the more highly publicized drug therapies. It is with these behavioral methods that we begin.

### Behavioral Therapies

If the problem is overeating, bedwetting, shyness, antisocial behavior, or anything else that can be described in behavioral terms, the chances are good that it can be modified by one of the behavioral therapies, derived from behavioral learning theories. **Behavioral therapy** (also called **behavior modification**) applies the well-established principles of conditioning and reinforcement to a wide range of undesirable behavior patterns that, in addition to those listed above, include fears, compulsions, depression, addictions, aggression, and delinquent behaviors. Unlike the therapist

**THE FAR SIDE** By GARY LARSON

Professor Gallagher and his controversial technique of simultaneously confronting the fear of heights, snakes and the dark.

who worked with Ken in our chapter-opening vignette, behavioral therapists focus on problem *behaviors* (rather than inner thoughts or emotions), examining how these behaviors might have been learned and, more importantly, how they can be eliminated and replaced by more effective patterns. We will look first at the techniques they borrow from classical conditioning.

**CLASSICAL CONDITIONING TECHNIQUES** The development of irrational fear responses and other undesirable emotionally based behaviors seems to follow the classical conditioning model. As you will recall, classical conditioning involves the association of a new stimulus with a powerful and familiar stimulus, so that the person responds the same way to both. For example, when a claustrophobic woman walks into an elevator (a conditioned stimulus), she may experience an anxiety response (e.g., shaking, turning pale), learned originally when she was trapped in a locked closet as a child (the frightening confinement served as the unconditioned stimulus for fear and anxiety).

When a problem behavior such as this arises from classical conditioning, a favored treatment is **counterconditioning,** a set of techniques designed to substitute a new response for the unwanted one. Counterconditioning is most often applied when an individual has an anxiety disorder such as a phobia, an irrational fear reaction directed at a harmless object or situation, such as a spider, a confined space, or social contact. From our discussion of classical conditioning, we know that *any* neutral stimulus may acquire the power to elicit strong conditioned reactions if it has

**Chapter 6: Learning and Remembering**

*The behavioral learning theories include* classical conditioning *and* operant conditioning.

**Chapter 6: Leaning and Remembering**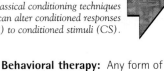

*Classical conditioning techniques can alter conditioned responses (CR) to conditioned stimuli (CS).*

**Behavioral therapy:** Any form of psychotherapy based on the principles of behavioral learning, especially operant conditioning and classical conditioning.

**Behavior modification:** Another term for behavioral therapy.

**Counterconditioning:** A set of classical conditioning techniques for substituting a new response for an unwanted response; used especially in treating phobias.

been associated with an unconditioned stimulus. To weaken the strength of these learned associations, behavioral therapists often use a form of therapeutic *extinction*. Let us see how this is done in a special form of counterconditioning called *reciprocal inhibition therapy*.

**Chapter 6:**
**Learning and Remembering**
*Classical extinction involves learning not to give the unwanted conditioned response to a conditioned stimulus.*

*RECIPROCAL INHIBITION AND SYSTEMATIC DESENSITIZATION* The nervous system cannot be relaxed and agitated or anxious at the same time because these two incompatible processes cannot be activated simultaneously. This simple notion is the basis for the technique of **reciprocal inhibition,** developed by South African psychiatrist Joseph Wolpe (1958, 1973).

Wolpe has used reciprocal inhibition extensively to treat fears and phobias. He begins with a training program that teaches his patients to relax their muscles and their minds. While they are in this deeply relaxed state, he *desensitizes* them to their fear by having them imagine the feared situation. They do so in gradual steps that move from remote associations of the feared situation to direct images of it. Wolpe calls this part of the treatment **systematic desensitization.**

In the process of desensitization, the therapist and client first identify the stimuli that provoke anxiety and arrange them in a *hierarchy* ranked from weakest to strongest (Shapiro, 1995). For example, a patient suffering from severe snake phobia constructed the hierarchy in Table 14.2. During desensitization, the relaxed client vividly imagines the *weakest* anxiety stimulus on the list. If the stimulus can be visualized without discomfort, the client goes on to the next stronger one. After a number of sessions, the client can imagine the most distressing situations on the list without anxiety—even situations that could not be faced originally (Lang & Lazovik, 1963). In some forms of desensitization, called **exposure therapy,** the therapist may actually have the patient confront the feared object, such as a snake, rather than simply imagining it.

A behavioral therapist uses exposure therapy and participant modeling to help a client overcome fear of flying.

A number of evaluation studies have shown that this behavioral therapy works remarkably well with most phobic patients (Smith & Glass, 1977). Desensitization has also been successfully applied to a variety of human concerns, including fears such as stage fright and anxiety about sexual performance (Kazdin, 1994; Kazdin & Wilcoxin, 1976).

*AVERSION THERAPY* Desensitization therapy helps clients deal with stimuli that they want to *avoid*. But what can be done to help those who are *attracted* to

TABLE 14.2: A Sample Anxiety Hierarchy

The following is typical of anxiety hierarchies that a therapist and a patient might develop during desensitization therapy. The therapist guides the deeply relaxed patient in imagining the following situations:

1. Seeing a picture of a snake
2. Watching a video of snake-handling
3. Knowing that the adjoining room contains a caged snake
4. A snake in a cage in this room
5. Observing someone, in the same room, handling a snake
6. A loose snake crawling toward me
7. Touching a snake held by someone else
8. Holding a snake in my hands
9. Having a snake wrapped around my neck and shoulders

**Reciprocal inhibition:** Joseph Wolpe's counterconditioning technique, involving relaxation training and systematic desensitization therapy.

**Systematic desensitization:** A behavioral therapy technique in which anxiety is extinguished by exposing the patient to an anxiety-provoking stimulus.

**Exposure therapy:** A form of desensitization therapy in which the patient directly confronts the anxiety-provoking stimulus (as opposed to imagining the stimulus).

**FIGURE 14.1:** Conditioning an Aversion for Cigarette Smoke

Aversion therapy for smoking might simultaneously pair a foul odor along with cigarette smoke blown in the smoker's face. The foul odor (such as the aversive smell of rotten eggs) produces nausea. This response then becomes the conditioned response associated with cigarette smoke.

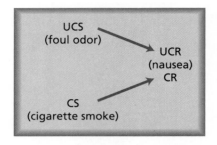

UCS
(foul odor)

UCR
(nausea)
CR

CS
(cigarette smoke)

A patient undergoes a simplified form of aversion therapy in which overexposure to smoke makes the patient nauseous. The smell of smoke and smoking behavior then take on unpleasant associations.

**Chapter 6:**
**Learning and Remembering**

*Most operant techniques are based on the manipulation of reinforcers.*

**Chapter 6:**
**Learning and Remembering**

*Social learning is a cognitive extension of operant conditioning that involves the expectation of rewards.*

stimuli that are harmful or illegal? For example, drug addiction, sexual perversions, and uncontrollable violence are human problems in which deviant behavior is elicited by tempting stimuli. A classical conditioning form of **aversion therapy** uses a counterconditioning procedure designed to make tempting stimuli less tempting by pairing the attractive stimuli with noxious (aversive) stimuli. These noxious stimuli might include electric shocks or nausea-producing drugs, whose effects are highly unpleasant but not in themselves destructive or dangerous to the client. In time, the negative reactions (unconditioned responses) associated with the aversive stimuli are elicited by the conditioned stimuli (such as an addictive drug), and the person develops an aversion that replaces the desire.

To give an example, persons who elect aversion therapy to help them quit smoking may be required to chain-smoke cigarettes (sometimes more than one cigarette at a time) while having a foul-smelling odor blown in their faces—until smoking is associated with nausea and vomiting (see Figure 14.1). A similar conditioning effect occurs in alcoholics who drink while taking the drug Antabuse. The drug has no side effects—unless the patient drinks even a small amount of alcohol; then he or she becomes severely nauseous. Often a daily dose of Antabuse is prescribed for alcoholics who want help with their resolve to quit drinking. With the single daily decision to take Antabuse, the patient can significantly strengthen the determination *not* to take a drink.

In some ways, aversion therapy resembles nothing so much as torture. So why would anyone submit voluntarily to it? Usually people do so only because they have tried other treatments and because they realize that the long-term consequences of continuing their maladaptive behavior will destroy their health or ruin their careers or family lives. In some cases, people may be required to enter aversion therapy by the courts or by institutional pressures, as in some prison treatment programs.

Critics are concerned that the painful procedures in aversion therapy may give too much power to the therapist, can be more punitive than therapeutic, and are most likely to be used in situations where people have the least freedom of choice about what is done to them. As a result of these concerns, the use of aversion therapy has become regulated by state laws and professional association guidelines for clinical treatment.

**OPERANT CONDITIONING TECHNIQUES** Johnny has a screaming fit when he goes to the grocery store with his parents and they refuse to buy him candy. His behavior is an example of a problem that has been acquired by *operant conditioning*—as the result of previously rewarded responses (his parents have occasionally given in to his demands) rather than by the paired association of classical conditioning. Accordingly, a therapist would most likely modify Johnny's behavior by *contingency management*. Contingency management involves using operant conditioning techniques to alter the rewards and punishers that have shaped the individual's behavior. In other cases, the problem behavior arises not from direct rewards but from observing someone else who is rewarded. This is an extension of operant learning known as *social learning*. Social learning therapy applies operant principles to people's expectations of reward and punishment by letting them observe the desired behavior in role models. Let us consider both of these techniques in more detail.

*CONTINGENCY MANAGEMENT* Changing behavior by modifying its consequences is the essence of **contingency management.** For example, Johnny's parents

## Behavior Self-Modification

Is there a behavior you would like to engage in more often than you do—studying, initiating conversations with others, exercising to keep fit? Write this in *behavioral terms* on the line below. (No fair using mentalistic words, such as "feeling" or "wanting." Behaviorists require that you keep things objective by specifying only an observable behavior.)

The desired new behavior:

_____

When or under what conditions would you like to engage in this new behavior? On the line below, write in the time or stimulus conditions when you want to initiate the behavior (for example: in class,

when relaxing with friends, or at a certain time every morning).

The time or conditions for the new behavior:

_____

To increase your likelihood of producing the desired response, apply some positive reinforcement therapy to yourself. Choose an appropriate reward that you will give yourself when you have produced the desired behavior at the appropriate time. Write the reward that you will give yourself on the line below.

Your reward:

_____

Give yourself feedback on your progress by keeping a daily record of the occurrence of your new behavior. This could be done, for example, on a calendar or a graph. In time, you will discover that the desired behavior has increased in frequency. You will also find that your new habit carries its own rewards, such as better grades or a more satisfying social life (Kazdin, 1994). Positive reinforcement strategies also have the advantage of building more pleasant and rewarding experiences into your life.

---

may agree that they will give him no attention when he throws his fit at the grocery store. They also agree that they will give him lots of attention when he is being good. Over time, the changing contingencies will work to extinguish the old, undesirable behaviors (throwing a fit) and help to keep the new ones in place.

A caution is in order: While some people misbehave merely because they aren't getting enough reinforcement in their lives, this is not always the case. For example, overzealous parents and teachers may be tempted to praise children lavishly, even when their performance has been mediocre—under the mistaken impression that the extra praise will increase low self-esteem and boost performance. But in such cases, increasing rewards inappropriately can actually aggravate behavior problems (Viken & McFall, 1994). How could this be? The subject may learn that more rewards can be "earned" by producing fewer and fewer desirable behaviors. One must, therefore, take care in simply piling on more rewards to encourage prosocial behaviors. The key to success lies not in giving more rewards but in tying rewards more closely to (making them *contingent* on) desirable behaviors.

*SOCIAL LEARNING THERAPY* "Monkey see—monkey do," we say. And sure enough, monkeys learn fears by observation and imitation. One study showed that young monkeys with no previous aversion to snakes could acquire a simian version of *ophidiophobia* by observing their parents reacting fearfully to real snakes and toy snakes. The more disturbed the parents were at the sight of the snakes, the greater the resulting fear in their offspring (Mineka et al., 1984). In a follow-up study, another group of young laboratory-raised monkeys showed little fear of snakes in a pretest, but they quickly acquired a fear of snakes after observing the reactions of adult monkeys to whom they were not related (See Figure 14.2.) This fear persisted but was less strong and more variable than that of the other young monkeys who had observed their own parents' fearful reactions (Cook et al., 1985).

**Aversion therapy:** As a classical conditioning procedure, aversive counterconditioning involves presenting individuals with an attractive stimulus paired with unpleasant (aversive) stimulation in order to condition a repulsive reaction.

**Contingency management:** An operant conditioning approach to changing behavior by altering the consequences, especially rewards and punishments, of behavior.

**Chapter 13:**
**Psychopathology**
Ophidiophobia *is the technical term for an extreme fear of snakes.*

## FIGURE 14.2: Fear Reactions in Monkeys

After young monkeys raised in laboratories observe unfamiliar adult monkeys showing a strong fear of snakes, they are vicariously conditioned to fear real snakes and toy snakes with an intensity that persists over time.

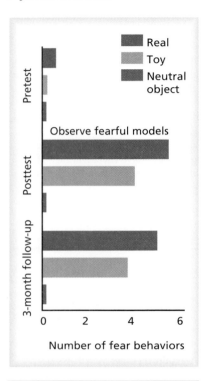

Like monkeys, we also learn by observing the behavior of others. Fears, in particular, are often learned in this way. **Social learning therapy** takes advantage of this capacity by having the client observe and imitate other persons—called *models*—while being reinforced for the desired response. This therapy has proved of special value in overcoming phobias and in building social skills.

Many new responses, especially complex ones, can be acquired more readily if a person can observe and imitate another person performing the desired behavior. In **participant modeling,** the therapist may model the behavior and encourage the client to imitate it. For example, in treating a phobia for snakes, a therapist might first approach a caged snake, then touch the snake, and so on. (Snake phobias have often been the subject of behavioral therapy demonstrations.) The client is urged and helped to imitate each modeled behavior, but at no time is the client forced to perform. Resistance at any level is overcome by having the client return to a previously successful, less-threatening approach behavior.

The power of participant modeling can be seen in a study that compared the participant modeling technique with several other approaches: (1) *symbolic modeling*, a technique in which subjects receive indirect exposure by watching a film or video in which models deal with a feared situation; (2) desensitization therapy, which, as you will remember, involves exposure to an imagined fearful stimulus; and (3) no therapeutic intervention (the control condition). As you can see in Figure 14.3, participant modeling was the most successful. A snake phobia was eliminated in 11 of the 12 subjects in the participant modeling group (Bandura, 1970).

*TOKEN ECONOMIES* A special form of reinforcement therapy called the **token economy** is applied to groups of people in classrooms and institutions (Ayllon &

## FIGURE 14.3: Participant Modeling Therapy

The subject shown in the photo first watches a model make a graduated series of snake-approach responses and then repeats them herself. Eventually, she is able to pick up the snake and let it move about on her. The graph compares the number of approach responses subjects made before and after receiving participant modeling therapy (most effective) with the behavior of those exposed to two other therapeutic techniques and a control group.

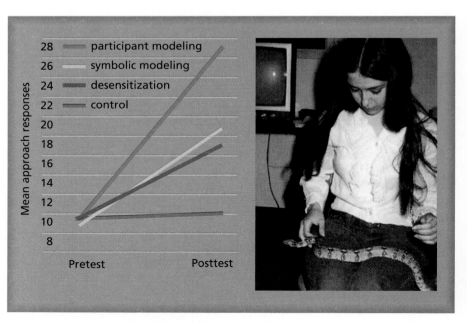

**Social learning therapy:** An approach to therapy based on social learning theory, which teaches that behavior is influenced by observation and imitation of others.

**Participant modeling:** A social learning technique in which a therapist demonstrates and encourages a client to imitate a desired behavior.

**Token economy:** An operant technique applied to groups, such as in classrooms or mental hospital wards, involving the distribution of "tokens" or other indicators of reinforcement contingent on desired behaviors. The tokens can later be exchanged for privileges, food, or other reinforcers.

Azrin, 1968). The therapy takes its name from the plastic tokens sometimes awarded by therapists (or teachers) as immediate reinforcers for desirable behaviors. Later, recipients may redeem the tokens for food, merchandise, or privileges. "Points" or other objects may be used in place of tokens. The important thing is that subjects receive *something* as a reinforcer immediately after giving desired responses. Immediate reward is the key to the success of token economies—or any reinforcement therapy, for that matter.

The token economy approach has been found to work especially well in encouraging prosocial behaviors among mental patients and prisoners (Schaefer & Martin, 1966). It also can stimulate academic performance among primary and secondary school students (Packard, 1970). And, it has been tried on college professors: At the institution where one of your authors teaches, the president has established a variation on the token economy to encourage staff participation in college events, such as athletic events and theatrical productions. Every staff member receives a special card, called a "college spirit pass." Then, those attending college-sponsored events receive "token" reinforcers in the form of punches in their spirit passes. At the end of the year, those having the most punches receive merchandise prizes from the campus store. It works.

## Insight Therapies

In contrast with the behavioral therapies, which focus on external behavior, the **insight therapies** attempt to change people on the *inside*—the way they think and feel. This is the sort of therapy that helped Ken, whom you read about at the beginning of the chapter. Sometimes called *talk therapies*, these methods share the assumption that distressed patients need to develop an understanding of the disordered thoughts, emotions, and motives that underlie their mental difficulties. That is, these therapies are designed to help patients achieve *insight* into their problems. A complete menu of insight therapies would list hundreds of options.

All the insight therapies offer techniques for revealing and changing a patient's disturbed mental processes through discussion and interpretation. Some, like Freudian psychoanalysis, assume that problems lie hidden deep in the unconscious, so they employ elaborate and time-consuming techniques to draw them out. Others, like Albert Ellis's *rational–emotive therapy*, assume that problems lie closer to the surface of awareness and, therefore, require correspondingly shorter and more direct courses of treatment. Because these therapies come in dozens of "brands," we will have space to examine only a sampling of the most influential ones, beginning with the legendary methods developed by Sigmund Freud.

**PSYCHODYNAMIC THERAPIES**  So called because they emphasize the *energy* within the personality, the **psychodynamic therapies** are based on the psychodynamic theories of personality that originated with Sigmund Freud. In the classic Freudian view, the psychological tension created by forbidden impulses and threatening memories locked in the unconscious cause the patient's problems. Therefore, Freudian therapy, known as **psychoanalysis,** requires intensive and prolonged exploration of patients' unconscious. Psychoanalytic techniques were designed to help neurotic, anxiety-ridden individuals to change their disruptive, often self-defeating patterns of thinking and acting by understanding the "true" causes of their problems. The major goal of psychoanalysis, therefore, is to reveal the unconscious mind's contents.

Of central importance to the psychoanalyst is understanding how a patient uses the ego defenses to handle conflicts, impulses, and memories. Symptoms are considered to be messages from the unconscious that something is wrong. But whatever the problem is, the ego blocks it from consciousness by repression. A psychoanalyst's task, then, is to help a patient overcome repression and bring these repressed thoughts to consciousness. By doing so, the patient gains *insight* into the relationship between the current symptoms and the repressed conflicts. In the final stages of psychoanalysis, patients

**Insight therapies:** Psychotherapies in which the therapist helps the patient understand (gain *insight* into) the causes of his or her problems.

**Psychodynamic therapies:** Any of the insight therapies based on the assumption that mental disorder is caused by powerful mental forces and conflicts. Freudian *psychoanalysis* was the first form of psychodynamic therapy to be developed.

**Psychoanalysis:** The form of psychodynamic therapy developed by Sigmund Freud. The goal of psychoanalysis is to release conflicts and memories from the unconscious.

**Chapter 10:
Personality**

*The psychodynamic theories include those developed by Freud, Jung, Adler, Horney, and Erikson.*

**Chapter 10:
Personality**

*Repression is the Freudian mechanism of forgetting by blocking threatening material in the unconscious.*

**Analysis of transference:** The Freudian technique of analyzing and interpreting the patient's relationship with the therapist, based on the assumption that this relationship mirrors unresolved conflicts in the patient's past.

**Post-Freudian psychodynamic therapies:** Therapies for mental disorder that were developed by psychodynamic theorists who disagreed with some aspects of Freud's theories and methods of treatment.

Sigmund Freud's study, including the famous couch (right), is housed in London's Freud Museum. The 82-year-old Freud fled to London in 1938 upon the Nazi occupation of Austria. He died there the following year.

**Chapter 10: Personality**

*Projection is the ego defense mechanism involved in attributing one's unconscious desires to someone else.*

**Chapter 3: States of Mind**

*Introspection is a subjective technique that involves describing one's own private mental processes.*

**Chapter 10: Personality**

*Adler, Jung, Horney, and Erikson all modified Freud's ideas about personality and mental disorder.*

learn how their relationship with the therapist reflects unresolved problems with their parents at earlier stages in their lives. This *projection* of parental attributes onto the therapist is called *transference*, and this final phase of therapy is known as the **analysis of transference.** According to psychoanalytic theory, patients will recover when they are "released" from repression established in early childhood (Munroe, 1955).

The goals of psychoanalysis are ambitious. They involve not just the elimination of the immediate symptoms of psychopathology but a reorganization of the personality. Because traditional psychoanalysis is an attempt to reconstruct long-standing repressed memories and then work through painful feelings to an effective resolution, it is a therapy that takes a long time. It thus requires patients who are highly motivated, introspective, verbally fluent, and able to bear the considerable expense in time and money. Classic psychoanalysis might involve three to five sessions of analysis per week over a period of years. Modern psychoanalytic techniques usually involve fewer sessions.

**POST-FREUDIAN PSYCHODYNAMIC THERAPIES** Freud's followers have retained some of his basic ideas and techniques but modified others. Classical Freudian psychoanalysis emphasizes the importance of three factors: unconscious motivation and conflict; the power of early childhood development; and the dynamics within one's personality. In contrast, **post-Freudian psychodynamic theories** generally emphasize the following:

- The importance of the individual's current social environment
- The ongoing influence of life experiences beyond childhood
- The role of social and interpersonal relationships
- The significance of one's conscious self-concept

These post-Freudian (or *neo-Freudian*) approaches include therapies developed by Adler, Jung, Horney, and Erikson.

**HUMANISTIC THERAPIES**    The primary symptoms for which college students seek therapy include low self-esteem, feelings of alienation, failure to achieve all they feel they should, and general dissatisfaction with their lives. These problems in everyday existence are commonly called *existential crises*. This term underscores the idea that many problems deal with questions about the meaning and purpose of one's existence. The humanistic psychologists have developed therapies aimed specifically at these problems.

Humanistic therapists dispute Freud's assumption of a personality divided into warring parts, dominated by a selfish id, and driven by hedonistic instincts and repressed conflicts. Instead, they emphasize the concept of a *whole person* who engages in a continual process of changing and becoming. Despite the restrictions of environment and heredity, we always remain free to choose what we will become by creating our own values and committing ourselves to them through our decisions. Along with this *freedom to choose*, however, comes the *burden of responsibility*. This burden may lead to anxiety and despair. We also suffer from guilt over lost opportunities to achieve our full potential. **Humanistic therapies** attempt to help clients confront these problems by recognizing their own freedom, enhancing their self-esteem, and realizing their fullest potential (see Schneider & May, 1995).

Among the most influential of the humanistic therapists, Carl Rogers (1951, 1977) developed a method called **person-centered therapy,** which begins with the assumption that all people have the need to self-actualize; that is, to realize their potential. Healthy development is hindered by a conflict between one's desire for a positive self-image and criticism by self and others. This conflict creates anxiety and unhappiness. The task of Rogerian therapy, then, is to create a nurturing environment that allows a client to learn how to think and act in order to achieve self-enhancement and self-actualization.

One of the main techniques used by Rogerian therapists involves **reflection of feeling** to help clients understand their emotions. With this technique therapists paraphrase their clients' words, attempting to capture the emotional tone expressed. In this fashion, the humanistic therapist may act as a sort of psychological "mirror" in which clients can see themselves. Notice how the Rogerian therapist uses reflection of feeling in the following segment extracted from a therapy session with a young woman: (Rogers, 1951, p. 152):

| | |
|---|---|
| Client: | It probably goes all the way back into my childhood. . . . My mother told me that I was the pet of my father. Although I never realized it—I mean, they never |

treated me as a pet at all. And other people always seemed to think I was sort of a privileged one in the family. . . . And as far as I can see looking back on it now, it's just that the family let the other kids get away with more than they usually did me. And it seems for some reason to have held me to a more rigid standard than they did the other children.

Therapist:  You're not so sure you were a pet in any sense, but more that the family situation seemed to hold you to pretty high standards.

Client:  M-hm. That's just what has occurred to me; and that the other people could sorta make mistakes, or do things as children that were naughty . . . but Alice wasn't supposed to do those things.

Therapist:  M-hm. With somebody else it would be just—oh, be a little naughtiness; but as far as you were concerned, it shouldn't be done.

**Humanistic therapies:** Treatment techniques based on the assumption that people have a tendency for positive growth and self-actualization, which may be blocked by an unhealthy environment that can include negative self-evaluation and criticism from others.

**Chapter 10: Personality**

*Humanistic theories of personality emphasize our potential for growth and actualization.*

**Chapter 10: Personality**

*Rogers's method of treatment is based on his person-centered theory of personality.*

Humanistic therapist Carl Rogers (right center) facilitates a therapy group.

**Person-centered therapy:** A humanistic approach to treatment developed by Carl Rogers, emphasizing an individual's tendency for healthy psychological growth through self-actualization.

**Reflection of feeling:** Carl Rogers's technique of paraphrasing clients' words, attempting to capture the emotional tone expressed.

Client: That's really the idea I've had. I think the whole business of my standards . . . is one that I need to think about rather carefully, since I've been doubting for a long time whether I even have any sincere ones.

Therapist: M-hm. Not sure whether you really have any deep values which you are sure of.

Client: M-hm. M-hm.

In Rogers's humanistic therapy, people are assumed to have basically healthy motives—which may be stifled by pressures from others. The therapist's task is mainly to help remove barriers that limit the expression of this natural positive tendency and help the client clarify and accept his or her own feelings. This is accomplished within an atmosphere of **unconditional positive regard**—nonjudgmental acceptance and respect for the client. In addition, the therapist tries to experience the client's feelings. Such total empathy requires that the therapist care for the client as a worthy, competent individual—not to be judged or evaluated but to be assisted in discovering his or her individuality (Meador & Rogers, 1979). Unlike practitioners of other therapies, who interpret, give answers, or instruct, the client-centered therapist is a supportive listener who reflects and, at times, restates the client's evaluative statements and feelings. Thus, person-centered therapy strives to be **nondirective** by having the client determine the direction of therapy. The therapist merely facilitates the patient's own search for self-awareness and self-acceptance.

**GROUP THERAPIES**    All the treatment approaches we have discussed so far involve one-to-one relationships between a patient or client and therapist. However, **group therapy** can have value in treating a variety of concerns, particularly problems with social behavior and relationships. This can be done in many ways, but a large number of therapy groups are based on the humanistic perspective. Humanistic therapies have most often made use of group contexts in order to provide clients with social support or evidence that they are not alone. Some other benefits of group therapy include opportunities to observe and imitate new social behaviors in a forgiving, supportive atmosphere. We will examine only a small sample of group therapies below: *self-help groups* and *marital and family therapy.*

*SELF-HELP GROUPS*    The most dramatic development in group therapy has been the surge of interest and participation in **self-help groups.** It is estimated that there are 500,000 such groups, which are attended by 15 million Americans every week (Leerhsen, 1990). Many of these group support sessions are free, especially those that are not directed by a health care professional. One of their biggest advantages is that these groups give people a chance to meet others with similar problems who are surviving and sometimes thriving (Christensen & Jacobson, 1994; Jacobs & Goodman, 1989).

One of the oldest, Alcoholics Anonymous (AA), pioneered the application of the self-help concept to community group settings, beginning in the mid-1930s. Central to the original AA structure was the concept of "twelve steps" to recovery from alcohol addiction, based not on psychological theory but on the trial-and-error experience of early AA members. The first step begins with recognizing that one has become powerless over alcohol; the second affirms that faith in a "greater power" is necessary for recovery. Most of the remaining steps refer to this greater power, or explicitly to God, and set goals for making amends to those who have been hurt by the addicted or disordered person's actions. In most twelve-step programs, members are urged and helped to accept as many of the steps as possible in order to maintain recovery.

**Unconditional positive regard:** Rogers's term for the therapist's attitude of nonjudgmental acceptance and respect for the client.

**Nondirective:** Rogers's term for a therapeutic approach in which the client, rather than the therapist, takes the lead in determining the direction of therapy.

**Group therapy:** Any form of psychotherapy done with more than one client/patient at a time. Group therapy is often done from a humanistic perspective.

**Self-help groups:** Therapy groups, such as Alcoholics Anonymous, that are organized and run by laypersons, rather than professional therapists.

In the United States, there are an estimated 500,000 self-help groups attended by 15 million people every week (Leerhsen, 1990).

The feminist consciousness-raising movement of the 1960s extended the reach of self-help groups beyond the arena of alcoholism. Today, such support groups deal with four basic categories of problems:

- Managing life transition or other crises, such as divorce or death of a child
- Coping with physical and mental disorders, such as depression or heart attack
- Dealing with addiction, such as alcohol, gambling, and drug dependency
- Handling the stress felt by relatives or friends of those who are dealing with addictions

Group therapy has also made valuable contributions to the treatment of terminally ill patients. The goals of such therapy are to help patients and their families live their lives as fully as possible during their illnesses, to cope realistically with impending death, and to adjust to the terminal illness (Adams, 1979; Yalom & Greaves, 1977). One general focus of such support groups for the terminally ill is to help them learn "how to live fully until you say goodbye" (Nungesser, 1990).

*MARITAL AND FAMILY THERAPY*    Sometimes the best group in which to learn about relationships is a group beset by problem relationships—as we see in groups composed of dysfunctional couples and families. *Couples counseling* (or therapy), for example, seeks to clarify the typical communication patterns of the partners and then to improve the quality of their interaction. By seeing a couple together (and sometimes videotaping and playing back their interactions) a therapist can help both partners appreciate the verbal and nonverbal styles they use to dominate, control, or confuse each other. Each party is taught how to reinforce desired responses in the other and withdraw reinforcement for undesirable reactions; they are also taught nondirective listening skills to help the other person clarify and express feelings and ideas (Dattilio & Padesky, 1990; O'Leary, 1987).

Couples therapy focuses not on the personalities involved but on the *processes* of their relationship, particularly their patterns of conflict and communication (Gottman, 1994; Greenberg & Johnson, 1988; Notarius & Markman, 1993). Ideally, both partners are willing to make some changes in the ways they think and behave and to take responsibility for their part in the relationship. Difficult as this may be, couples therapy can be much "easier" and more effective than efforts to change the basic personalities of the people involved. And, because both participants work together and support each other in reaching mutually desired goals, couples therapy is more effective in resolving marital problems and keeping marriages intact than is individual therapy with only one partner (Gottman, 1994).

In *family therapy*, the "client" is an entire nuclear family, and each family member is treated as a member of a *system* of relationships (Fishman, 1993). A family therapist works with troubled family members to help them perceive the issues or patterns that are creating problems for one or more of them. The focus is on altering the psychological "spaces" between people and the interpersonal *dynamics* of people acting as a unit, rather than on changing processes within maladjusted individuals (Foley, 1979; Schwebel & Fine, 1994).

A cognitive therapist would say that this student, depressed about a poor grade, may well stay depressed if he berates his own intelligence rather than reattributing the blame to the situation—a tough test.

Family therapy can reduce tensions within a family and improve the functioning of individual members by helping them recognize the positives as well as the negatives in their relationships. Virginia Satir, an innovative developer of family therapy approaches, noted that the family therapist plays many roles, acting as an interpreter and clarifier of the interactions that are taking place in the therapy session and as influence agent, mediator, and referee (Satir, 1983; Satir et al., 1991). Family therapists focus on the *situational* rather than the *dispositional* aspects of a family's problem—for example, how one family member's unemployment affects everyone's feelings and relationships, rather than seeking to assign blame or label anyone as lazy or selfish. The goal of a family therapy meeting is not to have a "gripe session" free-for-all of complaints, but to develop constructive, cooperative problem solving together.

**COGNITIVE THERAPY**  Most of the insight therapies emphasize changing people's emotional and motivational disturbances, while **cognitive therapy** sees rational *thinking* as the key to therapeutic change. Cognitive therapy does not neglect feelings or motives, but it does not focus on them directly. The underlying assumption of such therapy is that abnormal behavior patterns and emotional distress start with problems in *what* we think (cognitive content) and *how* we think (cognitive process). Cognitive therapy takes several different forms, but we will discuss only two examples here: Aaron Beck's *cognitive therapy for depression* and Albert Ellis's *rational–emotive therapy*.

**Chapter 13: Psychopathology**
*Along with bipolar disorder, depression is one of the mood disorders.*

*COGNITIVE THERAPY FOR DEPRESSION*  Depressed patients commonly repeat to themselves such self-destructive thoughts as, "I will never be as good as my brother," "Nobody would like me if they really knew me," and, "I'm not smart enough to make it in this competitive school." Aaron Beck believes that their depression occurs because of negative self-talk. If so, the treatment is simple: "The therapist helps the patient to identify his warped thinking and to learn more realistic ways to formulate his experiences" (Beck, 1976, p. 20). Beck and his followers may instruct depressed individuals to write down negative thoughts about themselves, figure out why these self-criticisms are unjustified, and come up with more realistic (and less destructive) self-cognitions. From here, cognitive therapists rely on specific tactics to change the cognitive foundation that supports the depression. These tactics include the following suggestions from Beck and his colleagues (1979):

**Cognitive therapy:** Emphasizes rational thinking (as opposed to subjective emotion, motivation, or repressed conflicts) as the key to treating mental disorder.

- Evaluating the *evidence* the patient has for and against these automatic thoughts ("But I always did well in math before; I can't be stupid")
- Reattributing blame to *situational factors* rather than to the patient's incompetence ("I had a disagreement with my roommate the night before the math test")
- Openly discussing *alternative solutions* to the problem ("I could study math between my two afternoon classes")
- Research shows that such an approach can be at least as effective in the treatment of depression as is medication (Antonuccio, 1995).

## Examining Your Own Beliefs

It may be obvious that the following are not healthy beliefs, but Albert Ellis finds that many people hold them. Do you? Be honest: Put a check mark beside each of the following statements that accurately describes how you feel about yourself.

_____ 1. I must be loved and approved by everyone.

_____ 2. I must be thoroughly competent, adequate, and achieving.

_____ 3. It is catastrophic when things do not go the way I want them to go.

_____ 4. Unhappiness results from forces over which I have no control.

_____ 5. People must always treat each other fairly and justly; those who don't are nasty and terrible people.

_____ 6. I must constantly be on my guard against dangers and things that could go wrong.

_____ 7. Life is full of problems, and I must always find quick solutions to them.

_____ 8. It is easier to evade my problems and responsibilities than to face them.

_____ 9. Unpleasant experiences in my past have had a profound influence on me. Therefore, they must continue to influence my current feelings and actions.

_____ 10. I can achieve happiness by just enjoying myself each day. The future will take care of itself.

In Ellis's view, all these statements are irrational beliefs that can cause mental problems. His cognitive approach to therapy, known as rational–emotive therapy, concentrates on helping people see that they "drive themselves crazy" with these irrational beliefs. For example, a person who is depressed about not landing a certain job probably holds irrational belief #3 above. You can obtain more information on Ellis's system from his books. (See If You're Interested at the end of this chapter for a recommendation.)

---

*RATIONAL–EMOTIVE THERAPY*    Another form of cognitive therapy is that developed by Albert Ellis (1962, 1987, 1990, 1996) to help a broad spectrum of unhappy clients eliminate ineffective, self-defeating thought patterns. Ellis dubbed his treatment **rational–emotive therapy (RET).** The name derives from its aim to change troubling emotional problems by attacking and modifying the client's basic "irrational" beliefs.

What are these irrational beliefs, and how do they lead to maladaptive feelings and actions? According to Ellis, maladjusted individuals base their lives on a set of warped values and unachievable goals. These "neurotic" goals and values lead people to hold unrealistic expectations that they should *always* succeed that they should *always* receive approval, that they should *always* be treated fairly, and that their experiences should *always* be pleasant. (You can see the most common irrational beliefs in the accompanying box, *Do It Yourself! Examining Your Own Beliefs.*) For example, in your own daily life, you may frequently tell yourself what you "should" get an A in math or that you "ought to" spend an hour exercising every day. If you seldom question this self-talk, it may come to control your actions or even prevent you from choosing the life you want. If you were to enter RET, your therapist would teach you to recognize such assumptions, question how rational they are, and replace faulty ideas with more valid ones. Don't "should" on yourself, says Ellis.

A rational–emotive therapist attempts to alter a client's irrational thinking by showing that an emotional reaction to an event may spring from unrecognized *beliefs* about the event, rather than the event itself. For example, a client behaves in a possessive and clingy way toward a romantic partner when that partner seems less interested or is distracted. According to Ellis, this emotional overreaction may be activated by a neurotic need for continual reminders of love and approval. Signs that

**Rational–emotive therapy (RET):** Albert Ellis's brand of cognitive therapy, based on the idea that irrational thinking is the cause of mental disorders.

Chapter 13:
Psychopathology

*The DSM-IV classifies
obsessive–compulsive disorder as
one of the anxiety disorders.*

the other person is pulling away are unreasonably interpreted to mean, "My partner will leave me if I don't take emergency action." Experiencing a real breakup may prompt the irrational thought that "Without this person to love me, I'll have no one in my life at all!" In RET, these beliefs are openly disputed through rational confrontation and examination of alternative reasons for the event.

By definition, the cognitive therapies rely on individuals to use their own *mental processes* to change *behavior*. Now research suggests that these treatments may enable the mind to change the brain itself, not only for problems with relationships, but for severe problems such as obsessive–compulsive disorder. Patients who suffered from obsessions about whether they had turned off their stoves and compulsions to wash and rewash their hands to expunge imaginary germs were given cognitive behavior modification (Schwartz et al., 1996). When they felt an urge to run home and check the stove or to wash their hands repeatedly, they were trained to *relabel* their experience as an obsession or compulsion—not a rational concern. They then focused on waiting out this "urge" rather than giving in to it, by distracting themselves with other activities for about 15 minutes (Begley & Biddle, 1996). Positron emission tomography (PET) scans of the brains of subjects who were trained in this relabeling-and-distracting technique indicated that, over time, the part of the brain responsible for that nagging fear or urge gradually became less active (Schwartz et al., 1996). Thus, the mind can apparently "fix the brain."

## ▌ FIGURE 14.4:    Therapies Compared

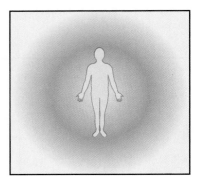

**Behavior therapy**
aims to change things *outside the individual*: rewards, punishments, and cues in the environment in order to change the person's external behaviors

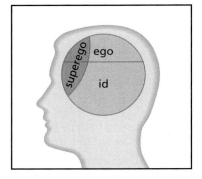

**Psychodynamic therapies**
aim to make changes *inside the person's mind*, especially the unconscious.

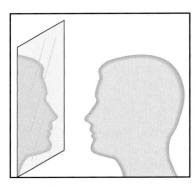

**Humanistic therapies**
aim to change the way people *see themselves.*

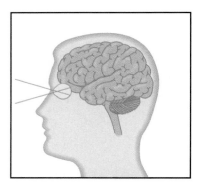

**Cognitive therapies**
aim to change the way people *think and perceive.*

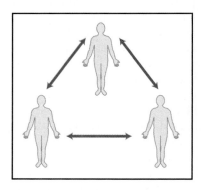

**Group therapies**
aim to change the way people *interact.*

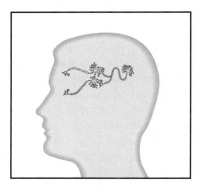

**Biomedical therapies**
aim to change the structure or function of the brain.

## Cognitive–Behavioral Therapy: A Synthesis

Suppose you are having difficulty controlling feelings of jealousy every time your mate is friendly with someone else. Chances are that the problem originates in your *cognitions* about yourself and the others involved ("Marty is stealing Terry away from me!") But these thoughts probably affect your *behavior,* too—making you act in ways that could drive Terry away from you. A dose of therapy aimed at *both* your cognitions and behaviors may be a better bet than either one alone. This is the two-pronged thrust of **cognitive–behavioral therapy.**

In brief, cognitive–behavioral therapy is a set of techniques that combines a cognitive emphasis on thoughts and attitudes with behavioral strategies for changing behavior by altering reinforcement contingencies. This approach assumes that an irrational *self-statement* is the cause of maladaptive behavior. For example, an addicted smoker might automatically tell himself, "One more cigarette won't hurt me," "I'll go crazy if I don't have a smoke now," or even "I can quit any time I want—I just don't want to." Before unacceptable behavior patterns can be modified, the individual's irrational self-statements must be changed or replaced with rational, constructive coping statements. ("It will be no easier to quit tomorrow than it is today. I can get through this craving if I distract myself with something else I like to do, like going to a movie.") Then, the therapist and client work together to set attainable goals, develop realistic strategies for attaining them, and evaluate the results realistically. In this way, people gradually develop a sense of mastery and *self-efficacy* (Bandura, 1986, 1992; Schwarzer, 1992).

In this combined therapeutic approach, the therapist and client must also focus on external conditions—situations in the client's environment that have encouraged the undesirable behavior. An example: For many smokers, alcohol is a trigger to light up. Thus, to stop smoking, the client may need to avoid drinking. Healthy new behaviors often need to be substituted for unhealthy old ones—so the smoker may be urged to take up a hobby, such as woodworking or sewing, that will occupy the hands. Practice attempts at these behaviors may be shaped and reinforced by the therapist, but the real payoff occurs when the new behavior patterns generate reinforcement by themselves—by working as desired in the world outside of therapy.

## Evaluating the Psychological Therapies

Now that we have looked at a variety of psychotherapies, let us step back and ask how well psychotherapy works. Does it make a difference? Are some kinds better than others? A half century ago, British psychologist Hans Eysenck (1952) shook the therapeutic world by giving a resounding "No!" on all counts—and providing data to back up his claim. Roughly two-thirds of all people with nonpsychotic problems recover spontaneously within two years of the onset of the problem, whether they get therapy or not, said Eysenck. If true, this meant that psychotherapy was essentially worthless—little better than no treatment at all. The evidence came from a review of several outcome studies of various kinds of insight therapy.

As you might expect, Eysenck's claim hit a raw nerve with therapists. But, right or wrong, it had a most important result: it stimulated therapists to respond with a flurry of research on the effectiveness of therapy. One of the main questions they put to the test was this: Does therapy *really* help—or do clients improve only because they hope and expect to receive special help? If the latter is true, then therapy is a kind of *placebo,* a behavioral sugar pill that only "works" because the individual expects it to be effective.

In fact, the placebo effect probably accounts for some of the success in therapy. After all, you would not expect most therapies to work if the subject did *not* believe in the therapy or the therapist. Many psychologists and psychiatrists believe that the key placebo ingredients in any therapy's success are a patient's belief that therapy will help and a therapist's social influence in conveying this suggestion (Fish, 1973). For psychiatrist Jerome Frank, the processes that occur in modern psychotherapy are

**Cognitive–behavioral therapy:** A newer form of psychotherapy that combines the techniques of cognitive therapy with those of behavioral therapy.

**Chapter 5:**
**Sensation and Perception**

*Placebos may imitate psychological treatments—not just drugs. Either way, they work because of expectations.*

essentially the same as those happening in religious revivalism, native healing ceremonies, and communist thought-reform programs (Frank, 1973, 1990; Frank & Frank, 1991). He argues that "belief is really crucial to all of these processes because without the belief the person does not participate in any real way. . . . Nothing happens unless they really believe that this could help them" (Frank, 1990).

Surveys of the existing studies on therapeutic effectiveness were reported in 1970 (by Meltzoff & Kornreich) and in 1975 (by Luborsky, Singer, & Luborsky). And by 1977, the list of outcome studies numbered some 375, all of which were surveyed in a monumental analysis by Smith and Glass. While their work substantiated Eysenck's estimate of improvement in two-thirds of the people undergoing therapy, Smith and Glass found that he had overestimated the improvement rate in no-therapy controls. Everything pointed to the conclusion that therapy is, after all, more effective than no therapy. By 1980 a consensus supporting the value of psychotherapy had emerged among researchers (Meredith, 1986; VandenBos, 1986). More recent evaluations of psychotherapy have also reported positive results in a variety of cultural settings throughout the world (Beutler & Machado, 1992; Lipsey & Wilson, 1993).

The new studies have, however, raised new issues. First, while they found that therapy is effective, they also found most forms of insight therapy essentially equivalent in their effectiveness. This may be because effective therapists share a common core of characteristics and methods. Carl Rogers (1957) suggested the "necessary and sufficient conditions" for therapy: warmth (*unconditional positive regard*), empathy, and genuineness. Others would add another requirement: An effective therapist helps clients organize their thoughts about their problems (Frank, 1973, 1982). Using the *meta-analysis* technique, which combines information from many studies, researchers find that a common element in successful therapy is a caring, hopeful relationship and a new way of looking at oneself and the world (Barker, Funk, & Houston, 1988; Jones, Cumming, & Horowitz, 1988). This conclusion has been supported by a more recent study which found that the effectiveness of therapy depended less on the specific *type* of therapy employed and more on the *quality of the relationship* between therapist and client (Blatt, Sanislow, & Pilkonis, 1996).

Based on their broad survey of the research, Smith and Glass (1977) awarded the behavioral therapies an advantage over insight therapies in the treatment of certain disorders. More recent evaluations suggest that behavioral techniques are especially well suited for treating phobias, certain sexual dysfunctions, and other problems in which desired behavior changes can be clearly identified (American Psychological Association, 1993; Giles, 1983; Masters et al., 1987). For example, we know that behavior modification is the most effective treatment for most cases of *enuresis* (bedwetting), and in 1992 the U.S. Agency for Health Care Policy and Research recommended behavior therapy as the first line of treatment for urinary incontinence in adults (1992). Cognitive–behavioral therapy also rivals drug treatment for depression (Antonuccio, 1995; Elkin et al., 1989; Muñoz et al., 1994; Young, Beck, & Weinberger, 1993) and for the treatment of panic disorder (Adler, 1991). Often, however, behavioral therapy and drug therapy may be combined (Craske & Barlow, 1993). Finally, although these cognitive–behavioral techniques by no means hold a cure for psychosis or mental retardation, they have been used widely and successfully to teach prosocial behaviors to people suffering from these afflictions (Wolpe, 1985).

On the other hand, behavior therapy has nothing much to offer the patient with nonspecific problems. For example, for a person seeking to make sense of a confusing relationship or make a difficult career choice, the therapist needs a repertoire that extends beyond behavior therapy techniques. In fact, most therapists who use behavior therapy use it as only one tool in their therapeutic kit.

Whatever the approach, most patients or clients seem to *like* therapy. This was shown in a novel study involving thousands of adults who responded to a survey distributed to subscribers of *Consumer Reports* (1995). Respondents indicated how much their treatment helped, their overall satisfaction with the therapist's treatment of their problems, their change in "overall emotional state" following therapy, as well as

**Chapter 8:
Emotion and Motivation**

*Masters and Johnson developed effective behavioral therapies for a variety of sexual disorders.*

details about the kind of therapy. Of the 7,000 respondents, about 3,000 just talked to friends, to relatives, or to clergy (as might be expected from our discussion earlier in this chapter), and 2,900 saw a mental health professional; the rest saw family doctors or support groups. The main results can be summarized as follows: (a) Therapy works—that is, it was perceived to have helped clients diminish or eliminate their psychological problems; (b) long-term therapy was better than short-term therapy; (c) psychotherapy plus medication was not better than psychotherapy alone; and (d) all forms of therapy were reported to be about equally effective for improving clients' problems (see Jacobson & Christensen, 1996; Kazdin, 1986; Seligman, 1995). We can't give a thumbs-up, however, to therapy merely because patients say they like it or that it helped them (Hollon, 1996). You will recall that cognitive dissonance theory predicts that people will come to like anything that they agree to suffer for.

**Chapter 12:**
**Social Psychology**
*Cognitive dissonance occurs when one's voluntary behavior conflicts with attitudes or beliefs.*

During the past decade, the American Psychological Association has sponsored a special task force charged with evaluating psychological therapies (Chambless et al., 1996; Nathan, 1998; "Task Force," 1993). The thrust of these reports is that more and more specific disorders—literally dozens of them—can be treated successfully by specific therapies, as demonstrated in well-designed experiments (Barlow, 1996). It is noteworthy that nearly all the therapies identified as effective are cognitive or behavioral. It is also noteworthy that all the disorders identified as treatable can be described in specific behavioral terms. Still, the number of disorders with clearly proven treatments is small, compared to the list in the *DSM-IV*. In addition, most people who seek psychotherapy do not do so because of one of the *DSM-IV* disorders but rather to find purpose and meaning in their lives (Strupp, 1996).

**TABLE 14.3:** Empirically Validated Cognitive and Behavioral Therapies

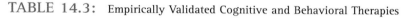

| TYPE OF DISORDER | TREATMENT |
|---|---|
| **ANXIETY AND MOOD** | |
| Panic disorder with and without agoraphobia | Cognitive–behavioral therapy |
| Generalized anxiety disorder | Cognitive–behavioral therapy |
| Social phobia | Group cognitive–behavioral therapy |
| Simple phobia | Systematic desensitization |
| Obsessive–compulsive disorder | Exposure and response prevention |
| Depression | Cognitive therapy |
| **PHYSICAL HEALTH PROBLEMS** | |
| Headache | Behavior modification therapy |
| Chronic pain | Cognitive–behavioral therapy |
| Bulimia | Cognitive–behavioral therapy |
| Enuresis (bed-wetting) | Behavior modification therapy |
| Female orgasmic dysfunction | Behavior modification therapy |
| Male erectile dysfunction | Behavior modification therapy |

According to an American Psychological Association task force on the effectiveness of psychological treatment, all the treatments for the specific disorders listed in this table have been clearly validated by at least two well-designed experiments (Chambless et al., 1996). A number of other treatments were found to be "probably efficacious," including:

- exposure treatment for posttraumatic stress disorder (PTSD)
- behavior therapy for drug dependence and abuse
- behavioral therapy for childhood obesity
- behavior modification for sex offenders

## Where Do Most People Get Help?

The effectiveness of psychotherapy for a variety of problems seems to be established beyond doubt. Having said that, we should again acknowledge that most people experiencing mental distress do not turn to professional therapists for help. Rather they turn to "just people" in the community (Wills & DePaulo, 1991). Those suffering from mental problems often look to friends, ministers, hairdressers, bartenders, and others with whom they have a trusting relationship. In fact, for some types of problems—perhaps the commonest problems of everyday living—a sympathetic friend may be just as effective as a trained professional therapist (Berman & Norton, 1985; Christensen & Jacobson, 1994). To put this in a different way: Most mental problems are not the crippling disorders that occupied the lion's share of the previous chapter. The psychological difficulties most of us face result from lives careening out of control: lost jobs, difficult marriages, misbehaving children, friendships gone sour, loved ones dying. . . In brief, the most familiar problems involve chaos, confusion, choice, frustration, stress, and loss. People who find themselves in the throes of these difficulties do not need extensive psychotherapy or medication or some other special form of treatment. They need someone who will help them sort through the pieces of their problems. Usually this means that they turn to someone like you.

So, what can you do when someone asks you for help? First, you should realize that some problems may require professional emergency treatment. These include a suicide threat or an indication of intent to harm others. You should not delay getting competent help for someone with such tendencies. Second, remember that some therapy methods *do* require special training, especially those methods that call for drugs, cognitive–behavioral therapy techniques, or for major intervention in peoples' lives and personalities, such as attempts to unveil unconscious conflicts. We urge you to learn as much as you can about these methods—but we strongly recommend that you leave them to the professionals. Some other very effective techniques, however, are simply extensions of good human relationships, and they fall well within the layperson's abilities for mental "first aid." Briefly, we will consider three of these generic helping skills that you can apply to help those who seek your assistance with ordinary problems, choices, and tensions of everyday living.

- *Listening*. You will rarely go wrong if you just listen. Sometimes listening is all the therapy a person in distress needs. It works by encouraging the speaker to organize a problem well enough to communicate it. As a result, those who talk out their problems frequently arrive at their own solutions. As an **active listener,** you take the role a step farther by giving the speaker *feedback*: nodding, maintaining an expression that shows interest, paraphrasing, and asking for clarification of points that you don't understand. Active listening lets the speaker know that you are interested and *empathetic* (in tune with the other person's feelings). At the same time, you will do well to avoid the temptation of advice-giving. Advice robs the recipient of the opportunity to work out his or her own solutions.

- *Acceptance*. Nondirective therapists call this a *nonjudgmental attitude*. It means accepting the person and the problem as they are. It also means suppressing shock, disgust, or condemnation that would create a hostile climate for problem-solving.

- *Exploration of alternatives*. People under stress may see only one course of action, so you can help by identifying other potential choices and helping them explore the consequences of each. (You can point out that *doing nothing* is also a choice.) Remember that, in the end, the choice of action is not up to you but to the individual who owns the problem.

Beyond these basic helping techniques lies the territory of the trained therapist. We strongly advise you against trying out the therapy techniques discussed in this chapter for any of the serious psychological disorders discussed in the previous chapter or listed in the *DSM-IV*.

**Active listener:** A person who gives the speaker feedback in such forms as nodding, paraphrasing, maintaining an expression that shows interest, and asking questions for clarification.

## Check Your Understanding

1. RECALL: *Counterconditioning is based on the principles of*
   a. operant conditioning.
   b. classical conditioning.
   c. social learning.
   d. cognitive learning.

2. **APPLICATION:** *You could use contingency management to change the behavior of a child who comes home late for dinner by*
   a. pairing food with electric shocks.
   b. having the child observe someone else coming home on time and being rewarded.
   c. refusing to let the child have dinner.
   d. having the child relax and imagine being home on time for dinner.

3. **RECALL:** *The primary goal of psychoanalysis is*
   a. to change behavior.
   b. to reveal problems in the unconscious.
   c. to overcome low self-esteem.
   d. to learn how to get along with others.

4. **RECALL:** *Carl Rogers invented a technique to help people see their own thinking more clearly. Using this technique, the therapist paraphrases the client's statements. Rogers called this*
   a. person-centered therapy.
   b. reflection of feeling.
   c. unconditional positive regard.
   d. self-actualization.

5. **RECALL:** *Which form of therapy directly confronts a client's self-defeating thought patterns?*
   a. humanistic therapy
   b. behavioral therapy

   c. social–learning therapy
   d. rational–emotive therapy

6. **RECALL:** *Eysenck caused a furor with his claim that people who receive psychotherapy*
   a. are just looking for a paid friend.
   b. really should seek medical treatment for their disorders.
   c. are usually just pampered rich people who have nothing better to do with their lives.
   d. get better no more often than people who receive no therapy at all.

7. **UNDERSTANDING THE CORE CONCEPT:** *A phobia would be best treated by _____, while a problem of choosing a major would be better suited for _____.*
   a. behavioral therapy/insight therapy
   b. cognitive therapy/psychoanalysis
   c. insight therapy/behavioral therapy
   d. humanistic therapy/behavioral therapy

**ANSWERS:** 1. b   2. c   3. b   4. b   5. d   6. d   7. a

---

 **HOW DO THE BIOMEDICAL THERAPIES APPROACH MENTAL DISORDERS?**

The ecology of the mind is held in a delicate biological balance. It can be upset by irregularities in our genes, hormones, enzymes, and metabolism, as well as by damage from accidents and disease. In the final analysis, behavior, thinking, and emotions—normal or abnormal—are products of brain mechanisms. When something goes wrong with the brain, we can see the consequences in abnormal patterns of behavior or peculiar cognitive and emotional reactions. Based on these assumptions, the biomedical therapies attempt to treat mental disorders by treating the dysfunctional brain. As our Core Concept says, they do this in three ways:

**CORE CONCEPT**

**The biomedical therapies alter the structure or function of the brain through drugs, surgery, or electrical stimulation.**

Each of the biomedical therapies emerges from the medical model of abnormal mental functioning, which assumes an organic basis for mental illnesses and treats them as diseases. We begin our examination of these biomedical therapies with the powerful arsenal of prescription psychoactive drugs.

 **Chapter 13: Psychopathology**

*The medical model approaches mental disorders much as medicine deals with physical diseases.*

### Drug Therapy

In the history of the treatment of mental disorder, nothing has ever rivaled the revolution created by the discovery of drugs that could calm anxious patients, restore contact with reality in withdrawn patients, and suppress hallucinations in psychotic patients. This new therapeutic era began in 1953 with the introduction of "tranquilizing" drugs, notably *chlorpromazine* (Thorazine), into mental hospital treatment

What will be the effect of prescribing mood-altering drugs such as Prozac to millions of people?

programs. As more psychoactive drugs came on line, unruly, assaultive patients became cooperative, calm, and sociable. Thought-disordered patients who had been absorbed in their delusions and hallucinations began to be responsive to the real physical and social environment around them. No longer did mental hospital staff have to act as guards, putting patients in seclusion or straitjackets. Staff morale also improved as efforts aimed at rehabilitation replaced mere custodial care of the mentally ill (Swazey, 1974).

The effectiveness of drug therapy had a pronounced effect on the census of the nation's mental hospitals. In 1955, over half a million Americans were living in mental institutions, staying an average of several years. Then, with the introduction of *chlorpromazine* and other drugs, the numbers began a steady decline. In just over ten years, less than half the country's mental patients actually resided in mental hospitals, and those who did were institutionalized for an average of only a few months.

No longer is drug therapy just a treatment for the institutionalized and the profoundly disturbed. It has long since steamrolled out of the mental hospital and into our everyday lives. Currently, millions of ordinary people take drugs for anxiety, stress, depression, hyperactivity, insomnia, fears and phobias, obsessions and compulsions, addictions, and numerous other problems.

Clearly, a drug-induced revolution occurred. But what are these miraculous drugs? You have probably heard of Prozac and Valium, but these are just two of scores of psychoactive drugs that can alter your mood, your perceptions, your desires, and perhaps your basic personality. Here we will consider four major categories of drugs are used today in drug therapy programs: *antipsychotics, antidepressants, antianxiety drugs,* and *stimulants.* As their names suggest, these drugs chemically alter specific brain functions that are responsible for psychotic symptoms, depression, extreme anxiety, or disturbances in activity level. We will look at each category in turn.

**Chapter 3:**
**States of Mind**

*All drugs used to treat mental disorders are psychoactive drugs.*

**Center 2:**
**Biopsychology**

*Dopamine is a transmitter used in many parts of the brain, notably the "pleasure centers."*

**Chapter 13:**
**Psychopathology**

*"Positive" symptoms of schizophrenia include active hallucinations, delusions, and extreme emotions.*

**Antipsychotic drugs:** Medicines that diminish psychotic symptoms, usually by their effect on the dopamine pathways in the brain.

**Tardive dyskinesia:** An incurable disorder of motor control, especially involving muscles of the face and head, resulting from long-term use of antipsychotic drugs.

**ANTIPSYCHOTIC DRUGS**   By dampening delusions, hallucinations, social withdrawal, and agitation, the **antipsychotic drugs** diminish the symptoms of psychosis (Gitlin, 1990; Holmes, 1994; Kane & Marder, 1993). Most work by reducing the activity of the neurotransmitter dopamine in the brain. Specifically, *chlorpromazine* (Thorazine) and *haloperidol* (Haldol), for example, are known to block dopamine receptors in the synapse between nerve cells. A new antipsychotic drug, *clozapine* (Clozaril), both decreases dopamine activity and increases the activity of another neurotransmitter, serotonin, which inhibits the dopamine system. Though these drugs reduce overall brain activity, they do not merely "tranquilize" the patient. They eliminate the positive symptoms of schizophrenia that we have listed, although they do little for the social distance, jumbled thoughts, and poor attention spans seen in patients with "negative" symptoms of schizophrenia (Wickelgren, 1998). Because of their powerful and wide-reaching effects on behavior and personality, these drugs are sometimes called "major tranquilizers."

Unfortunately, long-term administration of antipsychotic drugs has several negative side effects. For example, **tardive dyskinesia** is an incurable disturbance of motor control (especially of the facial muscles) caused by antipsychotic drugs. Although the newer drug, clozapine, has reduced motor side effects because of its more selective dopamine blocking, its use involves a small risk of causing *agranulocytosis,* a rare blood disease caused by bone marrow dysfunction. With the possibility of such side effects, are antipsychotic drugs worth the risk? There is no easy answer. The risks must be weighed against the severity of the patient's current suffering. And, while it is true that there is no *cure* for schizophrenia, appropriate drug treatments can promote great relief and symptom reduction in many cases.

**ANTIDEPRESSANT DRUGS** Another class of drugs reduces the symptoms of depression. These **antidepressant drugs** work by "turning up the volume" among neurons using the transmitters norepinephrine and serotonin (Holmes, 1994). *Tricyclic* compounds such as Tofranil and Elavil work by reducing the body's reabsorption of neurotransmitters after they have been released in the synapse between brain cells. The famous antidepressant, Prozac (fluoxetine), is part of a group of drugs that allow serotonin to work longer in the synapse. For many people, this prolonged serotonin effect dramatically lifts depressed moods (Kramer, 1993). But some critics warn it may also "relieve" patients of their personality and creativity (Breggin & Breggin, 1994). Another group of antidepressant drugs includes *monoamine oxidase (MAO) inhibitors,* which limit the activity of the enzyme MAO, a chemical that breaks down norepinephrine. When MAO is inhibited, more norepinephrine is available in the body.

**Chapter 2: Biopsychology**
*The synapse is a microscopic gap between a neuron and an organ or muscle.*

A simple chemical, **lithium carbonate** has proved highly effective in the treatment of bipolar disorder. Lithium is not just an antidepressant, because it affects both ends of the emotional spectrum, dampening swings of mood from uncontrollable periods of hyperexcitement to the lethargy and despair of depression. Lithium, unfortunately, has its drawbacks: In high concentrations, it has proved toxic. Physicians have learned that safe therapy requires that small doses be given to build up therapeutic concentrations of lithium in the blood over a period of a week or two. Then, as a precaution, patients must have periodic blood analyses to assure that lithium concentrations have not risen to dangerous levels. Additionally, the drug can cause stomach problems and other physical complications for some patients. Aside from these side effects, the other difficulty with lithium therapy is the reluctance of some patients to take their medicine. Why? Some enjoy the "high" feeling that accompanies manic excitement phase of their disorder.

**Chapter 13: Psychopathology**
*Bipolar disorder causes mood swings, from mania to depression.*

In a welcome new development, researchers have found a promising alternative to lithium for the treatment of bipolar disorder (Azar, 1994). A drug called *divalproex sodium* (sold under the brand name Depakote), originally developed to treat epilepsy, seems to be as effective as lithium, but with fewer dangerous side effects. The new use for Depakote is potentially of enormous significance because about one-third of all bipolar patients do not respond to lithium or cannot tolerate its side effects.

The wide and enthusiastic use of mood-altering medications, including those for depression and bipolar disorder, has provoked controversy. One study suggests that much of the effect of these drugs is not much more than a placebo effect (Kirsch & Sapirstein, 1998). Nevertheless, drug therapy has produced fundamental changes in the field of psychiatry by shifting the emphasis away from traditional psychotherapy, even for problems such as low self-esteem that may be more properly the province of talk therapy (Barondes, 1994). In his book *Listening to Prozac*, psychiatrist and Prozac advocate Peter Kramer (1993) encourages the use of the drug to deal not only with depression but with general feelings of social unease and fear of rejection. Such claims have brought heated replies from therapists who fear that drugs may merely mask the psychological problems that people need to face and resolve. Some worry that the wide use of antidepressants may produce fundamental changes in the personality structure of a huge segment of our population—changes that could bring unanticipated, and possibly unwelcome, social consequences (Sleek, 1994). With an estimated 900,000 prescriptions for Prozac filled in the United States each month (Brown & Epperson, 1993), we must ask: What are the potential dangers of altering the brain chemistry of large numbers of people over long periods of time? Do we really want large numbers of people to become more "laid back" and unperturbed? Do we really want people to become more homogeneous? Will mass personality changes through drug therapy rob our society of some of its energy, creativity, and diversity? Perhaps we shall see.

**Antidepressant drugs:** Medicines that affect depression, usually by their effect on the serotonin and/or norepinephrine pathways in the brain.

**Lithium carbonate:** A simple chemical compound that is highly effective in dampening the extreme mood swings of bipolar disorder.

**Chapter 9:**
**Stress, Health, and Well-Being**

*Stress can cause both physical and mental disorders.*

ANTIANXIETY DRUGS    To reduce stress and suppress anxiety associated with everyday hassles, untold millions of Americans take pills. In general, these **anti-anxiety drugs** work by sedating the user (Holmes, 1994; Schatzberg, 1991). Many psychologists believe that these drugs, like the antidepressants, are too often prescribed for problems that people should face, rather than mask with chemicals. Nevertheless, antianxiety compounds are extremely useful in helping people deal with specific situations, such as anxiety prior to major surgery. If used over long periods, however, these drugs can be physically and psychologically addicting.

Oddly, some antidepressant drugs have also been found useful for reducing the symptoms of certain anxiety disorders such as panic disorders, agoraphobia, and obsessive–compulsive disorder. Because these problems may arise from low levels of serotonin, they may also respond well to drugs like Prozac that specifically affect serotonin function. The most commonly prescribed classes of antianxiety compounds, however, are *barbiturates* and *benzodiazepines*. Barbiturates are central nervous system (CNS) depressants; they have a relaxing effect, but they can be dangerous if taken in excess or in combination with alcohol. Benzodiazepine drugs, such as Valium and Xanax, work by increasing the activity of the neurotransmitter GABA, thereby decreasing activity in brain regions more specifically involved in feelings of anxiety. The benzodiazepines are sometimes called "minor tranquilizers."

**Chapter 3:**
**States of Mind**

*Many critics believe that the "minor tranquilizers" are overprescribed by physicians.*

Here are some *cautions* to bear in mind about the antianxiety drugs—drugs that many students take on a prescription basis (Hecht, 1986):

- These medicines should not be taken to relieve anxieties that are part of the ordinary stresses of everyday life.
- When used for extreme anxiety, these drugs should not normally be taken for more than a week or two at a time. If used longer than this, their dosage should be gradually reduced by a physician. Abrupt cessation can lead to *withdrawal symptoms,* such as convulsions, tremors, and abdominal and muscle cramps.
- Because the antianxiety drugs depress the central nervous system, they can impair one's ability to drive, operate machinery, or perform other tasks that require alertness (such as studying or taking exams).
- In combination with alcohol (also a central nervous system depressant) or with sleeping pills, antianxiety drugs can lead to unconsciousness and even death.

STIMULANTS    We have noted that **stimulants** find some use in the treatment of *narcolepsy.* They also have an accepted niche in treating **attention-deficit/hyperactivity disorder (ADHD),** a common problem in children who have difficulty controlling their behavior and focusing their attention. While it may seem odd to prescribe stimulants for hyperactive children, studies comparing stimulant therapy with behavior therapy and with *placebos* have shown a clear advantage for stimulants (Henker & Whalen, 1989; Poling, Gadow, & Cleary, 1991; Welsh, Gullotta, & Rapoport, 1993). They may work in hyperactive children by increasing the availability of dopamine and/or serotonin in their brains (Barkley, 1998; Gainetdinov et al., 1999; Wu, 1998).

**Chapter 3:**
**States of Mind**

*Narcolepsy is a REM-sleep disorder involving sudden daytime sleep attacks.*

**Chapter 3:**
**States of Mind**

*Stimulants increase activity level in the brain.*

As you can imagine, the use of stimulants to treat hyperactive children has generated heated controversy among the general public (Whalen & Henker, 1991). Some of the objections, of course, stem from ignorance of the well-established calming effect that these drugs can have on hyperactive children. But some of the controversy also arises from the legitimate concern that the causes and boundaries of ADHD are vague and that a potential exists for excessive diagnosis (Alford & Bishop, 1991). Critics charge that any troublesome youngster risks being labeled with a diagnosis of attention-deficit/hyperactivity disorder and started on stimulant therapy. A further concern highlights the possibility that the prescription of stimulants might actually encourage drug abuse in children.

**Antianxiety drugs:** A category of drugs that includes the *barbiturates* and *benzodiazepines,* drugs that diminish feelings of anxiety.

**Stimulants:** Drugs that normally increase activity level by encouraging communication among neurons in the brain. Stimulants, however, have been found to suppress activity level in persons with attention-deficit/hyperactivity disorder.

**Attention–deficit/hyperactivity disorder (ADHD):** A common problem in children who have difficulty controlling their behavior and focusing their attention.

As with any drug therapy, it is important to monitor the patient's progress when prescribing stimulants to treat ADHD. For some, the drug will interfere with normal sleep patterns. For others, especially when the dosage is too high, the patient will become withdrawn and engage in repetitive, autistic-like behaviors (Solanto & Connors, 1982). Additionally, there is some controversial evidence that stimulant therapy might slow the growth of children taking these drugs (Klein et al., 1988).

**EVALUATING THE DRUG THERAPIES**   Again, there is no doubt that the drug therapies have caused a revolution in the treatment of severe mental disorders, starting in the 1950s, when virtually the only treatments available were talk therapies, hospitalization, restraints, "shock treatment," and lobotomies. They don't "cure" mental disorders, of course, but they sometimes alter the brain's chemistry to reduce or eliminate people's symptoms. The effects were, at first, most evident in the treatment of schizophrenia with the antipsychotic drugs. Soon, antidepressants and antianxiety agents became available and were prescribed extensively. (Stimulants have found much more limited uses.) Currently, millions of people have prescriptions for one of these drugs. Much as we saw with IQ testing, as more people use these drugs, public enthusiasm grows. Many cannot imagine facing their lives without their Prozac or Valium.

But is all the enthusiasm warranted? No, says neuroscientist Elliot Valenstein (Rolnick, 1998; Valenstein, 1998). The closer we look at the evidence supporting the biological theories of mental disorder and the use of drug therapy, the more gaps we find. Valenstein credits the wide acceptance of drug therapy to the huge investment drug companies have made in marketing their products, both to physicians and the general public. For many of the most common psychological problems, such as stress on the job or child-rearing difficulties, there are simply no effective drug therapies. For many other problems, such as depression and obsessive–compulsive disorder, purely psychological treatments may do as well or better than drugs (Barlow, 1996; Hollon, 1996). In fact, both approaches to treatment may have similar effects on the brain (Miller, 1995). The moral of the story—as it is written in the research so far—is not to put all your faith in drug therapies.

## Psychosurgery

The headline in the *Los Angeles Times* read, "Bullet in the Brain Cures Man's Mental Problem" (February 23, 1988). The article revealed that a 19-year-old man suffering from severe obsessive–compulsive disorder had shot a .22 caliber bullet through the front of his brain in a suicide attempt. Remarkably, he survived, his pathological symptoms were gone, and his intellectual capacity was not affected, even though some of the underlying causes of his problems remained.

This case illustrates the potential effects of physical intervention in the brain. With scalpels in place of bullets, surgeons have attempted to treat mental disorders by severing connections between parts of the brain or by removing small sections of brain. **Psychosurgery,** the general term for such procedures, is often considered a method of last resort to treat psychopathologies that have proven intractable with other, less extreme forms of therapy. There is an ongoing, heated controversy about their usefulness and their side effects, as well as the ethics of taking such drastic measures to change behavior.

Psychosurgery has a long history, dating back to Stone Age openings of the skull, presumably to release pressure caused by head wounds (Maher & Maher, 1985). In medieval times, surgeons opened the skull to cut "the stone of folly" from the brains of those suffering from madness, as shown vividly in engravings and paintings from that era. (There is, of course, no such "stone"—and there was no anesthetic for these procedures.) Miraculously, many of the patients survived these treatments.

In modern times, the best-known form of psychosurgery involved the now-abandoned prefrontal lobotomy—an operation that severed certain nerve fibers

**Psychosurgery:** The general term for surgical intervention in the brain to treat psychological disorders.

In medieval times, those suffering from madness were sometimes treated by cutting "the stone of folly" from their brains.

**Chapter 2:
Biopsychology**

*Phineas Gage survived—
with a changed personality—
after a steel rod was driven
through his frontal lobe.*

connecting the frontal lobes with deep brain structures, especially those of the thalamus and hypothalamus—much as Phineas Gage did to himself by accident. The original candidates for lobotomy were agitated schizophrenic patients and patients who were compulsive and anxiety ridden. The effects of this rather crude operation were often dramatic. A new personality emerged, with less intense emotional arousal. However, the operation permanently destroyed basic aspects of their mental functioning—and of their human nature. Lobotomized patients usually lost something special: their unique personalities. Specifically, the lobotomy resulted in inability to plan ahead, indifference to the opinions of others, childlike actions, and the intellectual and emotional flatness of a person without a coherent sense of self. Because the new drug therapies promised to control psychotic symptoms with less risk of permanent damage, the era of lobotomy came to a close in the 1950s (Valenstein, 1980).

Psychosurgery is still occasionally done, but it is now much more limited to precise and proven procedures. We have seen, for example, that severing the fibers of the corpus callosum can reduce violent seizures in certain cases of epilepsy, with few side effects. Psychosurgery is also done on portions of the brain involved in pain perception in cases of otherwise incurable pain. However, no *DSM-IV* diagnoses are routinely treated with psychosurgery.

**Chapter 2:
Biopsychology**

*The "split-brain" operation
severs the corpus callosum—
the fibers connecting the
cerebral hemispheres.*

## Electroconvulsive Therapy

Electrical stimulation of the brain in the form known as **electroconvulsive therapy (ECT)** is still widely used. The therapy consists of applying weak electric current (75 to 100 volts) to a patient's temples for a period of time from one-tenth to a full second, until a convulsion occurs. The convulsion usually runs its course in 45 to 60 seconds. Patients are prepared for this traumatic intervention by sedating them with a short-acting barbiturate and a muscle relaxant. This renders the patient unconscious and minimizes violent, uncontrolled physical spasms during the seizure (Abrams, 1992; Malitz & Sackheim, 1984). While ECT is not a panacea or cure-all, some studies have shown it to be useful in the treatment of certain psychiatric disorders, particularly severe depression.

One benefit of ECT, according to its practitioners, is that it works quickly: Typically the symptoms of depression are reduced in a three- or four-day course of treatment, in contrast with the one- to two-week period required for drug therapy to be effective. Speed can be a major concern in depression, where suicide is always a pos-

**Electroconvulsive therapy (ECT):**
A treatment used primarily for depression and involving the application of an electric current to the head, producing a generalized seizure. Sometimes called "shock treatment."

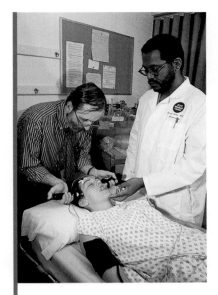

A sedated patient about to receive ECT. Electroconvulsive therapy applies a weak electrical current to a patient's temples, until a convulsion occurs. Some psychiatrists have found ECT successful in alleviating symptoms of severe depression, but it remains a treatment of last resort for most therapists.

sibility. Nonetheless, because of its occasional side effects, many therapists regard ECT with suspicion, reserving it for depressed patients for whom drug therapy is ineffective. Critics also fear it might be abused—used to silence dissent or punish patients who are uncooperative (Holmes, 1994). Among scientists themselves, suspicion of ECT comes from the fact that its effects are not well understood. To date no definitive theory "explains" why inducing a mild convulsion should alleviate disordered symptoms.

What are the unwanted side effects of ECT? They include temporary disorientation and a variety of memory deficits (Breggin, 1979, 1991). However, proponents claim that patients generally recover their specific memories within months of the treatment (Calev et al., 1991). One study found that patients who had received over 100 ECT treatments showed no deficit in functioning compared with those who had never received ECT (Devanand et al., 1991). To minimize even short-term side effects, however, ECT is now often administered "unilaterally" to only the right temple, in order to reduce the possibility of speech impairment (Scovern & Kilmann, 1980). In the face of such concerns, the National Institute of Mental Health (1985) investigated the use of ECT and gave it a cautious endorsement for treating a narrow range of disorders. In 1990, The American Psychiatric Association followed suit. In fact, its use is now limited largely to the treatment of depression.

## Hospitalization and the Alternatives

In modern times, mental hospitals have been a standard component of the medical arsenal for treating disorder. Originally they were designed as places of refuge—"asylums"—where disturbed people could escape the pressures of normal living. And, in fact, they often worked very well (Maher & Maher, 1985). But by the 20th century these hospitals had become overcrowded and, at best, little more than warehouses for the mentally ill. A feeble form of "group therapy" was often done with a whole ward—perhaps 50 patients—at a time. But too many patients and too few therapists meant little, if any, real therapy occurred. The drugs that so profoundly altered treatment in mental hospitals did not appear until the 1950s, so prior to that time institutionalized patients were often controlled by straitjackets and locked rooms.

**Therapeutic community:** Jones's term for a program of treating mental disorder by making the institutional environment supportive and humane for patients.

**THE THERAPEUTIC COMMUNITY**   Finally, in 1953—at about the time antipsychotic drugs were introduced—psychiatrist Maxwell Jones launched a frontal attack on this bankrupt mental hospital system. He proposed its replacement with a **therapeutic community** designed to interrupt the cycle of illness and institutionalization. Jones intended that the daily hospital routine could, itself, become a therapy designed to help patients learn to cope

Prior to the development of antipsychotic drugs, agitated patients were often restrained in straitjackets or locked rooms.

with the world outside. With this goal in mind, he began an experiment that abolished the dormitory accommodations that had been typical of mental hospitals, and in their place he gave patients more private living quarters that resembled apartments. He required that they make decisions about meals and daily activities. Then, as they were able to take more responsibilities, patients assumed the tasks of everyday living, including laundry, housekeeping, and maintenance. Further, Jones involved them in helping to plan their own treatment, which included not only group psychotherapy but occupational therapy and recreational therapy (Jones, 1953).

Eventually, variations on the therapeutic community concept were adopted across the United States, Canada, Britain, and Europe—often more on paper than in fact, as we saw in Rosenhan's "pseudopatient" study. But the changes did not come cheaply. And, while mental hospital populations have dropped, inpatient care costs have increased. The newer approach obviously required more staff and more costly facilities. The high costs led to a search for still another alternative, which came in the form of community-based treatment, rather than treatment based in remote mental hospitals. Thus more mental patients began entering psychiatric wards at general medical hospitals in their own communities. As a result, hospital care continued to consume most funding for mental health in the United States. Currently, mental patients account for about 25% of all hospital days (Kiesler, 1982a, 1982b, 1993).

And what has become of the therapeutic community? Most mental hospitals and mental wards in general hospitals have become holding places for patients whose medication is being adjusted. Although the abuse and gross neglect of earlier times is gone, very little nonmedical therapy occurs in most mental hospitals today.

### DEINSTITUTIONALIZATION AND COMMUNITY MENTAL HEALTH

For mental health professionals of all stripes, the goal of **deinstitutionalization,** begun in the 1950s, was to remove patients from mental hospitals as quickly as possible and return them to their communities. The concept of deinstitutionalization also gained popularity with politicians, who saw large sums of money being poured into mental hospitals (filled, incidentally, with nonvoting patients). Thus, a consensus formed among politicians and the mental health community that the major locus of treatment should shift from mental hospitals back to the community. There therapy would be dispensed from outpatient clinics, and recovering patients could live with their families, in foster homes, or in group homes. This vision became known as the **community mental health movement.**

Unfortunately, the reality did not match the vision (Torrey, 1996, 1997). Community mental health clinics—the centerpieces of the community mental health movement—never received full funding. Chronic patients were released from mental hospitals, but they often returned to communities that could offer them few therapeutic resources and to families ill-equipped to cope with still-disturbed individuals (Arnhoff, 1975; Smith et al., 1993). As a result, an estimated 150,000 patients, especially those with chronic schizophrenia, have ended up as homeless persons with no network of support (Torrey, 1997). Although estimates vary widely, up to 52% of homeless men and 71% of homeless women in the United States probably suffer from psychological disorders (Fischer & Breakey, 1991). Many also have problems with alcohol or other drugs (Drake, Osher, & Wallach, 1991). Under these conditions, they survive by shuttling from agency to agency. With no one to monitor their behavior, they usually stop taking their medication, and so their condition deteriorates until they require a period of rehospitalization. In fact, about 50% of all patients released from

**Chapter 13:**
**Psychopathology**

*None of Rosenhan's pseudopatients was ever discovered to be normal by any hospital staff member.*

**Deinstitutionalization:** The policy of removing patients, whenever possible, from mental hospitals.

**Community mental health movement:** An effort to deinstitutionalize mental patients and to provide therapy from outpatient clinics. Proponents of community mental health envisioned that recovering patients could live with their families, in foster homes, or in group homes.

Deinstitutionalization put mental patients back in the community—but often without adequate resources for continued treatment.

public mental hospitals find their way back to a hospital again within a year (Kiesling, 1983).

Despite this dismal picture, community treatment has not proved altogether unsuccessful. After a review of ten studies in which mental patients were randomly assigned to hospital treatment or to various community-based programs, Kiesler (1982a) reported that patients more often improved in the community treatment programs. Further, those given community-based treatment were less likely to be hospitalized at a later date. These results suggest that community treatment programs can work when they have been given the resources needed to extend a helping hand.

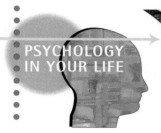

PSYCHOLOGY IN YOUR LIFE

## What Sort of Therapy Would You Recommend?

*N*ow that we have looked at both the psychological and medical therapies, consider the following situation. A friend begins to tell you about some personal problems he or she is having and requests your help in finding a therapist. Because you are studying psychology, reasons your friend, you might know what kind of treatment would be best. How do you respond?

First, you can lend a friendly ear, using the techniques of active listening, acceptance, and exploration of alternatives, which we discussed earlier in the chapter. In fact, this may be all that your troubled friend needs. But, if the situation looks in any way like one that requires professional assistance, you can use your knowledge of mental disorders and therapies to help your friend decide what sort of therapist might be most appropriate. To take some of the burden off your shoulders, both you and your friend should realize that any competent therapist will always refer the client elsewhere if the required therapy lies outside the therapist's specialty. Most cities and towns have specialists in marriage counseling, career counseling, treatment of phobic reactions, alcohol and drug treatment, sexual dysfunctions, and grief therapy.

A THERAPY CHECKLIST   Here, then, are some questions you will want to consider before you recommend a particular type of therapist.

- Is medical treatment needed? You might encourage your friend to see a psychiatrist for medical treatment if you suspect that the problem involves psychosis: schizophrenia, paranoia, a psychotic form of depression, mania, bipolar disorder, or the like. (*See Chapter 13, Psychopathology.*) Medical evaluation is also indicated if you suspect narcolepsy, sleep apnea, epilepsy, Alzheimer's disease, or other problems that have a known biological basis. If your suspicion is confirmed, the psychiatrist may employ a combination of drug therapy and psychotherapy.

  Even if you suspect a disorder that may need medical attention, however, it would not be amiss to refer your friend first to a clinical psychologist. Clinical psychologists all have extensive training in working on the psychological aspects of such problems. And most have established a working relationship with a physician, who can prescribe medication when necessary. You and your friend can get some guidance from *How to Choose a Psychologist*, a brochure published by the American Psychological Association (1995).

- Is there a specific behavioral problem? For example, does your friend want to eliminate a fear of spiders or a fear of flying? Is the problem a rebellious child? A sexual problem? Is she or he depressed—but not psychotic? If so, behavioral therapy (or cognitive–behavioral therapy) with a psychologist is probably the best bet. (Most psychia-

trists and other medical practitioners are not trained in these procedures.) Call the prospective therapist's office and ask for information on specific areas of training and specialization.

- Would group therapy be helpful? Many people find valuable help and support in a group setting, where they can learn not only from the therapist but also from other group members. Groups can be especially helpful in dealing with shyness, lack of assertiveness, addictions, and with complex problems of interpersonal relationships. (As a bonus, group therapy is often less expensive than individual therapy.) Professionals with training in several disciplines, including psychology, psychiatry, and social work, run therapy groups. Again, your best bet is a therapist who has had special training in this method and about whom you have heard good things from former clients.

- Is the problem one of stress, confusion, or choice? Most troubled people don't fall neatly into one of the categories that we have discussed in the previous paragraphs. More typically, they need help sorting through the chaos of their lives, finding a pattern, and developing a plan to cope. This is the territory of the insight therapies. If you decide to recommend an insight therapist for your friend, it does not seem to make much difference which form of insight therapy she or he receives. The important elements seem to be understanding, support, and a look at one's

*continued*

difficulties from a sensible new perspective.

SOME CAUTIONS   We now know enough about human biology, behavior, and mental processes to know some treatments to avoid. People with problems should be especially wary of therapies that may produce addictions or unwanted side effects. Some specifics follow.

- *Drug therapies to avoid.* Because of their addicting and sedating effects, the minor tranquilizers are too frequently prescribed for patients leading chronically stressful lives (Alford & Bishop, 1991). As we have said, these drugs should only be taken for short periods—if at all. Similarly, some physicians ignore the dangers of sleep-inducing medications for their patients who suffer from insomnia. While these drugs have legitimate uses, many such prescriptions actually cause more problems than they solve by risking the possibility of drug dependence and by interfering with the person's

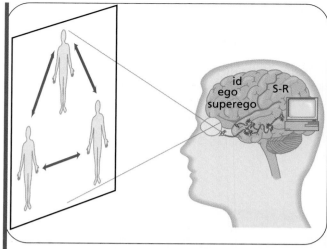

Which therapy would you recommend to a friend?

ability to alter the conditions that may have caused the original problem.

- *Advice and interpretations to avoid.* Although psychodynamic therapy can be helpful, patients should also be cautioned that some therapists may give ill-advised counsel in problems of anger management. Traditionally, Freudians have believed that individuals who are prone to angry or violent outbursts harbor deep-seated aggression that needs

to be vented. But, as we have seen, research shows that trying to empty one's aggressions through aggressive behavior, such as shouting or punching a pillow, may actually increase the likelihood of later aggressive behavior.

Another danger in some therapies lies in digging up the psychological bones of the patient's past and fixing blame on people for human frailties. A replay of our grievances can renew feelings of resentment and ill will toward parents, relatives, and friends. A good therapist will help patients work through such feelings. A good therapist will also remind patients of the *reconstructive* nature of memory, pointing out that memory is notoriously unreliable and that sudden recollections of "repressed" emotional material from childhood may not accurately reflect actual events.

1. APPLICATION: *Imagine that you are a psychiatrist. Which type of drug would you prescribe to a patient who has obsessive–compulsive disorder?*
   a. an antipsychotic drug
   b. lithium carbonate
   c. an antianxiety drug
   d. a stimulant
2. RECALL: *Which class of drugs blocks dopamine receptors in the brain?*
   a. antipsychotics
   b. antidepressants
   c. antianxiety drugs
   d. stimulants
3. RECALL: *A controversial treatment for attention-deficit/hyperactivity disorder involves*
   a. antipsychotics.
   b. antidepressants.

   c. antianxiety drugs.
   d. stimulants.
4. RECALL: *Which of the following medical treatments for mental disorder has now been largely abandoned as ineffective and dangerous?*
   a. electroconvulsive therapy
   b. lithium carbonate
   c. prefrontal lobotomy
   d. the "split-brain" operation
5. RECALL: *The community mental health movement followed a deliberate plan of* _____ *mental patients.*
   a. hospitalizing
   b. deinstitutionalizing
   c. administering insight therapy to
   d. removing stressful events in the lives of

**6.** UNDERSTANDING THE CORE CONCEPT: *Drug thera-pies, psychosurgery, and ECT all are methods of treating mental disorder*
   **a.** by changing the chemistry of the body.
   **b.** by removing stress in the patient's life.
   **c.** by directly altering the function of the brain.
   **d.** that have no scientific basis.

   ANSWERS:    1. c    2. b    3. d    4. c    5. b    6. c

## A PERSONAL ENDNOTE

We come to the end of our journey through *Psychology*. When you reflect on the lessons of this course (and ideally, when you take your final examination), you will realize just how much you have learned on the way. Yet we have barely scratched the surface of the excitement and challenges that await students of psychology, those curious people-watchers who choose to continue on to the next phase of the journey into more advanced realms of this discipline.

We hope you will be among them and that you may even go on to contribute to this dynamic enterprise as a scientific researcher or a clinical practitioner or by applying what is known in psychology to the solution of social and personal problems.

Playwright Tom Stoppard reminds us that "Every exit is an entry somewhere else." We would like to believe that the entry into the next phase of your life will be facilitated by what you have learned from *Psychology* and from your introductory psychology course. In that next journey, may you infuse new life into the study of human nature, while strengthening the human connections among all people you encounter. Till we meet again,

Phil Zimbardo

Ann Weber

Bob Johnson

# USING PSYCHOLOGY TO LEARN PSYCHOLOGY

## How Is Education Like Therapy?

Consider the ways in which psychotherapy is like your classroom experiences in college:

- Most therapists, like most professors, are professionals with special training in what they do.
- Most patients/clients are like students in that they are seeking professional help to change their lives in some way.
- Much of what happens in therapy and in the classroom involves learning: new ideas, new behaviors, new insights, new connections.

It may help you learn psychology (and other subjects, as well) to think of teaching and learning in therapeutic terms. As we have seen, therapy seems to work best when therapist and client have a good working relationship and when the client believes in the value of the experience—and the same is almost certainly true for the student–professor relationship. You can take the initiative in establishing a personal-but-professional relationship with your psychology professor by doing the following two things: (1) asking questions or otherwise participating in class (at appropriate times and without dominating, of course) and (2) seeking your instructor's help on points you don't understand or on course-related topics you would like to pursue in more detail (doing so during regular office hours). The result will be learning

more about psychology, because you will be taking a more active part in the learning process. Incidentally, an active approach to the course will also help you stand out from the crowd in the professor's mind, which could be helpful if you sometime need a faculty recommendation.

Now consider a parallel between education and group therapy. In group therapy, patients learn from each other, as well as from the therapist. Much the same can occur in your psychology course, if you consider other students as learning resources. As we noted earlier in this book, the most successful students often spend part of their study time sharing information in groups. (*See Chapter 6, Learning and Remembering.*)

One other tip for learning psychology we can borrow from the success of behavioral therapies: the importance of changing behavior, not just thinking. It is easy to "intellectualize" a fact or an idea passively when you read about it or hear about it in class. But you are likely to find that the idea makes little impact on you ("I know I *read* about it, but I can't *remember* it!") if you don't *use* it. The remedy is to do something with your new knowledge: Tell someone about it, come up with illustrations from your own experience, or try acting in a different way. For example, after reading about *active listening* in this chapter, try it the next time you talk to a friend. Educators sometimes speak of this as "active learning." And it works!

## CHAPTER SUMMARY

**KEY QUESTION** **WHAT IS THERAPY?**

- People seek therapy for a variety of problems. Treatment comes in many forms, both psychological and biomedical, but all involve diagnosing the problem, finding the

source of the problem, making a prognosis about probable outcomes with and without treatment, and carrying out treatment. A variety of professionals work under this model. In earlier times, treatments for those with mental problems were usually harsh and dehumanizing. Only recently in history have people with emotional problems been treated as individuals with "illnesses" or "problems" to be dealt with. This view of mental disorder has led to more humane treatment. Many cultures have their own ways of understanding and treating mental disorders, although some "universals" hold true for all forms of therapy.

 Therapy takes a variety of forms, but the common element is a relationship focused on altering behavior or mental processes.

 HOW DO PSYCHOLOGISTS TREAT MENTAL DISORDERS?

- Behavioral therapy attempts to apply the principles of learning to problem behaviors. Among the classical conditioning techniques, counterconditioning and systematic desensitization are commonly employed to treat fears. Aversion therapy may also be used for eliminating unwanted responses. Operant techniques include contingency management to modify behavior, primarily through positive reinforcement and extinction strategies. Social learning therapy involves the use of models and social skills training to help individuals gain confidence about their abilities.
- The first of the insight therapies, psychoanalysis grew out of Sigmund Freud's theory of personality. Its goal is to release repressed material from the unconscious. Neo-Freudians place more emphasis on the patient's current social situation, interpersonal relationships, and self-concept.
- Among other insight therapies, humanistic therapy focuses on individuals becoming more fully self-actualized. Therapists strive to be nondirective in helping their clients establish a positive self-image that can deal with external criticisms. Group therapy has many applications, including community self-help groups and support groups. Family and marital therapy concentrate on situational difficulties and interpersonal dynamics as a total system in need of improvement.
- Another form of insight therapy, cognitive therapy concentrates on changing negative or irrational thought patterns about oneself and one's social relationships. The client must learn more constructive thought patterns in reference to a problem and apply the new technique to other situations. Rational–emotive therapy helps clients recognize that their irrational beliefs about themselves

interfere with life and helps them learn how to change those thought patterns. In recent years a synthesis of cognitive and behavioral therapies has emerged, combining the techniques of insight therapy with methods based on learning theory.
- Research shows that psychotherapy is effective for a variety of psychological problems. Often it is more effective than drug therapy. As the research on mental disorders becomes more refined, we are learning to match specific psychotherapies to specific disorders.

 Psychologists employ two main forms of treatment: the behavioral therapies and the insight therapies.

 HOW DO THE BIOMEDICAL THERAPIES APPROACH MENTAL DISORDERS?

- Biomedical therapies concentrate on changing the physiological aspects of mental illness. Drug therapy includes antipsychotic, antidepressant, antianxiety, and stimulant medicines. Together these drugs have caused a revolution in the medical treatment of mental disorder, although critics warn of their abuse, particularly in treating the ordinary stress of daily living. Psychosurgery has lost much of its popularity in recent years because of its radical, irreversible side effects. Electroconvulsive therapy is undergoing a resurgence of use with depressed patients, but it remains controversial. In all of this, hospitalization has been a mainstay of medical treatment, although the trend is away from mental hospitals to community-based treatment. The policy of deinstitutionalization was based on the best of intentions, but it has resulted in many mental patients being turned back into their communities with few resources and little treatment. When the resources are available, however, community treatment is often successful.

 The biomedical therapies alter the structure or function of the brain through drugs, surgery, or electrical stimulation.

For each of the following items, choose the single correct or best answer. The answer key appears at the end of the test.

1. Despite the differences between various types of therapy, all therapeutic strategies are designed to
   a. make the client feel better about him- or herself.
   b. help the individual fit better into his or her society.
   c. change the individual's functioning in some way.
   d. educate the person without interfering with his or her usual patterns of behavior.

2. While professionals with somewhat different training and orientations can provide similar forms of therapy, only _____ on the list below are qualified to prescribe medications for the treatment of mental or behavioral disorders.
   a. psychiatrists
   b. psychiatric social workers
   c. psychologists
   d. psychotherapists

3. Because a central goal of the therapist is to guide a patient toward understanding the connections between past origins and present symptoms, psychodynamic therapy is often called _____ therapy.
   a. insight
   b. cognitive
   c. existential
   d. rational–emotive

4. A patient finds herself feeling personally fond of her therapist, who reminds her of her father. This is an example of the psychoanalytic process known as
   a. resistance.
   b. transference.
   c. countertransference.
   d. negative transference.

5. Lola has an irrational fear of speaking in front of others. With the support of her instructor and her entire psychology class, Lola confronts her fear by standing alone in front of her classmates and talking about her phobia. This strategy of placing the individual in the dreaded situation is called
   a. exposure therapy.
   b. catharsis.
   c. insight therapy.
   d. social-learning therapy.

6. To teach his young daughter not to be afraid to swim, a man tells her to "Watch me!" as he wades into the surf, then rolls with the waves, and finally invites her to join him if she wants to try. In behavioral therapy, this technique is known as
   a. clinical ecology.
   b. counterconditioning.
   c. behavioral rehearsal.
   d. participant modeling.

7. Which of the following problems might best be corrected through rational–emotive therapy (RET)?
   a. An addicted smoker wants to quit.
   b. A young man has an extreme fear of heights.
   c. An average-weight woman diets constantly, believing that she must be thin in order to have anyone love her.
   d. A patient complains of continual "voices" in his head telling him that people are trying to harm him.

8. Which of the following statements about electroconvulsive therapy (ECT) is true?
   a. Proper ECT applies a very strong electric current to a patient's brain without the interference or insulation of sedatives or anesthetic medication.
   b. Some studies have found ECT to be effective in the treatment of severe depression.
   c. It is known to work by increasing the stimulation of a particular neurotransmitter in the brain.
   d. It works best with manic patients.

9. Valium, a drug with a high "abuse potential," is classified as an _____ medication.
   a. antianxiety
   b. antidepressant
   c. antipsychotic
   d. antihistamine

10. Psychiatrist Jerome Frank argues that, like religious and political indoctrination programs, all healing processes rely on a common crucial element:
    a. deception.
    b. fear of authority.
    c. rejection of culture.
    d. belief in the experience.

ANSWERS:   1. c   2. a   3. a   4. b   5. a   6. d
7. c   8. b   9. a   10. d

## BOOKS

Berger, L., & Vuckovic, A. (1995). *Under observation: Life inside the McLean Psychiatric Hospital*. New York: Penguin Books.

> This vivid picture of life at psychiatric institutions across the country is illustrated with the case histories and personal stories of diverse patients who emerge as real people, some disturbingly familiar. The book dispels myths and challenges stereotypes about how the mentally ill are treated, leaving the reader both saddened and hopeful.

Ellis, A., & Lange, A. J. (1995). *How to keep people from pushing your buttons*. Secaucus, N.J.: Carol Press.

> Other people can't make you angry, depressed—or happy, for that matter. You do it to yourself with your own rational or irrational thoughts. Nevertheless, we do get into difficult situations with others, and this book explains how to defuse these situations without letting people "push your buttons." It's all based on the principles of rational thinking pioneered by Albert Ellis in his rational–emotive therapy.

Gillick, M. R. (1999). *Tangled minds: Understanding Alzheimer's disease and other dementias*. New York: Plume/Penguin.

> A Harvard medical school professor reviews the stages of Alzheimer's disease, its history, research into its causes, and treatments now in use to alleviate symptoms. She also offers advice about diagnosing dementia, caring for Alzheimer's patients, mediating its effects on family members, promoting public advocacy and funding, and preserving dignity and individuality in the face of debilitating loss of cognitive function.

Graham, H. (1998). *Discover color therapy: A first-step handbook to better health*. Berkeley, CA: Ulysses Press.

> This short, interesting approach to self-improvement is based on a topic that interests everyone—the colors of our world and our specific preferences for certain colors.

Imber-Black, E. (1998). *The secret life of families: Truth-telling, privacy, and reconciliation in a tell-all society*. New York: Bantam Doubleday Dell.

> The author, a psychiatry professor, critiques the phenomenon of indiscriminate self- and other-disclosure popularized by tabloids and talk shows, noting that every secret is different, and while some revelations may be relieving and inconsequential for others, other secrets create lasting pain and no relief. A valuable examination of the difference between therapy and "entertainment."

Kaysen, S. (1993). *Girl, interrupted*. New York: Turtle Bay Books.

> Susanna Kaysen's frank and vivid account tells of her two years, beginning in 1967 when she was 18, in McLean Hospital, a psychiatric hospital with a ward for teenage girls. Dark, funny stories of herself, her jumbled thinking, and the other patients are interspersed with pages from her medical record.

Keyes, D. (1981). *The minds of Billy Milligan*. New York: Bantam.

> This is a factual account of the life of William Stanley Milligan, the first person in the United States to be judged not guilty of major crimes by reason of insanity, because he possessed multiple personalities. The book explores whether Milligan fractionated into at least ten personalities as a result of childhood abuse. This is another work by the author of the book Flowers for Algernon, the basis for the 1968 film Charly (see "If You're Interested," Chapter 11).

Kramer, P. D. (1993). *Listening to Prozac: A psychiatrist explores antidepressant drugs and the remaking of the self*. New York: Viking.

> Probably no other mood-changing medication since Valium has so captivated the nation's attention and imagination as Prozac, an antidepressant that reputedly makes patients "better than well." Is it a wonder drug, releasing the real self from the pervasive burden of depression and disordered thinking? Or is it an artificial mask, an identity change in tablet form, a popular but ultimately limited form of self-deception? Through before-and-after interviews with patients who have embraced or rejected Prozac the author presents the case for and against Prozac, and speculates on the power and meaning of psychoactive medications.

Leahy, R. L. (1996). *Cognitive therapy: Basic principles and applications*. Northvale, NJ: Jason Aronson.

> With pressure from HMOs and government agencies to devise shorter courses of treatment for complex disorders, therapists are combining elements of cognitive and psychodynamic treatments—and achieving surprising success, according to Leahy's review of treatments for depression, anxiety, anger, and relationship conflict.

Schiller, L., & Bennett, A. (1996). *The quiet room: A journey out of the torment of madness*. New York: Warner Books.

> This vivid, acclaimed account is the true story of the first author's descent into schizophrenia and, with help from therapists and family, her return to reality.

Seligman, M. E. P. (1993). *What you can change and what you can't.* New York: Ballentine.

*This respected clinician tells us the good news that there are many previously unyielding mental disorders that can now be treated successfully—perhaps even cured—by psychological therapies. These include phobias, OCD, and other anxiety disorders, many sexual dysfunctions, depression, bulimia, anger, PTSD, and substance abuse.*

Valenstein, E. S. (1998). *Blaming the brain: The truth about drugs and mental health.* New York: Free Press.

*A neuroscientist who has spent more than 40 years looking at brain chemistry challenges the conventional wisdom that biochemistry is the royal road to understanding mental disorders. There are big gaps in the data supporting all our biological theories of psychopathology, Valenstein claims.*

## VIDEOS

*Amadeus.* (1984, color, 158 min.). Directed by Milos Forman; starring Tom Hulce, F. Murray Abraham, Elizabeth Berridge, Jeffrey Jones.

*This absorbing (and musically astounding) film is based on Peter Shaffer's play about the psychological rivalry between eighteenth-century composer Antonio Salieri and Wolfgang Amadeus Mozart, the young musical genius who seemed to be favored by God. Told in flashbacks, the story is framed by Salieri's retrospective confession from his asylum cell, surrounded by powerful scenes of the "therapies" of the day—the cages and restraints shackling the mentally ill, suicidal, and eccentric citizens of early modern Europe.*

*Analyze this.* (1999, color, 103 min.). Directed by Harold Ramis; starring Robert DeNiro, Billy Crystal, Lisa Kudrow.

*A normally arrogant mob boss becomes overwhelmed by life problems and seeks the help of a psychotherapist—but how much can he reveal without disclosing vital criminal secrets? This funny movie satirizes every gangster role DeNiro has played, counterpointed by Crystal's nervous and wry commentary.*

*Don Juan DeMarco.* (1995, color, 97 min.). Directed by Jeremy Leven; starring Marlon Brando, Johnny Depp, Faye Dunaway.

*A psychiatrist, treating a delusional young man who dresses like Zorro and believes he is the world's greatest lover, becomes affected by the patient's romantic and passionate approach to life.*

*Good Will Hunting.* (1997, color, 126 min.). Directed by Gus Van Sant; starring Matt Damon, Robin Williams, Ben Affleck, Minnie Driver, Stellan Skarsgård.

*A working-class youth with a genius for mathematics must confront a painful past and a belligerence about intimacy in order to hone his gifts, with the help of an MIT professor,*

*sympathetic friends, and a sensitive, offbeat psychotherapist (Williams in his Oscar-winning role).*

*The madness of King George.* (1994, color, 107 min.). Directed by Nicholas Hytner; starring Nigel Hawthorne, Helen Mirren, Ian Holm, Rupert Everett, John Wood, Amanda Donohoe.

*In the late eighteenth century, England's happy and benevolent George III (the very "tyrant" denounced in the American Declaration of Independence) becomes suddenly ill and irrational, prompting his friends, enemies, and physicians to take drastic actions. Based on Alan Bennett's play, the film vividly portrays the well-intentioned but utterly useless efforts of "medical science" at that time to treat mental illness.*

*Mr. Jones.* (1993, color, 114 min.). Directed by Mike Figgis; starring Richard Gere, Lena Olin, Anne Bancroft, Tom Irwin.

*A man with manic-depressive illness embarks on an unethical romance with his psychotherapist, a woman on the rebound. Some realistic issues of professional versus personal intimacy are mixed with unrealistically extreme (but cinematic) depictions of bipolar symptoms.*

*My name is Bill W.* (1989, color, 100 min.). Directed by Daniel Petrie; starring James Garner, James Woods, JoBeth Williams, Fritz Weaver, Gary Sinise.

*This is the story of the founding of Alcoholics Anonymous and the blueprint for many self-help programs and support groups. Set in the mid-1930s, the film shows how two alcoholics—stockbroker William Griffith Wilson ("Bill W.") and Dr. Robert Holbrook Smith ("Dr. Bob S.")—form a partnership to help each other quit drinking. With superb acting, the film explores the combination self-discipline, friendship, and support essential to therapeutic behavior change.*

*Ordinary people.* (1980, color, 123 min.). Directed by Robert Redford; starring Donald Sutherland, Mary Tyler Moore, Judd Hirsch, Timothy Hutton.

*Powerful film version of Judith Guest's novel about an upper-middle-class family's struggles to cope with the death of their older son, including the suicidal guilt of his surviving younger brother. This film presents an appealing portrayal of a psychotherapist as an important relationship in a troubled life.*

*The seven percent solution.* (1976, color, 113 min.). Directed by Herbert Ross; starring Nicol Williamson, Alan Arkin, Robert Duvall, Vanessa Redgrave, Laurence Olivier.

*What if fictional detective Sherlock Holmes sought the help of his real contemporary Sigmund Freud in overcoming his depression-triggered cocaine addiction? An entertaining film accurately portrays psychoanalytic principles—if not* the details and personality of the great analyst, who laughs and even dances in the film more than he may have done in real life—interwoven with a suspenseful mystery plot.

The snake pit. (1948, B&W, 108 min.). Directed by Anatole Litvak; starring Olivia de Havilland, Mark Stevens, Leo Genn.

This affecting film portrayal of a young woman's acute schizophrenia and gradual recovery through psychotherapy presents powerful images of what mental institutions were like in most of this country before the development of effective drug therapy for mental disorders.

Spellbound. (1945, B&W, 111 min.). Directed by Alfred Hitchcock; starring Gregory Peck, Ingrid Bergman, Leo G. Carroll.

This classic Hitchcock mystery blends psychoanalytic jargon and techniques with old-fashioned detective skills in solving the dilemma of an amnesiac suffering from a guilt complex. Compelling dream sequences were appropriately designed by surrealist artist Salvador Dali.

Stuart saves his family. (1995, color, 95 min.). Directed by Harold Ramis; starring Al Franken, Laura San Giacomo, Vincent D'Onofrio, Shirley Knight, Harris Yulin, Julia Sweeney.

Based on satirist Al Franken's character, Stuart Smalley, the chronic "twelve-stepper" and support group member on TV's "Saturday Night Live," this film pokes gentle fun at the New Age jargon and saccharine optimism of some self-improvement programs. Some uncanny, on-target depictions of difficult family dynamics make this film poignant and helpful as well as funny.

What about Bob? (1991, color, 99 min.). Directed by Frank Oz; starring Bill Murray, Richard Dreyfuss, Julie Hagerty.

A professional psychiatric patient proves the undoing of a pompous psychiatrist, pursued by the needy, neurotic man to his family summer vacation—where the patient proceeds to charm everyone, clarifying the psychiatrist's own inabilities as a father and husband. A sometimes disturbing comedy about the artificial barriers blocking the unique therapist–client relationship.

Appendix

# Understanding Graphs & Statistics: Analyzing Data & Forming Conclusions

## Outline

**Chapter 13: Psychopathology**

*Shyness may be a part of one's inborn temperament— or it may be learned.*

**Chapter 1: Mind, Behavior, and Science**

*Theories provide explanations for patterns observed or predicted in the data.*

hether they practice psychology, biology, chemistry, or astronomy, all scientists make measurements. In psychology, the measurements often describe people's behavior or other attributes, such as extraversion, romantic attraction, memory, aggression, or shyness. To look for patterns in their measurements, psychologists may put their data in visual form—as graphs. They also employ a set of mathematical techniques called **statistics** to organize the data and draw inferences from them. In the next few pages, we will give you a glimpse of graphic presentation and statistical analysis by walking you through the details of some real psychological research. For this purpose, we have selected a study designed to better understand people like Fred Cowan:

> Relatives, coworkers, and acquaintances described Fred Cowan as a "nice, quiet man," a "gentle man who loved children," and a "real pussycat." The principal of the parochial school Cowan had attended as a child reported that his former student had received A grades in courtesy, cooperation, and religion. According to a coworker, Cowan "never talked to anybody and was someone you could push around." Cowan, however, surprised everyone who knew him when, one Valentine's Day, he strolled into work toting a semiautomatic rifle and shot and killed four coworkers, a police officer, and, finally, himself.

How could a habitually "gentle man" suddenly become a murderer? A team of researchers had a hunch that there might be a link between violent behavior and certain personal characteristics, such as shyness (Lee et al., 1977). They reasoned that seemingly nonviolent people who suddenly commit murders might be individuals who keep strong passions and impulses under tight control. But, thought the researchers, these "sudden murderers" are probably also individuals who never learned how to deal comfortably with others. For most of their lives, they may suffer many silent injuries. But seldom, if ever, do they express anger, regardless of how angry they really feel. According to this theory, they appear unbothered on the outside, but on

**Chapter 1:**
**Mind, Behavior, and Science**

*A hypothesis is a statement*
*predicting the outcome*
*of a scientific study.*

the inside they may be fighting desperately to control their emotions. They give the impression that they are quiet, passive, responsible people, both as children and as adults. But because they are shy, they probably do not let others get close to them, so no one knows how they really feel. Then, suddenly, something "snaps." At the slightest provocation—one more small insult, one more little rejection, one more bit of social pressure—the fuse is lit, and they release the suppressed violence that has been building up for so long. Because they did not learn to deal with interpersonal conflicts through discussion and verbal negotiation, they are driven to act out their anger explosively and physically.

This line of reasoning led to three specific hypotheses: (1) A measure of impulse control should show that these *sudden murderers*—people who had engaged in homicide without any prior history of violence or antisocial behavior—usually exert higher levels of control over their impulses than would *habitual-criminal murderers*—those who had not only committed homicide but also had previous records of violent criminal behavior. (2) The researchers also hypothesized that shyness would be more characteristic of sudden murderers—who may have always felt themselves alienated from others—than it would be of habitual-criminal murderers. (3) Finally, the researchers suspected that sudden murderers would have personalities characterized by passivity and dependence. (Take a moment to decide which of these hypotheses you agree with.)

To test their hypotheses, the researchers administered three psychological questionnaires to inmates serving time for murder in California prisons. Nineteen inmates (all male) agreed to participate in the study. Prior to committing murder, some had committed a series of crimes, while the others had had no previous criminal record.

One questionnaire was a portion of the Minnesota Multiphasic Personality Inventory (MMPI), an instrument that was originally designed to measure many aspects of personality. The sudden-murderers study, however, used only the "ego-overcontrol" scale, which measures the degree to which a person controls impulses. The higher the score on this scale, the more the subject attempts to suppress, or "overcontrol," the urge to act on impulse.

To assess shyness, they used the Stanford Shyness Survey (Zimbardo, 1990). The most important item on this instrument simply asked if the subject considered himself to be shy. The answer could be either yes or no. Other items on the scale tapped degree and kinds of shyness and a variety of dimensions related to origins and triggers of shyness.

Finally, to assess passivity and dependence, the researchers used the Bem Sex-Role Inventory (BSRI). This instrument presents a list of adjectives, such as *aggressive* and *affectionate*, and asks how well each adjective describes the subject (Bem, 1974, 1981). Some adjectives are typically associated with being "feminine" because women more often use them to describe themselves than do men. The total score of these adjectives was a subject's femininity score. Other adjectives were considered "masculine," and the total score of those adjectives was a subject's masculinity score. The so-called "feminine" traits generally involve more passive and dependent characteristics than do the "masculine" traits. The final "sex-role difference score," which you see in Table A.1, was calculated by subtracting the masculinity score from the femininity score. If the researchers' hypothesis was correct, the sudden murderers should choose more feminine characteristics to describe themselves, and this should result in a higher sex-role difference score.

To summarize, the researchers predicted that sudden murderers would (1) score higher in ego overcontrol, (2) more often describe themselves as shy on the shyness survey, and (3) select more "feminine" traits than "masculine" ones on the sex-role scale. What did they discover? Before you find out, you need to understand some of the basic procedures that were used to analyze these data.

**Chapter 10:**
**Personality**

*The MMPI-2 is a widely*
*used trait inventory designed*
*to detect serious disorders.*

**Statistics:** A set of mathematical techniques used to organize data and to draw inferences from them. Numbers derived from these mathematical procedures are also called statistics.

## TABLE A.1    Raw Data from the Sudden-Murderers Study

| SUBJECT NUMBER | SHYNESS | BSRI (BEM SEX–ROLE INVENTORY) FEMININITY MINUS MASCULINITY | MMPI (MINNESOTA MULTIPHASIC PERSONALITY INVENTORY) EGO OVERCONTROL |
|---|---|---|---|
| *Group 1: Sudden Murderers* | | | |
| 1 | yes | +5 | 17 |
| 2 | no | −1 | 17 |
| 3 | yes | +4 | 13 |
| 4 | yes | +61 | 17 |
| 5 | yes | +19 | 13 |
| 6 | yes | +41 | 19 |
| 7 | no | −29 | 14 |
| 8 | yes | +23 | 9 |
| 9 | yes | −13 | 11 |
| 10 | yes | +5 | 14 |
| *Group 2: Habitual-Criminal Murderers* | | | |
| 11 | no | −12 | 15 |
| 12 | no | −14 | 11 |
| 13 | yes | −33 | 14 |
| 14 | no | −8 | 10 |
| 15 | no | −7 | 16 |
| 16 | no | +3 | 11 |
| 17 | no | −17 | 6 |
| 18 | no | +6 | 9 |
| 19 | no | −10 | 12 |

 KEY QUESTION

## HOW DO PSYCHOLOGISTS ANALYZE THEIR DATA?

For most researchers, analyzing the data is both an exciting and anxiety-provoking step. This is the point at which they discover whether their predictions were correct. Analysis of the data will tell them if their results will contribute to a better understanding of a particular aspect of behavior or if they have to go back to the drawing board and redesign their research or develop new hypotheses.

To illustrate how this process works, we will go step-by-step through an analysis of some of the data from the sudden-murderers study. You do not need to be highly skilled in math to be able to understand the concepts we will be discussing. You just need the courage to see a few graphical conventions and mathematical symbols for what they are—a shorthand for presenting ideas and conceptual operations.

### Graphic Representation

The **raw data**—the actual scores or other measures obtained—from the 19 inmates in the murderers study are listed in Table A.1. As you can see, there were ten inmates in the sudden-murderers group and nine in the habitual-criminal murderers group. When first glancing at these data, any researcher would feel what you probably feel: puzzled. What do all these scores mean? Do the two groups of murderers differ from one another on these various personality measures? It is difficult to know just by examining this disorganized array of numbers. For this reason, psychologists often

**Raw data:** The unanalyzed scores or other quantitative measures obtained from a study; the data on which statistical procedures are performed.

## TABLE A.2 Rank Ordering of Sex-Role Difference Scores

| SUDDEN MURDERERS | | HABITUAL-CRIMINAL MURDERERS |
|---|---|---|
| Highest | +61 | +6 |
| | +41 | +3 |
| | +23 | −7 |
| | +19 | −8 |
| | +5 | −10 |
| | +5 | −12 |
| | +4 | −14 |
| | −1 | −17 |
| | −13 | −33 |
| Lowest | −29 | |

Note: + scores are more "feminine"; − scores are more "masculine."

organize their data in graphic form so that they can get a visual impression of their results. To do so, they may begin with a *frequency distribution*.

**FREQUENCY DISTRIBUTIONS** A summary picture of the various scores can be quickly drawn from a **frequency distribution,** which shows how often each score occurs in the sample data. The first step in preparing a frequency distribution is to *rank order* the scores in each group from highest to lowest. The rank ordering for the sex-role scores is shown in Table A.2. The second step is to group these rank-ordered scores into a smaller number of categories called *intervals*. In the sudden-murderers study, 11 intervals were used, with each interval covering 10 possible scores. This gives us a frequency distribution table, listing the intervals from highest to lowest and noting the *frequencies*—the number of scores within each interval (see Table A.3). This frequency distribution shows us that the sex-role scores for both groups fall mainly between −20 and +9. You will notice, however, that different patterns appear in the data from the two groups. Of the sudden murderers, 70% (7 of the 10) chose adjectives that were more feminine than masculine (scores in the plus range). In comparison, only 22% of the habitual criminals (2 of 9) said that the feminine adjectives described them more accurately than did the masculine ones.

## TABLE A.3 Frequency Distribution of Sex-Role Difference Scores

| CATEGORY | SUDDEN MURDERERS FREQUENCY | HABITUAL–CRIMINAL MURDERERS FREQUENCY |
|---|---|---|
| +60 to +69 | 1 | 0 |
| +50 to +59 | 0 | 0 |
| +40 to +49 | 1 | 0 |
| +30 to +39 | 0 | 0 |
| +20 to +29 | 1 | 0 |
| +10 to +19 | 1 | 0 |
| 0 to +9 | 3 | 2 |
| −1 to −10 | 1 | 3 |
| −11 to −20 | 1 | 3 |
| −21 to −30 | 1 | 0 |
| −31 to −40 | 0 | 1 |

**Frequency distribution:** A summary chart, showing how frequently each of the various scores in a set of data occurs.

**TABLE A.4**   Frequency Distribution of Shyness in the Sudden-Murderers Study

| Shy: | SUDDEN MURDERERS | HABITUAL-CRIMINAL MURDERERS |
|------|:---:|:---:|
| Yes | 8 | 1 |
| No | 2 | 8 |

**TABLE A.5**   Frequency Distribution of Ego-Overcontrol Scores

| CATEGORY | SUDDEN MURDERERS FREQUENCY | HABITUAL-CRIMINAL MURDERERS FREQUENCY |
|:---:|:---:|:---:|
| 1 to  5 | 0 | 0 |
| 6 to 10 | 1 | 3 |
| 11 to 15 | 5 | 5 |
| 16 to 20 | 4 | 1 |

Constructing a frequency distribution for the shyness data is simpler than for the sex-role differences because there are only two "intervals": *yes* (shy) and *no* (not shy). As you can see in Table A.4, the sudden murderers and the habitual-criminal murderers do seem to differ on the shyness variable. In this sample, most sudden murderers described themselves as shy, while most habitual-criminal murderers did not. Of the 19 scores, we can see 9 *yes* and 10 *no* responses; almost all the *yes* responses are in Group 1 (the sudden murderers), and almost all the *no* responses are in Group 2 (the habitual-criminal murderers). (By comparison, 40% of people in the United States describe themselves as shy.) In addition, the researchers noticed a difference in the circumstances that precipitated the murders committed by the shy men. In virtually every case, the precipitating incidents for the sudden murderers were minor, compared with the incidents that triggered the violence of the habitual-criminal murderers.

Inspection of the ego-overcontrol scores of the two groups does not show a clear trend (see Table A.5). While sudden murderers scored higher in overcontrolling their impulses than did habitual-criminal murderers, their scores were not much higher (Lee et al., 1977). Clearly, we need more powerful techniques in order to tell whether the groups differ significantly in their overcontrol tendencies.

Although summaries of data such as this are compelling, we must look at a number of other analyses before we can state our conclusions with any certainty. The researchers' next step was to plot the distributions graphically.

**HISTOGRAMS AND BAR GRAPHS**   Distributions are often easier to understand when they are displayed in graphs. The simplest type of graph is a *bar graph*. We can use a bar graph to illustrate how many more sudden murderers than habitual-criminal murderers described themselves as shy (see Figure A.1). The bar graph reveals a striking difference in the number of shy inmates in each group—at least in the sample used for the study.

For a more complex array of data, such as the sex-role scores, we can use a *histogram*, as in Figure A.2. This sort of graph is similar to a bar graph except that the histogram's bars represent data *intervals*. That is, a histogram represents *number* categories (e.g., "−40 to −31" or "0 to +9") instead of the *name* categories used in the bar graph (e.g., "sudden murderers" or "habitual-criminal murderers"). More precisely, a histogram gives a visual picture of the number of scores falling in each interval of a distribution. It is easy to see from the sex-role scores

**FIGURE A.1:**   Shyness for Two Groups of Murderers (a Bar Graph)

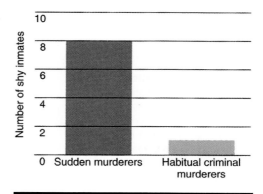

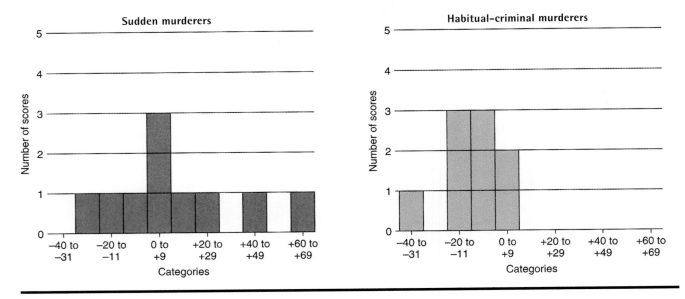

shown in the histograms in Figure A.2 that the distribution of scores differs in the two groups of murderers. Note how the sudden murderers are represented in almost every interval from –30 to +69, with a spike in the 0 to +9 interval. Habitual murderers, on the other hand, all cluster in the intervals below +9.

## Statistical Analysis

To complement this visual picture of the data, researchers customarily paint a mathematical picture, using two kinds of statistics. They begin with **descriptive statistics,** which involve a numerical *description* of their subjects' characteristics and responses. (If you have ever computed your grade-point average, you have used a descriptive statistic to summarize your grades.) Then, they use **inferential statistics** to assess whether the results of a study are reliable or whether they might be simply the result of chance. (Inferential statistics are often used to determine whether the scores from two or more groups are essentially the same or different.) Let's look first at descriptive statistics.

**DESCRIPTIVE STATISTICS**   Researchers form a summary picture of basic patterns in the data with *descriptive statistics*. Descriptive statistics may indicate the frequency of certain behaviors. Alternatively, descriptive statistics may summarize sets of scores collected from a group of subjects. These could be, for example, scores on a questionnaire or a personality test. Descriptive statistics may also be used to describe relationships among variables, such as grades and time spent studying. In general, you might think of descriptive statistics as a way to simplify the data. By using descriptive statistics, researchers don' t have to keep all the scores obtained by each of the subjects in mind.

Three kinds of descriptive statistics can help us understand and compare the data for the two groups in the sudden-murderers study. One kind indicates the scores that are most *typical* for each group. A second shows the extent to which the individual scores are spread out or clustered closely together. The third shows how closely related are the different measures used in the study—whether they are measuring the same traits or different traits. These three types of descriptive statistics are known as *measures of central tendency, measures of variability,* and *correlation*.

**Descriptive statistics:** Statistical procedures used to describe characteristics and responses of groups of subjects.

**Inferential statistics:** Statistical techniques (based on probability theory) used to assess whether the results of a study are reliable or whether they might be simply the result of chance. Inferential statistics are often used to determine whether two or more groups are essentially the same or different.

MEASURES OF CENTRAL TENDENCY   In order to compare the scores of sudden murderers with those of habitual-criminal murderers, it would be helpful to summarize each group with the one score on each scale that is most typical of the group as a whole. It would be much easier to compare the typical scores of the two groups than to compare their entire distributions. Such a single, *representative* score that can be used to describe a group of subjects is called a **measure of central tendency.** It is located near the center of the distribution, and other scores tend to cluster around it. Psychologists often use three different statistical measures of central tendency: the *mode*, the *median*, and the *mean*.

The simplest of these measures of central tendency is the **mode:** the score that occurs more often than any other. On the shyness variable, the modal response of the sudden murderers was *yes*: Eight out of ten said yes, they were shy. Among habitual-criminal murderers, the modal response was *no* (not shy). The sex-role scores for the sudden murderers had a mode of +5. Can you figure out what the modes of their ego-overcontrol scores are?

While the mode is the easiest index of central tendency to determine, it is often the least useful. You will see one reason for this relative lack of usefulness if you notice that only one overcontrol score lies above the mode of 17, while six lie below it. Although 17 is the score obtained most often, it may not fit your idea of "typical" or "central."

The **median** is more clearly a central score. It is the score that separates the upper half of the scores in a distribution from the lower half. The number of scores larger than the median is the same as the number that are smaller. If you look at the rank-ordering of the sex-role difference scores of the sudden murderers (Table A.2), you will see that the median score is +5 (in this case, the same as the mode, although this is not always true). Four scores are higher than +5, and four scores are lower. The median is quite simply the score in the middle of the distribution.

A big advantage in using the median is that it is not affected by extreme scores. For example, even if the highest sex-role score had been 129 instead of 61, the median value would still have been 5. That score would still separate the upper half of the data from the lower half.

The **mean** is what most people think of when they hear the word *average*. It is also the statistic most often used to describe sets of data. To calculate the mean, you add up all the scores in a distribution and divide by the total number of scores. The operation is summarized by the following formula:

$$M = \Sigma X \div N$$

In this formula, M is the mean, X is each individual score, $\Sigma$ (the Greek letter *sigma*) is the summation of what immediately follows it, and $N$ is the total number of scores. Because the summation of all the scores ($\Sigma X$) is 115 and the total number of scores ($N$) is 10, the mean (M) of the sex-role scores of the sudden murderers would be calculated as follows:

$$M = 115 \div 10 = +11.5$$

The mean sex-role score for the habitual murderers is

$$M = (-92) \div 9 = -10.22$$

You can see from these scores that there is a big difference between the two groups.

Unlike the median, the mean *is* affected by the specific values of all scores in the distribution. An extreme score *does* change the value of the mean. For example, if the sex-role score of inmate 4 happened to be 101 instead of 61, the mean for the whole group of sudden murderers would increase from 11.5 to 15.5.

Now try to calculate the mean overcontrol scores for the two groups yourself. You should find that the mean for the sudden murderers is 14.4. The mean for the habitual murderers is 11.56.

**Measure of central tendency:** A single, representative score that can be used as an index of the most typical score obtained by a group of subjects in a distribution. Measures of central tendency include the *mean*, *median*, and *mode*.

**Mode:** A measure of central tendency for a distribution, represented by the score that occurs more often than any other.

**Median:** A measure of central tendency for a distribution, represented by the score that separates the upper half of the scores in a distribution from the lower half.

**Mean:** The measure of central tendency most often used to describe a set of data—calculated by adding all the scores and dividing by the number of scores.

**Measures of variability:** Statistics that describe the distribution of scores around some measure of central tendency. Measures of variability include the *range* and the *standard deviation*.

**Range:** The simplest measure of variability, represented by the difference between the highest and the lowest values in a frequency distribution.

**Standard deviation:** A measure of variability that indicates the *average* difference between the scores and their mean.

**Correlation coefficient:** A measure of the relationship between two variables.

*MEASURES OF VARIABILITY* In addition to knowing which score is most representative of the distribution as a whole, it is useful to know how representative that measure of central tendency really is. Are most of the other scores fairly close to it or widely spread out? **Measures of variability** are statistics that describe the distribution of scores around some measure of central tendency.

Can you see why measures of variability are important? Another example may help. Suppose you are a second-grade teacher, and it is the beginning of the school year. Knowing that the average child in your class can now read a first-grade-level book will help you to plan your lessons. You could plan better, however, if you knew how *similar* or how *divergent* the reading abilities of the 30 children are. Do they all read at about the same level (low variability)? If so, then you can plan a fairly standard second-grade lesson. What if the group has high variability, with several that can read fourth-grade material and others that can barely read at all? Now the mean reading level is not so representative of the entire class, and you will have to plan a variety of lessons to meet the children's varied needs.

The simplest measure of variability is the **range,** the difference between the highest and the lowest values in a frequency distribution. Returning to the study of murderers, let us look at the range of scores in Table A.1. For the sudden murderers' sex-role scores, the range is 90: from +61 to −29. The range of their overcontrol scores is 10: from 19 to 9. To compute the range, you need to know only two of the scores: the highest and the lowest.

The range is simple to determine, but psychologists often prefer measures of variability that are more sensitive and that take into account all the scores in a distribution, not just the extremes. One widely used measure is the **standard deviation** (SD), a measure of variability that indicates an *average* difference between each score and the mean. To figure out the standard deviation of a distribution, you need to know the mean of the distribution, along with the individual scores. Although the arithmetic involved in calculating the standard deviation is easy, the formula is a bit more complicated than the one used to calculate the mean and, therefore, will not be presented here. (Many calculators have a button for computing the standard deviation of a set of scores.) The general procedure, however, involves subtracting the value of each individual score from the mean and then determining an average of those mean deviations.

The standard deviation tells us how variable a set of scores is. The larger the standard deviation, the more spread out the scores are. The standard deviation of the sex-role scores for the sudden murderers is 24.6 points, but the standard deviation for the habitual criminals is only 10.7. This shows that there was less variability in the habitual-criminals group. Their scores clustered more closely about their mean than did those of the sudden murderers. When the standard deviation is small, the mean is a good representative index of the entire distribution. When the standard deviation is large, the mean is less typical of the whole group.

*CORRELATION* Another useful tool in interpreting psychological data is the **correlation coefficient,** a measure of the relationship between two variables (such as height and weight). A correlation coefficient tells us the extent to which scores on one measure are associated with scores on the other. If people with high scores on one variable tend to have high scores on the other variable, the correlation coefficient will be positive (greater than 0). If, however, people with high scores on one variable tend to have *low* scores on the other variable, then the correlation coefficient will be negative (less than 0). If there is *no* consistent relationship between the scores, the correlation will be close to 0.

Correlation coefficients range from +1.00 (a perfect positive correlation) through 0 to −1.00 (a perfect negative correlation). The further a correlation coefficient lies from 0 in *either* direction, the more closely related the two variables are, positively or negatively. Higher coefficients permit better predictions of one variable, given knowledge of the other.

**Chapter 1:**
**Mind, Behavior, and Science**

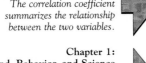

*The correlation coefficient summarizes the relationship between the two variables.*

**Chapter 1:**
**Mind, Behavior, and Science**

*Correlational research can show a relationship, but it cannot show which variable is the cause and which is the effect.*

In the sudden-murderers study, the correlation coefficient (symbolized as $r$) between the sex-role scores and the overcontrol scores turns out to be +0.35. The sex-role scores and the overcontrol scores are, thus, *positively correlated*: In general, subjects describing themselves in more feminine terms also tend to be higher in overcontrol. However, the correlation is modest compared with the highest possible value of +1.00. So we know that there are many exceptions to this relationship. (If we had also measured the self-esteem of these inmates and found a correlation of, say, −0.68 between overcontrol scores and self-esteem, it would mean that there was a *negative correlation*. If this were the case, we could say that the subjects who had high overcontrol scores tended to be lower in self-esteem. It would be a stronger relationship than the relationship between the sex-role scores and the overcontrol scores, because −0.68 is farther from 0, the point of no relationship, than is +0.35.)

**INFERENTIAL STATISTICS**   We have used several kinds of descriptive statistics to characterize the data from the sudden-murderers study, and now we have an idea of the pattern of results. We have compared the average responses and the variability in the two groups, and it appears that there are some differences between them. However, some basic questions remain unanswered. How do we know if the differences are large enough to be reliable or meaningful? To put it another way: If we repeated this study, with other samples of sudden murderers and habitual-criminal murderers, would we be likely to find the same patterns, or could these results have been merely the work of chance? Or, if we could somehow measure the entire population of sudden murderers and habitual-criminal murderers, would the means and standard deviations be essentially the same as those we found for these small samples?

*Inferential statistics* are used to answer these kinds of questions. They tell us what *inferences* we can make from our samples and which conclusions we can legitimately draw from our data. Inferential statistics use probability theory to determine the likelihood that a set of sample data occurred simply by chance variation.

*THE NORMAL CURVE*   In order to understand how inferential statistics work, we must look first at the properties of a special distribution called the *normal distribution*. A normal distribution occurs when data on a variable (height, IQ, or overcontrol, for example) collected from a large number of subjects fit a bell-shaped curve similar to that shown for IQ scores in Figure A.3 on page A-10. (This is essentially the same bell curve used by teachers who grade "on the curve.") Notice that the curve is symmetrical (the left half is a mirror image of the right) and bell shaped—high near the middle, where most scores are, and lower the farther you get from the mean. This type of curve is also called a **normal curve** because it describes a *normal distribution*. (By contrast, a *skewed* distribution is one in which scores cluster toward one end instead of around the middle.)

If the measurements you have made fit a normal curve, then the median, mode, and mean values are the same. Moreover, a specific percentage of the scores can be predicted to fall under different sections of the curve. Figure A.3 shows a normal curve generated by IQ scores on the Stanford-Binet Intelligence Test. These scores have a mean of 100 and a standard deviation of 16—telling us that most scores on this test cluster within 16 points on either side of 100. (Note: Many common IQ tests have a standard deviation that is slightly less, 15 points.) Specifically, if you mark off standard deviation units as distances from the mean along the baseline of the graph in Figure A.3, you find that about 68% of all the scores lie between the mean of 100 and 1 standard deviation above and below—between IQs of 84 and 116 on the Stanford-Binet. Roughly another 27% of the scores are found between the first and second standard deviations below the mean (IQ scores between 68 and 84) and above the mean (IQ scores between 116 and 132). Less than 5% of the scores fall in the third standard deviation above and below the mean, and *very* few scores fall beyond—only about 0.25%.

Using the statistics associated with the normal curve, researchers can judge whether two groups of scores have been drawn from groups that are truly different.

**Normal curve:** A bell-shaped curve that describes distributions of IQ scores in the general population, as well as other sets of data in which most subjects score near the center of the distribution and only a few have extreme scores.

**Chapter 11:
Intelligence and the Psychology of Differences**

*IQ stands for "intelligence quotient" and is an index of general intelligence.*

**Chapter 11:
Intelligence and the Psychology of Differences**

*The Stanford-Binet is a widely used IQ test developed at Stanford University and based on Binet's original intelligence test.*

**Chapter 11:
Intelligence and the Psychology of Differences**

*IQ scores falling more than two standard deviations from the mean are associated with "mental retardation" and "giftedness."*

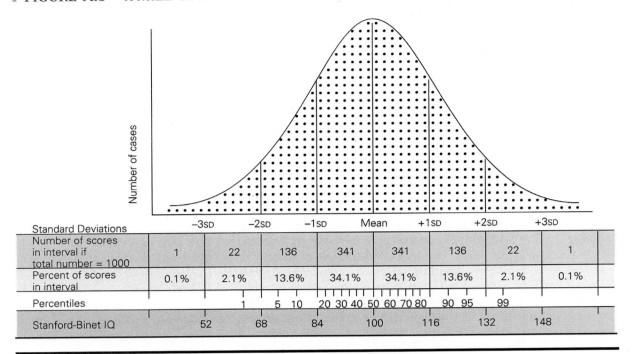

| Standard Deviations | | −3SD | −2SD | −1SD | Mean | +1SD | +2SD | +3SD | |
|---|---|---|---|---|---|---|---|---|---|
| Number of scores in interval if total number = 1000 | | 1 | 22 | 136 | 341 | 341 | 136 | 22 | 1 |
| Percent of scores in interval | | 0.1% | 2.1% | 13.6% | 34.1% | 34.1% | 13.6% | 2.1% | 0.1% |
| Percentiles | | | 1 | 5  10 | 20 30 40 50 60 70 80 | 90  95 | 99 | | |
| Stanford-Binet IQ | | 52 | 68 | 84 | 100 | 116 | 132 | 148 | |

Number of cases

That is, if each set of scores is a sample of a larger group described by a normal curve, and if the samples are different enough, the researchers can feel confidence in saying that the scores reflect a real difference between the larger groups.

For example, if you suspect that time spent studying is associated with the grades students receive, you could use means and standard deviations to compare the amount of study time in a sample of students with high grades and another sample of students with lower grades. To be sure that any differences between the two groups are real, however, you must look at the distribution of scores in both groups (do the sample scores approximate a normal distribution?) and you must factor in the size of the sample you used (is the sample large enough?). As you might expect, with a small sample, a relatively large difference between the two sample groups is required before you can conclude that the samples represent truly different populations. You will learn how to perform these statistical tests in a course on research design and statistics.

You must also, of course, make sure that your sample was selected in an unbiased manner. The safest way is to select subjects *at random*, by a method such as drawing names from a hat. Sometimes obtaining a **random sample** is not practicable (imagine trying to get a random sample of all college students). Then, a *representative sample* is often used. A **representative sample** is obtained in such a way that it reflects the important variables in the larger population in which you are interested—variables such as age, income level, ethnicity, and geographic distribution. Remarkably, a carefully selected representative sample of only a few hundred persons is often sufficient for public-opinion pollsters to obtain a highly accurate reflection of the political opinions of the entire population of a country. (A weakness in the sudden-murderers study is that the sample was not random. Nor do we know how representative it is of all sudden murderers and habitual-criminal murderers.)

*STATISTICAL SIGNIFICANCE*   As noted earlier, a researcher who finds a difference between the mean scores for two samples must ask if it represents a *real* difference between the two groups from which the samples were drawn, or if it occurred

**Random sample:** A sample group of subjects selected by chance (without biased selection techniques).

**Representative sample:** A sample obtained in such a way that it reflects the distribution of important variables in the larger population in which the researchers are interested—variables such as age, income level, ethnicity, and geographic distribution.

simply because of chance. A simple example will help illustrate the point. Suppose your psychology professor wants to see if the gender of a person proctoring a test makes a difference in the test scores obtained from male and female students. For this purpose, the professor randomly assigns half the students to a male proctor and half to a female proctor. The professor then compares the mean score of each group. If the proctor's gender makes *no* difference at all, then you would expect that the two mean scores would be fairly similar, and any slight difference the professor might find in the samples would be due to chance.

But, what if the difference between the scores for the two groups is large? As you have learned, less than a third of the scores in a normal distribution should be greater than one standard deviation above or below the mean (see Figure A.3). So, if there is no real difference between the male-proctor group and the female-proctor group (that is, if they come from the same larger group), the chances of getting a sample with a male-proctor mean score more than three standard deviations above or below the female-proctor mean would be very small. Thus, a researcher who *does* get a difference that great would feel fairly confident that the difference is a real one and is somehow related to the gender of the test proctor. The next question would be *how* that variable influences test scores.

If male and female students were randomly assigned to each type of proctor, it would be possible to analyze whether an overall difference found between the proctors was consistent across both student groups or was limited to only one sex. Imagine that the data show that male proctors grade female students higher than do female proctors, but both grade male students the same. Our professor could use a statistical inference procedure to estimate the probability that an observed difference could have occurred by chance. This computation is based on the sample size, the size of the difference, and the spread of the scores. (The details of this computation are beyond the scope of this book, but you will learn how to do the computation in an introductory statistics class.)

By common agreement, psychologists accept a difference between the groups as "real" when the probability that it might be due to chance is less than 5 in 100 (indicated by the notation $p < .05$). A **significant difference** is one that meets this criterion. However, in some cases, even stricter probability levels are used, such as $p < .01$ (less than 1 in 100) and $p < .001$ (less than 1 in 1000).

If we were to carry out the appropriate calculations on the murderers' data, we would find that the differences between the groups on their sex-role scores were *statistically significant*. That is, there is only a very slim possibility—less than 5 in 100 ($p < .05$) of our data being merely due to a chance. Therefore, we can feel more confident that there is a real difference between the two groups. The sudden murderers did rate themselves as more "feminine" than did the habitual-criminal murderers. Likewise, the difference in shyness, analyzed using another statistical test for frequency of scores, is highly significant, as we had suspected from inspection of the frequency distributions and graphs.

On the other hand, the difference between the two groups of murderers' over-control scores turns out *not* to be statistically significant ($p < .10$), so we must be more cautious in talking about this difference. There is a *trend* in the predicted direction—the difference in overcontrol scores is one that would occur by chance only 10 times in 100—but the difference is not within the accepted standard 5-in-100 range. This may mean that the notion of sudden murderers holding in their impulses is mistaken.

In this way, you can see that inferential statistics can help us answer some of the basic questions with which we began, and we are closer to understanding the psychology of people who suddenly change from mild-mannered, shy individuals into mass murderers. Any conclusion, however, is only a statement of the *probable* relationship between the events that were investigated; it is never one of absolute certainty. Truth in science is provisional, always open to revision by later data from better studies, developed from better hypotheses.

**Significant difference:** Psychologists accept a difference between the groups as "real," or *significant*, when the probability that it might be due to an atypical sample drawn by chance is less than 5 in 100 (indicated by the notation $p < .05$).

**Chapter 1:**
**Mind, Behavior, and Science**
*Only science bases its conclusions on empirical observations, which are subject to revision as new data become available.*

Now that we have considered the nature of statistics, how they are used, and what they mean, we should talk about how they can be misused. Many people accept unsupported "facts" when they are bolstered by the air of authority lent by a statistic. Others choose to believe or disbelieve what the statistics say without having any idea of how to question the numbers that are presented in support of a product, politician, or proposal.

Statistics can give a misleading impression in many ways. For example, characteristics of the group of subjects used in the research can make a large difference that can easily remain undetected when the results are reported. So, a survey of views on abortion rights will yield very different results if conducted in a small, conservative community in the South rather than a university in New York City. Likewise, a pro-life group surveying the opinions of its membership will very likely arrive at conclusions that differ from those obtained by the same survey conducted in a pro-choice group.

Even if the subjects are randomly selected, the statistics can produce misleading results if the necessary assumptions behind the statistics are violated. For example, suppose 20 people take an IQ test; 19 of them receive scores between 90 and 110, and 1 receives a score of 220. The mean of the group will be strongly elevated by that one outlying high score. With a data set like this one, the median or the mode would more accurately report the group's generally average intelligence, while the mean would make it look as if the average member of this group had a high IQ. This sort of bias is especially powerful in a small sample. If, on the other hand, the number of people in this group was 2000 instead of 20, the one extreme score would make virtually no difference, and the mean would be a legitimate summary of the group's intelligence.

One good way to avoid falling for this sort of deception is to check the size of the sample: Large samples are less likely to be misleading than small ones. Another method of checking is to look at the median or the mode as well as the mean—the results can be interpreted with more confidence if they are similar than if they are different.

Another way to guard against being misled by the misuse of statistics is to examine closely the methodology and results of the research reported. Check to see if the experimenters report their sample size and significance levels. Try to find out if the methods they used accurately and consistently measure whatever they claim to be investigating.

Statistics are the backbone of psychological research. They are used to understand observations and to determine whether findings are, in fact, correct and significant. Through the methods we have described, psychologists can prepare frequency distributions of their data and find the central tendencies and variability of the scores. They can use the correlation coefficient to determine the strength and direction of the association between sets of scores. Finally, psychological investigators can find out how representative the observations are and whether they are significantly different from what is observed among the general population. Statistics can also be used poorly or deceptively, misleading those who do not understand them. But when statistics are applied correctly and ethically, they allow researchers to expand the body of psychological knowledge.

# Glossary

**Absolute threshold:** The amount of stimulation necessary for the stimulus to be detected. In practice, this means being detected half the time over a number of trials.

**Access and retrieval:** Together these form the third basic function of memory, involving the location and recovery of information from memory.

**Accommodation:** A mental process that restructures existing schemes so that new information is better understood.

**Achievement test:** A test designed to measure current skills or how much an individual has learned.

**Acquisition:** The stage of classical conditioning in which a conditioned response is first elicited by the conditioned stimulus.

**Action potential:** The neural impulse—an electrical impulse that travels down the axon and carries the neural message.

**Activation-synthesis theory:** The theory that dreams begin with random electrical *activation* coming from the brain stem. Dreams, then, are the brain's attempt to make sense of—to *synthesize*—this random activity.

**Active listener:** A person who gives the speaker feedback in such forms as nodding, paraphrasing, maintaining an expression that shows interest, and asking questions for clarification.

**Acute stress:** A temporary pattern of arousal caused by a stressor with a clear onset and offset.

**Addiction:** A physical condition that produces withdrawal when the body lacks a certain drug.

**Adjustment disorders and other conditions that may be a focus of clinical attention:** A diverse group of relatively mild problems that do not fit under other headings. These categories include mild depression, physical complaints, marital problems, academic problems, job problems, parent–child problems, bereavement, malingering, and a number of other conditions.

**Adolescence:** In industrial societies, a developmental period beginning at puberty and ending (less clearly) at adulthood.

**Adoption studies:** An alternative to twin studies in which the adopted child's characteristics are compared to those of the biological family and of the adoptive family.

**Affect:** A term referring to emotion or mood.

**Affective disorders:** Abnormal disturbances in emotion or mood, including bipolar disorder and unipolar disorder.

**Afferent systems:** Sensory receptors and pathways that process information and carry it to the brain.

**Afterimages:** Sensations that linger after the stimulus is removed. Most visual afterimages are *negative afterimages*, which appear in reversed colors.

**Agoraphobia:** A fear of public places and open spaces, commonly accompanying panic disorder.

**Alarm reaction:** The first stage of the GAS, during which the body mobilizes its resources to cope with a stressor.

**Algorithms:** Problem-solving procedures or formulas that guarantee a correct outcome, if correctly applied.

**Ambiguity:** Capable of more than one interpretation. *Ambiguous figures* demonstrate important principles of perception.

**Ambivalence:** Having conflicting thoughts or feelings.

**Amnesia:** A loss of memory for personal information, such as one's identity or residence.

**Amplitude:** The physical strength of a wave. This is usually measured from peak (top) to trough (bottom) on a graph of the wave.

**Amygdala:** (a-MIG-da-la) A limbic system structure involved in memory and emotion, particularly aggression.

**Analysis of transference:** The Freudian technique of analyzing and interpreting the patient's relationship with the therapist, based on the assumption that this relationship mirrors unresolved conflicts in the patient's past.

**Anchoring bias:** A faulty heuristic caused by basing (anchoring) an estimate on a completely unrelated quantity.

**Anima:** The female archetype.

**Animistic thinking:** A preoperational mode of thought in which inanimate objects are imagined to have life and mental processes.

**Animus:** The male archetype.

**Anorexia nervosa:** An eating disorder involving persistent loss of appetite that endangers an individual's health and stemming from emotional or psychological reasons rather than from organic causes.

**Anterograde amnesia:** The inability to form memories for new information (as opposed to *retrograde amnesia*, which involves the inability to remember information previously stored in memory).

**Antianxiety drugs:** A category of drugs that includes the *barbiturates* and *benzodiazepines,* drugs that diminish feelings of anxiety.

**Antidepressant drugs:** Medicines that affect depression, usually by their effect on the serotonin and/or norepinephrine pathways in the brain.

**Antipsychotic drugs:** Medicines that diminish psychotic symptoms, usually by their effect on the dopamine pathways in the brain.

**Antisocial personality disorder:** Characterized by a long-standing pattern of irresponsible behavior indicating a lack of conscience and a diminished sense of responsibility to others.

**Anxiety disorders:** Mental problems characterized mainly by anxiety. Anxiety disorders include panic disorder, phobias, and obsessive–compulsive disorder.

**Applied psychologists:** Psychologists who use the knowledge developed by experimental psychologists to solve human problems.

**Applied research:** Research aimed at finding solutions to practical problems.

**Aptitude test:** A test designed to measure a person's potential for acquiring various skills—not necessarily present performance, but how well she or he will be able to perform in the future, with adequate training.

**Archetypes:** The ancient memory images in the collective unconscious. Archetypes appear and reappear in art, literature, and folk tales around the world.

**Artificial concepts:** Concepts defined by rules, such as word definitions and mathematical formulas.

**Asch effect:** A form of conformity in which a group majority influences individual judgments.

**Assimilation:** A mental process that modifies new information to fit it into existing schemes.

**Association cortex:** Cortical regions that combine information from various other parts of the brain.

**Attachment:** The enduring social-emotional relationship between a child and a parent or other regular caregiver.

**Attention-deficit/hyperactivity disorder (ADHD):** A common problem in children who have difficulty controlling their behavior and focusing their attention.

**Auditory cortex:** Portions of the temporal lobe involved in hearing.

**Auditory nerve:** The neural pathway connecting the ear and the brain.

**Autonomic nervous system:** The portion of the peripheral nervous system that sends messages to the internal organs and glands.

**Autonomy:** The ability to act independently.

**Availability heuristic:** A biased cognitive strategy that estimates probabilities based on information that can be recalled (made available) from personal experience.

**Aversion therapy:** As a classical conditioning procedure, aversive counterconditioning involves presenting individuals with an attractive stimulus paired with unpleasant (aversive) stimulation in order to condition a repulsive reaction.

**Aversive conditioning:** A type of classical conditioning in which the conditioned stimulus predicts the occurrence of an aversive or unpleasant unconditioned stimulus.

**Axon:** In a nerve cell, an extended fiber that conducts information from the cell body to the terminal buttons. Information travels along the axon in the form of an electric charge.

**Babbling stage:** The time during the first year of life when an infant produces a wide range of sounds but not functional words.

**Bait shyness:** An aversion to novel foods or to familiar foods in novel environments or conditions.

**Base rate:** A statistic that identifies the normal frequency, or probability, of a given event or process.

**Basic research:** Studies that focus on some process or phenomenon of interest to the researcher but with no practical application in mind.

**Basilar membrane:** A thin strip of tissue sensitive to vibrations in the cochlea. The basilar membrane contains hair cells connected to neurons, which accomplish the final step of converting sound waves to nerve impulses.

**Behavior genetics:** A new field bringing together geneticists and psychologists interested in the genetic basis of behavior and mental characteristics, such as intelligence, altruism, and psychological disorders.

**Behavior modification:** Another term for behavioral therapy.

**Behavioral learning:** Forms of learning, such as classical conditioning and operant conditioning, that can be described in terms of stimuli and responses.

**Behavioral measures:** Responses consisting of overt, observable, and recordable actions.

**Behavioral medicine:** The medical field specializing in the link between lifestyle and disease.

**Behavioral perspective:** The psychological view suggesting that abnormal behaviors can be acquired through behavioral learning, especially by operant conditioning and classical conditioning.

**Behavioral therapy:** Any form of psychotherapy based on the principles of behavioral learning, especially operant conditioning and classical conditioning.

**Behavioral view** or **behaviorism:** A psychological perspective that finds the source of our actions in environmental stimuli, rather than in inner mental processes.

**Big Five:** A group of apparently fundamental personality traits: Extraversion, Agreeableness, Conscientiousness, Emotional Stability, and Openness to New Experience.

**Binding problem:** A major unsolved mystery in cognitive psychology, concerning the physical processes used by the brain to combine many aspects of sensation into a single percept.

**Biofeedback:** A clinical procedure in which people are given information (feedback) on their biological responses (such as perspiration). Also, a therapy technique for learning relaxation and new visceral responses to stress, involving devices that sense small physical changes and provide immediate feedback to the individual.

**Biological view:** The psychological perspective that searches for the causes of behavior in the functioning of genes, the brain and nervous system, and the endocrine (hormone) system.

**Biomedical therapies:** Treatments that focus on altering the brain, especially with drugs, psychosurgery, or electroconvulsive therapy.

**Biopsychology:** The specialty in psychology that studies the interaction of biology, behavior, and the environment.

**Bipolar disorder:** A mental abnormality involving swings of mood from mania to depression.

**Blind spot:** The point where the optic nerve exits the eye and where there are no photoreceptors.

**Bottom-up processing:** Perceptual analysis that emphasizes characteristics of the stimulus, rather than internal concepts.

**Brain scans:** Recordings of the brain's electrical or biochemical activity at specific sites. Typically, the data are formed into visual images by computer. Common brain scanning devices include MRI, CT, and PET.

**Brain stem:** The most primitive of the brain's three major layers. It includes the medulla, pons, and the reticular activating system.

**Brain waves:** Patterns of electrical activity generated by the brain. The EEG records brain waves.

**Brightness:** A sensation caused by the intensity of light waves.

**Bulimia** (pronounced *boo-LEE-me-uh*): An eating disorder characterized by eating binges followed by "purges," induced by vomiting or laxatives; typically initiated as a weight-control measure.

**Burnout:** A syndrome of emotional exhaustion, depersonalization, and reduced personal accomplishment—often related to work.

**Cannabis:** A drug, derived from the hemp plant, whose effects include altered perception, sedation, pain relief, and mild euphoria. Cannabis is found in marijuana and hashish.

**Case study:** Research that involves only a single subject (or, at most, a few subjects).

**Cataplexy:** A sudden loss of muscle control that may occur just before a narcoleptic sleep attack. Cataplexy is a waking form of sleep paralysis.

**Catatonic type:** A form of schizophrenia involving stupor or extreme excitement.

**Cell body** or **soma:** The part of a cell (such as a neuron) containing the nucleus—which includes the chromosomes.

**Central fissure:** The prominent vertical groove in the cortex, separating the frontal from the parietal lobes in each hemisphere.

**Central nervous system:** The brain and the spinal cord.

**Centration:** A preoperational thought pattern involving the inability to take into account more than one factor at a time.

**Cerebellum:** The "little brain" attached to the brain stem. The cerebellum is responsible for coordinated movements.

**Cerebral cortex:** The thin grey-matter covering of the cerebrum, consisting of a ¼- inch layer dense with cell bodies of neurons. The cerebral cortex carries on the major portion of our "higher" mental processing, including thinking and perceiving.

**Cerebral dominance:** The tendency of each brain hemisphere to exert control over different functions, such as language or perception of spatial relationships.

**Cerebral hemispheres:** The two walnut-shaped halves of the cerebrum, connected by the corpus callosum.

**Cerebrum:** The topmost layer of the brain; the bulbous cap over the limbic system. The cerebrum, particularly the cerebral *cortex*, accounts for most of our thinking and processing of information from our environment.

**Chromosomes:** Tightly coiled threadlike structures along which the genes are organized, like beads on a necklace. Chromosomes consist primarily of DNA.

**Chronic stress:** A continuous state of stressful arousal persisting over time.

**Chronological age (CA):** The number of years since the individual's birth.

**Chunking:** Organizing pieces of information into a smaller number of meaningful units—a process which frees up space in working memory.

**Circadian rhythms:** Physiological patterns that repeat approximately every 24 hours—such as the sleep–wakefulness cycle.

**Classical conditioning:** A form of behavioral learning in which a previously neutral stimulus (CS) acquires the power to elicit the same innate reflex produced by another stimulus.

**Clinical psychologists:** Psychological practitioners who specialize in the treatment of mental disorders.

**Closure:** The Gestalt principle that identifies the tendency to fill in gaps in figures and to see incomplete figures as complete.

**Cochlea:** The primary organ of hearing; a coiled tube in the inner ear, where sound waves are transduced into nerve impulses.

**Cognition:** The mental processes involved in thinking, knowing, perceiving, learning, and remembering; also, the contents of these processes (e.g., thoughts, percepts, concepts).

**Cognitions:** Mental processes, such as thinking, memory, sensation, and perception.

**Cognitive:** A term referring to information processing in the brain. Cognitive functions include learning, memory, thinking, sensation, and perception.

**Cognitive–behavioral approach:** A psychological view that combines both the cognitive and the behavioral perspectives in attempting to understand behavior and mental processes.

**Cognitive–behavioral therapy:** A newer form of psychotherapy that combines the techniques of cognitive therapy with those of behavioral therapy.

**Cognitive development:** The process by which thinking changes over time.

**Cognitive dissonance:** A highly motivating state in which people have conflicting cognitions, especially when their voluntary *actions* conflict with their *attitudes*.

**Cognitive map:** A mental representation of physical space.

**Cognitive neuroscience:** A new, interdisciplinary field involving cognitive psychology, neuroscientists, computer scientists, and specialists from other fields who are interested in the connection between mental processes and the brain.

**Cognitive perspective:** The psychological view suggesting that abnormal behaviors are influenced by mental processes—by how people perceive or think about themselves and their relations with other people.

**Cognitive psychology:** The branch of psychology specializing in the scientific study of mental processes and mental structures.

**Cognitive science:** An interdisciplinary field that studies the variety of systems and processes that manipulate information.

**Cognitive therapy:** Emphasizes rational thinking (as opposed to subjective emotion, motivation, or repressed conflicts) as the key to treating mental disorder.

**Cognitive view:** The psychological perspective that emphasizes mental processing and interpretation of experience.

**Cohesiveness:** Solidarity, loyalty, and a sense of group membership.

**Cohort effects:** Selective influences that affect one group (cohort) more than another.

**Collective unconscious:** Jung's addition to the unconscious, involving a reservoir for instinctive "memories," including the archetypes, which exist in all people.

**Collectivism:** The view, common in Asia, Africa, Latin America, and the Middle East, that values group loyalty and pride over individual distinction.

**Color:** The psychological sensation derived from the wavelength of visible light. Color, itself, is not a property of the external world.

**Color blindness:** Typically a genetic disorder (although sometimes the result of trauma) that prevents an individual from discriminating certain colors. The most common form is red-green color blindness.

**Community mental health movement:** An effort to deinstitutionalize mental patients and to provide therapy from outpatient clinics. Proponents of community mental health envisioned that recovering patients could live with their families, in foster homes, or in group homes.

**Concept hierarchies:** Levels of concepts, from most general to most specific, in which a more general level includes more specific concepts—as the concept of "animal" includes "dog," "giraffe," and "butterfly."

**Concepts:** Mental representations of categories of items or ideas.

**Conceptual model:** In cognitive science, an explanatory metaphor that describes how information is detected, stored, and used by people and machines.

**Concordance rate:** The percentage of relatives who show the same trait.

**Concrete operational stage:** The third of Piaget's stages, when a child understands conservation, but still is incapable of abstract thought.

**Conditioned reinforcers:** Stimuli, such as tokens or money, that acquire their reinforcing power by a learned association with primary reinforcers.

**Conditioned response (CR):** In classical conditioning, a response elicited by a previously neutral stimulus that has become associated with the unconditioned stimulus.

**Conditioned stimulus (CS):** In classical conditioning, a previously neutral stimulus that comes to elicit the conditioned response.

**Cones:** Photoreceptors in the retina that are especially sensitive to colors but not to dim light.

**Conflict:** In social psychology, an interpersonal difficulty that occurs when people pursue opposing goals based on incompatible social realities.

**Conformity:** The tendency for people to adopt the behaviors, attitudes, and opinions of other members of a group.

**Confounding variables:** Factors that could be confused with the independent variable and thus distort the results of a study.

**Conscious motivation:** Having the desire to engage in an activity and being aware of the desire.

**Conservation:** The understanding that the physical properties of an object or substance do not change when appearances change but nothing is added or taken away.

**Contact comfort:** Stimulation and reassurance derived from the physical touch of a caregiver.

**Contingency management:** An operant conditioning approach to changing behavior by altering the consequences, especially rewards and punishments, of behavior.

**Continuity view:** The perspective that development is gradual and continuous—as opposed to the discontinuity (stage) view.

**Continuous reinforcement:** A type of reinforcement schedule by which all correct responses are reinforced.

**Control condition:** The stimulus conditions for the control group—conditions that are identical to the experimental condition in every respect, except for the special treatment given to the experimental group.

**Control group:** Those subjects who are used as a comparison for the experimental group. The control group is not given the special treatment of interest.

**Controlled test:** A part of the scientific method that involves gathering data under conditions that are designed to control potentially confounding variables.

**Convergent thinking:** A problem-solving process aimed at producing a single correct answer to a problem. Also, the form of intelligence, proposed by Guilford, that is used to find "correct" answers.

**Conversion disorder:** A type of somatoform disorder, marked by paralysis, weakness, or loss of sensation, but with no discernible physical cause.

**Coping strategies:** Ways of dealing with stressful situations.

**Corpus callosum:** The band of nerve cells that connects the two cerebral hemispheres.

**Correlation coefficient:** A statistic, *r*, that indicates the relationship between two variables. Correlation coefficients can range from −1.0 to 0 to +1.0.

**Correlational study:** A form of research in which the relationship between variables is studied, but without the experimental manipulation of an independent variable. Correlational studies cannot determine cause-and-effect relationships.

**Counseling psychologists:** Psychological practitioners who help people deal with a variety of problems, including relationships and vocational choice. Counseling psychologists are less likely than clinical psychologists to do long-term therapy with persons having severe mental disorders.

**Counterconditioning:** A set of classical conditioning techniques for substituting a new response for an unwanted response; used especially in treating phobias.

**Creativity:** A mental process that produces novel responses that contribute to the solutions of problems.

**Critical period:** A sensitive time in an organism's development, when it will acquire a particular behavior, such as language, if certain stimuli and experiences occur.

**Cross-sectional method:** A type of developmental research in which groups of subjects of different ages are observed and compared at the same time; usually an economical alternative to the longitudinal method.

**CT scanning** or **computerized tomography:** A computerized imaging technique that uses X rays passed through the brain at various angles and then combined into an image.

**Culture:** A term referring to a complex blend of language, beliefs, customs, values, and traditions developed by a group of people and shared with others in the same environment.

**Darwin, Charles:** The British naturalist who first described the evolutionary theory and provided overwhelming evidence for the process of natural selection.

**Data:** Information, especially information gathered by a researcher to be used in testing a hypothesis. (Singular: *datum*.)

**Daydreaming:** A mild form of consciousness alteration in which attention shifts to memories, expectations, desires, or fantasies and away from the immediate situation.

**Daytime sleepiness:** A sleep disorder, commonly caused by lifestyle or personal choice factors, which always comes from getting too little sleep.

**Declarative memory:** A division of LTM that stores explicit information; also known as *fact memory*. Declarative memory has two subdivisions: *episodic memory* and *semantic memory*.

**Deductive reasoning:** Drawing a conclusion intended to follow logically from a given set of assumptions (premises).

**Deinstitutionalization:** The policy of removing patients, whenever possible, from mental hospitals.

**Delusions:** Disorders of logical thinking. Delusions are the hallmark of paranoid disorders.

**Demographic:** Refers to population characteristics, such as age, gender, or income distribution.

**Demographics:** Population characteristics, such as the number of people at various income levels, from families of different sizes, and from various ethnic backgrounds.

**Dendrites:** Branched fibers that extend outward from the main cell body and carry information into the neuron.

**Denial:** Freud's ego defense mechanism that allows a person consciously to ignore a problem or to conclude that there is no problem at all.

**Dependent variable:** The measured outcome of a study; the responses of the subjects in a study.

**Depersonalization:** The denying or stripping away of a person's individual character; treating the person as a label or a stereotype.

**Depersonalization disorder:** An abnormality involving the sensation that mind and body have separated, as in an "out-of-body" experience.

**Depressants:** Drugs that slow down mental and physical activity by inhibiting transmission of nerve impulses in the central nervous system.

**Depression:** Pathological sadness or despair.

**Descriptive statistics:** Statistical procedures used to describe characteristics and responses of groups of subjects.

**Determinism:** The assumption that physical, behavioral, and mental events are determined by specific causal factors—as opposed to *free will*.

**Developmental psychology:** The psychological specialty that studies how organisms change over time as the result of biological and environmental influences.

**Developmental stages:** Periods of life initiated by significant transitions or changes in physical or psychological functioning.

**Diathesis–stress hypothesis:** In reference to schizophrenia, the proposal says that genetic factors place the individual at risk, but environmental stress factors transform this potential into an actual schizophrenic disorder.

**Difference threshold:** The smallest amount by which a stimulus can be changed and the difference be detected half the time.

**Differentiation:** The process by which cells in the embryo take on specialized functions.

**Diffusion of responsibility:** Dilution or weakening of each group member's obligation to act when responsibility is perceived to be shared with all group members.

**Discontinuity view:** The perspective that development proceeds in an uneven (discontinuous) fashion—as opposed to the continuity view.

**Discrimination:** A negative action taken against an individual as a result of his or her group membership.

**Disorganized type:** A form of schizophrenia featuring incoherent speech, hallucinations, delusions, and bizarre behavior.

**Displacement:** The ego defense mechanism by which we shift our reaction from the real source of distress to another individual or object.

**Display rules:** The permissible ways of displaying emotions in a particular society.

**Dissociative disorders:** A group of pathologies involving "fragmentation" of the personality, in which some parts of the personality have become detached, or dissociated from other parts. Forms of dissociative disorder include amnesia, fugue, depersonalization disorder, and dissociative identity disorder.

**Dissociative fugue:** Essentially the same as dissociative amnesia, but with the addition of "flight" from one's home, family, and job. "Fugue" means "flight."

**Dissociative identity disorder:** A condition in which an individual displays multiple identities, or personalities; formerly called "multiple personality disorder."

**Divergent thinking:** A problem-solving process aimed at producing many appropriate solutions to a single problem.

**Divergent thinking:** The form of intelligence, proposed by Guilford, that is used to generate creative responses.

**DNA:** A long, complex molecule that encodes genetic characteristics. The long name for DNA is *deoxyribonucleic acid.*

**Double-blind control:** An experimental procedure in which both researchers and subjects are uninformed about the nature of the independent variable being administered.

**Down syndrome:** A genetic disorder that produces one form of mental retardation.

**Drive:** Biologically instigated motivation.

**DSM-IV:** The latest revision of the *Diagnostic and Statistical Manual of Mental Disorders,* published by the American Psychiatric Association; the most widely accepted classification system in the United States.

**Duality of consciousness:** The condition in which a split-brain patient has a separate consciousness in each hemisphere. The intact brain does not exhibit this duality of consciousness.

**Eclectic:** Either switching theories to explain different situations or building one's own theory of personality from pieces borrowed from many perspectives.

**EEG** or **electroencephalograph:** A device for recording brain waves, typically by electrodes placed on the scalp. The record produced is known as an *electroencephalogram* (also called an *EEG*).

**Efferent systems:** Motor systems that process and carry information from the brain to muscles and glands.

**Ego:** In Freud's psychoanalytic theory, the conscious, rational part of the mind, charged with keeping peace between the superego and the id.

**Ego defense mechanisms:** According to Freud, these are unconscious strategies that we use to defend ourselves against threat and trauma, reduce internal conflict, and diminish anxiety.

**Ego-integrity:** In Erikson's theory, the ability to look back on life without regrets and to enjoy a sense of wholeness.

**Egocentrism:** In Piaget's theory, the self-centered inability to realize that there are other viewpoints beside one's own.

**Elaboration:** A form of encoding that adds meaning to information in working memory so that it can be more easily stored in long-term memory.

**Elaborative rehearsal:** A working-memory process in which information is actively reviewed and related to information already in long-term memory.

**Electroconvulsive therapy (ECT):** A treatment used primarily for depression and involving the application of an electric current to the head, producing a generalized seizure. Sometimes called "shock treatment."

**Electromagnetic spectrum:** The entire range of electromagnetic energy, including radio waves, X rays, microwaves, and visible light.

**Elicit:** Evoke or draw out.

**Embryo:** In humans, the name for the developing organism during the first eight weeks after conception.

**Emotional intelligence:** In Goleman's theory, the ability to understand and control emotional responses.

**Empirical:** Relying on direct sensory observation rather than subjective judgment.

**Empirical investigation:** An approach to research that relies on sensory experience and observation as research data.

**Encephalization:** An evolutionary increase in brain size and in the proportion of specialized brain tissue.

**Encoding:** One of the three basic functions of memory, involving the modification of information to fit the preferred format for the memory system.

**Endocrine system:** The hormone system—the body's chemical messenger system, including the following endocrine glands: pituitary, adrenals, gonads, thyroid, parathyroid, pancreas, ovaries, and testes.

**Engineering psychologists:** Applied psychologists who specialize in making objects and environments easier, more efficient, or more comfortable for people to use.

**Epilepsy:** A brain disorder that is often marked by seizures and loss of consciousness. Epilepsy is caused by out-of-control electrical activity in the brain.

**Episodic memory:** A subdivision of declarative memory that stores memory for personal events, or "episodes."

**Eros:** The unconscious force that drives people toward acts that are sexual, life-giving, and creative.

**Eugenics:** A philosophy and a political movement that encouraged biologically superior people to interbreed and sought to discourage biologically inferior people from having offspring.

**Eustress:** An optimum level of stress; "good" stress.

**Event-related potentials:** Brain waves shown on the EEG in response to stimulation.

**Evolution:** The gradual process of biological change that occurs in a species as it adapts to its environment.

**Evolutionary psychology:** A new emphasis in biological psychology that views behavior in terms of genetic adaptations for survival and reproduction.

**Expectancy-value theory:** A theory in social psychology that states how people decide whether or not to pursue a relationship by weighing the potential *value* of the relationship against their *expectation* of success in establishing the relationship.

**Experience-sampling method:** Another introspective technique that has subjects record what they are feeling at selected times—often signaled by the beeping of a pager.

**Experiential intelligence:** According to Sternberg, the form of intelligence that helps people see new relationships among concepts; involves insight and creativity.

**Experiment:** A kind of research in which the researcher controls all the conditions and directly manipulates the conditions, including the independent variable.

**Experimental condition:** The stimulus conditions involved in exposing those in the *experimental group* to the special treatment being investigated.

**Experimental group:** Those subjects in an experiment who are exposed to the treatment of interest.

**Experimental psychologists:** Psychologists who do research on basic psychological processes—as contrasted with *applied* psychologists.

**Experts:** Individuals who possess well-organized funds of knowledge, including the effective problem-solving strategies, in a field.

**Explicit memory:** Memory that has been processed with attention and can be consciously recalled.

**Exposure therapy:** A form of desensitization therapy in which the patient directly confronts the anxiety-provoking stimulus (as opposed to imagining the stimulus).

**Extinction:** In learning, the weakening of a conditioned association in the absence of an unconditioned stimulus or a reinforcer.

**Extraversion:** The Jungian personality dimension involving turning one's attention outward, toward others.

**Extrinsic motivation:** The desire to engage in an activity to achieve an external consequence, such as a reward.

**Feature detectors:** Cells in the cortex that specialize in extracting certain features of a stimulus.

**Fetus:** In humans, the term for the developing organism between the embryonic stage and birth.

**Fight-or-flight response:** A sequence of internal processes that prepares the organism for struggle or escape and is triggered when a situation is interpreted as threatening.

**Figure:** The part of a pattern that commands attention. The figure stands out against the ground.

**Fixation:** Occurs when psychosexual development is arrested at an immature stage.

**Fixed-action patterns:** Genetically based behaviors, seen across a species, that can be set off by a specific stimulus. The concept of fixed-action patterns has replaced the older notion of instinct.

**Flow:** In Csikszentmihalyi's theory, an intense focus on an activity, accompanied by increased creativity and near-ecstatic feelings. Flow involves intrinsic motivation.

**Forgetting curve:** A graph plotting the amount of retention and forgetting over time for a certain batch of material, such as a list of nonsense syllables. The typical forgetting curve is steep at first, becoming flatter as time goes on.

**Formal operational stage:** The last of Piaget's stages, during which abstract thought appears.

**Fovea:** The area of sharpest vision in the retina.

**Frames of mind:** A term sometimes used to refer to Gardner's seven forms of intelligence.

**Free will:** The power of a person to direct his or her own behavior. The concept of free will is the antithesis of *determinism*.

**Frequency:** The number of cycles completed by a wave in a given amount of time, usually a second.

**Frequency distribution:** A summary chart, showing how frequently each of the various scores in a set of data occurs.

**Freudian slip:** "Accidental" speech (a slip of the tongue) or behavior that reveals an unconscious desire.

**Frontal lobes:** Regions at the front of the brain that are especially involved in movement and in thinking.

**Fully functioning person:** Carl Rogers's term for a self-actualizing individual, who has a self-concept that is both positive and congruent with reality.

**Functional fixedness:** The inability to perceive a new use for an object associated with a different purpose; a form of mental set.

**Functionalism:** A historical school of psychology that believed mental processes could best be understood in terms of their adaptive purpose and function.

**Fundamental attribution error:** The assumption that another person's behavior, especially clumsy, inappropriate, or otherwise undesirable behavior, is the result of a flaw in the personality, rather than in the situation; the tendency to emphasize internal causes and ignore external pressures. The FAE is more common in individualistic cultures than in collectivistic cultures.

**g factor:** A general ability, proposed by Spearman as the main factor underlying all intelligent mental activity.

**General adaptation syndrome (GAS):** A general pattern of physical responses that takes essentially the same form in response to any serious, chronic stressor.

**Generativity:** In Erikson's theory, a process of making a commitment beyond oneself to family, work, society, or future generations.

**Genes:** Segments of a chromosome that encode the directions for the inherited physical and mental characteristics of an organism. Genes are the functional units of a chromosome.

**Genetics:** The study of the inheritance of physical and psychological traits.

**Genotype:** An organism's genetic makeup.

**Gestalt psychology:** A view of perception that originated in Germany. (*Gestalt* is a German word meaning "whole" or "form" or "configura-

tion.") The Gestaltists believed that much of perception is shaped by innate factors built into the brain.

**Giftedness:** Often conceived as representing the upper 2% of the IQ range, commencing about 30 points above average—at about 130 IQ points.

**Glial cells:** These cells bind the neurons together. Glial cells also provide an insulating covering (the myelin sheath) of the axon for some neurons, which facilitates the electrical impulse.

**Grammar:** The rules of a language, specifying how to use words, morphemes, and syntax to produce understandable sentences.

**Ground:** The part of a pattern that does not command attention; the background.

**Group therapy:** Any form of psychotherapy done with more than one client/patient at a time. Group therapy is often done from a humanistic perspective.

**Guilford's structure-of-intellect:** J. P. Guilford's model of intelligence, consisting of some 150 separate factors, generated by five kinds of mental *operations*, five classes of *contents*, and six types of intellectual *products*.

**Gustation:** The sense of taste.

**Hallucinations:** False perceptions that occur without external stimulation. Hallucinations may be the sign of drug states or of severe mental disorder.

**Hallucinogens** or **psychedelics:** Drugs that alter perceptions the external environment and inner awareness.

**Hardiness:** A resilient quality based on the "three Cs" of health: challenge (welcoming change), commitment (involvement in purposeful activity), and control (internal guide for actions).

**Hassles:** Situations that cause minor irritation or frustration.

**Head Start:** A program providing educational enrichment for children of poor families, launched in the 1960s as a part of the "war on poverty."

**Health psychology:** The psychological specialty devoted to understanding how people stay healthy, why they become ill, and how they respond when ill.

**Hedonic capacity:** The ability to experience pleasure and joy.

**Heritability:** The amount of trait variation *within a group*, raised under the same conditions, that can be attributed to genetic differences. Heritability tells us nothing about between-group differences.

**Heuristics:** Cognitive strategies or "rules of thumb" used as shortcuts to solve complex mental tasks. Unlike algorithms, heuristics do not guarantee a correct solution.

**Hippocampus:** A component of the limbic system, involved in establishing long-term memories.

**Homeostasis:** The body's tendency to maintain a biologically balanced condition, especially with regard to nutrients, water, and temperature.

**Hormones:** The chemical messengers used by the endocrine system. Many hormones also serve as neurotransmitters.

**Human Genome Project:** An international scientific effort to determine the complete human genetic code in all 23 pairs of chromosomes.

**Humanistic therapies:** Treatment techniques based on the assumption that people have a tendency for positive growth and self-actualization, which may be blocked by an unhealthy environment that can include negative self-evaluation and criticism from others.

**Humanistic view:** A viewpoint that emphasizes human ability, growth, potential, and free will.

**Humors:** Four body fluids—blood, phlegm, black bile, and yellow bile—that, according to an ancient theory, control personality by their relative abundance.

**Hypnosis:** An induced alternate state of awareness, characterized by heightened suggestibility and (usually) deep relaxation.

**Hypnotic analgesia:** Diminished sensitivity to pain while under hypnosis.

**Hypnotizability:** The degree to which an individual is responsive to hypnotic suggestions.

**Hypochondriasis:** A somatoform disorder involving excessive concern about health and disease.

**Hypothalamus:** A limbic structure that serves as the brain's blood-testing laboratory, constantly monitoring the blood to determine the condition of the body.

**Hypothesis:** A statement predicting the outcome of a scientific study; a statement describing the relationship among variables in a study.

**Hypothetical construct:** A characteristic that is not directly observable but is, instead, inferred from behavior.

**Id:** The primitive, unconscious portion of the personality that houses the most basic drives and stores repressed memories.

**Identity crisis:** In Erikson's theory, the developmental crisis of adolescence.

**Illusion:** The demonstrably incorrect experience of a stimulus pattern, shared by others in the same perceptual environment.

**Immunosuppression:** Diminished effectiveness of the immune system caused by impairment (suppression) of the immune response.

**Implicit memory:** A memory of which you are unaware but which can affect your behavior.

**Implicit personality theory:** Assumptions about personality that are held by people (especially nonpsychologists) to simplify the task of understanding others.

**Imprinting:** A primitive form of learning in which some young animals follow and form an attachment to the first moving object they see and hear.

**In-group:** The group with which an individual identifies.

**Incentive motivation:** Motivation aroused by external stimuli.

**Incentives:** External stimuli that activate motives.

**Incongruence:** Occurs when a negative emotional experience affects one's ability to perceive accurately.

**Independent variable:** A stimulus condition that is so named because the experimenter changes it *independently* of all the other carefully controlled experimental conditions.

**Individualism:** The view, common in the Euro-American world, that places a high value on individual achievement and distinction.

**Inductive reasoning:** Drawing a conclusion about the probability of an event or condition based on available, but incomplete, evidence and past experience.

**Industrial and organizational psychologists:** Applied psychologists who specialize in modifying the work environment to maximize productivity and morale. They are often called *I/O psychologists*.

**Infancy:** In humans, infancy spans the time between the end of the neonatal period and the establishment of language—usually at about 18 months to two years.

**Inferential statistics:** Statistical techniques (based on probability theory) used to assess whether the results of a study are reliable or whether they might be simply the result of chance. Inferential statistics are often used to determine whether two or more groups are essentially the same or different.

**Information-processing model:** A cognitive perspective that proposes that thinking and all other forms of cognition can be understood by analyzing them as a flow of information, as in a computer.

**Innate:** Inborn; present at birth; part of the organism's biological heritage.

**Innateness theory of language:** The view that children learn language mainly by following an inborn program for acquiring vocabulary and grammar.

**Insanity:** A legal term, not a psychological or psychiatric one, referring to a person who is unable, because of a mental disorder or defect, to conform his or her behavior to the law.

**Insight learning:** A form of cognitive learning, originally described by the Gestalt psychologists, involving a sudden reorganization of perceptions.

**Insight therapies:** Psychotherapies in which the therapist helps the patient understand (gain *insight* into) the causes of his or her problems.

**Insomnia:** A disorder that involves insufficient sleep, the inability to fall asleep quickly, frequent arousals, or early awakenings.

**Instinct theory:** The now outmoded view that certain behaviors are determined entirely by innate factors. The instinct theory was flawed because it overlooked the effects of learning and because it employed instincts merely as labels, rather than as explanations for behavior.

**Intelligence:** The mental capacity to acquire knowledge, reason, and solve problems effectively.

**Intelligence quotient (IQ):** A numerical score on an intelligence test, originally computed by dividing the person's mental age by chronological age and multiplying by 100.

**Interaction:** A process by which forces work together or influence each other—as in the interaction between the forces of heredity and environment.

**Interneurons:** Nerve cells that relay messages from between nerve cells, especially in the brain and spinal cord.

**Intervening variables:** Inner, unseen conditions that are assumed to function as the links between the observable stimulus and the individual's response.

**Intrinsic motivation:** The desire to engage in an activity for its own sake, rather than for some external consequence, such as a reward.

**Introspection:** The process of looking inside to observe one's own mental state and conscious experience.

**Introversion:** The Jungian dimension that focuses on inner experience—one's own thoughts and feelings, making the introvert less outgoing and sociable than the extravert.

**Intuition:** The ability to find solutions to problems without going laboriously through a conscious reasoning process. Intuition is based on heuristic strategies.

**Inverted "U" function:** Describes the relationship between arousal and performance. Both low and high levels of arousal produce lower performance than does a moderate level of arousal.

**James-Lange theory of emotion:** The theory that an emotion-provoking stimulus produces a physical response that, in turn, produces an emotion.

**Jet lag:** A biological and psychological disruption of the circadian rhythms produced by moving quickly across time zones and attempting to shift one's sleep-wakefulness cycle to the local time.

**Just noticeable difference (JND):** Same as the *difference threshold*.

**Kinesthetic sense:** The sense of body position and movement of body parts relative to each other (also called *kinesthesis*).

**Language acquisition device** or **LAD:** A biologically organized mental structure in the brain that facilitates the learning of language because (says Chomsky) it is innately programmed with some of the fundamental rules of grammar.

**Latent content:** In Freudian theory, the real and hidden meaning of a dream, disguised by symbolism.

**Lateral fissure:** The prominent horizontal groove separating the frontal and temporal lobes in each hemisphere.

**Lateralization of emotion:** Different influences of the two brain hemispheres on various emotions. The left hemisphere apparently influences positive emotions (for example, happiness), and the right hemisphere influences negative emotion (anger, for example).

**Law of common fate:** The Gestalt principle that we tend to group similar objects together that share a common motion or destination.

**Law of continuity:** The Gestalt principle that we prefer perceptions of connected and continuous figures to disconnected and disjointed ones.

**Law of effect:** Thorndike's law of learning, which states that the power of a stimulus to evoke a response is strengthened when the response is followed by a reward and weakened when it is not rewarded.

**Law of Prägnanz:** The most general Gestalt principle, which states that the simplest organization, requiring the least cognitive effort, will emerge as the figure.

**Law of proximity:** The Gestalt principle that we tend to group objects together when they are near each other.

**Law of similarity:** The Gestalt principle that we tend to group similar objects together in our perceptions.

**Laws of perceptual grouping:** The Gestalt principles of *similarity, proximity, continuation,* and *common fate.* These ideas suggest how stimulus elements are grouped together perceptually.

**Learned helplessness:** A pattern of not responding to noxious stimuli after an organism learns that its behavior has no effect.

**Learning:** A lasting change in behavior or mental processes that results from experience.

**Learning-based inference:** The view that perception is primarily shaped by learning (or experience), rather than innate factors.

**Lesions:** Tissue damage that results from disease or injury. To study the connection between brain and behavior, biopsychologists make precise lesions in the brains of experimental animals and observe the changes in the animals' behavior.

**Libido:** The Freudian concept of psychic energy that drives individuals to experience sensual pleasure.

**Limbic system:** The middle layer of the brain, involved in emotion and memory. The limbic system includes the amygdala, the hippocampus, the hypothalamus, and other structures.

**Lithium carbonate:** A simple chemical compound that is highly effective in dampening the extreme mood swings of bipolar disorder.

**Locus of control:** An individual's sense of where his or her life influences originate—internally or externally.

**Logical reasoning** (also called *componential intelligence*): According to Sternberg, this is the ability measured by most IQ tests; includes the ability to analyze problems and find correct answers.

**Long-term memory (LTM):** The third of three memory stages, with the largest capacity and longest duration; LTM stores material organized according to meaning.

**Longitudinal method:** A type of developmental research that involves repeated observations of the same individuals over a period of time.

**Loudness:** A sensory characteristic of sound produced by the amplitude (intensity) of the sound wave.

**Maintenance rehearsal:** A working-memory process in which information is merely repeated or reviewed to keep it from fading while in working memory. Maintenance rehearsal involves no active elaboration.

**Mania:** Pathologically excessive elation or manic excitement.

**Manifest content:** In Freudian theory, the superficial and obvious meaning of a dream.

**Matching hypothesis:** The prediction that most people will find friends and mates that are of about their same level of attractiveness.

**Maturation:** The process by which the genetic program manifests itself over time.

**Mean:** The measure of central tendency most often used to describe a set of data—calculated by adding all the scores and dividing by the number of scores.

**Measure of central tendency:** A single, representative score that can be used as an index of the most typical score obtained by a group of subjects in a distribution. Measures of central tendency include the *mean, median,* and *mode.*

**Measures of variability:** Statistics that describe the distribution of scores around some measure of central tendency. Measures of variability include the *range* and the *standard deviation.*

**Median:** A measure of central tendency for a distribution, represented by the score that separates the upper half of the scores in a distribution from the lower half.

**Medical model:** The view that mental disorders are diseases that, like ordinary physical diseases, have objective causes and require specific treatments.

**Meditation:** A form of consciousness change often induced by focusing on a repetitive behavior, assuming certain body positions, and minimizing external stimulation. Meditation is intended to enhance self-knowledge and well-being by reducing self-awareness.

**Medulla:** A brain-stem region that controls breathing and heart rate. The sensory and motor pathways connecting the brain to the body cross in the medulla.

**MEG** or **magnetoencephalography:** An imaging technique that measures magnetic fields generated by the electrical activity of the brain.

**Memory:** A mental system that encodes, stores, and retrieves information that has been learned.

**Menarche:** The onset of menstruation, which signals puberty in girls.

**Mental age (MA):** The average age at which normal (average) individuals achieve a particular score.

**Mental operations:** Solving problems by manipulating images in one's mind.

**Mental representation:** The ability to form internal images of objects and events.

**Mental retardation:** Often conceived as representing the lower 2% of the IQ range, commencing about 30 points below average (below about 70 points). More sophisticated definitions also take into account an individual's level of social functioning and other abilities.

**Mental set:** The tendency to respond to a new problem in the manner used for a previous problem.

**MMPI-2:** A widely used personality assessment instrument that gives scores on ten important clinical traits. Also called the *Minnesota Multiphasic Personality Inventory.*

**Mnemonics:** Techniques for improving memory.

**Mode:** A measure of central tendency for a distribution, represented by the score that occurs more often than any other.

**Morphemes:** The meaningful units of language that make up words. Some whole words are morphemes (example: "word"); other morphemes include grammatical components that alter a word's meaning (examples: "-ed," "-ing," and "un-").

**Motivation:** Refers to all the processes involved in starting, directing, and maintaining physical and psychological activities.

**Motive:** An internal mechanism that selects and directs behavior. The term "motive" is often used in the narrower sense of a motivational process that is learned, rather than biologically based (as are drives).

**Motor cortex:** A narrow vertical strip of cortex in the frontal lobes, just in front of the central fissure.

**Motor neurons** or **efferent neurons:** Nerve cells that carry messages away from the central nervous system toward the muscles and glands.

**Motor speech area:** A part of the left frontal lobe responsible for coordinating the muscles used in producing speech. It is often called Broca's area, after its discoverer.

**MRI** or **magnetic resonance imaging:** An imaging technique that relies on cells' responses in a high-intensity magnetic field.

**Mutations:** Genetic variations, which occur randomly, especially during the recombination of chromosomes in sexual reproduction.

**Mutual interdependence:** A shared sense that individuals or groups need each other in order to achieve common goals.

**Myelin sheath:** A fatty insulation coating some types of neural axons, which biochemically speeds the conduction of neural impulses.

**Myers-Briggs Type Indicator (MBTI):** A widely used personality test based on Jungian types.

**Narcissistic personality disorder:** Characterized by a grandiose sense of self-importance, a preoccupation with fantasies of success or power, and a need for constant attention or admiration.

**Narcolepsy:** A disorder of REM sleep, involving sudden REM-sleep attacks accompanied by cataplexy.

**Natural concepts:** Mental representations of objects and events drawn from our direct experience.

**Natural selection:** The driving force behind evolution—by which the environment "selects" the fittest organisms.

**Naturalistic observations:** A form of correlational research involving *behavioral measures* of people or animals in their home surroundings.

**Nature–nurture controversy:** The long-standing dispute over the relative importance of nature (heredity) and nurture (environment) in their influence on behavior and mental processes.

**Need for achievement (n Ach):** In Murray and McClelland's theory, a mental state that produces a psychological motive to excel or to reach some goal.

**Need:** In drive theory, a need is a biological imbalance (such as dehydration) that threatens survival, if the need is left unmet. Biological needs are believed to produce drives.

**Needs hierarchy:** In Maslow's theory, the notion that needs occur in priority order, with the biological needs as the most basic.

**Negative reinforcer:** The removal of an unpleasant or aversive stimulus, contingent upon a particular behavior. Compare with *punishment*.

**Negative schizophrenia:** Any form of schizophrenia distinguished by deficits, such as withdrawal and poverty of thought processes, rather than by active symptoms.

**Neonatal period:** In humans, the neonatal (newborn) period extends through the first month after birth.

**Nerve cells** or **neurons:** Cells specialized to receive and transmit information to other cells in the body. Bundles of many neurons are called *nerves*.

**Nervous system:** The entire network of neurons in the body, including the central nervous system, the peripheral nervous system, and their subdivisions.

**Neural impulse:** An electrochemical process generated in a nerve cell to carry the cell's neural message.

**Neural pathways:** Bundles of nerve cells that follow generally the same route and employ the same neurotransmitter.

**Neurotic disorder** or **neurosis:** Before the *DSM-IV*, these were terms used to describe a pattern of subjective distress or self-defeating behavior that did not show signs of brain abnormalities or grossly irrational thinking.

**Neurotransmitters:** Chemical messengers that relay neural messages across the synapse. Many neurotransmitters are also hormones.

**Neutral stimulus:** Any stimulus that produces no response prior to learning.

**Non-REM (NREM) sleep:** The recurring periods when a sleeper is not showing REM.

**Nonconscious processes:** Any brain process that does not involve conscious processing. Examples include regulation of the heart rate, breathing, and control of the internal organs and glands.

**Nondirective:** Rogers's term for a therapeutic approach in which the client, rather than the therapist, takes the lead in determining the direction of therapy.

**Normal curve:** A bell-shaped curve that describes distributions of IQ scores in the general population, as well as other sets of data in which most subjects score near the center of the distribution and only a few have extreme scores.

**Normal range:** Scores falling in (approximately) the middle two-thirds of a normal distribution.

**Normally distributed:** Spread through the population in varying degrees, so that few people fall into the high or low ranges, while most people cluster around the middle.

**Object permanence:** The knowledge that objects exist independently of one's own actions or awareness.

**Observational learning:** The process of learning new responses by watching others' behavior.

**Obsessive–compulsive disorder:** A condition characterized by patterns of persistent, unwanted thoughts and behaviors.

**Occipital lobes:** The cortical lobes at the back of the brain, containing the visual cortex.

**Oedipus complex:** According to Freud, a largely unconscious process whereby boys displace an erotic attraction toward their mother to females of their own age and, at the same time, identify with their fathers.

**Olfaction:** The sense of smell.

**Olfactory bulbs:** The brain sites of olfactory processing, located below the frontal lobes, where odor-sensitive receptors send their signals.

**One-word stage:** The first stage of true language, in which children communicate with single words, rather than sentences.

**Operant chamber:** A boxlike device that can be set up to deliver rewards or punishments contingent on specific behaviors, such as a food pellet for pressing a lever. Commonly, operant chambers are called "Skinner boxes."

**Operant conditioning:** A form of behavioral learning in which the probability of a response is changed by its consequences—that is, by the stimuli that follow the response.

**Operant extinction:** A form of extinction in which a response that has been learned by operant conditioning is weakened by removal of reinforcement.

**Operational definition:** A definition of a concept stated in terms of how the concept is measured or what operations are used to produce it.

**Opiates:** Highly addictive drugs, derived from opium, that can produce a profound sense of well-being and have strong pain-relieving properties.

**Optic nerve:** The bundle of neurons that carries visual information from the retina to the brain.

**Out-group:** Those outside the group with which an individual identifies.

**Overjustification:** The process by which extrinsic (external) rewards displace internal motivation, as when a child receives money for playing video games.

**Overregularization:** Applying a grammatical rule too widely and creating incorrect forms.

**Panic disorder:** A disturbance marked by panic attacks that have no connection with events in the person's present experience.

**Paranoid type:** A form of schizophrenia in which a combination of delusions and hallucinations is the prominent feature.

**Parasympathetic division:** The part of the autonomic nervous system that monitors the routine operations of the internal organs and returns the body to calmer functioning after arousal by the sympathetic division.

**Parietal lobes:** Cortical lobes lying in the upper back of the brain and involved in touch sensation and in perceiving spatial relationships (the relationships of objects in space).

**Partial reinforcement:** A type of reinforcement schedule by which some, but not all, correct responses are reinforced.

**Partial reinforcement effect:** The greater resistance to extinction produced by partial reinforcement, rather than continuous reinforcement.

**Participant modeling:** A social learning technique in which a therapist demonstrates and encourages a client to imitate a desired behavior.

**Penis envy:** According to Freud, the female desire to have a penis—a condition that usually results in their attraction to males.

**Percept:** The meaningful product of perception—often an image that has been associated with concepts, memories of events, emotions, and motives.

**Perception:** A process that makes sensory patterns meaningful and more elaborate. Perception draws heavily on memory, motivation, emotion, and other psychological processes.

**Perceptual constancy:** The ability to recognize the same object under different conditions, such as changes in illumination, distance, or location.

**Perceptual organization:** Refers to the mental processes by which sensory inputs are drawn together into a percept. The known aspects of perceptual organization include figure–ground, closure, and the Gestalt laws of perceptual grouping. The unknown details of how the brain accomplishes this are often referred to as the *binding problem*.

**Perceptual set:** Readiness to detect a particular stimulus in a given context.

**Peripheral nervous system:** All parts of the nervous system lying outside the central nervous system. The peripheral nervous system includes the autonomic and somatic nervous systems.

**Person-centered therapy:** A humanistic approach to treatment developed by Carl Rogers, emphasizing an individual's tendency for healthy psychological growth through self-actualization.

**Person–situation controversy:** A theoretical dispute concerning the relative contribution of personality factors and situational factors in controlling behavior.

**Personal unconscious:** Jung's term for that portion of the unconscious corresponding roughly to the Freudian id.

**Personality:** The psychological qualities that bring continuity to an individual's behavior in different situations and at different times

**Personality disorders:** Conditions involving a chronic, pervasive, inflexible, and maladaptive pattern of thinking, emotion, social relationships, or impulse control.

**PET scanning** or **positron emission tomography:** An imaging technique that relies on the detection of radioactive sugar consumed by active brain cells.

**Phenomenal field:** Our psychological reality, composed of perceptions.

**Phenotype:** An organism's observable physical characteristics.

**Pheromones:** Chemical signals released by organisms to communicate with other members of their species; often sexual attractors.

**Phobia** or **phobic disorder:** An anxiety disorder involving a pathological fear of a specific object or situation.

**Phosphenes:** Visual sensations that are not caused by light waves but by other forms of stimulation, such as pressure on the eyeball or electrical stimulation of the visual cortex.

**Photoreceptors:** Light-sensitive cells in the retina that convert light energy to neural impulses.

**Physiological dependence:** A process by which the body adjusts to, and becomes dependent on, a drug.

**Physiological measures:** Data based on subjects' biological responses to stimuli.

**Pitch:** A sensory characteristic of sound produced by the frequency of the sound wave.

**Pituitary gland:** The master gland that produces hormones influencing the secretions of all other endocrine glands, as well as a hormone that influences growth. The pituitary is attached to the brain's hypothalamus, from which it takes its orders.

**Place learning:** A type of cognitive learning in which the subject learns a cognitive map that it uses to get to a specific location or place, rather than just a sequence of behaviors.

**Placebo effect:** A response to a placebo (a fake drug), caused by subjects' belief that they are taking real drugs.

**Placebos:** Substances that appear to be drugs but are not.

**Placenta:** The organ separating the embryo or fetus and the mother. The placenta separates the bloodstreams, but it allows the exchange of nutrients and waste products.

**Plasticity:** The ability of the brain to be modified or to compensate for damage.

**Polygraph:** A device that records or graphs many ("poly") measures of physical arousal, such as heart rate, breathing, perspiration, and blood pressure. A polygraph is often called a "lie detector," even though it is really an arousal detector.

**Pons:** A brain-stem region that regulates brain activity during sleep and dreaming. *Pons* derives from the Latin word for "bridge."

**Positive reinforcer:** A stimulus, received after a response, that increases the probability of that response happening again.

**Positive schizophrenia:** Any form of schizophrenia in which the person displays active symptoms, such as delusions or hallucinations.

**Post-Freudian psychodynamic therapies:** Therapies for mental disorder that were developed by psychodynamic theorists who disagreed with some aspects of Freud's theories and methods of treatment.

**Posttraumatic stress disorder (PTSD):** A delayed stress reaction in which an individual involuntarily reexperiences emotional, cognitive, and behavioral aspects of past trauma.

**Practical intelligence** (also called *contextual intelligence*): According to Sternberg, this is the ability to cope with the environment; sometimes called "street smarts."

**Preconscious memories:** Memories accessible to consciousness only after something calls attention to them.

**Prejudice:** A negative *attitude* toward an individual based solely on his or her membership in a particular group.

**Premack principle:** The concept, developed by David Premack, that a more-preferred activity can be used to reinforce a less-preferred activity.

**Prenatal period:** The developmental period before birth.

**Preoperational stage:** The second stage in Piaget's theory, marked by well developed mental representation and the use of language.

**Preparedness hypothesis:** The notion that we have an innate tendency, acquired through natural selection, to respond quickly and automatically to stimuli that posed a survival threat to our ancestors.

**Primary reinforcers:** Reinforcers, such as food and sex, that have an innate basis because of their biological value to an organism.

**Principle of opposites:** A Jungian concept that portrays each personality as a balance between opposing pairs of unconscious tendencies, such as introversion and extroversion.

**Principle of proximity:** The notion that people at work will make more friends among those who are nearby—with whom they have the most contact. *Proximity* means "nearness."

**Proactive interference:** A cause of forgetting by which previously stored information prevents learning and remembering new information.

**Procedural memory:** A division of LTM that stores memories for how things are done.

**Prognosis:** Outlook, prediction.

**Projection:** The process by which people attribute their own unconscious motives, impulses, or fantasies to other people or objects. The concept of projection originally comes from Freud's theory.

**Projective test:** A personality assessment instrument based on Freud's concept of projection.

**Prompting:** Cuing a response in such a way that the subject knows what response is required. Prompting often involves touching or manipulating a body part to be moved in the desired response or modeling a part of the response.

**Prototype:** An ideal or most representative example of a conceptual category.

**Pseudomemory:** False memory of a new stimulus pattern because its components were previously experienced separately.

**Pseudoscience:** Any approach to explaining phenomena in the natural world that does not use empirical observation or other aspects of the scientific method.

**Psychiatrists:** Physicians who specialize in the treatment of mental disorders.

**Psychic determinism:** Freud's assumption that all mental and behavioral reactions are caused by earlier life experiences.

**Psychoactive drugs:** Chemicals that affect mental processes and behavior by their effects on the nervous system.

**Psychoanalysis:** The form of psychodynamic therapy developed by Sigmund Freud. The goal of psychoanalysis is to release conflicts and memories from the unconscious.

**Psychoanalysts:** Specialists (usually psychiatrists) who use Freudian methods of treating mental disorders.

**Psychodynamic therapies:** Any of the insight therapies based on the assumption that mental disorder is caused by powerful mental forces and conflicts. Freudian *psychoanalysis* was the first form of psychodynamic therapy to be developed.

**Psychodynamic view:** A viewpoint that emphasizes the understanding of mental disorders in terms of unconscious needs, desires, memories, and conflicts.

**Psychogenic:** Caused by psychological factors.

**Psychological dependence:** A pervasive desire to obtain or use a drug—but without physical addiction.

**Psychological therapies:** Therapies based on psychological principles (rather than on the biomedical approach); often called "psychotherapy."

**Psychology:** The science of individual behavior and mental processes.

**Psychometrics:** The field of mental testing.

**Psychoneuroimmunology:** A relatively new field that studies the influence of our mental states on the immune system.

**Psychopathology:** Any pattern of emotions, behaviors, or thoughts inappropriate to the situation and leading to personal distress or the inability to achieve important goals.

**Psychosexual stages:** Successive, instinctive patterns of associating pleasure with stimulation of specific bodily areas at different times of life.

**Psychosocial crises:** In Erikson's theory, any of the eight major developmental challenges across the life span, which require an individual to rethink his or her orientation to self and others.

**Psychosurgery:** The general term for surgical intervention in the brain to treat psychological disorders.

**Psychotherapy:** A term for any of the psychologically based therapies, including behavioral therapies and insight therapies.

**Psychotic disorder** or **psychosis:** A disorder involving profound disturbances in perception, rational thinking, or affect.

**Puberty:** The onset of sexual maturity.

**Punishment:** The application of an aversive stimulus after an undesirable response. Compare with *negative reinforcement*.

**Quantified:** Converted to numbers.

**Random:** Determined by chance.

**Random sample:** A sample group of subjects selected by chance (without biased selection techniques).

**Range:** The simplest measure of variability, represented by the difference between the highest and the lowest values in a frequency distribution.

**Rapid eye movements (REM):** Quick bursts of eye movements occurring (under closed eyelids) at periodic intervals during sleep. REM sleep periods are associated with dreaming.

**Rational–emotive therapy (RET):** Albert Ellis's brand of cognitive therapy, based on the idea that irrational thinking is the cause of mental disorders.

**Rationalization:** Giving socially acceptable reasons for actions that are really based on motives that the person believes to be unacceptable.

**Raw data:** The unanalyzed scores or other quantitative measures obtained from a study; the data on which statistical procedures are performed.

**Reaction formation:** The ego defense mechanism that makes us overreact in a manner opposite to our unconscious desires.

**Recall:** A retrieval method in which one must reproduce previously presented information.

**Receptors:** Specialized neurons that are activated by stimulation and transduce (convert) it into a nerve impulse.

**Reciprocal determinism:** The process in which the environment, cognition, and behavior mutually influence each other.

**Reciprocal inhibition:** Joseph Wolpe's counterconditioning technique, involving relaxation training and systematic desensitization therapy.

**Recognition:** A retrieval method in which one must identify present stimuli as having been previously presented.

**Reflection of feeling:** Carl Rogers's technique of paraphrasing clients' words, attempting to capture the emotional tone expressed.

**Reflexes:** Simple, unlearned responses triggered by stimuli—such as the knee-jerk reflex set off by tapping the tendon just below your kneecap.

**Regression:** The ego defense mechanism that makes us revert to immature behavior in the face of threat.

**Regression to the average:** A tendency for exceptional performances (either high or low) to be followed by more average performances—a concept often misunderstood, leading to faulty heuristic strategies.

**Rehabilitation psychologists:** Applied psychologists who treat patients with physical disorders.

**Reinforcement contingency:** A consistent relationship between a response and the changes it produces in the environment.

**Reinforcers:** Significant events that strengthen responses when they are delivered in connection with those responses.

**Relearning:** A technique, invented by Hermann Ebbinghaus, used in measuring memory retention by recording the number of trials necessary to relearn certain material. This is then compared with the number of trials necessary to learn the material originally (see *savings method*).

**Reliability:** An attribute of a psychological test that gives consistent results.

**REM rebound:** A condition of increased REM sleep following a period of REM-sleep deprivation.

**Representative sample:** A sample obtained in such a way that it reflects the distribution of important variables in the larger population in which the researchers are interested—variables such as age, income level, ethnicity, and geographic distribution.

**Representativeness heuristic:** A faulty cognitive strategy based on the presumption that, once a person or event is categorized, it shares all the features of other members in that category.

**Repression:** The Freudian defense mechanism of forgetting, by which painful or threatening material is blocked off in the unconscious and prevented from reaching consciousness.

**Residual type:** A diagnostic category used for individuals who have suffered from a past episode of schizophrenia but are currently free of positive symptoms.

**Reticular activating system (RAS):** A pencil-shaped structure in the brain stem, situated between the medulla and the pons. The RAS arouses the cortex to keep the brain alert and to attend to new stimulation.

**Retina:** The light-sensitive layer at the back of the eyeball.

**Retroactive interference:** A cause of forgetting by which newly learned information prevents retrieval of previously stored material.

**Reward theory of attraction:** A social learning view that says we like best those who give us maximum rewards at minimum cost.

**Rites of passage:** Social rituals that mark the transition between developmental stages, especially between childhood and adulthood.

**Rods:** Photoreceptors in the retina that are especially sensitive to dim light but not to colors.

**Romantic love:** A temporary and highly emotional condition based on infatuation and sexual desire.

**Rorschach test:** A projective technique requiring subjects to respond to a series of ten inkblots.

**Savant syndrome:** Found in individuals having a remarkable talent (such as the ability to multiply numbers quickly in their heads or to determine the day of the week for any given date) even though they are mentally slow in other domains.

**Savings method:** Ebbinghaus's approach to measuring memory retention by calculating "savings" in number of trials necessary for relearning after varying amounts of time.

**Scapegoating:** Blaming an innocent person or a group for one's own troubles.

**Schedule of reinforcement:** A plan for the timing and frequency of reinforcements.

**Schemas:** Knowledge clusters and general conceptual frameworks that provide expectations about topics, events, objects, people, and situations in one's life.

**Schemes:** In Piaget's theory, mental structures or programs that guide a developing child's thought.

**Schizophrenia** (pronounced *skits-o-FRENNY-a*): A psychotic disorder involving distortions in thoughts, perceptions, and/or emotions.

**School psychologists:** Applied psychologists with expertise in the problems of teaching and learning.

**Scientific method:** A five-step process for empirical investigation of a hypothesis under controlled conditions designed to control the observer's biases and subjectivity.

**Script:** A cluster of knowledge about sequences of events and actions expected to occur in particular settings.

**Seasonal affective disorder** or **SAD:** A form of depression believed to be caused by deprivation of sunlight.

**Selective social interaction:** Choosing to restrict the number of one's social contacts to those who are the most gratifying.

**Self-actualizing personalities:** Healthy individuals who have met their basic needs and are free to pursue an interest in "higher" ideals, such as truth, justice, and beauty.

**Self-fulfilling prophecy:** Observations or behaviors that result primarily from expectations.

**Self-help groups:** Therapy groups, such as Alcoholics Anonymous, that are organized and run by laypersons, rather than professional therapists.

**Self-report measures:** Verbal answers, either written or spoken, to questions posed by researchers.

**Self-serving bias:** An attributional pattern in which one takes credit for success but denies responsibility for failure. (Compare with the *fundamental attribution error*.)

**Semantic memory:** A subdivision of declarative memory that stores general knowledge, including the meanings of words and concepts.

**Sensation:** An early stage of perception in which neurons in a receptor create an internal pattern of nerve impulses that represent the conditions that stimulated it—either inside or outside the body.

**Sensation seekers:** In Zuckerman's theory, individuals who have a biological need for higher levels of stimulation than do other people.

**Sensorimotor intelligence:** The mental capacity shown in the first schemes an infant displays, which are mainly motor responses to stimuli, with a strong innate basis.

**Sensorimotor stage:** The first stage in Piaget's theory, during which the child relies heavily on innate motor responses to stimuli.

**Sensory adaptation:** Loss of responsiveness in receptor cells after stimulation has remained unchanged for a while.

**Sensory deprivation:** A procedure that minimizes sensation by creating an environment that contains very little stimulation.

**Sensory memory:** The first of three memory stages, preserving brief sensory impressions of stimuli; also called *sensory register*.

**Sensory neurons** or **afferent neurons:** Nerve cells that carry messages from sense receptors toward the central nervous system.

**Sensory pathway:** Bundles of neurons that carry information from the sense organs to the brain.

**Set point:** Refers to the tendency of the body to maintain a certain level of body fat and body weight.

**Sex chromosomes:** The X and Y chromosomes that determine our physical sex characteristics.

**Sexual orientation:** One's erotic attraction toward members of the same sex (a homosexual orientation), the opposite sex (heterosexual orientation), or both sexes (a bisexual orientation).

**Sexual response cycle:** The four-stage sequence of arousal, plateau, orgasm, and resolution occurring in both men and women.

**Sexual scripts:** Socially learned programs of sexual interpretation and responsiveness.

**Shadow:** The archetype representing the destructive and aggressive tendencies that we don't want to recognize in ourselves.

**Shaping:** An operant learning technique in which a new behavior is produced by reinforcing responses that approach the desired performance; also called *learning by successive approximations*.

**Shyness:** A distressing pattern of avoiding or withdrawing from social contact; not a *DSM-IV* disorder.

**Signal detection theory:** Explains perceptual judgment as a combination of sensation and decision-making processes. Signal detection theory adds observer characteristics to classical psychophysics.

**Significant difference:** Psychologists accept a difference between the groups as "real," or *significant*, when the probability that it might be due to an atypical sample drawn by chance is less than 5 in 100 (indicated by the notation $p < .05$).

**Similarity principle:** The notion that people are attracted to those who are most similar to themselves.

**Situationism:** The view that environmental conditions influence people's behavior as much or more than their personal dispositions do.

**Skin senses:** Sensory systems for processing touch, warmth, and cold.

**Sleep apnea:** A respiratory disorder in which the person intermittently stops breathing while asleep.

**Sleep paralysis:** A condition in which a sleeper is unable to move any of the voluntary muscles, except those controlling the eyes. Sleep paralysis normally occurs during REM sleep.

**Social distance:** The perceived difference or similarity between oneself and another person.

**Social learning** or **observational learning:** A form of cognitive learning in which new responses are acquired after watching others' behavior and the consequences of their behavior.

**Social learning therapy:** An approach to therapy based on social learning theory, which teaches that behavior is influenced by observation and imitation of others.

**Social norms:** A group's expectations regarding what is appropriate and acceptable for its members' attitudes and behaviors.

**Social psychology:** The branch of psychology that studies the effects of social variables and cognitions on individual behavior and social interactions.

**Social Readjustment Rating Scale (SRRS):** A psychological rating scale designed to measure stress levels by means of values attached to common life changes.

**Social reality:** An individual's subjective interpretation of other people and of relationships with them.

**Social role:** One of several socially defined patterns of behavior that are expected of persons in a given setting or group.

**Social support:** The resources others provide to help an individual cope with stress.

**Socialization:** The lifelong process of developing behavior patterns, values, standards, skills, attitudes, and motives that conform to those regarded as desirable in a society.

**Societal stressors:** Stressful conditions arising from our social and cultural environment.

**Sociocultural view:** A psychological perspective that emphasizes the importance of social interaction, social learning, and a multicultural perspective.

**Somatic nervous system:** A portion of the peripheral nervous system that sends voluntary messages to the body's skeletal muscles.

**Somatoform disorders:** Psychological problems appearing in the form of bodily symptoms or physical complaints, such as weakness or excessive worry about disease. The somatoform disorders include conversion disorder and hypochondriasis.

**Somatosensory cortex:** A strip of the parietal lobe lying just behind the central fissure. The somatosensory cortex is involved with sensations of touch.

**Spatial orientation:** (SPAY-shul) The process of locating one's body or other objects in space.

**Split-brain patients:** Individuals who have had the corpus callosum surgically severed, usually as a treatment for severe epilepsy.

**Spontaneous recovery:** The reappearance of an extinguished conditioned response after a time delay.

**Stage of exhaustion:** The third stage of the GAS, during which the body depletes its resources.

**Stage of resistance:** The second stage of the GAS, during which the body seems to adapt to the presence of the stressor.

**Standard deviation:** A measure of variability that indicates the *average* difference between the scores and their mean.

**Statistics:** A set of mathematical techniques used to organize data and to draw inferences from them. Numbers derived from these mathematical procedures are also called statistics.

**Stimulants:** Drugs that normally increase activity level by encouraging communication among neurons in the brain. Stimulants, however, have been found to suppress activity level in persons with attention-deficit/hyperactivity disorder.

**Stimulus–response psychology:** Another term for *behaviorism*.

**Stockholm syndrome:** A psychological reaction in which hostages and prisoners identify and sympathize with their captors.

**Storage:** One of the three basic functions of memory, involving the retention of encoded material over time.

**Stress:** A physical and mental response to a challenging or threatening situation.

**Stressors:** Stressful stimuli or situations.

**Stroke:** An interruption of blood supply to a part of the brain.

**Structuralism:** A historical school of psychology devoted to uncovering the basic structures that make up mind and thought. Structuralists sought the "elements" of conscious experience.

**Subconscious:** A store of information that was registered in memory without being consciously attended to.

**Subjective contours:** Boundaries that are perceived but do not appear in the stimulus pattern.

**Subjective well-being (SWB):** An individual's evaluative response to his or her life, including cognitive and emotional reactions.

**Superego:** The mind's storehouse of values, including moral attitudes learned from parents and from society; roughly the same as the common notion of the conscience.

**Surrogate mothers:** Mother substitutes, such as the cloth and wire dummies in Harlow's research.

**Survey:** A technique used in correlational research that typically involves seeking people's responses to a prepared set of verbal items.

**Syllogism:** A particular form of deductive reasoning involving a major premise, a minor premise, and a deductive conclusion.

**Sympathetic division:** The part of the autonomic nervous system that sends messages to internal organs and glands that help us respond to stressful and emergency situations.

**Synapse:** The junction between neurons or between a neuron and a muscle or gland. The synapse includes the terminal button, the synaptic cleft, and the receptor sites on the target cell. Neurotransmitters carry neural messages across the synaptic gap.

**Synaptic transmission:** The relaying of information across the synapse (from one neuron to another, for example) by means of chemical neurotransmitters.

**Syntax:** Grammatical rules for word order.

**Systematic desensitization:** A behavioral therapy technique in which anxiety is extinguished by exposing the patient to an anxiety-provoking stimulus.

**Tardive dyskinesia:** An incurable disorder of motor control, especially involving muscles of the face and head, resulting from long-term use of antipsychotic drugs.

**Taste-aversion learning:** A biological tendency in which an organism learns, after a single experience, to avoid a food with a certain taste, if eating it is followed by illness.

**Taste buds:** Receptors for taste, located primarily on the upper side of the tongue.

**Telegraphic speech:** Short, simple sentences, typical of young children, who omit plurals, tenses, and function words, such as "the" and "of"; so called because it sounds like a telegram.

**Temperament:** The basic, inherited personality dispositions that are apparent in early childhood and that establish the tempo and mood of the individual's behaviors.

**Temporal lobes:** Cortical lobes that process sounds, including speech. The temporal lobes are probably involved in storing long-term memories.

**Teratogen:** Any substance from the environment, including viruses, drugs, and other chemicals, that can damage the developing organism during the prenatal period.

**Terminal buttons:** Tiny bulblike structures at the end of the axon, which contain neurotransmitters that carry the neuron's message into the synapse.

**Thalamus:** The brain's central "relay station," situated just atop the brain stem. Nearly all the messages going into or out of the brain go through the thalamus.

**Thanatos:** The unconscious force that drives people toward aggressive and destructive behaviors.

**Thematic Apperception Test (TAT):** A projective test requiring subjects to make up stories that explain ambiguous pictures.

**Theory:** A body of interrelated principles used to explain or predict some psychological phenomenon.

**Therapeutic community:** Jones's term for a program of treating mental disorder by making the institutional environment supportive and humane for patients.

**Therapy:** A general term for any treatment process; in psychology and psychiatry, "therapy" refers to a variety of psychological and biomedical techniques.

**Think-aloud protocols:** An introspective technique that has subjects describe their thought processes as they carry out complex tasks, such as solving puzzles.

**Thinking:** The cognitive process involved in forming a new mental representation by manipulating available information.

**Tics:** Unwanted involuntary movements and twitches, such as exaggerated eye blinks.

**Timbre:** The quality of a sound wave that derives from the wave's complexity (combination of pure tones).

**Token economy:** An operant technique applied to groups, such as in classrooms or mental hospital wards, involving the distribution of "tokens" or other indicators of reinforcement contingent on desired behaviors. The tokens can later be exchanged for privileges, food, or other reinforcers.

**Tolerance:** The reduced effectiveness a drug has after repeated use.

**Top-down processing:** Perceptual analysis that emphasizes the perceiver's expectations, memories, and other cognitive factors, rather than being driven by the characteristics of the stimulus.

**Traits:** Stable personality characteristics that are presumed to exist within the individual and guide his or her thoughts and actions under various conditions.

**Transduction:** Transformation of one form of energy into another—especially the transformation of stimulus information into nerve impulses.

**Trial-and-error learning:** An operant form of learning, described by Thorndike, in which the learner gradually discovers the correct response by attempting many behaviors and noting which ones produce the desired consequences.

**Triangular theory of love:** A theory that describes various kinds of love in terms of three components: passion (erotic attraction), intimacy (sharing feelings and confidences), and commitment (dedication to putting this relationship first in one's life).

**Triarchic theory:** The term for Sternberg's theory; so called because it combines three main forms of intelligence.

**Twin studies:** Developmental investigations in which twins, especially identical twins, are compared in the search for genetic and environmental effects.

**Two-factor theory:** The proposal claiming that emotion results from the cognitive appraisal of both physical arousal (Factor #1) and an emotion-provoking stimulus (Factor #2).

**Two-word stage:** The second stage of true language, in which two words form rudimentary sentences—showing that the child is beginning to learn syntax.

**Tympanic membrane:** The eardrum.

**Type:** Refers to especially important dimensions or clusters of traits that are not only central to a person's personality but are found with essentially the same pattern in many people.

**Type A:** A behavior pattern characterized by an intense, angry, competitive, or perfectionistic response to life.

**Type B:** A behavior pattern characterized by a relaxed, unruffled response to life.

**Unconditional positive regard:** Love or caring without conditions attached; Rogers's term for the therapist's attitude of nonjudgmental acceptance and respect for the client.

**Unconditioned response (UCR):** In classical conditioning, the response elicited by an unconditioned stimulus without prior learning.

**Unconditioned stimulus (UCS):** In classical conditioning, the stimulus that elicits an unconditioned response.

**Unconscious:** In classic Freudian theory, a part of the mind that houses memories, desires, and feelings that would be threatening if brought to consciousness. Recently, many psychologists have come to believe in a simplified, "dumb" unconscious, which stores and processes some information outside of awareness.

**Unconscious motivation:** Having a desire to engage in an activity but being consciously unaware of the desire. Freud's psychoanalytic theory emphasized unconscious motivation.

**Undifferentiated type:** A category used to designate persons displaying a combination of schizophrenic symptoms that do not clearly fit in one of the other categories of schizophrenia.

**Unipolar depression:** A form of depression that does not alternate with mania.

**Validity:** An attribute of a psychological test that actually measures what it is being used to measure.

**Vestibular sense:** The sense of body orientation with respect to gravity.

**Vicarious trial-and-error:** Mentally trying alternative behaviors and thinking through their consequences before selecting a physical response. This concept was ridiculed by the behaviorists.

**Visible spectrum:** The tiny part of the electromagnetic spectrum to which our eyes are sensitive.

**Visual cortex:** The part of the brain—the occipital cortex—where visual sensations are processed.

**Weber's law:** This concept says that the size of a JND is proportional to the intensity of the stimulus; the JND is large when the stimulus intensity is high and small when the stimulus intensity is low.

**Withdrawal:** After addiction, a pattern of painful physical symptoms and cravings experienced when the level of drug is decreased or the drug is eliminated.

**Working backward:** A heuristic strategy that begins at the end (desired outcome) of the problem and proceeds backward.

**Working memory or short-term memory (STM):** The second of three memory stages, and most limited in capacity; preserves recently perceived events or experiences for less than a minute without rehearsal.

**Zygote:** A fertilized egg.

# References

ABC News. (1995). "My Family, Forgive Me." *20/20*, Transcript #1526, June 30, pp. 6–10. New York: American Broadcasting Companies, Inc.

Abelson, R. P. (1981). Psychological status of the script concept. *American Psychologist, 36*, 715–729.

Abrams, A. R. (1992). *Electroconvulsive therapy.* New York: Oxford University Press.

Abramson, L. Y., Metalsky, G. I., & Alloy, L. B. (1989). Hopelessness depression: A theory-based subtype. *Psychological Review, 96*, 358–372.

Achenbach, T.M. (1982). *Developmental psychopathology* (2nd ed.), New York: Wiley.

Ackerman, D. (1990). *A natural history of the senses.* New York: Vintage.

Adams, D. (Ed.). (1991). *The Seville statement on violence.* Washington, DC: Psychologists for Social Responsibility.

Adams, J. (1979). Mutual-help groups: Enhancing the coping ability of oncology clients. *Cancer Nursing, 2*, 95–98.

Adams, P. (1998). *House calls: How we can all heal the world one visit at a time.* San Francisco: Robert Reed Publisher.

Adams, P., & Mylander, M. (1998). *Gesundheit: Bringing good health to you, the medical system, and society through physician service, complementary therapies, humor and joy* (Rev. Ed.) Rochester, VT: Healing Arts Press.

Adams, P. R., & Adams, G. R. (1984). Mount Saint Helens' ashfall: Evidence for a disaster stress reaction. *American Psychologist, 39*, 252–260.

Ader, R., & Cohen, N. (1975). Behaviorally conditioned immuno-suppression. *Psychosomatic Medicine, 37*, 333–340.

Ader, R., & Cohen, N. (1993). Psychoneuroimmunology: Conditioning and stress. *Annual Review of Psychology, 44*, 53–85.

Adler, A. (1929). *The practice and theory of individual psychology.* New York: Harcourt, Brace & World.

Adler, J., & Salzhauer, A. (1995). Escaping the diet trap. *Newsweek, 126*(6), 54.

Adler, N. E., David, H. P., Major, B. N., Roth, S. H., Russo, N. F., & Wyatt, G. E. (1990). Psychological responses after abortion. *Science, 248*, 41–44.

Adler, T. (1991, November). Therapy may best treat panic disorder. *APA Monitor*, p. 10.

Adorno, T. W., Frenkel-Brunswick, E., Levinson, D. J., & Sanford, R. N. (1950). *The authoritarian personality.* New York: Harper.

Agency for Health Care Policy and Research. (1992). *Urinary incontinence in adults.* Silver Spring, MD: AHCPR Publications Clearinghouse.

Ahern, G. L., & Schwartz, G. E. (1985). Differential lateralization for positive and negative emotion in the human brain: EEG spectral analysis. *Neuropsychologia, 23*, 744–755.

Ahrons, C. R. (1994). *The good divorce: Keeping your family together when your marriage comes apart.* New York: HarperCollins.

Ainsworth, M. D. S. (1973). The development of infant–mother attachment. In B. M. Caldwell & H. N. Ricciuti (Eds.), *Review of child development research* (Vol. 3). Chicago: University of Chicago Press.

Ainsworth, M. D. S. (1989). Attachments beyond infancy. *American Psychologist, 44*, 709–716.

Ainsworth, M. D. S., Blehar, M., Water, E., & Wall, S. (1978). *Patterns of attachment.* Hillsdale, NJ: Erlbaum.

Ainsworth, M. D. S., & Wittig, B. A. (1969). Attachment and exploratory behavior of one-year-olds in a strange situation. In B. M. Foss (Ed.), *Determinants of infant behavior* (Vol. 4). London: Methuen.

Alford, G. S., & Bishop, A. C. (1991). Psychopharmacology. In M. Hersen, A. E. Kazdin, & A. S. Bellack (Eds.), *The clinical psychology handbook* (2nd ed., pp. 667–694). New York: Pergamon Press.

Alkon, D. L. (1983, July). Learning in a marine snail. *Scientific American, 249*, 70–84.

Alkon, D. L. (1984). Calcium-mediated reduction of ionic currents: A biophysical memory trace. *Science, 226*, 1037–1045.

Alkon, D. L. (1989, July). Memory storage and neural systems. *Scientific American, 261*, 42–50.

Allen, M. G. (1976). Twin studies of affective illness. *Archives of General Psychiatry, 33*, 1476–1478.

Allen, V. S., & Levine, J. M. (1969). Consensus and conformity. *Journal of Experimental Social Psychology, 5*, 389–399.

Allison, T., & Cicchetti, D. (1976). Sleep in mammals: Ecological and constitutional correlates. *Science, 194*, 732–734.

Allport, G. W., & Odbert, H. S. (1936). Trait-names, a psycho-lexical study. *Psychological Monographs, 47* (1, Whole No. 211).

Alper, J. (1993). Echo-planar MRI: Learning to read minds. *Science, 261*, 556.

Amabile, T. M. (1983). *The social psychology of creativity.* New York: Springer-Verlag.

Amabile, T. M. (1987). The motivation to be creative. In S. Isaksen (Ed.), *Frontiers in creativity: Beyond the basics.* Buffalo, NY: Bearly Limited.

American Psychiatric Association. (1990). *The practice of electroconvulsive therapy: Recommendations for treatment, training, and privileging.* Washington, DC: American Psychiatric Association.

American Psychiatric Association. (1994). *Diagnostic and statistical manual of mental disorders*, 4th edition. Washington, DC: American Psychiatric Association.

American Psychological Association. (1992). Ethical principles of psychologists and code of conduct. *American Psychologist, 47*, 1597–1611.

American Psychological Association. (1993). *Task force on promotion and dissemination of psychological procedures.* Washington, DC: Author.

American Psychological Association. (1995). *How to choose a psychologist.* Washington, DC: Author.

American Psychological Association. (1996). *Psychology: Careers for the twenty-first century.* Washington, DC: Author.

American Psychological Association. (1998). Association report. *American Psychologist, 53*, 836–853.

Anastasi, A. (1988). *Psychological testing* (6th ed.). New York: Macmillan.

Anch, A. M., Browman, C. P., Mitler, M. M., & Walsh, J. K. (1988). *Sleep: A scientific perspective.* Englewood Cliffs, NJ: Prentice Hall.

Anderson, A. E., & DiDomenico, L. (1992). Diet vs. shape content of popular male and female magazines: A dose-response relationship to the incidence of eating disorders? *International Journal of Eating Disorders, 11*, 283–287.

Anderson, J. R. (1976). *Language, memory, and thought*. Hillsdale, NJ: Erlbaum.

Anderson, J. R. (Ed.). (1981). *Cognitive skills and their acquisition*. Hillsdale, NJ: Erlbaum.

Anderson, J. R. (1982). Acquisition of cognitive skill. *Psychological Review, 89*, 369–406.

Andreasen, N. C., Rice, J., Endicott, J., Coryell, W., Grove, W. W., & Reich, T. (1987). Familial rates of affective disorder. *Archives of General Psychiatry, 44*, 461–472.

Andrews, J. D. W. (1967). The achievement motive and advancement in two types of organization. *Journal of Personality and Social Psychology, 6*, 163–168.

Angell, M. (1985). Disease as a reflection of the psyche. *New England Journal of Medicine, 312*, 1570–1572.

Antonuccio, D. (1995). Psychotherapy for depression: No stronger medicine. *American Psychologist, 50*, 450–452.

Antony, M. M., Brown, T. A., & Barlow, D. H. (1992). Current perspectives on panic and panic disorder. *Current Directions in Psychological Science, 1*, 79–82.

Archer, J. (1996). Sex differences in social behavior: Are the social role and evolutionary explanations compatible? *American Psychologist, 51*, 909–917.

Argyris, C. (1987). Bridging economics and psychology: The case of the economic theory of the firm. *American Psychologist, 42*, 456–463.

Arnhoff, F. N. (1975). Social consequences of policy toward mental illness. *Science, 188*, 1277–1281.

Arnsten, A. F. T. (1998, June 12). The biology of being frazzled. *Science, 280*, 1711–1712.

Aron, A., & Aron, E. (1994). Love. In A. L. Weber & J. H. Harvey (Eds.), *Perspectives on close relationships* (Chapter 7), pp. 131–152. Boston: Allyn & Bacon.

Aronson, E. (1995). *The Social Animal* (7th ed.). New York: W. H. Freeman.

Aronson, E., Helmreich, R., & LeFan, J. (1970). To err is humanizing—sometimes: Effects of self-esteem, competence, and a pratfall on interpersonal attraction. *Journal of Personality and Social Psychology, 16*, 259–264.

Aronson, E., Willerman, B., & Floyd, J. (1966). The effect of a pratfall on increasing interpersonal attractiveness. *Psychonomic Science, 4*, 227–228.

Asbell, B. (1995). *The Pill: A biography of the drug that changed the world*. New York: Random House.

Asch, S. E. (1940). Studies in the principles of judgments and attitudes: 11. Determination of judg-

ments by group and by ego standards. *Journal of Social Psychology, 12*, 433–465.

Asch, S. E. (1955). Opinions and social pressure. *Scientific American, 193*(5), 31–35.

Asch, S. E. (1956). Studies of independence and conformity: A minority of one against a unanimous majority. *Psychological Monographs, 70* (9, Whole No. 416).

Aserinsky, E., & Kleitman, N. (1953). Regularly occurring periods of eye mobility and concomitant phenomena during sleep. *Science, 118*, 273–274.

Auerbach, S. M., Kiesler, D. J., Strentz, T., & Schmidt, J. A. (1994). Interpersonal impacts and adjustment to the stress of simulated captivity: An empirical test of the Stockholm syndrome. *Journal of Social and Clinical Psychology, 13*, 207–221.

Averill, J. A.. (1980). A constructivist view of emotion. In R. Plutchik & H. Kellerman (Eds.), *Emotion: Theory, research, and experience: Vol. 1. Theories of emotion*. New York: Academic Press.

Axel, R. (1995, October). The molecular logic of smell. *Scientific American, 273*, 154–159.

Ayllon, T., & Azrin, N. H. (1965). The measurement and reinforcement of behavior of psychotics. *Journal of Experimental Analysis of Behavior, 8*, 357–383.

Ayllon, T., & Azrin, N. H. (1968). *The token economy: A motivational system for therapy and rehabilitation*. New York: Appleton-Century-Crofts.

Azar, B. (1994a, May). New mania treatment is major breakthrough. *APA Monitor*, p. 28.

Azar, B. (1994b, October). Seligman recommends a depression "vaccine." *APA Monitor*, p. 4.

Azar, B. (1995, June). New cognitive research makes waves. *APA Monitor*, p. 16.

Azar, B. (1996, November). Some forms of memory improve as people age. *APA Monitor*, p. 27.

Azar, B. (1997a, March). Human brain inspires new computer models. *APA Monitor*, p. 22.

Azar, B. (1997b, April). Do memories "play back," like films? *APA Monitor*, p. 27.

Azar, B. (1997c, May). Nature, nurture: Not mutually exclusive. *APA Monitor*, pp. 1, 28.

Azar, B. (1997d, May). Human traits defined by mix of environment, genes. *APA Monitor*, p. 27.

Azar, B. (1998a, January). Certain smells evoke stronger memories. *APA Monitor*, p. 10.

Azar, B. (1998b, January). Communicating through pheromones. *APA Monitor*, pp. 1, 12.

Baars, B. J. (1988). *A cognitive theory of consciousness*. Cambridge, England: Cambridge University Press.

Baars, B. J., & McGovern, K. (1994). Consciousness. *Encyclopedia of Human Behavior, 1*, 687–699. San Diego: Academic Press.

Baell, W. K., & Wertheim, E. H. (1992). Predictors of outcome in the treatment of bulimia nervosa. *British Journal of Clinical Psychology, 31*(3), 330–332.

Bailey, J. M., Bobrow, D., Wolfe, M, & Mikach, S. (1995). Sexual orientation of adult sons of gay fathers. *Developmental Psychology, 31*, 124–129.

Balch, P., & Ross, A. W. (1975). Predicting success in weight reduction as a function of locus of control: A uni-dimensional and multi-dimensional approach. *Journal of Consulting and Clinical Psychology, 43*, 119.

Balsam, P. D., & Tomie, A. (Eds.). (1985). *Context and learning*. Hillsdale, NJ: Erlbaum.

Baltes, M. M. (1995). Dependency in old age: Gains and losses. *Current Directions in Psychological Science, 4*, 14–19.

Baltes, P. B. (1987). Theoretical propositions on life-span developmental psychology: On the dynamics between growth and decline. *Developmental Psychology, 23*, 611–626.

Baltes, P. B. (1990, November). *Toward a psychology of wisdom*. Invited address presented at the annual convention of the Gerontological Society of America, Boston, MA.

Baltes, P. B. (1993). The aging mind: Potential and limits. *The Gerontologist, 33*, 580–594.

Baltes, P. B., & Kliegl, R. (1992). Further testing of limits of cognitive plasticity: Negative age differences in a mnemonic skill are robust. *Developmental Psychology, 28*, 121–125.

Bandura, A. (1970). Modeling therapy. In W. S. Sahakian (Ed.), *Psychopathology today: Experimentation, theory and research*. Itasca, IL: Peacock.

Bandura, A. (1981). In search of pure unidirectional determinants. *Behavior Therapy, 12*, 30–40.

Bandura, A. (1986). *Social foundations of thought and action: A social cognitive theory*. Englewood Cliffs, NJ: Prentice-Hall.

Bandura, A. (1992). Exercise of personal agency through the self-efficacy mechanism. In R. Schwarzer (Ed.), *Self-efficacy: Thought control of action* (pp. 3–38). Washington: Hemisphere.

Bandura, A., Ross, D., & Ross, S. A. (1963). Imitation of film-mediated aggressive models. *Journal of Abnormal and Social Psychology, 66*, 3–11.

Banks, M. S., & Bennet, P. J. (1988). Optical and photoreceptor immaturities limit the spatial and chromatic vision of human neonates. *Journal of the Optical Society of America, 5*, 2059–2079.

Barber, T. X. (1976). *Hypnosis: A scientific approach*. New York: Psychological Dimensions.

Barber, T. X. (1979). Suggested ("hypnotic") behavior: The trance paradigm versus an alternative paradigm. In E. Fromm & R. E. Shor (Eds.), *Hypnosis: Developments in research and new perspectives*. New York: Aldine.

Barber, T. X. (1986). Realities of stage hypnosis. In B. Zilbergeld, M. G. Edelstein, & D. L. Araoz (Eds.), *Hypnosis: Questions and answers*. New York: Norton.

Bard, M., & Sangrey, D. (1979). *The crime victim's book*. New York: Basic Books.

Barinaga, M. (1994, July 29). To sleep, perchance to . . . learn? New studies say yes. *Science, 265*, 603–604.

Barinaga, M. (1995, December 1). Brain researchers speak a common language. *Science, 270*, 1437–1438.

Barinaga, M. (1996, January 19). Social status sculpts activity of crayfish neurons. *Science, 271*, 290–291.

Barinaga, M. (1997, June 27). New imaging methods provide a better view into the brain. *Science, 276*, 1974–1976.

Barinaga, M. (1997, July 25). How jet-lag hormone does double duty in the brain. *Science, 277*, 480.

Barinaga, M. (1998, March 27). No-new-neurons dogma loses ground. *Science, 270*, 2041–2042.

Barinaga, M. (1998, July 24). How the brain sees in three dimensions. *Science, 281*, 500–501.

Barker, L. M., Best, M. R., & Domjan, M. (Eds.). (1978). *Learning mechanisms in food selection*. Houston: Baylor University Press.

Barker, S. L., Funk, S. C., & Houston, B. K. (1988). Psychological treatment versus nonspecific factors: A meta-analysis of conditions that engender comparable expectations for improvement. *Clinical Psychology Review, 8*, 579–594.

Barkley, R. A. (1998, September). Attention-deficit hyperactivity disorder. *Scientific American, 279*(9), 66–71.

Barlow, D. H. (1996). Health care policy, psychotherapy research, and the future of psychotherapy. *American Psychologist, 51*, 1050–1058.

Barnes, D. M. (1987). Biological issues in schizophrenia. *Science, 235*, 430–433.

Barnier, A. J., & McConkey, K. M. (1998). Posthypnotic responding away from the hypnotic setting. *Psychological Science, 9*, 256–262.

Barnouw, V. (1963). Culture and personality. Homewood, IL: Dorsey Press.

Baron, L., & Straus, M. A. (1985). *Four theories of rape in American society: A state-level analysis.* New Haven, CT: Yale University Press.

Barondes, S. H. (1994, February 25). Thinking about Prozac. *Science, 263,* 1102–1103.

Barron, F., & Harrington, D. M. (1981). Creativity, intelligence and personality. *Annual Review of Psychology, 32,* 439–476.

Barthe, D. G., & Hammen, C. L. (1981). The attributional model of depression: A naturalistic extension. *Personality & Social Psychology Bulletin, 7*(1), 53–58.

Bartoshuk, L. M. (1990, August–September). Psychophysiological insights on taste. *Science Agenda,* 12–13.

Bartoshuk, L. M. (1993). The biological basis of food perception and acceptance. *Food Quality and Preference, 4,* 21–32.

Bartoshuk, L. M., Duffy, V. B., & Miller, I. J. (1994). PCT/PROP tasting: Anatomy, psychophysics and sex effects. *Physiology and Behavior, 56, 1165–1171.*

Basic Behavioral Science Task Force of the National Advisory Mental Health Council (1996). Basic behavioral science research for mental health: Family processes and social networks. *American Psychologist, 51,* 622–630.

Baskett, L. (1985). Sibling status: Adult expectations. *Developmental Psychology, 21,* 441–445.

Batson, C. D. (1987). Prosocial motivation: Is it ever truly altruistic? In L. Berkowitz (Ed.), *Advances in experimental social psychology* (Vol. 20). Orlando, FL: Academic Press.

Baum, A. (1990). Stress, intrusive imagery, and chronic distress. *Health Psychology, 9,* 653–675.

Baum, W. M. (1994). *Understanding behaviorism: Science, behavior, and culture.* New York: HarperCollins.

Baumeister, A. A. (1987). Mental retardation: Some conceptions and dilemmas. *American Psychologist, 42,* 796–800.

Baumeister, R. F. (Ed.). (1993). *Self-esteem: The puzzle of low self-regard.* New York: Plenum.

Baumeister, R. F., & Leary, M. R. (1995). The need to belong: Desire for interpersonal attachments as a fundamental human motivation. *Psychological Bulletin, 117,* 427–529.

Baumeister, R. F., Stillwell, A. M., & Wotman, S. R. (1990). Victim and perpetrator accounts of interpersonal conflict: Autobiographical narratives about anger. *Journal of Personality and Social Psychology, 59,* 994–1005.

Baumrind, D. (1985). Research using intentional deception: Ethical issues revisited. *American Psychologist, 40,* 165–174.

Baynes, K., Eliassen, J. C., Lutsep, H. L., & Gazzaniga, M. S. (1998). Modular organization of cognitive systems masked by interhemispheric integration. *Science, 280,* 902–905.

Beall, A. E., & Sternberg, R. J. (1995). The social construction of love. *Journal of Social and Personal Relationships, 12* (3), 417–438.

Beaman, A. L., Barnes, P. J., Klentz, B., & McQuirk, B. (1978). Increasing helping rates through information dissemination: Teaching pays. *Personality and Social Psychology Bulletin, 4,* 406–411.

Beardsley, T. (1996, July). Waking up. *Scientific American, 14,* 18.

Beardsley, T. (1997, August). The machinery of thought. *Scientific American, 277,* 78–83.

Bechara, A., Damasio, H., Tranel, D., & Damasio, A. R. (1997, February 28). Deciding advantageously before knowing the advantageous strategy. *Science, 275,* 1293–1295.

Beck, A. T. (1976). *Cognitive therapy and emotional disorders.* New York: International Universities Press.

Beck, A. T., Rush, A. J., Shaw, B. F., & Emery, G. (1979). *Cognitive therapy of depression.* New York: Guilford Press.

Becker, M. H. (1993). A medical sociologist looks at health promotion. *Journal of Health and Social Behavior, 34,* 1–6.

Bédard, J., & Chi, M. T. H. (1992). Expertise. *Current Directions in Psychological Science, 1,* 135–139.

Bee, H. (1994). *Lifespan Development.* New York: HarperCollins.

Begley, S. (1995). Lights of madness. *Newsweek, CXXVI* (21), November 20, pp. 76–77.

Begley, S., & Biddle, N. (1996). For the obsessed, the mind can fix the brain. *Newsweek, Vol. CXXVII* (9), p. 60.

Bell, A. P., Weinberg, M. S., & Hammersmith, S. K. (1981). *Sexual preference.* Bloomington: Indiana University Press.

Bem, D. J., & Allen, A. (1974). On predicting some of the people some of the time: The search for cross-situational consistencies in behavior. *Psychological Review, 81*(6), 506–520.

Benassi, V. A., Sweeney, P. D., & Dufour, C. L. (1988). Is there a relation between locus of control orientation and depression? *Journal of Abnormal Psychology, 97,* 357–367.

Benedict, R. (1934). *Patterns of culture.* Boston: Houghton Mifflin.

Benedict, R. (1959). *Patterns of culture.* Boston: Houghton Mifflin.

Benjamin, L. T., Jr. (1986). Why don't they understand us? A history of psychology's public image. *American Psychologist, 41,* 941–946.

Benson, H. (1975). *The relaxation response.* New York: Morrow.

Berenbaum, H., & Connelly, J. (1993). The effect of stress on hedonic capacity. *Journal of Abnormal Psychology, 102,* 474–481.

Berk, L. (1996). The laughter–immune connection: New discoveries. *Humor and Health Journal, 5,* 1–5.

Berk, L. E. (1991). *Child development.* Boston: Allyn & Bacon.

Berk, L. E. (1994, November). Why children talk to themselves. *Scientific American, 271,* 78–83.

Berkman, L. F., & Syme, S. L. (1979). Social networks, host resistance, and mortality: A nine-year follow-up study of Alameda County residents. *American Journal of Epidemiology, 109,* 186–204.

Berlyne, D. E. (1960). *Conflict, arousal, and curiosity.* New York: McGraw-Hill.

Berman, J. S., & Norton, N. C. (1985). Does professional training make a therapist more effective? *Psychological Bulletin, 98,* 401–407.

Bernard, L. L. (1924). *Instinct.* New York: Holt, Rinehart & Winston.

Berndt, T. J. (1979). Developmental changes in conformity to peers and parents. *Developmental Psychology, 15,* 608–616.

Berndt, T. J. (1992). Friendship and friends' influence in adolescence. *Current Directions in Psychological Science, 1,* 156–159.

Bernstein, I. L. (1988). What does learning have to do with weight loss and cancer? *Proceedings of the Science and Public Policy Seminar of the Federation of Behavioral, Psychological and Cognitive Sciences.* Washington, DC.

Bernstein, I. L. (1990). Salt preference and development. *Developmental Psychology, 26,* 552–554.

Bernstein, I. L. (1991). Aversion conditioning in response to cancer and cancer treatment. *Clinical Psychology Review, 11,* 185–191.

Berry, J. (1992). Cree conceptions of cognitive competence. *International Journal of Psychology, 27,* 73–88.

Berry, J. W., Poortinga, Y. H., Segall, M. H., & Dasen, P. R. (1992). *Cross-cultural psychology: Research and applications.* New York: Cambridge University Press.

Berscheid, E. (1988). Some comments on love's anatomy: or, Whatever happened to old-fashioned lust? In R. J. Sternberg & M. L. Barnes (Eds.), *The psychology of love.* New Haven, CT: Yale University Press.

Beutler, L. E., & Machado, P. P. (1992). Research on psychotherapy. In M. R. Rosenzweig (Ed.), *International psychological science: Progress, problems, and prospects* (pp. 227–252). Washington, DC: American Psychological Association.

Biederman, I. (1989). Higher-level vision. In D. N. Osherson, H. Sasnik, S. Kosslyn, K. Hollerbach, E. Smith, & N. Block (Eds.), *An invitation to cognitive science.* Cambridge, MA: MIT Press.

Billings, A. G., & Moos, R. H. (1985). Life stressors and social resources affect posttreatment outcomes among depressed patients. *Journal of Abnormal Psychology, 94,* 140–153.

Binet, A. (1911). *Les idées modernes sur les enfants.* Paris: Flammarion.

Binitie, A. (1975). A factor-analytical study of depression across cultures (African and European). *British Journal of Psychiatry, 127,* 559–563.

Birenbaum, M., & Montag, I. (1986). On the location of the sensation seeking construct in the personality domain. *Multivariate Behavioral Research, 21,* 357–373.

Blacher, R. S. (1987). General surgery and anesthesia: The emotional experience. In R. S. Blacher (Ed.), *The psychological experience of surgery* (pp. 9–14). New York: Wiley.

Blass, E. M. (1990). Suckling: Determinants, changes, mechanisms, and lasting impressions. *Developmental Psychology, 26,* 520–533.

Blass, T. (1996). Experimental invention and controversy: The life and work of Stanley Milgram. *The General Psychologist, 32,* 47–55.

Blatt, S. J., Sanislow III, C. A., & Pilkonis, P. A. (1996). Characteristics of effective therapists: Further analyses of data from the National Institute of Mental Health treatment of depression collaborative research program. *Journal of Consulting and Clinical Psychology, 64,* 1276–1284.

Block, R. I., Ghoneim, M. M., Sum Ping, S. T., & Ali, M. A. (1991). Efficacy of therapeutic suggestions for improved postoperative recovery presented during general anesthesia. *Anesthesiology, 75,* 746–755.

Blum, D. (1994). *The monkey wars.* New York: Oxford University Press.

Bodmer, W. F., & Cavalli-Sforza, L. L. (1970, October). Intelligence and race. *Scientific American,* pp. 19–29.

Bolger, N., DeLongis, A., Kessler, R. C., & Schilling, E. A. (1989). Effects of daily stress on negative mood. *Journal of Personality and Social Psychology, 57,* 808–818.

Bond, C. F., & Brockett, D. R. (1987). A social context-personality index theory of memory for acquaintances. *Journal of Personality* and *Social Psychology*, *52*, 1110–1121.

Bond, M. H., Nakazato, H. S., & Shiraishi, D. (1975). Universality and distinctiveness in dimensions of Japanese person perception. *Journal of Cross-Cultural Psychology*, *6*, 346–355.

Bongiovanni, A. (1977). A review of research on the effects of punishment in the schools. *Conference on Child Abuse*, Children's Hospital National Medical Center, Washington, DC.

Boomsma, D., Anokhin, A., & de Geus, E. (1997, August). Genetics of electrophysiology: Linking genes, brain, and behavior. *Current Directions in Psychological Science*, *6*, 106–110.

Boone, D. E. (1994). Validity of the MMPI-2 depression content scale with psychiatric inpatients. *Psychological Reports*, *74*, 159–162.

Bootzin, R. R., & Nicasio, P. M. (1978). Behavioral treatments for insomnia. In M. Hersen, R. Eisler, & P. Miller (Eds.), *Progress in behavior modification*. New York: Academic Press.

Borkovec, T. D. (1982). Insomnia. *Journal of Consulting and Clinical Psychology*, *50*, 880–985.

Bornstein, R. F. (1989). Exposure and affect: Overview and meta-analysis of research, 1968–1987. *Psychological Bulletin*, *106*, 265–289.

Borod, C., Koff, E., Lorch, M. P., Nicholas, M., & Welkowitz, J. (1988). Emotional and non-emotional facial behavior in patients with unilateral brain damage. *Journal of Neurological and Neurosurgical Psychiatry*, *5*, 826–832.

Bouchard, T. J., Jr. (1994, June 17). Genes, environment, and personality. *Science*, *264*, 1700–1701.

Bouchard, T. J., Lykken, D. T., McGue, M., Segal, N. L., & Tellegen, A. (1990). Sources of human psychological differences: The Minnesota study of twins reared apart. *Science*, *250*, 223–228.

Bourguignon, E. (1979). *Psychological anthropology: An introduction to human nature and cultural differences*. New York: Holt, Rinehart and Winston.

Bower, B. (1992, August 22). Genetic clues to female homosexuality. *Science News*, *142*, 117.

Bower, B. (1995, March 4). Virus may trigger some mood disorders. *Science News*, *147*, 132.

Bower, B. (1996, April 27). Mom-child relations withstand day care. *Science News*, *149*, 261.

Bower, B. (1997, August 9). The ties that bond: Adult romantic and sexual styles may grow out of parent–child affiliations. *Science News*, *152*, 94–95.

Bower, B. (1998a). Dr. Freud goes to Washington. *Science News*, *154*, 347–349.

Bower, B. (1998b, April 25). The name game: Young kids grasp new words with intriguing dexterity. *Science News*, *153*, 268–269.

Bower, B. (1998c, June 20). Psychology's tangled web. *Science News*, *153*, 394–395.

Bower, B. (1998, September 12). Immigrants go from health to worse. *Science News*, *154*, 180.

Bower, G. H. (1972). A selective review of organizational factors in memory. In E. Tulving & W. Donaldson (Eds.), *Organization of memory*. New York: Academic Press.

Bower, G. H., & Morrow, D. G. (1990, January 5). Mental models in narrative comprehension. *Science*, *247*, 44–48.

Bowers, K. S. (1983). *Hypnosis for the seriously curious* (2nd ed.) New York: Norton.

Bowlby, J. (1969). *Attachment and loss: Vol. 1. Attachment*. New York: Basic Books.

Bowlby, J. (1973). *Attachment and loss: Vol. 2. Separation, anxiety and anger*. London: Hogarth.

Bradley, G. W. (1978). Self-serving biases in the attribution process: A re-examination of the fact or fiction question. *Journal of Personality and Social Psychology*, *35*, 56–71.

Bradshaw, G. (1992). The airplane and the logic of invention. In R. N. Giere (Ed.). *Minnesota studies in philosophy of science* (pp. 2239–250). Minneapolis: University of Minnesota Press.

Bradshaw, J. L. (1989). *Hemispheric specialization and psychological function*. New York: Wiley.

Braine, M. D. S. (1976). Children's first word combinations. *Monographs of the Society for Research in Child Development*, *41* (Serial No. 164).

Bransford, J., Sherwood, R., Vye, N., & Rieser, J. (1986). Teaching thinking and problem solving: Research foundations. *American Psychologist*, *41*, 1078–1089.

Bransford, J. D., & Franks, J. J. (1971). The abstraction of linguistic ideas. *Cognitive Psychology*, *2*, 331–350.

Breggin, P. R. (1979). *Electroshock: Its brain disabling effects*. New York: Springer.

Breggin, P. R. (1991). *Toxic psychiatry*. New York: St. Martin's Press.

Breggin, P. R., & Breggin, G. R. (1994). *Talking back to Prozac*. New York: St. Martin's Press.

Brehm, S. S. (1992). *Intimate relationships*, 2nd edition. Boston, MA: McGraw-Hill.

Brehm, S. S., & Kassin, S. M. (1990). *Social psychology*. Boston: Houghton Mifflin.

Brewer, M. B., Dull, V., and Lui, L. (1981). Perceptions of the elderly: Sterotypes and prototypes. *Journal of Personality and Social Psychology*, *41*, 656–670.

Brigham, J. C. (1980). Limiting conditions of the "physical attractiveness stereotype": Attributions about divorce. *Journal of Research in Personality*, *14*, 365–375.

Bringsjord, S. (1998, March/April). Chess is too easy. *Technology Review*, pp. 23–28.

Brislin, R. (1974). The Ponzo illusion: Additional cues, age, orientation, and culture. *Journal of Cross-Cultural Psychology*, *5*, 139–161.

Brislin, R. (1993). *Understanding culture's influence on behavior*. Fort Worth, TX: Harcourt Brace Jovanovich.

Brislin, R. W. (1981). *Cross-cultural encounters: Face-to-face interaction*. Boston: Allyn and Bacon.

Brody, J. (1994). Personal health: Feeling sleepy in the middle of the day? You're probably not getting enough rest at night. *The New York Times*, January 26.

Brody, N. (1985). The validity of tests of intelligence. In B. B. Wolman (Ed.), *Handbook of intelligence* (pp. 353–389). New York: Wiley.

Brody, R. V. (1986). Pain management in terminal disease. *Focus: A Review of AIDS Research*, *1*, 1–2

Broman, S. H., Nichols, P. I., & Kennedy, W. A. (1975). *Preschool IQ: Prenatal and early developmental correlates*. Hillsdale, NJ: Erlbaum.

Bronfenbrenner, U., & Ceci, S. J. (1994). Nature–nurture reconceptualized in developmental perspective: A bioecological model. *Psychological Review*, *101*, 568–586.

Brown, A. L., & Campione, J. C. (1986). Psychological theory and the study of learning disabilities. *American Psychologist*, *41*, 1059–1068.

Brown, A. M. (1990). *Human universals*. Unpublished manuscript, University of California, Santa Barbara.

Brown, D. E., & Epperson, S. E. (1993, October 11). The personality pill. *Time*, *142*, 61–62.

Brown, J. D. (1991). Accuracy and bias in self-knowledge. In C. R. Snyder & D. F. Forsyth (Eds.), *Handbook of social and clinical psychology: The health perspective*. New York: Pergamon.

Brown, J. L., & Pollitt, E. (1996, February). Malnutrition, poverty and intellectual development. *Scientific American*, *274* (2), 38–43.

Brownell, K. D., & Rodin, J. (1994). The dieting maelstrom: Is it possible and advisable to lose weight? *American Psychologist*, *49*, 781–789.

Bruch, H. (1978). *The golden cage: The enigma of anorexia nervosa*.

Cambridge, MA: Harvard University Press.

Bruck, M., & Ceci, S. (1997). The suggestibility of young children. *Current Directions in Psychological Science*, *6*, 75–79.

Brumberg, J. J. (1988). *Fasting girls: The history of anorexia nervosa*. New York: Plume.

Bruner, J. (1992). Another look at new look 1. *American psychologist*, *47*, 780–783.

Bruner, J. S. (1973). *Beyond the information given*. New York: Norton.

Bruner, J. S., Olver, R. R., & Greenfield, P. M. (1966). *Studies in cognitive growth*. New York: Wiley.

Brunner, H. G., Nelen, M., Breakefield, X. O., Ropers, H. H., & van Oost, B. A. (1993). Abnormal behavior associated with a point mutation in the structural gene for monoamine oxidase A. *Science*, *262*, 578.

Bryden, M. P. (1982). *Laterality: Functional asymmetry in the intact brain*. New York: Academic Press.

Buck, L., & Axel, R. (1991). A novel multigene family may encode odorant receptors: A molecular basis for odor recognition. *Cell*, *65*, 175–187.

Buie, J. (1988, July). "Control" studies bode better health in aging. *APA Monitor*, p. 20.

Bullock, M. (1995). What's so special about a longitudinal study? *Psychological Science Agenda*, *8*, 9–10.

Bushman, B. J., & Baumeister, R. F. (1998). Threatened egotism, narcissism, self-esteem, and direct and displaced aggression: Does self-love or self-hate lead to violence? *Journal of Personality and Social Psychology*, *75*, 219–229.

Buss, D. M., Haselton, M. G., Shackelford, T. K., Bleske, A. L., and Wakefield, J. C. (1998). Adaptations, exaptations, and spandrels. *American Psychologist*, *53*, 533–548.

Buss, D. M., & Schmitt, D. P. (1993). Sexual strategies theory: An evolutionary perspective on human mating. *Psychological Review*, *100*, 204–232.

Butcher, J. N., Graham, J. R., Williams, C. L., & Ben-Porath, Y. (1989). *Development and use of the MMPI-2 content scales*. Minneapolis: University of Minnesota Press.

Butcher, J. N., & Williams, C. L. (1992). *Essentials of MMPI-2 and MMPI-A interpretation*. Minneapolis: University of Minnesota Press.

Byne, W. (1995). The biological evidence challenged. *Scientific American*, *270*(5), 50–55.

Byrne, D. (1969). Attitudes and attraction. In L. Berkowitz (Ed.), *Advances in experimental social psychology* (Vol. 4). New York: Academic Press.

Byrne, D. (1981, August). Predicting human sexual behavior. G. Stanley Hall Lecture, meeting of American Psychological Association, Los Angeles, CA.

Caldwell, M. (1995, June). Kernel of fear. *Discover, 16,* 96–102.

Calev, A., Nigal, D., Shapira, B., Tubi, N., Chazan, S., Ben-Yehuda, Y., Kugelmass, S., & Lerer, B. (1991). Early and long-term effects of electroconvulsive therapy and depression on memory and other cognitive functions. *Journal of Nervous and Mental Disorders, 179,* 526–533.

Callahan, J. (1997, May/June). Hypnosis: Trick or treatment? *Health, 11* (1), 52–55.

Callaway, C. W. (1987). Obesity. *Public Health Reports Supplement, 102,* 26–29.

Calvert, J. D. (1988). Physical attractiveness: A review and reevaluation of its role in social skill research. *Behavioral Assessment, 10,* 29–42.

Calvin, W. H., & Ojemann, G. A. (1994). *Conversations with Neil's brain: The neural nature of thought and language.* Reading, MA: Addison-Wesley.

Campbell, S. S., & Murphy, P. J. (1998, January 16). Extraocular circadian phototransduction in humans. *Science, 279,* 396–399.

Campos, J. J., Barrett, K. C., Lamb, M. E., Goldsmith, H. H., & Stenberg, C. (1983). *Socioemotional development* (Vol. 2). New York: Wiley.

Candland, D. K. (1993). *Feral children and clever animals: Reflections on human nature.* New York: Oxford University Press.

Cann, A., Calhoun, L. G., Selby, J. W., & Kin, H. E. (Eds.). (1981). Rape. *Journal of Social Issues, 37* (Whole No. 4).

Caplow, T. (1982). *Middletown families: Fifty years of change and continuity.* Minneapolis: University of Minnesota Press.

Caporeal, L. R. (1976). Ergotism: The Satan loosed in Salem? *Science, 192,* 21–26.

Caprara, G. V., Barbaranelli, C., Borgoni, L., & Perugini, M. (1993). The Big Five Questionnaire: A new questionnaire for the measurement of the five-factor model. *Personality and Individual Differences, 15,* 281–288.

Carducci, B. J., & Zimbardo, P. G. (1995). Are you shy? *Psychology Today, 28,* 34–40ff.

Carey, S. (1978). The child as word learner. In M. Halle, J. Bresnan, & G. A. Miller (Eds.), *Linguistic theory and psychological reality* (pp. 265–293). Cambridge, MA: MIT Press.

Carlsson, A. (1978). Antipsychotic drugs, neurotransmitters, and schiz-

ophrenia. *American Journal of Psychiatry, 135,* 164–173.

Carmichael, L. (1970). The onset and early development of behavior. In P. H. Mussen (Ed.), *Carmichael's manual of child psychology* (3rd ed., Vol. 1). New York: Wiley.

Carpenter, G. C. (1973). Differential response to mother and stranger within the first month of life. *Bulletin of the British Psychological Society, 16,* 138.

Carson, R. C., Butcher, J. N., & Mineka, S. (1996). *Abnormal psychology and modern life,* 10th ed. New York: HarperCollins.

Carstensen, L. L. (1987). Age-related changes in social activity. In L. L. Carstensen & B. A. Edelstein (Eds.), *Handbook of clinical gerontology* (pp. 222–237). New York: Pergamon Press.

Carstensen, L. L. (1991). Selectivity theory: Social activity in life-span context. In K. W. Schaie (Ed.), *Annual Review of Geriatrics and Gerontology* (Vol. 11). New York: Springer.

Carstensen, L. L., and Freund, A. M. (1994). Commentary: The Resilience of the aging self. *Developmental Review, 14,* 81–92.

Cartwright, R. D. (1977). *Night life: Explorations in dreaming.* Englewood Cliffs, NJ: Prentice Hall.

Cartwright, R. D. (1978). *A primer on sleep and dreaming.* Reading, MA: Addison-Wesley.

Cartwright, R. D. (1982). The shape of dreams. In *1983 Yearbook of Science and the Future.* Chicago: Encyclopaedia Britannica.

Cartwright, R. D. (1984). Broken dreams: A study of the effects of divorce and depression on dream content. *Psychiatry, 47,* 251–259.

Carver, C. S., & Scheier, M. F. (1992). *Perspectives on personality.* Boston: Allyn and Bacon.

Casey, J. F., & Wilson, L. (1991). *The flock.* New York: Fawcett Columbine.

Cash, T. F., & Duncan, N. C. (1984). Physical attractiveness stereotyping among Black American college students. *Journal of Social Psychology, 122,* 71–77.

Cash, T. F., & Janda, L. H. (1984, December). The eye of the beholder. *Psychology Today, 18,* 46–52.

Cash, T. F., & Kilcullen, R. N. (1985). The aye of the beholder: Susceptibility to sexism and beautyism in the evaluation of managerial applicants. *Journal of Applied Social Psychology, 15,* 591–605.

Cassileth, B. R., Lusk, E. J., Miller, D. S., Brown, L. L., & Miller, C. (1985). Psychosocial correlates of survival in advanced malignant disease. *New England Journal of Medicine, 312,* 1551–1555.

Ceci, S. J., & Liker, J. K. (1986). A day at the races: A study of IQ, expertise, and cognitive complexity. *Journal of Experimental Psychology: General, 115,* 255–266.

Ceci, S. J., & Williams, W. M. (1997). Schooling, intelligence, and income. *American Psychologist, 52,* 1051–1058.

Chalmers, D. J. (1995, December). The puzzle of conscious experience. *Scientific American, 273*(6), 80–86.

Chamberlain, K., & Zika, S. (1990). The minor events approach to stress: Support for the use of daily hassles. *British Journal of Psychology, 81,* 469–481.

Chambless, D. L., Sanderson, W. C., Shoham, V., Johnson, S. B., Pope, K. S., Crits-Christoph, P., Baker, M., Johnson, B., Woody, S. R., Sue, S., Beutler, L., Williams, D. A., & McCurry, S. (1996). An update on empirically validated therapies. *The Clinical Psychologist, 49,* 5–18.

Chapman, P. D. (1988). *Schools as sorters: Lewis M. Terman, applied psychology, and the intelligence testing movement, 1890–1930.* New York: New York University Press.

Chi, M., Glaser, R., & Rees, E. (1982). Expertise in problem solving. In R. Sternberg (Ed.), *Advances in the psychology of human intelligence* (Vol. 1). Hillsdale, NJ: Erlbaum.

Chilman, C. S. (1983). *Adolescent sexuality in a changing American society* (2nd ed.). New York: Wiley.

Chomsky, N. (1957). *Syntactic structures.* The Hague: Mouton.

Chomsky, N. (1965). *Aspects of a theory of syntax.* Cambridge, MA: MIT Press.

Chomsky, N. (1972). *Language and mind.* New York: Harcourt Brace Jovanovich.

Chomsky, N. (1975). *Reflections on language.* New York: Pantheon Books.

Chorney, M. J., Chorney, K., Seese, N., Owen, M. J., Daniels, J., McGuffin, P., Thompson, L. A., Detterman, D. K., Benbow, C., Lubinski, D., Eley, T., & Plomin, R. (1998). A quantitative trait locus associated with cognitive ability in children. *Psychological Science, 9,* 159–166.

Christensen, A., & Jacobson, N. S. (1994). Who (or what) can do psychotherapy: The status and challenge of nonprofessional therapies. *Psychological Science, 5,* 8–14.

Churchland, P. M. (1995). *The engine of reason, the seat of the soul: A philosophical journey into the brain.* Cambridge, MA: MIT Press.

Clark, H. H., & Clark, E. V. (1977). *Psychology and language: An introduction to psycholinguistics.* New York: Harcourt Brace Jovanovich.

Clark, E.V. (1983). Meanings and concepts. In J. H. Flavell & E. M. Markman (Eds.), *Handbook of child psychology: Cognitive development* (Vol. 3) (pp. 787–840). New York: Wiley.

Clark, E.V. (1987). The principal of contrast: A constraint on language acquisition. In B. MacWhinney (Ed.), *Mechanisms of language acquisition* (pp. 1–34). Hillsdale, NJ: Erlbaum.

Clark, M. S., Mills, J. R., & Corcoran, D. M. (1989). Keeping track of needs and inputs of friends and strangers. *Personality and Social Psychology Bulletin, 15,* 533–542.

Clark, R. E., & Squire, L. R. (1998, April 3). Classical conditioning and brain systems: The role of awareness. *Science, 280,* 77–81.

Clarke-Stewart, K. A. (1989). Infant day care: Maligned or malignant? *American Psychologist, 44,* 266–273.

Clay, R. A. (1998, November). Preparing for the future: Practitioners seek training for prescribing medication. *APA Monitor,* p. 22–23.

Cleek, M. B., & Pearson, T. A. (1985). Perceived causes of divorce: An analysis of interrelationships. *Journal of Marriage and the Family, 47,* 179–191.

Cobb, S. (1976). Social support as a moderator of stress. *Psychosomatic Medicine, 35,* 375–389.

Cognitive–behavior therapy effective for panic disorder. (1991, November). *APS Observer,* p. 8.

Cohen, D. (1998). Culture, social organization, and patterns of violence. *Journal of Personality and Social Psychology, 75,* 408–419.

Cohen, D., Nisbett, R. E., Bowdle, B. F., & Schwarz, N. (1996). Insult, aggression, and the southern culture of honor: An "experimental ethnography." *Journal of Personality and Social Psychology, 70,* 945–960.

Cohen, M. N. (1998, April 17). Culture, not race, explains human diversity. *The Chronicle of Higher Education,* pp. B4–B5.

Cohen, R. E., & Ahearn, F. L., Jr. (1980). *Handbook for mental health care of disaster victims.* Baltimore: Johns Hopkins University Press.

Cohen, S. (1988). Psychosocial models of the role of social support in the etiology of physical disease. *Health Psychology, 7,* 269–297.

Cohen, S., & Girgus, J. S. (1973). Visual spatial illusions: Many explanations. *Science, 179,* 503–504.

Cohen, S., & McKay, G. (1983). Social support, stress, and the buffering hypotheses: A theoretical analysis. In A. Baum, S. E. Taylor, & J. Singer (Eds.), *Handbook of psychology and health* (Vol. 4). Hillsdale, NJ: Erlbaum.

Cohen, S., & Syme, S. L. (Eds.). (1985). *Social support and health*. Orlando, FL: Academic Press.

Cole, M. (1984). The world beyond our borders: What might our students need to know about it? *American Psychologist, 39,* 998–1005.

Coles, R., & Stokes, G. (1985). *Sex and the American teenager*. New York: Harper & Row.

Collins, N. L., & Read, S. J. (1990). Adult attachment, working models, and relationship quality in dating couples. *Journal of Personality and Social Psychology, 58,* 644–663.

Conger, J. J., & Peterson, A. C. (1984). *Adolescence and youth*, 3rd edition. New York: Harper & Row.

Conrad, R. (1964). Acoustic confusions in immediate memory. *British Journal of Psychology, 55,* 75–84.

*Consumer Reports*. (1995, November). Mental health: Does therapy help? 734–739.

Conway, J. K. (1992). *Written by herself: Autobiographies of American women: An anthology*. New York: Vintage.

Coon, D. J. (1992). Testing the limits of sense and science: American experimental psychologists combat spiritualism, 1880–1920. *American Psychologist, 47,* 143–151.

Cooper, J., & Fazio, R. H. (1984). A new look at dissonance theory. *Advances in Experimental Social Psychology, 17,* 229–266.

Cooper, M. J., & Fairburn, C. G. (1993). Demographic and clinical correlates of selective information processing in patients with bulimia nervosa. *International Journal of Eating Disorders, 13*(1), 109–116.

Cooper, W. H., (1983). An achievement motivation normological network. *Journal of Personality and Social Psychology, 44,* 841–861.

Costa, P. T., Jr., & McCrae, R. R. (1992a). Four ways five factors are basic. *Personality and Individual Differences, 13,* 653–665.

Costa, P. T., Jr., & McCrae, R. R. (1992b). *Revised NEO Personality Inventory (NEO-PI-R) and NEO Five-Factor Inventory (NEO-FFI) professional manual*. Odessa, FL: Psychological Assessment Resources.

Coughlin, E. K. (1994, October 26). Class, IQ, and heredity. *The Chronicle of Higher Education*, pp. A12, A20.

Cousins, N. (1979). *The anatomy of an illness as perceived by a patient: Reflections on healing and rejuvenation*. New York: Norton.

Cousins, N. (1989). *Head first: The biology of hope*. New York: Dutton.

Cowan, N. (1993). Activation, attention, and short-term memory. *Memory and Cognition, 21,* 162–167.

Cowan, P., & Cowan, P. A. (1988). Changes in marriage during the transition to parenthood. In G. Y. Michaels & W. A. Goldberg (Eds.), *The transition to parenthood: Current theory and research*. Cambridge: Cambridge University Press.

Cowan, P. A. (1988). Developmental psychopathology: A nine-cell map of the territory. In E. Nannis & P. A. Cowan (Eds.), *Developmental psychopathology and its treatment: New directions for child development* (No. 39, pp. 5–29). San Francisco: Jossey Bass.

Coyne, J. C., Burchill, S. A. L., & Stiles, W. B. (1991). An interactional perspective on depression. In C. R. Snyder & D. O. Forsyth (Eds.), *Handbook of social and clinical psychology: The health perspective* (pp. 327–349). New York: Pergamon Press.

Coyne, J. C., Wortman, C. B., & Lehman, D. R. (1988). The other side of support: Emotional overinvolvement and miscarried helping. In B. Gottlieb (Ed.), *Marshalling social support* (pp. 305–330). Newbury Park, CA: Sage.

Craig, A. D., & Reiman, E. M. (1996, November 21). Functional imaging of an illusion of pain. *Nature, 384,* 258–260.

Craske, M. G., & Barlow, D. H. (1993). Panic disorder and agoraphobia. In D. H. Barlow (Ed.), *Clinical handbook of psychological disorders: A step-by-step treatment manual* (2nd ed., pp. 1–47). New York: Guilford Press.

Crawford, C. B., & Anderson, J. L. (1989). Sociobiology: An environmentalist discipline? *American Psychologist, 44,* 1149–1459

Crick, F. (1994). *The astonishing hypothesis: The scientific search for the soul*. New York: Charles Scribner's Sons.

Crick, F., & Mitchison, G. (1983). The function of dream sleep. *Nature, 304,* 111–114.

Crocker, J., & Major, B. (1989). Social stigma and self-esteem: The self-protective properties of stigma. *Psychological Review, 96,* 608–630.

Crohan, S. E., Antonucci, T. C., Adelmann, P. K., & Coleman, L. M. (1989). Job characteristics and well-being at mid-life. *Psychology of Women Quarterly, 13,* 223–235.

Cromwell, R. L. (1993). Searching for the origins of schizophrenia. *Psychological Science, 4,* 276–279.

Csikszentmihalyi, M. (1990). *Flow: The psychology of optimal experience*. New York: Harper & Row.

Csikszentmihalyi, M. (1998). *Finding flow*. New York: Basic Books.

Csikszentmihalyi, M., Larson, R., & Prescott, S. (1977). The ecology of adolescent activity and experience. *Journal of Youth and Adolescence, 6,* 281–294.

Csikszentmihalyi, M., Rathunde, K. R., Whalen, S., & Wong, M. (1993). *Talented teenagers: The roots of success and failure*. New York: Cambridge University Press.

Cushman, P. (1990). Why the self is empty: Toward a historically situated psychology. *American Psychologist, 45,* 599–611.

Dackman, L. (1986). Everyday illusions. *Exploratorium Quarterly, 10,* 5–7.

Dahlstrom, W. G., Welsh, H. G., & Dahlstrom, L. E. (1975). *An MMPI handbook, Vol. 1: Clinical interpretation*. Minnesota: University of Minnesota Press.

Dakof, G. A., & Taylor, S. E. (1990). Victims' perceptions of social support: What is helpful from whom? *Journal of Personality and Social Psychology, 58,* 80–89.

Damasio, A. R. (1997, June). Thinking and feeling. *Scientific American*, pp. 140–141.

Damasio, H., Grabowski, T., Frank, R., Balaburda, A. M., & Damasio, A. R. (1994). The return of Phineas Gage: Clues about the brain from the skull of a famous patient. *Science, 264,* 1102–1105.

Dannefer, D., & Perlmutter, M. (1990). Developmental as a multidimensional process: Individual and social constituents. *Human Development, 33,* 108–137.

Darley, J. M., & Batson, C. D. (1973). From Jerusalem to Jericho: A study of situational and dispositional variables in helping behavior. *Journal of Personality and Social Psychology, 27,* 100–108.

Darley, J. M., & Latan, B. (1968) Bystander intervention in emergencies: Diffusion of responsibility. *Journal of Personality and Social Psychology, 8,* 377–383.

Darnton, R. (1968). *Mesmerism and the end of the Enlightenment in France*. Cambridge, MA: Harvard University Press.

Darwin, C. (1963). *On the origin of species*. London: Oxford University Press. (Original work published in 1859).

Darwin, C. (1998). *The expression of the emotions in man and animals* (3rd ed., with Introduction, Afterword, and Commentaries by P. Ekman). New York: Oxford University Press. (Original work published in 1862).

Darwin, C. J., Turvey, M. T., & Crowder, R. G. (1972). The auditory analogue of the Sperling partial report procedure: Evidence for brief auditory stage. *Cognitive Psychology, 3,* 255–267.

Dattilio, F. M., & Padesky, C. A. (1990). *Cognitive therapy with couples*. Sarasota, FL: Professional Resource Exchange.

Daum, I., & Schugens, M. M. (1996). On the cerebellum and classical conditioning. *Current Directions in Psychological Science, 5,* 58–61.

Davidson, J. M. (1980). The psychobiology of sexual experience. In J. M. Davidson & R. J. Davidson (Eds.), *The psychobiology of consciousness* (pp. 271–331). New York: Plenum.

Davidson, J. M. (1981). The psychobiology of sexual experience. In J. M. Davidson & R.J. Davidson (Eds.), *The psychobiology of consciousness* (pp. 271–331). New York: Plenum.

Davidson, R. J. (1984). Hemispheric asymmetry and emotion. In K. Scherer & P. Ekman (Eds.), *Approaches to emotion*. Hillsdale, NJ: Erlbaum.

Davidson, R. J. (1992a). Anterior cerebral asymmetry and the nature of emotion. *Brain and Cognition, 20,* 125–151.

Davidson, R. J. (1992b). Emotion and affective style: Hemispheric substrates. *Psychological Science, 3,* 39–43.

Davidson, R. J., & Cacioppo, J. T. (1992). New developments in the scientific study of emotion. *Psychological Science, 3,* 21–22.

Davis, H. P., Rosenzweig, M. R., Becker, L. A., & Sather, K. J. (1988). Biological psychology's relationships to psychology and neuroscience. *American Psychologist, 43,* 359–371.

Davis, I. P. (1985). *Adolescents: Theoretical and helping perspectives*. Boston: Kluwer-Nijhoff Publishing.

Deadwyler, S. A., & Hampson, R. E. (1995, November 24). Ensemble activity and behavior: What's the code? *Science, 270,* 1316–1318.

DeAngelis, T. (1997, January). Chromosomes contain clues on schizophrenia. *APA Monitor*, p. 26.

DeCasper, A. J., & Fifer, W. P. (1980). Of human bonding: Newborns prefer their mothers' voices. *Science, 208,* 1174–1176.

DeCasper, A.J., and Spence, M.J. (1986). Prenatal maternal speech influences newborns' perception of speech sounds. *Infant Behavior and Development, 9,* 133–150.

Deci, E. L. (1975). *Intrinsic motivation*. New York: Plenum.

de Groot, A. D. (1965). *Thought and choice in chess*. The Hague: Mouton.

Delgado, J. M. R. (1969). *Physical control of the mind: Toward a psychocivilized society*. New York: Harper & Row.

Dembroski, T. M., & Costa, P. T., Jr. (1987). Coronary prone behavior: Components of the Type A pattern and hostility. *Journal of Personality, 55,* 211–235.

Dembroski, T. M., Weiss, S. M., Shields, J. L. et al. (1978). *Coro-*

nary-prone behavior. New York: Springer-Verlag.

Dement, W. C. (1980). Some watch while some must sleep. San Francisco: San Francisco Book Co.

Dement, W. C., & Kleitman, N. (1957). Cyclic variations in EEG during sleep and their relations to eye movement, body mobility and dreaming. Electroencephalography and Clinical Neurophysiology, 9, 673–690.

Dennis, W. (1960). Causes of retardation among institutionalized children: Iran. Journal of Genetic Psychology, 96, 47–59.

Dennis, W., & Dennis, M. G. (1940). The effect of cradling practices upon the onset of walking in Hopi children. Journal of Genetic Psychology, 56, 77–86.

Denollet, J., & Sys, S. U. (1996, February 17). Personality as independent predictor of long-term mortality in patients with coronary heart disease. Lancet, 347, 417–421.

Deregowski, J. B. (1980). Illusions, patterns and pictures: A cross-cultural perspective (pp. 966–977). London: Academic Press.

Deutsch, M., & Collins, M. E. (1951). Interracial housing: A psychological evaluation of a social experiment. Minneapolis: University of Minnesota Press.

Deutsch, M., & Gerard, H. B. (1955). A study of normative and informational social influence upon individual judgment. Journal of Abnormal and Social Psychology, 51, 629–636.

Devanand, D. P., Verma, A. K., Tirumalasetti, F., & Sackheim, H. A. (1991). Absence of cognitive impairment after more than 100 lifetime ECT treatments. American Journal of Psychiatry, 148, 929–932.

Devereux, G. (1981). Mohave ethnopsychiatry and suicide: The psychiatric knowledge and psychic disturbances of an Indian tribe. Bureau of American Ethology Bulletin 175. Washington, DC: Smithsonian Institution.

Devine, P. G., & Zuwerink, J. R. (1994). Prejudice and guilt: The internal struggle to overcome prejudice. In W. J. Lonner & R. Malpass (Eds.), Psychology and culture (pp. 203–207). Boston: Allyn & Bacon.

Dewsbury, D. A. (1990). Early interactions between animal psychologists and animal activists and the founding of the APA Committee on Precautions in Animal Experimentation. American Psychologist, 45, 315–327.

Dewsbury, D. A. (1997). In celebration of the centennial of Ivan P. Pavlov's (1897/1902) The work of the digestive glands. American Psychologist, 52, 933–935.

Diamond, J. (1990). The great leap forward. Discover (Special Issue), pp. 66–77.

Diener, E. (1984). Subjective well-being. Psychological Bulletin, 95, 542–575.

Diener, E., & Diener, C. (1996). Most people are happy. Psychological Science, 7, 181–189.

Diener, E., Sandvik, E., Seidlitz, L., & Diener, M. (1993). The relationship between income and subjective well-being: Relative or absolute? Social Indicators Research, 28, 195–223.

Digman, J. M. (1990). Personality structure: Emergence of the five-factor model. Annual Review of Psychology, 41, 417–440.

Dillbeck, M. C., & Orme-Johnson, D. W. (1987). Physiological differences between transcendental meditation and rest. American Psychologist, 42 (9), 879–881.

Dion, K. K. (1986). Stereotyping based on physical attractiveness: Issues and conceptual perspectives. In C. P. Herman, M. P. Zanna, & E. T. Higgins (Eds.), Physical appearance, stigma, and social behavior: The Ontario symposium on personality and social psychology (Vol. 3). Hillsdale, NJ: Erlbaum.

Dirks, J. (1982). The effect of a commercial game on children's Block Design scores on the WISC-R test. Intelligence, 6, 109–123.

Discovering Psychology. (1990). PBS Video Series. Washington, D.C.: Annenberg/CPB Project.

Dixon, R. A., Kramer, D. A., & Baltes, P. B. (1985). Intelligence: A life-span developmental perspective. In B. B. Wolman (Ed.), Handbook of intelligence (pp. 301–352). New York: Wiley.

Dobbins, A. C., Jeo, R. M., Fiser, J., & Allman, J. M. (1998, July 24). Distance modulation of neural activity in the visual cortex. Science, 281, 552–555.

Dobelle, W. (1977). Current status of research on providing sight to the blind by electrical stimulation of the brain. Journal of Visual Impairment and Blindness, 71, 290–297.

Dohrenwend, B. P., & Shrout, P. E. (1985). "Hassles" in the conceptualization and measurement of life stress variables. American Psychologist, 40, 780–785.

Dohrenwend, B. S., & Dohrenwend, B. P. (1974). Stressful life events: Their nature and effects. New York: Wiley.

Dollard, J., & Miller, N. E. (1950). Personality and psychotherapy. New York: McGraw-Hill.

Domhoff, G. W. (1996). Finding meaning in dreams: A quantitative approach. New York: Plenum Press.

Donchin, E. (1975). On evoked potentials, cognition, and memory. Science, 790, 1004–1005.

Douglas, M. E. (1996, October). Creating eustress in the workplace: A supervisor's role. Supervision, 57, 6–9.

Dowling, J. E. (1992). Neurons and networks: An introduction to neuroscience. Cambridge, MA: Harvard University Press.

Draguns, J. (1980). Psychological disorders of clinical severity. In H. Triandis & J. Draguns (Eds.), Handbook of cross-cultural psychology, Vol. 6: Psychopathology (pp. 99–174). Boston: Allyn & Bacon.

Draguns, J. G. (1979). Culture and personality. In A. J. Marsella, R. G. Tharp, & T. J. Ciborowski (Eds.), Perspectives on cross-cultural psychology (pp. 179–207). New York: Academic Press.

Drake, R. E., Osher, F. C., & Wallach, M. A. (1991). Homelessness and dual diagnosis. American Psychologist, 46, 1149–1158.

Druckman, D., & Bjork, R. (Eds.) (1991). In the mind's eye: Enhancing human performance. Washington, D. C.: National Academy Press.

Druckman, D., & Bjork, R. A. (1991). In the mind's eye: Enhancing human performance. Washington, DC: National Academy Press.

Duck, S. (1992). Human relationships, 2nd edition. Newbury Park, CA: Sage.

Duncker, K. (1945). On problem solving. Psychological Monographs, 58 (No. 270).

Dunlap, J. (1998, June 5). Circadian rhythms: An end in the beginning. Science, 280, 1548–1549.

Dutton, D. G., & Aron, A. P. (1974). Some evidence for heightened sexual attraction under conditions of high anxiety. Journal of Personality and Social Psychology, 30, 510–517.

Dykema, J., Bergbower, K., & Peterson, C. (1995). Pessimistic explanatory style, stress, and illness. Journal of Social and Clinical Psychology, 14, 357–371.

Eagly, A. H., Ashmore, R. D., Makhijani, M. G., & Kennedy, L. C. (1991). What is beautiful is good, but. . . : A meta-analytic review of the social psychological literature. Psychological Bulletin, 100, 283–308.

Ebbinghaus, H. (1973). Psychology: An elementary textbook. New York: Arno Press. (Original work published 1908).

Eccles, J. S., Midgley, C., Wigfield, A., Buchanan, C. M., Reuman, D., Flanagan, C., & Mac Iver, D. (1993). Development during adolescence: The impact of stage-environment fit on young adolescents' experiences in schools and in families. American Psychologist, 48, 90–101.

Eckensberger, L. H. (1994). Moral development and its measurement across cultures. In W. J. Lonner & R. Malpass (Eds.), Psychology and culture (pp. 71–78). Boston, MA: Allyn & Bacon.

Educational Testing Service. (1990a, October 31). Background on the new SAT-I and SAT-II. Announcement at the College Board National Forum.

Educational Testing Service. (1990b). Manual and technical report for the School and College Ability Tests, Series III. Menlo Park, CA: Addison-Wesley.

Edwards, A. E., & Acker, L. E. (1962). A demonstration of the long-term retention of a conditioned galvanic skin response. Psychosomatic Medicine, 24, 459–463.

Edwards, R. (1995a, February). New tools help gauge marital success. APA Monitor.

Edwards, R. (1995b, February). Healthy divorces can lead to well-adjusted children. APA Monitor, p. 7.

Eichenbaum, H. (1997, July 18). How does the brain organize memories? Science, 277, 330–332.

Eichorn, D. H., & VandenBos, G. R. (1985). Dissemination of scientific and professional knowledge: Journal publication within the APA. American Psychologist, 40, 1309–1316.

Eisenberger, R., & Cameron, J. (1996). Detrimental effects of reward: Reality or myth? American Psychologist, 51, 1153–1166.

Ekman, P. (1984). Expression and the nature of emotion. In K. R. Scherer & P. Ekman (Eds.), Approaches to emotion. Hillsdale, NJ: Erlbaum.

Ekman, P. (1992). Facial expressions of emotion: New findings, new questions. Psychological Science, 3, 34–38.

Ekman, P. (1993). Facial expression and emotion. American Psychologist, 48, 384–392.

Ekman, P. (1994). Strong evidence for universals in facial expressions: A reply to Russell's mistaken critique. Psychological Bulletin, 115, 268–287.

Ekman, P., & Friesen, W. V. (1971). Constants across cultures in the face and emotion. Journal of Personality and Social Psychology, 17, 124–129.

Ekman, P., & Friesen, W. V. (1975). Unmasking the face: A guide to recognizing emotions from facial clues. Englewood Cliffs, NJ: Prentice-Hall.

Ekman, P., & Friesen, W. V. (1986). A new pan-cultural facial expression of emotion. Motivation and Emotion, 10, 159–168.

Ekman, P., Friesen, W. V., O'Sullivan, M., Chan, A., Diacoyanni-Tarlatzis, I., Heider, K., Krause, R.,

LeCompte, W. A., Pitcairn, T., Ricci-Bitti, P. E., Scherer, K., Tomita, M., & Tzavaras, A. (1987). Universal and cultural differences in the judgments of facial expressions of emotion. *Journal of Personality and Social Psychology, 53*, 712–717.

Ekman, P., Sorenson, E. R., & Friesen, W. V. (1969). Pan-cultural elements in facial displays in emotion. *Science, 764*, 86–88.

Elbert, T., Pantev, C., Wienbruch, C., Rockstroh, B., & Taub, E. (1995, October 13). Increased cortical representation of the fingers of the left hand in string players. *Science, 270*, 305–307.

Eley, T. C. (1997). General genes: A new theme in developmental psychopathology. *Current Directions in Psychological Science, 6*, 90–95.

Elkin, I., Shea, M. T., Watkins, J. T., Imber, S. D., Sotsky, S. M., Collins, J. F., Glass, D. R., Pilkonis, P. A., Leber, W. R., Kocherty, J. P., Fiester, S. J. & Parloff, M. B. (1989). National Institutes of Mental Health treatment of depression collaborative research program: General effectiveness of treatments. *Archives of General Psychiatry, 46*, 971–982.

Elliott, G. R., & Eisdorfer, C. (Eds.). (1982). *Stress and human health: Analysis and implications of research* (A study by the Institute of Medicine/National Academy of Sciences). New York: Springer.

Ellis, A. (1987). *The practice of rational emotive therapy (RET)*. New York: Springer.

Ellis A. (1990). *The essential Albert Ellis: Seminal writings on psychotherapy*. New York: Springer.

Ellis, A. (1996). *Better, deeper, and more enduring brief therapy: The rational emotive behavior therapy approach*. New York: Brunner/Mazel Publishers.

Ellis, A., & Grieger, R. (1986). *Handbook of rational emotive therapy* (Vol. 2). New York: Springer.

Ellison, J. (1984, June). The seven frames of mind. *Psychology Today, 18*, 21–24, 26.

Ellsworth, P. C. (1994). William James and emotion: Is a century of fame worth a century of misunderstanding? *Psychological Review, 101*, 222–229.

Emmelkamp, P. M. (1986). Behavior therapy with adults. In S. L. Garfield & A. E. Bergin (Eds.), *Handbook of psychotherapy and behavior change* (pp. 385–442). New York: Wiley.

Emmons, R. A. (1986). Personal strivings: An approach to personality and its subjective well being. *Journal of Personality and Social Psychology, 51*, 1058–1068.

Epstein, S. (1980). The stability of confusion: A reply to Mischel and

Peake. *Psychological Review, 90*, 179–184.

Epstein, S., & Feist, G. J. (1988). Relation between self- and other-acceptance and its moderation by identification. *Journal of Personality and Social Psychology, 54*, 309–315.

Erdberg, P. (1990). Rorschach assessment. In G. Goldstein & M. Hersen (Eds.), *Psychological assessment* (2nd ed.). New York: Pergamon.

Erdelyi, M. H. (1992). Psychodymanics and the unconscious. *American Psychologist, 47*, 784–787.

Ericsson, K. A., & Charness, N. (1994). Expert performance: Its structure and acquisition. *American Psychologist, 49*, 725–747.

Ericsson, K. A., Krampe, R. T., & Tesch-Römer, C. (1993). The role of deliberate practice in the acquisition of expert performance. *Psychological Review, 100*, 363–406.

Erikson, E. H. (1963). *Childhood and society* (2nd. ed.). New York: Norton.

Erikson, K. A., & Simon, H. A. (1993). Protocol analysis: Verbal reports as data (rev. ed.) Cambridge, MA: MIT Press.

Evans, C., & Richardson, P. H. (1988). Improved recovery and reduced post-operative stay after therapeutic suggestions during general anesthesia. *The Lancet, 2*, 491–493.

Exner, J. E., Jr. (1974). *The Rorschach: A comprehensive system: Vol. 1*. New York: Wiley.

Exner, J. E., Jr. (1978). *The Rorschach: A comprehensive system: Vol. 2: Current research and interpretation*. New York: Wiley.

Exner, J. E., Jr., & Weiner, I. B. (1982). *The Rorschach: A comprehensive system: Vol. 3: Assessment of children and adolescents*. New York: Wiley.

Eysenck, H. J. (1952). The effects of psychotherapy: An evaluation. *Journal of Consulting Psychology, 16*, 319–324.

Eysenck, H. J. (1967). *The biological basis of personality*. Springfield, IL: Charles C. Thomas.

Eysenck, H. J. (1992). Four ways five factors are *not* basic. *Personality and Individual Differences, 13*, 667–673.

Eysenck, H. J., & Eysenck, M. W. (1985). *Personality and individual differences: A natural science approach*. New York: Plenum.

Fajans, J. (1985). The person in social context: The social character of Baining "psychology." In G. M. White & J. Kirkpatrick (Eds.), *Person, self, and experience* (pp. 367–400). Berkeley: University of California Press.

Fallon, A., & Rozin, P. (1985). Sex differences in perceptions of desirable body states. *Journal of Abnormal Psychology, 94*, 102–105.

Fantz, R. L. (1963). Pattern vision in newborn infants. *Science, 140*, 296–297.

Farah, M. J. (1984). The neurological basis of mental imagery: A componential analysis. *Cognition, 18*, 245–272.

Farquhar, J. W., Maccoby, N., & Solomon, D. S. (1984). Community applications of behavioral medicine. In W. D. Gentry (Ed.), *Handbook of behavioral medicine* (pp. 437–478). New York: Guilford Press.

Featherman, D. L. (1980). Schooling and occupational careers: Constancy and change in worldly success. In O. G. Brim, Jr., and J. Kagan (Eds.), *Constancy and change in human development*. Cambridge, MA: Harvard University Press.

Fehr, B. (1988). How do I love thee? Let me consult my prototype. *Journal of Personality and Social Psychology, 55* (4), 557–579.

Fein, M. L. (1993). *I.A.M.: A common sense guide to coping with anger*. Westport, CT: Praeger/Greenwood.

Feingold, A. (1988). Matching for attractiveness in romantic partners and same-sex friends: A meta-analysis and theoretical critique. *Psychological Bulletin, 104*, 226–235.

Feingold, A. (1990). Gender differences in effects of physical attractiveness on romantic attraction: A comparison across five research paradigms. *Journal of Personality and Social Psychology, 59*, 981–993.

Ferster. D., & Spruston, N. (1995, November 3). Cracking the neuronal code. *Science, 270*, 756–757.

Festinger, L. (1957). *A theory of cognitive dissonance*. Stanford, CA: Stanford University Press.

Festinger, L., Schachter, S., & Back, K. (1950). *Social pressures in informal groups: A study of a housing community*. New York: Harper & Row.

Fetz, E. E. (1997, December 12). Temporal coding in neural populations? *Science, 278*, 1901–1902.

Feynman, R. P. (1985). *Surely you're joking, Mr. Feynman!* New York: W. W. Norton.

Field, T. (1990). In *Discovering Psychology*, Program 4 [PBS video series]. Washington, DC: Annenberg/CPB Project.

Field, T. F., & Schanberg, S. M. (1990). Massage alters growth and catecholamine production in preterm newborns. In N. Gunzenhauser (Ed.), *Advances in touch* (pp. 96–104). Skillman, NJ: Johnson & Johnson Co.

Fields, H. L. (1978, November). Secrets of the placebo. *Psychology Today*, p. 172.

Fields, H. L., & Levine, J. D. (1984). Placebo analgesia: A role for endorphins. *Trends in Neuroscience, 7*, 271–273.

Filsinger, E. E., & Fabes, R. A. (1985). Odor communication, pheromones, and human families. *Journal of Marriage and the Family, 47*, 349–359.

Findley, M. J., & Cooper, H. M. (1983). Locus of control and academic achievement: A literature review. *Journal of Personality and Social Psychology, 44*, 419–427.

Finer, B. (1980). Hypnosis and anaesthesia. In G. D. Burrows & L. Donnerstein (Eds.), *Handbook of hypnosis and psychosomatic medicine*. Amsterdam: Elsevier/North Holland Biomedical Press.

Fiorito, G., & Scotto, P. (1992). Observational learning in *Octopus vulgaris*. *Science, 256*, 545–547.

Fischer, A. H. (1993). Sex differences in emotionality: Fact or stereotype? *Feminism & Psychology, 3*, 303–318.

Fischer, P. C., Smith, R. J., Leonard, E., Fuqua, D. R., et al. (1993). Sex differences on affective dimensions: Continuing examination. *Journal of Counseling and Development, 71*, 440–443.

Fischer, P. J., & Breakey, W. R. (1991). The epidemiology of alcohol, drug, and mental disorders among homeless persons. *American Psychologist, 46*, 1115–1128.

Fish, J. M. (1973). *Placebo therapy*. San Francisco: Jossey-Bass.

Fisher, H. E. (1992). *Anatomy of love: The natural history of monogamy, adultery, and divorce*. New York: W. W. Norton and Company.

Fisher, S., & Greenberg, R. P. (1985). *The scientific credibility of Freud's theories and therapy*. New York: Columbia University Press.

Fishman, H. C. (1993). *Intensive structural therapy: Treating families in their social context*. New York: Basic Books.

Fiske, D. W., & Fogg, L. (1990). But the reviewers are making different criticisms of my paper! Diversity and uniqueness in reviewer comments. *American Psychologist, 45*, 591–598.

Fiske, S. T., & Neuberg, S. L. (1990). A continuum of impression formation, from category-based to individuating processes: Influences of information and motivation on attention and interpretation. In M. P. Zanna (Ed.), *Advances in experimental social psychology* (Vol. 23). San Diego, CA: Academic Press.

Flavell, J. H. (1985). *Cognitive development* (2nd ed.). Englewood Cliffs, NJ: Prentice-Hall.

Flavell, J. H. (1996). Piaget's legacy. *Psychological Science, 7*, 200–203.

Fletcher, G. J. O., & Ward, C. (1988). Attribution theory and processes: A cross-cultural perspective. In M. H. Bond (Ed.), *The cross-cultural challenge to social psychology* (pp. 230–244). Newbury Park, CA: Sage.

Fodor, J. (1983). *The modularity of mind*. Cambridge, MA: MIT Press.

Fogel, A. (1991). Movement and communication in human infancy: The social dynamics of development. *Human Movement Science, 11,* 387–423.

Foley, V. D. (1979). Family therapy. In R. J. Corsini (Ed.), *Current psychotherapies* (2nd ed., pp. 460–469). Itasca, IL: Peacock.

Folkes, V. S. (1982). Forming relationships and the matching hypothesis. *Journal of Personality and Social Psychology, 8,* 631–636.

Folkins, C. H., & Sime, W. (1981). Physical fitness training and mental health. *American Psychologist, 36,* 373–389.

Ford, C. S., & Beach, F. A. (1951). *Patterns of sexual behavior.* New York: Harper & Row.

Fowler, H. (1965). *Curiosity and exploratory behavior.* New York: Macmillan.

Frank, J. (1990). In *Discovering Psychology,* Program 2 [PBS video series]. Washington, DC: Annenberg/CPB Project.

Frank, J. D. (1973). *Persuasion and healing: A comparative study of psychotherapy* (Rev. ed.) Baltimore: Johns Hopkins University Press.

Frank, J. D. (1982). Therapeutic components shared by all psychotherapies. In J. H. Harvey & M. M. Parks (Eds.), *Psychotherapy research and behavior change.* Washington, DC: American Psychological Association.

Frank, J. D., & Frank, J. B. (1991). *Persuasion and healing: A comparative study of psychotherapy* (3rd ed.) Baltimore: Johns Hopkins University Press.

Fraser, S. (Ed.). (1995). *The bell curve wars: Race, intelligence, and the future of America.* New York: Basic Books.

Freedman, J. L. (1984) Effect of television violence on aggression. *Psychological Bulletin, 96,* 227–246.

Freedman, J. L. (1996, May). Violence in the mass media and violence in society: The link is unproven. *Harvard Mental Health Letter, 12* (11), 4–6.

French, E. G., & Thomas, F. H. (1958). The relation of achievement motivation to problem-solving effectiveness. *Journal of Abnormal and Social Psychology, 56,* 46-48.

Freud, S. (1915). Instincts and their vicissitudes. In S. Freud, *The collected papers.* New York: Collier.

Freud, S. (1925). The unconscious. In S. Freud, *The collected papers* (Vol. 4). London: Hogarth.

Freud, S. (1953). *The interpretation of dreams.* New York: Basic Books. (Original edition published in 1900).

Frey, W. H., II, Hoffman-Ahern, C., Johnson, R. A., Lydden, D. T., & Tuason, V. B. (1983). Crying behavior in the human adult. *Integrative Psychiatry, 1,* 94–98.

Fridlund, A. J. (1990). Evolution and facial action in reflex, social motive, and paralanguage. In P. K. Ackles, J. R. Jennings, & M. G. H. Coles (Eds.), *Advances in psychophysiology.* Greenwich, CT: JAI Press.

Friedman, H. S., & Booth-Kewley, S. (1988). Validity of the Type A construct: A reprise. *Psychological Bulletin, 104,* 381–384.

Friedman, H. S., Hawley, P. H., & Tucker, J. S. (1994). Personality, health, and longevity. *Current Directions in Psychological Science, 3,* 37–41.

Friedman, H. S., Tucker, J. S., Schwartz, J. E., Tomlinson-Keasey, C., Martin, L. R., Wingard, D. L., & Criqui, M. H. (1995). Psychosocial and behavioral predictors of longevity: The aging and death of the "termites." *American Psychologist, 50,* 69–78.

Friedman, M., & Rosenman, R. F. (1974). *Type A behavior and your heart.* New York: Knopf.

Friedman, M., Thoresen, C. E., & Gill, J. J. (1981). Type A behavior: Its possible role, detection, and alteration in patients with ischemic heart disease. In J. W. Hurst (Ed.), *The heart: Update V.* Hightstown, NJ: McGraw-Hill.

Friedman, M., & Ulmer, D. (1984). *Treating Type A behavior—and your heart.* New York: Knopf.

Friend, R., Rafferty, Y., & Bramel, D. (1990). A puzzling misinterpretation of the Asch "conformity" study. *European Journal of Social Psychology, 20,* 29–44.

Fromm, E., & Shor, R. E. (Eds.). (1979). *Hypnosis: Developments in research and new perspectives* (2nd ed.). Hawthorne, NY: Aldine.

Fujita, F., Diener, E., & Sandvik, E. (1991). Gender differences in dysphoria and well-being: The case for emotional intensity. *Journal of Personality and Social Psychology, 61,* 427–434.

Funder, D. C. (1983a). Three issues in predicting more of the people: A reply to Mischel & Peake. *Psychological Review, 90,* 283–289.

Funder, D. C. (1983b). The "consistency" controversy and the accuracy of personality judgments. *Journal of Personality, 51,* 346–359.

Funder, D. C., & Ozer, D. J. (1983). Behavior as a function of the situation. *Journal of Personality and Social Psychology, 44,* 107–112.

Furnham, A. (1982). Explanations for unemployment in Britain. *European Journal of Social Psychology, 12,* 335–352.

Gabbay, F. H. (January, 1992). Behavior-genetic strategies in the study of emotion. *Psychological Science, 3*(1), 50–54.

Gagnon, J. H. (1977). *Human sexualities.* Glenview, IL: Scott, Foresman.

Gainetdinov, R. R., Wetsel, W. C., Jones, S. R., Levin, E. D., Jaber, M., & Caron, M. G. (1999). Role of serotonin in the paradoxical calming effect of psychostimulants on hyperactivity. *Science, 283,* 397–401.

Galambos, N. L. (1992). Parent–adolescent relations. *Current Directions in Psychological Science, 1,* 146–149.

Gallagher, W. (1994, September). How we become what we are. *The Atlantic Monthly,* 39–55.

Gallo, P. S., & McClintock, C. G. (1965). Cooperative and competitive behavior in mixed-motive games. *Journal of Conflict Resolution, 9,* 68–78.

Galluscio, E. H. (1990). *Biological psychology.* New York: Macmillan.

Galton, F. (1869). *Hereditary genius.* London: Macmillan.

Galton, F. (1884). Measurement of character. *Fortnightly Review, 42,* 179–185.

Galton, F. (1907). *Inquiries into human faculty and its development.* London: Dent Publishers. (Original work published 1883).

Ganchrow, J. R., Steiner, J. E., & Daher, M. (1983). Neonatal facial expressions in response to different qualities and intensities of gustatory stimuli. *Infant Behavior and Development, 6,* 189–200.

Garcia, J. (1981). The logic and limits of mental aptitude testing. *American Psychologist, 36,* 1172–1180.

Garcia, J. (1990). Learning without memory. *Journal of Cognitive Neuroscience, 2,* 287–305.

Garcia, J. (1993). Misrepresentations of my criticisms of Skinner. *American Psychologist, 48,* 1158.

Garcia, J., & Koelling, R. A. (1966). The relation of cue to consequence in avoidance learning. *Psychonomic Science, 4,* 123–124.

Gardner, H. (1983). *Frames of mind.* New York: Basic Books.

Gardner, H. (1985). *The mind's new science: A history of the cognitive revolution.* New York: Basic Books.

Gardner, H. (1993). *Creating minds: An anatomy of creativity seen through the lives of Freud, Einstein, Picasso, Stravinsky, Eliot, Graham, and Gandhi.* New York: Basic Books.

Gardner, H. (1999, February). Who owns intelligence? *The Atlantic Monthly,* pp. 67–76.

Garland, A., & Zigler, E. (1993). Adolescent suicide prevention: Current research and social policy implications. *American Psychologist, 48,* 169–182.

Garnets, L., & Kimmel, D. (1991). Lesbian and gay male dimensions in the psychological study of human diversity. In J. D. Goodchilds (Ed.), *Psychological perspectives on human diversity in America* (pp. 137–189). Washington, DC: American Psychological Association.

Garnsey, S. M. (1993). Event-related brain potentials in the study of language: An introduction. *Language and Cognitive Processes, 8,* 337–356.

Gazzaniga, M. (1970). *The bisected brain.* New York: Appleton-Century-Crofts.

Gazzaniga, M. S. (1995). Consciousness and the cerebral hemispheres. In M. S. Gazzaniga (Ed.), *The cognitive neurosciences.* Cambridge, MA: MIT Press.

Gazzaniga, M. S. (1998, July). The split brain revisited. *Scientific American, 279,* 50–55.

Gazzaniga, M. S. (1998). *The Mind's Past.* Berkeley: University of California Press.

Gelernter, D. (1997, May 19). How hard is chess? *Time,* 72–73.

Gelernter, J. (1994, June 17). Behavioral genetics in transition. *Science, 264,* 1684–1689.

Gelman, S. A., & Wellman, H. M. (1991). Insides and essences: Early understandings of the non-obvious. *Cognition, 38,* 213–244.

Gentner, D., & Stevens, A. L. (1983). *Mental models.* Hillsdale, NJ: Erlbaum.

Gergen, K. J., Gulerce, A., Lock, A., & Misra, G. (1996). Psychological science in cultural context. *American Psychologist, 51,* 496–503.

Getzels, J. W., & Csikszentmihalyi, M. (1976). *The creative vision.* New York: Wiley.

Ghoneim, M. M., & Block, R. I. (1992). Learning and consciousness during general anesthesia. *Anesthesiology, 76,* 279–305.

Gibbons, A. (1998, September 4). Which of our genes make us human? *Science, 281,* 1432–1434.

Gibbs, W. W. (1995, March). Seeking the criminal element. *Scientific American,* pp. 100–107.

Gilbert, E. H., & DeBlassie, R. R. (1984). Anorexia nervosa: Adolescent starvation by choice. *Adolescence, 19,* 839–853.

Gilbert, R. M. (1992). *Extraordinary relationships: A new way of thinking about human interactions.* New York: Wiley.

Giles, T. R. (1983). Probable superiority of behavioral interventions—II: Empirical status of the equivalence of therapies hypothesis. *Journal of Behavior Therapy and Experimental Psychiatry, 14,* 189–196.

Gilligan, C. (1982). *In a different voice: Psychological theory and women's development.* Cambridge, MA: Harvard University Press.

Gitlin, M. J. (1990). *The psychotherapist's guide to psychopharmacology.* New York: The Free Press.

Givens, D. B. (1983). *Love signals: How to attract a mate.* New York: Crown.

Glaser, R. (1984). Education and thinking: The role of knowledge. *American Psychologist, 39,* 93–104.

Glaser, R. (1990). The reemergence of learning theory within instructional research. *American Psychologist, 45,* 29–39.

Goddard, C. R., & Stanley, J. R. (1995). Viewing the abusive parent and the abused child as captor and hostage: The application of hostage theory to the effects of child abuse. *Journal of Interpersonal Violence, 9,* 258–269.

Goddard, H. H. (1914). *The Kallikak family. A study of the heredity of feeble-mindedness.* New York: Macmillan.

Goddard, H. H. (1917). Mental tests and immigrants. *Journal of Delinquency, 2,* 243–277.

Goldberg, L. R. (1981). Language and individual differences: The search for universals in personality lexicons. In L. Wheeler (Ed.), *Review of personality and social psychology* (Vol. 2, pp. 141–165). Beverly Hills, CA: Sage.

Goldberg, L. R. (1993). The structure of phenotypic personality traits. *American Psychologist, 48,* 26–34.

Goldin-Meadow, S., & Mylander, C. (1990). Beyond the input given: The child's role in the acquisition of language. *Language, 66,* 323–355.

Goldman, S. L., Kraemer, D. T., & Salovey, P. (1996). Beliefs about mood moderate the relationship of stress to illness and symptom reporting. *Journal of Psychosomatic Research, 41,* 115–128.

Goldman-Rakic, P. S. (1992, September). Working memory and the mind. *Scientific American, 267,* 110–117.

Goleman, D. (1980, February). 1528 little geniuses and how they grew. *Psychology Today, 14,* 28–53.

Goleman, D. (1995). *Emotional intelligence.* New York: Bantam Books.

Golombok, S., & Tasker, F. (1996). Do parents influence the sexual orientation of their children? Findings from a longitudinal study of lesbian families. *Developmental Psychology, 32,* 3–11.

Gonzalvo, P., Cañas, J. J., & Bajo, M. (1994). Structural representations in knowledge acquisition. *Journal of Educational Psychology, 86,* 601–616.

Goodchilds, J. D. (Ed.). (1991). *Psychological perspectives on human diversity in America.* Washington, DC: American Psychological Association.

Gordon, L. (1990, September 2). Proposal to overhaul SAT to consider relevance, bias. *The Seattle Times/Post-Intelligencer.*

Gorman, J. (1999, January). The 11-year-old debunker. *Discover, 20*(1), 62–63.

Gottesman, I. I. (1991). *Schizophrenia genesis: The origins of madness.* New York: Freeman.

Gottlieb, B. H. (Ed.). (1981). *Social networks and social support.* Beverly Hills, CA: Sage.

Gottlieb, B. H. (1987). Marshalling social support for medical patients and their families. *Canadian Psychology, 28,* 201–217.

Gottman, J., & Silver, N. (1994). *Why marriages succeed or fail.* New York: Simon and Schuster.

Gottman, J. M. (1994). *What predicts divorce?* Hillsdale, NJ: Erlbaum.

Gottman, J. M. (1999). *Seven principles for making marriages work.* New York: Crown.

Gottman, J. M., & Krokoff, L. J. (1989). Marital interaction and satisfaction: A longitudinal view. *Journal of Consulting & Clinical Psychology, 57,* 47–52.

Gottman, J. M., & Levenson, R. W. (1986). Assessing the role of emotion in marriage. *Behavioral Assessment, 8,* 31–48.

Gould S. J. (1981). *The mismeasure of man.* New York: Norton.

Graham, J. R. (1990). *MMPI-2: Assessing personality and psychopathology.* New York: Oxford University Press.

Gray, P. (1993, November 29). The assault on Freud. *Time, 142* (23), 46–51.

Greeley, A., & Sheatsley, P. (1971). The acceptance of desegregation continues to advance. *Scientific American, 225*(6), 13–19.

Green, D. M. & Swets, J. A. (1966). *Signal detection theory and psychophysics.* New York: Wiley.

Greenberg, B. S. (1986). Minorities and the mass media. In J. Bryant & D. Zillman (Eds.), *Perspectives in media effects* (pp. 17–40). Hillsdale, NJ: Erlbaum.

Greenberg, L. S., & Johnson, S. (1988). *Emotionally focused therapy for couples.* New York: Guilford.

Greene, B. (1985). A testing time. In B. Greene, *Cheeseburgers* (pp. 56–61). New York: Ballantine.

Greene, R. L. (1991). *The MMPI-2/MMPI: An interpretive manual.* Boston: Allyn and Bacon.

Greeno, J. G. (1989). A perspective on thinking. *American Psychologist, 44,* 134–141.

Greenwald, A. G. (1992). New Look 3: Unconscious cognition reclaimed. *American Psychologist, 47* (6), 766–779.

Gregory, R. (1997). *Mirrors in mind.* New York: W. H. Freeman.

Grevert, P., & Goldstein, A. (1985). Placebo analgesia, naloxone, and the role of endogenous opioids. In L. White, B. Turks, & G. E. Schwartz (Eds.), *Placebo,* (pp. 332–351). New York: Guilford.

Guilford, J. P. (1967). *The nature of human intelligence.* New York: McGraw-Hill.

Guilford, J. P. (1973). Theories of intelligence. In B. B. Wolman (Ed.), *Handbook of general psychology* (pp. 630–643). Englewood Cliffs, NJ: Prentice-Hall.

Guilford, J. P. (1985). The Structure-of-Intellect model. In B. B. Wolman (Ed.), *Handbook of intelligence* (pp. 225–266). New York: Wiley.

Guilleminault, C. (1989). Clinical features and evaluation of obstructive sleep apnea. In M. Kryser, T. Roth, & W. C. Dement (Eds.), *Principles and practice of sleep medicine* (pp. 552–558). New York: Saunders Press.

Guisinger, S., & Blatt, S. J. (1994). Individuality and relatedness: Evolution of a fundamental dialectic. *American Psychologist, 49,* 104–111.

Gulya, M., Rovee-Collier, C., Galluccio, L., & Wilk, A. (1998). Memory processing of a serial list by young infants. *Psychological Science, 9,* 303–307.

Gur, R. E., & Pearlson, G. D. (1993). Neuroimaging in schizophrenia research. *Schizophrenia Bulletin, 19,* 337–353.

Gustafson, S. B., & Magnusson, D. (1991). *Female life careers: A pattern approach.* Hillsdale, NJ: Erlbaum.

Guthrie, G. M., & Bennett, A. B. (1970). Cultural differences in implicit personality theory. *International Journal of Psychology, 6,* 305–312.

Guthrie, R. V. (1998). *Even the rat was white.* Boston: Allyn & Bacon.

Hacker, A. (1986, February 13). The decline of higher learning. *The New York Review.*

Haimov, I., & Lavie, P. (1996). Melatonin—A soporific hormone. *Current Directions in Psychological Science, 5,* 106–111.

Hale, R. L. (1983). Intellectual assessment. In M. Hersen, A. E. Kazdin, & A. S. Bellack (Eds.), *The clinical psychology handbook* (pp. 345–376). New York: Pergamon.

Hall, C., (1951). What people dream about. *Scientific American, 184,* 60–63.

Hall, C. (1953/1966). *The meaning of dreams.* New York: Harper & Row/McGraw-Hill.

Hall, C., & Van de Castle, R. L. (1966). *The content analysis of dreams.* New York: Appleton-Century-Crofts.

Hall, C. C. I. (1997). Cultural malpractice: The growing obsolescence of psychology with the changing U.S. population. *American Psychologist, 52,* 642–651.

Hall, C. S. (1984). "A ubiquitous sex difference in dreams" revisited. *Journal of Personality and Social Psychology, 46,* 1109–1117.

Haller, E. (1992). Eating disorders: A review and update. *Western Journal of Medicine, 157,* 658–662.

Hamer, D. (1997). The search for personality genes: Adventures of a molecular biologist. *Current Directions in Psychological Science, 6,* 111–112.

Hamer, D. H., Hu, S., Magnuson, V. L., Hu, N., & Pattatucci, A. M. L. (1993, December 24). Male sexual orientation and genetic evidence. *Science, 261,* 2863–2865.

Haney, C., Banks, W. C., & Zimbardo, P. G. (1973). Interpersonal dynamics in a simulated prison. *International Journal of Criminology and Penology, 1,* 69–97.

Haney, C., & Zimbardo, P. (1998). The past and future of U.S. prison policy: Twenty-five years after the Stanford prison experiment. *American Psychologist, 53,* 709–727.

Haring, M. J., Stock, W. A., & Okun, M. A. (1984). A research synthesis of gender and social class as correlates of subjective well-being. *Human Relations, 37,* 645–657.

Harlow, H. F. (1965). Sexual behavior in the rhesus monkey. In F. Beach (Ed.), *Sex and behavior.* New York: Wiley.

Harlow, H. F., & Harlow, M. K. (1966). Learning to love. *American Scientist, 54,* 244–272.

Harris, B. (1979). Whatever happened to Little Albert? *American Psychologist, 34,* 151–160.

Harris, J. R. (1995). Where is the child's environment? A group socialization theory of development. *Psychological Review, 102,* 458–489.

Hart, R. A., & Moore, G. I. (1973). The development of spatial cognition: A review. In R. M. Downs & D. Stea (Eds.), *Image and environment.* Chicago: Aldine.

Hartmann, E. L. (1973). *The functions of sleep.* New Haven, CT: Yale University Press.

Harvey, J. H., Weber, A. L., & Orbuch, T. L. (1990). Interpersonal accounts: A social psychological perspective. Cambridge, MA: Basil Blackwell.

Harvey, P. H., & Krebs, J. R. (1990). Comparing brains. *Science, 249,* 140–146.

Harvey, S. M., & Spigner, C. (1995). Factors associated with sexual behavior among adolescents: A multivariate analysis. *Adolescence, 30,* 253–264.

Hass, A. (1979). *Teenage sexuality: A survey of teenage sexual behavior.* New York: Macmillan.

Hassebrauck, M. (1988). Beauty is more than "name" deep: The effect of women's first names on ratings of physical attractiveness and personality attributes. *Journal of Applied Social Psychology, 18,* 721–726.

Hatfield, E. (1988). Passionate and compassionate love. In R. J. Sternberg & M. L. Barnes (Eds.), *The psychology of love.* New Haven, CT: Yale University Press.

Hatfield, E., & Rapson, R. (1993). *Love, sex, and intimacy: Their psychology, biology, and history.* New York: HarperCollins.

Hatfield, E., & Sprecher, S. (1986). *Mirror, mirror: The importance of looks in everyday life.* New York: State University of New York Press.

Hayes, S. C., & Heiby, E. (1996). Psychology's drug problem: Do we need a fix or should we just say no? *American Psychologist, 51,* 198–206.

Haynes, S. G., & Feinleib, M. (1980). Women, work, and coronary heart disease: Prospective findings from the Framingham Heart Study. *American Journal of Public Health, 70,* 133–141.

Hazan, C., & Shaver, P.R. (1990). Love and work: An attachment-theoretical perspective. *Journal of Personality and Social Psychology, 59,* 270–280.

Hazan, C., & Shaver, P. R. (1992). Broken attachments: Relationship loss from the perspective of attachment theory. In T. L. Orbuch (Ed.), *Close relationship loss: Theoretical approaches* (pp. 90–108). New York: Springer Verlag.

Headey, B., & Wearing, A. (1992). *Understanding happiness: A theory of well-being.* Melbourne: Longman Cheshire.

Hearst, E. (1988). Fundamentals of learning and cognition. In R. C. Atkinson, R. J. Herrnstein, G. Lindzey, & R. D. Luce (Eds.), *Stevens' handbook of experimental psychology: Vol. 2. Learning and cognition* (2nd ed., pp. 3–109). New York: Wiley.

Hecht, A. (1986, April). A guide to the proper use of tranquilizers. *Healthline Newsletter,* pp. 5–6.

Heeger, D. J. (1994). The representation of visual stimuli in primary visual cortex. *Current Directions in Psychological Science, 3,* 159–163.

Heinrichs, R. W. (1993). Schizophrenia and the brain: conditions for a neuropsychology of madness. *American Psychologist, 48,* 221–233.

Helmes, E., & Reddon, J. R. (1993). A perspective on developments in assessing psychopathology: A critical review of the MMPI and MMPI-2. *Psychological Bulletin, 113,* 453–471.

Helms, J. E. (1992). Why is there no study of cultural equivalence in standardized cognitive ability testing? *American Psychologist, 47,* 1083–1101.

Hendrick, S. S., & Hendrick, C. (1992). *Liking, loving, and relating,* (2nd ed.) Pacific Grove, CA: Brooks/Cole.

Henig, R. M. (1998, May). Tempting fates. *Discover,* 58.

Henker, B., & Whalen, C. K. (1989). Hyperactivity and attention deficits. *American Psychologist, 44,* 216–223.

Henley, N. (1977). *Sexual politics: Power, sex, and nonverbal communication.* Englewood Cliffs, NJ: Prentice-Hall.

Hernstein, R. J., Nickerson, R. S., Sánchez, & Swets, J. A. (1986). Teaching thinking skills. *American Psychologist, 41,* 1279–1289.

Herrnstein, R. J., & Murray, C. (1994). *The bell curve.* New York: Free Press.

Heston, L. L. (1970). The genetics of schizophrenia and schizoid disease. *Science, 112,* 249–256.

Hersh, S. M. (1971). *My Lai 4: A report on the massacre and its aftermath.* New York: Random House.

Herzog, D. B. (1992). Eating disorders: New threats to health. *Psychosomatics, 33*(1), 10–15.

Herzog, D. B., Keller, M. B., Strober, & M., Yeh, C. (1992). The current status of treatment for anorexia nervosa and bulimia nervosa. *International Journal of Eating Disorders, 12*(2), 215–220.

Heston, L. L. (1970). The genetics of schizophrenic and schizoid disease. *Science, 167,* 249–256.

Hetherington, E. M., & Parke, R. D. (1975). *Child psychology: A contemporary viewpoint.* New York: McGraw-Hill.

Hetherington, M. M., Spalter, A. R., Bernat, A. S., Nelson, M. L. et al. (1993). Eating pathology in bulimia nervosa. *International Journal of Eating Disorders, 13*(1), 13–24.

Hicks, R. A. (1990). *The costs and benefits of normal insomnia.* Paper presented to the annual meeting of the Western Psychological Association, Los Angeles, CA.

Hilgard, E. R. (1968). *The experience of hypnosis.* New York: Harcourt Brace Jovanovich.

Hilgard, E. R. (1973). The domain of hypnosis with some comments on alternative paradigms. *American Psychologist, 28,* 972–982.

Hilts, P. J. (1995). *Memory's ghost: The strange tale of Mr. M. and the nature of memory.* New York: Simon & Schuster.

Hinton, G. E. (1992, September). How neural networks learn from experience. *Scientific American, 267,* 144–151.

Hinton, G. F., & Anderson, J. A. (1981). *Parallel models of associative memory.* Hillsdale, NJ: Erlbaum.

Hiroto, D. S. (1974). Locus of control and learned helplessness. *Journal of Experimental Psychology, 102,* 187–193.

Hirsch, J., Harrington, G., & Mehler, B. (1990). An irresponsible farewell gloss. *Educational Theory, 40,* 501–508.

Hirschfeld, R. M. A., & Goodwin, F. K. (1988). Mood disorders. In J. A. Talbott, R. E. Hales, & S. C. Yudofsky (Eds.), *The American Psychiatric Press textbook of psychiatry.* Washington, DC: American Psychiatric Press.

Hobson, J. A. (1988). *The dreaming brain.* New York: Basic Books.

Hobson, J. A. (1992). A new model of brain-mind state: Activation level, input source, and mode of processing (AIM). In J. S. Antrobus & M. Bertini (Eds.), *The neuropsychology of sleep and dreaming.* Hillsdale, NJ: Erlbaum Associates.

Hobson, J. A., & McCarley, R. W. (1977). The brain as a dream state generator: An activation-synthesis hypothesis of the dream process. *American Journal of Psychiatry, 134,* 1335–1348.

Hochwalder, J. (1995). On stability of the structure of implicit personality theory over situations. *Scandinavian Journal of Psychology, 36,* 386–398.

Hogan, R., Curphy, G. J., & Hogan, J. (1994). What we know about leadership: Effectiveness and personality. *American Psychologist, 49,* 493–504.

Hogan, R., Hogan, J., & Roberts, B. W. (1996). Personality measurement and employment decisions: Questions and answers. *American Psychologist, 51,* 469–477.

Holden, C. (1978). Patuxent: Controversial prison clings to belief in rehabilitation. *Science, 199,* 665–668.

Holden, C. (1996, July 5). New populations of old add to poor nations' burdens. *Science, 273,* 46–48

Holden, C. (1996, July 19). Sex and olfaction. *Science, 273,* 313.

Holden, C. (1997, October 3). A special place for faces in the brain. *Science, 278,* 41.

Hollis, K. L. (1997). Contemporary research on Pavlovian conditioning. *American Psychologist, 52,* 956–965.

Hollon, S. D. (1996). The efficacy and effectiveness of psychotherapy relative to medications. *American Psychologist, 51,* 1025–1030.

Holmes, D. S. (1984). Meditation and somatic arousal: A review of the experimental evidence. *American Psychologist, 39,* 1–10.

Holmes, D. S. (1994). *Abnormal psychology.* New York: HarperCollins.

Holmes, T. H. (1979). Development and application of a quantitative measure of life change magnitude. In J. E. Barrett, R. M. Rose, & G. L. Klerman (Eds.), *Stress and mental disorder.* New York: Raven.

Holmes, T. H., & Masuda, M. (1974). Life change and stress susceptibility. In B. S. Dohrenwend & B. P. Dohrenwend, (Eds.), *Stressful life events: Their nature and effects* (pp. 45–72). New York: Wiley.

Holmes, T. H., & Rahe, R. H. (1967). The social readjustment rating scale. *Journal of Psychosomatic Research, 11*(2), 213–218.

Holtzman, W. H. (1992). Health psychology. In M. A. Rosenzweig (Ed.), *International psychological science* (pp. 199–226). Washington, DC: American Psychological Association.

Holtzworth-Munroe, A., & Jacobson, N. S. (1985). Causal attributions of marital couples: When do they search for causes? What do they conclude when they do? *Journal of Personality and Social Psychology, 48,* 1398–1412.

Homme, L. E., de Baca, P. C., Devine, J. V., Steinhorst, R., & Rickert, E. J. (1963). Use of the Premack principle in controlling the behavior of nursery school children. *Journal of the Experimental Analysis of Behavior, 6,* 544.

Hopkins, B., & Westra, T. (1988). Maternal handling and motor development: An intracultural study. *Genetic, Social and General Psychology Monographs, 14,* 377–420.

Hopson, J. L. (1988, July–August). A pleasurable chemistry. *Psychology Today,* pp. 29–33.

Horgan, J. (1993, June). Eugenics revisited. *Scientific American,* pp. 122–131.

Horgan, J. (1995, November). Get smart, take a test: A long-term rise in IQ scores baffles intelligence experts. *Scientific American, 273,* 12, 14.

Horgan, J. (1996, November). Multicultural studies: Rates of depression vary widely throughout the world. *Scientific American, 275*(6), 24–25.

Horne, J. A. (1988). *Why we sleep: The functions of sleep in humans and other mammals.* Oxford, U. K.: Oxford University Press.

Horney, K. (1939). *New ways in psychoanalysis.* New York: Norton.

Horney, K. (1942). *Self-analysis.* New York: Norton.

Horvath, A. O., & Luborsky, L. (1993). The role of the therapeutic alliance in psychotherapy. *Journal of Consulting and Clinical Psychology, 61,* 561–573.

House, J. S., Landis, K. R., & Umberson, D. (1988). Social relationships and health. *Science, 241*, 540–545.

Hovland, C. I., & Sears, R. (1940). Minor studies of aggression: Correlation of lynchings with economic indices. *Journal of Psychology, 9*, 301–310.

Howes, C., Rodning, C., Galluzzo, D. C., & Myers, L. (1988). Attachment and child care: Relationships with mother and care-giver. *Early Childhood Research Quarterly, 3*, 403–416.

Hubel, D. H., & Wiesel, T. N. (1979, September). Brain mechanisms of vision. *Scientific American, 241*, 150–162.

Huesman, L. R., & Moise, J. (1996, June). Media violence: A demonstrated public health threat to children. *Harvard Mental Health Letter, 12*(12), 5–7.

Hull, C. L. (1943). *Principles of behavior: An introduction to behavior theory.* New York: Appleton-Century-Crofts.

Hull, C. L. (1952). *A behavior system: An introduction to behavior theory concerning the individual organism.* New Haven, CT: Yale University Press.

Humphrey, T. (1970). The development of human fetal activity and its relation to postnatal behavior. In H. W. Reese & L. P. Lipsitt (Eds.), *Advance in child development and behavior* (Vol. 5). New York: Academic Press.

Humphreys, L. G. (1988). Trends in levels of academic achievement of blacks and other minorities. *Intelligence, 12*, 231–260.

Hunt, E. (1989). Cognitive science: Definition, status, and questions. *Annual Review of Psychology, 40*, 603–629.

Hurlburt, R. T. (1979). Random sampling of cognitions and behavior. *Journal of Research in Personality, 13*, 103–111.

Huston, A. C., Watkins, B. A., & Kunkel, D. (1989). Public policy and children's television. *American Psychologist, 44*, 424–433

Huston, T. L., Ruggiero, M., Conner, R., & Geis, G. (1981). Bystander intervention into crime: A study based on naturally-occurring episodes. *Social Psychology Quarterly, 44*, 14–23.

Hyman, I. E., Jr., Husband, T. H., & Billings, F. J. (1995). False memories of childhood experiences. *Applied Cognitive Psychology, 9*, 181–197.

Hyman, R. (1989). The psychology of deception. *Annual Review of Psychology, 40*, 133–154.

Iacono, W. G., & Grove, W. M. (1993). Schizophrenia reviewed:

Toward an integrative genetic model. *Science, 4*, 273–276.

Ickes, W., & Layden, M. A. (1978). Attributional styles. In J. H. Harvey, W. Ickes, & R. F. Kidd (Eds.), *New directions in attributional research* (Vol. 2). Hillsdale, NJ: Erlbaum.

Ineichen, B. (1979). The social geography of marriage. In M. Cook & G. Wilson (Eds.), *Love and attraction.* New York: Pergamon Press.

Inglehart, R. (1990). *Culture shift in advanced industrial society.* Princeton, NJ: Princeton University Press.

Irwin, M., Daniels, M., Smith, T. L., Bloom, E., & Weiner, H. (1987). Impaired natural killer cell activity during bereavement. *Brain Behavior Immunology, 1*, 98–104.

Isay, R. A. (1990). Psychoanalytic theory and the therapy of gay men. In D. P. McWhirter, S. A. Sanders, & J. M. Reinisch (Eds.), *Homosexuality/heterosexuality: Concepts of sexual orientation* (pp. 283–303). New York: Oxford University Press.

Itard, J. M. G. (1962). *The wild boy of Aveyron* (G. & M. Humphrey, Trans.). New York: Appleton-Century-Crofts.

Izard, C. E. (1989). The structure and functions of emotions: Implications for cognition, motivation, and personality. In I. S. Cohen (Ed.), *The G. Stanley Hall lecture series* (Vol. 9, pp. 39–73). Washington, DC: American Psychological Association.

Izard, C. E. (1993). Four systems for emotion activation: Cognitive and noncognitive processes. *Psychological Review, 100*, 68–90.

Izard, C. E. (1994). Innate and universal facial expressions: Evidence from developmental and cross-cultural research. *Pschological Bulletin, 115*, 288–299.

Jackson, D. D. (1980, October). Reunion of identical twins, raised apart, reveals some astonishing similarities. *Smithsonian*, pp. 48–57.

Jacobs, B. L. (1987). How hallucinogenic drugs work. *American Scientist, 75*, 386–392.

Jacobs, M. K., & Goodman, G. (1989). Psychology and self-help groups: Predictions on a partnership. *American Psychologist, 44*, 536–545.

Jacobson, N. S., & Christensen, A. (1996). Studying the effectiveness of psychotherapy: How well can clinical trials do the job? *American Psychologist, 51*, 1031–1039.

Jacoby, L. L., Lindsay, D. S., Toth, J. P. (1992). Unconscious influences revealed: Attention, awareness, and control. *American Psychologist, 47*, 802–809.

Jacoby, L. L., Woloshyn, V., & Kelley, C. (1989). Becoming famous without being recognized: Unconscious influences of memory produced by divided attention. *Journal of Experi-*

*mental Psychology: General, 118* (2), 115–125.

James, W. (1950). *The principles of psychology* (2 vols.). New York: Holt, Rinehart & Winston. (Original work published 1890).

Janis, I. L., & Frick, F. (1943). The relationship between attitudes toward conclusions and errors in judging logical validity of syllogisms. *Journal of Experimental Psychology, 33*, 73–77.

Janoff-Bulman, R. (1989). The benefits of illusions, the threat of disillusionment, and the limitations of inaccuracy. *Journal of Social and Clinical Psychology, 8*, 158–175.

Janoff-Bulman, R. (1992). *Shattered assumptions: Towards a new psychology of trauma.* New York: The Free Press.

Jansen, A. S. P., Nguyen, X. V., Karpitskiy, V., Mettenleiter, T. C., & Loewy, A. D. (1995, October 27). Central command neurons of the sympathetic nervous system: Basis of the fight-or-flight response. *Science, 270*, 644–646.

Jeffery, R. W. (1987). Behavioral treatment of obesity. *Annals of Behavioral Medicine, 9*, 20–24.

Jenkins, C. D. (1976). Recent evidence supporting psychologic and social risk factors for coronary disease. *New England Journal of Medicine, 294*, 987–994, 1033–1038.

Jenkins, J. G., & Dallenbach, K. M. (1924). Oblivescence during sleep and waking. *The American Journal of Psychology, 35*, 605–612.

Jensen, A. R. (1969). How much can we boost IQ and scholastic achievement? *Harvard Educational Review, 39*, 1–123.

Jensen, A. R. (1980). *Bias in mental testing.* New York: Free Press.

Jensen, A. R. (1985). Methodological and statistical techniques for the chronometric study of mental abilities. In C. R. Reynolds & V. L. Wilson (Eds.), *Methodological and statistical advances in the study of individual difference* (pp. 51–116). New York: Plenum.

Jensen, A. R., & Figueroa, R. A. (1975). Forward and backward digit-span interaction with race and IQ: Predictions from Jensen's theory. *Journal of Educational Psychology, 67*, 882–893.

Johnson, D. L. (1989). Schizophrenia as a brain disease: Implications for psychologists and families. *American Psychologist, 44*, 553–555.

Johnson, J. H., & Sarason, I. B. (1979). Recent developments in research on life stress. In V. Hamilton & D. M. Warburton (Eds.), *Human stress and cognition: An information processing approach* (pp. 205–233) Chichester, England: Wiley.

Johnson-Laird, P. N., & Byrne, R. M. J. (1989). Only reasoning.

*Journal of Memory and Language, 28*, 313–330.

Johnston, L. D., O'Malley, P. M., & Bachman, J. G. (1989). *Drug use, drinking, and smoking: National survey results from high school, college, and young adult populations, 1975–1988.* Rockville, MD: U.S. Department of Health and Human Services.

Joiner, T. E., Jr., & Schmidt, N. B. (1995). Dimensions of perfectionism, life stress, and depressed and anxious symptoms: Prospective support for diathesis-stress but not specific vulnerability among male undergraduates. *Journal of Social and Clinical Psychology, 14*, 165–183.

Jones, E. E., Cumming, J. D., & Horowitz, M. J. (1988). Another look at the nonspecific hypothesis of therapeutic effectiveness. *Journal of Consulting and Clinical Psychology, 56*, 48–55.

Jones, J. M. (1991). Psychological models of race: What have they been and what should they be? In J. D. Goodchilds (Ed.), *Psychological perspectives on human diversity in America* (pp. 3–46). Washington, DC: American Psychological Association.

Jones, M. (1953). *The therapeutic community.* New York: Basic Books.

Joyce, L. (1989, Fall). Good genes, bad genes. *Stanford Medicine*, pp. 18–23.

Juliano, S. L. (1998, March 13). Mapping the sensory mosaic. *Science, 279*, 1653–1654.

Julien, R. M. (1995). *A primer of drug action: A concise, nontechnical guide to the actions, uses, and side effects of psychoactive drugs.* New York: W. H. Freeman.

Kagan, J. (1994a). *Galen's prophecy: Temperament in human nature.* New York: BasicBooks.

Kagan, J. (1994b, October 5). The realistic view of biology and behavior. *The Chronicle of Higher Education*, p. A64.

Kagan, J. (1996). Three pleasing ideas. *American Psychologist, 51*, 901–908.

Kagan, J. (1998). *Three seductive ideas.* Cambridge, MA: Harvard University Press.

Kagan, J., Reznick, J. S., & Snidman, N. (1986). Temperamental inhibition in early childhood. In R. Plomin & J. Dunn (Eds.), *The study of temperament: Changes, continuities, and challenges.* Hillsdale, NJ: Erlbaum.

Kagan, J., Reznick, J. S., & Snidman, N. (1988). Biological basis of childhood shyness. *Science, 20*, 167–171.

Kagan, J., & Snidman, N. (1991). Infant predictors of inhibited and uninhibited profiles. *Psychological Science, 2*, 40–44.

Kagan, J., Snidman, N., Arcus, D., and Reznick, J. S. (1994). *Galen's prophecy: Temperament in human nature*. New York: Basic Books.

Kamil, A. C., Krebs, J., & Pulliam, H. R. (1987). *Foraging behavior*. New York: Plenum.

Kamin, L. (1994, November 23). Intelligence, IQ tests, and race. *Chronicle of Higher Education*, p. B5.

Kamin, L. J. (1969). Predictability, surprise, attention, and conditioning. In B. A. Campbell & R. M. Church (Eds.), *Classical conditioning: A symposium*. New York: Appleton-Century-Crofts.

Kamin, L. J. (1974). *The science and politics of IQ*. Potomac, MD: Erlbaum.

Kamin, L. J. (1995, February). Book review: Behind the curve. *Scientific American, 272*, pp. 99–103.

Kandel, D. B. (1978). Similarity in real-life adolescent friendship pairs. *Journal of Personality and Social Psychology, 36*, 306–312.

Kandel, E. R., & Hawkins, R. D. (1992, September). The biological basis of learning and individuality. *Scientific American, 267*, 79–86

Kane, J. M., & Marder, S. R. (1993). Psychopharmacologic treatment of schizophrenia. *Schizophrenia Bulletin, 19*, 287–302.

Kantrowitz, B. (1992, January 27). A Head Start does not last. *Newsweek, 119*, 44–45.

Karni, A., Tanne, D., Rubenstein, B. S., Askenasy, J. J. M., & Sagi, D. (1994, July 29). Dependence on REM sleep of overnight improvement in perceptual skill. *Science, 265*, 679–682.

Kazdin, A. E. (1986). Comparative outcome studies of psychotherapy: Methodological issues and strategies. *Journal of Consulting and Clinical Psychology, 54*, 95–105.

Kazdin, A. E. (1994). *Behavior modification in applied settings* (5th ed.). Pacific Grove, CA: Brooks/Cole.

Kazdin, A. E., & Wilcoxin, L. A. (1976). Systematic desensitization and nonspecific treatment effects: A methodological evaluation. *Psychological Bulletin, 83*, 729–758.

Keating, C. F. (1994). World without words: Messages from face and body. In W. J. Lonner & R. Malpass (Eds.), *Psychology and culture* (pp. 175–182). Boston: Allyn and Bacon.

Keesey, R. E., & Powley, T. L. (1975). Hypothalamic regulation of body weight. *American Scientist, 63*, 558–565.

Kelley, H. H., Berscheid, E., Christensen, A., Harvey, J., Huston, T., Levinger, G., McClintock, E., Peplau, A., & Peterson, D. (1983). *Close relationships*. San Francisco: Freeman.

Kelman, H. C. (1997). Group processes in the resolution of international conflicts: Experiences from the Israeli-Palestinian case. *American Psychologist, 52*, 212–220.

Kelsoe, J. R., Ginns, E. I., Egeland, J. A., Gerhard, D. S., Goldstein, A. M., Bale, S. J., Pauls, D. L., Long, R. T., Kidd, K. K., Conte, G., Housman, D. E., & Paul, S. M. (1989). Reevaluation of the linkage relationship between chromosome 11p loci and the gene for bipolar affective disorder in the Old Order Amish. *Nature, 342*, 238–243.

Kempermann, G., & Gage, F. H. (1999, May). New nerve cells for the adult brain. *Scientific American, 280*, 48–53.

Kendler, K. S., & Diehl, S. R. (1993). The genetics of schizophrenia: A current, genetic–epidemiologic perspective. *Schizophrenia Bulletin, 19*, 261–285.

Kendler, K. S., & Gardner, C. O., Jr. (1998). Boundaries of major depression: An evaluation of DSM-IV criteria. *American Journal of Psychiatry, 155*, 172–177.

Kennedy, D. M. (1970). *Birth control in America: The career of Margaret Sanger*. New Haven, CT: Yale University Press.

Kennedy, S. H., & Garfinkel, P. E. (1992). Advances in diagnosis and treatment of anorexia nervosa and bulimia nervosa. *Canadian Journal of Psychiatry, 37*(5), 309–315.

Kenrick, D. T., & Funder, D. C. (1988). Profiting from controversy: Lessons from the person-situation debate. *American Psychologist, 43*, 23–34.

Kenrick, D. T., & Stringfield, D. O. (1980). Personality traits and the eye of the beholder: Crossing some traditional philosophical boundaries in the search for consistency in all of the people. *Psychological Review, 87*, 88–104.

Kerlinger, F. N. (1985). *Foundations of behavioral research* (3rd ed.). New York: Holt, Rinehart & Winston.

Kershner, J. R., & Ledger, G. (1985). Effect of sex, intelligence, and style of thinking on creativity: A comparison of gifted and average IQ children. *Journal of Personality and Social Psychology, 48*, 1033–1040.

Kesner, R., & Olton, D. S. (1990). *The neurobiology of comparative cognition*. Hillsdale, NJ: Erlbaum.

Kessler, S. (1980). The genetics of schizophrenia: A review. In S. J. Keith & L. R. Mosher (Eds.), *Special report: Schizophrenia, 1980* (pp. 14–26). Washington, DC: U.S. Government Printing Office.

Kiecolt-Glaser, J. K., & Glaser, R. (1987). Psychosocial moderators of immune function. *Annals of Behavioral Medicine, 9*, 16–20.

Kiesler, C. A. (1982a). Mental hospitals and alternative care: Noninstitutionalization as potential public policy for mental patients. *American Psychologist, 37*, 349–360.

Kiesler, C. A. (1982b). Public and professional myths about mental hospitalization. *American Psychologist, 37*, 1323–1339.

Kiesler, C. A. (1993). Mental health policy and mental hospitalization. *Current Directions in Psychological Science, 2*, 93–95.

Kiesling, R. (1983). Critique of Kiesler articles. *American Psychologist, 38*, 1127–1128.

Kiester, E. (1980, May/June). Images of the night. *Science 80*, pp. 36–42.

Kihlstrom, J. F. (1985). Hypnosis. *Annual Review of Psychology, 36*, 385–418.

Kihlstrom, J. F. (1987). The cognitive unconscious. *Science, 237*, 1445–1452.

Kihlstrom, J. F. (1990). The psychological unconscious. In L. Pervin (Ed.), *Handbook of personality: Theory and research* (pp. 445–464). New York: Guilford Press.

Kihlstrom, J. F., Barnhardt, T. M., & Tartaryn, D. J. (1992). The psychological unconscious: Found, lost, and regained. *American Psychologist, 47*, 788–791.

Kihlstrom, J. F., Schacter, D. L., Cork, R. C., Hurt, C. A., & Behr, S. E. (1990). Implicit and explicit memory following surgical anesthesia. *Psychological Science, 1*, 303–306.

Kim, J. J., Krupa, D. J., & Thompson, R. F. (1998, January 23). Inhibitory cerebello-olivary projections and blocking effect in classical conditioning. *Science, 279*, 570–573.

Kimmel, A. J. (1991). Predictable biases in the ethical decision making of American psychologists. *American Psychologist, 46*, 786–788.

Kinoshita, J. (1992, July). Dreams of a rat. *Discover, 13*, pp. 34–41.

Kinsey, A. C., Pomeroy, W. B., & Martin, C. E. (1948). *Sexual behavior in the human male*. Philadelphia: Saunders.

Kinsey, A. C., Pomeroy, W. B., Martin, C. E., & Gebhard, P. H. (1953). *Sexual behavior in the human female*. Philadelphia: Saunders.

Kintsch, W. (1981). Semantic memory: A tutorial. In R. S. Nickerson (Ed.), *Attention and performance* (Vol. 8 ). Hillsdale, NJ: Erlbaum.

Kipnis, D. (1987). Psychology and behavioral technology. *American Psychologist, 42*, 30–36.

Kirby, K. N., & Hernstein, R. J. (1995). Preference reversals due to myopic discounting of delayed reward. *Psychological Science, 6*, 83–89.

Kirkpatrick, L. A., & Shaver, P. R. (1992). An attachment-theoretical approach to romantic love and religious belief. *Personality and Social Psychology Bulletin, 18*, 266–275.

Kirsch, I., & Lynn, S. J. (1995). The altered state of hypnosis: Changes in the theoretical landscape. *American Psychologist, 50*, 846–858.

Kirsch, I., & Sapirstein, G. (1998, June 26). Listening to Prozac but hearing placebo: A meta-analysis of antidepressant medication. *Prevention & Treatment, 1*, Article 0002a. [http://journals.apa.org/prevention/volume1/pre0010002a.html]

Kitayama, S., & Markus, H. R. (1994). *Emotion and culture*. Washington, D.C.: American Psychological Association.

Klag, M. J., Whelton, P. K., Grim, C. E., & Kuller, L. H. (1991). The association of skin color with blood pressure in U.S. blacks with low socioeconomic status. *Journal of the American Medical Association, 265*, 599–602.

Klagsbrun, F. (1985). *Married people: Staying together in the age of divorce*. New York: Bantam Books.

Klein, K. E., & Wegmann, H. M. (1974). The resynchronization of human circadian rhythms after transmeridian flights as a result of flight direction and mode of activity. In L. E. Scheving, F. Halberg, & J. E. Pauly (Eds.), *Chronobiology* (pp. 564–570). Tokyo: Igaku.

Klein, R. G., Landa, B., Mattes, J. A., & Klein, D. F. (1988). Methylphenidate and growth in hyperactive children: A controlled withdrawal study. *Archives of General Psychiatry, 45*, 1127–1130.

Kleinfeld, J. (1994). Learning styles and culture. In Lonner, W. J. & Malpass, R. *Psychology and culture* (pp. 151–156). Boston: Allyn & Bacon.

Kleinke, C. (1975). *First impressions: The psychology of encountering others*. Englewood Cliffs: Prentice Hall.

Kleinman, A., & Cohen, A. (1997). Psychiatry's global challenge. *Scientific American, 276* (3), 86–89.

Klinger, E. (1987, May). The power of daydreams. *Psychology Today*, pp. 37–44.

Kobasa, S. O. (1984). How much stress can you survive? *American Health, 3*, 64–77.

Kobasa, S. O., Hilker, R. R., & Maddi, S. R. (1979). Who stays healthy under stress? *Journal of Occupational Medicine, 21*, 595–598.

Kohlberg, L. (1964). Development of moral character and moral ideology. In M. L. Hoffman & L. W. Hoffman (Eds.), *Review of child development research* (Vol. 1). New York: Russell Sage Foundation.

Kohlberg, L. (1981). *The philosophy of moral development*. New York: Harper & Row.

Köhler, W. (1925). *The mentality of apes*. New York: Harcourt Brace Jovanovich.

Kohn, P. M., Barnes, G. E., & Hoffman, F. M. (1979). Drug-use history and experience seeking among adult male correctional inmates. *Journal of Consulting and Clinical Psychology, 47*, 708–715.

Kolb, B. (1989). Development, plasticity, and behavior. *American Psychologist, 44*, 1203–1212.

Koob, G. F., & Le Moal, M. (1997, October 3). Drug abuse: Hedonic homeostatic dysregulation. *Science, 278*, 52–58.

Korkina, M. V., Tsivil'ko, M. A., Kareva, M. A., & Zhigalova, N. D. et al. (1992). Clinico-psychological correlations of mental rigidity in anorexia nervosa. *Journal of Russian and East European Psychiatry, 25*(2), 21–28.

Kosko, B., & Isaka, S. (1993, July). Fuzzy logic. *Scientific American, 269*, 76–81.

Kosslyn, S. M. (1976). Can imagery be distinguished from other forms of internal representation? Evidence from studies of information retrieval times. *Memory and Cognition, 4*, 291–297.

Kosslyn, S. M. (1983). *Ghosts in the mind's machine: Creating and using images in the brain*. New York: Norton.

Kramer, P. D. (1993). *Listening to Prozac: A psychiatrist explores antidepressant drugs and the remaking of the self*. New York: Viking.

Krampe, R. T., & Ericsson, K. A. (1996). Maintaining excellence: Deliberate practice and elite performance in young and older pianists. *Journal of Experimental Psychology: General, 125*, 331–359.

Krantz, D. S., Grunberg, N. E., & Baum, A. (1985). Health psychology. *Annual Review of Psychology, 36*, 349–383.

Kukla, A. (1989). Nonempirical issues in psychology. *American Psychologist, 44*, 785–794.

Lachman, R., Lachman, J. L., & Butterfield, E. C. (1979). *Cognitive psychology and information processing: An introduction*. Hillsdale, NJ: Erlbaum.

Lakoff, R. T. (1990). *Talking power*. New York: Basic Books.

Lambo, T. A. (1978). Psychotherapy in Africa. *Human Nature, 1*(3), 32–39.

Lampl, M., Veldhuis, J. D., & Johnson, M. L. (1992). Saltation and stasis: A model of human growth. *Science, 258*, 801–803.

Landesman, S., & Butterfield, E. C. (1987). Normalization and deinstitutionalization of mentally retarded individuals: Controversy and facts. *American Psychologist, 42*, 809–816.

Landry, D. W. (1997, February). Immunotherapy for cocaine addiction. *Scientific American*, 42–45.

Lang, F. R., & Carstensen, L. L. (1994). Close emotional relationships in late life: Further support for proactive aging in the social domain. *Psychology and Aging, 9*, 315–324.

Lang, P. J. (1995). The emotion probe. *American Psychologist, 50* (5), 372–385.

Lang, P. J., & Lazovik, D. A. (1963). The experimental desensitization of a phobia. *Journal of Abnormal and Social Psychology, 66*, 519–525.

Langlois, J. H., & Roggman, L. A. (1990). Attractive faces are only average. *Psychological Science, 1*, 115–121.

Langlois, J. H., Roggman, L. A., Casey, R. J., Ritter, J. M., Rieser-Danner, L. A., & Jenkins, V. Y. (1987). Infant preferences for attractive faces: Rudiments of a stereotype. *Developmental Psychology, 23*, 363–369.

Langlois, J. H., Roggman, L. A., & Musselman, L. (1994). What is average and what is not average about attractive faces? *Psychological Science, 5*, 214–220.

Larson, R. (1989). Is feeling "in control" related to happiness in daily life? *Psychological Reports, 64*, 775–784.

Latané, B., & Darley, J. M. (1968). Group inhibition of bystander intervention in emergencies. *Journal of Personality and Social Psychology, 10*, 215–221.

Laumann, E. O., Gagnon, J. H., Michael, R. T., & Michaels, S. (1994). *The social organization of sexuality: Sexual practices in the United States*. Chicago: University of Chicago Press.

Lazar, I., & Darlington, R. (1982). Lasting effects of early education: A report from the Consortium for Longitudinal Studies. *Monographs of the Society for Research in Child Development, 47*(2–3, Serial No. 195).

Lazarus, R. S. (1981, July). Little hassles can be hazardous to your health. *Psychology Today*, pp. 58–62.

Lazarus, R. S. (1984). On the primacy of cognition. *American Psychologist, 39*, 124–129.

Lazarus, R. S. (1991a). Cognition and motivation in emotion. *American Psychologist, 46*, 352–367.

Lazarus, R. S. (1991b). Progress on a cognitive-motivational-relational theory of emotion. *American Psychologist, 46*, 819–834.

Lazarus, R. S., DeLongis, A., Folkman, S., & Gruen, R. (1985). Stress and adaptational outcomes: The problem of confounded measures. *American Psychologist, 40*, 770–779.

LeDoux, J. E. (1994). Emotion, memory and the brain, *Scientific American, 270*(6), 50–57.

LeDoux, J. E. (1996). *The emotional brain: The mysterious underpinnings of emotional life*. New York: Simon & Schuster.

Lee, V. E., Brooks-Gunn, J., & Schnur, E. (1988). Does Head Start work? A 1-year follow-up of disadvantaged children attending Head Start, no preschool. *Developmental Psychology, 24*, 210–222.

Leeper, R. W., & Madison, P. (1959). *Toward understanding human personalities*. New York: Appleton-Century-Crofts.

Leerhsen, C. (1990, February 5). Unite and conquer: America's crazy for support groups. *Newsweek*, pp. 50–55.

Lefcourt, H. M., & Martin, R. A. (1986). *Humor and life stress: Antidote to adversity*. New York: Springer-Verlag.

Leiter, M. P., & Maslach, C. (1988). The impact of interpersonal environment on burnout and organizational commitment. *Journal of Organizational Behavior, 9*, 297–308.

Lempert, H., & Kinsbourne, M. (1982). Effect of laterality of orientation on verbal memory. *Neuropsychologia, 20*, 211–214.

Lennon, R. T. (1985). Group tests of intelligence. In B. B. Wolman (Ed.), *Handbook of intelligence* (pp. 825–847). New York: Wiley.

Leonard, J. (1998, May-June). Dreamcatchers: Understanding the biological basis of things that go bump in the night. *Harvard Magazine, 100*, 58–68.

Lepper, M. R. (1981). Intrinsic and extrinsic motivation in children: Detrimental effects of superfluous social controls. In U. A. Collins (Ed.), *Aspects of the development of competence: The Minnesota Symposium on Child Psychology* (Vol. 14, pp. 155–214). Hillsdale, NJ: Erlbaum.

Lepper, M. R., & Greene, D. (Eds.). (1978). *The hidden costs of reward*. Hillsdale, NJ: Erlbaum.

Lepper, M. R., Greene, D., & Nisbett, R. E. (1973). Undermining children's intrinsic interest with extrinsic reward: A test of the overjustification hypothesis. *Journal of Personality and Social Psychology, 28*(1), 129–137.

Lerner, R. M., Orlos, J. R., & Knapp, J. (1976). Physical attractiveness, physical effectiveness and self-concept in adolescents. *Adolescence, 11*, 313–326.

Leshner, A. I. (1997, October 3). Addiction is a brain disease, and it matters. *Science, 278*, 45–47.

Lesperance, F., & Frasure-Smith, N. (1996, February 17). Negative emotions and coronary heart disease: Getting to the heart of the matter. *Lancet, 347*, 414–415.

Lettvin, J. Y., Maturana, H. R., McCulloch, W. S., & Pitts, W. H. (1959). What the frog's eye tells the frog's brain. *Proceedings of the Institute of Radio Engineers, 47*, 1940–1951.

Leutwyler, K. (1994, March). Prosthetic vision: Workers resume the quest for a seeing-eye device. *Scientific American, 270*, 108.

Leutwyler, K. (1995, June). Depression's double standard. *Scientific American, 272*, 23–24.

LeVay, S. (1991). A difference in hypothalamic structure between heterosexual and homosexual men. *Science, 253*, 1034–1037.

LeVay, S., & Hamer, D. (1995). Evidence for a biological influence in male homosexuality. *Scientific American, 270* (5), 44–49.

Levenson, R. W. (1992). Autonomic nervous system differences among emotions. *Psychological Science, 3*, 23–27.

Leventhal, H., & Tomarken, A. J. (1986). Emotion: Today's problems. *Annual Review of Psychology, 37*, 565–610.

Levine, F. M., & Fasnacht, G. (1974). Token rewards may lead to token learning. *American Psychologist, 29*, 816–820.

Levine, M., & Perkins, D. V. (1987). *Principles of community psychology: Perspectives and applications*. New York: Oxford University.

Levinson, B. W. (1967). States of awareness during general anesthesia. In J. Lassner (Ed.), *Hypnosis and psychosomatic medicine* (pp. 200–207). New York: Springer-Verlag.

Levy, S. (1997a, May 19). Big Blue's hand of God. *Newsweek, 129*(20), 72.

Levy, S. (1997b, May 26). Garry sings the blues. *Newsweek, 129*(21), 84.

Lewine, R. R., Strauss, J. S., & Gift, T. E. (1981). Sex differences in age at first hospital admission for schizophrenia: Fact or artifact? *American Journal of Psychiatry, 138*, 440–444.

Lewinsohn, P. M., Clarke, G. N., Hops, H., & Andrews, J. A. (1990). Cognitive-behavioral treatment for depressed adolescents. *Behavior Therapy, 21*, 385–401.

Lewinsohn, P. M., Sullivan, J. M., & Grosscup, S. J. (1980). Changing reinforcing events: An approach to the treatment of depression. *Psychotherapy: Theory, Research and Practice, 17*, 322–334.

Lewy, A. J., Sack, R. L., Miller, S., & Hoban, T. M. (1987). Antidepressant and circadian phase-shifting effect of light. *Science, 235*, 352–354.

Liem, R., & Rayman, P. (1982). Health and social costs of unemployment: Research and policy considerations. *American Psychologist, 37*, 1116–1123.

Lillard, A. S. (1997). Other folks' theories of mind and behavior. *Psychological Science, 8*, 268–274.

Lindsay, D. S. (1990). Misleading suggestions can impair eyewitnesses' ability to remember event details. *Journal of Experimental Psychology: Learning, Memory, and Cognition, 16* (6), 1077–1083.

Lindsay, D. S. (1993). Eyewitness suggestibility. *Current Directions in Psychological Science, 2*, 86–89.

Lipsey, M. W., & Wilson, D. B. (1993). The efficacy of psychological, educational, and behavioral treatment: Confirmation from meta-analysis. *American Psychologist, 48*, 1181–1209.

Lipsitt, L. P., Reilly, B., Butcher, M. G., & Greenwood, M. M. (1976). The stability and interrelationships of newborn sucking and heart rate. *Developmental Psychobiology, 9*, 305–310.

Lloyd, P. (1993). Hedonistic long-range planning: The psychology of exercise. *The General Psychologist, 29*, 75–77.

Loehlin, J. C., Lindzey, G., & Spuhler, J. N. (1975). *Race differences in intelligence.* San Francisco: Freeman.

Loftus, E. (1998, September). Who is the cat that curiosity killed? *APS Observer*, pp. 3, 27.

Loftus, E. F. (1979). *Eyewitness testimony.* Cambridge, MA: Harvard University Press.

Loftus, E. F. (1984). The eyewitness on trial. In B. D. Sales & A. Alwork (Eds.), *With liberty and justice for all.* Englewood Cliffs, NJ: Prentice Hall.

Loftus, E. F. (1992). When a lie becomes memory's truth: Memory distortion after exposure to misinformation. *Current Directions in Psychological Science, 1*, 121–123.

Loftus, E. F. (1993). The reality of repressed memories. *American Psychologist, 48*, 518–537.

Loftus, E. F. (1997a, September). Creating false memories. *Scientific American, 227*, 70–75.

Loftus, E. F. (1997b). Memory for a past that never was. *Current Directions in Psychological Science, 6*, 60–65.

Loftus, E. F., & Ketcham, K. (1991). *Witness for the defense: The accused, the eyewitness, and the expert who puts memory on trial.* New York: St. Martin's Press.

Loftus, E. F., & Ketcham, K. (1994). *The myth of repressed memory: False memories and allegations of sexual abuse.* New York: St. Martin's Griffin.

Loftus, E. F., & Klinger, M. R. (1992). Is the unconscious smart or dumb? *American Psychologist, 47*, 761–765.

Loftus, E. F., & Palmer, J. C. (1973). Reconstruction of automobile destruction: An example of the interaction between language and memory. *Journal of Verbal Learning and Verbal Behavior, 13*, 585–589.

Loftus, G. R., Duncan, J., & Gehrig, P. (1992). On the time course of perceptual information that results from a brief visual presentation. *Journal of Experimental Psychology: Human Perception and Performance, 18* (2), 530–549.

London, K. A., Mosher, W. D., Pratt, W. F., & Williams, L. B. (1989, March). Preliminary findings from the National Survey of Family Growth, Cycle IV. Paper presented at the annual meeting of the Population Association of America, Baltimore, MD.

Long, B. C., & Kahn, S. E. (Eds.). (1993). *Women, work, and coping: A multidisciplinary approach to workplace stress.* Ottawa, Canada: McGill-Queen's.

Lonner, W. J. (1990). An overview of cross-cultural testing and assessment. In R. W. Brislin (Ed.), *Applied cross-cultural psychology.* Newbury Park, CA: Sage.

Loomis, A. L., Harvey, E. N., & Hobart, G. A. (1937). Cerebral states during sleep as studied by human brain potentials. *Journal of Experimental Psychology, 21*, 127–144.

*Los Angeles Times.* (1988, February 23). Bullet in the brain cures man's mental problem.

Lott, A. J., & Lott, B. E. (1961). Group cohesiveness, communication level, and conformity. *Journal of Abnormal and Social Psychology, 62*, 408–412.

Lovibond, S. H., Adams, M., & Adams, W. G. (1979). The effects of three experimental prison environments on the behavior of nonconflict volunteer subjects. *Australian Psychologist, 14*, 273–285.

Luborsky, L., Singer, B., & Luborsky, L. (1975). Comparative studies of psychotherapies: Is it true that everyone has won and all must have prizes? *Archives of General Psychiatry, 32*, 995–1008.

Lutz, C. (1988). *Unnatural emotions.* Chicago: University of Chicago Press.

Maccoby, N., Farquhar, J. W., Wood, P. D., & Alexander, J. K. (1977). Reducing the risk of cardiovascular disease: Effects of a community-based campaign on knowledge and behavior. *Journal of Community Health, 3*, 100–114.

MacLean, H. N. (1993). *Once upon a time: A true story of memory, murder, and the law.* New York: HarperCollins.

Macrae, C. N., Milne, A. B., & Bodenhausen, G. V. (1994). Stereotypes as energy-saving devices: A peek inside the cognitive toolbox.

*Journal of Personality and Social Psychology, 66*, 37–47.

Magee, W. J., Eaton, W. W., Wittchen, H.-U., McGonagle, K. A., Kessler, R. C. (1996). Agoraphobia, simple phobia, and social phobia in the national comorbidity survey. *Archives of General Psychiatry, 53*, 159–168.

Maher, W. B., & Maher, B. A. (1985). Psychopathology: I. From ancient times to the eighteenth century. In G. A. Kimble & K. Schlesinger (Eds.), *Topics in the history of psychology* (Vol. 2, pp. 251–294). Hillsdale, NJ: Erlbaum.

Maher, B. A., & Maher, W. B. (1985). Psychopathology: II. From the eighteenth century to modern times. In G. A. Kimble & K. Schlesinger (Eds.), *Topics in the history of psychology* (Vol. 2) (pp. 295–329). Hillsdale, NJ: Erlbaum.

Maher, B. A., & Ross, J. S. (1984). Delusions. In H. E. Adams & P. B. Sutker (Eds.), *Comprehensive handbook of psychopathology* (pp. 383–987). New York: Plenum.

Maier, S. F., Watkins, L. R., & Fleshner, M. (1994). Psychoneuroimmunology: The interface between behavior, brain, and immunity. *American Psychologist, 49*, 1004–1017.

Maisto, S. A., Galizio, M., & Connors, G. J. (1995). *Drug use and abuse* (2nd ed). Fort Worth, TX: Harcourt Brace.

Majewska, M. D., Harrison, N. L., Schwartz, R. D., Barker, J. L., & Paul, S. M. (1986). Steroid hormone metabolites are barbiturate-like modulators of the GABA receptor. *Science, 232*, 1004–1007.

Malatesta, V. J., Sutker, P. B., & Treiber, F. A. (1981). Sensation seeking and chronic public drunkenness. *Journal of Consulting and Clinical Psychology, 49*, 282–294.

Malinowski, B. (1927). *Sex and repression in savage society.* London: Humanities Press.

Malitz, S., & Sackheim, H. A. (1984). Low dosage ECT: Electrode placement and acute physiological and cognitive effects. *American Journal of Social Psychiatry, 4*, 47–53.

Manderscheid, R. W., Witkin, M. J., Rosenstein, M. J., Milazzo-Sayre, L. J., Bethel, H. E., & MacAskill, R. L. (1985). In C. A. Taube & S. A. Barrett (Eds.), *Mental Health, United States, 1985.* Washington, DC: National Institute of Mental Health.

Mandler, G. (1984). *Mind and body: The psychology of emotion and stress.* New York: Norton.

Manfredi, M., Bini, G., Cruccu, G., Accornero, N., Beradelli, A., & Medolago, L. (1981). Congenital absence of pain. *Archives of Neurology, 38*, 507–511.

Mann, C. C. (1994, June 17). Behavioral genetics in transition. *Science, 264*, 1686–1689.

Manschreck, T. C. (1989). Delusional (paranoid) disorders. In H. I. Kaplan & B. J. Sadock (Eds.), *Comprehensive textbook of psychiatry* (pp. 816–829). Baltimore: Williams & Wilkins.

Manson, S. M. (1994). Culture and depression: Discovering variations in the experience of illness. In W. J. Lonner & R. Malpass (Eds.), *Psychology and culture* (pp. 285–290). Boston: Allyn and Bacon.

Marcus, G. F. (1996). Why do children say "breaked"? *Current Directions in Psychological Science, 3*, 81–85.

Markman, H. J., & Notarius, C. I. (1993). *We can work it out.* Berkeley, CA: Berkeley Publishing Group.

Markus, H., & Kitayama, S. (1991). Culture and self: Implications for cognition, emotion and motivation. *Psychological Review, 98*, 224–253.

Markus, H. R., & Kitayama, S. (1994). The cultural construction of self and emotion: Implications for social behavior. In H. R. Markus & S. Kitayama (Eds.), *Emotion and culture: Empirical studies of mutual influence* (pp. 89–130). Washington, DC: American Psychological Association.

Marsh, P. (1988). Detecting insincerity. In Marsh, P. (Ed.), *Eye to eye: How people interact.* (Ch. 14, pp. 116–119). Oxford, England: Oxford Andromeda Ltd.

Marshall, G. D., & Zimbardo, P. G. (1979). Affective consequences of inadequately explained physiological arousal. *Journal of Personality and Social Psychology, 37*, 970–988.

Martin, J. A. (1981). A longitudinal study of the consequences of early mother-infant interaction: A microanalytic approach. *Monographs of the Society for Research in Child Development, 46* (203, Serial No. 190).

Martin, S. (1999, February). Drug use appears to be easing among teens. *APA Monitor*, p. 8.

Maruyama, G., & Miller, N. (1975). *Physical attractiveness and classroom acceptance* (Research Report 75–2). Los Angeles: University of Southern California, Social Science Research Institute.

Maslach, C. (1979). Negative emotional biasing of unexplained arousal. *Journal of Personality and Social Psychology, 37*, 953–969.

Maslach, C. (1982). *Burnout: The cost of caring.* Englewood Cliffs, NJ: Prentice-Hall.

Maslach, C. (1998, April). The truth about burnout. The G. Stanley Hall Lecture given at the Western Psychological Association convention in Albuquerque, NM.

Maslach, C., & Leiter, M. P. (1997). *The truth about burnout: How organizations cause personal stress and what to do about it.* San Francisco: Jossey-Bass Publishers.

Maslow, A. H. (1968). *Toward a psychology of being* (2nd ed.). New York: Van Nostrand.

Maslow, A. H. (1970). *Motivation and personality* (Rev. ed.). New York: Harper & Row.

Maslow, A. H. (1971). *Farther reaches of human nature.* New York: Viking Penguin.

Masters, J. C., Burish, T. G., Hollon, S. D., & Rimm, D. C. (1987). *Behavior therapy: Techniques and empirical findings* (3rd ed.). San Diego: Harcourt Brace Jovanovich.

Masters, W. H., & Johnson, V. E. (1966). *Human sexual response.* Boston: Little, Brown.

Masters, W. H., & Johnson, V. E. (1970). *Human sexual inadequacy.* Boston: Little, Brown.

Masters, W. H., & Johnson, V. E. (1979). *Homosexuality in perspective.* Boston: Little, Brown.

Matarazzo, J. D. (1980). Behavioral health and behavioral medicine: Frontiers for a new health psychology. *American Psychologist, 35,* 807–817.

Matlin, M. G. (1998). *Cognition* (4th ed.). Fort Worth, TX: Harcourt Brace.

Matossian, M. K. (1982). Ergot and the Salem witchcraft affair. *American Scientist, 70,* 355–357.

Matossian, M. K. (1989). *Poisons of the past: Molds, epidemics, and history.* New Haven: Yale University Press.

Matthews, K. A. (1982). Psychological perspectives on the Type-A behavior pattern. *Psychological Bulletin, 91,* 293–323.

Matthews, K. A. (1988). Coronary heart disease and Type A behavior: Update on an alternative to the Booth-Kewley and Friedman (1987) quantitative review. *Psychological Bulletin, 104,* 373–380.

Maunsell, J. H. R. (1995, November 3). The brain's visual world: Representation of visual targets in cerebral cortex. *Science, 270,* 764–769.

Mayer, D. J. (1979). Endogenous analgesia systems: Neural and behavioral mechanisms. In Bonica, J. J. (Ed.), *Advances in pain research and therapy* (Vol. 3). New York: Raven Press.

Mayer, R. E. (1983). *Thinking, problem solving, and cognition.* San Francisco: W. H. Freeman.

Mays, V. M., Rubin, J., Sabourin, M., & Walker, L. (1996). Moving toward a global psychology: Changing theories and practice to meet the needs of a changing world. *American Psychologist, 51,* 485–487.

McAdams, D. P. (1992). The five-factor model in personality: A critical appraisal. *Journal of Personality, 60,* 239–361.

McAdams, D. P., de St. Aubin, E., & Logan, R. L. (1993). Generativity among young, midlife, and older adults. *Psychology and Aging, 8,* 221–230.

McCann, I. L., & Holmes, D. S. (1984). Influence of aerobic exercise on depression. *Journal of Personality and Social Psychology, 46,* 1142–1147.

McCarley, N., & Carskadon, T. G. (1983). Test–retest reliabilities of scales and subscales of the Myers-Briggs Type Indicator and of criteria for clinical interpretive hypotheses involving them. *Research in Psychological Type, 6,* 24–36.

McCarthy, K. (1992, July). Hunt for memory traces takes 20 years. *APA Monitor,* pp. 18–19.

McClearn, G. E., Johansson, B., Berg, S., Pedersen, N. L., Ahern, F., Petrill, S. A., & Plomin, R. (1997, June 6). Substantial genetic influence on cognitive abilities in twins 80 or more years old. *Science, 276,* 1560–1563.

McClelland, D. C. (1961). *The achieving society.* Princeton, NJ: Van Nostrand.

McClelland, D. C. (1965). Achievement and entrepreneurship: A longitudinal study. *Journal of Personality and Social Psychology, 1,* 389–392.

McClelland, D. C. (1975). *Power: The inner experience.* New York: Irvington.

McClelland, D. C. (1987a). Characteristics of successful entrepreneurs. *The Journal of Creative Behavior, 21,* 219–233.

McClelland, D. C. (1987b). *Human motivation.* New York: Cambridge University Press.

McClelland, D. C. (1993). Intelligence is not the best predictor of job performance. *Current Directions in Psychological Science, 2,* 5–6.

McClelland, D. C., Atkinson, J. W., Clark, R. A., & Lowell, E. L. (1976). *The achievement motive* (2nd ed.). New York: Irvington.

McClelland, D. C., & Boyatzis, R. E. (1982). Leadership motive pattern and long-term success in management. *Journal of Applied Psychology, 67,* 737–743.

McDonald, K. A. (1998, August 14). Scientists consider new explanations for the impact of exercise on mood. *The Chronicle of Higher Education,* p. A15-A16.

McLintock, T. T. C., Aitken, H., Dowie, C. F. A., & Kenny, G. N. C. (1990). Post-operative analgesic requirements in patients exposed to positive intraoperative suggestions. *British Journal of Medicine, 301,* 788–790.

McNally, R. J. (1994, August). Cognitive bias in panic disorder. *Current Directions in Psychological Science, 3,* 129–132.

McPherson, K. S. (1985). On intelligence testing and immigration legislation. *American Psychologist, 40,* 242–243.

Mead, M. (1939). *From the South Seas: Studies of adolescence and sex in primitive societies.* New York: Morrow.

Meador, B. D., & Rogers, C. R. (1979). Person-centered therapy. In R. J. Corsini (Ed.), *Current psychotherapies* (2nd ed., pp. 131–184). Itasca, IL: Peacock.

Medin, D. L. (1989). Concepts and conceptual structure. *American Psychologist, 44,* 1469–1481.

Medin, D. L., & Ross, B. H. (1992). *Cognitive psychology.* Fort Worth, TX: Harcourt Brace Jovanovich.

Meier, R. P. (1991). Language acquisition by deaf children. *American Scientist, 79,* 60–70.

Mellinger, G. D., Balter, M. B., & Uhlenhuth, E. H. (1985). Insomnia and its treatment: Prevalence and correlates. *Archives of General Psychiatry, 42,* 225–232.

Meltzoff, A. N. (1998). *The nature of the preverbal mind: Towards a developmental cognitive science.* Paper presented at the Western Psychological Association/Rocky Mountain Psychological Association joint convention, Albuquerque, NM.

Meltzoff, A. N., & Moore, M. K. (1977). Imitation of facial and manual gestures by human neonates. *Science, 198,* 75–78.

Meltzoff, A. N., & Moore, M. K. (1983). Newborn infants imitate adult facial gestures. *Child Development, 54,* 702–709.

Meltzoff, A. N., & Moore, M. K. (1985). Cognitive foundations and social functions of imitation and intermodal representation in infancy. In J. Mehler & R. Fox (Eds.), *Neonate cognition: Beyond the blooming buzzing confusion* (pp. 139–156). Hillsdale, NJ: Erlbaum.

Meltzoff, A. N., & Moore, M. K. (1989). Imitation in newborn infants: Exploring the range of gestures imitated and the underlying mechanisms. *Developmental Psychology, 25,* 954–962.

Meltzoff, J., & Kornreich, M. (1970). *Research in psychotherapy.* New York: Atherton.

Melzack, R. (1990, February). The tragedy of needless pain. *Scientific American, 262,* 27–33.

Menzel, E. M. (1978). Cognitive mapping in chimpanzees. In S. H. Hulse, H. Fowler, & W. K. Honzig (Eds.), *Cognitive processes in animal behavior* (pp. 375–422). Hillsdale, NJ: Erlbaum.

Merikle, P. M., & Reingold, E. M. (1990). Recognition and lexical decision without detection: Unconscious perception? *Journal of Experimental Psychology: Human Perception & Performance, 16,* 574–583.

Meredith, N. (1986, June). Testing the talking cure. *Science 86, 7,* 30–37.

Mervis, C. B., & Rosch, E. (1981). Categorization of natural objects. *Annual Review of Psychology, 32,* 89–115.

Mesulam, M. M. (1990). Schizophrenia and the brain. *New England Journal of Medicine, 322,* 842–845

Meyer-Bahlburg, H. F. L. (1977). Sex hormones and female homosexuality: A critical examination. *Archives of Sexual Behavior, 8,* 297–326.

Meyer-Bahlburg, H. F. L. (1979). Sex hormones and female homosexuality: A critical examination. *Archives of Sexual Behavior, 8,* 101–120.

Michael, R. T., Gagnon, J. H., Laumann, E. O., & Kolata, G. (1994). *Sex in America: A definitive survey.* New York: Little, Brown.

Milgram, S. (1965). Some conditions of obedience and disobedience to authority. *Human Relations, 18,* 56–76.

Milgram, S. (1974). *Obedience to authority.* New York: Harper & Row.

Miller, A. G. (1986). *The obedience paradigm: A case study in controversy in social science.* New York: Praeger.

Miller, J. (1984). Culture and the development of everyday social explanation. *Journal of Personality and Social Psychology, 46,* 961–978.

Miller, M. E., & Bowers, K. S. (1993). Hypnotic analgesia: Dissociated experience of dissociated control? *Journal of Abnormal Psychology, 102,* 29–38.

Miller, M. W. (1993, December 2). Dark days: The staggering cost of depression. *The Wall Street Journal,* p. B1.

Miller, N. E. (1983). Behavioral medicine: Symbiosis between laboratory and clinic. *Annual Review of Psychology, 34,* 1–31.

Miller, N. E. (1995). Clinical–experimental interactions in the development of neuroscience: A primer for nonspecialists and lessons for young students. *American Psychologist, 50,* 901–911.

Miller, N. E., & Brucker, B. S. (1979). A learned visceral response apparently independent of skeletal ones in patients paralyzed by spinal lesions. In N. Birbaumer & H. D. Kimmel (Eds.), *Biofeedback and self-regulation.* Hillsdale, NJ: Erlbaum.

Miller, P. Y., & Simon, W. (1980). The development of sexuality in adolescence. In J. Adelson (Ed.), *Handbook of adolescent psychology.* New York: Wiley.

Miller, W. R., & Brown, S. A. (1997), Why psychologists should treat alcohol and drug problems. *American Psychologist, 52,* 1269–1279.

Miller-Jones, D. (1989). Culture and testing. *American Psychologist, 44,* 360–366.

Milner, B., Corkin, S., & Teuber, H. H. (1968) Further analysis of the hippocampal amnesic syndrome: 14-year follow-up study of H. M. *Neuropsychologia, 6,* 215–234.

Mineka, S., Davidson, M., Cook, M., & Keir, R. (1984). Observational conditioning of snake fear in rhesus monkeys. *Journal of Abnormal Psychology, 93,* 355–372.

Mintz, L. B., & Betz, N. E. (1986). Sex differences in the nature, realism, and correlates of body image. *Sex Roles, 15,* 185–195.

Mischel, W. (1961). Delay of gratification, need for achievement, and acquiescence in another culture. *Journal of Abnormal and Social Psychology, 62,* 543–552.

Mischel, W. (1968). *Personality and assessment.* New York: Wiley.

Mischel, W. (1973). Toward a cognitive social learning conceptualization of personality. *Psychological Review, 80,* 252–283.

Mischel, W. (1990). Personality dispositions revisited and revised: A view after three decades. In L. A. Pervin (Ed.), *Handbook of personality: Theory and research.* New York: Guilford Press.

Mischel, W. (1993). *Introduction to personality* (5th ed.). Fort Worth, TX: Harcourt Brace Jovanovich College Publishers.

Mischel, W., & Shoda, Y. (1995). A cognitive-affective system theory of personality: Reconceptualizing situations, dispositions, dynamics, and invariance in personality structure. *Psychological Review, 102,* 246–268.

Mizukami, K., Kobayashi, N., Ishii, T., and Iwata, H. (1990). First selective attachment begins in early infancy: A study using telethermography. *Infant Behavior and Development, 13,* 257–271.

Mlot, C. (1998, May 15). Probing the biology of emotion. *Science, 280,* 1005–1007.

Moar, I. (1980). The nature and acquisition of cognitive maps. In D. Cantor & T. Lee (Eds.), *Proceedings of the international conference on environmental psychology.* London: Architectural Press.

Mogilner, A., Grossman, J. A. I., & Ribary, W. (1993). Somatosensory cortical plasticity in adult humans revealed by magnetoencephalography. *Proceedings of the National Academy of Sciences, 90*(8), 3593–3597.

Monaghan, P. (1999, February 26). Lessons from the "marriage lab."

*The Chronicle of Higher Education,* p. A9.

Moncrieff, R. W. (1951). *The chemical senses.* London: Leonard Hill.

Money, J. (1987). Sin, sickness, or status? Homosexual gender identity and psychoneuroendocrinology. *American Psychologist, 42,* 384–399.

Monte, C. F. (1980). *Beneath the mask: An introduciton to theories of personality* (2nd ed.). New York: Holt, Rinehart and Winston.

Moore, J. S., Graziano, W. G., & Millar, M. G. (1987). Physical attractiveness, sex role orientation, and the evaluation of adults and children. *Personality and Social Psychology Bulletin, 13,* 95–102.

Moore-Ede, M. (1993). *The twenty-four-hour society: Understanding human limits in a world that never stops.* Reading, MA: Addison-Wesley.

Morgan, A. H., Hilgard, E. R., & Davert, E. C. (1970). The heritability of hypnotic susceptibility of twins: A preliminary report. *Behavior Genetics, 1,* 213–224.

Moriarity, T. (1975). Crime, commitment and the responsive bystander: Two field experiments. *Journal of Personality and Social Psychology, 31,* 370–376.

Morrell, E. M. (1986). Meditation and somatic arousal. *American Psychologist, 41*(6), 712–713.

Morris, D. (1967). *The naked ape.* New York: McGraw-Hill.

Morris, M. W., & Peng, K. (1994). Culture and cause: American and Chinese attributions for social and physical events. *Journal of Personality & Social Psychology, 8,* 949–971.

Morris, W. N., & Miller, R. S. (1975). The effects of consensus-breaking and consensus-preempting partners on reduction of conformity. *Journal of Experimental Social Psychology, 11,* 215–223.

Morrison-Bogorad, M., & Phelps, C. (1997, March 12). Alzheimer disease research comes of age. *JAMA: Journal of the American Medical Association, 277,* 837–840.

Moskowitz, H. (1985). Marihuana and driving. *Accident Analysis & Prevention, 17,* 323–345.

Mowrer, O. (1960). *Learning theory and symbolic processes.* New York: Wiley.

Mukerjee, M. (1995, October). Hidden scars: Sexual and other abuse may alter a brain region. *Scientific American, 273*(4), 14, 20.

Munakata, Y., McClelland, J. L., Johnson, M. H., & Siegler, R. S. (1997). Rethinking infant knowledge: Toward an adaptive process account of successes and failures in object permanence tasks. *Psychological Review, 104,* 686–713.

Muñoz, R. F., Hollon, S. D., Mc-Grath, E., Rehm, L. P., & Vanden-Bos, G. R. (1994). On the AHCPR *Depression in Primary Care* guidelines: Further considerations for practitioners. *American Psychologist, 49,* 42–61.

Munroe, R. L. (1955). *Schools of psychoanalytic thought.* New York: Dryden.

Murphy, G., & Murphy, L. B. (Eds.). (1968). *Asian psychology.* New York: Basic Books.

Murphy, J. M. (1976, March 12). Psychiatric labeling in cross-cultural perspective. *Science, 191,* 1019–1028.

Murray, B. (1995, October). Americans dream about food, Brazilians dream about sex. *APA Monitor,* p. 30.

Murray, B. (1997, September). Why aren't antidrug programs working? *APA Monitor,* 30.

Murray, J. P., & Kippax, S. (1979). Children's social behavior in three towns with differing television experience. *Journal of Communication, 28,* 19–29.

Musun-Miller, L. (1993). Sibling status effects: Parents' perceptions of their own children, *The Journal of Genetic Psychology, 154,* 189–198.

Myers, D. G. (1992). *The pursuit of happiness: Who is happy—and why.* New York: William Morrow and Company.

Myers, D. G., & Diener, E. (1995). Who is happy? *Psychological Science, 6,* 10–19.

Myers, I. B. (1962). *The Myers-Briggs type indicator.* Palo Alto, CA: Consulting Psychologists Press.

Myers, I. B. (1976). *Introduction to type* (2nd ed.). Gainesville, FL: Center for Applications of Psychological Type.

Myers, I. B. (1985). *Gifts differing.* Palo Alto, CA: Consulting Psychologists Press.

Myers, I. B. (1987). *Introduction to type: A description of the theory and applications of the Myers-Briggs Type Indicator.* Palo Alto, CA: Consulting Psychologists Press.

Myers, L. (1996). Europe's new criminal class: Under capitalism a violent crime wave is sweeping Central nations. *San Francisco Examiner,* January 7, p. A-8.

Myers, R. S., & Roth, D. L. (1997). Perceived benefits of and barriers to exercise and stage of exercise adoption in young adults. *Health Psychology, 16,* 277–283.

Nahemow, L., & Lawton, M. P. (1975). Similarity and propinquity in friendship formation. *Journal of Personality and Social Psychology, 32,* 205–213.

Naigles, L. (1990). Children use syntax to learn verb meanings. *Child language, 17,* 357–374.

Naigles, L. G., & Kako, E.T. (1993). First contact in verb acquisition: Defining a role for syntax. *Child Development, 64,* 1665–1687.

Nathan, P. E. (1998). Practice guidelines: Not yet ideal. *American Psychologist, 53,* 290–299.

National Institute of Mental Health. (1985). *Electroconvulsive therapy: Consensus Development Conference statement.* Bethesda, MD: U.S. Department of Health and Human Services.

National Institute on Alcohol Abuse and Alcoholism. (1993). *Alcohol and health: Eighth special report to the U.S. Congress.* Rockville, MD: Author.

National Press Club. (1999, Summer). Seligman on positive psychology: A session at the National Press Club. *The General Psychologist, 34*(2), 37–45.

National Public Radio. (1995a, June 25). The Stockholm syndrome: Empathy with captors discussed. *Weekend Edition.* Washington, DC: National Public Radio.

National Public Radio. (1995b, August 30). Americans are generally shy, and getting shyer. *Morning Edition.* Washington, DC: National Public Radio.

Nauta, W. J. H., & Feirtag, M. (1979). The organization of the brain. *Scientific American, 241* (9), 88–111.

Needleman, H., Schell, A., Belinger, D., Leviton, A., & Allred, E. (1990). The long-term effects of exposure to low doses of lead in childhood: An 11-year follow-up report. *New England Journal of Medicine, 322,* 83–88.

Neisser, U. (1967). *Cognitive psychology.* New York: Appleton-Century-Crofts.

Neisser, U., Boodoo, B., Bouchard, T. J., Jr., Boyukin, A. W., Brody, N., Ceci, S. J., Halpern, D. F., Loehlin, J. C., Perloff, R., Sternberg, R. J., & Urbina, S. (1996). Intelligence: Knowns and unknowns. *American Psychologist, 51,* 77–101.

Nelson, C. A. (1987). The recognition of facial expressions in the first two years of life: Mechanisms of development. *Child Development, 58,* 889–909.

Nelson, T. D. (1993). The hierarchical organization of behavior: A useful feedback model of self-regulation. *Current Directions in Psychological Science, 2,* 121–126.

Nemecek, S. (1998, September). Forestalling violence. *Scientific American, 278*(9), 15–16.

Nemacek, S. (1999, January). Unequal health. *Scientific American, 280*(1), 40–41.

Nemeroff, C. B. (1998, June). The neurobiology of depression. *Scientific American, 278,* 42–49.

Nesse, R. M., & Berridge, K. C. (1997, October 3). Psychoactive drug use in evolutionary perspective. *Science, 278,* 63–66.

Newcomb, M. D., & Bentler, P. M. (1988). *Consequences of adolescent drug use: Impact on the lives of young adults.* Newbury Park, CA: Sage.

Newcomb, T. M. (1943). *Personality and social change.* New York: Holt.

Newcomb, T. M., Koenig, D. E., Flacks, R., & Warwick, D. P. (1967). *Persistence and change: Bennington College and its students after twenty-five years.* New York: Wiley.

Newell, A., Shaw, J. C., & Simon, H. A. (1958). Elements of a theory of human problem solving. *Psychological Review, 65,* 152–166.

Newell, A., & Simon, H. A. (1972). *Human problem solving.* Englewood Cliffs, NJ: Prentice-Hall.

Newman, B. S., & Muzzonigro, P. G. (1993). The effects of traditional family values on the coming out process of gay male adolescents. *Adolescence, 28,* 213–226.

Nicol, S. E., & Gottesman, I. I. (1983). Clues to the genetics and neurobiology of schizophrenia. *American Scientist, 71,* 398–404.

Nicholls, J. G. (1972). Creativity in the person who will never produce anything original and useful: The concept of creativity as a normally distributed trait. *American Psychologist, 27,* 717–727.

Nisbett, R. E. (1972). Hunger, obesity, and the ventromedial hypothalamus. *Psychological Review, 79,* 433–453.

Nisbett, R. E. (1993). Violence and U.S. regional culture. *American Psychologist, 48,* 441–449.

Nobles, W. W. (1976). Black people in White insanity: An issue for Black community mental health. *Journal of Afro-American Issues, 4,* 21–27.

Nolen-Hoeksema, S. (1987). Sex differences in unipolar depression: Evidence and theory. *Psychological Bulletin, 101,* 259–282.

Nolen-Hoeksema, S. (1990). *Sex differences in depression.* Stanford, CA: Stanford University Press.

Norman, D. A., & Rumelhart, D. E. (1975). *Explorations in cognition.* San Francisco: Freeman.

Notarius, C.I. (1996). Marriage: Will I be happy or sad? In N. Vanzetti and S. Duck's *A lifetime of relationships.* New York: Brooks/Cole Publishing Company.

Notarius, C., & Markman, H. (1993). *We can work it out: Making sense of marital conflict.* New York: G. P. Putnam's Sons.

Novak, M. A., & Suomi, S. J. (1988). Psychological well-being of primates in captivity. *American Psychologist, 43,* 765–773.

Nungesser, L. G. (1990). *Axioms for survivors: How to live until you say goodbye.* Santa Monica, CA: IBS Press.

Nurmi, J.E. (1991). How do adolescents see their future? A review of the development of future orientation and planning. *Developmental Review, 11,* 1–59.

Nyman, L. (1995). The identification of birth order personality attributes. *The Journal of Psychology, 129,* 51–59.

Oakland, T., & Glutting, J. J. (1990). Examiner observations of children's WISC-R test-related behaviors: Possible socioeconomic status, race, and gender effects. *Psychological Assessment, 2,* 86–90.

Oatley, K., & Duncan, E. (1994). The experience of emotions in everyday life. *Cognition and Emotion, 8,* 369–381.

Oatley, K., & Jenkins, J. M. (1992). Human emotions: Function and dysfunction. *Annual Review of Psychology, 43,* 55–85.

Oden, G. C. (1987). Concept, knowledge, and thought. *Annual Review of Psychology, 38,* 203–227.

Oden, G. C. (1968). The fulfillment of promise: 40-year follow-up of the Terman gifted group. *Genetic Psychology Monographs, 77,* 3–93.

Offer, D., Ostrov, E., & Howard, K. I. (1981). *The adolescent: A psychological self-portrait.* New York: Basic Books.

Offer, D., Ostrov, E., Howard, K. I., & Atkinson, R. (1988). *The teenage world: Adolescents' self-image in ten countries.* New York: Plenum Medical.

Ofshe, R., & Watters, E. (1994). *Making monsters: False memories, psychotherapy, and sexual hysteria.* New York: Charles Scribner's Sons.

O'Leary, K. D. (Ed.). (1987). *Assessment of marital discord: An integration for research and clinical practice.* Hillsdale, NJ: Erlbaum.

Olton, D. S. (1979). Mazes, maxes, and memory. *American Psychologist, 34,* 583–596.

Olton, D. S. (1992). Tolman's cognitive analyses: Predecessors of current approaches in psychology. *Journal of Experimental Psychology: General, 121,* 427–428.

Oppel, J. J. (1854–55). Ueber geometrisch-optische Tauschungen. *Jahresbericht des physikalischen Vereins zu Frankfurt a. M.,* 34–47.

Opton, E. M. (1970). Lessons of My Lai. In N. Sanford & C. Comstock (Eds.), *Sanctions for evil.* San Francisco: Jossey-Bass.

Opton, E. M., Jr. (1973). "It never happened and besides they deserved it." In W. E. Henry & N. Sanford (Eds.), *Sanctions for evil* (pp. 49–70). San Francisco: Jossey-Bass.

Oren, D. A., & Terman, M. (1998, January 16). Tweaking the human circadian clock with light. *Science, 279,* 333–334.

Orne, M. T. (1980). Hypnotic control of pain: Toward a clarification of the different psychological processes involved. In J. J. Bonica (Ed.), *Pain* (pp. 155–172). New York: Raven Press.

Ornstein, R., & Sobel, D. (1989). *Healthy pleasures.* Reading, MA: Addison-Wesley.

Ornstein, R. E. (1986a). *Multimind: A new way of looking at human behavior.* Boston: Houghton Mifflin.

Ornstein, R. E. (1986b). *The psychology of consciousness* (Rev. ed.). New York: Penguin Books.

Osborn, A. (1953). *Applied imagination* (Rev. ed.). New York: Charles Scribner's Sons.

Osterhout, L., & Holcomb, P. J. (1992). Event-related brain potentials elicited by syntactic anomaly. *Journal of Memory and Language, 31,* 785–806.

Packard, R. G. (1970). The control of "classroom attention": A group contingency for complex behavior. *Journal of Applied Behavior Analysis, 3,* 13–28.

Paffenbarger, R. S., Jr., Hyde, R. T., Wing, A. L., & Hsieh, C-C. (1986). Physical activity, all-cause mortality, and longevity of college alumni. *New England Journal of Medicine, 314,* 605–612.

Page, T. L. (1994). Time is the essence: Molecular analysis of the biological clock. *Science, 263,* 1570–1572.

Paikoff, R. L., & Brooks-Gunn, J. (1991). Do parent–child relationships change during puberty? *Psychological Bulletin, 110,* 47–66.

Paivio, A. (1983). The empirical case for dual coding. In J. C. Yuille (Ed.), *Imagery, memory and cognition* (pp. 307–332). Hillsdale, NJ: Erlbaum.

Paivio, A. (1986). *Mental representations: A dual coding approach.* New York: Oxford University Press.

Pandey, J., Sinha, Y., Prakash, A., & Tripathi, R. C. (1982). Right-left political ideologies and attribution of the causes of poverty. *European Journal of Social Psychology, 12,* 327–331.

Papolos, D. F., & Papolos, J. (1987). *Overcoming depression.* New York: Harper & Row.

Parr, W. V., and Siegert, R. (1993). Adults' conceptions of everyday memory failures in others: Factors that mediate the effects of target age. *Psychology and Aging, 8,* 599–605.

Patrick, C. J., & Iacono, W. G. (1991). Validity of the control question polygraph test: The problem of

sampling bias. *Journal of Applied Psychology, 76,* 229–238.

Patterson, J. M. (1985). Critical factors affecting family compliance with home treatment for children with cystic fibrosis. *Family Relations, 34,* 74–89.

Pattie, F. A. (1994). *Mesmer and animal magnetism: A chapter in the history of medicine.* New York: Edmonston.

Patzer, G. L. (1985). *The physical attractiveness phenomena.* New York: Plenum Press.

Paul, S. M., Crawley, J. N., & Skolnick, P. (1986). The neurobiology of anxiety: The role of the GABA/benzodiazepine complex. In P. A. Berger & H. K. H. Brodie (Eds.), *American handbook on psychiatry: Biological psychology* (2nd ed.). New York: Basic Books.

Paunonen, S. P., Jackson, D. N., Trzebinski, J., & Fosterling, F. (1992). Personality structure across cultures: A multimethod evaluation. *Journal of Personality and Social Psychology, 62,* 447–456.

Pavlov, I. P. (1928). *Lectures on conditioned reflexes: Twenty-five years of objective study of higher nervous activity (behavior of animals)* (Vol. 1, W. H. Gantt, Trans.). New York: International Publishers.

Pavot, W., Diener, E., & Fujita, F. (1990). Extraversion and happiness. *Personality and Individual Differences, 1,* 1299–1306.

Pawlik, K., & d'Ydewalle, G. (1996). Psychology and the global commons: Perspectives of international psychology. *American Psychologist, 51,* 488–495.

Payne, D. G., Neuschatz, J. S., Lampinen, J. M., & Lynn, S. J. (1997). Compelling memory illusions: The qualitative characteristics of false memories. *Current Directions in Psychological Science, 6,* 56–60.

Pearman, R. R. (1991, November 13). Disputing a report on "Myers-Briggs" test. *Chronicle of Higher Education,* p. B7.

Pedersen, P. (1977). Asian personality theory. In R. J. Corsini (Ed.), *Current personality theories* (pp. 367–397). Itasca, IL: F. E. Peacock.

Pedersen, P. (1979). Non-Western psychology: The search for alternatives. In A. J. Marsella, R. G. Tharp, & T. J. Ciborowski (Eds.), *Perspectives on cross-cultural psychology* (pp. 77–98). New York: Academic Press.

Penfield, W., & Baldwin, M. (1952). Temporal lobe seizures and the technique of subtotal lobectomy. *Annals of Surgery, 136,* 625–634.

Pennebaker, J. W. (1990). *Opening up: The healing power of confiding in others.* New York: William Morrow.

Pennebaker, J. W., Barger, S. D., & Tiebout, J. (1989). Disclosure of traumas and health among Holocaust survivors. *Psychosomatic Medicine, 51,* 577–589.

Pennebaker, J. W., Dyer, M. A., Caulkins, R. J., Litowitz, D. L., Ackerman, P. L., Anderson, D. B., & McGraw, K. M. (1979). Don't the girls get prettier at closing time: A country and western application to psychology. *Personality and Social Psychology Bulletin, 5,* 122–125.

Pennebaker, J. W., & Harber, K. D. (1991, April). *Coping after the Loma Prieta earthquake: A preliminary report.* Paper presented at the Western Psychological Association Convention, San Francisco, CA.

Pennebaker, J. W., & Harber, K. D. (1993). A social stage model of collective coping: The Loma Prieta earthquake and the Persian Gulf war. *Journal of Social Issues, 49,* 125–145.

Pennisi, E. (1998, May 8). DNA sequencers' trial by fire. *Science, 280,* 814–817.

Peretz, L. (1993). *The enchanted world of sleep.* (Trans. by Anthony Berris). New Haven, CT: Yale University Press.

Perkins, D. F., & Lerner, R. M. (1995). Single and multiple indicators of physical attractiveness and psychosocial behaviors among young adolescents. *Journal of Early Adolescence, 15,* 268–297.

Perry, W. G., Jr. (1970). *Forms of intellectual and ethical development in the college years: A scheme.* New York: Holt, Rinehart and Winston.

Perry, W. J., Jr. (1994). Forms of intellectual and ethical development in the college years: A scheme. In Puka, B. (Ed.), *Defining perspectives in moral development: Vol. 1. Moral development: A compendium* (pp. 231–248). New York: Garland Publishing.

Pert, C. (1997). *Molecules of emotion.* New York: Scribner.

Pert, C. B., & Snyder, S. H. (1973). Opiate receptor: Demonstration in the nervous tissue. *Science, 179,* 1011–1014.

Pervin, L. A. (1985). Personality: Current controversies, issues, and directions. *Annual Review of Psychology, 36,* 83–114.

Peterson, C., & Barrett, L. C. (1987). Explanatory style and academic performance among university freshmen. *Journal of Personality and Social Psychology, 53,* 603–607.

Peterson, I. (1997, May 17). Computer triumphs over human champion. *Science News, 151*(20), 300.

Petrill, S. A., Plomin, R., Berg, S., Johansson, B., Pedersen, N. L., Ahern, F., & McClearn, G. E. (1998). Specific cognitive abilities in twins age 80 and older. *Psychological Science, 9,* 183–195.

Phelps, J. A., Davis, J. O., & Schartz, K. M. (1997). Nature, nurture, and twin research strategies. *Current Directions in Psychological Science, 6,* 117–121.

*Physician's desk reference* (53rd ed.). (1999). Montvale, NJ: Medical Economics Data Production Company.

Piaget, J. (1954). *The construction of reality in the child.* New York: Basic Books.

Pifer, A., & Bronte L. (Eds.). (1986). *Our aging society: Paradox and promise.* New York: Norton.

Pilisuk, M., & Parks, S. H. (1986). *The healing web: Social networks and human survival.* Hanover, NH: University Press of New England.

Pillard, R., & Bailey, M. (1991). A genetic study of male sexual orientation. *Archives of General Psychiatry, 48,* 1089–1096.

Pinker, S. (1994). *The language instinct.* New York: William Morrow.

Pion, G. M., Mednick, M. T., Astin, H. S., Hall, C. C. I., Kenkel, M. B., Keita, G. P., Kohout, J. L., & Kelleher, J. C. (1996). The shifting gender composition of psychology: Trends and implications for the discipline. *American Psychologist, 51,* 509–528.

Piotrowski, C., Keller, J. W., & Ogawa, T. (1993). Projective techniques: An international perspective. *Psychological Reports, 72,* 179–182.

Piotrowski, C., Sherry, D., & Keller, J. W. (1985). Psychodiagnostic test usage: A survey of the Society for Personality Assessment. *Journal of Personality Assessment, 49,* 115–119.

Piper, A., Jr. (1998, May/June). Multiple personality disorder: Witchcraft survives in the twentieth century. *Skeptical Inquirer, 22*(3), 44–50.

Pittenger, D. J. (1993). The utility of the Myers-Briggs Type Indicator. *Review of Educational Research, 63,* 467–488.

Plomin, R. (1989). Environment and genes: Determinants of behavior. *American Psychologist, 44,* 105–111.

Plomin, R. (1997, August). Current directions in behavioral genetics: Moving into the mainstream. *Current Directions in Psychological Science, 6,* 85.

Plomin, R., & McClearn, G. E. (Eds.). (1993). *Nature, nurture, and psychology.* Washington, DC: American Psychological Association.

Plomin, R., Owen, M. J., & McGuffin, P. (1994). The genetic basis of complex human behaviors. *Science, 264,* 1733–1739.

Plomin, R., & Rende, R. (1991). Human behavioral genetics. *Annual Review of Psychology, 42,* 161–190.

Plutchik, R. (1980). *Emotion: A psychoevolutionary synthesis.* New York: Harper & Row.

Plutchik, R. (1984). Emotions: A general psychoevolutionary theory. In K. Scherer & P. Ekman (Eds.), *Approaches to emotion.* Hillsdale, NJ: Erlbaum.

Polefrone, J. M., & Manuck, S. B. (1987). Gender differences in cardiovascular and neuroendocrine response to stressors. In R. C. Barnett, L. Biener, & G. K. Baruch (Eds.), *Gender and stress.* New York: Free Press.

Poling, A., Gadow, K. D., & Cleary, J. (1991). *Drug therapy for behavior disorders: An introduction.* New York: Pergamon Press.

Polivy, J., & Herman, C. P. (1993). Etiology of binge eating: Psychological mechanisms. In C. G. Fairburn & G. T. Wilson (Eds.), *Binge eating: Nature, assessment, and treatment* (pp. 173–205). New York: Guilford Press.

Pomerantz, J. R. (1994). On criteria for ethics in science: Commentary on Rosenthal. *Psychological Science, 5,* 135–136.

Pool, R. (1997, October). Portrait of a gene guy. *Discover,* pp. 51–55.

Poon, L. W. (1985). Differences in human memory with aging: Nature, causes, and clinical implications. In J. E. Birren & W. K. Schaie (Eds.), *Handbook of the psychology of aging* (pp. 427–462). New York: Van Nostrand Reinhold.

Popejoy, D. I. (1967). *The effects of a physical fitness program on selected psychological and physiological measures of anxiety.* Unpublished doctoral dissertation. University of Illinois.

Porter, L. S., & Stone, A. A. (1995). Are there really gender differences in coping? A reconsideration of previous data and results from a daily study. *Journal of Social and Clinical Psychology, 14,* 184–202.

Posner, M. I. (1993). Seeing the mind. *Science, 262,* 673–674.

Posner, M. I., & McCandliss, B. D. (1993). Converging methods for investigating lexical access. *Science, 4,* 305–309.

Posner, M. I., & Raichle, M. E. (1994). *Images of mind.* New York: W. H. Freeman.

Posner, M. I., Rothbart, M. K., & Harman, C. (1994). Cognitive science's contributions to culture and emotion. In S. Kitayama & H. R. Markus (Eds.), *Emotion and culture* (pp. 197–216). Washington, D.C.: American Psychological Association.

Powell, L. H., Shaker, L. A., & Jones, B. A. (1993). Psychosocial predictors of mortality in 83 women with premature acute myocardial infarction. *Psychosomatic Medicine, 55,* 426–433.

Premack, D. (1965). Reinforcement theory. In D. Levine (Ed.), *Nebraska Symposium on Motivation* (pp. 128–180). Lincoln: University of Nebraska Press.

Prentice, D. A., & Miller, D. T. (1993). Pluralistic ignorance and alcohol use on campus: Some consequences on misperceiving the social norm. *Journal of Personality and Social Psychology, 64,* 243–256.

Pribram, K. H. (1986). The cognitive revolution and mind/brain issues. *American Psychologist, 41,* 507–520.

Price, D. D., Rafii, A., Watkins, L. R., & Buckingham, B. (1984). A psychophysical analysis of acupuncture analgesia. *Pain, 19,* 27–42.

Priest, R. F., & Sawyer, J. (1967). Proximity and peership: Bases of balance in interpersonal attraction. *American Journal of Sociology, 72,* 633–649.

Primavera, L. H., & Herron, W. G. (1996). The effect of viewing television violence on aggression. *International Journal of Instructional Media, 23,* 91–104.

Prinzmetal, W. (1995). Visual feature integration in a world of objects. *Current Directions in Psychological Science, 5,* 90–94.

Putnam, F. W., Guroff, J. J., Silberman, E. K., Barban, L., & Post, R. M. (1986). The clinical phenomenology of multiple personality disorder: Review of 100 recent cases. *Journal of Clinical Psychiatry, 47,* 285–293.

Rabkin, J. G., & Struening, E. L. (1976). Life events, stress, and illness. *Science, 194,* 1013–1020.

Rachman, S. (1966). Sexual fetishism: An experimental analogue. *Psychological Record, 6,* 293–296.

Ragland, D. R., & Brand, R. J. (1988). Type A behavior and mortality from coronary heart disease. *New England Journal of Medicine, 318,* 65–69.

Rahe, R. H., & Arthur, R. J. (1978, March). Life change and illness studies: Past history and future directions. *Journal of Human Stress,* pp. 3–15.

Raichle, M. E. (1994). Visualizing the mind. *Scientific American, 270*(4), 58–64.

Rakic, P. (1985). Limits of neurogenesis in primates. *Science, 227,* 1054–1057.

Ramachandran, V. S. (1992). Filling in gaps in perception: Part 1. *Current Directions in Psychological Science, 1,* 199–205.

Ramey, C. T., & Ramey, S. L. (1998a). Early intervention and early experience. *American Psychologist, 53,* 109–120.

Ramey, C. T,. & Ramey, S. L. (1998b). In defense of special education. *American Psychologist, 53,* 1159–1160.

Rand, C. S., & Kuldau, J. M. (1992). Epidemiology of bulimia and symptoms in a general population: Sex, age, race, and socioeconomic status. *International Journal of Eating Disorders, 11,* 37–44.

Rapoport, J. L. (1989, March). The biology of obsessions and compulsions. *Scientific American, 263,* 83–89.

Raymond, C. (1989, September 20). Scientists examining behavior of a man who lost his memory gain new insights into the workings of the human mind. *The Chronicle of Higher Education,* pp. A4, A6.

Raymond, J. L., Lisberger, S. G., & Mauk, M. D. (1996, May 24). The cerebellum: A neuronal learning machine? *Science, 272,* 1126–1131.

Raynor, J. O. (1970). Relationships between achievement-related motives, future orientation, and academic performance. *Journal of Personality and Social Psychology, 15,* 28–33.

Raz, S., & Raz, N. (1990). Structural brain abnormalities in the major psychoses: A quantitative review of the evidence from computerized imaging. *Psychological Bulletin, 16,* 491–402.

Reber, A. S. (1993). *Implicit learning and tacit knowledge: An essay on the cognitive unconscious.* (Oxford Psychology Series No. 19). Oxford, U.K.: Oxford University Press.

Redelmeier, D. A., Rozin, P., & Kahneman, D. (1993). Understanding patients' decisions: Cognitive and emotional perspectives. *JAMA, 270,* 72–76.

Regier, D. A., Boyd, J. H, Burke, J. D., Rae, D. S., Myers, J. K., Kramer, M., Robins, L. N., George, L. K., Karno, M., & Locke, B. Z. (1988). One-month prevalence of mental disorders in the United States. *Archives of General Psychiatry, 45,* 977–986.

Regier, D. A., Narrow, W. E., Rae, D. S., Manderscheid, R. W., Locke, B. Z., & Goodwin, F. K. (1993). The de facto US mental and addictive disorders service system: Epidemiologic Catchment Area prospective 1-year-prevalence rates of disorders and services. *Archives of General Psychiatry, 50,* 85–94.

Reinisch, J. M. (1990). *The Kinsey Institute new report on sex: What you must know to be sexually literate.* New York: St. Martin's Press.

Reisenzein, R. (1983). The Schachter theory of emotion: Two decades later. *Psychological Bulletin, 94,* 239–264.

Reiser, B. J., Black, J. B., & Abelson, R. P. (1985). Knowledge structures in the organization and retrieval of autobiographical memories. *Cognitive Psychology, 17,* 89–137.

Rescorla, R. A. (1972). Information variables in Pavlovian conditioning. In G. Bower (Ed.), *The psychology of learning and motivation* (Vol. 6). New York: Academic Press.

Rescorla, R. A., & Wagner, A. R. (1972). A theory of Pavlovian conditioning: Variations in the effectiveness of reinforcement and nonreinforcement. In A. H. Black & W. F. Prokasy (Eds.), *Classical conditioning, II: Current research and theory* (pp. 64–94). New York: Appleton-Century-Crofts.

Resnick, S. M. (1992). Positron emission tomography in psychiatric illness. *Current Directions in Psychological Science, 1,* 92–98.

Rest, J. R., & Thoma, S. J. (1976). Relation of moral judgment development to formal education. *Developmental Psychology, 21,* 709–714.

Riddle, D., & Morin, S. (1977). Removing the stigma from individuals. *American Psychological Association Monitor, 16,* 28.

Riehle, A., Grün, S., Diesmann, M, & Aertsen, A. (1997, December 12). Spike synchronization and rate modulation differentially involved in motor cortical function. *Science, 278,* 1950–1953.

Rimland, B. (1982). The altruism paradox. *The Southern psychologist, 2*(1), 8–9.

Rips, L. J. (1990). *Annual Review of Psychology, 41,* 321–353.

Roberts, A. H. (1985). Biofeedback: Research, training, and clinical roles. *American Psychologist, 40,* 938–941.

Roberts, A. H., Kewman, D. G., Mercier, L., & Hovell, M. (1993). The power of nonspecific effects in healing: Implications for psychosocial and biological treatments. *Clinical Psychology Review, 13,* 373–391.

Robins, C. J. (1988). Attributions and depression: Why is the literature so inconsistent? *Journal of Personality and Social Psychology, 54,* 880–889.

Robins, L. N., Locke, B. Z., & Regier, D. A. (1991). An overview of psychiatric disorders in America. In L. N. Robins & D. A. Regier (Eds.), *Psychiatric disorders in America: The epidemiologic catchment area study.* New York: Free Press.

Rock, I., & Palmer, S. (1990, December). The legacy of Gestalt psychology. *Scientific American, 263,* 84–90.

Rodin, J. (1986). Aging and health: Effects of the sense of control. *Science, 233,* 1271–1276.

Rodin, J., & Salovey, P. (1989). Health psychology. *Annual Review of Psychology, 40,* 533–579.

Rodin, J., Striegel-Moore, R. H., & Silberstein, L. R. (1985, July). *A prospective study of bulimia among college students on three U. S. campuses.* Unpublished manuscript. New Haven: Yale University.

Roediger, H. L., III. (1990). Implicit memory: Retention without remembering. *American Psychologist, 45,* 1043–1056.

Rogers, C. R. (1951). *Client-centered therapy: Its current practice, implications and theory.* Boston: Houghton Mifflin.

Rogers, C. R. (1957). The necessary and sufficient conditions of therapeutic personality change. *Journal of Consulting Psychology, 21,* 95–103.

Rogers, C. R. (1961). *On becoming a person: A therapist's view of psychotherapy.* Boston: Houghton Mifflin.

Rogers, C. R. (1977). *On personal power: Inner strength and its revolutionary impact.* New York: Delacorte.

Rogers, C. R. (1980). *A way of being.* Boston: Houghton Mifflin.

Rogers, C. R. (1982, July/August) Roots of madness. In T. H. Carr & H. E. Fitzgerald (Eds.), *Psychology 83/84* (pp. 263–267). Guilford, CT: Dushkin. (Originally published in *Science 82,* July/August, 1982).

Rogoff, B. (1990). *Apprenticeship in thinking: Cognitive development in social context.* New York: Oxford University Press.

Roll, S., Hinton, R., & Glazer, M. (1974). Dreams and death: Mexican Americans vs. Anglo-Americans. *Interamerican Journal of Psychology, 8,* 111–115.

Rollman, G. B., & Harris, G. (1987). The detectability, discriminability, and perceived magnitude of painful electrical shock. *Perception & Psychophysics, 42,* 257–268.

Rolls, B. J., Federoff, I. C., & Guthrie, J. F. (1991). Gender differences in eating behavior and body weight regulation. *Health Psychology, 10,* 133–142.

Rolnick, J. (1998, December 4). Treating mental disorders: A neuroscientist says no to drugs. *The Chronicle of Higher Education,* A10.

Rorschach, H. (1942). *Psychodiagnostics: A diagnostic test based on perception.* New York: Grune & Stratton.

Rosa, L., Rosa, E., Sarner, L., & Barrett, S. (1998). A close look at therapeutic touch. *Journal of the American Medical Association, 279,* 1005–1010.

Rosch, E. H. (1973). Natural categories. *Cognitive Psychology, 4,* 328–350.

Rosch, E., & Mervis, C. B. (1975). Family resemblances: Studies in the internal structure of categories. *Cognitive Psychology, 7,* 573–605.

Rosch, E. H., Mervis, C. B., Gray, W. D., Johnson, D. M., & Boyes-Braem, P. (1976). Basic objects in natural categories. *Cognitive Psychology, 8,* 382–439.

Rosen, J. B., & Schulkin, J. (1998). From normal fear to pathological anxiety. *Psychological Review, 105,* 325–350.

Rosenblatt, P. C. (1966). A cross-cultural study of child-rearing and romantic love. *Journal of Personality and Social Psychology, 4,* 336–338.

Rosenhan, D. L. (1969). Some origins of concern for others. In P. Mussen, J. Langer, & M. Covington (Eds.), *Trends and issues in developmental psychology.* New York: Holt, Rinehart & Winston.

Rosenhan, D. L. (1973). On being sane in insane places. *Science, 179,* 250–258.

Rosenhan, D. L. (1975). The contextual nature of psychiatric diagnoses. *Journal of Abnormal Psychology, 84,* 462–474.

Rosenhan, D. L. (1983). Psychological abnormality and law. In C. J. Scheirer & B. C. Hammonds (Eds.), *The master lecture series: Vol. 2. Psychology and the law.* Washington, DC: American Psychological Association.

Rosenhan, D. L., & Seligman, M. E. P. (1995). *Abnormal psychology* (3rd ed.) New York: Norton.

Rosenthal, R. (1994). Science and ethics in conducting, analyzing, and reporting psychological research. *Psychological Science, 5,* 127–134.

Rosenthal, R., & Jacobson, L. F. (1968). Teacher expectations for the disadvantaged. *Scientific American, 218*(4), 19–23.

Rosenzweig, M. R. (1992a). Psychological science around the world. *American Psychologist, 47,* 718–722.

Rosenzweig, M. R. (1992b). Research on the neural bases of learning and memory. In M. R. Rosenzweig (Ed.), *International psychological science: Progress, problems, and prospects* (pp. 103–136). Washington, DC: American Psychological Association.

Ross, C. A., Miller, S. D., Reagor, P., Bjornson, L., Fraser, G. A., & Anderson, G. (1990). Structured interview data on 102 cases of multiple personality disorder from four centers. *American Journal of Psychiatry, 147,* 596–601.

Ross, C. A., Norton, G. R., & Wozney, K. (1989). Multiple personality disorder: An analysis of 236 cases. *Canadian Journal of Psychiatry, 34,* 413–418.

Ross, L. (1977). The intuitive psychologist and his shortcomings. In L. Berkowitz (Ed.), *Advances in ex-*

perimental social psychology (Vol. 10). New York: Academic Press.

Ross, L., & Nisbett, R. E. (1991). The person and the situation: Perspectives of social psychology. New York: McGraw-Hill.

Ross, P. E. (1992, July). Compulsive canines. Scientific American, 266 (5), 24–25.

Roth, T., Roehrs, T., Carskadon, M. A., & Dement, W. C. (1989). Daytime sleepiness and alertness. In M. Kryser, T. Roth, & W. C. Dement (Eds.), Principles and practice of sleep medicine (pp. 14–23). New York: Saunders.

Rotter, J. B. (1954). Social learning and clinical psychology. Englewood Cliffs, NJ: Prentice-Hall.

Rotter, J. B. (1966). Generalized expectancies for internal versus external control of reinforcement. Psychological Monographs, 80 (Whole no. 609).

Rotter, J. B. (1971, June). External control and internal control. Psychology Today, 4, 37–42, 58–59.

Rotter, J. B. (1990). Internal versus external control of reinforcement: A case history of a variable. American Psychologist, 45, 489–493.

Rottschaefer, W. A. (1991). Some philosophical implications of Bandura's social cognitive theory of human agency. American Psychologist, 46, 153–155.

Rouhana, N. N., & Kelman, H. C. (1994). Promoting joint thinking in international conflicts: An Israeli-Palestinian continuing workshop. Journal of Social Issues, 50, 157–168.

Roush, W. (1996, July 5). Live long and prosper? Science, 273, 42–46.

Rozin, P. (1976). The evolution of intelligence and access to the cognitive unconscious. In J. M. Sprague & A. A. Epstein (Eds.), Progress in psychobiology and physiological psychology (pp. 245–280). New York: Academic Press.

Rubin, Z. (1973). Liking and loving: An invitation to social psychology. New York: Holt, Rinehart and Winston.

Rusting, C. L., & Nolen-Hoeksema, S. (1998). Regulating responses to anger: Effects of rumination and distraction on angry mood. Journal of Personality and Social Psychology, 74, 790–803.

Rutter, M., Macdonald, H., Le Couteur, A., Harrington, R., Bolton, P., & Bailey, A. (1990). Genetic factors in child psychiatric disorders—II. Empirical findings. Journal of Child Psychology and Psychiatry, 31, 39–83.

Ryff, C. D. (1989). In the eye of the beholder: Views of psychological well-being among middle-aged and older adults. Psychology and Aging, 4, 195–210.

Saarinen, T. F. (1987). Centering of mental maps of the world: Discussion paper. Tucson: University of Arizona, Department of Geography and Regional Development.

Sacks, O. (1995). An anthropologist on Mars. New York: Random House.

Salter, S. (1993). "Buried Memories/ Broken Families," San Francisco Examiner, April 4, pp. A1,ff.

Saltzstein, H. D., & Sandberg, L. (1979). Indirect social influence: Change in judgmental processor anticipatory conformity. Journal of Experimental Social Psychology, 15, 209–216.

Sanger, M. (1971). Margaret Sanger: An autobiography. New York: W. W. Norton/Dover Publications, Inc. (Original work published in 1938).

Sapolsky, R. (1992, March). How big is yours? Discover, 13, 40–43.

Sapolsky, R. (1997, October). A gene for nothing. Discover, 40, 42–44, 46.

Sapolsky, R. M. (1990). Adrenocortical function, social rank, and personality among wild baboons. Biological Psychiatry, 28, pp. 1–17.

Sapolsky, R. M. (1992). Stress: The aging brain and the mechanisms of neuron death. Cambridge, MA: MIT Press.

Sarbin, T. R., & Coe, W. C. (1972). Hypnosis: A social psychological analysis of influence communication. New York: Holt, Rinehart & Winston.

Satir, V. (1967). Conjoint family therapy (Rev. ed.). Palo Alto, CA: Science and Behavior Books.

Satir, V. (1983). Conjoint family therapy (3rd ed.). Palo Alto, CA: Science and Behavior Books.

Satir, V., Banmen, J., Gerber, J., & Gomori, M. (1991). Satir model: Family therapy and beyond. Palo Alto, CA: Science & Behavior Books.

Sattler, J. M. (1970). Racial "experimenter effects" in experimentation, testing, interviewing, and psychotherapy. Psychological Bulletin, 73, 137–160.

Saudino, K. J. (1997, August). Moving beyond the heritability question: New directions in behavioral genetic studies of personality. Current Directions in Psychological Science, 6, 86–90.

Savitsky, J. C., & Lindblom, W. D. (1986). The impact of the guilty but mentally ill verdict on juror decisions: An empirical analysis. Journal of Applied Social Psychology.

Saxe, L. (1991). Lying: Thoughts of an applied social psychologist. American Psychologist, 46, 409–415.

Saxe, L. (1994). Detection of deception: Polygraph and integrity tests. Current Directions in Psychological Science, 3, 69–73.

Saxe, L. Dougherty, D., & Cross, T. (1985). The validity of polygraph

testing: Scientific analysis and public controversy. American Psychologist, 40, 355-366.

Scarr, S. (1988). Race and gender as psychological variables: Social and ethical issues. American Psychologist, 43, 56–59.

Scarr, S. (1997). Why child care has little impact on most children's development. Current Directions in Psychological Science, 6, 143–148.

Scarr, S. (1998). American child care today. American Psychologist, 53, 95–108.

Scarr, S., & Weinberg, R. (1976). IQ test performance of black children adopted by white families. American Psychologist, 31, 726–739.

Scarr, S., & Weinberg, R. A. (1978, April). Attitudes, interests, and IQ. Human Nature, pp. 29–36.

Schacter, D. L. (1992). Understanding implicit memory: A cognitive neuroscience approach. American Psychologist, 47, 559–569.

Schacter, D. L. (1996). Searching for memory: The brain, the mind, and the past. New York: Basic Books.

Schacter, D. L. (1999). The seven sins of memory: Insights from psychology and cognitive neuroscience. American Psychologist, 54, 182–203.

Schachter, S. (1971). Emotion, obesity and crime. New York: Academic Press.

Schachter, S. (1977). Nicotine regulation in heavy and light smokers. Journal of Experimental Psychology: General, 106, 5–12.

Schachter, S., & Singer, J. (1962). Cognitive, social and physiological determinants of emotional state. Psychological Review, 69, 379–399.

Schaefer, H. H., & Martin, P. L. (1966). Behavioral therapy for "apathy" of hospitalized patients. Psychological Reports, 19, 1147–1158.

Schank, R. C., & Abelson, R. (1977). Scripts, plans, goals and understanding: An inquiry into human knowledge and structures. Hillsdale, NJ: Erlbaum.

Schatzberg, A. F. (1991). Overview of anxiety disorders: Prevalence, biology, course, and treatment. Journal of Clinical Psychiatry, 42, 5–9.

Schaufeli, W. B., Maslach, C., & Marek, T. (Ed.) (1993). Professional burnout: Recent developments in theory and research. Washington, DC: Taylor & Francis.

Schleifer, S. J., Keller, S. E., Camerino, M., Thornton, J. C., & Stein, M. (1983). Suppression of lymphocyte stimulation following bereavement. Journal of the American Medical Association, 250, 374–377.

Schlenker, B. R., Weingold, M. F., Hallam, J. R. (1990). Self-serving attributions in social context: Ef-

fects of self-esteem and social pressure. Journal of Personality and Social Psychology, 58, 855–863.

Schmidt, W. E. (1987, June 7). Paddling in school: A tradition is under fire. The New York Times, pp. A1, A22.

Schneider, K., & May, R. (1995). The psychology of existence: An integrative, clinical perspective. New York: McGraw-Hill.

Schreiber, F. R. (1973). Sybil. New York: Warner Books.

Schroeder, D. A., Penner, L. A., Dovidio, J. F., & Piliavin, J. A. (1995). The psychology of helping and altruism. New York: McGraw-Hill.

Schroeder, D. A., & Prentice, D. A. (1995). Pluralistic ignorance and alcohol use on campus II: Correcting misperceptions of the social norm. Unpublished manuscript, Princeton University.

Schroeder, S. R., Schroeder, C. S., & Landesman, S. (1987). Psychological services in educational settings to persons with mental retardation. American Psychologist, 42, 805–808.

Schulkin, J. (1994). Melancholic depression and the hormones of adversity: A role for the amygdala. Current Directions in Psychological Science, 3, 41–44.

Schwartz, B. (1997). Psychology, idea technology, and ideology. Psychological Science, 8, 21–27.

Schwartz, P. (1994). Peer marriage: How love between equals really works. New York: The Free Press.

Schwartz, J. M., Stoessel, P. W., Baxter, L. R., Martin, K. M., & Phelps, M. E. (1996). Systematic changes in cerebral glucose metabolic rate after successful behavior modification treatment of obsessive–compulsive disorder. Archives of General Psychiatry, 53, 109–116.

Schwarzer, R. (Ed.). (1992). Self-efficacy: Thought control of action. Washington, DC: Hemisphere.

Schwebel, A. I., & Fine, M. A. (1994). Understanding and helping families: A cognitive behavioral approach. Hillsdale, NJ: Erlbaum.

Schweinhart, L. J., & Weikart, D. P. (1986, January). What do we know so far? A review of the Head Start Synthesis Project. Young Children, 41(2), 49–55.

Scott, J. P. (1963). The process of primary socialization in canine and human infants. Monographs of the Society for Research in Child Development, 28, 1–47.

Scott, K. G., & Carran, D. T. (1987). The epidemiology and prevention of mental retardation. American Psychologist, 42, 801–804.

Scovern, A. W., & Kilmann, P. R. (1980). Status of electro-convulsive therapy: Review of outcome literature. *Psychological Bulletin, 87,* 260–303.

Segall, M., Campbell, D., & Herskovits, M. (1966). *The influence of culture on visual perception.* Indianapolis: Bobbs-Merrill.

Segal, M. W. (1974). Alphabet and attraction: An unobtrusive measure of the effect of propinquity in a field setting. *Journal of Personality and Social Psychology, 30,* 654–657.

Segall, M. H. (1994). A cross-cultural research contribution to unraveling the nativist/empiricist controversy. In W. J. Lonner & R. Malpass, *Psychology and culture* (pp. 135–138). Boston: Allyn & Bacon.

Segall, M. H., Dasen, P. R., Berry, J. W., & Poortinga, Y. H. (1990). *Human behavior in global perspective: An introduction to cross-cultural psychology.* Boston: Allyn & Bacon.

Seger, C. A. (1994). Implicit learning. *Psychological Bulletin, 115* (2), 163–196.

Selfridge, O. G. (1955). Pattern recognition and modern computers. *Proceedings of the Western Joint Computer Conference.* New York: Institute of Electrical and Electronics Engineers.

Seligman, K. (1988, October 9). Educators are alarmed over testing frenzy. *San Francisco Examiner,* pp. B-1, B-5.

Seligman, M. E. P. (1971). Preparedness and phobias. *Behavior Therapy, 2,* 307–320.

Seligman, M. E. P. (1973, June). Fall into helplessness. *Psychology Today, 7,* 43–48

Seligman, M. E. P. (1975). *Helplessness: On depression, development and death.* San Francisco: Freeman.

Seligman, M. E. P. (1991). *Learned optimism.* New York: Knopf.

Seligman, M. E. P. (1995). The effectiveness of psychotherapy: The *Consumer Reports* study. *American Psychologist, 50,* 965–974.

Seligman, M. E. P., Abramson, L. Y., Semmel, A., & von Baeyer, C. (1979). Depressive attributional style. *Journal of Abnormal Psychology, 88,* 242–247.

Seligman, M. E. P., & Maier, S. F. (1967). Failure to escape traumatic shock. *Journal of Experimental Psychology, 74,* 1–9.

Seligson, S. V. (1994, November/December). Say good night to snoring. *Health, 8*(7), 89–93.

Selye, H. (1956). *The stress of life.* New York: McGraw-Hill.

Selye, H. (1974). *Stress without distress.* New York: New American Library.

Selye, H. (1976). *Stress in health and disease.* Reading, MA: Butterworth.

Selye, H. (1980). The stress concept today. In I. L. Kutash et al. (Eds.),

*Handbook on stress and anxiety.* San Francisco: Jossey-Bass.

Serpell, R. (1994). The cultural construction of intelligence. In Lonner, W. J. & Malpass, R. *Psychology and culture* (pp. 157–163). Boston: Allyn & Bacon.

Sexton, V. S., & Misiak, H. (1984). American psychologists and psychology abroad. *American Psychologist, 39,* 1026–1031.

Shapiro, D. H. (1985). Clinical use of meditation as a self-regulation strategy: Comments on Holmes's conclusions and implications. *American Psychologist, 40,* 719–722.

Shapiro, F. (1995). *Desensitization and reprocessing: Basic principles, protocols, and procedures.* New York: Guilford.

Shattuck, R. (1981). *The forbidden experiment: The story of the wild boy of Aveyron.* New York: Farrar, Straus & Giroux.

Shatz, M., Wellman, H. M., & Silber, S. (1983). The acquisition of mental verbs: A systematic investigation of the first reference to mental state. *Cognition, 14,* 301–321.

Shaver, P., & Hazan, C. (1987). Romantic love conceptualized as an attachment process. *Journal of Personality and Social Psychology, 52,* 511–524.

Shaver, P. R., & Hazan, C. (1993). Adult attachment: Theory and research. In W. Jones & D. Perlman (Eds.), *Advances in personal relationships,* Vol. 4, 29–70. London, England: Jessica Kingsley.

Shaver, P. R., & Hazan, C. (1994). Attachment. In A. L. Weber & J. H. Harvey (Eds.), *Perspectives on close relationships* (Chapter 6, 110–130). Boston: Allyn & Bacon.

Shea, C. (1996, September 27). Researchers try to understand why people are doing better on IQ tests. *The Chronicle of Higher Education,* p. A-18

Shea, C. (1998, January 30). Why depression strikes more women than men: "Ruminative coping" may provide answers. *The Chronicle of Higher Education,* p. 14.

Sheingold, K., & Tenney, Y. J. (1982). Memory for a salient childhood event. In U. Neisser (Ed.), *Memory observed.* San Francisco: Freeman.

Shepard, R. N. (1990). *Mind sights.* New York: W. H. Freeman.

Shepard, R. N., & Metzler, J. (1971). Mental rotation of three-dimensional objects. *Science, 171,* 701–703.

Sherif, C. W. (1981, August). *Social and psychological bases of social psychology.* The G. Stanley Hall Lecture on social psychology, presented at the annual convention of the American Psychological Association, Los Angeles, CA.

Sherif, M., Harvey, O. J., White, B. J., Hood, W., & Sherif, C. (1961). *Intergroup conflict and cooperation: The Robbers Cave experiment.* Norman, OK: University of Oklahoma Institute of Intergroup Relations.

Shields, S. A. (1991). Gender in the psychology of emotion: A selective research review. In K. T. Strongman (Ed.), *International review of studies on emotion* (Vol 1). New York: Wiley.

Shiffrin, R. M. (1993). Short-term memory: A brief commentary. *Memory and Cognition, 21* (2), 193–197.

Shimamura, A. P. (1996, September/October). Unraveling the mystery of the frontal lobes: Exlorations in cognitive neuroscience. *Psychological Science Agenda,* 8–9.

Shobe, K. K., & Kihlstrom, J. F. (1997). Is traumatic memory special? *Current Directions in Psychological Science, 6,* 70–74.

Siegel, B. (1988). Love, medicine & miracles. New York: Harper & Row.

Siegel, J. M. (1990). Stressful life events and use of physician services among the elderly: The moderating role of pet ownership. *Journal of Personality and Social Psychology, 58,* 1081–1086.

Siegel, R. K. (1980). The psychology of life after death. *American Psychologist, 35,* 911–931.

Siegel, R. K. (1992). *Fire in the brain.* New York: Dutton.

Siegler, R. S. (1994). Cognitive variability: A key to understanding cognitive development. *Current Directions in Psychological Science, 3,* 1–5.

Sigelman, C. K., Thomas, D. B., Sigelman, L., & Robich, F. D. (1986). Gender, physical attractiveness, and electability: An experimental investigation of voter biases. *Journal of Applied Social Psychology, 16,* 229–248.

Silbersweig, D. A., Stern, E., Frith, C., Cahill, C., Holmes, A., Grootoonk, S., Seaward, J., McKenna, P., Chua, S. E., Schnorr, L., Jones, T., & Frackowiak, R. S. J. (1995). A functional neuroanatomy of hallucinations in schizophrenia. *Nature, 378* (November 9), 176–179.

Silver, R. L. (1983). Coping with an undesirable life event: A study of early reactions to physical disability. *Dissertation Abstracts International, 43,* 3415.

Silver, R. L., Boon, C., & Stones, M. L. (1983). Searching for meaning in misfortune: Making sense of incest. *Journal of Social Issues, 39,* 81–101.

Silver, R. L., & Wortman, C. B. (1980). Coping with undesirable life events. In J. Garber & M. E. P. Seligman (Eds.), *Human helpless-*

*ness: Theory and application.* New York: Academic Press.

Simon, H. A. (1992). What is an "explanation" of behavior? *Psychological Science, 3,* 150–161.

Simpson, J. A. (1990). The influence of attachment styles on romantic relationships. *Journal of Personality and Social Psychology, 59,* 971–980.

Simpson, J. A., & Harris, B. A. (1994). Interpersonal attraction. In A. L. Weber & J. H. Harvey (Eds.), *Perspectives on close relationships* (pp. 45–66). Boston: Allyn & Bacon.

Sinclair, R. C., Hoffman, C., Mark, M. M., Martin L. L., & Pickering, T. L. (1994). Construct accessibility and the misattrbution of arousal: Schacter and Singer revisited. *Psychological Sciences, 5,* 15–18.

Singer, J. L. (1966). *Daydreaming: An introduction to the experimental study of inner experience.* New York: Random House.

Singer, J. L. (1975). Navigating the stream of consciousness: Research in daydreaming and related inner experience. *American Psychologist, 30,* 727–739.

Singer, J. L., & McCraven, V. J. (1961). Some characteristics of adult daydreaming. *Journal of Psychology, 51,* 151–164.

Singer, J. L., Singer, D. G., & Rapaczynski, W. S. (1984). Family patterns and television viewing as predictors of children's beliefs and aggression. *Journal of Communication, 34,* 73–89.

Singer, W. (1995, November 3). Development and plasticity of cortical processing architectures. *Science, 270,* 758–763.

Skinner, B. F. (1981). Selection by consequences. *Science, 213,* 501–504.

Skinner, B. F. (1987). Whatever happened to psychology as the science of behavior? *American Psychologist, 42,* 780–786.

Skinner, B. F. (1989). The origins of cognitive thought. *American Psychologist, 44,* 13–18.

Skinner, B. F. (1990). Can psychology be a science of mind? *American Psychologist, 45,* 1206–1210.

Skoog, I., Nilsson, L., Palmertz, B., Andreasson, L. A., & Svanborg, A. (1993). A population-based study of dementia in 85-year-olds. *New England Journal of Medicine, 328,* 153.

Sleek, S. (1994, April). Could Prozac replace demand for therapy? *APA Monitor,* p. 28.

Sleek, S. (1996, May). Shifting the paradigm for prescribing drugs. *APA Monitor,* pp. 1, 29.

Sleek, S. (1998, August). Experts scrambling on school shootings. *APA Monitor,* pp. 1, 35–36.

Slobin, D. I. (1979). *Psycholinguistics* (2nd ed.). Glenview, IL: Scott, Foresman.

Slobin, D. I. (1985a). Introduction: Why study acquisition crosslinguistically? In D.I. Slobin (Ed.), *The crosslinguistic study of language acquisition. Vol. 1: The data* (pp. 3–24). Hillsdale, NJ: Erlbaum.

Slobin, D. I. (1985b). Cross-linguistic evidence of the language making capacity. In D. I. Slobin (Ed.), *The crosslinguistic study of language acquisition. Vol. 2: Theoretical issues* (pp. 1157–1256). Hillsdale, NJ: Erlbaum.

Smith, C. A., & Ellsworth, P. C. (1987). Patterns of appraisal and emotion related to taking an exam. *Journal of Personality and Social Psychology, 52,* 475–488.

Smith, E. E., & Medin, D. L. (1981). *Cognitive Science Series: 4. Categories and concepts.* Cambridge, MA: Harvard University Press.

Smith, G. B., Schwebel, A. I., Dunn, R. L., & McIver, S. D. (1993). The role of psychologists in the treatment, management, and prevention of chronic mental illness. *American Psychologist, 48,* 966–971.

Smith, L. D. (1992). On prediction and control: B. F. Skinner and the technological ideal of science. *American Psychologist, 47,* 216–223.

Smith, M. L., & Glass, G. V. (1977). Meta-analysis of psychotherapy outcome studies. *American Psychologist, 32,* 752–760.

Smith, S. (1991, Spring). Two-generation program models: A new intervention strategy. *Social Policy Report of the Society for Research in Child Development, 5* (No. 1).

Snyder, S. H. (1986). *Drugs and the brain.* New York: Scientific American Books.

Sokol, M. M. (Ed.). (1987). *Psychological testing and American society, 1890–1930.* New Brunswick, NJ: Rutgers University Press.

Solanto, M. V., & Connors, C. K. (1982). A dose-response and time-action analysis of autonomic and behavioral effects of methylphenidate in attention deficit disorder with hyperactivity. *Psychophysiology, 19,* 658–667.

Solso, R. L. (1991). *Cognitive psychology* (3rd ed.). Boston: Allyn and Bacon.

Solso, R. L., & McCarthy, J. E. (1981). Prototype formation of faces: A case study of pseudomemory. *British Journal of Psychology, 72,* 499–503.

Solvason, H. B., Ghanta, V. K., & Hiramoto, R. N. (1988). Conditioned augmentation of natural killer cell activity: Independence from nociceptive effects and dependence on interferon-beta. *Journal of Immunology, 140,* 661–665.

Sorenson, R. C. (1973). *Adolescent sexuality in contemporary America.* Cleveland: World.

Sow, I. (1977). *Psychiatrie dynamique africaine*. Paris: Payot.

Spelke, E. S., and Owsley, C. J. (1979). Intermodal exploration and knowledge in infancy. *Infant Behavior and Development, 2,* 13–27.

Sperling, G. (1960). The information available in brief visual presentations. *Psychological Monographs, 74,* 1–29.

Sperling, G. (1963). A model for visual memory tasks. *Human Factors, 5,* 19–31.

Sperry, R. W. (1968). Mental unity following surgical disconnection of the cerebral hemispheres. *The Harvey Lectures,* Series 62. New York: Academic Press.

Sperry, R. W. (1982). Some effects of disconnecting the cerebral hemispheres. *Science, 217,* 1223–1226.

Sperry, R. W. (1988). Psychology's mentalist paradigm and the religion/science tension. *American Psychologist, 43,* 607–613.

Spiegel, D., & Cardeña, E. (1991). Disintegrated experience: The dissociate disorders revisited. *Psychological Bulletin, 100,* 366–378.

Spinweber, C. (1990). *Insomnias and parasomnias in young adults.* Paper presented at the annual meeting of the Western Psychological Association, Los Angeles, CA.

Spitzer, R. L., Gibbon, M., Skodol, A. E., Williams, J. B. W., & First, M. B. (1989). *DSM-III-R casebook.* Washington, DC: American Psychiatric Press.

Sprecher, S., & McKinney, K. (1994). Sexuality in close relationships. In A. L. Weber & J. H. Harvey (Eds.), *Perspectives on close relationships* (pp. 193–216). Boston: Allyn & Bacon.

Springer, S. P., & Deutsch, G. (1993). *Left brain, right brain* (4th ed.). New York: W. H. Freeman.

Sprock, J., & Blashfield, R. K. (1991). Classification and nosology. In M. Hersen, A. E. Kazdin, & A. S. Bellack (Eds.), *The clinical psychology handbook* (2nd ed., pp. 329–344). New York: Pergamon Press.

Squier, L. H., & Domhoff, G. W. (1998). The presentation of dreaming and dreams in introductory psychology textbooks: A critical examination with suggestions for textbook authors and course instructors. *Dreaming: Journal of the Association for the Study of Dreams, 8,* 149–168.

Squire, L. R. (1992). Memory and the hippocampus: A synthesis from findings with rats, monkeys, and humans. *Psychological Review, 99,* 195–231.

Squire, S. (1983). *The slender balance: Causes and cures for bulimia, anorexia, and the weight loss/weight gain seesaw.* New York: Putnam.

Staddon, J. E. R. (1992). Rationality, melioration, and law-of-effect models for choice. *Psychological Science, 3,* 136–141.

Stapley, J. C., & Haviland, J. M. (1989). Beyond depression: Gender differences in normal adolescents' emotional experiences. *Sex Roles, 20,* 295–308.

Stapp, J., Tucker, A. M., & VandenBos, G. R. (1985). Census of psychological personnel: 1983. *American Psychologist, 40,* 1317–1351.

Stavish, S. (1994, May/June). On the biology of temperament. *APS Observer, 7,* 35.

Stavish, S. (1994, Fall). Breathing room. *Stanford Medicine, 12*(1), 18–23.

Steele, C. M. (1997). A threat in the air: How stereotypes shape intellectual identity and performance. *American Psychologist, 52,* 613–629.

Stein, M. B., Walker, J. R., & Forde, D. R. (1996). Public-speaking fears in a community sample: Prevalence, impact on functioning, and diagnostic classification. *Archives of General Psychiatry, 53,* 169–174.

Steinmetz, J. E. (1998). The localization of a simple type of learning and memory: The cerebellum and classical eyeblink conditioning. *Current Directions in Psychological Science, 7,* 72–77.

Stern, J. A., Brown, M., Ulett, G. A., & Sletten, I. (1977). A comparison of hypnosis, acupuncture, morphine, valium, aspirin, and placebo in the management of experimentally induced pain. *Annals of the New York Academy of Sciences, 296,* 175–193.

Stern, W. (1914). The psychological methods of testing intelligence. *Educational Psychology Monographs* (No. 13).

Stern, W. C., & Morgane, P. S. (1974). Theoretical view of REM sleep function: Maintenance of catecholomine systems in the central nervous system. *Behavioral Biology, 11,* 1–32.

Sternberg, R. (1986). Inside intelligence. *American Scientist, 74,* 137–143.

Sternberg, R. J. (1994). A triarchic model for teaching and assessing students in general psychology. *The General Psychologist, 30,* 42–48.

Sternberg, R. J. (1998). *Cupid's arrow: The course of love through time.* New York: Cambridge University Press.

Sternberg, R. J., & Davidson, J. E. (1982, June). The mind of the puzzler. *Psychology Today,* pp. 37–44.

Sternberg, R. J., & Davidson, J. E. (1983). Insight in the gifted. *Educational Psychologist, 18,* 51–57.

Sternberg, R. J., & Lubart, T. I. (1991). An investment theory of creativity and its development. *Human Development, 34,* 1–31.

Sternberg, R. J., & Lubart, T. I. (1992). Buy low and sell high: An investment approach to creativity. *Current Directions in Psychological Science, 1,* 1–5.

Sternberg, R. J., Wagner, R. K., Williams, W. M., & Horvath, J. A. (1995). Testing common sense. *American Psychologist, 50,* 912–927.

Stevenson, H. W. (1992, December). Learning from Asian schools. *Scientific American, 267,* 70–76.

Stevenson, H. W., Chen, C., & Lee, S-Y. (1993). Mathematics achievement of Chinese, Japanese, and American children: Ten years later. *Science, 259,* 53–58.

Stevenson, J., Graham, P., Fredman, G., & McLoughlin, V. A. (1987). Twin study of genetic influences on reading and spelling ability and disability. *Journal of Child Psychiatry, 28,* 229–247.

Stock, M. B., & Smythe, P. M. (1963). Does undernutrition during infancy inhibit brain growth and subsequent intellectual development? *Archives of Disorders in Childhood, 38,* 546–552.

Storms, M. D. (1980). Theories of sexual orientation. *Journal of Personality and Social Psychology, 38,* 783–792.

Storms, M. D. (1981). A theory of erotic orientation development. *Psychological Review, 88,* 340–353.

Strauss, E. (1998). Writing, speech separated in split brain. *Science, 280,* 827.

Stress–illness link. (1987, January). *APA Monitor,* p. 8.

Strickland, B. R. (1992). Women and depression. *Current Directions in Psychological Science, 1,* 132–135.

Striegel-Moore, R. H., Silberstein, L. R., & Rodin, J. (1986). Toward an understanding of risk factors for bulimia. *American Psychologist, 41,* 246–263.

Striegel-Moore, R. H., Silberstein, L. R., & Rodin, J. (1993). The social self in bulimia nervosa: Public self-consciousness, social anxiety, and perceived fraudulence. *Journal of Abnormal Psychology, 102,* 297–303.

Strupp, H. H. (1996). The tripartite model and the *Consumer Reports* study. *American Psychologist, 51,* 1017–1024.

Styron, W. (1990). *Darkness visible: A memoir of madness.* New York: Random House.

Suchman, A. L., & Ader, R. (1989). Placebo response in humans can be shaped by prior pharmacologic experience. *Psychosomatic Medicine, 51,* 251.

Suddath, R. L., Christison, G. W., Torrey, E. F., Casanova, M. F., & Weinberger, D. R. (1990). Anatomical abnormalities in the brains of nonpsychotic twins discordant for schizophrenia. *New England Journal of Medicine, 322,* 789–794.

Sue, S. (1991). Ethnicity and culture in psychological research and practice. In J. D. Goodchilds (Ed.), *Psychological perspectives on human diversity in America* (pp. 47–86). Washington, DC: American Psychological Association.

Suedfeld, P. (1980). *Restricted environmental stimulation: Research and clinical applications.* New York: Wiley.

Sulloway, F. J. (1996). *Born to rebel: Birth order, family dynamics, and creative lives.* New York: Pantheon.

Suls, J., & Marco, C. A. (1990). Relationship between JAS- and FTAS-Type A behavior and non-CHD illness: A prospective study controlling for negative affectivity. *Health Psychology, 9,* 479–492.

Suls, J., & Sanders, G. S. (1988). Type A behavior as a general risk factor for physical disorder. *Journal of Behavioral Medicine, 11,* 201–226.

Svanum, S., McGrew, J., & Ehrman, L. (1994). Validity of the substance abuse scales of the MMPI-2 in a college student sample. *Journal of Personality Assessment, 62,* 427–439.

Swann, W. B., Jr., Hixon, J. G., & De La Ronde, C. (1992). Embracing the bitter "truth": Negative self-concepts and marital commitment. *Psychological Science, 3,* 118–121.

Swazey, J. P. (1974). *Chlorpromazine in psychiatry: A study of therapeutic innovation.* Cambridge, MA: MIT Press.

Sweeney, P. D., Anderson, K., & Bailey, S. (1986). Attributional style in depression: A meta-analytic review. *Journal of Personality and Social Psychology, 50,* 974–991.

Swets, J. A., & Bjork, R. A. (1990). Enhancing human performance: An evaluation of "new age" techniques considered by the U.S. Army. *Psychological Science, 1,* 85–96.

Szasz, T. S. (1961). *The myth of mental illness.* New York: Harper & Row.

Szasz, T. S. (1977). *The manufacture of models.* New York: Dell.

Task Force on Promotion and Dissemination of Psychological Procedures. (1993). *A report adopted by the Division 12 Board—October 1993.* Washington, D C: American Psychological Association, Division 12.

Tavris, C. (1983). *Anger: The misunderstood emotion.* New York: Simon & Schuster.

Tavris, C. (1991). The mismeasure of woman: Paradoxes and perspectives in the study of gender. In J. D. Goodchilds (Ed.), *Psychological perspectives on human diversity in America* (pp. 87–136). Washington, DC: American Psychological Association.

Tavris, C. (1995). From excessive rage to useful anger. *Contemporary Psychology, 40* (11), 1101-1102.

Taylor, S. E. (1986). *Health psychology.* New York: Random House.

Taylor, S. E. (1990). Health psychology: The science and the field. *American Psychologist, 45,* 40–50.

Taylor, S. E. (1992). *Health psychology* (3rd ed.). New York: Random House.

Taylor, S. E. (1995). *Health psychology* (3rd ed). New York: McGraw Hill.

Tellegen, A., Lykken, D. T., Bouchard, T. J., Wilcox, K. J., Segal, N. L., & Rich, S. (1988). Personality similarity in twins reared apart and together. *Journal of Personality and Social Psychology, 54,* 1031–1039.

Templin, M. (1957). Certain language skills in children: Their development and interrelationships. *Institute of Child Welfare Monograph,* Series No. 26. Minneapolis: University of Minnesota Press.

Terman, L., & Oden, M. H. (1959). *Genetic studies of genius: Vol 4. The gifted group at midlife.* Stanford, CA: Stanford University Press.

Terman, L. M. (1916). *The measurement of intelligence.* Boston: Houghton Mifflin.

Tesser, A., & Brodie, M. (1971). A note on the evaluation of a "computer date." *Psychonomic Science, 23,* 300.

Tesser, A., & Shaffer, D. R. (1990). Attitudes and attitude change. *Annual Review of Psychology, 41,* 479–523.

Thigpen, C. H., & Cleckley, H. A. (1957). *Three faces of Eve.* New York: McGraw-Hill.

Thill, G. (1998, Autumn). Blood on our hands. *Oregon Quarterly, 78*(1), pp. 16–19.

Thio, A. (1995). *Deviant behavior.* New York: HarperCollins.

Thomas, F. F. (1991). *Impact on teaching: Research with culturally diverse populations.* Symposium conducted at the Western Psychological Association Convention, San Francisco.

Thompson, J. K. (1986, April). Larger than life. *Psychology Today,* pp. 38–44.

Thomson, D. M. (1988). Context and false recognition. In G. M. Davies & D. M. Thomson (Eds.), *Memory in context: context in memory* (pp. 285–304). Chichester, England: Wiley.

Thoresen, C. E. (1990). *Recurrent coronary prevention project: Results after 8 ½ years.* Symposium presented at the First International Congress of Behavioral Medicine, Uppsala, Sweden.

Thoresen, C. E., & Eagleston, J. R. (1983). Chronic stress in children and adolescents [Special edition: Coping with stress]. *Theory into Practice, 22,* 48–56.

Thorndike, E. L. (1898). Animal intelligence. *Psychological Review Monograph Supplement, 2* (4, Whole No. 8).

Thorndike, R. L., & Hagen, E. (1978). *The cognitive abilities test.* Lombard, IL: Riverside.

Thorndyke, P. W., & Hayes-Roth, B. (1979). *Spatial knowledge acquisition from maps and navigation.* Paper presented at the Psychonomic Society Meeting, San Antonio, TX.

Tienari, P., Sorri, A., Lahti, I., Naarala, M., Wahlberg, K.-E., Moring, J., Pohjola, J., & Wynne, L. C. (1987). Genetic and psychosocial factors in schizophrenia: The Finnish adoptive family study. *Schizophrenia Bulletin, 13,* 476–483.

Todes, D. P. (1997). From the machine to the ghost within: Pavlov's transition from digestive physiology to conditional reflexes. *American Psychologist, 52,* 947–955.

Tolman, E. C. (1948). Cognitive maps in rats and men. *Psychological Review, 55,* 189–208.

Tolman, E. C., & Honzik, C. H. (1930). "Insight" in rats. *University of California Publications in Psychology, 4,* 215–232.

Tolman, E. C., Ritchie, B. G., & Kalish, D. (1946). Studies in spatial learning: I. Orientation and the short-cut. *Journal of Experimental Psychology, 36,* 13–24.

Tononi, G., & Edelman, G. M. (1998, December 4). Consciousness and complexity. *Science, 282,* 1846–1850.

Torrey, E. F. (1996). *Out of the shadows: Confronting America's mental illness crisis.* New York: Wiley.

Torrey, E. F. (1997). The release of the mentally ill from institutions: A well-intentioned disaster. *The Chronicle of Higher Education, B4–B5.*

Travis, J. (1998, October 31). Adult human brains add new cells. *Science News, 154,* 276.

Triandis, H. (1989). The self and social behavior in differing cultural contexts. *Psychological Review, 96,* 506–520.

Triandis, H. (1990). Cross-cultural studies of individualism and collectivism. In J. Berman (Ed.), *Nebraska Symposium on Motivation, 1989* (pp. 42–133). Lincoln: University of Nebraska Press.

Triandis, H. C. (1994). *Culture and social behavior.* New York: McGraw-Hill.

Triandis, H. C. (1995). *Individualism & collectivism.* Boulder, CO: Westview Press.

Triandis, H. C. (1996). The psychological measurement of cultural syndromes. *American Psychologist, 51,* 407–415.

Trinder, J. (1988). Subjective insomnia without objective findings: A pseudodiagnostic classification. *Psychological Bulletin, 103,* 87–94.

Tronick, E., Als, H., & Brazelton, T. B. (1980). Moradic phases: A structural description analysis of infant-mother face to face interaction. *Merrill-Palmer Quarterly, 26,* 3–24.

Trope, I., Rozin, P., Nelson, D. K., & Gur, R. C. (1992). Information processing in separated hemispheres of the callosotomy patients: Does the analytic–holistic dichotomy hold? *Brain and Cognition, 19,* 123–147.

Trotter, R. J. (1986, July). The mystery of mastery. *Psychology Today,* 32–38.

Tsai, M., & Uemura, A. (1988). Asian Americans: The struggles, the conflicts, and the successes. In P. Bronstein & K. Quina (Eds.), *Teaching a psychology of people: Resources for gender and sociocultural awareness.* Washington, DC: American Psychological Association.

Tsuang, M. T., & Faraone, S. V. (1990). *The genetics of mood disorders.* Baltimore, MD: Johns Hopkins University Press.

Tulving, E. (1983). *Elements of episodic memory.* Oxford, U.K.: Clarendon Press.

Turk, D. C. (1994). Perspectives on chronic pain: The role of psychological factors. *Current Directions in Psychological Science, 3,* 45–48.

Turk, D. C. (1995). Chronic pain and depression: Role of perceived impact and perceived control in different age cohorts. *Pain, 61,* 93–101.

Turkington, C. (1992, February). Depression? It's in the eye of the beholder. *APA Monitor,* pp. 14–15.

Turkington, C. (1993, January). New definition of retardation includes the need for support. *APA Monitor,* pp. 26–27.

Turner, J. C., & Oakes, P. J. (1989). Self-categorization theory and social influence. In P. B. Paulus (Ed.), *Psychology of group influence* (2nd ed.). Hillsdale, NJ: Earlbaum.

Tversky, A., & Kahneman, D. (1973). Availability: A heuristic for judging frequency and probability. *Cognitive Psychology, 5,* 207–232.

Tversky, A., & Kahneman, D. (1974). Judgment under uncertainty: Heuristics and biases. *Science, 185,* 1124–1131.

Tyler, L. (1988). Mental testing. In E. R. Hilgard (Ed.), *Fifty years of psychology* (pp. 127–138). Glenview, IL: Scott, Foresman.

Uleman, J. S., & Bargh, J. A. (1989). *Unintended thought.* New York: Guilford Press.

Ursano. R. J., McCaughey, B. G., & Fullerton, C. S. (Eds.). (1994). *Individual and community responses to trauma and disaster: The structure of human chaos*. Cambridge, England: Cambridge University Press.

Valenstein, E. S. (Ed.). (1980). *The psychosurgery debate*. New York: Freeman.

Valenstein, E. S. (1998). *Blaming the brain: The truth about drugs and mental health*. New York: The Free Press.

Vallee, B. L. (1998, June). Alcohol in the western world. *Scientific American, 278*(6), 80–85.

van Dam, L. (1996, October 1). Mindful healing: An interview with Herbert Benson. *Technology Review, 99*(7), 31–38.

Van de Castle, R. L. (1983). Animal figures in fantasy and dreams. In A. Katcher & A. Beck (Eds.), New perspectives on our lives with companion animals. Philadelphia: University of Pennsylvania Press.

Van de Castle, R. L. (1994). *Our dreaming mind*. New York: Ballantine Books.

VandenBos, G. R. (1986). Psychotherapy research: A special issue. *American Psychologist, 41*, 111–112.

van Goozen, S. H. M., van de Poll, N. E., & Sergeant, J. A. (Eds.). (1994). *Emotions: Essays on emotion theory*. Hillsdale, NJ: Erlbaum.

Vernon, P. E. (1969). *Intelligence and cultural environment*. London: Methuen.

Vernon, P. E. (1987). The demise of the Stanford-Binet Scale. *Canadian Psychology, 28*, 251–258.

Viken, R. J., & McFall, R. M. (1994). Paradox lost: Implications of contemporary reinforcement theory for behavior therapy. *Current Directions in Psychological Science, 3*, 121–125.

Vincent, K. R. (1991). Black/white IQ differences: Does age make a difference? *Journal of Clinical Psychology, 47*, 266–270.

Vincent, M., & Pickering, M. R. (1988). Multiple personality disorder in childhood. *Canadian Journal of Psychiatry, 33*, 524–529.

Vitaliano, P. P., Russo, J., Young, H. M., Becker, J., & Maiuro, R. D. (1991). The screen for caregiver burden. *The Gerontologist, 31*, 76–83.

Vogel, G. (1996, November 22). Illusion reveals pain locus in brain. *Science, 274*, 1301.

Vogel, G. (1997, February 28). Scientists probe feelings behind decision-making. *Science, 275*, 1269.

Vogel, G. (1997, October 3). Cocaine wreaks subtle damage on developing brains. *Science, 278*, 38–39.

von Hofsten, C., & Lindhagen, K. (1979). Observations on the development of reaching for moving objects. *Journal of Child Psychology, 28*, 158–173.

Wade, Nicholas (1998, March 10). The struggle to decipher human genes. *New York Times*, p. C1.

Wade, T. J. (1991). Race and sex differences in adolescent self-perceptions of physical attractiveness and level of self-esteem during early and late adolescence. *Journal of Personality and Individual Differences, 12*, 1319–1324.

Walker, E. F., & Diforio, D. (1997). Schizophrenia: A neural diathesis-stress model. *Psychological Review, 104*, 667–685.

Walker, L. J. (1989). A longitudinal study of moral reasoning. *Child Development, 60*, 157–166.

Walker, L. J. (1991). Sex differences in moral reasoning. In W. M. Kurtines & J. L. Gewirtz (Eds.), *Handbook of moral behavior and development: Research* (Vol. 2, pp. 333–364). Hillsdale, NJ: Erlbaum.

Walker, L. J., & de Vries, B. (1985). Moral stages/moral orientations: Do the sexes really differ? Paper presented at the annual meeting of the American Psychological Association, Los Angeles.

Walker, L. J., de Vries, B., & Trevethan, S. D. (1987). Moral stages and moral orientations in real-life and hypothetical dilemmas. *Child Development, 58*, 842–858.

Wallace, A. F. C. (1959). Cultural determinants of response to hallucinatory experience. *Archives of General Psychiatry, 1*, 58–69.

Wallbott, H. G., Ricci-Bitti, P., & Baenninger-Huber, E. (1986). Nonverbal reactions to emotional experiences. In K. R. Scherer, H. G. Wallbott, & A. B. Summerfield (Eds.), *Experiencing emotion: A cross-cultural study* (pp. 98–116). Cambridge, England: Cambridge University Press.

Wallis, C. (1984, June 11). Unlocking pain's secrets. *Time*, pp. 58–66.

Walsh, R. (1984). Asian psychologies. In R. Corsini (Ed.), *Encyclopedia of psychology* (pp. 90–94). New York: Wiley.

Walster (Hatfield), E., Aronson, V., Abrahams, D., & Rottman, L. (1966). Importance of physical attractiveness in dating behavior. *Journal of Personality and Social Psychology, 5*, 508–516.

Walters, C. C., & Grusec, J. E. (1977). *Punishment*. San Francisco: Freeman.

Walters, E. E., Neale, M. C., Eaves, L. J., Heath, A. C., Kessler, R. C., & Kendler, K. S. (1992). Bulimia nervosa and major depression: A study of common genetic and environmental factors. *Psychological Medicine, 22* (3), 617–622.

Watkins, L. R., & Mayer, D. J. (1982). Organization of the endogenous opiate and nonopiate

pain control systems. *Science, 216*, 1185–1193.

Wardle, J., Steptoe, A., Bellisle, F., Davou, B., Reschke, K., & Lappalainen, M. (1997). Healthy dietary practices among European students. *Health Psychology, 16*, 443–450.

Watson, J. B. (1928). *The ways of behaviorism*. New York: Harper & Brothers.

Watson, J. B., & Rayner, R. (1920). Conditioned emotional reactions. *Journal of Experimental Psychology, 3*, 1–14.

Watson, J. D. (1968). *The double helix*. New York: The New American Library.

Webb, W. B. (1974). Sleep as an adaptive response. *Perceptual and Motor Skills, 38*, 1023–1027.

Weber, A. L., & Harvey, J. H. (Eds.) (1994a). *Perspectives on close relationships*. Boston, MA: Allyn & Bacon.

Weber, A. L., & Harvey, J. H. (1994b). Accounts in coping with relationship loss. In A. L. Weber & J. H. Harvey (Eds.), *Perspectives on close relationships*, pp. 285–306. Boston: Allyn & Bacon.

Weber, R. J. (1992). *Forks, phonographs, and hot air balloons: A field guide to inventive thinking*. New York: Oxford University Press.

Wechsler, D. (1981). *Manual for the Wechsler Adult Intelligence Scale–Revised*. New York: Psychological Corporation.

Wegner, D. M. (1989). *White bears and other unwanted thoughts*. New York: Guilford.

Wegner, D. M., Schneider, D. J., Carter, S., III, & White, T. (1987). Paradoxical effects of thought suppression. *Journal of Personality and Social Psychology, 53*, 5–13.

Wehr, T. A., & Rosenthal, N. E. (1989). Seasonality and affective illness. *American Journal of Psychiatry, 146*, 829–839.

Weil, A. T. (1977). The marriage of the sun and the moon. In N. E. Zinberg (Ed.), *Alternate states of consciousness* (pp. 37–52). New York: Free Press.

Weinberger, M., Hiner, S. L., & Tierney, W. M. (1987). In support of hassles as a measure of stress in predicting health outcomes. *Journal of Behavioral Medicine, 10*, 19–31.

Weiner, J. (1994). *The beak of the finch*. New York: Vintage Books.

Weingardt, K. R., Loftus, E. F., & Lindsay, D. S. (1995). Misinformation revisited: New evidence on the suggestibility of memory. *Memory and Cognition, 23*, 72–82.

Weisberg, R. (1986). *Creativity, genius, and other myths*. New York: Freeman.

Weissman, M. M., Bland, R. C., Canino, G. J., Faravelli, C., Green-

wald, S., Hwu, H. G., Joyce, P. R., Karam, E. G., Lee, C. K., Lellouch, J., Lepine, J. P., Newman, S. C., Rubio-Stipec, M., Wells, J. E., Wickramaratne, P. J., Wittchen, H., Yeh, E. K. (1996, July 24–31). Cross-national epidemiology of major depression and bipolar disorder. *Journal of the American Medical Association, 276*, 293–299.

Weissman, M. M., Merikangas, K. R., Wickramaratne, P., Kidd, K. K., Prusoff, B. A., Leckman, J. F., & Pauls, D. L. (1986). Understanding the clinical heterogeneity of major depression using family data. *Archives of General Psychiatry, 43*, 430–434.

Weissman, W. W. (1987). Advances in psychiatric epidemiology: Rates and risks for depression. *American Journal of Public Health, 77*, 445–451.

Weisz, J. R., Rothbaum, F. M., & Blackburn, T. C. (1984). Standing out and standing in: The psychology of control in America and Japan. *American Psychologist, 39*, 955–969.

Wellman, H. M., & Estes, D. (1986). Early understanding of mental entities: A reexamination of childhood realism. *Child Development, 57*, 910–923.

Welsh, E. J., Gullotta, C., & Rapoport, J. (1993). Classroom academic performance: Improvement with both methylphenidate and dextroamphetamine in ADHD boys. *Journal of Child Psychology and Psychiatry and Allied Disciplines, 34*, 785–804.

Wertheimer, M. (1923). Untersuchungen zur Lehre von der Gestalt, II. *Psychologische Forschung, 4*, 301–350.

Wesson, D. R., Smith, D. E., & Seymour, R. B. (1992). Sedative-hypnotics and tricyclics. In J. H. Lowinson, P. Ruiz, R. B. Millman, & J. G. Langrod (Eds.), *Substance abuse: A comprehensive textbook* (2nd ed.) (pp. 271–279). Baltimore: Williams & Wilkins.

Whalen, C. K., & Henker, B. (1991). Therapies for hyperactive children: Comparisons, combinations, and compromises. *Journal of Consulting and Clinical Psychology, 59*, 126–137.

Whiteman, M. C., & Fowkes, F. G. R. (1997, August 16). Hostility and the heart. *British Medical Journal*, Issue 7105, 379–380.

Wickelgren, I. (1997, June 27). Marijuana: Harder than thought? *Science, 276*, 1967–1968.

Wickelgren, I. (1998a, June 26). Teaching the brain to take drugs. *Science, 280*, 2045–2047.

Wickelgren, I. (1998b, August 28). A new route to treating schizophrenia? *Science, 281*, 1264–1265.

Wickelgren, I. (1998c, September 11). The cerebellum: The brain's engine of agility. *Science, 281,* 1588–1590.

Wickelgren, I. (1999, March 19). Nurture helps mold able minds. *Science, 283,* 1832–1834.

Wickelgren, W. (1974). *How to solve problems: Elements of a theory of problems and problem solving.* San Francisco: W. H. Freeman.

Wiggins, J. S. (1973). *Personality and prediction: Principles of personality assessment.* Reading, MA: Addison-Wesley.

Williams, T. M. (Ed.). (1986). *The impact of television: A natural experiment in three communities.* Orlando, FL: Academic Press.

Williams, W. M., & Ceci, S. J. (1997). Are Americans becoming more or less alike? Trends in race, class, and ability differences in intelligence. *American Psychologist, 52,* 1226–1235.

Wills, T. A., & DePaulo, B. M. (1991). Interpersonal analysis of the help-seeking process. In C. R. Snyder & D. R. Forsyth (Eds.), *Handbook of social and clinical psychology: The health perspective* (pp. 350–375). New York: Pergamon Press.

Wilner, D., Walkley, R., & Cook, S. (1955). *Human relations in interracial housing.* Minneapolis: University of Minnesota Press.

Wilson, E. D., Reeves, A., & Culver, C. (1977). Cerebral commissurotomy for control of intractable seizures. *Neurology, 27,* 708–715.

Wilson, S. M., & Medora, N. P. (1990). Gender comparisons of college students' attitudes toward sexual behavior. *Adolescence, 25,* 615–627.

Windholz, G. (1997). Ivan P. Pavlov: An overview of his life and psychological work. *American Psychologist, 52,* 941–946.

Winson, J. (1990, November). The meaning of dreams. *Scientific American, 263,* 86–96.

Witkin, G., Tharp, M., Schrof, J. M., Toch, T., & Scattarella, C. (1998, June 1). Again. *U.S. News & World Report,* pp. 16–17.

Wolpe, J. (1958). *Psychotherapy by reciprocal inhibition.* Stanford, CA: Stanford University Press.

Wolpe, J. (1973). *The practice of behavior therapy* (2nd ed.). New York: Pergamon.

Wolpe, J. (1985). Existential problems and behavior therapy. *The Behavior Therapist, 8,* 126–127.

Wolpe, J., & Plaud, J. J. (1997). Pavlov's contributions to behavior therapy: The obvious and the not so obvious. *American Psychologist, 52,* 966–972.

Wong, M. M., & Csikszentmihalyi, M. (1991). Motivation and academic achievement: The effects of personality traits and the quality of experience. *Journal of Personality, 59,* 539–574.

Wood, J. M., Nezworski, M. T., & Stejskal, W. J. (1996). The comprehensive system for the Rorschach: A critical examination. *Psychological Science, 7,* 3–10.

Wood, J. V., Saltzberg, J. A., & Goldsamt, L. A. (1990a). Does affect induce self-focused attention? *Journal of Personality and Social Psychology, 58,* 899–908.

Wood, J. V., Saltzberg, J. A., Neale, J. M., Stone, A. A., & Rachmiel, T. B. (1990b). Self-focused attention, coping responses, and distressed mood in everyday life. *Journal of Personality and Social Psychology, 58,* 1027–1036.

Wooten, P. (1994). *Heart, humor and healing.* Salt Lake City, UT: Commune A Key Publishing.

Wooten, P. (1996). Humor: An antidote for stress. *Holistic Nursing Practice, 10,* 49–55.

World Health Organization (1973). *Report of the International Pilot Study of Schizophrenia* (Vol. 1). Geneva: Author.

World Health Organization (1979). *Schizophrenia: An international follow-up study.* New York: Wiley.

Wright, K., & Mahurin, M. (1997, October). Babies, bonds, and brains. *Discover,* 74–78.

Wright, L. (1988). The Type A behavior pattern and coronary artery disease: Quest for the active ingredients and the elusive mechanism. *American Psychologist, 43,* 2–14.

Wu, C. (1998, April 4). Ritalin may work better as a purer compound. *Science News, 153,* 213.

Wurtman, R. J. (1982, April). Nutrients that modify brain functions. *Scientific American, 242,* 50–59.

Wyatt, G. E., Peters, S. D., & Guthrie, D. (1988). Kinsey revisited, Part I: Comparisons of the sexual socialization and sexual behavior of white women over 33 years. *Archives of Sexual Behavior, 17,* 201–239.

Yalom, I. D., & Greaves, C. (1977). Group therapy with the terminally ill. *American Journal of Psychiatry, 134,* 396–400.

Yam, P. (1995). A skeptically inquiring mind. *Scientific American, 273* (1), 34–35.

Yerkes, R. M. (1921). Psychological examining in the United States Army. In R. M. Yerkes (Ed.), *Memoirs of the National Academy of Sciences: Vol. 15.* Washington, DC: U.S. Government Printing Office.

Young, J. E., Beck, A. T., & Weinberger, A. (1993). Depression. In D. H. Barlow (Ed.), *Clinical handbook of psychological disorders: A step-by-step treatment manual* (2nd ed., pp. 240–277). New York: Guilford Press.

Zajonc, R. B. (1980). Feeling and thinking: Preferences need no inferences. *American Psychologist, 35,* 151–175.

Zajonc, R. B., & Mullally, P. R. (1997). Birth order: Reconciling conflicting effects. *American Psychologist, 52,* 685–699.

Zeki, S. (1992, September). The visual image in mind and brain. *Scientific American, 267,* 68–76.

Zeman, N. (1990, Summer/Fall). The new rules of courtship (Special Edition). *Newsweek,* 24–27.

Zigler, E., & Muenchow, S. (1992). *Head Start: The inside story of America's most successful educational experiment.* New York: Basic Books.

Zigler, E., & Styfco, S. J. (1994). Head Start: Criticisms in a constructive context. *American Psychologist, 49,* 127–132.

Zilbergeld, B. (1986, June). Psychabuse. *Science 86, 7,* 48.

Zimbardo, P. G. (1973). On the ethics of investigation in human psychological research: With special reference to the Stanford Prison Experiment. *Cognition, 2,* 243–256.

Zimbardo, P. G. (1975). On transforming experimental research into advocacy for social change. In M. Deutsch & H. Hornstein (Eds.), *Applying social psychology: Implications for research, practice, and training* (pp. 33–66). Hillsdale, NJ: Erlbaum.

Zimbardo, P. G. (1990). *Shyness: What it is, what to do about it* (Rev. ed.). Reading, MA: Perseus Books. (Original work published 1977).

Zimbardo, P. G. (1995). *The psychology of time perspective:* Selected readings. Stanford, CA: Stanford University Custom Publishing.

Zimbardo, P. G., Andersen, S. M., & Kabat, L. (1981). Induced hearing deficit generates experimental paranoia. *Science, 212,* 1529–1531.

Zimbardo, P. G., & Leippe, M. (1991). *The psychology of attitude change and social influence.* New York: McGraw-Hill.

Zimbardo, P. G., Maslach, C., & Haney, C. (in press). Reflections on the Stanford prison experiment: Genesis, transformations, consequences. In T. Blass (Ed.), *Obedience to authority: Current perspectives on the Milgram paradigm.* Mahwah, NJ: Erlbaum.

Zimbardo, P. G., & Montgomery, K. D. (1957). The relative strengths of consummatory responses in hunger, thirst, and exploratory drive. *Journal of Comparative and Physiological Psychology, 50,* 504–508.

Zubeck, J. P., Pushkar, D., Sansom, W., & Gowing, J. (1961). Perceptual changes after prolonged sensory isolation (darkness and silence). *Canadian Journal of Psychology, 15,* 83–100.

Zucker, G. S., & Weiner, B. (1993). Conservatism and perceptions of poverty: An attributional analysis. *Journal of Applied Social Psychology, 23,* 925–943.

Zuckerman, M. (1971). Dimensions of sensation seeking. *Journal of Consulting and Clinical Psychology, 36,* 45-52.

Zuckerman, M. (1974). The sensation-seeking motive. In B. Maher (Ed.), *Progress in experimantal personality research* (Vol. 7). New York: Acadmeic Press.

Zuckerman, M. (1978, February). The search for high sensation. *Psychology Today, 12,* 38–46.

Zuckerman, M. (1979). *Sensation seeking: Beyond the optimal level of arousal.* Hillsdale, NJ: Erlbaum.

Zuckerman, M. (1990). Some dubious premises in research and theory on racial differences: Scientific, social, and ethical issues. *American Psychologist, 45,* 1297–1303.

Zuckerman, M., Buchsbaum, M. S., & Murphy, D. L. (1980). Sensation seeking and its biological correlates. *Psychological Buletin, 88,* 187–214.

Zuckerman, M., Eysenck, S., & Eysenck, H. J. (1978). Sensation seeking in England and America: Cross-cultural, age and sex comparisons. *Journal of Consulting and Clinical Psychology, 46,* 139–149.

# Credits

**Chapter 1:** p. 4, Dr. Mary Ainsworth; p. 7, Lawrence Migdale/Stock Boston; p. 9, Davis Barber/ PhotoEdit; p. 11, Archives of the History of American Psychology, University of Akron; p. 13, David Frazier/Photo Researchers, Inc.; p. 14, AP/Wide World Photos; p. 15, Spencer Grant/PhotoEdit; p. 19, AP/Wide World Photos; p. 20, Mark Richards/PhotoEdit; p. 21, R. Lord/ The Image Works; p. 22, Matthew McVay/Stock Boston; p. 25, Berkeley Police Department; p. 26, Sidney Harris; p. 27, V. Richard Haro/ Fort Collins Coloradoan; p. 29, Superstock, Inc.; p. 31, © The New Yorker Collection 1993 Donald Reilly from cartoonbank.com. All Rights Reserved; p. 32, from "The Cartoon Guide to Statistics" by Larry Gonick & Wollcott Smith; p. 33, Hugo Van Lawick/National Geographic Image Collection; p. 34, Sidney Harris; p. 37, P. Gontier/Explorer/Photo Researchers, Inc.

**Chapter 2:** p. 46 (top), AP/Wide World Photos; p. 46 (bottom), Pete Turner/Image Bank; p. 48, Tony Stone Images; p. 51 (top right), Nick Downes/ reprinted with permission from *Science* Vol. 238, 1989 copyright 1989 American Association for the Advancement of Science; p. 51 (top left), Greenlar/The Image Works; p. 51 (bottom), AP/Wide World; p. 55, Loren/Fisher/Liaison Agency; p. 56, Spanish National Tourist Office; p. 58, Carolina Kroon/Impact Visuals; p. 60, AP/Wide World Photos, Inc.; p. 65, Damasio H, Grabowski T, Frank R, Galaburda AM, Damasio AR: The return of Phineas Gage: Clues about the brain from a famous patient. *Science*, 264:1102–1105, 1994. Department of Neurology and Image Analysis Facility, University of Iowa; p. 66 (top), Peter Vanderwarker/Stock Boston; p. 66 (bottom), Courtesy of Monte S. Buchsbaum, M. D., Mt. Sinai School of Medicine, New York, NY.; p. 67, Courtesy of Professor Rodolfo Llinas; p. 67, Fig. 2.12, From *Psychology and Life*, 15th edition, by Philip G. Zimbardo and Richard J. Gerrig, copyright © 1999 by Philip G. Zimbardo, Inc., and Richard J. Gerrig, Addison-Wesley Educational Publishers, Inc.; p. 68, Joseph Sohm/ Stock Boston; p. 68, Fig. 2.13, From *Psychology and Life*, 15th edition, by Philip G. Zimbardo and Richard J. Gerrig, copyright © 1999 by Philip G. Zimbardo, Inc., and Richard J. Gerrig, Addison-Wesley Educational Publishers, Inc.; p. 69 (top), Esbin-Anderson/ The Image Works; p. 69 (bottom), Randi Anglin/ The Image Works; p. 69, Fig. 2.14, From *Psychology and Life*, 15th edition, by Philip G. Zimbardo and Richard J. Gerrig, copyright © 1999 by Philip G. Zimbardo, Inc., and Richard J. Gerrig, Addison-Wesley Educational Publishers, Inc.; p. 76, Fig. 2.20, From *The Harvey Lectures*, Series 62, by R. W. Sperry, Copyright © 1968 by Academic Press, Inc., reprinted by permission of the author and the publisher; p. 84, Chagall, Marc (1887–1986) Priere 1976 Coll. Privata St. Paul de Vence Scala/Art Resource.

**Chapter 3:** p. 85, Dr. Dennis Kunkel/Phototake; p. 86, Volker Steger/Peter Arnold, Inc.; p. 91, Rhoda Sidney/The Image Works; p. 95, Fig. 3.4, From "Ontogenetic Development of Human Sleep–Dream Cycle," by H. P. Roffwarg et al., in *Science*, April 1966, Vol. 152, No. 9, pages 604–619, copyright 1966 by American Association for the Advancement of Science, reprinted by permission of the American Association for the Advancement of Science; p. 96, Norman Kelly Tjampiginpa, Flying Ant Dreaming. Jennifer Steele/Art Resource, NY; p. 98, Ogust/The Image Works; p. 100, Tony Stone Images; p. 102, Amy Etra/PhotoEdit; p. 103, PhotoDisc, Inc.; p. 104, Stephen Frisch/Stock Boston; p. 105 (top), Superstock, Inc.; p. 105 (bottom), Michael Newman/PhotoEdit; p. 108, Mark M. Lawrence/Stock Market; p. 110, Images in Neuroscience, Carol A. Tamminga, M. D., Editor, Neuroimaging, XIII, SPECT Imaging of Synaptic Dopamine, Photographs courtesy of Dr. Innis, *Am J Psychiatry* 153:10, October 1996.

**Chapter 4:** p. 120, T. K. Wanstal/The Image Works; p. 121, Archive Photos; p. 124, Chemical Design LTD/Science Photo Library/Photo Researchers, Inc.; p. 125, from *A Child Is Born*, Lennart Nilsson/Bonnier-Fakta; p. 127, Fig. 4.2, From *The First Two Years* by Mary M. Shirley, reprinted by permission of the University of Minnesota Press; p. 127, Laura Dwight; p. 130, Liaison Agency; p. 132, Fig. 4.3, From "The Acquisition of Language" by Breyne Arlene Moskovitz, *Scientific American*, November 1978, page 94D, copyright © 1978 by Scientific American, Inc., all rights reserved, reprinted by permission of Gabor Kiss; p. 135, George Goodwin/Monkmeyer; p. 136, Lew Merrim/Monkmeyer; p. 137, Marcia Weinstein; p. 140, Will Hart; p. 141, Nina Leen/Life Magazine/Time Warner, Inc.; p. 142 (top), © 1996 Thomas Hoepker/Magnum Photos; p. 142 (bottom), Martin Roger/Tony Stone Images; p. 147, Christopher Langridge/Sygma; p. 148, Bob Daemmrich/Stock Boston; p. 149, Grantpix/Stock Boston; p. 151, Genaro Moline from *A Day in California*; p. 154, Bob Daemmrich/The Image Works.

**Chapter 5:** p. 163, Stephen Dalton/Animals, Animals; p. 165, Table 5.1, From "Sensation," page 254 of *The Encyclopedic Dictionary of Psychology*, Third Edition, copyright © 1986 by Dushkin/McGraw-Hill, A Division of The McGraw-Hill Companies, adapted by permission of the publisher; p. 166, Tony Freeman/PhotoEdit; p. 169, Chuck Fishman/Woodfin Camp & Associates; p. 173, Fig. 5.4, Adapted from *Seeing: Illusion, Brain and Mind* by John P. Frisby, copyright © 1979 by John P. Frisby, reprinted by permission; p. 173, Fitz Goro/Life Magazine/Time Inc.; p. 175, Fig. 5.6, From *Perception*, Third Edition, by B. Sekuler and R. Blake, copyright © 1994 by The McGraw-Hill Companies, reprinted by permission of the McGraw-Hill Companies; p. 177, Mac-Millan Science Company, Inc.; p. 180, From *New Directions in Psychology* by Roger Brown, Eugene Galanter, Eckhard H. Hess, page 97, copyright © 1962 by Holt, Rinehart and Winston, Inc., reprinted by permission of Dr. Eugene Galanter; p. 181, Fig. 5.12, From *The Science of Musical Sounds* by D. C. Miller, Figure 145, page 315, Macmillan Company, 1926, adapted by permission of Case Western Reserve University; p. 183, Fig. 5.13, From *Psychology and Life*, 15th edition, by Philip G. Zimbardo and Richard J. Gerrig, copyright © 1999 by Philip G. Zimbardo, Inc., and Richard J. Gerrig, Addison-Wesley Educational Publishers, Inc.; p. 184, Superstock, Inc.; p. 190, #66 Cataracts, 1967, (PVA on canvas) by Riley, Bridget (b.1931) Private Collection. The Bridgeman Art Library International; p. 192, Fig. 5.18, From *Fundamentals of Sensation and Perception* by M. W. Levine and J. Shefner, reprinted by permission of Michael W. Levine; p. 193 (left), by Victor Vasarely, Courtesy of the Artist; p. 193 (right), Cordon Art-Bam-Holland, M. C. Escher Heirs, collection of C. V. S. Roosevelt, Washington D.C.; p. 194, DeKeerle/Sygma; p. 195, Tate Gallery, London/Art Resource, NY 1999 © Artist Rights Society, New York; p. 19, Bob Daemmrich/Stock Boston; p. 198, "The Moment Before Death", Russell Sorgi, from *Life: The First Fifty Years, 1936–1986* (Little Brown); p. 202, Cary Wolinksy/Stock Boston.

**Chapter 6:** p. 210, Photofest; p. 212, The Far Side by Gary Larson, copyright 1986 Universal Press Syndicate; p. 213, CORBIS/Bettmann; p. 214, Fig. 6.1, From *Psychology and Life*, 15th edition, by Philip G. Zimbardo and Richard J. Gerrig, copyright © 1999 by Philip G. Zimbardo, Inc., and Richard J. Gerrig, Addison-Wesley Educational Publishers, Inc.; p. 215, Fig. 6.2, From *Psychology and Life*, 15th edition, by Philip G. Zimbardo and Richard J. Gerrig, copyright © 1999 by Philip G. Zimbardo, Inc., and Richard J. Gerrig, Addison-Wesley Educational Publishers, Inc.; p. 216, John Chiasson/The Liaison Agency; p. 217, Archives of the History of American Psychology, University of Akron; p. 218, PhotoEdit; p. 219, David Young-Wolff/PhotoEdit; p. 222, Life Magazine, Time Warner, Inc.; p. 223 (top), Esbin-Anderson/The Image Works; p. 223 (bottom), Jacob H. Bauchman; p. 224, Calvin & Hobbes by Bill Watterson/Universal Press Syndicate; p. 226, CORBIS/Bettmann; p. 227, Yerkes Regional Primate Research Center, Emory University; p. 228, Myrleen Ferguson/PhotoEdit; p. 228, Randy Taylor/Sygma; p. 231, © The New Yorker Collection 1994 Sam Gross from cartoonbank.com. All Rights Reserved; p. 232, Fig. 6.5, From "Degrees of Hunger, Reward and Nonreward, and Maze Learning in Rats" by E. C. Tolman and C. H. Honzik in *University of California Publication of Psychology*, Vol. 4, No. 16, December 1930, reprinted by permission of the University of California Press; p. 234, from A. Bandera and R. Walters/Photo Courtesy of Dr. Albert Bandera; p. 235, Tony Freeman/PhotoEdit; p. 236, AP/ Wide World; p. 237, From *Psychology and Life*, 15th edition, by Philip G. Zimbardo and Richard J. Gerrig, copyright © 1999 by Philip G. Zimbardo, Inc., and Richard J. Gerrig, Addison-Wesley Educational Publishers, Inc.; p. 238, From *Human Memory: Structures and Processes*, 2nd Edition, by Roberta Klatsky, copyright © 1975, 1980 by W. H. Freeman and Company, used with permissionl; p. 243 (bottom), Custom Medical Stock; p. 243 (top), Globe Photos, Inc.; p. 245, Corbis/Bettmann-UPI; p. 249, Will Hart/PhotoEdit.

**Chapter 7:** p. 258, Bonnie Kamin/PhotoEdit; p. 259, Fig. 7.1, From *Cognitive Psychology*, Fifth Edition, by Robert L. Solso, copyright © 1998 by Allyn and Bacon, reprinted by permission; p. 260, © Scott R. Goodwin, Inc.; p. 262, Science: Vol 275, 28 February 1997; p. 263, Courtesy of Marcus E. Raichle, M. D. Washington University School of Medicine; p. 267, Spencer Grant/Stock Boston; p. 267, Fig. 7.4, "Prototype formation of faces: A case study of pseudo-memory" by Robert L. Solso and Judity E. McCarthy, *British Journal of Psychology*, Volume 72, 1981, pages 499–503, reprinted by permission of The British Psychological Society; p. 269, Courtesy of H. Damasio, Human Neuroanatomy and Neuroimaging Laboratory, Department of Neurology, University of Iowa; p. 270, Figs. 7.6 and 7.7, From *Cognitive Psychology*, Fifth Edition, by Robert L. Solso, copyright © 1998 by Allyn and Bacon, reprinted by permission; p. 271, Frozen Images/The Image Works; p. 272 (right), Richard L/The Image Works; p. 272 (left), L. Kolvoord/The Image Works; p. 275, David Young-Wolff/PhotoEdit; p. 276, Jim Harrison/Stock Boston; p. 277 (left), Ken Eward/Photo Researchers, Inc.; p. 277 (right), Jan Butchofskyk-Houser/Corbis; p. 280, Fig. 7.12, and p. 281, Fig. 713, *From How to Solve Problems: Elements of a Theory of Problems and Problem Solving* by Wayne A. Wickelgren, copyright © 1974 by W. H. Freeman and Company, adapted by permission of Dover Publications Inc. and the author; p. 282, Mark C. Burnett/Stock Boston; p. 283 (left), Monkmeyer Press; p. 283 (right), Superstock, Inc.; p. 284, Deborah Davis/PhotoEdit; p. 285, Corbis.

**Chapter 8:** p. 296, Bonnie Kamin/PhotoEdit; p. 297, H. Gans/The Image Works; p. 298, Dr. Paul Ekman/ Human Interaction Laboratory; p. 299 (top left), Barry Lewis/Network/Matrix International, Inc.; p. 299 (top center), Erika Stone; p. 299 (top right), Ted Kerasote/Photo Researchers; p. 299 (bottom left), Francie Manning/Index Stock Photography; p. 299 (bottom center), John Giordano/SABA; p. 299 (bottom right), Dr. Paul Ekman, Human Interaction Laboratory; p. 300, Fig. 8.2, From "A Language for the Emotions" by Robert Plutchik, *Psychology Today*, February, 1980, reprinted with permission from Psychology Today Magazine, copyright © 1980 by Sussex Publishers, Inc.; p. 300, Wernher Krutein/The Liaison Agency; p. 301, From *Psychology*, Third Edition by Spencer A. Rathus, copyright © 1987 by Holt, Rinehart and Winston, Inc., adapted by permission of the publisher; p. 304, Courtesy of D. Silbersweig, M. D. and E. Stern, M. D. Functional Neuroimaging Laboratory, The New York Hospital-Cornell Medical Center. Appeared in: A Functional Neuroanatomy of Hallucinations in Schizophrenia D. Silbersweig, E. Stern et al. *Nature* 378: 176–179, 1995; p. 306, Barbara Brown/Adventure Photo; p. 307, Lauren Goodsmith/The Image Works; p. 308, Gogh, Vincent van. Sorrow. Giraudon/Art Resource, NY; p. 309, Fig. 8.5, Reprinted by permission of the author and the publisher from "Crying Behavior in the Human Adult" by William H. Frey, II, Ph. D. et al., in *Integrative Psychiatry*, September/October 1983, copyright © 1983 by Elsevier Science Publishing Company, Inc.; p. 313, Spencer Grant/ PhotoEdit; p. 314, Bob Daemmrich/Stock Boston; p. 315, Tony Stone Images; p. 320, David Young-Wolff/PhotoEdit; p. 325 (top), Olive R. Pierce/Stock Boston; p. 325 (middle) Sulli-

van/TexaStock; p. 325 (bottom), © Joel Gordon 1988; p. 327, Fig. 8.9, From page 207 of *Human Sexualities* by J. H. Gagnon, copyright © 1977 by Harper-Collins Publishers, Inc., reprinted by permission; p. 329, © 1998 Richard R. Renaldi/ Impact Visuals.

**Chapter 9:** p. 338, Tony Freeman/PhotoEdit; p. 340, J. Pat Carter/ The Liaison Agency; p. 342, Sep Seitz/ Woodfin Camp & Associates; p. 343, Chuck Nacke/Woodfin Camp & Associates; p. 344, Table 9.1, Adapted from Table 3, page 475, of "The Minor Events Approach to Stress: Support for the Use of Daily Hassles" by Kerry Chamberlain and Sheryl Zika, in *British Journal of Psychology*, 1990, Volume 81, reprinted by permission; p. 347, Susan Oristaglio/The Liaison Agency; p. 348, Steven Rubin/The Image Works; p. 349, Earth Scenes/Animals Animals; p. 351, Fig. 9.3, From Figure 7.10 of *Psychology* by Michael S. Gazzaniga, copyright © 1980 by Michael S. Gazzaniga, reprinted by permission of Harper-Collins Publishers, Inc.; table from Table 6.1, page 147 of *Health Psychology* by Michael Feurstein, copyright © 1986 by Plenum Publishing Corporation, reprinted by permission of the author and the publisher; p. 352, Mark Antman/The Image Works; p. 353, Ferry/The Liaison Agency; p. 354, Michael Gallacher/ The Liaison Agency; p. 357, AP/Wide World Photos; p. 358, Mulvehill/The Image Works; p. 360, Michael Newman/PhotoEdit; p. 364, Table 9.2, From *Morbidity and Mortality Weekly Report*, Volume 46, pages 1217–1220, Centers for Disease Control and Prevention, 1995; p. 364, Reuters/Win McNamee/Archive Photos; p. 365 (top), B. Bachmann/The Image Works; p. 365 (bottom), Superstock, Inc.; p. 366, Bob Daemmrich/The Image Works; p. 367, Courtesy of Patch Adams; p. 369, Scott Wachter/Photo Researchers; p. 370, Ferry/ The Liaison Agency; p. 372, Fig. 9.6, From *Health and Human Services*, Office of Disease Prevention and Health Promotion; p. 374, Chuck Savage/ Uniphoto.

**Chapter 10:** p. 383 (left), Frank Siteman/ Index Stock Photography; p. 383 (middle), Frank Siteman/Index Stock Photography; p. 383 (right), Frank Siteman/ Index Stock Photography; p. 384, Photograph by Max Halberstadt/ Courtesy of W. E. Freud. Sigmund Freud Copyrights. Mary Evans Picture Library; p. 385, Myrleen Ferguson/PhotoEdit; p. 387, 1970 Leonard Freed/Magnum Photos; p. 388, © Punch/Rothco; p. 390, reprinted by permission of the publishers from *Thematic Appreciation Test*, by Henry A. Murray, Cambridge MA: Harvard University Press, © 1943 by the President and Fellows of Harvard College: © 1971 by Henry A. Murray; p. 391, Scala/Art Resource; p. 393, CORBIS; p. 394, Franklin D. Roosevelt Library; p. 396, Bob Daemmrich/Stock Boston; p. 399, Bob Grant/ Fotos International/ Archive Photos; p. 402, David Young-Wolff/ PhotoEdit; p. 405, Bob Daemmrich/The Image Works; p. 406 (top), J. Greenberg/The Image Works; p. 406 (bottom), The Far Side by Gary Larson/Universal Press Syndicate; p. 410, Michael Newman/ PhotoEdit; p. 411, Robert Brenner/PhotoEdit.

**Chapter 11:** p. 421, Russell D. Curtis/Photo Researchers, Inc.; p. 430, Fig. 11.3, *From Wechsler's Measurement and Appraisal of Adult Intelligence*, Fifth Edition, by Joseph D. Matarazzo, copyright © 1972 by Oxford University Press, Inc. Adapted by permission of Oxford University Press, Inc.; p. 430, T. L. Litt/Impact Visuals; p. 436, Patrick Ward/Stock Boston; p. 438, Spencer Grant/Liaison Agency; p. 441, Archive Photos; p. 442, Aaron Haupt/ Stock Boston; p. 442, Table 11.1, "Familia Studies of Intelligence: A Review" by Bouchard and McGue from *Science*, 1981, Volume 212, pages 1055–1059, copyright © 1981 American Association for the Advancement of Science, reprinted with permission from American Association for the Advancement of Science; p. 444, Joan Clifford/Index Stock Photography; p. 448, Edward Clark/Life Magazine, Time Inc.

**Chapter 12:** p. 456, Courtesy Dr. Philip G. Zimbardo; p. 458 (bottom), Bob Daemmrich/Stock Boston;

p. 58 (top) Ted Horowitz/Stock Market; p. 459, Ted Goff; p. 462, Piet van Lier/Impact Visuals; p. 464, all from the film Obedience, copyright 1965 by Stanley Milgram, and distributed; p. 465, AP/Wide World Photos; p. 467, New York Times Pictures; p. 466, Fig. 12.2, From *The Obedience Experiments: A Case Study of Controversy in the Social Sciences* by A. G. Miller, copyright © 1986 by Praeger Publishers, reprinted by permission of Greenwood Publishing Group, Inc., Westport Connecticut; p. 468, Fig. 12.3, Adapted from "Bystander Intervention in Emergencies: Diffusion of Responsibilities" by Darley and Latane, in *Journal of Personality and Social Psychology*, 1968, Volume 8, Number 4, pages 377–384, copyright © 1968 by the American Psychological Association, adapted by permission of the author; p. 472, M. Ferguson/PhotoEdit; p. 473, B. Bachman/The Image Works; p. 474, D. Wells/The Image Works; p. 476, Scott Goodwin Photography; p. 477, © 1993 Tribune Media Services, Inc. All rights reserved; p. 478, John Marmaras/Woodfin Camp & Associates; p. 479, AP/ Wide World Photo; p. 481, David Stewart/Tony Stone Images; p. 483, Dr. O. J. Harvey, University of Colorado.

**Chapter 13:** p. 492, National Mental Health Association; p. 493, Fig. 13.1, From page 9 of *Mental Health for Canadians: Striking a Balance*, Minister of National Health and Welfare, 1988; p. 495, Courtesy Peabody Essex Museum, Salem, MA; p. 498, Michael Newman/PhotoEdit; p. 499, L. Fernandez/The Image Works; p. 503, CORBIS /Burstein Collection; p. 503, Table 13.2, From *Abnormal Psychology*, Third Edition, by David L. Rosenhan and Martin E. P. Seligman, copyright © 1995, 1989, 1984 by W. W. Norton & Company, Inc., adapted by permission of W. W. Norton & Company, Inc.; p. 504, Fig. 13.2, Adapted from "Seasonal Affective Disorder" by Rosental et al., from *Archives of General Psychiatry*, Volume 41, 1984, pages 72–80, copyright © 1984 American Medical Association, reprinted by permission; p. 505, Bill Aron/PhotoEdit; p. 509, © 1996 Margaret Ross/Stock Boston; p. 512, all Courtesy of Dr. Cormelia Wilbur; p. 515, Archive Photos; p. 516, Monkmeyer Press; p. 517, National Institute of Mental Health; p 518, Fig. 13.7, From *Schizophrenia Genesis* by Gottesman, copyright © 1991 by Irving I. Gottsman. Used with permission by W. H. Freeman and Company; p. 519, Reuters/ Archive Photos; p. 519, © the New Yorker Collection 1995 Bruce Eric Kaplan from cartoonbank.com. All Rights Reserved; p. 520, Bob Daemmrich/Stock Boston; p. 525, A. Ramey/PhotoEdit.

**Chapter 14:** p. 534, John Eastcott/Yva Momatiuk/ The Image Works; p. 535, © The New Yorker Collection 1995 Mick Stevens from cartoonbank.com. All Rights Reserved; p. 536, Cathy by Cathy Guisewite/Universal Press Syndicate; p. 539, Sir John Soane's Museum; p. 540, The Liaison Agency; p. 541, Dick Blume/The Image Works; p. 542, THE FAR SIDE © 1986 FARWORKS, Inc. Used by permission. All rights reserved; p. 543, Rick Freidman/Black Star; p. 543, Table 14.2, From The Practice of Behavior Therapy, Fourth Edition, by Joseph Wolpe, copyright © 1990 by Allyn & Bacon. p. 544, Lester Sloan/ Woodfin Camp & Associates; p. 546, Fig. 14.2, From page 603 of *Journal of Abnormal Psychology*, Volume 94, by Cook et al., copyright © 1985 by the American Psychological Association, adapted by permission; p. 546, Dr. Philip G. Zimbardo; p. 546, Fig. 14.3, From "Modeling Therapy" by Albert Bandura, reprinted by permission of the author; p. 548, Freud Museum, London; p. 549, Michael Rougier/Life Magazine ©; p. 551, Robert Nebecker/Leerhessen 1990; p. 552, David Young-Wolff/PhotoEdit; p. 560, Will & Deni McIntyre/Photo Researchers, Inc.; p. 564, Hieronymus Bosch, Extraction of the Stone of Folly, Prado Madrid, Giraudon/Art Resource; p. 565 (top), Najlah Feanny/Stock Boston; p. 565 (bottom), © 1999 John Launois/Black Star; p. 566, Michael Newman/PhotoEdit.

# Name Index

Heeger, D. J., 190
Heiby, E., 9
Heinrichs, R. W., 517
Helmes, E., 404
Helmholtz, Hermann von, 193, 194
Helmreich, R., 474
Helms, Janet E., 446
Hendrick, C., 472
Hendrick, S. S., 472
Henig, R. M., 52
Henker, B., 562
Henley, N., 185
Heracles, 391
Herman, C. P., 515
Hernstein, R. J., 11
Heron, W. G., 234
Herrnstein, Richard J., 285, 446–447
Hersh, S. M., 463
Herskovits, M., 201
Heslin, R., 328
Hess, Walter, 65
Heston, L. L., 517
Hetherington, E. M., 141
Hetherington, M. M., 515
Hicks, R. A., 99, 110
Hilgard, E. R., 102, 442
Hilker, R. R., 358
Hilts, P. J., 69, 243
Hinckley, John, 525
Hinton, G. E., 260
Hinton, G. F., 75
Hinton, R., 97
Hippocrates, 400–401, 494, 495
Hiramoto, R. N., 354
Hiroto, Donald S., 359
Hirsch, J., 448
Hirschfeld, R. M. A., 504
Hitler, Adolf, 463
Hixon, J. G., 474
Hobson, J. Allan, 98
Hochwalder, J., 409
Hoffman, Dustin, 295, 432
Hoffman, F. M., 301
Hogan, J., 343, 401
Hogan, R., 343, 401
Holcomb, P. J., 262
Holden, C., 71, 152, 184, 226–227
Hollis, K. L., 233
Hollon, S. D., 557, 563
Holmes, D. S., 103, 369, 501, 502, 516, 560, 561, 562, 565
Holmes, Thomas H., 345–346, 347
Holtzman, W. H., 371
Holtzworth-Munroe, A., 342
Homme, L. E., 227
Honzik, C. H., 231
Hopkins, B., 126
Hopson, J. L., 61
Horgan, J., 438, 503
Horne, J. A., 95
Horney, Karen, 392–393, 414, 547, 548
Horowitz, M. J., 556
Horvath, A. O., 537

House, J. S., 364
Houston, B. K., 556
Hovland, C. I., 478
Howard, K. I., 148
Howes, C., 144
Hubel, David H., 190, 260
Huesmann, L. R., 234
Hull, C. L., 317
Humphreys, L. G., 439
Hunt, E., 266
Hurlburt, R. T., 86
Husband, T. H., 235
Huston, A. C., 234
Huston, Ted L., 467–468
Hyman, I. E., Jr., 225, 235, 246
Hyman, R., 202

Iacono, W. G., 313, 517
Ickes, W., 477
Ineichen, B., 472
Inglehart, R., 373
Irwin, M., 354
Isaka, S., 266
Isay, R. A., 329
Izard, Carroll E., 298, 308

Jackson, D. D., 120, 121
Jacobs, B. L., 61, 105
Jacobs, M. K., 550
Jacobson, Lenore F., 33, 438–439
Jacobson, N. S., 342, 541, 550, 557, 558
Jacoby, L. L., 88, 315
James, William, 13, 18, 20, 126–127, 296, 305, 306
Janda, L. H., 472
Janis, I. L., 274
Janoff-Bulman, R., 373, 374
Jansen, A. S. P., 349
Jefferson, Thomas, 394
Jeffery, R. W., 325
Jenkins, C. D., 357
Jenkins, J. G., 248
Jenkins, J. M., 308
Jensen, Arthur R., 439, 443–444, 445, 450
Johnson, D. L., 517
Johnson, J. H., 346
Johnson, M. L., 126
Johnson, S., 551
Johnson, Virginia E., 185, 326–328, 556
Johnson-Laird, P. N., 274
Johnston, L. D., 105
Joiner, T. E., Jr., 357
Jones, B. A., 358
Jones, E. E., 556
Jones, J. M., 23, 423n
Jones, Maxwell, 565–566
Jones, Reverend Jim, 463
Jordan, Michael, 220
Joyce, L., 497
Juliano, S. L., 73
Julien, R. M., 104, 106, 107, 108
Jung, Carl, 391–392, 407, 409, 412, 414, 547, 548

Kabat, L., 102
Kagan, Jerome, 50, 140, 142, 147, 402, 412, 520
Kahn, S. E., 343
Kahneman, Daniel, 281–282, 308
Kako, E. T., 132
Kalish, D., 232
Kallikak, Martin, 440
Kamil, A. C., 232
Kamin, Leon J., 233, 447, 448
Kandel, D. B., 472
Kandel, Eric R., 233
Kane, J. M., 497, 560
Kantrowitz, B., 445
Karlsen, C. F., 494
Karni, A., 97
Kasparov, Garry, 45–46, 260
Kassin, S. M., 476
Katz, R. L., 84
Kazdin, A. E., 227, 543, 545, 557
Keating, C. F., 299
Keesey, R. E., 324
Keller, J. W., 389
Kelley, C., 88
Kelley, H. H., 319, 472
Kelman, Herbert C., 483–484
Kelsoe, J. R., 497
Kempermann, G., 56
Kendler, K. S., 497, 504
Kennedy, D. M., 382
Kennedy, John Fitzgerald, 460
Kennedy, W. A., 448
Kenrick, D. T., 406
Kerlinger, F. N., 7
Kershner, J. R., 287
Kesner, R., 231
Ketcham, K., 235, 245, 246, 390, 513
Kiecolt-Glaser, J. K., 354
Kiesler, C. A., 566, 567
Kiesling, R., 567
Kiester, E., 97
Kihlstrom, J. F., 84, 89, 103, 246, 315
Kilcullen, R. N., 473
Kilmann, P. R., 565
Kim, J. J., 233
Kimmel, A. J., 35
Kimmel, D., 23
King, Martin Luther, Jr., 19
Kinkel, Kip, 14, 15, 16, 19, 21, 22, 24, 33
Kinoshita, J., 97
Kinsbourne, M., 74
Kinsey, Alfred C., 326, 329
Kintsch, W., 266
Kipnis, D., 8
Kippax, S., 234
Kirby, K. N., 11
Kirkpatrick, L. A., 143
Kirsch, I., 102, 561
Kitayama, S., 22, 308, 409, 477
Klag, M. J., 342
Klagsbrun, F., 151
Klein, K. E., 92
Klein, R. G., 563
Kleinfeld, J., 436
Kleinke, C., 312
Kleinman, Arthur, 524

Kleitman, N., 92
Kliegl, R., 153
Kliegl, E., 91
Klinger, M. R., 315
Knapp, J., 148
Kobasa, Suzanne O., 358–359
Koelling, R. A., 218
Kohlberg, Lawrence, 138–139, 156
K'hler, Wolfgang, 230–231, 252
Kohn, P. M., 301
Kolb, B., 126
Koob, G. F., 109
Koresh, David, 463
Korkina, M. V., 515
Kornreich, M., 556
Kosko, B., 266
Kosslyn, Stephen M., 263, 264, 269
Kraemer, D. T., 308
Kramer, D. A., 443
Kramer, Peter D., 561
Krampe, R. T., 152, 153, 285
Krantz, D. S., 339
Krebs, J., 232
Krebs, J. R., 48
Krokoff, L. J., 309
Krupa, D. J., 233
Kukla, A., 8
Kuldau, J. M., 515
Kunkel, D., 234

Lachman, J. L., 273
Lachman, R., 273
Lakoff, R. T., 309
Lambo, T. A., 540
Lampl, M., 126
Landesman, S., 431
Landis, K. R., 364
Landry, D. W., 108
Lang, F. R., 154
Lang, P. J., 296, 297, 543
Lange, Carl, 305, 306
Langer, Ellen, 360
Langlois, J. H., 472, 473
Larson, Gary, 212
Larson, R., 149, 373
Latané, Bibb, 467
Laumann, E. O., 326
Lavie, P., 95
Lawton, M. P., 471
Layden, M. A., 477
Lazar, I., 445
Lazarus, Richard S., 308, 310, 339, 344, 345, 346
Lazovik, D. A., 543
Leary, M. R., 319
Ledger, G., 287
LeDoux, J. E., 296, 303
Lee, S.-Y., 447
Lee, V. E., 445
Leerhsen, C., 550, 551
LeFan, J., 474
Lefcourt, H. M., 367
Lehman, D. R., 365
Leippe, M., 371
Leiter, M. P., 343
Le Moal, M., 109
Lempert, H., 74

Lennon, R. T., 425, 428
Leonard, J., 97
Lepper, Mark R., 320
Lerner, R. M., 148
Leshner, A. I., 109
Lesperance, F., 358
Lettvin, Jerome Y., 190
Leutwyler, K., 182, 505
LeVay, Simon, 330
Levenson, R. W., 304, 309
Leventhal, H., 307
Levine, F. M., 320
Levine, J. D., 61, 186
Levine, J. M., 462
Levine, M., 524
Levinson, B. W., 84
Levy, S., 45, 46
Lewine, R. R., 516
Lewinsohn, Peter M., 504
Lewis, Jim, 120–121
Lewy, A. J., 504
Liem, R., 342
Liker, J. K., 435
Lillard, A. S., 409
Lincoln, Abraham, 394
Lindblom, W. D., 525
Lindhagen, K., 129
Lindsay, D. S., 245, 315
Lindzey, G., 447
Lipsey, M. W., 556
Lipsitt, L. P., 127
Lisberger, S. G., 68
Lloyd, P., 368
Locke, B. Z., 503
Loehlin, J. C., 447
Loftus, Elizabeth F., 210, 235, 245, 246, 315, 390, 513
Loftus, G. R., 239
Logan, R. L., 152
London, K. A., 149
Long, B. C., 343
Lonner, W. J., 404
Loomis, A. L., 92
Lorentz, Konrad, 141
Lott, A. J., 462
Lott, B. E., 462
Lovibond, S. H., 456
Lubart, Todd I., 286, 287
Luborsky, L., 537, 556
Lui, L., 154
Lutz, C., 410
Lynn, S. J., 102

Maccoby, N., 372
Machado, P. P., 556
Macrae, C. N., 409
Maddi, S. R., 358
Madonna, 493
Magee, W. J., 507, 508
Magnusson, D., 150
Maher, B. A., 153, 495, 563, 565
Maher, W. B., 495, 563, 565
Mahurin, M., 121
Maier, S. F., 354, 354, 359
Maisto, S. A., 107
Majewska, M. D., 305
Major, B., 374
Malatesta, V. J., 301
Malinowski, B., 96

Malitz, S., 564
Manderschied, R. W., 516
Mandler, G., 306
Manfredi, M., 186
Mann, C. C., 123
Manschreck, T. C., 153
Manson, S. M., 524
Manuck, S. B., 309
Marco, C. A., 357
Marcus, G. F., 133
Marder, S. R., 497, 560
Marek, T., 343
Markman, H. J., 151, 551
Markus, H. R., 22, 308, 409, 477
Marsh, P., 312
Marshall, G. D., 307
Martin, J. A., 129
Martin, P. L., 547
Martin, R. A., 367
Martin, S., 105
Maruyama, G., 473
Maslach, Christina, 307, 343, 456, 459
Maslow, Abraham H., 19, 151, 319–320, 394, 395, 412, 414
Masters, J. C., 556
Masters, William H., 185, 326–328, 556
Masuda, M., 345–346, 347
Matalsky, G. I., 504
Matarazzo, J. D., 371
Matlin, M. G., 271
Matossian, M. K., 495
Matthews, K. A., 351, 357
Mauk, M. D., 68
Maunsell, J. H. R., 172, 190
May, R., 549
Mayer, D. J., 61, 103, 186
Mayer, R. E., 261, 285
McAdams, D. P., 152, 405
McCandliss, B. D., 262
McCann, I. L., 369
McCarley, N., 407
McCarley, Robert W., 98
McCarthy, J. E., 266, 268
McCarthy, K., 233
McCaughey, B. G., 365
McClearn, G. E., 52, 442
McClelland, David C., 151, 322, 323, 331, 390
McClintock, C. G., 410
McConkey, K. M., 103
McCormick, Katharine, 382
McCrae, R. R., 404
McCraven, V. J., 91
McDonald, K. A., 368
McFall, R. M., 545
McGovern, K., 87, 88
McGrew, J., 404
McGue, M., 402
McGuffin, P., 50, 51, 121, 502, 504
McHugh, Paul, 210
McKay, G., 365
McKinney, K., 480
McLintock, T. T. C., 84
McNally, R. J., 507
McPherson, K. S., 440
Mead, Margaret, 317

Meador, B. D., 550
Medin, D. L., 263, 265, 266, 277
Medora, N. P., 148
Mehler, B., 448
Meier, R. P., 132
Mellinger, G. D., 98
Meltzoff, A. N., 129
Meltzoff, J., 556
Melzack, R., 107, 186
Menzel, E. M., 232
Meredith, N., 556
Merikle, P. M., 169
Mervis, C. B., 265, 266
Mesmer, Franz Anton, 496
Mesulam, M. M., 517
Metzler, Jacqueline, 263
Meyer-Bahlburg, H. F. L., 330
Michael, R. T., 326
Milgram, Stanley, 463–466
Millar, M. G., 473
Miller, A. G., 463
Miller, D. T., 460
Miller, I. J., 185
Miller, J., 409, 476
Miller, M. E., 102
Miller, M. W., 503
Miller, N., 473
Miller, N. E., 217, 366, 371, 563
Miller, P. Y., 149
Miller, R. S., 462
Miller, W. R., 109
Miller-Jones, D., 446
Mills, J. R., 471
Milner, Brenda, 243, 244
Mineka, S., 492, 545
Mintz, J., 514
Mischel, Walter, 322, 401, 405–406, 411, 412
Misiak, H., 21
Mitchison, Graeme, 94
Mizukami, K., 141
Mlot, C., 296
M'Naughten, Daniel, 525
Moar, I., 232
Mogilner, A., 65
Moise, J., 234
Monaghan, P., 481
Moncrieff, R. W., 183
Money, J., 329
Montag, I., 403
Monte, C. F., 393
Montgomery, K. D., 318
Moore, G. I., 269
Moore, J. S., 473
Moore, M. K., 129
Moore-Ede, M., 92
Moos, R. H., 364
Morgan, A. H., 442
Morgane, P. S., 94
Moriarity, Tom, 469–470
Morin, S., 149
Morrell, E. M., 103
Morris, D., 185
Morris, M. W., 409
Morris, W. N., 462
Morrison-Bogorad, M., 51
Morrow, D. G., 261, 263
Moskovitz, B. A., 132
Moskowitz, H., 106

Mowrer, O., 131
Muenchow, S., 445
Mukerjee, M., 73, 361
Mullally, P. R., 438
Munakata, Y., 137–138
MuZoz, R. F., 556
Munroe, R. L., 548
Murphy, D. L., 301
Murphy, G., 409
Murphy, Jane M., 524
Murphy, L. B., 409
Murphy, P. J., 504
Murray, B., 26, 97, 105
Murray, Charles, 446–447
Murray, Henry, 322, 323, 389
Murray, J. P., 234
Musselman, L., 473
Mussolini, Benito, 463
Musun-Miller, L., 118
Muzzonigro, P. G., 149
Myers, D. G., 150
Myers, David G., 319, 373, 374
Myers, I. B., 407
Myers, L., 343
Myers, R. S., 369
Mylander, C., 132
Mylander, M., 337, 354

Nahemow, L., 471
Naigles, L., 132
Naigles, L. G., 132
Nakazato, H. S., 403
Nathan, P. E., 557
National Institute of Mental Health, 565
National Institute on Alcohol Abuse and Alcoholism, 107
National Press Club, 505
National Public Radio, 360, 520
Nauta, W. J. H., 56
Needleman, H., 445
Neisser, U., 238, 422, 436, 438, 442, 443, 445
Nelson, C. A., 299
Nelson, T. D., 190
Nemecek, S., 14, 536
Nemeroff, C. B., 504
Nesse, R. M., 105
Neuberg, S. L., 409
Newcomb, Theodore M., 459–460
Newell, A., 86
Newell, Allen, 260
Newman, B. S., 149
Nezworski, M. T., 389
Nguyen, M. L., 328
Nguyen, T., 328
Nicasio, P. M., 98
Nicholls, John G., 286
Nichols, P. I., 448
Nicholson, Jack, 509
Nicol, S. E., 517, 518
Nisbett, R. E., 24, 320, 323, 349, 463
Nixon, Richard Milhous, 460
Nobles, W. W., 540
Nolen-Hoeksema, Susan, 309, 505
Norton, G. R., 512

Norton, N. C., 558
Notarius, C. I., 151, 551
Novak, M. A., 35
Nungesser, L. G., 551
Nurmi, J. E., 150
Nyman, L., 118

Oakes, P. J., 478
Oakland, T., 439
Oatley, K., 308, 309
Odbert, H. S., 403
Oden, G. C., 263
Oden, M. H., 431
Offer, D., 148, 149
Ofshe, Richard, 210, 513
Ogawa, T., 389
Okun, M. A., 373
O'Leary, K. D., 551
Olton, D. S., 231, 232
Olver, R. R., 137
O'Malley, P. M., 105
Opton, E. M., Jr., 463
Orbuch, T. L., 342
Oren, D. A., 504
Orlos, J. R., 148
Orme-Johnson, D. W., 103
Orne, M. T., 101, 102
Ornstein, R., 153
Ornstein, R. E., 75, 87
Orwell, George, 8, 241
Osborn, A., 286
Osher, F. C., 566
Osterhout, L., 262
Ostrov, E., 148
Owen, M. J., 50, 51, 121, 502, 504
Owsley, C. J., 128
Ozer, D. J., 406

Packard, R. G., 547
Padesky, C. A., 551
Paffenbarger, R. S., Jr., 369
Page, T. L., 92
Paikoff, R. L., 149
Paivio, A., 249, 269
Palmer, John C., 245
Palmer, S., 194
Pandey, J., 476
Papolos, D. F., 497
Papolos, J., 497
Parke, R. D., 141
Parks, S. H., 364, 365
Parr, W. V., 153
Patrick, C. J., 313
Patterson, J. M., 371
Pattie, F. A., 496
Patzer, G. L., 472
Paul, S. M., 61
Paunonen, S. P., 403
Pavlov, Ivan, 212–213, 214, 215, 216, 219, 220, 231, 296, 354
Pavot, W., 373
Pawlik, K., 21–22
Payne, D. G., 235
Pearlson, G. D., 497
Pearman, R. R., 407
Pearson, T. A., 151
Pederson, P., 409, 410
Peel, Robert, 525

Penfield, Wilder, 65
Peng, K., 409
Pennebaker, J. W., 341, 342
Pennisi, E., 51
Peretz, L., 92
Perkins, D. F., 148
Perkins, D. V., 524
Perlmutter, M., 120
Perry, William G., Jr., 155
Pert, C., 338, 354
Pert, C. B., 61
Pervin, L. A., 405
Peters, S. D., 148
Peterson ?, 367
Peterson, A. C., 515
Peterson, C., 345, 504
Peterson, I., 45
Petrill, S. A., 442
Phelps, C., 51
Phelps, J. A., 120
Phelps, M. E., 510
Piaget, Jean, 134–136, 137–138, 156, 232, 260, 271
Picasso, Pablo, 194, 195, 286–287, 435
Pickering, M. R., 512
Pifer, A., 152
Pilisuk, M., 364
Pilkonis, P. A., 556
Pillard, Richard, 330
Pillisuk, M., 365
Pincus, Gregory, 382
Pinker, S., 133
Pion, G. M., 23
Piotrowski, C., 389
Piper, A., Jr., 513
Pittenger, D. J., 407
Plato, 13
Plaud, J. J., 217
Plomin, R., 50, 51, 52, 121, 123, 442, 502, 504, 507, 517
Plutchik, Robert, 300
Polefrone, J. M., 309
Poling, A., 509, 562
Polivy, J., 515
Pollitt, E., 445
Pomerantz, J. R., 35
Pool, R., 121
Poon, L. W., 153
Popejoy, D. I., 369
Porter, L. S., 361
Posner, M. I., 65, 66, 74, 262, 308
Powell, L. H., 358
Powley, T. L., 324
Premack, David, 227
Prentice, D. A., 460
Prescott, S., 149
Pribram, K. H., 17
Price, D. D., 186
Priest, R. F., 471
Primavera, L. H., 234
Prinzmetal, W., 194
Pulliam, H. R., 232
Putnam, F. W., 512

Rabkin, J. G., 346
Rachman, S., 328
Rafferty, Y., 462
Ragland, D. R., 358

Rahe, Richard H., 345–346, 347
Raichle, M. E., 65, 66, 74, 262
Rakic, P., 56
Ramachandran, V. S., 196
Ramey, C. T., 445, 446
Ramey, S. L., 445, 446
Rand, C. S., 515
Randi, James "The Amazing," 348
Rapaczynski, W. S., 283
Rapoport, J., 562
Rapoport, Judith L., 509
Rapson, R., 148, 319, 472, 480, 481
Rapson, R. L., 480
Rayman, P., 342
Raymond, C., 243
Raymond, J. L., 68
Rayner, Rosalie, 216–217
Raynor, J. O., 322
Raz, N., 517
Raz, S., 517
Read, S. J., 142, 143
Reagan, Ronald Wilson, 121, 525
Reber, A. S., 169
Reddon, J. R., 404
Redelmeier, D. A., 308
Rees, E., 284
Reeve, Christopher, 54, 55
Reeves, J. L., 84
Reeves, A., 74–75
Regier, D. A., 492, 503, 506, 507, 509, 516, 519
Reiman, E. M., 185
Reingold, E. M., 169
Reinisch, J. M., 149
Reisenzein, R., 308
Reiser, B. J., 248
Remick, Dean, 295–296
Rende, R., 50
Rescorla, Robert A., 233
Resnick, S. M., 507, 509, 517
Rest, J. R., 139
Reznick, J. S., 140
Rice-Bitti, P., 309
Richardson, P. H., 84
Riddle, D., 149
Riley, Bridget, 190
Rimland, B., 319
Rips, L. J., 274
Ritchie, B. G., 232
Roberts, A. H., 33, 366
Roberts, B. W., 401
Robins, L. N., 503, 504
Rock, I., 194
Rodin, Judith, 325, 360, 371, 514, 515
Rodman, Dennis, 493
Roediger, H. L., 244
Rogers, Carl R., 19, 394–395, 412, 414, 536, 549–550, 556
Rogers, J. E., 516
Roggman, L. A., 473
Rogoff, B., 436
Roll, S., 97
Rollman, G. B., 186
Rolls, B. J., 148, 515
Rolnick, J., 563
Roosevelt, Eleanor, 394

Rorschach, H., 389
Rosa, Emily, 3–4, 5, 7, 26, 27, 28, 29, 30, 33
Rosa, L., 4, 30
Rosch, E., 265, 266
Rosch, E. H., 266
Rosen, J. B., 507
Rosenblatt, P. C., 410
Rosenhan, David L., 465, 491–493, 498, 522–523, 525
Rosenman, Ray F., 356–357
Rosenthal, N. E., 504
Rosenthal, Robert, 33, 35, 438–439
Rosenzweig, M. R., 10, 21–22, 243
Ross, A. W., 397
Ross, B. H., 277
Ross, C. A., 512
Ross, D., 234
Ross, J. S., 153
Ross, L., 463, 476
Ross, P. E., 510
Ross, S. A., 234
Roth, D. L., 369
Roth, T., 99
Rothbart, M. K., 308
Rothbaum, F. M., 9
Rotter, Julian B., 318–319, 397, 398, 412, 414
Rottschaefer, W. A., 17
Rouhana, N. N., 483
Roush, W., 152
Rozin, Paul, 87, 89, 308, 514, 515
Rubin, Zick, 5, 7
Rusting, C. L., 309
Rutter, M., 497
Ryff, C. D., 152

Saarinen, T. F., 269
Sachs, Jake, 381
Sachs, Sadie, 381, 382
Sackheim, H. A., 564
Sacks, Oliver, 161, 176–177
Salovey, P., 308, 371
Saltzberg, J. A., 504
Saltzstein, H. D., 462
Salzhauer, A., 324
Sandberg, L., 462
Sanders, G. S., 357
Sandvik, E., 373
Sanger, Margaret Higgins, 381–382, 391, 392, 393, 395, 397–398, 405
Sanger, Peggy, 382
Sangrey, D., 374
Sanislow, C. A., III, 556
Sapirstein, G., 561
Sapolsky, R., 121
Sapolsky, R. M., 73, 354, 402
Sarason, I. B., 346
Sarbin, T. R., 102
Sarner, L., 4
Satir, Virginia, 552
Sattler, J. M., 446
Saudino, K. J., 50
Savitsky, J. C., 525
Sawyer, J., 471
Saxe, L., 312, 313

Scarr, Sandra, 144, 442, 444, 448, 450
Schachter, S., 370, 472
Schachter, Stanley, 306
Schacter, Daniel L., 240, 244, 246, 248
Schaefer, H. H., 547
Schanberg, S. M., 185
Schank, R. C., 272
Schatzberg, A. F., 497, 562
Schaufeli, W. B., 343
Scheier, M. F., 391
Schleifer, S. J., 354
Schlenker, B. R., 477
Schmidt, N. B., 357
Schmidt, W. E., 225
Schmitt, D. P., 297, 329
Schneider, K., 549
Schnur, E., 445
Schreiber, F. R., 512
Schroeder, C. S., 431
Schroeder, D. A., 460, 470
Schroeder, S. R., 431
Schugens, M. M., 233
Schulkin, J., 353, 507
Schwartz, B., 446
Schwartz, G. E., 304
Schwartz, J. M., 510, 554
Schwartz, K. M., 120
Schwartz, P., 151
Schwarzer, R., 555
Schwebel, A. I., 552
Schweinhart, L. J., 445
Schweitzer, Albert, 394
Scott, J. P., 122
Scott, K. G., 430, 431
Scotto, P., 234
Scovern, A. W., 565
Sears, R., 478
Segal, M. W., 472
Segall, M., 201
Segall, M. H., 96, 201, 202, 410, 436
Seger, C. A., 244
Selfridge, O. G., 199
Seligman, K., 427
Seligman, Martin E. P., 359, 366, 367, 373, 498, 503, 504, 505–506, 508, 557
Seligson, S. V., 99
Selye, H., 354
Selye, Hans, 351, 352, 353, 355, 357, 370
Sergeant, J. A., 296
Serpell, R., 436
Sexton, V. S., 21
Seymour, R. B., 107
Shaffer, C. R., 365
Shaffer, D. R., 475
Shaker, L. A., 358
Shakespeare, William, 94–95
Shapiro, D. H., 103
Shapiro, F., 543
Shattuck, R., 119
Shatz, M., 134
Shaver, P. R., 142, 143, 309
Shaw, J. C., 260
Shea, C., 438, 505
Sheatsley, P., 478

Sheingold, K., 246
Shepard, Roger N., 263
Sherif, C. W., 457
Sherif, Muzafer, 482–483
Sherry, D., 389
Shields, S. A., 309
Shiffrin, R. M., 240
Shimamura, A. P., 71
Shiraishi, D., 403
Shobe, K. K., 246
Shoda, Y., 406
Shor, R. E., 102
Shrout, P. E., 345, 346
Siegel, B. S., 371
Siegel, J. M., 153
Siegel, R. K., 104, 512
Siegert, R., 153
Siegler, Robert S., 138
Sigelman, C. K., 473
Silber, S., 134
Silberstein, L. R., 514, 515
Silbersweig, D. A., 304
Silver, N., 481
Silver, R. L., 374
Sime, W., 369
Simon, Herbert A., 86, 260, 284, 285
Simon, ThJodore, 423–425, 426, 431, 449
Simon, W., 149
Simpson, J. A., 143, 471, 472
Sinclair, R. C., 307
Singer, B., 556
Singer, D. G., 283
Singer, J., 306
Singer, J. L., 91, 283
Singer, W., 73
Skinner, Burrhus Frederic, 20–21, 220–221, 222, 226, 228, 230, 251
Skolnick, P., 61
Skoog, I., 51
Sleek, S., 14, 537, 561
Slobin, D. I., 132, 133
Smith, C. A., 477
Smith, D. E., 107
Smith, Dan, 209–210
Smith, Donna, 209–210, 222–223, 235, 246
Smith, E. E., 265
Smith, G. B., 566
Smith, Helen, 19
Smith, Judee, 209–210
Smith, L. D., 8
Smith, M. L., 543, 556
Smith, S., 445
Smythe, P. M., 370
Snidman, N., 140
Snyder, S. H., 61, 517
Sobel, D., 153
Socrates, 13
Sokol, M. M., 420
Solanto, M. V., 563
Solomon, D. S., 372
Solso, R. L., 261, 262, 266, 268
Solvason, H. B., 354
Sorenson, E. R., 298–299
Sorenson, R. C., 148
Sow, I., 495, 540

Spearman, Charles, 433
Spelke, E. S., 128
Spence, M. J., 128
Sperling, George, 239
Sperry, Roger W., 17, 74, 75
Spiegel, D., 512
Spigner, C., 149
Spinweber, Cheryl, 110
Spitzer, R. L., 511
Sprague, Jeff, 14
Sprecher, S., 472, 473, 480
Springer, Jim, 120–121
Springer, S. P., 74
Sprock, J., 494, 524
Spruston, N., 59
Spuhler, J. N., 447
Squier, L. H., 96, 97
Squire, L. R., 69, 233
Squire, S., 515
Staddon, J. E. R., 11
Stanislavsky, Konstantin, 295–296, 297, 303, 305
Stanley, J. R., 361
Stapley, J. C., 309
Stapp, J., 10
Stavish, S., 99, 402
Steele, C. M., 446
Stein, M. B., 507
Steiner, J. E., 299
Steinmetz, J. E., 233
Stejskal, W. J., 389
Stern, J. A., 103
Stern, W. C., 94
Stern, William, 426
Sternberg, Robert J., 277, 286, 287, 434–435, 436, 438, 472, 480
Stevens, A. L., 285
Stevenson, H. W., 421, 447
Stevenson, J., 442
Stevenson, Robert Louis, 512
Stiles, W. B., 504
Stillwell, A. M., 309
Stock, M. B., 370
Stock, W. A., 373
Stoessel, P. W., 510
Stokes, G., 148
Stone, A. A., 361
Stones, M. L., 374
Stoppard, Tom, 569
Storms, M. D., 328
Straus, M. A., 361
Strauss, E., 75
Strauss, J. S., 516
Streep, Meryl, 295
Strickland, B. R., 505
Striegel-Moore, R. H., 514, 515
Stringfield, D. O., 406
Strong, Edward, 449
Struening, E. L., 346
Strupp, H. H., 557
Stryon, William, 503
Styfco, S. J., 445
Suchman, A. L., 349
Suddath, R. L., 517
Sue, Stanley, 23, 399
Suedfeld, P., 104
Sulloway, Frank J., 118, 150
Suls, J., 357

Suomi, S. J., 35
Sutker, P. B., 301
Svanum, S., 404
Swann, W. B., Jr., 474
Swazey, J. P., 560
Sweeney, P. D., 397, 504
Swets, J. A., 168, 366
Syme, S. L., 354, 364, 365
Sys, S. U., 358
Szasz, Thomas, 523, 524, 524, 536

Tartaryn, D. J., 89, 315
Tasker, F., 329
Tavris, C., 23, 313, 399
Taylor, Shelley E., 363, 365, 371
Tellegen, A., 442
Templin, M., 132
Tenney, Y. J., 246
Terman, Louis M., 123, 425, 426, 431, 438, 440
Terman, M., 504
Tesch-R'mer, C., 285
Tesser, A., 472, 475
Teuber, H. H., 243
Thigpen, C. H., 512
Thill, G., 14
Thio, A., 525
Thoma, S. J., 139
Thomas, F. F., 446
Thomas, F. H., 322
Thompson, J. K., 514
Thompson, R. F., 233
Thomson, Donald M., 249
Thoresen, C. E., 357, 358, 373
Thorndike, Edward L., 220–221, 230–231, 251, 425
Thorndike, R. L., 427
Thorndyke, P. W., 269
Tiebout, J., 342
Tienari, P., 517
Titchener, Edward, 18, 20
Tolman, Edward C., 231–232, 252, 269
Tomarken, A. J., 307
Tomie, A., 232
Tononi, G., 86
Torrey, E. F., 566
Toth, J. P., 315
Travis, J., 56
Trebek, Alex, 243
Treiber, F. A., 301
Trevethan, S. D., 139
Triandis, Harry C., 22, 22, 323, 399, 409, 412, 476, 540
Trinder, J., 98
Tronick, E., 129
Trope, I., 74
Trotter, R. J., 284
Tsai, M., 410
Tsuang, M. T., 503
Tucker, A. M., 10
Tucker, J. S., 358
Tulving, E., 242
Turk, D. C., 185, 186
Turkington, C., 430, 505
Turner, J. C., 478
Turvey, M. T., 239
Tversky, Amos, 281–282
Tyler, L., 420, 433

Uemura, A., 410
Uhlenhuth, E. H., 98
Uleman, J. S., 89
Ulmer, D., 357, 358
Umberson, D., 364
United States Agency for Health Care Policy and Research, 556
Ursano, R. J., 365

Valenstein, Elliot S., 563, 564
Vallee, B. L., 107, 108
van Dam, L., 103
Van de Castle, R. L., 96, 97
VandenBos, G. R., 10, 29–30, 556
van de Poll, N. E., 296
Van Gogh, Vincent, 308, 503
van Goozen, S. H. M., 296
Vasarely, Victor, 192, 193
Veldhuis, J. D., 126
Vernon, P. E., 426, 436
Vicary, James, 168–169
Viken, R. J., 545
Vincent, K. R., 439
Vincent, M., 512
Vitaliano, P. P., 374
Vogel, G., 108, 185, 262
von Hofsten, C., 129
von Neumann, John, 260

Wade, T. J., 51, 148
Wagner, A. R., 233
Walker, E. F., 518
Walker, J. R., 507
Walker, L. J., 139
Walkley, R., 479
Wallace, A. F. C., 540
Wallach, M. A., 566

Wallbott, H. G., 309
Wallis, C., 185
Walsh, R., 409
Walster (Hatfield), E., 473
Walters, E. E., 515
Ward, C., 476, 477
Wardle, J., 369
Watkins, B. A., 234
Watkins, L. R., 61, 103, 186, 354
Watson, James D., 277
Watson, John B., 20, 85, 127, 216–217, 231, 251, 508
Watters, E., 210, 513
Watterson, Bill, 224
Wearing, A., 374
Webb, W. B., 94
Weber, A. L., 319, 342
Weber, R. J., 286
Wechsler, David, 426–427
Wegmann, H. M., 92
Wegner, D. M., 91
Wehr, T. A., 504
Weikart, D. P., 445
Weil, A. T., 100
Weinberg, M. S., 148
Weinberg, Richard A., 444, 448, 450
Weinberger, A., 556
Weinberger, M., 344
Weiner, B., 476
Weiner, I. B., 389
Weiner, J., 48
Weingardt, K. R., 245
Weingold, M. F., 477
Weisberg, Robert, 286, 287
Weissman, M. M., 503, 504, 505
Weissman, W. W., 365

Weisz, J. R., 9
Wellman, H. M., 134, 138
Welsh, E. J., 562
Welsh, H. G., 404
Wertheim, E. H., 515
Wertheimer, Max, 196
Wesson, D. R., 107
Westra, T., 126
Whalen, C. K., 562
Whiteman, M. C., 357, 358
Wickelgren, I., 61, 68, 106, 109, 445, 560
Wickelgren, W., 276
Wiesel, Torsten N., 190, 260
Wiggins, J. S., 422
Wilcoxon, L. A., 543
Willerman, B., 474
Williams, C. L., 404, 405
Williams, Robin, 337, 493
Williams, T. M., 234
Williams, W. M., 438, 443
Wills, T. A., 558
Wilner, D., 479
Wilson, D. B., 556
Wilson, E. D., 74–75
Wilson, L., 512
Wilson, S. M., 148
Winson, J., 97
Witkin, G., 19, 22
Wittig, B. A., 141
Wolff, Patrick, 45
Woloshyn, V., 88
Wolpe, Joseph, 217, 543, 556
Wong, M. M., 431
Wood, J. M., 389
Wood, J. V., 504
Woods, Tiger, 479

Woodworth, R. S., 317
Wooten, P., 338, 368
World Health Organization, 524
Wortman, C. B., 365, 374
Wotman, S. R., 309
Wozney, K., 512
Wright, K., 121
Wright, L., 358
Wu, C., 562
Wundt, Wilhelm, 13, 18, 20, 39, 238
Wurtman, R. J., 370
Wyatt, G. E., 148

Yalom, I. D., 551
Yeltsin, Boris, 194
Yerkes, Robert M., 425
Young, J. E., 556

Zajonc, Robert B., 308, 438
Zeki, S., 176, 190
Zeman, N., 149
Zigler, E., 150, 445
Zika, S., 345
Zilbergeld, B., 541
Zimbardo, Philip G., 102, 150, 153, 307, 318, 371, 402, 456, 457, 459, 520, 520
Zubeck, J. P., 104
Zucker, G. S., 476
Zuckerman, Marvin, 301, 302, 312, 448
Zuwerink, J. R., 479

# Subject Index

Amacrine cells, in eye, 172
Ambiguity, in perception, 190–193
Ambiguous figures, perceiving, 191–193
Ambiguous situational cues
in bystander intervention experiments, 470
personality traits and, 406
Ambivalence, attachment and, 142, 143
American Association of Mental Retardation, definition of mental retardation by, 430
American Psychological Association (APA), 36
American Psychological Society (APS), 36
*American Psychologist, The* journal, 36
American Sign Language, 132
Amnesia
during anesthesia, 84
anterograde, 243–244, 511
in dissociative fugue, 511–512
retrograde, 243
Amphetamines
as psychoactive drug, 104–105
as stimulants, 108
Amplitude
of light waves, 175–176
of sound waves, 177, 180
Amygdala, 69, 497
long-term memory and, 243–244
violent behavior and, 15
Analgesic drugs, 186
Analogies, problem solving with, 277
Anal stage, in psychoanalytic theory, 387
Analysis of transference, 548
*Anatomy of an Illness, The* (Cousins), 367
Anchoring bias, as faulty heuristic, 281–282
Anesthesia
consciousness under, 83–84
Aglove," 510
unconsciousness under, 89
"Angel dust," as psychoactive drug, 105
Anger, 294, 298–300. *See also* Rage
biology of, 303
controlling, 313
Anima
consciousness and, 84–85
in Jungian theory, 392
Animal magnetism, 496
Animals. *See also* Laboratory animals
operant conditioning techniques to train, 228
Animistic thinking, among children, 136
Animus, in Jungian theory, 392
Anorexia, 324, 325

Anorexia nervosa, 325, 514–515, 528
Antabuse, 544
Anterior cingulate cortex, pain and, 185
Anterograde amnesia, 243–244, 511
Anthropology, psychology and, 11
Antianxiety drugs
coping with stress via, 370
as depressants, 107
in drug therapy, 562
Anticipation, 300
hunger and, 324
Anticipatory anxiety, 507
Antidepressant drugs, in drug therapy, 561
Antipsychotic drugs
in drug therapy, 560–561
schizophrenia and, 517
Antisocial behavior, 21
genetic basis of, 124
negative consequences of, 459
Antisocial personality disorder, 519
Anvil, 178
Anxiety, 7, 307, 308. *See also* Panic disorder
acute, 356
anticipatory, 507
attachment and, 142
hierarchy of, 543
neurotic patterns of dealing with, 392–393
as personality trait, 403
sexual, 328
test, 375, 413
Anxiety disorders, 501, 506–510, 527
*APA Monitor* newsletter, 36
Apperception, 390
Appetitive conditioning, 216
Applied psychology, 10–11
Applied research, in psychology, 10–11
Approximations, learning by successive, 227–228
Aptitude
of creative genius, 286–287
measuring, 419–421, 437
Aptitude tests, 437
Aqueous humor, 171
Archetypes, Jungian theory of, 391–392
Arousal, 331–332
biology of emotional, 303–305
in deception, 312
of emotions, 297, 332
gender and, 309
hormones and, 61
inverted "U" function and, 301
James-Lange theory of, 305–306, 307
in lie detection, 312–313
as obstacle to problem solving, 283–284
performance and, 294, 300–301
physical, 305–306, 307–308

sexual, 327
stress and, 338, 339–340, 348–349, 376
in test anxiety, 375
in two-factor theory of emotion, 306–308
Artificial concepts, 265, 266
Artificial intelligence (AI)
cognitive psychology and, 259
origins of, 260–261
Asch effect, 461
Asch experiments, 485
on conformity, 460–462
Asking for help, 469–470
Assertiveness, as personality trait, 403
Assimilation
of new information, 271
in Piaget's theory of cognitive development, 134, 135
Association cortex, 72–73
*Astonishing Hypothesis, The: The Scientific Search for the Soul* (Crick), 85
"Astonishing Hypothesis," 85
Astrology, as pseudoscience, 24
Asylums, 565. *See also* Hospitals; Mental hospitals
Athletes, Achoking" by, 300
Attachment
childhood influences on adult, 144–146
development of, 141–144
nature and nurture and, 140
styles of, 143
Attachment needs, in motivation, 319
Attention
behavioral view of, 21
children's intelligence and, 444
cognitive psychology and, 259
consciousness and, 87
emotions and, 308
in implicit and explicit memory, 244
Attention-deficit/hyperactivity disorder (ADHD)
stimulants for treating, 108, 562–563
Attitude, 6
prejudice as, 477
Attractiveness. *See* Physical attractiveness
among adolescents, 148
Attribution. *See also* Fundamental attribution error (FAE); Misattribution
in social reality, 475–477, 486
Auditory alertness, under anesthesia, 83–84
Auditory area, of brain, 70, 71
Auditory canal, speech and, 180
Auditory cortex, 71, 179
Auditory memory, 238–239
Auditory nerve, 179
Auditory sensations, conversion of sound into, 178–179

Australian Aboriginals, significance of dreaming among, 96
Authoritarian personality, 463
Authority, 485
obedience to, 462–463, 464–466
Autohypnosis, 101
Automatic action, as response to catastrophes, 341
Automation, as social force, 520
Autonomic nervous system (ANS), 55–56
alarm reaction and, 352–353
emotional arousal and, 304
Afight-or-flight" response and, 349–350
stress exhaustion and, 353–354
Autonomy, in psychosocial development, 145
Availability heuristic, 283–284
Average. *See also* Regression to the average
normal distribution and, 429
Aversion therapy, 543–544
Aversive conditioning, 216. *See also* Food aversion; Negative reinforcers; Punishments; Taste aversion
Aversive stimulus, 216
Avoidance, attachment and, 142, 143
Awareness, 112
consciousness and, 87, 100–101
Awe, 300
Axons, of neurons, 57, 59, 60

Babbling, in infancy, 131
Backgrounds, figures against, 195
"Backwards knowledge," 437
"Bad seed" concept, 440–441
Bait shyness, as food aversion, 218
Balance. *See* Equilibrium
Barbiturates
as depressants, 107
in drug therapy, 562
Base rate, in predictions, 8
Base rate information, in problem solving, 283
Basic anxiety, in psychodynamic perspective, 392–393
Basic levels, of concepts, 268–269
Basic research, in psychology, 10
Basilar membrane, 178–179
in pitch perception, 179–180
Beauty, quantification of, 422
Bedwetting, treatment of, 556
Behavior
altering hostile, 484
altering via therapy, 535
antisocial, 21, 459
biological view of, 15–16, 17
brain and, 78–79
cognitive dissonance and, 474–475
discrimination as, 477

eliminating undesirable, 223–224, 224–225
evolution of, 47–48
explaining unusual, 380
genetics and, 44, 50–51, 78
humanistic view of, 19–20
under hypnosis, 101–102
innate, 47
instinctive, 211
instincts and, 317
learning of, 210, 211
limbic system and, 68–69
during meditation, 103
motivation and, 316, 332
needs hierarchy and, 319–320
operant conditioning of, 220–229
personality traits and, 406
polyphasic, 357
prenatal, 125–126
in prison life, 455–457
pseudoscientific theories of, 24–25
psychology as study of, 5
punishing undesirable, 225
self-modification of, 545
sexual, 325–330
social situation and, 454
social standards of, 458–460
of split-brain patients, 74–76
Type A and Type B, 356–358
Type D, 358
unacceptable, 522–524
weakening of, 222
Behavioral learning, 212, 496, 497
cognitive psychology and, 233
Behavioral measures, in controlled tests, 28
Behavioral medicine, 376
coping with stress via, 371
preventing heart disease via, 372–373
Behavioral perspective, toward mental disorders, 496–497
Behavioral psychology, 2, 17, 20–21, 23, 39
Behavioral therapy, 21, 539, 542–547, 554, 571
biofeedback in, 366
counterconditioning as, 217
reinforcers in, 222
Behavior genetics, 50–51, 497
Behaviorism, 20–21, 211
cognitive psychology and, 231
consciousness and, 85
humanistic perspectives on, 394
mental disorders in, 496–497
Behaviorists, 20–21, 211, 220–221
cognitive scientists versus, 259–260, 290
humanistic psychology and, 396
Behavior modification, 542
*Bell Curve, The: Intelligence and Class Structure in American*

*Life* (Herrnstein & Murray), 446–447, 450
Belonging, in adult development, 151, 152
Bennington College, social norms at, 459–460
Benzodiazepines
as depressants, 107
in drug therapy, 562
Bias
anchoring, 281–282
fundamental attribution error as, 476
in IQ testing, 446
in psychological research, 33–34, 39
self-serving, 477
"Big Five Inventory," trait assessment with, 404
"Big Five" traits, 403, 414
genes and, 123
Bilingual people, concept formation by, 265
Binding problem, 205
in perception, 190, 194
Binet-Simon test, 423–425
"Binge-and-purge" eating, 515
Biofeedback, coping with stress via, 366
Biofeedback training, lie detection and, 313
*Biological Basis of Personality, The* (Eysenck), 403
"Biological clock," in depression, 504
Biological needs, in motivation, 319
Biological perspective, in psychology, 2, 15–16, 17, 23, 39, 45–78, 78–79
Biological rhythms. *See also* Biorhythm analysis; Circadian rhythms
in consciousness, 90–98
Biomedical therapies, 539, 554, 559–567, 571
Biopsychology, 45–78
of circadian rhythms, 92
computers and, 45–46
defined, 46
of endocrine and nervous systems, 53–63
of genes and behavior, 47–52
of human action, 46–47
madness in, 497
of mental processes, 64–78
of schizophrenia, 517–518
of sensation, 164–165
of sleep, 91–98
Biorhythm analysis, as pseudoscience, 25
Bipolar cells, in eye, 171, 172
Bipolar disorder, 502–503
cognitive therapy for, 552–553
Bipolar trait dimensions, 403
Birth control pill. *See* Oral contraceptive
Birth order, personality differences and, 117–119

Bisexuality, 329–330
Black bile, 494
melancholic personality and, 401
Blind spot, 171, 174, 196. *See also* Closure
"Blind" studies, removing bias with, 34
Blood, 494
sanguine personality and, 401
BoBo doll, learning violent behavior toward, 234
Bodily-kinesthetic ability, as form of intelligence, 435, 436
Body image, among adolescents, 148
Body sense area, of brain, 70, 71
Bottom-up processing, 190
Brain, 64–76, 78
behavior and, 78–79
biological view of, 15
cerebral dominance in, 73–74
color vision and, 161–162
computers and, 45–46
consciousness and, 84–87
dreaming and, 97–98
in emotional arousal, 303–304
endocrine system and, 63
evolution of, 48–49
evolution of human, 46–47
genetics and, 50–51, 51–52
hearing and, 177–181
innate language structures in, 131–132
instruments and techniques for studying, 65–66
learning and structural changes in, 73
mental processes and, 44, 64–65
nervous system and, 54, 55
operation of, 72–73, 78
patients with split, 74–76
perception and, 204–205
phosphenes and, 182
physical appearance of, 65
plasticity of, 77
position and movement and, 181–183
prenatal development of, 125–126
psychoactive drugs and, 63
psychology as study of, 5
sense organs and, 160, 163–164, 170–186, 204
seven intelligences in, 435–436
skin senses and, 185
smell and, 183–184
structure of, 63, 66–72, 79
taste and, 184–185
three layers of, 66–67, 79
vision and, 171–177
Brain damage, 6, 44, 73
affecting short-term and long-term memory, 243–244
behavior and, 76–77
mental retardation from, 430, 431
psychological changes from, 64

Brain hemispheres, 70
damage to, 44
in lateralization of emotion, 304
in visual system, 173
Brain scanning, 65–66, 78–79, 262
concept formation and, 265
diagnosing madness via, 497
Brain stem, 67–68, 79
Brainstorming, in creative thinking, 286
"Brainwashing," 8
Brain waves, 65
Branch Davidians community, 463
Brightness, in vision, 175–176
Broca's area, 70, 131
Buddhism, meditation in, 103
Bulimia, 324, 325, 515, 528
Burnout, 343–344
Bystander intervention studies, 35, 467–468, 468–469, 469–470
Bystander problem, 454, 466–470

Caffeine
as psychoactive drug, 104
as stimulant, 108
Campus culture, 459–460
conformity in, 460–462
Cannabis, as psychoactive drug, 104, 105–106
Captives, Stockholm syndrome among, 360–361
Careers, in psychology, 2, 9–12, 449, 485
Caregivers, attachment of children to, 141–144
CARL UnCover database, 36
Case studies
in Freudian theory, 391
in psychological research, 30, 32–33
Cataplexy, 99
*Cataracts* (Riley), 190
Catastrophes
defined, 341
as stressors, 340–342
Catatonic excitement, 516
Catatonic schizophrenia, 498, 516
Catatonic stupor, 516
Categorization
of concepts, 268–269
as faulty heuristic, 282–283
Caucasian Americans, IQ scores of, 440, 446
Caudal raphe nuclei, 63
Caudate nucleus, 63
Causation, correlation and, 31
Cell body, of neurons, 57
Cell division, of embryonic cells, 125
Cells, DNA and chromosomes in, 49–50
Central fissure, of brain, 70, 71
Central nervous system (CNS), 54–55, 78

Componential intelligence, IQ tests and, 435
Comprehension, among children, 138
Compromise, in resolving conflicts, 484
Compulsions, 509
Computerized tomography (CT) scans, 65–66, 260
Computer models, in cognitive science, 261
Computers
    in brain scanning, 65–66
    human mental processes and, 45–46
    in studying thought, 262
Computer science. *See also* Artificial intelligence (AI)
    cognitive science and, 259
    origins of, 260
Computer technology, as social force, 521
Concentration, measuring, 86
Concept formation, 265
Concept hierarchies, 268–269
Concepts, 256
    artificial, 265, 266
    defined, 265
    expertise and, 285
    "fuzzy," 266
    learning of, 210
    of mental disorder, 494–497
    natural, 265–266
    in perception, 190, 198–199
    prototypes for, 266–268
    for students and professors, 289–290
    thinking and, 258, 265–269
Conceptually driven processing, 190
Conceptual models, in cognitive science, 261
Conclusions, in syllogisms, 274
Concordance rate, for schizophrenia, 517–518
Concrete operational stage, in Piaget's theory of cognitive development, 135, 136–137, 138
Conditional love, in humanistic psychology, 395
Conditioned fear, 215, 216
    in "Little Albert" case, 216–217
Conditioned reflexes, 214
Conditioned reinforcers, 226–227
    motivation via, 318
Conditioned response (CR), 542
    in aversive conditioning, 216, 217
    in classical conditioning, 214–215, 233
    in food aversions, 217–218
Conditioned stimulus (CS), 542
    in aversive conditioning, 216, 217
    in classical conditioning, 214–215
    in food aversions, 217–218

informativeness of, 233
sexual, 328
Cones, 170–171, 172
Confidence, memory distortion and, 245, 268
Conflicts
    in cognitive dissonance, 474–475
    defined, 482
    resolving, 454, 475, 482–484, 486
    unconscious and, 384–385
Conformability, as personality trait, 403
Conformity, 460–462
    as cause of prejudice, 478
Confounding variables, in controlled tests, 27, 34
Conscience, superego and, 388
Conscientiousness, as personality trait, 403
Conscious motivation, 315
Consciousness, 82, 83–111, 111–112
    altered states of, 82, 100–108, 112, 328
    under anesthesia, 83–84
    brain and, 68
    cycles of, 82, 90–98, 111–112
    duality of, 75
    ego and, 84–85, 388
    emotions and, 308
    forms of, 100–108
    Freudian theory of, 84–85, 246
    functions of, 87–89
    levels of, 88–89
    motivation and, 315
    nature of, 84–86
    personality and, 385
    in post-Freudian theories, 393
    structures of, 88
    thalamus and, 68
    thinking and, 258
    tools for studying, 86–87
    unconscious and, 84–85, 88, 89
    working memory and, 240
Consequences, in operant conditioning, 220, 221–225
Conservation
    among children, 137, 138
    sleep as, 94–95
Constraint, as personality trait, 403
Construction, of subjective reality, 271
Constructive memory, 245, 246
Constructive thinking, relieving stress by, 366
Consummate love, 480–481
Contact comfort, 142–144
Contempt, 298–300
Contents, in structure-of-intellect, 433–434
Context
    in perception, 199
    for psychotherapy, 540
    of remembered material, 244–246, 248
    in social psychology, 457

Contextual intelligence, 434–435
Contingencies, 225
Contingency management, as therapy, 544–545
Contingent reinforcement, 226
Continuation, in perceptual grouping, 196–197
Continuity
    of personality, 383
    sensory memory and, 239
Continuity view, 156
    of children's development, 122
Continuous reinforcement, 226
Contours, perception of, 194, 195–196
Contraception, in early twentieth century, 381–382
Control
    of emotions, 294
    as goal of psychology, 5, 8–9
    in happiness and well-being, 373
    among hardy people, 358–359
    optimism and sense of, 366–367
    as personality trait, 403
Control conditions
    in psychological research, 30
    removing bias with, 34
Control groups, in controlled tests, 28, 30
Controlled tests, in scientific method, 27–28, 39
Convergent thinking, 286, 434
Conversation, childhood acquisition of skill in, 134
Conversion disorder, 384, 498, 510–511
Conversion hysteria, as MMPI-2 clinical scale, 404
Cooperation, in resolving group conflicts, 483, 484
Coping strategies, for stress, 344, 361, 363–374, 376
Cornea, 171
Corpus callosum, 70
    severing of, 74–76
Correlation
    causation and, 31
    between relationship and intelligence, 442
Correlational studies, in psychological research, 30–32
Correlation coefficient, 31–32
Cortex, 70
Couch, in psychotherapy, 535
Counseling psychologists, 538
Counseling psychology, 10
Counterconditioning therapy, 217, 542–543
Couples counseling, 551–552
Crack cocaine, as stimulant, 108
Creative genius, 256, 286–287, 291
Creativity, 286–287
    defined, 286
    as thinking, 265

Crime
    as social force, 520
    as societal stressor, 343
"Crimes of passion," 525
Critical periods
    identifying, 122–123
    for learning language, 119
Criticism, in scientific method, 29–30, 39
Cross-cultural psychology, 21–22, 23–24, 39
    implicit personality theories and, 409
    intelligence in, 436–437, 450
    perception in, 201–202
    personality in, 383, 412, 414
Cross-sectional method, 156
    identifying critical developmental periods via, 122, 123
Crying, gender and, 309
Cubism, 435
Cultural differences, 399
Culture
    achievement and, 323
    adolescence and, 147
    on campus, 459–462
    cognitive maps and, 269–273
    control and, 9
    defined, 21
    diagnostic labeling and, 524
    display rules and, 309
    dreams and, 97
    emotions and, 294, 309, 331–332
    fundamental attribution error and, 476
    implicit personality theories and, 409–411
    intelligence and, 436–437
    learning and memory and, 211–212
    meditation and, 103
    needs hierarchy in, 319–320
    perception and, 201–202
    personality and, 380
    psychoactive drugs and, 105
    in psychology, 2, 23–24
    psychotherapy and, 540
    race versus, 423n
    sexual orientation and, 329–330
    sociocultural view of, 21–22
    stress and, 339
"Culture of honor," 349
"Cupboard theory" of attachment, 142–143
*Curandeiros*, 540
Curiosity
    drives and, 318
    as personality trait, 403
*Current Directions in Psychological Science* journal, 36
Cycles. *See also* Sexual response cycle
    of consciousness, 90–98, 111–112
Cycles per second, 177

Ecological model, abnormality in, 524
Economic competition, as cause of prejudice, 478
Economics, psychology and, 11
Education, as therapy, 532, 570
Effect
    law of, 220
    partial reinforcement, 226
Efferent neurons, 56
Efferent systems, sensation and, 165
Ego
    consciousness and, 84–85, 388
    personality and, 385, 387–388
    self versus, 395
Egocentrism, among children, 136
Ego defense mechanisms, 388–389, 548
    fantasy as, 91
    in post-Freudian theories, 393
    projection as, 322
    under stress, 336, 362
Ego ideal, superego and, 388
Ego-integrity, in psychosocial development, 145, 152
Elaboration, in memory encoding, 237
Elaborative rehearsal, with working memory, 241
Elavil, in drug therapy, 561
Elderly. See Aged persons
Electroconvulsive therapy (ECT), 564–565, 571
Electroencephalograph (EEG), 28–29, 65
    studying consciousness with, 86
    studying emotions with, 304
    studying hypnosis with, 101
    studying sleep with, 92, 93
    studying thinking with, 262
Electromagnetic spectrum, 173, 175
Electronic resources, in psychology, 36
Embryo, 125
Emotion
    childhood expression of, 134
    in mental disorders, 493
Emotional control, 310–313
    as personality trait, 403
Emotional development, 139–146
Emotional expressions, 298–300
Emotional intelligence, 311–312, 332
Emotional stability, as personality trait, 403
Emotions, 79, 294, 295–313, 331–332
    in aversive conditioning, 216
    biology of, 303–305
    computers as lacking, 45–46
    creative genius and, 287
    deception and, 312–313
    evolution of, 297–298
    function of, 297
    generation of, 305–308
    lateralization of, 304

limbic system and, 69–70
motivation and, 295–296
negative, 297
personal control over, 310–313, 332
personality and, 397–398
positive, 297
psychology as study of, 5
responses associated with, 305
in romantic love, 480
stress and, 338–339
theories of, 305–309
thinking and, 308
two-factor theory of, 306–308
types of, 297, 300
Emotion wheel, 300
Empirical approach
    in defining reinforcers, 222
    to intelligence testing, 424
    to studying unconscious, 89
Empirical data, in controlled tests, 28
Empirical investigation, in psychology, 25–26
Employment
    burnout in, 343–344
    stressors in, 355
Encephalization, evolution of, 48–49
Encoding
    of memory, 237, 252
    in working memory, 240
Endocrine system, 44, 53–54, 61, 62, 63, 78
    alarm reaction and, 352–353
    biological view of, 15
    in emotional arousal, 303, 332
    hypothalamus and, 69–70
    immune system and, 354
Endorphins, 6
    hypnosis and, 102–103
    as neurotransmitters, 61
    opiates and, 106
    relieving pain with, 186
Engineering psychology, 10
Enuresis, treatment of, 556
Environment. See also Nature–nurture interaction
    in adoption studies, 121
    behavior and, 20
    evolution and, 47–48
    instinct and motivation and, 316–317
    intelligence and, 440, 442–443, 446–447, 450
    in psychological development, 118, 119–121
    raising IQ via, 445–446
    temperament and, 402
    in twin studies, 120–121
Epilepsy, 65, 77. See also H. M. case
    hallucinations during, 104
    split-brain patients and, 74–75
Epinephrin. See Adrenalin
Episodic memory, 193, 242–243
    forgetting and, 246
    in H. M. case, 243–244

Equal status contact, overcoming prejudice with, 479
Equilibrium, fundamental features of, 165
Erectile disorder, 327–328
Erikson's theory of psychosocial development, 144–146, 156
    for adulthood, 149–152
Eros, in psychoanalytic theory, 385
Esteem needs, in motivation, 319
*Ethical Principles of Psychologists and Code of Conduct* (American Psychological Association), 34–35
Ethics, in psychological research, 34–36, 39
"Ethnic cleansing," eugenics movement and, 423
Etiology, in therapy, 537
Eugenics, 423
Eugenics movement, 422–423
Euphoria
    from opiates, 106
    from stimulants, 108
Europe
    alcoholism in, 107–108
    history of psychology in, 13
Eustress, 336, 354, 355
    exercise as, 369
    test anxiety as, 375
Evaluation, in structure-of-intellect, 433
*Even the Rat Was White* (Guthrie), 33
Event-related potentials, 262
Evil, situational context of, 465–466
Evolution, 47–49, 78
    of brain structure, 67
    defined, 47
    of emotions, 297–298
    of hearing and speech, 180
    of human brain, 46–47
    learning and, 211
    mutations in, 49
    natural selection and, 220
    psychology and, 16
    sexuality and, 328–329
Evolutionary psychology, 16
Excitement, 307
Excitement phase, of sexual response cycle, 327
Exemplar faces, 266–267
Exercise, coping with stress via, 368–369, 376
Exhaustion stage, in general adaptation syndrome, 351, 353–354, 376
Expanded Academic Index database, 36
Expectancy, in cognitive learning, 232
Expectancy bias, in psychological research, 33, 39

Expectancy-value theory, 486
    reward theory of attractiveness and, 474
Expectations
    in cognitive psychology, 16–18, 230
    influence on IQ, 438–439
    in perception, 199
    in reward theory of attraction, 473–474
    in social learning, 22
    in social psychology, 457
    of successful relationship, 474
Experience
    dreaming and, 97
    intelligence and, 437
    in learning and in memory, 210
    sexual, 328
    temperament and, 402
Experience-sampling method, examining consciousness via, 86
Experiential intelligence, 435
Experimental conditions, in psychological research, 30
Experimental groups, in controlled tests, 28, 30
Experimental psychology, 10
    origins of, 13
Experiments
    correlational studies versus, 30–31
    in psychological research, 30
Expertise, 284–285
    aging and, 153
    of creative genius, 286
    structural changes in brain as, 73
Experts, 284, 290–291
Explanation
    as goal of psychology, 5, 7–8
    with trait theories, 405
Explicit memory, 244, 252
Exploration, drives and, 318
Exploration of alternatives, as therapy, 558
Exposure therapy, 543
Expressions, emotional, 298–300
External influences, as source of bias, 33, 39
External locus of control, 318–319, 397, 413
Extinction, 208, 215, 216, 225, 229, 543
    of operant behaviors, 223–224
Extinguishment, of operant behaviors, 223–224, 228, 229
Extraversion, 407
    in Jungian theory, 392
    as personality trait, 403
Extraverts, 392
Extrinsic motivation, 315, 320–321, 332
Eye, anatomy of, 170–171
Eyewitnesses
    memory distortion by, 245
    prototype faces for, 266–267
    recognition by, 238

Faces
emotions and, 134, 140, 299
exemplar and prototype, 266–267
Failure, fundamental attribution error and, 476–477
"Faith healing," placebo bias in, 33
False memories, 209–210, 252. See also Pseudomemory
creation of, 235–236
Falsification, in scientific method, 27
Familiarity, in reward theory of attraction, 472
Families
in adult development, 151–152
development of children in, 117–119
diagnosing, 527
group therapy for, 551–552
personality and, 398–399
Family context, for psychotherapy, 540
Family planning, origins of, 381–382
Family structure changes, as social force, 520
Family systems theory, personality in, 398–399
Family therapy, 552
Fantasy, daydreaming as, 91
Fat, hunger and, 323–325
Faulty heuristics, as problem solving obstacle, 281–284, 290
Fear, 296, 297, 298–300, 497
behavioral view of, 20
conditioned, 8, 215, 216
counterconditioning therapy for, 217
Feature detectors, in perceptual systems, 190, 260
Feedback, 366. See also Biofeedback
Feeling, cultural differences in, 410
Female orgasmic disorder, 328
Feminine Psychology (Horney), 393
Feminism
in psychodynamic psychology, 392–393
self-help groups and, 551
Feral children, 119
Fetal alcohol syndrome, mental retardation in, 430
Fetishism, 328
Fetus, prenatal development of, 125–126
Fever, hallucinations during, 104
"Fight-or-flight" response, 296, 303
defined, 349
to stress, 349–350, 376
sympathetic nervous system and, 56
Figure and ground, in images, 194–195

Firstborns, psychological development of, 117–118
Five-factor trait theory, 403
Fixations, in psychoanalytic theory, 386–387
Fixed-action patterns, instincts as, 317
"Flashbulb" memories, 235–236
Flock, The (Casey & Wilson), 512
Flow, in motivation, 331
Fluoxetine, in drug therapy, 561
"Folk theories"
of dreaming, 95–96
of personality, 408–409
Food, as reinforcer, 228
Food aversion, 208, 212, 217–218
during chemotherapy, 219
Forced choice tests, Internal-External Locus of Control Scale as, 398
Foreplay, 328
Forgetting, 6, 246–249, 252
repression and, 388
Forgetting curve, 236
Formal operational stage, in Piaget's theory of cognitive development, 135, 137
Formal reasoning, 274–275
Fortune telling, 24–25
Fovea, 171
"Fragmentation," 511
Frames of mind, intelligence and, 435–436
France, intelligence testing in, 423–424
Free will, 15–16
Frequency
and pitch of sound, 179–180
of sound waves, 177
Frequency theory, of pitch perception, 180
Freudian dream analysis, 96
Freudian personality theory, 384–391
criticisms of, 390–391
feminist modifications to, 392–393
Jungian theory and, 391–392
theories following from, 393
Freudian slips, 386
Freudian theory of consciousness, 246
Freudian theory of memory, 235
Freud Museum, 548
Friendly compliance, as personality trait, 403
Friendship
in adult development, 151
love and, 480
of therapist, 536–537
as therapy, 558
Frontal lobes, 70, 71, 72, 183, 262
Frowns, 298, 299
Fugue, dissociative, 511–512
Fully functioning persons, humanistic perspectives on, 394–395
Functional fixedness, as problem solving obstacle, 279–280

Functionalism, 17, 18, 39
Fundamental attribution error (FAE), 316, 476–477, 486
in implicit personality theories, 409
"Fuzzy concepts," 266

GABA (gamma-amino butyric acid), as neurotransmitter, 61
Ganglia, 57
Ganglion cells, in eye, 171, 172
Gardner's frames of mind, intelligence and, 435–436
Gay adolescents, 148–149
Gender. See also Men; Women
dreams and, 97
personality and, 399
Gender roles
emotions and, 309
evolution of, 16
in happiness and well-being, 373
stress and, 361, 376
General adaptation syndrome (GAS), 350, 351–354, 376
defined, 351
General intelligence, 433
Generativity
in adult development, 151, 152
in psychosocial development, 145, 152
Genes, 49
behavior and, 44, 78
in chromosomes, 49–50
development and, 116, 123–124
emotions and, 298, 299
hunger and, 325
inheritance via, 49–52
personality traits and, 402–403
psychology and, 15–16
sexuality and, 328–329
temperament and, 402
Genetic manipulation, of humans, 51–52
Genetics, 49. See also Nature–nurture interaction
adoption studies and, 121
in bipolar disorder, 502–503
intelligence and, 440, 441–442
mental retardation and, 430
in psychological development, 118, 119–121
in schizophrenia, 517–518
twins' IQ and, 442
Genetic therapy, for mental retardation, 430
Genital stage, in psychoanalytic theory, 387
Genius. See also Creative genius
quantification of, 422–423
Genotype, 49, 50
Gestalt Bleue (Vasarely), 192, 193
Gestalt principles of perceptual grouping, 196–197
Gestalt psychologists, 194
in cognitive revolution, 260, 261

Gestalt theory of perception, 193, 194
Gesundheit Institute, 337
g factor, intelligence and, 433, 450
Giftedness, 430, 431
measuring, 429
Glial cells, 58
"Glove anesthesia," 510
Good Samaritan parable, 468–469
Graduate school, social psychology of getting into, 485
Grammar
childhood acquisition of, 132–133
defined, 132
innate rules of, 131–132
learning rules of, 133
Grandpa Salvatore story, 257–258
Graphology, as pseudoscience, 25
Grasping reflex, of newborns, 128
Great Britain, civil service testing in, 421–422
Ground, figure and, 194–195
Group achievement, 323
in collectivist societies, 409
Group cohesiveness, 482–483
Group pressure, in conformity experiments, 460–462
Groups. See also Control groups; Experimental groups; In-groups; Out-groups
bystanders in, 466–468
differences in intelligence among, 440–448, 450
obedience of, 462–466
of perceptual elements, 194, 196–197
prejudice and, 477–478
testing intelligence of, 427, 440
Group therapies, 550–552, 554
Growth
of infants, 126
maturation and, 126
prenatal, 125–126
Guilford's structure-of-intellect, 433–434
Guilt
humanistic perspectives on, 395
in psychosocial development, 146
Guinness Book of World Records, The, 4
Gullibility, 25
among children, 137
Gustation. See Taste

Haldol, in drug therapy, 560
Hallucinations, 103–104, 112
in mental disorders, 493
in schizophrenia, 304
Hallucinogenic drugs, 61, 112
altered states of consciousness and, 105–106
Haloperidol, in drug therapy, 560
Hammer, 178

Happiness, 298–300, 336, 376
coping with stress and, 363
measuring, 373–374
relationships and, 319
selfishness and, 319
"Hard" determinism, 15, 16
Hardiness, 358–359, 497
Hashish, as psychoactive drug, 105–106
Hassles, 338
defined, 344
as stressors, 344–345
Head Start program, 443, 445, 450
Health
burnout as affecting, 343–344
exercise and, 368–369
happiness and well-being and, 337–338
lifestyle choices and, 363
nutrition and diet and, 369–370
positive attitudes and, 367–368
problem solving and, 283–284
sleep disorders and, 82
stress as affecting, 337–338, 342
Health psychology, 376
coping with stress via, 371
preventing heart disease via, 372–373
Hearing, 71, 72, 204
aging and, 153
under anesthesia, 83–84
biophysics of, 177–181
fundamental features of, 165
vision and, 181
Heartbeat, initiation of fetal, 125
Heart disease
behavioral medicine to prevent, 372–373
among Type A personalities, 357–358
among Type D personalities, 358
Heart of Darkness (Conrad), 89
Heaven's Gate community, 463
Hedonic capacity, stress and diminished, 360, 361
Helping, 454
asking for, 469–470
in bystander intervention studies, 468–469
psychotherapy as, 558
training for, 467–468
Helplessness
learned, 359–360
punishment and, 225
Hereditary Genius (Galton), 422
Heredity. See also Genetics; Inheritance; Nature–nurture interaction
in psychological development, 118, 119–121, 123–124
in twin studies, 120–121
Heritability
defined, 443
of intelligence within groups, 443–447

Hermann grid, 191, 192
Heroin
as opiate, 106
as psychoactive drug, 104–105
Hertz (cycles per second), 177
Heterosexuality
among adolescents, 148–149
homosexuality versus, 329–330
Heuristics
faulty, 281–284, 290
problem solving with, 276–278, 290, 291
Hierarchies
of anxieties, 543
of concepts, 268–269
of needs, 319–320, 332, 394
High n Ach persons, 322
Hippocampus, 63, 69
long-term memory and, 243–244
History
of psychology, 12–14
psychology and, 11
of significance of dreaming, 95–96
H. M. case, 243–244
hippocampus in, 69
Homeostasis, 332
drives and, 317
general adaptation syndrome and, 351
hypothalamus and, 70
Homicide, school-related, 14–15
Homosexuality
among adolescents, 148–149
heterosexuality versus, 329–330
Horizontal cells, in eye, 172
Hormones, 53, 78
in alarm reaction, 352–353
biological view of, 15
in emotional arousal, 304, 305
hypothalamus and, 69–70
immune system and, 354
of major endocrine glands (table), 62
as neurotransmitters, 60, 61
stress exhaustion and, 353–354
"Horse sense," 435
Hospitals, 565–567
Hostages, Stockholm syndrome among, 360–361, 376
Hostility, among Type A personalities, 357
Housewives, burnout among, 343
How to Choose a Psychologist (American Psychological Association), 567
Human contact, developmental importance of, 119–120, 126
"Human energy field," 3–4
debunking of, 29
"Human error," in engineering psychology, 10
Human Genome Project, 50, 51–52
Human intelligence. See Intelligence

Humanistic psychology, 2, 17, 19–20, 23, 39
criticisms of, 395–396
personality in, 380, 383, 384, 393–396, 412, 413–414
unusual personalities in, 399–400
Humanistic theory of motivation, 319–320
Humanistic therapies, 539, 549–550, 554, 571
Humanities
archetypes in, 391–392
impact of Freudian psychology on, 386
Jungian influence on, 392
Human mind
behavioral view of, 20
cognition by, 16–17
creativity of, 286–287
generation of emotions by, 305–308
intuition of, 284–285
neural activity of, 260–261
philosophy of, 259
problem solving by, 275–284
psychodynamic view of, 19
reasoning by, 274–275
talents of, 258
Human sexuality, 325–330, 332
scientific study of, 326–328
Humor
coping with stress via, 363, 367, 376
health and, 337
Humors, four classical, 400–401, 494
Hunger, 294, 321, 323–325, 332
arousal and, 300–301
as drive, 315
hypothalamus and, 69–70
Huntington's disease, genetic basis of, 124
Hypnosis, 101–103, 112
mesmerism and, 496
relieving hysteria with, 384
treating pain via, 186
uses of, 102–103
Hypnotherapy, 102–103
Hypnotic analgesia, 101
Hypnotizability, 101
Hypochondriasis, 511
as MMPI-2 clinical scale, 404
Hypomania, as MMPI-2 clinical scale, 404
Hypothalamus, 67, 69
in alarm reaction, 352
endocrine system and, 63
"fight-or-flight" response and, 349–350
in hunger, 323, 324
pituitary gland and, 53
Hypothesis, in scientific method, 26–27, 39
Hypothesis acceptance, in scientific method, 29
Hypothetical construct, intelligence as, 422

Hysteria, 384
as MMPI-2 clinical scale, 404
psychic determinism and, 386
in Salem witch trials, 494–495
"Hysterical neurosis," 510

IBM corporation, Deep Blue chessplaying computer by, 45–46
Iconic memory, 238
Id, personality and, 385, 387–388
Identity
development of, 396
in psychosocial development, 145
Identity crisis, among adolescents, 149–150
"Idiots," 425
Illicit drugs, coping with stress via, 370
Illnesses
faking, 520
among hardy people, 358–359
among Type A personalities, 357
Illusions
of context and expectation, 198–201
culture and, 201–202
defined, 191
hallucinations versus, 104
of magicians and politicians, 202–203
perceptual, 191–193
Images, 256. See also Mental images; Visual imagery
cognitive psychology and, 259
figure and ground in, 194–195
thinking and, 258
Imagination, emotions and, 308
"Imbeciles," 425
Imitation, in social learning, 22
Immigrants, intelligence testing of, 425, 440–442
Immigration Restriction Act of 1924, 440
Immune system, stress and, 354–355, 376
Immunosuppression, 354–355
Implicit memory, 244, 252
Implicit personality theories, 383, 408–409, 412, 414
cultural differences in, 409–411
Imprinting, 141
Impulses
id and, 388
neural, 58–59
unconscious and, 384–385
Impulsiveness
emotional intelligence and, 311
as personality trait, 403
sensation seeking and, 301
Incentive motivation, 318
Income levels, IQ test scores and, 440
Incongruence, in humanistic psychology, 394

Independence
in conformity experiments, 461–462
of creative genius, 287
as personality trait, 403
Independent variables
in bystander experiments, 467
in controlled tests, 27
Individual achievement, 323, 409
humanistic perspectives on, 393–394
Individualism
achievement and, 323
collectivism versus, 22, 399
fundamental attribution error and, 409, 476
Individuals
attributions and, 475–477
intelligence of, 441–442, 443, 447–448
labeling of, 522–524
Inductive reasoning, 274–275, 290
Industrial and organizational (I/O) psychology, 10
Inescapable punishment, 225
Infant attachment, 141–142
Infants
babbling of, 131
developmental standards for, 129–130
sensorimotor developmental stage of, 135–136
taste sensitivity of, 185
Infatuation, love and, 480
Inferences
learning-based, 193–194
in psychology, 7
schemas in, 271
Inferiority, in psychosocial development, 146
Information
assimilation of new, 271
base rate, 283
in blood stream, 61
declarative memory of, 242–243
in implicit and explicit memory, 244
lost by working memory, 240–241
memory and, 236
in mental processes, 46
overcoming prejudice with, 479
received during anesthesia, 83–84
in sensation, 165
sensory, 170
sensory memory and, 239
in stimuli, 233
Informational support, coping with stress via, 365
Information-processing models, in cognitive science, 261
Informativeness, of conditioned stimuli, 233
In-groups, prejudice and, 477–478

Inheritance
evolution and, 48
genes and, 49–52
of group intelligence, 443–447
of intelligence, 440–442, 446–447, 450
in psychological development, 118, 119–121
Initiative, in psychosocial development, 146
Innate behavior, 47
of newborn infants, 126–130
Innateness theory of language, 131–132
Inoperable tumor problem, 275
Inquiring intellect, as personality trait, 403
"Insane asylum," 494
Insanity. See also Mental disorders; Psychopathology; Schizophrenia
as legal term, 525
Insanity plea, 490, 522, 525
Insecurity
attachment and, 143
as societal stressor, 343
Insight learning, 230–231
defined, 231
Insight therapies, 547–554, 571
Insomnia, 82, 98–99, 112
Instincts
learning and, 211
in motivation theory, 316–317
in psychoanalytic theory, 385
terminological vagueness of, 317
Instinct theory, motivation in, 316–317
Institute on Violence and Destructive Behavior, 14
Integrated Anger Management (I.A.M.), 313
Intellect
IQ and, 432–433
as personality trait, 403
quantification of, 433–434
Intelligence, 6, 418, 419–448, 449–450. See also Artificial intelligence (AI); Human mind
aging and, 153
in American education, 421
cognitive psychology and, 259, 434–436
componential, 435
components of, 418, 432–438, 450
contextual, 434–435
creative genius and, 287
cultural definitions of, 436–437
defined, 422
emotional, 311–312, 332
environment and, 442–443
eugenics movement and, 422–423
exceptional children and, 418
experiential, 435
general, 433
genetic influence on, 121, 123

group differences in, 418, 440–448
as hypothetical construct, 422
inheritance of, 440–442
measuring, 418, 419–421, 449–450
mental abilities related to, 437–438
practical, 434–435
psychometric theories of, 433–434
quantification of, 422
sensorimotor, 136
seven forms of, 435–436
testing, 423–431
Intelligence quotient (IQ), 418, 449–450
calculating for children versus adults, 429–430
defined, 426
effect of adoption on, 444
environment and, 442–443
giftedness and, 430, 431
group differences in, 440, 443–446, 446–447, 447–448
group testing of, 427
heritability of, 440–442, 443–447
history of, 423–425
intellectual ability and, 432–433
in mental retardation, 430–431
race and, 443–447
rising test scores and, 438
sample test questions from, 428
SAT and, 438
social class and, 444–446
testing, 425–427
testing biases in, 446
test scores as self-fulfilling prophecy, 438–439
Intentions, as concepts, 265
Interaction
aging and social, 153–154
of children with others, 139–146
in family systems theory, 398–399
of heredity and environment, 124
mental disorders and, 497
of nature and nurture, 119, 120–121
in psychological development, 119
in social psychology, 457
Intercourse. See Sexual intercourse
Interdependence, mutual, 483
Interest
of creative genius, 287
measuring, 449
Interference, forgetting via, 247–248, 252
Internal-External Locus of Control Scale, 397, 398
Internal locus of control, 318–319, 397, 413

Internal mental states, motivation and, 316
Internet, 36
as social force, 521
Interneurons, 56, 58
Interpersonal ability, as form of intelligence, 436
Interpersonal attraction, 471–475
Interpersonal involvement, as personality trait, 403
Interpretation
cognition and, 16
consciousness as, 87
in constructing social reality, 485–486
hardiness and, 359
illusions of, 192
in learning and in memory, 210
of memories, 209–210, 245
in perception, 163, 187–188
*Interpretation of Dreams, The* (Freud), 96
Intervening tasks, in retroactive interference, 248
Intervening variables, in psychology, 7
Intimacy
in adult development, 151–152
in love, 480–481
in psychosocial development, 145
Intrapersonal ability, as form of intelligence, 436
Intrinsic motivation, 315, 320, 331
Introspection, 548
examining consciousness via, 85, 86
in structuralism, 18
Introversion, 407
in Jungian theory, 392
as MMPI-2 clinical scale, 404
as personality trait, 403
Introverts, 392
Intuition
defined, 284
localizing in the brain, 262
in thinking, 284–285
Inverted "U" function, in arousal and performance, 294, 301
Iris, 171
Irrationality, as indicator of mental disorder, 498, 499
Isolation
in adult development, 151–152
in psychosocial development, 145

James-Lange theory of physical arousal, 305–306, 307
Japan, control concept in, 9
Jensen controversy, 443–444, 450
*Jeopardy* game show, 243
Jet lag, 92
Jews, Nazi scapegoating of, 478
"Jonathan I." case, 161–162, 175, 176–177
Jonestown community, 463

Observational learning, 208
  defined, 235, 396
  personality and, 396–397
  of violent behavior, 234
Observer bias, in psychological
  research, 33, 39
Observer discomfort, as indicator
  of mental disorder, 498,
  499
Obsession, 509
Obsessive–compulsive disorder
  (OCD), 508–510
  genetic basis of, 124
  rational–emotive therapy
    (RET) for, 554
Occipital lobes, 70, 71
  in visual system, 173–174
Occupational choices, of
  adolescents, 150
*Occupational Outlook Handbook*
  (U.S. Department of Labor),
  9
Octopus, observational learning
  by, 234
Odors, communication by,
  183–184
Oedipus complex, 386, 392
Olfaction. *See* Smell
Olfactory bulbs, 183
Olfactory epithelium, 183
Olfactory nerves, 183
"On Being Sane in Insane Places"
  (Rosenhan), 492
One-word stage, of vocabulary
  development, 132
Only-borns, psychological
  development of, 118
*On the Origin of Species* (Darwin),
  16, 47
On-time condition, in bystander
  intervention studies, 469
Openness to experience, as
  personality trait, 403
Operant behaviors
  conditioning of, 222
  eliminating, 223
  of newborns, 128–130
Operant chamber, 222, 228
Operant conditioning, 140, 208,
  212, 214, 220–229, 251,
  251–252, 496
  classical conditioning versus,
    220
  cognitive psychology and, 232,
    233
  consequences in, 221–225
  defined, 221
  therapy via, 544–547
Operant extinction, 223–224
Operant responses, 221
Operants, 221
Operational definitions
  of absolute threshold, 166
  Freudian theory as lacking,
    390
  in psychology, 5–7
  in scientific method, 26–27
Operations, in structure-of-
  intellect, 433–434

Ophidiophobia, 505, 508
  among monkeys, 546
  social learning therapy for, 545
Opiates, 61, 106–107, 112
Opium, as psychoactive drug, 104
Optic nerve, 171, 172
Optimism, 300
  coping with stress via,
    366–367, 376
  in happiness and well-being,
    373, 374
Oral contraceptive, history of,
  381–382
Oral stage, in psychoanalytic
  theory, 386–387
Orgasm phase, of sexual response
  cycle, 327
Orienting response, 214
Out-groups, prejudice and, 478
Ovaries, hormones of, 62
Overjustification, in motivation,
  320
Overregularization, grammatical
  rules and, 133

Pacific Islanders
  intelligence among, 436
  significance of dreaming
    among, 96
Pain, 160, 181, 185–186
  controlling with hypnosis,
    102–103
  fundamental features of, 165
  opiates for, 106
Pain withdrawal reflex, 58
Palmistry, as pseudoscience,
  24–25
Pancreas, hormones of, 62
Panic attack, 507
Panic disorder, 308, 309, 498,
  506–507. *See also* Anxiety
  genetic basis of, 124
Papillae, 184–185
Paranoia, as MMPI-2 clinical
  scale, 404
Paranoid schizophrenia, 516
Paranormal phenomena, 348
  altered states of consciousness
    and, 101
  testing, 3–4, 24–25
Paraprofessionals, therapy by, 532,
  540–541
Parasympathetic nervous system,
  55, 56, 57
  emotional arousal and, 304
Parathyroid glands, hormones of,
  62
Parents
  adolescents and, 150
  killing of, 19
  love from, 395
  in psychoanalytic theory,
    386–387
Parietal lobes, 70, 71, 72, 183,
  185
Parkinson's disease, 60
Partial reinforcement, 226
Partial reinforcement effect, 226
Participant modeling, 546

Passion, in love, 480–481
Pastoral counselors, 538
*Patch Adams*, 337
Path analysis, of cognitive maps,
  289
Patriotism test, 176
Pattern recognition, cognitive
  psychology and, 259
PCP (phencyclidine), as
  psychoactive drug, 105
Peer groups, among adolescents,
  149–150
"Peer marriages," 151
Penis envy, 386, 390
Peoples Temple community, 463
Perception, 210
  aging and, 153
  ambiguity in and distortion of,
    190–193
  cognitive psychology and,
    16–18, 259
  defined, 162–163
  emotions and, 308
  Gestalt psychologists and, 260
  Gestalt theory of, 193, 194
  memory and, 236
  memory distortion and, 245
  memory encoding and, 237
  sensation and, 160, 164–165,
    187–203, 205
  sensory memory and, 239
  sensory thresholds in, 166–167
  stress and, 336, 356
  theoretical explanations for,
    193–194
Percepts, 188
Perceptual constancy, 189
Perceptual grouping, 196–197
Perceptual organization, 194–197
Perceptual processing, 188–190
Perceptual sets, 199–201
Perceptual system
  "feature detectors" in, 260
  in learning and in memory, 210
Perfectionism, among Type A
  personalities, 357
Performance
  arousal and, 294, 300–301
  Binet-Simon test and, 424
  inverted "U" function and, 301
  in Wechsler intelligence scales,
    426–427
Peripheral nervous system, 54–56,
  78
Perseverance, motivation and,
  316
Persistence
  of high *n Ach* persons, 322
  in motivation, 314–315
Personal bias, in psychological
  research, 33, 39
Personality, 380, 381–413,
  413–414
  attributions and, 475–477
  authoritarian, 463
  childhood influences on adult,
    144–146
  cognitive theories of, 396–398
  of creative genius, 286–287

culture and, 380, 409–411
  defined, 383
  development of, 116, 117–119
  emotion and, 397–398
  in family systems theory,
    398–399
  Freudian theory of, 384–391
  gender and, 399
  hassles and, 344–345
  humanistic theories of,
    393–396
  implicit theories of, 383,
    408–409
  of Margaret Sanger, 381–382
  origins of, 382–383
  patterns in, 400–406
  personal theories of, 380,
    408–411
  person-centered theory of,
    394–395
  post-Freudian theories of,
    391–393
  pseudoscientific theories of,
    24–25
  psychodynamic view of, 19
  psychology as study of, 5
  self-actualizing, 394
  social learning and, 396–397
  stress and, 336, 338–339, 356
  theories of, 380, 412
Personality disorders, 501,
  518–519, 528
Personality structure, in
  psychoanalytic theory,
  384–385, 387–388
Personality tests, 437
Personality theory. *See also*
    Freudian personality theory;
    Jungian personality theory
  cognitive, 396–398
  current, 398–399
  humanistic, 393–396
  post-Freudian, 391–393
  unusual behavior in, 380,
    399–400
Personality types, 356–358, 380,
  383, 401, 407, 412, 414
  in Jungian theory, 392
  reliability of, 407
Personal unconscious, 391
Person-centered theory, of
  personality, 394–395
Person-centered therapy, 549
Person–situation controversy,
  405–406, 414
Persuasion
  changing deleterious lifestyles
    via, 371
  among Native Americans, 437
  to prevent heart disease, 372
  subliminal, 168–169
Pessimism, optimism versus, 366
Phallic stage, in psychoanalytic
  theory, 387
Phenomenal field, in humanistic
  psychology, 395
Phenotype, 49, 50
Pheromones, 184
Phlegm, 494

Phlegmatic personality, mucus and, 401
Phobias, 498, 507–508
  behavioral view of, 20
  counterconditioning therapy for, 217
  hypnosis in treating, 103
  learning of, 8
  misattribution of emotions and, 306
  psychoanalysis for treating, 385
  sexual, 328
  snake, 505
  social, 507–508
  specific, 508
  table of, 508
Phosphenes, 181, 182
Photoreceptors, 170–171, 172
Physical arousal, 305–306, 307–308
  sexual, 326–328
  from stress, 336
Physical attractiveness
  anorexia nervosa and, 514–515
  love and, 480
  in matching hypothesis, 473–474
  in reward theory of attraction, 471, 472–473
Physical maturation, 148
Physiological dependance, 109
Physiological measures, in controlled tests, 28, 29
Piaget's theory of cognitive development, 134–138, 156
Pill, the. See Oral contraceptive
Pi spirits, 495
Pitch, sound frequency and, 179–180
Pituitary gland, 53
  hormones of, 62, 63
PKU (phenylketonuria), mental retardation in, 430, 431
Placebo bias
  double-blind controls and, 34
  in psychological research, 33, 39
Placebo effect, treating pain via, 186
Placebos, 349, 555, 562
  in controlled tests, 27
  neurotransmitters and, 61
Place learning, 231
Placenta, 125
Place theory, of pitch perception, 179–180
Plasticity, of brain, 77
Plateau phase, of sexual response cycle, 327
Play, drives and, 318
Pleasure
  limbic system and, 69
  sex and, 325
"Poker face," 312
Political science, psychology and, 11
Politicians, perceptual illusions of, 202–203
Polygraph, 6, 312–313

Polyphasic behavior, 357
Pons, 68
Ponzo illusion, 201–202
Position, sense of, 181–182
Positive afterimages, 176
Positive emotions, 297
  in happiness and well-being, 373
  health and, 367–368
  left brain hemisphere and, 304
Positive experiences, fully functioning persons and, 394
Positive reinforcers, 222, 223, 225, 229
Positive schizophrenia, 517
Positron emission tomography (PET) scans, 65–66, 260
  studying consciousness with, 86
  studying schizophrenia with, 304
  studying thinking with, 262
Positrons, 66
Possession, 494–495
Post-Freudian personality theories, 391–393
Post-Freudian psychotherapy, 548
Posthypnotic suggestions, 103
Postsynaptic neurons, 60
Posttraumatic stress disorder (PTSD), 73, 361, 376
Postural reflex, of newborns, 128
Poverty, IQ and, 444–445, 446–447, 447–448
Power
  as personality trait, 403
  psychodynamic perspective on, 393
  of situation, 482–484
Practical intelligence, 434–435
Practice, expertise and, 285
Pr"gnanz, in perceptual grouping, 197
Preconscious memories, 88
Preconsciousness, 111
  consciousness and, 88
  personality and, 385
Prediction
  by Freudian theory, 390
  as goal of psychology, 5, 8
  with trait theories, 405
Preferred activities, 226, 227
  motivation and, 314
  in social psychology, 457
Prefrontal lobotomy, 563–564
Pregnancy, 329
  in early twentieth century, 381
Prejudice
  causes of, 477–479
  combating, 479–480
  defined, 477
  in social reality, 477–480
Premack principle, 227, 251
Premature ejaculation, 328
Premises, in syllogisms, 274
Prenatal period, human development during, 125–126

Preoperational stage, in Piaget's theory of cognitive development, 135, 136, 138
Preparedness hypothesis, phobias and, 508
Presynaptic neurons, 60
Primary reinforcers, 226
Priming
  probing unconscious with, 86
  studying memory by, 244
Princeton Theological Seminary, bystander studies at, 468–469
Principle of attractiveness, in reward theory of attraction, 473
Principle of opposites, in Jungian theory, 392
Principle of proximity, in reward theory of attraction, 472
Principles of Psychology, The (James), 13
Prison life, 455–457
Proactive interference
  forgetting via, 247–248
  functional fixedness and, 279
Problem identification, in therapy, 537
Problems in living, mental disorders as, 536
Problem solving, 275–284, 290–291
  by breaking big problems into smaller ones, 277–278
  childhood development of, 137
  cognitive psychology and, 259
  by creative genius, 287
  by experts, 284–285
  identifying problems in, 275
  obstacles to, 278–284, 290–291
  selecting strategies for, 276–278
Procedural memory, 242, 252
  forgetting and, 246–247
  in H. M. case, 243–244
Procedures, as concepts, 265
Process. See also Mental processes
  in family systems theory, 399
Products, in structure-of-intellect, 433–434
Professors, cognitive maps of, 289–290
Prognosis, 54
  in therapy, 537
Projection, 323, 548
  as ego defense mechanism, 389
  of needs, 322
  as response to stressors, 362, 376
Projective tests, 389–390
  defined, 389
Promiscuity, evolution of, 329
Prompting, 227–228
Proofreading, law of Pr"gnanz and, 197
Properties, as concepts, 265
Prototypes, in concepts, 266–268

Proximity
  in perceptual grouping, 196–197
  in reward theory of attraction, 471–472
Prozac, 61, 63, 563
  in drug therapy, 561
Prudence, as personality trait, 403
Pseudomemory, 268
Pseudopatients case, 491–493, 566
Pseudoscience, 24–25
Psilocybin, as psychoactive drug, 105–106
Psychasthenia, as MMPI-2 clinical scale, 404
Psychedelics, 105–106
Psychiatric nurse practitioners, 538
Psychiatrists, 538
  pseudopatients and, 491–493
  psychoanalysts versus, 11–12
Psychic determinism, 385–386
Psychic energy, 317
Psychic numbing
  in learning violent behavior, 234
  posttraumatic stress disorder and, 361
  as response to catastrophes, 341
  stress and, 360
"Psychic secretions," 213
PsychInfo database, 36
PsychLit database, 36
Psychoactive drugs, 63, 112
  altered states of consciousness and, 104–108
  brain and, 54
  hallucinations from, 104
  neural effects of, 59, 60
  side effects of, 44
Psychoanalysis, 11–12, 19, 384–391, 539, 547–548, 571
  case studies in, 32–33
  defined, 384
  dreaming and, 96
  as therapy for mental disorders, 496
Psychoanalysts, 538
  psychiatrists versus, 11–12
Psychodynamic perspective
  on personality, 380, 383, 384–393, 412, 413–414
  post-Freudian therapy in, 548
  in psychology, 2, 17, 19, 23, 39
  on therapy, 554
  therapy in, 539, 547–548
  unusual personalities in, 400
Psychogenic disorders, 496
Psycholinguistics, 261
Psychological Common-Sense Test, 5, 6
Psychological dependance, 109
Psychological development. See Developmental psychology
Psychological models, of mental disorders, 495–498
Psychological Science journal, 36